THE ROTHNER FAMILY EDITION

THE KOREN NCSY SIDDUR

סידור לימות החול ולשבת

DEVELOPED BY

Ms. Debbie Stone and Rabbi Dr. Daniel Rose

•

KOREN PUBLISHERS JERUSALEM
OU PRESS

The Koren NCSY Siddur
First Hebrew/English Ashkenaz Edition, 2017
Combined American/Canadian Edition

Koren Publishers Jerusalem Ltd.
POB 4044, Jerusalem 9104001, ISRAEL
POB 8531, New Milford, CT 06776, USA
www.korenpub.com

OU Press, an imprint of the Orthodox Union
11 Broadway, New York, NY 10004
www.oupress.org

The English translation in this edition is based on the English translation first published in Great Britain in 2006 in the Authorised Daily Prayer Book of the United Hebrew Congregations of the Commonwealth: New Translation and Commentary by Chief Rabbi Jonathan Sacks, (Fourth Edition, Compilation © United Synagogue) by Collins, a division of HarperCollins Publishers, London.

Photograph Credits are listed in the Appendix "Guide to the Images" on p. 1152.

The creation of this Siddur was made possible with the generous support of Torah Education in Israel.

Printed in the PRC

Standard Size, Hardcover, ISBN 978 965 301 831 0

AT3A01

בני בנים הרי הם כבנים

In honor of our grandchildren,
each of whom strives for
a unique relationship with the Almighty.

May this סידור *serve as a companion*
as you deepen your connection to Hashem
throughout your lifetimes.

With love and pride,

Eric and Gale Rothner

וְשִׁנַּנְתָּם לְבָנֶיךָ

Dedicated to my wife,
Debra צביה אהובה
and our children,
Elijah Matthew מנחם מנדל
Zachary Noah יצחק אבנר
Sydney Rachel אלקה שיינה
Lexie Belle רחל לאה

In celebration
of our joint and individual journeys
toward a better understanding of Torah
and our relationship to Hashem.

David Magerman

In honor of

Willfred "Moe" *and* **Lois Lefkovich** a"h

Two individuals
who found the beauty of Judaism later in life
and created a beautiful Jewish legacy.

David and Chaya Tova Hartman

CONTENTS

PREFACE

It is with great excitement that we present to you the Rothner Family Edition of *The Koren NCSY Weekday and Shabbat Siddur*, an engaging and thoughtful siddur for the inquiring young person. This Siddur is part of the Magerman Educational Siddur Series of appropriately designed siddurim for students from first to twelfth grade, and beyond. Each siddur has been created to inspire and develop connections to prayer and to God. These goals are achieved through encouraging personal reflection, spiritual and emotional connection, and cognitive learning.

It is always a privilege to collaborate on a project with those who share our commitment and enthusiasm for bringing out the beauty of *Tefilla*. We are grateful to the Rothner family and Debra and David Magerman, for their critical support and encouragement, and for enabling the creation of this volume in the series. On behalf of the students who will use this Siddur, we are forever in your debt.

We are fortunate to benefit from a world-class Educational Editorial Board assisting us in the building of this program. We would like to thank the Board's Chairman, Dr. Scott Goldberg of Yeshiva University; Rabbi Adam Englander of the Hillel Day School of Boca Raton; Rabbi Dr. Jay Goldmintz of the Azrieli Graduate School; Rabbi Boruch Sufrin of the Harkham Hillel Hebrew Academy of Beverly Hills; and Rabbi Benjy Levy of Sydney, Australia. Their broad knowledge and experience provided the framework to structure the program.

We wish to thank Rabbi Micah Greenland, NCSY International Director, for his foreword and support for this project. Special thanks go to Debbie Stone and NCSY/OU Press for their partnership in this exciting endeavor. The small but highly professional team at Koren was led by Rabbi Dr. Daniel Rose, Director of Educational Projects, and included

◂ Avishai

Avishai Magence who managed the project; Esther Be'er who designed and typeset the text; Rachel Meghnagi, our Language Editor; and Tani Bayer, our Art Director.

It is our sincere hope and prayer that this Siddur will provide a platform for the educational and spiritual growth of present and upcoming generations of committed Jews.

Matthew Miller, Publisher
Jerusalem, 5778 (2018)

FOREWORD

In some ways, connecting with others is easier today than it has ever been before. Technology, and social media in particular, provides us with both a platform to distribute information to others, as well as incredible speed with which to share it. The sheer number of contacts we each have, in many cases from all over the world, is at an all-time high.

It would stand to reason then, that relationships today would be unprecedentedly strong. Friendships should be closer, parent-child dynamics should be excellent, marriages should be nearly unbreakable, and even interactions with relatively simple acquaintances should be deeper and more meaningful.

Yet, that is unquestionably not the case. Somehow, in an age when making connections seems easier than ever, we still struggle to build and strengthen genuine relationships. In the worst cases, marriages flounder, families crumble, and friendships collapse. But even in the best of cases, we struggle to find the sort of closeness that we long for in our relationships.

We can intuitively understand why this is the case. Fleeting interactions, often through an electronic medium, don't lend themselves to deep, intimate communication. The more adept we have become at simultaneously conducting multiple conversations over our electronic devices, the less proficient or comfortable we are at fully opening up and building meaningful relationships that require deeper communication. Quantity of distinct contacts is no replacement for quality of individual relationships.

Successful prayer – real, genuine, תפילה – is at its core a relationship building exercise. Our aim is to communicate, to open up, and to express to God our deepest wishes and aspirations, as well as gratitude for the

◂ many gifts

many gifts that we enjoy and rely upon. The more we bare our souls before Hashem, the stronger our relationship with Him can become.

Not surprisingly, it is all the more difficult today, when even relationships with actual "flesh-and-blood" human beings are so challenging. We struggle so mightily to communicate successfully even with friends and family members, so how can we expect our "one-sided" conversations with an invisible God to go any better? Moreover, a relationship with the Almighty seems difficult to contemplate even under the best of circumstances, and all the more so with today's unique challenges. Yet, that is precisely what we are striving to establish or strengthen each time we pray.

And therefore: this Siddur.

God, metaphorically, "wears many hats" in His relationship dynamic with us. The Torah and the Prophets at times refer to God as: "our Father," "our King," "our Shepherd," "our Creator," and many others. Each of these "hats" or names reflects a different dimension of how we as Jews can develop our relationship with God. By presenting Himself to us in such varied ways, Hashem is inviting us relate to Him in the model that most resonates with our individual circumstance and situation.

Similarly, each of us as human beings is completely unique. What one person finds is a very meaningful avenue towards connecting with God, may not work for others. Some connect through stories, others through contemplation, and others through visual cues or thought-provoking questions. Relationship building rightly happens in a distinct way for each person, and there are a multitude of ways in which meaningful תפילה is achieved for different individuals as well.

The Koren NCSY Siddur is a powerful tool to help each of us in establishing our own unique connection with God. Through an exceptional collaboration between NCSY and Koren Publishing, two outstanding educators – Debbie Stone from NCSY and Rabbi Dr. Daniel Rose from Koren – have developed this Siddur to serve as a companion as you forge your own one-of-a-kind relationship with the Almighty. I am deeply appreciative of their countless hours invested in bringing this to fruition, as I am of Matthew Miller, Publisher at Koren and NCSY's valued partner. I express gratitude to the lay and professional leadership of the Orthodox Union, NCSY's parent organization, for their constant encouragement and assistance in fostering the Siddur project.

◂ I am

I am most thankful for the support provided by Mr. Eric Rothner and family. Without their generosity and vision, this volume would not have been possible, and I am profoundly grateful for their partnership and friendship.

May it be God's will that this Siddur be successful in achieving its sacred mission: bringing each of us closer to Hashem.

Rabbi Micah Greenland
International Director, NCSY
Chicago, 5778 (2018)

INTRODUCTION

The Koren NCSY Siddur

Imagine a shul. A gorgeous tall building with beautiful stained-glass windows, marble floors, and an exquisitely designed *aron kodesh*. The chazzan and the accompanying choir sing sublime melodies in perfect pitch and harmony. When you sit in such a shul, you look around mesmerized by its beauty. All you want to do is watch it all and soak up the experience.

Imagine a second shul. This shul has nothing memorable in its décor. It's a simple *shtiebel,* clean and comfortable but not remarkable in any way. The *ba'al tefilla* in this shul sings well known tunes. He's not a gifted singer or trained chazzan, but his voice is familiar and inviting. In this shul you don't just want to sit back and listen to the tefilla – you want to sing together. The tunes, the people and the shul move you to participate and be part of the melody.

Commentaries on prayer are much like these different shuls. Each different commentary has its own feel and evokes different responses. Some commentaries are so elegant and pristine, all you want to do is passively read them, undisturbed and uninterrupted. This commentary is not that. This commentary is about singing along, finding your emotions and joining in with the *ba'al tefilla*. This is not reading material to follow along with the choir, but a tool to develop your own voice and a window to share your own experiences within prayer. Don't just read the commentary - sing along with it. We want the teen soul to discover its voice within the prayer experience.

Davening can be hard. Writing about davening hasn't made it any easier. The experience of reading and writing about prayer for over a year has been both gratifying and challenging. Reading and learning about tefilla can provide beautiful ideas, but there is a constant struggle to balance the application of the ideas and concepts I have read, while still preserving the genuine feeling and spontaneity of my personal prayer

◂ experience

experience. Everyone grapples with tefilla, we are tasked with balancing the fixed text and language of prayer with our individual volatile emotional experience. Praying is about exploring the worlds beneath the words - and integrating your world with Judaism's words. Words of prayer remain static, even as our feelings and experiences constantly change.

This siddur has a fixed text, but it also has an innovative commentary – distinctive with personalized questions and pictures. We are hoping to give you an opportunity to react to the messages of the text. We are hoping that this siddur will be the bridge between the fixed text and the unique emotional experience that each individual brings to his or her tefillah. We want you to sing along with prayer.

There is an old Hasidic story about two students who didn't know how to approach the High Holy Days. They went to their rebbe and asked for his guidance.

> "At the far end of the village lives a man who can teach you how to approach these holy days. Go, watch him, and learn."
>
> So the two students traveled to this man and watched him go through his day. They saw him rise early in the morning and work hard into the night. He ate very simply, lived alone, and was obviously poor.
>
> Late in the evening, the students watched as the man fervently prayed. Then, he took out a list. He said, "God in Heaven, please forgive me for these sins, Your requests that I have not fulfilled!" And he read out a long list of his wrongdoings.
>
> When he finished, he put that list away. Then, he took out another list.
>
> "God in Heaven, these are the requests I have made of You that You have not yet answered."
>
> He went on to list all the prayers and hopes he had sent to heaven that had remained unanswered.
>
> The man spread his arms heavenward and said, "God, I will make you a deal. Forgive me for my list of sins, and in return, I will forgive you for not answering my requests!"

All voices, even those that may challenge God, are a part of the prayer experience. The teen years are a time when people form their own ideas and identities. It is especially important for their questions, reflections

◂ and responses

and responses to prayers to be heard and validated. This siddur encourages such dialogue between each person and God.

Some books and commentaries are so beautiful and graceful you find enjoyment and inspiration from reading the words, allowing them to wash over you. The educational components in this Siddur are not like that. They require active participation, thoughtful responding to the ideas contained herein, connecting, self-introspection. This Siddur commentary is about joining in with the song of your people. Finding and expressing your own soul and its emotions, connecting to your community and your people, and contributing your own harmony to their melody. With these ideas in mind several educational elements have been included in the Siddur, in order to place the user at the center of the tefilla experience, and facilitate the identity- and relationship-forming potential of tefilla.

TYPESETTING

As with all Koren siddurim, much thought and attention has been paid to the typesetting of the liturgical text. Not only in the beautiful aesthetic that has come to be expected from Koren publications, but in the pedagogic factors that have also been taken into account during the typesetting process. The Koren NCSY Siddur has been typeset in an intuitive way where each tefilla unit stands on its own, aiding the user in their tefilla experience and in their understanding of the tefilla text.

TRANSLATION AND RUBRICS

The translation found in the Koren NCSY Siddur, based on the translation by Rabbi Jonathan Sacks in the Koren Siddur has been adapted in a developmentally appropriate manner for the users of this Siddur. Explanatory rubrics have also been written in developmentally appropriate language.

EDUCATIONAL COMMENTARY

This Siddur follows the format of the Koren Magerman Educational Siddur series which have reflection, connection, and learning at their core. We chose to use these three processes as the basis for the categories of our educational commentary, and added a pictorial commentary, to complete the four categories of commentary found in the Koren NCSY Siddur.

◂ Each category

Each category uses color coding, and when appropriate, the text of the tefilla that the commentary is connected to will be highlighted in the same color. This increases the power and impact of the text of the commentary and helps the pray-er to connect it to the tefilla.

The four categories are:

- REFLECTION – Reflection and thought questions, sometimes preceded by a relevant and meaningful quote.
- CONNECTION – This section contains stories, narratives and quotes to help the pray-er to connect to the themes of the tefilla text.
- LEARNING – A Biur Tefilla section where historical, philosophical or halakhic explanation helps the pray-er to understand the full context and ritual norms of the tefilla.
- ... A THOUSAND WORDS – They say the power of a picture is worth a thousand words, and this is the most unique element of the Koren NCSY Siddur. A photographic commentary on the tefilla that creates connections between the tefilla and the world around us. Photographs and images from the world closest to us, as well as from the broader universe, connect the pray-er to the themes of the *tefillot*.

TORAH READING SUMMARIES

The first aliya of each of the weekday Torah readings is found with a short summary to help focus the pray-er during Keriat HaTorah.

GUIDE TO THE IMAGES – PHOTOGRAPH CREDITS AND SUMMARY

As an appendix, all photograph and image credits are found together with a short summary elucidation, in order to help the pray-er to find the full impact of the message of the image in the context of the text of the tefilla.

Acknowledgements

This siddur has benefited from many voices, harmonies and accompaniments. It is with deep gratitude that we would like to thank Matthew Miller and all at Koren Publishers for the opportunity to work on this wonderful project. Esther Be'er and Tani Bayer deserve specific thanks

◂ for the beautiful

for the beautiful typesetting and aesthetic of the siddur, and Aryeh Grossman for being a constant educational sounding board throughout the process. For his tremendous support and guidance throughout this project, thank you to Allen Fagin, Executive Vice President of the Orthodox Union. Special appreciation to Rabbi Micah Greenland, International Director of NCSY for his constant support, advice and encouragement. We are extremely grateful to the Rothner Family for their generous support to NCSY in this endeavor.

Thank you to Rabbi Dovid Bashevkin of NCSY who has provided constant support, guidance and creativity at every stage of the creation of this siddur. Thanks also to Rabbi Simon Posner, Rabbi Eliyahu Krakowski, and Rabbi Menachem Genack at OU Press for their care and attention to all details. Thank you to Rachel First for her careful review. Thanks to Dayan Chanoch Ehrentreu, Rabbi Tzvi Hersh Weinreb, Rabbi David Block and Rabbi Simcha Willig for contributing scholarly and analytical eyes, and for giving us a nuanced and mindful perspective.

Finally, special thanks goes to Rabbi Dr. Jay Goldmintz, a world renowned expert on Tefilla Education, a mentor, role model and friend to us both. Rabbi Goldmintz has had an inestimable impact on this project from its genesis in the Koren offices at the beginning of 2013, until his significant role with this siddur. His influence can be found on every page of each of the siddurim in the Koren Magerman Educational Siddurim series.

Rabbi Sacks describes tefilla as a "profoundly transformative experience." It is our hope that this siddur will be a catalyst for "self-acquisition and self-discovery," for personal growth and identity formation, and as an aide to develop and nurture a relationship with God, through meaningful engagements with tefilla. From there, not only will the pray-er be transformed for the better, but the whole world, because "prayer changes the world because it changes us."[1]

Debbie Stone
New York City,
Daniel Rose
Jerusalem,
5778 (2018)

1. "Understanding Jewish Prayer," Introduction to the Koren Sacks Siddur.

THE KOREN NCSY SIDDUR
סידור לימות החול ולשבת

ימי חול

WEEKDAYS

Shaḥarit

ON WAKING

On waking, our first thought should be that we are in the presence of God. Since we are forbidden to speak God's name until we have washed our hands, the following prayer is said, which, without mentioning God's name, acknowledges His presence and gives thanks for a new day and for the gift of life.

מוֹדֶה I thank You, living and eternal King,
for giving me back my soul in mercy.
Great is Your faith in us.

Wash hands and say the following blessings.

בָּרוּךְ Blessed are You, Lord our God, King of the Universe,
who has made us holy through His commandments,
and has commanded us about washing hands.

CONNECTION

Close your eyes and relax. What do you have to be thankful for today? Who do you need to be thankful to for these things?

Think about all the people who have helped and will help you in some way today. From your parents at home from the moment you wake up, to the bus driver, to the janitor at your school. How many people will help you in some way today? What will each one do for you? How would your day be different without them in your life? Now choose one of them to thank today, and choose two to thank tomorrow.

Now take a moment to think about what you have to thank Hashem for.

Now say מוֹדֶה אֲנִי.

... A THOUSAND WORDS

שחרית

השכמת הבוקר

On waking, our first thought should be that we are in the presence of God. Since we are forbidden to speak God's name until we have washed our hands, the following prayer is said, which, without mentioning God's name, acknowledges His presence and gives thanks for a new day and for the gift of life.

men מוֹדֶה/ *women* מוֹדָה/ אֲנִי לְפָנֶיךָ מֶלֶךְ חַי וְקַיָּם
שֶׁהֶחֱזַרְתָּ בִּי נִשְׁמָתִי בְּחֶמְלָה
רַבָּה אֱמוּנָתֶךָ.

Wash hands and say the following blessings.

בָּרוּךְ אַתָּה יהוה אֱלֹהֵינוּ מֶלֶךְ הָעוֹלָם
אֲשֶׁר קִדְּשָׁנוּ בְּמִצְוֹתָיו וְצִוָּנוּ עַל נְטִילַת יָדָיִם.

REFLECTION

"The darkest hour is just before the dawn."

Yesterday is behind us. Today is a new beginning. What do you want to achieve today?

What experiences did you have yesterday that make you a new you today?

LEARNING

The halakha obligates us to wash our hands as soon as we wake up. Some identified this need with a "*ruaḥ ra'a*," a negative spirit, that was acquired during sleep, perhaps an ancient equivalent of a spiritual bacteria or perhaps simply an association with the seemingly lifeless state that comes with death. Others view it as a requirement to wash our hands whenever we pray, reminiscent of the Kohanim as they began their service in the *Beit HaMikdash*. Regardless, we view this as an opportunity for renewal, a way to begin one's day with a sense of higher purpose for our bodies and our souls.

According to some, there is also an obligation to wash our hands before *tefilla*. If you said the blessing for washing after waking up, then do not repeat it again here. It is best to wash your hands with a cup, and the custom is to pour water from the cup onto the right hand and then the left, and then repeat, a total of three times.

בָּרוּךְ Blessed are You, Lord our God, King of the Universe,
who formed man with wisdom
and created in him many openings and cavities.
It is revealed and known before the throne of Your glory
that were one of them to be ruptured or blocked,
it would be impossible to survive and stand before You.
Blessed are You, Lord,
Healer of all flesh
who does miracles.

REFLECTION

"We forget that we have a holy body no less than a holy spirit."
(Rav Kook, *Orot HaTeḥiya* 33)

Is your body a highly efficient scientific machine or a miracle from God? Can it be both?

Does your human body help you to believe in God?

If your human body is a gift from God, how would that change the way you treat your body?

CONNECTION

"The human body contains 100 trillion cells. Within each cell is a nucleus. Within each nucleus is a double copy of the human genome. Each genome contains 3.1 billion letters of genetic code, enough if transcribed to fill a library of five thousand books. Each cell, in other words, contains a blueprint of the entire body of which it is a part. The cumulative force of these scientific discoveries is nothing short of wondrous. In ways undreamt of by our ancestors, we now know to what extent the microcosm is a map of the macrocosm. From a single cell, it may be possible to reconstruct an entire organism."

(Rabbi Jonathan Sacks, *Covenant & Conversation, Emor* 5768)

LEARNING

This *berakha* is said after every visit to the restroom, to thank Hashem for the intricate wonders of the human body. It is recommended to go to the restroom immediately after washing your hands in the morning, and then say both the *berakha* of *Netilat Yadayim* and *Asher Yatzar*.

בָּרוּךְ אַתָּה יהוה אֱלֹהֵינוּ מֶלֶךְ הָעוֹלָם
אֲשֶׁר יָצַר אֶת הָאָדָם בְּחָכְמָה
וּבָרָא בוֹ נְקָבִים נְקָבִים, חֲלוּלִים חֲלוּלִים.
גָּלוּי וְיָדוּעַ לִפְנֵי כִסֵּא כְבוֹדֶךָ
שֶׁאִם יִפָּתֵחַ אֶחָד מֵהֶם
אוֹ יִסָּתֵם אֶחָד מֵהֶם
אִי אֶפְשַׁר לְהִתְקַיֵּם וְלַעֲמֹד לְפָנֶיךָ.
בָּרוּךְ אַתָּה יהוה
רוֹפֵא כָל בָּשָׂר וּמַפְלִיא לַעֲשׂוֹת.

... A THOUSAND WORDS

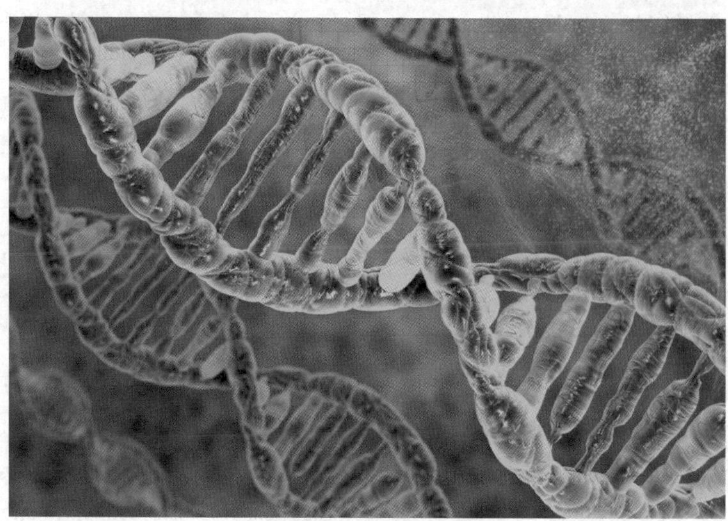

אֱלֹהַי My God,
the soul You placed within me is pure.
You created it, You formed it, You breathed it into me,
and You guard it while it is within me.
One day You will take it from me,
and restore it to me in the time to come.
As long as the soul is within me, I will thank You,
LORD my God and God of my ancestors,
Master of all works, LORD of all souls.
Blessed are You, LORD, who restores souls to lifeless bodies.

TZITZIT

The following blessing is said before putting on tzitzit. Neither it nor the following prayer is said by those who wear a tallit. The blessing over the latter exempts the former.

בָּרוּךְ Blessed are You, LORD our God, King of the Universe,
who has made us holy through His commandments,
and has commanded us about the command of tzitzit.

After putting on tzitzit, say:

יְהִי רָצוֹן May it be Your will, LORD my God and God of my ancestors, that the commandment of the tzitzit be considered before You as if I had fulfilled it in all its specifics, details and intentions, as well as the 613 commandments dependent on it, Amen, Selah.

REFLECTION

וַיִּיצֶר יהוה אֱלֹהִים אֶת־הָאָדָם, עָפָר מִן־הָאֲדָמָה, וַיִּפַּח בְּאַפָּיו, נִשְׁמַת חַיִּים; וַיְהִי הָאָדָם, לְנֶפֶשׁ חַיָּה.

"Then the LORD God formed man, dust of the ground; He breathed breath of life into his nostrils; and man became a living creature." (Bereshit 2:7)

What does having a soul mean to you?

Your body inherits genetics from your ancestors. Do you think your soul does too?

What is in your soul's DNA?

CONNECTION

One of the disciples of the Hasidic master Rebbe Bunam explained his greatness: "Remember what happened to Elisha? Elisha was a simple shepherd who spoke to his cattle, not to humans. Then one day he met the prophet Elijah and from then on he was another person: his soul had caught fire. Rebbe Bunam? You want to know about Rebbe Bunam? Simple. No matter how hardened, how icy your soul may be, at his touch it will burst into flames."

(Elie Wiesel, *Souls on Fire*)

אֱלֹהַי
נְשָׁמָה שֶׁנָּתַתָּ בִּי טְהוֹרָה הִיא.
אַתָּה בְרָאתָהּ, אַתָּה יְצַרְתָּהּ, אַתָּה נְפַחְתָּהּ בִּי
וְאַתָּה מְשַׁמְּרָהּ בְּקִרְבִּי, וְאַתָּה עָתִיד לִטְּלָהּ מִמֶּנִּי
וּלְהַחֲזִירָהּ בִּי לֶעָתִיד לָבוֹא.
כָּל זְמַן שֶׁהַנְּשָׁמָה בְקִרְבִּי, *men* מוֹדֶה / *women* מוֹדָה/ אֲנִי לְפָנֶיךָ
יהוה אֱלֹהַי וֵאלֹהֵי אֲבוֹתַי, רִבּוֹן כָּל הַמַּעֲשִׂים, אֲדוֹן כָּל הַנְּשָׁמוֹת.
בָּרוּךְ אַתָּה יהוה, הַמַּחֲזִיר נְשָׁמוֹת לִפְגָרִים מֵתִים.

לבישת ציצית

The following blessing is said before putting on a טלית קטן. *Neither it nor* יְהִי רָצוֹן *is said by those who wear a* טלית. *The blessing over the latter exempts the former.*

בָּרוּךְ אַתָּה יהוה אֱלֹהֵינוּ מֶלֶךְ הָעוֹלָם
אֲשֶׁר קִדְּשָׁנוּ בְּמִצְוֹתָיו וְצִוָּנוּ עַל מִצְוַת צִיצִית.

After putting on the טלית קטן*, say:*

יְהִי רָצוֹן מִלְּפָנֶיךָ, יהוה אֱלֹהַי וֵאלֹהֵי אֲבוֹתַי, שֶׁתְּהֵא חֲשׁוּבָה מִצְוַת צִיצִית לְפָנֶיךָ, כְּאִלּוּ קִיַּמְתִּיהָ בְּכָל פְּרָטֶיהָ וְדִקְדּוּקֶיהָ וְכַוָּנוֹתֶיהָ, וְתַרְיַ״ג מִצְוֹת הַתְּלוּיוֹת בָּהּ, אָמֵן סֶלָה.

LEARNING

It is a mitzva from the Torah to wear tzitzit on any four-cornered garment. Since most garments today are not four cornered, the generally accepted custom is to wear a special *tallit katan* all day long and a *tallit gadol* during Shaharit. This *berakha* is for the *tallit katan* (the *berakha* for *tallit gadol* can be found on page 15). If you are going to put on a *tallit gadol* later then do not say this *berakha* when you put on a *tallit katan*. There are various traditions in how we tie the four strings to form the tzitzit. The majority Ashkenazi practice is Rashi's method, which doubles the four strings over to make eight, and has five knots, which added together with the numerical value of the word **ציצית** (600) totals 613. This is the number of mitzvot in the Torah, and according to Rashi hints at the intended purpose of the tzitzit as specified in the Torah – a sign to remind us of the 613 mitzvot in the Torah (*Bemidbar* 15:39–40).

BLESSINGS OVER THE TORAH

In Judaism, study is greater even than prayer. So, before beginning to pray, we engage in a brief act of study, after saying the blessings. The blessings are followed by brief selections from Scripture, Mishna and Gemara, the three foundational texts of Judaism.

בָּרוּךְ Blessed are You, LORD our God, King of the Universe,
who has made us holy through His commandments,
and has commanded us to be involved
in the study of the words of Torah.
Please, LORD our God, make the words of Your Torah
sweet in our mouths and in the mouths of Your people,
the house of Israel,
so that we, our descendants (and their descendants)
and the descendants of Your people, the house of Israel,
may all know Your name and study Your Torah for its own sake.
Blessed are You, LORD, who teaches Torah to His people Israel.

בָּרוּךְ Blessed are You, LORD our God, King of the Universe,
who has chosen us from all the peoples and given us His Torah.
Blessed are You, LORD, Giver of the Torah.

LEARNING

There is a mitzva in the Torah to learn Torah every day. Like most other mitzvot, we make a *berakha* before performing this mitzva. Since learning Torah is a mitzva that we are charged with fulfilling all day every day, we say the *berakhot* first thing in the morning for all the Torah we will learn that day.

While the word "Torah" often refers to the Five Books of Moses, it is commonly used in its widest sense, to include the rest of Tanakh, as well as the written formulations of the Oral Torah – the Talmud (Mishna and Gemara), and beyond.

In order to avoid an interruption between saying these *berakhot* and fulfilling the mitzva of *talmud Torah*, we immediately learn representative excerpts of these three foundational texts of Judaism – Tanakh, Mishna, with Gemara following shortly thereafter.

...A THOUSAND WORDS

ברכות התורה

In Judaism, study is greater even than prayer. So, before beginning to pray, we engage in a brief act of study, after saying the blessings. The blessings are followed by brief selections from תנ״ך*,* משנה *and* גמרא*, the three foundational texts of Judaism.*

בָּרוּךְ אַתָּה יהוה אֱלֹהֵינוּ מֶלֶךְ הָעוֹלָם
אֲשֶׁר קִדְּשָׁנוּ בְּמִצְוֹתָיו וְצִוָּנוּ לַעֲסֹק בְּדִבְרֵי תוֹרָה.
וְהַעֲרֶב נָא יהוה אֱלֹהֵינוּ אֶת דִּבְרֵי תוֹרָתְךָ
בְּפִינוּ וּבְפִי עַמְּךָ בֵּית יִשְׂרָאֵל
וְנִהְיֶה אֲנַחְנוּ וְצֶאֱצָאֵינוּ (וְצֶאֱצָאֵי צֶאֱצָאֵינוּ)
וְצֶאֱצָאֵי עַמְּךָ בֵּית יִשְׂרָאֵל
כֻּלָּנוּ יוֹדְעֵי שְׁמֶךָ וְלוֹמְדֵי תוֹרָתֶךָ לִשְׁמָהּ.
בָּרוּךְ אַתָּה יהוה, הַמְלַמֵּד תּוֹרָה לְעַמּוֹ יִשְׂרָאֵל.

בָּרוּךְ אַתָּה יהוה אֱלֹהֵינוּ מֶלֶךְ הָעוֹלָם
אֲשֶׁר בָּחַר בָּנוּ מִכָּל הָעַמִּים, וְנָתַן לָנוּ אֶת תּוֹרָתוֹ.
בָּרוּךְ אַתָּה יהוה, נוֹתֵן הַתּוֹרָה.

REFLECTION

"Rabbi Yishmael would say: One who studies Torah in order to teach will be given the opportunity to both study and to teach. One who studies in order to practice will be given the opportunity to study, to teach, to observe, and to practice." (Avot 4:6)

Why do you learn Torah?

How many generations do you think have been learning the same Torah you are going to learn today? How does that make you feel? Are you going to learn it exactly the same way or differently from them? How?

CONNECTION

The great Rabbi Akiva was 40 years old before he had studied any Torah. He was once standing by a well and noticed a rock with a hole carved in it. He asked his fellow shepherds: Who carved the hole in the rock? They replied to him that it had been formed by the steady dripping of water from the well over many, many years. Rabbi Akiva realized that if the soft water can chisel a hole in the hard rock, then words of Torah that are hard as iron can certainly make an impression on my heart of flesh and blood! He dedicated his life to learning Torah from then on.

(Adapted from *Avot DeRabbi Natan* 6:2)

יְבָרֶכְךָ May the LORD bless you and protect you. *Num. 6*
May the LORD make His face shine on you and be generous to you.
May the LORD turn His face toward you and give you peace.

אֵלּוּ These are the things for which there is no fixed measure: *Mishna Pe'ah 1:1*
the mitzvah of the corner of the field, first-fruits,
appearing before the LORD [on festivals, with offerings],
acts of kindness and the study of Torah.

אֵלּוּ These are the things whose fruits we eat in this world *Shabbat 127a*
but whose full reward waits for us in the World to Come:
honoring parents; acts of kindness;
arriving early at the house of study morning and evening;
hospitality to strangers; visiting the sick;
helping the needy bride; attending to the dead;
devotion in prayer;
and bringing peace between people –
but the study of Torah is equal to them all.

---

against Ra'avad. In his defense the student expresses himself rashly, too outspoken in his critique of Ra'avad. Young boys are wont to speak in such a fashion. So I correct him and suggest more restrained tones. Another boy jumps up with a new idea. Rashba smiles gently. I try to analyze what the young boy meant. Another boy intervenes. Rabbeinu Tam is called upon to express his opinion, and suddenly a symposium of generations comes into existence. Young students debate earlier generations with an air of daring familiarity, and a crescendo of discussion ensues.

We enjoy each other's company, speak one language, and pursue one goal. All are committed to a common vision, and all operate with the same halakhic categories. A mesora collegiality is achieved. It is a friendship, a comradeship of young and old, spanning antiquity, the Middle Ages, and modern times.

This joining of the generations, this merger of identities will ultimately bring about the redemption of the Jewish People. It will fulfill the words of the last of the Hebrew prophets, Malakhi...

After a two- or three-hour shiur, the rebbe emerges from the chamber young and rejuvenated. He has defeated age. The students look exhausted. In the mesora experience, years play no role. Hands, however parchment-dry and wrinkled, embrace warm and supple hands in a commonality, bridging the gap which separates the generations.

(Rabbi J.B. Soloveitchik, *Reflections of the Rav*, Vol. 2)

יְבָרֶכְךָ יהוה וְיִשְׁמְרֶךָ: במדבר ו

יָאֵר יהוה פָּנָיו אֵלֶיךָ וִיחֻנֶּךָּ:

יִשָּׂא יהוה פָּנָיו אֵלֶיךָ וְיָשֵׂם לְךָ שָׁלוֹם:

אֵלּוּ דְבָרִים שֶׁאֵין לָהֶם שִׁעוּר משנה, פאה א:א

הַפֵּאָה וְהַבִּכּוּרִים וְהָרֵאָיוֹן, וּגְמִילוּת חֲסָדִים וְתַלְמוּד תּוֹרָה.

אֵלּוּ דְבָרִים שֶׁאָדָם אוֹכֵל פֵּרוֹתֵיהֶם בָּעוֹלָם הַזֶּה שבת קכז.

וְהַקֶּרֶן קַיֶּמֶת לוֹ לָעוֹלָם הַבָּא, וְאֵלּוּ הֵן

כִּבּוּד אָב וָאֵם, וּגְמִילוּת חֲסָדִים

וְהַשְׁכָּמַת בֵּית הַמִּדְרָשׁ שַׁחֲרִית וְעַרְבִית

וְהַכְנָסַת אוֹרְחִים, וּבִקּוּר חוֹלִים

וְהַכְנָסַת כַּלָּה, וּלְוָיַת הַמֵּת, וְעִיּוּן תְּפִלָּה

וַהֲבָאַת שָׁלוֹם בֵּין אָדָם לַחֲבֵרוֹ

וְתַלְמוּד תּוֹרָה כְּנֶגֶד כֻּלָּם.

CONNECTION

As I enter the classroom, I am filled with despair and pessimism. I always ask myself: Can there be a dialogue between an old teacher and young students, between a rebbe in his Indian summer and boys enjoying the spring of their lives? I start the shiur without knowing what the conclusion will be.

As I start the shiur, the door opens and another old man walks in and sits down. My students call me the Rav. He is older than the Rav. He is the grandfather of the Rav. His name is Rav Chaim of Brisk. Without his method of study, no shiur could be delivered nowadays. Then the door opens quietly again and another old man comes in. He is older than Rav Chaim because he lived in the seventeenth century. His name is Rav Shabbetai HaKohen, the famous Shakh.... Then more visitors show up, some from the eleventh, twelfth, or thirteenth centuries. Some even lived in antiquity. Among them are Rabbi Akiva, Rashi, Rabbeinu Tam, Ra'avad, and Rashba. More and more keep on coming in.

What do I do? I introduce them to my pupils, and the dialogue commences. Maimonides states a halakha, and Ra'avad disagrees sharply. At times Ra'avad utilizes harsh language against Maimonides. A boy jumps up to defend Maimonides

TALLIT

Some say the following paragraphs to prepare themselves before putting on the tallit.

בָּרְכִי נַפְשִׁי Bless the Lord, my soul. Lord, my God, You are very great, clothed in majesty and splendor, wrapped in a robe of light, spreading out the heavens like a tent. *Ps. 104*

Some say:

For the sake of the unification of the Holy One, blessed be He, and His Divine Presence, with fear and love, to unify the name *Yod-Heh* with *Vav-Heh* in perfect unity in the name of all Israel.

I am about to wrap myself in this tallit. So may my soul, my 248 limbs and 365 sinews be wrapped in the light of *hatzitzit* which amounts to 613 [commandments]. And just as I cover myself with a tallit in this world, so may I be worthy of rabbinical dress and a fine garment in the World to Come in the Garden of Eden. Through the commandment of tzitzit may my life's-breath, spirit, soul and prayer be saved from external obstacles, and may the tallit spread its wings over them like an eagle stirring up its nest, hovering over its young. May the commandment of tzitzit be considered before the Holy One, blessed be He, as if I had fulfilled it in all its specifics, details and intentions, as well as the 613 commandments dependent on it, Amen, Selah. *Deut. 32*

LEARNING

... A THOUSAND WORDS

The mitzva in the Torah to wear tzitzit on any four-cornered garment is mentioned in the third paragraph of the Shema.

The generally accepted custom is to wear a special *tallit katan* all day long; some people, such as married men, wear a *tallit gadol* during Shaḥarit.

In some communities (many Sephardic, and some Ashkenazic communities that follow the German custom) the custom is to wear a *tallit* from the age of Bar Mitzva (or even earlier). This *berakha* is for the *tallit gadol* (the *berakha* for *tallit katan* can be found on page 9). Those people who wear a *tallit gadol* do not say the *berakha* when putting on a *tallit katan*.

עטיפת טלית

Some say the following paragraphs to prepare themselves before putting on the טלית.

תהלים קד
בָּרְכִי נַפְשִׁי אֶת־יהוה, יהוה אֱלֹהַי גָּדַלְתָּ מְּאֹד, הוֹד וְהָדָר לָבָשְׁתָּ: עֹטֶה־אוֹר כַּשַּׂלְמָה, נוֹטֶה שָׁמַיִם כַּיְרִיעָה:

Some say:

לְשֵׁם יִחוּד קֻדְשָׁא בְּרִיךְ הוּא וּשְׁכִינְתֵּהּ בִּדְחִילוּ וּרְחִימוּ, לְיַחֵד שֵׁם י״ה בו״ה בְּיִחוּדָא שְׁלִים בְּשֵׁם כָּל יִשְׂרָאֵל.

הֲרֵינִי מִתְעַטֵּף בְּצִיצִית. כֵּן תִּתְעַטֵּף נִשְׁמָתִי וּרְמַ״ח אֵבָרַי וּשְׁסָ״ה גִידַי בְּאוֹר הַצִּיצִית הָעוֹלָה תַּרְיַ״ג. וּכְשֵׁם שֶׁאֲנִי מִתְכַּסֶּה בְטַלִּית בָּעוֹלָם הַזֶּה, כָּךְ אֶזְכֶּה לַחֲלוּקָא דְרַבָּנָן וּלְטַלִּית נָאָה לָעוֹלָם הַבָּא בְּגַן עֵדֶן. וְעַל יְדֵי מִצְוַת צִיצִית תִּנָּצֵל נַפְשִׁי רוּחִי וְנִשְׁמָתִי וּתְפִלָּתִי מִן הַחִיצוֹנִים. וְהַטַּלִּית תִּפְרֹשׂ כְּנָפֶיהָ עֲלֵיהֶם וְתַצִּילֵם,
דברים לב
כְּנֶשֶׁר יָעִיר קִנּוֹ, עַל גּוֹזָלָיו יְרַחֵף: וּתְהֵא חֲשׁוּבָה מִצְוַת צִיצִית לִפְנֵי הַקָּדוֹשׁ בָּרוּךְ הוּא, כְּאִלּוּ קִיַּמְתִּיהָ בְּכָל פְּרָטֶיהָ וְדִקְדּוּקֶיהָ וְכַוָּנוֹתֶיהָ וְתַרְיַ״ג מִצְוֹת הַתְּלוּיוֹת בָּהּ, אָמֵן סֶלָה.

LEARNING

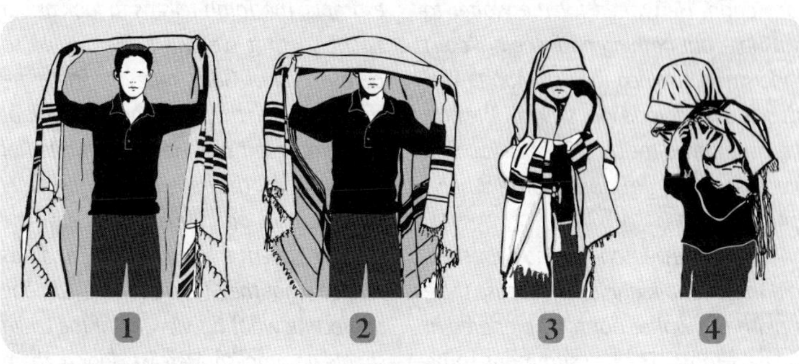

1 The tallit is held spread above one's head and the berakha is recited.

2 The tallit is placed upon one's head.

3 The tallit is rolled up upon one's shoulders.

4 The part of the tallit which has been rolled up is draped over one shoulder and held there for a short period.

Before wrapping oneself in the tallit, say:

בָּרוּךְ Blessed are You, Lord our God, King of the Universe, who has made us holy through His commandments, and has commanded us to wrap ourselves in tzitzit.

According to the Shela (R. Isaiah Horowitz), one should say these verses after wrapping oneself in the tallit:

מַה־יָּקָר How precious is Your loving-kindness, O God, *Ps. 36*
and the children of men find refuge
under the shadow of Your wings.
They are filled with the rich plenty of Your House.
You give them drink from Your river of delights.
For with You is the fountain of life;
in Your light, we see light.
Continue Your loving-kindness to those who know You,
and Your righteousness to the upright in heart.

---

conviction. He waited for the waiter to walk in – but nothing happened! "I don't understand it! When the rich man tinkled his bell, all that food was served!" The next day he returned the bell. "The bell you sold me is useless. I got no response when I rang it."

"The obvious reason nothing happened," said the Dubno Maggid, "is because there is neither a waiter nor food prepared in the next room. The bell summons something that is there to be summoned. Much preparation is necessary before the bell can accomplish anything."

"In some ways many of us are like this man," continued the Dubno Maggid. "For example, the Torah tells us to look at our tzitzit so that we will be reminded to perform all of God's mitzvot. There are many people, though, who can look at a pair of tzitzit and not be reminded of anything. All they see are strings. Only if one studies and understands how the tzitzit represent the 613 mitzvot, and has studied what the 613 mitzvot are, can one appreciate what his viewing of the tzitzit should accomplish. Merely to look at them without any preparation is like tinkling a bell without having arranged for anyone to respond."

(Rabbi Paysach Krohn, *Around the Maggid's Table*)

Before wrapping oneself in the טלית, say:

בָּרוּךְ אַתָּה יהוה אֱלֹהֵינוּ מֶלֶךְ הָעוֹלָם
אֲשֶׁר קִדְּשָׁנוּ בְּמִצְוֹתָיו
וְצִוָּנוּ לְהִתְעַטֵּף בַּצִּיצִית.

According to the Shela (R. Isaiah Horowitz), one should say these verses after wrapping oneself in the טלית:

תהלים לו

מַה־יָּקָר חַסְדְּךָ אֱלֹהִים
וּבְנֵי אָדָם בְּצֵל כְּנָפֶיךָ יֶחֱסָיוּן:
יִרְוְיֻן מִדֶּשֶׁן בֵּיתֶךָ
וְנַחַל עֲדָנֶיךָ תַשְׁקֵם:
כִּי־עִמְּךָ מְקוֹר חַיִּים
בְּאוֹרְךָ נִרְאֶה־אוֹר:
מְשֹׁךְ חַסְדְּךָ לְיֹדְעֶיךָ
וְצִדְקָתְךָ לְיִשְׁרֵי־לֵב:

CONNECTION

A certain poor fellow, Rabbi Yona, was invited to a meal at a wealthy man's house. When all the diners were finished with their portions, the rich man, who sat at the head of the table, tinkled a bell. Almost at once, waiters came in to remove the dishes and bring in the next course. Rabbi Yona was amazed. He had never seen anything like that before.

After the second course was completed, the host again tinkled the bell, and again the waiters removed the plates and brought in yet more food. Rabbi Yona was immensely impressed. When the meal was finally over, he went out to get such a bell for his home as well.

He ran home excitedly to his wife. "We're going to have unlimited food and waiters. Wait until you see what I brought home!" He immediately placed the bell on the table and told his family to take their regular seats. He then tinkled the bell with

TEFILLIN

Some say the following paragraphs to prepare themselves before putting on the tefillin.

For the sake of the unification of the Holy One, blessed be He, and His Divine Presence, with fear and love, to unify the name *Yod-Heh* with *Vav-Heh* in perfect unity in the name of all Israel.

By putting on the tefillin I hereby intend to fulfill the commandment of my Creator who commanded us to wear tefillin, as it is written in His Torah: "Bind them as a sign on your hand, and they shall be a symbol on the center of your head." *Deut. 6* They contain these four sections of the Torah: one beginning with *Shema* [Deut. 6:4–9]; another with *Vehaya im shamo'a* [ibid. 11:13–21]; the third with *Kadesh Li* [Ex. 13:1–10]; and the fourth with *Vehaya ki yevi'akha* [ibid. 13:11–16]. These declare the uniqueness and unity of God, blessed be His name in the world. They also remind us of the miracles and wonders which He did for us when He brought us out of Egypt, and that He has the power and the dominion over the highest and the lowest to deal with them as He pleases. He commanded us to place one of the tefillin on the arm in memory of His "outstretched arm" (of redemption), setting it opposite the heart, to force the desires and thoughts of our heart to His service, blessed be His name. The other is to be on the head, opposite the brain, so that my mind, whose seat is in the brain, together with my other senses and abilities, may be forced to His service, blessed be His name. May the spiritual influence of the commandment of the tefillin be with me so that I may have a long life, a flow of holiness, and sacred thoughts, free from any suggestion of sin or wrongdoing. May the evil inclination neither tempt nor provoke us, but leave us to serve the LORD, as it is in our hearts to do.

And may it be Your will, LORD our God and God of our ancestors, that the commandment of tefillin be considered before You as if I had fulfilled it in all its specifics, details and intentions, as well as the 613 commandments dependent on it, Amen, Selah.

The *tefillin shel yad* is placed on the arm that represents action, and the *tefillin shel rosh* is placed on the head that represents thought.

What are the differences between thought and action?

What thought are you going to have today that will lead you to action?

הנחת תפילין

Some say the following paragraphs to prepare themselves before putting on the תפילין.

לְשֵׁם יִחוּד קֻדְשָׁא בְּרִיךְ הוּא וּשְׁכִינְתֵּהּ בִּדְחִילוּ וּרְחִימוּ, לְיַחֵד שֵׁם י״ה בו״ה בְּיִחוּדָא שְׁלִים בְּשֵׁם כָּל יִשְׂרָאֵל.

הִנְנִי מְכַוֵּן בַּהֲנָחַת תְּפִלִּין לְקַיֵּם מִצְוַת בּוֹרְאִי, שֶׁצִּוָּנוּ לְהָנִיחַ
תְּפִלִּין, כַּכָּתוּב בְּתוֹרָתוֹ: וּקְשַׁרְתָּם לְאוֹת עַל־יָדֶךָ, וְהָיוּ לְטֹטָפֹת בֵּין דברים ו
עֵינֶיךָ: וְהֵן אַרְבַּע פָּרָשִׁיּוֹת אֵלּוּ, שְׁמַע, וְהָיָה אִם שָׁמֹעַ, קַדֶּשׁ לִי, וְהָיָה כִּי יְבִאֲךָ, שֶׁיֵּשׁ בָּהֶם יִחוּדוֹ וְאַחְדוּתוֹ יִתְבָּרַךְ שְׁמוֹ בָּעוֹלָם, וְשֶׁנִּזְכֹּר נִסִּים וְנִפְלָאוֹת שֶׁעָשָׂה עִמָּנוּ בְּהוֹצִיאוֹ אוֹתָנוּ מִמִּצְרַיִם, וַאֲשֶׁר לוֹ הַכֹּחַ וְהַמֶּמְשָׁלָה בָּעֶלְיוֹנִים וּבַתַּחְתּוֹנִים לַעֲשׂוֹת בָּהֶם כִּרְצוֹנוֹ. וְצִוָּנוּ לְהָנִיחַ עַל הַיָּד לְזִכְרוֹן זְרוֹעַ הַנְּטוּיָה, וְשֶׁהִיא נֶגֶד הַלֵּב, לְשַׁעְבֵּד בָּזֶה תַּאֲווֹת וּמַחְשְׁבוֹת לִבֵּנוּ לַעֲבוֹדָתוֹ יִתְבָּרַךְ שְׁמוֹ. וְעַל הָרֹאשׁ נֶגֶד הַמֹּחַ, שֶׁהַנְּשָׁמָה שֶׁבְּמֹחִי עִם שְׁאָר חוּשַׁי וְכֹחוֹתַי כֻּלָּם יִהְיוּ מְשֻׁעְבָּדִים לַעֲבוֹדָתוֹ, יִתְבָּרַךְ שְׁמוֹ. וּמִשֶּׁפַע מִצְוַת תְּפִלִּין יִתְמַשֵּׁךְ עָלַי לִהְיוֹת לִי חַיִּים אֲרוּכִים וְשֶׁפַע קֹדֶשׁ וּמַחֲשָׁבוֹת קְדוֹשׁוֹת בְּלִי הִרְהוּר חֵטְא וְעָוֹן כְּלָל, וְשֶׁלֹּא יְפַתֵּנוּ וְלֹא יִתְגָּרֶה בָּנוּ יֵצֶר הָרָע, וְיַנִּיחֵנוּ לַעֲבֹד אֶת יהוה כַּאֲשֶׁר עִם לְבָבֵנוּ.

וִיהִי רָצוֹן מִלְּפָנֶיךָ, יהוה אֱלֹהֵינוּ וֵאלֹהֵי אֲבוֹתֵינוּ, שֶׁתְּהֵא חֲשׁוּבָה מִצְוַת הֲנָחַת תְּפִלִּין לִפְנֵי הַקָּדוֹשׁ בָּרוּךְ הוּא, כְּאִלּוּ קִיַּמְתִּיהָ בְּכָל פְּרָטֶיהָ וְדִקְדּוּקֶיהָ וְכַוָּנוֹתֶיהָ וְתַרְיַ״ג מִצְוֹת הַתְּלוּיוֹת בָּהּ, אָמֵן סֶלָה.

REFLECTION

"God so loved Israel that He surrounded them with mitzvot. Tefillin on the arm and head, tzitzit on their clothes, and a mezuza on their door." (*Menaḥot* 43b)

Are there any other mitzvot you can think of that "surround us"?

What does it feel like to you to be surrounded by mitzvot?

Stand and place the hand-tefillin on the biceps of the left arm (or right arm if you are left-handed), angled toward the heart, and before tightening the strap, say:

בָּרוּךְ Blessed are You, Lord our God, King of the Universe, who has made us holy through His commandments, and has commanded us to put on tefillin.

Wrap the strap of the hand-tefillin seven times around the arm. Place the head-tefillin above the hairline, centered between the eyes, and say quietly:

בָּרוּךְ Blessed are You, Lord our God, King of the Universe, who has made us holy through His commandments, and has commanded us about the commandment of tefillin.

Adjust the head-tefillin and say:

בָּרוּךְ Blessed be the name of His glorious kingdom for ever and all time.

Some say:

From Your wisdom, God most high, give me [wisdom], and from Your understanding, give me understanding. May You increase Your loving-kindness upon me, and in Your might may my enemies and those who rise against me be subdued. Pour Your goodly oil on the seven branches of the menora so that Your good flows down upon Your creatures. You open Your hand, and satisfy every living thing with favor. *Ps. 145*

Wind the strap of the hand-tefillin three times around the middle finger, saying:

וְאֵרַשְׂתִּיךְ I will betroth you to Me for ever; I will betroth you to Me in righteousness and justice, loving-kindness and compassion; I will betroth you to Me in loyalty; and you shall know the Lord. *Hos. 2*

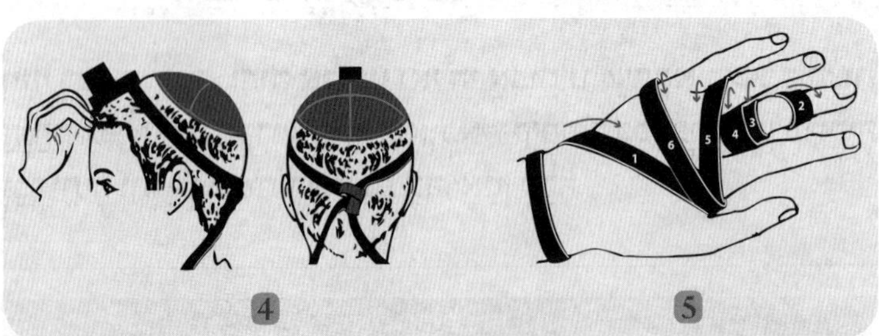

times. Without speaking, one places the *tefillin shel rosh* on the head above the hairline, centered over the nose, and says the blessing עַל מִצְוַת תְּפִלִּין. One then adjusts the straps, so that the knot rests at the base of the skull and the two straps hang down the front of one's chest, and says: בָּרוּךְ שֵׁם כְּבוֹד מַלְכוּתוֹ לְעוֹלָם וָעֶד. Finally, one wraps the strap of the *tefillin shel yad* around the fingers, while saying וְאֵרַשְׂתִּיךְ. (This diagram is based on the most common Ashkenazi practice.)

Stand and place the תפילין של יד *on the biceps of the left arm (or right arm if you are left-handed), angled toward the heart, and before tightening the strap, say:*

בָּרוּךְ אַתָּה יהוה אֱלֹהֵינוּ מֶלֶךְ הָעוֹלָם
אֲשֶׁר קִדְּשָׁנוּ בְּמִצְוֹתָיו, וְצִוָּנוּ לְהָנִיחַ תְּפִלִּין.

Wrap the strap of the תפילין של יד *seven times around the arm.*
Place the תפילין של ראש *above the hairline, centered between the eyes, and say quietly:*

בָּרוּךְ אַתָּה יהוה אֱלֹהֵינוּ מֶלֶךְ הָעוֹלָם
אֲשֶׁר קִדְּשָׁנוּ בְּמִצְוֹתָיו, וְצִוָּנוּ עַל מִצְוַת תְּפִלִּין.

Adjust the תפילין של ראש *and say:*

בָּרוּךְ שֵׁם כְּבוֹד מַלְכוּתוֹ לְעוֹלָם וָעֶד

Some say:

וּמֵחָכְמָתְךָ אֵל עֶלְיוֹן תַּאֲצִיל עָלַי, וּמִבִּינָתְךָ תְּבִינֵנִי, וּבְחַסְדְּךָ תַּגְדִּיל
עָלַי, וּבִגְבוּרָתְךָ תַּצְמִית אוֹיְבַי וְקָמַי. וְשֶׁמֶן הַטּוֹב תָּרִיק עַל שִׁבְעָה קְנֵי
הַמְּנוֹרָה, לְהַשְׁפִּיעַ טוּבְךָ לִבְרִיּוֹתֶיךָ. פּוֹתֵחַ אֶת־יָדֶךָ וּמַשְׂבִּיעַ לְכָל־חַי רָצוֹן: תהלים קמה

Wind the strap of the תפילין של יד *three times around the middle finger, saying:*

וְאֵרַשְׂתִּיךְ לִי לְעוֹלָם, וְאֵרַשְׂתִּיךְ לִי בְּצֶדֶק וּבְמִשְׁפָּט וּבְחֶסֶד הושע ב
וּבְרַחֲמִים: וְאֵרַשְׂתִּיךְ לִי בֶּאֱמוּנָה, וְיָדַעַתְּ אֶת־יהוה:

LEARNING

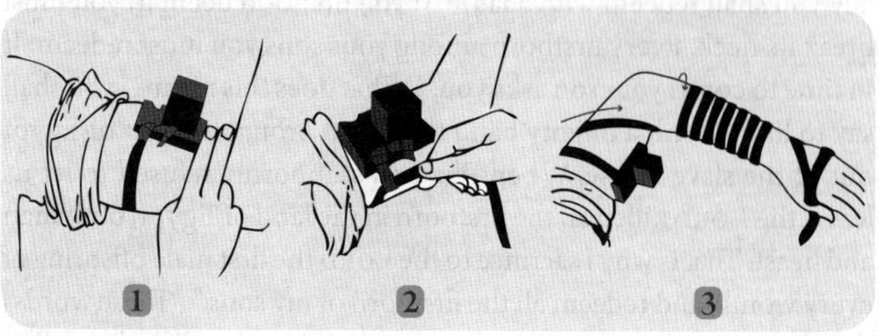

The *tefillin shel yad* is put on first, by placing the box on the biceps near the elbow joint, angled toward the heart, and saying the blessing לְהָנִיחַ תְּפִלִּין. Then one tightens the strap around the muscle and wraps the strap around the forearm seven

After putting on the tefillin, say the following:

וַיְדַבֵּר The Lord spoke to Moses, saying, "Make holy to Me every firstborn male. The first offspring of every womb among the Israelites, whether man or beast, belongs to Me." Then Moses said to the people, "Remember this day on which you left Egypt, the slave-house, when the Lord brought you out of it with a mighty hand. No leaven shall be eaten. You are leaving on this day, in the month of Aviv. When the Lord brings you into the land of the Canaanites, Hittites, Amorites, Hivites and Jebusites, the land He swore to your ancestors to give you, a land flowing with milk and honey, you are to observe this service in this same month. For seven days you shall eat unleavened bread, and make the seventh day a festival to the Lord. Unleavened bread shall be eaten throughout the seven days. No leavened bread may be seen in your possession, and no leaven shall be seen anywhere within your borders. On that day you shall tell your son, 'This is because of what the Lord did for me when I left Egypt.' [These words] shall also be a sign on your hand, and a reminder above your forehead, so that the Lord's Torah may always be in your mouth, because with a mighty hand the Lord brought you out of Egypt. You shall therefore keep this law at its appointed time from year to year." *Ex. 13*

וְהָיָה After the Lord has brought you into the land of the Canaanites, as He swore to you and your ancestors, and He has given it to you, you shall set apart for the Lord the first offspring of every womb. All the firstborn males of your cattle belong to the Lord. Every firstling donkey you shall redeem with a lamb. If you do not redeem it, you must break its neck. Every firstborn among your sons you must redeem. If, in time to come, your son asks you, "What does this mean?" you shall say to him, "With a mighty hand the Lord brought us out of Egypt, out of the slave-house. When Pharaoh stubbornly refused to let us leave, the Lord killed all the firstborn in the land of Egypt, both man and beast. That is why I sacrifice to the Lord the first male offspring of every womb, and redeem all the firstborn of my sons." [These words] shall be a sign on your hand and as a symbol above your forehead, that with a mighty hand the Lord brought us out of Egypt.

After putting on the תפילין*, say the following:*

שמות יג וַיְדַבֵּר יהוה אֶל־מֹשֶׁה לֵּאמֹר: קַדֶּשׁ־לִי כָל־בְּכוֹר, פֶּטֶר כָּל־רֶחֶם
בִּבְנֵי יִשְׂרָאֵל, בָּאָדָם וּבַבְּהֵמָה, לִי הוּא: וַיֹּאמֶר מֹשֶׁה אֶל־הָעָם,
זָכוֹר אֶת־הַיּוֹם הַזֶּה, אֲשֶׁר יְצָאתֶם מִמִּצְרַיִם מִבֵּית עֲבָדִים, כִּי
בְּחֹזֶק יָד הוֹצִיא יהוה אֶתְכֶם מִזֶּה, וְלֹא יֵאָכֵל חָמֵץ: הַיּוֹם אַתֶּם
יֹצְאִים, בְּחֹדֶשׁ הָאָבִיב: וְהָיָה כִי־יְבִיאֲךָ יהוה אֶל־אֶרֶץ הַכְּנַעֲנִי
וְהַחִתִּי וְהָאֱמֹרִי וְהַחִוִּי וְהַיְבוּסִי, אֲשֶׁר נִשְׁבַּע לַאֲבֹתֶיךָ לָתֶת לָךְ,
אֶרֶץ זָבַת חָלָב וּדְבָשׁ, וְעָבַדְתָּ אֶת־הָעֲבֹדָה הַזֹּאת בַּחֹדֶשׁ הַזֶּה:
שִׁבְעַת יָמִים תֹּאכַל מַצֹּת, וּבַיּוֹם הַשְּׁבִיעִי חַג לַיהוה: מַצּוֹת יֵאָכֵל
אֵת שִׁבְעַת הַיָּמִים, וְלֹא־יֵרָאֶה לְךָ חָמֵץ וְלֹא־יֵרָאֶה לְךָ שְׂאֹר,
בְּכָל־גְּבֻלֶךָ: וְהִגַּדְתָּ לְבִנְךָ בַּיּוֹם הַהוּא לֵאמֹר, בַּעֲבוּר זֶה עָשָׂה
יהוה לִי בְּצֵאתִי מִמִּצְרָיִם: וְהָיָה לְךָ לְאוֹת עַל־יָדְךָ וּלְזִכָּרוֹן בֵּין
עֵינֶיךָ, לְמַעַן תִּהְיֶה תּוֹרַת יהוה בְּפִיךָ, כִּי בְּיָד חֲזָקָה הוֹצִאֲךָ יהוה
מִמִּצְרָיִם: וְשָׁמַרְתָּ אֶת־הַחֻקָּה הַזֹּאת לְמוֹעֲדָהּ, מִיָּמִים יָמִימָה:

וְהָיָה כִּי־יְבִאֲךָ יהוה אֶל־אֶרֶץ הַכְּנַעֲנִי כַּאֲשֶׁר נִשְׁבַּע לְךָ וְלַאֲבֹתֶיךָ,
וּנְתָנָהּ לָךְ: וְהַעֲבַרְתָּ כָל־פֶּטֶר־רֶחֶם לַיהוה, וְכָל־פֶּטֶר שֶׁגֶר בְּהֵמָה
אֲשֶׁר יִהְיֶה לְךָ הַזְּכָרִים, לַיהוה: וְכָל־פֶּטֶר חֲמֹר תִּפְדֶּה בְשֶׂה, וְאִם־
לֹא תִפְדֶּה וַעֲרַפְתּוֹ, וְכֹל בְּכוֹר אָדָם בְּבָנֶיךָ תִּפְדֶּה: וְהָיָה כִּי־יִשְׁאָלְךָ
בִנְךָ מָחָר, לֵאמֹר מַה־זֹּאת, וְאָמַרְתָּ אֵלָיו, בְּחֹזֶק יָד הוֹצִיאָנוּ יהוה
מִמִּצְרַיִם מִבֵּית עֲבָדִים: וַיְהִי כִּי־הִקְשָׁה פַרְעֹה לְשַׁלְּחֵנוּ, וַיַּהֲרֹג
יהוה כָּל־בְּכוֹר בְּאֶרֶץ מִצְרַיִם, מִבְּכֹר אָדָם וְעַד־בְּכוֹר בְּהֵמָה, עַל־
כֵּן אֲנִי זֹבֵחַ לַיהוה כָּל־פֶּטֶר רֶחֶם הַזְּכָרִים, וְכָל־בְּכוֹר בָּנַי אֶפְדֶּה:
וְהָיָה לְאוֹת עַל־יָדְכָה וּלְטוֹטָפֹת בֵּין עֵינֶיךָ, כִּי בְּחֹזֶק יָד הוֹצִיאָנוּ
יהוה מִמִּצְרָיִם:

PREPARATION FOR PRAYER

On entering the synagogue:

HOW GOODLY are your tents, Jacob *Num. 24*
your dwelling places, Israel.
As for me, in Your great loving-kindness, *Ps. 5*
I will come into Your House.
I will bow down to Your holy Temple in awe of You.
LORD, I love the habitation of Your House, *Ps. 26*
the place where Your glory is present.

As for me, I will bow in worship;
I will bend the knee before the LORD my Maker.

As for me, may my prayer come to You, LORD, *Ps. 69*
at a time of favor.
God, in Your great loving-kindness,
answer me with Your faithful salvation.

REFLECTION

What makes a building a Jewish building?

If you were building a "Jewish building" what would it look like?

Can you design a building with values? How?

…A THOUSAND WORDS

הכנה לתפילה

On entering the בית כנסת:

במדבר כד
מַה־טֹּבוּ אֹהָלֶיךָ יַעֲקֹב
מִשְׁכְּנֹתֶיךָ יִשְׂרָאֵל:

תהלים ה
וַאֲנִי בְּרֹב חַסְדְּךָ אָבוֹא בֵיתֶךָ
אֶשְׁתַּחֲוֶה אֶל־הֵיכַל־קָדְשְׁךָ, בְּיִרְאָתֶךָ:

תהלים כו
יהוה אָהַבְתִּי מְעוֹן בֵּיתֶךָ
וּמְקוֹם מִשְׁכַּן כְּבוֹדֶךָ:

וַאֲנִי אֶשְׁתַּחֲוֶה
וְאֶכְרָעָה, אֶבְרְכָה לִפְנֵי יהוה עֹשִׂי.

תהלים סט
וַאֲנִי תְפִלָּתִי־לְךָ יהוה
עֵת רָצוֹן, אֱלֹהִים בְּרָב־חַסְדֶּךָ
עֲנֵנִי בֶּאֱמֶת יִשְׁעֶךָ:

LEARNING

This *tefilla* is known as "*Ma Tovu*" after the first and most famous of the verses from it. This verse (*Bemidbar* 24:5) is the climax of the story of the non-Jewish prophet Balaam, who, at the behest of Balak the king of Moab, attempted to curse the Children of Israel. Instead, however, these beautiful words of praise and blessing were uttered: "How goodly are your tents Jacob, your dwelling places, Israel." This *tefilla* is not really one single prayer but rather a collection of verses from Tanakh. They are all appropriately themed to inspire us and prepare us for entering the synagogue and begin our *tefilla*. They generally speak about Jewish buildings, including the *Beit HaMikdash*, and about worshiping Hashem.

Lord of the universe,

who reigned before the birth of any thing –
When by His will all things were made
then was His name declared King.
And when all things shall cease to be
He alone will reign in awe.
He was, He is, and He shall be
glorious for evermore.
He is One, there is none else,
alone, unique, beyond compare;
Without beginning, without end,
His might, His rule are everywhere.
He is my God; my Redeemer lives.
He is the Rock on whom I rely –
My banner and my safe retreat,
my cup, my portion when I cry.
Into His hand my soul I place,
when I awake and when I sleep.
The Lord is with me, I shall not fear;
body and soul from harm will He keep.

CONNECTION

"And you?" Rebbe Levi-Yitzḥak of Berditchev was asked. "What did you discover at the Great Maggid's school?" – "I discovered that God exists, that He is of this world, of all worlds." – "But, Rebbe, everybody knows that!" – "No," answered the illustrious Rebbe of Berditchev. "They say it everywhere, but in Mezeritch they know it."

(Elie Wiesel, *Souls on Fire*)

... A THOUSAND WORDS

Do you think God exists or do you know He exists? How can you go from just saying it to knowing it?

אֲדוֹן עוֹלָם

אֲשֶׁר מָלַךְ בְּטֶרֶם כָּל־יְצִיר נִבְרָא.

לְעֵת נַעֲשָׂה בְחֶפְצוֹ כֹּל אֲזַי מֶלֶךְ שְׁמוֹ נִקְרָא.

וְאַחֲרֵי כִּכְלוֹת הַכֹּל לְבַדּוֹ יִמְלֹךְ נוֹרָא.

וְהוּא הָיָה וְהוּא הֹוֶה וְהוּא יִהְיֶה בְּתִפְאָרָה.

וְהוּא אֶחָד וְאֵין שֵׁנִי לְהַמְשִׁיל לוֹ לְהַחְבִּירָה.

בְּלִי רֵאשִׁית בְּלִי תַכְלִית וְלוֹ הָעֹז וְהַמִּשְׂרָה.

וְהוּא אֵלִי וְחַי גּוֹאֲלִי וְצוּר חֶבְלִי בְּעֵת צָרָה.

וְהוּא נִסִּי וּמָנוֹס לִי מְנָת כּוֹסִי בְּיוֹם אֶקְרָא.

בְּיָדוֹ אַפְקִיד רוּחִי בְּעֵת אִישַׁן וְאָעִירָה.

וְעִם רוּחִי גְּוִיָּתִי יהוה לִי וְלֹא אִירָא.

LEARNING

Adon Olam is a poem written in the Middle Ages summarizing various statements of Jewish faith. These include:

- God is the creator of the universe.
- God is sovereign of the universe.
- God is eternal.
- God is one indivisible unity.
- God is infinite and limitless.
- God is a personal God active in one's individual life.

REFLECTION

Where can you see evidence that God created the world?

Where can you see evidence that God rules the world?

Where can you see evidence that God plays a role in your life?

GREAT

is the living God and praised.
He exists, and His existence is beyond time.

He is One, and there is no unity like His.
Unfathomable, His oneness is infinite.

He has neither bodily form nor substance;
His holiness is beyond compare.

He preceded all that was created.
He was first: there was no beginning to His beginning.

Behold He is Master of the Universe; and every creature
shows His greatness and majesty.

The rich flow of His prophecy He gave
to His treasured people in whom He gloried.

---

3. Belief in God's incorporeality
4. Belief in God's eternity
5. Belief that God alone should be the object of worship
6. Belief in revelation through God's prophets
7. Belief in the preeminence of Moses among the prophets
8. Belief that the Torah that we have today is the one dictated to Moses by God
9. Belief that the Torah given by Moses will not be replaced and that nothing may be added to or removed from it
10. Belief in God's awareness of all human actions and thoughts
11. Belief in the reward of good and punishment of evil
12. Belief in the coming of the Messiah
13. Belief in the resurrection of the dead

REFLECTION

What do you have to believe in to be a good Jew?

What is the source of your faith?

Now that we no longer have prophecy, where do you go to listen to God?

What do you think the world will look like during the messianic age? How would you like it to look?

יִגְדַּל

אֱלֹהִים חַי וְיִשְׁתַּבַּח
נִמְצָא וְאֵין עֵת אֶל מְצִיאוּתוֹ.

אֶחָד וְאֵין יָחִיד כְּיִחוּדוֹ
נֶעְלָם וְגַם אֵין סוֹף לְאַחְדּוּתוֹ.

אֵין לוֹ דְּמוּת הַגּוּף וְאֵינוֹ גוּף
לֹא נַעֲרֹךְ אֵלָיו קְדֻשָּׁתוֹ.

קַדְמוֹן לְכָל דָּבָר אֲשֶׁר נִבְרָא
רִאשׁוֹן וְאֵין רֵאשִׁית לְרֵאשִׁיתוֹ.

הִנּוֹ אֲדוֹן עוֹלָם
וְכָל נוֹצָר יוֹרֶה גְדֻלָּתוֹ וּמַלְכוּתוֹ.

שֶׁפַע נְבוּאָתוֹ נְתָנוֹ
אֶל־אַנְשֵׁי סְגֻלָּתוֹ וְתִפְאַרְתּוֹ.

LEARNING

Yigdal, believed to be written by Rabbi Yehuda ben Daniel in the fourteenth century, is a poem based on Rambam's Thirteen Principles of Faith. Rambam (Maimonides) is perhaps the most famous Jewish philosopher-halakhist of medieval times. Born in Spain in 1135, he fled Muslim persecution in Spain and settled in Egypt where he became physician to the sultan, making him the most prominent doctor in the land. He died in 1204 and was buried in Tiberias, where his grave can still be visited today.

While some of Rambam's formulations have generated controversy, his enumeration of the 13 core principles of the Jewish faith has nevertheless been widely accepted. These are:

1. Belief in the existence of God
2. Belief in God's unity and indivisibility into elements

Never in Israel has there arisen another like Moses,
a prophet who beheld God's image.

God gave His people a Torah of truth
by the hand of His prophet, most faithful of His House.

God will not alter or change His law
for any other, for eternity.

He sees and knows our secret thoughts;
as soon as something is begun, He foresees its end.

He rewards people with loving-kindness according to their deeds;
He punishes the wicked according to his wickedness.

At the end of days He will send our Messiah
to redeem those who await His final salvation.

God will revive the dead in His great loving-kindness.
Blessed for evermore is His glorious name!

Akiva], "How do you know this?" and he replied, "This is the law given to Moses at Sinai"; and his strength returned.

(*Menahot* 29b)

We believe in the truth of Moses' prophecy. But Moses himself believed in the truth of Rabbi Akiva and his interpretation of the Torah. Judaism is all about the transmission of tradition.

לֹא קָם בְּיִשְׂרָאֵל כְּמֹשֶׁה
עוֹד נָבִיא וּמַבִּיט אֶת תְּמוּנָתוֹ.

תּוֹרַת אֱמֶת נָתַן לְעַמּוֹ אֵל
עַל יַד נְבִיאוֹ נֶאֱמַן בֵּיתוֹ.

לֹא יַחֲלִיף הָאֵל וְלֹא יָמִיר דָּתוֹ
לְעוֹלָמִים לְזוּלָתוֹ.

צוֹפֶה וְיוֹדֵעַ סְתָרֵינוּ
מַבִּיט לְסוֹף דָּבָר בְּקַדְמָתוֹ.

גּוֹמֵל לְאִישׁ חֶסֶד כְּמִפְעָלוֹ
נוֹתֵן לְרָשָׁע רָע כְּרִשְׁעָתוֹ.

יִשְׁלַח לְקֵץ יָמִין מְשִׁיחֵנוּ
לִפְדּוֹת מְחַכֵּי קֵץ יְשׁוּעָתוֹ.

מֵתִים יְחַיֶּה אֵל בְּרֹב חַסְדּוֹ
בָּרוּךְ עֲדֵי עַד שֵׁם תְּהִלָּתוֹ.

CONNECTION

When Moses reached heaven he found the Holy One, blessed be He, fixing tiny crowns to the letters of the Sefer Torah. Moses asked God, "Lord of the Universe, what compels You to do this?" God replied, "There will one day be a man, at the end of many generations, Akiva ben Yosef will be his name, who will deduce heaps and heaps of laws from every tiny point [of every crown of every letter]." "Lord of the Universe," Moses said, "let me see this man." God replied, "Turn around." Moses went and sat eight rows back [and listened to the discussion in the beit midrash of Rabbi Akiva]. But he was not able to follow and became faint because of it. Until they came to discuss a certain subject and the students asked [Rabbi

MORNING BLESSINGS

The following blessings are said aloud by the Leader, but each individual should say them quietly as well. It is our custom to say them standing.

בָּרוּךְ Blessed are You, Lord our God,
King of the Universe,
who gives the heart understanding
to distinguish day from night.

Blessed are You, Lord our God,
King of the Universe,
who has not made me a gentile.

Blessed are You, Lord our God,
King of the Universe,
who has not made me a slave.

CONNECTION

Have you ever wondered why God designed it that humans need sleep? Why did He create us to require a sleep mode?

We've all had one of those days: you oversleep because your alarm clock fails to wake you. As you stumble out of bed, you stub your toe. You hobble to the bathroom to find it occupied by your sister, who seems to have no concept of time. You finally make it downstairs to discover there is no milk left for your cereal, it is raining, and now you've missed the bus. In school it just gets worse: in the rush this morning you forgot your homework, your teacher yells at you and it's only 9 a.m.! On a day when everything seems to go wrong and everything just seems miserable, how are you going to feel better?

Often, just the simple magic of a good night's sleep will help. Sleep mode, shutting everything off, somehow makes us feel better when we wake up the next morning. The creation of night and sleep and the ability to separate between each day is a gift; every day can offer us a fresh start.

LEARNING

טוֹב לְהֹדוֹת לַיהוה, וּלְזַמֵּר לְשִׁמְךָ עֶלְיוֹן. לְהַגִּיד בַּבֹּקֶר חַסְדֶּךָ, וֶאֱמוּנָתְךָ בַּלֵּילוֹת

"It is good to give thanks to the Lord, and to sing to Your name, Most High, to relate Your kindness in the morning, and Your trustworthiness in the evening." (*Tehillim* 92:2)

Rashi explains that the day represents good times, light, clarity – we can clearly see God's kindness and it is easy to be thankful. Night represents hard times, darkness, when we cannot see God. It is during these times that we need to trust and have faith that all will be good eventually.

ברכות השחר

The following blessings are said aloud by the שליח ציבור*, but each individual should say them quietly as well. It is our custom to say them standing.*

בָּרוּךְ אַתָּה יהוה אֱלֹהֵינוּ מֶלֶךְ הָעוֹלָם
אֲשֶׁר נָתַן לַשֶּׂכְוִי בִינָה
לְהַבְחִין בֵּין יוֹם וּבֵין לָיְלָה.

בָּרוּךְ אַתָּה יהוה אֱלֹהֵינוּ מֶלֶךְ הָעוֹלָם
שֶׁלֹּא עָשַׂנִי גּוֹי.

בָּרוּךְ אַתָּה יהוה אֱלֹהֵינוּ מֶלֶךְ הָעוֹלָם
שֶׁלֹּא עָשַׂנִי עָבֶד.

REFLECTION

"It is a common experience that a problem difficult at night is resolved in the morning after the committee of sleep has worked on it."
(John Steinbeck)

Have you ever lost a night's sleep? How did it make you feel?

Why do people say "It will feel better in the morning"?

Notice the blessings that are written in the negative. What situations are you grateful not to be in?

... A THOUSAND WORDS

Blessed are You, Lord our God,
King of the Universe,
men: who has not made me a woman.
women: who has made me according to His will.

Blessed are You, Lord our God,
King of the Universe,
who gives sight to the blind.

Blessed are You, Lord our God,
King of the Universe,
who clothes the naked.

CONNECTION

A group of American schoolchildren was asked to list what they thought were the present "Seven Wonders of the World." Though there were some disagreements, the following received the most votes: Egypt's Great Pyramids, the Taj Mahal, the Grand Canyon, the Panama Canal, the Empire State Building, St. Peter's Basilica, and the Great Wall of China.

While gathering the votes, the teacher noted that one student had not finished her paper yet. So she asked the girl if she was having trouble with her list. The little girl replied, "Yes, a little. I couldn't quite make up my mind because there are so many." The teacher said, "Well, tell us what you have, and maybe we can help." The girl hesitated, then read, "I think the 'Seven Wonders of the World' are:

To see
To hear
To touch
To taste
To feel
To laugh
To love."

The room was so quiet you could hear a pin drop. The things we overlook as simple and ordinary and that we take for granted are truly wondrous. A gentle reminder – that the most precious things in life cannot be built by hand or bought by man.

בָּרוּךְ אַתָּה יהוה אֱלֹהֵינוּ מֶלֶךְ הָעוֹלָם
men שֶׁלֹּא עָשַׂנִי אִשָּׁה.
women שֶׁעָשַׂנִי כִּרְצוֹנוֹ.

בָּרוּךְ אַתָּה יהוה אֱלֹהֵינוּ מֶלֶךְ הָעוֹלָם
פּוֹקֵחַ עִוְרִים.

בָּרוּךְ אַתָּה יהוה אֱלֹהֵינוּ מֶלֶךְ הָעוֹלָם
מַלְבִּישׁ עֲרֻמִּים.

... A THOUSAND WORDS

REFLECTION

What is the most beautiful thing you have ever seen?

In what areas of your life would you like to ask God for more clarity?

Clothes show people who we are: what do your clothes say about you?

LEARNING

וַיִּפְקַח אֱלֹהִים אֶת עֵינֶיהָ וַתֵּרֶא בְּאֵר מָיִם

"And God opened her eyes and she saw a well of water."
(*Bereshit* 21:19)

Seforno explains that Hagar was not blind; rather God widened Hagar's perspective and gave her the ability to "see" that which she could not previously see. God allowed her to recognize where she was and what she needed to see.

Blessed are You, LORD our God,
King of the Universe,
who sets captives free.

Blessed are You, LORD our God,
King of the Universe,
who raises those bowed down.

...A THOUSAND WORDS

This is the bowing stage of development, where we bend ourselves in an attempt to destroy the problematic elements within us.

However, teaches Rav Kook, subjugation and self-negation are only preparatory stages of development. "The goal is to shine with the light of God, with an abundance of strength and joy. Then, all of the powers of the soul straighten up and endure with much courage and an elevated and lofty life force." First we bow, but then we straighten up.

בָּרוּךְ אַתָּה יהוה אֱלֹהֵינוּ מֶלֶךְ הָעוֹלָם
מַתִּיר אֲסוּרִים.

בָּרוּךְ אַתָּה יהוה אֱלֹהֵינוּ מֶלֶךְ הָעוֹלָם
זוֹקֵף כְּפוּפִים.

CONNECTION

A little boy once found a cocoon of a butterfly. One day a small opening appeared. He sat and watched for hours as the butterfly struggled to squeeze itself out through the tiny hole. Then it stopped, as if it could go no further. The little boy decided to help the poor butterfly. He took a tiny pair of scissors and snipped off the remaining bit of the cocoon. The butterfly emerged easily but it had a swollen body and shriveled wings. The boy waited, expecting that any minute the wings would expand to support the butterfly. Nothing happened. The butterfly spent the rest of its life dragging its swollen body around; it was never able to fly.

In his haste and kindness to help the butterfly, the little boy failed to understand that the struggle that the butterfly had to go through to push through the small hole in the cocoon was nature's way of forcing the extra fluid from its body and strengthening its wings.

Only by struggling through the hole would the butterfly be ready for flight.

Sometimes struggles are exactly what we need in our lives. If we did not struggle, we would not have the strength to fly.

REFLECTION

Have you ever felt unable to move physically or emotionally?

How do you want God to support you?

Do you have any areas in your life that make you feel trapped?

LEARNING

Rav Kook (*Siddur Olat Re'iya*, vol. 1): Bowing and straightening up are a metaphor for two stages of personal development. People begin with all sorts of negative forces they need to weed out, suppress, and destroy. This is difficult work that demands a lot of subjugation – of one's ego, and of negative inner forces in general.

Blessed are You, LORD our God,
King of the Universe,
who spreads the earth above the waters.

Blessed are You, LORD our God,
King of the Universe,
who has provided me with all I need.

Blessed are You, LORD our God,
King of the Universe,
who makes firm the steps of man.

CONNECTION

One night I dreamed a dream.
As I was walking along the beach with the LORD.
Across the dark sky flashed scenes from my life.
For each scene, I noticed two sets of footprints in the sand,
One belonging to me and one to the LORD.
After the last scene of my life flashed before me,
I looked back at the footprints in the sand.
I noticed that at many times along the path of my life,
especially at the very lowest and saddest times,
there was only one set of footprints.
This really troubled me,
so I asked the LORD about it.
"LORD, You said once I decided to follow You,
You'd walk with me all the way.
But I noticed that during the saddest and most troublesome times of my life,
there was only one set of footprints.
I don't understand why, when I needed You the most, You would leave me."
He whispered,
"My precious child, I love you and will never leave you.
Never, ever, during your trials and testings.
When you saw only one set of footprints,
It was then that I carried you."

בָּרוּךְ אַתָּה יהוה אֱלֹהֵינוּ מֶלֶךְ הָעוֹלָם
רוֹקַע הָאָרֶץ עַל הַמָּיִם.

בָּרוּךְ אַתָּה יהוה אֱלֹהֵינוּ מֶלֶךְ הָעוֹלָם
שֶׁעָשָׂה לִי כָּל צְרָכִי.

בָּרוּךְ אַתָּה יהוה אֱלֹהֵינוּ מֶלֶךְ הָעוֹלָם
הַמֵּכִין מִצְעֲדֵי גָבֶר.

REFLECTION

Have you ever seen a flood or witnessed water overflowing its boundaries? What boundaries do you have in your life that you are careful not to cross?

What is lacking in your life and what do you need to ask God for?

How is God guiding your steps? What path are you going to choose today?

... A THOUSAND WORDS

LEARNING

The Gemara (*Bava Batra* 17a) explains that three people lived as if they were in the World to Come. This is proven by the use of the word כָּל in describing them. The word כָּל is all-encompassing, it includes all things. Avraham, Yitzḥak, and Yaakov were all blessed with the perception that they possessed all they could possibly need. This perception and appreciation allows a person to live in a state of tranquil bliss, as if already in *Olam HaBa*. Are you able to look at your life and see how much you have rather than how much you are lacking?

Blessed are You, LORD our God,
King of the Universe,
who binds Israel with strength.

Blessed are You, LORD our God,
King of the Universe,
who crowns Israel with glory.

Blessed are You, LORD our God,
King of the Universe,
who gives strength to the tired.

LEARNING

"The tefillin *serve as a sign of dignity. The word* 'tiferet' (*used in reference to the* tefillin) *indicates that it is an item that elevates us from our natural state into a Godly dignity. All items described with the word* 'tiferet' *serve a similar purpose; the garments of the Kohen in the Temple, the Temple itself,* and tefillin. *The sages say that the* tefillin *are the glory of the Jewish People because wearing them shows that we are with Hashem and inheritors of His Torah."* (*HaKtav VeHaKabbala Shemot* 13:14)

REFLECTION

Are you tired today? What makes you most tired?

Aside from lack of sleep, what else makes you tired? Why?

Can you think of ways to help yourself be really awake today?

CONNECTION

In 1992 Derek Redmond was favored to win a medal in the Olympic 400-meter sprint. After a lightning start, about 150 meters in, Redmond felt a searing pain; in agony he fell to the ground with a torn hamstring. Not willing to give up, determined to finish the race, he continued, half running, half hopping along the track, tears of agony and exertion pouring down his face.

Breaking through security, a man came to Derek's side. It was his father. "You don't have to do this," he told him. "Yes, I do," Derek cried. "Well then, we are going to finish this together."

Arm in arm, leaning heavily on his father, Derek limped, sobbing, along the track. Together, father and son continued. Just before the finish line, Derek's father let him go to complete his race, receiving a standing ovation from a crowd of over 65,000.

בָּרוּךְ אַתָּה יהוה אֱלֹהֵינוּ מֶלֶךְ הָעוֹלָם
אוֹזֵר יִשְׂרָאֵל בִּגְבוּרָה.

בָּרוּךְ אַתָּה יהוה אֱלֹהֵינוּ מֶלֶךְ הָעוֹלָם
עוֹטֵר יִשְׂרָאֵל בְּתִפְאָרָה.

בָּרוּךְ אַתָּה יהוה אֱלֹהֵינוּ מֶלֶךְ הָעוֹלָם
הַנּוֹתֵן לַיָּעֵף כֹּחַ.

... A THOUSAND WORDS

REFLECTION

"Who is strong? He who conquers his evil inclination."
(*Pirkei Avot* 4:1)

What is your greatest strength?

When have you shown strength? When have the Jewish People shown strength? What do the Jewish People need strength for?

How do you behave with dignity?

How can the Jewish People show dignity and glory?

CONNECTION

The Jewish People's strength is a unique strength. It is a strength that is manifest not through the conquering of others, by overpowering them or destroying them; rather, it is a strength that comes from the ability of man to conquer himself. This is a strength of the divine soul, the ability of man to conquer his physicality and his base desires, which is thousands of times greater than the strength to take over a city.

This is the strength that girds the Jewish People, the foundation of pure morality and the pinnacle of man that raises him above the animals.

(Rav Kook, *Olat Re'iya*)

בָּרוּךְ Blessed are You, LORD our God, King of the Universe,
who removes sleep from my eyes and slumber from my eyelids.
And may it be Your will, LORD our God
and God of our ancestors, to accustom us to Your Torah,
and make us attached to Your commandments.
Lead us not into error,
sin, wrongdoing, temptation or disgrace.
Do not let the evil instinct dominate us.
Keep us far from a bad person and a bad friend.
Help us attach ourselves to the good instinct and to good deeds
and bend our instincts to be subservient to You.
Give us, this day and every day, grace, loving-kindness
and compassion in Your eyes
and in the eyes of all who see us,
and act with loving-kindness toward us.
Blessed are You, LORD,
who acts with loving-kindness toward His people Israel.

יְהִי רָצוֹן May it be Your will, LORD my God and God of my ancestors,
to save me today and every day, from the arrogant and from arrogance itself, *Berakhot 16b*
from a bad person, a bad friend, a bad neighbor,
a bad mishap, a destructive enemy,
a harsh trial and a harsh opponent,
whether or not he is a son of the covenant.

LEARNING

"A person should get up like a lion in the morning to serve his Creator."
(*Shulḥan Arukh* 1:1)

The *Mishna Berura* expands: if your *yetzer hara* entices you to stay in bed you must strengthen yourself against it and not listen. You must say, "If I were needed to serve a human king, how enthusiastic and excited would I be to get up early to prepare for this service? How much more so for the King of kings – God Himself."

בָּרוּךְ אַתָּה יהוה אֱלֹהֵינוּ מֶלֶךְ הָעוֹלָם
הַמַּעֲבִיר שֵׁנָה מֵעֵינַי וּתְנוּמָה מֵעַפְעַפָּי.
וִיהִי רָצוֹן מִלְּפָנֶיךָ יהוה אֱלֹהֵינוּ וֵאלֹהֵי אֲבוֹתֵינוּ
שֶׁתַּרְגִּילֵנוּ בְּתוֹרָתֶךָ
וְדַבְּקֵנוּ בְּמִצְוֹתֶיךָ
וְאַל תְּבִיאֵנוּ לֹא לִידֵי חֵטְא
וְלֹא לִידֵי עֲבֵרָה וְעָוֹן
וְלֹא לִידֵי נִסָּיוֹן וְלֹא לִידֵי בִזָּיוֹן
וְאַל תַּשְׁלֶט בָּנוּ יֵצֶר הָרָע
וְהַרְחִיקֵנוּ מֵאָדָם רָע וּמֵחָבֵר רָע
וְדַבְּקֵנוּ בְּיֵצֶר הַטּוֹב וּבְמַעֲשִׂים טוֹבִים
וְכֹף אֶת יִצְרֵנוּ לְהִשְׁתַּעְבֶּד לָךְ
וּתְנֵנוּ הַיּוֹם וּבְכָל יוֹם לְחֵן וּלְחֶסֶד וּלְרַחֲמִים
בְּעֵינֶיךָ, וּבְעֵינֵי כָל רוֹאֵינוּ
וְתִגְמְלֵנוּ חֲסָדִים טוֹבִים.
בָּרוּךְ אַתָּה יהוה
גּוֹמֵל חֲסָדִים טוֹבִים לְעַמּוֹ יִשְׂרָאֵל.

יְהִי רָצוֹן מִלְּפָנֶיךָ יהוה אֱלֹהַי וֵאלֹהֵי אֲבוֹתַי ברכות טז:
שֶׁתַּצִּילֵנִי הַיּוֹם וּבְכָל יוֹם מֵעַזֵּי פָנִים וּמֵעַזּוּת פָּנִים
מֵאָדָם רָע, וּמֵחָבֵר רָע, וּמִשָּׁכֵן רָע
וּמִפֶּגַע רָע, וּמִשָּׂטָן הַמַּשְׁחִית
מִדִּין קָשֶׁה, וּמִבַּעַל דִּין קָשֶׁה
בֵּין שֶׁהוּא בֶן בְּרִית וּבֵין שֶׁאֵינוֹ בֶן בְּרִית.

THE BINDING OF ISAAC

On the basis of Jewish mystical tradition, some have the custom of saying daily the biblical passage describing the Binding of Isaac, the trial of faith in which Abraham demonstrated his love of God above all other loves.

Our God and God of our ancestors, remember us with a favorable memory, and recall us with a remembrance of salvation and compassion from the highest of high heavens. Remember, LORD our God, on our behalf, the love of the ancients, Abraham, Isaac and Yisrael Your servants; the covenant, the loving-kindness, and the oath You swore to Abraham our father on Mount Moriah, and the Binding, when he bound Isaac his son on the altar, as is written in Your Torah:

It happened after these things that God tested Abraham. He said to him, "Abraham!" "Here I am," he replied. He said, "Take your son, your only son, Isaac, whom you love, and go to the land of Moriah and offer him there as a burnt-offering on one of the mountains which I shall say to you." Early the next morning Abraham rose and saddled his donkey and took his two lads with him, and Isaac his son, and he cut wood for the burnt-offering, and he set out for the place of which God had told him. On the third day Abraham looked up and saw the place from afar. Abraham said to his lads, "Stay here with the donkey while I and the boy go on ahead. We will worship and we will return to you." Abraham took the wood for the burnt-offering and placed it on Isaac his son, and he took in his hand the fire and the knife, and the two of them went together. Isaac said to Abraham his father, "Father?" and he said "Here I am, my son." And he said, "Here are the fire and the wood, but where is the sheep for the burnt-offering?" Abraham said, "God will see to the sheep for the burnt-offering, my son." And the two of them went together. They came to the place God had told him about, *Gen. 22*

פרשת העקדה

On the basis of Jewish mystical tradition, some have the custom of saying daily the biblical passage describing the Binding of Isaac, the trial of faith in which Abraham demonstrated his love of God above all other loves.

אֱלֹהֵינוּ וֵאלֹהֵי אֲבוֹתֵינוּ, זׇכְרֵנוּ בְּזִכָּרוֹן טוֹב לְפָנֶיךָ, וּפׇקְדֵנוּ בִּפְקֻדַּת יְשׁוּעָה וְרַחֲמִים מִשְּׁמֵי שְׁמֵי קֶדֶם, וּזְכׇר לָנוּ יהוה אֱלֹהֵינוּ, אַהֲבַת הַקַּדְמוֹנִים אַבְרָהָם יִצְחָק וְיִשְׂרָאֵל עֲבָדֶיךָ, אֶת הַבְּרִית וְאֶת הַחֶסֶד וְאֶת הַשְּׁבוּעָה שֶׁנִּשְׁבַּעְתָּ לְאַבְרָהָם אָבִינוּ בְּהַר הַמּוֹרִיָּה, וְאֶת הָעֲקֵדָה שֶׁעָקַד אֶת יִצְחָק בְּנוֹ עַל גַּבֵּי הַמִּזְבֵּחַ, כַּכָּתוּב בְּתוֹרָתֶךָ:

וַיְהִי אַחַר הַדְּבָרִים הָאֵלֶּה, וְהָאֱלֹהִים נִסָּה אֶת־אַבְרָהָם, בראשית כב
וַיֹּאמֶר אֵלָיו אַבְרָהָם, וַיֹּאמֶר הִנֵּנִי: וַיֹּאמֶר קַח־נָא אֶת־בִּנְךָ
אֶת־יְחִידְךָ אֲשֶׁר־אָהַבְתָּ, אֶת־יִצְחָק, וְלֶךְ־לְךָ אֶל־אֶרֶץ
הַמֹּרִיָּה, וְהַעֲלֵהוּ שָׁם לְעֹלָה עַל אַחַד הֶהָרִים אֲשֶׁר אֹמַר
אֵלֶיךָ: וַיַּשְׁכֵּם אַבְרָהָם בַּבֹּקֶר, וַיַּחֲבֹשׁ אֶת־חֲמֹרוֹ, וַיִּקַּח אֶת־
שְׁנֵי נְעָרָיו אִתּוֹ וְאֵת יִצְחָק בְּנוֹ, וַיְבַקַּע עֲצֵי עֹלָה, וַיָּקׇם וַיֵּלֶךְ
אֶל־הַמָּקוֹם אֲשֶׁר־אָמַר־לוֹ הָאֱלֹהִים: בַּיּוֹם הַשְּׁלִישִׁי וַיִּשָּׂא
אַבְרָהָם אֶת־עֵינָיו וַיַּרְא אֶת־הַמָּקוֹם מֵרָחֹק: וַיֹּאמֶר אַבְרָהָם
אֶל־נְעָרָיו, שְׁבוּ־לָכֶם פֹּה עִם־הַחֲמוֹר, וַאֲנִי וְהַנַּעַר נֵלְכָה עַד־
כֹּה, וְנִשְׁתַּחֲוֶה וְנָשׁוּבָה אֲלֵיכֶם: וַיִּקַּח אַבְרָהָם אֶת־עֲצֵי הָעֹלָה
וַיָּשֶׂם עַל־יִצְחָק בְּנוֹ, וַיִּקַּח בְּיָדוֹ אֶת־הָאֵשׁ וְאֶת־הַמַּאֲכֶלֶת,
וַיֵּלְכוּ שְׁנֵיהֶם יַחְדָּו: וַיֹּאמֶר יִצְחָק אֶל־אַבְרָהָם אָבִיו, וַיֹּאמֶר
אָבִי, וַיֹּאמֶר הִנֶּנִּי בְנִי, וַיֹּאמֶר, הִנֵּה הָאֵשׁ וְהָעֵצִים, וְאַיֵּה
הַשֶּׂה לְעֹלָה: וַיֹּאמֶר אַבְרָהָם, אֱלֹהִים יִרְאֶה־לּוֹ הַשֶּׂה לְעֹלָה,
בְּנִי, וַיֵּלְכוּ שְׁנֵיהֶם יַחְדָּו: וַיָּבֹאוּ אֶל־הַמָּקוֹם אֲשֶׁר אָמַר־לוֹ

and Abraham built there an altar and arranged the wood and bound Isaac his son and laid him on the altar on top of the wood. He reached out his hand and took the knife to slay his son. Then an angel of the LORD called out to him from heaven, "Abraham! Abraham!" He said, "Here I am." He said, "Do not reach out your hand against the boy; do not do anything to him, for now I know that you fear God, because you have not held back your son, your only son, from Me." Abraham looked up and there he saw a ram caught in a thicket by its horns, and Abraham went and took the ram and offered it as a burnt-offering instead of his son. Abraham called that place "The LORD will see," as is said to this day, "On the mountain of the LORD He will be seen." The angel of the LORD called to Abraham a second time from heaven, and said, "By Myself I swear, declares the LORD, that because you have done this and have not held back your son, your only son, I will greatly bless you and greatly multiply your descendants, as the stars of heaven and the sand of the seashore, and your descendants shall take possession of the gates of their enemies. Through your descendants, all the nations of the earth will be blessed, because you have listened to My voice." Then Abraham returned to his lads, and they rose and went together to Beersheba, and Abraham stayed in Beersheba.

Master of the Universe, just as Abraham our father suppressed his compassion to do Your will wholeheartedly, so may Your compassion suppress Your anger from us and may Your compassion prevail over Your other attributes. Deal with us, LORD our God, with the attributes of loving-kindness and compassion, and in Your great goodness may Your anger be turned away from Your people, Your city, Your land and Your inheritance. Fulfill in us, LORD our God, the promise You made in Your Torah through the hand of Moses Your servant, as it is said: "I will remember My covenant with Jacob, *Lev. 26*
and also My covenant with Isaac, and also My covenant with Abraham I will remember, and the land I will remember."

הָאֱלֹהִים, וַיִּבֶן שָׁם אַבְרָהָם אֶת־הַמִּזְבֵּחַ וַיַּעֲרֹךְ אֶת־הָעֵצִים, וַיַּעֲקֹד אֶת־יִצְחָק בְּנוֹ, וַיָּשֶׂם אֹתוֹ עַל־הַמִּזְבֵּחַ מִמַּעַל לָעֵצִים: וַיִּשְׁלַח אַבְרָהָם אֶת־יָדוֹ, וַיִּקַּח אֶת־הַמַּאֲכֶלֶת, לִשְׁחֹט אֶת־בְּנוֹ: וַיִּקְרָא אֵלָיו מַלְאַךְ יהוה מִן־הַשָּׁמַיִם, וַיֹּאמֶר אַבְרָהָם אַבְרָהָם, וַיֹּאמֶר הִנֵּנִי: וַיֹּאמֶר אַל־תִּשְׁלַח יָדְךָ אֶל־הַנַּעַר, וְאַל־תַּעַשׂ לוֹ מְאוּמָה, כִּי עַתָּה יָדַעְתִּי כִּי־יְרֵא אֱלֹהִים אַתָּה, וְלֹא חָשַׂכְתָּ אֶת־בִּנְךָ אֶת־יְחִידְךָ מִמֶּנִּי: וַיִּשָּׂא אַבְרָהָם אֶת־עֵינָיו, וַיַּרְא וְהִנֵּה־אַיִל, אַחַר נֶאֱחַז בַּסְּבַךְ בְּקַרְנָיו, וַיֵּלֶךְ אַבְרָהָם וַיִּקַּח אֶת־הָאַיִל, וַיַּעֲלֵהוּ לְעֹלָה תַּחַת בְּנוֹ: וַיִּקְרָא אַבְרָהָם שֵׁם־הַמָּקוֹם הַהוּא יהוה יִרְאֶה, אֲשֶׁר יֵאָמֵר הַיּוֹם בְּהַר יהוה יֵרָאֶה: וַיִּקְרָא מַלְאַךְ יהוה אֶל־אַבְרָהָם שֵׁנִית מִן־הַשָּׁמָיִם: וַיֹּאמֶר, בִּי נִשְׁבַּעְתִּי נְאֻם־יהוה, כִּי יַעַן אֲשֶׁר עָשִׂיתָ אֶת־הַדָּבָר הַזֶּה, וְלֹא חָשַׂכְתָּ אֶת־בִּנְךָ אֶת־יְחִידֶךָ: כִּי־בָרֵךְ אֲבָרֶכְךָ, וְהַרְבָּה אַרְבֶּה אֶת־זַרְעֲךָ כְּכוֹכְבֵי הַשָּׁמַיִם, וְכַחוֹל אֲשֶׁר עַל־שְׂפַת הַיָּם, וְיִרַשׁ זַרְעֲךָ אֵת שַׁעַר אֹיְבָיו: וְהִתְבָּרְכוּ בְזַרְעֲךָ כֹּל גּוֹיֵי הָאָרֶץ, עֵקֶב אֲשֶׁר שָׁמַעְתָּ בְּקֹלִי: וַיָּשָׁב אַבְרָהָם אֶל־נְעָרָיו, וַיָּקֻמוּ וַיֵּלְכוּ יַחְדָּו אֶל־בְּאֵר שָׁבַע, וַיֵּשֶׁב אַבְרָהָם בִּבְאֵר שָׁבַע:

רִבּוֹנוֹ שֶׁל עוֹלָם, כְּמוֹ שֶׁכָּבַשׁ אַבְרָהָם אָבִינוּ אֶת רַחֲמָיו לַעֲשׂוֹת רְצוֹנְךָ בְּלֵבָב שָׁלֵם, כֵּן יִכְבְּשׁוּ רַחֲמֶיךָ אֶת כַּעַסְךָ מֵעָלֵינוּ וְיִגֹּלּוּ רַחֲמֶיךָ עַל מִדּוֹתֶיךָ. וְתִתְנַהֵג עִמָּנוּ יהוה אֱלֹהֵינוּ בְּמִדַּת הַחֶסֶד וּבְמִדַּת הָרַחֲמִים, וּבְטוּבְךָ הַגָּדוֹל יָשׁוּב חֲרוֹן אַפְּךָ מֵעַמְּךָ וּמֵעִירְךָ וּמֵאַרְצְךָ וּמִנַּחֲלָתֶךָ. וְקַיֶּם לָנוּ יהוה אֱלֹהֵינוּ אֶת הַדָּבָר שֶׁהִבְטַחְתָּנוּ בְּתוֹרָתֶךָ עַל יְדֵי מֹשֶׁה עַבְדֶּךָ, כָּאָמוּר: וְזָכַרְתִּי אֶת־בְּרִיתִי יַעֲקוֹב וְאַף אֶת־בְּרִיתִי יִצְחָק, וְאַף אֶת־בְּרִיתִי אַבְרָהָם אֶזְכֹּר, וְהָאָרֶץ אֶזְכֹּר: ויקרא כו

ACCEPTING THE SOVEREIGNTY OF HEAVEN

לְעוֹלָם A person should always be God-fearing, privately and publicly, acknowledging the truth and speaking it in his heart. He should rise early and say: *Tanna DeVei Eliyahu, ch. 21*

Master of all worlds,
not because of our righteousness *Dan. 9*
do we lay our pleas before You,
but because of Your great compassion.

What are we? What are our lives?
What is our loving-kindness?
What is our righteousness?
What is our salvation?
What is our strength? What is our might?
What shall we say before You,
LORD our God and God of our ancestors?
Are not all the mighty like nothing before You,
the men of fame as if they had never been,
the wise as if they know nothing,
and the understanding as if they lack intelligence?
For their many works are in vain,
and the days of their lives like a fleeting breath before You.
The pre-eminence of man over the animals is nothing, *Eccl. 3*
for all is but a fleeting breath.

אֲבָל Yet we are Your people, the children of Your covenant,
the children of Abraham, Your beloved,
to whom You made a promise on Mount Moriah;
the offspring of Isaac his only one who was bound on the altar;
the congregation of Jacob Your firstborn son
whom – because of the love with which You loved him
and the joy with which You rejoiced in him –
You called Yisrael and Yeshurun.

קבלת עול מלכות שמים

לְעוֹלָם יְהֵא אָדָם יְרֵא שָׁמַיִם בְּסֵתֶר וּבְגָלוּי
וּמוֹדֶה עַל הָאֱמֶת, וְדוֹבֵר אֱמֶת בִּלְבָבוֹ
וְיַשְׁכֵּם וְיֹאמַר

תנא דבי אליהו, פרק כא

רִבּוֹן כָּל הָעוֹלָמִים
לֹא עַל־צִדְקוֹתֵינוּ אֲנַחְנוּ מַפִּילִים תַּחֲנוּנֵינוּ לְפָנֶיךָ
כִּי עַל־רַחֲמֶיךָ הָרַבִּים:

דניאל ט

מָה אָנוּ, מֶה חַיֵּינוּ
מֶה חַסְדֵּנוּ, מַה צִּדְקוֹתֵינוּ
מַה יְּשׁוּעָתֵנוּ, מַה כֹּחֵנוּ, מַה גְּבוּרָתֵנוּ
מַה נֹּאמַר לְפָנֶיךָ, יהוה אֱלֹהֵינוּ וֵאלֹהֵי אֲבוֹתֵינוּ
הֲלֹא כָּל הַגִּבּוֹרִים כְּאַיִן לְפָנֶיךָ
וְאַנְשֵׁי הַשֵּׁם כְּלֹא הָיוּ
וַחֲכָמִים כִּבְלִי מַדָּע, וּנְבוֹנִים כִּבְלִי הַשְׂכֵּל
כִּי רֹב מַעֲשֵׂיהֶם תֹּהוּ, וִימֵי חַיֵּיהֶם הֶבֶל לְפָנֶיךָ
וּמוֹתַר הָאָדָם מִן־הַבְּהֵמָה אָיִן
כִּי הַכֹּל הָבֶל:

קהלת ג

אֲבָל אֲנַחְנוּ עַמְּךָ בְּנֵי בְרִיתֶךָ
בְּנֵי אַבְרָהָם אֹהַבְךָ שֶׁנִּשְׁבַּעְתָּ לּוֹ בְּהַר הַמּוֹרִיָּה
זֶרַע יִצְחָק יְחִידוֹ שֶׁנֶּעֱקַד עַל גַּבֵּי הַמִּזְבֵּחַ
עֲדַת יַעֲקֹב בִּנְךָ בְּכוֹרֶךָ
שֶׁמֵּאַהֲבָתְךָ שֶׁאָהַבְתָּ אוֹתוֹ, וּמִשִּׂמְחָתְךָ שֶׁשָּׂמַחְתָּ בּוֹ
קָרָאתָ אֶת שְׁמוֹ יִשְׂרָאֵל וִישֻׁרוּן.

לְפִיכָךְ Therefore it is our duty
to thank You, and to praise, glorify, bless, sanctify
and give praise and thanks to Your name.
Happy are we, how good is our portion,
how lovely our fate, how beautiful our heritage.

▸ Happy are we who, early and late,
evening and morning,
say twice each day –

Listen, Israel: the LORD is our God, the LORD is One. *Deut. 6*

Quietly: Blessed be the name of His glorious kingdom for ever and all time.

Some congregations say the entire first paragraph of the Shema (below) at this point. If there is a concern that the Shema will not be recited within the prescribed time, then all three paragraphs should be said.

Love the LORD your God with all your heart, with all your soul, and with all your might. These words which I command you today shall be on your heart. Teach them repeatedly to your children, speaking of them when you sit at home and when you travel on the way, when you lie down and when you rise. Bind them as a sign on your hand, and they shall be a symbol between your eyes. Write them on the doorposts of your house and gates.

אַתָּה הוּא It was You who existed
before the world was created,
it is You now that the world has been created.
It is You in this world
and You in the World to Come.
▸ Sanctify Your name
through those who sanctify Your name,
and sanctify Your name
throughout Your world.
By Your salvation may our pride be elevated;
raise high our pride.
Blessed are You, LORD,
who sanctifies His name among the multitudes.

לְפִיכָךְ אֲנַחְנוּ חַיָּבִים
לְהוֹדוֹת לְךָ וּלְשַׁבֵּחֲךָ וּלְפָאֶרְךָ
וּלְבָרֵךְ וּלְקַדֵּשׁ וְלָתֵת שֶׁבַח וְהוֹדָיָה לִשְׁמֶךָ.
אַשְׁרֵינוּ, מַה טּוֹב חֶלְקֵנוּ
וּמַה נָּעִים גּוֹרָלֵנוּ, וּמַה יָּפָה יְרֻשָּׁתֵנוּ.

◂ אַשְׁרֵינוּ, שֶׁאֲנַחְנוּ מַשְׁכִּימִים וּמַעֲרִיבִים עֶרֶב וָבֹקֶר
וְאוֹמְרִים פַּעֲמַיִם בְּכָל יוֹם

דברים ו

שְׁמַע יִשְׂרָאֵל, יהוה אֱלֹהֵינוּ, יהוה אֶחָד:

Quietly בָּרוּךְ שֵׁם כְּבוֹד מַלְכוּתוֹ לְעוֹלָם וָעֶד.

Some congregations say the entire first paragraph of the שמע *(below) at this point. If there is a concern that the* שמע *will not be recited within the prescribed time, then all three paragraphs should be said.*

וְאָהַבְתָּ אֵת יהוה אֱלֹהֶיךָ, בְּכָל־לְבָבְךָ, וּבְכָל־נַפְשְׁךָ, וּבְכָל־מְאֹדֶךָ: וְהָיוּ הַדְּבָרִים הָאֵלֶּה, אֲשֶׁר אָנֹכִי מְצַוְּךָ הַיּוֹם, עַל־לְבָבֶךָ: וְשִׁנַּנְתָּם לְבָנֶיךָ, וְדִבַּרְתָּ בָּם, בְּשִׁבְתְּךָ בְּבֵיתֶךָ, וּבְלֶכְתְּךָ בַדֶּרֶךְ, וּבְשָׁכְבְּךָ וּבְקוּמֶךָ: וּקְשַׁרְתָּם לְאוֹת עַל־יָדֶךָ וְהָיוּ לְטֹטָפֹת בֵּין עֵינֶיךָ: וּכְתַבְתָּם עַל־מְזֻזוֹת בֵּיתֶךָ וּבִשְׁעָרֶיךָ:

אַתָּה הוּא עַד שֶׁלֹּא נִבְרָא הָעוֹלָם
אַתָּה הוּא מִשֶּׁנִּבְרָא הָעוֹלָם.
אַתָּה הוּא בָּעוֹלָם הַזֶּה
וְאַתָּה הוּא לָעוֹלָם הַבָּא.
◂ קַדֵּשׁ אֶת שִׁמְךָ עַל מַקְדִּישֵׁי שְׁמֶךָ
וְקַדֵּשׁ אֶת שִׁמְךָ בְּעוֹלָמֶךָ
וּבִישׁוּעָתְךָ תָּרוּם וְתַגְבִּיהַּ קַרְנֵנוּ.
בָּרוּךְ אַתָּה יהוה, הַמְקַדֵּשׁ אֶת שִׁמְךָ בָּרַבִּים.

אַתָּה הוּא You are the LORD our God
in heaven and on earth,
and in the highest heaven of heavens.
Truly, You are the first
and You are the last,
and besides You there is no god.
Gather those who hope in You
from the four quarters of the earth.
May all mankind recognize and know
that You alone are God
over all the kingdoms on earth.

You made the heavens and the earth,
the sea and all they contain.
Who among all the works of Your hands,
above and below,
can tell You what to do?

Heavenly Father,
deal kindly with us
for the sake of Your great name
by which we are called,
and fulfill for us,
LORD our God,
that which is written:

"At that time I will bring you home, *Zeph. 3*
and at that time I will gather you,
for I will give you fame and praise
among all the peoples of the earth
when I bring back your exiles
before your eyes,
says the LORD."

אַתָּה הוּא יהוה אֱלֹהֵינוּ
בַּשָּׁמַיִם וּבָאָרֶץ
וּבִשְׁמֵי הַשָּׁמַיִם הָעֶלְיוֹנִים.
אֱמֶת, אַתָּה הוּא רִאשׁוֹן
וְאַתָּה הוּא אַחֲרוֹן
וּמִבַּלְעָדֶיךָ אֵין אֱלֹהִים.
קַבֵּץ קוֶֹיךָ מֵאַרְבַּע כַּנְפוֹת הָאָרֶץ.
יַכִּירוּ וְיֵדְעוּ כָּל בָּאֵי עוֹלָם
כִּי אַתָּה הוּא הָאֱלֹהִים לְבַדְּךָ לְכֹל מַמְלְכוֹת הָאָרֶץ.

אַתָּה עָשִׂיתָ אֶת הַשָּׁמַיִם וְאֶת הָאָרֶץ
אֶת הַיָּם וְאֶת כָּל אֲשֶׁר בָּם
וּמִי בְּכָל מַעֲשֵׂי יָדֶיךָ בָּעֶלְיוֹנִים אוֹ בַתַּחְתּוֹנִים
שֶׁיֹּאמַר לְךָ מַה תַּעֲשֶׂה.

אָבִינוּ שֶׁבַּשָּׁמַיִם
עֲשֵׂה עִמָּנוּ חֶסֶד
בַּעֲבוּר שִׁמְךָ הַגָּדוֹל שֶׁנִּקְרָא עָלֵינוּ
וְקַיֶּם לָנוּ יהוה אֱלֹהֵינוּ
מַה שֶּׁכָּתוּב:

בָּעֵת הַהִיא אָבִיא אֶתְכֶם, וּבָעֵת קַבְּצִי אֶתְכֶם צפניה ג
כִּי־אֶתֵּן אֶתְכֶם לְשֵׁם וְלִתְהִלָּה בְּכֹל עַמֵּי הָאָרֶץ
בְּשׁוּבִי אֶת־שְׁבוּתֵיכֶם לְעֵינֵיכֶם
אָמַר יהוה:

OFFERINGS

The sages held that, in the absence of the Temple, studying the laws of sacrifices is the equivalent of offering them. Hence the following texts. There are different customs as to how many passages are to be said, and one should follow the custom of one's congregation. The minimum requirement is to say the verses relating to The Daily Sacrifice on the next page.

THE BASIN

The Lord spoke to Moses, saying: Make a bronze basin, with its bronze stand for washing, and place it between the Tent of Meeting and the altar, and put water in it. From it, Aaron and his sons are to wash their hands and feet. When they enter the Tent of Meeting, they shall wash with water so that they will not die; likewise when they approach the altar to minister, presenting a fire-offering to the Lord. They must wash their hands and feet so that they will not die. This shall be an everlasting ordinance for Aaron and his descendants throughout their generations. *Ex. 30*

TAKING OF THE ASHES

The Lord spoke to Moses, saying: Instruct Aaron and his sons, saying, This is the law of the burnt-offering. The burnt-offering shall remain on the altar hearth throughout the night until morning, and the altar fire shall be kept burning on it. The priest shall then put on his linen garments, and linen breeches next to his body, and shall remove the ashes of the burnt-offering that the fire has consumed on the altar and place them beside the altar. Then he shall take off these clothes and put on others, and carry the ashes outside the camp to a clean place. The fire on the altar must be kept burning; it must not go out. Each morning the priest shall burn wood on it, and prepare on it the burnt-offering and burn the fat of the peace-offerings. A perpetual fire must be kept burning on the altar; it must not go out. *Lev. 6*

May it be Your will, Lord our God and God of our ancestors, that You have compassion on us and pardon us all our sins, grant atonement for all our iniquities and forgive all our transgressions. May You rebuild the Temple swiftly in our days so that we may offer You the continual-offering that it may atone for us as You have prescribed for us in Your Torah through Moses Your servant, from the mouthpiece of Your glory, as it is said:

סדר הקרבנות

חז״ל held that, in the absence of the Temple, studying the laws of sacrifices is the equivalent of offering them. Hence the following texts. There are different customs as to how many passages are to be said, and one should follow the custom of one's congregation. The minimum requirement is to say the verses relating to the קרבן תמיד *on the next page.*

פרשת הכיור

וַיְדַבֵּר יהוה אֶל־מֹשֶׁה לֵּאמֹר: וְעָשִׂיתָ כִּיּוֹר נְחֹשֶׁת וְכַנּוֹ נְחֹשֶׁת לְרָחְצָה, שמות ל
וְנָתַתָּ אֹתוֹ בֵּין־אֹהֶל מוֹעֵד וּבֵין הַמִּזְבֵּחַ, וְנָתַתָּ שָׁמָּה מָיִם: וְרָחֲצוּ אַהֲרֹן
וּבָנָיו מִמֶּנּוּ אֶת־יְדֵיהֶם וְאֶת־רַגְלֵיהֶם: בְּבֹאָם אֶל־אֹהֶל מוֹעֵד יִרְחֲצוּ־
מַיִם, וְלֹא יָמֻתוּ, אוֹ בְגִשְׁתָּם אֶל־הַמִּזְבֵּחַ לְשָׁרֵת, לְהַקְטִיר אִשֶּׁה לַיהוה:
וְרָחֲצוּ יְדֵיהֶם וְרַגְלֵיהֶם וְלֹא יָמֻתוּ, וְהָיְתָה לָהֶם חָק־עוֹלָם, לוֹ וּלְזַרְעוֹ
לְדֹרֹתָם:

פרשת תרומת הדשן

וַיְדַבֵּר יהוה אֶל־מֹשֶׁה לֵּאמֹר: צַו אֶת־אַהֲרֹן וְאֶת־בָּנָיו לֵאמֹר, זֹאת ויקרא ו
תּוֹרַת הָעֹלָה, הִוא הָעֹלָה עַל מוֹקְדָה עַל־הַמִּזְבֵּחַ כָּל־הַלַּיְלָה עַד־
הַבֹּקֶר, וְאֵשׁ הַמִּזְבֵּחַ תּוּקַד בּוֹ: וְלָבַשׁ הַכֹּהֵן מִדּוֹ בַד, וּמִכְנְסֵי־בַד יִלְבַּשׁ
עַל־בְּשָׂרוֹ, וְהֵרִים אֶת־הַדֶּשֶׁן אֲשֶׁר תֹּאכַל הָאֵשׁ אֶת־הָעֹלָה, עַל־
הַמִּזְבֵּחַ, וְשָׂמוֹ אֵצֶל הַמִּזְבֵּחַ: וּפָשַׁט אֶת־בְּגָדָיו, וְלָבַשׁ בְּגָדִים אֲחֵרִים,
וְהוֹצִיא אֶת־הַדֶּשֶׁן אֶל־מִחוּץ לַמַּחֲנֶה, אֶל־מָקוֹם טָהוֹר: וְהָאֵשׁ עַל־
הַמִּזְבֵּחַ תּוּקַד־בּוֹ, לֹא תִכְבֶּה, וּבִעֵר עָלֶיהָ הַכֹּהֵן עֵצִים בַּבֹּקֶר בַּבֹּקֶר,
וְעָרַךְ עָלֶיהָ הָעֹלָה, וְהִקְטִיר עָלֶיהָ חֶלְבֵי הַשְּׁלָמִים: אֵשׁ, תָּמִיד תּוּקַד
עַל־הַמִּזְבֵּחַ, לֹא תִכְבֶּה:

יְהִי רָצוֹן מִלְּפָנֶיךָ יהוה אֱלֹהֵינוּ וֵאלֹהֵי אֲבוֹתֵינוּ, שֶׁתְּרַחֵם עָלֵינוּ, וְתִמְחֹל לָנוּ עַל כָּל
חַטֹּאתֵינוּ וּתְכַפֵּר לָנוּ עַל כָּל עֲוֹנוֹתֵינוּ וְתִסְלַח לָנוּ עַל כָּל פְּשָׁעֵינוּ, וְתִבְנֶה בֵּית הַמִּקְדָּשׁ
בִּמְהֵרָה בְיָמֵינוּ, וְנַקְרִיב לְפָנֶיךָ קָרְבַּן הַתָּמִיד שֶׁיְּכַפֵּר בַּעֲדֵנוּ, כְּמוֹ שֶׁכָּתַבְתָּ עָלֵינוּ בְּתוֹרָתֶךָ
עַל יְדֵי מֹשֶׁה עַבְדֶּךָ מִפִּי כְבוֹדֶךָ, כָּאָמוּר

THE DAILY SACRIFICE

וַיְדַבֵּר The Lord said to Moses, "Command the Israelites and tell them: 'Be careful to offer to Me at the appointed time My food-offering consumed by fire, as an aroma pleasing to Me.' Tell them: 'This is the fire-offering you shall offer to the Lord – two lambs a year old without blemish, as a regular burnt-offering each day. Prepare one lamb in the morning and the other toward evening, together with a meal-offering of a tenth of an ephah of fine flour mixed with a quarter of a hin of oil from pressed olives. This is the regular burnt-offering instituted at Mount Sinai as a pleasing aroma, a fire-offering made to the Lord. Its libation is to be a quarter of a hin [of wine] with each lamb, poured in the Sanctuary as a libation of strong drink to the Lord. Prepare the second lamb in the afternoon, along with the same meal-offering and libation as in the morning. This is a fire-offering, an aroma pleasing to the Lord.'" *Num. 28*

CONNECTION

*The Gemara (*Sota 49b*) recalls that when the Greek army besieged Jerusalem, the Kohanim would lower a purse full of money over the walls, and the Greeks, in return, sent over two lambs for the* korban tamid *sacrifices. One day an evil elderly man saw this and said to the Greeks, "As long as the Jews continue to offer the* korban tamid *sacrifice, you will never defeat them!" The next day, as usual, the Kohanim lowered a bag full of money over the wall in anticipation of a lamb for their* korban. *In return, instead of a lamb, the Greeks sent a pig. From that day on, the* korban tamid *could no longer be brought and soon thereafter the Temple was destroyed.*

... A THOUSAND WORDS

פרשת קרבן התמיד

במדבר כח

וַיְדַבֵּר יהוה אֶל־מֹשֶׁה לֵּאמֹר: צַו אֶת־בְּנֵי יִשְׂרָאֵל וְאָמַרְתָּ אֲלֵהֶם, אֶת־קׇרְבָּנִי לַחְמִי לְאִשַּׁי, רֵיחַ נִיחֹחִי, תִּשְׁמְרוּ לְהַקְרִיב לִי בְּמוֹעֲדוֹ: וְאָמַרְתָּ לָהֶם, זֶה הָאִשֶּׁה אֲשֶׁר תַּקְרִיבוּ לַיהוה, כְּבָשִׂים בְּנֵי־שָׁנָה תְמִימִם שְׁנַיִם לַיּוֹם, עֹלָה תָמִיד: אֶת־הַכֶּבֶשׂ אֶחָד תַּעֲשֶׂה בַבֹּקֶר, וְאֵת הַכֶּבֶשׂ הַשֵּׁנִי תַּעֲשֶׂה בֵּין הָעַרְבָּיִם: וַעֲשִׂירִית הָאֵיפָה סֹלֶת לְמִנְחָה, בְּלוּלָה בְּשֶׁמֶן כָּתִית רְבִיעִת הַהִין: עֹלַת תָּמִיד, הָעֲשֻׂיָה בְּהַר סִינַי, לְרֵיחַ נִיחֹחַ אִשֶּׁה לַיהוה: וְנִסְכּוֹ רְבִיעִת הַהִין לַכֶּבֶשׂ הָאֶחָד, בַּקֹּדֶשׁ הַסֵּךְ נֶסֶךְ שֵׁכָר לַיהוה: וְאֵת הַכֶּבֶשׂ הַשֵּׁנִי תַּעֲשֶׂה בֵּין הָעַרְבָּיִם, כְּמִנְחַת הַבֹּקֶר וּכְנִסְכּוֹ תַּעֲשֶׂה, אִשֵּׁה רֵיחַ נִיחֹחַ לַיהוה:

LEARNING

"Other religions and belief systems focus almost entirely on spiritual peaks – on those exceptional bursts of upliftment, enlightenment, and elevation, on the once-a-year celebration. We, too, have our celebrations, our pinnacles and peaks, but these are not the essence of our spiritual growth. Judaism focuses particularly on the everyday, the common, regular, mundane activities which comprise the bulk of our lives…. From the very beginning of the Tabernacle's function and every day thereafter, a new foundation is laid – a foundation consisting of the most regular, the most plain, daily sacrifice. In order to build any building, to create any framework, one needs to focus not on the one-time opening ceremony, but rather on the daily routine, the ordinary, gray, unnoticed things which form the framework's basis. It is these things which define the context and matrix in which all actions, all thoughts and all other development take place." (Rav Aharon Lichtenstein, *The Daily Sacrifice – "A Great Principle of the Torah"*)

REFLECTION

What are you committed to doing every single day?

What is the value of doing the same thing every day?

Are there areas in your relationship with God in which you could be more consistent?

וְשָׁחַט He shall slaughter it at the north side of the altar before the LORD, and Aaron's sons the priests shall sprinkle its blood against the altar on all sides. *Lev. 1*

May it be Your will, LORD our God and God of our ancestors, that this recitation be considered accepted and favored before You as if we had offered the daily sacrifice at its appointed time and place, according to its laws.

It is You, LORD our God, to whom our ancestors offered fragrant incense when the Temple stood, as You commanded them through Moses Your prophet, as is written in Your Torah:

THE INCENSE

The LORD said to Moses: Take fragrant spices – balsam, onycha, galbanum and pure frankincense, all in equal amounts – and make a fragrant blend of incense, the work of a perfumer, well mixed, pure and holy. Grind it very finely and place it in front of the [Ark of] Testimony in the Tent of Meeting, where I will meet with you. It shall be most holy to you. *Ex. 30*

And it is said:

Aaron shall burn fragrant incense on the altar every morning when he cleans the lamps. He shall burn incense again when he lights the lamps toward evening so that there will be incense before the LORD at all times, throughout your generations.

The rabbis taught: How was the incense prepared? It weighed 368 manehs, 365 corresponding to the number of days in a solar year, a maneh for each day, half to be offered in the morning and half in the afternoon, and three additional manehs from which the High Priest took two handfuls on Yom Kippur. These were put back into the mortar on the day before Yom Kippur and ground again very thoroughly so as to be extremely fine. The incense contained eleven kinds of spices: balsam, onycha, galbanum and frankincense, each weighing seventy manehs; myrrh, cassia, spikenard and saffron, each weighing sixteen manehs; twelve manehs of costus, three of aromatic bark; nine of cinnamon; nine kabs of Carsina lye; three seahs and three kabs of Cyprus wine. If Cyprus wine was not available, old white wine might be used. A quarter of a kab of Sodom salt, and a minute amount of a smoke-raising herb. Rabbi Nathan the Babylonian says: also a minute amount of Jordan amber. If one added honey to the mixture, he rendered it unfit for sacred use. If he omitted any one of its ingredients, he is guilty of a capital offence. *Keritot 6a*

Rabban Simeon ben Gamliel says: "Balsam" refers to the sap that drips from the balsam tree. The Carsina lye was used for bleaching the onycha to improve it. The Cyprus wine was used to soak the onycha in it to make it pungent. Though urine is suitable for this purpose, it is not brought into the Temple out of respect.

וְשָׁחַט אֹתוֹ עַל יֶרֶךְ הַמִּזְבֵּחַ צָפֹנָה לִפְנֵי יהוה, וְזָרְקוּ בְּנֵי אַהֲרֹן הַכֹּהֲנִים אֶת־דָּמוֹ עַל־הַמִּזְבֵּחַ, סָבִיב: ויקרא א

יְהִי רָצוֹן מִלְּפָנֶיךָ, יהוה אֱלֹהֵינוּ וֵאלֹהֵי אֲבוֹתֵינוּ, שֶׁתְּהֵא אֲמִירָה זוֹ חֲשׁוּבָה וּמְקֻבֶּלֶת וּמְרֻצָּה לְפָנֶיךָ, כְּאִלּוּ הִקְרַבְנוּ קָרְבַּן הַתָּמִיד בְּמוֹעֲדוֹ וּבִמְקוֹמוֹ וּכְהִלְכָתוֹ.

אַתָּה הוּא יהוה אֱלֹהֵינוּ שֶׁהִקְטִירוּ אֲבוֹתֵינוּ לְפָנֶיךָ אֶת קְטֹרֶת הַסַּמִּים בִּזְמַן שֶׁבֵּית הַמִּקְדָּשׁ הָיָה קַיָּם, כַּאֲשֶׁר צִוִּיתָ אוֹתָם עַל יְדֵי מֹשֶׁה נְבִיאֶךָ, כַּכָּתוּב בְּתוֹרָתֶךָ:

פרשת הקטורת

וַיֹּאמֶר יהוה אֶל־מֹשֶׁה, קַח־לְךָ סַמִּים נָטָף וּשְׁחֵלֶת וְחֶלְבְּנָה, סַמִּים וּלְבֹנָה זַכָּה, בַּד בְּבַד יִהְיֶה: וְעָשִׂיתָ אֹתָהּ קְטֹרֶת, רֹקַח מַעֲשֵׂה רוֹקֵחַ, מְמֻלָּח, טָהוֹר קֹדֶשׁ: וְשָׁחַקְתָּ מִמֶּנָּה הָדֵק, וְנָתַתָּה מִמֶּנָּה לִפְנֵי הָעֵדֻת בְּאֹהֶל מוֹעֵד אֲשֶׁר אִוָּעֵד לְךָ שָׁמָּה, קֹדֶשׁ קָדָשִׁים תִּהְיֶה לָכֶם: שמות ל

וְנֶאֱמַר

וְהִקְטִיר עָלָיו אַהֲרֹן קְטֹרֶת סַמִּים, בַּבֹּקֶר בַּבֹּקֶר בְּהֵיטִיבוֹ אֶת־הַנֵּרֹת יַקְטִירֶנָּה: וּבְהַעֲלֹת אַהֲרֹן אֶת־הַנֵּרֹת בֵּין הָעַרְבַּיִם יַקְטִירֶנָּה, קְטֹרֶת תָּמִיד לִפְנֵי יהוה לְדֹרֹתֵיכֶם:

תָּנוּ רַבָּנָן: פִּטּוּם הַקְּטֹרֶת כֵּיצַד, שְׁלֹשׁ מֵאוֹת וְשִׁשִּׁים וּשְׁמוֹנָה מָנִים הָיוּ בָהּ. שְׁלֹשׁ מֵאוֹת וְשִׁשִּׁים וַחֲמִשָּׁה כְּמִנְיַן יְמוֹת הַחַמָּה, מָנֶה לְכָל יוֹם, פְּרַס בְּשַׁחֲרִית וּפְרַס בֵּין הָעַרְבַּיִם, וּשְׁלֹשָׁה מָנִים יְתֵרִים שֶׁמֵּהֶם מַכְנִיס כֹּהֵן גָּדוֹל מְלֹא חָפְנָיו בְּיוֹם הַכִּפּוּרִים, וּמַחֲזִירָן לְמַכְתֶּשֶׁת בְּעֶרֶב יוֹם הַכִּפּוּרִים וְשׁוֹחֲקָן יָפֶה יָפֶה, כְּדֵי שֶׁתְּהֵא דַקָּה מִן הַדַּקָּה. וְאַחַד עָשָׂר סַמָּנִים הָיוּ בָהּ, וְאֵלּוּ הֵן: הַצְּרִי, וְהַצִּפֹּרֶן, וְהַחֶלְבְּנָה, וְהַלְּבוֹנָה מִשְׁקַל שִׁבְעִים שִׁבְעִים מָנֶה, מֹר, וּקְצִיעָה, שִׁבֹּלֶת נֵרְדְּ, וְכַרְכֹּם מִשְׁקַל שִׁשָּׁה עָשָׂר שִׁשָּׁה עָשָׂר מָנֶה, הַקֹּשְׁטְ שְׁנֵים עָשָׂר, קִלּוּפָה שְׁלֹשָׁה, קִנָּמוֹן תִּשְׁעָה, בֹּרִית כַּרְשִׁינָה תִּשְׁעָה קַבִּין, יֵין קַפְרִיסִין סְאִין תְּלָת וְקַבִּין תְּלָתָא, וְאִם לֹא מָצָא יֵין קַפְרִיסִין, מֵבִיא חֲמַר חִוַּרְיָן עַתִּיק. מֶלַח סְדוֹמִית רֹבַע, מַעֲלֶה עָשָׁן כָּל שֶׁהוּא. רַבִּי נָתָן הַבַּבְלִי אוֹמֵר: אַף כִּפַּת הַיַּרְדֵּן כָּל שֶׁהוּא, וְאִם נָתַן בָּהּ דְּבַשׁ פְּסָלָהּ, וְאִם חִסַּר אַחַת מִכָּל סַמָּנֶיהָ, חַיָּב מִיתָה. כריתות ו.

רַבָּן שִׁמְעוֹן בֶּן גַּמְלִיאֵל אוֹמֵר: הַצְּרִי אֵינוֹ אֶלָּא שְׂרָף הַנּוֹטֵף מֵעֲצֵי הַקְּטָף. בֹּרִית כַּרְשִׁינָה שֶׁשָּׁפִין בָּהּ אֶת הַצִּפֹּרֶן כְּדֵי שֶׁתְּהֵא נָאָה, יֵין קַפְרִיסִין שֶׁשּׁוֹרִין בּוֹ אֶת הַצִּפֹּרֶן כְּדֵי שֶׁתְּהֵא עַזָּה, וַהֲלֹא מֵי רַגְלַיִם יָפִין לָהּ, אֶלָּא שֶׁאֵין מַכְנִיסִין מֵי רַגְלַיִם בַּמִּקְדָּשׁ מִפְּנֵי הַכָּבוֹד.

It was taught, Rabbi Nathan says: While it was being ground, another would say, "Grind well, well grind," because the [rhythmic] sound is good for spices. If it was mixed in half-quantities, it is fit for use, but we have not heard whether this applies to a third or a quarter. Rabbi Judah said: The general rule is that if it was made in the correct proportions, it is fit for use even if made in half-quantity, but if he omitted any one of its ingredients, he is guilty of a capital offense.

It was taught, Bar Kappara says: Once every sixty or seventy years, the accumulated surpluses amounted to half the yearly quantity. Bar Kappara also taught: If a minute quantity of honey had been mixed into the incense, no one could have resisted the scent. Why did they not put honey into it? Because the Torah says, "For you are not to burn any leaven or honey in a fire-offering made to the LORD." *JT Yoma 4:5* *Lev. 2*

The following three verses are each said three times:

The LORD of multitudes is with us; the God of Jacob is our stronghold, Selah. *Ps. 46*
LORD of multitudes, happy is the one who trusts in You. *Ps. 84*
LORD, save! May the King answer us on the day we call. *Ps. 20*

You are my hiding place; You will protect me from distress and surround me with songs of salvation, Selah. Then the offering of Judah and Jerusalem will be pleasing to the LORD as in the days of old and as in former years. *Ps. 32* *Mal. 3*

THE ORDER OF THE PRIESTLY FUNCTIONS

Abaye related the order of the daily priestly functions in the name of tradition and in accordance with Abba Shaul: The large pile [of wood] comes before the second pile for the incense; the second pile for the incense precedes the laying in order of the two logs of wood; the laying in order of the two logs of wood comes before the removing of ashes from the inner altar; the removing of ashes from the inner altar precedes the cleaning of the five lamps; the cleaning of the five lamps comes before the blood of the daily offering; the blood of the daily offering precedes the cleaning of the [other] two lamps; the cleaning of the two lamps comes before the incense-offering; the incense-offering precedes the burning of the limbs; the burning of the limbs comes before the meal-offering; the meal-offering precedes the pancakes; the pancakes come before the wine-libations; the wine-libations precede the additional offerings; the additional offerings come before the [frankincense] censers; the censers precede the daily afternoon offering; as it is said, "On it he shall arrange burnt-offerings, and on it he shall burn the fat of the peace-offerings" – "on it" [the daily offering] all the offerings were completed. *Yoma 33a* *Lev. 6*

Please, by the power of Your great right hand, set the captive nation free. Accept Your people's prayer. Strengthen us, purify us, You who are feared. Please, Mighty One, guard like the pupil of the eye those who seek Your unity. Bless them, cleanse them, have compassion on them, give them Your righteousness always. Mighty One, Holy One, in Your great goodness guide Your congregation. Only One, elevated One, turn to Your people, who declare Your holiness. Accept our plea and listen to our cry, You who know all secret thoughts.

Blessed be the name of His glorious kingdom for ever and all time.

תַּנְיָא, רַבִּי נָתָן אוֹמֵר: כְּשֶׁהוּא שׁוֹחֵק אוֹמֵר, הָדֵק הֵיטֵב הֵיטֵב הָדֵק, מִפְּנֵי שֶׁהַקּוֹל יָפֶה לַבְּשָׂמִים. פִּטְּמָהּ לַחֲצָאִין כְּשֵׁרָה, לִשְׁלִישׁ וְלִרְבִיעַ לֹא שָׁמַעְנוּ. אָמַר רַבִּי יְהוּדָה: זֶה הַכְּלָל, אִם כְּמִדָּתָהּ כְּשֵׁרָה לַחֲצָאִין, וְאִם חִסַּר אֶחָד מִכָּל סַמָּנֶיהָ חַיָּב מִיתָה.

תַּנְיָא, בַּר קַפָּרָא אוֹמֵר: אַחַת לְשִׁשִּׁים אוֹ לְשִׁבְעִים שָׁנָה הָיְתָה בָאָה שֶׁל שִׁירַיִם לַחֲצָאִין. וְעוֹד תָּנֵי בַּר קַפָּרָא: אִלּוּ הָיָה נוֹתֵן בָּהּ קוֹרְטוֹב שֶׁל דְּבַשׁ אֵין אָדָם יָכוֹל לַעֲמֹד מִפְּנֵי רֵיחָהּ, וְלָמָּה אֵין מְעָרְבִין בָּהּ דְּבַשׁ, מִפְּנֵי שֶׁהַתּוֹרָה אָמְרָה: כִּי כָל־שְׂאֹר וְכָל־דְּבַשׁ לֹא־תַקְטִירוּ מִמֶּנּוּ אִשֶּׁה לַיהוה: ירושלמי יומא ד, הלכה ה; ויקרא ב

The following three verses are each said three times:

יהוה צְבָאוֹת עִמָּנוּ, מִשְׂגָּב לָנוּ אֱלֹהֵי יַעֲקֹב סֶלָה: תהלים מו

יהוה צְבָאוֹת, אַשְׁרֵי אָדָם בֹּטֵחַ בָּךְ: תהלים פד

יהוה הוֹשִׁיעָה, הַמֶּלֶךְ יַעֲנֵנוּ בְיוֹם־קָרְאֵנוּ: תהלים כ

אַתָּה סֵתֶר לִי, מִצַּר תִּצְּרֵנִי, רָנֵּי פַלֵּט תְּסוֹבְבֵנִי סֶלָה: תהלים לב

וְעָרְבָה לַיהוה מִנְחַת יְהוּדָה וִירוּשָׁלָםִ, כִּימֵי עוֹלָם וּכְשָׁנִים קַדְמֹנִיּוֹת: מלאכי ג

סדר המערכה

אַבַּיֵּי הֲוָה מְסַדֵּר סֵדֶר הַמַּעֲרָכָה מִשְּׁמָא דִגְמָרָא, וְאַלִּבָּא דְאַבָּא שָׁאוּל: מַעֲרָכָה גְדוֹלָה קוֹדֶמֶת לְמַעֲרָכָה שְׁנִיָּה שֶׁל קְטֹרֶת, וּמַעֲרָכָה שְׁנִיָּה שֶׁל קְטֹרֶת קוֹדֶמֶת לְסִדּוּר שְׁנֵי גִזְרֵי עֵצִים, וְסִדּוּר שְׁנֵי גִזְרֵי עֵצִים קוֹדֵם לְדִשּׁוּן מִזְבֵּחַ הַפְּנִימִי, וְדִשּׁוּן מִזְבֵּחַ הַפְּנִימִי קוֹדֵם לַהֲטָבַת חָמֵשׁ נֵרוֹת, וַהֲטָבַת חָמֵשׁ נֵרוֹת קוֹדֶמֶת לְדַם הַתָּמִיד, וְדַם הַתָּמִיד קוֹדֵם לַהֲטָבַת שְׁתֵּי נֵרוֹת, וַהֲטָבַת שְׁתֵּי נֵרוֹת קוֹדֶמֶת לִקְטֹרֶת, וּקְטֹרֶת קוֹדֶמֶת לְאֵבָרִים, וְאֵבָרִים לְמִנְחָה, וּמִנְחָה לַחֲבִתִּין, וַחֲבִתִּין לִנְסָכִין, וּנְסָכִין לְמוּסָפִין, וּמוּסָפִין לְבָזִיכִין, וּבָזִיכִין קוֹדְמִין לְתָמִיד שֶׁל בֵּין הָעַרְבָּיִם. שֶׁנֶּאֱמַר: וְעָרַךְ עָלֶיהָ הָעֹלָה, וְהִקְטִיר עָלֶיהָ חֶלְבֵי הַשְּׁלָמִים: עָלֶיהָ הַשְׁלֵם כָּל הַקָּרְבָּנוֹת כֻּלָּם. יומא לג.; ויקרא ו

אָנָּא, בְּכֹחַ גְּדֻלַּת יְמִינְךָ, תַּתִּיר צְרוּרָה.\
קַבֵּל רִנַּת עַמְּךָ, שַׂגְּבֵנוּ, טַהֲרֵנוּ, נוֹרָא.\
נָא גִבּוֹר, דּוֹרְשֵׁי יִחוּדְךָ כְּבָבַת שָׁמְרֵם.\
בָּרְכֵם, טַהֲרֵם, רַחֲמֵם, צִדְקָתְךָ תָּמִיד גָּמְלֵם.\
חֲסִין קָדוֹשׁ, בְּרֹב טוּבְךָ נַהֵל עֲדָתֶךָ.\
יָחִיד גֵּאֶה, לְעַמְּךָ פְּנֵה, זוֹכְרֵי קְדֻשָּׁתֶךָ.\
שַׁוְעָתֵנוּ קַבֵּל וּשְׁמַע צַעֲקָתֵנוּ, יוֹדֵעַ תַּעֲלוּמוֹת.\
בָּרוּךְ שֵׁם כְּבוֹד מַלְכוּתוֹ לְעוֹלָם וָעֶד.

Master of the Universe, You have commanded us to offer the daily sacrifice at its appointed time with the priests at their service, the Levites on their platform, and the Israelites at their post. Now, because of our sins, the Temple is destroyed and the daily sacrifice discontinued, and we have no priest at his service, no Levite on his platform, no Israelite at his post. But You said: "We will offer in place of bullocks [the prayer of] our lips." Therefore may it be Your will, Lord our God and God of our ancestors, that the prayer of our lips be considered, accepted and favored before You as if we had offered the daily sacrifice at its appointed time and place, according to its laws. *Hos. 14*

On Shabbat:

וּבְיוֹם הַשַּׁבָּת On the Shabbat day, make an offering of two lambs a year old, without blemish, together with two-tenths of an ephah of fine flour mixed with oil as a meal-offering, and its appropriate libation. This is the burnt-offering for every Shabbat, in addition to the regular daily burnt-offering and its libation. *Num. 28*

On Rosh Hodesh:

וּבְרָאשֵׁי חָדְשֵׁיכֶם On your new moons, present as a burnt-offering to the Lord, two young bulls, one ram, and seven yearling lambs without blemish. There shall be a meal-offering of three-tenths of an ephah of fine flour mixed with oil for each bull, two-tenths of an ephah of fine flour mixed with oil for the ram, and one-tenth of an ephah of fine flour mixed with oil for each lamb. This is the burnt-offering – a fire-offering of pleasing aroma to the Lord. Their libations shall be: half a hin of wine for each bull, a third of a hin for the ram, and a quarter of a hin for each lamb. This is the monthly burnt-offering to be made at each new moon throughout the year. One male goat should be offered as a sin-offering to God, in addition to the regular daily burnt-offering and its libation. *Num. 28*

LAWS OF OFFERINGS, MISHNA ZEVAHIM

אֵיזֶהוּ מְקוֹמָן What is the location for sacrifices? The holiest offerings were slaughtered on the north side. The bull and he-goat of Yom Kippur were slaughtered on the north side. Their blood was received in a sacred vessel on the north side, and had to be sprinkled between the poles [of the Ark], toward the veil [screening the Holy of Holies], and on the golden altar. [The omission of] one of these sprinklings invalidated [the atonement ceremony]. The leftover blood was to be poured onto the western base of the outer altar. If this was not done, however, the omission did not invalidate [the ceremony]. *Zevahim Ch. 5*

The bulls and he-goats that were completely burnt were slaughtered on the north side, their blood was received in a sacred vessel on the north side, and had to be sprinkled toward the veil and on the golden altar. [The omission of] one of these sprinklings invalidated [the ceremony]. The leftover blood was to be poured onto the western base of the outer altar. If this was not done, however, the omission did not invalidate [the ceremony]. All these offerings were burnt where the altar ashes were deposited.

רִבּוֹן הָעוֹלָמִים, אַתָּה צִוִּיתָנוּ לְהַקְרִיב קָרְבַּן הַתָּמִיד בְּמוֹעֲדוֹ וְלִהְיוֹת כֹּהֲנִים בַּעֲבוֹדָתָם וּלְוִיִּם בְּדוּכָנָם וְיִשְׂרָאֵל בְּמַעֲמָדָם, וְעַתָּה בַּעֲוֹנוֹתֵינוּ חָרַב בֵּית הַמִּקְדָּשׁ וּבָטַל הַתָּמִיד וְאֵין לָנוּ לֹא כֹהֵן בַּעֲבוֹדָתוֹ וְלֹא לֵוִי בְּדוּכָנוֹ וְלֹא יִשְׂרָאֵל בְּמַעֲמָדוֹ,
וְאַתָּה אָמַרְתָּ: וּנְשַׁלְּמָה פָרִים שְׂפָתֵינוּ: לָכֵן יְהִי רָצוֹן מִלְּפָנֶיךָ יהוה אֱלֹהֵינוּ וֵאלֹהֵי אֲבוֹתֵינוּ, שֶׁיְּהֵא שִׂיחַ שִׂפְתוֹתֵינוּ חָשׁוּב וּמְקֻבָּל וּמְרֻצֶּה לְפָנֶיךָ, כְּאִלּוּ הִקְרַבְנוּ קָרְבַּן הַתָּמִיד בְּמוֹעֲדוֹ וּבִמְקוֹמוֹ וּכְהִלְכָתוֹ. הושע יד

בשבת וּבְיוֹם הַשַּׁבָּת שְׁנֵי־כְבָשִׂים בְּנֵי־שָׁנָה תְּמִימִם, וּשְׁנֵי עֶשְׂרֹנִים סֹלֶת מִנְחָה בְּלוּלָה בַשֶּׁמֶן, וְנִסְכּוֹ: עֹלַת שַׁבַּת בְּשַׁבַּתּוֹ, עַל־עֹלַת הַתָּמִיד וְנִסְכָּהּ: במדבר כח

בראש חודש: וּבְרָאשֵׁי חָדְשֵׁיכֶם תַּקְרִיבוּ עֹלָה לַיהוה, פָּרִים בְּנֵי־בָקָר שְׁנַיִם, וְאַיִל אֶחָד, כְּבָשִׂים בְּנֵי־שָׁנָה שִׁבְעָה, תְּמִימִם: וּשְׁלֹשָׁה עֶשְׂרֹנִים סֹלֶת מִנְחָה בְּלוּלָה בַשֶּׁמֶן לַפָּר הָאֶחָד, וּשְׁנֵי עֶשְׂרֹנִים סֹלֶת מִנְחָה בְּלוּלָה בַשֶּׁמֶן לָאַיִל הָאֶחָד: וְעִשָּׂרֹן עִשָּׂרוֹן סֹלֶת מִנְחָה בְּלוּלָה בַשֶּׁמֶן לַכֶּבֶשׂ הָאֶחָד, עֹלָה רֵיחַ נִיחֹחַ, אִשֶּׁה לַיהוה: וְנִסְכֵּיהֶם, חֲצִי הַהִין יִהְיֶה לַפָּר, וּשְׁלִישִׁת הַהִין לָאַיִל, וּרְבִיעִת הַהִין לַכֶּבֶשׂ, יָיִן, זֹאת עֹלַת חֹדֶשׁ בְּחָדְשׁוֹ לְחָדְשֵׁי הַשָּׁנָה: וּשְׂעִיר עִזִּים אֶחָד לְחַטָּאת לַיהוה, עַל־עֹלַת הַתָּמִיד יֵעָשֶׂה, וְנִסְכּוֹ: במדבר כח

דיני זבחים

אֵיזֶהוּ מְקוֹמָן שֶׁל זְבָחִים. קָדְשֵׁי קָדָשִׁים שְׁחִיטָתָן בַּצָּפוֹן. פַּר וְשָׂעִיר שֶׁל יוֹם הַכִּפּוּרִים, שְׁחִיטָתָן בַּצָּפוֹן, וְקִבּוּל דָּמָן בִּכְלֵי שָׁרֵת בַּצָּפוֹן, וְדָמָן טָעוּן הַזָּיָה עַל בֵּין הַבַּדִּים, וְעַל הַפָּרֹכֶת, וְעַל מִזְבַּח הַזָּהָב. מַתָּנָה אַחַת מֵהֶן מְעַכָּבֶת. שְׁיָרֵי הַדָּם הָיָה שׁוֹפֵךְ עַל יְסוֹד מַעֲרָבִי שֶׁל מִזְבֵּחַ הַחִיצוֹן, אִם לֹא נָתַן לֹא עִכֵּב. זבחים פרק ה

פָּרִים הַנִּשְׂרָפִים וּשְׂעִירִים הַנִּשְׂרָפִים, שְׁחִיטָתָן בַּצָּפוֹן, וְקִבּוּל דָּמָן בִּכְלֵי שָׁרֵת בַּצָּפוֹן, וְדָמָן טָעוּן הַזָּיָה עַל הַפָּרֹכֶת וְעַל מִזְבַּח הַזָּהָב. מַתָּנָה אַחַת מֵהֶן מְעַכָּבֶת. שְׁיָרֵי הַדָּם הָיָה שׁוֹפֵךְ עַל יְסוֹד מַעֲרָבִי שֶׁל מִזְבֵּחַ הַחִיצוֹן, אִם לֹא נָתַן לֹא עִכֵּב. אֵלּוּ וָאֵלּוּ נִשְׂרָפִין בְּבֵית הַדָּשֶׁן.

The communal and individual sin-offerings – these are the communal sin-offerings: the he-goats offered on Rosh Ḥodesh and Festivals were slaughtered on the north side, their blood was received in a sacred vessel on the north side, and required four sprinklings, one on each of the four corners of the altar. How was this done? The priest ascended the ramp and turned [right] onto the surrounding ledge. He came to the southeast corner, then went to the northeast, then to the northwest, then to the southwest. The leftover blood he poured onto the southern base. [The meat of these offerings], prepared in any manner, was eaten within the [courtyard] curtains, by males of the priest-hood, on that day and the following night, until midnight.

The burnt-offering was among the holiest of sacrifices. It was slaughtered on the north side, its blood was received in a sacred vessel on the north side, and required two sprinklings [at opposite corners of the altar], making four in all. The offering had to be flayed, dismembered and wholly consumed by fire.

The communal peace-offerings and the guilt-offerings – these are the guilt-offerings: the guilt-offering for robbery; the guilt-offering for profane use of a sacred object; the guilt-offering [for violating] a betrothed maidservant; the guilt-offering of a Nazirite [who had become defiled by a corpse]; the guilt-offering of a leper [at his cleansing]; and the guilt-offering in case of doubt. All these were slaughtered on the north side, their blood was received in a sacred vessel on the north side, and required two sprinklings [at opposite corners of the altar], making four in all. [The meat of these offerings], prepared in any manner, was eaten within the [courtyard] curtains, by males of the priesthood, on that day and the following night, until midnight.

The thanksgiving-offering and the ram of a Nazirite were offerings of lesser holiness. They could be slaughtered anywhere in the Temple court, and their blood required two sprinklings [at opposite corners of the altar], making four in all. The meat of these offerings, prepared in any manner, was eaten anywhere within the city [Jerusalem], by anyone during that day and the following night until midnight. This also applied to the portion of these sacrifices [given to the priests], except that the priests' portion was only to be eaten by the priests, their wives, children and servants.

Peace-offerings were [also] of lesser holiness. They could be slaughtered anywhere in the Temple court, and their blood required two sprinklings [at opposite corners of the altar], making four in all. The meat of these offerings, prepared in any manner, was eaten anywhere within the city [Jerusalem], by anyone, for two days and one night. This also applied to the portion of these sacrifices [given to the priests], except that the priests' portion was only to be eaten by the priests, their wives, children and servants.

The firstborn and tithe of cattle and the Pesaḥ lamb were sacrifices of lesser holiness. They could be slaughtered anywhere in the Temple court, and their blood required only one sprinkling, which had to be done at the base of the altar. They differed in their consumption: the firstborn was eaten only by priests, while the tithe could be eaten by anyone. Both could be eaten anywhere within the city, prepared in any manner, during two days and one night. The Pesaḥ lamb had to be eaten that night until midnight. It could only be eaten by those who had been numbered for it, and eaten only roasted.

חַטֹּאת הַצִּבּוּר וְהַיָּחִיד. אֵלּוּ הֵן חַטֹּאת הַצִּבּוּר: שְׂעִירֵי רָאשֵׁי חֳדָשִׁים וְשֶׁל מוֹעֲדוֹת. שְׁחִיטָתָן בַּצָּפוֹן, וְקִבּוּל דָּמָן בִּכְלִי שָׁרֵת בַּצָּפוֹן, וְדָמָן טָעוּן אַרְבַּע מַתָּנוֹת עַל אַרְבַּע קְרָנוֹת. כֵּיצַד, עָלָה בַכֶּבֶשׁ, וּפָנָה לַסּוֹבֵב, וּבָא לוֹ לְקֶרֶן דְּרוֹמִית מִזְרָחִית, מִזְרָחִית צְפוֹנִית, צְפוֹנִית מַעֲרָבִית, מַעֲרָבִית דְּרוֹמִית. שְׁיָרֵי הַדָּם הָיָה שׁוֹפֵךְ עַל יְסוֹד דְּרוֹמִי. וְנֶאֱכָלִין לִפְנִים מִן הַקְּלָעִים, לְזִכְרֵי כְהֻנָּה, בְּכָל מַאֲכָל, לְיוֹם וָלַיְלָה עַד חֲצוֹת.

הָעוֹלָה קֹדֶשׁ קָדָשִׁים. שְׁחִיטָתָהּ בַּצָּפוֹן, וְקִבּוּל דָּמָהּ בִּכְלִי שָׁרֵת בַּצָּפוֹן, וְדָמָהּ טָעוּן שְׁתֵּי מַתָּנוֹת שֶׁהֵן אַרְבַּע, וּטְעוּנָה הֶפְשֵׁט וְנִתּוּחַ, וְכָלִיל לָאִשִּׁים.

זִבְחֵי שַׁלְמֵי צִבּוּר וַאֲשָׁמוֹת. אֵלּוּ הֵן אֲשָׁמוֹת: אֲשַׁם גְּזֵלוֹת, אֲשַׁם מְעִילוֹת, אֲשַׁם שִׁפְחָה חֲרוּפָה, אֲשַׁם נָזִיר, אֲשַׁם מְצֹרָע, אָשָׁם תָּלוּי. שְׁחִיטָתָן בַּצָּפוֹן, וְקִבּוּל דָּמָן בִּכְלִי שָׁרֵת בַּצָּפוֹן, וְדָמָן טָעוּן שְׁתֵּי מַתָּנוֹת שֶׁהֵן אַרְבַּע. וְנֶאֱכָלִין לִפְנִים מִן הַקְּלָעִים, לְזִכְרֵי כְהֻנָּה, בְּכָל מַאֲכָל, לְיוֹם וָלַיְלָה עַד חֲצוֹת.

הַתּוֹדָה וְאֵיל נָזִיר קָדָשִׁים קַלִּים. שְׁחִיטָתָן בְּכָל מָקוֹם בָּעֲזָרָה, וְדָמָן טָעוּן שְׁתֵּי מַתָּנוֹת שֶׁהֵן אַרְבַּע, וְנֶאֱכָלִין בְּכָל הָעִיר, לְכָל אָדָם, בְּכָל מַאֲכָל, לְיוֹם וָלַיְלָה עַד חֲצוֹת. הַמּוּרָם מֵהֶם כַּיּוֹצֵא בָהֶם, אֶלָּא שֶׁהַמּוּרָם נֶאֱכָל לַכֹּהֲנִים, לִנְשֵׁיהֶם, וְלִבְנֵיהֶם וּלְעַבְדֵיהֶם.

שְׁלָמִים קָדָשִׁים קַלִּים. שְׁחִיטָתָן בְּכָל מָקוֹם בָּעֲזָרָה, וְדָמָן טָעוּן שְׁתֵּי מַתָּנוֹת שֶׁהֵן אַרְבַּע, וְנֶאֱכָלִין בְּכָל הָעִיר, לְכָל אָדָם, בְּכָל מַאֲכָל, לִשְׁנֵי יָמִים וְלַיְלָה אֶחָד. הַמּוּרָם מֵהֶם כַּיּוֹצֵא בָהֶם, אֶלָּא שֶׁהַמּוּרָם נֶאֱכָל לַכֹּהֲנִים, לִנְשֵׁיהֶם, וְלִבְנֵיהֶם וּלְעַבְדֵיהֶם.

הַבְּכוֹר וְהַמַּעֲשֵׂר וְהַפֶּסַח קָדָשִׁים קַלִּים. שְׁחִיטָתָן בְּכָל מָקוֹם בָּעֲזָרָה, וְדָמָן טָעוּן מַתָּנָה אֶחָת, וּבִלְבַד שֶׁיִּתֵּן כְּנֶגֶד הַיְסוֹד. שִׁנָּה בַאֲכִילָתָן, הַבְּכוֹר נֶאֱכָל לַכֹּהֲנִים וְהַמַּעֲשֵׂר לְכָל אָדָם, וְנֶאֱכָלִין בְּכָל הָעִיר, בְּכָל מַאֲכָל, לִשְׁנֵי יָמִים וְלַיְלָה אֶחָד. הַפֶּסַח אֵינוֹ נֶאֱכָל אֶלָּא בַלַּיְלָה, וְאֵינוֹ נֶאֱכָל אֶלָּא עַד חֲצוֹת, וְאֵינוֹ נֶאֱכָל אֶלָּא לִמְנוּיָו, וְאֵינוֹ נֶאֱכָל אֶלָּא צָלִי.

THE INTERPRETIVE PRINCIPLES OF RABBI YISHMAEL

רַבִּי יִשְׁמָעֵאל Rabbi Yishmael says:
The Torah is expounded by thirteen principles:

1. An inference from a lenient law to a strict one, and vice versa.
2. An inference drawn from identical words in two passages.
3. A general principle derived from one text or two related texts.
4. A general law followed by specific examples
   [where the law applies exclusively to those examples].
5. A specific example followed by a general law
   [where the law applies to everything implied in the general statement].
6. A general law followed by specific examples and concluding with a general law:
   here you may infer only cases similar to the examples.
7. When a general statement requires clarification by a specific example,
   or a specific example requires clarification by a general statement
   [then rules 4 and 5 do not apply].
8. When a particular case, already included in the general statement,
   is expressly mentioned to teach something new, that special provision
   applies to all other cases included in the general statement.
9. When a particular case, though included in the general statement,
   is expressly mentioned with a provision similar to the general law,
   such a case is singled out to lessen the severity of the law, not to increase it.
10. When a particular case, though included in the general statement,
    is explicitly mentioned with a provision differing from the general law,
    it is singled out to lessen in some respects,
    and in others to increase, the severity of the law.
11. When a particular case, though included in the general statement,
    is explicitly mentioned with a new provision,
    the terms of the general statement no longer apply to it,
    unless Scripture indicates explicitly that they do apply.
12. A matter elucidated from its context, or from the following passage.
13. ▸ Also, when two passages [seem to] contradict each other,
    [they are to be elucidated by] a third passage that reconciles them.

May it be Your will, Lord our God and God of our ancestors, that the Temple be speedily rebuilt in our days, and give us our share in Your Torah. And may we serve You there in reverence, as in the days of old and as in former years.

ברייתא דרבי ישמעאל

רַבִּי יִשְׁמָעֵאל אוֹמֵר: בִּשְׁלֹשׁ עֶשְׂרֵה מִדּוֹת הַתּוֹרָה נִדְרֶשֶׁת

א מִקַּל וָחֹמֶר

ב וּמִגְּזֵרָה שָׁוָה

ג מִבִּנְיַן אָב מִכָּתוּב אֶחָד, וּמִבִּנְיַן אָב מִשְּׁנֵי כְתוּבִים

ד מִכְּלָל וּפְרָט

ה מִפְּרָט וּכְלָל

ו כְּלָל וּפְרָט וּכְלָל, אִי אַתָּה דָן אֶלָּא כְּעֵין הַפְּרָט

ז מִכְּלָל שֶׁהוּא צָרִיךְ לִפְרָט, וּמִפְּרָט שֶׁהוּא צָרִיךְ לִכְלָל

ח כָּל דָּבָר שֶׁהָיָה בִּכְלָל, וְיָצָא מִן הַכְּלָל לְלַמֵּד
לֹא לְלַמֵּד עַל עַצְמוֹ יָצָא
אֶלָּא לְלַמֵּד עַל הַכְּלָל כֻּלּוֹ יָצָא

ט כָּל דָּבָר שֶׁהָיָה בִּכְלָל, וְיָצָא לִטְעֹן טֹעַן אֶחָד שֶׁהוּא כְעִנְיָנוֹ
יָצָא לְהָקֵל וְלֹא לְהַחֲמִיר

י כָּל דָּבָר שֶׁהָיָה בִּכְלָל, וְיָצָא לִטְעֹן טֹעַן אַחֵר שֶׁלֹּא כְעִנְיָנוֹ
יָצָא לְהָקֵל וּלְהַחֲמִיר

יא כָּל דָּבָר שֶׁהָיָה בִּכְלָל, וְיָצָא לִדּוֹן בַּדָּבָר הֶחָדָשׁ
אִי אַתָּה יָכוֹל לְהַחֲזִירוֹ לִכְלָלוֹ
עַד שֶׁיַּחֲזִירֶנּוּ הַכָּתוּב לִכְלָלוֹ בְּפֵרוּשׁ

יב דָּבָר הַלָּמֵד מֵעִנְיָנוֹ, וְדָבָר הַלָּמֵד מִסּוֹפוֹ

יג וְכֵן שְׁנֵי כְתוּבִים הַמַּכְחִישִׁים זֶה אֶת זֶה
עַד שֶׁיָּבוֹא הַכָּתוּב הַשְּׁלִישִׁי וְיַכְרִיעַ בֵּינֵיהֶם.

יְהִי רָצוֹן מִלְּפָנֶיךָ, יהוה אֱלֹהֵינוּ וֵאלֹהֵי אֲבוֹתֵינוּ, שֶׁיִּבָּנֶה בֵּית הַמִּקְדָּשׁ בִּמְהֵרָה בְיָמֵינוּ, וְתֵן חֶלְקֵנוּ בְּתוֹרָתֶךָ, וְשָׁם נַעֲבָדְךָ בְּיִרְאָה כִּימֵי עוֹלָם וּכְשָׁנִים קַדְמוֹנִיּוֹת.

THE RABBIS' KADDISH

The following prayer, said by mourners, requires the presence of a minyan. A transliteration can be found on page 1150.

Mourner: יִתְגַּדַּל Magnified and sanctified
may His great name be,
in the world He created by His will.
May He establish His kingdom in your lifetime
and in your days,
and in the lifetime of all the house of Israel,
swiftly and soon –
and say: Amen.

All: May His great name be blessed for ever and all time.

Mourner: Blessed and praised, glorified and elevated,
raised and honored, uplifted and praised
be the name of the Holy One,
blessed be He,
beyond any blessing,
song, praise and consolation
uttered in the world –
and say: Amen.

LEARNING

Kaddish marks the end of a section of the service. This Kaddish marks the end of *Birkhot HaShaḥar* and *Korbanot*. There are four versions of the Kaddish prayer: the Rabbis' Kaddish, the Mourner's Kaddish, the Full Kaddish, and the Half Kaddish.

The Rabbis' Kaddish (*Kaddish DeRabbanan*), which honors Torah scholars, is recited by mourners after Torah study. The *Birkhot HaShaḥar* section of Shaḥarit, which concludes with *Korbanot*, contains verses from Tanakh and studies from Talmudic passages and is therefore followed by the recitation of *Kaddish DeRabbanan*.

Kaddish is written mostly in Aramaic, the everyday language of the Jews of Talmudic times.

קדיש דרבנן

The following prayer, said by mourners, requires the presence of a מנין*.*
A transliteration can be found on page 1150.

A transliteration can be found on page 1150.

אבל: **יִתְגַּדַּל וְיִתְקַדַּשׁ שְׁמֵהּ רַבָּא** (קהל: אָמֵן)
בְּעָלְמָא דִּי בְרָא כִרְעוּתֵהּ
וְיַמְלִיךְ מַלְכוּתֵהּ
בְּחַיֵּיכוֹן וּבְיוֹמֵיכוֹן וּבְחַיֵּי דְכָל בֵּית יִשְׂרָאֵל
בַּעֲגָלָא וּבִזְמַן קָרִיב
וְאִמְרוּ אָמֵן. (קהל: אָמֵן)

קהל ואבל: **יְהֵא שְׁמֵהּ רַבָּא מְבָרַךְ לְעָלַם וּלְעָלְמֵי עָלְמַיָּא.**

אבל: **יִתְבָּרַךְ וְיִשְׁתַּבַּח וְיִתְפָּאַר וְיִתְרוֹמַם וְיִתְנַשֵּׂא**
וְיִתְהַדָּר וְיִתְעַלֶּה וְיִתְהַלָּל
שְׁמֵהּ דְּקֻדְשָׁא בְּרִיךְ הוּא (קהל: בְּרִיךְ הוּא)
לְעֵלָּא מִן כָּל בִּרְכָתָא
/ בעשרת ימי תשובה: **לְעֵלָּא לְעֵלָּא מִכָּל בִּרְכָתָא**/
וְשִׁירָתָא, תֻּשְׁבְּחָתָא וְנֶחֱמָתָא
דַּאֲמִירָן בְּעָלְמָא
וְאִמְרוּ אָמֵן. (קהל: אָמֵן)

REFLECTION

"The parent brings the child into the life of this world, whereas the teacher, who teaches him wisdom, brings him into the life of the World to Come."

(*Bava Metzia* 33a)

Take a minute to think about which teachers most impacted your life.

How do you honor them?

To Israel, to the teachers, their disciples
and their disciples' disciples,
and to all who engage in the study of Torah,
in this (*in Israel add:* holy) place or elsewhere,
may there come to them and you great peace,
grace, kindness and compassion,
long life, abundant sustenance and deliverance,
from their Father in Heaven –
and say: Amen.

May there be great peace from heaven,
and (good) life for us and all Israel –
and say: Amen.

Bow, take three steps back, as if taking leave of the Divine Presence, then bow, first left, then right, then center, while saying:

May He who makes peace in His high places,
in His compassion make peace
for us and all Israel –
and say: Amen.

On Shabbat, Hoshana Raba, and in many communities on Yom HaAtzma'ut and Yom Yerushalayim, continue Shaḥarit on page 528.

---

spiritual father, I was tearing my clothes for him… Rabbi Auerbach remains an example to me. I think about him often, missing him as a scholar, educator, and mainly, as a person. Even now, years after his death, his spirit remains close to my heart, and his absence has left a void that cannot be filled."

(Rabbi Yisrael Meir Lau, *Out of the Depths*)

...A THOUSAND WORDS

עַל יִשְׂרָאֵל וְעַל רַבָּנָן וְעַל תַּלְמִידֵיהוֹן
וְעַל כָּל תַּלְמִידֵי תַלְמִידֵיהוֹן
וְעַל כָּל מָאן דְּעָסְקִין בְּאוֹרַיְתָא
דִּי בְאַתְרָא (בארץ ישראל: **קַדִּישָׁא**) **הָדֵין, וְדִי בְּכָל אֲתַר וַאֲתַר**
יְהֵא לְהוֹן וּלְכוֹן שְׁלָמָא רַבָּא
חִנָּא וְחִסְדָּא, וְרַחֲמֵי
וְחַיֵּי אֲרִיכֵי, וּמְזוֹנֵי רְוִיחֵי
וּפֻרְקָנָא מִן קֳדָם אֲבוּהוֹן דִּי בִשְׁמַיָּא
וְאִמְרוּ אָמֵן. (קהל: אָמֵן)

יְהֵא שְׁלָמָא רַבָּא מִן שְׁמַיָּא
וְחַיִּים (טוֹבִים) עָלֵינוּ וְעַל כָּל יִשְׂרָאֵל
וְאִמְרוּ אָמֵן. (קהל: אָמֵן)

Bow, take three steps back, as if taking leave of the Divine Presence, then bow, first left, then right, then center, while saying:

עֹשֶׂה שָׁלוֹם/ בעשרת ימי תשובה: **הַשָּׁלוֹם/ בִּמְרוֹמָיו**
הוּא יַעֲשֶׂה בְרַחֲמָיו שָׁלוֹם, עָלֵינוּ וְעַל כָּל יִשְׂרָאֵל
וְאִמְרוּ אָמֵן. (קהל: אָמֵן)

On שבת, הושענא רבה, *and in many communities on* יום העצמאות *and* יום ירושלים, *continue* שחרית *on page 529.*

CONNECTION

"When Rabbi Shlomo Zalman [Auerbach] died, I followed the tradition of tearing my clothing, as a son would do for his father. He was the only person for whom I have ever done so. Someone saw me and, noticing my torn suit, asked in a worried voice what had happened. I answered that I had not had the opportunity to tear my clothing for my biological father. Because Rabbi Shlomo Zalman was my

A PSALM BEFORE VERSES OF PRAISE

מִזְמוֹר שִׁיר A psalm of David. A song for the dedication of the House. Ps. 30
I will elevate You, Lord, for You have lifted me up, and not let my enemies rejoice over me. Lord, my God, I cried to You for help and You healed me. Lord, You lifted my soul from the grave; You spared me from going down to the pit. Sing to the Lord, you His devoted ones, and give thanks to His holy name. For His anger is for a moment, but His favor for a lifetime. At night there may be weeping, but in the morning there is joy. When I felt secure, I said, "I shall never be shaken." Lord, when You favored me, You made me stand firm as a mountain, but when You hid Your face, I was terrified. To You, Lord, I called; I pleaded with my Lord: "What gain would there be if I died and went down to the grave? Can dust thank You? Can it declare Your truth? Hear, Lord, and be generous to me; Lord, be my help." ▸ You have turned my sorrow into dancing. You have removed my sackcloth and clothed me with joy, so that my soul may sing to You and not be silent. Lord my God, for ever will I thank You.

LEARNING

A theme of this *perek* is the contrast between negativity and positivity. The author explores the depths of despair and heights of joy and the thin line between them. The chapter teaches us that turning to God is how we can transcend from despair to hope. When we are able to turn to God in our hardest times and recognize His power to help, the door to hope opens. It is critical that we understand and internalize this idea before we begin the first section of *tefilla*: *Pesukei DeZimra*. The chapter shows us the power of *tefilla*. When we turn to God, the contrast between pain and hope becomes powerfully real for us. This is a chapter of hope, transition, and inspiration.

CONNECTION

Ordeal leads to transcendence. In the paradox of facing crisis with a lion's strength and yet inwardly knowing that only Hashem manifests here, we reveal Him openly. What is possible and what is impossible is not our concern. The Alter of Kelm used to say, "Ask not if a thing is possible, ask only if it is necessary." Our concern is to rise to that partnership with the Divine which invites Him, as it were, to reach down to us.

(Rabbi Akiva Tatz, *Living Inspired*)

מזמור לפני פסוקי דזמרה

מִזְמוֹר שִׁיר־חֲנֻכַּת הַבַּיִת לְדָוִד: אֲרוֹמִמְךָ יהוה כִּי דִלִּיתָנִי, תהלים ל
וְלֹא־שִׂמַּחְתָּ אֹיְבַי לִי: יהוה אֱלֹהָי, שִׁוַּעְתִּי אֵלֶיךָ וַתִּרְפָּאֵנִי:
יהוה, הֶעֱלִיתָ מִן־שְׁאוֹל נַפְשִׁי, חִיִּיתַנִי מִיָּרְדִי־בוֹר: זַמְּרוּ לַיהוה
חֲסִידָיו, וְהוֹדוּ לְזֵכֶר קָדְשׁוֹ: כִּי רֶגַע בְּאַפּוֹ, חַיִּים בִּרְצוֹנוֹ, בָּעֶרֶב
יָלִין בֶּכִי וְלַבֹּקֶר רִנָּה: וַאֲנִי אָמַרְתִּי בְשַׁלְוִי, בַּל־אֶמּוֹט לְעוֹלָם:
יהוה, בִּרְצוֹנְךָ הֶעֱמַדְתָּה לְהַרְרִי עֹז, הִסְתַּרְתָּ פָנֶיךָ הָיִיתִי נִבְהָל:
אֵלֶיךָ יהוה אֶקְרָא, וְאֶל־אֲדֹנָי אֶתְחַנָּן: מַה־בֶּצַע בְּדָמִי, בְּרִדְתִּי
אֶל שָׁחַת, הֲיוֹדְךָ עָפָר, הֲיַגִּיד אֲמִתֶּךָ: שְׁמַע־יהוה וְחָנֵּנִי, יהוה
הֱיֵה־עֹזֵר לִי: ◂ הָפַכְתָּ מִסְפְּדִי לְמָחוֹל לִי, פִּתַּחְתָּ שַׂקִּי, וַתְּאַזְּרֵנִי
שִׂמְחָה: לְמַעַן יְזַמֶּרְךָ כָבוֹד וְלֹא יִדֹּם, יהוה אֱלֹהַי, לְעוֹלָם אוֹדֶךָּ:

… A THOUSAND WORDS

REFLECTION

Can you think of a time when your pain transitioned into a time of joy?

How can you ask God to help you? How does asking for help provide hope?

MOURNER'S KADDISH

The following prayer, said by mourners, requires the presence of a minyan. A transliteration can be found on page 1151.

Mourner: יִתְגַּדַּל Magnified and sanctified may His great name be,
in the world He created by His will.
May He establish His kingdom
in your lifetime and in your days,
and in the lifetime of all the house of Israel,
swiftly and soon – and say: Amen.

All: May His great name be blessed for ever and all time.

Mourner: Blessed and praised, glorified and elevated,
raised and honored, uplifted and praised
be the name of the Holy One,
blessed be He,
beyond any blessing,
song, praise and consolation
uttered in the world – and say: Amen.

May there be great peace from heaven,
and life for us and all Israel – and say: Amen.

Bow, take three steps back, as if taking leave of the Divine Presence, then bow, first left, then right, then center, while saying:

May He who makes peace in His high places,
make peace for us and all Israel – and say: Amen.

REFLECTION

How can you carry someone else's memory?

How can you show that you accept God's judgment?

Do you know anyone saying this Kaddish? What do you think they are thinking about?

...A THOUSAND WORDS

קדיש יתום

The following prayer, said by mourners, requires the presence of a מנין*.*
A transliteration can be found on page 1151.

אבל: יִתְגַּדַּל וְיִתְקַדַּשׁ שְׁמֵהּ רַבָּא (קהל: אָמֵן)
בְּעָלְמָא דִּי בְרָא כִרְעוּתֵהּ, וְיַמְלִיךְ מַלְכוּתֵהּ
בְּחַיֵּיכוֹן וּבְיוֹמֵיכוֹן וּבְחַיֵּי דְכָל בֵּית יִשְׂרָאֵל
בַּעֲגָלָא וּבִזְמַן קָרִיב, וְאִמְרוּ אָמֵן. (קהל: אָמֵן)

קהל ואבל: יְהֵא שְׁמֵהּ רַבָּא מְבָרַךְ לְעָלַם וּלְעָלְמֵי עָלְמַיָּא.

אבל: יִתְבָּרַךְ וְיִשְׁתַּבַּח וְיִתְפָּאַר
וְיִתְרוֹמַם וְיִתְנַשֵּׂא וְיִתְהַדָּר וְיִתְעַלֶּה וְיִתְהַלָּל
שְׁמֵהּ דְּקֻדְשָׁא בְּרִיךְ הוּא (קהל: בְּרִיךְ הוּא)
לְעֵלָּא מִן כָּל בִּרְכָתָא / בעשרת ימי תשובה: לְעֵלָּא לְעֵלָּא מִכָּל בִּרְכָתָא/
וְשִׁירָתָא, תֻּשְׁבְּחָתָא וְנֶחֱמָתָא
דַּאֲמִירָן בְּעָלְמָא, וְאִמְרוּ אָמֵן. (קהל: אָמֵן)

יְהֵא שְׁלָמָא רַבָּא מִן שְׁמַיָּא
וְחַיִּים, עָלֵינוּ וְעַל כָּל יִשְׂרָאֵל, וְאִמְרוּ אָמֵן. (קהל: אָמֵן)

Bow, take three steps back, as if taking leave of the Divine Presence, then bow, first left, then right, then center, while saying:

עֹשֶׂה שָׁלוֹם/ בעשרת ימי תשובה: הַשָּׁלוֹם/ בִּמְרוֹמָיו
הוּא יַעֲשֶׂה שָׁלוֹם עָלֵינוּ וְעַל כָּל יִשְׂרָאֵל, וְאִמְרוּ אָמֵן. (קהל: אָמֵן)

LEARNING

The custom of reciting Kaddish as an atonement for the soul of a departed family member is first recorded in the thirteenth century by Rabbi Yitzḥak ben Moshe of Vienna in his *Or Zarua*. Rabbi Ḥayyim ben Bezalel (*Sefer HaḤayyim*) explains that when a child's parent has been taken from him and despite his pain and mourning, the child is able to stand up and pronounce God's greatness in public, the departed soul receives atonement. The child, in overcoming his anguish and publicly praising God, becomes a credit to the departed parent and for this reason the soul derives benefit and merit.

PESUKEI DEZIMRA

The introductory blessing to the Pesukei DeZimra (Verses of Praise) is said standing. There is a custom to hold the two front tzitziot of the tallit until the end of the blessing at "songs of praise" *(on page 78)* *after which they are kissed and released. From the beginning of this prayer to the end of the Amida, conversation is forbidden.*

Some say:

I hereby prepare my mouth to thank, praise and applaud my Creator, for the sake of the unification of the Holy One, blessed be He, and His Divine Presence, through that which is hidden and concealed, in the name of all Israel.

BLESSED IS HE WHO SPOKE
and the world came into being, blessed is He.
Blessed is He who creates the universe.
Blessed is He who speaks and acts.
Blessed is He who decrees and fulfills.
Blessed is He who shows compassion to the earth.
Blessed is He who shows compassion to all creatures.
Blessed is He who gives a good reward
to those who fear Him.
Blessed is He who lives for ever and exists to eternity.
Blessed is He who redeems and saves.
Blessed is His name.

Pesukei DeZimra is a stand-alone section of the *tefilla* service and is bracketed by two *berakhot* – *Yishtabaḥ* at the end and *Barukh SheAmar* at the beginning. *Barukh SheAmar* can be divided into two parts. The first contains ten praises of God, each beginning with the word "*Barukh*." They attest to the way He created the world and remains involved in it on a constant basis, and correspond to the ten times the word "*vayomer*" is found in the first chapter of *Bereshit* as God creates the world with words and speech. The second section is a statement of intent and serves as an introduction to *Pesukei DeZimra* – we will now use the words of David HaMelekh from *Tehillim* to praise Hashem.

REFLECTION

"By ten acts of speech the world was created."
(*Avot* 5:1)

How can speech create worlds?

When did you last use words for the power of good?

When did you last use words for the power of bad?

פסוקי דזמרה

The introductory blessing to the פסוקי דזמרה *is said standing. There is a custom to hold the two front* ציציות *of the* טלית *until the end of the blessing at* בַּתִּשְׁבָּחוֹת *(on page 79) after which they are kissed and released. From the beginning of this prayer to the end of the* עמידה*, conversation is forbidden.*

Some say:

הֲרֵינִי מְזַמֵּן אֶת פִּי לְהוֹדוֹת וּלְהַלֵּל וּלְשַׁבֵּחַ אֶת בּוֹרְאִי, לְשֵׁם יִחוּד קֻדְשָׁא בְּרִיךְ הוּא וּשְׁכִינְתֵּהּ, עַל יְדֵי הַהוּא טָמִיר וְנֶעְלָם בְּשֵׁם כָּל יִשְׂרָאֵל.

בָּרוּךְ שֶׁאָמַר
וְהָיָה הָעוֹלָם, בָּרוּךְ הוּא.
בָּרוּךְ עוֹשֶׂה בְרֵאשִׁית
בָּרוּךְ אוֹמֵר וְעוֹשֶׂה
בָּרוּךְ גּוֹזֵר וּמְקַיֵּם
בָּרוּךְ מְרַחֵם עַל הָאָרֶץ
בָּרוּךְ מְרַחֵם עַל הַבְּרִיּוֹת
בָּרוּךְ מְשַׁלֵּם שָׂכָר טוֹב לִירֵאָיו
בָּרוּךְ חַי לָעַד וְקַיָּם לָנֶצַח
בָּרוּךְ פּוֹדֶה וּמַצִּיל
בָּרוּךְ שְׁמוֹ

LEARNING

Have you ever needed to psych yourself up before an important event or performance? To get your mind in the right zone? *Pesukei DeZimra* is designed to do just that. Through the reciting of verses from Tanakh that describe God's magnificent universe and the way He created it, and His majestic role in history, *Pesukei DeZimra* aims to inspire us and lift us to a place where we are ready to stand before Hashem and open our souls to Him. Like an athlete who listens to music before entering the arena, we say "verses of song" before we enter the ultimate arena and stand before Hashem.

Blessed are You, Lord our God, King of the Universe,
God, compassionate Father,
celebrated by the mouth of His people,
praised and glorified by the tongue of His devoted ones
and those who serve Him.
With the songs of Your servant David
we will praise You, O Lord our God.
With praises and psalms
we will magnify and praise You, glorify You,
Speak Your name and declare Your kingship,
our King, our God, ‣ the only One, Giver of life to the worlds,
the King whose great name is praised
and glorified to all eternity.
Blessed are You, Lord,
the King celebrated with songs of praise.

"Four score and seven years ago our fathers brought forth on this continent a new nation, conceived in liberty, and dedicated to the proposition that all men are created equal. Now we are engaged in a great civil war, testing whether that nation, or any nation so conceived and so dedicated, can long endure. We are met on a great battlefield of that war. We have come to dedicate a portion of that field, as a final resting place for those who here gave their lives that that nation might live.... The brave men, living and dead, who struggled here, have consecrated it, far above our poor power to add or detract. The world will little note, nor long remember what we say here, but it can never forget what they did here. "

(Abraham Lincoln,
The Gettysburg Address)

"I have a dream that one day this nation will rise up and live out the true meaning of its creed: 'We hold these truths to be self-evident, that all men are created equal.'

I have a dream that one day on the red hills of Georgia, the sons of former slaves and the sons of former slave owners will be able to sit down together at the table of brotherhood.

I have a dream that one day even the state of Mississippi, a state sweltering with the heat of injustice, sweltering with the heat of oppression, will be transformed into an oasis of freedom and justice.

I have a dream that my four little children will one day live in a nation where they will not be judged by the color of their skin but by the content of their character."

(Martin Luther King,
delivered August 28, 1963, at the
Lincoln Memorial, Washington D.C.)

בָּרוּךְ אַתָּה יהוה אֱלֹהֵינוּ מֶלֶךְ הָעוֹלָם
הָאֵל הָאָב הָרַחֲמָן הַמְהֻלָּל בְּפִי עַמּוֹ
מְשֻׁבָּח וּמְפֹאָר בִּלְשׁוֹן חֲסִידָיו וַעֲבָדָיו
וּבְשִׁירֵי דָוִד עַבְדֶּךָ נְהַלֶּלְךָ יהוה אֱלֹהֵינוּ.
בִּשְׁבָחוֹת וּבִזְמִירוֹת, נְגַדֶּלְךָ וּנְשַׁבֵּחֲךָ וּנְפָאֶרְךָ
וְנַזְכִּיר שִׁמְךָ וְנַמְלִיכְךָ מַלְכֵּנוּ אֱלֹהֵינוּ, ◂ יָחִיד חֵי הָעוֹלָמִים
מֶלֶךְ, מְשֻׁבָּח וּמְפֹאָר עֲדֵי עַד שְׁמוֹ הַגָּדוֹל
בָּרוּךְ אַתָּה יהוה, מֶלֶךְ מְהֻלָּל בַּתִּשְׁבָּחוֹת.

REFLECTION

"[Music's] language is a language which the soul alone understands, but which the soul can never translate."
(Arnold Bennett)

When do you listen to music? Why?

When do you sing? Why?

... A THOUSAND WORDS

CONNECTION

SPEECHES THAT CHANGED THE WORLD

"Even though large tracts of Europe and many old and famous States have fallen or may fall into the grip of the Gestapo and all the odious apparatus of Nazi rule, we shall not flag or fail. We shall go on to the end, we shall fight in France, we shall fight on the seas and oceans, we shall fight with growing confidence and growing strength in the air, we shall defend our Island, whatever the cost may be, we shall fight on the beaches, we shall fight on the landing grounds, we shall fight in the fields and in the streets, we shall fight in the hills; we shall never surrender."

(Winston Churchill, Address to the House of Commons, June 4, 1940)

הוֹדוּ לַיהוה Thank the LORD, call on His name, make His acts known among the peoples. Sing to Him, make music to Him, tell of all His wonders. Glory in His holy name; let the hearts of those who seek the LORD rejoice. Search out the LORD and His strength; seek His presence at all times. Remember the wonders He has done, His miracles, and the judgments He pronounced. Descendants of Yisrael His servant, sons of Jacob His chosen ones: He is the LORD our God. His judgments are throughout the earth. Remember His covenant for ever, the word He commanded for a thousand generations. He made it with Abraham, vowed it to Isaac, and confirmed it to Jacob as a law and to Israel as an everlasting covenant, saying, "To you I will give the land of Canaan as your heritage." You were then small in number, few, strangers there, wandering from nation to nation, from one kingdom to another, but He let no man oppress them, and for their sake He rebuked kings: "Do not touch My anointed ones, and do My prophets no harm." Sing to the LORD, all the earth; tell of His salvation daily. Declare His glory among the nations, His wonders among all the peoples. For great is the LORD and greatly to be praised; He is awesome beyond all heavenly powers. ▸ For all the gods of the peoples are mere idols; it was the LORD who made the heavens. *I Chr. 16*

CONNECTION

"There is an inner connection between music and the spirit...

Words are the language of the mind. Music is the language of the soul.

So when we seek to express or evoke emotion we turn to melody. Deborah sang after Israel's victory over the forces of Siserah. Hannah sang when she had a child. When Saul was depressed, David would play for him and his spirit would be restored. David himself was known as the 'sweet singer of Israel.' Elisha called for a harpist to play so that the prophetic spirit could rest upon him. The Levites sang in the Temple. Every day, in Judaism, we preface our morning prayers with Pesukei DeZimra, *the 'Verses of Song' with their magnificent crescendo, Psalm 150, in which instruments and the human voice combine to sing God's praises."*

(Rabbi Jonathan Sacks, *Covenant & Conversation*, Beshalaḥ, 5772)

דברי הימים א, טז

הוֹדוּ לַיהוה קִרְאוּ בִשְׁמוֹ, הוֹדִיעוּ בָעַמִּים עֲלִילֹתָיו: שִׁירוּ לוֹ,
זַמְּרוּ־לוֹ, שִׂיחוּ בְּכָל־נִפְלְאוֹתָיו: הִתְהַלְלוּ בְּשֵׁם קָדְשׁוֹ, יִשְׂמַח לֵב
מְבַקְשֵׁי יהוה: דִּרְשׁוּ יהוה וְעֻזּוֹ, בַּקְּשׁוּ פָנָיו תָּמִיד: זִכְרוּ נִפְלְאֹתָיו
אֲשֶׁר עָשָׂה, מֹפְתָיו וּמִשְׁפְּטֵי־פִיהוּ: זֶרַע יִשְׂרָאֵל עַבְדּוֹ, בְּנֵי יַעֲקֹב
בְּחִירָיו: הוּא יהוה אֱלֹהֵינוּ בְּכָל־הָאָרֶץ מִשְׁפָּטָיו: זִכְרוּ לְעוֹלָם
בְּרִיתוֹ, דָּבָר צִוָּה לְאֶלֶף דּוֹר: אֲשֶׁר כָּרַת אֶת־אַבְרָהָם, וּשְׁבוּעָתוֹ
לְיִצְחָק: וַיַּעֲמִידֶהָ לְיַעֲקֹב לְחֹק, לְיִשְׂרָאֵל בְּרִית עוֹלָם: לֵאמֹר,
לְךָ אֶתֵּן אֶרֶץ־כְּנָעַן, חֶבֶל נַחֲלַתְכֶם: בִּהְיוֹתְכֶם מְתֵי מִסְפָּר,
כִּמְעַט וְגָרִים בָּהּ: וַיִּתְהַלְּכוּ מִגּוֹי אֶל־גּוֹי, וּמִמַּמְלָכָה אֶל־עַם
אַחֵר: לֹא־הִנִּיחַ לְאִישׁ לְעָשְׁקָם, וַיּוֹכַח עֲלֵיהֶם מְלָכִים: אַל־
תִּגְּעוּ בִּמְשִׁיחָי, וּבִנְבִיאַי אַל־תָּרֵעוּ: שִׁירוּ לַיהוה כָּל־הָאָרֶץ,
בַּשְּׂרוּ מִיּוֹם־אֶל־יוֹם יְשׁוּעָתוֹ: סַפְּרוּ בַגּוֹיִם אֶת־כְּבוֹדוֹ, בְּכָל־
הָעַמִּים נִפְלְאֹתָיו: כִּי גָדוֹל יהוה וּמְהֻלָּל מְאֹד, וְנוֹרָא הוּא עַל־
כָּל־אֱלֹהִים: › כִּי כָּל־אֱלֹהֵי הָעַמִּים אֱלִילִים, וַיהוה שָׁמַיִם עָשָׂה:

REFLECTION

What miracles
in Jewish history
inspire you?

Have you
or anyone in your family
lived through any miracles
in Jewish history?

Ask your parents
and grandparents
this question
next time
you see them.

... A THOUSAND WORDS

Before Him are majesty and splendor; there is strength and beauty in His holy place. Give to the LORD, families of the peoples, give to the LORD honor and might. Give to the LORD the glory due to His name; bring an offering and come before Him; bow down to the LORD in the splendor of holiness. Tremble before Him, all the earth; the world stands firm, it will not be shaken. Let the heavens rejoice and the earth be glad; let them declare among the nations, "The LORD is King." Let the sea roar, and all that is in it; let the fields be jubilant, and all they contain. Then the trees of the forest will sing for joy before the LORD, for He is coming to judge the earth. Thank the LORD for He is good; His loving-kindness is for ever. Say: "Save us, God of our salvation; gather us and rescue us from the nations, to acknowledge Your holy name and glory in Your praise. Blessed is the LORD, God of Israel, from this world to eternity." And let all the people say "Amen" and "Praise the LORD."

▸ Elevate the LORD our God and bow before His footstool: He is holy. Elevate the LORD our God and bow at His holy mountain; for holy is the LORD our God. *Ps. 99*

...A THOUSAND WORDS

הוד וְהָדָר לְפָנָיו, עֹז וְחֶדְוָה בִּמְקֹמוֹ: הָבוּ לַיהוה מִשְׁפְּחוֹת עַמִּים, הָבוּ לַיהוה כָּבוֹד וָעֹז: הָבוּ לַיהוה כְּבוֹד שְׁמוֹ, שְׂאוּ מִנְחָה וּבֹאוּ לְפָנָיו, הִשְׁתַּחֲווּ לַיהוה בְּהַדְרַת־קֹדֶשׁ: חִילוּ מִלְּפָנָיו כָּל־הָאָרֶץ, אַף־תִּכּוֹן תֵּבֵל בַּל־תִּמּוֹט: יִשְׂמְחוּ הַשָּׁמַיִם וְתָגֵל הָאָרֶץ, וְיֹאמְרוּ בַגּוֹיִם יהוה מָלָךְ: יִרְעַם הַיָּם וּמְלוֹאוֹ, יַעֲלֹץ הַשָּׂדֶה וְכָל־אֲשֶׁר־בּוֹ: אָז יְרַנְּנוּ עֲצֵי הַיָּעַר, מִלִּפְנֵי יהוה, כִּי־בָא לִשְׁפּוֹט אֶת־הָאָרֶץ: הוֹדוּ לַיהוה כִּי טוֹב, כִּי לְעוֹלָם חַסְדּוֹ: וְאִמְרוּ, הוֹשִׁיעֵנוּ אֱלֹהֵי יִשְׁעֵנוּ, וְקַבְּצֵנוּ וְהַצִּילֵנוּ מִן־הַגּוֹיִם, לְהֹדוֹת לְשֵׁם קָדְשֶׁךָ, לְהִשְׁתַּבֵּחַ בִּתְהִלָּתֶךָ: בָּרוּךְ יהוה אֱלֹהֵי יִשְׂרָאֵל מִן־הָעוֹלָם וְעַד־הָעֹלָם, וַיֹּאמְרוּ כָל־הָעָם אָמֵן, וְהַלֵּל לַיהוה:

תהלים צט ‹ רוֹמְמוּ יהוה אֱלֹהֵינוּ וְהִשְׁתַּחֲווּ לַהֲדֹם רַגְלָיו, קָדוֹשׁ הוּא: רוֹמְמוּ יהוה אֱלֹהֵינוּ וְהִשְׁתַּחֲווּ לְהַר קָדְשׁוֹ, כִּי־קָדוֹשׁ יהוה אֱלֹהֵינוּ:

CONNECTION

There's music in the sighing of a reed;
There's music in the gushing of a rill;
There's music in all things,
if men had ears:

Their earth is but an echo
of the spheres.

(Lord Byron)

REFLECTION

"Earth laughs in flowers."
(Ralph Waldo Emerson)

Close your eyes. Can you hear nature? What is it saying? Is it praising God?

Have you ever seen a natural phenomenon that took your breath away? What was it?

Think of it now as you say this *tefilla*.

He is compassionate. He forgives wrongdoing and does not *Ps. 78*
destroy. Repeatedly He suppresses His anger, not rousing His
full fury. You, LORD: do not withhold Your compassion from me. *Ps. 40*
May Your loving-kindness and truth always guard me. Remember, *Ps. 25*
LORD, Your acts of compassion and love, for they have existed for
ever. Ascribe power to God, whose majesty is over Israel and whose *Ps. 68*
might is in the skies. You are awesome, God, in Your holy places.
It is the God of Israel who gives might and strength to the people,
may God be blessed. God of retribution, LORD, God of retribu- *Ps. 94*
tion, appear. Arise, Judge of the earth, to repay the arrogant their
just deserts. Salvation belongs to the LORD; may Your blessing rest *Ps. 3*
upon Your people, Selah! ▸ The LORD of multitudes is with us, the *Ps. 46*
God of Jacob is our stronghold, Selah! LORD of multitudes, happy *Ps. 84*
is the one who trusts in You. LORD, save! May the King answer us *Ps. 20*
on the day we call.

Save Your people and bless Your heritage; tend them and carry *Ps. 28*
them for ever. Our soul longs for the LORD; He is our Help and *Ps. 33*
Shield. For in Him our hearts rejoice, for in His holy name we have
trusted. May Your loving-kindness, LORD, be upon us, as we have
put our hope in You. Show us, LORD, Your loving-kindness and *Ps. 85*
give us Your salvation. Arise, help us and redeem us for the sake of *Ps. 44*
Your love. I am the LORD your God who brought you up from the *Ps. 81*
land of Egypt: open your mouth wide and I will fill it. Happy is the *Ps. 144*
people for whom this is so; happy is the people whose God is the
LORD. ▸ As for me, I trust in Your loving-kindness; my heart rejoices *Ps. 13*
in Your salvation. I will sing to the LORD for He has been good to me.

CONNECTION

Close your eyes. Consider for a moment whom you trust most in the world. Perhaps your best friend? Your sibling? Your parents? Think about how it feels to place your life in their hands. Do you trust them with your life? Does that feel safe or does that make you feel vulnerable? Now take a moment to think about your relationship with God. Do you feel vulnerable or safe in the knowledge that your life is in His hands? How does it feel to know that your every waking moment is dependent on Him and His kindness?

וְהוּא רַחוּם, יְכַפֵּר עָוֹן וְלֹא־יַשְׁחִית, וְהִרְבָּה לְהָשִׁיב אַפּוֹ, תהלים עח
וְלֹא־יָעִיר כָּל־חֲמָתוֹ: אַתָּה יהוה לֹא־תִכְלָא רַחֲמֶיךָ מִמֶּנִּי, חַסְדְּךָ תהלים מ
וַאֲמִתְּךָ תָּמִיד יִצְּרוּנִי: זְכֹר־רַחֲמֶיךָ יהוה וַחֲסָדֶיךָ, כִּי מֵעוֹלָם תהלים כה
הֵמָּה: תְּנוּ עֹז לֵאלֹהִים, עַל־יִשְׂרָאֵל גַּאֲוָתוֹ, וְעֻזּוֹ בַּשְּׁחָקִים: תהלים סח
נוֹרָא אֱלֹהִים מִמִּקְדָּשֶׁיךָ, אֵל יִשְׂרָאֵל הוּא נֹתֵן עֹז וְתַעֲצֻמוֹת
לָעָם, בָּרוּךְ אֱלֹהִים: אֵל־נְקָמוֹת יהוה, אֵל נְקָמוֹת הוֹפִיעַ: הִנָּשֵׂא תהלים צד
שֹׁפֵט הָאָרֶץ, הָשֵׁב גְּמוּל עַל־גֵּאִים: לַיהוה הַיְשׁוּעָה, עַל־עַמְּךָ תהלים ג
בִרְכָתֶךָ סֶּלָה: ‧ יהוה צְבָאוֹת עִמָּנוּ, מִשְׂגָּב לָנוּ אֱלֹהֵי יַעֲקֹב תהלים מו
סֶלָה: יהוה צְבָאוֹת, אַשְׁרֵי אָדָם בֹּטֵחַ בָּךְ: יהוה הוֹשִׁיעָה, הַמֶּלֶךְ תהלים פד תהלים כ
יַעֲנֵנוּ בְיוֹם־קָרְאֵנוּ:

הוֹשִׁיעָה אֶת־עַמֶּךָ, וּבָרֵךְ אֶת־נַחֲלָתֶךָ, וּרְעֵם וְנַשְּׂאֵם עַד־ תהלים כח
הָעוֹלָם: נַפְשֵׁנוּ חִכְּתָה לַיהוה, עֶזְרֵנוּ וּמָגִנֵּנוּ הוּא: כִּי־בוֹ יִשְׂמַח תהלים לג
לִבֵּנוּ, כִּי בְשֵׁם קָדְשׁוֹ בָטָחְנוּ: יְהִי־חַסְדְּךָ יהוה עָלֵינוּ, כַּאֲשֶׁר
יִחַלְנוּ לָךְ: הַרְאֵנוּ יהוה חַסְדֶּךָ, וְיֶשְׁעֲךָ תִּתֶּן־לָנוּ: קוּמָה עֶזְרָתָה תהלים פה תהלים מד
לָּנוּ, וּפְדֵנוּ לְמַעַן חַסְדֶּךָ: אָנֹכִי יהוה אֱלֹהֶיךָ הַמַּעַלְךָ מֵאֶרֶץ תהלים פא
מִצְרָיִם, הַרְחֶב־פִּיךָ וַאֲמַלְאֵהוּ: אַשְׁרֵי הָעָם שֶׁכָּכָה לּוֹ, אַשְׁרֵי תהלים קמד
הָעָם שֶׁיהוה אֱלֹהָיו: ‧ וַאֲנִי בְּחַסְדְּךָ בָטַחְתִּי, יָגֵל לִבִּי בִּישׁוּעָתֶךָ, תהלים יג
אָשִׁירָה לַיהוה, כִּי גָמַל עָלָי:

REFLECTION

Do you have faith in God?
Why?

Do you think God has faith in us?

... A THOUSAND WORDS

The following psalm recalls the thanksgiving-offering in Temple times.
It is not said on Erev Pesaḥ, on Ḥol HaMo'ed Pesaḥ, or Erev Yom Kippur
since no thanksgiving-offerings were brought on these days.
To emphasize its sacrificial nature, the custom is to say it standing.

מִזְמוֹר A psalm of thanksgiving. Shout joyously to the LORD, all the earth. Serve the LORD with joy. Come before Him with celebration. Know that the LORD is God. He made us and we are His. We are His people and the flock He tends. Enter His gates with thanksgiving, His courts with praise. Thank Him and bless His name. ▸ For the LORD is good, His loving-kindness is everlasting, and His trustworthiness is for every generation. *Ps. 100*

CONNECTION

During a time when Jews had a curfew and were barred from the streets of Russia at night, a holy Hasid of the Rebbe of Karlin risked his life to be close to his rebbe and braved the streets in order to bathe in the light and warmth of the rebbe's service of Hashem. Grasping his tiny book of Tehillim *in his hand the Hasid ran wildly through the streets of Karlin in order to reach the home of the rebbe, until his path was blocked by a Russian policeman. He was grabbed and dragged to jail, and his book of* Tehillim *was confiscated. Weeping silently in his cell, the Hasid said to himself, "They have taken away my opportunity to be close to my rebbe tonight, and snatched my* Tehillim, *but they can't stop me from being a Jew." And with that he jumped to his feet with joy and tears in his eyes, and he began to dance a jubilant dance. The prison guard stared at him with disbelief and amusement in equal measure as he gave way to hysterical laughing at the bizarre sight of the dancing Jew. With that he opened the cell and sent the Jew on his way, shouting after him, "There is no room in this jail for mentally imbalanced people!" As the Hasid arrived at the rebbe's house he was greeted with a warm knowing smile and the words, "If one is truly happy to be a Jew and part of the Jewish People, then one can be rescued from anything!"*

REFLECTION

"מִצְוָה גְּדוֹלָה
לִהְיוֹת בְּשִׂמְחָה"

"It is a great mitzva to always be happy."
(Rabbi Naḥman of Breslov)

What makes you happy?

Does believing in God make you feel happy?

How can we serve Hashem with happiness?

The following psalm recalls the קרבן תודה *in Temple times.*
It is not said on ערב פסח, חול המועד פסח *or* ערב יום כיפור,
since no קרבנות תודה *were brought on these days.*
To emphasize its sacrificial nature, the custom is to say it standing.

מִזְמוֹר לְתוֹדָה, הָרִיעוּ לַיהוה כָּל־הָאָרֶץ: עִבְדוּ אֶת־ תהלים ק
יהוה בְּשִׂמְחָה, בֹּאוּ לְפָנָיו בִּרְנָנָה: דְּעוּ כִּי־יהוה הוּא
אֱלֹהִים, הוּא עָשָׂנוּ וְלוֹ אֲנַחְנוּ, עַמּוֹ וְצֹאן מַרְעִיתוֹ: בֹּאוּ
שְׁעָרָיו בְּתוֹדָה, חֲצֵרֹתָיו בִּתְהִלָּה, הוֹדוּ לוֹ, בָּרְכוּ שְׁמוֹ:
‹ כִּי־טוֹב יהוה, לְעוֹלָם חַסְדּוֹ, וְעַד־דֹּר וָדֹר אֱמוּנָתוֹ:

... A THOUSAND WORDS

LEARNING

This Psalm of Thanksgiving was said in the *Beit HaMikdash* when the *korban toda* (thanksgiving offering) was brought. This happened when a person survived life-threatening ordeal such as a hazardous journey, an illness, or being subjected to captivity. We include this chapter from *Tehillim* here to further proclaim our mood of thanksgiving as we consider Hashem's role in the world.

יְהִי כְבוֹד May the Lord's glory be for ever; may the Lord rejoice Ps. 104
in His works. May the Lord's name be blessed, now and for ever. Ps. 113
From the rising of the sun to its setting, may the Lord's name be
praised. The Lord is high above all nations; His glory is above the
heavens. Lord, Your name is for ever. Your reputation, Lord, is for Ps. 135
all generations. The Lord has established His throne in heaven; Ps. 103
His kingdom rules all. Let the heavens rejoice and the earth be 1 Chr. 16
glad. Let them say among the nations, "The Lord is King." The
Lord is King, the Lord was King, the Lord will be King for ever
and all time. The Lord is King for ever and all time; nations will Ps. 10
perish from His land. The Lord foils the plans of nations; He Ps. 33
frustrates the intentions of peoples. Many are the intentions in a Prov. 19
person's mind, but the Lord's plan prevails. The Lord's plan shall Ps. 33
stand for ever, His mind's intent for all generations. For He spoke
and it was; He commanded and it stood firm. For the Lord has Ps. 132
chosen Zion; He desired it for His dwelling. For the Lord has Ps. 135
chosen Jacob as His own, Israel as His special treasure. For the Ps. 94
Lord will not abandon His people; nor will He abandon His
heritage. ▸ He is compassionate. He forgives wrongdoing and does Ps. 78
not destroy. Repeatedly He suppresses His anger, not rousing His
full fury. Lord, save! May the King answer us on the day we call. Ps. 20

...A THOUSAND WORDS

יְהִי כְבוֹד יהוה לְעוֹלָם, יִשְׂמַח יהוה בְּמַעֲשָׂיו: יְהִי שֵׁם יהוה מְבֹרָךְ, תהלים קד / תהלים קיג
מֵעַתָּה וְעַד־עוֹלָם: מִמִּזְרַח־שֶׁמֶשׁ עַד־מְבוֹאוֹ, מְהֻלָּל שֵׁם יהוה:
רָם עַל־כָּל־גּוֹיִם יהוה, עַל הַשָּׁמַיִם כְּבוֹדוֹ: יהוה שִׁמְךָ לְעוֹלָם, תהלים קלה
יהוה זִכְרְךָ לְדֹר־וָדֹר: יהוה בַּשָּׁמַיִם הֵכִין כִּסְאוֹ, וּמַלְכוּתוֹ בַּכֹּל תהלים קג
מָשָׁלָה: יִשְׂמְחוּ הַשָּׁמַיִם וְתָגֵל הָאָרֶץ, וְיֹאמְרוּ בַגּוֹיִם יהוה מָלָךְ: דברי הימים א׳ טז
יהוה מֶלֶךְ, יהוה מָלָךְ, יהוה יִמְלֹךְ לְעוֹלָם וָעֶד. יהוה מֶלֶךְ עוֹלָם תהלים י
וָעֶד, אָבְדוּ גוֹיִם מֵאַרְצוֹ: יהוה הֵפִיר עֲצַת־גּוֹיִם, הֵנִיא מַחְשְׁבוֹת תהלים לג
עַמִּים: רַבּוֹת מַחֲשָׁבוֹת בְּלֶב־אִישׁ, וַעֲצַת יהוה הִיא תָקוּם: משלי יט
עֲצַת יהוה לְעוֹלָם תַּעֲמֹד, מַחְשְׁבוֹת לִבּוֹ לְדֹר וָדֹר: כִּי הוּא אָמַר תהלים לג
וַיֶּהִי, הוּא־צִוָּה וַיַּעֲמֹד: כִּי־בָחַר יהוה בְּצִיּוֹן, אִוָּהּ לְמוֹשָׁב לוֹ: תהלים קלב
כִּי־יַעֲקֹב בָּחַר לוֹ יָהּ, יִשְׂרָאֵל לִסְגֻלָּתוֹ: כִּי לֹא־יִטֹּשׁ יהוה עַמּוֹ, תהלים קלה / תהלים צד
וְנַחֲלָתוֹ לֹא יַעֲזֹב: › וְהוּא רַחוּם, יְכַפֵּר עָוֹן וְלֹא־יַשְׁחִית, וְהִרְבָּה תהלים עח
לְהָשִׁיב אַפּוֹ, וְלֹא־יָעִיר כָּל־חֲמָתוֹ: יהוה הוֹשִׁיעָה, הַמֶּלֶךְ יַעֲנֵנוּ תהלים כ
בְיוֹם־קָרְאֵנוּ:

REFLECTION

וַיְבִאֵנוּ אֶל־הַמָּקוֹם הַזֶּה; וַיִּתֶּן־לָנוּ אֶת־הָאָרֶץ הַזֹּאת, אֶרֶץ זָבַת חָלָב וּדְבָשׁ.

"He brought us to this place and gave us this land, a land flowing with milk and honey."
(*Devarim* 26:9)

What is special about *Eretz Yisrael*?

Why do you think God chose it for our homeland?

Do we need a homeland at all? Why?

Does it matter where this is?

CONNECTION

"I will insist that the Hebrews have done more to civilize men than any other nation. If I were an atheist, and believed in blind eternal fate, I should still believe that fate had ordained the Jews to be the most essential instrument for civilizing the nations. If I were an atheist of the other sect, who believe or pretend to believe that all is ordered by chance, I should believe that chance had ordered the Jews to preserve and propagate to all mankind the doctrine of a supreme, intelligent, wise, almighty sovereign of the universe, which I believe to be the great essential principle of all morality, and consequently of all civilization."

(President John Adams, 1809)

The line beginning with "You open Your hand" should be said with special concentration, representing as it does the key idea of this psalm, and of Pesukei DeZimra as a whole, that God is the creator and sustainer of all. Some have the custom to touch the hand-tefillin at °, and the head-tefillin at °°.

אַשְׁרֵי Happy are those who live in Your House; *Ps. 84*
they shall continue to praise You, Selah!
Happy are the people for whom this is so; *Ps. 144*
happy are the people whose God is the Lord.

A song of praise by David. *Ps. 145*
א I will elevate You, my God, the King,
and bless Your name for ever and all time.
ב Every day I will bless You,
and praise Your name for ever and all time.
ג Great is the Lord and greatly to be praised;
His greatness is unfathomable.
ד One generation will praise Your works to the next,
and tell of Your mighty deeds.
ה On the glorious splendor of Your majesty I will meditate,
and on the acts of Your wonders.
ו They shall talk of the power of Your awesome deeds,
and I will tell of Your greatness.
ז They shall recite the record of Your great goodness,
and sing with joy of Your righteousness.
ח The Lord is generous and compassionate,
slow to anger and great in loving-kindness.
ט The Lord is good to all,
and His compassion extends to all His works.
י All Your works shall thank You, Lord,
and Your devoted ones shall bless You.
כ They shall talk of the glory of Your kingship,
and speak of Your might.

---

we have available to us. In truth, the entire *alef-beit* is not represented here. Can you see which letter is missing? This is because it would represent "*nefila*" and refer to the fall of man. Instead we choose to focus on the opposite when the very next verse refers to God supporting and carrying those that fall.

The line beginning with פּוֹתֵחַ אֶת יָדֶךָ *should be said with special concentration, representing as it does the key idea of this psalm, and of* פסוקי דזמרה *as a whole, that God is the creator and sustainer of all. Some have the custom to touch the* תפילין של יד *at* °, *and the* תפילין של ראש *at* °°.

תהלים פד
אַשְׁרֵי יוֹשְׁבֵי בֵיתֶךָ, עוֹד יְהַלְלְוּךָ סֶּלָה:
תהלים קמד
אַשְׁרֵי הָעָם שֶׁכָּכָה לּוֹ, אַשְׁרֵי הָעָם שֶׁיהוה אֱלֹהָיו:
תהלים קמה
תְּהִלָּה לְדָוִד

אֲרוֹמִמְךָ אֱלוֹהַי הַמֶּלֶךְ, וַאֲבָרְכָה שִׁמְךָ לְעוֹלָם וָעֶד:
בְּכָל־יוֹם אֲבָרְכֶךָּ, וַאֲהַלְלָה שִׁמְךָ לְעוֹלָם וָעֶד:
גָּדוֹל יהוה וּמְהֻלָּל מְאֹד, וְלִגְדֻלָּתוֹ אֵין חֵקֶר:
דּוֹר לְדוֹר יְשַׁבַּח מַעֲשֶׂיךָ, וּגְבוּרֹתֶיךָ יַגִּידוּ:
הֲדַר כְּבוֹד הוֹדֶךָ, וְדִבְרֵי נִפְלְאֹתֶיךָ אָשִׂיחָה:
וֶעֱזוּז נוֹרְאֹתֶיךָ יֹאמֵרוּ, וּגְדוּלָּתְךָ אֲסַפְּרֶנָּה:
זֵכֶר רַב־טוּבְךָ יַבִּיעוּ, וְצִדְקָתְךָ יְרַנֵּנוּ:
חַנּוּן וְרַחוּם יהוה, אֶרֶךְ אַפַּיִם וּגְדָל־חָסֶד:
טוֹב־יהוה לַכֹּל, וְרַחֲמָיו עַל־כָּל־מַעֲשָׂיו:
יוֹדְוּךָ יהוה כָּל־מַעֲשֶׂיךָ, וַחֲסִידֶיךָ יְבָרְכוּכָה:
כְּבוֹד מַלְכוּתְךָ יֹאמֵרוּ, וּגְבוּרָתְךָ יְדַבֵּרוּ:

LEARNING

This is the first of three times that we say *Ashrei* in our daily *tefillot*. We first say *Ashrei* here as the centerpiece of *Pesukei DeZimra*, and then repeat it toward the end of Shaḥarit, and then again as a "mini-*Pesukei DeZimra*" at the beginning of Minḥa. The Talmud states (*Berakhot* 4b) that whoever says *Ashrei* three times every day is guaranteed a place in the World to Come. Maybe this is because *Ashrei* describes a perfect world, and ideal state in which all the world is in harmony.

This chapter of *Tehillim* is written with an *alef-beit* acrostic. This is a classic literary technique, and has some obvious advantages such as ease of memorization, and the simple beauty of the *alef-beit* format. However, there is also a deeper message here: we praise Hashem with every sound, every letter and every form of speech that

ל To make known to mankind His mighty deeds
and the glorious majesty of His kingship.
מ Your kingdom is an everlasting kingdom,
and Your reign is for all generations.
ס The LORD supports all who fall,
and raises all who are bowed down.
ע All raise their eyes to You in hope,
and You give them their food in due season.
פ °You open Your hand, °°and satisfy every living thing with favor.
צ The LORD is righteous in all His ways, and kind in all He does.
ק The LORD is close to all who call on Him,
to all who call on Him in truth.
ר He fulfills the will of those who fear Him;
He hears their cry and saves them.
ש The LORD guards all who love Him,
but all the wicked He will destroy.
ת ▸ My mouth shall speak the praise of the LORD,
and all creatures shall bless His holy name for ever and all time.
We will bless the LORD now and for ever. Halleluya! *Ps. 115*

REFLECTION

Can you think of something amazing about the world beginning with every letter of the alphabet?

Do you feel close to Hashem right now?

How do you think you could get closer?

CONNECTION

Joseph Gitler made aliya from New Jersey in the year 2000. In 2002, he read a report from Israel's National Insurance Institute that told a bleak story of Israel's poor and unemployed. This together with witnessing himself tremendous food wastage in Israel – from social events, restaurants, and stores, and from unharvested farm fields – inspired him to found Leket in 2003 – Israel's largest national food bank and food-rescue. With the help of thousands of volunteers each year, Leket salvages 115 tons of food every week that would otherwise be destroyed. It delivers this excess food to hundreds of thousands of needy Israelis through its partnership with non-profit agencies throughout the country. Joseph Gitler saw a desperate need in Israel that went unaddressed and stood up and took responsibility, to help the poor of Israel.

לְהוֹדִיעַ לִבְנֵי הָאָדָם גְּבוּרֹתָיו, וּכְבוֹד הֲדַר מַלְכוּתוֹ:
מַלְכוּתְךָ מַלְכוּת כָּל־עֹלָמִים, וּמֶמְשַׁלְתְּךָ בְּכָל־דּוֹר וָדֹר:
סוֹמֵךְ יהוה לְכָל־הַנֹּפְלִים, וְזוֹקֵף לְכָל־הַכְּפוּפִים:
עֵינֵי־כֹל אֵלֶיךָ יְשַׂבֵּרוּ, וְאַתָּה נוֹתֵן־לָהֶם אֶת־אָכְלָם בְּעִתּוֹ:
°פּוֹתֵחַ אֶת־יָדֶךָ, °°וּמַשְׂבִּיעַ לְכָל־חַי רָצוֹן:
צַדִּיק יהוה בְּכָל־דְּרָכָיו, וְחָסִיד בְּכָל־מַעֲשָׂיו:
קָרוֹב יהוה לְכָל־קֹרְאָיו, לְכֹל אֲשֶׁר יִקְרָאֻהוּ בֶאֱמֶת:
רְצוֹן־יְרֵאָיו יַעֲשֶׂה, וְאֶת־שַׁוְעָתָם יִשְׁמַע, וְיוֹשִׁיעֵם:
שׁוֹמֵר יהוה אֶת־כָּל־אֹהֲבָיו, וְאֵת כָּל־הָרְשָׁעִים יַשְׁמִיד:
◂ תְּהִלַּת יהוה יְדַבֶּר פִּי, וִיבָרֵךְ כָּל־בָּשָׂר שֵׁם קָדְשׁוֹ לְעוֹלָם וָעֶד:
וַאֲנַחְנוּ נְבָרֵךְ יָהּ מֵעַתָּה וְעַד־עוֹלָם, הַלְלוּיָהּ: תהלים קטו

... A THOUSAND WORDS

הַלְלוּיָהּ Halleluya! Praise the LORD, my soul. I will praise the LORD all my life; I will sing to my God as long as I live. Put not your trust in princes, or in mortal man who cannot save. His breath expires, he returns to the earth; on that day his plans come to an end. Happy is he whose help is the God of Jacob, whose hope is in the LORD his God who made heaven and earth, the sea and all they contain; He who keeps faith for ever. He secures justice for the oppressed. He gives food to the hungry. The LORD sets captives free. The LORD gives sight to the blind. The LORD raises those bowed down. The LORD loves the righteous. The LORD protects the stranger. He gives courage to the orphan and widow. He defeats the way of the wicked. ▸ The LORD shall reign for ever. He is your God, Zion, for all generations. Halleluya! *Ps. 146*

REFLECTION

Who is weak in your society?

How does God protect them?

How do you protect them?

CONNECTION

Not like the brazen giant of Greek fame,
With conquering limbs astride from land to land;
Here at our sea-washed, sunset gates shall stand
A mighty woman with a torch, whose flame
Is the imprisoned lightning, and her name
Mother of Exiles. From her beacon-hand
Glows world-wide welcome; her mild eyes command
The air-bridged harbor that twin cities frame.

"Keep, ancient lands, your storied pomp!" cries she
With silent lips. "Give me your tired, your poor,
Your huddled masses yearning to breathe free,
The wretched refuse of your teeming shore.
Send these, the homeless, tempest-tost to me,
I lift my lamp beside the golden door!"

(Emma Lazarus, *The New Colossus*, engraved inside the pedestal of the Statue of Liberty)

הַלְלוּיָהּ, הַלְלִי נַפְשִׁי אֶת־יהוה: אֲהַלְלָה יהוה בְּחַיָּי, אֲזַמְּרָה תהלים קמו
לֵאלֹהַי בְּעוֹדִי: אַל־תִּבְטְחוּ בִנְדִיבִים, בְּבֶן־אָדָם שֶׁאֵין לוֹ
תְשׁוּעָה: תֵּצֵא רוּחוֹ, יָשֻׁב לְאַדְמָתוֹ, בַּיּוֹם הַהוּא אָבְדוּ עֶשְׁתֹּנֹתָיו:
אַשְׁרֵי שֶׁאֵל יַעֲקֹב בְּעֶזְרוֹ, שִׂבְרוֹ עַל־יהוה אֱלֹהָיו: עֹשֶׂה שָׁמַיִם
וָאָרֶץ, אֶת־הַיָּם וְאֶת־כָּל־אֲשֶׁר־בָּם, הַשֹּׁמֵר אֱמֶת לְעוֹלָם: עֹשֶׂה
מִשְׁפָּט לָעֲשׁוּקִים, נֹתֵן לֶחֶם לָרְעֵבִים, יהוה מַתִּיר אֲסוּרִים: יהוה
פֹּקֵחַ עִוְרִים, יהוה זֹקֵף כְּפוּפִים, יהוה אֹהֵב צַדִּיקִים: יהוה שֹׁמֵר
אֶת־גֵּרִים, יָתוֹם וְאַלְמָנָה יְעוֹדֵד, וְדֶרֶךְ רְשָׁעִים יְעַוֵּת: ‹ יִמְלֹךְ
יהוה לְעוֹלָם, אֱלֹהַיִךְ צִיּוֹן לְדֹר וָדֹר, הַלְלוּיָהּ:

... A THOUSAND WORDS

הַלְלוּיָהּ Halleluya! How good it is to sing songs to our God; how pleasant and fitting to praise Him. The LORD rebuilds Jerusalem. He gathers the scattered exiles of Israel. He heals the brokenhearted and binds up their wounds. He counts the number of the stars, calling each by name. Great is our LORD and mighty in power; His understanding has no limit. The LORD gives courage to the humble, but casts the wicked to the ground. Sing to the LORD in thanks; make music to our God on the harp. He covers the sky with clouds. He provides the earth with rain and makes grass grow on the hills. He gives food to the cattle and to the ravens when they cry. He does not take delight in the strength of horses nor pleasure in the fleetness of man. The LORD takes pleasure in those who fear Him, who put their hope in His loving care. Praise the LORD, Jerusalem; sing to your God, Zion, for He has strengthened the bars of your gates and blessed your children in your midst. He has brought peace to your borders, and satisfied you with the finest wheat. He sends His commandment to earth; swiftly runs His word. He spreads snow like fleece, sprinkles frost like ashes, scatters hail like crumbs. Who can stand His cold? He sends His word and melts them; He makes the wind blow and the waters flow. ▸ He has declared His words to Jacob, His statutes and laws to Israel. He has done this for no other nation; such laws they do not know. Halleluya! *Ps. 147*

REFLECTION

"A change in the weather is sufficient to recreate the world and ourselves."
(Marcel Proust)

Have you ever felt God in the weather? When?

Look outside. Can you find God in the weather today?

Think about it now as you say this *tefilla*.

... A THOUSAND WORDS

הַלְלוּיָהּ, כִּי־טוֹב זַמְּרָה אֱלֹהֵינוּ, כִּי־נָעִים נָאוָה תְהִלָּה: בּוֹנֵה תהלים קמז
יְרוּשָׁלַםִ יהוה, נִדְחֵי יִשְׂרָאֵל יְכַנֵּס: הָרוֹפֵא לִשְׁבוּרֵי לֵב, וּמְחַבֵּשׁ
לְעַצְּבוֹתָם: מוֹנֶה מִסְפָּר לַכּוֹכָבִים, לְכֻלָּם שֵׁמוֹת יִקְרָא: גָּדוֹל
אֲדוֹנֵינוּ וְרַב־כֹּחַ, לִתְבוּנָתוֹ אֵין מִסְפָּר: מְעוֹדֵד עֲנָוִים יהוה,
מַשְׁפִּיל רְשָׁעִים עֲדֵי־אָרֶץ: עֱנוּ לַיהוה בְּתוֹדָה, זַמְּרוּ לֵאלֹהֵינוּ
בְכִנּוֹר: הַמְכַסֶּה שָׁמַיִם בְּעָבִים, הַמֵּכִין לָאָרֶץ מָטָר, הַמַּצְמִיחַ
הָרִים חָצִיר: נוֹתֵן לִבְהֵמָה לַחְמָהּ, לִבְנֵי עֹרֵב אֲשֶׁר יִקְרָאוּ: לֹא
בִגְבוּרַת הַסּוּס יֶחְפָּץ, לֹא־בְשׁוֹקֵי הָאִישׁ יִרְצֶה: רוֹצֶה יהוה אֶת־
יְרֵאָיו, אֶת־הַמְיַחֲלִים לְחַסְדּוֹ: שַׁבְּחִי יְרוּשָׁלַםִ אֶת־יהוה, הַלְלִי
אֱלֹהַיִךְ צִיּוֹן: כִּי־חִזַּק בְּרִיחֵי שְׁעָרָיִךְ, בֵּרַךְ בָּנַיִךְ בְּקִרְבֵּךְ: הַשָּׂם־
גְּבוּלֵךְ שָׁלוֹם, חֵלֶב חִטִּים יַשְׂבִּיעֵךְ: הַשֹּׁלֵחַ אִמְרָתוֹ אָרֶץ, עַד־
מְהֵרָה יָרוּץ דְּבָרוֹ: הַנֹּתֵן שֶׁלֶג כַּצָּמֶר, כְּפוֹר כָּאֵפֶר יְפַזֵּר: מַשְׁלִיךְ
קַרְחוֹ כְפִתִּים, לִפְנֵי קָרָתוֹ מִי יַעֲמֹד: יִשְׁלַח דְּבָרוֹ וְיַמְסֵם, יַשֵּׁב
רוּחוֹ יִזְּלוּ־מָיִם: › מַגִּיד דְּבָרָו לְיַעֲקֹב, חֻקָּיו וּמִשְׁפָּטָיו לְיִשְׂרָאֵל:
לֹא עָשָׂה כֵן לְכָל־גּוֹי, וּמִשְׁפָּטִים בַּל־יְדָעוּם, הַלְלוּיָהּ:

CONNECTION

"Once it happened that it didn't rain for almost the whole of winter in Eretz Yisrael. *The people were desperate and so they sent for Ḥoni to whom they knew Hashem would listen. Ḥoni drew a circle with a stick in the dirt and cried out to Hashem: 'Hashem, have mercy on Your children and let it rain. I won't leave this circle until You do!' At once a few drops of rain began to fall but nothing more than a drizzle. Ḥoni cried out to Hashem again: 'I didn't pray to You for rain like this. Your children need real rain that will fill their wells and reservoirs.' Immediately torrents of rain began to pour, threatening to flood the towns and villages. Once again Ḥoni cried to Hashem: 'I didn't pray to You, Hashem, for rain like this. This rain will destroy the world! Your children need rain of love and kindness.' Finally the rains calmed to a normal level, the wind began to blow and the clouds dispersed and the sun shone, and the people were saved. They ran out into the fields and gathered mushrooms and truffles."*

(*Ta'anit* 23a)

הַלְלוּיָהּ Halleluya! Praise the LORD from the heavens, praise Him in the heights. Praise Him, all His angels; praise Him, all His multitudes. Praise Him, sun and moon; praise Him, all shining stars. Praise Him, highest heavens and the waters above the heavens. Let them praise the name of the LORD, for He commanded and they were created. He established them for ever and all time, issuing a decree that will never change. Praise the LORD from the earth: sea monsters and all the deep seas; fire and hail, snow and mist, storm winds that obey His word; mountains and all hills, fruit trees and all cedars; wild animals and all cattle, creeping things and winged birds; kings of the earth and all nations, princes and all judges on earth; youths and maidens, old and young. ▸ Let them praise the name of the LORD, for His name alone is sublime; His majesty is above earth and heaven. He has raised the pride of His people, for the glory of all His devoted ones, the children of Israel, the people close to Him. Halleluya! Ps. 148

... A THOUSAND WORDS

תהלים קמח

הַלְלוּיָהּ, הַלְלוּ אֶת־יהוה מִן־הַשָּׁמַיִם, הַלְלְוּהוּ בַּמְּרוֹמִים:
הַלְלְוּהוּ כָל־מַלְאָכָיו, הַלְלְוּהוּ כָּל־צְבָאָו: הַלְלְוּהוּ שֶׁמֶשׁ וְיָרֵחַ,
הַלְלְוּהוּ כָּל־כּוֹכְבֵי אוֹר: הַלְלְוּהוּ שְׁמֵי הַשָּׁמָיִם, וְהַמַּיִם אֲשֶׁר
מֵעַל הַשָּׁמָיִם: יְהַלְלוּ אֶת־שֵׁם יהוה, כִּי הוּא צִוָּה וְנִבְרָאוּ:
וַיַּעֲמִידֵם לָעַד לְעוֹלָם, חָק־נָתַן וְלֹא יַעֲבוֹר: הַלְלוּ אֶת־יהוה
מִן־הָאָרֶץ, תַּנִּינִים וְכָל־תְּהֹמוֹת: אֵשׁ וּבָרָד שֶׁלֶג וְקִיטוֹר, רוּחַ
סְעָרָה עֹשָׂה דְבָרוֹ: הֶהָרִים וְכָל־גְּבָעוֹת, עֵץ פְּרִי וְכָל־אֲרָזִים:
הַחַיָּה וְכָל־בְּהֵמָה, רֶמֶשׂ וְצִפּוֹר כָּנָף: מַלְכֵי־אֶרֶץ וְכָל־לְאֻמִּים,
שָׂרִים וְכָל־שֹׁפְטֵי אָרֶץ: בַּחוּרִים וְגַם־בְּתוּלוֹת, זְקֵנִים עִם־נְעָרִים:
◂ יְהַלְלוּ אֶת־שֵׁם יהוה, כִּי־נִשְׂגָּב שְׁמוֹ לְבַדּוֹ, הוֹדוֹ עַל־אֶרֶץ
וְשָׁמָיִם: וַיָּרֶם קֶרֶן לְעַמּוֹ, תְּהִלָּה לְכָל־חֲסִידָיו, לִבְנֵי יִשְׂרָאֵל
עַם קְרֹבוֹ, הַלְלוּיָהּ:

REFLECTION

Can you find a way to praise God in a large way (like the vastness of the cosmos) and a tiny way (like the beauty of each blade of grass)?

Imagine the amazing things that nature has witnessed over time – what would it highlight?

What part are you playing in the orchestra of creation? What is your unique contribution?

CONNECTION

"The best remedy for those who are afraid, lonely, or unhappy is to go outside, somewhere where they can be quite alone with the heavens, nature, and God. Because only then does one feel that all is as it should be and that God wishes to see people happy, amidst the simple beauty of nature. As long as this exists, and it certainly always will, I know that then there will always be comfort for every sorrow, whatever the circumstances may be. And I firmly believe that nature brings solace in all troubles."

(Anne Frank, *The Diary of a Young Girl*)

הַלְלוּיָהּ Halleluya! Sing to the LORD a new song, His praise in the assembly of the devoted. Let Israel rejoice in its Maker; let the children of Zion delight in their King. Let them praise His name with dancing; sing praises to Him with drum and harp. For the LORD delights in His people; He adorns the humble with salvation. Let the devoted celebrate in glory; let them sing for joy on their beds. Let high praises of God be in their throats, and a two-edged sword in their hand: to impose retribution on the nations, punishment on the peoples, ▸ binding their kings with chains, their nobles with iron shackles, carrying out the judgment written against them. This is the glory of all His devoted ones. Halleluya! *Ps. 149*

REFLECTION

"A generation in which the Temple is not built is considered as if it was one in which it was destroyed."

(Yerushalmi, *Yoma* 1:1)

What would you like to see in the time of the final *geula*? What can you do to help perfect the world?

How are you contributing to the rebuilding of the Temple?

...A THOUSAND WORDS

תהלים קמט

הַלְלוּיָהּ, שִׁירוּ לַיהוה שִׁיר חָדָשׁ, תְּהִלָּתוֹ בִּקְהַל חֲסִידִים:
יִשְׂמַח יִשְׂרָאֵל בְּעֹשָׂיו, בְּנֵי־צִיּוֹן יָגִילוּ בְמַלְכָּם: יְהַלְלוּ שְׁמוֹ
בְמָחוֹל, בְּתֹף וְכִנּוֹר יְזַמְּרוּ־לוֹ: כִּי־רוֹצֶה יהוה בְּעַמּוֹ, יְפָאֵר
עֲנָוִים בִּישׁוּעָה: יַעְלְזוּ חֲסִידִים בְּכָבוֹד, יְרַנְּנוּ עַל־מִשְׁכְּבוֹתָם:
רוֹמְמוֹת אֵל בִּגְרוֹנָם, וְחֶרֶב פִּיפִיּוֹת בְּיָדָם: לַעֲשׂוֹת נְקָמָה בַּגּוֹיִם,
תּוֹכֵחוֹת בַּלְאֻמִּים: ◂ לֶאְסֹר מַלְכֵיהֶם בְּזִקִּים, וְנִכְבְּדֵיהֶם בְּכַבְלֵי
בַרְזֶל: לַעֲשׂוֹת בָּהֶם מִשְׁפָּט כָּתוּב, הָדָר הוּא לְכָל־חֲסִידָיו,
הַלְלוּיָהּ:

CONNECTION

Several years after the destruction of the Holy Temple, Rabban Gamliel, Rabbi Eliezer ben Azarya, Rabbi Yehoshua, and Rabbi Akiva were going up to Jerusalem. When they reached Mount Scopus, the site of the Temple came into view, and they tore their garments in mourning. When they reached the Temple Mount, they saw a fox dart out from the spot where the Holy of Holies had stood in the Holy Temple. The rabbis began to weep, but Rabbi Akiva laughed. They said to him: "Akiva, you never cease to amaze us. We are crying, and you laugh!" But Rabbi Akiva said, "And you, why are you crying?"

The rabbis responded: "What? Shall we not weep? The place about which Scripture states (Bemidbar 1:51), 'And the stranger who draws close shall die,' has become a den of foxes! Indeed, this is a fulfillment of the verse, 'For Mount Zion which lies desolate, foxes prowl over it' (Eikha 5:18)."

Rabbi Akiva answered them: "This is exactly why I laugh. For just as we have seen the prophecies of Jerusalem's destruction have come to pass, so too, know that the prophecies of her future consolation shall also be fulfilled. I laughed because I remembered the verses (Zekharya 8:4–5), 'Old men and old women will once again sit in the streets of Jerusalem, each with his staff in his hand because of advanced age; and the city will be filled with boys and girls playing in its streets.' The Holy One, blessed be He, has declared that just as the first prophecies have been fulfilled, so shall the latter. I am joyous that the first have already come to pass, for the latter shall be fulfilled in the future."

Said the rabbis, "You have comforted us, Akiva, you have comforted us. May you be comforted by the footsteps of the Messiah."

(Adapted from *Midrash Raba Eikha*, 5)

Ps. 150

הַלְלוּיָהּ Halleluya! Praise God in His holy place;
praise Him in the heavens of His power.
Praise Him for His mighty deeds;
praise Him for His immense greatness.
Praise Him with blasts of the shofar;
praise Him with the harp and lyre.
Praise Him with drum and dance;
praise Him with strings and flute.
Praise Him with clashing cymbals;
praise Him with resounding cymbals.
▸ Let all that breathes praise the Lord. Halleluya!
Let all that breathes praise the Lord. Halleluya!

REFLECTION

"And David was dancing with full might before the Lord, and David was wearing a linen ephod." (*Shmuel Beit* 6:14)

How can you use your mind, heart, hands, and mouth to praise God?

Have you ever felt music speak to you in ways that words could not?

Can you think of other ways to connect to God other than prayer?

... A THOUSAND WORDS

תהלים קנ

הַלְלוּיָהּ, הַלְלוּ־אֵל בְּקָדְשׁוֹ
הַלְלוּהוּ בִּרְקִיעַ עֻזּוֹ:
הַלְלוּהוּ בִגְבוּרֹתָיו
הַלְלוּהוּ כְּרֹב גֻּדְלוֹ:
הַלְלוּהוּ בְּתֵקַע שׁוֹפָר
הַלְלוּהוּ בְּנֵבֶל וְכִנּוֹר:
הַלְלוּהוּ בְתֹף וּמָחוֹל
הַלְלוּהוּ בְּמִנִּים וְעוּגָב:
הַלְלוּהוּ בְצִלְצְלֵי־שָׁמַע
הַלְלוּהוּ בְּצִלְצְלֵי תְרוּעָה:
◂ כֹּל הַנְּשָׁמָה תְּהַלֵּל יָהּ, הַלְלוּיָהּ:
כֹּל הַנְּשָׁמָה תְּהַלֵּל יָהּ, הַלְלוּיָהּ:

LEARNING

The Midrash *Yalkut Shimoni* (*Tehillim* 889) says that when King David finished writing *Sefer Tehillim,* he felt proud and said to God, "Is there any other creature You created in Your world that can recite song and praise more than I do?" At that moment a frog said to King David, "David, don't be so proud, I sing songs and praise more than you do. Not only that, but for every song that I sing, three thousand parables can be derived from it."

CONNECTION

The Rabbi of Karlin was asked the following question: "Why do Hasidim dance so much?"

The rabbi smiled and answered, "Ah, you see, when a person dances, his feet are a few of inches off the ground. This means that while a person is dancing, he is a few inches closer to heaven."

בָּרוּךְ Blessed be the LORD for ever. Ps. 89
Amen and Amen.
Blessed from Zion be the LORD Ps. 135
who is present in Jerusalem. Halleluya!
Blessed be the LORD, God of Israel, Ps. 72
who alone does wonders.
▸ Blessed be His glorious name for ever,
and may all the earth be filled with His glory.
Amen and Amen.

---

be more important than reciting an entire blessing to Hashem?

Imagine an official of the king, who praises the king warmly in front of a large gathering. If people ignore the official's words, it is incredibly disrespectful to the king. It is an indication that no one really agrees with his praise. On the other hand, if the gathering breaks out into hearty applause, this confirms the praise and proves that the king is worthy of honor.

... A THOUSAND WORDS

תהלים פט
בָּרוּךְ יהוה לְעוֹלָם
אָמֵן וְאָמֵן:

תהלים קלה
בָּרוּךְ יהוה מִצִּיּוֹן
שֹׁכֵן יְרוּשָׁלָםִ, הַלְלוּיָהּ:

תהלים עב
בָּרוּךְ יהוה אֱלֹהִים אֱלֹהֵי יִשְׂרָאֵל
עֹשֵׂה נִפְלָאוֹת לְבַדּוֹ:
← וּבָרוּךְ שֵׁם כְּבוֹדוֹ לְעוֹלָם
וְיִמָּלֵא כְבוֹדוֹ אֶת־כָּל־הָאָרֶץ
אָמֵן וְאָמֵן:

REFLECTION

How do you show you agree with something?

Can you think of ways to emphasize something you really believe in when you're talking to someone?

What things have you said that you can imagine God saying "Amen" to you?

CONNECTION

In the book "Mofet HaDor," *the biography of Reb Yechezkel Levenstein, it is said that he once saw a grandchild of Reb Yisrael Salanter crying.*

He asked the boy of five years old, "Why are you crying, sweet one?"

The child said, "Because I want to eat."

"Why don't you eat?" Reb Yechezkel asked him.

"Because I need first to recite a blessing," the child answered.

"Do you not know the blessing to be recited over this food?" Reb Yechezkel asked.

"Yes, I know it," the child responded, "but there is no one to answer 'Amen' after my blessing. How can I say it?"

LEARNING

The Gemara tells us – "Answering Amen is greater than reciting a blessing" (*Berakhot* 53b). At first, this may seem surprising. How can saying one short, simple word

Stand until after "Bless the Lord" on page 120.

וַיְבָרֶךְ David blessed the Lord in front of the entire assembly. David *1 Chr. 29*
said, "Blessed are You, Lord, God of our father Yisrael, for ever and ever. Yours, Lord, are the greatness and the power, the glory, majesty and splendor, for everything in heaven and earth is Yours. Yours, Lord, is the kingdom; You are great as Head over all. Both riches and honor are in Your gift and You reign over all things. In Your hand are strength and might. It is in Your power to make great and give strength to all. Therefore, our God, we thank You
and praise Your glorious name." You alone are the Lord. *Neh. 9*

REFLECTION

"Tzedaka and acts of kindness are the equivalent of all the mitzvot of the Torah." (Yerushalmi, *Pe'ah* 1:1)

How do you dedicate your money toward God?

How will you be generous today?

Do you make God proud in how you use your money?

... A THOUSAND WORDS

Stand until after בָּרְכוּ *on page 121.*

וַיְבָֽרֶךְ דָּוִיד אֶת־יהוה לְעֵינֵי כָּל־הַקָּהָל, וַיֹּֽאמֶר דָּוִיד, בָּרוּךְ דברי הימים א, כט
אַתָּה יהוה, אֱלֹהֵי יִשְׂרָאֵל אָבִֽינוּ, מֵעוֹלָם וְעַד־עוֹלָם: לְךָ יהוה
הַגְּדֻלָּה וְהַגְּבוּרָה וְהַתִּפְאֶֽרֶת וְהַנֵּֽצַח וְהַהוֹד, כִּי־כֹל בַּשָּׁמַֽיִם
וּבָאָֽרֶץ, לְךָ יהוה הַמַּמְלָכָה וְהַמִּתְנַשֵּׂא לְכֹל לְרֹאשׁ: וְהָעְשֶׁר
וְהַכָּבוֹד מִלְּפָנֶֽיךָ, וְאַתָּה מוֹשֵׁל בַּכֹּל, וּבְיָדְךָ כֹּֽחַ וּגְבוּרָה, וּבְיָדְךָ
לְגַדֵּל וּלְחַזֵּק לַכֹּל: וְעַתָּה אֱלֹהֵֽינוּ מוֹדִים אֲנַֽחְנוּ לָךְ, וּמְהַלְלִים
לְשֵׁם תִּפְאַרְתֶּֽךָ: אַתָּה־הוּא יהוה לְבַדֶּֽךָ, אַתָּ עָשִֽׂיתָ נחמיה ט

CONNECTION

There was once a boy called Tommy. He was actually known as "Tommy Doesn't Give" because despite that fact that Tommy was a sweet, polite, and charming young man, he lived with his motto "Tommy doesn't give." Tommy never gave anything to anyone. One day, Tommy went swimming and found himself caught in a whirlpool. He struggled to stay afloat and waved for the attention of a lifeguard. The lifeguard approached on a small boat. "Tommy," he yelled, "give me your hand."

Tommy, struggling to keep his head above the waves, shouted back, "Tommy doesn't give!" The lifeguard exasperatedly tried again, but each time his plea was answered with Tommy's staunch refusal to cooperate.

Finally the lifeguard cried, "OK Tommy, take my hand." Automatically Tommy reached out and took the lifeguard's hand to safety.

Sometimes, we lose sight of the fact that giving is actually the most important way of receiving.

LEARNING

This verse was recited by King David when he had amassed all of his wealth and was dedicating it to build the *Beit HaMikdash*. The Talmud (*Gittin* 7b) says: "Even a poor person who receives *tzedaka* must give from what he or she receives." This is telling us that an individual's sense of *kavod*, his or her self-dignity, is expressed through giving. Freeing a person from the responsibility of giving is actually taking away a privilege. It is therefore a widely accepted custom to give some *tzedaka* at this point in the *tefilla*.

You made the heavens, even the highest heavens, and all their multitudes, the earth and all that is on it, the seas and all they contain. You give life to them all, and the multitudes of heaven worship You. ▸ You are the LORD God who chose Abram and brought him out of Ur of the Chaldees, changing his name to Abraham. You found his heart faithful toward You, ◂ and You made a covenant with him to give to his descendants the land of the Canaanites, Hittites, Amorites, Perizzites, Jebusites and Girgashites. You fulfilled Your promise for You are righteous. You saw the suffering of our ancestors in Egypt. You heard their cry at the Sea of Reeds. You sent signs and wonders against Pharaoh, all his servants and all the people of his land, because You knew how arrogantly the Egyptians treated them. You created for Yourself reputation that remains to this day. ▸ You divided the sea before them, so that they passed through the sea on dry land, but You cast their pursuers into the depths, like a stone into mighty waters.

... A THOUSAND WORDS

REFLECTION

How are you connected to your ancestors?

What is the greatest thing God has done for you?

How do your memories affect you?

אֶת־הַשָּׁמַיִם, שְׁמֵי הַשָּׁמַיִם וְכׇל־צְבָאָם, הָאָרֶץ וְכׇל־אֲשֶׁר עָלֶיהָ, הַיַּמִּים וְכׇל־אֲשֶׁר בָּהֶם, וְאַתָּה מְחַיֶּה אֶת־כֻּלָּם, וּצְבָא הַשָּׁמַיִם לְךָ מִשְׁתַּחֲוִים: ‹ אַתָּה הוּא יהוה הָאֱלֹהִים אֲשֶׁר בָּחַרְתָּ בְּאַבְרָם, וְהוֹצֵאתוֹ מֵאוּר כַּשְׂדִּים, וְשַׂמְתָּ שְּׁמוֹ אַבְרָהָם: וּמָצָאתָ אֶת־לְבָבוֹ נֶאֱמָן לְפָנֶיךָ, ‹ וְכָרוֹת עִמּוֹ הַבְּרִית לָתֵת אֶת־אֶרֶץ הַכְּנַעֲנִי הַחִתִּי הָאֱמֹרִי וְהַפְּרִזִּי וְהַיְבוּסִי וְהַגִּרְגָּשִׁי, לָתֵת לְזַרְעוֹ, וַתָּקֶם אֶת־דְּבָרֶיךָ, כִּי צַדִּיק אָתָּה: וַתֵּרֶא אֶת־עֳנִי אֲבֹתֵינוּ בְּמִצְרָיִם, וְאֶת־זַעֲקָתָם שָׁמַעְתָּ עַל־יַם־סוּף: וַתִּתֵּן אֹתֹת וּמֹפְתִים בְּפַרְעֹה וּבְכׇל־עֲבָדָיו וּבְכׇל־עַם אַרְצוֹ, כִּי יָדַעְתָּ כִּי הֵזִידוּ עֲלֵיהֶם, וַתַּעַשׂ־לְךָ שֵׁם כְּהַיּוֹם הַזֶּה: ‹ וְהַיָּם בָּקַעְתָּ לִפְנֵיהֶם, וַיַּעַבְרוּ בְתוֹךְ־הַיָּם בַּיַּבָּשָׁה, וְאֶת־רֹדְפֵיהֶם הִשְׁלַכְתָּ בִמְצוֹלֹת כְּמוֹ־אֶבֶן, בְּמַיִם עַזִּים:

CONNECTION

"There is a profound difference between history and memory. History is his story – an event that happened sometime else to someone else. Memory is my story – something that happened to me and is part of who I am. History is information. Memory, by contrast, is part of identity. I can study the history of other peoples, cultures and civilizations. They deepen my knowledge and broaden my horizons. But they do not make a claim on me. They are the past as past. Memory is the past as present, as it lives on in me. Without memory there can be no identity."

(The Jonathan Sacks Haggada)

LEARNING

This section of prayers originated at a time when the Temple was still in ruins and the Jewish nation was returning from captivity in Babylon. It was important to re-inspire the nation with a renewed consciousness of its origin and destiny and to persuade it to make sacrifices for the fulfillment of its mission. (Rabbi S.R. Hirsch)

וַיּוֹשַׁע That day the Lord saved Israel from the hands of the Egyptians, and Israel saw the Egyptians lying dead on the seashore. Ex. 14
▸ When Israel saw the great power the Lord had displayed against the Egyptians, the people feared the Lord, and believed in the Lord and in His servant, Moses.

LEARNING

"The people feared the Lord, and believed in the Lord." By seeing with their own eyes and witnessing the hand of God, the Jewish People internalized their faith. This group of people who left Egypt was the beginning of the Jewish nation. Their faith became deeply rooted in the nature of the nation and its traditions and therefore all subsequent generations can tap into this faith and loyalty forever. (Rabbi Avigdor Miller)

CONNECTION

A young man once came to Rabbi Akiva. The student seemed troubled and asked to be taught about the nature of faith. The rabbi brought the student over to a sprout in the ground and said, "Pull it up." The student bent over and did so without any trouble. The two of them walked over to a sapling. The sage pointed and said to the student, "All right, now pull that one up." The sapling took more effort but the student was able to do it. Rabbi Akiva took the student to a shrub. The same command was given, and this time the student used all his strength to pull the shrub out of the ground. Finally, Rabbi Akiva took the young man to a fully grown tree. "Now," the rabbi said, "uproot it." The young student put both his hands around the tree and pulled as hard as he could, but the tree would not move.

Rabbi Akiva spoke to the student: "That is how it is with faith. If the roots of our faith are deep, if our religious views are mature and developed, our faith cannot be uprooted even by someone trying very hard to do so. Always remember that the strength of your faith first depends on the strength of its roots."

שמות יד

וַיּוֹשַׁע יהוה בַּיּוֹם הַהוּא אֶת־יִשְׂרָאֵל מִיַּד מִצְרָיִם, וַיַּרְא יִשְׂרָאֵל
אֶת־מִצְרַיִם מֵת עַל־שְׂפַת הַיָּם: › וַיַּרְא יִשְׂרָאֵל אֶת־הַיָּד הַגְּדֹלָה
אֲשֶׁר עָשָׂה יהוה בְּמִצְרַיִם, וַיִּירְאוּ הָעָם אֶת־יהוה, וַיַּאֲמִינוּ
בַּיהוה וּבְמֹשֶׁה עַבְדּוֹ:

REFLECTION

Do you feel a deep sense of faith? How can you deepen it?

How did you develop your faith in the first place?

How do you show faith as an individual?

How can the Jewish People show faith as a nation?

... A THOUSAND WORDS

אָז יָשִׁיר־מֹשֶׁה Then Moses and the Israelites sang this song to the Lord, saying: Ex. 15

I will sing to the Lord, for He has triumphed gloriously;
horse and rider He has hurled into the sea.
The Lord is my strength and song; He has become my salvation.
This is my God, and I will beautify Him,
my father's God, and I will elevate Him.
The Lord is a Master of war; Lord is His name.
Pharaoh's chariots and army He cast into the sea;
the best of his officers drowned in the Sea of Reeds.
The deep waters covered them;
they went down to the depths like a stone.
Your right hand, Lord, is majestic in power.
Your right hand, Lord, shatters the enemy.
In the greatness of Your majesty, You overthrew those who rose against You.
You sent out Your fury; it consumed them like straw.
By the blast of Your nostrils the waters piled up.
The surging waters stood straight like a wall;
the deeps congealed in the heart of the sea.
The enemy said, "I will pursue. I will overtake. I will divide the spoil.
My desire shall have its fill of them.
I will draw my sword. My hand will destroy them."
You blew with Your wind; the sea covered them.
They sank in the mighty waters like lead.
Who is like You, Lord, among the mighty?
Who is like You – majestic in holiness, awesome in glory, working wonders?

REFLECTION

"In Israel, in order to be a realist you must believe in miracles." (David Ben-Gurion)

Have you ever experienced a miracle?
Would seeing a miracle change how you understand God?
Have you ever had a moment of seeing God's hand?

אָז יָשִׁיר־מֹשֶׁה וּבְנֵי יִשְׂרָאֵל אֶת־הַשִּׁירָה הַזֹּאת לַיהוה, וַיֹּאמְרוּ שמות טו
לֵאמֹר, אָשִׁירָה לַּיהוה כִּי־גָאֹה גָּאָה, סוּס
וְרֹכְבוֹ רָמָה בַיָּם: עָזִּי וְזִמְרָת יָהּ וַיְהִי־לִי
לִישׁוּעָה, זֶה אֵלִי וְאַנְוֵהוּ, אֱלֹהֵי
אָבִי וַאֲרֹמְמֶנְהוּ: יהוה אִישׁ מִלְחָמָה, יהוה
שְׁמוֹ: מַרְכְּבֹת פַּרְעֹה וְחֵילוֹ יָרָה בַיָּם, וּמִבְחַר
שָׁלִשָׁיו טֻבְּעוּ בְיַם־סוּף: תְּהֹמֹת יְכַסְיֻמוּ, יָרְדוּ בִמְצוֹלֹת כְּמוֹ־
אָבֶן: יְמִינְךָ יהוה נֶאְדָּרִי בַּכֹּחַ, יְמִינְךָ
יהוה תִּרְעַץ אוֹיֵב: וּבְרֹב גְּאוֹנְךָ תַּהֲרֹס
קָמֶיךָ, תְּשַׁלַּח חֲרֹנְךָ יֹאכְלֵמוֹ כַּקַּשׁ: וּבְרוּחַ
אַפֶּיךָ נֶעֶרְמוּ מַיִם, נִצְּבוּ כְמוֹ־נֵד
נֹזְלִים, קָפְאוּ תְהֹמֹת בְּלֶב־יָם: אָמַר
אוֹיֵב אֶרְדֹּף, אַשִּׂיג, אֲחַלֵּק שָׁלָל, תִּמְלָאֵמוֹ
נַפְשִׁי, אָרִיק חַרְבִּי, תּוֹרִישֵׁמוֹ יָדִי: נָשַׁפְתָּ
בְרוּחֲךָ כִּסָּמוֹ יָם, צָלֲלוּ כַּעוֹפֶרֶת בְּמַיִם
אַדִּירִים: מִי־כָמֹכָה בָּאֵלִם יהוה, מִי
כָּמֹכָה נֶאְדָּר בַּקֹּדֶשׁ, נוֹרָא תְהִלֹּת עֹשֵׂה

LEARNING

The Gemara (*Pesaḥim* 118a and *Sota* 2a) teaches that "finding a marriage partner and making a living are as difficult as splitting the sea."

How do we understand that the splitting of the sea was difficult for God? Is anything difficult for God?

Perhaps a solution is that in all these challenges – making a living, finding a soulmate, and the splitting of the sea – there are clear instances where God plays such an open role in supporting us that His natural hiddenness is revealed. God is supposed to be hidden, so that we have space to choose to believe. It is not that His actions are difficult for Him, but it is difficult that His power is so clearly revealed, which leaves us little room to doubt His role.

You stretched out Your right hand, the earth swallowed them.
In Your loving-kindness, You led the people You redeemed.
In Your strength, You guided them to Your holy abode.
Nations heard and trembled;
terror gripped Philistia's inhabitants.
The chiefs of Edom were dismayed,
Moab's leaders were seized with trembling,
the people of Canaan melted away.
Fear and dread fell upon them.
By the power of Your arm, they were still as stone –
until Your people crossed, LORD,
until the people You acquired crossed over.
You will bring them and plant them
on the mountain of Your heritage –
the place, LORD, You made for Your presence,
the Sanctuary, LORD, Your hands established.
The LORD will reign for ever and all time.

The LORD will reign for ever and all time.
The LORD's kingship is established for ever and to all eternity.

When Pharaoh's horses, chariots and riders went into the sea,
the LORD brought the waters of the sea back over them,
but the Israelites walked on dry land through the sea.

▸ For kingship is the LORD's *Ps. 22*
and He rules over the nations.
Saviors shall go up to Mount Zion *Ob. 1*
to judge Mount Esau,
and the LORD's shall be the kingdom.

Then the LORD shall be King over all the earth; *Zech. 14*
on that day the LORD shall be One and His name One,

(as it is written in Your Torah, saying:
Listen, Israel: the LORD is our God, the LORD is One.) *Deut. 6*

פֶלֶא: נָטִיתָ יְמִינְךָ תִּבְלָעֵמוֹ אָרֶץ: נָחִיתָ
בְחַסְדְּךָ עַם־זוּ גָּאָלְתָּ, נֵהַלְתָּ בְעָזְּךָ אֶל־נְוֵה
קָדְשֶׁךָ: שָׁמְעוּ עַמִּים יִרְגָּזוּן, חִיל
אָחַז יֹשְׁבֵי פְּלָשֶׁת: אָז נִבְהֲלוּ אַלּוּפֵי
אֱדוֹם, אֵילֵי מוֹאָב יֹאחֲזֵמוֹ רָעַד, נָמֹגוּ
כֹּל יֹשְׁבֵי כְנָעַן: תִּפֹּל עֲלֵיהֶם אֵימָתָה
וָפַחַד, בִּגְדֹל זְרוֹעֲךָ יִדְּמוּ כָּאָבֶן, עַד־
יַעֲבֹר עַמְּךָ יהוה, עַד־יַעֲבֹר עַם־זוּ
קָנִיתָ: תְּבִאֵמוֹ וְתִטָּעֵמוֹ בְּהַר נַחֲלָתְךָ, מָכוֹן
לְשִׁבְתְּךָ פָּעַלְתָּ יהוה, מִקְּדָשׁ אֲדֹנָי כּוֹנְנוּ
יָדֶיךָ: יהוה יִמְלֹךְ לְעֹלָם וָעֶד:

יהוה יִמְלֹךְ לְעֹלָם וָעֶד.
יהוה מַלְכוּתֵהּ קָאֵם לְעָלַם וּלְעָלְמֵי עָלְמַיָּא.

כִּי
בָא סוּס פַּרְעֹה בְּרִכְבּוֹ וּבְפָרָשָׁיו בַּיָּם, וַיָּשֶׁב יהוה עֲלֵהֶם אֶת־מֵי
הַיָּם, וּבְנֵי יִשְׂרָאֵל הָלְכוּ בַיַּבָּשָׁה בְּתוֹךְ הַיָּם:

‹ כִּי לַיהוה הַמְּלוּכָה וּמֹשֵׁל בַּגּוֹיִם: תהלים כב
וְעָלוּ מוֹשִׁעִים בְּהַר צִיּוֹן לִשְׁפֹּט אֶת־הַר עֵשָׂו עובדיה א
וְהָיְתָה לַיהוה הַמְּלוּכָה:
וְהָיָה יהוה לְמֶלֶךְ עַל־כָּל־הָאָרֶץ זכריה יד
בַּיּוֹם הַהוּא יִהְיֶה יהוה אֶחָד וּשְׁמוֹ אֶחָד:
(וּבְתוֹרָתְךָ כָּתוּב לֵאמֹר, שְׁמַע יִשְׂרָאֵל, יהוה אֱלֹהֵינוּ יהוה אֶחָד:) דברים ו

יִשְׁתַּבַּח May Your name be praised
for ever, our King,
the great and holy God,
King in heaven and on earth.
For to You, LORD our God and God of our ancestors,
it is right to offer
song and praise, hymn and psalm,
strength and dominion,
eternity, greatness and power,
song of praise and glory,
holiness and kingship,
▸ blessings and thanks, from now and for ever.
Blessed are You, LORD,
God and King, great in praises,
God of thanksgivings,
Master of wonders,
who delights in hymns of song,
King, God, Giver of life to the worlds.

REFLECTION

What do you want to praise God for today?

Can you think of fifteen blessings God has given you?

Can you think of fifteen things God would praise you for?

LEARNING

There are fifteen expressions of praise in *Yishtabaḥ*. The number fifteen is a very significant number in Judaism – Tu BiShvat, Sukkot, Pesaḥ, and Tu B'av all fall on the fifteenth of their respective Hebrew months. Beyond the calendrical concentration, the number fifteen features prominently in the Pesaḥ Seder: the fifteen stages of the Seder, the fifteen events described in the song *Dayeinu* which culminate in the building of the *Beit HaMikdash*. The fifteen steps of the Seder are modeled on the fifteen steps leading up to the courtyard of the *Beit HaMikdash* where the *Levi'im* would sing the fifteen psalms beginning *Shir HaMa'alot*. In the siddur *Avodat Yisrael* in the name of the Shela we find a parallel drawn to the fifteen words of *Birkat Kohanim* (the priestly blessing). God blesses us with fifteen, so we too bless Him with fifteen.

יִשְׁתַּבַּח

שִׁמְךָ לָעַד, מַלְכֵּנוּ
הָאֵל הַמֶּלֶךְ הַגָּדוֹל וְהַקָּדוֹשׁ בַּשָּׁמַיִם וּבָאָרֶץ
כִּי לְךָ נָאֶה, יהוה אֱלֹהֵינוּ וֵאלֹהֵי אֲבוֹתֵינוּ
שִׁיר וּשְׁבָחָה, הַלֵּל וְזִמְרָה
עֹז וּמֶמְשָׁלָה, נֶצַח, גְּדֻלָּה וּגְבוּרָה
תְּהִלָּה וְתִפְאֶרֶת, קְדֻשָּׁה וּמַלְכוּת
◂ בְּרָכוֹת וְהוֹדָאוֹת, מֵעַתָּה וְעַד עוֹלָם.
בָּרוּךְ אַתָּה יהוה
אֵל מֶלֶךְ גָּדוֹל בַּתִּשְׁבָּחוֹת
אֵל הַהוֹדָאוֹת, אֲדוֹן הַנִּפְלָאוֹת
הַבּוֹחֵר בְּשִׁירֵי זִמְרָה, מֶלֶךְ, אֵל, חֵי הָעוֹלָמִים.

CONNECTION

The Rebbe of Kotzk explained the following about Yishtabaḥ*: The prayer states that God "chooses musical songs." The Hebrew word for "songs" –* shirim *– shares a root with the word* shirayim *– meaning "remains." God chooses not "songs" but what remains after that song is over. If the song is true, it does not fade; if the feeling is genuine, it will leave a resonance. These "remains" are not necessarily something intellectual or even emotional; they are merely an impression of something that had been. And the indication of whether the experience left such an impression is whether some change has been wrought in the individual. If the answer is yes, that is all the proof that is needed to show that this was indeed a genuine experience.*

(Rabbi Adin Steinsaltz)

... A THOUSAND WORDS

Between Rosh HaShana and Yom Kippur, and on Hoshana Raba, many congregations open the Ark and say this psalm responsively, verse by verse.

שִׁיר הַמַּעֲלוֹת A song of ascents. From the depths I have called to You, LORD. *Ps. 130*
LORD, hear my voice; let Your ears be attentive to my plea. If You, LORD, should keep account of sins, O LORD, who could stand? But with You there is forgiveness, that You may be held in awe. I wait for the LORD, my soul waits, and in His word I put my hope. My soul waits for the LORD more than watchmen wait for the morning, more than watchmen wait for the morning. Israel, put your hope in the LORD, for with the LORD there is loving-kindness, and great is His power to redeem. It is He who will redeem Israel from all their sins.

HALF KADDISH

Leader: יִתְגַּדַּל Magnified and sanctified may His great name be,
in the world He created by His will.
May He establish His kingdom
in your lifetime and in your days,
and in the lifetime of all the house of Israel,
swiftly and soon – and say: Amen.

All: May His great name be blessed for ever and all time.

Leader: Blessed and praised, glorified and elevated,
raised and honored, uplifted and praised
be the name of the Holy One, blessed be He,
beyond any blessing, song, praise and consolation
uttered in the world – and say: Amen.

This is what is meant in *Tehillim* 130 by the double expression of 'hear' and 'be attentive.' When a Jew prays and he is answered, his subsequent prayers are even stronger and he is stimulated to greater passion. But now we have not been answered, and the situation has become even more grievous. We have sunk from one depth to another, as King David said: 'From the depths I have called to You.' That is, I called not just from one depth, but from two depths. Though I called upon You when I fell into the first crisis, not only was I not answered and rescued, but I plunged even deeper into crisis – depth within depth. Nevertheless, I take strength and call upon You again."

REFLECTION

When were you most angry or upset in your life?

What do you want to ask forgiveness for?

What do you need God's help with?

During the עשרת ימי תשובה*, and on* הושענא רבה*,*
many congregations open the ארון קודש *and say this psalm responsively, verse by verse.*

שִׁיר הַמַּעֲלוֹת, מִמַּעֲמַקִּים קְרָאתִיךָ יהוה: אֲדֹנָי שִׁמְעָה בְקוֹלִי, תִּהְיֶינָה תהלים קל
אָזְנֶיךָ קַשֻּׁבוֹת לְקוֹל תַּחֲנוּנָי: אִם־עֲוֹנוֹת תִּשְׁמָר־יָהּ, אֲדֹנָי מִי יַעֲמֹד: כִּי־
עִמְּךָ הַסְּלִיחָה, לְמַעַן תִּוָּרֵא: קִוִּיתִי יהוה קִוְּתָה נַפְשִׁי, וְלִדְבָרוֹ הוֹחָלְתִּי:
נַפְשִׁי לַאדֹנָי, מִשֹּׁמְרִים לַבֹּקֶר, שֹׁמְרִים לַבֹּקֶר: יַחֵל יִשְׂרָאֵל אֶל יהוה, כִּי־
עִם־יהוה הַחֶסֶד, וְהַרְבֵּה עִמּוֹ פְדוּת: וְהוּא יִפְדֶּה אֶת־יִשְׂרָאֵל, מִכֹּל עֲוֹנֹתָיו:

חצי קדיש

ש״ץ: יִתְגַּדַּל וְיִתְקַדַּשׁ שְׁמֵהּ רַבָּא (קהל: אָמֵן)
בְּעָלְמָא דִּי בְרָא כִרְעוּתֵהּ, וְיַמְלִיךְ מַלְכוּתֵהּ
בְּחַיֵּיכוֹן וּבְיוֹמֵיכוֹן וּבְחַיֵּי דְכָל בֵּית יִשְׂרָאֵל
בַּעֲגָלָא וּבִזְמַן קָרִיב, וְאִמְרוּ אָמֵן. (קהל: אָמֵן)

קהל וש״ץ: יְהֵא שְׁמֵהּ רַבָּא מְבָרַךְ לְעָלַם וּלְעָלְמֵי עָלְמַיָּא.

ש״ץ: יִתְבָּרַךְ וְיִשְׁתַּבַּח וְיִתְפָּאַר וְיִתְרוֹמַם וְיִתְנַשֵּׂא
וְיִתְהַדָּר וְיִתְעַלֶּה וְיִתְהַלָּל
שְׁמֵהּ דְּקֻדְשָׁא בְּרִיךְ הוּא (קהל: בְּרִיךְ הוּא)
לְעֵלָּא מִן כָּל בִּרְכָתָא / בעשרת ימי תשובה: לְעֵלָּא לְעֵלָּא מִכָּל בִּרְכָתָא/
וְשִׁירָתָא, תֻּשְׁבְּחָתָא וְנֶחֱמָתָא
דַּאֲמִירָן בְּעָלְמָא, וְאִמְרוּ אָמֵן. (קהל: אָמֵן)

LEARNING

The *Eish Kodesh* (Rabbi Kalonymous Kalmish Shapira, also known as the Piaseczner Rebbe), was living through the horrors of the Warsaw Ghetto. Writing before *Shabbat Shuva* in 1942, he comments as follows on this chapter of *Tehillim*: "When we pray out loud, the sound arouses greater intention. And with greater intention there is also a stronger voice. But alas, what can we do when they do not allow us to cry out or gather together to pray? Only secretly can we approach Hashem, but nonetheless our prayers are from the depths of our heart.

BLESSINGS OF THE SHEMA

The following blessing and response are said only in the presence of a minyan. They represent a formal summons to the congregation to engage in an act of collective prayer.

The Leader says the following, bowing at "Bless," standing straight at "the LORD." The congregation, followed by the Leader, responds, bowing at "Bless," standing straight at "the LORD."

Leader: **BLESS**
the LORD, the blessed One.

Congregation: Bless the LORD, the blessed One,
for ever and all time.

Leader: Bless the LORD, the blessed One,
for ever and all time.

The custom is to sit from this point until the Amida, since the primary emotion of this section of the prayers is love rather than awe. Conversation is forbidden until after the Amida.

בָּרוּךְ Blessed are You, LORD our God, King of the Universe,
who forms light and creates darkness, makes peace and creates all. *Is. 45*

REFLECTION

"Unless we believe that God renews creation every day, our prayers grow habitual and tedious."
(Ba'al Shem Tov)

What can you do with your new day?

What will you do with your new day?

What specific blessings has God brought you today?

What goodness can you find in the darkness?

... A THOUSAND WORDS

קריאת שמע וברכותיה

The following blessing and response are said only in the presence of a מנין.
They represent a formal summons to the קהל *to engage in an act of collective prayer.*
The שליח ציבור *says the following, bowing at* בָּרְכוּ, *standing straight at* ה׳. *The* קהל,
followed by the שליח ציבור, *responds, bowing at* בָּרוּךְ, *standing straight at* ה׳.

ש״ץ: **בָּרְכוּ**
אֶת יהוה הַמְבֹרָךְ.

קהל: **בָּרוּךְ יהוה הַמְבֹרָךְ לְעוֹלָם וָעֶד.**

ש״ץ: **בָּרוּךְ יהוה הַמְבֹרָךְ לְעוֹלָם וָעֶד.**

The custom is to sit from this point until the עמידה, *since the primary*
emotion of this section of the prayers is love rather than awe.
Conversation is forbidden until after the עמידה.

בָּרוּךְ אַתָּה יהוה אֱלֹהֵינוּ מֶלֶךְ הָעוֹלָם
יוֹצֵר אוֹר וּבוֹרֵא חֹשֶׁךְ, עֹשֶׂה שָׁלוֹם וּבוֹרֵא אֶת הַכֹּל. ישעיה מה

CONNECTION

Our masters taught: When Adam, on the day of his creation, saw the sun sinking in the sky before him, he said, "Woe is me! Because I acted offensively, the world is darkening for me and is about to return to darkness and desolation – indeed, this is the death that Heaven has decreed for me." So he sat down to fast and to weep throughout the night, while Eve wept beside him. But when the dawn began slowly rising like a column, he said, "Such is the way of nature," and then proceeded to offer up a bull. (*Avoda Zara* 8a)

Adam thought that the end of the day meant the end of the world. When the sun came up he realized that he would be able to begin again, and so he offered a sacrifice to express his profound gratitude. How do you feel at the beginning of a new day?

הַמֵּאִיר In compassion He gives light to the earth and its inhabitants,
and in His goodness continually renews the work of creation,
day after day.
How numerous are Your works, LORD; *Ps. 104*
You made them all in wisdom;
the earth is full of Your creations.
He is the King great alone since the beginning of time –
praised, glorified and elevated since the world began.
Eternal God,
in Your great compassion, have compassion on us,
LORD of our strength, Rock of our refuge,
Shield of our salvation, You are our stronghold.

CONNECTION

Avram didn't grow up in a home that knew about God. Avram had to go out and find God on his own. As a boy, he looked up at the vast sky and wondered, "Who created this magnificent world? Who created the stars and the sky and the earth on which we walk? Who created me?" At first he was certain it was the sun. "The sun must be the creator of all; it is so powerful, it shines light on the world and heats all living things." So Avram spent the day praying to the sun. However, in the evening as the sun set, slowly disappearing in the west as the moon rose in the east, Avram said, "Forgive me, Moon, I was mistaken. You must be the creator of the heavens and the earth. Those beautiful shining stars must be your crown." Little Avram stayed up all night praying to the moon. In the morning, the moon sank in the west and the sun rose in the east once again. Avram realized: "Neither the sun nor the moon could have created the world, neither is powerful enough, there must be an even greater power, God, who created the sun, moon, and stars and everything else." So Avram began to pray to God, the Master of creation.

(*Midrash HaGadol, Bereshit* 11:28)

LEARNING

Rav Tzaddok explains the words "the earth is full of Your creations" mean not simply that the world is filled with God's possessions, but instead that the world is filled with things with which we can "possess" God. How can you use the world to access God? What inspires you to seek out God?

הַמֵּאִיר לָאָרֶץ וְלַדָּרִים עָלֶיהָ בְּרַחֲמִים
וּבְטוּבוֹ מְחַדֵּשׁ בְּכָל יוֹם תָּמִיד מַעֲשֵׂה בְרֵאשִׁית.
תהלים קד מָה־רַבּוּ מַעֲשֶׂיךָ יהוה
כֻּלָּם בְּחָכְמָה עָשִׂיתָ
מָלְאָה הָאָרֶץ קִנְיָנֶךָ:
הַמֶּלֶךְ הַמְרוֹמָם לְבַדּוֹ מֵאָז
הַמְשֻׁבָּח וְהַמְפֹאָר וְהַמִּתְנַשֵּׂא מִימוֹת עוֹלָם.
אֱלֹהֵי עוֹלָם
בְּרַחֲמֶיךָ הָרַבִּים רַחֵם עָלֵינוּ
אֲדוֹן עֻזֵּנוּ
צוּר מִשְׂגַּבֵּנוּ
מָגֵן יִשְׁעֵנוּ
מִשְׂגָּב בַּעֲדֵנוּ.

REFLECTION

Have you ever looked at creation and seen the beauty of God's work? How did it make you feel?

When you look up at the multitude of stars what do you think about?

... A THOUSAND WORDS

The blessed God, great in knowledge,
prepared and made the rays of the sun.
He who is good formed glory for His name,
surrounding His power with radiant stars.
The leaders of His multitudes, the holy ones,
elevate the Almighty,
constantly declaring God's glory and holiness.
Be blessed, LORD our God,
for the magnificence of Your handiwork
and for the radiant lights You have made.
May they glorify You, Selah!

REFLECTION

What do you want to ask God about the world?

How many words can you think of to describe God?

...A THOUSAND WORDS

אֵל בָּרוּךְ גְּדוֹל דֵּעָה
הֵכִין וּפָעַל זָהֳרֵי חַמָּה
טוֹב יָצַר כָּבוֹד לִשְׁמוֹ
מְאוֹרוֹת נָתַן סְבִיבוֹת עֻזּוֹ
פִּנּוֹת צְבָאָיו קְדוֹשִׁים, רוֹמְמֵי שַׁדַּי
תָּמִיד מְסַפְּרִים כְּבוֹד אֵל וּקְדֻשָּׁתוֹ.
תִּתְבָּרַךְ יהוה אֱלֹהֵינוּ
עַל שֶׁבַח מַעֲשֵׂה יָדֶיךָ.
וְעַל מְאוֹרֵי אוֹר שֶׁעָשִׂיתָ
יְפָאֲרוּךָ סֶּלָה.

LEARNING

בְּרֵאשִׁית בָּרָא אֱלֹהִים
אֵת הַשָּׁמַיִם וְאֵת הָאָרֶץ

"In the beginning God created the heavens and the earth."
(*Bereshit* 1:1)

A kabbalistic reading of this passage is, "*Bereshit bara Elokim ET* [*alef-tav*]" signifying the entire *alef-beit*. The Hebrew letters, *alef, beit, gimmel*... they are living things. They are the building blocks of creation. Like oxygen and hydrogen, God formed the world through combinations of the Hebrew letters. God used the primal forces contained in these letters as the instruments of all further creation.

CONNECTION

There was a simple shepherd boy who was passing by a synagogue and heard people inside praying. He came inside to join them. The only problem was they were all praying from prayer books. The shepherd, however, did not know how to read, though he did know how to say the letters of the Hebrew alphabet. Not knowing what else to do, he stood in the back of the synagogue and yelled out "Alef! Beit! Gimmel!" *until he finished the entire alphabet.*

Two of the worshipers were so offended that they went over to the shepherd boy and were about to escort him outside, when the rabbi told them: "Stop! That boy's shouting was more precious than any other prayers said here today! His prayer went straight up to Heaven!"

תִּתְבָּרַךְ May You be blessed,
our Rock, King and Redeemer, Creator of holy beings.
May Your name be praised for ever,
our King, Creator of the ministering angels,
all of whom stand in the universe's heights,
declaring together, in awe, aloud,
the words of the living God, the eternal King.
They are all beloved, all pure, all mighty,
and all perform in awe and fear the will of their Maker.
▸ All open their mouths in holiness and purity,
with song and psalm,
and bless, praise, glorify,
fear, sanctify and declare the sovereignty of – ◂

...A THOUSAND WORDS

תִּתְבָּרַךְ
צוּרֵנוּ מַלְכֵּנוּ וְגוֹאֲלֵנוּ, בּוֹרֵא קְדוֹשִׁים
יִשְׁתַּבַּח שִׁמְךָ לָעַד
מַלְכֵּנוּ, יוֹצֵר מְשָׁרְתִים
וַאֲשֶׁר מְשָׁרְתָיו כֻּלָּם עוֹמְדִים בְּרוּם עוֹלָם
וּמַשְׁמִיעִים בְּיִרְאָה יַחַד בְּקוֹל
דִּבְרֵי אֱלֹהִים חַיִּים וּמֶלֶךְ עוֹלָם.
כֻּלָּם אֲהוּבִים, כֻּלָּם בְּרוּרִים, כֻּלָּם גִּבּוֹרִים
וְכֻלָּם עוֹשִׂים בְּאֵימָה וּבְיִרְאָה רְצוֹן קוֹנָם
◂ וְכֻלָּם פּוֹתְחִים אֶת פִּיהֶם בִּקְדֻשָּׁה וּבְטָהֳרָה
בְּשִׁירָה וּבְזִמְרָה
וּמְבָרְכִים וּמְשַׁבְּחִים וּמְפָאֲרִים
וּמַעֲרִיצִים וּמַקְדִּישִׁים וּמַמְלִיכִים ◂

LEARNING

Why do we want to be like angels? Typically we embrace humanity with its unique ability for creativity and ingenuity. What is it about angels that we are trying to emulate? The Maharal of Prague, in his commentary on *Bereshit* 18:2, says that the essence of what it means to be an angel is to act on someone else's behalf. This is the underlying angelic value we aspire to; the selflessness that angels embody.

REFLECTION

How can you be angelic today?

What does it mean to be angelic? Are angels the only beings that can achieve selflessness?

What selfless thing will you do today?

CONNECTION

Today, I watched a teenage boy help an elderly woman with a cane onto the city bus I was riding. He was so careful with her, assisting her every step of the way. The woman had the biggest smile on her face. They both sat directly across from me, and just as I was about to compliment her on having a wonderful grandson, the boy looked at her and said, "My name is Jonathan. What's your name, ma'am?"

The name of the great, mighty and awesome God and King,
holy is He.
▸ All accept on themselves, one from another,
the yoke of the kingdom of heaven,
giving permission to one another
to sanctify the One who formed them, in peaceful spirit,
pure speech and sweet melody.
All, as one, declare His holiness,
saying in awe:

All say aloud: Holy, holy, holy is the Lord of multitudes; *Is. 6*
the whole world is filled with His glory.

▸ Then the Ophanim and the Holy Ḥayyot, with a roar of noise,
raise themselves toward the Seraphim and,
facing them, give praise, saying:

All say aloud: Blessed is the Lord's glory from His place. *Ezek. 3*

... A THOUSAND WORDS

REFLECTION

What does holiness mean to you?

Are there places where you feel more close to God?

What does it mean that God has a place?

CONNECTION

"O Lord, where shall I find You?
All-hidden and exalted is Your place;
And where shall I not find You?
Full of Your glory is the infinite space."

(Rabbi Yehuda HaLevi)

אֶת שֵׁם הָאֵל הַמֶּלֶךְ הַגָּדוֹל, הַגִּבּוֹר וְהַנּוֹרָא
קָדוֹשׁ הוּא.

◂ וְכֻלָּם מְקַבְּלִים עֲלֵיהֶם עֹל מַלְכוּת שָׁמַיִם זֶה מִזֶּה
וְנוֹתְנִים רְשׁוּת זֶה לָזֶה
לְהַקְדִּישׁ לְיוֹצְרָם בְּנַחַת רוּחַ
בְּשָׂפָה בְרוּרָה וּבִנְעִימָה
קְדֻשָּׁה כֻּלָּם כְּאֶחָד
עוֹנִים וְאוֹמְרִים בְּיִרְאָה

ישעיה ו *All say aloud* קָדוֹשׁ, קָדוֹשׁ, קָדוֹשׁ יהוה צְבָאוֹת
מְלֹא כָל־הָאָרֶץ כְּבוֹדוֹ:

◂ וְהָאוֹפַנִּים וְחַיּוֹת הַקֹּדֶשׁ
בְּרַעַשׁ גָּדוֹל מִתְנַשְּׂאִים לְעֻמַּת שְׂרָפִים
לְעֻמָּתָם מְשַׁבְּחִים וְאוֹמְרִים

יחזקאל ג *All say aloud* בָּרוּךְ כְּבוֹד־יהוה מִמְּקוֹמוֹ:

LEARNING

The first time God speaks to Moshe is at the burning bush in the desert. This encounter, according to the sages, took place at Mount Horeb or Mount Sinai, the place where the Torah would be given to the Jewish People.

> The Lord saw that he turned to see, and God called to him from within the bush, and He said: "Moses, Moses," and he said: "Here I am!" He said: "Do not approach here; remove your shoes from your feet, as the place upon which you are standing is sacred ground." (*Shemot* 3:4–5)

There are some places that are more conducive to holiness, and God is more easily accessible there. The place where Moshe first encounters God was a considered and planned location. It was a place where the largest mass revelation of God in the world would take place, Mount Sinai – a place imbued with holiness.

לָאֵל To the blessed God they offer melodies.
To the King, living and eternal God,
they say psalms and declare praises.

For it is He alone
who does mighty deeds
and creates new things,
who is Master of battles,
and sows righteousness,
who makes salvation grow
and creates cures,
who is feared in praises,
Lord of wonders,

who in His goodness, continually renews the work of creation,
day after day, as it is said:

"[Praise] Him who made the great lights, *Ps. 136*
for His love endures for ever."

▸ May You make a new light shine over Zion,
and may we all soon be worthy of its light.
Blessed are You, Lord, who forms the radiant lights.

CONNECTION

In 1997, Mr. Rogers, an icon of American children's entertainment and education, walked on stage to accept the Emmy Lifetime Achievement Award. In front of all the soap-opera stars he made his small bow and said into the microphone, "All of us have special ones who have loved us into being. Would you just take, along with me, ten seconds to think of the people who have helped you become who you are.... Ten seconds of silence." And then he lifted his wrist, and looked at the audience, and looked at his watch, and said softly, "I'll watch the time." There was, at first, a small whoop from the crowd, a giddy, strangled hiccup of laughter, as people realized that he wasn't kidding, that Mr. Rogers was an authority figure who actually expected them to do what he asked... and so they did. One second, two seconds, three seconds... and now the jaws clenched, and the chests heaved, and the mascara ran, and the tears fell upon the bejeweled gathering like rain leaking down a crystal chandelier, and Mr. Rogers finally looked up from his watch and said, "May God be with you."

לָאֵל בָּרוּךְ נְעִימוֹת יִתֵּנוּ, לַמֶּלֶךְ אֵל חַי וְקַיָּם
זְמִירוֹת יֹאמֵרוּ וְתִשְׁבָּחוֹת יַשְׁמִיעוּ
כִּי הוּא לְבַדּוֹ
פּוֹעֵל גְּבוּרוֹת, עוֹשֶׂה חֲדָשׁוֹת
בַּעַל מִלְחָמוֹת, זוֹרֵעַ צְדָקוֹת
מַצְמִיחַ יְשׁוּעוֹת, בּוֹרֵא רְפוּאוֹת
נוֹרָא תְהִלּוֹת, אֲדוֹן הַנִּפְלָאוֹת
הַמְחַדֵּשׁ בְּטוּבוֹ בְּכָל יוֹם תָּמִיד מַעֲשֵׂה בְרֵאשִׁית
כָּאָמוּר
תהלים קלו לְעֹשֵׂה אוֹרִים גְּדֹלִים, כִּי לְעוֹלָם חַסְדּוֹ:
▸ אוֹר חָדָשׁ עַל צִיּוֹן תָּאִיר וְנִזְכֶּה כֻלָּנוּ מְהֵרָה לְאוֹרוֹ.
בָּרוּךְ אַתָּה יהוה, יוֹצֵר הַמְּאוֹרוֹת.

REFLECTION

What is the best compliment you have ever received?

What is the best compliment you have ever given?

How do you find the appropriate accolades to praise God?

Has someone ever taken your compliment badly?

LEARNING

Silence is the greatest form of praising God. "To You silence is praise" (*Tehillim* 65:2). As the Gemara (*Berakhot* 33b) relates: A man came in front of Rabbi Ḥanina and praised God using every possible adjective he could think of. When he finished, the rabbi asked him, "Have you no praises left for your Master?! Why did you say so many? We can say the praises that we do only because Moshe said them; otherwise, it's like a mortal king who had millions of gold coins, and someone was praising him for having silver! What an insult!"

This is why we stop – to make sure we are focusing on the right things. The particular language of the *tefilla* is worded very carefully when it comes to praising God. Look at the words chosen to praise God. Why do you think these are the compliments we use to praise God?

אַהֲבָה You have loved us with great love, Lord our God,
and with immense compassion have You had compassion on us.
Our Father, our King,
for the sake of our ancestors who trusted in You,
and to whom You taught the laws of life,
be generous also to us and teach us.
Our Father, compassionate Father, ever compassionate,
have compassion on us.
Instill in our hearts the desire to understand and discern,
to listen, learn and teach, to observe, perform and fulfill
all the teachings of Your Torah in love.
Enlighten our eyes in Your Torah
and let our hearts cling to Your commandments.
Unite our hearts to love and fear Your name,
so that we may never be ashamed.
And because we have trusted in Your holy, great and feared name,
may we be glad and rejoice in Your salvation.

At this point, gather the four tzitziot of the tallit, holding them in the left hand.

Bring us back in peace from the four quarters of the earth
and lead us upright to our land.
▸ For You are a God who performs acts of salvation,
and You chose us from all peoples and tongues,
bringing us close to Your great name for ever in truth,
that we may thank You and declare Your oneness in love.
Blessed are You, Lord, who chooses His people Israel in love.

---

studies Torah, his mind meets and communicates with the mind of God. This compares well to a mother and her child looking at a family album together. The mother is like God, the child is like the Jew. Their perspectives of the album are certainly different, but a deep bond is nonetheless created.

(Rabbi Adin Steinsaltz)

REFLECTION

Who teaches you Torah?

Do you feel more connected to your Judaism or to God when you learn Torah?

How has the Torah impacted the Jewish People?

What is your favorite Torah teaching?

אַהֲבָה רַבָּה אֲהַבְתָּנוּ, יהוה אֱלֹהֵינוּ
חֶמְלָה גְדוֹלָה וִיתֵרָה חָמַלְתָּ עָלֵינוּ.
אָבִינוּ מַלְכֵּנוּ, בַּעֲבוּר אֲבוֹתֵינוּ שֶׁבָּטְחוּ בְךָ
וַתְּלַמְּדֵם חֻקֵּי חַיִּים, כֵּן תְּחָנֵּנוּ וּתְלַמְּדֵנוּ.
אָבִינוּ, הָאָב הָרַחֲמָן, הַמְרַחֵם
רַחֵם עָלֵינוּ
וְתֵן בְּלִבֵּנוּ לְהָבִין וּלְהַשְׂכִּיל
לִשְׁמֹעַ, לִלְמֹד וּלְלַמֵּד, לִשְׁמֹר וְלַעֲשׂוֹת, וּלְקַיֵּם
אֶת כָּל דִּבְרֵי תַלְמוּד תּוֹרָתֶךָ בְּאַהֲבָה.
וְהָאֵר עֵינֵינוּ בְּתוֹרָתֶךָ, וְדַבֵּק לִבֵּנוּ בְּמִצְוֹתֶיךָ
וְיַחֵד לְבָבֵנוּ לְאַהֲבָה וּלְיִרְאָה אֶת שְׁמֶךָ
וְלֹא נֵבוֹשׁ לְעוֹלָם וָעֶד.
כִּי בְשֵׁם קָדְשְׁךָ הַגָּדוֹל וְהַנּוֹרָא בָּטָחְנוּ
נָגִילָה וְנִשְׂמְחָה בִּישׁוּעָתֶךָ.

At this point, gather the four ציציות *of the* טלית*, holding them in the left hand.*

וַהֲבִיאֵנוּ לְשָׁלוֹם מֵאַרְבַּע כַּנְפוֹת הָאָרֶץ
וְתוֹלִיכֵנוּ קוֹמְמִיּוּת לְאַרְצֵנוּ.
◂ כִּי אֵל פּוֹעֵל יְשׁוּעוֹת אָתָּה, וּבָנוּ בָחַרְתָּ מִכָּל עַם וְלָשׁוֹן
וְקֵרַבְתָּנוּ לְשִׁמְךָ הַגָּדוֹל סֶלָה, בֶּאֱמֶת
לְהוֹדוֹת לְךָ וּלְיַחֶדְךָ בְּאַהֲבָה.
בָּרוּךְ אַתָּה יהוה, הַבּוֹחֵר בְּעַמּוֹ יִשְׂרָאֵל בְּאַהֲבָה.

CONNECTION

Why would God want us to study? You might say, it is a way to commune with Him. Perhaps, the study of Torah is best defined as a meeting of minds. When a Jew

The Shema must be said with intense concentration. In the first paragraph one should accept, with love, the sovereignty of God; in the second, the mitzvot as the will of God. The end of the third paragraph constitutes fulfillment of the mitzva to remember, morning and evening, the exodus from Egypt.

When not praying with a minyan, say:

God, faithful King!

The following verse should be said aloud, while covering the eyes with the right hand:

Listen, Israel: the LORD is our God, the LORD is One. *Deut. 6*

Quietly: Blessed be the name of His glorious kingdom for ever and all time.

Touch the hand-tefillin at ° and the head-tefillin at °°.

וְאָהַבְתָּ Love the LORD your God with all your heart, with all your soul, and with all your might. These words which I command you today shall be on your heart. Teach them repeatedly to your children, speaking of them when you sit at home and when you travel on the way, when you lie down and when you rise. °Bind them as a sign on your hand, and °°they shall be a symbol between your eyes. Write them on the doorposts of your house and gates. *Deut. 6*

LEARNING

Despite many people believing the *Shema* is the most important prayer, it is in fact not a prayer at all, but a declaration of Jewish belief. That is why we call it *Keriat Shema* ("the reading of the *Shema*") instead of *Tefillat Shema*. Much like a national anthem, we say it as much for ourselves as for anyone else.

The first paragraph focuses on our accepting God as the ultimate Ruler in our lives. The second paragraph focuses on our acceptance of the responsibility to do mitzvot, and the reward and punishment that comes with that responsibility. The third paragraph focuses on the daily mitzva to recall the exodus from Egypt – a basic tenet of Jewish faith. The thematic progression between the three paragraphs goes from God as King of the universe, to the Jewish People's unique relationship with God, to God's role in Jewish history.

The שמע must be said with intense concentration. In the first paragraph one should accept, with love, the sovereignty of God; in the second, the מצוות as the will of God. The end of the third paragraph constitutes fulfillment of the מצווה to remember, morning and evening, the exodus from Egypt.

When not praying with a מנין, say:

אֵל מֶלֶךְ נֶאֱמָן

The following verse should be said aloud, while covering the eyes with the right hand:

דברים ו
שְׁמַע יִשְׂרָאֵל, יהוה אֱלֹהֵינוּ, יהוה | אֶחָד:

Quietly בָּרוּךְ שֵׁם כְּבוֹד מַלְכוּתוֹ לְעוֹלָם וָעֶד.

Touch the תפילין של יד *at* ° *and the* תפילין של ראש *at* °°.

דברים ו
וְאָהַבְתָּ אֵת יהוה אֱלֹהֶיךָ, בְּכָל־לְבָבְךָ וּבְכָל־נַפְשְׁךָ וּבְכָל־
מְאֹדֶךָ: וְהָיוּ הַדְּבָרִים הָאֵלֶּה, אֲשֶׁר אָנֹכִי מְצַוְּךָ הַיּוֹם, עַל־לְבָבֶךָ:
וְשִׁנַּנְתָּם לְבָנֶיךָ וְדִבַּרְתָּ בָּם, בְּשִׁבְתְּךָ בְּבֵיתֶךָ וּבְלֶכְתְּךָ בַדֶּרֶךְ,
וּבְשָׁכְבְּךָ וּבְקוּמֶךָ: °וּקְשַׁרְתָּם לְאוֹת עַל־יָדֶךָ °°וְהָיוּ לְטֹטָפֹת
בֵּין עֵינֶיךָ: וּכְתַבְתָּם עַל־מְזֻזוֹת בֵּיתֶךָ וּבִשְׁעָרֶיךָ:

CONNECTION

It once happened on the battlefield between two warring nations, that Jew faced Jew in mortal combat. As one of the Jewish soldiers ran for cover into a foxhole, the other called out, "Surrender, or I'll shoot." The hiding soldier, quivering in fear, closed his eyes, and crying, recited the familiar words from his childhood: "Shema Yisrael, Hashem Elokeinu, Hashem Eḥad." *As the other soldier heard these words, he responded with surprise and emotion,* "Barukh shem kevod malkhuto le'olam va'ed." *As he laid down his gun he extended a hand to his former enemy, and they embraced as brothers.*

... A THOUSAND WORDS

Touch the hand-tefillin at ° and the head-tefillin at °°.

וְהָיָה If you indeed follow My commandments with which I charge you today, to love the LORD your God and worship Him with all your heart and with all your soul, I will give rain in your land in its season, the early and late rain; and you shall gather in your grain, wine and oil. I will give grass in your field for your cattle, and you shall eat and be satisfied. Be careful lest your heart be tempted and you go astray and worship other gods, bowing down to them. Then the LORD's anger will flare against you and He will close the heavens so that there will be no rain. The land will not yield its crops, and you will perish swiftly from the good land that the LORD is giving you. Therefore, set these, My words, on your heart and soul. °Bind them as a sign on your hand, °°and they shall be a symbol between your eyes. Teach them to your children, speaking of them when you sit at home and when you travel on the way, when you lie down and when you rise. Write them on the doorposts of your house and gates, so that you and your children may live long in the land that the LORD swore to your ancestors to give them, for as long as the heavens are above the earth. *Deut. 11*

REFLECTION

"Run to do even a minor mitzva, and flee from sin, for one mitzva leads to another, and one sin leads to another – for the reward of a mitzva is another mitzva, and the punishment of a sin is another sin." (Avot 4:2)

What is more important, believing in Hashem or keeping mitzvot?

What extra mitzva will you do today?

...A THOUSAND WORDS

Touch the תפילין של יד *at* ° *and the* תפילין של ראש *at* °°.

וְהָיָה אִם־שָׁמֹעַ תִּשְׁמְעוּ אֶל־מִצְוֺתַי אֲשֶׁר אָנֹכִי מְצַוֶּה אֶתְכֶם דברים יא
הַיּוֹם, לְאַהֲבָה אֶת־יהוה אֱלֹהֵיכֶם וּלְעָבְדוֹ, בְּכָל־לְבַבְכֶם וּבְכָל־
נַפְשְׁכֶם: וְנָתַתִּי מְטַר־אַרְצְכֶם בְּעִתּוֹ, יוֹרֶה וּמַלְקוֹשׁ, וְאָסַפְתָּ
דְגָנֶךָ וְתִירֹשְׁךָ וְיִצְהָרֶךָ: וְנָתַתִּי עֵשֶׂב בְּשָׂדְךָ לִבְהֶמְתֶּךָ, וְאָכַלְתָּ
וְשָׂבָעְתָּ: הִשָּׁמְרוּ לָכֶם פֶּן־יִפְתֶּה לְבַבְכֶם, וְסַרְתֶּם וַעֲבַדְתֶּם
אֱלֹהִים אֲחֵרִים וְהִשְׁתַּחֲוִיתֶם לָהֶם: וְחָרָה אַף־יהוה בָּכֶם, וְעָצַר
אֶת־הַשָּׁמַיִם וְלֹא־יִהְיֶה מָטָר, וְהָאֲדָמָה לֹא תִתֵּן אֶת־יְבוּלָהּ,
וַאֲבַדְתֶּם מְהֵרָה מֵעַל הָאָרֶץ הַטֹּבָה אֲשֶׁר יהוה נֹתֵן לָכֶם:
וְשַׂמְתֶּם אֶת־דְּבָרַי אֵלֶּה עַל־לְבַבְכֶם וְעַל־נַפְשְׁכֶם, °וּקְשַׁרְתֶּם
אֹתָם לְאוֹת עַל־יֶדְכֶם, °°וְהָיוּ לְטוֹטָפֹת בֵּין עֵינֵיכֶם: וְלִמַּדְתֶּם
אֹתָם אֶת־בְּנֵיכֶם לְדַבֵּר בָּם, בְּשִׁבְתְּךָ בְּבֵיתֶךָ וּבְלֶכְתְּךָ בַדֶּרֶךְ,
וּבְשָׁכְבְּךָ וּבְקוּמֶךָ: וּכְתַבְתָּם עַל־מְזוּזוֹת בֵּיתֶךָ וּבִשְׁעָרֶיךָ: לְמַעַן
יִרְבּוּ יְמֵיכֶם וִימֵי בְנֵיכֶם עַל הָאֲדָמָה אֲשֶׁר נִשְׁבַּע יהוה לַאֲבֹתֵיכֶם
לָתֵת לָהֶם, כִּימֵי הַשָּׁמַיִם עַל־הָאָרֶץ:

LEARNING

The major philosophical theme of the second paragraph of the *Shema* is reward and punishment for keeping and transgressing mitzvot. This is the eleventh of Rambam's Thirteen Principles of Jewish Faith: "I believe with perfect faith that the Creator, blessed be His name, rewards those who keep His commandments and punishes those who transgress them."

CONNECTION

"To defend a land, you need an army. But to defend freedom, you need education. You need families and schools to ensure that your ideals are passed on to the next generation and never lost, or despaired of, or obscured. The citadels of liberty are houses of study. Its heroes are teachers, its passion is education and the life of the mind. Moses realized that a people achieves immortality not by building temples or mausoleums, but by engraving their values on the hearts of their children, and they on theirs, and so on until the end of time."

(Rabbi Jonathan Sacks, *A Letter in the Scroll*)

Hold the tzitziot in the right hand also (some transfer to the right hand), kissing them at °.

וַיֹּאמֶר The LORD spoke to Moses, saying: Speak to the Israelites and tell them to make °tzitzit on the corners of their garments for all generations. They shall attach to the °tzitzit at each corner a thread of blue. This shall be your °tzitzit, and you shall see it and remember all of the LORD's commandments and keep them, not straying after your heart and after your eyes, following your own sinful desires. Thus you will be reminded to keep all My commandments, and be holy to your God. I am the LORD your God, who brought you out of the land of Egypt to be your God. I am the LORD your God. Num. 15

°True –

The Leader repeats:

▸ The LORD your God is true –

REFLECTION

לֹא תַטֶּה מִשְׁפַּט גֵּר יָתוֹם וְלֹא תַחֲבֹל בֶּגֶד אַלְמָנָה: וְזָכַרְתָּ כִּי עֶבֶד הָיִיתָ בְּמִצְרַיִם וַיִּפְדְּךָ יהוה אֱלֹהֶיךָ מִשָּׁם עַל־כֵּן אָנֹכִי מְצַוְּךָ לַעֲשׂוֹת אֶת־הַדָּבָר הַזֶּה:
(דברים כד יז-יח)

"You shall not pervert the judgment of a stranger, or an orphan; you shall not take a widow's garment as a pledge. And you shall remember that you were a slave in Egypt, and the LORD your God redeemed you from there; therefore, I command you to do this thing."
(*Devarim* 24:17–18)

Why do you think the history of the Jewish People begins with slavery in Egypt?

Why do you think there is a mitzva to remember the exodus every day?

LEARNING

If you are wearing tzitzit then at the beginning of the third paragraph of the *Shema* you should transfer them to your right hand. Some have the custom to kiss the tzitzit every time the word **צִיצִת** is mentioned (three times) and then again at the word **אֱמֶת** at the end of the paragraph. This is to demonstrate our love for this mitzva. The tzitzit should also be passed before the eyes and stared at, at the mention of the words **וּרְאִיתֶם אוֹתוֹ** – "and you shall see it." This reflects the emphasis on the visual aspect of this mitzva – i.e., the tzitzit are a visual reminder of all the other mitzvot. (The numerical value of the word **צִיצִת** comes to 600. If you add the number of strings [8] and knots [5] to 600 you arrive at 613, the number of mitzvot found in the Torah.)

Hold the ציציות *in the right hand also (some transfer to the right hand), kissing them at °.*

וַיֹּאמֶר יהוה אֶל־מֹשֶׁה לֵּאמֹר: דַּבֵּר אֶל־בְּנֵי יִשְׂרָאֵל וְאָמַרְתָּ במדבר טו
אֲלֵהֶם, וְעָשׂוּ לָהֶם °צִיצִת עַל־כַּנְפֵי בִגְדֵיהֶם לְדֹרֹתָם, וְנָתְנוּ °עַל־
צִיצִת הַכָּנָף פְּתִיל תְּכֵלֶת: וְהָיָה לָכֶם °לְצִיצִת, וּרְאִיתֶם אֹתוֹ
וּזְכַרְתֶּם אֶת־כָּל־מִצְוֹת יהוה וַעֲשִׂיתֶם אֹתָם, וְלֹא תָתוּרוּ אַחֲרֵי
לְבַבְכֶם וְאַחֲרֵי עֵינֵיכֶם, אֲשֶׁר־אַתֶּם זֹנִים אַחֲרֵיהֶם: לְמַעַן תִּזְכְּרוּ
וַעֲשִׂיתֶם אֶת־כָּל־מִצְוֹתָי, וִהְיִיתֶם קְדֹשִׁים לֵאלֹהֵיכֶם: אֲנִי יהוה
אֱלֹהֵיכֶם, אֲשֶׁר הוֹצֵאתִי אֶתְכֶם מֵאֶרֶץ מִצְרַיִם, לִהְיוֹת לָכֶם
לֵאלֹהִים, אֲנִי יהוה אֱלֹהֵיכֶם:

°אֱמֶת

The שליח ציבור *repeats:*

◂ יהוה אֱלֹהֵיכֶם אֱמֶת

CONNECTION

Three hundred years ago a ship called the Mayflower *set sail to the New World. This was a great event in the history of England. Yet I wonder if there is one Englishman who knows at what time the ship set sail? Do the English know how many people embarked on this voyage? What quality of bread did they eat? Yet more than 3,300 years ago, before the* Mayflower *set sail, the Jews left Egypt. Every Jew in the world, even in America or Soviet Russia, knows on exactly what date they left – the fifteenth of the month of Nisan. Everyone knows what kind of bread they ate. Even today the Jews worldwide eat matza on the fifteenth of Nisan. They retell the story of the exodus and all the troubles Jews have endured since being exiled. They conclude this evening with two statements:* This year slaves. Next year, free men. This year here. Next year in Jerusalem, in Zion, in Eretz Yisrael. *That is the nature of the Jews.*

(David Ben-Gurion)

...A THOUSAND WORDS

וְיַצִּיב And firm, established and enduring, right, faithful,
beloved, cherished, delightful, pleasant,
awesome, mighty, perfect, accepted, good and beautiful
is this faith for us for ever.

True is the eternal God, our King,
Rock of Jacob, Shield of our salvation.
He exists and His name exists through all generations.
His throne is established,
His kingship and trustworthiness endure for ever.

At °, kiss the tzitziot and release them.

His words live and persist, faithful and desirable
°for ever and all time.

▸ So they were for our ancestors, so they are for us,
and so they will be for our children and all our generations
and for all future generations
of the seed of Israel, Your servants. ◂

CONNECTION

"It once happened that Ḥoni the Circle Drawer was walking along the way and he saw an old man planting a young fruit tree. Ḥoni asked the man how long it would take until the tree would produce fruit. 'Seventy years,' the old man answered him. 'Do you really think you will be alive for another seventy years so you can enjoy the fruit from this tree?' Ḥoni asked the man with wonder. The man replied, 'Just as I was born into a world with fully grown fruit trees that were planted by my ancestors, so I plant a tree for my children.'"

(*Ta'anit* 23a)

... A THOUSAND WORDS

REFLECTION

"On three things does the world stand – on truth, justice, and peace."
(*Avot* 1:18)

What are you sure is absolutely true in your world?

Who is loyal to you?
Who are you loyal to?

Who is God loyal to?

וְיַצִּיב, וְנָכוֹן וְקַיָּם, וְיָשָׁר וְנֶאֱמָן
וְאָהוּב וְחָבִיב, וְנֶחְמָד וְנָעִים
וְנוֹרָא וְאַדִּיר, וּמְתֻקָּן וּמְקֻבָּל
וְטוֹב וְיָפֶה
הַדָּבָר הַזֶּה עָלֵינוּ לְעוֹלָם וָעֶד.

אֱמֶת אֱלֹהֵי עוֹלָם מַלְכֵּנוּ
צוּר יַעֲקֹב מָגֵן יִשְׁעֵנוּ
לְדוֹר וָדוֹר הוּא קַיָּם וּשְׁמוֹ קַיָּם
וְכִסְאוֹ נָכוֹן
וּמַלְכוּתוֹ וֶאֱמוּנָתוֹ לָעַד קַיֶּמֶת.

At °, kiss the ציציות *and release them.*

וּדְבָרָיו חָיִים וְקַיָּמִים, נֶאֱמָנִים וְנֶחֱמָדִים
°לָעַד וּלְעוֹלְמֵי עוֹלָמִים
◂ עַל אֲבוֹתֵינוּ וְעָלֵינוּ
עַל בָּנֵינוּ וְעַל דּוֹרוֹתֵינוּ
וְעַל כָּל דּוֹרוֹת זֶרַע יִשְׂרָאֵל עֲבָדֶיךָ. ◂

LEARNING

The siddur is most likely the first book of Jewish philosophy that any Jew finds in his hands. On its pages are numerous examples of deep principles of Jewish faith and theology, sometimes expressed directly and sometimes only implied. This *tefilla*, commencing with a burst of descriptive terms, proclaims the absolute and everlasting truth of God's message to us that is embodied in the *Shema*, and expresses our faith in God's redemption of the Jewish People. Stressing the importance of these concepts, the Gemara tells us, "Whoever has not recited *Emet Ve-yatziv* in *Shaharit* and *Emet Ve-emuna* in *Arvit* has not fulfilled his obligation" (*Berakhot* 12a). Rashi comments that *Emet Ve-yatziv* acknowledges God's past redemption of the Jews from Egypt, and *Emet Ve-emuna*, recited in *Ma'ariv*, confirms our faith in God's redemption of the Jews in the future.

For the early
and the later generations
this faith has proved good and enduring for ever –

True and faithful, an irrevocable law.

True You are the LORD: our God and God of our ancestors,
▸ our King and King of our ancestors,
our Redeemer and Redeemer of our ancestors,
our Maker, Rock of our salvation,
our Deliverer and Rescuer:
this has ever been Your name.
There is no God but You.

REFLECTION

"If I have seen further, it is by standing on the shoulders of giants."
(Sir Isaac Newton)

What knowledge have your ancestors passed along to you about God?

How do you imagine God?

Think about your ancestors, and about their relationship to God. How does it compare to yours?

CONNECTION

There once was a severe drought, and the people of the town had no water to drink. The rabbi called everyone together to pray for rain. The people gathered in the center of the town and cried out with emotion and sincerity to ask Hashem to send the rains they so desperately needed. Among the crowd was a small girl and her father. She tugged on her father's hand and asked him, "Abba, if we have all come to pray to Hashem for rain, then why has nobody brought an umbrella?"

LEARNING

Rambam wrote the thirteen things every Jew must believe in a list that is known as his Thirteen Principles of Faith. The first one is:

I believe with perfect faith that the Creator, blessed be His name, is the Creator and Guide of everything that has been created; He alone has made, does make, and will make all things.

The twelfth one is:

I believe with perfect faith in the coming of the Messiah; and even though he may be delayed, nonetheless, I wait every day for his coming.

עַל הָרִאשׁוֹנִים
וְעַל הָאַחֲרוֹנִים
דָּבָר טוֹב וְקַיָּם לְעוֹלָם וָעֶד
אֱמֶת וֶאֱמוּנָה, חֹק וְלֹא יַעֲבֹר.

אֱמֶת שָׁאַתָּה הוּא יהוה אֱלֹהֵינוּ וֵאלֹהֵי אֲבוֹתֵינוּ
◂ מַלְכֵּנוּ מֶלֶךְ אֲבוֹתֵינוּ
גּוֹאֲלֵנוּ גּוֹאֵל אֲבוֹתֵינוּ
יוֹצְרֵנוּ צוּר יְשׁוּעָתֵנוּ
פּוֹדֵנוּ וּמַצִּילֵנוּ מֵעוֹלָם שְׁמֶךָ
אֵין אֱלֹהִים זוּלָתֶךָ.

... A THOUSAND WORDS

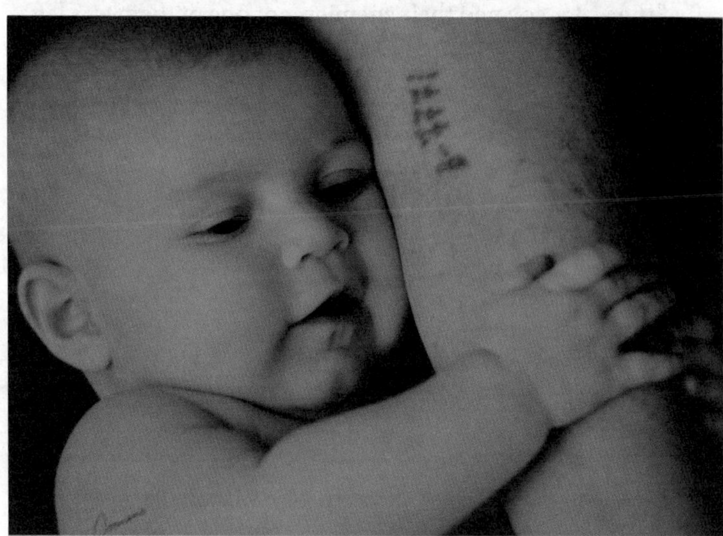

עֶזְרַת You have always been the help of our ancestors,
Shield and Savior of their children after them
in every generation.
Your presence is in the heights of the universe,
and Your judgments and righteousness
reach to the ends of the earth.
Happy is the one who obeys Your commandments
and takes to heart Your teaching and Your word.

True You are the Master of Your people
and a mighty King who pleads their cause.

True You are the first and You are the last.
Besides You, we have no king, redeemer or savior.
From Egypt You redeemed us, LORD our God,
and from the slave-house You saved us.
All their firstborn You killed,
but Your firstborn You redeemed.
You split the Sea of Reeds and drowned the arrogant.
You brought Your beloved ones across.
The water covered their enemies, not one of them was left. *Ps. 106*

REFLECTION

"[My] faith [in God] has been persistently reinforced by Jewish history.... 'These are His awesome effects, for were it not for awe of God, how could one nation survive among the nations?' (Yoma, 69b) ... Our singular history has provided much reinforcement."
(Rabbi Aharon Lichtenstein)

...A THOUSAND WORDS

What is your favorite period of Jewish history? Why? What role do you think God played then?

Does your understanding of Jewish history help your belief in God or hinder it?

עֶזְרַת אֲבוֹתֵינוּ אַתָּה הוּא מֵעוֹלָם
מָגֵן וּמוֹשִׁיעַ לִבְנֵיהֶם אַחֲרֵיהֶם בְּכָל דּוֹר וָדוֹר.
בְּרוּם עוֹלָם מוֹשָׁבֶךָ
וּמִשְׁפָּטֶיךָ וְצִדְקָתְךָ עַד אַפְסֵי אָרֶץ.
אַשְׁרֵי אִישׁ שֶׁיִּשְׁמַע לְמִצְוֹתֶיךָ
וְתוֹרָתְךָ וּדְבָרְךָ יָשִׂים עַל לִבּוֹ.

אֱמֶת אַתָּה הוּא אָדוֹן לְעַמֶּךָ
וּמֶלֶךְ גִּבּוֹר לָרִיב רִיבָם.

אֱמֶת אַתָּה הוּא רִאשׁוֹן וְאַתָּה הוּא אַחֲרוֹן
וּמִבַּלְעָדֶיךָ אֵין לָנוּ מֶלֶךְ גּוֹאֵל וּמוֹשִׁיעַ.
מִמִּצְרַיִם גְּאַלְתָּנוּ, יהוה אֱלֹהֵינוּ
וּמִבֵּית עֲבָדִים פְּדִיתָנוּ
כָּל בְּכוֹרֵיהֶם הָרָגְתָּ, וּבְכוֹרְךָ גָּאָלְתָּ
וְיַם סוּף בָּקַעְתָּ, וְזֵדִים טִבַּעְתָּ, וִידִידִים הֶעֱבַרְתָּ
וַיְכַסּוּ־מַיִם צָרֵיהֶם, אֶחָד מֵהֶם לֹא נוֹתָר: תהלים קו

CONNECTION

"First the knock of the Beloved was heard in the political arena. No one can deny that from the standpoint of international relations, the establishment of the State of Israel, in a political sense, was an almost supernatural occurrence. Both Russia and the Western countries jointly supported the idea of the establishment of the State. This was perhaps the only proposal where East and West were united. I am inclined to believe that the United Nations organization was created specifically for this purpose – in order to carry out the mission which divine providence had set for it…

"Second, the knocking of the Beloved could be heard on the battlefield. The small Israeli defense forces defeated the mighty armies of the Arab countries. The miracle of 'the many in the hands of the few' took place before our very eyes…"

(Rabbi J.B. Soloveitchik, *Kol Dodi Dofek*)

For this, the beloved ones praised and great God,
the cherished ones sang psalms, songs and praises,
blessings and thanksgivings to the King,
the living and enduring God.
High and elevated, great and awesome,
He humbles the arrogant and raises the lowly,
freeing captives and redeeming those in need, helping the poor
and answering His people when they cry out to Him.

Stand in preparation for the Amida. Take three steps back before beginning the Amida.

▸ Praises to God Most High, the Blessed One who is blessed.
Moses and the children of Israel
recited to You a song with great joy,
and they all exclaimed:
"Who is like You, Lord, among the mighty? *Ex. 15*
Who is like You, majestic in holiness,
awesome in praises, doing wonders?"

▸ With a new song, the redeemed people praised
Your name at the seashore.
Together they all gave thanks, proclaimed Your kingship,
and declared:
"The Lord shall reign for ever and ever." *Ex. 15*

CONNECTION

"[The Ba'al Shem Tov] explained to them that abstract erudition is not the sole vessel of truth or the sole path leading to saintliness. And that saintliness is not the only link between man and the eternity he carries inside him. Song is more precious than words, intention more important than formulas. And since it is given to every man to acquire all the powers, why despair? Why give up the fight? One tear, one prayer can change the course of events; one fragment of melody can contain all the joy in the world, and by letting it go free, influence fate. And no elite has a monopoly on song or tears; God listens to the shepherd playing his flute as readily as He listens to the saint renouncing his earthly attachments. The prisoner's craving equals the wise man's: the one, like the other, has a bearing on the essence of man."

(Elie Wiesel, *Souls on Fire*)

עַל זֹאת שִׁבְּחוּ אֲהוּבִים, וְרוֹמְמוּ אֵל
וְנָתְנוּ יְדִידִים זְמִירוֹת, שִׁירוֹת וְתִשְׁבָּחוֹת
בְּרָכוֹת וְהוֹדָאוֹת לַמֶּלֶךְ אֵל חַי וְקַיָּם
רָם וְנִשָּׂא, גָּדוֹל וְנוֹרָא
מַשְׁפִּיל גֵּאִים וּמַגְבִּיהַּ שְׁפָלִים
מוֹצִיא אֲסִירִים, וּפוֹדֶה עֲנָוִים וְעוֹזֵר דַּלִּים
וְעוֹנֶה לְעַמּוֹ בְּעֵת שַׁוְּעָם אֵלָיו.

Stand in preparation for the עמידה*. Take three steps back before beginning the* עמידה*.*

◂ תְּהִלּוֹת לְאֵל עֶלְיוֹן, בָּרוּךְ הוּא וּמְבֹרָךְ
מֹשֶׁה וּבְנֵי יִשְׂרָאֵל, לְךָ עָנוּ שִׁירָה בְּשִׂמְחָה רַבָּה
וְאָמְרוּ כֻלָּם
מִי־כָמֹכָה בָּאֵלִם, יהוה שמות טו
מִי כָּמֹכָה נֶאְדָּר בַּקֹּדֶשׁ, נוֹרָא תְהִלֹּת, עֹשֵׂה פֶלֶא:
◂ שִׁירָה חֲדָשָׁה שִׁבְּחוּ גְאוּלִים
לְשִׁמְךָ עַל שְׂפַת הַיָּם
יַחַד כֻּלָּם הוֹדוּ וְהִמְלִיכוּ
וְאָמְרוּ
יהוה יִמְלֹךְ לְעֹלָם וָעֶד: שמות טו

... A THOUSAND WORDS

REFLECTION

Can you think of a time in modern history when God has answered His people when they have cried out to Him?

For what in Jewish history do you want to show gratitude to God?

Congregants should end the following blessing together with the Leader so as to be able to move directly from the words "redeemed Israel" to the Amida, without the interruption of saying Amen.

צוּר יִשְׂרָאֵל Rock of Israel! Arise to the help of Israel.
Deliver, as You promised, Judah and Israel.
Our Redeemer, the Lord of multitudes is His name, *Is. 47*
the Holy One of Israel.
Blessed are You, Lord, who redeemed Israel.

LEARNING

INTRODUCTION TO *AMIDA*

The *Amida* prayer is the central prayer of the *tefilla* service, to which everything up until this point has been building up. The *Amida* encompasses within it all the elements of prayer. Originally composed by the Men of the Great Assembly, the *Amida* consisted of eighteen blessings, hence its other name, *Shemoneh Esreh* (Eighteen). Later, in Talmudic times, a nineteenth prayer was added (the thirteenth *berakha* according to our number – Against Informers).

The *Amida* has its own internal logical structure. The first three *berakhot* are blessings of praise (*shevaḥ*), followed by thirteen requests (*bakashot*), and then the *Amida* concludes with three blessings of thanks (*hoda'a)*. Within the thirteen (originally twelve) *berakhot* of requests, the first six focus on personal needs, and the remaining six (now seven) focus on our national needs.

We derive many of the laws for how to conduct ourselves when saying the *Amida* prayer from a woman called Ḥana. Ḥana was married for many years and despite her many prayers, she was unable to have children. One Rosh HaShana, Ḥana prayed at the *Mishkan*. So powerful and devout were her prayers that she was granted a child. Not just any child, but the next leader of the Jewish People; the future prophet Shmuel. Ḥana prayed silently; only her lips moved, audible only to herself. We therefore pray in quiet devotion just as Ḥana did, standing and supplicating God for our deepest desires.

Before we begin our *Amida* prayer, we take a few moments to focus and take stock. Facing Jerusalem, we take three steps back and remove all foreign and distracting thoughts from our minds. We then slowly take three steps forward and in doing so, we show our readiness to approach the Master of the Universe.

Take a moment to disconnect from everything; as you take your three steps back, focus your mind, think about what you are about to do. Remember that as you approach God, you are seizing a special opportunity to stand before Him in a personal audience and speak directly to Him. If the conversation seems difficult to start, remember that **אֲדֹנָי, שְׂפָתַי תִּפְתָּח** is the prayer to be able to pray.

The קהל *should end the following blessing together with the* שליח ציבור *so as to be able to move directly from the words* גָּאַל יִשְׂרָאֵל *to the* עמידה*, without the interruption of saying* אמן.

צוּר יִשְׂרָאֵל, קוּמָה בְּעֶזְרַת יִשְׂרָאֵל
וּפְדֵה כִנְאֻמֶךָ יְהוּדָה וְיִשְׂרָאֵל.
גֹּאֲלֵנוּ יהוה צְבָאוֹת שְׁמוֹ, קְדוֹשׁ יִשְׂרָאֵל: ישעיה מז
בָּרוּךְ אַתָּה יהוה, גָּאַל יִשְׂרָאֵל.

LEARNING

The halakha forbids any interruption between the conclusion of the *berakha* גָּאַל יִשְׂרָאֵל and the beginning of the *Amida*. This includes any kind of speech, and according to some even the response "Amen" to that *berakha*. Many people have the custom to be careful to complete the *berakha* at the same time as the leader so there is no opportunity to say Amen.

A possible reason for our insistence that this *berakha* and the *Amida* are juxtaposed without interruption – In halakhic terminology סְמִיכַת גְּאֻלָּה לִתְפִלָּה – is because the *berakha* represents the link between the *tefillot* that speak about the previous redemption from Egypt (in the third paragraph of the *Shema*) and the future redemption (Mashiaḥ) in the *Amida*. This is a declaration of faith that just as Hashem redeemed us previously, He will redeem us again and bring the Mashiaḥ.

REFLECTION

אָבִינוּ שֶׁבַּשָּׁמַיִם, צוּר יִשְׂרָאֵל וְגוֹאֲלוֹ,
בָּרֵךְ אֶת מְדִינַת יִשְׂרָאֵל,
רֵאשִׁית צְמִיחַת גְּאֻלָּתֵנוּ.

"Heavenly Father, Israel's Rock and Redeemer, bless the State of Israel, the first flowering of our redemption."

Close your eyes. Think about when the Mashiaḥ comes. What will the world look like? How will it be different from your world today?

What can you do today to make your world closer to the Messianic one?

CONNECTION

It is said that Napoleon, passing a synagogue on Tisha B'Av, was struck by the sounds of lament coming from the building. "What," he asked one of his officers, "are the Jews crying for?" "For Jerusalem," came the reply. "How long ago did they lose Jerusalem?" "More than seventeen hundred years ago." Napoleon was silent for a moment and then said, "A people that can remember Jerusalem for so long will one day have it restored to them." So it has come to pass in our time.

THE AMIDA

The Amida until "in former years" on page 198, is said standing with feet together. The Amida is said silently, following the precedent of Hannah when she prayed for a child (1 Sam. 1:13). If there is a minyan, it is repeated aloud by the Leader. Take three steps forward, as if formally entering the place of the Divine Presence.

O Lord, open my lips, Ps. 51
so that my mouth may declare Your praise.

CONNECTION

For many of us, instead of opening our hearts to prayer, something silences our natural instinct to pray. It's like the story of a simple shepherd, who every day would offer his personal prayer to God: "God, I love You so much, that if You were here, I would give You half of my sheep. If it was raining and You were cold, I would share my blanket with You."

One day a man was walking by the field, and he heard the shepherd praying. He said "Do you call that praying? Are you kidding? What would God do with your sheep? Of what use would a blanket be to God? Here, let me show you to pray properly before you further desecrate God's holy name!" The man then took out a siddur, and proceeded to lecture the poor illiterate shepherd on the structure and meaning of the various prayers.

As soon as the man left, the shepherd sat there dumbfounded. He didn't understand a word of it. But he knew the man was quite upset that his prayers were not proper. So he stopped praying.

For too many of us, that's where the story ends. Fortunately for the shepherd, there is more to his story.

Up in heaven, God noticed the silence, and said, "What happened to the beautiful prayers of My humble shepherd?" He sent down an angel to find out what was wrong.

The angel found the shepherd, and the shepherd told him the whole story of his meeting with the man. The angel said, "What does that man know? Would you like to see how we pray in heaven?" The shepherd instantly agreed and the angel whisked him off to heaven, where he saw an angel standing and proclaiming: "God, I love You so much, that if You were here, I would give You half of my sheep. If it was raining and You were cold, I would share my blanket with You." The shepherd happily went back to his prayers, and God happily listened.

עמידה

The עמידה *until* קָדְמֹנִיּוֹת *on page 199, is said standing with feet together. The* עמידה *is said silently, following the precedent of Hannah when she prayed for a child* (שמואל א׳ א, יג)*. If there is a* מנין*, it is repeated aloud by the* שליח ציבור*. Take three steps forward, as if formally entering the place of the Divine Presence.*

אֲדֹנָי, שְׂפָתַי תִּפְתָּח, וּפִי יַגִּיד תְּהִלָּתֶךָ׃ תהלים נא

REFLECTION

A prayer to be able to pray...

Have you ever struggled to start a conversation? How did you overcome it?

Do you need help starting a conversation with God? What are you scared to say?

What do you want to praise God for?

...A THOUSAND WORDS

LEARNING

On his own, it is impossible for a person to fully understand his own needs and formulate them into a clear prayer. His mouth is inarticulate, his tongue fails. A person requires divine assistance not only for his basic needs but also to recognize his limitations and to arrange his words. Not only are we dependent on God to fulfill our needs, but also to recognize and express them. So the *Amida* opens with the introductory phrase, **אֲדֹנָי שְׂפָתַי תִּפְתָּח**, "O Lord, open my lips." We cannot contemplate prayer unless we seek God's assistance in formulating our pleas. (Based on the commentary of Rabbi J.B. Soloveitchik, in the Koren Mesorat Harav Siddur, 120–121.)

PATRIARCHS

בָּרוּךְ Blessed are You,
LORD our God and God of our fathers,
God of Abraham, God of Isaac and God of Jacob;
the great, mighty and awesome God, God Most High,
who acts with loving-kindness and creates all,
who remembers the loving-kindness of the fathers
and will bring a Redeemer to their children's children
for the sake of His name, in love.

Between Rosh HaShana & Yom Kippur: Remember us for life, O King who desires life,
and write us in the book of life –
for Your sake, O God of life.

King, Helper, Savior, Shield:
Blessed are You, LORD, Shield of Abraham.

REFLECTION

What merits of our ancestors would you like to "borrow"?

What message would you like our forefathers to give God on your behalf?

How are you going to be kind today?

...A THOUSAND WORDS

LEARNING

The *berakha* says God of Avraham, God of Yitzḥak, and God of Yaakov individually instead of God of all three to teach us a profound lesson. A person is required to find his individual connection to God and not simply rely on the belief taught to him by his forefathers. Each of us have an opportunity to forge our own individual relationships with God, learning from but not merely copying our ancestors.

(Rabbi Meir Eisenstadt, *Panim Me'irot*)

אבות

בָּרוּךְ אַתָּה יהוה, אֱלֹהֵינוּ וֵאלֹהֵי אֲבוֹתֵינוּ
אֱלֹהֵי אַבְרָהָם, אֱלֹהֵי יִצְחָק, וֵאלֹהֵי יַעֲקֹב
הָאֵל הַגָּדוֹל הַגִּבּוֹר וְהַנּוֹרָא, אֵל עֶלְיוֹן
גּוֹמֵל חֲסָדִים טוֹבִים, וְקוֹנֵה הַכֹּל
וְזוֹכֵר חַסְדֵי אָבוֹת
וּמֵבִיא גוֹאֵל לִבְנֵי בְנֵיהֶם לְמַעַן שְׁמוֹ בְּאַהֲבָה.

בעשרת ימי תשובה: **זָכְרֵנוּ לְחַיִּים, מֶלֶךְ חָפֵץ בַּחַיִּים**
וְכָתְבֵנוּ בְּסֵפֶר הַחַיִּים
לְמַעַנְךָ אֱלֹהִים חַיִּים.

מֶלֶךְ עוֹזֵר וּמוֹשִׁיעַ וּמָגֵן.
בָּרוּךְ אַתָּה יהוה, מָגֵן אַבְרָהָם.

CONNECTION

While in the Janowska Road Concentration Camp, Nazi SS officers forced the Bluzhever Rebbe and fellow prisoners on a death march. The Rebbe walked with a maskil *(free thinker) whom he befriended, a man who did not believe in God. As they approached several huge ditches, the prisoners were ordered to jump across, an almost impossible feat. If they landed in the ditch, they would be summarily shot.*

"Well Spira," said the maskil *to the Rebbe, "it looks like we've reached our end." "Just hold onto my coat and we'll jump across together," replied the Rebbe. They closed their eyes and jumped. They opened their eyes alive on the other side. Shocked, the* maskil *turned to the Rebbe and asked, "Rebbe, we're alive, we're alive because of you! There must be a God! How did you do it Rebbe?" The Rebbe replied, "I had* zekhut avot *(ancestral merit). I held on to the* bekeshe *of my father and his father and all of my ancestors. But tell me," the Rebbe asked the* maskil*, "how did you reach the other side?" The* maskil *answered, "I was holding on to you!"*

(Hasidic Tales of the Holocaust)

DIVINE MIGHT

אַתָּה גִּבּוֹר You are eternally mighty, LORD.
You give life to the dead and have great power to save.

The phrase "He makes the wind blow and the rain fall" is said from Simḥat Torah until Pesaḥ. In Israel the phrase "He causes the dew to fall" is said from Pesaḥ until Shemini Atzeret.

In fall & winter: He makes the wind blow and the rain fall.
In Israel, in spring & summer: He causes the dew to fall.

He sustains the living with loving-kindness,
and with great compassion revives the dead.
He supports the fallen, heals the sick, sets captives free,
and keeps His faith with those who sleep in the dust.
Who is like You, Master of might,
and who can compare to You,
O King who brings death and gives life, and makes salvation grow?

Between Rosh HaShana & Yom Kippur: Who is like You, compassionate Father,
who remembers His creatures in compassion, for life?

Faithful are You to revive the dead.
Blessed are You, LORD, who revives the dead.

When saying the Amida silently, continue with "You are holy" on page 158.

CONNECTION

According to early scientific thought, the bumblebee's body was too heavy and its wingspan too small. Aerodynamically, it was thought, the bumblebee should not be able to fly. But the bumblebee has no idea of this and it keeps flying. When you don't know your limitations, you go out and surprise yourself. In hindsight, you wonder if you had any limitations. Often, the only limitations a person has are those that are self-imposed. How can you find your own inner strength?

LEARNING

We mention the resurrection of the dead three times in this blessing. The first is to reflect on God's kindness in returning our souls to us each day. The second refers to rainfall which revives the ground and the third refers to the final actual resurrection of the dead in the times of Mashiaḥ. (Abudraham)

גבורות

אַתָּה גִּבּוֹר לְעוֹלָם, אֲדֹנָי
מְחַיֵּה מֵתִים אַתָּה, רַב לְהוֹשִׁיעַ

The phrase מַשִּׁיב הָרְוּחַ *is said from* שמחת תורה *until* פסח.
In ארץ ישראל *the phrase* מוֹרִיד הַטָּל *is said from* פסח *until* שמיני עצרת.

בחורף: **מַשִּׁיב הָרְוּחַ וּמוֹרִיד הַגֶּשֶׁם** / בארץ ישראל בקיץ: **מוֹרִיד הַטָּל**

מְכַלְכֵּל חַיִּים בְּחֶסֶד, מְחַיֵּה מֵתִים בְּרַחֲמִים רַבִּים
סוֹמֵךְ נוֹפְלִים, וְרוֹפֵא חוֹלִים, וּמַתִּיר אֲסוּרִים
וּמְקַיֵּם אֱמוּנָתוֹ לִישֵׁנֵי עָפָר.
מִי כָמְוֹךָ, בַּעַל גְּבוּרוֹת, וּמִי דְּוֹמֶה לָּךְ
מֶלֶךְ, מֵמִית וּמְחַיֶּה וּמַצְמִיחַ יְשׁוּעָה.

בעשרת ימי תשובה: **מִי כָמְוֹךָ אַב הָרַחֲמִים, זוֹכֵר יְצוּרָיו לְחַיִּים בְּרַחֲמִים.**

וְנֶאֱמָן אַתָּה לְהַחֲיוֹת מֵתִים.
בָּרוּךְ אַתָּה יהוה, מְחַיֵּה הַמֵּתִים.

When saying the עמידה *silently, continue with* אַתָּה קָדוֹשׁ *on page 159.*

REFLECTION

Are you trying to find the inner strength to help yourself?

What area of your life would you like to turn around?

Where do you feel like you need help picking yourself up, healing, and freeing yourself?

... A THOUSAND WORDS

KEDUSHA

During the Leader's Repetition, the following is said standing with feet together, rising on the toes at the words indicated by ▲.

Cong. then Leader: נְקַדֵּשׁ We will sanctify Your name on earth,
as they sanctify it in the highest heavens,
as is written by Your prophet,
"And they [the angels] call to one another saying: *Is. 6*

Cong. then Leader: ▲Holy, ▲holy, ▲holy is the LORD of multitudes
the whole world is filled with His glory."
Those facing them say "Blessed – "

Cong. then Leader: ▲"Blessed is the LORD's glory from His place." *Ezek. 3*
And in Your holy Writings it is written thus:

Cong. then Leader: ▲"The LORD shall reign for ever. He is your God, Zion, *Ps. 146*
from generation to generation, Halleluya!"

Leader: From generation to generation we will speak of Your greatness,
and we will declare Your holiness for evermore.
Your praise, our God, shall not leave our mouth forever,
for You, God, are a great and holy King. Blessed are You, LORD,
the holy God. / *Between Rosh HaShana & Yom Kippur:* the holy King./

The Leader continues with "You grace humanity" on page 160.

CONNECTION

The Kotzker Rebbe once asked his students where God was to be found; they answered that "He fills all the world with His glory." He shook his head and said, "No, I asked where is He to be found, not where He is." The students looked at the rabbi with confusion and exasperation. "Did we not already say that He is everywhere?" "No, no," the Kotzker smiled at them. "You must understand that God is to be found in the place that you open up your hearts and let Him in!"

... A THOUSAND WORDS

קדושה

During חזרת הש״ץ*, the following is said standing with feet together, rising on the toes at the words indicated by* ▴.

then קהל ש״ץ: נְקַדֵּשׁ אֶת שִׁמְךָ בָּעוֹלָם
כְּשֵׁם שֶׁמַּקְדִּישִׁים אוֹתוֹ בִּשְׁמֵי מָרוֹם
כַּכָּתוּב עַל יַד נְבִיאֶךָ, וְקָרָא זֶה אֶל־זֶה וְאָמַר — ישעיה ו

then קהל ש״ץ: ▴קָדוֹשׁ, ▴קָדוֹשׁ, ▴קָדוֹשׁ, יהוה צְבָאוֹת
מְלֹא כָל־הָאָרֶץ כְּבוֹדוֹ:
לְעֻמָּתָם בָּרוּךְ יֹאמֵרוּ

then קהל ש״ץ: ▴בָּרוּךְ כְּבוֹד־יהוה מִמְּקוֹמוֹ: — יחזקאל ג
וּבְדִבְרֵי קָדְשְׁךָ כָּתוּב לֵאמֹר

then קהל ש״ץ: ▴יִמְלֹךְ יהוה לְעוֹלָם, אֱלֹהַיִךְ צִיּוֹן לְדֹר וָדֹר, הַלְלוּיָהּ: — תהלים קמו

ש״ץ: לְדוֹר וָדוֹר נַגִּיד גָּדְלֶךָ, וּלְנֵצַח נְצָחִים קְדֻשָּׁתְךָ נַקְדִּישׁ
וְשִׁבְחֲךָ אֱלֹהֵינוּ מִפִּינוּ לֹא יָמוּשׁ לְעוֹלָם וָעֶד
כִּי אֵל מֶלֶךְ גָּדוֹל וְקָדוֹשׁ אָתָּה.
בָּרוּךְ אַתָּה יהוה, הָאֵל הַקָּדוֹשׁ./ בעשרת ימי תשובה: הַמֶּלֶךְ הַקָּדוֹשׁ./

The שליח ציבור *continues with* אַתָּה חוֹנֵן *on page 161.*

LEARNING

The first verse we recite in the *Kedusha* prayer is what the prophet Isaiah heard the angels singing before God every morning. According to Jewish tradition, the angels cannot recite *Kedusha* in their heavenly realm until the Jewish People recite *Kedusha* on earth (*Ḥullin* 91b).

REFLECTION

"The virtue of angels is that they cannot deteriorate;
their flaw is that they cannot improve.
Humanity's flaw is that we can deteriorate;
but our virtue is that we can improve."
(Hasidic proverb)

What does holiness mean to you?

Can you think of a way you can act like an angel today?

Think about how you act on Yom Kippur – how can you act like that for one moment today?

HOLINESS

אַתָּה קָדוֹשׁ You are holy and Your name is holy,
and holy ones praise You daily, Selah!
Blessed are You, LORD,
the holy God. / *Between Rosh HaShana & Yom Kippur:* the holy King./

(*If forgotten, repeat the Amida.*)

CONNECTION

Imagine a city in the middle of a war. The dirt flying in the air. Missiles overhead. Everything in chaos. The smell of chemicals permeating the thick fog that has become the sky and civilians running through the streets in confusion, in panic – a living nightmare. A doctor runs across the blood-stained streets looking for people he can help, wounds he can heal just enough to get people back on their feet so they can keep running, keep living. He tends to a man bleeding from a piece of shrapnel, when he suddenly hears someone call out, "Doctor."

A short distance away he sees the woman calling out. She is hurt and in need of immediate attention. But as soon as he runs toward her, he hears another voice: "David!" He looks over to see his neighbor on the ground with a serious injury. No sooner than two steps to the neighbor's direction, a small voice pierces through the sweaty air and whispers, "Dad." The doctor is paralyzed for a moment before looking for his son amidst the rubble.

"Hashem" is the Jewish People's way of saying Dad.

To most people, the man in the story was an anonymous person running around the streets – until someone saw him performing a medical act. Then he became "Doctor." To his neighbor, however, he was "David," a name that suggests an attachment that forced him to care just a little bit more. And when he heard "Dad" come through the thick fog, he was paralyzed.

This is the power of a name. It defines the relationship we have with the person and forces us to treat him in a particular way.

"Hashem" is the Jewish People's way of saying Dad. Dad is not the person's legal name, it's not their Hebrew name, it's not their business title. It's shorthand. It's a way to say that we, as Jews, have a nickname for You, God. It's a nickname that suggests both intimacy and respect, like the appellation "Dad." It's a way to tell your father that you love him, but that you still understand he's the father, he's in charge.

Likewise with Hashem: we love You and feel close to You. And at the same time we recognize our distance and who is really in charge.

(Jon Dabach)

קדושת השם

אַתָּה קָדוֹשׁ וְשִׁמְךָ קָדוֹשׁ
וּקְדוֹשִׁים בְּכָל יוֹם יְהַלְלוּךָ סֶּלָה.
בָּרוּךְ אַתָּה יהוה, הָאֵל הַקָּדוֹשׁ./ בעשרת ימי תשובה: **הַמֶּלֶךְ הַקָּדוֹשׁ.**/

(*If forgotten, repeat the* עמידה.)

REFLECTION

How can I behave today
in a way that reflects
my inner holiness?

Am I behaving
in a way that makes
a ***kiddush Hashem***?

What will you do today
to bring holiness
into the world?

LEARNING

"A person will have to answer for everything that his eye beheld and he did not consume." (Yerushalmi, *Kiddushin* 4:12) In Judaism, holiness does not mean denying the physical, rather enjoying that which is permitted to us and uplifting it to make it spiritual. *Kedusha* is the transformation and the elevation of the mundane to the holy and spiritual.

... A THOUSAND WORDS

KNOWLEDGE

אַתָּה חוֹנֵן You grace humanity with knowledge
and teach mortals understanding.
Grace us with the knowledge, understanding
and insight that come from You.
Blessed are You, LORD,
who generously gives knowledge.

...A THOUSAND WORDS

we grow wise and are able to say all that we say, but not because we are greater than they.'"

(Rabbi Isaiah di Trani)

"When I went to the moon I was a pragmatic test pilot. But when I saw the planet Earth floating in the vastness of space, the presence of divinity became almost palpable and I knew that life in the universe was not just an accident."

(Edgar Mitchell, Apollo 14 Astronaut)

דעת

אַתָּה חוֹנֵן לְאָדָם דַּעַת
וּמְלַמֵּד לֶאֱנוֹשׁ בִּינָה.
חָנֵּנוּ מֵאִתְּךָ דֵּעָה בִּינָה וְהַשְׂכֵּל.
בָּרוּךְ אַתָּה יהוה
חוֹנֵן הַדָּעַת.

LEARNING

On Saturday night we insert Havdala into this *berakha*. Havdala is when we make distinctions and separations, between holy and unholy, between light and dark, between Shabbat and the rest of the week. Being able to distinguish between one thing and another is a type of wisdom, therefore Havdala is included in the *berakha* about wisdom. The word **בִּינָה** also hints to **בְּשָׂמִים, יַיִן, נֵר, הַבְדָּלָה**, the four blessings of the Havdala service. (*Mishna Berura* 115:1)

REFLECTION

"You can't help respecting anybody who can spell TUESDAY, even if he doesn't spell it right."
(A.A. Milne)

What do you wish you could know?

Which is more impressive to you, someone who already has knowledge or someone who continuously tries to gain more knowledge?

Have you ever wished to understand something more? What do you most want to understand?

CONNECTION

"The wisest of the philosophers asked: 'We admit that our predecessors were wiser than we. At the same time we criticize their comments, often rejecting them and claiming that the truth rests with us. How is this possible?' The wise philosopher responded: 'Who sees further, a dwarf or a giant? Surely a giant for his eyes are situated at a higher level than those of the dwarf. But if the dwarf is placed on the shoulders of the giant who sees further?... So too we are dwarfs astride the shoulders of giants. We master their wisdom and move beyond it. Due to their wisdom

REPENTANCE

הֲשִׁיבֵנוּ Bring us back, our Father, to Your Torah.
Draw us near, our King, to Your service.
Lead us back to You in perfect repentance.
Blessed are You, LORD,
who desires repentance.

CONNECTION

Rabbi Yisrael Salanter was returning home very late one night. As he walked through the dark alleyways, he suddenly noticed that a light was still burning in the home of the shoemaker. He knocked on the door and entered his home.

"Why are you still sitting and working at such a late hour?" asked Rabbi Salanter.

"As long as the candle burns," replied the shoemaker, "it is still possible to repair."

Those words made a great impression upon Rabbi Salanter and, from then on, he repeated them on many occasions.

"Do you hear?" Rabbi Salanter would ask. "As long as the candle burns, it is still possible to repair! As long as a person is alive and his soul is within him, he can still rectify his deeds."

REFLECTION

In what respect
do you want God
to treat you
as His child?

Have you moved
away from God?
How are you trying
to return?

Have you asked Him
to help you
to rekindle
your connection?

CONNECTION

"For a righteous person may fall
seven times and rise up..."
(*Mishlei* 24:16)

"God gave Adam a secret –
and that secret was not how to begin,
but how to begin again."
(Elie Wiesel)

"In a place where one
who has achieved teshuva stands
even the perfectly righteous
cannot stand."
(*Berakhot* 34b)

תשובה

הֲשִׁיבֵנוּ אָבִינוּ לְתוֹרָתֶךָ
וְקָרְבֵנוּ מַלְכֵּנוּ לַעֲבוֹדָתֶךָ
וְהַחֲזִירֵנוּ בִּתְשׁוּבָה שְׁלֵמָה לְפָנֶיךָ.
בָּרוּךְ אַתָּה יהוה
הָרוֹצֶה בִּתְשׁוּבָה.

... A THOUSAND WORDS

FORGIVENESS

Strike the left side of the chest at °.

סְלַח לָנוּ Forgive us, our Father,
for we have °sinned.
Pardon us, our King,
for we have °transgressed;
for You pardon and forgive.
Blessed are You, Lord,
the generous One who repeatedly forgives.

...A THOUSAND WORDS

סליחה

Strike the left side of the chest at °.

סְלַח לָנוּ אָבִינוּ כִּי °חָטָאנוּ
מְחַל לָנוּ מַלְכֵּנוּ כִּי °פָשָׁעְנוּ
כִּי מוֹחֵל וְסוֹלֵחַ אָתָּה.
בָּרוּךְ אַתָּה יהוה
חַנּוּן הַמַּרְבֶּה לִסְלֹחַ.

REFLECTION

Are all sins forgivable?

What would you like to erase?

In what area would you like a second chance?

What do you need to apologize for?

LEARNING

"Such is the power of *teshuva* that you can even turn purposeful sins into merits." (*Yoma* 86b)

Complete *teshuva* can even turn an evil act into a merit. This is even more powerful than conquering your inclination and never doing the act. Such is the power of *teshuva*. (Rav Tzaddok of Lublin)

CONNECTION

There once was a rabbi on a train who was meditating peacefully, when a salesman shoved him to the next car because of his aloofness, not knowing that he was the rabbi of Brisk. Upon arrival at the station, a large entourage greeted the rabbi. The salesman, embarrassed at having insulted the great rabbi asked for forgiveness but the rabbi said no. The salesman came to the rabbi's house and asked for forgiveness, but again, the rabbi refused. The rabbi's son heard that his father refused to forgive a man who visited, and asked him why. He answered, "I cannot forgive him. He did not know who I was. He offended a common man. Let the salesman go to him and ask for forgiveness."

REDEMPTION

רְאֵה Look on our suffering, plead our cause,
and redeem us soon for Your name's sake,
for You are a powerful Redeemer.
Blessed are You, LORD, the Redeemer of Israel.

On Fast Days the Leader adds:

עֲנֵנוּ Answer us, LORD, answer us on our Fast Day, for we are in great distress. Look not at our wickedness. Do not hide Your face from us and do not ignore our plea. Be near to our cry; please let Your loving-kindness comfort us. Even before we call to You, answer us, as is said, "Before they call, I will answer. While they are still speaking, I will hear." For You, LORD, are the One who answers in time of distress, redeems and rescues in all times of trouble and anguish. Blessed are You, LORD, who answers in time of distress. *Is. 65*

LEARNING

The beginning of this *berakha* asks God to "see our suffering." In this blessing about personal redemption the first stage of deliverance is a recognition of suffering. This marks the beginning of our redemption. We ask God to see us, to look upon what is causing us pain, and to rescue us.

"And God saw the Children of Israel and God knew." (*Shemot* 2:25)

The Jews in Egypt were enslaved with backbreaking labor and afflictions. The Egyptians would find ways to abuse them sometimes openly and sometimes discreetly. Therefore the text tells us, "And God saw." He saw and He knew about everything.

REFLECTION

"The salvation of God is like the blink of an eye."
(*Pesikta Zutrata, Ester* 4:17)

What affliction or emotional pain do you want God to see in your life?

How do you show others that you see their pain and struggles?

What is your biggest challenge each day?
What do you need personal help overcoming?

CONNECTION

"Challenges make life interesting; however, overcoming them is what makes life meaningful."
(Mark Twain)

גאולה

רְאֵה בְעָנְיֵנוּ, וְרִיבָה רִיבֵנוּ
וּגְאָלֵנוּ מְהֵרָה לְמַעַן שְׁמֶךָ
כִּי גּוֹאֵל חָזָק אָתָּה.
בָּרוּךְ אַתָּה יהוה, גּוֹאֵל יִשְׂרָאֵל.

On Fast Days the שליח ציבור *adds:*

עֲנֵנוּ יהוה עֲנֵנוּ בְּיוֹם צוֹם תַּעֲנִיתֵנוּ, כִּי בְצָרָה גְדוֹלָה אֲנָחְנוּ. אַל תֵּפֶן אֶל
רִשְׁעֵנוּ, וְאַל תַּסְתֵּר פָּנֶיךָ מִמֶּנּוּ, וְאַל תִּתְעַלַּם מִתְּחִנָּתֵנוּ. הֱיֵה נָא קָרוֹב
לְשַׁוְעָתֵנוּ, יְהִי נָא חַסְדְּךָ לְנַחֲמֵנוּ, טֶרֶם נִקְרָא אֵלֶיךָ עֲנֵנוּ, כַּדָּבָר שֶׁנֶּאֱמַר:
וְהָיָה טֶרֶם יִקְרָאוּ וַאֲנִי אֶעֱנֶה, עוֹד הֵם מְדַבְּרִים וַאֲנִי אֶשְׁמָע: כִּי אַתָּה ישעיה סה
יהוה הָעוֹנֶה בְּעֵת צָרָה, פּוֹדֶה וּמַצִּיל בְּכָל עֵת צָרָה וְצוּקָה. בָּרוּךְ אַתָּה
יהוה, הָעוֹנֶה בְּעֵת צָרָה.

... A THOUSAND WORDS

HEALING

רְפָאֵנוּ Heal us, LORD, and we shall be healed.
Save us and we shall be saved,
for You are our praise.
Bring complete recovery for all our illnesses,

The following prayer for a sick person may be said here:
May it be Your will, O LORD my God and God of my ancestors, that You speedily send a complete recovery from heaven, a healing of both soul and body, to the patient (*name*), son/daughter of (*mother's name*) among the other sick of Israel.

for You, God, King,
are a faithful and compassionate Healer.
Blessed are You, LORD,
Healer of the sick of His people Israel.

CONNECTION

A 24-year-old man staring out from the train's window shouted, "Dad, look the trees are falling behind us!"

Dad smiled while a young couple sitting nearby looked at the 24-year-old's childish behavior with pity. Suddenly the boy again exclaimed, "Dad, look the clouds are running with us!"

The couple couldn't resist and said to the old man, "Why don't you take your son to a good doctor?"

The old man smiled and said, "I did, and we are just coming from the hospital. My son was blind from birth; he just got his eyes today."

LEARNING

In *Bereshit* 21:1, we find the story of our matriarch Sara finally becoming pregnant directly after the incident of Avraham praying on behalf of King Avimelekh to be healed. Avimelekh and his household were stricken by a plague as a punishment for Sara's abduction. This plague caused Sara and Avraham to be unable to have children. Upon Sara's release, Avraham promised to pray for Avimelekh's recovery. Rashi explains that if one prays on behalf of someone else for something that he himself needs, his own prayer will be answered first.

רפואה

רְפָאֵנוּ יהוה וְנֵרָפֵא
הוֹשִׁיעֵנוּ וְנִוָּשֵׁעָה
כִּי תְהִלָּתֵנוּ אָתָּה
וְהַעֲלֵה רְפוּאָה שְׁלֵמָה לְכָל מַכּוֹתֵינוּ

The following prayer for a sick person may be said here:

יְהִי רָצוֹן מִלְּפָנֶיךָ יהוה אֱלֹהַי וֵאלֹהֵי אֲבוֹתַי, שֶׁתִּשְׁלַח מְהֵרָה רְפוּאָה שְׁלֵמָה מִן הַשָּׁמַיִם רְפוּאַת הַנֶּפֶשׁ וּרְפוּאַת הַגּוּף לַחוֹלֶה/לַחוֹלָה *name of patient* בֶּן/בַּת *mother's name* בְּתוֹךְ שְׁאָר חוֹלֵי יִשְׂרָאֵל.

כִּי אֵל מֶלֶךְ רוֹפֵא נֶאֱמָן וְרַחֲמָן אָתָּה.
בָּרוּךְ אַתָּה יהוה, רוֹפֵא חוֹלֵי עַמּוֹ יִשְׂרָאֵל.

REFLECTION

Do you know someone who is sick?

Are you suffering physically, emotionally, or spiritually?

From what would you like God to heal you?

… A THOUSAND WORDS

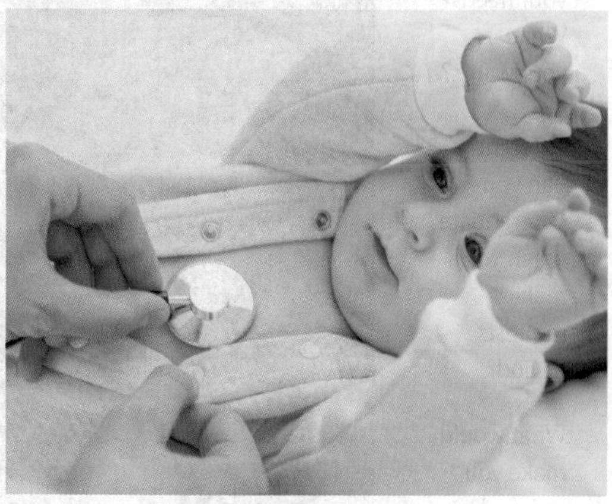

PROSPERITY

The phrase "Give dew and rain as a blessing" is said from December 5th (in the year before a civil leap year, December 6th) until Pesaḥ. In Israel, it is said from the 7th of Marḥeshvan. The phrase "Give blessing" is said from Ḥol HaMo'ed Pesaḥ until December 4th (in the year before a civil leap year, December 5th). In Israel it is said through the 6th of Marḥeshvan.

בָּרֵךְ Bless this year for us, LORD our God,
and all its types of produce for good.

In winter: Give dew and rain as a blessing
In other seasons: Give blessing

on the face of the earth,
and from its goodness satisfy us,
blessing our year as the best of years.
Blessed are You, LORD,
who blesses the years.

REFLECTION

What are your needs? What are your wants? Are they different? Can you differentiate when you make requests of God?

What would make you satisfied?

... A THOUSAND WORDS

ברכת השנים

The phrase וְתֵן טַל וּמָטָר לִבְרָכָה *is said from December 5th (in the year before a civil leap year, December 6th) until* פסח. *In* ארץ ישראל, *it is said from* ז׳ מרחשון. *The phrase* וְתֵן בְּרָכָה *is said from* חול המועד פסח *until December 4th (in the year before a civil leap year, December 5th). In* ארץ ישראל *it is said through* ו׳ מרחשון.

בָּרֵךְ עָלֵינוּ יהוה אֱלֹהֵינוּ אֶת הַשָּׁנָה הַזֹּאת
וְאֶת כָּל מִינֵי תְבוּאָתָהּ, לְטוֹבָה
בחורף: **וְתֵן טַל וּמָטָר לִבְרָכָה** / בקיץ: **וְתֵן בְּרָכָה**
עַל פְּנֵי הָאֲדָמָה, וְשַׂבְּעֵנוּ מִטּוּבָהּ
וּבָרֵךְ שְׁנָתֵנוּ כַּשָּׁנִים הַטּוֹבוֹת.
בָּרוּךְ אַתָּה יהוה, מְבָרֵךְ הַשָּׁנִים.

CONNECTION

The naḥash, *snake, was punished for inciting Adam and Eve to eat from the Tree of Knowledge by having to eat the dust of the earth (*Bereshit 3:14*). Rabbi Menachem Mendel of Kotzk is bothered by this choice of punishment; after all, it resulted in the fact that the snake is never lacking sustenance. While other creatures must struggle to find food, the snake never experiences that problem. This appears to be a great blessing; how is this a punishment?*

He suggested that the very fact that the snake is never lacking is itself the punishment because there is, therefore, no need for the snake to be dependent on Hashem. And when there is no dependence there is also no relationship. The absence of a relationship with God is the ultimate curse that any creature can receive.

LEARNING

The Talmud (*Yoma* 74b) teaches, "The blind eat but are not satisfied." The commentators explain that a blind person cannot be truly satisfied by his food because he cannot see his food. What does it mean to be "blind" when it comes to eating? What does it mean to be unable to "see" one's food? Perhaps this statement is not to be taken literally; it has a spiritual meaning as well. If we cannot see the blessings and the bounty that we are being given, if we cannot recognize it, it will never bring us satisfaction.

INGATHERING OF EXILES

תְּקַע Sound the great shofar for our freedom,
raise high the banner to gather our exiles,
and gather us together from the four quarters of the earth.
Blessed are You, Lord,
who gathers the dispersed of His people Israel.

REFLECTION

לִבִּי בְמִזְרָח וְאָנֹכִי בְּסוֹף מַעֲרָב

*"My heart is in the east,
and I in the uttermost west."*
(Rabbi Yehuda HaLevi)

How did the Jewish People come to be scattered all over the world?

How and when will we be gathered together again?

Has this process already started?

... A THOUSAND WORDS

קבוץ גלויות

תְּקַע בְּשׁוֹפָר גָּדוֹל לְחֵרוּתֵנוּ
וְשָׂא נֵס לְקַבֵּץ גָּלֻיּוֹתֵינוּ
וְקַבְּצֵנוּ יַחַד מֵאַרְבַּע כַּנְפוֹת הָאָרֶץ.
בָּרוּךְ אַתָּה יהוה, מְקַבֵּץ נִדְחֵי עַמּוֹ יִשְׂרָאֵל.

LEARNING

The language of this *berakha* is based on the verse from *Yeshayahu* (27:13):

וְהָיָה בַּיּוֹם הַהוּא,
יִתָּקַע בְּשׁוֹפָר גָּדוֹל,
וּבָאוּ הָאֹבְדִים בְּאֶרֶץ אַשּׁוּר,
וְהַנִּדָּחִים בְּאֶרֶץ מִצְרָיִם;
וְהִשְׁתַּחֲווּ לַיהוה
בְּהַר הַקֹּדֶשׁ, בִּירוּשָׁלָםִ.

"It shall be on that day that a great shofar will be blown and the lost in the land of Assyria and the dispersed in the land of Egypt will come; and they will prostrate themselves before the Lord on the holy mountain, in Jerusalem."

This *berakha* signals the transition from individual requests and hopes to collective and national ones.

CONNECTION

The national flag of the State of Israel was formally adopted on October 28, 1948, five months after the establishment of the State. But its history dates much further back than that. Based on a design that was adopted at the First Zionist Congress in Basel, Switzerland, in 1897, the blue stripes and Star of David design first appeared in 1885 in Rishon LeTziyon, one of the earliest modern Zionist settlements in Eretz Yisrael, *as a banner to lead an agricultural procession in the village. The two blue stripes on the flag were inspired by the stripes on the tallit, often black, but light blue/turquoise was chosen for the color of the flag to represent the color of* tekhelet, *the color of the dyed longer string in the tzitzit that takes its color from the sea snail, the* ḥilazon. *This color has much spiritual significance in Judaism, representing the color of the heavens, Aharon's staff, and some say the* Luḥot HaBrit *on which the Ten Commandments were written. The color was also found on the* Kohen Gadol's *clothes, and considered to be the color of purity and holiness. In time, blue and white became the national colors of the Jewish People, and then in 1948, together with the* Magen David, *these colors became the national flag of the Jewish People.*

Fun Fact: The Guinness Book of Records *records that the largest flag in the world was a giant Israeli flag unfurled at the ancient Jewish desert fortress of Masada in 2007.*

JUSTICE

הָשִׁיבָה Restore our judges as at first,
and our advisors as at the beginning,
and remove from us sorrow and sighing.
May You alone, LORD, reign over us
with loving-kindness and compassion,
and vindicate us in justice.
Blessed are You, LORD,
the King who loves righteousness and justice.

/ *Between Rosh HaShana & Yom Kippur, end the blessing:* the King of justice./

REFLECTION

"Rabban Shimon ben Gamliel used to say:
On three things does the world stand –
on truth, justice, and peace."
(*Avot* 1:18)

What is justice? Who decides what is just?

How do you live your life by the value of justice?

How will you practice justice today?

LEARNING

This *berakha* follows the last thematically – asking for our exiles to be ingathered and the establishment of a Jewish State is not enough. That State must also be based on the Torah values of justice and compassion.

CONNECTION

"The State of Israel will be open for Jewish immigration and for the Ingathering of the Exiles; it will foster the development of the country for the benefit of all its inhabitants; it will be based on freedom, justice and peace as envisaged by the prophets of Israel; it will ensure complete equality of social and political rights to all its inhabitants irrespective of religion, race or sex; it will guarantee freedom of religion, conscience, language, education and culture; it will safeguard the Holy Places of all religions; and it will be faithful to the principles of the Charter of the United Nations."

(The Declaration of the Establishment of the State of Israel, May 14, 1948)

השבת המשפט

הָשִֽׁיבָה שׁוֹפְטֵֽינוּ כְּבָרִאשׁוֹנָה
וְיוֹעֲצֵֽינוּ כְּבַתְּחִלָּה
וְהָסֵר מִמֶּֽנּוּ יָגוֹן וַאֲנָחָה
וּמְלֹךְ עָלֵֽינוּ אַתָּה יהוה לְבַדְּךָ בְּחֶֽסֶד וּבְרַחֲמִים
וְצַדְּקֵֽנוּ בַּמִּשְׁפָּט.
בָּרוּךְ אַתָּה יהוה
מֶֽלֶךְ אוֹהֵב צְדָקָה וּמִשְׁפָּט. / בעשרת ימי תשובה: הַמֶּֽלֶךְ הַמִּשְׁפָּט./

... A THOUSAND WORDS

AGAINST INFORMERS

וְלַמַּלְשִׁינִים For the slanderers let there be no hope,
and may all wickedness perish in an instant.
May all Your people's enemies swiftly be cut down.
May You swiftly uproot, crush, cast down
and humble the arrogant
swiftly in our days.
Blessed are You, LORD,
who destroys enemies and humbles the arrogant.

... A THOUSAND WORDS

ברכת המינים

וְלַמַּלְשִׁינִים אַל תְּהִי תִקְוָה
וְכָל הָרִשְׁעָה כְּרֶגַע תֹּאבֵד
וְכָל אוֹיְבֵי עַמְּךָ מְהֵרָה יִכָּרֵתוּ
וְהַזֵּדִים מְהֵרָה תְעַקֵּר וּתְשַׁבֵּר וּתְמַגֵּר וְתַכְנִיעַ
בִּמְהֵרָה בְיָמֵינוּ.
בָּרוּךְ אַתָּה יהוה, שׁוֹבֵר אוֹיְבִים וּמַכְנִיעַ זֵדִים.

LEARNING

The *Shemoneh Esreh* is known by this name because it originally contained eighteen *berakhot*. But this *berakha* was added as the nineteenth blessing at a later time to address those (Jews) who worked against the Jewish community in Roman times. Since those times it has come to be considered a *tefilla* against all enemies of the Jewish People.

REFLECTION

"Each maḥloket that is in the name of heaven will have enduring value; but one that is not in the name of heaven will not have enduring value."
(*Avot* 5:21)

Why do you think Jews fight?

How do we stop Jews from fighting?

How can you respect someone you disagree with? When and how will you do that today?

CONNECTION

*There were thugs in Rabbi Meir's neighborhood who distressed him greatly. Rabbi Meir prayed to Hashem that they should die. His wife Beruria asked him, "What are you thinking? Is this the verse that inspired you to do this? 'Let sins cease from the land' (*Tehillim *104:35)? But does it say sins or sinners? It says "sins," not "sinners"! You should pray to Hashem that He should help them do* teshuva *and repent!" Rabbi Meir admitted that Beruria was in fact correct, and he changed his prayer that Hashem should have mercy on them and they should repent. And they did!*

(*Berakhot* 10a)

THE RIGHTEOUS

עַל הַצַּדִּיקִים To the righteous, the pious,
the elders of Your people the house of Israel,
the surviving scholars,
the righteous converts, and to us,
may Your compassion be aroused, LORD our God.
Give a good reward to all who sincerely trust in Your name.
Set our lot with them,
so that we may never be ashamed,
for in You we trust.
Blessed are You, LORD,
who is the support and trust of the righteous.

If you can make one heap of all your winnings
And risk it on one turn of pitch-and-toss,
And lose, and start again at your beginnings
And never breathe a word about your loss;
If you can force your heart and nerve and sinew
To serve your turn long after they are gone,
And so hold on when there is nothing in you
Except the Will which says to them: "Hold on!"

If you can talk with crowds and keep your virtue,
Or walk with Kings – nor lose the common touch,
If neither foes nor loving friends can hurt you,
If all men count with you, but none too much;
If you can fill the unforgiving minute
With sixty seconds' worth of distance run,
Yours is the Earth and everything that's in it,
And – which is more – you'll be a Man, my son.

(Rudyard Kipling, 1895)

REFLECTION

"We are all called on to be leaders. But we are also called on to be followers. In Judaism the two concepts are not opposites as they are in many cultures. They are part of the same process.... A leader is one who challenges a follower. A follower is one who challenges a leader."

(Rabbi Jonathan Sacks, *Lessons in Leadership*)

What does it take to be a good leader?

Are you a good leader?
Are you a good follower?

How will you lead today?

על הצדיקים

עַל הַצַּדִּיקִים וְעַל הַחֲסִידִים
וְעַל זִקְנֵי עַמְּךָ בֵּית יִשְׂרָאֵל
וְעַל פְּלֵיטַת סוֹפְרֵיהֶם, וְעַל גֵּרֵי הַצֶּדֶק, וְעָלֵינוּ
יֶהֱמוּ רַחֲמֶיךָ יהוה אֱלֹהֵינוּ
וְתֵן שָׂכָר טוֹב לְכָל הַבּוֹטְחִים בְּשִׁמְךָ בֶּאֱמֶת
וְשִׂים חֶלְקֵנוּ עִמָּהֶם, וּלְעוֹלָם לֹא נֵבוֹשׁ כִּי בְךָ בָּטָחְנוּ.
בָּרוּךְ אַתָּה יהוה, מִשְׁעָן וּמִבְטָח לַצַּדִּיקִים.

LEARNING

Glossary:

צַדִּיקִים – The truly righteous who serve Hashem in every possible way.

חֲסִידִים – The pious, who push themselves to do more than is expected.

זִקְנֵי יִשְׂרָאֵל – The elders of Israel, not necessarily just in age, but in wisdom born of life experience.

סוֹפְרֵיהֶם – The scholars who teach.

גֵּרֵי הַצֶּדֶק – The converts to Judaism who join the Jewish People because they believe in the truth of the Torah.

עָלֵינוּ – We, the everyday ordinary Jews. Everyone has a contribution to make.

CONNECTION

If

If you can keep your head when all about you
Are losing theirs and blaming it on you,
If you can trust yourself when all men doubt you,
But make allowance for their doubting too;
If you can wait and not be tired by waiting,
Or being lied about, don't deal in lies,
Or being hated, don't give way to hating,
And yet don't look too good, nor talk too wise:

If you can dream – and not make dreams your master;
If you can think – and not make thoughts your aim;
If you can meet with Triumph and Disaster
And treat those two impostors just the same;
If you can bear to hear the truth you've spoken
Twisted by knaves to make a trap for fools,
Or watch the things you gave your life to, broken,
And stoop and build 'em up with worn-out tools:

REBUILDING JERUSALEM

וְלִירוּשָׁלַיִם To Jerusalem, Your city, may You return in compassion, and may You rest Your presence in it as You promised.

May You rebuild it rapidly in our days
as an everlasting structure,

and install within it soon the throne of David.

Blessed are You, LORD, who builds Jerusalem.

REFLECTION

לַשָּׁנָה הַבָּאָה בִּירוּשָׁלַיִם הַבְּנוּיָה

Should we still say this ***berakha*** if Jerusalem has been rebuilt?

Have you ever been to Jerusalem? Go there now in your mind.

When will Jerusalem be fully rebuilt? How can we help make that happen?

LEARNING

A very brief Jerusalem timeline:

1000 BCE: King David conquers Jerusalem, makes it Jewish capital.
960 BCE: King Solomon builds First Temple.
586 BCE: First Temple destroyed by Babylonian army.
516 BCE: Second Temple built and Jews return with permission from Cyrus.
332 BCE: Alexander the Great conquers Jerusalem.
70 CE: Second Temple destroyed by Roman army.
135: Jerusalem rebuilt as a Roman city.
638–1099: First Muslim Period.
1099–1187: Crusader Period.
1187–1516: Second Muslim Period.
1516–1917: Ottoman Period.
1860: Mishkenot Sha'ananim built – first Jewish neighborhood outside the walls of the old city.
1917: British capture Jerusalem – the beginning of the British Mandate Period.
1948: The Old City of Jerusalem falls to the Jordanian Legion. West Jerusalem declared the capital of the State of Israel.
1967: Jerusalem reunited as East Jerusalem and the Old City are conquered in the Six-Day War.

בניין ירושלים

וְלִירוּשָׁלַיִם עִירְךָ בְּרַחֲמִים תָּשׁוּב, וְתִשְׁכֹּן בְּתוֹכָהּ כַּאֲשֶׁר דִּבַּרְתָּ
וּבְנֵה אוֹתָהּ בְּקָרוֹב בְּיָמֵינוּ בִּנְיַן עוֹלָם
וְכִסֵּא דָוִד מְהֵרָה לְתוֹכָהּ תָּכִין.
בָּרוּךְ אַתָּה יהוה, בּוֹנֵה יְרוּשָׁלָיִם.

CONNECTION

THE PARATROOPERS CRY

This Kotel *has heard many prayers*
This Kotel *has seen many walls fall*
This Kotel *has felt wailing women's hands and notes pressed between its stones*
This Kotel *has seen Rabbi Yehuda HaLevi trampled in front of it*
This Kotel *has seen Caesars rising and falling*
But this Kotel *has never before seen paratroopers cry.*
This Kotel *has seen them tired and exhausted*
This Kotel *has seen them wounded and scratched-up*
Running toward it with beating hearts, with cries and with silence
Pouncing out like predators from the alleyways of the Old City
And they're dust-covered and dry-lipped
And they're whispering: if I forget you, if I forget you, O Jerusalem
And they are lighter than eagles and more tenacious then lions
And their tanks are the fiery chariot of Elijah the Prophet
And they pass like lightning
And they pass in fury
And they remember the thousands of terrible years in which we didn't even have a Kotel *in front of which we could cry.*
And here they are standing in front of it and breathing deeply
And here they are looking at it with the sweet pain
And the tears fall and they look awkwardly at each other
How is it that paratroopers cry?
How is it that they touch the wall with feeling?
How is it that from crying they move to singing?
Maybe it's because these 19-year-olds were born with the birth of Israel
Carrying on their backs – 2,000 years.

(Haim Hefer)

KINGDOM OF DAVID

אֶת צֶמַח May the offshoot of Your servant David soon flower, and may his pride be raised high by Your salvation, for we wait for Your salvation all day. Blessed are You, Lord, who makes the glory of salvation flourish.

REFLECTION

״אֲנִי מַאֲמִין בֶּאֱמוּנָה שְׁלֵמָה, בְּבִיאַת הַמָּשִׁיחַ,
וְאַף עַל פִּי שֶׁיִּתְמַהְמֵהַּ,
עִם כָּל זֶה אֲחַכֶּה לּוֹ בְּכָל יוֹם שֶׁיָּבוֹא״

"I believe with perfect faith in the coming of the Messiah, and though he may delay, I wait daily for him to come."

What can you do today to bring the Mashiaḥ one step closer?

Can you see any signs in the world that we are closer to the coming of the Mashiaḥ than previous generations?

... A THOUSAND WORDS

מלכות בית דוד

אֶת צֶמַח דָּוִד עַבְדְּךָ מְהֵרָה תַצְמִיחַ
וְקַרְנוֹ תָּרוּם בִּישׁוּעָתֶךָ
כִּי לִישׁוּעָתְךָ קִוִּינוּ כָּל הַיּוֹם.
בָּרוּךְ אַתָּה יהוה, מַצְמִיחַ קֶרֶן יְשׁוּעָה.

CONNECTION

Once upon a time, Hashem called for the Melekh HaMashiaḥ *to tell Him that the time had come for the final redemption. So the Mashiaḥ got dressed in his very best clothes, and entered the first beit knesset he came to, to announce the good news. Everyone there immediately stopped their learning and stared at him in disbelief. One person called out, "That cannot be the Mashiaḥ. Just look at his hat… it has pinches and the brim is down!" So the Mashiaḥ changed his hat, and put the brim up, and traveled to the next* shul *on the way. But there he was also received with surprise. "What a strange thought, Mashiaḥ wearing a hat!" they said. "If you were really the Mashiaḥ you would have a knitted* kippa*!" So the Mashiaḥ took off his hat and placed a knitted* kippa *on his head, for he didn't mind what he wore on his head. At the next shul they said to him, "Whoever heard of a Mashiaḥ without a black hat?" "But I have a black hat," he replied. And as he placed it on his head they all laughed and said, "The Mashiaḥ wearing a hat with pinches and the brim down!" With sadness in his eyes the Mashiaḥ realized that his time had not yet come, and he began his journey back to heaven. As he was leaving, Jews of every type ran after him crying, "Wait! Don't leave. It was their fault!" But the Mashiaḥ just continued slowly and sadly walking, saying, "Don't you see? Hashem loves each and every one of you. But my time will only come when you do too!"*

LEARNING

The word צֶמַח means offshoot or growth, and in this context refers to the descendant of King David who Jewish tradition tells us will be the Mashiaḥ – the redeemer who will herald the Messianic period. This term could be used because this process will be a slow and incremental one just like the flowering and growth of a plant. This may also be the reason why this term was used to describe the Messianic dimension of the establishment of the State of Israel in the prayer for the State of Israel (page 655).

RESPONSE TO PRAYER

שְׁמַע קוֹלֵנוּ Listen to our voice, LORD our God.
Spare us and have compassion on us,
and in compassion and favor accept our prayer,
for You, God, listen to prayers and pleas.
Do not turn us away, O our King,
empty-handed from Your presence,*

*In times of drought in Israel, some add "And answer us" on page 1064.

for You listen with compassion to the prayer of Your people Israel.
Blessed are You, LORD, who listens to prayer.

REFLECTION

"The man who persists in knocking will succeed in entering."
(Ibn Ezra)

Is there something you want to ask God for that you cannot put into words?

How well do you listen to others?

What do you want God to listen to you about?

LEARNING

The *Shulḥan Arukh* (*Oraḥ Ḥayyim* 101:2) teaches us that a person must hear his own voice when he prays, though he must not disturb those around him. So important is the voice of our prayer, that the *Siftei Ḥayyim* says that we ask God to hear our prayer based on the sound of our voice alone even if we lack the proper and complete intention or wording that would render our prayers worthy of His attention.

CONNECTION

"We are often taught that if we just pray hard enough and well enough, God will grant us our wishes, but it is not like that. Our relationship with God is more complicated.

How do we educate our children to pray with all their hearts and souls, but in parallel to also know that the response to all those prayers might be 'No'? This is one of the most difficult challenges of faith – and yet we just have to accept that we have no right to make demands. All we can do is be confident that our prayers are heard. Faith is stronger than us. What is incredible is that we continue to believe, despite everything."

(Rachelle Fraenkel, mother of Naftali Fraenkel HY"D, who was one of the three boys kidnapped from a bus stop on their way home from school in the summer of 2014, and murdered by Hamas)

שומע תפילה

שְׁמַע קוֹלֵנוּ יהוה אֱלֹהֵינוּ
חוּס וְרַחֵם עָלֵינוּ
וְקַבֵּל בְּרַחֲמִים וּבְרָצוֹן אֶת תְּפִלָּתֵנוּ
כִּי אֵל שׁוֹמֵעַ תְּפִלּוֹת וְתַחֲנוּנִים אָתָּה
וּמִלְּפָנֶיךָ מַלְכֵּנוּ רֵיקָם אַל תְּשִׁיבֵנוּ*

*In times of drought in ארץ ישראל, some add וַעֲנֵנוּ on page 1065.

כִּי אַתָּה שׁוֹמֵעַ תְּפִלַּת עַמְּךָ יִשְׂרָאֵל בְּרַחֲמִים.
בָּרוּךְ אַתָּה יהוה, שׁוֹמֵעַ תְּפִלָּה.

...A THOUSAND WORDS

TEMPLE SERVICE

רְצֵה Find favor, LORD our God,
in Your people Israel and their prayer.
Restore the service to Your most holy House,
and accept in love and favor
the fire-offerings of Israel and their prayer.
May the service of Your people Israel always find favor with You.

On Rosh Ḥodesh and Ḥol HaMo'ed, say:

אֱלֹהֵינוּ Our God and God of our ancestors, may there rise, come, reach, appear, be favored, heard, regarded and remembered before You, our recollection and remembrance, as well as the remembrance of our ancestors, and of the Messiah son of David Your servant, and of Jerusalem Your holy city, and of all Your people the house of Israel – for deliverance and well-being, grace, loving-kindness and compassion, life and peace, on this day of:

On Rosh Ḥodesh: Rosh Ḥodesh.
On Pesaḥ: the Festival of Matzot.
On Sukkot: the Festival of Sukkot.

On it remember us, LORD our God, for good; recollect us for blessing, and save us for life. In accord with Your promise of salvation and compassion, spare us and be generous to us; have compassion on us and save us, for our eyes are turned to You because You, God, are a generous and compassionate King.

וְתֶחֱזֶינָה And may our eyes witness
Your return to Zion in compassion.
Blessed are You, LORD, who restores His Presence to Zion.

LEARNING

In the Gemara (*Berakhot* 26b) there is a disagreement as to the source for our *tefillot* in their current form. Rabbi Yossi ben Ḥanina says that our *tefillot* were instituted by our forefathers, whereas Rabbi Yehoshua ben Levi says our *tefillot* correspond to the daily sacrifices in the Temple. The conclusion of the Gemara is that both are true, and the theme of the *korbanot* runs all the way through our *tefillot*. This *berakha* is a further example of this.

עבודה

רְצֵה יהוה אֱלֹהֵינוּ בְּעַמְּךָ יִשְׂרָאֵל וּבִתְפִלָּתָם
וְהָשֵׁב אֶת הָעֲבוֹדָה לִדְבִיר בֵּיתֶךָ
וְאִשֵּׁי יִשְׂרָאֵל וּתְפִלָּתָם בְּאַהֲבָה תְקַבֵּל בְּרָצוֹן
וּתְהִי לְרָצוֹן תָּמִיד עֲבוֹדַת יִשְׂרָאֵל עַמֶּךָ.

On ראש חודש *and* חול המועד*, say:*

אֱלֹהֵינוּ וֵאלֹהֵי אֲבוֹתֵינוּ, יַעֲלֶה וְיָבוֹא וְיַגִּיעַ, וְיֵרָאֶה וְיֵרָצֶה וְיִשָּׁמַע, וְיִפָּקֵד וְיִזָּכֵר זִכְרוֹנֵנוּ וּפִקְדוֹנֵנוּ וְזִכְרוֹן אֲבוֹתֵינוּ, וְזִכְרוֹן מָשִׁיחַ בֶּן דָּוִד עַבְדֶּךָ, וְזִכְרוֹן יְרוּשָׁלַיִם עִיר קָדְשֶׁךָ, וְזִכְרוֹן כָּל עַמְּךָ בֵּית יִשְׂרָאֵל, לְפָנֶיךָ, לִפְלֵיטָה לְטוֹבָה, לְחֵן וּלְחֶסֶד וּלְרַחֲמִים, לְחַיִּים וּלְשָׁלוֹם בְּיוֹם

בראש חודש: רֹאשׁ הַחֹדֶשׁ / בפסח: חַג הַמַּצּוֹת / בסוכות: חַג הַסֻּכּוֹת

הַזֶּה. זָכְרֵנוּ יהוה אֱלֹהֵינוּ בּוֹ לְטוֹבָה, וּפָקְדֵנוּ בוֹ לִבְרָכָה, וְהוֹשִׁיעֵנוּ בוֹ לְחַיִּים. וּבִדְבַר יְשׁוּעָה וְרַחֲמִים, חוּס וְחָנֵּנוּ וְרַחֵם עָלֵינוּ וְהוֹשִׁיעֵנוּ, כִּי אֵלֶיךָ עֵינֵינוּ, כִּי אֵל מֶלֶךְ חַנּוּן וְרַחוּם אָתָּה.

וְתֶחֱזֶינָה עֵינֵינוּ בְּשׁוּבְךָ לְצִיּוֹן בְּרַחֲמִים.
בָּרוּךְ אַתָּה יהוה, הַמַּחֲזִיר שְׁכִינָתוֹ לְצִיּוֹן.

REFLECTION

What can you do in your life instead of bringing sacrifices?

Have you ever been in Israel for *Ḥag*? Was it special? How?

... A THOUSAND WORDS

THANKSGIVING

מוֹדִים We give thanks to You,
for You are the LORD our God
and God of our ancestors
for ever and all time.
You are the Rock of our lives,
Shield of our salvation
from generation to generation.
We will thank You and
declare Your praise for our lives,
which are entrusted into Your hand;
for our souls,
which are placed in Your charge;
for Your miracles
which are with us every day;
and for Your wonders and favors
at all times, evening,
morning and midday.
You are good –
for Your compassion never fails.
You are compassionate –
for Your loving-kindnesses never cease.
We have always placed our hope in You.

During the Leader's Repetition, the congregation says quietly:

מוֹדִים We give thanks
to You, for You are
the LORD our God
and God of our ancestors,
God of all flesh,
who formed us
and formed the universe.
Blessings and thanks are due
to Your great and holy name
for giving us life
and sustaining us.
May You continue
to give us life and sustain us;
and may You gather
our exiles to Your holy courts,
to keep Your decrees,
do Your will and serve You
with a perfect heart,
for it is for us
to give You thanks.
Blessed be God to whom
thanksgiving is due.

REFLECTION

"God gave you a gift of 86,400 seconds today. Have you used one to say thank you?"
(William Arthur Ward)

What do you want to thank God for in your life?
What little miracles in your life can you recognize?
What can you thank God for today that you did not thank Him for yesterday?

...A THOUSAND WORDS

הודאה

During חזרת הש״ץ, *the* קהל *says quietly:*

מוֹדִים אֲנַחְנוּ לָךְ
שָׁאַתָּה הוּא יהוה אֱלֹהֵינוּ
וֵאלֹהֵי אֲבוֹתֵינוּ
אֱלֹהֵי כָל בָּשָׂר
יוֹצְרֵנוּ, יוֹצֵר בְּרֵאשִׁית.
בְּרָכוֹת וְהוֹדָאוֹת
לְשִׁמְךָ הַגָּדוֹל וְהַקָּדוֹשׁ
עַל שֶׁהֶחֱיִיתָנוּ וְקִיַּמְתָּנוּ.
כֵּן תְּחַיֵּנוּ וּתְקַיְּמֵנוּ
וְתֶאֱסֹף גָּלֻיּוֹתֵינוּ
לְחַצְרוֹת קָדְשֶׁךָ, לִשְׁמֹר חֻקֶּיךָ
וְלַעֲשׂוֹת רְצוֹנֶךָ וּלְעָבְדְּךָ
בְּלֵבָב שָׁלֵם
עַל שֶׁאֲנַחְנוּ מוֹדִים לָךְ.
בָּרוּךְ אֵל הַהוֹדָאוֹת.

מוֹדִים אֲנַחְנוּ לָךְ
שָׁאַתָּה הוּא יהוה אֱלֹהֵינוּ
וֵאלֹהֵי אֲבוֹתֵינוּ לְעוֹלָם וָעֶד.
צוּר חַיֵּינוּ, מָגֵן יִשְׁעֵנוּ
אַתָּה הוּא לְדוֹר וָדוֹר.
נוֹדֶה לְּךָ וּנְסַפֵּר תְּהִלָּתֶךָ
עַל חַיֵּינוּ הַמְּסוּרִים בְּיָדֶךָ
וְעַל נִשְׁמוֹתֵינוּ הַפְּקוּדוֹת לָךְ
וְעַל נִסֶּיךָ שֶׁבְּכָל יוֹם עִמָּנוּ
וְעַל נִפְלְאוֹתֶיךָ וְטוֹבוֹתֶיךָ
שֶׁבְּכָל עֵת, עֶרֶב וָבֹקֶר וְצָהֳרָיִם.
הַטּוֹב, כִּי לֹא כָלוּ רַחֲמֶיךָ
וְהַמְרַחֵם, כִּי לֹא תַמּוּ חֲסָדֶיךָ
מֵעוֹלָם קִוִּינוּ לָךְ.

LEARNING

The Gemara (*Berakhot* 7b) says: "From the day that God created the world there was no person who offered thanks to Him until Leah came and thanked Him." Leah our matriarch thanked God by naming her fourth child Yehuda. She saw through prophecy that her husband Yaakov would have twelve sons through his four wives. Upon giving birth to her fourth child, Leah realized that she would have more than the other wives and immediately thanked God for her extra bounty. Leah teaches that real gratitude comes from seeing something as a gift, undeserved and a blessing. When Leah thanked God for her fourth child, her gratitude was so genuine because she never expected to receive him. The name Yehuda is the source of our national name. As Jews, *Yehudim*, gratitude and thanksgiving are an integral part of our national DNA.

On Ḥanukka:

עַל הַנִּסִּים [We thank You also] for the miracles, the redemption, the mighty deeds, the salvations, and the victories in battle which You performed for our ancestors in those days, at this time.

בִּימֵי מַתִּתְיָהוּ In the days of Mattityahu, son of Yoḥanan, the High Priest, the Hasmonean, and his sons, the wicked Greek kingdom rose up against Your people Israel to make them forget Your Torah and to force them to transgress the laws of Your will. It was then that You in Your great compassion stood by them in the time of their distress. You championed their cause, judged their claim, and avenged their wrong. You delivered the strong into the hands of the weak, the many into the hands of the few, the impure into the hands of the pure, the wicked into the hands of the righteous, and the arrogant into the hands of those who were engaged in the study of Your Torah. You made for Yourself a great and holy reputation in Your world, and for Your people Israel You performed a great salvation and redemption as of this very day. Your children then entered the holiest part of Your House, cleansed Your Temple, purified Your Sanctuary, kindled lights in Your holy courts, and designated these eight days of Ḥanukka for giving thanks and praise to Your great name.

Continue with "For all these things" on page 194.

LEARNING

Each of the *Al HaNisim* prayers thanks God for the salvation of the Jewish People. The threats of each story were very different. In the times of Mattityahu the threat was spiritual, the enemy wanted to force us to abandon our Torah. In the times of Mordekhai and Ester, there was a genocidal threat, to kill every man, woman, and child. Enemies sometimes want to destroy who we are, sometimes they want to destroy what we do. God intervened in both stories saving the Jewish People both from physical and spiritual annihilation.

CONNECTION

"The Egyptian, the Babylonian, and the Persian rose, filled the planet with sound and splendor, then faded to dream-stuff and passed away; the Greek and the Roman followed, and made a vast noise, and they are gone; other peoples have sprung up and held their torch high for a time, but it burned out, and they sit in twilight now, or have vanished. The Jew saw them all, beat them all, and is now what he always was.... All things are mortal but the Jew; all other forces pass, but he remains. What is the secret of his immortality?"

(Mark Twain)

בחנוכה:

עַל הַנִּסִּים וְעַל הַפֻּרְקָן וְעַל הַגְּבוּרוֹת וְעַל הַתְּשׁוּעוֹת וְעַל הַמִּלְחָמוֹת שֶׁעָשִׂיתָ לַאֲבוֹתֵינוּ בַּיָּמִים הָהֵם בַּזְּמַן הַזֶּה.

בִּימֵי מַתִּתְיָהוּ בֶּן יוֹחָנָן כֹּהֵן גָּדוֹל חַשְׁמוֹנַאי וּבָנָיו, כְּשֶׁעָמְדָה מַלְכוּת יָוָן הָרְשָׁעָה עַל עַמְּךָ יִשְׂרָאֵל לְהַשְׁכִּיחָם תּוֹרָתֶךָ וּלְהַעֲבִירָם מֵחֻקֵּי רְצוֹנֶךָ, וְאַתָּה בְּרַחֲמֶיךָ הָרַבִּים עָמַדְתָּ לָהֶם בְּעֵת צָרָתָם, רַבְתָּ אֶת רִיבָם, דַּנְתָּ אֶת דִּינָם, נָקַמְתָּ אֶת נִקְמָתָם, מָסַרְתָּ גִבּוֹרִים בְּיַד חַלָּשִׁים, וְרַבִּים בְּיַד מְעַטִּים, וּטְמֵאִים בְּיַד טְהוֹרִים, וּרְשָׁעִים בְּיַד צַדִּיקִים, וְזֵדִים בְּיַד עוֹסְקֵי תוֹרָתֶךָ, וּלְךָ עָשִׂיתָ שֵׁם גָּדוֹל וְקָדוֹשׁ בְּעוֹלָמֶךָ, וּלְעַמְּךָ יִשְׂרָאֵל עָשִׂיתָ תְּשׁוּעָה גְדוֹלָה וּפֻרְקָן כְּהַיּוֹם הַזֶּה. וְאַחַר כֵּן בָּאוּ בָנֶיךָ לִדְבִיר בֵּיתֶךָ, וּפִנּוּ אֶת הֵיכָלֶךָ, וְטִהֲרוּ אֶת מִקְדָּשֶׁךָ, וְהִדְלִיקוּ נֵרוֹת בְּחַצְרוֹת קָדְשֶׁךָ, וְקָבְעוּ שְׁמוֹנַת יְמֵי חֲנֻכָּה אֵלּוּ, לְהוֹדוֹת וּלְהַלֵּל לְשִׁמְךָ הַגָּדוֹל.

Continue with וְעַל כֻּלָּם *on page 195*.

... A THOUSAND WORDS

REFLECTION

"There are only two ways to live your life. One is as though nothing is a miracle. The other is as though everything is a miracle."
(Albert Einstein)

Think about the miracle of Jewish survival through the millennia. How are you helping to maintain its survival?

How can holiness triumph over impurity?

How are you bringing light into the world?

On Purim:

עַל הַנִּסִּים [We thank You also] for the miracles, the redemption, the mighty deeds, the salvations, and the victories in battle which You performed for our ancestors in those days, at this time.

בִּימֵי מָרְדְּכַי In the days of Mordekhai and Esther, in Shushan the capital, the wicked Haman rose up against them and sought to destroy, slay *Esther 3* and exterminate all the Jews, young and old, children and women, on one day, the thirteenth day of the twelfth month, which is the month of Adar, and to plunder their possessions. Then You in Your great compassion defeated his counsel, frustrated his plans, and caused his scheme to recoil on his own head, so that they hanged him and his sons on the gallows.

Continue with "For all these things" on the next page.

REFLECTION

How do you find God hidden in your life?

Have you experienced a miracle?

How do you protest against genocides of other peoples?

CONNECTION

The book of Esther *is the only book in the whole of Tanakh which does not mention God's name. If one chooses to do so, he could read the book as series of unconnected events culminating in an extraordinary turn of events. The Jewish survival could be looked at as a fortuitous coincidence if one chooses to ignore the hidden hand of God. The omission of God's name is not a sign that God was uninvolved in the events of Purim; rather He orchestrated everything from behind the scenes. The book of* Esther *means the book of concealment. The hidden nature of God's role in this story is a challenge to us, to look beneath the surface and to search for God even when we cannot see Him clearly. The miracles of the Purim story teach us to look for God in our natural lives. Every baby born, every sick person recovering, every terror attack survivor, the very existence of the Jewish People are all modern-day Purim miracles, miracles that require us to look closer and not just see.*

בפורים:

עַל הַנִּסִּים וְעַל הַפֻּרְקָן וְעַל הַגְּבוּרוֹת וְעַל הַתְּשׁוּעוֹת וְעַל הַמִּלְחָמוֹת שֶׁעָשִׂיתָ לַאֲבוֹתֵינוּ בַּיָּמִים הָהֵם בִּזְּמַן הַזֶּה.

בִּימֵי מָרְדְּכַי וְאֶסְתֵּר בְּשׁוּשַׁן הַבִּירָה, כְּשֶׁעָמַד עֲלֵיהֶם הָמָן הָרָשָׁע,
בִּקֵּשׁ לְהַשְׁמִיד לַהֲרֹג וּלְאַבֵּד אֶת־כָּל־הַיְּהוּדִים מִנַּעַר וְעַד־זָקֵן טַף אסתר ג
וְנָשִׁים בְּיוֹם אֶחָד, בִּשְׁלוֹשָׁה עָשָׂר לְחֹדֶשׁ שְׁנֵים־עָשָׂר, הוּא־חֹדֶשׁ אֲדָר, וּשְׁלָלָם לָבוֹז: וְאַתָּה בְּרַחֲמֶיךָ הָרַבִּים הֵפַרְתָּ אֶת עֲצָתוֹ, וְקִלְקַלְתָּ אֶת מַחֲשַׁבְתּוֹ, וַהֲשֵׁבוֹתָ לּוֹ גְּמוּלוֹ בְּרֹאשׁוֹ, וְתָלוּ אוֹתוֹ וְאֶת בָּנָיו עַל הָעֵץ.

Continue with וְעַל כֻּלָּם *on the next page.*

... A THOUSAND WORDS

וְעַל כֻּלָּם For all these things may Your name be blessed and elevated, our King, continually, for ever and all time.

Between Rosh HaShana & Yom Kippur: And write, for a good life, all the children of Your covenant.

Let all that lives thank You, Selah! and praise Your name in truth, God, our Savior and Help, Selah!
Blessed are You, LORD,
whose name is "the Good" and to whom thanks are due.

The following is said by the Leader during the Repetition of the Amida, except in a house of mourning and on Tisha B'Av. In Israel, if Kohanim bless the congregation, *turn to page 1064.*

Our God and God of our fathers, bless us with the threefold blessing in the Torah, written by the hand of Moses Your servant and pronounced by Aaron and his sons the priests, Your holy people, as it is said:

May the LORD bless you and protect you. *Num. 6*
Cong: May it be Your will.
May the LORD make His face shine on you and be generous to you.
Cong: May it be Your will.
May the LORD turn His face toward you, and give you peace.
Cong: May it be Your will.

REFLECTION

"Gratitude is not only the greatest of virtues, but the parent of all others."
(Cicero)

Why thank?

Why bow? How does it feel to bow?

Who are you going to thank today and for what?

LEARNING

It is a positive mitzva from the Torah for the Kohen to bless the congregation with the famous words given by Hashem to Aharon in *Bemidbar* 6:24–26 every day when there is a *minyan* of ten men present during Shaḥarit, and also during Musaf on those days when it is said. However, it has become the custom outside of Israel in Ashkenazi communities for the *Ḥazan* to say אֱלֹהֵינוּ וֵאלֹהֵי אֲבוֹתֵינוּ instead.

וְעַל כֻּלָּם יִתְבָּרַךְ וְיִתְרוֹמַם שִׁמְךָ מַלְכֵּנוּ תָּמִיד לְעוֹלָם וָעֶד.

בעשרת ימי תשובה: **וּכְתֹב לְחַיִּים טוֹבִים כָּל בְּנֵי בְרִיתֶךָ.**

וְכֹל הַחַיִּים יוֹדוּךָ סֶּלָה, וִיהַלְלוּ אֶת שִׁמְךָ בֶּאֱמֶת הָאֵל יְשׁוּעָתֵנוּ וְעֶזְרָתֵנוּ סֶלָה.

בָּרוּךְ אַתָּה יהוה, הַטּוֹב שִׁמְךָ וּלְךָ נָאֶה לְהוֹדוֹת.

The following is said by the שליח ציבור *during* חזרת הש״ץ, *except in a house of mourning and on* תשעה באב. *In* ארץ ישראל *if* כוהנים *say* ברכת כוהנים *turn to page 1065.*

אֱלֹהֵינוּ וֵאלֹהֵי אֲבוֹתֵינוּ, בָּרְכֵנוּ בַבְּרָכָה הַמְשֻׁלֶּשֶׁת בַּתּוֹרָה, הַכְּתוּבָה עַל יְדֵי מֹשֶׁה עַבְדֶּךָ, הָאֲמוּרָה מִפִּי אַהֲרֹן וּבָנָיו כֹּהֲנִים עַם קְדוֹשֶׁיךָ, כָּאָמוּר

במדבר ו

יְבָרֶכְךָ יהוה וְיִשְׁמְרֶךָ: קהל: כֵּן יְהִי רָצוֹן

יָאֵר יהוה פָּנָיו אֵלֶיךָ וִיחֻנֶּךָּ: קהל: כֵּן יְהִי רָצוֹן

יִשָּׂא יהוה פָּנָיו אֵלֶיךָ וְיָשֵׂם לְךָ שָׁלוֹם: קהל: כֵּן יְהִי רָצוֹן

CONNECTION

We had recently arrived in Atlanta, our new home for two years. This was our first journey on the Georgia State Route 400, when we saw the signs warning that the toll plaza was approaching. So I prepared 50 cents to pay to the toll collector, only to be shocked to find out that the car in front of us had already paid our toll for us. Rather than accept the 50 cents change for their dollar bill they asked the toll collector to use it for our toll. Dumbfounded, I looked up at the toll collector and couldn't even think of what to ask so she could help me understand what had just happened. "She paid it forward. Georgians have been doing that for twenty years on this road. That's just the way we roll down here in the south!" she said with a smile. And so, in a small anonymous act of kindness two sets of strangers became connected. "But I want to thank them," I said to the toll lady. "Well you can't... but you can pay it forward too. That's the best way to thank them!" And she was so right of course. So I did, and smiled to myself as I looked in the rear view mirror at the strangers in the car behind us as I drove away.

PEACE

שִׂים שָׁלוֹם Give peace, goodness and blessing,
grace, loving-kindness and compassion
to us and all Israel Your people.
Bless us, our Father, all as one,
with the light of Your face,
for by the light of Your face
You have given us, LORD our God,
the Torah of life and love of kindness,
righteousness, blessing, compassion, life and peace.
May it be good in Your eyes to bless Your people Israel
at every time, in every hour, with Your peace.

Between Rosh HaShana & Yom Kippur: In the book of life, blessing, peace and prosperity,
may we and all Your people the house of Israel
be remembered and written before You
for a good life, and for peace.*

Blessed are You, LORD, who blesses His people Israel with peace.

**Between Rosh HaShana and Yom Kippur outside Israel, many end the blessing:*
Blessed are You, LORD, who makes peace.

The following verse concludes the Leader's Repetition of the Amida. Some also say it here as part of the silent Amida.

May the words of my mouth and the inner thoughts of my heart *Ps. 19*
find favor before You, LORD, my Rock and Redeemer.

REFLECTION

"Her ways are ways of pleasantness, and all her paths are peace." (*Mishlei* 3:17)

Is peace the most important value?

How can we achieve peace?

How will you bring some peace to your world today?

... A THOUSAND WORDS

שלום

שִׂים שָׁלוֹם טוֹבָה וּבְרָכָה

חֵן וָחֶסֶד וְרַחֲמִים עָלֵינוּ וְעַל כָּל יִשְׂרָאֵל עַמֶּךָ.
בָּרְכֵנוּ אָבִינוּ כֻּלָּנוּ כְּאֶחָד בְּאוֹר פָּנֶיךָ
כִּי בְאוֹר פָּנֶיךָ נָתַתָּ לָּנוּ יהוה אֱלֹהֵינוּ
תּוֹרַת חַיִּים וְאַהֲבַת חֶסֶד
וּצְדָקָה וּבְרָכָה וְרַחֲמִים וְחַיִּים וְשָׁלוֹם.
וְטוֹב בְּעֵינֶיךָ לְבָרֵךְ אֶת עַמְּךָ יִשְׂרָאֵל
בְּכָל עֵת וּבְכָל שָׁעָה בִּשְׁלוֹמֶךָ.

בעשרת ימי תשובה: בְּסֵפֶר חַיִּים, בְּרָכָה וְשָׁלוֹם, וּפַרְנָסָה טוֹבָה
נִזָּכֵר וְנִכָּתֵב לְפָנֶיךָ, אֲנַחְנוּ וְכָל עַמְּךָ בֵּית יִשְׂרָאֵל
לְחַיִּים טוֹבִים וּלְשָׁלוֹם.*

בָּרוּךְ אַתָּה יהוה, הַמְבָרֵךְ אֶת עַמּוֹ יִשְׂרָאֵל בַּשָּׁלוֹם.

During the עשרת ימי תשובה in חוץ לארץ, many end the blessing:

בָּרוּךְ אַתָּה יהוה, עוֹשֵׂה הַשָּׁלוֹם.

The following verse concludes the חזרת הש״ץ.
Some also say it here as part of the silent עמידה.

יִהְיוּ לְרָצוֹן אִמְרֵי־פִי וְהֶגְיוֹן לִבִּי לְפָנֶיךָ, יהוה צוּרִי וְגוֹאֲלִי: תהלים יט

CONNECTION

When Hashem was about to create man, the angels in heaven arranged themselves into two groups, one shouting, "Don't do it!" and the other shouting, "Do it!" Some used kindness as their argument, and said, "Let man be created because he will do acts of kindness." Others used truth and said, "Don't create man because he will bring lies into the world." Others used righteousness and argued, "Let him be created because he will do righteous acts." And others used peace and said, "Don't create him because he will only fight!" When Hashem heard the angels arguing these points He took truth and threw it to the ground, showing them that loving-kindness, righteousness, and peace were more important.

(Bereshit Raba 8:5)

אֱלֹהַי My God, Berakhot 17a
guard my tongue from evil and my lips from dishonest speech.
To those who curse me, let my soul be silent;
may my soul be to all like the dust.
Open my heart to Your Torah
and let my soul pursue Your commandments.
As for all who plan evil against me,
swiftly defeat their counsel and frustrate their plans.
Act for the sake of Your name; act for the sake of Your right hand;
act for the sake of Your holiness; act for the sake of Your Torah.
That Your beloved ones may be rescued, Ps. 60
save with Your right hand and answer me.
May the words of my mouth and the inner thoughts of my heart Ps. 19
find favor before You, LORD, my Rock and Redeemer.

Bow, take three steps back, then bow, first left, then right, then center, while saying:

May He who makes peace in His high places,
make peace for us and all Israel – and say: Amen.

יְהִי רָצוֹן May it be Your will, LORD our God and God of our ancestors, that the Temple be rebuilt speedily in our days, and give us a share in Your Torah. And there we will serve You with fear, as in the days of old and as in former years. Then Mal. 3
the offering of Judah and Jerusalem will be pleasing to the LORD as in the days of old and as in former years.

When praying with a minyan, the Amida is repeated aloud by the Leader.

On days when Tahanun is said (see page 206), start Taḥanun on page 214. On Mondays and Thursdays start Taḥanun on page 206.

On fast days (except Tisha B'Av) most congregations say Seliḥot on page 968 before Avinu Malkenu on the next page.

Between Rosh HaShana and Yom Kippur (but not on Erev Yom Kippur, unless it falls on Friday), say Avinu Malkenu on the next page.

On Rosh Ḥodesh, Ḥanukka, Ḥol HaMo'ed, Yom HaAtzma'ut and Yom Yerushalayim, say Hallel on page 822.

On other days when Taḥanun is not said (see page 206), the Leader says Half Kaddish on page 218.

LEARNING

The verse beginning יִהְיוּ לְרָצוֹן signifies the end of the *Amida*. Once you have reached this point, you may answer responsive prayers such as Kaddish and *Kedusha*.

ברכות יז.

אֱלֹהַי
נְצֹר לְשׁוֹנִי מֵרָע וּשְׂפָתַי מִדַּבֵּר מִרְמָה
וְלִמְקַלְלַי נַפְשִׁי תִדֹּם, וְנַפְשִׁי כֶּעָפָר לַכֹּל תִּהְיֶה.
פְּתַח לִבִּי בְּתוֹרָתֶךָ, וּבְמִצְוֹתֶיךָ תִּרְדֹּף נַפְשִׁי.
וְכָל הַחוֹשְׁבִים עָלַי רָעָה, מְהֵרָה הָפֵר עֲצָתָם וְקַלְקֵל מַחֲשַׁבְתָּם.
עֲשֵׂה לְמַעַן שְׁמֶךָ, עֲשֵׂה לְמַעַן יְמִינֶךָ
עֲשֵׂה לְמַעַן קְדֻשָּׁתֶךָ, עֲשֵׂה לְמַעַן תּוֹרָתֶךָ.
תהלים ס לְמַעַן יֵחָלְצוּן יְדִידֶיךָ, הוֹשִׁיעָה יְמִינְךָ וַעֲנֵנִי:
תהלים יט יִהְיוּ לְרָצוֹן אִמְרֵי־פִי וְהֶגְיוֹן לִבִּי לְפָנֶיךָ, יהוה צוּרִי וְגֹאֲלִי:

Bow, take three steps back, then bow, first left, then right, then center, while saying:

עֹשֶׂה שָׁלוֹם/ בעשרת ימי תשובה: הַשָּׁלוֹם/ בִּמְרוֹמָיו
הוּא יַעֲשֶׂה שָׁלוֹם עָלֵינוּ וְעַל כָּל יִשְׂרָאֵל, וְאִמְרוּ אָמֵן.

יְהִי רָצוֹן מִלְּפָנֶיךָ יהוה אֱלֹהֵינוּ וֵאלֹהֵי אֲבוֹתֵינוּ, שֶׁיִּבָּנֶה בֵּית הַמִּקְדָּשׁ בִּמְהֵרָה בְיָמֵינוּ, וְתֵן חֶלְקֵנוּ בְּתוֹרָתֶךָ, וְשָׁם נַעֲבָדְךָ בְּיִרְאָה כִּימֵי עוֹלָם וּכְשָׁנִים קַדְמֹנִיּוֹת.
מלאכי ג וְעָרְבָה לַיהוה מִנְחַת יְהוּדָה וִירוּשָׁלָםִ כִּימֵי עוֹלָם וּכְשָׁנִים קַדְמֹנִיּוֹת:

When praying with a מנין*, the* עמידה *is repeated aloud by the* שליח ציבור.

On days when תחנון *is said (see page 207), start* תחנון *on page 215.*
On Mondays and Thursdays start תחנון *on page 207.*

On fast days (except תשעה באב*) most congregations say* סליחות
on page 969 before אבינו מלכנו *on the next page.*

During the עשרת ימי תשובה *(but not on* ערב יום כיפור*,*
unless it falls on Friday), say אבינו מלכנו *on the next page.*

On ראש חודש, חנוכה, חול המועד, יום העצמאות *and* יום ירושלים, *say* הלל *on page 823.*

On other days when תחנון *is not said (see page 207), the* שליח ציבור *says* חצי קדיש *on page 219.*

REFLECTION

What might the connection be between peace and ***lashon hara***?

What good will you accomplish with your words today?

What damage might you do with your words today? How can you avoid that?

How will you build with your words today and not destroy?

How can you achieve peace today with your words?

AVINU MALKENU

On fast days (except Tisha B'Av) most congregations say Seliḥot on page 968 before Avinu Malkenu.

Between Rosh HaShana and Yom Kippur (but not on Erev Yom Kippur, unless it falls on Friday), say Avinu Malkenu below.

The Ark is opened.

אָבִינוּ מַלְכֵּנוּ Our Father, our King, we have sinned before You.

Our Father, our King, we have no king but You.

Our Father, our King, deal kindly with us for the sake of Your name.

Our Father our King, /*bless us with / a good year.

/ **Between Rosh HaShana & Yom Kippur:* renew for us/

Our Father, our King, nullify all harsh decrees against us.

Our Father, our King, nullify the plans of those who hate us.

Our Father, our King, defeat the counsel of our enemies.

Our Father, our King, rid us of every oppressor and enemy.

Our Father, our King, close the mouths of our enemies and accusers.

Our Father, our King, eradicate disease, sword, famine, captivity and destruction, wrongdoing and eradication from the people of Your covenant.

Our Father, our King, withhold the plague from Your heritage.

Our Father, our King, forgive and pardon all our wrongdoing.

Our Father, our King, wipe away and remove our crimes and sins from Your sight.

Our Father, our King, erase in Your great mercy all records of our sins.

The Gemara in *Ta'anit* 25b relates that there was a terrible drought in the Land of Israel. Rabbi Eliezer stepped before the ark to lead the congregation in prayer and recited the *Amida* and six extra *berakhot* for times of drought and his prayer was not answered. Rabbi Akiva stepped before the ark after him and exclaimed:

Our Father, our King! We have no king but You!

Our Father, our King! For Your sake, have compassion for us!

Finally rain fell.

אבינו מלכנו

On fast days (except תשעה באב*) most congregations say* סליחות *on page 969 before* אבינו מלכנו.

During the עשרת ימי תשובה *(but not on* ערב יום כיפור*, unless it falls on Friday), say* אבינו מלכנו *below.*

The ארון קודש *is opened.*

אָבִינוּ מַלְכֵּנוּ, חָטָאנוּ לְפָנֶיךָ.
אָבִינוּ מַלְכֵּנוּ, אֵין לָנוּ מֶלֶךְ אֶלָּא אָתָּה.
אָבִינוּ מַלְכֵּנוּ, עֲשֵׂה עִמָּנוּ לְמַעַן שְׁמֶךָ.
אָבִינוּ מַלְכֵּנוּ, בָּרֵךְ/ בעשרת ימי תשובה: חַדֵּשׁ/ עָלֵינוּ שָׁנָה טוֹבָה.
אָבִינוּ מַלְכֵּנוּ, בַּטֵּל מֵעָלֵינוּ כָּל גְּזֵרוֹת קָשׁוֹת.
אָבִינוּ מַלְכֵּנוּ, בַּטֵּל מַחְשְׁבוֹת שׂוֹנְאֵינוּ.
אָבִינוּ מַלְכֵּנוּ, הָפֵר עֲצַת אוֹיְבֵינוּ.
אָבִינוּ מַלְכֵּנוּ, כַּלֵּה כָּל צַר וּמַשְׂטִין מֵעָלֵינוּ.
אָבִינוּ מַלְכֵּנוּ, סְתֹם פִּיּוֹת מַשְׂטִינֵנוּ וּמְקַטְרְגֵנוּ.
אָבִינוּ מַלְכֵּנוּ, כַּלֵּה דֶּבֶר וְחֶרֶב וְרָעָב וּשְׁבִי וּמַשְׁחִית וְעָוֹן וּשְׁמַד מִבְּנֵי בְרִיתֶךָ.
אָבִינוּ מַלְכֵּנוּ, מְנַע מַגֵּפָה מִנַּחֲלָתֶךָ.
אָבִינוּ מַלְכֵּנוּ, סְלַח וּמְחַל לְכָל עֲוֹנוֹתֵינוּ.
אָבִינוּ מַלְכֵּנוּ, מְחֵה וְהַעֲבֵר פְּשָׁעֵינוּ וְחַטֹּאתֵינוּ מִנֶּגֶד עֵינֶיךָ.
אָבִינוּ מַלְכֵּנוּ, מְחֹק בְּרַחֲמֶיךָ הָרַבִּים כָּל שִׁטְרֵי חוֹבוֹתֵינוּ.

LEARNING

This special prayer is recited on Rosh HaShana, the *Aseret Yemei Teshuva*, and Yom Kippur, as well as fast days. This *tefilla* uses language of intense pleading and supplication, uniquely suitable for these days.

The following nine sentences are said responsively, first by the Leader, then by the congregation:

Our Father, our King, bring us back to You in perfect repentance.

Our Father, our King, send a complete healing to the sick of Your people.

Our Father, our King, tear up the evil decree against us.

Our Father, our King, remember us with a memory of favorable deeds before You.

Between Rosh HaShana and Yom Kippur:

Our Father, our King, write us in the book of good life.

Our Father, our King, write us in the book of redemption and salvation.

Our Father, our King, write us in the book of livelihood and sustenance.

Our Father, our King, write us in the book of merit.

Our Father, our King, write us in the book of pardon and forgiveness.

On Fast Days:

Our Father, our King, remember us for a good life.

Our Father, our King, remember us for redemption and salvation.

Our Father, our King, remember us for livelihood and sustenance.

Our Father, our King, remember us for merit.

Our Father, our King, remember us for pardon and forgiveness.

End of responsive reading.

REFLECTION

What would you like to ask your parent for?

What would you like to ask your king for?

What would you like to ask Hashem for?

What is the most important thing you are asking for?

What does a "good life" look like?

The following nine sentences are said responsively, first by the שליח ציבור*, then by the* קהל*:*

אָבִינוּ מַלְכֵּנוּ, הַחֲזִירֵנוּ בִּתְשׁוּבָה שְׁלֵמָה לְפָנֶיךָ.
אָבִינוּ מַלְכֵּנוּ, שְׁלַח רְפוּאָה שְׁלֵמָה לְחוֹלֵי עַמֶּךָ.
אָבִינוּ מַלְכֵּנוּ, קְרַע רֹעַ גְּזַר דִּינֵנוּ.
אָבִינוּ מַלְכֵּנוּ, זָכְרֵנוּ בְּזִכָּרוֹן טוֹב לְפָנֶיךָ.

During the עשרת ימי תשובה*:*

אָבִינוּ מַלְכֵּנוּ, כָּתְבֵנוּ בְּסֵפֶר חַיִּים טוֹבִים.
אָבִינוּ מַלְכֵּנוּ, כָּתְבֵנוּ בְּסֵפֶר גְּאֻלָּה וִישׁוּעָה.
אָבִינוּ מַלְכֵּנוּ, כָּתְבֵנוּ בְּסֵפֶר פַּרְנָסָה וְכַלְכָּלָה.
אָבִינוּ מַלְכֵּנוּ, כָּתְבֵנוּ בְּסֵפֶר זְכֻיּוֹת.
אָבִינוּ מַלְכֵּנוּ, כָּתְבֵנוּ בְּסֵפֶר סְלִיחָה וּמְחִילָה.

On Fast Days:

אָבִינוּ מַלְכֵּנוּ, זָכְרֵנוּ לְחַיִּים טוֹבִים.
אָבִינוּ מַלְכֵּנוּ, זָכְרֵנוּ לִגְאֻלָּה וִישׁוּעָה.
אָבִינוּ מַלְכֵּנוּ, זָכְרֵנוּ לְפַרְנָסָה וְכַלְכָּלָה.
אָבִינוּ מַלְכֵּנוּ, זָכְרֵנוּ לִזְכֻיּוֹת.
אָבִינוּ מַלְכֵּנוּ, זָכְרֵנוּ לִסְלִיחָה וּמְחִילָה.

End of responsive reading.

... A THOUSAND WORDS

Our Father, our King, let salvation soon flourish for us.
Our Father, our King, raise the honor of Your people Israel.
Our Father, our King, raise the honor of Your anointed.
Our Father, our King, fill our hands with Your blessings.
Our Father, our King, fill our storehouses with abundance.
Our Father, our King, hear our voice, pity and be compassionate to us.
Our Father, our King, accept, with compassion and favor, our prayer.
Our Father, our King, open the gates of heaven to our prayer.
Our Father, our King, remember that we are dust.
Our Father, our King, please do not turn us away from You empty-handed.
Our Father, our King, may this moment be a moment of compassion and a time of favor before You.
Our Father, our King, have pity on us, our children and our infants.
Our Father, our King, act for the sake of those who were killed for Your holy name.
Our Father, our King, act for the sake of those who were slaughtered for declaring Your Unity.
Our Father, our King, act for the sake of those who went through fire and water to sanctify Your name.
Our Father, our King, avenge before our eyes the spilt blood of Your servants.
Our Father, our King, act for Your sake, if not for ours.
Our Father, our King, act for Your sake, and save us.
Our Father, our King, act for the sake of Your great compassion.
Our Father, our King, act for the sake of Your great, mighty and awesome name by which we are called.
▸ Our Father, our King, be generous to us and answer us, though we have no worthy deeds; act with us in charity and loving-kindness and save us.

The Ark is closed.

---

boat pass so I can wave my flag to the captain and he will wave his flag back to me."

The older fellow chuckled, "Young man, any boat that passes on this ocean is likely to be a huge ship and the busy captain won't be able to see you, a small child sitting on the beach."

"Oh no, the captain of the ship will see me," the boy replied.

"How can you be so sure?" asked the man.

"Because the captain is my father," answered the boy.

אָבִינוּ מַלְכֵּנוּ, הַצְמַח לָנוּ יְשׁוּעָה בְּקָרוֹב.
אָבִינוּ מַלְכֵּנוּ, הָרֵם קֶרֶן יִשְׂרָאֵל עַמֶּךָ.
אָבִינוּ מַלְכֵּנוּ, הָרֵם קֶרֶן מְשִׁיחֶךָ.
אָבִינוּ מַלְכֵּנוּ, מַלֵּא יָדֵינוּ מִבִּרְכוֹתֶיךָ.
אָבִינוּ מַלְכֵּנוּ, מַלֵּא אֲסָמֵינוּ שָׂבָע.
אָבִינוּ מַלְכֵּנוּ, שְׁמַע קוֹלֵנוּ, חוּס וְרַחֵם עָלֵינוּ.
אָבִינוּ מַלְכֵּנוּ, קַבֵּל בְּרַחֲמִים וּבְרָצוֹן אֶת תְּפִלָּתֵנוּ.
אָבִינוּ מַלְכֵּנוּ, פְּתַח שַׁעֲרֵי שָׁמַיִם לִתְפִלָּתֵנוּ.
אָבִינוּ מַלְכֵּנוּ, זְכֹר כִּי עָפָר אֲנָחְנוּ.
אָבִינוּ מַלְכֵּנוּ, נָא אַל תְּשִׁיבֵנוּ רֵיקָם מִלְּפָנֶיךָ.
אָבִינוּ מַלְכֵּנוּ, תְּהֵא הַשָּׁעָה הַזֹּאת שְׁעַת רַחֲמִים
וְעֵת רָצוֹן מִלְּפָנֶיךָ.
אָבִינוּ מַלְכֵּנוּ, חֲמֹל עָלֵינוּ וְעַל עוֹלָלֵינוּ וְטַפֵּנוּ.
אָבִינוּ מַלְכֵּנוּ, עֲשֵׂה לְמַעַן הֲרוּגִים עַל שֵׁם קָדְשֶׁךָ.
אָבִינוּ מַלְכֵּנוּ, עֲשֵׂה לְמַעַן טְבוּחִים עַל יִחוּדֶךָ.
אָבִינוּ מַלְכֵּנוּ, עֲשֵׂה לְמַעַן בָּאֵי בָאֵשׁ וּבַמַּיִם עַל קִדּוּשׁ שְׁמֶךָ.
אָבִינוּ מַלְכֵּנוּ, נְקֹם לְעֵינֵינוּ נִקְמַת דַּם עֲבָדֶיךָ הַשָּׁפוּךְ.
אָבִינוּ מַלְכֵּנוּ, עֲשֵׂה לְמַעַנְךָ אִם לֹא לְמַעֲנֵנוּ.
אָבִינוּ מַלְכֵּנוּ, עֲשֵׂה לְמַעַנְךָ וְהוֹשִׁיעֵנוּ.
אָבִינוּ מַלְכֵּנוּ, עֲשֵׂה לְמַעַן רַחֲמֶיךָ הָרַבִּים.
אָבִינוּ מַלְכֵּנוּ, עֲשֵׂה לְמַעַן שִׁמְךָ הַגָּדוֹל הַגִּבּוֹר וְהַנּוֹרָא, שֶׁנִּקְרָא עָלֵינוּ.
◂ אָבִינוּ מַלְכֵּנוּ, חָנֵּנוּ וַעֲנֵנוּ, כִּי אֵין בָּנוּ מַעֲשִׂים
עֲשֵׂה עִמָּנוּ צְדָקָה וָחֶסֶד וְהוֹשִׁיעֵנוּ.

The ארון קודש *is closed.*

CONNECTION

A little boy was playing on an open beach. A man approached the boy and asked him, "Young man, why are you playing here all alone? Why don't you join the other children?" The boy looked up and responded innocently, "Because I want to see the big

TAḤANUN

On Mondays and Thursdays, when Taḥanun is said, begin with "He is compassionate" below. On other days when Taḥanun is said, begin with "David said" on page 214.

Taḥanun is not said on: Rosh Ḥodesh, Ḥanukka, Tu BiShvat, the 14th and 15th of Adar I, Purim and Shushan Purim, in the month of Nisan, Yom HaAtzma'ut, the 14th of Iyar (Pesaḥ Sheni), Lag BaOmer, Yom Yerushalayim, from Rosh Ḥodesh Sivan through the day after Shavuot (in Israel through 12th of Sivan), Tisha B'Av, Tu B'Av, Erev Rosh HaShana, and from Erev Yom Kippur through the day after Simḥat Torah (in Israel through Rosh Ḥodesh Marḥeshvan).

Taḥanun is also not said: on the morning of a Brit Mila, either where the brit will take place or where the father, Sandek or Mohel are present; if a groom is present (and some say a bride) on the day of his wedding or during the week of Sheva Berakhot; in a house of mourning.

The following until "David said" on page 214 is said standing.

וְהוּא רַחוּם He is compassionate. He forgives wrongdoing and does not de- *Ps. 78*
stroy. Repeatedly He suppresses His anger, not rousing His full fury. LORD, do not withhold Your compassion from us. May Your loving-kindness and
truth always protect us. Save us, LORD our God, and gather us from among *Ps. 106*
the nations, that we may give thanks to Your holy name and glory in Your
praise. If You, LORD, should keep account of sins, O LORD, who could *Ps. 130*
stand? But with You is forgiveness, that You may be feared. Do not deal *Jer. 14*
with us according to our sins; do not repay us according to our wrongdoing. Though our wrongdoings testify against us, LORD, act for Your name's
sake. Remember, LORD, Your compassion and loving-kindness, for they *Ps. 25*

---

loves with a diamond ring outstretched before her? What is a toddler telling his parents as he lies face down on the floor screaming because he dropped his ice cream? Sometimes words are not enough.

This helps us to understand the act of *nefilat apayim* – "falling down on one's face" – that we do here during *Taḥanun*. We just spent a serious amount of time pouring our hearts out before Hashem. And yet there is still a feeling that we just haven't done enough. Haven't said enough. So we throw ourselves down in front of the Creator of the Universe who knows and understands everything, and have faith that He understands.

Mondays and Thursdays – long Taḥanun

On Mondays and Thursdays an extended version of *Taḥanun* is said. Tradition has it that Mondays and Thursdays are days that are favorable for prayers being answered. Moshe ascended to receive the second *Luḥot HaBrit* on a Thursday and descended with them on a Monday. Since then, many have the custom to fast and to add additional requests for forgiveness.

סדר תחנון

On Mondays and Thursdays, when תחנון *is said, begin with* וְהוּא רַחוּם *below.*
On other days when תחנון *is said, begin with* וַיֹּאמֶר דָּוִד *on page 215.*

תחנון *is not said on:* ראש חודש, חנוכה, ט״ו בשבט, *the 14th and 15th of* אדר א׳, פורים *and* שושן פורים, *in the month of* ניסן, יום העצמאות, *the 14th of* אייר (פסח שני), ל״ג בעומר, יום ירושלים, *from* ראש חודש סיון *through the day after* שבועות (*in* ארץ ישראל *through* י״ב סיון), תשעה באב, ט״ו באב, ראש השנה, ערב ראש השנה, *and from* ערב יום כיפור *through the day after* שמחת תורה (*in* ארץ ישראל *through* ראש חודש מרחשון).

תחנון *is also not said: on the morning of a* ברית מילה, *either where the* ברית *will take place or where the father,* סנדק *or* מוהל *are present; if a* חתן *is present (and some say a* כלה*) on the day of his wedding or during the week of* שבע ברכות*; in a house of mourning.*

The following until וַיֹּאמֶר דָּוִד *on page 215 is said standing.*

תהלים עח וְהוּא רַחוּם, יְכַפֵּר עָוֹן וְלֹא־יַשְׁחִית, וְהִרְבָּה לְהָשִׁיב אַפּוֹ וְלֹא־יָעִיר
כָּל־חֲמָתוֹ: אַתָּה יהוה לֹא־תִכְלָא רַחֲמֶיךָ מִמֶּנּוּ, חַסְדְּךָ וַאֲמִתְּךָ תָּמִיד
תהלים קו יִצְּרוּנוּ. הוֹשִׁיעֵנוּ יהוה אֱלֹהֵינוּ וְקַבְּצֵנוּ מִן־הַגּוֹיִם, לְהוֹדוֹת לְשֵׁם קָדְשֶׁךָ,
תהלים קל לְהִשְׁתַּבֵּחַ בִּתְהִלָּתֶךָ: אִם־עֲוֺנוֹת תִּשְׁמָר־יָהּ, אֲדֹנָי מִי יַעֲמֹד: כִּי־עִמְּךָ
הַסְּלִיחָה לְמַעַן תִּוָּרֵא: לֹא כַחֲטָאֵינוּ תַּעֲשֶׂה לָנוּ, וְלֹא כַעֲוֺנוֹתֵינוּ תִּגְמֹל
ירמיה יד / תהלים כה עָלֵינוּ. אִם־עֲוֺנֵינוּ עָנוּ בָנוּ, יהוה עֲשֵׂה לְמַעַן שְׁמֶךָ: זְכֹר־רַחֲמֶיךָ יהוה

LEARNING

Tahanun signifies a return to private prayer following a break to pray as a community with the repetition of the *Amida*. As the *tefilla* service draws to a close, *Tahanun*, which means "plea," is one last chance for an intimate audience with Hashem, where we can bare our soul one last time.

The meaning of the word Tahanun

The word *Tahanun* comes from the root **ח-נ-נ** which means "to show favor, to be generous, to forgive." But what is unique about *Tahanun* is how honest we are about our failings. We make no attempt to hide them or sugar-coat them. We just ask for Hashem's understanding and mercy.

Nefilat Apayim – body language

You can say so much without words – just with your body. What statement is a serviceman making when he stands with his chest puffed out, hand on heart, during the national anthem? What emotion does a mother express as she envelops her child with a protective hug? What powerful message is a man making when he kneels at the feet of the woman he

are everlasting. May the LORD answer us when we are in distress; may the name of Jacob's God protect us. LORD, save! May the King answer us when we call. Our Father, our King, be generous to us and answer us, though we have no worthy deeds; act charitably with us for Your name's sake. LORD our God, hear the sound of our pleas. Remember for us the covenant of our ancestors, and save us for Your name's sake. *Ps. 20*

וְעַתָּה And now, My LORD, our God, who took Your people out of the land of Egypt with a mighty hand, creating for Yourself reputation to this day: we have sinned and acted wrongly. LORD, in keeping with all Your righteousness, please turn Your rage and anger away from Jerusalem, Your holy mountain. Because of our sins and the wrongdoing of our ancestors, Jerusalem and Your people have become the scorn of all those around us. And now, our God, listen to Your servant's prayer and pleas, and let Your face shine on Your desolate Sanctuary, for Your sake, O LORD. Incline Your ear, my God, and hear. Open Your eyes and see our desolation and that of the city called by Your name. Not because of our righteousness do we lay our pleas before You, but because of Your great compassion. LORD, hear! LORD, forgive! LORD, listen and act! Do not delay – for Your sake, my God, because Your city and Your people are called by Your name. *Dan. 9*

אָבִינוּ Our Father, compassionate Father, show us a sign for good, and gather our scattered ones from the four quarters of the earth. Let all the nations recognize and know that You are the LORD our God. And now, *Is. 64* LORD, You are our Father. We are the clay and You are our Potter; we are all the work of Your hand. Save us for the sake of Your name, our Rock, our King and our Redeemer. Pity Your people, LORD. Let not Your heritage *Joel 2* become an object of scorn, a byword among nations. Why should they say among the peoples, "Where is their God?" We know we have sinned and that there is no one to stand up for us. Let Your great name stand up for us in time of trouble. We know we have no merits of our own: therefore deal with us charitably for Your name's sake. As a father has compassion on his children, so, LORD, have compassion on us, and save us for the sake of Your name. Have mercy on Your people; have compassion for Your heritage; take pity in Your great compassion. Be generous to us and answer us, for righteousness is Yours, LORD. Always You do miracles.

וַחֲסָדֶיךָ, כִּי מֵעוֹלָם הֵמָּה: יַעֲנֵנוּ יהוה בְּיוֹם צָרָה, יְשַׂגְּבֵנוּ שֵׁם אֱלֹהֵי
יַעֲקֹב. יהוה הוֹשִׁיעָה, הַמֶּלֶךְ יַעֲנֵנוּ בְיוֹם־קָרְאֵנוּ: אָבִינוּ מַלְכֵּנוּ, חָנֵּנוּ תהלים כ
וַעֲנֵנוּ, כִּי אֵין בָּנוּ מַעֲשִׂים, צְדָקָה עֲשֵׂה עִמָּנוּ לְמַעַן שְׁמֶךָ. אֲדוֹנֵינוּ
אֱלֹהֵינוּ, שְׁמַע קוֹל תַּחֲנוּנֵינוּ, וּזְכָר לָנוּ אֶת בְּרִית אֲבוֹתֵינוּ וְהוֹשִׁיעֵנוּ
לְמַעַן שְׁמֶךָ.

וְעַתָּה אֲדֹנָי אֱלֹהֵינוּ, אֲשֶׁר הוֹצֵאתָ אֶת־עַמְּךָ מֵאֶרֶץ מִצְרַיִם בְּיָד חֲזָקָה דניאל ט
וַתַּעַשׂ־לְךָ שֵׁם כַּיּוֹם הַזֶּה, חָטָאנוּ רָשָׁעְנוּ: אֲדֹנָי, כְּכָל־צִדְקֹתֶךָ יָשָׁב־
נָא אַפְּךָ וַחֲמָתְךָ, מֵעִירְךָ יְרוּשָׁלַםִ הַר־קָדְשֶׁךָ, כִּי בַחֲטָאֵינוּ וּבַעֲוֹנוֹת
אֲבֹתֵינוּ, יְרוּשָׁלַםִ וְעַמְּךָ לְחֶרְפָּה לְכָל־סְבִיבֹתֵינוּ: וְעַתָּה שְׁמַע אֱלֹהֵינוּ
אֶל־תְּפִלַּת עַבְדְּךָ וְאֶל־תַּחֲנוּנָיו, וְהָאֵר פָּנֶיךָ עַל־מִקְדָּשְׁךָ הַשָּׁמֵם,
לְמַעַן אֲדֹנָי: הַטֵּה אֱלֹהַי אָזְנְךָ וּשְׁמָע, פְּקַח עֵינֶיךָ וּרְאֵה שֹׁמְמֹתֵינוּ
וְהָעִיר אֲשֶׁר־נִקְרָא שִׁמְךָ עָלֶיהָ, כִּי לֹא עַל־צִדְקֹתֵינוּ אֲנַחְנוּ מַפִּילִים
תַּחֲנוּנֵינוּ לְפָנֶיךָ, כִּי עַל־רַחֲמֶיךָ הָרַבִּים: אֲדֹנָי שְׁמָעָה, אֲדֹנָי סְלָחָה, אֲדֹנָי
הַקְשִׁיבָה וַעֲשֵׂה אַל־תְּאַחַר, לְמַעַנְךָ אֱלֹהַי, כִּי־שִׁמְךָ נִקְרָא עַל־עִירְךָ
וְעַל־עַמֶּךָ:

אָבִינוּ הָאָב הָרַחֲמָן, הַרְאֵנוּ אוֹת לְטוֹבָה וְקַבֵּץ נְפוּצוֹתֵינוּ מֵאַרְבַּע
כַּנְפוֹת הָאָרֶץ. יַכִּירוּ וְיֵדְעוּ כָּל הַגּוֹיִם כִּי אַתָּה יהוה אֱלֹהֵינוּ: וְעַתָּה ישעיה סד
יהוה אָבִינוּ אַתָּה, אֲנַחְנוּ הַחֹמֶר וְאַתָּה יֹצְרֵנוּ וּמַעֲשֵׂה יָדְךָ כֻּלָּנוּ.
הוֹשִׁיעֵנוּ לְמַעַן שְׁמֶךָ, צוּרֵנוּ מַלְכֵּנוּ וְגוֹאֲלֵנוּ. חוּסָה יהוה עַל־עַמֶּךָ, יואל ב
וְאַל־תִּתֵּן נַחֲלָתְךָ לְחֶרְפָּה לִמְשָׁל־בָּם גּוֹיִם, לָמָּה יֹאמְרוּ בָעַמִּים אַיֵּה
אֱלֹהֵיהֶם: יָדַעְנוּ כִּי חָטָאנוּ וְאֵין מִי יַעֲמֹד בַּעֲדֵנוּ, שִׁמְךָ הַגָּדוֹל יַעֲמָד
לָנוּ בְּעֵת צָרָה. יָדַעְנוּ כִּי אֵין בָּנוּ מַעֲשִׂים, צְדָקָה עֲשֵׂה עִמָּנוּ לְמַעַן
שְׁמֶךָ. כְּרַחֵם אָב עַל בָּנִים כֵּן תְּרַחֵם יהוה עָלֵינוּ, וְהוֹשִׁיעֵנוּ לְמַעַן
שְׁמֶךָ. חֲמֹל עַל עַמֶּךָ, רַחֵם עַל נַחֲלָתֶךָ, חוּסָה נָּא כְּרֹב רַחֲמֶיךָ, חָנֵּנוּ
וַעֲנֵנוּ. כִּי לְךָ יהוה הַצְּדָקָה, עֹשֵׂה נִפְלָאוֹת בְּכָל עֵת.

הַבֵּט נָא Please look, please swiftly have compassion for Your people for Your name's sake. In Your great compassion, LORD our God, have pity and compassion, and rescue the flock You tend. Let us not be ruled by fury, for our eyes are turned toward You. Save us for Your name's sake. Have compassion on us for the sake of Your covenant. Look and answer us in time of trouble, for Yours, LORD, is the power to save. Our hope is in You, God of forgiveness. Please forgive, good and forgiving God, for You are a generous, compassionate God and King.

אָנָּא מֶלֶךְ Please, generous and compassionate King, remember and call to mind the Covenant between the Pieces [with Abraham] and let the binding of his only son [Isaac] appear before You for Israel's sake. Our Father, our King, be generous to us and answer us, for we are called by Your great name. You who work miracles at all times, deal with us according to Your loving-kindness. Generous and compassionate One, look and answer us in time of trouble, for salvation is Yours, LORD. Our Father, our King, our Refuge, do not act with us according to our evil deeds. Remember, LORD, Your tender mercies and Your love. Save us in Your great goodness, and have mercy on us, for we have no other god but You, our Rock. Do not abandon us, LORD our God, do not be distant from us, for we are worn out by the sword and captivity, disease and plague, and by every trouble and sorrow. Rescue us, for in You lies our hope. Put us not to shame, LORD our God. Let Your face shine upon us. Remember for us the covenant of our ancestors and save us for Your name's sake. See our troubles and listen to the voice of our prayer, for You listen to the prayer of every mouth.

אֵל רַחוּם וְחַנּוּן O Compassionate and generous God, have compassion on us and on all Your works, for there is none like You, LORD our God. Please, we beg You, forgive our sins, our Father, our King, our Rock, our Redeemer, living and eternal God, mighty in strength, loving and good to all Your works, for You are the LORD our God. O God, slow to anger and full of compassion, act with us according to Your great compassion and save us for Your name's sake. Hear our prayer, our King, and save us from our enemies' hands. Listen to our prayer, our King, and save us from all distress and sorrow. You are our Father, our King. We are called by Your name. Do not desert us. Do not abandon us, our Father. Do not cast us away, our Creator. Do not forget us, our Maker – for You are a generous and compassionate God and King.

הַבֶּט נָא, רַחֵם נָא עַל עַמְּךָ מְהֵרָה לְמַעַן שְׁמֶךָ בְּרַחֲמֶיךָ הָרַבִּים יהוה אֱלֹהֵינוּ. חוּס וְרַחֵם וְהוֹשִׁיעָה צֹאן מַרְעִיתֶךָ, וְאַל יִמְשָׁל בָּנוּ קֶצֶף, כִּי לְךָ עֵינֵינוּ תְלוּיוֹת. הוֹשִׁיעֵנוּ לְמַעַן שְׁמֶךָ. רַחֵם עָלֵינוּ לְמַעַן בְּרִיתֶךָ. הַבִּיטָה וַעֲנֵנוּ בְּעֵת צָרָה, כִּי לְךָ יהוה הַיְשׁוּעָה. בְּךָ תוֹחַלְתֵּנוּ אֱלוֹהַּ סְלִיחוֹת, אָנָּא סְלַח נָא אֵל טוֹב וְסַלָּח, כִּי אֵל מֶלֶךְ חַנּוּן וְרַחוּם אָתָּה.

אָנָּא מֶלֶךְ חַנּוּן וְרַחוּם, זְכֹר וְהַבֵּט לִבְרִית בֵּין הַבְּתָרִים, וְתֵרָאֶה לְפָנֶיךָ עֲקֵדַת יָחִיד לְמַעַן יִשְׂרָאֵל. אָבִינוּ מַלְכֵּנוּ, חָנֵּנוּ וַעֲנֵנוּ, כִּי שִׁמְךָ הַגָּדוֹל נִקְרָא עָלֵינוּ. עֹשֵׂה נִפְלָאוֹת בְּכָל עֵת, עֲשֵׂה עִמָּנוּ כְּחַסְדֶּךָ. חַנּוּן וְרַחוּם, הַבִּיטָה וַעֲנֵנוּ בְּעֵת צָרָה, כִּי לְךָ יהוה הַיְשׁוּעָה. אָבִינוּ מַלְכֵּנוּ מַחְסֵנוּ, אַל תַּעַשׂ עִמָּנוּ כְּרֹעַ מַעֲלָלֵינוּ. זְכֹר רַחֲמֶיךָ יהוה וַחֲסָדֶיךָ, וּכְרֹב טוּבְךָ הוֹשִׁיעֵנוּ, וַחֲמָל נָא עָלֵינוּ, כִּי אֵין לָנוּ אֱלוֹהַּ אַחֵר מִבַּלְעָדֶיךָ צוּרֵנוּ. אַל תַּעַזְבֵנוּ יהוה אֱלֹהֵינוּ אַל תִּרְחַק מִמֶּנּוּ. כִּי נַפְשֵׁנוּ קְצָרָה, מֵחֶרֶב וּמִשְּׁבִי וּמִדֶּבֶר וּמִמַּגֵּפָה. וּמִכָּל צָרָה וְיָגוֹן הַצִּילֵנוּ, כִּי לְךָ קִוִּינוּ. וְאַל תַּכְלִימֵנוּ יהוה אֱלֹהֵינוּ, וְהָאֵר פָּנֶיךָ בָּנוּ, וּזְכָר לָנוּ אֶת בְּרִית אֲבוֹתֵינוּ וְהוֹשִׁיעֵנוּ לְמַעַן שְׁמֶךָ. רְאֵה בְצָרוֹתֵינוּ, וּשְׁמַע קוֹל תְּפִלָּתֵנוּ, כִּי אַתָּה שׁוֹמֵעַ תְּפִלַּת כָּל פֶּה.

אֵל רַחוּם וְחַנּוּן, רַחֵם עָלֵינוּ וְעַל כָּל מַעֲשֶׂיךָ, כִּי אֵין כָּמוֹךָ יהוה אֱלֹהֵינוּ. אָנָּא שָׂא נָא פְשָׁעֵינוּ, אָבִינוּ מַלְכֵּנוּ צוּרֵנוּ וְגוֹאֲלֵנוּ, אֵל חַי וְקַיָּם הַחֲסִין בַּכֹּחַ, חָסִיד וָטוֹב עַל כָּל מַעֲשֶׂיךָ, כִּי אַתָּה הוּא יהוה אֱלֹהֵינוּ. אֵל אֶרֶךְ אַפַּיִם וּמָלֵא רַחֲמִים, עֲשֵׂה עִמָּנוּ כְּרֹב רַחֲמֶיךָ, וְהוֹשִׁיעֵנוּ לְמַעַן שְׁמֶךָ. שְׁמַע מַלְכֵּנוּ תְּפִלָּתֵנוּ, וּמִיַּד אוֹיְבֵינוּ הַצִּילֵנוּ. שְׁמַע מַלְכֵּנוּ תְּפִלָּתֵנוּ, וּמִכָּל צָרָה וְיָגוֹן הַצִּילֵנוּ. אָבִינוּ מַלְכֵּנוּ אָתָּה, וְשִׁמְךָ עָלֵינוּ נִקְרָא. אַל תַּנִּחֵנוּ, אַל תַּעַזְבֵנוּ אָבִינוּ וְאַל תִּטְּשֵׁנוּ בּוֹרְאֵנוּ וְאַל תִּשְׁכָּחֵנוּ יוֹצְרֵנוּ, כִּי אֵל מֶלֶךְ חַנּוּן וְרַחוּם אָתָּה.

אֵין כָּמְוֹךָ There is none like You in grace and compassion, Lord our God. There is none like You, God, slow to anger and abounding in loving-kindness and truth. Save us in Your great compassion; rescue us from storm and turmoil. Remember Your servants Abraham, Isaac and Jacob; do not attend to our stubbornness, wickedness and sinfulness. Turn from Your fierce anger, and relent from the evil meant for Your people. Remove from us the curse of death, for You are compassionate. This is Your way, to show unearned loving-kindness to every generation. Have pity on Your people, Lord, and save us from Your fury. Remove from us the curse of plague and the harsh decree, for You are the Guardian of Israel. You are right, my Lord, and we are shamefaced. How can we complain? What can we say? What can we plead? How can we justify ourselves? Let us search our ways and examine them and return to You, for Your right hand is outstretched to receive those who return. Please, Lord, please save. Please, Lord, please send success. Please, Lord, answer us when we call. For You, Lord, we wait. For You, Lord, we hope. For You, Lord, we long. Do not be silent while we suffer, for the nations are saying, "Their hope is lost." To You alone every knee must bend, and those who hold themselves high bow down.

Ex. 32 *Dan. 9* *Ps. 118*

הַפּוֹתֵחַ יָד You who hold out an open hand of repentance to receive transgressors and sinners – our soul is overwhelmed by our great sorrow. Do not forget us for ever. Arise and save us, for we seek refuge in You. Our Father, our King, though we lack righteousness and good deeds, remember for us the covenant of our fathers, and our testimonies daily that "The Lord is One." Look on our suffering, for many are our sufferings and heartaches. Have pity on us, Lord, in the land of our captivity. Do not pour out Your fury on us, for we are Your people, the children of Your covenant. God, see how low our glory has sunk among the nations. They hate us as if we were impure. How long will Your strength be captive, and Your glory in the hand of the enemy? Arouse Your strength and zeal against Your enemies. Let them be shamed and deprived of power. Let not our hardships seem small to You. Swiftly may Your compassion reach us in the day of our distress. If not for our sake, act for Yours, so that the memory of our survivors be not destroyed. Be generous to the nation who, in constant love, declare twice daily the unity of Your name, saying, "Listen, Israel, the Lord is our God, the Lord is One."

Deut. 6

אֵין כָּמְוֹךָ חַנּוּן וְרַחוּם יהוה אֱלֹהֵינוּ, אֵין כָּמְוֹךָ אֵל אֶרֶךְ אַפַּיִם וְרַב
חֶסֶד וֶאֱמֶת. הוֹשִׁיעֵנוּ בְּרַחֲמֶיךָ הָרַבִּים, מֵרַעַשׁ וּמֵרֹגֶז הַצִּילֵנוּ. זְכֹר
לַעֲבָדֶיךָ לְאַבְרָהָם לְיִצְחָק וּלְיַעֲקֹב, אַל תֵּפֶן אֶל קְשְׁיֵנוּ וְאֶל רִשְׁעֵנוּ
וְאֶל חַטָּאתֵנוּ. שׁוּב מֵחֲרוֹן אַפֶּךָ, וְהִנָּחֵם עַל־הָרָעָה לְעַמֶּךָ: וְהָסֵר שמות לב
מִמֶּנּוּ מַכַּת הַמָּוֶת כִּי רַחוּם אָתָּה, כִּי כֵן דַּרְכֶּךָ, עֹשֶׂה חֶסֶד חִנָּם בְּכָל
דּוֹר וָדוֹר. חוּסָה יהוה עַל עַמֶּךָ וְהַצִּילֵנוּ מִזַּעְמֶךָ, וְהָסֵר מִמֶּנּוּ מַכַּת
הַמַּגֵּפָה וּגְזֵרָה קָשָׁה, כִּי אַתָּה שׁוֹמֵר יִשְׂרָאֵל. לְךָ אֲדֹנָי הַצְּדָקָה וְלָנוּ דניאל ט
בֹּשֶׁת הַפָּנִים: מַה נִּתְאוֹנֵן, מַה נֹּאמַר, מַה נְּדַבֵּר וּמַה נִּצְטַדָּק. נַחְפְּשָׂה
דְרָכֵינוּ וְנַחְקֹרָה וְנָשׁוּבָה אֵלֶיךָ, כִּי יְמִינְךָ פְשׁוּטָה לְקַבֵּל שָׁבִים. אָנָּא תהלים קיח
יהוה הוֹשִׁיעָה נָּא, אָנָּא יהוה הַצְלִיחָה נָא: אָנָּא יהוה עֲנֵנוּ בְיוֹם
קָרְאֵנוּ. לְךָ יהוה חִכִּינוּ, לְךָ יהוה קִוִּינוּ, לְךָ יהוה נְיַחֵל. אַל תֶּחֱשֶׁה
וּתְעַנֵּנוּ, כִּי נָאֲמוּ גוֹיִם, אָבְדָה תִקְוָתָם. כָּל בֶּרֶךְ וְכָל קוֹמָה, לְךָ לְבַד
תִּשְׁתַּחֲוֶה.

הַפּוֹתֵחַ יָד בִּתְשׁוּבָה לְקַבֵּל פּוֹשְׁעִים וְחַטָּאִים, נִבְהֲלָה נַפְשֵׁנוּ מֵרֹב
עִצְּבוֹנֵנוּ. אַל תִּשְׁכָּחֵנוּ נֶצַח, קוּמָה וְהוֹשִׁיעֵנוּ כִּי חָסִינוּ בָךְ. אָבִינוּ
מַלְכֵּנוּ, אִם אֵין בָּנוּ צְדָקָה וּמַעֲשִׂים טוֹבִים, זְכָר לָנוּ אֶת בְּרִית אֲבוֹתֵינוּ
וְעֵדוֹתֵנוּ בְּכָל יוֹם יהוה אֶחָד. הַבִּיטָה בְעָנְיֵנוּ, כִּי רַבּוּ מַכְאוֹבֵינוּ וְצָרוֹת
לְבָבֵנוּ. חוּסָה יהוה עָלֵינוּ בְּאֶרֶץ שִׁבְיֵנוּ, וְאַל תִּשְׁפֹּךְ חֲרוֹנְךָ עָלֵינוּ,
כִּי אֲנַחְנוּ עַמְּךָ בְּנֵי בְרִיתֶךָ. אֵל, הַבִּיטָה, דַּל כְּבוֹדֵנוּ בַּגּוֹיִם וְשִׁקְּצוּנוּ
כְּטֻמְאַת הַנִּדָּה. עַד מָתַי עֻזְּךָ בַּשְּׁבִי, וְתִפְאַרְתְּךָ בְּיַד צָר. עוֹרְרָה גְבוּרָתְךָ
וְקִנְאָתְךָ עַל אוֹיְבֶיךָ. הֵם יֵבוֹשׁוּ וְיֵחַתּוּ מִגְּבוּרָתָם. וְאַל יִמְעֲטוּ לְפָנֶיךָ
תְּלָאוֹתֵינוּ, מַהֵר יְקַדְּמוּנוּ רַחֲמֶיךָ בְּיוֹם צָרָתֵנוּ. וְאִם לֹא לְמַעֲנֵנוּ, לְמַעַנְךָ
פְעַל, וְאַל תַּשְׁחִית זֵכֶר שְׁאֵרִיתֵנוּ, וְחֹן אֹם הַמְיַחֲדִים שִׁמְךָ פַּעֲמַיִם
בְּכָל יוֹם תָּמִיד בְּאַהֲבָה, וְאוֹמְרִים, שְׁמַע יִשְׂרָאֵל, יהוה אֱלֹהֵינוּ, דברים ו
יהוה אֶחָד:

LOWERING THE HEAD

On Sundays, Tuesdays, Wednesdays and Fridays, begin Taḥanun here. The following, until "We do not know" on page 218, is said sitting. When praying in a place where there is a Torah scroll, one should lean forward, resting one's head on the left arm (unless you are wearing tefillin on the left arm, in which case rest on the right arm out of respect for the tefillin), until in "sudden shame."

וַיֹּאמֶר דָּוִד David said to Gad, "I am in great distress. *II Sam. 24*
Let us fall into God's hand, for His mercy is great;
but do not let me fall into the hand of man."

Compassionate and generous One,
I have sinned before You.
Lord, full of compassion,
have compassion on me and accept my pleas.

Lord, do not rebuke me in Your anger or chastise me in Your fury. Be generous to me, Lord, for I am weak. Heal me, Lord, for my bones are in agony. My soul is in anguish, and You, O Lord – how long? Turn, Lord, set my soul free; save me for the sake of Your love. For no one remembers You when he is dead. Who can praise You from the grave? I am tired with my sighing. Every night I drench my bed, I soak my couch with my tears. My eye grows dim from grief, worn out because of all my enemies. Leave me, all you evildoers, for the Lord has heard the sound of my weeping. The Lord has heard my pleas. The Lord will accept my prayer. All my enemies will be shamed and utterly dismayed. They will turn back in sudden shame. *Ps. 6*

Sit upright.

REFLECTION

"Fie, fie upon her!
There's language
in her eye, her cheek, her lip,
Nay, her foot speaks;
her wanton spirits look out
At every joint and motive
of her body."
(William Shakespeare)

When are words not enough?

What can you say
with your body
that you can't say
with your words?

What are you saying
with your body right now?

נפילת אפיים

On Sundays, Tuesdays, Wednesdays and Fridays, begin תחנון *here.*
The following, until וַאֲנַחְנוּ לֹא נֵדַע *on page 219, is said sitting. When praying in a place where there is a* ספר תורה*, one should lean forward, resting one's head on the left arm (unless you are wearing* תפילין *on the left arm, in which case rest on the right arm out of respect for the* תפילין*), until* יֵבֹשׁוּ רָגַע*.*

שמואל ב, כד

וַיֹּאמֶר דָּוִד אֶל־גָּד, צַר־לִי מְאֹד
נִפְּלָה־נָּא בְיַד־יהוה, כִּי רַבִּים רַחֲמָו, וּבְיַד־אָדָם אַל־אֶפֹּלָה:

רַחוּם וְחַנּוּן, חָטָאתִי לְפָנֶיךָ.
יהוה מָלֵא רַחֲמִים, רַחֵם עָלַי וְקַבֵּל תַּחֲנוּנָי.

תהלים ו

יהוה, אַל־בְּאַפְּךָ תוֹכִיחֵנִי, וְאַל־בַּחֲמָתְךָ תְיַסְּרֵנִי: חָנֵּנִי יהוה, כִּי אֻמְלַל אָנִי, רְפָאֵנִי יהוה, כִּי נִבְהֲלוּ עֲצָמָי: וְנַפְשִׁי נִבְהֲלָה מְאֹד, וְאַתְּ יהוה, עַד־מָתָי: שׁוּבָה יהוה, חַלְּצָה נַפְשִׁי, הוֹשִׁיעֵנִי לְמַעַן חַסְדֶּךָ: כִּי אֵין בַּמָּוֶת זִכְרֶךָ, בִּשְׁאוֹל מִי יוֹדֶה־לָּךְ: יָגַעְתִּי בְּאַנְחָתִי, אַשְׂחֶה בְכָל־לַיְלָה מִטָּתִי, בְּדִמְעָתִי עַרְשִׂי אַמְסֶה: עָשְׁשָׁה מִכַּעַס עֵינִי, עָתְקָה בְּכָל־צוֹרְרָי: סוּרוּ מִמֶּנִּי כָּל־פֹּעֲלֵי אָוֶן, כִּי שָׁמַע יהוה קוֹל בִּכְיִי: שָׁמַע יהוה תְּחִנָּתִי, יהוה תְּפִלָּתִי יִקָּח: יֵבֹשׁוּ וְיִבָּהֲלוּ מְאֹד כָּל־אֹיְבָי, יָשֻׁבוּ יֵבֹשׁוּ רָגַע:

Sit upright.

LEARNING

This part of *Taḥanun*, called נְפִילַת אַפַּיִם, literally, lowering of the head, should be said sitting down, with your head lowered against your weaker arm. If you are wearing tefillin you should rest your head on your other arm. Only lower your head onto your arm when you are in the presence of a *Sefer Torah*. However, in Yerushalayim the custom is to always lower the head, as it is considered as if you are in the presence of the *Aron* of Hashem.

... A THOUSAND WORDS

On Mondays and Thursdays, say the following.
On other days, continue with "Guardian of Israel" below.

Lord, God of Israel, turn away from Your fierce anger,
and relent from the evil against Your people.

Look down from heaven and see how we have become an object of scorn and derision among the nations. We are regarded as sheep led to the slaughter, to be killed, destroyed, beaten and humiliated. Yet, despite all this, we have not forgotten Your name. Please do not forget us.

Lord, God of Israel, turn away from Your fierce anger,
and relent from the evil against Your people.

Strangers say, "You have no hope or expectation." Be generous to the nation whose hope is in Your name. O Pure One, bring our deliverance close. We are exhausted. We are given no rest. May Your compassion suppress Your anger against us. Please turn away from Your fierce anger, and have compassion on the people You chose as Your own.

Lord, God of Israel, turn away from Your fierce anger,
and relent from the evil against Your people.

Have pity on us, Lord, in Your compassion, and do not hand us over to cruel oppressors. Why should the nations say, "Where is their God now?" For Your own sake, deal kindly with us, and do not delay. Please turn away from Your fierce anger, and have compassion on the people You chose as Your own.

Lord, God of Israel, turn away from Your fierce anger,
and relent from the evil against Your people.

Listen to our voice and be generous. Do not abandon us into the hand of our enemies to blot out our name. Remember what You promised our fathers: "I will make your descendants as many as the stars of heaven" – yet now we are only a few left from many. Yet, despite all this, we have not forgotten Your name. Please do not forget us.

Lord, God of Israel, turn away from Your fierce anger,
and relent from the evil against Your people.

Help us, God of our salvation, for the sake of the glory of Your name. Save us and *Ps. 79*
pardon our sins for Your name's sake.

Lord, God of Israel, turn away from Your fierce anger,
and relent from the evil against Your people.

On all days continue here:

שׁוֹמֵר יִשְׂרָאֵל Guardian of Israel, guard the survivors of Israel,
and let not Israel perish, who declare, "Listen, Israel."

Guardian of a unique nation, guard the survivors of a unique people,
and let not that unique nation perish, who declare the unity
of Your name [saying], "The Lord is our God, the Lord is One."

On Mondays and Thursdays, say the following.
On other days, continue with שׁוֹמֵר יִשְׂרָאֵל *below.*

יהוה אֱלֹהֵי יִשְׂרָאֵל, שׁוּב מֵחֲרוֹן אַפֶּךָ וְהִנָּחֵם עַל הָרָעָה לְעַמֶּךָ.

הַבֵּט מִשָּׁמַיִם וּרְאֵה כִּי הָיִינוּ לַעַג וָקֶלֶס בַּגּוֹיִם, נֶחְשַׁבְנוּ כַּצֹּאן לַטֶּבַח יוּבָל, לַהֲרֹג וּלְאַבֵּד וּלְמַכָּה וּלְחֶרְפָּה. וּבְכָל זֹאת שִׁמְךָ לֹא שָׁכָחְנוּ, נָא אַל תִּשְׁכָּחֵנוּ.

יהוה אֱלֹהֵי יִשְׂרָאֵל, שׁוּב מֵחֲרוֹן אַפֶּךָ וְהִנָּחֵם עַל הָרָעָה לְעַמֶּךָ.

זָרִים אוֹמְרִים אֵין תּוֹחֶלֶת וְתִקְוָה, חֹן אֹם לְשִׁמְךָ מְקַוֶּה, טָהוֹר יְשׁוּעָתֵנוּ קָרְבָה, יָגַעְנוּ וְלֹא הוּנַח לָנוּ, רַחֲמֶיךָ יִכְבְּשׁוּ אֶת כַּעַסְךָ מֵעָלֵינוּ. אָנָּא שׁוּב מֵחֲרוֹנְךָ וְרַחֵם סְגֻלָּה אֲשֶׁר בָּחָרְתָּ.

יהוה אֱלֹהֵי יִשְׂרָאֵל, שׁוּב מֵחֲרוֹן אַפֶּךָ וְהִנָּחֵם עַל הָרָעָה לְעַמֶּךָ.

חוּסָה יהוה עָלֵינוּ בְּרַחֲמֶיךָ, וְאַל תִּתְּנֵנוּ בִּידֵי אַכְזָרִים. לָמָּה יֹאמְרוּ הַגּוֹיִם אַיֵּה נָא אֱלֹהֵיהֶם, לְמַעַנְךָ עֲשֵׂה עִמָּנוּ חֶסֶד וְאַל תְּאַחַר. אָנָּא שׁוּב מֵחֲרוֹנְךָ וְרַחֵם סְגֻלָּה אֲשֶׁר בָּחָרְתָּ.

יהוה אֱלֹהֵי יִשְׂרָאֵל, שׁוּב מֵחֲרוֹן אַפֶּךָ וְהִנָּחֵם עַל הָרָעָה לְעַמֶּךָ.

קוֹלֵנוּ תִשְׁמַע וְתָחֹן, וְאַל תִּטְּשֵׁנוּ בְּיַד אֹיְבֵינוּ לִמְחוֹת אֶת שְׁמֵנוּ. זְכֹר אֲשֶׁר נִשְׁבַּעְתָּ לַאֲבוֹתֵינוּ כְּכוֹכְבֵי הַשָּׁמַיִם אַרְבֶּה אֶת זַרְעֲכֶם, וְעַתָּה נִשְׁאַרְנוּ מְעַט מֵהַרְבֵּה. וּבְכָל זֹאת שִׁמְךָ לֹא שָׁכָחְנוּ, נָא אַל תִּשְׁכָּחֵנוּ.

יהוה אֱלֹהֵי יִשְׂרָאֵל, שׁוּב מֵחֲרוֹן אַפֶּךָ וְהִנָּחֵם עַל הָרָעָה לְעַמֶּךָ.

עָזְרֵנוּ אֱלֹהֵי יִשְׁעֵנוּ עַל־דְּבַר כְּבוֹד־שְׁמֶךָ, וְהַצִּילֵנוּ וְכַפֵּר עַל־חַטֹּאתֵינוּ לְמַעַן שְׁמֶךָ׃ תהלים עט

יהוה אֱלֹהֵי יִשְׂרָאֵל, שׁוּב מֵחֲרוֹן אַפֶּךָ וְהִנָּחֵם עַל הָרָעָה לְעַמֶּךָ.

On all days continue here:

שׁוֹמֵר יִשְׂרָאֵל, שְׁמֹר שְׁאֵרִית יִשְׂרָאֵל, וְאַל יֹאבַד יִשְׂרָאֵל
הָאוֹמְרִים שְׁמַע יִשְׂרָאֵל.

שׁוֹמֵר גּוֹי אֶחָד, שְׁמֹר שְׁאֵרִית עַם אֶחָד, וְאַל יֹאבַד גּוֹי אֶחָד
הַמְיַחֲדִים שִׁמְךָ, יהוה אֱלֹהֵינוּ יהוה אֶחָד.

Guardian of a holy nation, guard the survivors of that holy people,
and let not the holy nation perish, who three times repeat
the threefold declaration of holiness to the Holy One.

You who are conciliated by calls for compassion and placated by pleas,
be conciliated and placated toward an afflicted generation,
for there is no other help.

Our Father, our King, be generous to us and answer us,
though we have no worthy deeds;
act with us in charity and loving-kindness and save us.

Stand at ▴.

וַאֲנַחְנוּ We do not know ▴what to do, but our eyes are turned to You. Remember, Lord, Your compassion and loving-kindness, for they are everlasting. May Your loving-kindness, Lord, be with us, for we have put our hope in You. Do not hold against us the sins of those who came before us. May Your mercies meet us swiftly, for we have been brought very low. Be generous to us, Lord, be generous to us, for we are full with contempt. In fury, remember mercy. He knows our nature; He remembers that we are dust. ▸ Help us, God of our salvation, for the sake of the glory of Your name. Save us and give atonement for our sins for Your name's sake.

II Chr. 12
Ps. 25
Ps. 33
Ps. 79
Ps. 123
Hab. 3
Ps. 103
Ps. 79

HALF KADDISH

Leader: יִתְגַּדַּל Magnified and sanctified may His great name be,
in the world He created by His will.
May He establish His kingdom
in your lifetime and in your days,
and in the lifetime of all the house of Israel,
swiftly and soon –
and say: Amen.

All: May His great name be blessed for ever and all time.

Leader: Blessed and praised, glorified and elevated,
raised and honored, uplifted and praised
be the name of the Holy One,
blessed be He,
beyond any blessing, song, praise and consolation
uttered in the world –
and say: Amen.

שׁוֹמֵר גּוֹי קָדוֹשׁ, שְׁמֹר שְׁאֵרִית עַם קָדוֹשׁ, וְאַל יֹאבַד גּוֹי קָדוֹשׁ
הַמְשַׁלְּשִׁים בְּשָׁלֹשׁ קְדֻשּׁוֹת לְקָדוֹשׁ.

מִתְרַצֶּה בְּרַחֲמִים וּמִתְפַּיֵּס בְּתַחֲנוּנִים, הִתְרַצֵּה וְהִתְפַּיֵּס לְדוֹר עָנִי
כִּי אֵין עוֹזֵר.

אָבִינוּ מַלְכֵּנוּ, חָנֵּנוּ וַעֲנֵנוּ, כִּי אֵין בָּנוּ מַעֲשִׂים
עֲשֵׂה עִמָּנוּ צְדָקָה וָחֶסֶד וְהוֹשִׁיעֵנוּ.

Stand at ▴.

וַאֲנַחְנוּ לֹא נֵדַע ▴מַה־נַּעֲשֶׂה, כִּי עָלֶיךָ עֵינֵינוּ: זְכֹר־רַחֲמֶיךָ יהוה וַחֲסָדֶיךָ, דברי הימים ב׳ כ תהלים כה
כִּי מֵעוֹלָם הֵמָּה: יְהִי־חַסְדְּךָ יהוה עָלֵינוּ, כַּאֲשֶׁר יִחַלְנוּ לָךְ: אַל־תִּזְכָּר־לָנוּ תהלים לג תהלים עט
עֲוֹנֹת רִאשֹׁנִים, מַהֵר יְקַדְּמוּנוּ רַחֲמֶיךָ, כִּי דַלּוֹנוּ מְאֹד: חָנֵּנוּ יהוה חָנֵּנוּ, תהלים קכג
כִּי־רַב שָׂבַעְנוּ בוּז: בְּרֹגֶז רַחֵם תִּזְכּוֹר: כִּי־הוּא יָדַע יִצְרֵנוּ, זָכוּר כִּי־עָפָר חבקוק ג תהלים קג
אֲנָחְנוּ: ◂ עָזְרֵנוּ אֱלֹהֵי יִשְׁעֵנוּ עַל־דְּבַר כְּבוֹד־שְׁמֶךָ, וְהַצִּילֵנוּ וְכַפֵּר עַל־ תהלים עט
חַטֹּאתֵינוּ לְמַעַן שְׁמֶךָ:

חצי קדיש

ש״ץ: יִתְגַּדַּל וְיִתְקַדַּשׁ שְׁמֵהּ רַבָּא (קהל: אָמֵן)
בְּעָלְמָא דִּי בְרָא כִרְעוּתֵהּ
וְיַמְלִיךְ מַלְכוּתֵהּ
בְּחַיֵּיכוֹן וּבְיוֹמֵיכוֹן וּבְחַיֵּי דְכָל בֵּית יִשְׂרָאֵל
בַּעֲגָלָא וּבִזְמַן קָרִיב, וְאִמְרוּ אָמֵן. (קהל: אָמֵן)

קהל וש״ץ: יְהֵא שְׁמֵהּ רַבָּא מְבָרַךְ לְעָלַם וּלְעָלְמֵי עָלְמַיָּא.

ש״ץ: יִתְבָּרַךְ וְיִשְׁתַּבַּח וְיִתְפָּאַר וְיִתְרוֹמַם וְיִתְנַשֵּׂא
וְיִתְהַדָּר וְיִתְעַלֶּה וְיִתְהַלָּל
שְׁמֵהּ דְּקֻדְשָׁא בְּרִיךְ הוּא (קהל: בְּרִיךְ הוּא)
לְעֵלָּא מִן כָּל בִּרְכָתָא / בעשרת ימי תשובה: לְעֵלָּא לְעֵלָּא מִכָּל בִּרְכָתָא/
וְשִׁירָתָא, תֻּשְׁבְּחָתָא וְנֶחֱמָתָא
דַּאֲמִירָן בְּעָלְמָא, וְאִמְרוּ אָמֵן. (קהל: אָמֵן)

REMOVING THE TORAH FROM THE ARK

On Mondays and Thursdays, Rosh Ḥodesh, Ḥol HaMo'ed, Ḥanukka, Purim and Fast Days, the Torah is read when a minyan is present. On Yom HaAtzma'ut that is not Thursday, the Haftara on page 962 is read. On all other days, continue with "Happy are those" on page 236.

Before taking the Torah out of the Ark, on Mondays and Thursdays, stand while reciting "God, slow to anger." It is not said on Rosh Ḥodesh, Ḥol HaMo'ed, Erev Pesaḥ, Ḥanukka, the 14th and 15th of Adar I, Purim and Shushan Purim, Yom HaAtzma'ut, Yom Yerushalayim, Tisha B'Av or in a house of mourning, and in Israel on Isru Ḥag. Most people say both paragraphs; some say only the first.

God, slow to anger, abounding
in loving-kindness and truth,
do not rebuke us in Your anger.
Have pity on Your people, LORD,
and save us from all evil.
We have sinned against You, LORD.
Please forgive in accordance with
Your great compassion, God.

God, slow to anger, full of compassion,
do not hide Your face from us.
Have pity on the survivors of Israel
Your people, LORD,
and deliver us from all evil.
We have sinned against You, LORD.
Please forgive in accordance with
Your great compassion, God.

The Ark is opened and the congregation stands. All say:

וַיְהִי בִּנְסֹעַ Whenever the Ark set out, Moses would say, *Num. 10*
"Arise, LORD, and may Your enemies be scattered.
May those who hate You flee before You."
For the Torah shall come forth from Zion, *Is. 2*
and the word of the LORD from Jerusalem.
Blessed is He who in His holiness
gave the Torah to His people Israel.

REFLECTION

"So says the LORD of Multitudes : "In those days it will be that ten men of all the languages of the nations will grasp; they will grasp the hem of a Judean man, saying: 'We will go with you, for we have heard that God is with you.'"

(*Zekharia* 8:23)

Does the Torah
and the word of Hashem
emanate from Yerushalayim
to all over the world today?

How is your religious life
influenced by Israel
and Israelis?

הוצאת ספר תורה

On Mondays and Thursdays, ראש חודש, חול המועד, חנוכה, פורים *and Fast Days, the* תורה *is read when a* מנין *is present. On* יום העצמאות *that is not Thursday, the* הפטרה *on page 963 is read. On all other days, continue with* אשרי *on page 237.*

Before taking the תורה *out of the* ארון קודש*, on Mondays and Thursdays, stand while reciting* אֵל אֶרֶךְ אַפַּיִם*. It is not said on:* ראש חודש, חול המועד, ערב פסח, חנוכה*, the 14th and 15th of* אדר א׳, פורים *and* שושן פורים, יום העצמאות, יום ירושלים, תשעה באב *or in a house of mourning, and in* ארץ ישראל *on* אסרו חג*. Most people say both paragraphs, some say only the first.*

אֵל אֶרֶךְ אַפַּיִם וְרַב חֶסֶד וֶאֱמֶת
אַל בְּאַפְּךָ תוֹכִיחֵנוּ.
חוּסָה יהוה עַל עַמֶּךָ
וְהוֹשִׁיעֵנוּ מִכָּל רָע.
חָטָאנוּ לְךָ אָדוֹן
סְלַח נָא כְּרֹב רַחֲמֶיךָ אֵל.

אֵל אֶרֶךְ אַפַּיִם וּמָלֵא רַחֲמִים
אַל תַּסְתֵּר פָּנֶיךָ מִמֶּנּוּ.
חוּסָה יהוה עַל שְׁאֵרִית יִשְׂרָאֵל עַמֶּךָ
וְהַצִּילֵנוּ מִכָּל רָע.
חָטָאנוּ לְךָ אָדוֹן
סְלַח נָא כְּרֹב רַחֲמֶיךָ אֵל.

The ארון קודש *is opened and the* קהל *stands. All say:*

במדבר י
וַיְהִי בִּנְסֹעַ הָאָרֹן וַיֹּאמֶר מֹשֶׁה
קוּמָה יהוה וְיָפֻצוּ אֹיְבֶיךָ וְיָנֻסוּ מְשַׂנְאֶיךָ מִפָּנֶיךָ:
ישעיה ב
כִּי מִצִּיּוֹן תֵּצֵא תוֹרָה וּדְבַר־יהוה מִירוּשָׁלָםִ:
בָּרוּךְ שֶׁנָּתַן תּוֹרָה לְעַמּוֹ יִשְׂרָאֵל בִּקְדֻשָּׁתוֹ.

LEARNING

On Mondays and Thursdays, Rosh Ḥodesh, Ḥol HaMo'ed, Ḥanukka, Purim, and Fast Days, the Torah is read if there is a *minyan* present. Together with Shabbat and *Ḥagim*, these are the times when the community comes together to experience, hear, and learn from the Torah. Even if you are not able to read or understand the words of the Torah, this public reading allows you to experience it as a microcosm of the original experience of the giving of the Torah. In this act, the *beit knesset* becomes a *beit midrash*, and we focus not on our words to God, but on His words to us.

CONNECTION

"[The] people of Israel must have their own social and political state and a national kingdom with its own culture… In order that this nation can teach the world that living in the way of God is available not just to the very wise and holy people who live according to this divine notion privately, but that it is accessible to entire peoples…[who] are able to live in the way of God and become upright and moral."

(Rav Kook, *Orot*)

Blessed is the name of the Master of the Universe. Blessed is Your crown and Your place. May Your favor always be with Your people Israel. Show Your people the salvation of Your right hand in Your Temple. Give us the gift of Your good light, and accept our prayers in mercy. May it be Your will to prolong our life in goodness. May I be counted among the righteous, so that You will have compassion on me and protect me and all that is mine and all that is Your people Israel's. You feed all; You sustain all; You rule over all; You rule over kings, for sovereignty is Yours. I am a servant of the Holy One, blessed be He, before whom and before whose glorious Torah I bow at all times. Not in man do I trust, nor on any angel do I rely, but on the God of heaven who is the God of truth, whose Torah is truth, whose prophets speak truth, and who abounds in acts of love and truth. ▸ In Him I trust, and to His holy and glorious name I offer praises. May it be Your will to open my heart to the Torah, and to fulfill the wishes of my heart and of the hearts of all Your people Israel for good, for life, and for peace.

Zohar, Vayak-hel

CONNECTION

כִּי־אֵשֵׁב בַּחֹשֶׁךְ יהוה אוֹר לִי

"When I sat in the darkness the Lord was a light for me." (*Mikha* 7:8)

The Ba'al Shem Tov explains that this does not mean that Hashem was a light to me in darkness but rather because of the time I spent in darkness I was able to appreciate and understand the light of God. Both darkness and light serve a purpose in spiritual development. Sometimes when things seem dark and hopeless, there is an opportunity to learn and to grow; this is the light that can be found in the darkness.

LEARNING

According to Rabbi Aharon Lichtenstein, *talmud Torah* can be seen on three different religious levels. First and foremost it is the halakhic fulfillment of a mitzva obligation. Secondly, *talmud Torah* is a value, encouraging the gaining of knowledge and broadening of religious horizons, as well as having a moral educational impact, encouraging ethical behavior. Finally *talmud Torah* has cosmic and spiritual impact on the individual, the collective, and the universe as a whole.

That the siddur makes the mitzva of *talmud Torah* a recurring theme makes a profound statement on its importance and value to our everyday life.

זוהר ויקהל

בְּרִיךְ שְׁמֵהּ דְּמָרֵא עָלְמָא, בְּרִיךְ כִּתְרָךְ וְאַתְרָךְ. יְהֵא רְעוּתָךְ עִם עַמָּךְ יִשְׂרָאֵל לְעָלַם, וּפֻרְקַן יְמִינָךְ אַחֲזִי לְעַמָּךְ בְּבֵית מַקְדְּשָׁךְ, וּלְאַמְטוֹיֵי לַנָא מִטּוּב נְהוֹרָךְ, וּלְקַבֵּל צְלוֹתַנָא בְּרַחֲמִין. יְהֵא רַעֲוָא קֳדָמָךְ דְּתוֹרִיךְ לַן חַיִּין בְּטִיבוּ, וְלֶהֱוֵי אֲנָא פְקִידָא בְּגוֹ צַדִּיקַיָּא, לְמִרְחַם עָלַי וּלְמִנְטַר יָתִי וְיַת כָּל דִּי לִי וְדִי לְעַמָּךְ יִשְׂרָאֵל. אַנְתְּ הוּא זָן לְכֹלָּא וּמְפַרְנֵס לְכֹלָּא, אַנְתְּ הוּא שַׁלִּיט עַל כֹּלָּא, אַנְתְּ הוּא דְּשַׁלִּיט עַל מַלְכַיָּא, וּמַלְכוּתָא דִּילָךְ הִיא. אֲנָא עַבְדָּא דְקֻדְשָׁא בְּרִיךְ הוּא, דְּסָגֵדְנָא קַמֵּהּ וּמִקַּמֵּי דִּיקַר אוֹרַיְתֵהּ בְּכָל עִדָּן וְעִדָּן. לָא עַל אֱנָשׁ רָחִיצְנָא וְלָא עַל בַּר אֱלָהִין סָמִיכְנָא, אֶלָּא בֶּאֱלָהָא דִשְׁמַיָּא, דְּהוּא אֱלָהָא קְשׁוֹט, וְאוֹרַיְתֵהּ קְשׁוֹט, וּנְבִיאוֹהִי קְשׁוֹט, וּמַסְגֵּא לְמֶעְבַּד טַבְוָן וּקְשׁוֹט. ◂ בֵּהּ אֲנָא רָחִיץ, וְלִשְׁמֵהּ קַדִּישָׁא יַקִּירָא אֲנָא אֵמַר תֻּשְׁבְּחָן. יְהֵא רַעֲוָא קֳדָמָךְ דְּתִפְתַּח לִבַּאי בְּאוֹרַיְתָא, וְתַשְׁלִים מִשְׁאֲלִין דְּלִבַּאי וְלִבָּא דְכָל עַמָּךְ יִשְׂרָאֵל לְטָב וּלְחַיִּין וְלִשְׁלָם.

REFLECTION

What language is this *tefilla* written in?

Why do you think it is written in a language that is not Hebrew?

Do you prefer to pray in Hebrew or English? What are the benefits of each?

... A THOUSAND WORDS

The Leader takes the Torah scroll in his right arm, bows toward the Ark and says:

Magnify the LORD with me, and let us elevate His name together. *Ps. 34*

The Ark is closed. The Leader carries the Torah scroll to the bima and the congregation says:

לְךָ Yours, LORD, are the greatness and the power, the glory and the majesty and splendor, for everything in heaven and earth is Yours. Yours, LORD, is the kingdom; You are elevated as Head over all. *1 Chr. 29*

רוֹמְמוּ Elevate the LORD our God and bow to His footstool; He is holy. Elevate thE Lord our God, and bow at His holy mountain, for holy is the LORD our God. *Ps. 99*

אַב הָרַחֲמִים May the Father of compassion have compassion on the people borne by Him. May He remember the covenant with the mighty [patriarchs], and save us from evil times. May He reproach the evil instinct in the people carried by Him, and generously grant that we be an everlasting remnant. May He fulfill in good measure our requests for salvation and compassion.

The Torah scroll is placed on the bima and the Gabbai calls a Kohen to the Torah.

May His kingship over us be soon revealed and made seen. May He be generous to our surviving remnant, the survivors of His people the house of Israel in grace, loving-kindness, compassion and favor, and let us say: Amen. Let us all give greatness to our God and give honor to the Torah. *Let the Kohen come forward. Arise (*name* son of *father's name*), the Kohen.

**If no Kohen is present, a Levi or Yisrael is called up as follows:*

/As there is no Kohen, arise (*name* son of *father's name*) in place of a Kohen./

Blessed is He who, in His holiness, gave the Torah to His people Israel.

Congregation followed by the Gabbai:

You who cling to the LORD your God are all alive today. *Deut. 4*

The appropriate Torah portions are to be found from page 1070.

CONNECTION

"The public reading of the Torah is as ancient an institution as prayer itself. The synagogue thus became not only a house of prayer but also a house of study. The result is a dynamic tension between speaking and listening. In prayer, we speak to God. In study we listen to God speaking to us, His word unchanged and undiminished across the centuries."

(Rabbi Jonathan Sacks)

The שליח ציבור *takes the* ספר תורה *in his right arm, bows toward the* ארון קודש *and says:*

גַּדְּלוּ לַיהוה אִתִּי וּנְרוֹמְמָה שְׁמוֹ יַחְדָּו: תהלים לד

The ארון קודש *is closed. The* שליח ציבור *carries the* ספר תורה *to the* בימה *and the* קהל *says:*

לְךָ יהוה הַגְּדֻלָּה וְהַגְּבוּרָה וְהַתִּפְאֶרֶת וְהַנֵּצַח וְהַהוֹד, כִּי־כֹל בַּשָּׁמַיִם וּבָאָרֶץ, לְךָ יהוה הַמַּמְלָכָה וְהַמִּתְנַשֵּׂא לְכֹל לְרֹאשׁ: דברי הימים א, כט

רוֹמְמוּ יהוה אֱלֹהֵינוּ וְהִשְׁתַּחֲווּ לַהֲדֹם רַגְלָיו, קָדוֹשׁ הוּא: רוֹמְמוּ יהוה אֱלֹהֵינוּ וְהִשְׁתַּחֲווּ לְהַר קָדְשׁוֹ, כִּי־קָדוֹשׁ יהוה אֱלֹהֵינוּ: תהלים צט

אַב הָרַחֲמִים הוּא יְרַחֵם עַם עֲמוּסִים, וְיִזְכֹּר בְּרִית אֵיתָנִים, וְיַצִּיל נַפְשׁוֹתֵינוּ מִן הַשָּׁעוֹת הָרָעוֹת, וְיִגְעַר בְּיֵצֶר הָרָע מִן הַנְּשׂוּאִים, וְיָחֹן אוֹתָנוּ לִפְלֵיטַת עוֹלָמִים, וִימַלֵּא מִשְׁאֲלוֹתֵינוּ בְּמִדָּה טוֹבָה יְשׁוּעָה וְרַחֲמִים.

The ספר תורה *is placed on the* שולחן *and the* גבאי *calls a* כהן *to the* תורה.

וְתִגָּלֶה וְתֵרָאֶה מַלְכוּתוֹ עָלֵינוּ בִּזְמַן קָרוֹב, וְיָחֹן פְּלֵיטָתֵנוּ וּפְלֵיטַת עַמּוֹ בֵּית יִשְׂרָאֵל לְחֵן וּלְחֶסֶד וּלְרַחֲמִים וּלְרָצוֹן וְנֹאמַר אָמֵן. הַכֹּל הָבוּ גֹדֶל לֵאלֹהֵינוּ וּתְנוּ כָבוֹד לַתּוֹרָה.

*כֹּהֵן קְרַב, יַעֲמֹד (פלוני בֶּן פלוני) הַכֹּהֵן.

**If no* כהן *is present, a* לוי *or* ישראל *is called up as follows:*

/אֵין כָּאן כֹּהֵן, יַעֲמֹד (פלוני בֶּן פלוני) בִּמְקוֹם כֹּהֵן./

בָּרוּךְ שֶׁנָּתַן תּוֹרָה לְעַמּוֹ יִשְׂרָאֵל בִּקְדֻשָּׁתוֹ.

קהל *followed by the* גבאי:

וְאַתֶּם הַדְּבֵקִים בַּיהוה אֱלֹהֵיכֶם חַיִּים כֻּלְּכֶם הַיּוֹם: דברים ד

The appropriate תורה *portions are to be found from page 1070.*

REFLECTION

"Keriat HaTorah *is a reenactment of the original experience of* Matan Torah."

(Rabbi J.B. Soloveitchik)

Is there a significant difference between reading the Torah at the following times?

- Together in public in the *beit knesset*.
- On our own at home.
- With a *ḥavruta* in the *beit midrash*.

The Reader shows the oleh the section to be read. The oleh touches the scroll at that place with the tzitzit of his tallit, which he then kisses. Holding the handles of the scroll, he says:

Oleh: Bless the LORD, the blessed One.

Cong: Bless the LORD, the blessed One, for ever and all time.

Oleh: Bless the LORD, the blessed One, for ever and all time.

Blessed are You, LORD our God, King of the Universe,
who has chosen us from all peoples
and has given us His Torah.
Blessed are You, LORD, Giver of the Torah.

After the reading, the oleh says:

Oleh: Blessed are You, LORD our God, King of the Universe,
who has given us the Torah of truth,
planting everlasting life in our midst.
Blessed are You, LORD, Giver of the Torah.

One who has survived a situation of danger says:

Blessed are You, LORD our God, King of the Universe,
who bestows good on the unworthy, who has bestowed on me much good.

The congregation responds:

Amen. May He who bestowed much good on you
continue to bestow on you much good, Selah.

After a Bar Mitzva boy has finished the Torah blessing, his father says aloud:

Blessed is He who has released me from the responsibility for this child.

---

should hold the handles of the *Sefer Torah*, and take care to look away from the *Sefer Torah* so it doesn't look like he is reading the *berakha* from the *Sefer Torah*.

4. Originally the custom was that each *oleh* would read the section that he was called up for. But so as not to embarrass those who cannot, generally one person (the *ba'al keria*) reads all the sections. However, the *oleh* should read along in a whisper the verses that are being read from the *Sefer Torah*.

5. After saying the *berakha* after the reading, the *oleh* should remain at the *bima*, either alongside the next *oleh* or on the other side of the reader (depending on the community's custom), for the following *aliya*, so as to show honor to the Torah and not appear as if he is trying to escape as quickly as possible.

The קורא *shows the* עולה *the section to be read. The* עולה *touches the* ספר תורה *at that place with the* ציצית *of his* טלית*, which he then kisses. Holding the handles of the* ספר תורה*, he says:*

עולה: **בָּרְכוּ אֶת יהוה הַמְבֹרָךְ.**

קהל: בָּרוּךְ יהוה הַמְבֹרָךְ לְעוֹלָם וָעֶד.

עולה: **בָּרוּךְ יהוה הַמְבֹרָךְ לְעוֹלָם וָעֶד.**
בָּרוּךְ אַתָּה יהוה, אֱלֹהֵינוּ מֶלֶךְ הָעוֹלָם
אֲשֶׁר בָּחַר בָּנוּ מִכָּל הָעַמִּים, וְנָתַן לָנוּ אֶת תּוֹרָתוֹ.
בָּרוּךְ אַתָּה יהוה, נוֹתֵן הַתּוֹרָה.

After the קריאת התורה*, the* עולה *says:*

עולה: **בָּרוּךְ אַתָּה יהוה אֱלֹהֵינוּ מֶלֶךְ הָעוֹלָם**
אֲשֶׁר נָתַן לָנוּ תּוֹרַת אֱמֶת, וְחַיֵּי עוֹלָם נָטַע בְּתוֹכֵנוּ.
בָּרוּךְ אַתָּה יהוה, נוֹתֵן הַתּוֹרָה.

One who has survived a situation of danger says:

בָּרוּךְ אַתָּה יהוה אֱלֹהֵינוּ מֶלֶךְ הָעוֹלָם
הַגּוֹמֵל לְחַיָּבִים טוֹבוֹת, שֶׁגְּמָלַנִי כָּל טוֹב.

The קהל *responds:*

אָמֵן. מִי שֶׁגְּמָלְךָ כָּל טוֹב הוּא, יִגְמָלְךָ כָּל טוֹב, סֶלָה.

After a בר מצווה *has finished the* תורה *blessing, his father says aloud:*

בָּרוּךְ שֶׁפְּטָרַנִי מֵעָנְשׁוֹ שֶׁלָּזֶה.

LEARNING

A guide to getting an *aliya*:

Since it is a mitzva to read from the Torah publicly, each section of the reading is preceded and followed by *berakhot* said by the one who is called up (the "*oleh*").

1. To show his love of this mitzva and not to delay the community the *oleh* should take the shortest, most direct route to the *bima*.
2. The *oleh* should be shown by the reader where the section to be read starts. Some have the custom to kiss the first words with the *tzitzit* of their tallit before making the *berakha*.
3. While making the *berakha*, the *oleh*

Special blessings and memorial prayers may be said at this point (below).

FOR A SICK MAN

May He who blessed our fathers, Abraham, Isaac and Jacob, Moses and Aaron, David and Solomon, bless and heal one who is ill, (*sick person's name*, son of *mother's name*), on whose behalf (*name of the one making the offering*) is making a contribution to charity. As a reward for this, may the Holy One, blessed be He, be filled with compassion for him, to restore his health, cure him, strengthen and revive him, sending him a swift and full recovery from heaven to all his 248 organs and 365 sinews, amongst the other sick ones in Israel, a healing of the spirit and a healing of the body, now, swiftly and soon, and let us say: Amen.

FOR A SICK WOMAN

May He who blessed our fathers, Abraham, Isaac and Jacob, Moses and Aaron, David and Solomon, bless and heal one who is ill, (*sick person's name*, daughter of *mother's name*), on whose behalf (*name of the one making the offering*) is making a contribution to charity. As a reward for this, may the Holy One, blessed be He, be filled with compassion for her, to restore her health, cure her, strengthen and revive her, sending her a swift and full recovery from heaven to all her organs and sinews, amongst the other sick ones in Israel, a healing of the spirit and a healing of the body, now, swiftly and soon, and let us say: Amen.

For a male close relative:

אֵל מָלֵא רַחֲמִים God, full of mercy, who is on high, give fitting rest on the wings of the Divine Presence, in the heights of the holy and the pure who shine like the radiance of heaven, to the soul of (*name* son of *father's name*) who has gone to his eternal home, and to this I pledge (without formal vow) to give charity in his memory, may his resting place be in the Garden of Eden. Therefore, Master of compassion, shelter him in the shadow of Your wings forever and bind his soul in the bond of everlasting life. The LORD is his heritage; may he rest in peace, and let us say: Amen.

For a female close relative:

אֵל מָלֵא רַחֲמִים God, full of mercy, who is on high, give fitting rest on the wings of the Divine Presence, in the heights of the holy and the pure who shine like the radiance of heaven, to the soul of (*name* daughter of *father's name*) who has gone to her eternal home, and to this I pledge (without formal vow) to give charity in her memory, may her resting place be in the Garden of Eden. Therefore, Master of compassion, shelter her in the shadow of Your wings forever and bind her soul in the bond of everlasting life. The LORD is her heritage; may she rest in peace, and let us say: Amen.

Special מי שבירך *and memorial prayers may be said at this point (below).*

מי שבירך לחולה

מִי שֶׁבֵּרַךְ אֲבוֹתֵינוּ אַבְרָהָם יִצְחָק וְיַעֲקֹב, מֹשֶׁה וְאַהֲרֹן דָּוִד וּשְׁלֹמֹה הוּא יְבָרֵךְ וִירַפֵּא אֶת הַחוֹלֶה (פלוני בֶּן פלונית) בַּעֲבוּר שֶׁ(פלוני בֶּן פלוני) נוֹדֵר צְדָקָה בַּעֲבוּרוֹ. בִּשְׂכַר זֶה הַקָּדוֹשׁ בָּרוּךְ הוּא יִמָּלֵא רַחֲמִים עָלָיו לְהַחֲלִימוֹ וּלְרַפְּאֹתוֹ וּלְהַחֲזִיקוֹ וּלְהַחֲיוֹתוֹ וְיִשְׁלַח לוֹ מְהֵרָה רְפוּאָה שְׁלֵמָה מִן הַשָּׁמַיִם לִרְמַ״ח אֵבָרָיו וּשְׁסָ״ה גִּידָיו בְּתוֹךְ שְׁאָר חוֹלֵי יִשְׂרָאֵל, רְפוּאַת הַנֶּפֶשׁ וּרְפוּאַת הַגּוּף, הַשְׁתָּא בַּעֲגָלָא וּבִזְמַן קָרִיב, וְנֹאמַר אָמֵן.

מי שבירך לחולָה

מִי שֶׁבֵּרַךְ אֲבוֹתֵינוּ אַבְרָהָם יִצְחָק וְיַעֲקֹב, מֹשֶׁה וְאַהֲרֹן דָּוִד וּשְׁלֹמֹה הוּא יְבָרֵךְ וִירַפֵּא אֶת הַחוֹלָה (פלונית בַּת פלונית) בַּעֲבוּר שֶׁ(פלוני בֶּן פלוני) נוֹדֵר צְדָקָה בַּעֲבוּרָהּ. בִּשְׂכַר זֶה הַקָּדוֹשׁ בָּרוּךְ הוּא יִמָּלֵא רַחֲמִים עָלֶיהָ לְהַחֲלִימָהּ וּלְרַפְּאֹתָהּ וּלְהַחֲזִיקָהּ וּלְהַחֲיוֹתָהּ וְיִשְׁלַח לָהּ מְהֵרָה רְפוּאָה שְׁלֵמָה מִן הַשָּׁמַיִם לְכָל אֵבָרֶיהָ וּלְכָל גִּידֶיהָ בְּתוֹךְ שְׁאָר חוֹלֵי יִשְׂרָאֵל, רְפוּאַת הַנֶּפֶשׁ וּרְפוּאַת הַגּוּף, הַשְׁתָּא בַּעֲגָלָא וּבִזְמַן קָרִיב, וְנֹאמַר אָמֵן.

For a male close relative:

אֵל מָלֵא רַחֲמִים, שׁוֹכֵן בַּמְּרוֹמִים, הַמְצֵא מְנוּחָה נְכוֹנָה עַל כַּנְפֵי הַשְּׁכִינָה, בְּמַעֲלוֹת קְדוֹשִׁים וּטְהוֹרִים, כְּזֹהַר הָרָקִיעַ מַזְהִירִים, לְנִשְׁמַת (פלוני בֶּן פלוני) שֶׁהָלַךְ לְעוֹלָמוֹ, בַּעֲבוּר שֶׁבְּלִי נֶדֶר אֶתֵּן צְדָקָה בְּעַד הַזְכָּרַת נִשְׁמָתוֹ, בְּגַן עֵדֶן תְּהֵא מְנוּחָתוֹ. לָכֵן, בַּעַל הָרַחֲמִים יַסְתִּירֵהוּ בְּסֵתֶר כְּנָפָיו לְעוֹלָמִים, וְיִצְרֹר בִּצְרוֹר הַחַיִּים אֶת נִשְׁמָתוֹ, יהוה הוּא נַחֲלָתוֹ, וְיָנוּחַ בְּשָׁלוֹם עַל מִשְׁכָּבוֹ, וְנֹאמַר אָמֵן.

For a female close relative:

אֵל מָלֵא רַחֲמִים, שׁוֹכֵן בַּמְּרוֹמִים, הַמְצֵא מְנוּחָה נְכוֹנָה עַל כַּנְפֵי הַשְּׁכִינָה, בְּמַעֲלוֹת קְדוֹשִׁים וּטְהוֹרִים, כְּזֹהַר הָרָקִיעַ מַזְהִירִים, לְנִשְׁמַת (פלונית בַּת פלוני) שֶׁהָלְכָה לְעוֹלָמָהּ, בַּעֲבוּר שֶׁבְּלִי נֶדֶר אֶתֵּן צְדָקָה בְּעַד הַזְכָּרַת נִשְׁמָתָהּ, בְּגַן עֵדֶן תְּהֵא מְנוּחָתָהּ. לָכֵן, בַּעַל הָרַחֲמִים יַסְתִּירֶהָ בְּסֵתֶר כְּנָפָיו לְעוֹלָמִים, וְיִצְרֹר בִּצְרוֹר הַחַיִּים אֶת נִשְׁמָתָהּ, יהוה הוּא נַחֲלָתָהּ, וְתָנוּחַ בְּשָׁלוֹם עַל מִשְׁכָּבָהּ, וְנֹאמַר אָמֵן.

HALF KADDISH

After the Reading of the Torah, the Reader says Half Kaddish:

Reader: יִתְגַּדַּל Magnified and sanctified may His great name be,
in the world He created by His will.
May He establish His kingdom in your lifetime and in your days,
and in the lifetime of all the house of Israel,
swiftly and soon – and say: Amen.

All: May His great name be blessed for ever and all time.

Reader: Blessed and praised, glorified and elevated,
raised and honored, uplifted and praised
be the name of the Holy One, blessed be He,
beyond any blessing, song, praise and consolation
uttered in the world – and say: Amen.

The Torah scroll is lifted and the congregation says:

וְזֹאת הַתּוֹרָה This is the Torah *Deut. 4*
that Moses placed before the children of Israel,
at the LORD's commandment, by the hand of Moses. *Num. 9*

Some add: It is a tree of life to those who grasp it, and those who uphold it are happy. Its ways are ways of pleasantness, and all its paths are peace. Long life is at its right hand; at its left, riches and honor. It pleased the LORD for the sake of [Israel's] righteousness, to make the Torah great and glorious. *Prov. 3* *Is. 42*

... A THOUSAND WORDS

חצי קדיש

After the קריאת התורה*, the* קורא *says* חצי קדיש*:*

קורא: **יִתְגַּדַּל וְיִתְקַדַּשׁ שְׁמֵהּ רַבָּא** (קהל: אָמֵן)
בְּעָלְמָא דִּי בְרָא כִרְעוּתֵהּ
וְיַמְלִיךְ מַלְכוּתֵהּ
בְּחַיֵּיכוֹן וּבְיוֹמֵיכוֹן
וּבְחַיֵּי דְכָל בֵּית יִשְׂרָאֵל
בַּעֲגָלָא וּבִזְמַן קָרִיב
וְאִמְרוּ אָמֵן. (קהל: אָמֵן)

קורא וקהל: **יְהֵא שְׁמֵהּ רַבָּא מְבָרַךְ לְעָלַם וּלְעָלְמֵי עָלְמַיָּא.**

קורא: **יִתְבָּרַךְ וְיִשְׁתַּבַּח וְיִתְפָּאַר וְיִתְרוֹמַם וְיִתְנַשֵּׂא**
וְיִתְהַדָּר וְיִתְעַלֶּה וְיִתְהַלָּל
שְׁמֵהּ דְּקֻדְשָׁא בְּרִיךְ הוּא (קהל: בְּרִיךְ הוּא)
לְעֵלָּא מִן כָּל בִּרְכָתָא
/בעשרת ימי תשובה: **לְעֵלָּא לְעֵלָּא מִכָּל בִּרְכָתָא**/
וְשִׁירָתָא, תֻּשְׁבְּחָתָא וְנֶחֱמָתָא
דַּאֲמִירָן בְּעָלְמָא
וְאִמְרוּ אָמֵן. (קהל: אָמֵן)

The ספר תורה *is lifted and the* קהל *says:*

וְזֹאת הַתּוֹרָה אֲשֶׁר־שָׂם מֹשֶׁה לִפְנֵי בְּנֵי יִשְׂרָאֵל: דברים ד
עַל־פִּי יהוה בְּיַד־מֹשֶׁה: במדבר ט

Some add עֵץ־חַיִּים הִיא לַמַּחֲזִיקִים בָּהּ וְתֹמְכֶיהָ מְאֻשָּׁר: משלי ג
דְּרָכֶיהָ דַרְכֵי־נֹעַם וְכָל־נְתִיבוֹתֶיהָ שָׁלוֹם:
אֹרֶךְ יָמִים בִּימִינָהּ, בִּשְׂמֹאולָהּ עֹשֶׁר וְכָבוֹד:
יהוה חָפֵץ לְמַעַן צִדְקוֹ יַגְדִּיל תּוֹרָה וְיַאְדִּיר: ישעיה מב

On those Mondays and Thursdays when Taḥanun is said,
the Leader says the following while the Torah scroll is being bound:

יְהִי רָצוֹן May it be the will of our Father in heaven
to establish (the Temple), home of our life,
and to restore His Presence to our midst, swiftly in our days –
and let us say: Amen.

יְהִי רָצוֹן May it be the will of our Father in heaven
to have compassion on us and our remnant,
and to keep destruction and plague away from us
and from all His people the house of Israel –
and let us say: Amen.

יְהִי רָצוֹן May it be the will of our Father in heaven
to preserve among us the sages of Israel:
them, their wives, their sons and daughters,
their disciples and their disciples' disciples,
in all their dwelling places –
and let us say: Amen.

יְהִי רָצוֹן May it be the will of our Father in heaven
that we may hear and be given good tidings
of salvation and consolation,
and that our dispersed be gathered
from the four quarters of the earth –
and let us say: Amen.

All:

אַחֵינוּ As for our brothers of the whole house of Israel
who are in distress or captivity, on sea or land,
may the All-Present have compassion on them
and lead them from distress to relief,
from darkness to light, and from oppression to freedom,
now, swiftly and soon –
and let us say: Amen.

The prayers for the welfare of the American and Canadian governments and for
the safety of the American and Canadian militaries, can be found on pages 650–652.
The prayer for the State of Israel, and for the Israel Defence Forces,
can be found on pages 654–656.

On those Mondays and Thursdays when תחנון *is said,*
the שליח ציבור *says the following while the* ספר תורה *is being bound:*

יְהִי רָצוֹן מִלִּפְנֵי אָבִינוּ שֶׁבַּשָּׁמַיִם
לְכוֹנֵן אֶת בֵּית חַיֵּינוּ
וּלְהָשִׁיב אֶת שְׁכִינָתוֹ בְּתוֹכֵנוּ
בִּמְהֵרָה בְיָמֵינוּ, וְנֹאמַר אָמֵן.

יְהִי רָצוֹן מִלִּפְנֵי אָבִינוּ שֶׁבַּשָּׁמַיִם
לְרַחֵם עָלֵינוּ וְעַל פְּלֵיטָתֵנוּ
וְלִמְנֹעַ מַשְׁחִית וּמַגֵּפָה מֵעָלֵינוּ
וּמֵעַל כָּל עַמּוֹ בֵּית יִשְׂרָאֵל, וְנֹאמַר אָמֵן.

יְהִי רָצוֹן מִלִּפְנֵי אָבִינוּ שֶׁבַּשָּׁמַיִם
לְקַיֶּם בָּנוּ חַכְמֵי יִשְׂרָאֵל
הֵם וּנְשֵׁיהֶם וּבְנֵיהֶם וּבְנוֹתֵיהֶם
וְתַלְמִידֵיהֶם וְתַלְמִידֵי תַלְמִידֵיהֶם
בְּכָל מְקוֹמוֹת מוֹשְׁבוֹתֵיהֶם, וְנֹאמַר אָמֵן.

יְהִי רָצוֹן מִלִּפְנֵי אָבִינוּ שֶׁבַּשָּׁמַיִם
שֶׁנִּשְׁמַע וְנִתְבַּשֵּׂר בְּשׂוֹרוֹת טוֹבוֹת, יְשׁוּעוֹת וְנֶחָמוֹת
וִיקַבֵּץ נִדָּחֵינוּ מֵאַרְבַּע כַּנְפוֹת הָאָרֶץ, וְנֹאמַר אָמֵן.

All:

אַחֵינוּ כָּל בֵּית יִשְׂרָאֵל
הַנְּתוּנִים בְּצָרָה וּבְשִׁבְיָה, הָעוֹמְדִים בֵּין בַּיָּם וּבֵין בַּיַּבָּשָׁה
הַמָּקוֹם יְרַחֵם עֲלֵיהֶם וְיוֹצִיאֵם מִצָּרָה לִרְוָחָה
וּמֵאֲפֵלָה לְאוֹרָה, וּמִשִּׁעְבּוּד לִגְאֻלָּה
הַשְׁתָּא בַּעֲגָלָא וּבִזְמַן קָרִיב
וְנֹאמַר אָמֵן.

The prayers for the welfare of the American and Canadian governments and for the safety of the American and Canadian militaries, can be found on pages 651–653.
The prayer for the State of Israel, and for the Israel Defence Forces, can be found on pages 655–657.

RETURNING THE TORAH TO THE ARK

The Ark is opened. The Leader takes the Torah scroll and says:

יְהַלְלוּ Let them praise the name of the LORD, *Ps. 148*
for His name alone is sublime.

The congregation responds:

הוֹדוֹ His majesty is above earth and heaven.
He has raised the horn of His people,
for the glory of all His devoted ones,
the children of Israel, the people close to Him. Halleluya!

As the Torah scroll is returned to the Ark, say:

לְדָוִד מִזְמוֹר A psalm of David. The earth is the LORD's and all it contains, *Ps. 24* the world and all who live in it. For He founded it on the seas and established it on the streams. Who may climb the mountain of the LORD? Who may stand in His holy place? He who has clean hands and a pure heart, who has not taken My name in vain, or sworn falsely. He shall receive blessing from the LORD, and just reward from God, his salvation. This is a generation of those who seek Him, the descendants of Jacob who seek Your presence, Selah! Lift up your heads, O gates; be uplifted, eternal doors, so that the King of glory may enter. Who is the King of glory? It is the LORD, strong and mighty, the LORD mighty in battle. Lift up your heads, O gates; lift them up, eternal doors, so that the King of glory may enter. Who is He, the King of glory? The LORD of multitudes, He is the King of glory, Selah!

As the Torah scroll is placed into the Ark, say:

וּבְנֻחֹה יֹאמַר When the Ark came to rest, Moses would say: "Return, *Num. 10* O LORD, to the countless thousands of Israel." Advance, LORD, to *Ps. 132* Your resting place, You and Your mighty Ark. Your priests are clothed in righteousness, and Your devoted ones sing in joy. For the sake of Your servant David, do not reject Your anointed one. For I give you *Prov. 4* good instruction; do not abandon My Torah. It is a tree of life to those *Prov. 3* who grasp it, and those who uphold it are happy. Its ways are ways of pleasantness, and all its paths are peace. ▸ Turn us back, O LORD, to *Lam. 5* You, and we will return. Renew our days as of old.

The Ark is closed.

הכנסת ספר תורה

The ארון קודש *is opened. The* שליח ציבור *takes the* ספר תורה *and says:*

יְהַלְלוּ אֶת־שֵׁם יהוה, כִּי נִשְׂגָּב־שְׁמוֹ, לְבַדּוֹ תהלים קמח

The קהל *responds:*

הוֹדוֹ עַל־אֶרֶץ וְשָׁמָיִם:
וַיָּרֶם קֶרֶן לְעַמּוֹ, תְּהִלָּה לְכָל־חֲסִידָיו
לִבְנֵי יִשְׂרָאֵל עַם קְרֹבוֹ, הַלְלוּיָהּ:

As the ספר תורה *is returned to the* ארון קודש*, say:*

לְדָוִד מִזְמוֹר, לַיהוה הָאָרֶץ וּמְלוֹאָהּ, תֵּבֵל וְיֹשְׁבֵי בָהּ: כִּי־הוּא עַל־ תהלים כד
יַמִּים יְסָדָהּ, וְעַל־נְהָרוֹת יְכוֹנְנֶהָ: מִי־יַעֲלֶה בְהַר־יהוה, וּמִי־יָקוּם
בִּמְקוֹם קָדְשׁוֹ: נְקִי כַפַּיִם וּבַר־לֵבָב, אֲשֶׁר לֹא־נָשָׂא לַשָּׁוְא נַפְשִׁי
וְלֹא נִשְׁבַּע לְמִרְמָה: יִשָּׂא בְרָכָה מֵאֵת יהוה, וּצְדָקָה מֵאֱלֹהֵי יִשְׁעוֹ:
זֶה דּוֹר דֹּרְשָׁו, מְבַקְשֵׁי פָנֶיךָ, יַעֲקֹב, סֶלָה: שְׂאוּ שְׁעָרִים רָאשֵׁיכֶם,
וְהִנָּשְׂאוּ פִּתְחֵי עוֹלָם, וְיָבוֹא מֶלֶךְ הַכָּבוֹד: מִי זֶה מֶלֶךְ הַכָּבוֹד, יהוה
עִזּוּז וְגִבּוֹר, יהוה גִּבּוֹר מִלְחָמָה: שְׂאוּ שְׁעָרִים רָאשֵׁיכֶם, וּשְׂאוּ פִּתְחֵי
עוֹלָם, וְיָבֹא מֶלֶךְ הַכָּבוֹד: מִי הוּא זֶה מֶלֶךְ הַכָּבוֹד, יהוה צְבָאוֹת
הוּא מֶלֶךְ הַכָּבוֹד, סֶלָה:

As the ספר תורה *is placed into the* ארון קודש*, say:*

וּבְנֻחֹה יֹאמַר, שׁוּבָה יהוה רִבְבוֹת אַלְפֵי יִשְׂרָאֵל: קוּמָה יהוה במדבר י / תהלים קלב
לִמְנוּחָתֶךָ, אַתָּה וַאֲרוֹן עֻזֶּךָ: כֹּהֲנֶיךָ יִלְבְּשׁוּ־צֶדֶק, וַחֲסִידֶיךָ יְרַנֵּנוּ:
בַּעֲבוּר דָּוִד עַבְדֶּךָ אַל־תָּשֵׁב פְּנֵי מְשִׁיחֶךָ: כִּי לֶקַח טוֹב נָתַתִּי משלי ד
לָכֶם, תּוֹרָתִי אַל־תַּעֲזֹבוּ: עֵץ־חַיִּים הִיא לַמַּחֲזִיקִים בָּהּ, וְתֹמְכֶיהָ משלי ג
מְאֻשָּׁר: דְּרָכֶיהָ דַרְכֵי־נֹעַם וְכָל־נְתִיבֹתֶיהָ שָׁלוֹם: ◂ הֲשִׁיבֵנוּ יהוה איכה ה
אֵלֶיךָ וְנָשׁוּבָה, חַדֵּשׁ יָמֵינוּ כְּקֶדֶם:

The ארון קודש *is closed.*

CONCLUSION OF THE SERVICE

Some have the custom to touch the hand-tefillin at °, and the head-tefillin at °°.

אַשְׁרֵי Happy are those who live in Your House; *Ps. 84*
they shall continue to praise You, Selah!
Happy are the people for whom this is so; *Ps. 144*
happy are the people whose God is the LORD.

A song of praise by David. *Ps. 145*

א I will elevate You, my God, the King, and bless Your name for ever and all time. ב Every day I will bless You, and praise Your name for ever and all time. ג Great is the LORD and greatly to be praised; His greatness is unfathomable. ד One generation will praise Your works to the next, and tell of Your mighty deeds. ה On the glorious splendor of Your majesty I will meditate, and on the acts of Your wonders. ו They shall talk of the power of Your awesome deeds, and I will tell of Your greatness. ז They shall recite the record of Your great goodness, and sing with joy of Your righteousness. ח The LORD is generous and compassionate, slow to anger and great in loving-kindness. ט The LORD is good to all, and His compassion extends to all His works. י All Your works shall thank You, LORD, and Your devoted ones shall bless You. כ They shall talk of the glory of Your kingship, and speak of Your might. ל To make known to mankind His mighty deeds and the glorious majesty of His kingship. מ Your kingdom is an everlasting kingdom, and Your reign is for all generations. ס The LORD supports all who fall, and raises all who are bowed down. ע All raise their eyes to You in hope, and You give them their food in due season. פ °You open Your hand, °°and satisfy every living thing with favor. צ The LORD is righteous in all His ways, and kind in all He does. ק The LORD is close to all who call on Him, to all who call on Him in truth. ר He fulfills the will of those who fear Him; He hears their cry and saves them.

סיום התפילה

Some have the custom to touch the תפילין של יד *at* °, *and the* תפילין של ראש *at* °°.

אַשְׁרֵי יוֹשְׁבֵי בֵיתֶךָ, עוֹד יְהַלְלְוּךָ סֶּלָה: תהלים פד

אַשְׁרֵי הָעָם שֶׁכָּכָה לּוֹ, אַשְׁרֵי הָעָם שֶׁיהוה אֱלֹהָיו: תהלים קמד

תְּהִלָּה לְדָוִד תהלים קמה

אֲרוֹמִמְךָ אֱלוֹהַי הַמֶּלֶךְ, וַאֲבָרְכָה שִׁמְךָ לְעוֹלָם וָעֶד:

בְּכָל־יוֹם אֲבָרְכֶךָּ, וַאֲהַלְלָה שִׁמְךָ לְעוֹלָם וָעֶד:

גָּדוֹל יהוה וּמְהֻלָּל מְאֹד, וְלִגְדֻלָּתוֹ אֵין חֵקֶר:

דּוֹר לְדוֹר יְשַׁבַּח מַעֲשֶׂיךָ, וּגְבוּרֹתֶיךָ יַגִּידוּ:

הֲדַר כְּבוֹד הוֹדֶךָ, וְדִבְרֵי נִפְלְאֹתֶיךָ אָשִׂיחָה:

וֶעֱזוּז נוֹרְאֹתֶיךָ יֹאמֵרוּ, וּגְדוּלָּתְךָ אֲסַפְּרֶנָּה:

זֵכֶר רַב־טוּבְךָ יַבִּיעוּ, וְצִדְקָתְךָ יְרַנֵּנוּ:

חַנּוּן וְרַחוּם יהוה, אֶרֶךְ אַפַּיִם וּגְדָל־חָסֶד:

טוֹב־יהוה לַכֹּל, וְרַחֲמָיו עַל־כָּל־מַעֲשָׂיו:

יוֹדְוּךָ יהוה כָּל־מַעֲשֶׂיךָ, וַחֲסִידֶיךָ יְבָרְכוּכָה:

כְּבוֹד מַלְכוּתְךָ יֹאמֵרוּ, וּגְבוּרָתְךָ יְדַבֵּרוּ:

לְהוֹדִיעַ לִבְנֵי הָאָדָם גְּבוּרֹתָיו, וּכְבוֹד הֲדַר מַלְכוּתוֹ:

מַלְכוּתְךָ מַלְכוּת כָּל־עֹלָמִים, וּמֶמְשַׁלְתְּךָ בְּכָל־דּוֹר וָדֹר:

סוֹמֵךְ יהוה לְכָל־הַנֹּפְלִים, וְזוֹקֵף לְכָל־הַכְּפוּפִים:

עֵינֵי־כֹל אֵלֶיךָ יְשַׂבֵּרוּ, וְאַתָּה נוֹתֵן־לָהֶם אֶת־אָכְלָם בְּעִתּוֹ:

°פּוֹתֵחַ אֶת־יָדֶךָ, °°וּמַשְׂבִּיעַ לְכָל־חַי רָצוֹן:

צַדִּיק יהוה בְּכָל־דְּרָכָיו, וְחָסִיד בְּכָל־מַעֲשָׂיו:

קָרוֹב יהוה לְכָל־קֹרְאָיו, לְכֹל אֲשֶׁר יִקְרָאֻהוּ בֶאֱמֶת:

רְצוֹן־יְרֵאָיו יַעֲשֶׂה, וְאֶת־שַׁוְעָתָם יִשְׁמַע, וְיוֹשִׁיעֵם:

ש The LORD guards all who love Him, but all the wicked He will destroy. ת ▸ My mouth shall speak the praise of the LORD, and all creatures shall bless His holy name for ever and all time.

We will bless the LORD now and for ever. Halleluya! Ps. 115

Omit on Rosh Hodesh, Hol HaMo'ed, Erev Pesah, Erev Yom Kippur, Hanukka, the 14th and 15th of Adar I, Purim and Shushan Purim, Yom HaAtzma'ut, Yom Yerushalayim, Tisha B'Av, or in a house of mourning, and in Israel on Isru Hag.

לַמְנַצֵּחַ For the conductor of music. A psalm of David. May the LORD answer you when you are in distress; may the name of Jacob's God protect you. May He send you help from the Sanctuary and support from Zion. May He remember all your meal-offerings and accept your burnt-offerings, Selah! May He give you your heart's desire and make all your plans succeed. We will shout for joy at Your salvation and lift a banner in the name of our God. May the LORD fulfill all your requests. Now I know that the LORD saves His anointed; He answers him from His holy heaven with the saving power of His right hand. Some trust in chariots, others in horses, but we call on the name of the LORD our God. They were brought to their knees and fell, but we rose up and stood firm. ▸ LORD, save! May the King answer us on the day we call. Ps. 20

CONNECTION

There was once a man sitting in his house when a hurricane struck. As the house and neighborhood flooded, he ran upstairs to the roof. Suddenly a helicopter flew by and the people inside it threw down a ladder. They shouted down to him, "Grab on."

"No. Go away. I trust that God will save me," he refused.

A boat came and threw him a life saver. The sailor said, "Grab on."

"No. Go away. I trust that God will save me," he shouted as the water kept rising.

The man drowned. When he entered heaven, he turned to God and said, "Hashem, I trusted in You that You would save me. Why didn't You save me?"

God turned to him and said, "Who do you think sent you the helicopter and the boat?"

שׁוֹמֵר יהוה אֶת־כָּל־אֹהֲבָיו, וְאֵת כָּל־הָרְשָׁעִים יַשְׁמִיד:
› תְּהִלַּת יהוה יְדַבֶּר פִּי, וִיבָרֵךְ כָּל־בָּשָׂר שֵׁם קָדְשׁוֹ לְעוֹלָם וָעֶד:
תהלים קטו וַאֲנַחְנוּ נְבָרֵךְ יָהּ מֵעַתָּה וְעַד־עוֹלָם, הַלְלוּיָהּ:

Omit on ראש חודש, חול המועד, ערב פסח, ערב יום כיפור, חנוכה,
the 14th and 15th of אדר א׳, פורים *and* שושן פורים, יום העצמאות,
אסרו חג *on* ארץ ישראל, תשעה באב, *or in a house of mourning, and in* יום ירושלים.

תהלים כ לַמְנַצֵּחַ מִזְמוֹר לְדָוִד: יַעַנְךָ יהוה בְּיוֹם צָרָה, יְשַׂגֶּבְךָ שֵׁם אֱלֹהֵי
יַעֲקֹב: יִשְׁלַח־עֶזְרְךָ מִקֹּדֶשׁ, וּמִצִּיּוֹן יִסְעָדֶךָּ: יִזְכֹּר כָּל־מִנְחֹתֶיךָ,
וְעוֹלָתְךָ יְדַשְּׁנֶה סֶלָה: יִתֶּן־לְךָ כִלְבָבֶךָ וְכָל־עֲצָתְךָ יְמַלֵּא: נְרַנְּנָה
בִּישׁוּעָתֶךָ, וּבְשֵׁם־אֱלֹהֵינוּ נִדְגֹּל, יְמַלֵּא יהוה כָּל־מִשְׁאֲלוֹתֶיךָ:
עַתָּה יָדַעְתִּי כִּי הוֹשִׁיעַ יהוה מְשִׁיחוֹ, יַעֲנֵהוּ מִשְּׁמֵי קָדְשׁוֹ,
בִּגְבֻרוֹת יֵשַׁע יְמִינוֹ: אֵלֶּה בָרֶכֶב וְאֵלֶּה בַסּוּסִים, וַאֲנַחְנוּ בְּשֵׁם־
יהוה אֱלֹהֵינוּ נַזְכִּיר: הֵמָּה כָּרְעוּ וְנָפָלוּ, וַאֲנַחְנוּ קַּמְנוּ וַנִּתְעוֹדָד:
› יהוה הוֹשִׁיעָה, הַמֶּלֶךְ יַעֲנֵנוּ בְיוֹם־קָרְאֵנוּ:

LEARNING

This *mizmor* was originally composed when David sent his captain Yoav with the army to confront the massive forces that Avshalom had assembled against David's kingdom (*Shmuel Beit* 18). On this occasion David chose not to accompany his army. He felt that he would be more effective if he stayed in Jerusalem and prayed for the success of his army.

This *mizmor* is a prayer, although he presented it in the form of a blessing to the men who were about to face the danger of fighting and who would desperately need God's help. In the *mizmor* David emphasizes our belief that God will respond to our supplications.

REFLECTION

"Sometimes one must look into ashes to find a solitary spark"
(Rabbi Dov Ber of Mezeritch)

How has God supported you in difficult times?

What difficulties in your life have made you turn to God?

In a house of mourning and on Tisha B'Av omit the verse beginning "As for Me" and continue with "You are the Holy One."

וּבָא לְצִיּוֹן גּוֹאֵל "A redeemer will come to Zion, to those in Jacob who repent of their sins," declares the LORD. *Is. 59*

"As for Me, this is My covenant with them," says the LORD. "My spirit, that is on you, and My words I have placed in your mouth will not depart from your mouth, or from the mouth of your children, or from the mouth of their descendants from this time on and for ever," says the LORD.

▸ You are the Holy One, enthroned on the praises of Israel. And (the angels) call to one another, saying, "Holy, holy, holy is the LORD of multitudes; the whole world is filled with His glory." *Ps. 22* *Is. 6*

And they receive permission from one another, saying: "Holy in the highest heavens, home of His Presence; holy on earth, the work of His strength; holy for ever and all time is the LORD of multitudes; the whole earth is full of His radiant glory." *Targum Yonatan Is. 6*

▸ Then a wind lifted me up and I heard behind me the sound of a great noise, saying, "Blessed is the LORD's glory from His place." *Ezek. 3*

Then a wind lifted me up and I heard behind me the sound of a great tempest of those who uttered praise, saying, "Blessed is the LORD's glory from the place of the home of His Presence." *Targum Yonatan Ezek. 3*

The LORD shall reign for ever and all time. *Ex. 15*

The LORD's kingdom is established for ever and all time. *Targum Onkelos Ex. 15*

---

to *hol*, from the presence of God to the mundane world outside. The answer of the sages in constructing the morning prayer is to "learn a little bit of Torah." After prayer, one must engage in learning. When you have finished praying, it is truly over. But when you finish learning, the Torah accompanies you because it is part of you. In other words, even though the Torah is the word of the living God and an intimate encounter with Him, it can accompany us in the everyday world.

CONNECTION

The Maggid of Kosznitz once turned to a little boy and said to him, "I'll give you a ruble if you can tell me where God is."

The little boy paused thoughtfully and with a smile replied to the Maggid, "I'll give you two if you can tell me where He isn't."

The little boy became the first Hasidic Gerer Rebbe.

In a house of mourning and on תשעה באב *omit the verse beginning* וַאֲנִי זֹאת בְּרִיתִי *and continue with* וְאַתָּה קָדוֹשׁ.

ישעיה נט

וּבָא לְצִיּוֹן גּוֹאֵל, וּלְשָׁבֵי פֶשַׁע בְּיַעֲקֹב, נְאֻם יהוה:
וַאֲנִי זֹאת בְּרִיתִי אוֹתָם, אָמַר יהוה, רוּחִי אֲשֶׁר עָלֶיךָ וּדְבָרַי
אֲשֶׁר־שַׂמְתִּי בְּפִיךָ, לֹא־יָמוּשׁוּ מִפִּיךָ וּמִפִּי זַרְעֲךָ וּמִפִּי זֶרַע זַרְעֲךָ,
אָמַר יהוה, מֵעַתָּה וְעַד־עוֹלָם:

תהלים כב
ישעיה ו

▸ וְאַתָּה קָדוֹשׁ יוֹשֵׁב תְּהִלּוֹת יִשְׂרָאֵל: וְקָרָא זֶה אֶל־זֶה וְאָמַר
קָדוֹשׁ, קָדוֹשׁ, קָדוֹשׁ, יהוה צְבָאוֹת, מְלֹא כָל־הָאָרֶץ כְּבוֹדוֹ:

תרגום יונתן ישעיה ו

וּמְקַבְּלִין דֵּין מִן דֵּין וְאָמְרִין, קַדִּישׁ בִּשְׁמֵי מְרוֹמָא עִלָּאָה בֵּית שְׁכִינְתֵהּ,
קַדִּישׁ עַל אַרְעָא עוֹבַד גְּבוּרְתֵהּ, קַדִּישׁ לְעָלַם וּלְעָלְמֵי עָלְמַיָּא, יהוה צְבָאוֹת,
מַלְיָא כָל אַרְעָא זִיו יְקָרֵהּ.

יחזקאל ג

▸ וַתִּשָּׂאֵנִי רוּחַ, וָאֶשְׁמַע אַחֲרַי קוֹל רַעַשׁ גָּדוֹל, בָּרוּךְ כְּבוֹד־יהוה
מִמְּקוֹמוֹ:

תרגום יונתן יחזקאל ג

וּנְטָלַתְנִי רוּחָא, וּשְׁמָעִית בַּתְרַי קָל זִיעַ סַגִּיא, דִּמְשַׁבְּחִין וְאָמְרִין, בְּרִיךְ יְקָרָא
דַיהוה מֵאֲתַר בֵּית שְׁכִינְתֵהּ.

שמות טו

יהוה יִמְלֹךְ לְעֹלָם וָעֶד:

תרגום אונקלוס שמות טו

יהוה מַלְכוּתֵהּ קָאֵם לְעָלַם וּלְעָלְמֵי עָלְמַיָּא.

LEARNING

The *Kedusha* in the beginning of *Uva LeTziyon* is known as *Kedusha deSidra*. The Gemara (*Sota* 49a) asks: "On what does the world endure? On the *Kedusha deSidra* and on the *Yeheh shemeh raba* of *aggadeta*."

Rashi explains that *Kedusha deSidra* contains two elements, the sanctification of the name and the study of Torah. These two points interrelate and combine to create something unique.

The morning prayer is now basically complete. *Tefilla* ends with *Taḥanun*. What we are doing now is answering an important question: What do we do, how do we live, when we depart from *tefilla*, from the presence of God? This is a very difficult transition, from *kodesh*

יהוה LORD, God of Abraham, Isaac and Yisrael, our ancestors, may You keep this for ever so that it forms the thoughts in Your people's heart, and directs their heart toward You. He is compassionate. He forgives wrongdoing and does not destroy. Repeatedly He suppresses His anger, not rousing His full fury. For You, my LORD, are good and forgiving, generously kind to all who call on You. Your righteousness is eternally righteous, and Your Torah is truth. Give truth to Jacob, loving-kindness to Abraham, as You promised our ancestors in ancient times. Blessed is my LORD for day after day He burdens us [with His blessings]; God is our salvation, Selah! The LORD of multitudes is with us; the God of Jacob is our refuge, Selah! LORD of multitudes, happy is the one who trusts in You. LORD, save! May the King answer us on the day we call.

1 Chr. 29 · *Ps. 78* · *Ps. 86* · *Ps. 119* · *Mic. 7* · *Ps. 46* · *Ps. 84* · *Ps. 20*

בָּרוּךְ Blessed is He, our God, who created us for His glory, separating us from those who go astray; who gave us the Torah of truth, planting within us eternal life. May He open our heart to His Torah, imbuing our heart with the love and awe of Him, that we may do His will and serve Him with a perfect heart, so that we neither toil in vain nor give birth to confusion.

יְהִי רָצוֹן May it be Your will, O LORD our God and God of our ancestors, that we keep Your laws in this world, and thus be worthy to live, see and inherit goodness and blessing in the Messianic Age and in the life of the World to Come. So that my soul may sing to You and not be silent. LORD, my God, for ever I will thank You. Blessed is the man who trusts in the LORD, whose trust is in the LORD alone. Trust in the LORD for evermore, for God, the LORD, is an everlasting Rock. ▸ Those who know Your name trust in You, for You, LORD, do not abandon those who seek You. The LORD desired, for the sake of Israel's merit, to make the Torah great and glorious.

Ps. 30 · *Jer. 17* · *Is. 26* · *Ps. 9* · *Is. 42*

On Rosh Ḥodesh and Ḥol HaMo'ed, the Leader says Half Kaddish, page 230. The service then continues with Musaf for Rosh Ḥodesh on page 836, and for Ḥol HaMo'ed on page 858.

On other days, the Leader continues with Full Kaddish on the next page.

---

that he would like to buy a sizable amount of furs. However, it was the set learning time of Rav Kotler. His wife knocked on the door of his room, once, twice, and three times, and urged her husband to utilize this opportunity for his business.

Rav Kotler answered from behind the door, "Go tell him that if he's willing to wait until I finish my learning, good! If not – he should go in peace. A person's livelihood is determined on Rosh HaShana until Rosh HaShana. If it was decreed that I will sell the merchandise, I'll find a buyer!"

Rav Aharon concluded his story, "My father's wondrous mesirat nefesh *for Torah instilled in us the basic belief, 'When you learn Torah, you never lose out!' All of my* mesirat nefesh *for Torah – I acquired from him!"*

יהוה אֱלֹהֵי אַבְרָהָם יִצְחָק וְיִשְׂרָאֵל אֲבֹתֵינוּ, שָׁמְרָה־זֹּאת לְעוֹלָם — דברי הימים א׳ כט
לְיֵצֶר מַחְשְׁבוֹת לְבַב עַמֶּךָ, וְהָכֵן לְבָבָם אֵלֶיךָ: וְהוּא רַחוּם יְכַפֵּר עָוֹן — תהלים עח
וְלֹא־יַשְׁחִית, וְהִרְבָּה לְהָשִׁיב אַפּוֹ, וְלֹא־יָעִיר כָּל־חֲמָתוֹ: כִּי־אַתָּה אֲדֹנָי — תהלים פו
טוֹב וְסַלָּח, וְרַב־חֶסֶד לְכָל־קֹרְאֶיךָ: צִדְקָתְךָ צֶדֶק לְעוֹלָם וְתוֹרָתְךָ — תהלים קיט
אֱמֶת: תִּתֵּן אֱמֶת לְיַעֲקֹב, חֶסֶד לְאַבְרָהָם, אֲשֶׁר־נִשְׁבַּעְתָּ לַאֲבֹתֵינוּ — מיכה ז
מִימֵי קֶדֶם: בָּרוּךְ אֲדֹנָי יוֹם יוֹם יַעֲמָס־לָנוּ, הָאֵל יְשׁוּעָתֵנוּ סֶלָה: יהוה — תהלים סח
צְבָאוֹת עִמָּנוּ, מִשְׂגָּב לָנוּ אֱלֹהֵי יַעֲקֹב סֶלָה: יהוה צְבָאוֹת, אַשְׁרֵי אָדָם — תהלים פד
בֹּטֵחַ בָּךְ: יהוה הוֹשִׁיעָה, הַמֶּלֶךְ יַעֲנֵנוּ בְיוֹם־קָרְאֵנוּ: — תהלים כ

בָּרוּךְ הוּא אֱלֹהֵינוּ שֶׁבְּרָאָנוּ לִכְבוֹדוֹ, וְהִבְדִּילָנוּ מִן הַתּוֹעִים, וְנָתַן לָנוּ תּוֹרַת אֱמֶת, וְחַיֵּי עוֹלָם נָטַע בְּתוֹכֵנוּ. הוּא יִפְתַּח לִבֵּנוּ בְּתוֹרָתוֹ, וְיָשֵׂם בְּלִבֵּנוּ אַהֲבָתוֹ וְיִרְאָתוֹ וְלַעֲשׂוֹת רְצוֹנוֹ וּלְעָבְדוֹ בְּלֵבָב שָׁלֵם, לְמַעַן לֹא נִיגַע לָרִיק וְלֹא נֵלֵד לַבֶּהָלָה.

יְהִי רָצוֹן מִלְּפָנֶיךָ יהוה אֱלֹהֵינוּ וֵאלֹהֵי אֲבוֹתֵינוּ, שֶׁנִּשְׁמֹר חֻקֶּיךָ בָּעוֹלָם
הַזֶּה, וְנִזְכֶּה וְנִחְיֶה וְנִרְאֶה וְנִירַשׁ טוֹבָה וּבְרָכָה, לִשְׁנֵי יְמוֹת הַמָּשִׁיחַ
וּלְחַיֵּי הָעוֹלָם הַבָּא. לְמַעַן יְזַמֶּרְךָ כָבוֹד וְלֹא יִדֹּם, יהוה אֱלֹהַי, לְעוֹלָם — תהלים ל
אוֹדֶךָּ: בָּרוּךְ הַגֶּבֶר אֲשֶׁר יִבְטַח בַּיהוה, וְהָיָה יהוה מִבְטַחוֹ: בִּטְחוּ — ירמיה יז / ישעיה כו
בַיהוה עֲדֵי־עַד, כִּי בְּיָהּ יהוה צוּר עוֹלָמִים: ◂ וְיִבְטְחוּ בְךָ יוֹדְעֵי שְׁמֶךָ, כִּי — תהלים ט
לֹא־עָזַבְתָּ דֹרְשֶׁיךָ, יהוה: יהוה חָפֵץ לְמַעַן צִדְקוֹ, יַגְדִּיל תּוֹרָה וְיַאְדִּיר: — ישעיה מב

On ראש חודש *and* חול המועד*, the* שליח ציבור *says* חצי קדיש*,* *page 231.* *The service then continues with* מוסף *for* ראש חודש *on page 837**, and for* חול המועד *on page 859.*

On other days the שליח ציבור *continues with* קדיש שלם *on the next page.*

CONNECTION

Rav Aharon Kotler told a story about his father's mesirat nefesh *(self sacrifice) for Torah. His father was a fur merchant in Lithuania. At a certain period, his business dwindled, and it reached a point where his family was lacking food to sustain themselves.*

Every day after Shaḥarit, his father would learn Torah for two hours, and was very particular to maintain this learning schedule his entire life. One day, a wealthy merchant knocked on the door of the Kotler family home, and informed them

FULL KADDISH

Leader: יִתְגַּדַּל Magnified and sanctified may His great name be,
in the world He created by His will.
May He establish His kingdom in your lifetime
and in your days, and in the lifetime
of all the house of Israel,
swiftly and soon –
and say: Amen.

All: May His great name be blessed
for ever and all time.

Leader: Blessed and praised,
glorified and elevated,
raised and honored,
uplifted and praised
be the name of the Holy One,
blessed be He,
beyond any blessing,
song, praise and consolation
uttered in the world –
and say: Amen.

On Tisha B'Av, omit the next verse and continue with "May there be great peace."

May the prayers and pleas of all Israel
be accepted by their Father in heaven –
and say: Amen.

May there be great peace from heaven,
and life for us and all Israel –
and say: Amen.

Bow, take three steps back, as if taking leave of the Divine Presence, then bow, first left, then right, then center, while saying:

May He who makes peace in His high places,
make peace for us and all Israel –
and say: Amen.

קדיש שלם

ש״ץ: יִתְגַּדַּל וְיִתְקַדַּשׁ שְׁמֵהּ רַבָּא (קהל: אָמֵן)
בְּעָלְמָא דִּי בְרָא כִרְעוּתֵהּ
וְיַמְלִיךְ מַלְכוּתֵהּ
בְּחַיֵּיכוֹן וּבְיוֹמֵיכוֹן וּבְחַיֵּי דְכָל בֵּית יִשְׂרָאֵל
בַּעֲגָלָא וּבִזְמַן קָרִיב, וְאִמְרוּ אָמֵן. (קהל: אָמֵן)

קהל וש״ץ: יְהֵא שְׁמֵהּ רַבָּא מְבָרַךְ לְעָלַם וּלְעָלְמֵי עָלְמַיָּא.

ש״ץ: יִתְבָּרַךְ וְיִשְׁתַּבַּח וְיִתְפָּאַר
וְיִתְרוֹמַם וְיִתְנַשֵּׂא וְיִתְהַדָּר וְיִתְעַלֶּה וְיִתְהַלָּל
שְׁמֵהּ דְּקֻדְשָׁא בְּרִיךְ הוּא (קהל: בְּרִיךְ הוּא)
לְעֵלָּא מִן כָּל בִּרְכָתָא
/בעשרת ימי תשובה: לְעֵלָּא לְעֵלָּא מִכָּל בִּרְכָתָא/
וְשִׁירָתָא, תֻּשְׁבְּחָתָא וְנֶחֱמָתָא
דַּאֲמִירָן בְּעָלְמָא, וְאִמְרוּ אָמֵן. (קהל: אָמֵן)

On תשעה באב*, omit the next verse and continue with* יְהֵא שְׁלָמָא.

תִּתְקַבַּל צְלוֹתְהוֹן וּבָעוּתְהוֹן דְּכָל יִשְׂרָאֵל
קֳדָם אֲבוּהוֹן דִּי בִשְׁמַיָּא, וְאִמְרוּ אָמֵן. (קהל: אָמֵן)

יְהֵא שְׁלָמָא רַבָּא מִן שְׁמַיָּא
וְחַיִּים, עָלֵינוּ וְעַל כָּל יִשְׂרָאֵל, וְאִמְרוּ אָמֵן. (קהל: אָמֵן)

Bow, take three steps back, as if taking leave of the Divine Presence, then bow, first left, then right, then center, while saying:

עֹשֶׂה שָׁלוֹם/בעשרת ימי תשובה: הַשָּׁלוֹם/ בִּמְרוֹמָיו
הוּא יַעֲשֶׂה שָׁלוֹם
עָלֵינוּ וְעַל כָּל יִשְׂרָאֵל, וְאִמְרוּ אָמֵן. (קהל: אָמֵן)

Stand while saying Aleinu.

עָלֵינוּ It is our duty to praise the Master of all,
and ascribe greatness to the Author of creation,
who has not made us like the nations of the lands
nor placed us like the families of the earth;
who has not made our portion like theirs,
nor our destiny like all their multitudes.
(For they worship vanity and emptiness,
and pray to a god who cannot save.)
But we bow in worship and thank the Supreme King of kings,
the Holy One, blessed be He,
who extends the heavens and establishes the earth,
whose throne of glory is in the heavens above,
and whose power's Presence is in the highest of heights.
He is our God; there is no other.
Truly He is our King, there is none else, as it is written in His Torah:
"You shall know and take to heart this day *Deut. 4*
that the LORD is God, in heaven above and on earth below.
There is no other."

CONNECTION

"Yes I do accept the Chosen People concept as affirmed by Judaism in its holy writ, its prayers and its millennial tradition. In fact, I believe every people – and indeed in a more limited way, every individual – is 'chosen' or destined for some distinct purpose in advancing the designs of Providence. Only, some fulfill their assignment and others do not.

Maybe the Greeks were chosen for their unique contributions to art and philosophy, the Romans for their pioneering services in law and government, the British for bringing parliamentary rule into the world, and the Americans for piloting democracy in a pluralistic society.

The Jews were chosen by God to be 'special unto Me' as the pioneers of religion and morality: that was and is their national purpose."

(Rabbi Immanuel Jakobovits)

Stand while saying עָלֵינוּ.

עָלֵינוּ לְשַׁבֵּחַ לַאֲדוֹן הַכֹּל, לָתֵת גְּדֻלָּה לְיוֹצֵר בְּרֵאשִׁית
שֶׁלֹּא עָשָׂנוּ כְּגוֹיֵי הָאֲרָצוֹת, וְלֹא שָׂמָנוּ כְּמִשְׁפְּחוֹת הָאֲדָמָה
שֶׁלֹּא שָׂם חֶלְקֵנוּ כָּהֶם וְגוֹרָלֵנוּ כְּכָל הֲמוֹנָם.
(שֶׁהֵם מִשְׁתַּחֲוִים לְהֶבֶל וָרִיק וּמִתְפַּלְלִים אֶל אֵל לֹא יוֹשִׁיעַ.)
וַאֲנַחְנוּ כּוֹרְעִים וּמִשְׁתַּחֲוִים וּמוֹדִים
לִפְנֵי מֶלֶךְ מַלְכֵי הַמְּלָכִים, הַקָּדוֹשׁ בָּרוּךְ הוּא
שֶׁהוּא נוֹטֶה שָׁמַיִם וְיוֹסֵד אָרֶץ
וּמוֹשַׁב יְקָרוֹ בַּשָּׁמַיִם מִמַּעַל, וּשְׁכִינַת עֻזּוֹ בְּגָבְהֵי מְרוֹמִים.
הוּא אֱלֹהֵינוּ, אֵין עוֹד.
אֱמֶת מַלְכֵּנוּ, אֶפֶס זוּלָתוֹ
כַּכָּתוּב בְּתוֹרָתוֹ, וְיָדַעְתָּ הַיּוֹם וַהֲשֵׁבֹתָ אֶל־לְבָבֶךָ דברים ד
כִּי יהוה הוּא הָאֱלֹהִים בַּשָּׁמַיִם מִמַּעַל וְעַל־הָאָרֶץ מִתָּחַת
אֵין עוֹד:

REFLECTION

"And now, if you will heed My voice and observe My covenant, and you shall be a distinction for Me from among all the peoples; as all the earth is Mine. And you shall be for Me a kingdom of priests and a holy nation. These are the words that you shall speak to the Children of Israel." (*Shemot* 19:5–6)

What does being a chosen nation mean to you?

What do you think you personally have been chosen for?

What does it mean to you to be a Jew?

What does it mean to you to be part of the Jewish People?

LEARNING

The *Aleinu* prayer is from the Rosh HaShana liturgy where it is used as an introduction to the *berakha* of *Malkhiyot* (Kingship) in Musaf. The text of the *tefilla* declares Hashem's sovereignty in the world, and this was considered so central to what it means to see the world through Jewish eyes that it was later chosen as the conclusion to all *tefilla* services in the siddur as the closing message.

Therefore, we place our hope in You, LORD our God,
that we may soon see the glory of Your power,
when You will remove abominations from the earth,
and idols will be utterly destroyed,
when the world will be perfected
under the sovereignty of the Almighty,
when all humanity will call on Your name,
to turn all the earth's wicked toward You.
All the world's inhabitants will realize and know
that to You every knee must bow and every tongue swear loyalty.
Before You, LORD our God, they will kneel and bow down
and give honor to Your glorious name.
They will all accept the yoke of Your kingdom,
and You will reign over them soon and for ever.
For the kingdom is Yours, and to all eternity You will reign in glory,
as it is written in Your Torah: "The LORD will reign for ever and ever." *Ex. 15*
▸ And it is said: "Then the LORD shall be King over all the earth; *Zech. 14*
on that day the LORD shall be One and His name One."

Some add:

Have no fear of sudden terror or of the ruin when it overtakes the wicked. *Prov. 3*
Devise your strategy, but it will be defeated, propose your plan, *Is. 8*
but it will not stand, for God is with us.
When you grow old, I will still be the same. *Is. 46*
When your hair turns gray, I will still carry you.
I made you, I will bear you, I will carry you, and I will rescue you.

LEARNING

The two paragraphs of the prayer *Aleinu* represent two distinct but related themes. The first paragraph explores our chosenness in the eyes of Hashem, while the second speaks of our mission in the world – to improve it (*tikkun olam*), which is the reason why we have been chosen. In the words of Rabbi Jonathan Sacks: "No prayer more eloquently expresses the dual nature of the Jewish People: its singular history as the nation chosen to be God's witness on earth, and its universal aspiration for the time when all the inhabitants of earth will recognize the God in whose image we are formed."

עַל כֵּן נְקַוֶּה לְּךָ יהוה אֱלֹהֵינוּ, לִרְאוֹת מְהֵרָה בְּתִפְאֶרֶת עֻזֶּךָ
לְהַעֲבִיר גִּלּוּלִים מִן הָאָרֶץ, וְהָאֱלִילִים כָּרוֹת יִכָּרֵתוּן
לְתַקֵּן עוֹלָם בְּמַלְכוּת שַׁדַּי.
וְכָל בְּנֵי בָשָׂר יִקְרְאוּ בִשְׁמֶךָ לְהַפְנוֹת אֵלֶיךָ כָּל רִשְׁעֵי אָרֶץ.
יַכִּירוּ וְיֵדְעוּ כָּל יוֹשְׁבֵי תֵבֵל
כִּי לְךָ תִּכְרַע כָּל בֶּרֶךְ, תִּשָּׁבַע כָּל לָשׁוֹן.
לְפָנֶיךָ יהוה אֱלֹהֵינוּ יִכְרְעוּ וְיִפֹּלוּ
וְלִכְבוֹד שִׁמְךָ יְקָר יִתֵּנוּ
וִיקַבְּלוּ כֻלָּם אֶת עֹל מַלְכוּתֶךָ
וְתִמְלֹךְ עֲלֵיהֶם מְהֵרָה לְעוֹלָם וָעֶד.
כִּי הַמַּלְכוּת שֶׁלְּךָ הִיא וּלְעוֹלְמֵי עַד תִּמְלֹךְ בְּכָבוֹד
כַּכָּתוּב בְּתוֹרָתֶךָ, יהוה יִמְלֹךְ לְעֹלָם וָעֶד: שמות טו
► וְנֶאֱמַר, וְהָיָה יהוה לְמֶלֶךְ עַל־כָּל־הָאָרֶץ זכריה יד
בַּיּוֹם הַהוּא יִהְיֶה יהוה אֶחָד וּשְׁמוֹ אֶחָד:

Some add:

אַל־תִּירָא מִפַּחַד פִּתְאֹם וּמִשֹּׁאַת רְשָׁעִים כִּי תָבֹא: משלי ג
עֻצוּ עֵצָה וְתֻפָר, דַּבְּרוּ דָבָר וְלֹא יָקוּם, כִּי עִמָּנוּ אֵל: ישעיה ח
וְעַד־זִקְנָה אֲנִי הוּא, וְעַד־שֵׂיבָה אֲנִי אֶסְבֹּל, אֲנִי עָשִׂיתִי וַאֲנִי אֶשָּׂא וַאֲנִי אֶסְבֹּל וַאֲמַלֵּט: ישעיה מו

REFLECTION

"[Hillel says]: That which is hateful to you, do not do to your friend. That is the entire Torah. The rest is just explanation. Go and study it!" (*Shabbat* 31a)

How would you sum up Judaism in one sentence?

... A THOUSAND WORDS

MOURNER'S KADDISH

The following prayer, said by mourners, requires the presence of a minyan.
A transliteration can be found on page 1151.

Mourner: יִתְגַּדַּל Magnified and sanctified
may His great name be,
in the world He created by His will.
May He establish His kingdom
in your lifetime and in your days,
and in the lifetime of all the house of Israel,
swiftly and soon –
and say: Amen.

All: May His great name be blessed
for ever and all time.

Mourner: Blessed and praised,
glorified and elevated,
raised and honored,
uplifted and praised
be the name of the Holy One,
blessed be He,
beyond any blessing, song,
praise and consolation
uttered in the world –
and say: Amen.

May there be great peace from heaven,
and life for us and all Israel –
and say: Amen.

Bow, take three steps back, as if taking leave of the Divine Presence,
then bow, first left, then right, then center, while saying:

May He who makes peace in His high places,
make peace for us and all Israel –
and say: Amen.

קדיש יתום

The following prayer, said by mourners, requires the presence of a מנין*.*
A transliteration can be found on page 1151.

אבל: יִתְגַּדַּל וְיִתְקַדַּשׁ שְׁמֵהּ רַבָּא (קהל: אָמֵן)
בְּעָלְמָא דִּי בְרָא כִרְעוּתֵהּ
וְיַמְלִיךְ מַלְכוּתֵהּ
בְּחַיֵּיכוֹן וּבְיוֹמֵיכוֹן וּבְחַיֵּי דְכָל בֵּית יִשְׂרָאֵל
בַּעֲגָלָא וּבִזְמַן קָרִיב
וְאִמְרוּ אָמֵן. (קהל: אָמֵן)

קהל ואבל: יְהֵא שְׁמֵהּ רַבָּא מְבָרַךְ לְעָלַם וּלְעָלְמֵי עָלְמַיָּא.

אבל: יִתְבָּרַךְ וְיִשְׁתַּבַּח וְיִתְפָּאַר
וְיִתְרוֹמַם וְיִתְנַשֵּׂא וְיִתְהַדָּר וְיִתְעַלֶּה וְיִתְהַלָּל
שְׁמֵהּ דְּקֻדְשָׁא בְּרִיךְ הוּא (קהל: בְּרִיךְ הוּא)
לְעֵלָּא מִן כָּל בִּרְכָתָא
/בעשרת ימי תשובה: לְעֵלָּא לְעֵלָּא מִכָּל בִּרְכָתָא/
וְשִׁירָתָא, תֻּשְׁבְּחָתָא וְנֶחֱמָתָא
דַּאֲמִירָן בְּעָלְמָא
וְאִמְרוּ אָמֵן. (קהל: אָמֵן)

יְהֵא שְׁלָמָא רַבָּא מִן שְׁמַיָּא
וְחַיִּים, עָלֵינוּ וְעַל כָּל יִשְׂרָאֵל
וְאִמְרוּ אָמֵן. (קהל: אָמֵן)

Bow, take three steps back, as if taking leave of the Divine Presence, then bow, first left, then right, then center, while saying:

עֹשֶׂה שָׁלוֹם/בעשרת ימי תשובה: הַשָּׁלוֹם/ בִּמְרוֹמָיו
הוּא יַעֲשֶׂה שָׁלוֹם עָלֵינוּ וְעַל כָּל יִשְׂרָאֵל
וְאִמְרוּ אָמֵן. (קהל: אָמֵן)

THE DAILY PSALM

One of the following psalms is said on the appropriate day of the week as indicated. After the psalm, the Mourner's Kaddish on page 250 is said.

After the Daily Psalm, on Rosh Ḥodesh, add Barekhi Nafshi, page 264 (in Israel, some only say Barekhi Nafshi). On Ḥanukka, add Psalm 30, page 72 followed by Mourner's Kaddish. From the second day of Rosh Ḥodesh Elul through Shemini Atzeret (in Israel, through Hoshana Raba), add Psalm 27 on page 268. In a house of mourning the service concludes on page 270.

Sunday: Today is the first day of the week,
on which the Levites used to say this psalm in the Temple:

לְדָוִד מִזְמוֹר A psalm of David. The earth is the LORD's and all it contains, the world and all who live in it. For He founded it on the seas and established it on the streams. Who may climb the mountain of the LORD? Who may stand in His holy place? He who has clean hands and a pure heart, who has not taken My name in vain or sworn falsely. He shall receive a blessing from the LORD, and just reward from the God of his salvation. This is a generation of those who seek Him, the descendants of Jacob who seek Your presence, Selah! Lift up your heads, O gates; be uplifted, eternal doors, so that the King of glory may enter. Who is the King of glory? It is the LORD, strong and mighty, the LORD mighty in battle. Lift up your heads, O gates; lift them up, eternal doors, that the King of glory may enter. ▸ Who is He, the King of glory? The LORD of multitudes, He is the King of glory, Selah! *Ps. 24*

Mourner's Kaddish (page 250)

REFLECTION

Have you ever wondered why God created the world?

What did you come up with?

How are you going to aspire to come close to God this week?

What do you think God wants you to do with your time in the world?

LEARNING

During the times of the *Beit HaMikdash*, the *Levi'im* would sing a psalm each day which related to the significance of that particular day of the week (*Tamid* 7:4). Furthermore, mentioning each day, *Yom Rishon, Sheni, Shelishi… beShabbat*, helps us build up anticipation for Shabbat. By mentioning the day of the week in relation to Shabbat, we fulfill the commandment to remember Shabbat every day and eagerly anticipate it.

שיר של יום

One of the following psalms is said on the appropriate day of the week as indicated.
After the psalm, קדיש יתום *on page 251 is said.*
After שיר של יום, *on* ראש חודש, *add* בָּרְכִי נַפְשִׁי, *page 265 (in* ארץ ישראל, *some only say* בָּרְכִי נַפְשִׁי). *On* חנוכה, *add* מִזְמוֹר שִׁיר־חֲנֻכַּת הַבַּיִת, *page 73 followed by* קדיש יתום. *From the second day of* ראש חודש אלול *through* שמיני עצרת *(in* ארץ ישראל, *through* הושענא רבה), *add* לְדָוִד, יהוה אוֹרִי *on page 269. In a house of mourning the service concludes on page 271.*

Sunday הַיּוֹם יוֹם רִאשׁוֹן בְּשַׁבָּת, שֶׁבּוֹ הָיוּ הַלְוִיִּם אוֹמְרִים בְּבֵית הַמִּקְדָּשׁ:

לְדָוִד מִזְמוֹר, לַיהוה הָאָרֶץ וּמְלוֹאָהּ, תֵּבֵל וְיֹשְׁבֵי בָהּ: כִּי־הוּא עַל־יַמִּים תהלים כד
יְסָדָהּ, וְעַל־נְהָרוֹת יְכוֹנְנֶהָ: מִי־יַעֲלֶה בְהַר־יהוה, וּמִי־יָקוּם בִּמְקוֹם
קָדְשׁוֹ: נְקִי כַפַּיִם וּבַר־לֵבָב, אֲשֶׁר לֹא־נָשָׂא לַשָּׁוְא נַפְשִׁי, וְלֹא נִשְׁבַּע
לְמִרְמָה: יִשָּׂא בְרָכָה מֵאֵת יהוה, וּצְדָקָה מֵאֱלֹהֵי יִשְׁעוֹ: זֶה דּוֹר דֹּרְשָׁו,
מְבַקְשֵׁי פָנֶיךָ יַעֲקֹב סֶלָה: שְׂאוּ שְׁעָרִים רָאשֵׁיכֶם, וְהִנָּשְׂאוּ פִּתְחֵי עוֹלָם,
וְיָבוֹא מֶלֶךְ הַכָּבוֹד: מִי זֶה מֶלֶךְ הַכָּבוֹד, יהוה עִזּוּז וְגִבּוֹר, יהוה גִּבּוֹר
מִלְחָמָה: שְׂאוּ שְׁעָרִים רָאשֵׁיכֶם, וּשְׂאוּ פִּתְחֵי עוֹלָם, וְיָבֹא מֶלֶךְ הַכָּבוֹד:
‹ מִי הוּא זֶה מֶלֶךְ הַכָּבוֹד, יהוה צְבָאוֹת הוּא מֶלֶךְ הַכָּבוֹד סֶלָה:

קדיש יתום *(page 251)*

... A THOUSAND WORDS

CONNECTION

"He looks for the image of God not in the mathematical formula or the natural relational law but in every beam of light, in every bud and blossom, in the morning breeze and the stillness of a star-lit evening. In a word, Adam [the Second] explores not the scientific abstract universe but the irresistibly fascinating qualitative world where he establishes an intimate relation with God."

(Rabbi J.B. Soloveitchik, *Lonely Man of Faith*)

Monday: Today is the second day of the week,
on which the Levites used to say this psalm in the Temple:

שִׁיר מִזְמוֹר A song. A psalm of the sons of Korah. Great is the LORD and greatly to be praised in the city of God, on His holy mountain – beautiful in its heights, joy of all the earth, Mount Zion on its northern side, city of the great King. In its castles God is known as a stronghold. See how the kings joined forces, advancing together. They saw, they were astounded, they panicked, they fled. There fear seized them, like the pains of a woman giving birth, like ships of Tarshish wrecked by an eastern wind. What we had heard, now we have seen, in the city of the LORD of multitudes, in the city of our God. May God preserve it for ever, Selah! In the midst of Your Temple, God, we meditate on Your love. As is Your name, God, so is Your praise: it reaches to the ends of the earth. Your right hand is filled with righteousness. Let Mount Zion rejoice, let the towns of Judah be glad, because of Your judgments. Walk around Zion and encircle it. Count its towers, note its strong walls, view its castles, so that you may tell a future generation ▸ that this is God, our God, for ever and ever. He will guide us for evermore. *Ps. 48*

Mourner's Kaddish (page 250)

REFLECTION

Where
in your life
do you feel
conflicted?

How
do you
make choices
in those areas?

Can
conflict
ever be good?

... A THOUSAND WORDS

Monday הַיּוֹם יוֹם שֵׁנִי בְּשַׁבָּת, שֶׁבּוֹ הָיוּ הַלְוִיִּם אוֹמְרִים בְּבֵית הַמִּקְדָּשׁ:

שִׁיר מִזְמוֹר לִבְנֵי־קֹרַח: גָּדוֹל יהוה וּמְהֻלָּל מְאֹד, בְּעִיר אֱלֹהֵינוּ, הַר־ תהלים מח
קָדְשׁוֹ: יְפֵה נוֹף מְשׂוֹשׂ כָּל־הָאָרֶץ, הַר־צִיּוֹן יַרְכְּתֵי צָפוֹן, קִרְיַת מֶלֶךְ
רָב: אֱלֹהִים בְּאַרְמְנוֹתֶיהָ נוֹדַע לְמִשְׂגָּב: כִּי־הִנֵּה הַמְּלָכִים נוֹעֲדוּ, עָבְרוּ
יַחְדָּו: הֵמָּה רָאוּ כֵּן תָּמָהוּ, נִבְהֲלוּ נֶחְפָּזוּ: רְעָדָה אֲחָזָתַם שָׁם, חִיל
כַּיּוֹלֵדָה: בְּרוּחַ קָדִים תְּשַׁבֵּר אֳנִיּוֹת תַּרְשִׁישׁ: כַּאֲשֶׁר שָׁמַעְנוּ כֵּן רָאִינוּ,
בְּעִיר־יהוה צְבָאוֹת, בְּעִיר אֱלֹהֵינוּ, אֱלֹהִים יְכוֹנְנֶהָ עַד־עוֹלָם סֶלָה:
דִּמִּינוּ אֱלֹהִים חַסְדֶּךָ, בְּקֶרֶב הֵיכָלֶךָ: כְּשִׁמְךָ אֱלֹהִים כֵּן תְּהִלָּתְךָ עַל־
קַצְוֵי־אֶרֶץ, צֶדֶק מָלְאָה יְמִינֶךָ: יִשְׂמַח הַר־צִיּוֹן, תָּגֵלְנָה בְּנוֹת יְהוּדָה,
לְמַעַן מִשְׁפָּטֶיךָ: סֹבּוּ צִיּוֹן וְהַקִּיפוּהָ, סִפְרוּ מִגְדָּלֶיהָ: שִׁיתוּ לִבְּכֶם לְחֵילָה,
פַּסְּגוּ אַרְמְנוֹתֶיהָ, לְמַעַן תְּסַפְּרוּ לְדוֹר אַחֲרוֹן: ‹ כִּי זֶה אֱלֹהִים אֱלֹהֵינוּ
עוֹלָם וָעֶד, הוּא יְנַהֲגֵנוּ עַל־מוּת:

קדיש יתום (*page 251*)

CONNECTION

*There was once a wise man whom people visited from far and wide to seek his counsel. One day a cynical boy visited the man hoping to catch him out and prove him no wiser than anyone else. He approached the wise man with cupped hands in front of him. "I hold a butterfly in my hand; tell me, wise master, is it alive or dead?" He smirked to himself, if the man says dead, I will release the butterfly, if he says alive, I will squash it that moment. The man would be wrong no matter what he said. The wise man sighed and looked at the young boy and said, "*hakol beyadekha *– it's all in your hands."*

The smirk vanished from the boy's face as he realized the man's wisdom and the greater lesson behind his words. Indeed, the butterfly's life rested in his own very hands, but on a deeper level, so much more rests in our hands. We can make choices and decide which path to take.

LEARNING

The Gemara in *Rosh HaShana* 31a teaches us the reason why each day's psalm was chosen for that specific day. On the second day of Creation, God separated between the waters above and below, and distinguished heaven. *Resisei Laila* comments that by separating the physical and spiritual realms, God set off the continual strife that would exist between the two; Rabbeinu Baḥya actually cites this as the source of all subsequent conflict. That is why the *Levi'im* chose a psalm composed by the *Benei Koraḥ*, since Koraḥ initiated a rebellion against Moshe's authority as the medium between the nation and God's word, part of the perpetuation of this strife. By singing this psalm we can remind ourselves of the consequences of strife and conflict.

Tuesday: Today is the third day of the week,
on which the Levites used to say this psalm in the Temple:

מִזְמוֹר לְאָסָף A psalm of Asaph. God stands in the divine assembly. Among *Ps. 82*
the judges He delivers judgment. How long will you judge unjustly, showing favor to the wicked? Selah. Do justice to the weak and the orphaned. Vindicate the poor and destitute. Rescue the weak and needy. Save them from the hand of the wicked. They do not know nor do they understand. They walk about in darkness while all the earth's foundations shake. I once said, "You are like gods, all of you are sons of the Most High." But you shall die like mere men, you will fall like any prince. ▸ Arise, O Lord, judge the earth, for all the nations are Your possession.

Mourner's Kaddish (page 250)

... A THOUSAND WORDS

Tuesday הַיּוֹם יוֹם שְׁלִישִׁי בְּשַׁבָּת, שֶׁבּוֹ הָיוּ הַלְוִיִּם אוֹמְרִים בְּבֵית הַמִּקְדָּשׁ:

תהלים פב מִזְמוֹר לְאָסָף, אֱלֹהִים נִצָּב בַּעֲדַת־אֵל, בְּקֶרֶב אֱלֹהִים יִשְׁפֹּט: עַד־מָתַי
תִּשְׁפְּטוּ־עָוֶל, וּפְנֵי רְשָׁעִים תִּשְׂאוּ־סֶלָה: שִׁפְטוּ־דָל וְיָתוֹם, עָנִי וָרָשׁ
הַצְדִּיקוּ: פַּלְּטוּ־דַל וְאֶבְיוֹן, מִיַּד רְשָׁעִים הַצִּילוּ: לֹא יָדְעוּ וְלֹא יָבִינוּ,
בַּחֲשֵׁכָה יִתְהַלָּכוּ, יִמּוֹטוּ כָּל־מוֹסְדֵי אָרֶץ: אֲנִי־אָמַרְתִּי אֱלֹהִים אַתֶּם,
וּבְנֵי עֶלְיוֹן כֻּלְּכֶם: אָכֵן כְּאָדָם תְּמוּתוּן, וּכְאַחַד הַשָּׂרִים תִּפֹּלוּ: ‹ קוּמָה
אֱלֹהִים שָׁפְטָה הָאָרֶץ, כִּי־אַתָּה תִנְחַל בְּכָל־הַגּוֹיִם:

קדיש יתום (*page 251*)

LEARNING

On the third day of Creation the waters that covered the earth were withdrawn and dry land appeared. Thus, the world became habitable. Just like the careful balance of dry land and water borders needs to constantly be maintained and monitored, so, too, the continued existence of our world depends on the maintenance of justice which must always be exact and monitored.

REFLECTION

"There may be times when we are powerless to prevent injustice, but there must never be a time when we fail to protest."

(Elie Wiesel)

Why do you think justice is so important?

Do you act fairly and judge people fairly?

How do you stand up for people who cannot stand up for themselves?

CONNECTION

We have a positive mitzva to judge our fellow man with righteousness. Rabbi Shlomo Wolbe in Alei Shur *explains: Someone who judges others favorably really hopes that his fellow man is guiltless. He seeks ways of understanding the other's actions as good.*

This is the extent to which one must regard another person with a positive attitude, and wish to see his actions as issuing from a good source. We should search out another's positive qualities. This is the opposite of what most people usually do, which is to immediately notice another person's shortcomings and ignore his strong points.

(*Alei Shur*, vol. II)

Wednesday: Today is the fourth day of the week,
on which the Levites used to say this psalm in the Temple:

אֵל־נְקָמוֹת God of retribution, Lord, God of retribution, appear! Rise up, Judge of the earth. Repay to the arrogant what they deserve. How long shall the wicked, Lord, how long shall the wicked triumph? They pour out insolent words. All the evildoers are full of boasting. They crush Your people, Lord, and oppress Your inheritance. They kill the widow and the stranger. They murder the orphaned. They say, "The Lord does not see. The God of Jacob pays no heed." Take heed, you most brutish people. You fools, when will you grow wise? Will He who implants the ear not hear? Will He who formed the eye not see? Will He who disciplines nations – He who teaches man knowledge – not punish? The Lord knows that the thoughts of man are a mere fleeting breath. Happy is the man whom You discipline, Lord, the one You instruct in Your Torah, giving him tranquility in days of trouble, until a pit is dug for the wicked. For the Lord will not abandon His people, nor abandon His heritage. Judgment shall again accord with justice, and all the upright in heart will follow it. Who will rise up for me against the wicked? Who will stand up for me against wrongdoers? Had the Lord not been my help, I would soon have dwelt in death's silence. When I thought my foot was slipping, Your loving-kindness, Lord, gave me support. When I was filled with anxiety, Your consolations soothed my soul. Can a corrupt throne be allied with You? Can injustice be framed into law? They join forces against the life of the righteous, and condemn the innocent to death. But the Lord is my stronghold, my God is the Rock of my refuge. He will bring back on them their wickedness, and destroy them for their evil deeds. The Lord our God will destroy them. *Ps. 94*

▸ Come, let us sing for joy to the Lord; let us shout aloud to the Rock of our salvation. Let us greet Him with thanksgiving, shout aloud to Him with songs of praise. For the Lord is the great God, the King great above all powers. *Ps. 95*

Mourner's Kaddish (page 250)

LEARNING

On the fourth day we say, "God, He is a God of retribution," because on this day God created the sun, moon, and stars to benefit mankind with their light and radiance. Though they were intended for this purpose, mankind took to worshiping them as gods. God is not pleased with those who foolishly believe that any of His creations are to be worshiped and God will not tolerate this evil. Eventually He will vengefully remove all idolatry from the world.

Wednesday הַיּוֹם יוֹם רְבִיעִי בְּשַׁבָּת, שֶׁבּוֹ הָיוּ הַלְוִיִּם אוֹמְרִים בְּבֵית הַמִּקְדָּשׁ:

תהלים צד
אֵל־נְקָמוֹת יהוה, אֵל נְקָמוֹת הוֹפִיעַ: הִנָּשֵׂא שֹׁפֵט הָאָרֶץ, הָשֵׁב גְּמוּל עַל־גֵּאִים: עַד־מָתַי רְשָׁעִים, יהוה, עַד־מָתַי רְשָׁעִים יַעֲלֹזוּ: יַבִּיעוּ יְדַבְּרוּ עָתָק, יִתְאַמְּרוּ כָּל־פֹּעֲלֵי אָוֶן: עַמְּךָ יהוה יְדַכְּאוּ, וְנַחֲלָתְךָ יְעַנּוּ: אַלְמָנָה וְגֵר יַהֲרֹגוּ, וִיתוֹמִים יְרַצֵּחוּ: וַיֹּאמְרוּ לֹא יִרְאֶה־יָּהּ, וְלֹא־יָבִין אֱלֹהֵי יַעֲקֹב: בִּינוּ בֹּעֲרִים בָּעָם, וּכְסִילִים מָתַי תַּשְׂכִּילוּ: הֲנֹטַע אֹזֶן הֲלֹא יִשְׁמָע, אִם־יֹצֵר עַיִן הֲלֹא יַבִּיט: הֲיֹסֵר גּוֹיִם הֲלֹא יוֹכִיחַ, הַמְלַמֵּד אָדָם דָּעַת: יהוה יֹדֵעַ מַחְשְׁבוֹת אָדָם, כִּי־הֵמָּה הָבֶל: אַשְׁרֵי הַגֶּבֶר אֲשֶׁר־תְּיַסְּרֶנּוּ יָּהּ, וּמִתּוֹרָתְךָ תְלַמְּדֶנּוּ: לְהַשְׁקִיט לוֹ מִימֵי רָע, עַד יִכָּרֶה לָרָשָׁע שָׁחַת: כִּי לֹא־יִטֹּשׁ יהוה עַמּוֹ, וְנַחֲלָתוֹ לֹא יַעֲזֹב: כִּי־עַד־צֶדֶק יָשׁוּב מִשְׁפָּט, וְאַחֲרָיו כָּל־יִשְׁרֵי־לֵב: מִי־יָקוּם לִי עִם־מְרֵעִים, מִי־יִתְיַצֵּב לִי עִם־פֹּעֲלֵי אָוֶן: לוּלֵי יהוה עֶזְרָתָה לִּי, כִּמְעַט שָׁכְנָה דוּמָה נַפְשִׁי: אִם־אָמַרְתִּי מָטָה רַגְלִי, חַסְדְּךָ יהוה יִסְעָדֵנִי: בְּרֹב שַׂרְעַפַּי בְּקִרְבִּי, תַּנְחוּמֶיךָ יְשַׁעַשְׁעוּ נַפְשִׁי: הַיְחָבְרְךָ כִּסֵּא הַוּוֹת, יֹצֵר עָמָל עֲלֵי־חֹק: יָגוֹדּוּ עַל־נֶפֶשׁ צַדִּיק, וְדָם נָקִי יַרְשִׁיעוּ: וַיְהִי יהוה לִי לְמִשְׂגָּב, וֵאלֹהַי לְצוּר מַחְסִי: וַיָּשֶׁב עֲלֵיהֶם אֶת־אוֹנָם, וּבְרָעָתָם יַצְמִיתֵם, יַצְמִיתֵם יהוה אֱלֹהֵינוּ:

תהלים צה
› לְכוּ נְרַנְּנָה לַיהוה, נָרִיעָה לְצוּר יִשְׁעֵנוּ: נְקַדְּמָה פָנָיו בְּתוֹדָה, בִּזְמִרוֹת נָרִיעַ לוֹ: כִּי אֵל גָּדוֹל יהוה, וּמֶלֶךְ גָּדוֹל עַל־כָּל־אֱלֹהִים:

קדיש יתום (*page 251*)

REFLECTION

"Right is right, even if everyone is against it, and wrong is wrong, even if everyone is for it."
(William Penn)

Have you ever seen injustice that you want God to avenge?

Why do you think God sometimes seems to fail to stop wrongdoing?

Have you ever stood up to injustice? What did you do?

... A THOUSAND WORDS

Thursday: Today is the fifth day of the week,
on which the Levites used to say this psalm in the Temple:

לַמְנַצֵּחַ For the conductor of music. On the Gittit. By Asaph. Sing for joy to God, our strength. Shout aloud to the God of Jacob. Raise a song, beat the drum, play the sweet harp and lyre. Sound the shofar on the new moon, on our feast day when the moon is hidden. For it is a law for Israel, an ordinance of the God of Jacob. He established it as a testimony for Joseph when He went forth against the land of Egypt, where I heard a language that I did not know. I relieved his shoulder of the burden. His hands were freed from the builder's basket. In distress you called and I rescued you. I answered you from the secret place of thunder; I tested you at the waters of Meribah, Selah! Hear, My people, and I will warn you. Israel, if you would only listen to Me! Let there be no strange god among you. Do not bow down to an alien god. I am the LORD your God who brought you out of the land of Egypt. Open your mouth wide and I will fill it. But My people would not listen to Me. Israel would have none of Me. So I left them to their stubborn hearts, letting them follow their own devices. If only My people would listen to Me, if Israel would walk in My ways, I would soon subdue their enemies, and turn My hand against their foes. Those who hate the LORD would cower before Him and their doom would last for ever. ▸ He would feed Israel with the finest wheat – with honey from the rock I would satisfy you. *Ps. 81*

Mourner's Kaddish (page 250)

REFLECTION

How do you serve God with joy?

How do you share joy with others?

... A THOUSAND WORDS

LEARNING

The Gemara in *Shabbat* 156a states that a person born on the fifth day of the week will be a person who shares joy with others. Rashi explains this is because the fish and birds, also "born" on the fifth day, were blessed with abundant food supplies enabling them to shift their focus away from the extreme effort usually required to obtain food. So, too, people born on the fifth day of the week will have excess energy to expend with and for others.

Thursday הַיּוֹם יוֹם חֲמִישִׁי בְּשַׁבָּת, שֶׁבּוֹ הָיוּ הַלְוִיִּם אוֹמְרִים בְּבֵית הַמִּקְדָּשׁ:

לַמְנַצֵּחַ עַל־הַגִּתִּית לְאָסָף: הַרְנִינוּ לֵאלֹהִים עוּזֵּנוּ, הָרִיעוּ לֵאלֹהֵי תהלים פא
יַעֲקֹב: שְׂאוּ־זִמְרָה וּתְנוּ־תֹף, כִּנּוֹר נָעִים עִם־נָבֶל: תִּקְעוּ בַחֹדֶשׁ שׁוֹפָר,
בַּכֶּסֶה לְיוֹם חַגֵּנוּ: כִּי חֹק לְיִשְׂרָאֵל הוּא, מִשְׁפָּט לֵאלֹהֵי יַעֲקֹב: עֵדוּת
בִּיהוֹסֵף שָׂמוֹ, בְּצֵאתוֹ עַל־אֶרֶץ מִצְרָיִם, שְׂפַת לֹא־יָדַעְתִּי אֶשְׁמָע:
הֲסִירוֹתִי מִסֵּבֶל שִׁכְמוֹ, כַּפָּיו מִדּוּד תַּעֲבֹרְנָה: בַּצָּרָה קָרָאתָ וָאֲחַלְּצֶךָּ,
אֶעֶנְךָ בְּסֵתֶר רַעַם, אֶבְחָנְךָ עַל־מֵי מְרִיבָה סֶלָה: שְׁמַע עַמִּי וְאָעִידָה
בָּךְ, יִשְׂרָאֵל אִם־תִּשְׁמַע־לִי: לֹא־יִהְיֶה בְךָ אֵל זָר, וְלֹא תִשְׁתַּחֲוֶה לְאֵל
נֵכָר: אָנֹכִי יהוה אֱלֹהֶיךָ, הַמַּעַלְךָ מֵאֶרֶץ מִצְרָיִם, הַרְחֶב־פִּיךָ וַאֲמַלְאֵהוּ:
וְלֹא־שָׁמַע עַמִּי לְקוֹלִי, וְיִשְׂרָאֵל לֹא־אָבָה לִי: וָאֲשַׁלְּחֵהוּ בִּשְׁרִירוּת
לִבָּם, יֵלְכוּ בְּמוֹעֲצוֹתֵיהֶם: לוּ עַמִּי שֹׁמֵעַ לִי, יִשְׂרָאֵל בִּדְרָכַי יְהַלֵּכוּ:
כִּמְעַט אוֹיְבֵיהֶם אַכְנִיעַ, וְעַל־צָרֵיהֶם אָשִׁיב יָדִי: מְשַׂנְאֵי יהוה יְכַחֲשׁוּ־
לוֹ, וִיהִי עִתָּם לְעוֹלָם: ◂ וַיַּאֲכִילֵהוּ מֵחֵלֶב חִטָּה, וּמִצּוּר, דְּבַשׁ אַשְׂבִּיעֶךָ:

קדיש יתום (*page 251*)

CONNECTION

A SMILE COSTS NOTHING, BUT GIVES MUCH

It enriches those who receive, without making poorer those who give.
It takes but a moment, but the memory of it sometimes lasts forever.

None is so rich or mighty that he can get along without it,
and none is so poor but that he can be made rich by it.

A smile creates happiness in the home, fosters good will in business,
and is the countersign of friendship.

It brings rest to the weary, cheer to the discouraged,
sunshine to the sad, and is nature's best antidote for trouble.

Yet it cannot be bought, begged, borrowed, or stolen,
for it is something that is of no value to anyone until it is given away.

Some people are too tired to give you a smile.
Give them one of yours,
as none needs a smile so much as he who has no more to give.

Friday: Today is the sixth day of the week,
on which the Levites used to say this psalm in the Temple:

יהוה מָלָךְ The LORD reigns. He is robed in majesty. The LORD is robed, clothed with strength. The world is firmly established; it cannot be moved. Your throne stands firm as of old; You are eternal. Rivers lift up, LORD, rivers lift up their voice, rivers lift up their crashing waves. Mightier than the noise of many waters, than the mighty waves of the sea is the LORD on high. ▸ Your testimonies are very sure; holiness adorns Your House, LORD, for evermore. *Ps. 93*

Mourner's Kaddish (page 250)

LEARNING

On the sixth day of the week, Erev Shabbat, we prepare ourselves and don our finest clothing in honor of Shabbat. God "robed in majesty" is like the preparation we do for Shabbat by donning our finest clothing. We read about God in this psalm with very human descriptions and imagery to connect God and humanity, just as Friday connects the holy day of Shabbat to the rest of the week.

REFLECTION

How do you imagine God?
What imagery of God
does this psalm paint for you?

How do you experience
the transition of Friday
into Shabbat?

What do you do
to prepare for Shabbat?
How do you help your family
prepare for Shabbat?

CONNECTION

The Midrash (Mekhilta Shemot *20:7) describes Shammai's method of shopping for Shabbat. Whenever he would see a fine food, he would buy it and set it aside for Shabbat. If he would subsequently find something better, he would buy that for Shabbat and eat the earlier, lesser food. In this way, he turned his weekdays into a search for the best items with which to sanctify Shabbat.*

Friday הַיּוֹם יוֹם שִׁשִּׁי בְּשַׁבָּת, שֶׁבּוֹ הָיוּ הַלְוִיִּם אוֹמְרִים בְּבֵית הַמִּקְדָּשׁ

תהלים צג
יהוה מָלָךְ, גֵּאוּת לָבֵשׁ, לָבֵשׁ יהוה עֹז הִתְאַזָּר, אַף־תִּכּוֹן תֵּבֵל בַּל־
תִּמּוֹט: נָכוֹן כִּסְאֲךָ מֵאָז, מֵעוֹלָם אָתָּה: נָשְׂאוּ נְהָרוֹת יהוה, נָשְׂאוּ נְהָרוֹת
קוֹלָם, יִשְׂאוּ נְהָרוֹת דָּכְיָם: מִקֹּלוֹת מַיִם רַבִּים, אַדִּירִים מִשְׁבְּרֵי־יָם,
אַדִּיר בַּמָּרוֹם יהוה: ‹ עֵדֹתֶיךָ נֶאֶמְנוּ מְאֹד, לְבֵיתְךָ נַאֲוָה־קֹדֶשׁ, יהוה
לְאֹרֶךְ יָמִים:

קדיש יתום (*page 251*)

... A THOUSAND WORDS

On Rosh Hodesh, the following psalm is said:

בָּרְכִי נַפְשִׁי Bless the LORD, my soul. LORD, my God, You are very great, clothed in majesty and splendor, wrapped in a robe of light. You have spread out the heavens like a tent. He has laid the beams of His lofts in the waters. He makes the clouds His chariot, riding on the wings of the wind. He makes the winds His messengers, flames of fire His ministers. He has fixed the earth on its foundations so that it will never be shaken. You covered it with the deep like a cloak; the waters stood above the mountains. At Your rebuke they fled; at the sound of Your thunder they rushed away, flowing over the hills, pouring down into the valleys to the place You appointed for them. You fixed a boundary they were not to pass, so that they would never cover the earth again. He makes springs flow in the valleys; they make their way between the hills, giving drink to all the beasts of the field; the wild donkeys quench their thirst. The birds of the sky live beside them, singing among the foliage. He waters the mountains from His lofts: the earth is full with the fruit of Your work. He makes grass grow for the cattle, and plants for the use of man, that he may produce bread from the earth, wine to cheer the heart of man, oil to make the face shine, and bread to *Ps. 104*

LEARNING

Barekhi Nafshi is recited on Rosh Hodesh. Rabbi Soloveitchik explains that the Jew can identify personally with the moon. Just like our people, the moon is regularly revived from an almost nonexistent state and its illumination always returns from a state of darkness. Rosh Hodesh speaks to this eternal faith in redemption yet to come, in the coming light though it is yet dark. Rosh Hodesh, when the moon itself teaches us about the concept of renewal and rebirth, reminds the Jewish People to hope and have faith.

The Gemara in *Menahot* states in the name of Rabbi Yishmael: God told Moshe, "Observe the moon and recognize that from darkness shall emanate light. The moon will teach you and all future Jewish generations that Israel will be renewed and revitalized, just as the moon is. Just as at certain times of the month it is impossible to contemplate or even imagine a moon, at certain points of history it will be hard to imagine Jews and Judaism. But I promise you, Moshe, *kazeh re'eh vekadesh*, like this, see and sanctify, precisely when the moon is so tiny, hidden, and insignificant, sanctify it and renew your hopes in its capacity to shine." (Rabbi Eliyahu Safran)

On ראש חודש*, the following psalm is said:*

תהלים קד
בָּרְכִי נַפְשִׁי אֶת־יהוה, יהוה אֱלֹהַי גָּדַלְתָּ מְּאֹד, הוֹד וְהָדָר לָבָשְׁתָּ:
עֹטֶה־אוֹר כַּשַּׂלְמָה, נוֹטֶה שָׁמַיִם כַּיְרִיעָה: הַמְקָרֶה בַמַּיִם עֲלִיּוֹתָיו,
הַשָּׂם־עָבִים רְכוּבוֹ, הַמְהַלֵּךְ עַל־כַּנְפֵי־רוּחַ: עֹשֶׂה מַלְאָכָיו רוּחוֹת,
מְשָׁרְתָיו אֵשׁ לֹהֵט: יָסַד־אֶרֶץ עַל־מְכוֹנֶיהָ, בַּל־תִּמּוֹט עוֹלָם וָעֶד:
תְּהוֹם כַּלְּבוּשׁ כִּסִּיתוֹ, עַל־הָרִים יַעַמְדוּ־מָיִם: מִן־גַּעֲרָתְךָ יְנוּסוּן, מִן־
קוֹל רַעַמְךָ יֵחָפֵזוּן: יַעֲלוּ הָרִים, יֵרְדוּ בְקָעוֹת, אֶל־מְקוֹם זֶה יָסַדְתָּ
לָהֶם: גְּבוּל־שַׂמְתָּ בַּל־יַעֲבֹרוּן, בַּל־יְשׁוּבוּן לְכַסּוֹת הָאָרֶץ: הַמְשַׁלֵּחַ
מַעְיָנִים בַּנְּחָלִים, בֵּין הָרִים יְהַלֵּכוּן: יַשְׁקוּ כָּל־חַיְתוֹ שָׂדָי, יִשְׁבְּרוּ
פְרָאִים צְמָאָם: עֲלֵיהֶם עוֹף־הַשָּׁמַיִם יִשְׁכּוֹן, מִבֵּין עֳפָאיִם יִתְּנוּ־קוֹל:
מַשְׁקֶה הָרִים מֵעֲלִיּוֹתָיו, מִפְּרִי מַעֲשֶׂיךָ תִּשְׂבַּע הָאָרֶץ: מַצְמִיחַ
חָצִיר לַבְּהֵמָה, וְעֵשֶׂב לַעֲבֹדַת הָאָדָם, לְהוֹצִיא לֶחֶם מִן־הָאָרֶץ: וְיַיִן

... A THOUSAND WORDS

sustain man's heart. The trees of the LORD drink their fill, the cedars of Lebanon which He planted. There, birds build their nests; the stork makes its home in the cypresses. High hills are for the wild goats; crags are shelter for the badgers. He made the moon to mark the seasons, and makes the sun know when to set. You bring darkness and it is night; then all the beasts of the forests stir. The young lions roar for prey, seeking their food from God. When the sun rises, they slink away and seek rest in their lairs. Man goes out to his work and his labor until evening. How numerous are Your works, LORD; You made them all in wisdom; the earth is full of Your creations. There is the vast, immeasurable sea with its countless swarming creatures, living things great and small. There ships sail. There is Leviathan You formed to sport there. All of them look to You in hope, to give them their food when it is due. What You give them, they gather up. When You open Your hand, they are filled with good. When You hide Your face, they are dismayed. When You take away their breath, they die and return to dust. When You send back Your breath, they are created, giving new life to the earth. May the glory of the LORD be for ever; may the LORD rejoice in His works. When He looks at the earth, it trembles. When He touches the mountains, they pour forth smoke. I will sing to the LORD as long as I live; I will sing psalms to my God all my life. ▸ May my prayers be pleasing to Him; I shall rejoice in the LORD. May sinners vanish from the earth, and the wicked be no more. Bless the LORD, my soul. Halleluya!

Mourner's Kaddish (page 250)

... A THOUSAND WORDS

יְשַׂמַּח לְבַב־אֱנוֹשׁ, לְהַצְהִיל פָּנִים מִשָּׁמֶן, וְלֶחֶם לְבַב־אֱנוֹשׁ יִסְעָד:
יִשְׂבְּעוּ עֲצֵי יהוה, אַרְזֵי לְבָנוֹן אֲשֶׁר נָטָע: אֲשֶׁר־שָׁם צִפֳּרִים יְקַנֵּנוּ,
חֲסִידָה בְּרוֹשִׁים בֵּיתָהּ: הָרִים הַגְּבֹהִים לַיְּעֵלִים, סְלָעִים מַחְסֶה
לַשְׁפַנִּים: עָשָׂה יָרֵחַ לְמוֹעֲדִים, שֶׁמֶשׁ יָדַע מְבוֹאוֹ: תָּשֶׁת־חֹשֶׁךְ
וִיהִי לָיְלָה, בּוֹ־תִרְמֹשׂ כָּל־חַיְתוֹ־יָעַר: הַכְּפִירִים שֹׁאֲגִים לַטָּרֶף,
וּלְבַקֵּשׁ מֵאֵל אָכְלָם: תִּזְרַח הַשֶּׁמֶשׁ יֵאָסֵפוּן, וְאֶל־מְעוֹנֹתָם יִרְבָּצוּן:
יֵצֵא אָדָם לְפָעֳלוֹ, וְלַעֲבֹדָתוֹ עֲדֵי־עָרֶב: מָה־רַבּוּ מַעֲשֶׂיךָ יהוה,
כֻּלָּם בְּחָכְמָה עָשִׂיתָ, מָלְאָה הָאָרֶץ קִנְיָנֶךָ: זֶה הַיָּם גָּדוֹל וּרְחַב
יָדָיִם, שָׁם־רֶמֶשׂ וְאֵין מִסְפָּר, חַיּוֹת קְטַנּוֹת עִם־גְּדֹלוֹת: שָׁם אֳנִיּוֹת
יְהַלֵּכוּן, לִוְיָתָן זֶה־יָצַרְתָּ לְשַׂחֶק־בּוֹ: כֻּלָּם אֵלֶיךָ יְשַׂבֵּרוּן, לָתֵת
אָכְלָם בְּעִתּוֹ: תִּתֵּן לָהֶם יִלְקֹטוּן, תִּפְתַּח יָדְךָ יִשְׂבְּעוּן טוֹב: תַּסְתִּיר
פָּנֶיךָ יִבָּהֵלוּן, תֹּסֵף רוּחָם יִגְוָעוּן, וְאֶל־עֲפָרָם יְשׁוּבוּן: תְּשַׁלַּח רוּחֲךָ
יִבָּרֵאוּן, וּתְחַדֵּשׁ פְּנֵי אֲדָמָה: יְהִי כְבוֹד יהוה לְעוֹלָם, יִשְׂמַח יהוה
בְּמַעֲשָׂיו: הַמַּבִּיט לָאָרֶץ וַתִּרְעָד, יִגַּע בֶּהָרִים וְיֶעֱשָׁנוּ: אָשִׁירָה
לַיהוה בְּחַיָּי, אֲזַמְּרָה לֵאלֹהַי בְּעוֹדִי: ‹ יֶעֱרַב עָלָיו שִׂיחִי, אָנֹכִי
אֶשְׂמַח בַּיהוה: יִתַּמּוּ חַטָּאִים מִן־הָאָרֶץ, וּרְשָׁעִים עוֹד אֵינָם,
בָּרְכִי נַפְשִׁי אֶת־יהוה, הַלְלוּיָהּ:

קדיש יתום (*page 251*)

REFLECTION

"The more we understand of the complexity of life, the more we appreciate 'How numerous are Your works, Lord; You made them all in wisdom; the earth is full of Your creations.'"

(*Tehillim* 104:24)

(Rabbi Jonathan Sacks, Koren Sacks Siddur)

How do you see God in nature?

Why do we focus on God's mastery over nature at the beginning of each new month?

What would you like to renew this month?

How would you like to start again?

During the month of Elul (except Erev Rosh HaShana), the shofar is sounded (some sound the shofar after the psalm below). From the second day of Rosh Hodesh Elul through Shemini Atzeret (in Israel through Hoshana Raba), the following psalm is said:

לְדָוִד By David. The LORD is my light and my salvation – whom then shall I fear? The LORD is the stronghold of my life – of whom shall I be afraid? When evil men close in on me to devour my flesh, it is they, my enemies and foes, who stumble and fall. Should an army besiege me, my heart would not fear. Should war break out against me, still I would be confident. One thing I ask of the LORD, only this do I seek: to live in the House of the LORD all the days of my life, to gaze on the beauty of the LORD and worship in His Temple. For He will keep me safe in His pavilion on the day of trouble. He will hide me under the cover of His tent. He will set me high upon a rock. Now my head is high above my enemies who surround me. I will sacrifice in His tent with shouts of joy. I will sing and chant praises to the LORD. LORD, hear my voice when I call. Be generous to me and answer me. On Your behalf my heart says, "Seek My face." Your face, LORD, will I seek. Do not hide Your face from me. Do not turn Your servant away in anger. You have been my help. Do not reject or abandon me, God, my Savior. Were my father and my mother to abandon me, the LORD would take me in. Teach me Your way, LORD, and lead me on a level path, because of my oppressors. Do not abandon me to the will of my enemies, for false witnesses have risen against me, breathing violence. ▸ Were it not for my faith that I shall see the LORD's goodness in the land of the living. Hope in the LORD. Be strong and of good courage, and hope in the LORD! Ps. 27

Mourner's Kaddish (page 250)

CONNECTION

Think *ought*.

Not what *is* a Jew, but what *ought* a Jew to be.

Not what *is* a synagogue, but what *ought* a synagogue to be.

Not what prayer *is*, but what prayer *ought* to be.

Not what ritual *is*, but what ritual *ought* to be.

Focus from *is* to *ought*, and our mindset is affected. *Is* faces me toward the present; *ought* turns me to the future. *Ought* challenges my creative imagination and opens me to the realm of possibilities and responsibilities to realize yesterday's dream.

Ought and *is* are complementary. Without an *is*, the genius of our past and present collective wisdom is forgotten. Without an *ought*, the great visions of tomorrow fade.

Ought demands not only a knowledge of history but of exciting expectation. *Is* is a being, *ought* is a becoming.

Ought emancipates me from status quo thinking.

Ought is the freedom of spirit.

Ought we not *Ought*?

(Harold Schulweis)

During the month of אלול *(except* ערב ראש השנה*), the* שופר *is sounded (some sound the* שופר *after the psalm below). From the second day of* ראש חודש אלול *through* שמיני עצרת *(in* ארץ ישראל *through* הושענא רבה*), the following psalm is said:*

לְדָוִד, יהוה אוֹרִי וְיִשְׁעִי, מִמִּי אִירָא, יהוה מָעוֹז־חַיַּי, מִמִּי אֶפְחָד: תהלים כז
בִּקְרֹב עָלַי מְרֵעִים לֶאֱכֹל אֶת־בְּשָׂרִי, צָרַי וְאֹיְבַי לִי, הֵמָּה כָשְׁלוּ
וְנָפָלוּ: אִם־תַּחֲנֶה עָלַי מַחֲנֶה, לֹא־יִירָא לִבִּי, אִם־תָּקוּם עָלַי מִלְחָמָה,
בְּזֹאת אֲנִי בוֹטֵחַ: אַחַת שָׁאַלְתִּי מֵאֵת־יהוה, אוֹתָהּ אֲבַקֵּשׁ, שִׁבְתִּי
בְּבֵית־יהוה כָּל־יְמֵי חַיַּי, לַחֲזוֹת בְּנֹעַם־יהוה, וּלְבַקֵּר בְּהֵיכָלוֹ: כִּי
יִצְפְּנֵנִי בְּסֻכֹּה בְּיוֹם רָעָה, יַסְתִּרֵנִי בְּסֵתֶר אָהֳלוֹ, בְּצוּר יְרוֹמְמֵנִי:
וְעַתָּה יָרוּם רֹאשִׁי עַל אֹיְבַי סְבִיבוֹתַי, וְאֶזְבְּחָה בְאָהֳלוֹ זִבְחֵי תְרוּעָה,
אָשִׁירָה וַאֲזַמְּרָה לַיהוה: שְׁמַע־יהוה קוֹלִי אֶקְרָא, וְחָנֵּנִי וַעֲנֵנִי: לְךָ
אָמַר לִבִּי בַּקְּשׁוּ פָנָי, אֶת־פָּנֶיךָ יהוה אֲבַקֵּשׁ: אַל־תַּסְתֵּר פָּנֶיךָ מִמֶּנִּי,
אַל תַּט־בְּאַף עַבְדֶּךָ, עֶזְרָתִי הָיִיתָ, אַל־תִּטְּשֵׁנִי וְאַל־תַּעַזְבֵנִי, אֱלֹהֵי
יִשְׁעִי: כִּי־אָבִי וְאִמִּי עֲזָבוּנִי, וַיהוה יַאַסְפֵנִי: הוֹרֵנִי יהוה דַּרְכֶּךָ, וּנְחֵנִי
בְּאֹרַח מִישׁוֹר, לְמַעַן שׁוֹרְרָי: אַל־תִּתְּנֵנִי בְּנֶפֶשׁ צָרָי, כִּי קָמוּ־בִי
עֵדֵי־שֶׁקֶר, וִיפֵחַ חָמָס: ‹ לוּלֵא הֶאֱמַנְתִּי לִרְאוֹת בְּטוּב־יהוה בְּאֶרֶץ
חַיִּים: קַוֵּה אֶל־יהוה, חֲזַק וְיַאֲמֵץ לִבֶּךָ, וְקַוֵּה אֶל־יהוה:

קדיש יתום (page 251)

REFLECTION

What is David's central request in this psalm?

If you could ask God for only one thing, what would it be?

What do you pray for most?

LEARNING

This *mizmor* is said every day in the month of Elul and until Shemini Atzeret. The custom is based on a midrash (*Vayikra Raba* 21) that explains that "*Ori* – my light" refers to Rosh HaShana and "*Yishi* – my salvation" refers to Yom Kippur. While there is no mention of repentance in this psalm, the theme of the Days of Awe is clear. David focuses on his main request: to be close to God. This is surely an apt theme for the Days of Awe, returning to God and becoming close with Him.

After the regular service, the following psalm is read in a house of mourning during the shiva week. On those days on which Taḥanun is not said, Psalm 16 (below) is substituted.

לַמְנַצֵּחַ For the conductor of music. Of the sons of Koraḥ. A sacred song. Hear this, all you peoples. Listen, all inhabitants of the world, low and high, rich and poor alike. My mouth will speak words of wisdom; the utterance of my heart will give understanding. I listen with care to a parable; I expound my mystery to the music of the harp. Why should I fear when evil days come, when the wickedness of my enemies surrounds me, trusting in their wealth, boasting of their great riches? No man can redeem his brother or pay God the price of his release, for the ransom of a life is costly; no payment is ever enough that would let him live for ever, never seeing the grave. For all can see that wise men die, that the foolish and senseless all perish and leave their wealth to others. They think their houses will remain for ever, their dwellings for all generations; they give their names to their estates. But man, despite his splendor, does not endure; he is like the beasts that perish. Such is the fate of the foolish and their followers who approve their words, Selah. Like sheep they are destined for the grave: death will be their shepherd. The upright will rule over them in the morning. Their forms will decay in the grave, far from their mansions. But God will redeem my life from the grave; He will surely take me to Himself, Selah. Do not be overawed when a man grows rich, when the glory of his house increases, for he will take nothing with him when he dies; his wealth will not descend with him. Though while he lived he counted himself blessed – men always praise you when you prosper – he will join the generation of his ancestors who will never again see the light. A man who, despite his splendor, lacks understanding, is like the beasts that perish. *Ps. 49*

Mourner's Kaddish (page 250)

On those days on which Taḥanun is not said, substitute:

מִכְתָּם לְדָוִד A musical composition of David. Protect me, God, for in You I have found refuge. I have said to the Lord: You are my Lord: from You alone comes the good I enjoy. All my delight is in the holy ones, the mighty in the land. Those who run after other gods multiply their sorrows. I shall never offer them libations of blood, nor will their names pass my lips. The Lord is my portion and my cup: You direct my fate. The lines have fallen for me in pleasant places; I am well content with my inheritance. I will bless the Lord who has guided me; at night my innermost being rebukes me. I have set the Lord before me at all times. He is at my right hand: I shall not be shaken. Therefore my heart is glad, my spirit rejoices, and my body rests secure. For You will not abandon me to the grave, nor let Your faithful one see the pit. You will teach me the path of life. In Your presence is fullness of joy; at Your right hand, bliss for evermore. *Ps. 16*

Mourner's Kaddish (page 250)

After the regular service, the following psalm is read in a house of mourning during the שבעה *week. On those days on which* תחנון *is not said,* תהלים טז *(below) is substituted.*

תהלים מט

לַמְנַצֵּחַ לִבְנֵי־קֹרַח מִזְמוֹר: שִׁמְעוּ־זֹאת כׇּל־הָעַמִּים, הַאֲזִינוּ כׇּל־יֹשְׁבֵי חָלֶד: גַּם־בְּנֵי אָדָם, גַּם־בְּנֵי־אִישׁ, יַחַד עָשִׁיר וְאֶבְיוֹן: פִּי יְדַבֵּר חׇכְמוֹת, וְהָגוּת לִבִּי תְבוּנוֹת: אַטֶּה לְמָשָׁל אׇזְנִי, אֶפְתַּח בְּכִנּוֹר חִידָתִי: לָמָּה אִירָא בִּימֵי רָע, עֲוֺן עֲקֵבַי יְסֻבֵּנִי: הַבֹּטְחִים עַל־חֵילָם, וּבְרֹב עׇשְׁרָם יִתְהַלָּלוּ: אָח לֹא־פָדֹה יִפְדֶּה אִישׁ, לֹא־יִתֵּן לֵאלֹהִים כׇּפְרוֹ: וְיֵקַר פִּדְיוֹן נַפְשָׁם, וְחָדַל לְעוֹלָם: וִיחִי־עוֹד לָנֶצַח, לֹא יִרְאֶה הַשָּׁחַת: כִּי יִרְאֶה חֲכָמִים יָמוּתוּ, יַחַד כְּסִיל וָבַעַר יֹאבֵדוּ, וְעָזְבוּ לַאֲחֵרִים חֵילָם: קִרְבָּם בָּתֵּימוֹ לְעוֹלָם, מִשְׁכְּנֹתָם לְדוֹר וָדֹר, קָרְאוּ בִשְׁמוֹתָם עֲלֵי אֲדָמוֹת: וְאָדָם בִּיקָר בַּל־יָלִין, נִמְשַׁל כַּבְּהֵמוֹת נִדְמוּ: זֶה דַרְכָּם, כֵּסֶל לָמוֹ, וְאַחֲרֵיהֶם בְּפִיהֶם יִרְצוּ סֶלָה: כַּצֹּאן לִשְׁאוֹל שַׁתּוּ, מָוֶת יִרְעֵם, וַיִּרְדּוּ בָם יְשָׁרִים לַבֹּקֶר, וְצוּרָם לְבַלּוֹת שְׁאוֹל מִזְּבֻל לוֹ: אַךְ־אֱלֹהִים יִפְדֶּה נַפְשִׁי מִיַּד שְׁאוֹל, כִּי יִקָּחֵנִי סֶלָה: אַל־תִּירָא כִּי־יַעֲשִׁר אִישׁ, כִּי־יִרְבֶּה כְּבוֹד בֵּיתוֹ: כִּי לֹא בְמוֹתוֹ יִקַּח הַכֹּל, לֹא־יֵרֵד אַחֲרָיו כְּבוֹדוֹ: כִּי־נַפְשׁוֹ בְּחַיָּיו יְבָרֵךְ, וְיוֹדֻךָ כִּי־תֵיטִיב לָךְ: תָּבוֹא עַד־דּוֹר אֲבוֹתָיו, עַד־נֵצַח לֹא יִרְאוּ־אוֹר: אָדָם בִּיקָר וְלֹא יָבִין, נִמְשַׁל כַּבְּהֵמוֹת נִדְמוּ:

קדיש יתום (*page 251*)

On those days on which תחנון *is not said, substitute:*

תהלים טז

מִכְתָּם לְדָוִד, שָׁמְרֵנִי אֵל כִּי־חָסִיתִי בָךְ: אָמַרְתְּ לַיהוה, אֲדֹנָי אָתָּה, טוֹבָתִי בַּל־עָלֶיךָ: לִקְדוֹשִׁים אֲשֶׁר־בָּאָרֶץ הֵמָּה, וְאַדִּירֵי כׇּל־חֶפְצִי־בָם: יִרְבּוּ עַצְּבוֹתָם אַחֵר מָהָרוּ, בַּל־אַסִּיךְ נִסְכֵּיהֶם מִדָּם, וּבַל־אֶשָּׂא אֶת־שְׁמוֹתָם עַל־שְׂפָתָי: יהוה, מְנָת־חֶלְקִי וְכוֹסִי, אַתָּה תּוֹמִיךְ גּוֹרָלִי: חֲבָלִים נָפְלוּ־לִי בַּנְּעִמִים, אַף־נַחֲלָת שָׁפְרָה עָלָי: אֲבָרֵךְ אֶת־יהוה אֲשֶׁר יְעָצָנִי, אַף־לֵילוֹת יִסְּרוּנִי כִלְיוֹתָי: שִׁוִּיתִי יהוה לְנֶגְדִּי תָמִיד, כִּי מִימִינִי בַּל־אֶמּוֹט: לָכֵן שָׂמַח לִבִּי וַיָּגֶל כְּבוֹדִי, אַף־בְּשָׂרִי יִשְׁכֹּן לָבֶטַח: כִּי לֹא־תַעֲזֹב נַפְשִׁי לִשְׁאוֹל, לֹא־תִתֵּן חֲסִידְךָ לִרְאוֹת שָׁחַת: תּוֹדִיעֵנִי אֹרַח חַיִּים, שֹׂבַע שְׂמָחוֹת אֶת־פָּנֶיךָ, נְעִמוֹת בִּימִינְךָ נֶצַח:

קדיש יתום (*page 251*)

Minḥa for Weekdays

אַשְׁרֵי Happy are those who live in Your House; *Ps. 84*
they shall continue to praise You, Selah!
Happy are the people for whom this is so; *Ps. 144*
happy are the people whose God is the Lord.

A song of praise by David. *Ps. 145*

א I will elevate You, my God, the King, and bless Your name for ever and all time. ב Every day I will bless You, and praise Your name for ever and all time. ג Great is the Lord and greatly to be praised; His greatness is unfathomable. ד One generation will praise Your works to the next, and tell of Your mighty deeds. ה On the glorious splendor of Your majesty I will meditate, and on the acts of Your wonders. ו They shall talk of the power of Your awesome deeds, and I will tell of Your greatness. ז They shall recite the record of Your great goodness, and sing with joy of Your righteousness. ח The Lord is generous and compassionate, slow to anger and great in loving-kindness. ט The Lord is good to all, and His compassion extends to all His works. י All Your works shall thank You, Lord, and Your devoted ones shall bless You. כ They shall talk of the glory of Your kingship, and speak of Your might. ל To make known to mankind His mighty deeds and the glorious majesty of

---

hands like the afternoon offering (*minḥat arev*)."

The Minḥa service consists of a highly abridged version of Shaḥarit. *Ashrei* serves as a mini-*Pesukei DeZimra*. Then comes the *Amida* as the central *tefilla* as with all other prayer services. *Taḥanun* serves as another opportunity for supplication, and then *Aleinu* as the conclusion. Minḥa is the shortest of the three daily *tefillot*, perhaps because it comes at a time when we are the busiest – in the middle of the hours of our productivity. There is a tradition, however, that this is a time when our *tefillot* can be most effective. This was the time when Eliyahu HaNavi cried to Hashem, "Answer me! Answer me!" and his prayers were answered (*Melakhim Alef* 18:36–38). Perhaps it is because Minḥa comes at the busiest part of our day, and because it is the easiest *tefilla* to forget or skip, that Minḥa has this potency. Minḥa is the prayer service where it becomes most critical to push ourselves to break up our day with reflection, introspection, and time for God.

מנחה לחול

אַשְׁרֵי יוֹשְׁבֵי בֵיתֶךָ, עוֹד יְהַלְלוּךָ סֶּלָה: תהלים פד

אַשְׁרֵי הָעָם שֶׁכָּכָה לּוֹ, אַשְׁרֵי הָעָם שֶׁיהוה אֱלֹהָיו: תהלים קמד

תְּהִלָּה לְדָוִד תהלים קמה

אֲרוֹמִמְךָ אֱלוֹהַי הַמֶּלֶךְ, וַאֲבָרְכָה שִׁמְךָ לְעוֹלָם וָעֶד:

בְּכָל־יוֹם אֲבָרְכֶךָּ, וַאֲהַלְלָה שִׁמְךָ לְעוֹלָם וָעֶד:

גָּדוֹל יהוה וּמְהֻלָּל מְאֹד, וְלִגְדֻלָּתוֹ אֵין חֵקֶר:

דּוֹר לְדוֹר יְשַׁבַּח מַעֲשֶׂיךָ, וּגְבוּרֹתֶיךָ יַגִּידוּ:

הֲדַר כְּבוֹד הוֹדֶךָ, וְדִבְרֵי נִפְלְאֹתֶיךָ אָשִׂיחָה:

וֶעֱזוּז נוֹרְאֹתֶיךָ יֹאמֵרוּ, וּגְדוּלָּתְךָ אֲסַפְּרֶנָּה:

זֵכֶר רַב־טוּבְךָ יַבִּיעוּ, וְצִדְקָתְךָ יְרַנֵּנוּ:

חַנּוּן וְרַחוּם יהוה, אֶרֶךְ אַפַּיִם וּגְדָל־חָסֶד:

טוֹב־יהוה לַכֹּל, וְרַחֲמָיו עַל־כָּל־מַעֲשָׂיו:

יוֹדְוּךָ יהוה כָּל־מַעֲשֶׂיךָ, וַחֲסִידֶיךָ יְבָרְכוּכָה:

כְּבוֹד מַלְכוּתְךָ יֹאמֵרוּ, וּגְבוּרָתְךָ יְדַבֵּרוּ:

לְהוֹדִיעַ לִבְנֵי הָאָדָם גְּבוּרֹתָיו, וּכְבוֹד הֲדַר מַלְכוּתוֹ:

LEARNING

INTRODUCTION TO MINḤA:

The word *minḥa* (מִנְחָה) meaning an offering, refers to the meal-offering, and is the term used to denote the afternoon *tefilla* and sacrificial service. The Talmud debates whether our three *tefillot* services were instituted by our forefathers, the *Avot*, or correspond to the sacrificial services in the *Beit HaMikdash* (*Berakhot* 26b). Minḥa takes its name from the daily afternoon sacrifice (*Bemidbar* 28:4). Although the meal offering (the *minḥa*) was not unique to the afternoon service, the name may have become associated with it because of this verse in *Tehillim* (141:2): "May my prayer be like incense before You, the lifting up of my

His kingship. מ Your kingdom is an everlasting kingdom, and Your reign is for all generations. ס The LORD supports all who fall, and raises all who are bowed down. ע All raise their eyes to You in hope, and You give them their food in due season. פ You open Your hand, and satisfy every living thing with favor. צ The LORD is righteous in all His ways, and kind in all He does. ק The LORD is close to all who call on Him, to all who call on Him in truth. ר He fulfills the will of those who fear Him; He hears their cry and saves them. ש The LORD guards all who love Him, but all the wicked He will destroy. ת ▸ My mouth shall speak the praise of the LORD, and all creatures shall bless His holy name for ever and all time.

We will bless the LORD now and for ever. Halleluya! *Ps. 115*

HALF KADDISH

Leader: יִתְגַּדַּל Magnified and sanctified may His great name be,
in the world He created by His will.
May He establish His kingdom
in your lifetime and in your days,
and in the lifetime of all the house of Israel,
swiftly and soon –
and say: Amen.

All: May His great name be blessed for ever and all time.

Leader: Blessed and praised, glorified and elevated,
raised and honored, uplifted and praised
be the name of the Holy One,
blessed be He,
beyond any blessing,
song, praise and consolation
uttered in the world –
and say: Amen.

On fast days, turn to Removing the Torah from the Ark on page 220. The Torah reading and Haftara for fast days are on page 1120. After the Torah is returned to the Ark, the Leader says Half Kaddish.

מַלְכוּתְךָ מַלְכוּת כָּל־עֹלָמִים, וּמֶמְשַׁלְתְּךָ בְּכָל־דּוֹר וָדֹר:
סוֹמֵךְ יהוה לְכָל־הַנֹּפְלִים, וְזוֹקֵף לְכָל־הַכְּפוּפִים:
עֵינֵי־כֹל אֵלֶיךָ יְשַׂבֵּרוּ, וְאַתָּה נוֹתֵן־לָהֶם אֶת־אָכְלָם בְּעִתּוֹ:
פּוֹתֵחַ אֶת־יָדֶךָ, וּמַשְׂבִּיעַ לְכָל־חַי רָצוֹן:
צַדִּיק יהוה בְּכָל־דְּרָכָיו, וְחָסִיד בְּכָל־מַעֲשָׂיו:
קָרוֹב יהוה לְכָל־קֹרְאָיו, לְכֹל אֲשֶׁר יִקְרָאֻהוּ בֶאֱמֶת:
רְצוֹן־יְרֵאָיו יַעֲשֶׂה, וְאֶת־שַׁוְעָתָם יִשְׁמַע, וְיוֹשִׁיעֵם:
שׁוֹמֵר יהוה אֶת־כָּל־אֹהֲבָיו, וְאֵת כָּל־הָרְשָׁעִים יַשְׁמִיד:
› תְּהִלַּת יהוה יְדַבֶּר פִּי, וִיבָרֵךְ כָּל־בָּשָׂר שֵׁם קָדְשׁוֹ לְעוֹלָם וָעֶד:
וַאֲנַחְנוּ נְבָרֵךְ יָהּ מֵעַתָּה וְעַד־עוֹלָם, הַלְלוּיָהּ: תהלים קטו

חצי קדיש

ש״ץ: יִתְגַּדַּל וְיִתְקַדַּשׁ שְׁמֵהּ רַבָּא (קהל: אָמֵן)
בְּעָלְמָא דִּי בְרָא כִרְעוּתֵהּ
וְיַמְלִיךְ מַלְכוּתֵהּ
בְּחַיֵּיכוֹן וּבְיוֹמֵיכוֹן וּבְחַיֵּי דְכָל בֵּית יִשְׂרָאֵל
בַּעֲגָלָא וּבִזְמַן קָרִיב, וְאִמְרוּ אָמֵן. (קהל: אָמֵן)

קהל וש״ץ: יְהֵא שְׁמֵהּ רַבָּא מְבָרַךְ לְעָלַם וּלְעָלְמֵי עָלְמַיָּא.

ש״ץ: יִתְבָּרַךְ וְיִשְׁתַּבַּח וְיִתְפָּאַר וְיִתְרוֹמַם וְיִתְנַשֵּׂא
וְיִתְהַדָּר וְיִתְעַלֶּה וְיִתְהַלָּל
שְׁמֵהּ דְּקֻדְשָׁא בְּרִיךְ הוּא (קהל: בְּרִיךְ הוּא)
לְעֵלָּא מִן כָּל בִּרְכָתָא / בעשרת ימי תשובה: לְעֵלָּא לְעֵלָּא מִכָּל בִּרְכָתָא/
וְשִׁירָתָא, תֻּשְׁבְּחָתָא וְנֶחֱמָתָא
דַּאֲמִירָן בְּעָלְמָא, וְאִמְרוּ אָמֵן. (קהל: אָמֵן)

On fast days, turn to הוצאת ספר תורה *on page 221. The* תורה *reading and* הפטרה *for fast days are on page 1120. After the* תורה *is returned to the* ארון קודש*, the* שליח ציבור *says* חצי קדיש.

THE AMIDA

The Amida, until "in former years" on page 296, is said silently, standing with feet together. If there is a minyan, the Amida is repeated aloud by the Leader. Take three steps forward as if formally entering the place of the Divine Presence.

When I declare the LORD's name, give glory to our God. *Deut. 32*
O LORD, open my lips, so that my mouth may declare Your praise. *Ps. 51*

PATRIARCHS

בָּרוּךְ Blessed are You,
LORD our God and God of our fathers,
God of Abraham, God of Isaac and God of Jacob;
the great, mighty and awesome God, God Most High,
who acts with loving-kindness and creates all,
who remembers the loving-kindness of the fathers
and will bring a Redeemer to their children's children
for the sake of His name, in love.

Between Rosh HaShana & Yom Kippur: Remember us for life, O King who desires life,
and write us in the book of life –
for Your sake, O God of life.

King, Helper, Savior, Shield:
Blessed are You, LORD, Shield of Abraham.

DIVINE MIGHT

אַתָּה גִּבּוֹר You are eternally mighty, LORD.
You give life to the dead and have great power to save.

The phrase "He makes the wind blow and the rain fall" is added from Simḥat Torah until Pesaḥ. In Israel the phrase "He causes the dew to fall" is added from Pesaḥ until Shemini Atzeret.

In fall & winter: He makes the wind blow and the rain fall.
In Israel, in spring & summer: He causes the dew to fall.

He sustains the living with loving-kindness,
and with great compassion revives the dead.
He supports the fallen, heals the sick, sets captives free,
and keeps His faith with those who sleep in the dust.

עמידה

The עמידה*, until* קַדְמֹנִיּוֹת *on page 297, is said silently, standing with feet together.*
If there is a מנין*, the* עמידה *is repeated aloud by the* שליח ציבור*.*
Take three steps forward as if formally entering
the place of the Divine Presence.

כִּי שֵׁם יהוה אֶקְרָא, הָבוּ גֹדֶל לֵאלֹהֵינוּ: דברים לב
אֲדֹנָי, שְׂפָתַי תִּפְתָּח, וּפִי יַגִּיד תְּהִלָּתֶךָ: תהלים נא

אבות

בָּרוּךְ אַתָּה יהוה, אֱלֹהֵינוּ וֵאלֹהֵי אֲבוֹתֵינוּ
אֱלֹהֵי אַבְרָהָם, אֱלֹהֵי יִצְחָק, וֵאלֹהֵי יַעֲקֹב
הָאֵל הַגָּדוֹל הַגִּבּוֹר וְהַנּוֹרָא, אֵל עֶלְיוֹן
גּוֹמֵל חֲסָדִים טוֹבִים, וְקוֹנֵה הַכֹּל, וְזוֹכֵר חַסְדֵּי אָבוֹת
וּמֵבִיא גוֹאֵל לִבְנֵי בְנֵיהֶם לְמַעַן שְׁמוֹ בְּאַהֲבָה.

בעשרת ימי תשובה: זָכְרֵנוּ לְחַיִּים, מֶלֶךְ חָפֵץ בַּחַיִּים
וְכָתְבֵנוּ בְּסֵפֶר הַחַיִּים, לְמַעַנְךָ אֱלֹהִים חַיִּים.

מֶלֶךְ עוֹזֵר וּמוֹשִׁיעַ וּמָגֵן.
בָּרוּךְ אַתָּה יהוה, מָגֵן אַבְרָהָם.

גבורות

אַתָּה גִּבּוֹר לְעוֹלָם, אֲדֹנָי
מְחַיֵּה מֵתִים אַתָּה, רַב לְהוֹשִׁיעַ

The phrase מַשִּׁיב הָרוּחַ *is added from* שמחת תורה *until* פסח*.*
In ארץ ישראל *the phrase* מוֹרִיד הַטָּל *is added from* פסח *until* שמיני עצרת*.*

בחורף: **מַשִּׁיב הָרְוּחַ וּמוֹרִיד הַגֶּשֶׁם** / בארץ ישראל בקיץ: **מוֹרִיד הַטָּל**

מְכַלְכֵּל חַיִּים בְּחֶסֶד, מְחַיֵּה מֵתִים בְּרַחֲמִים רַבִּים
סוֹמֵךְ נוֹפְלִים, וְרוֹפֵא חוֹלִים, וּמַתִּיר אֲסוּרִים
וּמְקַיֵּם אֱמוּנָתוֹ לִישֵׁנֵי עָפָר.

Who is like You, Master of might,
and who can compare to You,
O King who brings death and gives life,
and makes salvation grow?

Between Rosh HaShana & Yom Kippur: Who is like You, compassionate Father,
who remembers His creatures
in compassion, for life?

Faithful are You to revive the dead.
Blessed are You, Lord, who revives the dead.

When saying the Amida silently, continue with "You are holy" on the next page.

KEDUSHA

During the Leader's Repetition, the following is said standing with feet together, rising on the toes at the words indicated by ▴.

Cong. then Leader: נְקַדֵּשׁ We will sanctify Your name on earth,
as they sanctify it in the highest heavens,
as is written by Your prophet,
"And they [the angels] call to one another saying: *Is. 6*

Cong. then Leader: ▴Holy, ▴holy, ▴holy is the Lord of multitudes
the whole world is filled with His glory."
Those facing them say "Blessed – "

Cong. then Leader: ▴"Blessed is the Lord's glory from His place." *Ezek. 3*
And in Your holy Writings it is written thus:

Cong. then Leader: ▴"The Lord shall reign for ever. He is your God, Zion, *Ps. 146*
from generation to generation, Halleluya!"

Leader: From generation to generation
we will speak of Your greatness,
and we will declare Your holiness for evermore.
Your praise, our God, shall not leave our mouth forever,
for You, God, are a great and holy King.
Blessed are You, Lord,
the holy God. / *Between Rosh HaShana & Yom Kippur:* the holy King./

The Leader continues with "You grace humanity" on the next page.

מִי כָמְוֹךָ, בַּעַל גְּבוּרוֹת
וּמִי דּוֹמֶה לָּךְ
מֶלֶךְ, מֵמִית וּמְחַיֶּה וּמַצְמִיחַ יְשׁוּעָה.

בעשרת ימי תשובה: מִי כָמְוֹךָ אַב הָרַחֲמִים
זוֹכֵר יְצוּרָיו לְחַיִּים בְּרַחֲמִים.

וְנֶאֱמָן אַתָּה לְהַחֲיוֹת מֵתִים.
בָּרוּךְ אַתָּה יהוה, מְחַיֵּה הַמֵּתִים.

When saying the עמידה *silently, continue with* אַתָּה קָדוֹשׁ *on the next page.*

קדושה

During the חזרת הש״ץ, *the following is said standing with feet together, rising on the toes at the words indicated by* ˄.

קהל *then* ש״ץ: נְקַדֵּשׁ אֶת שִׁמְךָ בָּעוֹלָם, כְּשֵׁם שֶׁמַּקְדִּישִׁים אוֹתוֹ בִּשְׁמֵי מָרוֹם
כַּכָּתוּב עַל יַד נְבִיאֶךָ:
וְקָרָא זֶה אֶל־זֶה וְאָמַר ישעיה ו

קהל *then* ש״ץ: ˄קָדוֹשׁ, ˄קָדוֹשׁ, ˄קָדוֹשׁ, יהוה צְבָאוֹת, מְלֹא כָל־הָאָרֶץ כְּבוֹדוֹ:
לְעֻמָּתָם בָּרוּךְ יֹאמֵרוּ

קהל *then* ש״ץ: ˄בָּרוּךְ כְּבוֹד־יהוה מִמְּקוֹמוֹ: יחזקאל ג
וּבְדִבְרֵי קָדְשְׁךָ כָּתוּב לֵאמֹר

קהל *then* ש״ץ: ˄יִמְלֹךְ יהוה לְעוֹלָם, אֱלֹהַיִךְ צִיּוֹן לְדֹר וָדֹר, הַלְלוּיָהּ: תהלים קמו

ש״ץ: לְדוֹר וָדוֹר נַגִּיד גָּדְלֶךָ, וּלְנֵצַח נְצָחִים קְדֻשָּׁתְךָ נַקְדִּישׁ
וְשִׁבְחֲךָ אֱלֹהֵינוּ מִפִּינוּ לֹא יָמוּשׁ לְעוֹלָם וָעֶד
כִּי אֵל מֶלֶךְ גָּדוֹל וְקָדוֹשׁ אָתָּה.
בָּרוּךְ אַתָּה יהוה, הָאֵל הַקָּדוֹשׁ. /בעשרת ימי תשובה: הַמֶּלֶךְ הַקָּדוֹשׁ./

The שליח ציבור *continues with* אַתָּה חוֹנֵן *on the next page.*

HOLINESS

אַתָּה קָדוֹשׁ You are holy and Your name is holy,
and holy ones praise You daily, Selah!
Blessed are You, LORD,
the holy God. / *Between Rosh HaShana & Yom Kippur:* the holy King./

(*If forgotten, repeat the Amida.*)

KNOWLEDGE

אַתָּה חוֹנֵן You grace humanity with knowledge
and teach mortals understanding.
Grace us with the knowledge, understanding
and insight that come from You.
Blessed are You, LORD,
who generously gives knowledge.

REPENTANCE

הֲשִׁיבֵנוּ Bring us back, our Father, to Your Torah.
Draw us near, our King, to Your service.
Lead us back to You in perfect repentance.
Blessed are You, LORD,
who desires repentance.

FORGIVENESS

Strike the left side of the chest at °.

סְלַח לָנוּ Forgive us, our Father, for we have °sinned.
Pardon us, our King, for we have °transgressed;
for You pardon and forgive.
Blessed are You, LORD,
the generous One who repeatedly forgives.

REDEMPTION

רְאֵה Look on our suffering, plead our cause,
and redeem us soon for Your name's sake,
for You are a powerful Redeemer.
Blessed are You, LORD,
the Redeemer of Israel.

קדושת השם

אַתָּה קָדוֹשׁ וְשִׁמְךָ קָדוֹשׁ
וּקְדוֹשִׁים בְּכָל יוֹם יְהַלְלוּךָ סֶּלָה.
בָּרוּךְ אַתָּה יהוה, הָאֵל הַקָּדוֹשׁ. / בעשרת ימי תשובה: הַמֶּלֶךְ הַקָּדוֹשׁ./
(*If forgotten, repeat the* עמידה.)

דעת

אַתָּה חוֹנֵן לְאָדָם דַּעַת, וּמְלַמֵּד לֶאֱנוֹשׁ בִּינָה.
חָנֵּנוּ מֵאִתְּךָ דֵּעָה בִּינָה וְהַשְׂכֵּל.
בָּרוּךְ אַתָּה יהוה, חוֹנֵן הַדָּעַת.

תשובה

הֲשִׁיבֵנוּ אָבִינוּ לְתוֹרָתֶךָ, וְקָרְבֵנוּ מַלְכֵּנוּ לַעֲבוֹדָתֶךָ
וְהַחֲזִירֵנוּ בִּתְשׁוּבָה שְׁלֵמָה לְפָנֶיךָ.
בָּרוּךְ אַתָּה יהוה, הָרוֹצֶה בִּתְשׁוּבָה.

סליחה

Strike the left side of the chest at °.

סְלַח לָנוּ אָבִינוּ כִּי °חָטָאנוּ
מְחַל לָנוּ מַלְכֵּנוּ כִּי °פָשָׁעְנוּ
כִּי מוֹחֵל וְסוֹלֵחַ אָתָּה.
בָּרוּךְ אַתָּה יהוה, חַנּוּן הַמַּרְבֶּה לִסְלֹחַ.

גאולה

רְאֵה בְעָנְיֵנוּ, וְרִיבָה רִיבֵנוּ
וּגְאָלֵנוּ מְהֵרָה לְמַעַן שְׁמֶךָ
כִּי גּוֹאֵל חָזָק אָתָּה.
בָּרוּךְ אַתָּה יהוה, גּוֹאֵל יִשְׂרָאֵל.

On fast days the Leader adds:

עֲנֵנוּ Answer us, LORD, answer us on our Fast Day, for we are in great distress. Look not at our wickedness. Do not hide Your face from us and do not ignore our plea. Be near to our cry; please let Your loving-kindness comfort us. Even before we call to You, answer us, as it is said, "Before they call, I will answer. While they are still speaking, I will hear." For You, LORD, are the One who answers in time of distress, redeems and rescues in all times of trouble and anguish. Blessed are You, LORD, who answers in time of distress. *Is. 65*

HEALING

רְפָאֵנוּ Heal us, LORD, and we shall be healed.
Save us and we shall be saved, for You are our praise.
Bring complete recovery for all our illnesses,

The following prayer for a sick person may be said here:

May it be Your will, O LORD my God and God of my ancestors, that You speedily send a complete recovery from heaven, a healing of both soul and body, to the patient (*name*), son/daughter of (*mother's name*) among the other sick of Israel.

for You, God, King, are a faithful and compassionate Healer.
Blessed are You, LORD, Healer of the sick of His people Israel.

PROSPERITY

The phrase "Give dew and rain as a blessing" is said from December 5th (in the year before a civil leap year, December 6th) until Pesaḥ. In Israel, it is said from the 7th of Marḥeshvan. The phrase "Give blessing" is said from Ḥol HaMo'ed Pesaḥ until December 4th (in the year before a civil leap year, December 5th). In Israel it is said through the 6th of Marḥeshvan.

בָּרֵךְ Bless this year for us, LORD our God,
and all its types of produce for good.

In winter: Give dew and rain as a blessing
In other seasons: Give blessing

on the face of the earth,
and from its goodness satisfy us,
blessing our year as the best of years.
Blessed are You, LORD, who blesses the years.

On fast days the שליח ציבור *adds:*

עֲנֵנוּ יהוה עֲנֵנוּ בְּיוֹם צוֹם תַּעֲנִיתֵנוּ, כִּי בְצָרָה גְדוֹלָה אֲנָחְנוּ. אַל תֵּפֶן אֶל רִשְׁעֵנוּ, וְאַל תַּסְתֵּר פָּנֶיךָ מִמֶּנּוּ, וְאַל תִּתְעַלַּם מִתְּחִנָּתֵנוּ. הֱיֵה נָא קָרוֹב לְשַׁוְעָתֵנוּ, יְהִי נָא חַסְדְּךָ לְנַחֲמֵנוּ, טֶרֶם נִקְרָא אֵלֶיךָ עֲנֵנוּ, כַּדָּבָר שֶׁנֶּאֱמַר: וְהָיָה טֶרֶם יִקְרָאוּ וַאֲנִי אֶעֱנֶה, עוֹד הֵם מְדַבְּרִים וַאֲנִי אֶשְׁמָע: כִּי אַתָּה יהוה הָעוֹנֶה בְּעֵת צָרָה, פּוֹדֶה וּמַצִּיל בְּכָל עֵת צָרָה וְצוּקָה. בָּרוּךְ אַתָּה יהוה, הָעוֹנֶה בְּעֵת צָרָה. ישעיה סה

רפואה

רְפָאֵנוּ יהוה וְנֵרָפֵא, הוֹשִׁיעֵנוּ וְנִוָּשֵׁעָה, כִּי תְהִלָּתֵנוּ אָתָּה וְהַעֲלֵה רְפוּאָה שְׁלֵמָה לְכָל מַכּוֹתֵינוּ

The following prayer for a sick person may be said here:

יְהִי רָצוֹן מִלְּפָנֶיךָ יהוה אֱלֹהַי וֵאלֹהֵי אֲבוֹתַי, שֶׁתִּשְׁלַח מְהֵרָה רְפוּאָה שְׁלֵמָה מִן הַשָּׁמַיִם רְפוּאַת הַנֶּפֶשׁ וּרְפוּאַת הַגּוּף לַחוֹלֶה/לַחוֹלָה *name of patient* בֶּן/בַּת *mother's name* בְּתוֹךְ שְׁאָר חוֹלֵי יִשְׂרָאֵל.

כִּי אֵל מֶלֶךְ רוֹפֵא נֶאֱמָן וְרַחֲמָן אָתָּה.
בָּרוּךְ אַתָּה יהוה, רוֹפֵא חוֹלֵי עַמּוֹ יִשְׂרָאֵל.

ברכת השנים

The phrase וְתֵן טַל וּמָטָר לִבְרָכָה *is said from December 5th (in the year before a civil leap year, December 6th) until* פסח. *In* ארץ ישראל*, it is said from* ז׳ מרחשון.
The phrase וְתֵן בְּרָכָה *is said from* חול המועד פסח *until December 4th (in the year before a civil leap year, December 5th). In* ארץ ישראל *it is said through* ו׳ מרחשון.

בָּרֵךְ עָלֵינוּ יהוה אֱלֹהֵינוּ אֶת הַשָּׁנָה הַזֹּאת
וְאֶת כָּל מִינֵי תְבוּאָתָהּ, לְטוֹבָה
בחורף: **וְתֵן טַל וּמָטָר לִבְרָכָה** / בקיץ: **וְתֵן בְּרָכָה**
עַל פְּנֵי הָאֲדָמָה, וְשַׂבְּעֵנוּ מִטּוּבָהּ
וּבָרֵךְ שְׁנָתֵנוּ כַּשָּׁנִים הַטּוֹבוֹת.
בָּרוּךְ אַתָּה יהוה, מְבָרֵךְ הַשָּׁנִים.

INGATHERING OF EXILES

תְּקַע Sound the great shofar for our freedom,
raise high the banner to gather our exiles,
and gather us together from the four quarters of the earth.
Blessed are You, LORD,
who gathers the dispersed of His people Israel.

JUSTICE

הָשִׁיבָה Restore our judges as at first,
and our advisors as at the beginning,
and remove from us sorrow and sighing.
May You alone, LORD,
reign over us with loving-kindness and compassion,
and vindicate us in justice.
Blessed are You, LORD,
the King who loves righteousness and justice.
/*Between Rosh HaShana & Yom Kippur, end the blessing:* the King of justice./

AGAINST INFORMERS

וְלַמַּלְשִׁינִים For the slanderers let there be no hope,
and may all wickedness perish in an instant.
May all Your people's enemies swiftly be cut down.
May You swiftly uproot, crush, cast down
and humble the arrogant swiftly in our days.
Blessed are You, LORD,
who destroys enemies and humbles the arrogant.

THE RIGHTEOUS

עַל הַצַּדִּיקִים To the righteous, the pious,
the elders of Your people the house of Israel,
the surviving scholars,
the righteous converts, and to us,
may Your compassion be aroused, LORD our God.

קבוץ גלויות

תְּקַע בְּשׁוֹפָר גָּדוֹל לְחֵרוּתֵנוּ
וְשָׂא נֵס לְקַבֵּץ גָּלֻיּוֹתֵינוּ
וְקַבְּצֵנוּ יַחַד מֵאַרְבַּע כַּנְפוֹת הָאָרֶץ.
בָּרוּךְ אַתָּה יהוה, מְקַבֵּץ נִדְחֵי עַמּוֹ יִשְׂרָאֵל.

השבת המשפט

הָשִׁיבָה שׁוֹפְטֵינוּ כְּבָרִאשׁוֹנָה וְיוֹעֲצֵינוּ כְּבַתְּחִלָּה
וְהָסֵר מִמֶּנּוּ יָגוֹן וַאֲנָחָה
וּמְלֹךְ עָלֵינוּ אַתָּה יהוה לְבַדְּךָ בְּחֶסֶד וּבְרַחֲמִים
וְצַדְּקֵנוּ בַּמִּשְׁפָּט.
בָּרוּךְ אַתָּה יהוה
מֶלֶךְ אוֹהֵב צְדָקָה וּמִשְׁפָּט. / בעשרת ימי תשובה: הַמֶּלֶךְ הַמִּשְׁפָּט./

ברכת המינים

וְלַמַּלְשִׁינִים אַל תְּהִי תִקְוָה, וְכָל הָרִשְׁעָה כְּרֶגַע תֹּאבֵד
וְכָל אוֹיְבֵי עַמְּךָ מְהֵרָה יִכָּרֵתוּ
וְהַזֵּדִים מְהֵרָה תְעַקֵּר וּתְשַׁבֵּר וּתְמַגֵּר וְתַכְנִיעַ בִּמְהֵרָה בְיָמֵינוּ.
בָּרוּךְ אַתָּה יהוה, שׁוֹבֵר אוֹיְבִים וּמַכְנִיעַ זֵדִים.

על הצדיקים

עַל הַצַּדִּיקִים וְעַל הַחֲסִידִים
וְעַל זִקְנֵי עַמְּךָ בֵּית יִשְׂרָאֵל
וְעַל פְּלֵיטַת סוֹפְרֵיהֶם
וְעַל גֵּרֵי הַצֶּדֶק, וְעָלֵינוּ
יֶהֱמוּ רַחֲמֶיךָ יהוה אֱלֹהֵינוּ

Give a good reward to all who sincerely trust in Your name.
Set our lot with them,
so that we may never be ashamed, for in You we trust.
Blessed are You, LORD,
who is the support and trust of the righteous.

REBUILDING JERUSALEM

וְלִירוּשָׁלַיִם To Jerusalem, Your city, may You return in compassion,
and may You rest Your presence in it as You promised.
May You rebuild it rapidly in our days
as an everlasting structure,
and install within it soon the throne of David.
*Blessed are You, LORD,
who builds Jerusalem.

**On Tisha B'Av all conclude as follows:*

נַחֵם Console, O LORD our God, the mourners of Zion and the mourners of Jerusalem, and the city that is in sorrow, laid waste, scorned and desolate; that grieves for the loss of its children, that is laid waste of its dwellings, robbed of its glory, desolate without inhabitants. She sits with her head covered like a barren childless woman. Legions have devoured her; idolaters have taken possession of her; they have put Your people Israel to the sword and deliberately killed the devoted followers of the Most High. Therefore Zion weeps bitterly, and Jerusalem raises her voice. My heart, my heart grieves for those they killed; I am in anguish, I am in anguish for those they killed. For You, O LORD, consumed it with fire, and with fire You will rebuild it in the future, as is said, "And I Myself will be a wall of fire around it, says the LORD, and I will be its glory within." Blessed are You, LORD, who consoles Zion and rebuilds Jerusalem. *Zech. 2*

Continue with "May the offshoot" below.

KINGDOM OF DAVID

אֶת צֶמַח May the offshoot of Your servant David soon flower,
and may his pride be raised high by Your salvation,
for we wait for Your salvation all day.
Blessed are You, LORD,
who makes the glory of salvation flourish.

וְתֵן שָׂכָר טוֹב לְכָל הַבּוֹטְחִים בְּשִׁמְךָ בֶּאֱמֶת
וְשִׂים חֶלְקֵנוּ עִמָּהֶם
וּלְעוֹלָם לֹא נֵבוֹשׁ כִּי בְךָ בָּטָחְנוּ.
בָּרוּךְ אַתָּה יהוה, מִשְׁעָן וּמִבְטָח לַצַּדִּיקִים.

בניין ירושלים

וְלִירוּשָׁלַיִם עִירְךָ בְּרַחֲמִים תָּשׁוּב
וְתִשְׁכֹּן בְּתוֹכָהּ כַּאֲשֶׁר דִּבַּרְתָּ
וּבְנֵה אוֹתָהּ בְּקָרוֹב בְּיָמֵינוּ בִּנְיַן עוֹלָם
וְכִסֵּא דָוִד מְהֵרָה לְתוֹכָהּ תָּכִין.
*בָּרוּךְ אַתָּה יהוה, בּוֹנֵה יְרוּשָׁלָיִם.

**On* תשעה באב, *all conclude as follows:*

נַחֵם יהוה אֱלֹהֵינוּ אֶת אֲבֵלֵי צִיּוֹן וְאֶת אֲבֵלֵי יְרוּשָׁלָיִם, וְאֶת הָעִיר הָאֲבֵלָה וְהֶחֳרֵבָה וְהַבְּזוּיָה וְהַשּׁוֹמֵמָה. הָאֲבֵלָה מִבְּלִי בָנֶיהָ, וְהֶחֳרֵבָה מִמְּעוֹנוֹתֶיהָ, וְהַבְּזוּיָה מִכְּבוֹדָהּ, וְהַשּׁוֹמֵמָה מֵאֵין יוֹשֵׁב. וְהִיא יוֹשֶׁבֶת וְרֹאשָׁהּ חָפוּי, כְּאִשָּׁה עֲקָרָה שֶׁלֹּא יָלָדָה. וַיְבַלְּעוּהָ לִגְיוֹנוֹת, וַיִּירָשׁוּהָ עוֹבְדֵי פְסִילִים, וַיָּטִילוּ אֶת עַמְּךָ יִשְׂרָאֵל לֶחָרֶב, וַיַּהַרְגוּ בְזָדוֹן חֲסִידֵי עֶלְיוֹן. עַל כֵּן צִיּוֹן בְּמַר תִּבְכֶּה, וִירוּשָׁלַיִם תִּתֵּן קוֹלָהּ. לִבִּי לִבִּי עַל חַלְלֵיהֶם, מֵעַי מֵעַי עַל חַלְלֵיהֶם, כִּי אַתָּה יהוה בָּאֵשׁ הִצַּתָּהּ, וּבָאֵשׁ אַתָּה עָתִיד לִבְנוֹתָהּ. כָּאָמוּר: וַאֲנִי אֶהְיֶה־לָּהּ, זכריה ב
נְאֻם־יהוה, חוֹמַת אֵשׁ סָבִיב, וּלְכָבוֹד אֶהְיֶה בְתוֹכָהּ: בָּרוּךְ אַתָּה יהוה, מְנַחֵם צִיּוֹן וּבוֹנֵה יְרוּשָׁלָיִם.

Continue with אֶת צֶמַח *below.*

משיח בן דוד

אֶת צֶמַח דָּוִד עַבְדְּךָ מְהֵרָה תַצְמִיחַ
וְקַרְנוֹ תָּרוּם בִּישׁוּעָתֶךָ
כִּי לִישׁוּעָתְךָ קִוִּינוּ כָּל הַיּוֹם.
בָּרוּךְ אַתָּה יהוה, מַצְמִיחַ קֶרֶן יְשׁוּעָה.

RESPONSE TO PRAYER

שְׁמַע קוֹלֵנוּ Listen to our voice, LORD our God.
Spare us and have compassion on us,
and in compassion and favor accept our prayer,
for You, God, listen to prayers and pleas.
Do not turn us away, O our King,
empty-handed from Your presence,*
for You listen with compassion
to the prayer of Your people Israel.
Blessed are You, LORD,
who listens to prayer.

**At this point on fast days, the congregation adds "Answer us" below.*
In times of drought in Israel, say "And answer us" on page 1064.

עֲנֵנוּ Answer us, LORD, answer us on our Fast Day, for we are in great distress. Look not at our wickedness. Do not hide Your face from us and do not ignore our plea. Be near to our cry; please let Your loving-kindness comfort us. Even before we call to You, answer us, as is said, "Before they call, I will answer. While they are still speaking, I will hear." For You, LORD, are the One who answers in time of distress, redeems and rescues in all times of trouble and anguish.

Continue with "for You listen" above.

TEMPLE SERVICE

רְצֵה Find favor, LORD our God,
in Your people Israel and their prayer.
Restore the service to Your most holy House,
and accept in love and favor
the fire-offerings of Israel and their prayer.
May the service of Your people Israel always find favor with You.

On Rosh Ḥodesh and Ḥol HaMo'ed, say:

אֱלֹהֵינוּ Our God and God of our ancestors, may there rise, come, reach, appear, be favored, heard, regarded and remembered before You, our recollection and remembrance, as well as the remembrance of our ancestors, and of the Messiah son of David Your servant, and of Jerusalem Your holy city, and of all Your people the house of Israel – for deliverance and

שומע תפילה

שְׁמַע קוֹלֵנוּ יהוה אֱלֹהֵינוּ
חוּס וְרַחֵם עָלֵינוּ
וְקַבֵּל בְּרַחֲמִים וּבְרָצוֹן אֶת תְּפִלָּתֵנוּ
כִּי אֵל שׁוֹמֵעַ תְּפִלּוֹת וְתַחֲנוּנִים אָתָּה
וּמִלְּפָנֶיךָ מַלְכֵּנוּ רֵיקָם אַל תְּשִׁיבֵנוּ*
כִּי אַתָּה שׁוֹמֵעַ תְּפִלַּת עַמְּךָ יִשְׂרָאֵל בְּרַחֲמִים.
בָּרוּךְ אַתָּה יהוה, שׁוֹמֵעַ תְּפִלָּה.

**At this point on fast days, the* קהל *adds* עֲנֵנוּ *below.*
In times of drought in ארץ ישראל*, say* וַעֲנֵנוּ *on page 1065.*

עֲנֵנוּ יהוה עֲנֵנוּ בְּיוֹם צוֹם תַּעֲנִיתֵנוּ, כִּי בְצָרָה גְדוֹלָה אֲנָחְנוּ. אַל תֵּפֶן אֶל רִשְׁעֵנוּ, וְאַל תַּסְתֵּר פָּנֶיךָ מִמֶּנּוּ, וְאַל תִּתְעַלַּם מִתְּחִנָּתֵנוּ. הֱיֵה נָא קָרוֹב לְשַׁוְעָתֵנוּ, יְהִי נָא חַסְדְּךָ לְנַחֲמֵנוּ, טֶרֶם נִקְרָא אֵלֶיךָ עֲנֵנוּ, כַּדָּבָר שֶׁנֶּאֱמַר: וְהָיָה טֶרֶם יִקְרָאוּ וַאֲנִי אֶעֱנֶה, עוֹד הֵם מְדַבְּרִים וַאֲנִי אֶשְׁמָע: כִּי אַתָּה יהוה הָעוֹנֶה בְּעֵת צָרָה, פּוֹדֶה וּמַצִּיל בְּכָל עֵת צָרָה וְצוּקָה.

Continue with כִּי אַתָּה שׁוֹמֵעַ *above.*

עבודה

רְצֵה יהוה אֱלֹהֵינוּ בְּעַמְּךָ יִשְׂרָאֵל וּבִתְפִלָּתָם
וְהָשֵׁב אֶת הָעֲבוֹדָה לִדְבִיר בֵּיתֶךָ
וְאִשֵּׁי יִשְׂרָאֵל וּתְפִלָּתָם בְּאַהֲבָה תְקַבֵּל בְּרָצוֹן
וּתְהִי לְרָצוֹן תָּמִיד עֲבוֹדַת יִשְׂרָאֵל עַמֶּךָ.

On ראש חודש *and* חול המועד*, say:*

אֱלֹהֵינוּ וֵאלֹהֵי אֲבוֹתֵינוּ, יַעֲלֶה וְיָבוֹא וְיַגִּיעַ, וְיֵרָאֶה וְיֵרָצֶה וְיִשָּׁמַע, וְיִפָּקֵד וְיִזָּכֵר זִכְרוֹנֵנוּ וּפִקְדוֹנֵנוּ וְזִכְרוֹן אֲבוֹתֵינוּ, וְזִכְרוֹן מָשִׁיחַ בֶּן דָּוִד עַבְדֶּךָ, וְזִכְרוֹן יְרוּשָׁלַיִם עִיר קָדְשֶׁךָ, וְזִכְרוֹן כָּל עַמְּךָ בֵּית

well-being, grace, loving-kindness and compassion, life and peace, on this day of:

On Rosh Ḥodesh: Rosh Ḥodesh.
On Pesaḥ: the Festival of Matzot.
On Sukkot: the Festival of Sukkot.

On it remember us, LORD our God, for good; recollect us for blessing, and save us for life. In accord with Your promise of salvation and compassion, spare us and be generous to us; have compassion on us and save us, for our eyes are turned to You because You, God, are a generous and compassionate King.

וְתֶחֱזֶינָה And may our eyes witness Your return to Zion in compassion. Blessed are You, LORD, who restores His Presence to Zion.

THANKSGIVING

מוֹדִים We give thanks to You,
for You are the LORD our God
and God of our ancestors
for ever and all time.
You are the Rock of our lives,
Shield of our salvation
from generation to generation.
We will thank You and
declare Your praise for our lives,
which are entrusted into Your hand;
for our souls,
which are placed in Your charge;
for Your miracles
which are with us every day;
and for Your wonders and favors
at all times, evening, morning and midday.
You are good –
for Your compassion never fails.
You are compassionate –
for Your loving-kindnesses never cease.
We have always placed our hope in You.

During the Leader's Repetition, the congregation says quietly:
מוֹדִים We give thanks
to You, for You are
the LORD our God
and God of our ancestors,
God of all flesh,
who formed us
and formed the universe.
Blessings and thanks
are due to Your great
and holy name for giving us
life and sustaining us.
May You continue
to give us life and sustain us;
and may You gather our
exiles to Your holy courts,
to keep Your decrees,
do Your will and serve You
with a perfect heart,
for it is for us
to give You thanks.
Blessed be God to whom
thanksgiving is due.

יִשְׂרָאֵל, לְפָנֶיךָ, לִפְלֵיטָה לְטוֹבָה, לְחֵן וּלְחֶסֶד וּלְרַחֲמִים, לְחַיִּים וּלְשָׁלוֹם בְּיוֹם

בראש חודש: רֹאשׁ הַחֹדֶשׁ / בפסח: חַג הַמַּצּוֹת / בסוכות: חַג הַסֻּכּוֹת

הַזֶּה. זָכְרֵנוּ יהוה אֱלֹהֵינוּ בּוֹ לְטוֹבָה, וּפָקְדֵנוּ בוֹ לִבְרָכָה, וְהוֹשִׁיעֵנוּ בוֹ לְחַיִּים. וּבִדְבַר יְשׁוּעָה וְרַחֲמִים, חוּס וְחָנֵּנוּ וְרַחֵם עָלֵינוּ וְהוֹשִׁיעֵנוּ, כִּי אֵלֶיךָ עֵינֵינוּ, כִּי אֵל מֶלֶךְ חַנּוּן וְרַחוּם אָתָּה.

וְתֶחֱזֶינָה עֵינֵינוּ בְּשׁוּבְךָ לְצִיּוֹן בְּרַחֲמִים.
בָּרוּךְ אַתָּה יהוה, הַמַּחֲזִיר שְׁכִינָתוֹ לְצִיּוֹן.

הודאה

מוֹדִים אֲנַחְנוּ לָךְ
שָׁאַתָּה הוּא יהוה אֱלֹהֵינוּ
וֵאלֹהֵי אֲבוֹתֵינוּ לְעוֹלָם וָעֶד.
צוּר חַיֵּינוּ, מָגֵן יִשְׁעֵנוּ
אַתָּה הוּא לְדוֹר וָדוֹר.
נוֹדֶה לְּךָ וּנְסַפֵּר תְּהִלָּתֶךָ
עַל חַיֵּינוּ הַמְּסוּרִים בְּיָדֶךָ
וְעַל נִשְׁמוֹתֵינוּ הַפְּקוּדוֹת לָךְ
וְעַל נִסֶּיךָ שֶׁבְּכָל יוֹם עִמָּנוּ
וְעַל נִפְלְאוֹתֶיךָ וְטוֹבוֹתֶיךָ
שֶׁבְּכָל עֵת, עֶרֶב וָבֹקֶר וְצָהֳרָיִם.
הַטּוֹב, כִּי לֹא כָלוּ רַחֲמֶיךָ
וְהַמְרַחֵם, כִּי לֹא תַמּוּ חֲסָדֶיךָ
מֵעוֹלָם קִוִּינוּ לָךְ.

During חזרת הש״ץ, *the* קהל *says quietly:*

מוֹדִים אֲנַחְנוּ לָךְ
שָׁאַתָּה הוּא יהוה אֱלֹהֵינוּ
וֵאלֹהֵי אֲבוֹתֵינוּ
אֱלֹהֵי כָל בָּשָׂר
יוֹצְרֵנוּ, יוֹצֵר בְּרֵאשִׁית.
בְּרָכוֹת וְהוֹדָאוֹת
לְשִׁמְךָ הַגָּדוֹל וְהַקָּדוֹשׁ
עַל שֶׁהֶחֱיִיתָנוּ וְקִיַּמְתָּנוּ.
כֵּן תְּחַיֵּנוּ וּתְקַיְּמֵנוּ
וְתֶאֱסֹף גָּלֻיּוֹתֵינוּ
לְחַצְרוֹת קָדְשֶׁךָ
לִשְׁמֹר חֻקֶּיךָ וְלַעֲשׂוֹת רְצוֹנֶךָ
וּלְעָבְדְּךָ בְּלֵבָב שָׁלֵם
עַל שֶׁאֲנַחְנוּ מוֹדִים לָךְ.
בָּרוּךְ אֵל הַהוֹדָאוֹת.

On Ḥanukka:

עַל הַנִּסִּים [We thank You also] for the miracles, the redemption, the mighty deeds, the salvations, and the victories in battle which You performed for our ancestors in those days, at this time.

בִּימֵי מַתִּתְיָהוּ In the days of Mattityahu, son of Yoḥanan, the High Priest, the Hasmonean, and his sons, the wicked Greek kingdom rose up against Your people Israel to make them forget Your Torah and to force them to transgress the laws of Your will. It was then that You in Your great compassion stood by them in the time of their distress. You championed their cause, judged their claim, and avenged their wrong. You delivered the strong into the hands of the weak, the many into the hands of the few, the impure into the hands of the pure, the wicked into the hands of the righteous, and the arrogant into the hands of those who were engaged in the study of Your Torah. You made for Yourself a great and holy reputation in Your world, and for Your people Israel You performed a great salvation and redemption as of this very day. Your children then entered the holiest part of Your House, cleansed Your Temple, purified Your Sanctuary, kindled lights in Your holy courts, and designated these eight days of Ḥanukka for giving thanks and praise to Your great name.

Continue with "For all these things."

On Purim:

עַל הַנִּסִּים [We thank You also] for the miracles, the redemption, the mighty deeds, the salvations, and the victories in battle which You performed for our ancestors in those days, at this time.

בִּימֵי מָרְדְּכַי In the days of Mordekhai and Esther, in Shushan the capital, the
wicked Haman rose up against them and sought to destroy, slay and exterminate *Esther 3*
all the Jews, young and old, children and women, on one day, the thirteenth day of the twelfth month, which is the month of Adar, and to plunder their possessions. Then You in Your great compassion defeated his counsel, frustrated his plans, and caused his scheme to recoil on his own head, so that they hanged him and his sons on the gallows.

Continue with "For all these things."

וְעַל כֻּלָּם For all these things may Your name be blessed and elevated, our King, continually, for ever and all time.

Between Rosh HaShana & Yom Kippur: And write, for a good life,
all the children of Your covenant.

Let all that lives thank You, Selah! and praise Your name in truth,
God, our Savior and Help, Selah!
Blessed are You, Lord,
whose name is "the Good" and to whom thanks are due.

בחנוכה:

עַל הַנִּסִּים וְעַל הַפֻּרְקָן וְעַל הַגְּבוּרוֹת וְעַל הַתְּשׁוּעוֹת וְעַל הַמִּלְחָמוֹת שֶׁעָשִׂיתָ לַאֲבוֹתֵינוּ בַּיָּמִים הָהֵם בִּזְּמַן הַזֶּה.

בִּימֵי מַתִּתְיָהוּ בֶּן יוֹחָנָן כֹּהֵן גָּדוֹל חַשְׁמוֹנַאי וּבָנָיו, כְּשֶׁעָמְדָה מַלְכוּת יָוָן הָרְשָׁעָה עַל עַמְּךָ יִשְׂרָאֵל לְהַשְׁכִּיחָם תּוֹרָתֶךָ וּלְהַעֲבִירָם מֵחֻקֵּי רְצוֹנֶךָ, וְאַתָּה בְּרַחֲמֶיךָ הָרַבִּים עָמַדְתָּ לָהֶם בְּעֵת צָרָתָם, רַבְתָּ אֶת רִיבָם, דַּנְתָּ אֶת דִּינָם, נָקַמְתָּ אֶת נִקְמָתָם, מָסַרְתָּ גִבּוֹרִים בְּיַד חַלָּשִׁים, וְרַבִּים בְּיַד מְעַטִּים, וּטְמֵאִים בְּיַד טְהוֹרִים, וּרְשָׁעִים בְּיַד צַדִּיקִים, וְזֵדִים בְּיַד עוֹסְקֵי תוֹרָתֶךָ, וּלְךָ עָשִׂיתָ שֵׁם גָּדוֹל וְקָדוֹשׁ בְּעוֹלָמֶךָ, וּלְעַמְּךָ יִשְׂרָאֵל עָשִׂיתָ תְּשׁוּעָה גְדוֹלָה וּפֻרְקָן כְּהַיּוֹם הַזֶּה. וְאַחַר כֵּן בָּאוּ בָנֶיךָ לִדְבִיר בֵּיתֶךָ, וּפִנּוּ אֶת הֵיכָלֶךָ, וְטִהֲרוּ אֶת מִקְדָּשֶׁךָ, וְהִדְלִיקוּ נֵרוֹת בְּחַצְרוֹת קָדְשֶׁךָ, וְקָבְעוּ שְׁמוֹנַת יְמֵי חֲנֻכָּה אֵלּוּ, לְהוֹדוֹת וּלְהַלֵּל לְשִׁמְךָ הַגָּדוֹל.

Continue with וְעַל כֻּלָּם.

בפורים:

עַל הַנִּסִּים וְעַל הַפֻּרְקָן וְעַל הַגְּבוּרוֹת וְעַל הַתְּשׁוּעוֹת וְעַל הַמִּלְחָמוֹת שֶׁעָשִׂיתָ לַאֲבוֹתֵינוּ בַּיָּמִים הָהֵם בִּזְּמַן הַזֶּה.

בִּימֵי מָרְדְּכַי וְאֶסְתֵּר בְּשׁוּשַׁן הַבִּירָה, כְּשֶׁעָמַד עֲלֵיהֶם הָמָן הָרָשָׁע, בִּקֵּשׁ לְהַשְׁמִיד לַהֲרֹג וּלְאַבֵּד אֶת־כָּל־הַיְּהוּדִים מִנַּעַר וְעַד־זָקֵן טַף וְנָשִׁים בְּיוֹם אֶחָד, בִּשְׁלוֹשָׁה עָשָׂר לְחֹדֶשׁ שְׁנֵים־עָשָׂר, הוּא־חֹדֶשׁ אֲדָר, וּשְׁלָלָם לָבוֹז: אסתר ג
וְאַתָּה בְּרַחֲמֶיךָ הָרַבִּים הֵפַרְתָּ אֶת עֲצָתוֹ, וְקִלְקַלְתָּ אֶת מַחֲשַׁבְתּוֹ, וַהֲשֵׁבוֹתָ לּוֹ גְּמוּלוֹ בְּרֹאשׁוֹ, וְתָלוּ אוֹתוֹ וְאֶת בָּנָיו עַל הָעֵץ.

Continue with וְעַל כֻּלָּם.

וְעַל כֻּלָּם יִתְבָּרַךְ וְיִתְרוֹמַם שִׁמְךָ מַלְכֵּנוּ תָּמִיד לְעוֹלָם וָעֶד.

בעשרת ימי תשובה: וּכְתֹב לְחַיִּים טוֹבִים כָּל בְּנֵי בְרִיתֶךָ.

וְכֹל הַחַיִּים יוֹדוּךָ סֶּלָה, וִיהַלְלוּ אֶת שִׁמְךָ בֶּאֱמֶת הָאֵל יְשׁוּעָתֵנוּ וְעֶזְרָתֵנוּ סֶלָה.

בָּרוּךְ אַתָּה יהוה, הַטּוֹב שִׁמְךָ וּלְךָ נָאֶה לְהוֹדוֹת.

On public fast days only, the following is said by the Leader during the Repetition of the Amida, except in a house of mourning. In Israel, on Fast Days, if Kohanim bless the congregation, *turn to page 1064.*

Our God and God of our fathers, bless us with the threefold blessing in the Torah, written by the hand of Moses Your servant and pronounced by Aaron and his sons the priests, Your holy people, as it is said:

May the LORD bless you and protect you. *Num. 6*
Cong: May it be Your will.
May the LORD make His face shine on you and be generous to you.
Cong: May it be Your will.
May the LORD turn His face toward you, and give you peace.
Cong: May it be Your will.

PEACE

שָׁלוֹם רָב Give great peace to Your people Israel for ever, for You are the sovereign LORD of all peace; and may it be good in Your eyes to bless Your people Israel at every time, at every hour, with Your peace.

In Minḥa on fast days:
שִׂים שָׁלוֹם Give peace, goodness and blessing,
grace, loving-kindness and compassion
to us and all Israel Your people.
Bless us, our Father, all as one,
with the light of Your face,
for by the light of Your face
You have given us, LORD our God,
the Torah of life and love of kindness,
righteousness, blessing, compassion,
life and peace.
May it be good in Your eyes
to bless Your people Israel
at every time, in every hour,
with Your peace.

Between Rosh HaShana & Yom Kippur: In the book of life, blessing, peace and prosperity, may we and all Your people the house of Israel be remembered and written before You for a good life, and for peace.*

Blessed are You, LORD, who blesses His people Israel with peace.

**Between Rosh HaShana and Yom Kippur outside Israel, many end the blessing:*
Blessed are You, LORD, who makes peace.

The following verse concludes the Leader's Repetition of the Amida. Some also say it here as part of the silent Amida.

May the words of my mouth and the inner thoughts of my heart *Ps. 19*
find favor before You, LORD, my Rock and Redeemer.

On public fast days only, the following is said by the שליח ציבור *during the* חזרת הש״ץ *except in a house of mourning. In* ארץ ישראל*, on Fast Days, if* כוהנים *say* ברכת כוהנים *turn to page 1065.*

אֱלֹהֵינוּ וֵאלֹהֵי אֲבוֹתֵינוּ, בָּרְכֵנוּ בַּבְּרָכָה הַמְשֻׁלֶּשֶׁת בַּתּוֹרָה הַכְּתוּבָה עַל יְדֵי מֹשֶׁה עַבְדֶּךָ, הָאֲמוּרָה מִפִּי אַהֲרֹן וּבָנָיו כֹּהֲנִים עַם קְדוֹשֶׁיךָ, כָּאָמוּר

במדבר ו יְבָרֶכְךָ יהוה וְיִשְׁמְרֶךָ: קהל: כֵּן יְהִי רָצוֹן
יָאֵר יהוה פָּנָיו אֵלֶיךָ וִיחֻנֶּךָּ: קהל: כֵּן יְהִי רָצוֹן
יִשָּׂא יהוה פָּנָיו אֵלֶיךָ וְיָשֵׂם לְךָ שָׁלוֹם: קהל: כֵּן יְהִי רָצוֹן

ברכת שלום

שָׁלוֹם רָב עַל יִשְׂרָאֵל עַמְּךָ
תָּשִׂים לְעוֹלָם
כִּי אַתָּה הוּא מֶלֶךְ אָדוֹן
לְכָל הַשָּׁלוֹם.
וְטוֹב בְּעֵינֶיךָ
לְבָרֵךְ אֶת עַמְּךָ יִשְׂרָאֵל
בְּכָל עֵת וּבְכָל שָׁעָה
בִּשְׁלוֹמֶךָ.

In מנחה *on fast days:*

שִׂים שָׁלוֹם טוֹבָה וּבְרָכָה
חֵן וָחֶסֶד וְרַחֲמִים
עָלֵינוּ וְעַל כָּל יִשְׂרָאֵל עַמֶּךָ.
בָּרְכֵנוּ אָבִינוּ כֻּלָּנוּ כְּאֶחָד בְּאוֹר פָּנֶיךָ
כִּי בְאוֹר פָּנֶיךָ נָתַתָּ לָּנוּ יהוה אֱלֹהֵינוּ
תּוֹרַת חַיִּים וְאַהֲבַת חֶסֶד
וּצְדָקָה וּבְרָכָה וְרַחֲמִים וְחַיִּים וְשָׁלוֹם.
וְטוֹב בְּעֵינֶיךָ לְבָרֵךְ אֶת עַמְּךָ יִשְׂרָאֵל
בְּכָל עֵת וּבְכָל שָׁעָה בִּשְׁלוֹמֶךָ.

בעשרת ימי תשובה: בְּסֵפֶר חַיִּים, בְּרָכָה וְשָׁלוֹם, וּפַרְנָסָה טוֹבָה נִזָּכֵר וְנִכָּתֵב לְפָנֶיךָ, אֲנַחְנוּ וְכָל עַמְּךָ בֵּית יִשְׂרָאֵל לְחַיִּים טוֹבִים וּלְשָׁלוֹם.*

בָּרוּךְ אַתָּה יהוה, הַמְבָרֵךְ אֶת עַמּוֹ יִשְׂרָאֵל בַּשָּׁלוֹם.

**During the* עשרת ימי תשובה *in* חוץ לארץ*, many end the blessing:*

בָּרוּךְ אַתָּה יהוה, עוֹשֵׂה הַשָּׁלוֹם.

The following verse concludes the חזרת הש״ץ.
Some also say it here as part of the silent עמידה.

תהלים יט יִהְיוּ לְרָצוֹן אִמְרֵי־פִי וְהֶגְיוֹן לִבִּי לְפָנֶיךָ, יהוה צוּרִי וְגֹאֲלִי:

אֱלֹהַי My God, *Berakhot 17a*
guard my tongue from evil and my lips from dishonest speech.
To those who curse me, let my soul be silent;
may my soul be to all like the dust.
Open my heart to Your Torah and let my soul
pursue Your commandments.
As for all who plan evil against me,
swiftly defeat their counsel and frustrate their plans.
Act for the sake of Your name;
act for the sake of Your right hand;
act for the sake of Your holiness;
act for the sake of Your Torah.
That Your beloved ones may be rescued, *Ps. 60*
save with Your right hand and answer me.
May the words of my mouth and the inner thoughts of my heart *Ps. 19*
find favor before You, Lord, my Rock and Redeemer.

Bow, take three steps back, then bow, first left, then right, then center, while saying:

May He who makes peace in His high places,
make peace for us and all Israel –
and say: Amen.

יְהִי רָצוֹן May it be Your will, Lord our God and God of our ancestors,
that the Temple be rebuilt speedily in our days,
and give us a share in Your Torah.
And there we will serve You with fear,
as in the days of old and as in former years.
Then the offering of Judah and Jerusalem *Mal. 3*
will be pleasing to the Lord
as in the days of old and as in former years.

On days when Taḥanun is not said, the Leader says Full Kaddish on page 304.

ברכות יז.

אֱלֹהַי

נְצֹר לְשׁוֹנִי מֵרָע וּשְׂפָתַי מִדַּבֵּר מִרְמָה

וְלִמְקַלְלַי נַפְשִׁי תִדֹּם, וְנַפְשִׁי כֶּעָפָר לַכֹּל תִּהְיֶה.

פְּתַח לִבִּי בְּתוֹרָתֶךָ, וּבְמִצְוֹתֶיךָ תִּרְדֹּף נַפְשִׁי.

וְכָל הַחוֹשְׁבִים עָלַי רָעָה

מְהֵרָה הָפֵר עֲצָתָם וְקַלְקֵל מַחֲשַׁבְתָּם.

עֲשֵׂה לְמַעַן שְׁמֶךָ

עֲשֵׂה לְמַעַן יְמִינֶךָ

עֲשֵׂה לְמַעַן קְדֻשָּׁתֶךָ

עֲשֵׂה לְמַעַן תּוֹרָתֶךָ.

לְמַעַן יֵחָלְצוּן יְדִידֶיךָ, הוֹשִׁיעָה יְמִינְךָ וַעֲנֵנִי: תהלים ס

יִהְיוּ לְרָצוֹן אִמְרֵי־פִי וְהֶגְיוֹן לִבִּי לְפָנֶיךָ, יהוה צוּרִי וְגֹאֲלִי: תהלים יט

Bow, take three steps back, then bow, first left, then right, then center, while saying:

עֹשֶׂה שָׁלוֹם/ בעשרת ימי תשובה: הַשָּׁלוֹם/ בִּמְרוֹמָיו

הוּא יַעֲשֶׂה שָׁלוֹם עָלֵינוּ וְעַל כָּל יִשְׂרָאֵל

וְאִמְרוּ אָמֵן.

יְהִי רָצוֹן מִלְּפָנֶיךָ יהוה אֱלֹהֵינוּ וֵאלֹהֵי אֲבוֹתֵינוּ

שֶׁיִּבָּנֶה בֵּית הַמִּקְדָּשׁ בִּמְהֵרָה בְיָמֵינוּ

וְתֵן חֶלְקֵנוּ בְּתוֹרָתֶךָ

וְשָׁם נַעֲבָדְךָ בְּיִרְאָה כִּימֵי עוֹלָם וּכְשָׁנִים קַדְמוֹנִיּוֹת.

וְעָרְבָה לַיהוה מִנְחַת יְהוּדָה וִירוּשָׁלָםִ כִּימֵי עוֹלָם וּכְשָׁנִים קַדְמוֹנִיּוֹת: מלאכי ג

On days when תחנון *is not said, the* שליח ציבור *says* קדיש שלם *on page 305.*

AVINU MALKENU

Between Rosh HaShana and Yom Kippur and on fast days, except days when Taḥanun is not said (see list on page 302), Avinu Malkenu is said.

The Ark is opened.

אָבִינוּ מַלְכֵּנוּ Our Father, our King, we have sinned before You.
Our Father, our King, we have no king but You.
Our Father, our King, deal kindly with us for the sake of Your name.
Our Father our King, /*bless us with / a good year.
/ *Between Rosh HaShana & Yom Kippur:* renew for us/
Our Father, our King, nullify all harsh decrees against us.
Our Father, our King, nullify the plans of those who hate us.
Our Father, our King, defeat the counsel of our enemies.
Our Father, our King, rid us of every oppressor and enemy.
Our Father, our King, close the mouths of our enemies and accusers.
Our Father, our King, eradicate disease, sword, famine, captivity and destruction, wrongdoing and eradication from the people of Your covenant.
Our Father, our King, withhold the plague from Your heritage.
Our Father, our King, forgive and pardon all our wrongdoing.
Our Father, our King, wipe away and emove our crimes and sins from Your sight.
Our Father, our King, erase in Your great mercy all records of our sins.

The following nine sentences are said responsively, first by the Leader, then by the congregation:

Our Father, our King, bring us back to You in perfect repentance.
Our Father, our King, send a complete healing to the sick of Your people.
Our Father, our King, tear up the evil decree against us.
Our Father, our King, remember us with a memory of favorable deeds before You.

Between Rosh HaShana and Yom Kippur:

Our Father, our King, write us in the book of good life.
Our Father, our King, write us in the book of redemption and salvation.
Our Father, our King, write us in the book of livelihood and sustenance.
Our Father, our King, write us in the book of merit.
Our Father, our King, write us in the book of pardon and forgiveness.

אבינו מלכנו

During the עשרת ימי תשובה *and on fast days, except days when* תחנון *is not said (**see list on page 303**),* אבינו מלכנו *is said.*

The ארון קודש *is opened.*

אָבִינוּ מַלְכֵּנוּ, חָטָאנוּ לְפָנֶיךָ.
אָבִינוּ מַלְכֵּנוּ, אֵין לָנוּ מֶלֶךְ אֶלָּא אָתָּה.
אָבִינוּ מַלְכֵּנוּ, עֲשֵׂה עִמָּנוּ לְמַעַן שְׁמֶךָ.
אָבִינוּ מַלְכֵּנוּ, בָּרֵךְ/ בעשרת ימי תשובה: חַדֵּשׁ/ עָלֵינוּ שָׁנָה טוֹבָה.
אָבִינוּ מַלְכֵּנוּ, בַּטֵּל מֵעָלֵינוּ כָּל גְּזֵרוֹת קָשׁוֹת.
אָבִינוּ מַלְכֵּנוּ, בַּטֵּל מַחְשְׁבוֹת שׂוֹנְאֵינוּ.
אָבִינוּ מַלְכֵּנוּ, הָפֵר עֲצַת אוֹיְבֵינוּ.
אָבִינוּ מַלְכֵּנוּ, כַּלֵּה כָּל צַר וּמַשְׂטִין מֵעָלֵינוּ.
אָבִינוּ מַלְכֵּנוּ, סְתֹם פִּיּוֹת מַשְׂטִינֵנוּ וּמְקַטְרְגֵינוּ.
אָבִינוּ מַלְכֵּנוּ, כַּלֵּה דֶּבֶר וְחֶרֶב וְרָעָב וּשְׁבִי וּמַשְׁחִית וְעָוֹן וּשְׁמַד מִבְּנֵי בְרִיתֶךָ.
אָבִינוּ מַלְכֵּנוּ, מְנַע מַגֵּפָה מִנַּחֲלָתֶךָ.
אָבִינוּ מַלְכֵּנוּ, סְלַח וּמְחַל לְכָל עֲוֹנוֹתֵינוּ.
אָבִינוּ מַלְכֵּנוּ, מְחֵה וְהַעֲבֵר פְּשָׁעֵינוּ וְחַטֹּאתֵינוּ מִנֶּגֶד עֵינֶיךָ.
אָבִינוּ מַלְכֵּנוּ, מְחֹק בְּרַחֲמֶיךָ הָרַבִּים כָּל שִׁטְרֵי חוֹבוֹתֵינוּ.

The following nine sentences are said responsively, first by the שליח ציבור*, then by the* קהל*:*

אָבִינוּ מַלְכֵּנוּ, הַחֲזִירֵנוּ בִּתְשׁוּבָה שְׁלֵמָה לְפָנֶיךָ.
אָבִינוּ מַלְכֵּנוּ, שְׁלַח רְפוּאָה שְׁלֵמָה לְחוֹלֵי עַמֶּךָ.
אָבִינוּ מַלְכֵּנוּ, קְרַע רֹעַ גְּזַר דִּינֵנוּ.
אָבִינוּ מַלְכֵּנוּ, זָכְרֵנוּ בְּזִכָּרוֹן טוֹב לְפָנֶיךָ.

During the עשרת ימי תשובה*:*

אָבִינוּ מַלְכֵּנוּ, כָּתְבֵנוּ בְּסֵפֶר חַיִּים טוֹבִים.
אָבִינוּ מַלְכֵּנוּ, כָּתְבֵנוּ בְּסֵפֶר גְּאֻלָּה וִישׁוּעָה.
אָבִינוּ מַלְכֵּנוּ, כָּתְבֵנוּ בְּסֵפֶר פַּרְנָסָה וְכַלְכָּלָה.
אָבִינוּ מַלְכֵּנוּ, כָּתְבֵנוּ בְּסֵפֶר זְכֻיּוֹת.
אָבִינוּ מַלְכֵּנוּ, כָּתְבֵנוּ בְּסֵפֶר סְלִיחָה וּמְחִילָה.

On Fast Days:

Our Father, our King, remember us for a good life.
Our Father, our King, remember us for redemption and salvation.
Our Father, our King, remember us for livelihood and sustenance.
Our Father, our King, remember us for merit.
Our Father, our King, remember us for pardon and forgiveness.

End of responsive reading.

Our Father, our King, let salvation soon flourish for us.
Our Father, our King, raise the honor of Your people Israel.
Our Father, our King, raise the honor of Your anointed.
Our Father, our King, fill our hands with Your blessings.
Our Father, our King, fill our storehouses with abundance.
Our Father, our King, hear our voice, pity and be compassionate to us.
Our Father, our King, accept, with compassion and favor, our prayer.
Our Father, our King, open the gates of heaven to our prayer.
Our Father, our King, remember that we are dust.
Our Father, our King, please do not turn us away from You empty-handed.
Our Father, our King, may this moment be a moment of compassion and a time of favor before You.
Our Father, our King, have pity on us, our children and our infants.
Our Father, our King, act for the sake of those who were killed for Your holy name.
Our Father, our King, act for the sake of those who were slaughtered for declaring Your Unity.
Our Father, our King, act for the sake of those who went through fire and water to sanctify Your name.
Our Father, our King, avenge before our eyes the spilt blood of Your servants.
Our Father, our King, act for Your sake, if not for ours.
Our Father, our King, act for Your sake, and save us.
Our Father, our King, act for the sake of Your great compassion.
Our Father, our King, act for the sake of Your great, mighty and awesome name by which we are called.
▸ Our Father, our King, be generous to us and answer us, though we have no worthy deeds; act with us in charity and loving-kindness and save us.

The Ark is closed.

On Fast Days:

אָבִינוּ מַלְכֵּנוּ, זָכְרֵנוּ לְחַיִּים טוֹבִים.
אָבִינוּ מַלְכֵּנוּ, זָכְרֵנוּ לִגְאֻלָּה וִישׁוּעָה.
אָבִינוּ מַלְכֵּנוּ, זָכְרֵנוּ לְפַרְנָסָה וְכַלְכָּלָה.
אָבִינוּ מַלְכֵּנוּ, זָכְרֵנוּ לִזְכֻיּוֹת.
אָבִינוּ מַלְכֵּנוּ, זָכְרֵנוּ לִסְלִיחָה וּמְחִילָה.

End of responsive reading.

אָבִינוּ מַלְכֵּנוּ, הַצְמַח לָנוּ יְשׁוּעָה בְּקָרוֹב.
אָבִינוּ מַלְכֵּנוּ, הָרֵם קֶרֶן יִשְׂרָאֵל עַמֶּךָ.
אָבִינוּ מַלְכֵּנוּ, הָרֵם קֶרֶן מְשִׁיחֶךָ.
אָבִינוּ מַלְכֵּנוּ, מַלֵּא יָדֵינוּ מִבִּרְכוֹתֶיךָ.
אָבִינוּ מַלְכֵּנוּ, מַלֵּא אֲסָמֵינוּ שָׂבָע.
אָבִינוּ מַלְכֵּנוּ, שְׁמַע קוֹלֵנוּ, חוּס וְרַחֵם עָלֵינוּ.
אָבִינוּ מַלְכֵּנוּ, קַבֵּל בְּרַחֲמִים וּבְרָצוֹן אֶת תְּפִלָּתֵנוּ.
אָבִינוּ מַלְכֵּנוּ, פְּתַח שַׁעֲרֵי שָׁמַיִם לִתְפִלָּתֵנוּ.
אָבִינוּ מַלְכֵּנוּ, זְכֹר כִּי עָפָר אֲנָחְנוּ.
אָבִינוּ מַלְכֵּנוּ, נָא אַל תְּשִׁיבֵנוּ רֵיקָם מִלְּפָנֶיךָ.
אָבִינוּ מַלְכֵּנוּ, תְּהֵא הַשָּׁעָה הַזֹּאת שְׁעַת רַחֲמִים וְעֵת רָצוֹן מִלְּפָנֶיךָ.
אָבִינוּ מַלְכֵּנוּ, חֲמֹל עָלֵינוּ וְעַל עוֹלָלֵינוּ וְטַפֵּנוּ.
אָבִינוּ מַלְכֵּנוּ, עֲשֵׂה לְמַעַן הֲרוּגִים עַל שֵׁם קָדְשֶׁךָ.
אָבִינוּ מַלְכֵּנוּ, עֲשֵׂה לְמַעַן טְבוּחִים עַל יִחוּדֶךָ.
אָבִינוּ מַלְכֵּנוּ, עֲשֵׂה לְמַעַן בָּאֵי בָאֵשׁ וּבַמַּיִם עַל קִדּוּשׁ שְׁמֶךָ.
אָבִינוּ מַלְכֵּנוּ, נְקֹם לְעֵינֵינוּ נִקְמַת דַּם עֲבָדֶיךָ הַשָּׁפוּךְ.
אָבִינוּ מַלְכֵּנוּ, עֲשֵׂה לְמַעַנְךָ אִם לֹא לְמַעֲנֵנוּ.
אָבִינוּ מַלְכֵּנוּ, עֲשֵׂה לְמַעַנְךָ וְהוֹשִׁיעֵנוּ.
אָבִינוּ מַלְכֵּנוּ, עֲשֵׂה לְמַעַן רַחֲמֶיךָ הָרַבִּים.
אָבִינוּ מַלְכֵּנוּ, עֲשֵׂה לְמַעַן שִׁמְךָ הַגָּדוֹל הַגִּבּוֹר וְהַנּוֹרָא שֶׁנִּקְרָא עָלֵינוּ.
◂ אָבִינוּ מַלְכֵּנוּ, חָנֵּנוּ וַעֲנֵנוּ, כִּי אֵין בָּנוּ מַעֲשִׂים
עֲשֵׂה עִמָּנוּ צְדָקָה וָחֶסֶד וְהוֹשִׁיעֵנוּ.

The ארון קודש *is closed.*

TAḤANUN

Taḥanun is not said on Erev Shabbat and Erev Yom Tov. It is also not said on the following days: Rosh Ḥodesh, Ḥanukka, Tu BiShvat, the 14th and 15th of Adar I, Purim and Shushan Purim, Yom HaAtzma'ut, Lag BaOmer, Yom Yerushalayim, Tisha B'Av, Tu B'Av, and the preceding afternoons, the month of Nisan, the 14th of Iyar (Pesaḥ Sheni), from Rosh Ḥodesh Sivan through the day after Shavuot (in Israel through 12th of Sivan), and from Erev Yom Kippur through the day after Simḥat Torah (in Israel through Rosh Ḥodesh Marḥeshvan). Taḥanun is also not said: on the occasion of a Brit Mila, either where the brit will take place or where the father, Sandek or Mohel are present; if a groom is present (and some say, a bride) on the day of his wedding or during the week of Sheva Berakhot; in a house of mourning.

LOWERING THE HEAD

Say while sitting; in the presence of a Torah scroll say until "in sudden shame," leaning forward and resting one's head on the left arm.

וַיֹּאמֶר דָּוִד David said to Gad, "I am in great distress. *II Sam. 24*
Let us fall into God's hand, for His mercy is great;
but do not let me fall into the hand of man."

Compassionate and generous One, I have sinned before You.
Lord, full of compassion, have compassion on me
and accept my pleas.

Lord, do not rebuke me in Your anger or chastise me in Your fury. *Ps. 6*
Be generous to me, Lord, for I am weak.
Heal me, Lord, for my bones are in agony.
My soul is in anguish, and You, O Lord – how long?
Turn, Lord, set my soul free; save me for the sake of Your love.
For no one remembers You when he is dead.
Who can praise You from the grave? I am tired with my sighing.
Every night I drench my bed, I soak my couch with my tears.
My eye grows dim from grief, worn out because of all my enemies.
Leave me, all you evildoers,
for the Lord has heard the sound of my weeping.
The Lord has heard my pleas. The Lord will accept my prayer.
All my enemies will be shamed and utterly dismayed.
They will turn back in sudden shame.

Sit upright.

סדר תחנון

תחנון is not said on ערב שבת and ערב יום טוב. It is also not said on the following days: ראש חודש, חנוכה, ט״ו בשבט, the 14th and 15th of אדר א׳, פורים and שושן פורים, יום העצמאות, ל״ג בעומר, יום ירושלים, תשעה באב, ט״ו באב, and the preceding afternoons, the month of ניסן, the 14th of אייר (פסח שני), from ראש חודש סיון through the day after שבועות (in ארץ ישראל through י״ב סיון), and from ערב יום כיפור through the day after שמחת תורה (in ארץ ישראל through ראש חודש מרחשון). תחנון is also not said: on the occasion of a ברית מילה, either where the ברית will take place or where the father, סנדק or מוהל are present; if a חתן is present (and some say, a כלה) on the day of his wedding or during the week of שבע ברכות; in a house of mourning.

נפילת אפיים

Say while sitting; in the presence of a ספר תורה say until יֵבֹשׁוּ רָגַע, leaning forward and resting one's head on the left arm.

וַיֹּאמֶר דָּוִד אֶל־גָּד, צַר־לִי מְאֹד שמואל ב׳ כד
נִפְּלָה־נָּא בְיַד־יהוה, כִּי רַבִּים רַחֲמָו, וּבְיַד־אָדָם אַל־אֶפֹּלָה:

רַחוּם וְחַנּוּן, חָטָאתִי לְפָנֶיךָ.
יהוה מָלֵא רַחֲמִים, רַחֵם עָלַי וְקַבֵּל תַּחֲנוּנָי.

יהוה, אַל־בְּאַפְּךָ תוֹכִיחֵנִי, וְאַל־בַּחֲמָתְךָ תְיַסְּרֵנִי: תהלים ו
חָנֵּנִי יהוה, כִּי אֻמְלַל אָנִי, רְפָאֵנִי יהוה, כִּי נִבְהֲלוּ עֲצָמָי:
וְנַפְשִׁי נִבְהֲלָה מְאֹד, וְאַתָּ יהוה, עַד־מָתָי:
שׁוּבָה יהוה, חַלְּצָה נַפְשִׁי, הוֹשִׁיעֵנִי לְמַעַן חַסְדֶּךָ:
כִּי אֵין בַּמָּוֶת זִכְרֶךָ, בִּשְׁאוֹל מִי יוֹדֶה־לָּךְ:
יָגַעְתִּי בְּאַנְחָתִי, אַשְׂחֶה בְכָל־לַיְלָה מִטָּתִי, בְּדִמְעָתִי עַרְשִׂי אַמְסֶה:
עָשְׁשָׁה מִכַּעַס עֵינִי, עָתְקָה בְּכָל־צוֹרְרָי:
סוּרוּ מִמֶּנִּי כָּל־פֹּעֲלֵי אָוֶן, כִּי־שָׁמַע יהוה קוֹל בִּכְיִי:
שָׁמַע יהוה תְּחִנָּתִי, יהוה תְּפִלָּתִי יִקָּח:
יֵבֹשׁוּ וְיִבָּהֲלוּ מְאֹד כָּל־אֹיְבָי, יָשֻׁבוּ יֵבֹשׁוּ רָגַע:

Sit upright.

שׁוֹמֵר יִשְׂרָאֵל Guardian of Israel,
guard the survivors of Israel,
and let not Israel perish, who declare, "Listen, Israel."
Guardian of a unique nation, guard the survivors of a unique people,
and let not that unique nation perish, who declare the unity of Your name [saying], "The LORD is our God, the LORD is One."
Guardian of a holy nation, guard the survivors of that holy people,
and let not the holy nation perish, who three times repeat
the threefold declaration of holiness to the Holy One.
You who are conciliated by calls for compassion and placated by pleas,
be conciliated and placated toward an afflicted generation,
for there is no other help.
Our Father, our King, be generous to us and answer us,
though we have no worthy deeds;
act with us in charity and loving-kindness and save us.

Stand at ▲.

וַאֲנַחְנוּ We do not know ▲what to do, but our eyes are turned to You. *II Chr. 12*
Remember, LORD, Your compassion and loving-kindness, for they are *Ps. 25*
everlasting. May Your loving-kindness, LORD, be with us, for we have put *Ps. 33*
our hope in You. Do not hold against us the sins of those who came before *Ps. 79*
us. May Your mercies meet us swiftly, for we have been brought very low.
Be generous to us, LORD, be generous to us, for we are full with contempt. *Ps. 123*
In fury, remember mercy. He knows our nature; He remembers that we *Hab. 3* *Ps. 103*
are dust. ▸ Help us, God of our salvation, for the sake of the glory of Your *Ps. 79*
name. Save us and give atonement for our sins for Your name's sake.

FULL KADDISH

Leader: יִתְגַּדַּל Magnified and sanctified may His great name be,
in the world He created by His will.
May He establish His kingdom
in your lifetime and in your days,
and in the lifetime of all the house of Israel,
swiftly and soon – and say: Amen.

All: May His great name be blessed for ever and all time.

שׁוֹמֵר יִשְׂרָאֵל, שְׁמֹר שְׁאֵרִית יִשְׂרָאֵל, וְאַל יֹאבַד יִשְׂרָאֵל
הָאוֹמְרִים שְׁמַע יִשְׂרָאֵל.
שׁוֹמֵר גּוֹי אֶחָד, שְׁמֹר שְׁאֵרִית עַם אֶחָד, וְאַל יֹאבַד גּוֹי אֶחָד
הַמְיַחֲדִים שִׁמְךָ, יהוה אֱלֹהֵינוּ יהוה אֶחָד.
שׁוֹמֵר גּוֹי קָדוֹשׁ, שְׁמֹר שְׁאֵרִית עַם קָדוֹשׁ, וְאַל יֹאבַד גּוֹי קָדוֹשׁ
הַמְשַׁלְּשִׁים בְּשָׁלֹשׁ קְדֻשּׁוֹת לְקָדוֹשׁ.
מִתְרַצֶּה בְּרַחֲמִים וּמִתְפַּיֵּס בְּתַחֲנוּנִים, הִתְרַצֶּה וְהִתְפַּיֵּס לְדוֹר עָנִי
כִּי אֵין עוֹזֵר.
אָבִינוּ מַלְכֵּנוּ, חָנֵּנוּ וַעֲנֵנוּ, כִּי אֵין בָּנוּ מַעֲשִׂים
עֲשֵׂה עִמָּנוּ צְדָקָה וָחֶסֶד וְהוֹשִׁיעֵנוּ.

Stand at ▲.

וַאֲנַחְנוּ לֹא נֵדַע ▲מַה־נַּעֲשֶׂה, כִּי עָלֶיךָ עֵינֵינוּ: זְכֹר־רַחֲמֶיךָ יהוה — דברי הימים ב׳ יב, תהלים כה
וַחֲסָדֶיךָ, כִּי מֵעוֹלָם הֵמָּה: יְהִי־חַסְדְּךָ יהוה עָלֵינוּ, כַּאֲשֶׁר יִחַלְנוּ לָךְ: — תהלים לג
אַל־תִּזְכָּר־לָנוּ עֲוֹנֹת רִאשֹׁנִים, מַהֵר יְקַדְּמוּנוּ רַחֲמֶיךָ, כִּי דַלּוֹנוּ מְאֹד: — תהלים עט
חָנֵּנוּ יהוה חָנֵּנוּ, כִּי־רַב שָׂבַעְנוּ בוּז: בְּרֹגֶז רַחֵם תִּזְכּוֹר: כִּי־הוּא יָדַע — תהלים קכג, חבקוק ג, תהלים קג
יִצְרֵנוּ, זָכוּר כִּי־עָפָר אֲנָחְנוּ: ◂ עָזְרֵנוּ אֱלֹהֵי יִשְׁעֵנוּ עַל־דְּבַר כְּבוֹד־ — תהלים עט
שְׁמֶךָ, וְהַצִּילֵנוּ וְכַפֵּר עַל־חַטֹּאתֵינוּ לְמַעַן שְׁמֶךָ:

קדיש שלם

ש״ץ: יִתְגַּדַּל וְיִתְקַדַּשׁ שְׁמֵהּ רַבָּא (קהל: אָמֵן)
בְּעָלְמָא דִּי בְרָא כִרְעוּתֵהּ
וְיַמְלִיךְ מַלְכוּתֵהּ
בְּחַיֵּיכוֹן וּבְיוֹמֵיכוֹן וּבְחַיֵּי דְכָל בֵּית יִשְׂרָאֵל
בַּעֲגָלָא וּבִזְמַן קָרִיב, וְאִמְרוּ אָמֵן. (קהל: אָמֵן)

קהל וש״ץ: יְהֵא שְׁמֵהּ רַבָּא מְבָרַךְ לְעָלַם וּלְעָלְמֵי עָלְמַיָּא.

Leader: Blessed and praised, glorified and elevated,
raised and honored, uplifted and praised
be the name of the Holy One,
blessed be He,
beyond any blessing,
song, praise and consolation
uttered in the world –
and say: Amen.

May the prayers and pleas of all Israel
be accepted by their Father in heaven –
and say: Amen.

May there be great peace from heaven,
and life for us and all Israel –
and say: Amen.

Bow, take three steps back, as if taking leave of the Divine Presence, then bow, first left, then right, then center, while saying:

May He who makes peace in His high places,
make peace for us and all Israel –
and say: Amen.

Stand while saying Aleinu.

עָלֵינוּ It is our duty to praise the Master of all,
and ascribe greatness to the Author of creation,
who has not made us like the nations of the lands
nor placed us like the families of the earth;
who has not made our portion like theirs,
nor our destiny like all their multitudes.
(For they worship vanity and emptiness,
and pray to a god who cannot save.)
But we bow in worship
and thank the Supreme King of kings,
the Holy One, blessed be He,

ש״ץ: יִתְבָּרַךְ וְיִשְׁתַּבַּח וְיִתְפָּאַר
וְיִתְרוֹמַם וְיִתְנַשֵּׂא וְיִתְהַדָּר וְיִתְעַלֶּה וְיִתְהַלָּל
שְׁמֵהּ דְּקֻדְשָׁא בְּרִיךְ הוּא (קהל: בְּרִיךְ הוּא)
לְעֵלָּא מִן כָּל בִּרְכָתָא
/בעשרת ימי תשובה: לְעֵלָּא לְעֵלָּא מִכָּל בִּרְכָתָא/
וְשִׁירָתָא, תֻּשְׁבְּחָתָא וְנֶחֱמָתָא
דַּאֲמִירָן בְּעָלְמָא וְאִמְרוּ אָמֵן. (קהל: אָמֵן)

תִּתְקַבַּל צְלוֹתְהוֹן וּבָעוּתְהוֹן דְּכָל יִשְׂרָאֵל
קֳדָם אֲבוּהוֹן דִּי בִשְׁמַיָּא, וְאִמְרוּ אָמֵן. (קהל: אָמֵן)

יְהֵא שְׁלָמָא רַבָּא מִן שְׁמַיָּא
וְחַיִּים, עָלֵינוּ וְעַל כָּל יִשְׂרָאֵל
וְאִמְרוּ אָמֵן. (קהל: אָמֵן)

Bow, take three steps back, as if taking leave of the Divine Presence, then bow, first left, then right, then center, while saying:

עֹשֶׂה שָׁלוֹם/ בעשרת ימי תשובה: הַשָּׁלוֹם/ בִּמְרוֹמָיו
הוּא יַעֲשֶׂה שָׁלוֹם עָלֵינוּ
וְעַל כָּל יִשְׂרָאֵל, וְאִמְרוּ אָמֵן. (קהל: אָמֵן)

Stand while saying עָלֵינוּ.

עָלֵינוּ לְשַׁבֵּחַ לַאֲדוֹן הַכֹּל, לָתֵת גְּדֻלָּה לְיוֹצֵר בְּרֵאשִׁית
שֶׁלֹּא עָשָׂנוּ כְּגוֹיֵי הָאֲרָצוֹת, וְלֹא שָׂמָנוּ כְּמִשְׁפְּחוֹת הָאֲדָמָה
שֶׁלֹּא שָׂם חֶלְקֵנוּ כָּהֶם וְגוֹרָלֵנוּ כְּכָל הֲמוֹנָם.
(שֶׁהֵם מִשְׁתַּחֲוִים לְהֶבֶל וָרִיק וּמִתְפַּלְּלִים אֶל אֵל לֹא יוֹשִׁיעַ.)
ק וַאֲנַחְנוּ כּוֹרְעִים וּמִשְׁתַּחֲוִים וּמוֹדִים
לִפְנֵי מֶלֶךְ מַלְכֵי הַמְּלָכִים, הַקָּדוֹשׁ בָּרוּךְ הוּא

who extends the heavens and establishes the earth,
whose throne of glory is in the heavens above,
and whose power's Presence is in the highest of heights.
He is our God; there is no other.
Truly He is our King, there is none else,
as it is written in His Torah:
"You shall know and take to heart this day that the LORD is God, *Deut. 4*
in heaven above and on earth below. There is no other."

Therefore, we place our hope in You, LORD our God,
that we may soon see the glory of Your power,
when You will remove abominations from the earth,
and idols will be utterly destroyed,
when the world will be perfected
under the sovereignty of the Almighty,
when all humanity will call on Your name,
to turn all the earth's wicked toward You.
All the world's inhabitants will realize and know
that to You every knee must bow
and every tongue swear loyalty.
Before You, LORD our God, they will kneel and bow down
and give honor to Your glorious name.
They will all accept the yoke of Your kingdom,
and You will reign over them soon and for ever.
For the kingdom is Yours,
and to all eternity You will reign in glory,
as it is written in Your Torah:
"The LORD will reign for ever and ever." *Ex. 15*
▸ And it is said: "Then the LORD shall be King over all the earth; *Zech. 14*
on that day the LORD shall be One and His name One."

Some add:

Have no fear of sudden terror or of the ruin when it overtakes the wicked. *Prov. 3*
Devise your strategy, but it will be defeated, propose your plan, *Is. 8*
but it will not stand, for God is with us.
When you grow old, I will still be the same. *Is. 46*
When your hair turns gray, I will still carry you.
I made you, I will bear you, I will carry you, and I will rescue you.

שֶׁהוּא נוֹטֶה שָׁמַיִם וְיוֹסֵד אָרֶץ, וּמוֹשַׁב יְקָרוֹ בַּשָּׁמַיִם מִמַּעַל
וּשְׁכִינַת עֻזּוֹ בְּגָבְהֵי מְרוֹמִים.
הוּא אֱלֹהֵינוּ, אֵין עוֹד.
אֱמֶת מַלְכֵּנוּ, אֶפֶס זוּלָתוֹ
כַּכָּתוּב בְּתוֹרָתוֹ
דברים ד וְיָדַעְתָּ הַיּוֹם וַהֲשֵׁבֹתָ אֶל־לְבָבֶךָ
כִּי יהוה הוּא הָאֱלֹהִים בַּשָּׁמַיִם מִמַּעַל וְעַל־הָאָרֶץ מִתָּחַת
אֵין עוֹד:

עַל כֵּן נְקַוֶּה לְּךָ יהוה אֱלֹהֵינוּ, לִרְאוֹת מְהֵרָה בְּתִפְאֶרֶת עֻזֶּךָ
לְהַעֲבִיר גִּלּוּלִים מִן הָאָרֶץ, וְהָאֱלִילִים כָּרוֹת יִכָּרֵתוּן
לְתַקֵּן עוֹלָם בְּמַלְכוּת שַׁדַּי.
וְכָל בְּנֵי בָשָׂר יִקְרְאוּ בִשְׁמֶךָ לְהַפְנוֹת אֵלֶיךָ כָּל רִשְׁעֵי אָרֶץ.
יַכִּירוּ וְיֵדְעוּ כָּל יוֹשְׁבֵי תֵבֵל
כִּי לְךָ תִּכְרַע כָּל בֶּרֶךְ, תִּשָּׁבַע כָּל לָשׁוֹן.
לְפָנֶיךָ יהוה אֱלֹהֵינוּ יִכְרְעוּ וְיִפֹּלוּ, וְלִכְבוֹד שִׁמְךָ יְקָר יִתֵּנוּ
וִיקַבְּלוּ כֻלָּם אֶת עֹל מַלְכוּתֶךָ
וְתִמְלֹךְ עֲלֵיהֶם מְהֵרָה לְעוֹלָם וָעֶד.
כִּי הַמַּלְכוּת שֶׁלְּךָ הִיא וּלְעוֹלְמֵי עַד תִּמְלֹךְ בְּכָבוֹד
שמות טו כַּכָּתוּב בְּתוֹרָתֶךָ, יהוה יִמְלֹךְ לְעֹלָם וָעֶד:
זכריה יד ◂ וְנֶאֱמַר, וְהָיָה יהוה לְמֶלֶךְ עַל־כָּל־הָאָרֶץ
בַּיּוֹם הַהוּא יִהְיֶה יהוה אֶחָד וּשְׁמוֹ אֶחָד:

Some add:

משלי ג אַל־תִּירָא מִפַּחַד פִּתְאֹם וּמִשֹּׁאַת רְשָׁעִים כִּי תָבֹא:
ישעיה ח עֻצוּ עֵצָה וְתֻפָר, דַּבְּרוּ דָבָר וְלֹא יָקוּם, כִּי עִמָּנוּ אֵל:
ישעיה מו וְעַד־זִקְנָה אֲנִי הוּא, וְעַד־שֵׂיבָה אֲנִי אֶסְבֹּל
אֲנִי עָשִׂיתִי וַאֲנִי אֶשָּׂא וַאֲנִי אֶסְבֹּל וַאֲמַלֵּט:

MOURNER'S KADDISH

The following prayer, said by mourners, requires the presence of a minyan. A transliteration can be found on page 1151.

Mourner: יִתְגַּדַּל Magnified and sanctified
may His great name be,
in the world He created by His will.
May He establish His kingdom
in your lifetime
and in your days,
and in the lifetime
of all the house of Israel,
swiftly and soon –
and say: Amen.

All: May His great name be blessed for ever and all time.

Mourner: Blessed and praised,
glorified and elevated,
raised and honored,
uplifted and praised
be the name of the Holy One,
blessed be He,
beyond any blessing,
song, praise and consolation
uttered in the world –
and say: Amen.

May there be great peace from heaven,
and life for us and all Israel –
and say: Amen.

Bow, take three steps back, as if taking leave of the Divine Presence, then bow, first left, then right, then center, while saying:

May He who makes peace in His high places,
make peace for us and all Israel –
and say: Amen.

קדיש יתום

The following prayer, said by mourners, requires the presence of a מנין*.*
A transliteration can be found on page 1151.

אבל: **יִתְגַּדַּל וְיִתְקַדַּשׁ שְׁמֵהּ רַבָּא** (קהל: אָמֵן)
בְּעָלְמָא דִּי בְרָא כִרְעוּתֵהּ
וְיַמְלִיךְ מַלְכוּתֵהּ
בְּחַיֵּיכוֹן וּבְיוֹמֵיכוֹן וּבְחַיֵּי דְכָל בֵּית יִשְׂרָאֵל
בַּעֲגָלָא וּבִזְמַן קָרִיב
וְאִמְרוּ אָמֵן. (קהל: אָמֵן)

קהל ואבל: **יְהֵא שְׁמֵהּ רַבָּא מְבָרַךְ לְעָלַם וּלְעָלְמֵי עָלְמַיָּא.**

אבל: **יִתְבָּרַךְ וְיִשְׁתַּבַּח וְיִתְפָּאַר**
וְיִתְרוֹמַם וְיִתְנַשֵּׂא וְיִתְהַדָּר וְיִתְעַלֶּה וְיִתְהַלָּל
שְׁמֵהּ דְּקֻדְשָׁא בְּרִיךְ הוּא (קהל: בְּרִיךְ הוּא)
לְעֵלָּא מִן כָּל בִּרְכָתָא
/בעשרת ימי תשובה: **לְעֵלָּא לְעֵלָּא מִכָּל בִּרְכָתָא**/
וְשִׁירָתָא, תֻּשְׁבְּחָתָא וְנֶחֱמָתָא
דַּאֲמִירָן בְּעָלְמָא
וְאִמְרוּ אָמֵן. (קהל: אָמֵן)

יְהֵא שְׁלָמָא רַבָּא מִן שְׁמַיָּא
וְחַיִּים, עָלֵינוּ וְעַל כָּל יִשְׂרָאֵל
וְאִמְרוּ אָמֵן. (קהל: אָמֵן)

Bow, take three steps back, as if taking leave of the Divine Presence, then bow, first left, then right, then center, while saying:

עֹשֶׂה שָׁלוֹם/ בעשרת ימי תשובה: **הַשָּׁלוֹם/ בִּמְרוֹמָיו**
הוּא יַעֲשֶׂה שָׁלוֹם עָלֵינוּ וְעַל כָּל יִשְׂרָאֵל
וְאִמְרוּ אָמֵן. (קהל: אָמֵן)

Ma'ariv for Weekdays

On Motza'ei Shabbat, many congregations recite Psalms 144 and 67 before Ma'ariv (page 366).

וְהוּא רַחוּם He is compassionate. *Ps. 78*
He forgives wrongdoing and does not destroy.
Repeatedly He suppresses His anger, not rousing His full fury.
LORD, save! May the King, answer us on the day we call. *Ps. 20*

BLESSINGS OF THE SHEMA

The Leader says the following, bowing at "Bless," standing straight at "the LORD"; the congregation, followed by the Leader, responds, bowing at "Bless," standing straight at "the LORD":

Leader: **BLESS**
the LORD, the blessed One.

Congregation: Bless the LORD, the blessed One,
for ever and all time.

Leader: Bless the LORD, the blessed One,
for ever and all time.

---

there were those who held that Ma'ariv was not obligatory. However, due to its widespread observance it became obligatory, and is seen this way today. Because it was not originally instituted as an obligatory prayer, the *Amida* is not repeated by the leader as it is in Shaḥarit and Minḥa (Rambam, *Hilkhot Tefilla* 9:9).

It has been suggested that the three daily services reflect the characters of their originators. Avraham was a courageous pioneer, associated with a brand new day and the morning service of Shaḥarit. Yitzḥak, who never left *Eretz Yisrael* (unlike his father, Avraham, and son, Yaakov), represents continuity, and the afternoon *tefilla* of Minḥa. Our tradition tells us that it is Yaakov who instituted Ma'ariv. Yaakov had much uncertainty in his life, and faced many trials and tribulations. He also had his most intense religious experiences at night, such as his dream with angels ascending and descending a ladder. It is fitting therefore that it is Yaakov who established the *tefilla* we say before we embark on the sometimes uncertain and insecure nighttime.

מעריב לחול

On מוצאי שבת*, many congregations recite Psalms 144 and 67 before* מעריב *(page 367).*

וְהוּא רַחוּם, יְכַפֵּר עָוֹן וְלֹא־יַשְׁחִית תהלים עח
וְהִרְבָּה לְהָשִׁיב אַפּוֹ, וְלֹא־יָעִיר כָּל־חֲמָתוֹ:
יהוה הוֹשִׁיעָה, הַמֶּלֶךְ יַעֲנֵנוּ בְיוֹם־קָרְאֵנוּ: תהלים כ

קריאת שמע וברכותיה

The שליח ציבור *says the following, bowing at* בָּרְכוּ*, standing straight at* ה'*; the* קהל*, followed by the* שליח ציבור*, responds, bowing at* בָּרוּךְ*, standing straight at* ה'*:*

ש״ץ: 

אֶת יהוה הַמְבֹרָךְ.

קהל: בָּרוּךְ יהוה הַמְבֹרָךְ לְעוֹלָם וָעֶד.

ש״ץ: בָּרוּךְ יהוה הַמְבֹרָךְ לְעוֹלָם וָעֶד.

LEARNING

INTRODUCTION TO MA'ARIV

As previously mentioned, our *tefillot* services correspond either to the *Avot* who instituted them, or to the daily sacrificial services in the *Beit HaMikdash* (*Berakhot* 26b). While this discussion is left somewhat open in the Gemara, we learn the halakhic times of our *tefillot* from the sacrificial service. Ma'ariv, the third daily *tefilla* service, does not have a corresponding sacrificial service, as there were no sacrifices at night. Instead, Ma'ariv corresponds to the burning of the remainders of the daily sacrifices, which continued to burn on the altar all night, until daybreak. Since Ma'ariv does not correspond to an actual sacrifice,

בָּרוּךְ Blessed are You, Lord our God, King of the Universe,
who by His word brings on evenings,
by His wisdom opens the gates of heaven,
with understanding makes time change and the seasons rotate,
and by His will orders the stars in their constellations in the sky.
He creates day and night,
rolling away the light before the darkness,
and darkness before the light.
▸ He makes the day pass and brings on night,
distinguishing day from night:
the Lord of multitudes is His name.
May the living and forever enduring God rule over us for all time.
Blessed are You, Lord, who brings on evenings.

CONNECTION

To every thing there is a season,
a time to every purpose under the heaven:

A time to be born, and a time to die;
A time to plant, and a time to uproot that which was planted.

A time to kill, and a time to heal;
A time to break, and a time to build.

A time to weep, and a time to laugh;
A time of mourning and a time of dancing.

A time to cast away stones,
and a time to gather stones.

A time to embrace,
and a time to refrain from embracing.

A time to seek, and a time to lose;
A time to keep, and a time to cast away.

A time to rend, and a time to sew;
A time to keep silence, and a time to speak.

A time to love, and a time to hate;
A time of war, and a time of peace.

(*Kohelet* 3:1–7)

בָּרוּךְ אַתָּה יהוה אֱלֹהֵינוּ מֶלֶךְ הָעוֹלָם
אֲשֶׁר בִּדְבָרוֹ מַעֲרִיב עֲרָבִים
בְּחָכְמָה פּוֹתֵחַ שְׁעָרִים
וּבִתְבוּנָה מְשַׁנֶּה עִתִּים וּמַחֲלִיף אֶת הַזְּמַנִּים
וּמְסַדֵּר אֶת הַכּוֹכָבִים בְּמִשְׁמְרוֹתֵיהֶם בָּרָקִיעַ כִּרְצוֹנוֹ.
בּוֹרֵא יוֹם וָלָיְלָה, גּוֹלֵל אוֹר מִפְּנֵי חֹשֶׁךְ וְחֹשֶׁךְ מִפְּנֵי אוֹר
◂ וּמַעֲבִיר יוֹם וּמֵבִיא לָיְלָה, וּמַבְדִּיל בֵּין יוֹם וּבֵין לָיְלָה
יהוה צְבָאוֹת שְׁמוֹ.
אֵל חַי וְקַיָּם תָּמִיד, יִמְלֹךְ עָלֵינוּ לְעוֹלָם וָעֶד.
בָּרוּךְ אַתָּה יהוה, הַמַּעֲרִיב עֲרָבִים.

LEARNING

While the natural rhythm of our day has the evening as the time when our day begins to wind down, and the descent toward sleep begins, culminating in a night of shutdown and reboot, in Jewish tradition it is in fact considered to be the beginning of the day. The Jewish date changes with nightfall, and all other halakhic definitions to do with time begin then or before then with sunset, such as the beginning of Shabbat and *Ḥagim*, or the birth date of a child. This is due to the terminology used in the account of the creation of the world found in *Bereshit*. At the end of each day of creation God says, "And there was evening, and there was morning, one day" (*Bereshit* 1:4). Evening here precedes morning, indicating that according to this account the day begins with nightfall. Perhaps an inspiring message is contained in this way of looking at daily time. In the Jewish day, light conquers darkness, day conquers night. Every day! No matter how dark our world seems, there is always light to come.

REFLECTION

וַיְהִי־עֶרֶב וַיְהִי־בֹקֶר יוֹם אֶחָד.

"And it was evening and it was morning, one day."
(*Bereshit* 1:4)

Is dark
the absence of light
or something tangible
in its own right?

Is night
the absence of day,
or does it
have significance
in its own right?

How did you
spend your day?

How will you
spend your night?

אַהֲבַת עוֹלָם With everlasting love
have You loved Your people, the house of Israel.
You have taught us Torah and commandments,
decrees and laws of justice.
Therefore, LORD our God, when we lie down and when we rise up
we will speak of Your decrees, rejoicing in the words of Your Torah
and Your commandments for ever.
▸ For they are our life and the length of our days;
on them will we meditate day and night.
May You never take away Your love from us.
Blessed are You, LORD, who loves His people Israel.

REFLECTION

"One who studies Torah at night is blessed with a 'thread of kindness.'"
(*Avoda Zara* 3b)

"One who learns Torah at night will have long life."
(*Ta'anit* 31a)

"Even though it is a mitzva to study during the day and at night, it is only at night that a person acquires most of his wisdom."
(Rambam, *Hilkhot Talmud Torah* 3:13)

When do you prefer to study, during the day or at night?

Why do you think there is a special reward for learning Torah at night?

What Torah will you learn tonight?

LEARNING

One should establish a fixed time to learn after *tefilla*. If one has a great need that one must leave for, one should learn at least one *pasuk* or one halakha. (*Kitzur Shulḥan Arukh* 27:1) There's a special practice to "join the day and night" with learning or *davening* by learning during sunset and sunrise. (*Kitzur Shulḥan Arukh* 1:6)

In the morning, when we recite *Ahava Raba* before *Shema,* we ask Hashem to "Instill in our hearts understanding to listen, learn and teach" and to "illuminate our eyes in Your Torah." But in this blessing before the nighttime *Shema*, we do not ask Hashem to grant us enlightenment – instead we proclaim that "*we* will speak of Your decrees, and *we* will rejoice in the words of Your Torah…because they are our life." If daytime represents God-given clarity, night is a time of darkness when we must struggle on our own to achieve understanding. Perhaps this explains the special qualities ascribed to nighttime study.

אַהֲבַת עוֹלָם בֵּית יִשְׂרָאֵל עַמְּךָ אָהָבְתָּ
תּוֹרָה וּמִצְוֹת, חֻקִּים וּמִשְׁפָּטִים, אוֹתָֽנוּ לִמַּדְתָּ
עַל כֵּן יהוה אֱלֹהֵינוּ
בְּשָׁכְבֵנוּ וּבְקוּמֵנוּ נָשִׂיחַ בְּחֻקֶּיךָ
וְנִשְׂמַח בְּדִבְרֵי תוֹרָתֶךָ
וּבְמִצְוֹתֶיךָ לְעוֹלָם וָעֶד
◂ כִּי הֵם חַיֵּינוּ וְאֹֽרֶךְ יָמֵינוּ
וּבָהֶם נֶהְגֶּה יוֹמָם וָלָֽיְלָה.
וְאַהֲבָתְךָ אַל תָּסִיר מִמֶּנּוּ לְעוֹלָמִים.
בָּרוּךְ אַתָּה יהוה, אוֹהֵב עַמּוֹ יִשְׂרָאֵל.

... A THOUSAND WORDS

CONNECTION

"Night is purer than day; it is better for thinking and loving and dreaming. At night everything is more intense, more true. The echo of words that have been spoken during the day takes on a new and deeper meaning..."

(Elie Wiesel, *Dawn*)

The Shema must be said with intense concentration.

When not with a minyan, say:

God, faithful King!

The following verse should be said aloud, while covering the eyes with the right hand:

Listen, Israel: the LORD is our God, the LORD is One.

Deut. 6

Quietly: Blessed be the name of His glorious kingdom for ever and all time.

וְאָהַבְתָּ Love the LORD your God with all your heart, with all your soul, and with all your might. These words which I command you today shall be on your heart. Teach them repeatedly to your children, speaking of them when you sit at home and when you travel on the way, when you lie down and when you rise. Bind them as a sign on your hand, and they shall be a symbol between your eyes. Write them on the doorposts of your house and gates. Deut. 6

וְהָיָה If you indeed follow My commandments with which I charge you today, to love the LORD your God and worship Him with all your heart and with all your soul, I will give rain in your land in its season, the early and late rain; and you shall gather in your grain, wine and oil. I will give grass in your field for your cattle, and you shall eat and be satisfied. Be careful lest your heart be tempted and you go astray and worship other gods, bowing down to them. Then the LORD's anger will flare against you and He will close the heavens so that there will be no rain. The land will not yield its crops, and you will perish swiftly from the good land that the LORD is giving you. Therefore, set these, My words, on your heart and soul. Bind them as a sign on your hand, and they shall be a symbol between your eyes. Teach them to your children, speaking of them when you sit at home and when you travel on the way, when you lie down and when you rise. Deut. 11

The שמע must be said with intense concentration.

When not with a מנין, say:

אֵל מֶלֶךְ נֶאֱמָן

The following verse should be said aloud, while covering the eyes with the right hand:

דברים ו **שְׁמַע יִשְׂרָאֵל, יהוה אֱלֹהֵינוּ, יהוה ׀ אֶחָד:**

Quietly בָּרוּךְ שֵׁם כְּבוֹד מַלְכוּתוֹ לְעוֹלָם וָעֶד.

דברים ו וְאָהַבְתָּ אֵת יהוה אֱלֹהֶיךָ, בְּכׇל־לְבָבְךָ וּבְכׇל־נַפְשְׁךָ וּבְכׇל־
מְאֹדֶךָ: וְהָיוּ הַדְּבָרִים הָאֵלֶּה, אֲשֶׁר אָנֹכִי מְצַוְּךָ הַיּוֹם, עַל־לְבָבֶךָ:
וְשִׁנַּנְתָּם לְבָנֶיךָ וְדִבַּרְתָּ בָּם, בְּשִׁבְתְּךָ בְּבֵיתֶךָ וּבְלֶכְתְּךָ בַדֶּרֶךְ,
וּבְשׇׁכְבְּךָ וּבְקוּמֶךָ: וּקְשַׁרְתָּם לְאוֹת עַל־יָדֶךָ וְהָיוּ לְטֹטָפֹת בֵּין
עֵינֶיךָ: וּכְתַבְתָּם עַל־מְזֻזוֹת בֵּיתֶךָ וּבִשְׁעָרֶיךָ:

דברים יא וְהָיָה אִם־שָׁמֹעַ תִּשְׁמְעוּ אֶל־מִצְוֺתַי אֲשֶׁר אָנֹכִי מְצַוֶּה אֶתְכֶם
הַיּוֹם, לְאַהֲבָה אֶת־יהוה אֱלֹהֵיכֶם וּלְעׇבְדוֹ, בְּכׇל־לְבַבְכֶם וּבְכׇל־
נַפְשְׁכֶם: וְנָתַתִּי מְטַר־אַרְצְכֶם בְּעִתּוֹ, יוֹרֶה וּמַלְקוֹשׁ, וְאָסַפְתָּ
דְגָנֶךָ וְתִירֹשְׁךָ וְיִצְהָרֶךָ: וְנָתַתִּי עֵשֶׂב בְּשָׂדְךָ לִבְהֶמְתֶּךָ, וְאָכַלְתָּ
וְשָׂבָעְתָּ: הִשָּׁמְרוּ לָכֶם פֶּן־יִפְתֶּה לְבַבְכֶם, וְסַרְתֶּם וַעֲבַדְתֶּם
אֱלֹהִים אֲחֵרִים וְהִשְׁתַּחֲוִיתֶם לָהֶם: וְחָרָה אַף־יהוה בָּכֶם, וְעָצַר
אֶת־הַשָּׁמַיִם וְלֹא־יִהְיֶה מָטָר, וְהָאֲדָמָה לֹא תִתֵּן אֶת־יְבוּלָהּ,
וַאֲבַדְתֶּם מְהֵרָה מֵעַל הָאָרֶץ הַטֹּבָה אֲשֶׁר יהוה נֹתֵן לָכֶם:
וְשַׂמְתֶּם אֶת־דְּבָרַי אֵלֶּה עַל־לְבַבְכֶם וְעַל־נַפְשְׁכֶם, וּקְשַׁרְתֶּם
אֹתָם לְאוֹת עַל־יֶדְכֶם, וְהָיוּ לְטוֹטָפֹת בֵּין עֵינֵיכֶם: וְלִמַּדְתֶּם
אֹתָם אֶת־בְּנֵיכֶם לְדַבֵּר בָּם, בְּשִׁבְתְּךָ בְּבֵיתֶךָ וּבְלֶכְתְּךָ בַדֶּרֶךְ,

Write them on the doorposts of your house and gates, so that you and your children may live long in the land that the LORD swore to your ancestors to give them, for as long as the heavens are above the earth.

וַיֹּאמֶר The LORD spoke to Moses, saying: Speak to the Israelites and tell them to make tzitzit on the corners of their garments for all generations. They shall attach to the tzitzit at each corner a thread of blue. This shall be your tzitzit, and you shall see it and remember all of the LORD's commandments and keep them, not straying after your heart and after your eyes, following your own sinful desires. Thus you will be reminded to keep all My commandments, and be holy to your God. I am the LORD your God, who brought you out of the land of Egypt to be your God. I am the LORD your God. *Num. 15*

True –

The Leader repeats:

▸ The LORD your God is true –

וֶאֱמוּנָה – and faithful is all this,
and firmly established for us
that He is the LORD our God,
and there is none besides Him,
and that we, Israel, are His people.
He is our King,
who redeems us from the hand of kings
and delivers us from the grasp of all tyrants.
He is our God,
who on our behalf repays our foes
and brings just retribution
on our mortal enemies;

וּבְשָׁכְבְּךָ֖ וּבְקוּמֶֽךָ׃ וּכְתַבְתָּ֛ם עַל־מְזוּז֥וֹת בֵּיתֶ֖ךָ וּבִשְׁעָרֶֽיךָ׃ לְמַ֨עַן
יִרְבּ֤וּ יְמֵיכֶם֙ וִימֵ֣י בְנֵיכֶ֔ם עַ֚ל הָֽאֲדָמָ֔ה אֲשֶׁ֨ר נִשְׁבַּ֧ע יְהוָ֛ה לַאֲבֹתֵיכֶ֖ם
לָתֵ֣ת לָהֶ֑ם, כִּימֵ֥י הַשָּׁמַ֖יִם עַל־הָאָֽרֶץ׃

במדבר טו וַיֹּ֥אמֶר יְהוָ֖ה אֶל־מֹשֶׁ֥ה לֵּאמֹֽר׃ דַּבֵּ֞ר אֶל־בְּנֵ֤י יִשְׂרָאֵל֙ וְאָמַרְתָּ֣
אֲלֵהֶ֔ם, וְעָשׂ֨וּ לָהֶ֥ם צִיצִ֛ת עַל־כַּנְפֵ֥י בִגְדֵיהֶ֖ם לְדֹרֹתָ֑ם, וְנָ֥תְנ֛וּ
עַל־צִיצִ֥ת הַכָּנָ֖ף פְּתִ֥יל תְּכֵֽלֶת׃ וְהָיָ֣ה לָכֶם֮ לְצִיצִת֒, וּרְאִיתֶ֣ם אֹת֗וֹ
וּזְכַרְתֶּם֙ אֶת־כׇּל־מִצְוֺ֣ת יְהוָ֔ה וַעֲשִׂיתֶ֖ם אֹתָ֑ם, וְלֹֽא־תָת֜וּרוּ אַחֲרֵ֤י
לְבַבְכֶם֙ וְאַחֲרֵ֣י עֵֽינֵיכֶ֔ם, אֲשֶׁר־אַתֶּ֥ם זֹנִ֖ים אַחֲרֵיהֶֽם׃ לְמַ֣עַן תִּזְכְּר֔וּ
וַעֲשִׂיתֶ֖ם אֶת־כׇּל־מִצְוֺתָ֑י, וִהְיִיתֶ֥ם קְדֹשִׁ֖ים לֵאלֹהֵיכֶֽם׃ אֲנִ֞י יְהוָ֣ה
אֱלֹֽהֵיכֶ֗ם, אֲשֶׁ֨ר הוֹצֵ֤אתִי אֶתְכֶם֙ מֵאֶ֣רֶץ מִצְרַ֔יִם, לִהְי֥וֹת לָכֶ֖ם
לֵאלֹהִ֑ים, אֲנִ֖י יְהוָ֥ה אֱלֹהֵיכֶֽם׃

אֱמֶת

The שליח ציבור *repeats:*

› יהוה אֱלֹהֵיכֶם אֱמֶת

וֶאֱמוּנָה כׇּל זֹאת וְקַיָּם עָלֵינוּ
כִּי הוּא יהוה אֱלֹהֵינוּ וְאֵין זוּלָתוֹ
וַאֲנַחְנוּ יִשְׂרָאֵל עַמּוֹ.
הַפּוֹדֵנוּ מִיַּד מְלָכִים
מַלְכֵּנוּ הַגּוֹאֲלֵנוּ מִכַּף כׇּל הֶעָרִיצִים.
הָאֵל הַנִּפְרָע לָנוּ מִצָּרֵינוּ
וְהַמְשַׁלֵּם גְּמוּל לְכׇל אוֹיְבֵי נַפְשֵׁנוּ.

who performs great deeds beyond understanding
and wonders beyond number;
who kept us alive, not letting our foot slip; *Ps. 66*
who led us on the high places of our enemies,
raising our pride above all our foes;
who did miracles for us
and brought vengeance against Pharaoh;
who performed signs and wonders
in the land of Ham's children;
who smote in His fury all the firstborn of Egypt,
and brought out His people Israel from their midst
into everlasting freedom;
who led His children through the divided Reed Sea,
plunging their pursuers and enemies into the depths.
When His children saw His might,
they gave praise and thanks to His name,
▸ and willingly accepted His Sovereignty.
Moses and the children of Israel
then sang a song to You with great joy,
and they all exclaimed:

מִי־כָמֹכָה "Who is like You, Lord, among the mighty? *Ex. 15*
Who is like You, majestic in holiness,
awesome in praises, doing wonders?"

▸ Your children beheld Your majesty
as You parted the sea before Moses.
"This is my God!" they responded,
and then said:

"The Lord shall reign for ever and ever." *Ex. 15*

▸ And it is said,

"For the Lord has redeemed Jacob *Jer. 31*
and rescued him from a power stronger than his own."

Blessed are You, Lord, who redeemed Israel.

הָעוֹשֶׂה גְדוֹלוֹת עַד אֵין חֵקֶר, וְנִפְלָאוֹת עַד אֵין מִסְפָּר
הַשָּׂם נַפְשֵׁנוּ בַּחַיִּים תהלים סו
וְלֹא־נָתַן לַמּוֹט רַגְלֵנוּ:
הַמַּדְרִיכֵנוּ עַל בָּמוֹת אוֹיְבֵינוּ
וַיָּרֶם קַרְנֵנוּ עַל כָּל שׂוֹנְאֵינוּ.
הָעוֹשֶׂה לָּנוּ נִסִּים וּנְקָמָה בְּפַרְעֹה
אוֹתוֹת וּמוֹפְתִים בְּאַדְמַת בְּנֵי חָם.
הַמַּכֶּה בְעֶבְרָתוֹ כָּל בְּכוֹרֵי מִצְרָיִם
וַיּוֹצֵא אֶת עַמּוֹ יִשְׂרָאֵל מִתּוֹכָם לְחֵרוּת עוֹלָם.
הַמַּעֲבִיר בָּנָיו בֵּין גִּזְרֵי יַם סוּף
אֶת רוֹדְפֵיהֶם וְאֶת שׂוֹנְאֵיהֶם בִּתְהוֹמוֹת טִבַּע
וְרָאוּ בָנָיו גְּבוּרָתוֹ, שִׁבְּחוּ וְהוֹדוּ לִשְׁמוֹ
◂ וּמַלְכוּתוֹ בְּרָצוֹן קִבְּלוּ עֲלֵיהֶם.
מֹשֶׁה וּבְנֵי יִשְׂרָאֵל, לְךָ עָנוּ שִׁירָה בְּשִׂמְחָה רַבָּה
וְאָמְרוּ כֻלָּם

מִי־כָמֹכָה בָּאֵלִם יהוה שמות טו
מִי כָּמֹכָה נֶאְדָּר בַּקֹּדֶשׁ
נוֹרָא תְהִלֹּת עֹשֵׂה פֶלֶא:

◂ מַלְכוּתְךָ רָאוּ בָנֶיךָ, בּוֹקֵעַ יָם לִפְנֵי מֹשֶׁה
זֶה אֵלִי עָנוּ, וְאָמְרוּ
יהוה יִמְלֹךְ לְעֹלָם וָעֶד: שמות טו
◂ וְנֶאֱמַר
כִּי־פָדָה יהוה אֶת־יַעֲקֹב, וּגְאָלוֹ מִיַּד חָזָק מִמֶּנּוּ: ירמיהו לא
בָּרוּךְ אַתָּה יהוה, גָּאַל יִשְׂרָאֵל.

הַשְׁכִּיבֵנוּ Help us lie down, O Lord our God, in peace,
and rise up, O our King, to life.
Spread over us Your canopy of peace.
Direct us with Your good counsel,
and save us for the sake of Your name.
Shield us and remove from us every enemy,
plague, sword, famine and sorrow.
Remove the enemy from before and behind us.
Shelter us in the shadow of Your wings,
for You, God, are our Guardian and Deliverer;
You, God, are a generous and compassionate King.
▸ Guard our going out and our coming in,
for life and peace, from now and for ever.
Blessed are You, Lord,
who guards His people Israel for ever.

REFLECTION

What do you need protecting from?

What do you think your nation needs protecting from?

Spend a moment now thinking about this as you say this *berakha*.

... A THOUSAND WORDS

הַשְׁכִּיבֵנוּ יהוה אֱלֹהֵינוּ לְשָׁלוֹם
וְהַעֲמִידֵנוּ מַלְכֵּנוּ לְחַיִּים
וּפְרֹשׂ עָלֵינוּ סֻכַּת שְׁלוֹמֶךָ
וְתַקְּנֵנוּ בְּעֵצָה טוֹבָה מִלְּפָנֶיךָ
וְהוֹשִׁיעֵנוּ לְמַעַן שְׁמֶךָ.
וְהָגֵן בַּעֲדֵנוּ, וְהָסֵר מֵעָלֵינוּ אוֹיֵב, דֶּבֶר וְחֶרֶב וְרָעָב וְיָגוֹן
וְהָסֵר שָׂטָן מִלְּפָנֵינוּ וּמֵאַחֲרֵינוּ, וּבְצֵל כְּנָפֶיךָ תַּסְתִּירֵנוּ
כִּי אֵל שׁוֹמְרֵנוּ וּמַצִּילֵנוּ אָתָּה, כִּי אֵל מֶלֶךְ חַנּוּן וְרַחוּם אָתָּה.
◂ וּשְׁמֹר צֵאתֵנוּ וּבוֹאֵנוּ לְחַיִּים וּלְשָׁלוֹם מֵעַתָּה וְעַד עוֹלָם.
בָּרוּךְ אַתָּה יהוה, שׁוֹמֵר עַמּוֹ יִשְׂרָאֵל לָעַד.

CONNECTION

In 1973, during the Yom Kippur War, the People of Israel owed its existence to the Seventh Armored Brigade, who with their meager 100 tanks managed to hold off an attack on the Golan Heights from the superior 500 Syrian tanks, buying vital time until the IDF could call up more reservists and ultimately hold on to the heights and win the war. Within the Seventh Armored Brigade was a tiny force of four tanks commanded by Lieutenant Zvi Greengold, nicknamed "Force Zvika" after him. They were charged with stopping the Syrian advance along the Tapline Route parallel to a maintenance road that ran along a pipeline in the Golan. As a column of 30 Syrian tanks approached, Zvika took out the lead tank but in the process damaged his communication equipment and lost communication with his three support tanks. Alone and in mortal danger he devised a tactic whereby his tank hid behind a hill and emerged to take out Syrian tanks one by one, retreating behind the hill each time, playing a deadly game of hide and seek. After several direct hits the superior Syrian force inexplicably retreated. Whether they just believed they were facing a stronger force, or whether, as some Syrian soldiers reported, they even saw an image of hundreds of Israeli tanks, what is clear is that the miracle of "Force Zvika" saved the day and saved the Golan.

In Israel and in some communities outside Israel the service continues with Half Kaddish on the next page.

בָּרוּךְ Blessed be the Lord for ever. Amen and Amen. *Ps. 89*
Blessed from Zion be the Lord *Ps. 135*
who is present in Jerusalem. Halleluya!
Blessed be the Lord, God of Israel, *Ps. 72*
who alone does miracles.
Blessed be His glorious name for ever,
and may the whole earth
be filled with His glory. Amen and Amen.
May the glory of the Lord endure for ever; *Ps. 104*
may the Lord rejoice in His works.
May the name of the Lord *Ps. 113*
be blessed now and for all time.
For the sake of His great name *I Sam. 12*
the Lord will not abandon His people,
for the Lord vowed to make you a people of His own.
When all the people saw [God's wonders] they fell on their faces *I Kings 18*
and said: "The Lord, He is God; the Lord, He is God."
Then the Lord shall be King over all the earth; *Zech. 14*
on that day the Lord shall be One and His name One.
May Your love, Lord, be upon us, as we have put our hope in You. *Ps. 33*
Save us, Lord our God, gather us *Ps. 106*
and deliver us from the nations,
to thank Your holy name, and glory in Your praise.
All the nations You made shall come and bow before You, Lord, *Ps. 86*
and pay honor to Your name,
for You are great and You perform wonders:
You alone are God.
We, Your people, the flock of Your pasture, will praise You for ever. *Ps. 79*
For all generations we will relate Your praise.

בָּרוּךְ Blessed is the Lord by day, blessed is the Lord by night.
Blessed is the Lord when we lie down;
blessed is the Lord when we rise.

In ארץ ישראל *and in some communities outside* ארץ ישראל
the service continues with חצי קדיש *on the next page.*

בָּרוּךְ יהוה לְעוֹלָם, אָמֵן וְאָמֵן: תהלים פט

בָּרוּךְ יהוה מִצִּיּוֹן, שֹׁכֵן יְרוּשָׁלָםִ, הַלְלוּיָהּ: תהלים קלה

בָּרוּךְ יהוה אֱלֹהִים אֱלֹהֵי יִשְׂרָאֵל, עֹשֵׂה נִפְלָאוֹת לְבַדּוֹ: תהלים עב

וּבָרוּךְ שֵׁם כְּבוֹדוֹ לְעוֹלָם

וְיִמָּלֵא כְבוֹדוֹ אֶת־כֹּל־הָאָרֶץ, אָמֵן וְאָמֵן:

יְהִי כְבוֹד יהוה לְעוֹלָם, יִשְׂמַח יהוה בְּמַעֲשָׂיו: תהלים קד

יְהִי שֵׁם יהוה מְבֹרָךְ מֵעַתָּה וְעַד־עוֹלָם: תהלים קיג

כִּי לֹא־יִטֹּשׁ יהוה אֶת־עַמּוֹ בַּעֲבוּר שְׁמוֹ הַגָּדוֹל שמואל א, יב

כִּי הוֹאִיל יהוה לַעֲשׂוֹת אֶתְכֶם לוֹ לְעָם:

וַיַּרְא כָּל־הָעָם וַיִּפְּלוּ עַל־פְּנֵיהֶם מלכים א, יח

וַיֹּאמְרוּ, יהוה הוּא הָאֱלֹהִים, יהוה הוּא הָאֱלֹהִים:

וְהָיָה יהוה לְמֶלֶךְ עַל־כָּל־הָאָרֶץ זכריה יד

בַּיּוֹם הַהוּא יִהְיֶה יהוה אֶחָד וּשְׁמוֹ אֶחָד:

יְהִי־חַסְדְּךָ יהוה עָלֵינוּ, כַּאֲשֶׁר יִחַלְנוּ לָךְ: תהלים לג

הוֹשִׁיעֵנוּ יהוה אֱלֹהֵינוּ, וְקַבְּצֵנוּ מִן־הַגּוֹיִם תהלים קו

לְהוֹדוֹת לְשֵׁם קָדְשֶׁךָ, לְהִשְׁתַּבֵּחַ בִּתְהִלָּתֶךָ:

כָּל־גּוֹיִם אֲשֶׁר עָשִׂיתָ, יָבוֹאוּ וְיִשְׁתַּחֲווּ לְפָנֶיךָ, אֲדֹנָי תהלים פו

וִיכַבְּדוּ לִשְׁמֶךָ:

כִּי־גָדוֹל אַתָּה וְעֹשֵׂה נִפְלָאוֹת, אַתָּה אֱלֹהִים לְבַדֶּךָ:

וַאֲנַחְנוּ עַמְּךָ וְצֹאן מַרְעִיתֶךָ, נוֹדֶה לְּךָ לְעוֹלָם תהלים עט

לְדוֹר וָדֹר נְסַפֵּר תְּהִלָּתֶךָ:

בָּרוּךְ יהוה בַּיּוֹם, בָּרוּךְ יהוה בַּלָּיְלָה

בָּרוּךְ יהוה בְּשָׁכְבֵנוּ, בָּרוּךְ יהוה בְּקוּמֵנוּ.

כִּי בְיָדְךָ נַפְשׁוֹת הַחַיִּים וְהַמֵּתִים.

For in Your hand are the souls of the living and the dead,
[as it is written:] "In His hand is every living soul, *Job 12*
and the breath of all mankind."
Into Your hand I entrust my spirit: *Ps. 31*
You redeemed me, LORD, God of truth.
Our God in heaven, bring unity to Your name,
establish Your kingdom constantly
and reign over us for ever and all time.

יִרְאוּ May our eyes see, our hearts rejoice,
and our souls be glad in Your true salvation,
when Zion is told, "Your God reigns."
The LORD is King, the LORD was King,
the LORD will be King for ever and all time.
▸ For sovereignty is Yours,
and to all eternity You will reign in glory,
for we have no king but You.
Blessed are You, LORD,
the King who in His constant glory will reign over us
and all His creation for ever and all time.

HALF KADDISH

Leader: יִתְגַּדַּל Magnified and sanctified may His great name be,
in the world He created by His will.
May He establish His kingdom
in your lifetime and in your days,
and in the lifetime of all the house of Israel,
swiftly and soon – and say: Amen.

All: May His great name be blessed for ever and all time.

Leader: Blessed and praised, glorified and elevated,
raised and honored, uplifted and praised
be the name of the Holy One, blessed be He,
beyond any blessing, song, praise and consolation
uttered in the world – and say: Amen.

אֲשֶׁר בְּיָדוֹ נֶפֶשׁ כׇּל־חָי, וְרוּחַ כׇּל־בְּשַׂר־אִישׁ: איוב יב

בְּיָדְךָ אַפְקִיד רוּחִי, פָּדִיתָה אוֹתִי יהוה אֵל אֱמֶת: תהלים לא

אֱלֹהֵינוּ שֶׁבַּשָּׁמַיִם, יַחֵד שִׁמְךָ וְקַיֵּם מַלְכוּתְךָ תָּמִיד
וּמְלֹךְ עָלֵינוּ לְעוֹלָם וָעֶד.

יִרְאוּ עֵינֵינוּ וְיִשְׂמַח לִבֵּנוּ, וְתָגֵל נַפְשֵׁנוּ בִּישׁוּעָתְךָ בֶּאֱמֶת
בֶּאֱמֹר לְצִיּוֹן מָלַךְ אֱלֹהָיִךְ.
יהוה מֶלֶךְ, יהוה מָלָךְ, יהוה יִמְלֹךְ לְעֹלָם וָעֶד.
◂ כִּי הַמַּלְכוּת שֶׁלְּךָ הִיא, וּלְעוֹלְמֵי עַד תִּמְלֹךְ בְּכָבוֹד
כִּי אֵין לָנוּ מֶלֶךְ אֶלָּא אָתָּה.
בָּרוּךְ אַתָּה יהוה
הַמֶּלֶךְ בִּכְבוֹדוֹ תָּמִיד, יִמְלֹךְ עָלֵינוּ לְעוֹלָם וָעֶד, וְעַל כׇּל מַעֲשָׂיו.

חצי קדיש

ש״ץ: יִתְגַּדַּל וְיִתְקַדַּשׁ שְׁמֵהּ רַבָּא (קהל: אָמֵן)
בְּעָלְמָא דִּי בְרָא כִרְעוּתֵהּ
וְיַמְלִיךְ מַלְכוּתֵהּ
בְּחַיֵּיכוֹן וּבְיוֹמֵיכוֹן וּבְחַיֵּי דְכׇל בֵּית יִשְׂרָאֵל
בַּעֲגָלָא וּבִזְמַן קָרִיב, וְאִמְרוּ אָמֵן. (קהל: אָמֵן)

קהל וש״ץ: יְהֵא שְׁמֵהּ רַבָּא מְבָרַךְ לְעָלַם וּלְעָלְמֵי עָלְמַיָּא.

ש״ץ: יִתְבָּרַךְ וְיִשְׁתַּבַּח וְיִתְפָּאַר וְיִתְרוֹמַם וְיִתְנַשֵּׂא
וְיִתְהַדָּר וְיִתְעַלֶּה וְיִתְהַלָּל
שְׁמֵהּ דְּקֻדְשָׁא בְּרִיךְ הוּא (קהל: בְּרִיךְ הוּא)
לְעֵלָּא מִן כׇּל בִּרְכָתָא / בעשרת ימי תשובה: לְעֵלָּא לְעֵלָּא מִכׇּל בִּרְכָתָא/
וְשִׁירָתָא, תֻּשְׁבְּחָתָא וְנֶחֱמָתָא
דַּאֲמִירָן בְּעָלְמָא, וְאִמְרוּ אָמֵן. (קהל: אָמֵן)

THE AMIDA

The following prayer, until "in former years" on page 348, is said silently, standing with feet together. Take three steps forward as if formally entering the place of the Divine Presence.

O Lord, open my lips, so that my mouth may declare Your praise. *Ps. 51*

PATRIARCHS

בָּרוּךְ Blessed are You,
Lord our God and God of our fathers,
God of Abraham, God of Isaac and God of Jacob;
the great, mighty and awesome God, God Most High,
who acts with loving-kindness and creates all,
who remembers the loving-kindness of the fathers
and will bring a Redeemer to their children's children
for the sake of His name, in love.

Between Rosh HaShana & Yom Kippur: Remember us for life, O King who desires life,
and write us in the book of life –
for Your sake, O God of life.

King, Helper, Savior, Shield:
Blessed are You, Lord, Shield of Abraham.

DIVINE MIGHT

אַתָּה גִּבּוֹר You are eternally mighty, Lord.
You give life to the dead and have great power to save.

The phrase "He makes the wind blow and the rain fall" is added from Simḥat Torah until Pesaḥ. In Israel the phrase "He causes the dew to fall" is added from Pesaḥ until Shemini Atzeret.

In fall & winter: He makes the wind blow and the rain fall.
In Israel, in spring & summer: He causes the dew to fall.

He sustains the living with loving-kindness,
and with great compassion revives the dead.
He supports the fallen, heals the sick, sets captives free,
and keeps His faith with those who sleep in the dust.

עמידה

The following prayer, until קַדְמֹנִיּוֹת *on page 349, is said silently, standing with feet together. Take three steps forward as if formally entering the place of the Divine Presence.*

אֲדֹנָי, שְׂפָתַי תִּפְתָּח, וּפִי יַגִּיד תְּהִלָּתֶךָ: תהלים נא

אבות

בָּרוּךְ אַתָּה יהוה, אֱלֹהֵינוּ וֵאלֹהֵי אֲבוֹתֵינוּ
אֱלֹהֵי אַבְרָהָם, אֱלֹהֵי יִצְחָק, וֵאלֹהֵי יַעֲקֹב
הָאֵל הַגָּדוֹל הַגִּבּוֹר וְהַנּוֹרָא, אֵל עֶלְיוֹן
גּוֹמֵל חֲסָדִים טוֹבִים, וְקוֹנֵה הַכֹּל
וְזוֹכֵר חַסְדֵי אָבוֹת
וּמֵבִיא גוֹאֵל לִבְנֵי בְנֵיהֶם לְמַעַן שְׁמוֹ בְּאַהֲבָה.

בעשרת ימי תשובה: זָכְרֵנוּ לְחַיִּים, מֶלֶךְ חָפֵץ בַּחַיִּים
וְכָתְבֵנוּ בְּסֵפֶר הַחַיִּים, לְמַעַנְךָ אֱלֹהִים חַיִּים.

מֶלֶךְ עוֹזֵר וּמוֹשִׁיעַ וּמָגֵן.
בָּרוּךְ אַתָּה יהוה, מָגֵן אַבְרָהָם.

גבורות

אַתָּה גִּבּוֹר לְעוֹלָם, אֲדֹנָי
מְחַיֵּה מֵתִים אַתָּה, רַב לְהוֹשִׁיעַ

The phrase מַשִּׁיב הָרְוּחַ *is added from* שמחת תורה *until* פסח. *In* ארץ ישראל *the phrase* מוֹרִיד הַטָּל *is added from* פסח *until* שמיני עצרת.

בחורף: מַשִּׁיב הָרְוּחַ וּמוֹרִיד הַגֶּשֶׁם / בארץ ישראל בקיץ: מוֹרִיד הַטָּל

מְכַלְכֵּל חַיִּים בְּחֶסֶד, מְחַיֵּה מֵתִים בְּרַחֲמִים רַבִּים
סוֹמֵךְ נוֹפְלִים, וְרוֹפֵא חוֹלִים, וּמַתִּיר אֲסוּרִים
וּמְקַיֵּם אֱמוּנָתוֹ לִישֵׁנֵי עָפָר.

Who is like You, Master of might,
and who can compare to You,
O King who brings death and gives life,
and makes salvation grow?

Between Rosh HaShana & Yom Kippur: Who is like You, compassionate Father,
who remembers His creatures in compassion, for life?

Faithful are You to revive the dead.
Blessed are You, LORD, who revives the dead.

HOLINESS

אַתָּה קָדוֹשׁ You are holy and Your name is holy,
and holy ones praise You daily, Selah!
Blessed are You, LORD,
the holy God. / *Between Rosh HaShana & Yom Kippur:* the holy King./

(*If forgotten, repeat the Amida.*)

KNOWLEDGE

אַתָּה חוֹנֵן You grace humanity with knowledge
and teach mortals understanding.

On Motza'ei Shabbat and Motza'ei Yom Tov say:

אַתָּה חוֹנַנְתָּנוּ You have graced us with the knowledge of Your Torah, and taught us to perform the laws of Your will. You have distinguished, LORD our God, between sacred and profane, light and darkness, Israel and the nations, and between the seventh day and the six days of work. Our Father, our King, may the days approaching us bring peace; may we be free from all sin, cleansed from all wrongdoing, holding fast to our fear of You. And

---

Grace us with the knowledge, understanding
and insight that come from You.
Blessed are You, LORD, who generously gives knowledge.

REPENTANCE

הֲשִׁיבֵנוּ Bring us back, our Father, to Your Torah.
Draw us near, our King, to Your service.
Lead us back to You in perfect repentance.
Blessed are You, LORD, who desires repentance.

מִי כָמְוֹךָ, בַּעַל גְּבוּרוֹת, וּמִי דּוֹמֶה לָּךְ
מֶלֶךְ, מֵמִית וּמְחַיֶּה וּמַצְמִיחַ יְשׁוּעָה.

בעשרת ימי תשובה: מִי כָמְוֹךָ אַב הָרַחֲמִים, זוֹכֵר יְצוּרָיו לְחַיִּים בְּרַחֲמִים.

וְנֶאֱמָן אַתָּה לְהַחֲיוֹת מֵתִים.
בָּרוּךְ אַתָּה יהוה, מְחַיֵּה הַמֵּתִים.

קדושת השם

אַתָּה קָדוֹשׁ וְשִׁמְךָ קָדוֹשׁ
וּקְדוֹשִׁים בְּכָל יוֹם יְהַלְלְוּךָ סֶּלָה.
בָּרוּךְ אַתָּה יהוה, הָאֵל הַקָּדוֹשׁ./ בעשרת ימי תשובה: הַמֶּלֶךְ הַקָּדוֹשׁ./

(*If forgotten, repeat the* עמידה.)

דעת

אַתָּה חוֹנֵן לְאָדָם דַּעַת
וּמְלַמֵּד לֶאֱנוֹשׁ בִּינָה.

On מוצאי שבת *and* מוצאי יום טוב *say:*

אַתָּה חוֹנַנְתָּנוּ לְמַדַּע תּוֹרָתֶךָ, וַתְּלַמְּדֵנוּ לַעֲשׂוֹת חֻקֵּי רְצוֹנֶךָ, וַתַּבְדֵּל יהוה אֱלֹהֵינוּ בֵּין קֹדֶשׁ לְחוֹל, בֵּין אוֹר לְחֹשֶׁךְ, בֵּין יִשְׂרָאֵל לָעַמִּים, בֵּין יוֹם הַשְּׁבִיעִי לְשֵׁשֶׁת יְמֵי הַמַּעֲשֶׂה. אָבִינוּ מַלְכֵּנוּ, הָחֵל עָלֵינוּ הַיָּמִים הַבָּאִים לִקְרָאתֵנוּ לְשָׁלוֹם, חֲשׂוּכִים מִכָּל חֵטְא וּמְנֻקִּים מִכָּל עָוֹן וּמְדֻבָּקִים בְּיִרְאָתֶךָ. וְ

חָנֵּנוּ מֵאִתְּךָ דֵּעָה בִּינָה וְהַשְׂכֵּל.
בָּרוּךְ אַתָּה יהוה, חוֹנֵן הַדָּעַת.

תשובה

הֲשִׁיבֵנוּ אָבִינוּ לְתוֹרָתֶךָ, וְקָרְבֵנוּ מַלְכֵּנוּ לַעֲבוֹדָתֶךָ
וְהַחֲזִירֵנוּ בִּתְשׁוּבָה שְׁלֵמָה לְפָנֶיךָ.
בָּרוּךְ אַתָּה יהוה, הָרוֹצֶה בִּתְשׁוּבָה.

FORGIVENESS

Strike the left side of the chest at °.

סְלַח לָנוּ Forgive us, our Father,
for we have °sinned.
Pardon us, our King,
for we have °transgressed;
for You pardon and forgive.
Blessed are You, LORD,
the generous One who repeatedly forgives.

REDEMPTION

רְאֵה Look on our suffering,
plead our cause,
and redeem us soon for Your name's sake,
for You are a powerful Redeemer.
Blessed are You, LORD,
the Redeemer of Israel.

HEALING

רְפָאֵנוּ Heal us, LORD, and we shall be healed.
Save us and we shall be saved,
for You are our praise.
Bring complete recovery for all our illnesses,

The following prayer for a sick person may be said here:
May it be Your will, O LORD my God and God of my ancestors, that You speedily send a complete recovery from heaven, a healing of both soul and body, to the patient (*name*), son/daughter of (*mother's name*) among the other sick of Israel.

---

for You, God, King, are a faithful and compassionate Healer.
Blessed are You, LORD,
Healer of the sick of His people Israel.

סליחה

Strike the left side of the chest at °.

סְלַח לָנוּ אָבִינוּ כִּי °חָטָאנוּ
מְחַל לָנוּ מַלְכֵּנוּ כִּי °פָשָׁעְנוּ
כִּי מוֹחֵל וְסוֹלֵחַ אָתָּה.
בָּרוּךְ אַתָּה יהוה, חַנּוּן הַמַּרְבֶּה לִסְלֹחַ.

גאולה

רְאֵה בְעָנְיֵנוּ, וְרִיבָה רִיבֵנוּ
וּגְאָלֵנוּ מְהֵרָה לְמַעַן שְׁמֶךָ
כִּי גּוֹאֵל חָזָק אָתָּה.
בָּרוּךְ אַתָּה יהוה, גּוֹאֵל יִשְׂרָאֵל.

רפואה

רְפָאֵנוּ יהוה וְנֵרָפֵא
הוֹשִׁיעֵנוּ וְנִוָּשֵׁעָה
כִּי תְהִלָּתֵנוּ אָתָּה
וְהַעֲלֵה רְפוּאָה שְׁלֵמָה לְכָל מַכּוֹתֵינוּ

The following prayer for a sick person may be said here:

יְהִי רָצוֹן מִלְּפָנֶיךָ יהוה אֱלֹהַי וֵאלֹהֵי אֲבוֹתַי, שֶׁתִּשְׁלַח מְהֵרָה רְפוּאָה שְׁלֵמָה
מִן הַשָּׁמַיִם רְפוּאַת הַנֶּפֶשׁ וּרְפוּאַת הַגּוּף לַחוֹלֶה/לַחוֹלָה *name of patient*
בֶּן/בַּת *mother's name* בְּתוֹךְ שְׁאָר חוֹלֵי יִשְׂרָאֵל.

כִּי אֵל מֶלֶךְ רוֹפֵא נֶאֱמָן וְרַחֲמָן אָתָּה.
בָּרוּךְ אַתָּה יהוה, רוֹפֵא חוֹלֵי עַמּוֹ יִשְׂרָאֵל.

PROSPERITY

The phrase "Give dew and rain as a blessing" is said from December 4th (in the year before a civil leap year, December 5th) until Pesaḥ. In Israel, it is said from the 7th of Marḥeshvan. The phrase "Give blessing" is said from Ḥol HaMo'ed Pesaḥ until December 3rd (in the year before a civil leap year, December 4th). In Israel it is said through the 6th of Marḥeshvan.

בָּרֵךְ Bless this year for us, Lord our God,
and all its types of produce for good.
In winter: Give dew and rain as a blessing
In other seasons: Give blessing
on the face of the earth,
and from its goodness satisfy us,
blessing our year as the best of years.
Blessed are You, Lord,
who blesses the years.

INGATHERING OF EXILES

תְּקַע Sound the great shofar for our freedom,
raise high the banner to gather our exiles,
and gather us together from the four quarters of the earth.
Blessed are You, Lord,
who gathers the dispersed of His people Israel.

JUSTICE

הָשִׁיבָה Restore our judges as at first,
and our advisors as at the beginning,
and remove from us sorrow and sighing.
May You alone, Lord,
reign over us with loving-kindness and compassion,
and vindicate us in justice.
Blessed are You, Lord,
the King who loves righteousness and justice.
/*Between Rosh HaShana & Yom Kippur, end the blessing:* the King of justice./

ברכת השנים

The phrase וְתֵן טַל וּמָטָר לִבְרָכָה *is said from December 4th (in the year before a civil leap year, December 5th) until* פסח. *In* ארץ ישראל, *it is said from* ז׳ מרחשון. *The phrase* וְתֵן בְּרָכָה *is said from* חול המועד פסח *until December 3rd (in the year before a civil leap year, December 4th). In* ארץ ישראל *it is said through* ו׳ מרחשון.

בָּרֵךְ עָלֵינוּ יהוה אֱלֹהֵינוּ אֶת הַשָּׁנָה הַזֹּאת
וְאֶת כָּל מִינֵי תְבוּאָתָהּ, לְטוֹבָה
בחורף: וְתֵן טַל וּמָטָר לִבְרָכָה / בקיץ: וְתֵן בְּרָכָה
עַל פְּנֵי הָאֲדָמָה, וְשַׂבְּעֵנוּ מִטּוּבָהּ
וּבָרֵךְ שְׁנָתֵנוּ כַּשָּׁנִים הַטּוֹבוֹת.
בָּרוּךְ אַתָּה יהוה, מְבָרֵךְ הַשָּׁנִים.

קבוץ גלויות

תְּקַע בְּשׁוֹפָר גָּדוֹל לְחֵרוּתֵנוּ
וְשָׂא נֵס לְקַבֵּץ גָּלֻיּוֹתֵינוּ
וְקַבְּצֵנוּ יַחַד מֵאַרְבַּע כַּנְפוֹת הָאָרֶץ.
בָּרוּךְ אַתָּה יהוה, מְקַבֵּץ נִדְחֵי עַמּוֹ יִשְׂרָאֵל.

השבת המשפט

הָשִׁיבָה שׁוֹפְטֵינוּ כְּבָרִאשׁוֹנָה
וְיוֹעֲצֵינוּ כְּבַתְּחִלָּה
וְהָסֵר מִמֶּנּוּ יָגוֹן וַאֲנָחָה
וּמְלֹךְ עָלֵינוּ אַתָּה יהוה לְבַדְּךָ בְּחֶסֶד וּבְרַחֲמִים
וְצַדְּקֵנוּ בַּמִּשְׁפָּט.
בָּרוּךְ אַתָּה יהוה
מֶלֶךְ אוֹהֵב צְדָקָה וּמִשְׁפָּט. / בעשרת ימי תשובה: הַמֶּלֶךְ הַמִּשְׁפָּט./

AGAINST INFORMERS

וְלַמַּלְשִׁינִים For the slanderers let there be no hope,
and may all wickedness perish in an instant.
May all Your people's enemies swiftly be cut down.
May You swiftly uproot, crush, cast down
and humble the arrogant swiftly in our days.
Blessed are You, Lord,
who destroys enemies and humbles the arrogant.

THE RIGHTEOUS

עַל הַצַּדִּיקִים To the righteous, the pious,
the elders of Your people the house of Israel,
the surviving scholars,
the righteous converts, and to us,
may Your compassion be aroused, Lord our God.
Give a good reward to all
who sincerely trust in Your name.
Set our lot with them,
so that we may never be ashamed,
for in You we trust.
Blessed are You, Lord,
who is the support and trust of the righteous.

REBUILDING JERUSALEM

וְלִירוּשָׁלַיִם To Jerusalem, Your city,
may You return in compassion,
and may You rest Your presence in it as You promised.
May You rebuild it rapidly in our days
as an everlasting structure,
and install within it soon the throne of David.
Blessed are You, Lord,
who builds Jerusalem.

ברכת המינים

וְלַמַּלְשִׁינִים אַל תְּהִי תִקְוָה
וְכָל הָרִשְׁעָה כְּרֶגַע תֹּאבֵד
וְכָל אוֹיְבֵי עַמְּךָ מְהֵרָה יִכָּרֵתוּ
וְהַזֵּדִים מְהֵרָה תְעַקֵּר וּתְשַׁבֵּר וּתְמַגֵּר וְתַכְנִיעַ
בִּמְהֵרָה בְיָמֵינוּ.
בָּרוּךְ אַתָּה יהוה, שׁוֹבֵר אוֹיְבִים וּמַכְנִיעַ זֵדִים.

על הצדיקים

עַל הַצַּדִּיקִים וְעַל הַחֲסִידִים
וְעַל זִקְנֵי עַמְּךָ בֵּית יִשְׂרָאֵל
וְעַל פְּלֵיטַת סוֹפְרֵיהֶם
וְעַל גֵּרֵי הַצֶּדֶק, וְעָלֵינוּ
יֶהֱמוּ רַחֲמֶיךָ יהוה אֱלֹהֵינוּ
וְתֵן שָׂכָר טוֹב לְכָל הַבּוֹטְחִים בְּשִׁמְךָ בֶּאֱמֶת
וְשִׂים חֶלְקֵנוּ עִמָּהֶם
וּלְעוֹלָם לֹא נֵבוֹשׁ כִּי בְךָ בָּטָחְנוּ.
בָּרוּךְ אַתָּה יהוה, מִשְׁעָן וּמִבְטָח לַצַּדִּיקִים.

בניין ירושלים

וְלִירוּשָׁלַיִם עִירְךָ בְּרַחֲמִים תָּשׁוּב
וְתִשְׁכֹּן בְּתוֹכָהּ כַּאֲשֶׁר דִּבַּרְתָּ
וּבְנֵה אוֹתָהּ בְּקָרוֹב בְּיָמֵינוּ בִּנְיַן עוֹלָם
וְכִסֵּא דָוִד מְהֵרָה לְתוֹכָהּ תָּכִין.
בָּרוּךְ אַתָּה יהוה, בּוֹנֵה יְרוּשָׁלָיִם.

KINGDOM OF DAVID

אֶת צֶמַח May the offshoot of Your servant David soon flower,
and may his pride be raised high by Your salvation,
for we wait for Your salvation all day.
Blessed are You, LORD,
who makes the glory of salvation flourish.

RESPONSE TO PRAYER

שְׁמַע קוֹלֵנוּ Listen to our voice, LORD our God.
Spare us and have compassion on us,
and in compassion and favor accept our prayer,
for You, God, listen to prayers and pleas.
Do not turn us away, O our King,
empty-handed from Your presence,*

**At this point, in times of drought in Israel, some add "And answer us" on page 1064.*

for You listen with compassion
to the prayer of Your people Israel.
Blessed are You, LORD,
who listens to prayer.

TEMPLE SERVICE

רְצֵה Find favor, LORD our God,
in Your people Israel and their prayer.
Restore the service to Your most holy House,
and accept in love and favor
the fire-offerings of Israel and their prayer.
May the service of Your people Israel always find favor with You.

On Rosh Ḥodesh and Ḥol HaMo'ed say:

אֱלֹהֵינוּ Our God and God of our ancestors, may there rise, come, reach, appear, be favored, heard, regarded and remembered before You, our recollection and remembrance, as well as the remembrance of our ancestors, and of the Messiah son of David Your servant, and of Jerusalem Your holy city, and of all Your people the house of

משיח בן דוד

אֶת צֶמַח דָּוִד עַבְדְּךָ מְהֵרָה תַצְמִיחַ
וְקַרְנוֹ תָּרוּם בִּישׁוּעָתֶךָ
כִּי לִישׁוּעָתְךָ קִוִּינוּ כָּל הַיּוֹם.
בָּרוּךְ אַתָּה יהוה, מַצְמִיחַ קֶרֶן יְשׁוּעָה.

שומע תפילה

שְׁמַע קוֹלֵנוּ יהוה אֱלֹהֵינוּ
חוּס וְרַחֵם עָלֵינוּ
וְקַבֵּל בְּרַחֲמִים וּבְרָצוֹן אֶת תְּפִלָּתֵנוּ
כִּי אֵל שׁוֹמֵעַ תְּפִלּוֹת וְתַחֲנוּנִים אָתָּה
וּמִלְּפָנֶיךָ מַלְכֵּנוּ רֵיקָם אַל תְּשִׁיבֵנוּ*

**At this point, in times of drought in ארץ ישראל, some add וַעֲנֵנוּ on page 1065.*

כִּי אַתָּה שׁוֹמֵעַ תְּפִלַּת עַמְּךָ יִשְׂרָאֵל בְּרַחֲמִים.
בָּרוּךְ אַתָּה יהוה, שׁוֹמֵעַ תְּפִלָּה.

עבודה

רְצֵה יהוה אֱלֹהֵינוּ בְּעַמְּךָ יִשְׂרָאֵל וּבִתְפִלָּתָם
וְהָשֵׁב אֶת הָעֲבוֹדָה לִדְבִיר בֵּיתֶךָ
וְאִשֵּׁי יִשְׂרָאֵל וּתְפִלָּתָם בְּאַהֲבָה תְקַבֵּל בְּרָצוֹן
וּתְהִי לְרָצוֹן תָּמִיד עֲבוֹדַת יִשְׂרָאֵל עַמֶּךָ.

On ראש חודש *and* חול המועד *say:*

אֱלֹהֵינוּ וֵאלֹהֵי אֲבוֹתֵינוּ, יַעֲלֶה וְיָבוֹא וְיַגִּיעַ, וְיֵרָאֶה וְיֵרָצֶה וְיִשָּׁמַע, וְיִפָּקֵד וְיִזָּכֵר זִכְרוֹנֵנוּ וּפִקְדוֹנֵנוּ וְזִכְרוֹן אֲבוֹתֵינוּ, וְזִכְרוֹן מָשִׁיחַ בֶּן דָּוִד עַבְדֶּךָ, וְזִכְרוֹן יְרוּשָׁלַיִם עִיר קָדְשֶׁךָ, וְזִכְרוֹן כָּל עַמְּךָ בֵּית

Israel – for deliverance and well-being, grace, loving-kindness and compassion, life and peace, on this day of:

On Rosh Ḥodesh: Rosh Ḥodesh.
On Pesaḥ: the Festival of Matzot.
On Sukkot: the Festival of Sukkot.

On it remember us, Lord our God, for good; recollect us for blessing, and save us for life. In accord with Your promise of salvation and compassion, spare us and be generous to us; have compassion on us and save us, for our eyes are turned to You because You, God, are a generous and compassionate King.

וְתֶחֱזֶינָה And may our eyes witness Your return
to Zion in compassion.
Blessed are You, Lord,
who restores His Presence to Zion.

THANKSGIVING

מוֹדִים We give thanks to You,
for You are the Lord our God and God of our ancestors
for ever and all time.
You are the Rock of our lives,
Shield of our salvation from generation to generation.
We will thank You and declare Your praise for our lives,
which are entrusted into Your hand;
for our souls, which are placed in Your charge;
for Your miracles which are with us every day;
and for Your wonders and favors
at all times, evening, morning and midday.
You are good –
for Your compassion never fails.
You are compassionate –
for Your loving-kindnesses never cease.
We have always placed our hope in You.

יִשְׂרָאֵל, לְפָנֶיךָ, לִפְלֵיטָה לְטוֹבָה, לְחֵן וּלְחֶסֶד וּלְרַחֲמִים, לְחַיִּים וּלְשָׁלוֹם בְּיוֹם

בראש חודש: רֹאשׁ הַחֹדֶשׁ / בפסח: חַג הַמַּצּוֹת / בסוכות: חַג הַסֻּכּוֹת

הַזֶּה. זָכְרֵנוּ יהוה אֱלֹהֵינוּ בּוֹ לְטוֹבָה, וּפָקְדֵנוּ בוֹ לִבְרָכָה, וְהוֹשִׁיעֵנוּ בוֹ לְחַיִּים. וּבִדְבַר יְשׁוּעָה וְרַחֲמִים, חוּס וְחָנֵּנוּ וְרַחֵם עָלֵינוּ וְהוֹשִׁיעֵנוּ, כִּי אֵלֶיךָ עֵינֵינוּ, כִּי אֵל מֶלֶךְ חַנּוּן וְרַחוּם אָתָּה.

וְתֶחֱזֶינָה עֵינֵינוּ בְּשׁוּבְךָ לְצִיּוֹן בְּרַחֲמִים.
בָּרוּךְ אַתָּה יהוה
הַמַּחֲזִיר שְׁכִינָתוֹ לְצִיּוֹן.

הודאה

מוֹדִים אֲנַחְנוּ לָךְ
שָׁאַתָּה הוּא יהוה אֱלֹהֵינוּ וֵאלֹהֵי אֲבוֹתֵינוּ לְעוֹלָם וָעֶד.
צוּר חַיֵּינוּ, מָגֵן יִשְׁעֵנוּ
אַתָּה הוּא לְדוֹר וָדוֹר.
נוֹדֶה לְּךָ וּנְסַפֵּר תְּהִלָּתֶךָ
עַל חַיֵּינוּ הַמְּסוּרִים בְּיָדֶךָ
וְעַל נִשְׁמוֹתֵינוּ הַפְּקוּדוֹת לָךְ
וְעַל נִסֶּיךָ שֶׁבְּכָל יוֹם עִמָּנוּ
וְעַל נִפְלְאוֹתֶיךָ וְטוֹבוֹתֶיךָ
שֶׁבְּכָל עֵת, עֶרֶב וָבֹקֶר וְצָהֳרָיִם.
הַטּוֹב, כִּי לֹא כָלוּ רַחֲמֶיךָ וְהַמְרַחֵם
כִּי לֹא תַמּוּ חֲסָדֶיךָ
מֵעוֹלָם קִוִּינוּ לָךְ.

On Ḥanukka:

עַל הַנִּסִּים [We thank You also] for the miracles, the redemption, the mighty deeds, the salvations, and the victories in battle which You performed for our ancestors in those days, at this time.

בִּימֵי מַתִּתְיָהוּ In the days of Mattityahu, son of Yoḥanan, the High Priest, the Hasmonean, and his sons, the wicked Greek kingdom rose up against Your people Israel to make them forget Your Torah and to force them to transgress the laws of Your will. It was then that You in Your great compassion stood by them in the time of their distress. You championed their cause, judged their claim, and avenged their wrong. You delivered the strong into the hands of the weak, the many into the hands of the few, the impure into the hands of the pure, the wicked into the hands of the righteous, and the arrogant into the hands of those who were engaged in the study of Your Torah. You made for Yourself a great and holy reputation in Your world, and for Your people Israel You performed a great salvation and redemption as of this very day. Your children then entered the holiest part of Your House, cleansed Your Temple, purified Your Sanctuary, kindled lights in Your holy courts, and designated these eight days of Ḥanukka for giving thanks and praise to Your great name.

Continue with "For all these things."

On Purim:

עַל הַנִּסִּים [We thank You also] for the miracles, the redemption, the mighty deeds, the salvations, and the victories in battle which You performed for our ancestors in those days at this time.

בִּימֵי מָרְדְּכַי In the days of Mordekhai and Esther, in Shushan the capital, the
wicked Haman rose up against them and sought to destroy, slay and exterminate *Esther 3*
all the Jews, young and old, children and women, on one day, the thirteenth day of the twelfth month, which is the month of Adar, and to plunder their possessions. Then You in Your great compassion defeated his counsel, frustrated his plans, and caused his scheme to recoil on his own head, so that they hanged him and his sons on the gallows.

Continue with "For all these things."

וְעַל כֻּלָּם For all these things may Your name be blessed and elevated, our King, continually, for ever and all time.

Between Rosh HaShana & Yom Kippur: And write, for a good life, all the children of Your covenant.

Let all that lives thank You, Selah! and praise Your name in truth, God, our Savior and Help, Selah!
Blessed are You, LORD,
whose name is "the Good" and to whom thanks are due.

בחנוכה:

עַל הַנִּסִּים וְעַל הַפֻּרְקָן וְעַל הַגְּבוּרוֹת וְעַל הַתְּשׁוּעוֹת וְעַל הַמִּלְחָמוֹת שֶׁעָשִׂיתָ לַאֲבוֹתֵינוּ בַּיָּמִים הָהֵם בַּזְּמַן הַזֶּה.

בִּימֵי מַתִּתְיָהוּ בֶּן יוֹחָנָן כֹּהֵן גָּדוֹל חַשְׁמוֹנַאי וּבָנָיו, כְּשֶׁעָמְדָה מַלְכוּת יָוָן הָרְשָׁעָה עַל עַמְּךָ יִשְׂרָאֵל לְהַשְׁכִּיחָם תּוֹרָתֶךָ וּלְהַעֲבִירָם מֵחֻקֵּי רְצוֹנֶךָ, וְאַתָּה בְּרַחֲמֶיךָ הָרַבִּים עָמַדְתָּ לָהֶם בְּעֵת צָרָתָם, רַבְתָּ אֶת רִיבָם, דַּנְתָּ אֶת דִּינָם, נָקַמְתָּ אֶת נִקְמָתָם, מָסַרְתָּ גִבּוֹרִים בְּיַד חַלָּשִׁים, וְרַבִּים בְּיַד מְעַטִּים, וּטְמֵאִים בְּיַד טְהוֹרִים, וּרְשָׁעִים בְּיַד צַדִּיקִים, וְזֵדִים בְּיַד עוֹסְקֵי תוֹרָתֶךָ, וּלְךָ עָשִׂיתָ שֵׁם גָּדוֹל וְקָדוֹשׁ בְּעוֹלָמֶךָ, וּלְעַמְּךָ יִשְׂרָאֵל עָשִׂיתָ תְּשׁוּעָה גְדוֹלָה וּפֻרְקָן כְּהַיּוֹם הַזֶּה. וְאַחַר כֵּן בָּאוּ בָנֶיךָ לִדְבִיר בֵּיתֶךָ, וּפִנּוּ אֶת הֵיכָלֶךָ, וְטִהֲרוּ אֶת מִקְדָּשֶׁךָ, וְהִדְלִיקוּ נֵרוֹת בְּחַצְרוֹת קָדְשֶׁךָ, וְקָבְעוּ שְׁמוֹנַת יְמֵי חֲנֻכָּה אֵלּוּ, לְהוֹדוֹת וּלְהַלֵּל לְשִׁמְךָ הַגָּדוֹל.

Continue with וְעַל כֻּלָּם.

בפורים:

עַל הַנִּסִּים וְעַל הַפֻּרְקָן וְעַל הַגְּבוּרוֹת וְעַל הַתְּשׁוּעוֹת וְעַל הַמִּלְחָמוֹת שֶׁעָשִׂיתָ לַאֲבוֹתֵינוּ בַּיָּמִים הָהֵם בַּזְּמַן הַזֶּה.

בִּימֵי מָרְדְּכַי וְאֶסְתֵּר בְּשׁוּשַׁן הַבִּירָה, כְּשֶׁעָמַד עֲלֵיהֶם הָמָן הָרָשָׁע, בִּקֵּשׁ לְהַשְׁמִיד לַהֲרֹג וּלְאַבֵּד אֶת־כָּל־הַיְּהוּדִים מִנַּעַר וְעַד־זָקֵן טַף וְנָשִׁים בְּיוֹם אֶחָד, בִּשְׁלוֹשָׁה עָשָׂר לְחֹדֶשׁ שְׁנֵים־עָשָׂר, הוּא־חֹדֶשׁ אֲדָר, וּשְׁלָלָם לָבוֹז: אסתר ג וְאַתָּה בְּרַחֲמֶיךָ הָרַבִּים הֵפַרְתָּ אֶת עֲצָתוֹ, וְקִלְקַלְתָּ אֶת מַחֲשַׁבְתּוֹ, וַהֲשֵׁבוֹתָ לּוֹ גְּמוּלוֹ בְּרֹאשׁוֹ, וְתָלוּ אוֹתוֹ וְאֶת בָּנָיו עַל הָעֵץ.

Continue with וְעַל כֻּלָּם.

וְעַל כֻּלָּם יִתְבָּרַךְ וְיִתְרוֹמַם שִׁמְךָ מַלְכֵּנוּ תָּמִיד לְעוֹלָם וָעֶד.

בעשרת ימי תשובה: וּכְתֹב לְחַיִּים טוֹבִים כָּל בְּנֵי בְרִיתֶךָ.

וְכֹל הַחַיִּים יוֹדוּךָ סֶּלָה, וִיהַלְלוּ אֶת שִׁמְךָ בֶּאֱמֶת
הָאֵל יְשׁוּעָתֵנוּ וְעֶזְרָתֵנוּ סֶלָה.

בָּרוּךְ אַתָּה יהוה, הַטּוֹב שִׁמְךָ וּלְךָ נָאֶה לְהוֹדוֹת.

PEACE

שָׁלוֹם רָב Give great peace to Your people Israel for ever,
for You are the sovereign LORD of all peace;
and may it be good in Your eyes
to bless Your people Israel
at every time, at every hour, with Your peace.

Between Rosh HaShana & Yom Kippur: In the book of life, blessing, peace and prosperity,
may we and all Your people the house of Israel be remembered
and written before You for a good life, and for peace.*

Blessed are You, LORD, who blesses His people Israel with peace.

**Between Rosh HaShana and Yom Kippur outside Israel, many end the blessing:*
Blessed are You, LORD, who makes peace.

Some say the following verse:

May the words of my mouth and the inner thoughts of my heart *Ps. 19*
find favor before You, LORD, my Rock and Redeemer.

אֱלֹהַי My God, *Berakhot 17a*
guard my tongue from evil and my lips from dishonest speech.
To those who curse me, let my soul be silent;
may my soul be to all like the dust.
Open my heart to Your Torah
and let my soul pursue Your commandments.
As for all who plan evil against me,
swiftly defeat their counsel and frustrate their plans.
Act for the sake of Your name; act for the sake of Your right hand;
act for the sake of Your holiness; act for the sake of Your Torah.
That Your beloved ones may be rescued, *Ps. 60*
save with Your right hand and answer me.
May the words of my mouth *Ps. 19*
and the inner thoughts of my heart find favor before You,
LORD, my Rock and Redeemer.

Bow, take three steps back, then bow, first left, then right, then center, while saying:

May He who makes peace in His high places,
make peace for us and all Israel – and say: Amen.

ברכת שלום

שָׁלוֹם רָב עַל יִשְׂרָאֵל עַמְּךָ תָּשִׂים לְעוֹלָם
כִּי אַתָּה הוּא מֶלֶךְ אָדוֹן לְכָל הַשָּׁלוֹם.
וְטוֹב בְּעֵינֶיךָ לְבָרֵךְ אֶת עַמְּךָ יִשְׂרָאֵל
בְּכָל עֵת וּבְכָל שָׁעָה בִּשְׁלוֹמֶךָ.

בעשרת ימי תשובה: בְּסֵפֶר חַיִּים, בְּרָכָה וְשָׁלוֹם, וּפַרְנָסָה טוֹבָה
נִזָּכֵר וְנִכָּתֵב לְפָנֶיךָ, אֲנַחְנוּ וְכָל עַמְּךָ בֵּית יִשְׂרָאֵל
לְחַיִּים טוֹבִים וּלְשָׁלוֹם.*

בָּרוּךְ אַתָּה יהוה, הַמְבָרֵךְ אֶת עַמּוֹ יִשְׂרָאֵל בַּשָּׁלוֹם.

During the עשרת ימי תשובה in חוץ לארץ, many end the blessing:

בָּרוּךְ אַתָּה יהוה, עוֹשֶׂה הַשָּׁלוֹם.

Some say the following verse:

יִהְיוּ לְרָצוֹן אִמְרֵי־פִי וְהֶגְיוֹן לִבִּי לְפָנֶיךָ, יהוה צוּרִי וְגֹאֲלִי: תהלים יט

אֱלֹהַי ברכות יז.
נְצֹר לְשׁוֹנִי מֵרָע וּשְׂפָתַי מִדַּבֵּר מִרְמָה
וְלִמְקַלְלַי נַפְשִׁי תִדֹּם, וְנַפְשִׁי כֶּעָפָר לַכֹּל תִּהְיֶה.
פְּתַח לִבִּי בְּתוֹרָתֶךָ, וּבְמִצְוֺתֶיךָ תִּרְדֹּף נַפְשִׁי.
וְכָל הַחוֹשְׁבִים עָלַי רָעָה, מְהֵרָה הָפֵר עֲצָתָם וְקַלְקֵל מַחֲשַׁבְתָּם.
עֲשֵׂה לְמַעַן שְׁמֶךָ, עֲשֵׂה לְמַעַן יְמִינֶךָ
עֲשֵׂה לְמַעַן קְדֻשָּׁתֶךָ, עֲשֵׂה לְמַעַן תּוֹרָתֶךָ.
לְמַעַן יֵחָלְצוּן יְדִידֶיךָ, הוֹשִׁיעָה יְמִינְךָ וַעֲנֵנִי: תהלים ס
יִהְיוּ לְרָצוֹן אִמְרֵי־פִי וְהֶגְיוֹן לִבִּי לְפָנֶיךָ, יהוה צוּרִי וְגֹאֲלִי: תהלים יט

Bow, take three steps back, then bow, first left, then right, then center, while saying:

עֹשֶׂה שָׁלוֹם/ בעשרת ימי תשובה: הַשָּׁלוֹם/ בִּמְרוֹמָיו
הוּא יַעֲשֶׂה שָׁלוֹם עָלֵינוּ וְעַל כָּל יִשְׂרָאֵל, וְאִמְרוּ אָמֵן.

יְהִי רָצוֹן May it be Your will, LORD our God and God of our ancestors,
that the Temple be rebuilt speedily in our days, and give us a share in Your Torah.
And there we will serve You with fear,
as in the days of old and as in former years.
Then the offering of Judah and Jerusalem *Mal. 3*
will be pleasing to the LORD as in the days of old and as in former years.

On Motza'ei Shabbat (except when Yom Tov or Erev Pesaḥ falls in the following week), the Leader continues with Half Kaddish on page 368, then "May the pleasantness" on page 368.
On Motza'ei Shabbat when Yom Tov falls in the following week, the service continues on page 374.
On other evenings the Leader says Full Kaddish:

FULL KADDISH

Leader: יִתְגַּדַּל Magnified and sanctified may His great name be,
in the world He created by His will.
May He establish His kingdom
in your lifetime and in your days,
and in the lifetime of all the house of Israel,
swiftly and soon – and say: Amen.

All: May His great name be blessed for ever and all time.

Leader: Blessed and praised, glorified and elevated,
raised and honored, uplifted and praised
be the name of the Holy One, blessed be He,
beyond any blessing, song, praise and consolation
uttered in the world – and say: Amen.

May the prayers and pleas of all Israel
be accepted by their Father in heaven –
and say: Amen.

May there be great peace from heaven,
and life for us and all Israel –
and say: Amen.

Bow, take three steps back, as if taking leave of the Divine Presence, then bow, first left, then right, then center, while saying:

May He who makes peace in His high places,
make peace for us and all Israel –
and say: Amen.

יְהִי רָצוֹן מִלְּפָנֶיךָ יהוה אֱלֹהֵינוּ וֵאלֹהֵי אֲבוֹתֵינוּ
שֶׁיִּבָּנֶה בֵּית הַמִּקְדָּשׁ בִּמְהֵרָה בְיָמֵינוּ, וְתֵן חֶלְקֵנוּ בְּתוֹרָתֶךָ
וְשָׁם נַעֲבָדְךָ בְּיִרְאָה כִּימֵי עוֹלָם וּכְשָׁנִים קַדְמֹנִיּוֹת.
וְעָרְבָה לַיהוה מִנְחַת יְהוּדָה וִירוּשָׁלָםִ כִּימֵי עוֹלָם וּכְשָׁנִים קַדְמֹנִיּוֹת: מלאכי ג

On מוצאי שבת *(except when* ערב פסח *or* יום טוב *falls in the following week), the* שליח ציבור *continues with* חצי קדיש *on page 369, then* וִיהִי נֹעַם *on page 369.*

On מוצאי שבת *when* יום טוב *falls in the following week, the service continues on page 375.*

On other evenings the שליח ציבור *says* קדיש שלם*:*

קדיש שלם

ש״ץ: יִתְגַּדַּל וְיִתְקַדַּשׁ שְׁמֵהּ רַבָּא (קהל: אָמֵן)
בְּעָלְמָא דִּי בְרָא כִרְעוּתֵהּ, וְיַמְלִיךְ מַלְכוּתֵהּ
בְּחַיֵּיכוֹן וּבְיוֹמֵיכוֹן וּבְחַיֵּי דְכָל בֵּית יִשְׂרָאֵל
בַּעֲגָלָא וּבִזְמַן קָרִיב, וְאִמְרוּ אָמֵן. (קהל: אָמֵן)

קהל וש״ץ: יְהֵא שְׁמֵהּ רַבָּא מְבָרַךְ לְעָלַם וּלְעָלְמֵי עָלְמַיָּא.

ש״ץ: יִתְבָּרַךְ וְיִשְׁתַּבַּח וְיִתְפָּאַר וְיִתְרוֹמַם וְיִתְנַשֵּׂא
וְיִתְהַדָּר וְיִתְעַלֶּה וְיִתְהַלָּל
שְׁמֵהּ דְּקֻדְשָׁא בְּרִיךְ הוּא (קהל: בְּרִיךְ הוּא)
לְעֵלָּא מִן כָּל בִּרְכָתָא / בעשרת ימי תשובה: לְעֵלָּא לְעֵלָּא מִכָּל בִּרְכָתָא/
וְשִׁירָתָא, תֻּשְׁבְּחָתָא וְנֶחֱמָתָא
דַּאֲמִירָן בְּעָלְמָא, וְאִמְרוּ אָמֵן. (קהל: אָמֵן)
תִּתְקַבַּל צְלוֹתְהוֹן וּבָעוּתְהוֹן דְּכָל יִשְׂרָאֵל
קֳדָם אֲבוּהוֹן דִּי בִשְׁמַיָּא, וְאִמְרוּ אָמֵן. (קהל: אָמֵן)
יְהֵא שְׁלָמָא רַבָּא מִן שְׁמַיָּא
וְחַיִּים, עָלֵינוּ וְעַל כָּל יִשְׂרָאֵל, וְאִמְרוּ אָמֵן. (קהל: אָמֵן)

Bow, take three steps back, as if taking leave of the Divine Presence, then bow, first left, then right, then center, while saying:

עֹשֶׂה שָׁלוֹם/ בעשרת ימי תשובה: הַשָּׁלוֹם/ בִּמְרוֹמָיו
הוּא יַעֲשֶׂה שָׁלוֹם עָלֵינוּ וְעַל כָּל יִשְׂרָאֵל, וְאִמְרוּ אָמֵן. (קהל: אָמֵן)

On Yom HaAtzma'ut in many communities the service continues with "Listen, Israel" on page 958.

From the second night of Pesaḥ until the night before Shavuot, the Omer is counted here (page 356).

On Purim, Megillat Esther is read; on Tisha B'Av, Megillat Eikha is read.

Stand while saying Aleinu.

עָלֵינוּ It is our duty to praise the Master of all,
and ascribe greatness to the Author of creation,
who has not made us like the nations of the lands
nor placed us like the families of the earth;
who has not made our portion like theirs,
nor our destiny like all their multitudes.
(For they worship vanity and emptiness,
and pray to a god who cannot save.)
But we bow in worship and thank the Supreme King of kings,
the Holy One, blessed be He,
who extends the heavens and establishes the earth,
whose throne of glory is in the heavens above,
and whose power's Presence is in the highest of heights.
He is our God; there is no other.
Truly He is our King, there is none else,
as it is written in His Torah:
"You shall know and take to heart this day *Deut. 4*
that the Lord is God, in heaven above and on earth below.
There is no other."

Therefore, we place our hope in You, Lord our God,
that we may soon see the glory of Your power,
when You will remove abominations from the earth,
and idols will be utterly destroyed,
when the world will be perfected
under the sovereignty of the Almighty,
when all humanity will call on Your name,
to turn all the earth's wicked toward You.
All the world's inhabitants will realize and know
that to You every knee must bow and every tongue swear loyalty.

On יום העצמאות *in many communities the service continues with* שְׁמַע יִשְׂרָאֵל *on page 959.*
From the second night of פסח *until the night before* שבועות*, the* עומר *is counted here (page 357).*
On פורים*,* מגילת אסתר *is read; on* תשעה באב*,* מגילת איכה *is read.*

Stand while saying עָלֵינוּ.

עָלֵינוּ לְשַׁבֵּחַ לַאֲדוֹן הַכֹּל, לָתֵת גְּדֻלָּה לְיוֹצֵר בְּרֵאשִׁית
שֶׁלֹּא עָשָׂנוּ כְּגוֹיֵי הָאֲרָצוֹת, וְלֹא שָׂמָנוּ כְּמִשְׁפְּחוֹת הָאֲדָמָה
שֶׁלֹּא שָׂם חֶלְקֵנוּ כָּהֶם וְגוֹרָלֵנוּ כְּכָל הֲמוֹנָם.
(שֶׁהֵם מִשְׁתַּחֲוִים לְהֶבֶל וָרִיק וּמִתְפַּלְלִים אֶל אֵל לֹא יוֹשִׁיעַ.)
וַאֲנַחְנוּ כּוֹרְעִים וּמִשְׁתַּחֲוִים וּמוֹדִים
לִפְנֵי מֶלֶךְ מַלְכֵי הַמְּלָכִים, הַקָּדוֹשׁ בָּרוּךְ הוּא
שֶׁהוּא נוֹטֶה שָׁמַיִם וְיוֹסֵד אָרֶץ
וּמוֹשַׁב יְקָרוֹ בַּשָּׁמַיִם מִמַּעַל, וּשְׁכִינַת עֻזּוֹ בְּגָבְהֵי מְרוֹמִים.
הוּא אֱלֹהֵינוּ, אֵין עוֹד.
אֱמֶת מַלְכֵּנוּ, אֶפֶס זוּלָתוֹ
כַּכָּתוּב בְּתוֹרָתוֹ
דברים ד וְיָדַעְתָּ הַיּוֹם וַהֲשֵׁבֹתָ אֶל־לְבָבֶךָ
כִּי יהוה הוּא הָאֱלֹהִים בַּשָּׁמַיִם מִמַּעַל וְעַל־הָאָרֶץ מִתָּחַת
אֵין עוֹד:

עַל כֵּן נְקַוֶּה לְּךָ יהוה אֱלֹהֵינוּ
לִרְאוֹת מְהֵרָה בְּתִפְאֶרֶת עֻזֶּךָ
לְהַעֲבִיר גִּלּוּלִים מִן הָאָרֶץ, וְהָאֱלִילִים כָּרוֹת יִכָּרֵתוּן
לְתַקֵּן עוֹלָם בְּמַלְכוּת שַׁדַּי.
וְכָל בְּנֵי בָשָׂר יִקְרְאוּ בִשְׁמֶךָ לְהַפְנוֹת אֵלֶיךָ כָּל רִשְׁעֵי אָרֶץ.
יַכִּירוּ וְיֵדְעוּ כָּל יוֹשְׁבֵי תֵבֵל
כִּי לְךָ תִּכְרַע כָּל בֶּרֶךְ, תִּשָּׁבַע כָּל לָשׁוֹן.

Before You, Lord our God, they will kneel and bow down
and give honor to Your glorious name.
They will all accept the yoke of Your kingdom,
and You will reign over them soon and for ever.
For the kingdom is Yours, and to all eternity You will reign in glory,
as it is written in Your Torah:
"The Lord will reign for ever and ever." *Ex. 15*
▸ And it is said: "Then the Lord shall be King over all the earth; *Zech. 14*
on that day the Lord shall be One and His name One."

Some add:

Have no fear of sudden terror or of the ruin when it overtakes the wicked. *Prov. 3*
Devise your strategy, but it will be defeated, propose your plan, *Is. 8*
but it will not stand, for God is with us.
When you grow old, I will still be the same. *Is. 46*
When your hair turns gray, I will still carry you.
I made you, I will bear you, I will carry you, and I will rescue you.

MOURNER'S KADDISH

The following prayer, said by mourners, requires the presence of a minyan.
A transliteration can be found on page 1151.

Mourner: יִתְגַּדַּל Magnified and sanctified
may His great name be,
in the world He created by His will.
May He establish His kingdom
in your lifetime and in your days,
and in the lifetime of all the house of Israel,
swiftly and soon –
and say: Amen.

All: May His great name be blessed for ever and all time.

Mourner: Blessed and praised, glorified and elevated,
raised and honored, uplifted and praised
be the name of the Holy One,
blessed be He,

לְפָנֶיךָ יהוה אֱלֹהֵינוּ יִכְרְעוּ וְיִפֹּלוּ, וְלִכְבוֹד שִׁמְךָ יְקָר יִתֵּנוּ
וִיקַבְּלוּ כֻלָּם אֶת עֹל מַלְכוּתֶךָ
וְתִמְלֹךְ עֲלֵיהֶם מְהֵרָה לְעוֹלָם וָעֶד.
כִּי הַמַּלְכוּת שֶׁלְּךָ הִיא וּלְעוֹלְמֵי עַד תִּמְלֹךְ בְּכָבוֹד
כַּכָּתוּב בְּתוֹרָתֶךָ, יהוה יִמְלֹךְ לְעֹלָם וָעֶד: שמות טו
◂ וְנֶאֱמַר, וְהָיָה יהוה לְמֶלֶךְ עַל־כָּל־הָאָרֶץ זכריה יד
בַּיּוֹם הַהוּא יִהְיֶה יהוה אֶחָד וּשְׁמוֹ אֶחָד:

Some add:

אַל־תִּירָא מִפַּחַד פִּתְאֹם וּמִשֹּׁאַת רְשָׁעִים כִּי תָבֹא: משלי ג
עֻצוּ עֵצָה וְתֻפָר, דַּבְּרוּ דָבָר וְלֹא יָקוּם, כִּי עִמָּנוּ אֵל: ישעיה ח
וְעַד־זִקְנָה אֲנִי הוּא, וְעַד־שֵׂיבָה אֲנִי אֶסְבֹּל ישעיה מו
אֲנִי עָשִׂיתִי וַאֲנִי אֶשָּׂא וַאֲנִי אֶסְבֹּל וַאֲמַלֵּט:

קדיש יתום

The following prayer, said by mourners, requires the presence of a מנין.
A transliteration can be found on page 1151.

אבל: יִתְגַּדַּל וְיִתְקַדַּשׁ שְׁמֵהּ רַבָּא (קהל: אָמֵן)
בְּעָלְמָא דִּי בְרָא כִרְעוּתֵהּ
וְיַמְלִיךְ מַלְכוּתֵהּ
בְּחַיֵּיכוֹן וּבְיוֹמֵיכוֹן וּבְחַיֵּי דְכָל בֵּית יִשְׂרָאֵל
בַּעֲגָלָא וּבִזְמַן קָרִיב
וְאִמְרוּ אָמֵן. (קהל: אָמֵן)

קהל ואבל: יְהֵא שְׁמֵהּ רַבָּא מְבָרַךְ לְעָלַם וּלְעָלְמֵי עָלְמַיָּא.

אבל: יִתְבָּרַךְ וְיִשְׁתַּבַּח וְיִתְפָּאַר
וְיִתְרוֹמַם וְיִתְנַשֵּׂא וְיִתְהַדָּר וְיִתְעַלֶּה וְיִתְהַלָּל
שְׁמֵהּ דְּקֻדְשָׁא בְּרִיךְ הוּא (קהל: בְּרִיךְ הוּא)

beyond any blessing, song, praise and consolation
uttered in the world –
and say: Amen.

May there be great peace from heaven,
and life for us and all Israel –
and say: Amen.

Bow, take three steps back, as if taking leave of the Divine Presence, then bow, first left, then right, then center, while saying:

May He who makes peace in His high places,
make peace for us and all Israel –
and say: Amen.

From the second day of Rosh Ḥodesh Elul through Shemini Atzeret (in Israel through Hoshana Raba), the following psalm is said:

לְדָוִד By David. The LORD is my light and my salvation – whom then shall I fear? The LORD is the stronghold of my life – of whom shall I be afraid? When evil men close in on me to devour my flesh, it is they, my enemies and foes, who stumble and fall. Should an army besiege me, my heart would not fear. Should war break out against me, still I would be confident. One thing I ask of the LORD, only this do I seek: to live in the House of the LORD all the days of my life, to gaze on the beauty of the LORD and worship in His Temple. For He will keep me safe in His pavilion on the day of trouble. He will hide me under the cover of His tent. He will set me high upon a rock. Now my head is high above my enemies who surround me. I will sacrifice in His tent with shouts of joy. I will sing and chant praises to the LORD. LORD, hear my voice when I call. Be generous to me and answer me. On Your behalf my heart says, "Seek My face." Your face, LORD, will I seek. Do not hide Your face from me. Do not turn Your servant away in anger. You have been my help. Do not reject or abandon me, God, my Savior. Were my father and my mother to abandon me, the LORD would take me in. Teach me Your way, LORD, and lead me on a level path, because of my oppressors. Do not abandon me to the will of my enemies, for false witnesses have risen against me, breathing violence. ▸ Were it not for my faith that I shall see the LORD's goodness in the land of the living. Hope in the LORD. Be strong and of good courage, and hope in the LORD! *Ps. 27*

Mourner's Kaddish *(on previous page)*

In a house of mourning the service continues on page 270.

לְעֵלָּא מִן כָּל בִּרְכָתָא / בעשרת ימי תשובה: לְעֵלָּא לְעֵלָּא מִכָּל בִּרְכָתָא/
וְשִׁירָתָא, תֻּשְׁבְּחָתָא וְנֶחֱמָתָא
דַּאֲמִירָן בְּעָלְמָא, וְאִמְרוּ אָמֵן. (קהל: אָמֵן)

יְהֵא שְׁלָמָא רַבָּא מִן שְׁמַיָּא
וְחַיִּים, עָלֵינוּ וְעַל כָּל יִשְׂרָאֵל, וְאִמְרוּ אָמֵן. (קהל: אָמֵן)

Bow, take three steps back, as if taking leave of the Divine Presence, then bow, first left, then right, then center, while saying:

עֹשֶׂה שָׁלוֹם/ בעשרת ימי תשובה: הַשָּׁלוֹם/ בִּמְרוֹמָיו
הוּא יַעֲשֶׂה שָׁלוֹם
עָלֵינוּ וְעַל כָּל יִשְׂרָאֵל, וְאִמְרוּ אָמֵן. (קהל: אָמֵן)

From the second day of ראש חודש אלול *through* שמיני עצרת
(*in* ארץ ישראל *through* הושענא רבה), *the following psalm is said:*

לְדָוִד, יהוה אוֹרִי וְיִשְׁעִי, מִמִּי אִירָא, יהוה מָעוֹז־חַיַּי, מִמִּי אֶפְחָד: בִּקְרֹב תהלים כז
עָלַי מְרֵעִים לֶאֱכֹל אֶת־בְּשָׂרִי, צָרַי וְאֹיְבַי לִי, הֵמָּה כָשְׁלוּ וְנָפָלוּ: אִם־
תַּחֲנֶה עָלַי מַחֲנֶה, לֹא־יִירָא לִבִּי, אִם־תָּקוּם עָלַי מִלְחָמָה, בְּזֹאת אֲנִי
בוֹטֵחַ: אַחַת שָׁאַלְתִּי מֵאֵת־יהוה, אוֹתָהּ אֲבַקֵּשׁ, שִׁבְתִּי בְּבֵית־יהוה
כָּל־יְמֵי חַיַּי, לַחֲזוֹת בְּנֹעַם־יהוה, וּלְבַקֵּר בְּהֵיכָלוֹ: כִּי יִצְפְּנֵנִי בְּסֻכֹּה בְּיוֹם
רָעָה, יַסְתִּרֵנִי בְּסֵתֶר אָהֳלוֹ, בְּצוּר יְרוֹמְמֵנִי: וְעַתָּה יָרוּם רֹאשִׁי עַל אֹיְבַי
סְבִיבוֹתַי, וְאֶזְבְּחָה בְאָהֳלוֹ זִבְחֵי תְרוּעָה, אָשִׁירָה וַאֲזַמְּרָה לַיהוה: שְׁמַע־
יהוה קוֹלִי אֶקְרָא, וְחָנֵּנִי וַעֲנֵנִי: לְךָ אָמַר לִבִּי בַּקְּשׁוּ פָנָי, אֶת־פָּנֶיךָ יהוה
אֲבַקֵּשׁ: אַל־תַּסְתֵּר פָּנֶיךָ מִמֶּנִּי, אַל תַּט־בְּאַף עַבְדֶּךָ, עֶזְרָתִי הָיִיתָ, אַל־
תִּטְּשֵׁנִי וְאַל־תַּעַזְבֵנִי, אֱלֹהֵי יִשְׁעִי: כִּי־אָבִי וְאִמִּי עֲזָבוּנִי, וַיהוה יַאַסְפֵנִי:
הוֹרֵנִי יהוה דַּרְכֶּךָ, וּנְחֵנִי בְּאֹרַח מִישׁוֹר, לְמַעַן שׁוֹרְרָי: אַל־תִּתְּנֵנִי בְּנֶפֶשׁ
צָרָי, כִּי קָמוּ־בִי עֵדֵי־שֶׁקֶר, וִיפֵחַ חָמָס: ‹ לוּלֵא הֶאֱמַנְתִּי לִרְאוֹת בְּטוּב־
יהוה בְּאֶרֶץ חַיִּים: קַוֵּה אֶל־יהוה, חֲזַק וְיַאֲמֵץ לִבֶּךָ, וְקַוֵּה אֶל־יהוה:

קדיש יתום (*on previous page*)

In a house of mourning the service continues on page 271.

COUNTING OF THE OMER

The Omer is counted each night from the second night of Pesaḥ until the night before Shavuot.

Some say the following meditation before the blessing:

For the sake of the unification of the Holy One, blessed be He,
and His Divine Presence, with fear and love,
to unify the name *Yod-Heh* with *Vav-Heh*
in perfect unity in the name of all Israel.

הִנְנִי I am prepared and ready to fulfill the positive commandment of Counting the Omer, as is written in the Torah, "You shall count seven complete weeks from the day following the [Pesaḥ] rest day, when you brought the Omer as a wave-offering. To the day after the seventh week you shall count fifty days. Then you shall present a meal-offering of new grain to the LORD." *Lev. 23*
May the pleasantness of the LORD our God be upon us. Establish for us the work of our hands, O establish the work of our hands. *Ps. 90*

בָּרוּךְ Blessed are You, LORD our God, King of the Universe,
who has made us holy through His commandments,
and has commanded us about counting the Omer.

16 Nisan

1. Today is the first day of the Omer.

17 Nisan

2. Today is the second day of the Omer.

18 Nisan

3. Today is the third day of the Omer.

19 Nisan

4. Today is the fourth day of the Omer.

20 Nisan

5. Today is the fifth day of the Omer.

21 Nisan

6. Today is the sixth day of the Omer.

22 Nisan

7. Today is the seventh day, making one week of the Omer.

23 Nisan

8. Today is the eighth day, making one week and one day of the Omer.

24 Nisan

9. Today is the ninth day, making one week and two days of the Omer.

סדר ספירת העומר

The עומר *is counted each night from the second night of* פסח *until the night before* שבועות*.*

Some say the following meditation before the blessing:

לְשֵׁם יִחוּד קֻדְשָׁא בְּרִיךְ הוּא וּשְׁכִינְתֵּהּ בִּדְחִילוּ וּרְחִימוּ לְיַחֵד שֵׁם י״ה בו״ה בְּיִחוּדָא שְׁלִים בְּשֵׁם כָּל יִשְׂרָאֵל.

הִנְנִי מוּכָן וּמְזֻמָּן לְקַיֵּם מִצְוַת עֲשֵׂה שֶׁל סְפִירַת הָעֹמֶר. כְּמוֹ שֶׁכָּתוּב בַּתּוֹרָה, וּסְפַרְתֶּם לָכֶם מִמָּחֳרַת הַשַּׁבָּת, מִיּוֹם הֲבִיאֲכֶם אֶת־עֹמֶר הַתְּנוּפָה, שֶׁבַע שַׁבָּתוֹת תְּמִימֹת תִּהְיֶינָה: עַד מִמָּחֳרַת הַשַּׁבָּת הַשְּׁבִיעִת תִּסְפְּרוּ חֲמִשִּׁים יוֹם, וְהִקְרַבְתֶּם מִנְחָה חֲדָשָׁה לַיהוה: וִיהִי נֹעַם אֲדֹנָי אֱלֹהֵינוּ עָלֵינוּ, וּמַעֲשֵׂה יָדֵינוּ כּוֹנְנָה עָלֵינוּ, וּמַעֲשֵׂה יָדֵינוּ כּוֹנְנֵהוּ:

(ויקרא כג; תהלים צ)

בָּרוּךְ אַתָּה יהוה אֱלֹהֵינוּ מֶלֶךְ הָעוֹלָם
אֲשֶׁר קִדְּשָׁנוּ בְּמִצְוֹתָיו וְצִוָּנוּ עַל סְפִירַת הָעֹמֶר.

טז בניסן

1. הַיּוֹם יוֹם אֶחָד בָּעֹמֶר.

חסד שבחסד

יז בניסן

2. הַיּוֹם שְׁנֵי יָמִים בָּעֹמֶר.

גבורה שבחסד

יח בניסן

3. הַיּוֹם שְׁלֹשָׁה יָמִים בָּעֹמֶר.

תפארת שבחסד

יט בניסן

4. הַיּוֹם אַרְבָּעָה יָמִים בָּעֹמֶר.

נצח שבחסד

כ בניסן

5. הַיּוֹם חֲמִשָּׁה יָמִים בָּעֹמֶר.

הוד שבחסד

כא בניסן

6. הַיּוֹם שִׁשָּׁה יָמִים בָּעֹמֶר.

יסוד שבחסד

כב בניסן

7. הַיּוֹם שִׁבְעָה יָמִים שֶׁהֵם שָׁבוּעַ אֶחָד בָּעֹמֶר.

מלכות שבחסד

כג בניסן

8. הַיּוֹם שְׁמוֹנָה יָמִים שֶׁהֵם שָׁבוּעַ אֶחָד וְיוֹם אֶחָד בָּעֹמֶר.

חסד שבגבורה

כד בניסן

9. הַיּוֹם תִּשְׁעָה יָמִים שֶׁהֵם שָׁבוּעַ אֶחָד וּשְׁנֵי יָמִים בָּעֹמֶר.

גבורה שבגבורה

25 Nisan

10. Today is the tenth day,
making one week and three
days of the Omer.

26 Nisan

11. Today is the eleventh day,
making one week
and four days
of the Omer.

27 Nisan

12. Today is the twelfth day,
making one week
and five days
of the Omer.

28 Nisan

13. Today is the thirteenth day,
making one week
and six days
of the Omer.

29 Nisan

14. Today is the fourteenth day,
making two weeks
of the Omer.

30 Nisan, 1st day Rosh Ḥodesh

15. Today is the fifteenth day,
making two weeks
and one day
of the Omer.

1 Iyar, 2nd day Rosh Ḥodesh

16. Today is the sixteenth day,
making two weeks
and two days
of the Omer.

2 Iyar

17. Today is the seventeenth day,
making two weeks
and three days
of the Omer.

3 Iyar

18. Today is the eighteenth day,
making two weeks
and four days
of the Omer.

4 Iyar

19. Today is the nineteenth day,
making two weeks
and five days
of the Omer.

5 Iyar, Yom HaAtzma'ut

20. Today is the twentieth day,
making two weeks
and six days
of the Omer.

6 Iyar

21. Today is the twenty-first day,
making three weeks
of the Omer.

7 Iyar

22. Today is the twenty-second day,
making three weeks
and one day
of the Omer.

8 Iyar

23. Today is the twenty-third day,
making three weeks
and two days
of the Omer.

כה בניסן

10. הַיּוֹם עֲשָׂרָה יָמִים
שֶׁהֵם שָׁבוּעַ אֶחָד וּשְׁלֹשָׁה
יָמִים בָּעֹמֶר. תפארת שבגבורה

כו בניסן

11. הַיּוֹם אַחַד עָשָׂר יוֹם
שֶׁהֵם שָׁבוּעַ אֶחָד וְאַרְבָּעָה
יָמִים בָּעֹמֶר. נצח שבגבורה

כז בניסן

12. הַיּוֹם שְׁנֵים עָשָׂר יוֹם
שֶׁהֵם שָׁבוּעַ אֶחָד וַחֲמִשָּׁה
יָמִים בָּעֹמֶר. הוד שבגבורה

כח בניסן

13. הַיּוֹם שְׁלֹשָׁה עָשָׂר יוֹם
שֶׁהֵם שָׁבוּעַ אֶחָד וְשִׁשָּׁה יָמִים
בָּעֹמֶר. יסוד שבגבורה

כט בניסן

14. הַיּוֹם אַרְבָּעָה עָשָׂר יוֹם
שֶׁהֵם שְׁנֵי שָׁבוּעוֹת
בָּעֹמֶר. מלכות שבגבורה

ל בניסן, א׳ דראש חודש

15. הַיּוֹם חֲמִשָּׁה עָשָׂר יוֹם
שֶׁהֵם שְׁנֵי שָׁבוּעוֹת וְיוֹם אֶחָד
בָּעֹמֶר. חסד שבתפארת

א באייר, ב׳ דראש חודש

16. הַיּוֹם שִׁשָּׁה עָשָׂר יוֹם
שֶׁהֵם שְׁנֵי שָׁבוּעוֹת וּשְׁנֵי יָמִים
בָּעֹמֶר. גבורה שבתפארת

ב באייר

17. הַיּוֹם שִׁבְעָה עָשָׂר יוֹם
שֶׁהֵם שְׁנֵי שָׁבוּעוֹת וּשְׁלֹשָׁה
יָמִים בָּעֹמֶר. תפארת שבתפארת

ג באייר

18. הַיּוֹם שְׁמוֹנָה עָשָׂר יוֹם
שֶׁהֵם שְׁנֵי שָׁבוּעוֹת וְאַרְבָּעָה
יָמִים בָּעֹמֶר. נצח שבתפארת

ד באייר

19. הַיּוֹם תִּשְׁעָה עָשָׂר יוֹם
שֶׁהֵם שְׁנֵי שָׁבוּעוֹת וַחֲמִשָּׁה
יָמִים בָּעֹמֶר. הוד שבתפארת

ה באייר, יום העצמאות

20. הַיּוֹם עֶשְׂרִים יוֹם
שֶׁהֵם שְׁנֵי שָׁבוּעוֹת וְשִׁשָּׁה
יָמִים בָּעֹמֶר. יסוד שבתפארת

ו באייר

21. הַיּוֹם אֶחָד וְעֶשְׂרִים יוֹם
שֶׁהֵם שְׁלֹשָׁה שָׁבוּעוֹת בָּעֹמֶר.
מלכות שבתפארת

ז באייר

22. הַיּוֹם שְׁנַיִם וְעֶשְׂרִים יוֹם
שֶׁהֵם שְׁלֹשָׁה שָׁבוּעוֹת
וְיוֹם אֶחָד בָּעֹמֶר. חסד שבנצח

ח באייר

23. הַיּוֹם שְׁלֹשָׁה וְעֶשְׂרִים יוֹם
שֶׁהֵם שְׁלֹשָׁה שָׁבוּעוֹת
וּשְׁנֵי יָמִים בָּעֹמֶר. גבורה שבנצח

9 Iyar

24. Today is the twenty-fourth day,
making three weeks
and three days
of the Omer.

10 Iyar

25. Today is the twenty-fifth day,
making three weeks
and four days
of the Omer.

11 Iyar

26. Today is the twenty-sixth day,
making three weeks
and five days
of the Omer.

12 Iyar

27. Today is the twenty-seventh
day, making three weeks
and six days
of the Omer.

13 Iyar

28. Today is the twenty-eighth day,
making four weeks
of the Omer.

14 Iyar, Pesaḥ Sheni

29. Today is the twenty-ninth day,
making four weeks
and one day
of the Omer.

15 Iyar

30. Today is the thirtieth day,
making four weeks
and two days
of the Omer.

16 Iyar

31. Today is the thirty-first day,
making four weeks
and three days
of the Omer.

17 Iyar

32. Today is the thirty-second day,
making four weeks
and four days
of the Omer.

18 Iyar, Lag BaOmer

33. Today is the thirty-third day,
making four weeks
and five days
of the Omer.

19 Iyar

34. Today is the thirty-fourth day,
making four weeks
and six days
of the Omer.

20 Iyar

35. Today is the thirty-fifth day,
making five weeks
of the Omer.

21 Iyar

36. Today is the thirty-sixth day,
making five weeks
and one day
of the Omer.

22 Iyar

37. Today is the thirty-seventh day,
making five weeks
and two days
of the Omer.

ט באייר

24. הַיּוֹם אַרְבָּעָה וְעֶשְׂרִים יוֹם
שֶׁהֵם שְׁלֹשָׁה שָׁבוּעוֹת
וּשְׁלֹשָׁה יָמִים בָּעֹמֶר.

תפארת שבנצח

י באייר

25. הַיּוֹם חֲמִשָּׁה וְעֶשְׂרִים יוֹם
שֶׁהֵם שְׁלֹשָׁה שָׁבוּעוֹת
וְאַרְבָּעָה יָמִים בָּעֹמֶר. נצח שבנצח

יא באייר

26. הַיּוֹם שִׁשָּׁה וְעֶשְׂרִים יוֹם
שֶׁהֵם שְׁלֹשָׁה שָׁבוּעוֹת
וַחֲמִשָּׁה יָמִים בָּעֹמֶר. הוד שבנצח

יב באייר

27. הַיּוֹם שִׁבְעָה וְעֶשְׂרִים יוֹם
שֶׁהֵם שְׁלֹשָׁה שָׁבוּעוֹת
וְשִׁשָּׁה יָמִים בָּעֹמֶר. יסוד שבנצח

יג באייר

28. הַיּוֹם שְׁמוֹנָה וְעֶשְׂרִים יוֹם
שֶׁהֵם אַרְבָּעָה שָׁבוּעוֹת
בָּעֹמֶר. מלכות שבנצח

יד באייר, פסח שני

29. הַיּוֹם תִּשְׁעָה וְעֶשְׂרִים יוֹם
שֶׁהֵם אַרְבָּעָה שָׁבוּעוֹת
וְיוֹם אֶחָד בָּעֹמֶר. חסד שבהוד

טו באייר

30. הַיּוֹם שְׁלֹשִׁים יוֹם
שֶׁהֵם אַרְבָּעָה שָׁבוּעוֹת
וּשְׁנֵי יָמִים בָּעֹמֶר. גבורה שבהוד

טז באייר

31. הַיּוֹם אֶחָד וּשְׁלֹשִׁים יוֹם
שֶׁהֵם אַרְבָּעָה שָׁבוּעוֹת
וּשְׁלֹשָׁה יָמִים בָּעֹמֶר.

תפארת שבהוד

יז באייר

32. הַיּוֹם שְׁנַיִם וּשְׁלֹשִׁים יוֹם
שֶׁהֵם אַרְבָּעָה שָׁבוּעוֹת
וְאַרְבָּעָה יָמִים בָּעֹמֶר. נצח שבהוד

יח באייר, לג בעומר

33. הַיּוֹם שְׁלֹשָׁה וּשְׁלֹשִׁים יוֹם
שֶׁהֵם אַרְבָּעָה שָׁבוּעוֹת
וַחֲמִשָּׁה יָמִים בָּעֹמֶר. הוד שבהוד

יט באייר

34. הַיּוֹם אַרְבָּעָה וּשְׁלֹשִׁים יוֹם
שֶׁהֵם אַרְבָּעָה שָׁבוּעוֹת
וְשִׁשָּׁה יָמִים בָּעֹמֶר. יסוד שבהוד

כ באייר

35. הַיּוֹם חֲמִשָּׁה וּשְׁלֹשִׁים יוֹם
שֶׁהֵם חֲמִשָּׁה שָׁבוּעוֹת
בָּעֹמֶר. מלכות שבהוד

כא באייר

36. הַיּוֹם שִׁשָּׁה וּשְׁלֹשִׁים יוֹם
שֶׁהֵם חֲמִשָּׁה שָׁבוּעוֹת
וְיוֹם אֶחָד בָּעֹמֶר. חסד שביסוד

כב באייר

37. הַיּוֹם שִׁבְעָה וּשְׁלֹשִׁים יוֹם
שֶׁהֵם חֲמִשָּׁה שָׁבוּעוֹת
וּשְׁנֵי יָמִים בָּעֹמֶר. גבורה שביסוד

23 Iyar

38. Today is the thirty-eighth day,
making five weeks
and three days
of the Omer.

24 Iyar

39. Today is the thirty-ninth day,
making five weeks
and four days
of the Omer.

25 Iyar

40. Today is the fortieth day,
making five weeks
and five days
of the Omer.

26 Iyar

41. Today is the forty-first day,
making five weeks
and six days
of the Omer.

27 Iyar

42. Today is the forty-second day,
making six weeks
of the Omer.

28 Iyar, Yom Yerushalayim

43. Today is the forty-third day,
making six weeks and one day
of the Omer.

29 Iyar

44. Today is the forty-fourth day,
making six weeks
and two days
of the Omer.

1 Sivan, Rosh Ḥodesh

45. Today is the forty-fifth day,
making six weeks
and three days
of the Omer.

2 Sivan

46. Today is the forty-sixth day,
making six weeks and four
days of the Omer.

3 Sivan

47. Today is the forty-seventh day,
making six weeks and five days
of the Omer.

4 Sivan

48. Today is the forty-eighth day,
making six weeks and six days
of the Omer.

5 Sivan, Erev Shavuot

49. Today is the forty-ninth day,
making seven weeks of the
Omer.

הָרַחֲמָן May the Compassionate One
restore the Temple service to its place speedily in our days.
Amen, Selah.

כג באייר

38. הַיּוֹם שְׁמוֹנָה וּשְׁלֹשִׁים יוֹם שֶׁהֵם חֲמִשָּׁה שָׁבוּעוֹת וּשְׁלֹשָׁה יָמִים בָּעֹמֶר. תפארת שביסוד

כד באייר

39. הַיּוֹם תִּשְׁעָה וּשְׁלֹשִׁים יוֹם שֶׁהֵם חֲמִשָּׁה שָׁבוּעוֹת וְאַרְבָּעָה יָמִים בָּעֹמֶר. נצח שביסוד

כה באייר

40. הַיּוֹם אַרְבָּעִים יוֹם שֶׁהֵם חֲמִשָּׁה שָׁבוּעוֹת וַחֲמִשָּׁה יָמִים בָּעֹמֶר. הוד שביסוד

כו באייר

41. הַיּוֹם אֶחָד וְאַרְבָּעִים יוֹם שֶׁהֵם חֲמִשָּׁה שָׁבוּעוֹת וְשִׁשָּׁה יָמִים בָּעֹמֶר. יסוד שביסוד

כז באייר

42. הַיּוֹם שְׁנַיִם וְאַרְבָּעִים יוֹם שֶׁהֵם שִׁשָּׁה שָׁבוּעוֹת בָּעֹמֶר. מלכות שביסוד

כח באייר, יום ירושלים

43. הַיּוֹם שְׁלֹשָׁה וְאַרְבָּעִים יוֹם שֶׁהֵם שִׁשָּׁה שָׁבוּעוֹת וְיוֹם אֶחָד בָּעֹמֶר. חסד שבמלכות

כט באייר

44. הַיּוֹם אַרְבָּעָה וְאַרְבָּעִים יוֹם שֶׁהֵם שִׁשָּׁה שָׁבוּעוֹת וּשְׁנֵי יָמִים בָּעֹמֶר. גבורה שבמלכות

א בסיון, ראש חודש

45. הַיּוֹם חֲמִשָּׁה וְאַרְבָּעִים יוֹם שֶׁהֵם שִׁשָּׁה שָׁבוּעוֹת וּשְׁלֹשָׁה יָמִים בָּעֹמֶר. תפארת שבמלכות

ב בסיון

46. הַיּוֹם שִׁשָּׁה וְאַרְבָּעִים יוֹם שֶׁהֵם שִׁשָּׁה שָׁבוּעוֹת וְאַרְבָּעָה יָמִים בָּעֹמֶר. נצח שבמלכות

ג בסיון

47. הַיּוֹם שִׁבְעָה וְאַרְבָּעִים יוֹם שֶׁהֵם שִׁשָּׁה שָׁבוּעוֹת וַחֲמִשָּׁה יָמִים בָּעֹמֶר. הוד שבמלכות

ד בסיון

48. הַיּוֹם שְׁמוֹנָה וְאַרְבָּעִים יוֹם שֶׁהֵם שִׁשָּׁה שָׁבוּעוֹת וְשִׁשָּׁה יָמִים בָּעֹמֶר. יסוד שבמלכות

ה בסיון, ערב שבועות

49. הַיּוֹם תִּשְׁעָה וְאַרְבָּעִים יוֹם שֶׁהֵם שִׁבְעָה שָׁבוּעוֹת בָּעֹמֶר. מלכות שבמלכות

הָרַחֲמָן הוּא יַחֲזִיר לָנוּ עֲבוֹדַת בֵּית הַמִּקְדָּשׁ לִמְקוֹמָהּ בִּמְהֵרָה בְיָמֵינוּ, אָמֵן סֶלָה.

Some add:

לַמְנַצֵּחַ For the conductor of music. With stringed instruments. A psalm, a song. May God be generous to us and bless us. May He make His face shine on us, Selah. Then will Your way be known on earth, Your salvation among all the nations. Let the peoples praise You, God; let all peoples praise You. Let nations rejoice and sing for joy, for You judge the peoples fairly, and guide the nations of the earth, Selah. Let the peoples praise You, God; let all peoples praise You. The earth has yielded its harvest. May God, our God, bless us. God will bless us, and all the ends of the earth will fear Him. *Ps. 67*

אָנָּא Please, by the power of Your great right hand, set the captive nation free.
Accept Your people's prayer. Strengthen us, purify us, You who are feared.
Please, mighty One, guard like the pupil of the eye those who seek Your unity.
Bless them, cleanse them, have compassion on them, give them Your righteousness always.
Mighty One, Holy One, in Your great goodness guide Your congregation.
Only One, elevated One, turn to Your people, who declare Your holiness.
Accept our plea and listen to our cry, You who know all secret thoughts.
Blessed be the name of His glorious kingdom for ever and all time.

רִבּוֹנוֹ שֶׁל עוֹלָם Master of the Universe, You commanded us through Your servant Moses to count the Omer, to cleanse our shells and impurities, as You have written in Your Torah: "You shall count seven complete weeks from the day following the [Pesaḥ] rest day, when you brought the Omer as a wave-offering. To the day after the seventh week, you shall count fifty days." *Lev. 23* This is so that the souls of Your people Israel may be purified from their uncleanliness. May it also be Your will, Lord our God and God of our ancestors, that in the merit of the Omer count that I have counted today, there may be rectified any defect on my part in the counting of (*insert the appropriate sefira for each day*). May I be cleansed and sanctified with Your holiness on high, and through this may there flow a rich stream through all worlds, to rectify our lives, spirits and souls from any dross and defect, purifying and sanctifying us with Your sublime holiness. Amen, Selah.

The service continues with Aleinu on page 350.

Some add:

לַמְנַצֵּחַ בִּנְגִינֹת, מִזְמוֹר שִׁיר: אֱלֹהִים יְחָנֵּנוּ וִיבָרְכֵנוּ, יָאֵר פָּנָיו אִתָּנוּ סֶלָה: תהלים סז
לָדַעַת בָּאָרֶץ דַּרְכֶּךָ, בְּכָל־גּוֹיִם יְשׁוּעָתֶךָ: יוֹדְוּךָ עַמִּים אֱלֹהִים, יוֹדְוּךָ עַמִּים
כֻּלָּם: יִשְׂמְחוּ וִירַנְּנוּ לְאֻמִּים, כִּי־תִשְׁפֹּט עַמִּים מִישֹׁר, וּלְאֻמִּים בָּאָרֶץ תַּנְחֵם
סֶלָה: יוֹדְוּךָ עַמִּים אֱלֹהִים, יוֹדְוּךָ עַמִּים כֻּלָּם: אֶרֶץ נָתְנָה יְבוּלָהּ, יְבָרְכֵנוּ
אֱלֹהִים אֱלֹהֵינוּ: יְבָרְכֵנוּ אֱלֹהִים, וְיִירְאוּ אוֹתוֹ כָּל־אַפְסֵי־אָרֶץ:

אָנָּא, בְּכֹחַ גְּדֻלַּת יְמִינְךָ, תַּתִּיר צְרוּרָה.
קַבֵּל רִנַּת עַמְּךָ, שַׂגְּבֵנוּ, טַהֲרֵנוּ, נוֹרָא.
נָא גִבּוֹר, דּוֹרְשֵׁי יִחוּדְךָ כְּבָבַת שָׁמְרֵם.
בָּרְכֵם, טַהֲרֵם, רַחֲמֵם, צִדְקָתְךָ תָּמִיד גָּמְלֵם.
חֲסִין קָדוֹשׁ, בְּרֹב טוּבְךָ נַהֵל עֲדָתֶךָ.
יָחִיד גֵּאֶה, לְעַמְּךָ פְּנֵה, זוֹכְרֵי קְדֻשָּׁתֶךָ.
שַׁוְעָתֵנוּ קַבֵּל וּשְׁמַע צַעֲקָתֵנוּ, יוֹדֵעַ תַּעֲלוּמוֹת.
בָּרוּךְ שֵׁם כְּבוֹד מַלְכוּתוֹ לְעוֹלָם וָעֶד.

רִבּוֹנוֹ שֶׁל עוֹלָם, אַתָּה צִוִּיתָנוּ עַל יְדֵי מֹשֶׁה עַבְדְּךָ לִסְפֹּר סְפִירַת הָעֹמֶר,
כְּדֵי לְטַהֲרֵנוּ מִקְּלִפּוֹתֵינוּ וּמִטֻּמְאוֹתֵינוּ. כְּמוֹ שֶׁכָּתַבְתָּ בְּתוֹרָתֶךָ: וּסְפַרְתֶּם ויקרא כג
לָכֶם מִמָּחֳרַת הַשַּׁבָּת, מִיּוֹם הֲבִיאֲכֶם אֶת־עֹמֶר הַתְּנוּפָה, שֶׁבַע שַׁבָּתוֹת
תְּמִימֹת תִּהְיֶינָה: עַד מִמָּחֳרַת הַשַּׁבָּת הַשְּׁבִיעִת תִּסְפְּרוּ חֲמִשִּׁים יוֹם:
כְּדֵי שֶׁיִּטָּהֲרוּ נַפְשׁוֹת עַמְּךָ יִשְׂרָאֵל מִזֻּהֲמָתָם. וּבְכֵן יְהִי רָצוֹן מִלְּפָנֶיךָ יהוה
אֱלֹהֵינוּ וֵאלֹהֵי אֲבוֹתֵינוּ, שֶׁבִּזְכוּת סְפִירַת הָעֹמֶר שֶׁסָּפַרְתִּי הַיּוֹם, יְתֻקַּן מַה
שֶּׁפָּגַמְתִּי בִּסְפִירָה (*insert appropriate* ספירה *for each day*) וְאֶטָּהֵר וְאֶתְקַדֵּשׁ
בִּקְדֻשָּׁה שֶׁל מַעְלָה, וְעַל יְדֵי זֶה יֻשְׁפַּע שֶׁפַע רַב בְּכָל הָעוֹלָמוֹת, לְתַקֵּן
אֶת נַפְשׁוֹתֵינוּ וְרוּחוֹתֵינוּ וְנִשְׁמוֹתֵינוּ מִכָּל סִיג וּפְגַם, וּלְטַהֲרֵנוּ וּלְקַדְּשֵׁנוּ
בִּקְדֻשָּׁתְךָ הָעֶלְיוֹנָה, אָמֵן סֶלָה.

The service continues with עָלֵינוּ *on page 351.*

MOTZA'EI SHABBAT

In many congregations, the following two psalms are sung before Ma'ariv at the end of Shabbat.

לְדָוִד Of David. Blessed is the LORD, my Rock, who trains my hands for war, my fingers for battle. He is my Benefactor, my Fortress, my Stronghold and my Refuge, my Shield in whom I trust, He who subdues nations under me. LORD, what is man that You care for him, what are mortals that You think of them? Man is no more than a breath, his days like a fleeting shadow. LORD, part Your heavens and come down; touch the mountains so that they pour forth smoke. Flash forth lightning and scatter them; shoot Your arrows and panic them. Reach out Your hand from on high; deliver me and rescue me from the mighty waters, from the hands of strangers, whose every word is worthless, whose right hands are raised in falsehood. To You, God, I will sing a new song; to You I will play music on a ten-stringed harp. He who gives salvation to kings, who saved His servant David from the cruel sword: may He deliver me and rescue me from the hands of strangers, whose every word is worthless, whose right hands are raised in falsehood. Then our sons will be like saplings, well nurtured in their youth. Our daughters will be like pillars carved for a palace. Our barns will be filled with every kind of provision. Our sheep will increase by thousands, even tens of thousands in our fields. Our oxen will draw heavy loads. There will be no breach in the walls, no going into captivity, no cries of distress in our streets. Happy are the people for whom this is so; happy are the people whose God is the LORD. *Ps. 144*

לַמְנַצֵּחַ For the conductor of music. With stringed instruments. A psalm, a song. May God be generous to us and bless us. May He make His face shine on us, Selah. Then will Your way be known on earth, Your salvation among all the nations. Let the peoples praise You, God; let all peoples praise You. Let nations rejoice and sing for joy, for You judge the peoples fairly, and guide the nations of the earth, Selah. Let the peoples praise You, God; let all peoples praise You. The earth has yielded its harvest. May God, our God, bless us. God will bless us, and all the ends of the earth will fear Him. *Ps. 67*

The service continues with Ma'ariv for Weekdays on page 312.

סדר מוצאי שבת

In many congregations, the following two psalms are sung before מעריב *on* מוצאי שבת*.*

תהלים קמד

לְדָוִד, בָּרוּךְ יהוה צוּרִי, הַמְלַמֵּד יָדַי לַקְרָב, אֶצְבְּעוֹתַי לַמִּלְחָמָה: חַסְדִּי וּמְצוּדָתִי מִשְׂגַּבִּי וּמְפַלְטִי לִי, מָגִנִּי וּבוֹ חָסִיתִי, הָרוֹדֵד עַמִּי תַחְתָּי: יהוה מָה־אָדָם וַתֵּדָעֵהוּ, בֶּן־אֱנוֹשׁ וַתְּחַשְּׁבֵהוּ: אָדָם לַהֶבֶל דָּמָה, יָמָיו כְּצֵל עוֹבֵר: יהוה הַט־שָׁמֶיךָ וְתֵרֵד, גַּע בֶּהָרִים וְיֶעֱשָׁנוּ: בְּרוֹק בָּרָק וּתְפִיצֵם, שְׁלַח חִצֶּיךָ וּתְהֻמֵּם: שְׁלַח יָדֶיךָ מִמָּרוֹם, פְּצֵנִי וְהַצִּילֵנִי מִמַּיִם רַבִּים, מִיַּד בְּנֵי נֵכָר: אֲשֶׁר פִּיהֶם דִּבֶּר־שָׁוְא, וִימִינָם יְמִין שָׁקֶר: אֱלֹהִים שִׁיר חָדָשׁ אָשִׁירָה לָּךְ, בְּנֵבֶל עָשׂוֹר אֲזַמְּרָה־לָּךְ: הַנּוֹתֵן תְּשׁוּעָה לַמְּלָכִים, הַפּוֹצֶה אֶת־דָּוִד עַבְדּוֹ מֵחֶרֶב רָעָה: פְּצֵנִי וְהַצִּילֵנִי מִיַּד בְּנֵי נֵכָר, אֲשֶׁר פִּיהֶם דִּבֶּר־שָׁוְא, וִימִינָם יְמִין שָׁקֶר: אֲשֶׁר בָּנֵינוּ כִּנְטִעִים, מְגֻדָּלִים בִּנְעוּרֵיהֶם, בְּנוֹתֵינוּ כְזָוִיּוֹת, מְחֻטָּבוֹת תַּבְנִית הֵיכָל: מְזָוֵינוּ מְלֵאִים, מְפִיקִים מִזַּן אֶל־זַן, צֹאונֵנוּ מַאֲלִיפוֹת מְרֻבָּבוֹת בְּחוּצוֹתֵינוּ: אַלּוּפֵינוּ מְסֻבָּלִים, אֵין פֶּרֶץ וְאֵין יוֹצֵאת, וְאֵין צְוָחָה בִּרְחוֹבֹתֵינוּ: אַשְׁרֵי הָעָם שֶׁכָּכָה לּוֹ, אַשְׁרֵי הָעָם שֶׁיהוה אֱלֹהָיו:

תהלים סז

לַמְנַצֵּחַ בִּנְגִינֹת, מִזְמוֹר שִׁיר: אֱלֹהִים יְחָנֵּנוּ וִיבָרְכֵנוּ, יָאֵר פָּנָיו אִתָּנוּ סֶלָה: לָדַעַת בָּאָרֶץ דַּרְכֶּךָ, בְּכָל־גּוֹיִם יְשׁוּעָתֶךָ: יוֹדוּךָ עַמִּים אֱלֹהִים, יוֹדוּךָ עַמִּים כֻּלָּם: יִשְׂמְחוּ וִירַנְּנוּ לְאֻמִּים, כִּי־תִשְׁפֹּט עַמִּים מִישֹׁר, וּלְאֻמִּים בָּאָרֶץ תַּנְחֵם סֶלָה: יוֹדוּךָ עַמִּים אֱלֹהִים, יוֹדוּךָ עַמִּים כֻּלָּם: אֶרֶץ נָתְנָה יְבוּלָהּ, יְבָרְכֵנוּ אֱלֹהִים אֱלֹהֵינוּ: יְבָרְכֵנוּ אֱלֹהִים, וְיִירְאוּ אוֹתוֹ כָּל־אַפְסֵי־אָרֶץ:

The service continues with מעריב לחול *on page 313.*

MOTZA'EI SHABBAT

At the conclusion of the Amida on Motza'ei Shabbat (except when Yom Tov or Erev Pesaḥ falls in the following week), the Leader continues with Half Kaddish below, then "May the pleasantness."

HALF KADDISH

Leader: יִתְגַּדַּל Magnified and sanctified may His great name be,
in the world He created by His will.
May He establish His kingdom
in your lifetime and in your days,
and in the lifetime of all the house of Israel,
swiftly and soon –
and say: Amen.

All: May His great name be blessed for ever and all time.

Leader: Blessed and praised, glorified and elevated,
raised and honored, uplifted and praised
be the name of the Holy One,
blessed be He,
beyond any blessing, song,
praise and consolation
uttered in the world –
and say: Amen.

וִיהִי נֹעַם May the pleasantness of the Lord our God be upon us. *Ps. 90*
Establish for us the work of our hands, O establish the work of our hands.

יֹשֵׁב He who lives in the shelter of the Most High lives in the shadow *Ps. 91*
of the Almighty. I say of the Lord, my Refuge and Stronghold, my God in whom I trust, that He will save you from the hunter's trap and the deadly disease. With His outstretched limbs He will cover you, and beneath His wings you will find shelter; His truthfulness is an encircling shield. You need not fear terror by night, nor the

מוצאי שבת

At the conclusion of the עמידה *on* מוצאי שבת *(except when* יום טוב *or* ערב פסח *falls in the following week), the* שליח ציבור *continues with* חצי קדיש *below, then* וִיהִי נֹעַם.

חצי קדיש

ש״ץ: יִתְגַּדַּל וְיִתְקַדַּשׁ שְׁמֵהּ רַבָּא (קהל: אָמֵן)
בְּעָלְמָא דִּי בְרָא כִרְעוּתֵהּ
וְיַמְלִיךְ מַלְכוּתֵהּ
בְּחַיֵּיכוֹן וּבְיוֹמֵיכוֹן וּבְחַיֵּי דְכָל בֵּית יִשְׂרָאֵל
בַּעֲגָלָא וּבִזְמַן קָרִיב, וְאִמְרוּ אָמֵן. (קהל: אָמֵן)

קהל וש״ץ: יְהֵא שְׁמֵהּ רַבָּא מְבָרַךְ לְעָלַם וּלְעָלְמֵי עָלְמַיָּא.

ש״ץ: יִתְבָּרַךְ וְיִשְׁתַּבַּח וְיִתְפָּאַר וְיִתְרוֹמַם וְיִתְנַשֵּׂא
וְיִתְהַדָּר וְיִתְעַלֶּה וְיִתְהַלָּל
שְׁמֵהּ דְּקֻדְשָׁא בְּרִיךְ הוּא (קהל: בְּרִיךְ הוּא)
לְעֵלָּא מִן כָּל בִּרְכָתָא
/בעשרת ימי תשובה: לְעֵלָּא לְעֵלָּא מִכָּל בִּרְכָתָא/
וְשִׁירָתָא, תֻּשְׁבְּחָתָא וְנֶחָמָתָא
דַּאֲמִירָן בְּעָלְמָא, וְאִמְרוּ אָמֵן. (קהל: אָמֵן)

וִיהִי נֹעַם אֲדֹנָי אֱלֹהֵינוּ עָלֵינוּ וּמַעֲשֵׂה יָדֵינוּ כּוֹנְנָה עָלֵינוּ וּמַעֲשֵׂה תהלים צ
יָדֵינוּ כּוֹנְנֵהוּ:

ישֵׁב בְּסֵתֶר עֶלְיוֹן, בְּצֵל שַׁדַּי יִתְלוֹנָן: אֹמַר לַיהוה מַחְסִי וּמְצוּדָתִי, תהלים צא
אֱלֹהַי אֶבְטַח־בּוֹ: כִּי הוּא יַצִּילְךָ מִפַּח יָקוּשׁ, מִדֶּבֶר הַוּוֹת:
בְּאֶבְרָתוֹ יָסֶךְ לָךְ, וְתַחַת־כְּנָפָיו תֶּחְסֶה, צִנָּה וְסֹחֵרָה אֲמִתּוֹ:
לֹא־תִירָא מִפַּחַד לָיְלָה, מֵחֵץ יָעוּף יוֹמָם: מִדֶּבֶר בָּאֹפֶל יַהֲלֹךְ,

arrow that flies by day; not the disease that stalks in darkness, nor the plague that ravages at noon. A thousand may fall at your side, ten thousand at your right hand, but it will not come near you. You will only look with your eyes and see the punishment of the wicked. Because you said, "The LORD is my Refuge," taking the Most High as your shelter, no harm will befall you, no plague come near your tent, for He will command His angels about you, to guard you in all your ways. They will lift you in their hands, lest your foot stumble on a stone. You will tread on lions and vipers; you will trample on young lions and snakes. [God says:] "Because he loves Me, I will rescue him; I will protect him, because he acknowledges My name. When he calls on Me, I will answer him; I will be with him in distress, I will deliver him and bring him honor.
▸ With long life I will satisfy him and show him My salvation.
With long life I will satisfy him and show him My salvation.

▸ You are the Holy One, enthroned on the praises of Israel. *Ps. 22*
And [the angels] call to one another, saying,
"Holy, holy, holy is the LORD of multitudes; *Is. 6*
the whole world is filled with His glory."

And they receive permission from one another, saying: *Targum Yonatan Is. 6*
"Holy in the highest heavens, home of His Presence;
holy on earth, the work of His strength;
holy for ever and all time is the LORD of multitudes;
the whole earth is full of His radiant glory."

▸ Then a wind lifted me up *Ezek. 3*
and I heard behind me the sound of a great noise, saying,
"Blessed is the LORD's glory from His place."

Then a wind lifted me up and I heard behind me *Targum Yonatan Ezek. 3*
the sound of a great tempest of those who uttered praise, saying,
"Blessed is the LORD's glory from the place of the home of His Presence."

The LORD shall reign for ever and all time. *Ex. 15*
The LORD's kingdom is established for ever and all time. *Targum Onkelos Ex. 15*

מִקֶּטֶב יָשׁוּד צָהֳרָיִם: יִפֹּל מִצִּדְּךָ אֶלֶף, וּרְבָבָה מִימִינֶךָ, אֵלֶיךָ
לֹא יִגָּשׁ: רַק בְּעֵינֶיךָ תַבִּיט, וְשִׁלֻּמַת רְשָׁעִים תִּרְאֶה: כִּי־אַתָּה
יהוה מַחְסִי, עֶלְיוֹן שַׂמְתָּ מְעוֹנֶךָ: לֹא־תְאֻנֶּה אֵלֶיךָ רָעָה, וְנֶגַע
לֹא־יִקְרַב בְּאָהֳלֶךָ: כִּי מַלְאָכָיו יְצַוֶּה־לָּךְ, לִשְׁמָרְךָ בְּכָל־דְּרָכֶיךָ:
עַל־כַּפַּיִם יִשָּׂאוּנְךָ, פֶּן־תִּגֹּף בָּאֶבֶן רַגְלֶךָ: עַל־שַׁחַל וָפֶתֶן תִּדְרֹךְ,
תִּרְמֹס כְּפִיר וְתַנִּין: כִּי בִי חָשַׁק וַאֲפַלְּטֵהוּ, אֲשַׂגְּבֵהוּ כִּי־יָדַע
שְׁמִי: יִקְרָאֵנִי וְאֶעֱנֵהוּ, עִמּוֹ אָנֹכִי בְצָרָה, אֲחַלְּצֵהוּ וַאֲכַבְּדֵהוּ:
◂ אֹרֶךְ יָמִים אַשְׂבִּיעֵהוּ, וְאַרְאֵהוּ בִּישׁוּעָתִי:
אֹרֶךְ יָמִים אַשְׂבִּיעֵהוּ, וְאַרְאֵהוּ בִּישׁוּעָתִי:

◂ וְאַתָּה קָדוֹשׁ יוֹשֵׁב תְּהִלּוֹת יִשְׂרָאֵל: תהלים כב
וְקָרָא זֶה אֶל־זֶה וְאָמַר
קָדוֹשׁ, קָדוֹשׁ, קָדוֹשׁ, יהוה צְבָאוֹת, מְלֹא כָל־הָאָרֶץ כְּבוֹדוֹ: ישעיה ו
וּמְקַבְּלִין דֵּין מִן דֵּין וְאָמְרִין תרגום יונתן ישעיה ו
קַדִּישׁ בִּשְׁמֵי מְרוֹמָא עִלָּאָה בֵּית שְׁכִינְתֵהּ
קַדִּישׁ עַל אַרְעָא עוֹבַד גְּבוּרְתֵהּ
קַדִּישׁ לְעָלַם וּלְעָלְמֵי עָלְמַיָּא
יהוה צְבָאוֹת, מַלְיָא כָל אַרְעָא זִיו יְקָרֵהּ.

◂ וַתִּשָּׂאֵנִי רוּחַ, וָאֶשְׁמַע אַחֲרַי קוֹל רַעַשׁ גָּדוֹל יחזקאל ג
בָּרוּךְ כְּבוֹד־יהוה מִמְּקוֹמוֹ:
וּנְטָלַתְנִי רוּחָא, וְשִׁמְעֵית בַּתְרַי קָל זִיעַ סַגִּיא, דִּמְשַׁבְּחִין וְאָמְרִין תרגום יונתן יחזקאל ג
בְּרִיךְ יְקָרָא דַיהוה מֵאֲתַר בֵּית שְׁכִינְתֵהּ.

יהוה יִמְלֹךְ לְעֹלָם וָעֶד: שמות טו
יהוה מַלְכוּתֵהּ קָאֵם לְעָלַם וּלְעָלְמֵי עָלְמַיָּא. תרגום אונקלוס שמות טו

יהוה Lord, God of Abraham, Isaac and Yisrael, our ancestors, may *1 Chr. 29*
You keep this for ever so that it forms the thoughts in Your people's
heart, and directs their heart toward You. He is compassionate. He *Ps. 78*
forgives wrongdoing and does not destroy. Repeatedly He sup-
presses His anger, not rousing His full fury. For You, my Lord, are *Ps. 86*
good and forgiving, generously kind to all who call on You. Your *Ps. 119*
righteousness is eternally righteous, and Your Torah is truth. Give *Micah 7*
truth to Jacob, loving-kindness to Abraham, as You promised our
ancestors in ancient times. Blessed is my Lord for day after day *Ps. 68*
He burdens us [with His blessings]; God is our salvation, Selah!
The Lord of multitudes is with us; the God of Jacob is our refuge, *Ps. 46*
Selah! Lord of multitudes, happy is the one who trusts in You. *Ps. 84*
Lord, save! May the King answer us on the day we call. *Ps. 20*

בָּרוּךְ Blessed is He, our God, who created us for His glory, separating us from those who go astray; who gave us the Torah of truth, planting within us eternal life. May He open our heart to His Torah, imbuing our heart with the love and awe of Him, that we may do His will and serve Him with a perfect heart, so that we neither toil in vain nor give birth to confusion.

יְהִי רָצוֹן May it be Your will, O Lord our God and God of our ances-
tors, that we keep Your laws in this world, and thus be worthy to
live, see and inherit goodness and blessing in the Messianic Age
and in the life of the World to Come. So that my soul may sing to *Ps. 30*
You and not be silent. Lord, my God, for ever I will thank You.
Blessed is the man who trusts in the Lord, whose trust is in the *Jer. 17*
Lord alone. Trust in the Lord for evermore, for God, the Lord, is *Is. 26*
an everlasting Rock. ▸ Those who know Your name trust in You, for *Ps. 9*
You, Lord, do not abandon those who seek You. The Lord desired, *Is. 42*
for the sake of Israel's merit, to make the Torah great and glorious.

יהוה אֱלֹהֵי אַבְרָהָם יִצְחָק וְיִשְׂרָאֵל אֲבֹתֵינוּ, שָׁמְרָה־זֹּאת לְעוֹלָם   דברי הימים א׳ כט
לְיֵצֶר מַחְשְׁבוֹת לְבַב עַמֶּךָ, וְהָכֵן לְבָבָם אֵלֶיךָ: וְהוּא רַחוּם יְכַפֵּר   תהלים עח
עָוֹן וְלֹא־יַשְׁחִית, וְהִרְבָּה לְהָשִׁיב אַפּוֹ, וְלֹא־יָעִיר כָּל־חֲמָתוֹ:
כִּי־אַתָּה אֲדֹנָי טוֹב וְסַלָּח, וְרַב־חֶסֶד לְכָל־קֹרְאֶיךָ: צִדְקָתְךָ   תהלים פו תהלים קיט
צֶדֶק לְעוֹלָם וְתוֹרָתְךָ אֱמֶת: תִּתֵּן אֱמֶת לְיַעֲקֹב, חֶסֶד לְאַבְרָהָם,   מיכה ז
אֲשֶׁר־נִשְׁבַּעְתָּ לַאֲבֹתֵינוּ מִימֵי קֶדֶם: בָּרוּךְ אֲדֹנָי יוֹם יוֹם יַעֲמָס־   תהלים סח
לָנוּ, הָאֵל יְשׁוּעָתֵנוּ סֶלָה: יהוה צְבָאוֹת עִמָּנוּ, מִשְׂגָּב לָנוּ אֱלֹהֵי   תהלים מו
יַעֲקֹב סֶלָה: יהוה צְבָאוֹת, אַשְׁרֵי אָדָם בֹּטֵחַ בָּךְ: יהוה הוֹשִׁיעָה,   תהלים פד תהלים כ
הַמֶּלֶךְ יַעֲנֵנוּ בְיוֹם־קָרְאֵנוּ:

בָּרוּךְ הוּא אֱלֹהֵינוּ שֶׁבְּרָאָנוּ לִכְבוֹדוֹ, וְהִבְדִּילָנוּ מִן הַתּוֹעִים, וְנָתַן לָנוּ תּוֹרַת אֱמֶת, וְחַיֵּי עוֹלָם נָטַע בְּתוֹכֵנוּ. הוּא יִפְתַּח לִבֵּנוּ בְּתוֹרָתוֹ, וְיָשֵׂם בְּלִבֵּנוּ אַהֲבָתוֹ וְיִרְאָתוֹ וְלַעֲשׂוֹת רְצוֹנוֹ וּלְעָבְדוֹ בְּלֵבָב שָׁלֵם, לְמַעַן לֹא נִיגַע לָרִיק וְלֹא נֵלֵד לַבֶּהָלָה.

יְהִי רָצוֹן מִלְּפָנֶיךָ יהוה אֱלֹהֵינוּ וֵאלֹהֵי אֲבוֹתֵינוּ, שֶׁנִּשְׁמֹר חֻקֶּיךָ
בָּעוֹלָם הַזֶּה, וְנִזְכֶּה וְנִחְיֶה וְנִרְאֶה וְנִירַשׁ טוֹבָה וּבְרָכָה, לִשְׁנֵי
יְמוֹת הַמָּשִׁיחַ וּלְחַיֵּי הָעוֹלָם הַבָּא. לְמַעַן יְזַמֶּרְךָ כָבוֹד וְלֹא יִדֹּם,   תהלים ל
יהוה אֱלֹהַי, לְעוֹלָם אוֹדֶךָּ: בָּרוּךְ הַגֶּבֶר אֲשֶׁר יִבְטַח בַּיהוה,   ירמיה יז
וְהָיָה יהוה מִבְטַחוֹ: בִּטְחוּ בַיהוה עֲדֵי־עַד, כִּי בְּיָהּ יהוה צוּר   ישעיה כו
עוֹלָמִים: ‹ וְיִבְטְחוּ בְךָ יוֹדְעֵי שְׁמֶךָ, כִּי לֹא־עָזַבְתָּ דֹרְשֶׁיךָ, יהוה: תהלים ט
יהוה חָפֵץ לְמַעַן צִדְקוֹ, יַגְדִּיל תּוֹרָה וְיַאְדִּיר: ישעיה מב

FULL KADDISH

Leader: יִתְגַּדַּל Magnified and sanctified may His great name be,
in the world He created by His will.
May He establish His kingdom in your lifetime
and in your days,
and in the lifetime of all the house of Israel,
swiftly and soon –
and say: Amen.

All: May His great name be blessed for ever and all time.

Leader: Blessed and praised,
glorified and elevated,
raised and honored,
uplifted and praised
be the name of the Holy One,
blessed be He,
beyond any blessing,
song, praise and consolation uttered in the world –
and say: Amen.

On Purim and Tisha B'Av, omit the next verse and continue with "May there be great peace."

May the prayers and pleas of all Israel
be accepted by their Father in heaven –
and say: Amen.

May there be great peace from heaven,
and life for us and all Israel –
and say: Amen.

Bow, take three steps back, as if taking leave of the Divine Presence, then bow, first left, then right, then center, while saying:

May He who makes peace in His high places,
make peace for us and all Israel –
and say: Amen.

קדיש שלם

ש״ץ: יִתְגַּדַּל וְיִתְקַדַּשׁ שְׁמֵהּ רַבָּא (קהל: אָמֵן)
בְּעָלְמָא דִּי בְרָא כִרְעוּתֵהּ
וְיַמְלִיךְ מַלְכוּתֵהּ
בְּחַיֵּיכוֹן וּבְיוֹמֵיכוֹן וּבְחַיֵּי דְכָל בֵּית יִשְׂרָאֵל
בַּעֲגָלָא וּבִזְמַן קָרִיב, וְאִמְרוּ אָמֵן. (קהל: אָמֵן)

קהל וש״ץ: יְהֵא שְׁמֵהּ רַבָּא מְבָרַךְ לְעָלַם וּלְעָלְמֵי עָלְמַיָּא.

ש״ץ: יִתְבָּרַךְ וְיִשְׁתַּבַּח וְיִתְפָּאַר
וְיִתְרוֹמַם וְיִתְנַשֵּׂא וְיִתְהַדָּר וְיִתְעַלֶּה וְיִתְהַלָּל
שְׁמֵהּ דְּקֻדְשָׁא בְּרִיךְ הוּא (קהל: בְּרִיךְ הוּא)
לְעֵלָּא מִן כָּל בִּרְכָתָא
/בעשרת ימי תשובה: לְעֵלָּא לְעֵלָּא מִכָּל בִּרְכָתָא/
וְשִׁירָתָא, תֻּשְׁבְּחָתָא וְנֶחֱמָתָא
דַּאֲמִירָן בְּעָלְמָא, וְאִמְרוּ אָמֵן. (קהל: אָמֵן)

On פורים *and* תשעה באב*, omit the next verse and continue with* יְהֵא שְׁלָמָא*.*

תִּתְקַבַּל צְלוֹתְהוֹן וּבָעוּתְהוֹן דְּכָל יִשְׂרָאֵל
קֳדָם אֲבוּהוֹן דִּי בִשְׁמַיָּא, וְאִמְרוּ אָמֵן. (קהל: אָמֵן)

יְהֵא שְׁלָמָא רַבָּא מִן שְׁמַיָּא
וְחַיִּים, עָלֵינוּ וְעַל כָּל יִשְׂרָאֵל, וְאִמְרוּ אָמֵן. (קהל: אָמֵן)

Bow, take three steps back, as if taking leave of the Divine Presence, then bow, first left, then right, then center, while saying:

עֹשֶׂה שָׁלוֹם/ בעשרת ימי תשובה: הַשָּׁלוֹם/ בִּמְרוֹמָיו
הוּא יַעֲשֶׂה שָׁלוֹם עָלֵינוּ וְעַל כָּל יִשְׂרָאֵל
וְאִמְרוּ אָמֵן. (קהל: אָמֵן)

Between Pesaḥ and Shavuot the Omer is counted at this point on page 356.
On Ḥanukka, the candles are lit at this point, page 940.
On Tisha B'Av, the following prayers are omitted
and the service continues with Aleinu on page 386.

BIBLICAL VERSES OF BLESSING

וַיִּתֶּן־לְךָ May God give you dew from heaven and the richness of the earth, and *Gen. 27*
corn and wine in plenty. May peoples serve you and nations bow down to you.
Be lord over your brothers, and may your mother's sons bow down to you. A
curse on those who curse you, but a blessing on those who bless you.

וְאֵל שַׁדַּי May God Almighty bless you; may He make you fruitful and numerous *Gen. 28*
until you become an assembly of peoples. May He give you and your descen-
dants the blessing of Abraham, that you may possess the land where you are
now staying, the land God gave to Abraham. This comes from the God of your *Gen. 49*
father – may He help you – and from the Almighty – may He bless you with
blessings of the heaven above and the blessings of the deep that lies below, the
blessings of breast and womb. The blessings of your father surpass the blessings
of my fathers to the bounds of the endless hills. May they rest on the head of
Joseph, on the brow of the prince among his brothers. He will love you and bless *Deut. 7*
you and increase your numbers. He will bless the fruit of your womb and the
fruit of your land: your corn, your wine and oil, the calves of your herds and
the lambs of your flocks, in the land He swore to your fathers to give you. You
will be blessed more than any other people. None of your men or women will
be childless, nor any of your livestock without young. The LORD will keep you
free from any disease. He will not inflict on you the terrible diseases you knew
in Egypt, but He will inflict them on those who hate you.

הַמַּלְאָךְ May the angel who rescued me from all harm, bless these boys. May they *Gen. 48*
be called by my name and the names of my fathers Abraham and Isaac, and may
they increase greatly on the earth. The LORD your God has increased your num- *Deut. 1*
bers so that today you are as many as the stars in the sky. May the LORD, God of
your fathers, increase you a thousand times, and bless you as He promised you.

בָּרוּךְ You will be blessed in the city, and blessed in the field. You will be blessed *Deut. 28*
when you come in, and blessed when you go out. Your basket and your kneading
trough will be blessed. The fruit of your womb will be blessed, and the crops
of your land, and the young of your livestock, the calves of your herds and the
lambs of your flocks. The LORD will send a blessing on your barns, and on ev-
erything you put your hand to. The LORD your God will bless you in the land
He is giving you. The LORD will open for you the heavens, the storehouse of
His bounty, to send rain on your land in season, and to bless all the work of your
hands. You will lend to many nations but will borrow from none. For the LORD *Deut. 15*

Between פסח and שבועות the עומר is counted at this point on page 357.

On חנוכה, the candles are lit at this point, page 941.

On תשעה באב, the following prayers are omitted
and the service continues with עָלֵינוּ on page 387.

פסוקי ברכה

בראשית כז וְיִתֶּן־לְךָ הָאֱלֹהִים מִטַּל הַשָּׁמַיִם וּמִשְׁמַנֵּי הָאָרֶץ, וְרֹב דָּגָן וְתִירֹשׁ: יַעַבְדוּךָ
עַמִּים וְיִשְׁתַּחֲוֻ לְךָ לְאֻמִּים, הֱוֵה גְבִיר לְאַחֶיךָ וְיִשְׁתַּחֲווּ לְךָ בְּנֵי אִמֶּךָ,
אֹרְרֶיךָ אָרוּר וּמְבָרְכֶיךָ בָּרוּךְ:

בראשית כח וְאֵל שַׁדַּי יְבָרֵךְ אֹתְךָ וְיַפְרְךָ וְיַרְבֶּךָ, וְהָיִיתָ לִקְהַל עַמִּים: וְיִתֶּן־לְךָ אֶת־
בִּרְכַּת אַבְרָהָם, לְךָ וּלְזַרְעֲךָ אִתָּךְ, לְרִשְׁתְּךָ אֶת־אֶרֶץ מְגֻרֶיךָ אֲשֶׁר־נָתַן
בראשית מט אֱלֹהִים לְאַבְרָהָם: מֵאֵל אָבִיךָ וְיַעְזְרֶךָּ וְאֵת שַׁדַּי וִיבָרְכֶךָּ, בִּרְכֹת שָׁמַיִם
מֵעָל, בִּרְכֹת תְּהוֹם רֹבֶצֶת תָּחַת, בִּרְכֹת שָׁדַיִם וָרָחַם: בִּרְכֹת אָבִיךָ גָּבְרוּ
עַל־בִּרְכֹת הוֹרַי עַד־תַּאֲוַת גִּבְעֹת עוֹלָם, תִּהְיֶיןָ לְרֹאשׁ יוֹסֵף וּלְקָדְקֹד
דברים ז נְזִיר אֶחָיו: וַאֲהֵבְךָ וּבֵרַכְךָ וְהִרְבֶּךָ, וּבֵרַךְ פְּרִי־בִטְנְךָ וּפְרִי־אַדְמָתֶךָ, דְּגָנְךָ
וְתִירֹשְׁךָ וְיִצְהָרֶךָ, שְׁגַר־אֲלָפֶיךָ וְעַשְׁתְּרֹת צֹאנֶךָ, עַל הָאֲדָמָה אֲשֶׁר־נִשְׁבַּע
לַאֲבֹתֶיךָ לָתֶת לָךְ: בָּרוּךְ תִּהְיֶה מִכָּל־הָעַמִּים, לֹא־יִהְיֶה בְךָ עָקָר וַעֲקָרָה
וּבִבְהֶמְתֶּךָ: וְהֵסִיר יהוה מִמְּךָ כָּל־חֹלִי, וְכָל־מַדְוֵי מִצְרַיִם הָרָעִים אֲשֶׁר
יָדַעְתָּ, לֹא יְשִׂימָם בָּךְ, וּנְתָנָם בְּכָל־שֹׂנְאֶיךָ:

בראשית מח הַמַּלְאָךְ הַגֹּאֵל אֹתִי מִכָּל־רָע יְבָרֵךְ אֶת־הַנְּעָרִים, וְיִקָּרֵא בָהֶם שְׁמִי וְשֵׁם
דברים א אֲבֹתַי אַבְרָהָם וְיִצְחָק, וְיִדְגּוּ לָרֹב בְּקֶרֶב הָאָרֶץ: יהוה אֱלֹהֵיכֶם הִרְבָּה
אֶתְכֶם, וְהִנְּכֶם הַיּוֹם כְּכוֹכְבֵי הַשָּׁמַיִם לָרֹב: יהוה אֱלֹהֵי אֲבוֹתֵכֶם יֹסֵף
עֲלֵיכֶם כָּכֶם אֶלֶף פְּעָמִים, וִיבָרֵךְ אֶתְכֶם כַּאֲשֶׁר דִּבֶּר לָכֶם:

דברים כח בָּרוּךְ אַתָּה בָּעִיר, וּבָרוּךְ אַתָּה בַּשָּׂדֶה: בָּרוּךְ אַתָּה בְּבֹאֶךָ, וּבָרוּךְ אַתָּה
בְּצֵאתֶךָ: בָּרוּךְ טַנְאֲךָ וּמִשְׁאַרְתֶּךָ: בָּרוּךְ פְּרִי־בִטְנְךָ וּפְרִי אַדְמָתְךָ וּפְרִי
בְהֶמְתֶּךָ, שְׁגַר אֲלָפֶיךָ וְעַשְׁתְּרוֹת צֹאנֶךָ: יְצַו יהוה אִתְּךָ אֶת־הַבְּרָכָה
בַּאֲסָמֶיךָ וּבְכֹל מִשְׁלַח יָדֶךָ, וּבֵרַכְךָ בָּאָרֶץ אֲשֶׁר־יהוה אֱלֹהֶיךָ נֹתֵן לָךְ:
יִפְתַּח יהוה לְךָ אֶת־אוֹצָרוֹ הַטּוֹב אֶת־הַשָּׁמַיִם, לָתֵת מְטַר־אַרְצְךָ בְּעִתּוֹ,
דברים טו וּלְבָרֵךְ אֵת כָּל־מַעֲשֵׂה יָדֶךָ, וְהִלְוִיתָ גּוֹיִם רַבִּים וְאַתָּה לֹא תִלְוֶה: כִּי־יהוה

your God will bless you as He has promised: you will lend to many nations but
will borrow from none. You will rule over many nations, but none will rule over
you. Happy are you, Israel! Who is like you, a people saved by the LORD? He *Deut. 33*
is your Shield and Helper and your glorious Sword. Your enemies will cower
before you, and you will tread on their high places.

מָחִיתִי I have wiped away your crimes like a cloud, your sins like the morning *Is. 44*
mist. Return to Me for I have redeemed you. Sing for joy, O heavens, for the
LORD has done this; shout aloud, you depths of the earth; burst into song, you
mountains, you forests and all your trees, for the LORD has redeemed Jacob,
and will glory in Israel. Our Redeemer, the LORD of multitudes is His name, *Is. 47*
the Holy One of Israel.

יִשְׂרָאֵל Israel is saved by the LORD with everlasting salvation. You will never be *Is. 45*
ashamed or disgraced to time everlasting. You will eat your fill and praise the *Joel 2*
name of the LORD your God, who has worked wonders for you. Never again
shall My people be shamed. Then you will know that I am in the midst of Israel,
that I am the LORD your God, and there is no other. Never again will My people
be shamed. You will go out in joy and be led out in peace. The mountains and *Is. 55*
hills will burst into song before you, and all the trees of the field will clap their
hands. Behold, God is my salvation, I will trust and not be afraid. The LORD, *Is. 12*
the LORD, is my strength and my song. He has become my salvation. With
joy you will draw water from the springs of salvation. On that day you will say,
"Thank the LORD, declare His name, make His deeds known among the nations."
Declare that His name is great. Sing to the LORD, for He has done glorious
things; let this be known throughout the world. Shout aloud and sing for joy,
you who live in Zion, for great in your midst is the Holy One of Israel. On that *Is. 25*
day they will say, "See, this is our God; we set our hope in Him and He saved us.
This is the LORD in whom we hoped; let us rejoice and be glad in His salvation."

בֵּית Come, house of Jacob: let us walk in the light of the LORD. He will be the *Is. 2* *Is. 32*
sure foundation of your times; a rich store of salvation, wisdom and knowl-
edge – the fear of the LORD is a person's treasure. In everything he did, David *1 Sam. 18*
was successful, for the LORD was with him.

פָּדָה He redeemed my soul in peace from the battle waged against me, for the *Ps. 55*
sake of the many who were with me. The people said to Saul, "Shall Jonathan *1 Sam. 14*
die – he who has brought about this great deliverance in Israel? Heaven forbid!
As surely as the LORD lives, not a hair of his head shall fall to the ground, for he
did this today with God's help." So the people rescued Jonathan and he did not
die. Those redeemed by the LORD shall return; they will enter Zion singing; *Is. 35*
everlasting joy will crown their heads. Gladness and joy will overtake them, and
sorrow and sighing will flee away.

אֱלֹהֶיךָ בֵּרַכְךָ כַּאֲשֶׁר דִּבֶּר־לָךְ, וְהַעֲבַטְתָּ גּוֹיִם רַבִּים וְאַתָּה לֹא תַעֲבֹט,
וּמָשַׁלְתָּ בְּגוֹיִם רַבִּים וּבְךָ לֹא יִמְשֹׁלוּ: אַשְׁרֶיךָ יִשְׂרָאֵל, מִי כָמוֹךָ, עַם דברים לג
נוֹשַׁע בַּיהוה, מָגֵן עֶזְרֶךָ וַאֲשֶׁר־חֶרֶב גַּאֲוָתֶךָ, וְיִכָּחֲשׁוּ אֹיְבֶיךָ לָךְ, וְאַתָּה
עַל־בָּמוֹתֵימוֹ תִדְרֹךְ:

מָחִיתִי כָעָב פְּשָׁעֶיךָ וְכֶעָנָן חַטֹּאותֶיךָ, שׁוּבָה אֵלַי כִּי גְאַלְתִּיךָ: רָנּוּ שָׁמַיִם ישעיה מד
כִּי־עָשָׂה יהוה, הָרִיעוּ תַּחְתִּיּוֹת אָרֶץ, פִּצְחוּ הָרִים רִנָּה, יַעַר וְכָל־עֵץ בּוֹ,
כִּי־גָאַל יהוה יַעֲקֹב וּבְיִשְׂרָאֵל יִתְפָּאָר: גֹּאֲלֵנוּ, יהוה צְבָאוֹת שְׁמוֹ, קְדוֹשׁ ישעיה מז
יִשְׂרָאֵל:

יִשְׂרָאֵל נוֹשַׁע בַּיהוה תְּשׁוּעַת עוֹלָמִים, לֹא־תֵבֹשׁוּ וְלֹא־תִכָּלְמוּ עַד־עוֹלְמֵי ישעיה מה
עַד: וַאֲכַלְתֶּם אָכוֹל וְשָׂבוֹעַ, וְהִלַּלְתֶּם אֶת־שֵׁם יהוה אֱלֹהֵיכֶם אֲשֶׁר־עָשָׂה יואל ב
עִמָּכֶם לְהַפְלִיא, וְלֹא־יֵבֹשׁוּ עַמִּי לְעוֹלָם: וִידַעְתֶּם כִּי בְקֶרֶב יִשְׂרָאֵל
אָנִי, וַאֲנִי יהוה אֱלֹהֵיכֶם וְאֵין עוֹד, וְלֹא־יֵבֹשׁוּ עַמִּי לְעוֹלָם: כִּי־בְשִׂמְחָה ישעיה נה
תֵצֵאוּ וּבְשָׁלוֹם תּוּבָלוּן, הֶהָרִים וְהַגְּבָעוֹת יִפְצְחוּ לִפְנֵיכֶם רִנָּה, וְכָל־עֲצֵי
הַשָּׂדֶה יִמְחֲאוּ־כָף: הִנֵּה אֵל יְשׁוּעָתִי אֶבְטַח, וְלֹא אֶפְחָד, כִּי־עָזִּי וְזִמְרָת ישעיה יב
יָהּ יהוה, וַיְהִי־לִי לִישׁוּעָה: וּשְׁאַבְתֶּם־מַיִם בְּשָׂשׂוֹן, מִמַּעַיְנֵי הַיְשׁוּעָה:
וַאֲמַרְתֶּם בַּיּוֹם הַהוּא, הוֹדוּ לַיהוה קִרְאוּ בִשְׁמוֹ, הוֹדִיעוּ בָעַמִּים עֲלִילֹתָיו,
הַזְכִּירוּ כִּי נִשְׂגָּב שְׁמוֹ: זַמְּרוּ יהוה כִּי גֵאוּת עָשָׂה, מוּדַעַת זֹאת בְּכָל־
הָאָרֶץ: צַהֲלִי וָרֹנִּי יוֹשֶׁבֶת צִיּוֹן, כִּי־גָדוֹל בְּקִרְבֵּךְ קְדוֹשׁ יִשְׂרָאֵל: וְאָמַר ישעיה כה
בַּיּוֹם הַהוּא, הִנֵּה אֱלֹהֵינוּ זֶה קִוִּינוּ לוֹ וְיוֹשִׁיעֵנוּ, זֶה יהוה קִוִּינוּ לוֹ, נָגִילָה
וְנִשְׂמְחָה בִּישׁוּעָתוֹ:

בֵּית יַעֲקֹב לְכוּ וְנֵלְכָה בְּאוֹר יהוה: וְהָיָה אֱמוּנַת עִתֶּיךָ, חֹסֶן יְשׁוּעֹת חָכְמַת ישעיה ב ישעיה לב
וָדָעַת, יִרְאַת יהוה הִיא אוֹצָרוֹ: וַיְהִי דָוִד לְכָל־דְּרָכָו מַשְׂכִּיל, וַיהוה עִמּוֹ: שמואל א׳ יח

פָּדָה בְשָׁלוֹם נַפְשִׁי מִקְּרָב־לִי, כִּי־בְרַבִּים הָיוּ עִמָּדִי: וַיֹּאמֶר הָעָם אֶל־ תהלים נה שמואל א׳ יד
שָׁאוּל, הֲיוֹנָתָן יָמוּת אֲשֶׁר עָשָׂה הַיְשׁוּעָה הַגְּדוֹלָה הַזֹּאת בְּיִשְׂרָאֵל,
חָלִילָה, חַי־יהוה אִם־יִפֹּל מִשַּׂעֲרַת רֹאשׁוֹ אַרְצָה, כִּי־עִם־אֱלֹהִים עָשָׂה
הַיּוֹם הַזֶּה, וַיִּפְדּוּ הָעָם אֶת־יוֹנָתָן וְלֹא־מֵת: וּפְדוּיֵי יהוה יְשֻׁבוּן וּבָאוּ צִיּוֹן ישעיה לה
בְּרִנָּה, וְשִׂמְחַת עוֹלָם עַל־רֹאשָׁם, שָׂשׂוֹן וְשִׂמְחָה יַשִּׂיגוּ, וְנָסוּ יָגוֹן וַאֲנָחָה:

הָפַכְתָּ You have turned my sorrow into dancing. You have removed my sackcloth *Ps. 30*
and clothed me with joy. The LORD your God refused to listen to Balaam; in- *Deut. 23*
stead the LORD your God turned the curse into a blessing, for the LORD your
God loves you. Then maidens will dance and be glad; so too will young men and *Jer. 31*
old together; I will turn their mourning into gladness; I will give them comfort
and joy instead of sorrow.

בּוֹרֵא I create the speech of lips: Peace, peace to those far and near, says the LORD, *Is. 57*
and I will heal them. Then the spirit came upon Amasai, chief of the captains, *1 Chr. 12*
and he said: "We are yours, David! We are with you, son of Jesse! Peace, peace to
you, and peace to those who help you; for your God will help you." Then David
received them and made them leaders of his troop. And you shall say: "To life! *1 Sam. 25*
Peace be to you, peace to your household, and peace to all that is yours!" The *Ps. 29*
LORD will give strength to His people; the LORD will bless His people with peace.

אָמַר Rabbi Yoḥanan said: Wherever you find the greatness of the Holy One, *Megilla 31a*
blessed be He, there you find His humility. This is written in the Torah, repeated
in the Prophets, and stated a third time in the Writings. It is written in the
Torah: "For the LORD your God is God of gods and LORD of lords, the great, *Deut. 10*
mighty and awe-inspiring God, who shows no favoritism and accepts no bribe."
Immediately afterwards it is written, "He upholds the cause of the orphan and
widow, and loves the stranger, giving him food and clothing." It is repeated in
the Prophets, as it says: "So says the High and Great One, who lives for ever and *Is. 57*
whose name is Holy: I live in a high and holy place, but also with the contrite
and lowly in spirit, to revive the spirit of the lowly, and to revive the heart of
the contrite." It is stated a third time in the Writings: "Sing to God, make music *Ps. 68*
for His name, extol Him who rides the clouds – the LORD is His name – and
celebrate before Him." Immediately afterwards it is written: "Father of the orphans and Justice of widows, is God in His holy habitation."

יְהִי May the LORD our God be with us, as He was with our ancestors. May He *1 Kings 8*
never abandon us or forsake us. You who cleave to the LORD your God are all *Deut. 4*
alive this day. For the LORD will comfort Zion, He will comfort all her ruins; *Is. 51*
He will make her wilderness like Eden, and her desert like a garden of the LORD.
Joy and gladness will be found there, thanksgiving and the sound of singing. It *Is. 42*
pleased the LORD for the sake of [Israel's] righteousness to make the Torah
great and glorious.

שִׁיר הַמַּעֲלוֹת A song of ascents. Happy are all who fear the LORD, who walk in His *Ps. 128*
ways. When you eat the fruit of your labor, happy and fortunate are you. Your wife shall be like a fruitful vine within your house; your sons like olive saplings around your table. So shall the man who fears the LORD be blessed. May the LORD bless you from Zion; may you see the good of Jerusalem all the days of your life; and may you live to see your children's children. Peace be on Israel!

הָפַכְתָּ מִסְפְּדִי לְמָחוֹל לִי, פִּתַּחְתָּ שַׂקִּי, וַתְּאַזְּרֵנִי שִׂמְחָה: וְלֹא־אָבָה יהוה (תהלים ל / דברים כג)
אֱלֹהֶיךָ לִשְׁמֹעַ אֶל־בִּלְעָם, וַיַּהֲפֹךְ יהוה אֱלֹהֶיךָ לְּךָ אֶת־הַקְּלָלָה לִבְרָכָה,
כִּי אֲהֵבְךָ יהוה אֱלֹהֶיךָ: אָז תִּשְׂמַח בְּתוּלָה בְּמָחוֹל, וּבַחֻרִים וּזְקֵנִים יַחְדָּו, (ירמיה לא)
וְהָפַכְתִּי אֶבְלָם לְשָׂשׂוֹן, וְנִחַמְתִּים, וְשִׂמַּחְתִּים מִיגוֹנָם:

בּוֹרֵא נִיב שְׂפָתָיִם, שָׁלוֹם שָׁלוֹם לָרָחוֹק וְלַקָּרוֹב אָמַר יהוה, וּרְפָאתִיו: וְרוּחַ (ישעיה נז / דברי הימים א׳ יב)
לָבְשָׁה אֶת־עֲמָשַׂי רֹאשׁ הַשָּׁלִישִׁים, לְךָ דָוִיד וְעִמְּךָ בֶן־יִשַׁי, שָׁלוֹם שָׁלוֹם
לְךָ וְשָׁלוֹם לְעֹזְרֶךָ, כִּי עֲזָרְךָ אֱלֹהֶיךָ, וַיְקַבְּלֵם דָּוִיד וַיִּתְּנֵם בְּרָאשֵׁי הַגְּדוּד:
וַאֲמַרְתֶּם כֹּה לֶחָי, וְאַתָּה שָׁלוֹם וּבֵיתְךָ שָׁלוֹם וְכֹל אֲשֶׁר־לְךָ שָׁלוֹם: יהוה (שמואל א׳ כה / תהלים כט)
עֹז לְעַמּוֹ יִתֵּן, יהוה יְבָרֵךְ אֶת־עַמּוֹ בַשָּׁלוֹם:

אָמַר רַבִּי יוֹחָנָן: בְּכָל מָקוֹם שֶׁאַתָּה מוֹצֵא גְּדֻלָּתוֹ שֶׁל הַקָּדוֹשׁ בָּרוּךְ (מגילה לא.)
הוּא, שָׁם אַתָּה מוֹצֵא עַנְוְתָנוּתוֹ. דָּבָר זֶה כָּתוּב בַּתּוֹרָה, וְשָׁנוּי בַּנְּבִיאִים,
וּמְשֻׁלָּשׁ בַּכְּתוּבִים. כָּתוּב בַּתּוֹרָה: כִּי יהוה אֱלֹהֵיכֶם הוּא אֱלֹהֵי הָאֱלֹהִים (דברים י)
וַאֲדֹנֵי הָאֲדֹנִים, הָאֵל הַגָּדֹל הַגִּבֹּר וְהַנּוֹרָא, אֲשֶׁר לֹא־יִשָּׂא פָנִים וְלֹא יִקַּח
שֹׁחַד: וּכְתִיב בַּתְרֵהּ: עֹשֶׂה מִשְׁפַּט יָתוֹם וְאַלְמָנָה, וְאֹהֵב גֵּר לָתֶת לוֹ לֶחֶם
וְשִׂמְלָה: שָׁנוּי בַּנְּבִיאִים, דִּכְתִיב: כִּי כֹה אָמַר רָם וְנִשָּׂא שֹׁכֵן עַד וְקָדוֹשׁ (ישעיה נז)
שְׁמוֹ, מָרוֹם וְקָדוֹשׁ אֶשְׁכּוֹן, וְאֶת־דַּכָּא וּשְׁפַל־רוּחַ, לְהַחֲיוֹת רוּחַ שְׁפָלִים
וּלְהַחֲיוֹת לֵב נִדְכָּאִים: מְשֻׁלָּשׁ בַּכְּתוּבִים, דִּכְתִיב: שִׁירוּ לֵאלֹהִים, זַמְּרוּ (תהלים סח)
שְׁמוֹ, סֹלּוּ לָרֹכֵב בָּעֲרָבוֹת בְּיָהּ שְׁמוֹ, וְעִלְזוּ לְפָנָיו: וּכְתִיב בַּתְרֵהּ: אֲבִי
יְתוֹמִים וְדַיַּן אַלְמָנוֹת, אֱלֹהִים בִּמְעוֹן קָדְשׁוֹ:

יְהִי יהוה אֱלֹהֵינוּ עִמָּנוּ כַּאֲשֶׁר הָיָה עִם־אֲבֹתֵינוּ, אַל־יַעַזְבֵנוּ וְאַל־יִטְּשֵׁנוּ: (מלכים א׳ ח)
וְאַתֶּם הַדְּבֵקִים בַּיהוה אֱלֹהֵיכֶם, חַיִּים כֻּלְּכֶם הַיּוֹם: כִּי־נִחַם יהוה צִיּוֹן, נִחַם (דברים ד / ישעיה נא)
כָּל־חָרְבֹתֶיהָ, וַיָּשֶׂם מִדְבָּרָהּ כְּעֵדֶן וְעַרְבָתָהּ כְּגַן־יהוה, שָׂשׂוֹן וְשִׂמְחָה יִמָּצֵא
בָהּ, תּוֹדָה וְקוֹל זִמְרָה: יהוה חָפֵץ לְמַעַן צִדְקוֹ, יַגְדִּיל תּוֹרָה וְיַאְדִּיר: (ישעיה מב)

שִׁיר הַמַּעֲלוֹת, אַשְׁרֵי כָּל־יְרֵא יהוה, הַהֹלֵךְ בִּדְרָכָיו: יְגִיעַ כַּפֶּיךָ כִּי תֹאכֵל, (תהלים קכח)
אַשְׁרֶיךָ וְטוֹב לָךְ: אֶשְׁתְּךָ כְּגֶפֶן פֹּרִיָּה בְּיַרְכְּתֵי בֵיתֶךָ, בָּנֶיךָ כִּשְׁתִלֵי זֵיתִים,
סָבִיב לְשֻׁלְחָנֶךָ: הִנֵּה כִי־כֵן יְבֹרַךְ גָּבֶר יְרֵא יהוה: יְבָרֶכְךָ יהוה מִצִּיּוֹן, וּרְאֵה
בְּטוּב יְרוּשָׁלָםִ, כֹּל יְמֵי חַיֶּיךָ: וּרְאֵה־בָנִים לְבָנֶיךָ, שָׁלוֹם עַל־יִשְׂרָאֵל:

HAVDALA

Some congregations begin Havdala at "Please pay attention" on the next page.
On Motza'ei Yom Tov that is not a Motza'ei Shabbat, the blessings for the spices and flame are omitted. At the end of Yom Kippur, only the blessing for the spices is omitted.

The Leader takes the cup of wine in his right hand, and says:

הִנֵּה Behold, God is my salvation. *Is. 12*
I will trust and not be afraid.
The LORD, the LORD, is my strength and my song.
He has become my salvation.
With joy you will draw water from the springs of salvation.
Salvation is the LORD's; *Ps. 3*
on Your people is Your blessing, Selah.
The LORD of multitudes is with us, *Ps. 46*
the God of Jacob is our stronghold, Selah.
LORD of multitudes: happy is the one who trusts in You. *Ps. 84*
LORD, save! May the King answer us on the day we call. *Ps. 20*
For the Jews there was light and gladness, joy and honor – *Esther 8*
so may it be for us.
I will lift the cup of salvation *Ps. 116*
and call on the name of the LORD.

LEARNING

Havdala is the separation ceremony which marks the end of Shabbat and the beginning of the week ahead. We recite Havdala with a glass of wine, sweet-smelling spices, and a multi-wicked flame. Most Jewish rituals are performed over wine to symbolize the importance of elevating physical things. The kabbalists explain that we smell the spices to revive ourselves from the loss of our extra soul that we receive on Shabbat. The flame represents unity and new light for the new week; just as Adam made fire after the loss of light from the first Shabbat in creation we light a candle to light the way for the new week ahead. Additionally, we use a candle with more than one wick. When Shabbat came in we lit two separate candles; we light a multi-wicked candle at the end of Shabbat as a symbol of hope Shabbat has helped us achieve. We hope that by the end of Shabbat we have taken all of our own separate candles and lights and merged them into one unified light.

הבדלה

Some congregations begin הבדלה *at* סַבְרִי מָרָנָן *on the next page.*
On מוצאי יום טוב *that is not a* מוצאי שבת*, the blessings for the spices and flame are omitted. At the end of* יום כפור*, only the blessing for the spices is omitted.*

The שליח ציבור *takes the cup of wine in his right hand, and says:*

ישעיה יב הִנֵּה אֵל יְשׁוּעָתִי אֶבְטַח, וְלֹא אֶפְחָד
כִּי־עָזִּי וְזִמְרָת יָהּ יהוה, וַיְהִי־לִי לִישׁוּעָה:
וּשְׁאַבְתֶּם־מַיִם בְּשָׂשׂוֹן, מִמַּעַיְנֵי הַיְשׁוּעָה:
תהלים ג לַיהוה הַיְשׁוּעָה, עַל־עַמְּךָ בִרְכָתֶךָ סֶּלָה:
תהלים מו יהוה צְבָאוֹת עִמָּנוּ, מִשְׂגָּב לָנוּ אֱלֹהֵי יַעֲקֹב סֶלָה:
תהלים פד יהוה צְבָאוֹת, אַשְׁרֵי אָדָם בֹּטֵחַ בָּךְ:
תהלים כ יהוה הוֹשִׁיעָה, הַמֶּלֶךְ יַעֲנֵנוּ בְיוֹם־קָרְאֵנוּ:
אסתר ח לַיְּהוּדִים הָיְתָה אוֹרָה וְשִׂמְחָה וְשָׂשֹׂן וִיקָר:
כֵּן תִּהְיֶה לָּנוּ.
תהלים קטז כּוֹס־יְשׁוּעוֹת אֶשָּׂא, וּבְשֵׁם יהוה אֶקְרָא:

... A THOUSAND WORDS

Please pay attention, my masters.

Blessed are You, Lord our God, King of the Universe,
who creates the fruit of the vine.

Holding the spice box, the Leader says:

Blessed are You, Lord our God, King of the Universe,
who creates the various spices.

The Leader smells the spices and puts the spice box down.

He lifts his hands toward the flame of the Havdala candle, and says:

Blessed are You, Lord our God, King of the Universe,
who creates the lights of fire.

He lifts the cup of wine in his right hand, and says:

Blessed are You, Lord our God, King of the Universe,
who distinguishes between sacred and secular,
between light and darkness, between Israel and the nations,
between the seventh day and the six days of work.
Blessed are You, Lord,
who distinguishes between sacred and secular.

On Sukkot, if Havdala is made in the sukka, add:

Blessed are You, Lord our God, King of the Universe,
who has made us holy through his commandments
and has commanded us to live in the sukka.

---

spaces and pockets of air within the straw. All this time the youngest brother had not been busy at all, lounging around watching his brothers toil in their task. When his turn came, he took his father by the hand and led him into an empty barn. His father became upset, that he had not taken the challenge seriously, but at that moment the son took a small candle from his pocket and lit it. Instantly, the barn became filled, from the floor to the roof, in every nook and cranny, with light.

REFLECTION

What do you hope to achieve this week?

How can you bring
some of the holiness
of Shabbat
into the week ahead?

What do you separate
in your life to keep it special?

סַבְרִי מָרָנָן

בָּרוּךְ אַתָּה יהוה אֱלֹהֵינוּ מֶלֶךְ הָעוֹלָם, בּוֹרֵא פְּרִי הַגָּפֶן.

Holding the spice box, the שליח ציבור *says:*

בָּרוּךְ אַתָּה יהוה אֱלֹהֵינוּ מֶלֶךְ הָעוֹלָם, בּוֹרֵא מִינֵי בְשָׂמִים.

The שליח ציבור *smells the spices and puts the spice box down.*

He lifts his hands toward the flame of the הבדלה *candle, and says:*

בָּרוּךְ אַתָּה יהוה אֱלֹהֵינוּ מֶלֶךְ הָעוֹלָם, בּוֹרֵא מְאוֹרֵי הָאֵשׁ.

He lifts the cup of wine in his right hand, and says:

בָּרוּךְ אַתָּה יהוה אֱלֹהֵינוּ מֶלֶךְ הָעוֹלָם
הַמַּבְדִּיל בֵּין קֹדֶשׁ לְחֹל
בֵּין אוֹר לְחֹשֶׁךְ, בֵּין יִשְׂרָאֵל לָעַמִּים
בֵּין יוֹם הַשְּׁבִיעִי לְשֵׁשֶׁת יְמֵי הַמַּעֲשֶׂה.
בָּרוּךְ אַתָּה יהוה, הַמַּבְדִּיל בֵּין קֹדֶשׁ לְחֹל.

On סוכות*, if* הבדלה *is made in the* סוכה*, add:*

בָּרוּךְ אַתָּה יהוה אֱלֹהֵינוּ מֶלֶךְ הָעוֹלָם
אֲשֶׁר קִדְּשָׁנוּ בְּמִצְוֹתָיו וְצִוָּנוּ לֵישֵׁב בַּסֻּכָּה.

CONNECTION

There once was a wealthy businessman who had three sons. He wanted the cleverest of his sons to inherit all his wealth, and to discover which one that would be he set them a task to prove their intelligence. He showed them a barn on his estate, and challenged his sons to fill the barn to the fullest. Whoever best succeeded in this task would win the entire inheritance. The eldest son worked day and night gathering rocks and pebbles of all shapes and sizes to fill the barn from the floor to the roof. His father was most impressed with his effort, but he found many spaces in between the rocks and stones. The second son used straw, and packed the barn from floor to roof with the straw that was compact and fit tightly. However, the father still found

Stand while saying Aleinu.

עָלֵינוּ It is our duty to praise the Master of all,
and ascribe greatness to the Author of creation,
who has not made us like the nations of the lands
nor placed us like the families of the earth;
who has not made our portion like theirs,
nor our destiny like all their multitudes.
(For they worship vanity and emptiness,
and pray to a god who cannot save.)
But we bow in worship and thank the Supreme King of kings,
the Holy One, blessed be He,
who extends the heavens and establishes the earth,
whose throne of glory is in the heavens above,
and whose power's Presence is in the highest of heights.
He is our God; there is no other.
Truly He is our King, there is none else, as it is written in His Torah:
"You shall know and take to heart this day that the LORD is God, *Deut. 4*
in heaven above and on earth below. There is no other."

Therefore, we place our hope in You, LORD our God,
that we may soon see the glory of Your power,
when You will remove abominations from the earth,
and idols will be utterly destroyed,
when the world will be perfected under the sovereignty of the Almighty,
when all humanity will call on Your name,
to turn all the earth's wicked toward You.
All the world's inhabitants will realize and know
that to You every knee must bow and every tongue swear loyalty.
Before You, LORD our God, they will kneel and bow down
and give honor to Your glorious name.
They will all accept the yoke of Your kingdom,
and You will reign over them soon and for ever.
For the kingdom is Yours, and to all eternity You will reign in glory,
as it is written in Your Torah:
"The LORD will reign for ever and ever." *Ex. 15*
▸ And it is said: "Then the LORD shall be King over all the earth; *Zech. 14*
on that day the LORD shall be One and His name One."

Stand while saying עָלֵינוּ.

עָלֵינוּ לְשַׁבֵּחַ לַאֲדוֹן הַכֹּל, לָתֵת גְּדֻלָּה לְיוֹצֵר בְּרֵאשִׁית
שֶׁלֹּא עָשָׂנוּ כְּגוֹיֵי הָאֲרָצוֹת, וְלֹא שָׂמָנוּ כְּמִשְׁפְּחוֹת הָאֲדָמָה
שֶׁלֹּא שָׂם חֶלְקֵנוּ כָּהֶם וְגוֹרָלֵנוּ כְּכָל הֲמוֹנָם.
(שֶׁהֵם מִשְׁתַּחֲוִים לְהֶבֶל וָרִיק וּמִתְפַּלְלִים אֶל אֵל לֹא יוֹשִׁיעַ.)
וַאֲנַחְנוּ כּוֹרְעִים וּמִשְׁתַּחֲוִים וּמוֹדִים
לִפְנֵי מֶלֶךְ מַלְכֵי הַמְּלָכִים, הַקָּדוֹשׁ בָּרוּךְ הוּא
שֶׁהוּא נוֹטֶה שָׁמַיִם וְיוֹסֵד אָרֶץ
וּמוֹשַׁב יְקָרוֹ בַּשָּׁמַיִם מִמַּעַל
וּשְׁכִינַת עֻזּוֹ בְּגָבְהֵי מְרוֹמִים.
הוּא אֱלֹהֵינוּ, אֵין עוֹד.
אֱמֶת מַלְכֵּנוּ, אֶפֶס זוּלָתוֹ, כַּכָּתוּב בְּתוֹרָתוֹ
וְיָדַעְתָּ הַיּוֹם וַהֲשֵׁבֹתָ אֶל־לְבָבֶךָ דברים ד
כִּי יהוה הוּא הָאֱלֹהִים בַּשָּׁמַיִם מִמַּעַל וְעַל־הָאָרֶץ מִתָּחַת, אֵין עוֹד:

עַל כֵּן נְקַוֶּה לְּךָ יהוה אֱלֹהֵינוּ, לִרְאוֹת מְהֵרָה בְּתִפְאֶרֶת עֻזֶּךָ
לְהַעֲבִיר גִּלּוּלִים מִן הָאָרֶץ, וְהָאֱלִילִים כָּרוֹת יִכָּרֵתוּן
לְתַקֵּן עוֹלָם בְּמַלְכוּת שַׁדַּי.
וְכָל בְּנֵי בָשָׂר יִקְרְאוּ בִשְׁמֶךָ לְהַפְנוֹת אֵלֶיךָ כָּל רִשְׁעֵי אָרֶץ.
יַכִּירוּ וְיֵדְעוּ כָּל יוֹשְׁבֵי תֵבֵל, כִּי לְךָ תִּכְרַע כָּל בֶּרֶךְ, תִּשָּׁבַע כָּל לָשׁוֹן.
לְפָנֶיךָ יהוה אֱלֹהֵינוּ יִכְרְעוּ וְיִפֹּלוּ, וְלִכְבוֹד שִׁמְךָ יְקָר יִתֵּנוּ
וִיקַבְּלוּ כֻלָּם אֶת עֹל מַלְכוּתֶךָ וְתִמְלֹךְ עֲלֵיהֶם מְהֵרָה לְעוֹלָם וָעֶד.
כִּי הַמַּלְכוּת שֶׁלְּךָ הִיא וּלְעוֹלְמֵי עַד תִּמְלֹךְ בְּכָבוֹד
כַּכָּתוּב בְּתוֹרָתֶךָ
יהוה יִמְלֹךְ לְעֹלָם וָעֶד: שמות טו
◄ וְנֶאֱמַר, וְהָיָה יהוה לְמֶלֶךְ עַל־כָּל־הָאָרֶץ זכריה יד
בַּיּוֹם הַהוּא יִהְיֶה יהוה אֶחָד וּשְׁמוֹ אֶחָד:

Some add:

Have no fear of sudden terror or of the ruin when it overtakes the wicked. *Prov. 3*
Devise your strategy, but it will be defeated, propose your plan, *Is. 8*
but it will not stand, for God is with us. When you grow old, I will still be the same. *Is. 46*
When your hair turns gray, I will still carry you. I made you, I will bear you,
I will carry you, and I will rescue you.

MOURNER'S KADDISH

The following prayer, said by mourners, requires the presence of a minyan.
A transliteration can be found on page 1151.

Mourner: יִתְגַּדַּל Magnified and sanctified
may His great name be,
in the world He created by His will.
May He establish His kingdom
in your lifetime and in your days,
and in the lifetime of all the house of Israel,
swiftly and soon –
and say: Amen.

All: May His great name be blessed for ever and all time.

Mourner: Blessed and praised, glorified and elevated,
raised and honored, uplifted and praised
be the name of the Holy One,
blessed be He,
beyond any blessing,
song, praise and consolation
uttered in the world –
and say: Amen.

May there be great peace from heaven,
and life for us and all Israel – and say: Amen.

Bow, take three steps back, as if taking leave of the Divine Presence,
then bow, first left, then right, then center, while saying:

May He who makes peace in His high places,
make peace for us and all Israel –
and say: Amen.

Some add:

אַל־תִּירָא מִפַּחַד פִּתְאֹם וּמִשֹּׁאַת רְשָׁעִים כִּי תָבֹא: משלי ג

עֻצוּ עֵצָה וְתֻפָר, דַּבְּרוּ דָבָר וְלֹא יָקוּם, כִּי עִמָּנוּ אֵל: ישעיה ח

וְעַד־זִקְנָה אֲנִי הוּא, וְעַד־שֵׂיבָה אֲנִי אֶסְבֹּל ישעיה מו

אֲנִי עָשִׂיתִי וַאֲנִי אֶשָּׂא וַאֲנִי אֶסְבֹּל וַאֲמַלֵּט:

קדיש יתום

The following prayer, said by mourners, requires the presence of a מנין.
A transliteration can be found on page 1151.

אבל: יִתְגַּדַּל וְיִתְקַדַּשׁ שְׁמֵהּ רַבָּא (קהל: אָמֵן)

בְּעָלְמָא דִּי בְרָא כִרְעוּתֵהּ

וְיַמְלִיךְ מַלְכוּתֵהּ

בְּחַיֵּיכוֹן וּבְיוֹמֵיכוֹן וּבְחַיֵּי דְכָל בֵּית יִשְׂרָאֵל

בַּעֲגָלָא וּבִזְמַן קָרִיב, וְאִמְרוּ אָמֵן. (קהל: אָמֵן)

קהל ואבל: יְהֵא שְׁמֵהּ רַבָּא מְבָרַךְ לְעָלַם וּלְעָלְמֵי עָלְמַיָּא.

אבל: יִתְבָּרַךְ וְיִשְׁתַּבַּח וְיִתְפָּאַר

וְיִתְרוֹמַם וְיִתְנַשֵּׂא וְיִתְהַדָּר וְיִתְעַלֶּה וְיִתְהַלָּל

שְׁמֵהּ דְּקֻדְשָׁא בְּרִיךְ הוּא (קהל: בְּרִיךְ הוּא)

לְעֵלָּא מִן כָּל בִּרְכָתָא / בעשרת ימי תשובה: לְעֵלָּא לְעֵלָּא מִכָּל בִּרְכָתָא/

וְשִׁירָתָא, תֻּשְׁבְּחָתָא וְנֶחֱמָתָא

דַּאֲמִירָן בְּעָלְמָא, וְאִמְרוּ אָמֵן. (קהל: אָמֵן)

יְהֵא שְׁלָמָא רַבָּא מִן שְׁמַיָּא

וְחַיִּים, עָלֵינוּ וְעַל כָּל יִשְׂרָאֵל, וְאִמְרוּ אָמֵן. (קהל: אָמֵן)

Bow, take three steps back, as if taking leave of the Divine Presence,
then bow, first left, then right, then center, while saying:

עֹשֶׂה שָׁלוֹם/ בעשרת ימי תשובה: הַשָּׁלוֹם / בִּמְרוֹמָיו

הוּא יַעֲשֶׂה שָׁלוֹם עָלֵינוּ וְעַל כָּל יִשְׂרָאֵל

וְאִמְרוּ אָמֵן. (קהל: אָמֵן)

From the second day of Rosh Ḥodesh Elul through Shemini Atzeret (in Israel through Hoshana Raba), the following psalm is said:

לְדָוִד By David. The LORD is my light and my salvation – whom then shall I fear? The LORD is the stronghold of my life – of whom shall I be afraid? When evil men close in on me to devour my flesh, it is they, my enemies and foes, who stumble and fall. Should an army besiege me, my heart would not fear. Should war break out against me, still I would be confident. One thing I ask of the LORD, only this do I seek: to live in the House of the LORD all the days of my life, to gaze on the beauty of the LORD and worship in His Temple. For He will keep me safe in His pavilion on the day of trouble. He will hide me under the cover of His tent. He will set me high upon a rock. Now my head is high above my enemies who surround me. I will sacrifice in His tent with shouts of joy. I will sing and chant praises to the LORD. LORD, hear my voice when I call. Be generous to me and answer me. On Your behalf my heart says, "Seek My face." Your face, LORD, will I seek. Do not hide Your face from me. Do not turn Your servant away in anger. You have been my help. Do not reject or abandon me, God, my Savior. Were my father and my mother to abandon me, the LORD would take me in. Teach me Your way, LORD, and lead me on a level path, because of my oppressors. Do not abandon me to the will of my enemies, for false witnesses have risen against me, breathing violence. ▸ Were it not for my faith that I shall see the LORD's goodness in the land of the living. Hope in the LORD. Be strong and of good courage, and hope in the LORD! *Ps. 27*

Mourner's Kaddish (previous page)

From the second day of ראש חודש אלול *through* שמיני עצרת
(*in* ארץ ישראל *through* הושענא רבה), *the following psalm is said:*

תהלים כז
לְדָוִד, יהוה אוֹרִי וְיִשְׁעִי, מִמִּי אִירָא, יהוה מָעוֹז־חַיַּי, מִמִּי אֶפְחָד: בִּקְרֹב עָלַי מְרֵעִים לֶאֱכֹל אֶת־בְּשָׂרִי, צָרַי וְאֹיְבַי לִי, הֵמָּה כָשְׁלוּ וְנָפָלוּ: אִם־תַּחֲנֶה עָלַי מַחֲנֶה, לֹא־יִירָא לִבִּי, אִם־תָּקוּם עָלַי מִלְחָמָה, בְּזֹאת אֲנִי בוֹטֵחַ: אַחַת שָׁאַלְתִּי מֵאֵת־יהוה, אוֹתָהּ אֲבַקֵּשׁ, שִׁבְתִּי בְּבֵית־יהוה כָּל־יְמֵי חַיַּי, לַחֲזוֹת בְּנֹעַם־יהוה, וּלְבַקֵּר בְּהֵיכָלוֹ: כִּי יִצְפְּנֵנִי בְּסֻכֹּה בְּיוֹם רָעָה, יַסְתִּרֵנִי בְּסֵתֶר אָהֳלוֹ, בְּצוּר יְרוֹמְמֵנִי: וְעַתָּה יָרוּם רֹאשִׁי עַל אֹיְבַי סְבִיבוֹתַי, וְאֶזְבְּחָה בְאָהֳלוֹ זִבְחֵי תְרוּעָה, אָשִׁירָה וַאֲזַמְּרָה לַיהוה: שְׁמַע־יהוה קוֹלִי אֶקְרָא, וְחָנֵּנִי וַעֲנֵנִי: לְךָ אָמַר לִבִּי בַּקְּשׁוּ פָנָי, אֶת־פָּנֶיךָ יהוה אֲבַקֵּשׁ: אַל־תַּסְתֵּר פָּנֶיךָ מִמֶּנִּי, אַל תַּט־בְּאַף עַבְדֶּךָ, עֶזְרָתִי הָיִיתָ, אַל־תִּטְּשֵׁנִי וְאַל־תַּעַזְבֵנִי, אֱלֹהֵי יִשְׁעִי: כִּי־אָבִי וְאִמִּי עֲזָבוּנִי, וַיהוה יַאַסְפֵנִי: הוֹרֵנִי יהוה דַּרְכֶּךָ, וּנְחֵנִי בְּאֹרַח מִישׁוֹר, לְמַעַן שׁוֹרְרָי: אַל־תִּתְּנֵנִי בְּנֶפֶשׁ צָרָי, כִּי קָמוּ־בִי עֵדֵי־שֶׁקֶר, וִיפֵחַ חָמָס: ‹ לוּלֵא הֶאֱמַנְתִּי לִרְאוֹת בְּטוּב־יהוה בְּאֶרֶץ חַיִּים: קַוֵּה אֶל־יהוה, חֲזַק וְיַאֲמֵץ לִבֶּךָ, וְקַוֵּה אֶל־יהוה:

קדיש יתום (*previous page*)

BLESSING OF THE NEW MOON

Kiddush Levana, the Blessing of the New Moon, is said between the third day and the middle day of each month. If possible, it should be said at the end of Shabbat, under the open sky, and in the presence of a minyan.

הַלְלוּיָהּ Halleluya! Praise the LORD from the heavens, praise Him in the heights. Praise Him, all His angels; praise Him, all His multitudes. Praise Him, sun and moon; praise Him, all shining stars. Praise Him, highest heavens and the waters above the heavens. Let them praise the name of the LORD, for He commanded and they were created. He established them for ever and all time, issuing a decree that will never change. *Ps. 148*

כִּי־אֶרְאֶה When I see Your heavens, the work of Your fingers, the moon and the stars which You have set in place: What is man that You are mindful of him, the son of man that You care for him? *Ps. 8*

Look at the moon, then say:

בָּרוּךְ Blessed are You, LORD our God, King of the Universe who by His word created the heavens, and by His breath all their multitudes. He set for them laws and times, so that they should not deviate from their appointed task. They are joyous and glad to perform the will of their Owner, the Worker of truth whose work is truth. To the moon He said that it should renew itself as a crown of beauty for those He carried from the womb [Israel], for they are destined to be renewed like it, and to praise their Creator for the sake of His glorious majesty. Blessed are You, LORD, who renews the months.

The following five verses are each said three times:

Blessed is He who formed you; blessed is He who made you;
blessed is He who owns you; blessed is He who created you.

The following verse is said rising on the toes.

Just as I leap toward you but cannot touch you,
so may none of my enemies be able to touch me to do me harm.

May fear and dread fall upon them; *Ex. 15*
by the power of Your arm may they be still as stone.

May they be still as stone through the power of Your arm,
when dread and fear fall upon them.

David, King of Israel, lives and endures.

קידוש לבנה

קידוש לבנה, the Blessing of the New Moon, is said between the third day and the middle day of each month. If possible, it should be said at the end of שבת, under the open sky, and in the presence of a מנין.

תהלים קמח
הַלְלוּיָהּ, הַלְלוּ אֶת־יהוה מִן־הַשָּׁמַיִם, הַלְלוּהוּ בַּמְּרוֹמִים: הַלְלוּהוּ כָל־מַלְאָכָיו, הַלְלוּהוּ כָּל־צְבָאָו: הַלְלוּהוּ שֶׁמֶשׁ וְיָרֵחַ, הַלְלוּהוּ כָּל־כּוֹכְבֵי אוֹר: הַלְלוּהוּ שְׁמֵי הַשָּׁמָיִם, וְהַמַּיִם אֲשֶׁר מֵעַל הַשָּׁמָיִם: יְהַלְלוּ אֶת־שֵׁם יהוה, כִּי הוּא צִוָּה וְנִבְרָאוּ: וַיַּעֲמִידֵם לָעַד לְעוֹלָם, חָק־נָתַן וְלֹא יַעֲבוֹר:

תהלים ח
כִּי־אֶרְאֶה שָׁמֶיךָ מַעֲשֵׂה אֶצְבְּעֹתֶיךָ, יָרֵחַ וְכוֹכָבִים אֲשֶׁר כּוֹנָנְתָּה: מָה־אֱנוֹשׁ כִּי־תִזְכְּרֶנּוּ, וּבֶן־אָדָם כִּי תִפְקְדֶנּוּ:

Look at the moon, then say:

בָּרוּךְ אַתָּה יהוה אֱלֹהֵינוּ מֶלֶךְ הָעוֹלָם, אֲשֶׁר בְּמַאֲמָרוֹ בָּרָא שְׁחָקִים, וּבְרוּחַ פִּיו כָּל צְבָאָם, חֹק וּזְמַן נָתַן לָהֶם שֶׁלֹּא יְשַׁנּוּ אֶת תַּפְקִידָם. שָׂשִׂים וּשְׂמֵחִים לַעֲשׂוֹת רְצוֹן קוֹנָם, פּוֹעֵל אֱמֶת שֶׁפְּעֻלָּתוֹ אֱמֶת. וְלַלְּבָנָה אָמַר שֶׁתִּתְחַדֵּשׁ, עֲטֶרֶת תִּפְאֶרֶת לַעֲמוּסֵי בָטֶן, שֶׁהֵם עֲתִידִים לְהִתְחַדֵּשׁ כְּמוֹתָהּ וּלְפָאֵר לְיוֹצְרָם עַל שֵׁם כְּבוֹד מַלְכוּתוֹ. בָּרוּךְ אַתָּה יהוה, מְחַדֵּשׁ חֳדָשִׁים.

The following five verses are each said three times.

בָּרוּךְ יוֹצְרֵךְ, בָּרוּךְ עוֹשֵׂךְ, בָּרוּךְ קוֹנֵךְ, בָּרוּךְ בּוֹרְאֵךְ.

The following verse is said rising on the toes.

כְּשֵׁם שֶׁאֲנִי רוֹקֵד כְּנֶגְדֵּךְ וְאֵינִי יָכוֹל לִנְגֹּעַ בָּךְ
כָּךְ לֹא יוּכְלוּ כָּל אוֹיְבַי לִנְגֹּעַ בִּי לְרָעָה.

שמות טו
תִּפֹּל עֲלֵיהֶם אֵימָתָה וָפַחַד, בִּגְדֹל זְרוֹעֲךָ יִדְּמוּ כָּאָבֶן:
כָּאָבֶן יִדְּמוּ זְרוֹעֲךָ בִּגְדֹל, וָפַחַד אֵימָתָה עֲלֵיהֶם תִּפֹּל.

דָּוִד מֶלֶךְ יִשְׂרָאֵל חַי וְקַיָּם.

Turn to three people and say to each:

Peace upon you.

They respond:

Upon you, peace.

Say three times:

May it be a good sign and a good omen for us and all Israel.
Amen.

קוֹל Hark! My beloved! Here he comes, leaping over the mountains, bounding over the hills. My beloved is like a gazelle, like a young deer. There he stands outside our wall, peering in through the windows, gazing through the lattice. *Song. 2*

שִׁיר לַמַּעֲלוֹת A song of ascents. I lift my eyes up to the hills; from where will my help come? My help comes from the LORD, Maker of heaven and earth. He will not let your foot stumble; He who guards you does not slumber. See: the Guardian of Israel neither slumbers nor sleeps. The LORD is your Guardian; the LORD is your Shade at your right hand. The sun will not strike you by day, nor the moon by night. The LORD will guard you from all harm; He will guard your life. The LORD will guard your going and coming, now and for evermore. *Ps. 121*

הַלְלוּיָהּ Halleluya! Praise God in His holy place; praise Him in the heavens of His power. Praise Him for His mighty deeds; praise Him for His immense greatness. Praise Him with blasts of the ram's horn; praise Him with the harp and lyre. Praise Him with drum and dance; praise Him with strings and flute. Praise Him with clashing cymbals; praise Him with resounding cymbals. Let all that breathes praise the LORD. Halleluya! *Ps. 150*

תָּנָא In the academy of Rabbi Yishmael it was taught: Were the people of Israel privileged to greet the presence of their heavenly Father only once a month, it would have been sufficient for them. Abaye said: Therefore it [the blessing of the moon] should be said standing. Who is this coming up from the desert, leaning on her beloved? *Sanhedrin 42a* *Song. 8*

Turn to three people and say to each:

שָׁלוֹם עֲלֵיכֶם.

They respond:

עֲלֵיכֶם שָׁלוֹם.

Say three times:

סִימָן טוֹב וּמַזָּל טוֹב יְהֵא לָנוּ וּלְכָל יִשְׂרָאֵל
אָמֵן.

שיר השירים ב קוֹל דּוֹדִי הִנֵּה־זֶה בָּא, מְדַלֵּג עַל־הֶהָרִים, מְקַפֵּץ עַל־הַגְּבָעוֹת: דּוֹמֶה דוֹדִי לִצְבִי אוֹ לְעֹפֶר הָאַיָּלִים, הִנֵּה־זֶה עוֹמֵד אַחַר כָּתְלֵנוּ, מַשְׁגִּיחַ מִן־הַחַלֹּנוֹת, מֵצִיץ מִן־הַחֲרַכִּים:

תהלים קכא שִׁיר לַמַּעֲלוֹת, אֶשָּׂא עֵינַי אֶל־הֶהָרִים, מֵאַיִן יָבֹא עֶזְרִי: עֶזְרִי מֵעִם יהוה, עֹשֵׂה שָׁמַיִם וָאָרֶץ: אַל־יִתֵּן לַמּוֹט רַגְלֶךָ, אַל־יָנוּם שֹׁמְרֶךָ: הִנֵּה לֹא־יָנוּם וְלֹא יִישָׁן, שׁוֹמֵר יִשְׂרָאֵל: יהוה שֹׁמְרֶךָ, יהוה צִלְּךָ עַל־יַד יְמִינֶךָ: יוֹמָם הַשֶּׁמֶשׁ לֹא־יַכֶּכָּה, וְיָרֵחַ בַּלָּיְלָה: יהוה יִשְׁמָרְךָ מִכָּל־רָע, יִשְׁמֹר אֶת־נַפְשֶׁךָ: יהוה יִשְׁמָר־צֵאתְךָ וּבוֹאֶךָ, מֵעַתָּה וְעַד־עוֹלָם:

תהלים קנ הַלְלוּיָהּ, הַלְלוּ־אֵל בְּקָדְשׁוֹ, הַלְלוּהוּ בִּרְקִיעַ עֻזּוֹ: הַלְלוּהוּ בִגְבוּרֹתָיו, הַלְלוּהוּ כְּרֹב גֻּדְלוֹ: הַלְלוּהוּ בְּתֵקַע שׁוֹפָר, הַלְלוּהוּ בְּנֵבֶל וְכִנּוֹר: הַלְלוּהוּ בְתֹף וּמָחוֹל, הַלְלוּהוּ בְּמִנִּים וְעוּגָב: הַלְלוּהוּ בְצִלְצְלֵי־שָׁמַע, הַלְלוּהוּ בְּצִלְצְלֵי תְרוּעָה: כֹּל הַנְּשָׁמָה תְּהַלֵּל יָהּ, הַלְלוּיָהּ:

סנהדרין מב. תָּנָא דְבֵי רַבִּי יִשְׁמָעֵאל: אִלְמָלֵי לֹא זָכוּ יִשְׂרָאֵל אֶלָּא לְהַקְבִּיל פְּנֵי אֲבִיהֶם שֶׁבַּשָּׁמַיִם פַּעַם אַחַת בַּחֹדֶשׁ, דַּיָּם. אָמַר אַבַּיֵּי: הִלְכָּךְ צָרִיךְ לְמֵימְרָא מְעֻמָּד.

שיר השירים ח מִי זֹאת עֹלָה מִן־הַמִּדְבָּר, מִתְרַפֶּקֶת עַל־דּוֹדָהּ:

וִיהִי May it be Your will, LORD my God and God of my ancestors, to make good the deficiency of the moon, so that it is no longer in its diminished state. May the light of the moon be like the light of the sun and like the light of the seven days of creation as it was before it was diminished, as it says, "The two great luminaries." And may there be fulfilled for us the verse: "They shall seek the LORD their God, and David their king." Amen.

Gen. 1
Hos. 3

לַמְנַצֵּחַ For the conductor of music. With stringed instruments, a psalm. A song. May God be generous to us and bless us. May He make His face shine on us, Selah. Then will Your way be known on earth, Your salvation among all the nations. Let the peoples praise You, God; let all peoples praise You. Let nations rejoice and sing for joy, for You judge the peoples fairly, and guide the nations of the earth, Selah. Let the peoples praise You, God; let all peoples praise You. The earth has yielded its harvest. May God, our God, bless us. God will bless us, and all the ends of the earth will fear Him.

Ps. 67

The service continues with Aleinu (page 386)
and Mourner's Kaddish (page 388)
followed by "Good are the radiant stars" below.

All sing:

טוֹבִים Good are the radiant stars our God created;
He formed them with knowledge,
understanding and thought.
He gave them strength and might
to rule throughout the world.

Full of splendor, radiating light,
beautiful is their splendor throughout the world.
Glad as they go forth, joyous as they return,
they fulfill with awe their Creator's will.

Glory and honor they give to His name,
celebration and song at the mention of His majesty.
He called the sun into being and it shone with light.
He looked and fashioned the form of the moon.

וִיהִי רָצוֹן מִלְּפָנֶיךָ יהוה אֱלֹהַי וֵאלֹהֵי אֲבוֹתַי, לְמַלֹּאת פְּגִימַת הַלְּבָנָה וְלֹא יִהְיֶה בָּהּ שׁוּם מִעוּט. וִיהִי אוֹר הַלְּבָנָה כְּאוֹר הַחַמָּה וּכְאוֹר שִׁבְעַת יְמֵי בְרֵאשִׁית, כְּמוֹ שֶׁהָיְתָה קֹדֶם מִעוּטָהּ, שֶׁנֶּאֱמַר: אֶת־שְׁנֵי הַמְּאֹרֹת הַגְּדֹלִים: וְיִתְקַיֵּם בָּנוּ מִקְרָא שֶׁכָּתוּב: וּבִקְשׁוּ אֶת־יהוה אֱלֹהֵיהֶם וְאֵת דָּוִיד מַלְכָּם: אָמֵן. בראשית א הושע ג

לַמְנַצֵּחַ בִּנְגִינֹת, מִזְמוֹר שִׁיר: אֱלֹהִים יְחָנֵּנוּ וִיבָרְכֵנוּ, יָאֵר פָּנָיו אִתָּנוּ סֶלָה: לָדַעַת בָּאָרֶץ דַּרְכֶּךָ, בְּכָל־גּוֹיִם יְשׁוּעָתֶךָ: יוֹדוּךָ עַמִּים אֱלֹהִים, יוֹדוּךָ עַמִּים כֻּלָּם: יִשְׂמְחוּ וִירַנְּנוּ לְאֻמִּים, כִּי־תִשְׁפֹּט עַמִּים מִישֹׁר, וּלְאֻמִּים בָּאָרֶץ תַּנְחֵם סֶלָה: יוֹדוּךָ עַמִּים אֱלֹהִים, יוֹדוּךָ עַמִּים כֻּלָּם: אֶרֶץ נָתְנָה יְבוּלָהּ, יְבָרְכֵנוּ אֱלֹהִים אֱלֹהֵינוּ: יְבָרְכֵנוּ אֱלֹהִים, וְיִירְאוּ אוֹתוֹ כָּל־אַפְסֵי־אָרֶץ: תהלים סז

The service continues with עָלֵינוּ *(page 387) and* קדיש יתום *(page 389) followed by* טוֹבִים מְאוֹרוֹת *below.*

All sing:

טוֹבִים מְאוֹרוֹת שֶׁבָּרָא אֱלֹהֵינוּ
יְצָרָם בְּדַעַת בְּבִינָה וּבְהַשְׂכֵּל
כֹּחַ וּגְבוּרָה נָתַן בָּהֶם
לִהְיוֹת מוֹשְׁלִים בְּקֶרֶב תֵּבֵל.

מְלֵאִים זִיו וּמְפִיקִים נֹגַהּ
נָאֶה זִיוָם בְּכָל הָעוֹלָם
שְׂמֵחִים בְּצֵאתָם וְשָׂשִׂים בְּבוֹאָם
עוֹשִׂים בְּאֵימָה רְצוֹן קוֹנָם.

פְּאֵר וְכָבוֹד נוֹתְנִים לִשְׁמוֹ
צָהֳלָה וְרִנָּה לְזֵכֶר מַלְכוּתוֹ
קָרָא לַשֶּׁמֶשׁ וַיִּזְרַח אוֹר
רָאָה וְהִתְקִין צוּרַת הַלְּבָנָה.

SHEMA BEFORE SLEEP AT NIGHT

הֲרֵינִי I hereby forgive anyone who has angered or provoked me or sinned against me, physically or financially or by failing to give me due respect, or in any other matter relating to me, involuntarily or willingly, inadvertently or deliberately, whether in word or deed: let no one incur punishment because of me.

בָּרוּךְ Blessed are You, Lord our God, King of the Universe,
who makes the bonds of sleep fall on my eyes, and slumber on my eye-lids.
May it be Your will, Lord my God and God of my fathers,
that You make me lie down in peace and arise in peace.
Let not my imagination, bad dreams or troubling thoughts disturb me.
May my bed be flawless before You.
Enlighten my eyes lest I sleep the sleep of death,
for it is You who illuminates the pupil of the eye.
Blessed are You, Lord, who gives light to the whole world in His glory.

REFLECTION

"Dreams are one-sixtieth of prophecy."
(*Berakhot* 57b)

"A person is only shown in his dreams the thoughts of his heart."
(*Berakhot* 55b)

Do you dream?

Do you think dreams mean something?

What was the last dream you had?
What do you think it means?

CONNECTION

When I was a month I could barely stay awake for a few minutes at a time.
When I was 3 years old I would fight sleep with all my might.
When I was 9 years old I could sleep in almost any place.
When I was 16 years old I would sleep all day and stay awake all night.
When I was 23 I had no time to sleep. There was too much to do.
When I was 34 I dreamed of sleep all the time. Sleep was a gift.
When I was 42 I found I did not need to sleep that much at all.
When I was 55 I would trade in sleep for experiencing the new dawn each morning.
When I was 71 I would only sleep in small increments. Day and night. In almost any place.
When I was 83 I would fight to stay awake and enjoy the life I had left.
When I was 96 I slept peacefully.

Sleep. Hope or hindrance? Essential or extraneous? Blessing or blight?

קריאת שמע על המיטה

הֲרֵינִי מוֹחֵל לְכָל מִי שֶׁהִכְעִיס וְהִקְנִיט אוֹתִי אוֹ שֶׁחָטָא כְּנֶגְדִּי, בֵּין בְּגוּפִי בֵּין בְּמָמוֹנִי בֵּין בִּכְבוֹדִי בֵּין בְּכָל אֲשֶׁר לִי, בֵּין בְּאֹנֶס בֵּין בְּרָצוֹן, בֵּין בְּשׁוֹגֵג בֵּין בְּמֵזִיד, בֵּין בְּדִבּוּר בֵּין בְּמַעֲשֶׂה, וְלֹא יֵעָנֵשׁ שׁוּם אָדָם בְּסִבָּתִי.

בָּרוּךְ אַתָּה יהוה אֱלֹהֵינוּ מֶלֶךְ הָעוֹלָם
הַמַּפִּיל חֶבְלֵי שֵׁנָה עַל עֵינַי וּתְנוּמָה עַל עַפְעַפָּי.
וִיהִי רָצוֹן מִלְּפָנֶיךָ, יהוה אֱלֹהַי וֵאלֹהֵי אֲבוֹתַי
שֶׁתַּשְׁכִּיבֵנִי לְשָׁלוֹם וְתַעֲמִידֵנִי לְשָׁלוֹם
וְאַל יְבַהֲלְוּנִי רַעְיוֹנַי וַחֲלוֹמוֹת רָעִים וְהִרְהוּרִים רָעִים
וּתְהֵא מִטָּתִי שְׁלֵמָה לְפָנֶיךָ
וְהָאֵר עֵינַי פֶּן אִישַׁן הַמָּוֶת
כִּי אַתָּה הַמֵּאִיר לְאִישׁוֹן בַּת עָיִן.
בָּרוּךְ אַתָּה יהוה, הַמֵּאִיר לָעוֹלָם כֻּלּוֹ בִּכְבוֹדוֹ.

LEARNING

It says in the first paragraph of the *Shema*, "Teach [these words] repeatedly to your children, speaking of them when you sit at home and when you travel on the way, when you lie down and when you rise" (*Devarim* 6:7). From this we learn that the *Shema* should be said in both the Shaḥarit and Ma'ariv *tefillot*. However, the Talmud (*Berakhot* 4b) says that this first paragraph should also be said literally as you lie down, at night, just before you go to sleep. It is preceded by a special *berakha* before going to sleep known as *HaMapil*. After the first paragraph of the *Shema*, there are additional *tefillot* that form an expansion of the request for protection during the night.

... A THOUSAND WORDS

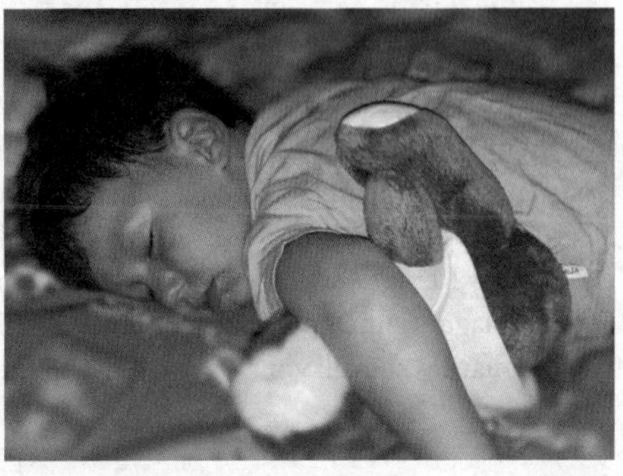

When saying all three paragraphs of Shema, say:
God, faithful King!

The following verse should be said aloud, while covering the eyes with the right hand:

Listen, Israel: the LORD is our God, the LORD is One. *Deut. 6*

Quietly: Blessed be the name of His glorious kingdom for ever and all time.

וְאָהַבְתָּ Love the LORD your God with all your heart, with all your soul, and with all your might. These words which I command you today shall be on your heart. Teach them repeatedly to your children, speaking of them when you sit at home and when you travel on the way, when you lie down and when you rise. Bind them as a sign on your hand, and they shall be a symbol between your eyes. Write them on the doorposts of your house and gates. *Deut. 6*

וִיהִי May the pleasantness of the LORD our God be upon us. Establish for us the work of our hands, O establish the work of our hands. *Ps. 90*

יֹשֵׁב He who lives in the shelter of the Most High lives in the shadow of the Almighty. I say of God, my Refuge and Stronghold, my LORD in whom I trust, that He will save you from the hunter's trap and the deadly disease. With His outstretched limbs He will cover you, and beneath His wings you will find shelter; His truthfulness is an encircling shield. You need not fear terror by night, nor the arrow that flies by day; not the disease that stalks in darkness, nor the plague that ravages at noon. A thousand may fall at your side, ten thousand at your right hand, but it will not come near you. You will only look with your eyes and see the punishment of the wicked. Because you said, "The LORD is my Refuge," taking the Most High as your shelter, no harm will befall you, no plague come near your tent, for He will command His angels about you, to guard you in all your ways. They will lift you in their hands, lest your *Ps. 91*

---

into Christian orphanages in convents, but after the war the nuns would not often admit to this in the hope that they could bring up these Jewish children as Christians. When the Mother Superior would deny there were any Jewish children in their home, Rabbi Schonfeld would walk directly to the dormitories and begin to softly say the Shema. When several small voices were heard joining in with these ancient words, he refused to leave without these Jewish souls.

When saying all three paragraphs of שמע*, say:*

אֵל מֶלֶךְ נֶאֱמָן

The following verse should be said aloud, while covering the eyes with the right hand:

דברים ו

שְׁמַע יִשְׂרָאֵל, יהוה אֱלֹהֵינוּ, יהוה אֶחָד:

Quietly בָּרוּךְ שֵׁם כְּבוֹד מַלְכוּתוֹ לְעוֹלָם וָעֶד.

דברים ו
וְאָהַבְתָּ אֵת יהוה אֱלֹהֶיךָ, בְּכָל־לְבָבְךָ וּבְכָל־נַפְשְׁךָ וּבְכָל־
מְאֹדֶךָ: וְהָיוּ הַדְּבָרִים הָאֵלֶּה, אֲשֶׁר אָנֹכִי מְצַוְּךָ הַיּוֹם, עַל־לְבָבֶךָ:
וְשִׁנַּנְתָּם לְבָנֶיךָ וְדִבַּרְתָּ בָּם, בְּשִׁבְתְּךָ בְּבֵיתֶךָ וּבְלֶכְתְּךָ בַדֶּרֶךְ,
וּבְשָׁכְבְּךָ וּבְקוּמֶךָ: וּקְשַׁרְתָּם לְאוֹת עַל־יָדֶךָ וְהָיוּ לְטֹטָפֹת בֵּין
עֵינֶיךָ: וּכְתַבְתָּם עַל־מְזֻזוֹת בֵּיתֶךָ וּבִשְׁעָרֶיךָ:

תהלים צ
וִיהִי נֹעַם אֲדֹנָי אֱלֹהֵינוּ עָלֵינוּ וּמַעֲשֵׂה יָדֵינוּ כּוֹנְנָה עָלֵינוּ וּמַעֲשֵׂה יָדֵינוּ
כּוֹנְנֵהוּ:

תהלים צא
יֹשֵׁב בְּסֵתֶר עֶלְיוֹן, בְּצֵל שַׁדַּי יִתְלוֹנָן: אֹמַר לַיהוה מַחְסִי וּמְצוּדָתִי,
אֱלֹהַי אֶבְטַח־בּוֹ: כִּי הוּא יַצִּילְךָ מִפַּח יָקוּשׁ, מִדֶּבֶר הַוּוֹת: בְּאֶבְרָתוֹ
יָסֶךְ לָךְ, וְתַחַת־כְּנָפָיו תֶּחְסֶה, צִנָּה וְסֹחֵרָה אֲמִתּוֹ: לֹא־תִירָא מִפַּחַד
לָיְלָה, מֵחֵץ יָעוּף יוֹמָם: מִדֶּבֶר בָּאֹפֶל יַהֲלֹךְ, מִקֶּטֶב יָשׁוּד צָהֳרָיִם:
יִפֹּל מִצִּדְּךָ אֶלֶף, וּרְבָבָה מִימִינֶךָ, אֵלֶיךָ לֹא יִגָּשׁ: רַק בְּעֵינֶיךָ תַבִּיט,
וְשִׁלֻּמַת רְשָׁעִים תִּרְאֶה: כִּי־אַתָּה יהוה מַחְסִי, עֶלְיוֹן שַׂמְתָּ מְעוֹנֶךָ:
לֹא־תְאֻנֶּה אֵלֶיךָ רָעָה, וְנֶגַע לֹא־יִקְרַב בְּאָהֳלֶךָ: כִּי מַלְאָכָיו יְצַוֶּה־לָּךְ,
לִשְׁמָרְךָ בְּכָל־דְּרָכֶיךָ: עַל־כַּפַּיִם יִשָּׂאוּנְךָ, פֶּן־תִּגֹּף בָּאֶבֶן רַגְלֶךָ: עַל־

CONNECTION

Rabbi Schonfeld threw himself in to the task of saving Jewish orphans from Europe after the Shoah, and worked tirelessly to bring them to England and find them homes with Jewish families. Many children had survived by being smuggled

foot stumble on a stone. You will tread on lions and vipers; you will trample on young lions and snakes. [God says:] "Because he loves Me, I will rescue him; I will protect him, because he acknowledges My name. When he calls on Me, I will answer him; I will be with him in distress, I will deliver him and bring him honor. With long life I will satisfy him and show him My salvation.

With long life I will satisfy him and show him My salvation.

יהוה Lord, how numerous are my enemies, how many rise against me. *Ps. 3* Many say of me: "There is no help for him in God," Selah. But You, Lord, are a shield around me. You are my glory; You raise my head high. I cry aloud to the Lord, and He answers me from His holy mountain, Selah. I lie down to sleep and I wake again, for the Lord supports me. I will not fear the countless forces ranged against me on all sides. Arise, Lord, save me, O my God; strike all my enemies across the cheek; break the teeth of the wicked. From the Lord comes deliverance; may Your blessing rest upon Your people, Selah.

הַשְׁכִּיבֵנוּ Help us lie down, O Lord our God, in peace, and rise up, O our King, to life. Spread over us Your canopy of peace. Direct us with Your good counsel, and save us for the sake of Your name. Shield us and remove from us every enemy, plague, sword, famine and sorrow. Remove the enemy from before and behind us. Shelter us in the shadow of Your wings, for You, God, are our Guardian and Deliverer; You, God, are a generous and compassionate King. Guard our going out and our coming in, for life and peace, from now and for ever.

בָּרוּךְ Blessed is the Lord by day, blessed is the Lord by night. Blessed is the Lord when we lie down; blessed is the Lord when we rise. For in Your hand are the souls of the living and the dead, [as it is written:] "In His hand is every living soul, and the breath of all mankind." Into *Job 12* Your hand I entrust my spirit: You redeemed me, Lord, God of truth. *Ps. 31* Our God in heaven, bring unity to Your name, establish Your kingdom constantly and reign over us for ever and all time.

יִרְאוּ May our eyes see, our hearts rejoice, and our souls be glad in Your true salvation, when Zion is told, "Your God reigns." The Lord is King, the Lord was King, and the Lord will be King for ever and all time. For sovereignty is Yours, and to all eternity You will reign in glory, for we have no king but You.

שַׁחַל וָפֶתֶן תִּדְרֹךְ, תִּרְמֹס כְּפִיר וְתַנִּין: כִּי בִי חָשַׁק וַאֲפַלְּטֵהוּ, אֲשַׂגְּבֵהוּ כִּי־יָדַע שְׁמִי: יִקְרָאֵנִי וְאֶעֱנֵהוּ, עִמּוֹ־אָנֹכִי בְצָרָה, אֲחַלְּצֵהוּ וַאֲכַבְּדֵהוּ:
אֹרֶךְ יָמִים אַשְׂבִּיעֵהוּ, וְאַרְאֵהוּ בִּישׁוּעָתִי:
אֹרֶךְ יָמִים אַשְׂבִּיעֵהוּ, וְאַרְאֵהוּ בִּישׁוּעָתִי:

תהלים ג יהוה מָה־רַבּוּ צָרָי, רַבִּים קָמִים עָלָי: רַבִּים אֹמְרִים לְנַפְשִׁי, אֵין יְשׁוּעָתָה לּוֹ בֵאלֹהִים, סֶלָה: וְאַתָּה יהוה מָגֵן בַּעֲדִי, כְּבוֹדִי וּמֵרִים רֹאשִׁי: קוֹלִי אֶל־יהוה אֶקְרָא, וַיַּעֲנֵנִי מֵהַר קָדְשׁוֹ, סֶלָה: אֲנִי שָׁכַבְתִּי וָאִישָׁנָה, הֱקִיצוֹתִי כִּי יהוה יִסְמְכֵנִי: לֹא־אִירָא מֵרִבְבוֹת עָם, אֲשֶׁר סָבִיב שָׁתוּ עָלָי: קוּמָה יהוה, הוֹשִׁיעֵנִי אֱלֹהַי, כִּי־הִכִּיתָ אֶת־כָּל־אֹיְבַי לֶחִי, שִׁנֵּי רְשָׁעִים שִׁבַּרְתָּ: לַיהוה הַיְשׁוּעָה, עַל־עַמְּךָ בִרְכָתֶךָ סֶּלָה:

הַשְׁכִּיבֵנוּ, יהוה אֱלֹהֵינוּ, לְשָׁלוֹם. וְהַעֲמִידֵנוּ, מַלְכֵּנוּ, לְחַיִּים. וּפְרֹשׂ עָלֵינוּ סֻכַּת שְׁלוֹמֶךָ, וְתַקְּנֵנוּ בְּעֵצָה טוֹבָה מִלְּפָנֶיךָ, וְהוֹשִׁיעֵנוּ לְמַעַן שְׁמֶךָ. וְהָגֵן בַּעֲדֵנוּ, וְהָסֵר מֵעָלֵינוּ אוֹיֵב, דֶּבֶר וְחֶרֶב וְרָעָב וְיָגוֹן. וְהָסֵר שָׂטָן מִלְּפָנֵינוּ וּמֵאַחֲרֵינוּ, וּבְצֵל כְּנָפֶיךָ תַּסְתִּירֵנוּ, כִּי אֵל שׁוֹמְרֵנוּ וּמַצִּילֵנוּ אָתָּה, כִּי אֵל מֶלֶךְ חַנּוּן וְרַחוּם אָתָּה. וּשְׁמֹר צֵאתֵנוּ וּבוֹאֵנוּ לְחַיִּים וּלְשָׁלוֹם מֵעַתָּה וְעַד עוֹלָם.

בָּרוּךְ יהוה בַּיּוֹם, בָּרוּךְ יהוה בַּלָּיְלָה, בָּרוּךְ יהוה בְּשָׁכְבֵנוּ, בָּרוּךְ
איוב יב יהוה בְּקוּמֵנוּ. כִּי בְיָדְךָ נַפְשׁוֹת הַחַיִּים וְהַמֵּתִים. אֲשֶׁר בְּיָדוֹ נֶפֶשׁ
תהלים לא כָּל־חָי, וְרוּחַ כָּל־בְּשַׂר־אִישׁ: בְּיָדְךָ אַפְקִיד רוּחִי, פָּדִיתָה אוֹתִי יהוה
אֵל אֱמֶת: אֱלֹהֵינוּ שֶׁבַּשָּׁמַיִם, יַחֵד שִׁמְךָ וְקַיֵּם מַלְכוּתְךָ תָּמִיד, וּמְלֹךְ עָלֵינוּ לְעוֹלָם וָעֶד.

יִרְאוּ עֵינֵינוּ וְיִשְׂמַח לִבֵּנוּ, וְתָגֵל נַפְשֵׁנוּ בִּישׁוּעָתְךָ בֶּאֱמֶת, בֶּאֱמֹר לְצִיּוֹן מָלַךְ אֱלֹהָיִךְ. יהוה מֶלֶךְ, יהוה מָלָךְ, יהוה יִמְלֹךְ לְעוֹלָם וָעֶד. כִּי הַמַּלְכוּת שֶׁלְּךָ הִיא, וּלְעוֹלְמֵי עַד תִּמְלֹךְ בְּכָבוֹד, כִּי אֵין לָנוּ מֶלֶךְ אֶלָּא אָתָּה.

הַמַּלְאָךְ May the angel who rescued me from all harm, bless these boys. Gen. 48
May they be called by my name and the names of my fathers Abraham and Isaac, and may they increase greatly on the earth.

וַיֹּאמֶר He said, "If you listen carefully to the voice of the LORD your Ex. 15
God and do what is right in His eyes, if you pay attention to His commandments and keep all His laws, I will not bring on you any of the diseases I brought on the Egyptians, for I am the LORD who heals you."
The LORD said to the accuser, "The LORD shall rebuke you, accuser. Zech. 3
The LORD who has chosen Jerusalem shall rebuke you! Is not this man
a burning stick snatched from the fire?" Look! It is Solomon's bed, es- Song. 3
corted by sixty warriors, the noblest of Israel, all of them wearing the sword, experienced in battle, each with his sword at his side, prepared for the terror of the nights.

Say three times:

יְבָרֶכְךָ May the LORD bless you and protect you. Num. 6
May the LORD make His face shine on you
and be generous to you.
May the LORD turn His face toward you
and give you peace.

Say three times:

הִנֵּה See – the Guardian of Israel Ps. 121
neither slumbers nor sleeps.

Say three times:

לִישׁוּעָתְךָ For Your salvation I hope, LORD. Gen. 49
I hope, LORD, for Your salvation.
LORD, for Your salvation I hope.

Say three times:

בְּשֵׁם In the name of the LORD, God of Israel:
may Michael be at my right hand,
Gabriel, at my left;
in front of me, Uriel,
behind me, Raphael;
and above my head the Presence of God.

בראשית מח הַמַּלְאָךְ הַגֹּאֵל אֹתִי מִכָּל־רָע יְבָרֵךְ אֶת־הַנְּעָרִים, וְיִקָּרֵא בָהֶם שְׁמִי
וְשֵׁם אֲבֹתַי אַבְרָהָם וְיִצְחָק, וְיִדְגּוּ לָרֹב בְּקֶרֶב הָאָרֶץ:

שמות טו וַיֹּאמֶר אִם־שָׁמוֹעַ תִּשְׁמַע לְקוֹל יהוה אֱלֹהֶיךָ, וְהַיָּשָׁר בְּעֵינָיו תַּעֲשֶׂה,
וְהַאֲזַנְתָּ לְמִצְוֺתָיו וְשָׁמַרְתָּ כָּל־חֻקָּיו, כָּל־הַמַּחֲלָה אֲשֶׁר־שַׂמְתִּי
זכריה ג בְמִצְרַיִם לֹא־אָשִׂים עָלֶיךָ, כִּי אֲנִי יהוה רֹפְאֶךָ: וַיֹּאמֶר יהוה אֶל־
הַשָּׂטָן, יִגְעַר יהוה בְּךָ הַשָּׂטָן, וְיִגְעַר יהוה בְּךָ הַבֹּחֵר בִּירוּשָׁלָםִ,
הֲלוֹא זֶה אוּד מֻצָּל מֵאֵשׁ: הִנֵּה מִטָּתוֹ שֶׁלִּשְׁלֹמֹה, שִׁשִּׁים גִּבֹּרִים
שיר השירים ג סָבִיב לָהּ, מִגִּבֹּרֵי יִשְׂרָאֵל: כֻּלָּם אֲחֻזֵי חֶרֶב, מְלֻמְּדֵי מִלְחָמָה, אִישׁ
חַרְבּוֹ עַל־יְרֵכוֹ מִפַּחַד בַּלֵּילוֹת:

Say three times:

במדבר ו יְבָרֶכְךָ יהוה וְיִשְׁמְרֶךָ:
יָאֵר יהוה פָּנָיו אֵלֶיךָ וִיחֻנֶּךָּ:
יִשָּׂא יהוה פָּנָיו אֵלֶיךָ וְיָשֵׂם לְךָ שָׁלוֹם:

Say three times:

תהלים קכא הִנֵּה לֹא־יָנוּם וְלֹא יִישָׁן שׁוֹמֵר יִשְׂרָאֵל:

Say three times:

בראשית מט לִישׁוּעָתְךָ קִוִּיתִי יהוה:
קִוִּיתִי יהוה לִישׁוּעָתְךָ
יהוה לִישׁוּעָתְךָ קִוִּיתִי

Say three times:

בְּשֵׁם יהוה אֱלֹהֵי יִשְׂרָאֵל
מִימִינִי מִיכָאֵל
וּמִשְּׂמֹאלִי גַּבְרִיאֵל
וּמִלְּפָנַי אוּרִיאֵל
וּמֵאֲחוֹרַי רְפָאֵל
וְעַל רֹאשִׁי שְׁכִינַת אֵל.

שִׁיר הַמַּעֲלוֹת A song of ascents. Ps. 128
Happy are all who fear the LORD, who walk in His ways.
When you eat the fruit of your labor, happy and fortunate are you.
Your wife shall be like a fruitful vine within your house;
your sons like olive saplings around your table.
So shall the man who fears the LORD be blessed.
May the LORD bless you from Zion;
may you see the good of Jerusalem all the days of your life;
and may you live to see your children's children. Peace be on Israel!

Say three times:

רִגְזוּ Tremble, and do not sin. Ps. 4
Search your heart as you lie on your bed, and be silent. Selah.

אֲדוֹן עוֹלָם LORD of the Universe,
who reigned before the birth of any thing;
when by His will all things were made,
then was His name declared King.
And when all things shall cease to be,
He alone will reign in awe.
He was, He is, and He shall be glorious for evermore.
He is One, there is none else, alone, unique, beyond compare;
Without beginning, without end, His might, His rule are everywhere.
He is my God; my Redeemer lives.
He is the Rock on whom I rely –
my banner and my safe retreat, my cup, my portion when I cry.
Into His hand my soul I place, when I awake and when I sleep.
The LORD is with me, I shall not fear;
body and soul from harm will He keep.

תהלים קכח

שִׁיר הַמַּעֲלוֹת, אַשְׁרֵי כָּל־יְרֵא יהוה, הַהֹלֵךְ בִּדְרָכָיו:
יְגִיעַ כַּפֶּיךָ כִּי תֹאכֵל, אַשְׁרֶיךָ וְטוֹב לָךְ:
אֶשְׁתְּךָ כְּגֶפֶן פֹּרִיָּה בְּיַרְכְּתֵי בֵיתֶךָ
בָּנֶיךָ כִּשְׁתִלֵי זֵיתִים, סָבִיב לְשֻׁלְחָנֶךָ:
הִנֵּה כִי־כֵן יְבֹרַךְ גָּבֶר יְרֵא יהוה:
יְבָרֶכְךָ יהוה מִצִּיּוֹן, וּרְאֵה בְּטוּב יְרוּשָׁלָםִ, כֹּל יְמֵי חַיֶּיךָ:
וּרְאֵה־בָנִים לְבָנֶיךָ, שָׁלוֹם עַל־יִשְׂרָאֵל:

Say three times:

תהלים ד

רִגְזוּ וְאַל־תֶּחֱטָאוּ
אִמְרוּ בִלְבַבְכֶם עַל־מִשְׁכַּבְכֶם, וְדֹמּוּ סֶלָה:

אֲדוֹן עוֹלָם אֲשֶׁר מָלַךְ בְּטֶרֶם כָּל־יְצִיר נִבְרָא.
לְעֵת נַעֲשָׂה בְחֶפְצוֹ כֹּל אֲזַי מֶלֶךְ שְׁמוֹ נִקְרָא.
וְאַחֲרֵי כִּכְלוֹת הַכֹּל לְבַדּוֹ יִמְלֹךְ נוֹרָא.
וְהוּא הָיָה וְהוּא הֹוֶה וְהוּא יִהְיֶה בְּתִפְאָרָה.
וְהוּא אֶחָד וְאֵין שֵׁנִי לְהַמְשִׁיל לוֹ לְהַחְבִּירָה.
בְּלִי רֵאשִׁית בְּלִי תַכְלִית וְלוֹ הָעֹז וְהַמִּשְׂרָה.
וְהוּא אֵלִי וְחַי גּוֹאֲלִי וְצוּר חֶבְלִי בְּעֵת צָרָה.
וְהוּא נִסִּי וּמָנוֹס לִי מְנָת כּוֹסִי בְּיוֹם אֶקְרָא.
בְּיָדוֹ אַפְקִיד רוּחִי בְּעֵת אִישַׁן וְאָעִירָה.
וְעִם רוּחִי גְּוִיָּתִי יהוה לִי וְלֹא אִירָא.

שבת
SHABBAT

Erev Shabbat

EIRUV TEḤUMIN

On Shabbat and Yom Tov it is forbidden to walk more than 2000 cubits (about 3000 feet) beyond the boundary (teḥum) of the town where you live or are staying when the day begins. By placing food sufficient for two meals, before nightfall, at a point within 2000 cubits from the town limits, you confer on that place the status of a dwelling for the next day, and are then permitted to walk 2000 cubits from there.

בָּרוּךְ Blessed are You, Lord our God, King of the Universe,
who has made us holy through His commandments,
and has commanded us about the mitzva of Eiruv.

By this Eiruv may we be permitted to walk from this place,
2000 cubits in any direction.

EIRUV ḤATZEROT

On Shabbat it is forbidden to carry objects from one private domain to another, or from a private domain into space shared by others, such as a communal staircase, corridor or courtyard. An Eiruv Ḥatzerot is created when each of the Jewish households in a court or apartment block, before Shabbat, places a loaf of bread or matza in one of the homes. The entire court or block then becomes a single private domain within which it is permitted to carry.

בָּרוּךְ Blessed are You, Lord our God, King of the Universe,
who has made us holy through His commandments,
and has commanded us about the mitzva of Eiruv.

By this Eiruv may we be permitted to move, carry out and carry in
from the houses to the courtyard, or from the courtyard to the houses,
or from house to house, for all the houses within the courtyard.

---

girls, the men on their way to the synagogue. When my town shall fade into the abyss of time, I will continue to remember the light and the warmth it radiated on Shabbat. (Elie Wiesel, *A Jew Today*)

LEARNING

"The Shabbat mood begins with its preparation. The Commandment says, "Remember the Shabbat Day to keep it holy." Our sages teach us that in order to truly keep it holy, we must remember it all week long and prepare for it. If you see something you will enjoy on Shabbat, by all means set it aside for use on Shabbat. (*Beitzah* 15b)

ערב שבת

עירוב תחומין

On שבת and יום טוב it is forbidden to walk more than 2000 cubits (about 3000 feet) beyond the boundary (תחום) of the town where you live or are staying when the day begins. By placing food sufficient for two meals, before nightfall, at a point within 2000 cubits from the town limits, you confer on that place the status of a dwelling for the next day, and are then permitted to walk 2000 cubits from there.

בָּרוּךְ אַתָּה יהוה אֱלֹהֵינוּ מֶלֶךְ הָעוֹלָם
אֲשֶׁר קִדְּשָׁנוּ בְּמִצְוֹתָיו וְצִוָּנוּ עַל מִצְוַת עֵרוּב.

בְּדֵין עֵרוּבָא יְהֵא שְׁרֵא לִי לְמֵיזַל מֵאַתְרָא הָדֵין
תְּרֵין אַלְפִין אַמִּין לְכָל רוּחָא.

עירוב חצרות

On שבת it is forbidden to carry objects from one private domain to another, or from a private domain into space shared by others, such as a communal staircase, corridor or courtyard. An עירוב חצרות is created when each of the Jewish households in a court or apartment block, before שבת, places a loaf of bread or matza in one of the homes. The entire court or block then becomes a single private domain within which it is permitted to carry.

בָּרוּךְ אַתָּה יהוה אֱלֹהֵינוּ מֶלֶךְ הָעוֹלָם
אֲשֶׁר קִדְּשָׁנוּ בְּמִצְוֹתָיו וְצִוָּנוּ עַל מִצְוַת עֵרוּב.

בְּדֵין עֵרוּבָא יְהֵא שְׁרֵא לַנָא לְטַלְטוּלֵי וּלְאַפּוּקֵי וּלְעַיּוּלֵי
מִן הַבָּתִּים לֶחָצֵר וּמִן הֶחָצֵר לַבָּתִּים
וּמִבַּיִת לְבַיִת לְכָל הַבָּתִּים שֶׁבֶּחָצֵר.

CONNECTION

I shall never forget Shabbat in my town. When I shall have forgotten everything else, my memory will still retain the atmosphere of holiday, of serenity pervading even the poorest houses; the white tablecloth, the candles, the meticulously combed little

CANDLE LIGHTING

On Erev Shabbat, cover the eyes with the hands after lighting the candles, and say:

בָּרוּךְ Blessed are You, Lord our God, King of the Universe, who has made us holy through His commandments, and has commanded us to light the Sabbath light.

Prayer after candlelighting (add the words in parentheses as appropriate):

יְהִי May it be Your will, Lord my God and God of my ancestors, that You give me grace – me (and my husband/and my father/and my mother/and my sons and my daughters) and all those close to me, and give us and all Israel good and long lives. And remember us with a memory that brings goodness and blessing; come to us with compassion and bless us with great blessings. Build our homes until they are complete, and allow Your Presence to live among us. And may I merit to raise children and grandchildren, each one wise and understanding, loving the Lord and in awe of God, people of truth, holy children, who will cling on to the Lord and light up the world with Torah and with good actions, and with all the kinds of work that serve the Creator. Please, hear my pleading at this time, by the merit of Sarah and Rebecca, Rachel and Leah our mothers, and light our candle that it should never go out, and light up Your face, so that we shall be saved, Amen.

REFLECTION

Rava said: If one must choose between Shabbat candles and the Hanukka candles (because he can only afford one), he chooses the Shabbat candles because they bring *shalom bayit* (peace in the home). Furthermore, if we have to choose between Shabbat candles or wine for Kiddush, the candles take precedence, on account of *shalom bayit*. (Shabbat 23b)

Close your eyes and think about everything you achieved this week. Everything you worked hard at. All the good and bad that happened to you. Now let it go. Feel it wash away from you as Shabbat begins. Can you feel the stress of the week being replaced with the tranquility of Shabbat?

... A THOUSAND WORDS

Take a look at the Shabbat candles – how do you contribute to *shalom bayit* in your home on Shabbat?

הדלקת נרות

On ערב שבת, cover the eyes with the hands after lighting the candles, and say:

בָּרוּךְ אַתָּה יהוה אֱלֹהֵינוּ מֶלֶךְ הָעוֹלָם
אֲשֶׁר קִדְּשָׁנוּ בְּמִצְוֹתָיו וְצִוָּנוּ לְהַדְלִיק נֵר שֶׁל שַׁבָּת.

Prayer after candlelighting (add the words in parentheses as appropriate):

יְהִי רָצוֹן מִלְּפָנֶיךָ יהוה אֱלֹהַי וֵאלֹהֵי אֲבוֹתַי, שֶׁתְּחוֹנֵן אוֹתִי (וְאֶת אִישִׁי/ וְאֶת אָבִי/ וְאֶת אִמִּי/ וְאֶת בָּנַי וְאֶת בְּנוֹתַי) וְאֶת כָּל קְרוֹבַי, וְתִתֶּן לָנוּ וּלְכָל יִשְׂרָאֵל חַיִּים טוֹבִים וַאֲרֻכִּים, וְתִזְכְּרֵנוּ בְּזִכְרוֹן טוֹבָה וּבְרָכָה, וְתִפְקְדֵנוּ בִּפְקֻדַּת יְשׁוּעָה וְרַחֲמִים, וּתְבָרְכֵנוּ בְּרָכוֹת גְּדוֹלוֹת, וְתַשְׁלִים בָּתֵּינוּ וְתַשְׁכֵּן שְׁכִינָתְךָ בֵּינֵינוּ. וְזַכֵּנִי לְגַדֵּל בָּנִים וּבְנֵי בָנִים חֲכָמִים וּנְבוֹנִים, אוֹהֲבֵי יהוה יִרְאֵי אֱלֹהִים, אַנְשֵׁי אֱמֶת זֶרַע קֹדֶשׁ, בַּיהוה דְּבֵקִים וּמְאִירִים אֶת הָעוֹלָם בַּתּוֹרָה וּבְמַעֲשִׂים טוֹבִים וּבְכָל מְלֶאכֶת עֲבוֹדַת הַבּוֹרֵא. אָנָּא שְׁמַע אֶת תְּחִנָּתִי בָּעֵת הַזֹּאת בִּזְכוּת שָׂרָה וְרִבְקָה וְרָחֵל וְלֵאָה אִמּוֹתֵינוּ, וְהָאֵר נֵרֵנוּ שֶׁלֹּא יִכְבֶּה לְעוֹלָם וָעֶד, וְהָאֵר פָּנֶיךָ וְנִוָּשֵׁעָה. אָמֵן.

LEARNING

Shabbat is the day that brings illumination to our world, which can so often seem to be dark and negative. Candles are a metaphor for Torah and for the human soul, and represent the light and holiness we bring to the world.

The first woman to light Shabbat candles was our matriarch Sara. While the mitzva of lighting Shabbat candles rests upon all members of the household, women have been charged with the actual lighting. This is one of the three special mitzvot for women. The time of candle-lighting is an especially auspicious occasion for private prayer.

In Sara's tent, a special miracle proclaimed that the Divine Presence dwelled therein: the lamp she lit every Friday evening, in honor of the divine day of rest, miraculously kept burning all week, until the next Friday eve. When Sara died the miracle of her Shabbat lamp ceased. But when Rivka was brought to Sara's tent as the destined wife of Sara's son, Yitzḥak, the miracle of the lamp returned. Once again, the light of Shabbat filled the tent of the matriarch of Israel and radiated its holiness to the entire week. (*Bereshit Raba* 60)

The service starts with Minḥa for Weekdays on page 272.
Most congregations sing "Beloved of the soul" before the Kabbalat Shabbat service.
On Yom Tov or Motza'ei Yom Tov falling on Shabbat, or on Shabbat Ḥol HaMo'ed, the service begins with Psalm 92 on page 440.

יְדִיד Beloved of the soul, Father of compassion,
draw Your servant close to Your will.
Like a deer will Your servant run
and bow before Your beauty.
To him Your love is sweeter
than honey from the comb, than any taste.

הָדוּר Glorious, beautiful, radiance of the world,
my soul is sick with love for You.
Please, God, heal her now
by showing her Your tender radiance.
Then she will recover her strength and be healed,
Be Your servant for eternity.

...A THOUSAND WORDS

between Friday and Shabbat, during which the final moments of Friday and the first stirrings of *Shabbat Kodesh* intertwine) is such a time. When such an encounter inevitably draws to a close, and the prospect of renewed separation imminently looms, on Shabbat afternoon, we sing this song again. (*Rabbi Simcha Willig*)

The service starts with מנחה לחול *on page 273.*
Most congregations sing יְדִיד נֶפֶשׁ *at this point before* קבלת שבת.
On מוצאי יום טוב *falling on* שבת, *or on* שבת חול המועד,
the service begins with מִזְמוֹר שִׁיר *on page 441.*

יְדִיד נֶפֶשׁ, אָב הָרַחֲמָן, מְשֹׁךְ עַבְדְּךָ אֶל רְצוֹנֶךָ
יָרוּץ עַבְדְּךָ כְּמוֹ אַיָּל, יִשְׁתַּחֲוֶה מוּל הֲדָרֶךָ
כִּי יֶעֱרַב לוֹ יְדִידוּתֶךָ, מִנֹּפֶת צוּף וְכָל טָעַם.

הָדוּר, נָאֶה, זִיו הָעוֹלָם, נַפְשִׁי חוֹלַת אַהֲבָתֶךָ
אָנָּא, אֵל נָא, רְפָא נָא לָהּ, בְּהַרְאוֹת לָהּ נֹעַם זִיוֶךָ
אָז תִּתְחַזֵּק וְתִתְרַפֵּא, וְהָיְתָה לָךְ שִׁפְחַת עוֹלָם.

REFLECTION

כִּי־יִבְעַל בָּחוּר בְּתוּלָה יִבְעָלוּךְ בָּנָיִךְ
וּמְשׂוֹשׂ חָתָן עַל־כַּלָּה יָשִׂישׂ עָלַיִךְ אֱלֹהָיִךְ:

As a young man marries a maiden,
so will your children settle with you,
and like a bridegroom's rejoicing
over his bride,
so will your God rejoice over you.
(*Yeshayahu* 62:5)

With whom do you most value spending time?

Think about the most special relationship you have.
What makes it special?

Have you ever felt sick with love?

Is your relationship with God loving?

LEARNING

In the most poetic language we talk of our lovesickness for God, but in the following line we ask that He heal us. Are we trying to rid ourselves of our lovesickness?

Lovesickness comes from being apart from the person you love. When we ask God to heal us, we are asking to be close to Him so that we may love Him without the sickness.

Even one who is deeply in love does not always express his admiration for his beloved at all times. There are moments, though, when his love pours out, without distraction, in great intensity. Among such occasions are the times when he is first reunited with his beloved after a period of separation. In this case, *erev Shabbat, bein hashemashot* (the twilight period

וָתִיק Ancient of Days, let Your mercy be aroused;
please have pity on Your beloved child.
How long have I yearned
to see the glory of Your strength.
Please, my God, my heart's desire –
be quick; do not hide Yourself.

הִגָּלֵה Reveal Yourself, beloved, and spread over me
the canopy of Your peace.
Let the earth shine with Your glory,
let us be overjoyed and rejoice in You.
Hurry, beloved, for the appointed time has come,
and be gracious to me as in the times of old.

David mailed the letter with a knot in his stomach.

The coming days and weeks brought new acquaintances and adventures as David hitchhiked with cars, vans, trucks, and freight trains, all the time edging closer to his home in Maryland.

Finally, as he ascended the passenger train that would be the last leg of his journey homeward, the knot returned and firmly lodged itself in his core. He could hardly bring himself to imagine the apple tree in the pasture of his childhood home, for fear it would be bereft of the white cloth, even in his imagination.

As he sat down next to the window that would deliver his fate, an elderly gentleman sat in the seat beside him. As day turned to night, and once again back to day, the travel companions shared their stories. As David regaled his neighbor with stories of the West Coast, Canada, and even Mexico, he realized that in just a short while the train tracks would take a gentle bend to the right, and there would be the farm on which he grew up, with its south-facing pasture, and the old apple tree which he used to climb as a child. He couldn't look. He was too afraid the cloth would not be there – too afraid he would find, staring back at him, just another tree, just another field – so he turned quickly away.

Desperately, he nudged his travel companion beside him. "Mister, will you do me a favor? Around this bend on the right, you'll see an apple tree. I wonder if you'll tell me if you see a white cloth tied to one of its branches."

"Son," the man said in a voice slow with wonder, "I see a white cloth tied on almost every twig."

(Based on *"Somebody's Son"*
by Richard Pindell)

וָתִיק, יֶהֱמוּ רַחֲמֶיךָ, וְחוּס נָא עַל בֵּן אוֹהֲבָךְ.
כִּי זֶה כַּמָּה נִכְסֹף נִכְסַף לִרְאוֹת בְּתִפְאֶרֶת עֻזָּךְ
אָנָּא, אֵלִי, מַחְמַד לִבִּי, חוּשָׁה נָּא, וְאַל תִּתְעַלָּם.

הִגָּלֶה נָא וּפְרֹשׂ, חָבִיב, עָלַי אֶת סֻכַּת שְׁלוֹמָךְ
תָּאִיר אֶרֶץ מִכְּבוֹדָךְ, נָגִילָה וְנִשְׂמְחָה בָּךְ.
מַהֵר, אָהוּב, כִּי בָא מוֹעֵד, וְחָנֵּנִי כִּימֵי עוֹלָם.

CONNECTION

As David sat on the side of the road in the Dakota plains, waiting for his next ride, he wrote:

Dear Mom,

If Dad will permit it I would like to come home. I know there's little chance he will. I'm not going to kid myself. I remember he said once, if I ever ran off, I might as well keep going.

All I can say is that I felt like leaving home was something I had to do. I wanted to find out more about life and about me, and the best way for us (life and me) to live with each other.

You won't be able to reach me by mail, because I don't know where I will be next. But in a few days, I hope to be passing our place. If there's any chance Dad will have me back, please ask him to tie a white cloth to the apple tree in the south pasture. I'll be going by on the train. If there's no cloth on the tree, I'll just quietly, and without any hard feelings toward Dad, keep going.

Love,

David

Kabbalat Shabbat

Mourners during the week of Shiva leave the synagogue at this point, returning after "Come, my Beloved" on page 440.

Ps. 95

לְכוּ נְרַנְּנָה Come, let us sing for joy to the LORD, let us shout aloud to the Rock of our salvation. Let us greet Him with thanksgiving, shout aloud to Him with songs of praise. For the LORD is the great God, the King great above all powers. In His hand are the depths of the earth, and the mountain peaks are His. The sea is His, for He made it; the dry land too, for His hands formed it. Come, let us bow in worship and bend the knee before the LORD our Maker. For He is our God, and we are the people of His pasture, the flock He tends – today, if you would listen to His voice. Do not harden your hearts as you did at Meribah, as you did that day at Massah in the desert, when your ancestors tested and tried Me though they had seen My deeds. ▸ For forty years I struggled with that generation. I said, "They are a people whose hearts go astray, who have not understood My ways." So I swore in My anger, "They shall not enter My place of rest."

REFLECTION

How do you transform yourself from the mindset of the week to a Shabbat state of mind?

Think about a piece of music that moved you. How can music transition your mood?

Are you ready to transition to Shabbat?

LEARNING

This psalm was originally composed by Moshe Rabbeinu and subsequently incorporated into *Tehillim* by King David. This *mizmor* is addressed to a generation in *galut* (exile), such as our own. However, the *mizmor* diverts us from the sad thoughts of suffering in exile by portraying our present experience as a second journey through the desert to which we ourselves can put an end at any time through our own efforts at observing the Torah and mitzvot.

There are two central themes in this psalm which reflect two central themes of Shabbat: the first half talks of creation and the second of the exodus from Egypt. These themes are found in the Kiddush for Friday night.

קבלת שבת

Mourners during the week of שבעה *leave the* בית כנסת *at this point, returning after* לְכָה דוֹדִי *on page 441.*

לְכוּ נְרַנְּנָה לַיהוה, נָרִיעָה לְצוּר יִשְׁעֵנוּ: נְקַדְּמָה פָנָיו בְּתוֹדָה, תהלים צה
בִּזְמִרוֹת נָרִיעַ לוֹ: כִּי אֵל גָּדוֹל יהוה, וּמֶלֶךְ גָּדוֹל עַל־כָּל־אֱלֹהִים:
אֲשֶׁר בְּיָדוֹ מֶחְקְרֵי־אָרֶץ, וְתוֹעֲפוֹת הָרִים לוֹ: אֲשֶׁר־לוֹ הַיָּם וְהוּא
עָשָׂהוּ, וְיַבֶּשֶׁת יָדָיו יָצָרוּ: בֹּאוּ נִשְׁתַּחֲוֶה וְנִכְרָעָה, נִבְרְכָה לִפְנֵי־יהוה
עֹשֵׂנוּ: כִּי הוּא אֱלֹהֵינוּ, וַאֲנַחְנוּ עַם מַרְעִיתוֹ וְצֹאן יָדוֹ, הַיּוֹם אִם־
בְּקֹלוֹ תִשְׁמָעוּ: אַל־תַּקְשׁוּ לְבַבְכֶם כִּמְרִיבָה, כְּיוֹם מַסָּה בַּמִּדְבָּר:
אֲשֶׁר נִסּוּנִי אֲבוֹתֵיכֶם, בְּחָנוּנִי גַּם רָאוּ פָעֳלִי: ◂ אַרְבָּעִים שָׁנָה אָקוּט
בְּדוֹר, וָאֹמַר עַם תֹּעֵי לֵבָב הֵם, וְהֵם לֹא־יָדְעוּ דְרָכָי: אֲשֶׁר־נִשְׁבַּעְתִּי
בְאַפִּי, אִם־יְבֹאוּן אֶל מְנוּחָתִי:

INTRODUCTION TO *KABBALAT SHABBAT*

Can you think of something really important to you that took a lot of preparation? Exams, a recital, the big game, or perhaps your Bar or Bat Mitzva? What kind of preparation did it take? Physical, mental, or emotional preparation? Sometimes weekly or even daily events and activities take just as much preparation if they are important enough to us. The authors of the siddur understood that and built this process into the siddur in several places. The first you encounter is the "verses of song" in *Pesukei DeZimra* that prepare you mentally, emotionally, and spiritually for the critical parts of the Shaḥarit *tefilla* service which are the *Shema* and *Amida*. In much the same way, the *Kabbalat Shabbat* (literally "Receiving the Sabbath") section of the Shabbat evening service prepares us not only for the critical parts of the evening *tefilla* service, but for actually accepting Shabbat as our holiest day of rest.

Kabbalat Shabbat is a later addition to the siddur, dating from the sixteenth century, and originating in the practice of the kabbalists who lived in Tzefat. These mystics, creative in their worship of Hashem, would literally leave the synagogue for the fields surrounding their homes to greet the Shabbat Queen as the sun set behind the hills of northern Israel. They would recite the seven psalms that comprise the *Kabbalat Shabbat* service as they did this. Six for the six days of creation and the six days of the work week, and the seventh for the holy Shabbat.

What do you take care to prepare for? How can you prepare yourself to welcome Shabbat?

שִׁירוּ Sing to the LORD a new song; sing to the LORD all the earth. Ps. 96
Sing to the LORD, bless His name; declare his deliverance day after day. Declare His glory among the nations, His wonders among all peoples. For great is the LORD and greatly to be praised; He is awesome beyond all heavenly powers. For all the gods of the peoples are mere idols: it was the LORD who made the heavens. Before Him are majesty and splendor; there are strength and beauty in His holy place. Give to the LORD, O families of the peoples; give to the LORD glory and might. Give to the LORD the glory due to His name; bring an offering and come into His courts. Bow down to the LORD in the splendor of holiness. Tremble before Him, all the earth. Say among the nations, "The LORD is King." The world stands firm, it will not be shaken. He will judge the peoples fairly. ▸ Let the heavens rejoice and the earth be glad. Let the sea roar, and all that is in it; let the fields be jubilant, and all they contain. Then the trees of the forest will sing for joy before the LORD, for He is coming to judge the earth. He will judge the world with justice, and the peoples with His trustworthiness.

LEARNING

The word כל is repeated seven times in this psalm. When Eisav and Yaakov were reunited following a long feud, each tells the other of his fortune. Eisav says, "I have plenty, רב." Yaakov by contrast says, "I have everything, כל." Someone who sees what he has as a lot will always look for more. Yaakov teaches us that when you see what you have as all encompassing, as everything you need, you learn to appreciate everything that you have and you cease to concern yourself with what is missing. This is the secret to contentment and fulfillment. When we think about having everything we need we can sing this song to God from a different perspective.

REFLECTION

Why sing a new song?

What areas in your life do you want to start over?

Can you think of something new to sing about this Shabbat?

שִׁירוּ לַיהוה שִׁיר חָדָשׁ, שִׁירוּ לַיהוה כָּל־הָאָרֶץ: שִׁירוּ לַיהוה, תהלים צו
בָּרְכוּ שְׁמוֹ, בַּשְּׂרוּ מִיּוֹם־לְיוֹם יְשׁוּעָתוֹ: סַפְּרוּ בַגּוֹיִם כְּבוֹדוֹ,
בְּכָל־הָעַמִּים נִפְלְאוֹתָיו: כִּי גָדוֹל יהוה וּמְהֻלָּל מְאֹד, נוֹרָא הוּא
עַל־כָּל־אֱלֹהִים: כִּי כָּל־אֱלֹהֵי הָעַמִּים אֱלִילִים, וַיהוה שָׁמַיִם
עָשָׂה: הוֹד־וְהָדָר לְפָנָיו, עֹז וְתִפְאֶרֶת בְּמִקְדָּשׁוֹ: הָבוּ לַיהוה
מִשְׁפְּחוֹת עַמִּים, הָבוּ לַיהוה כָּבוֹד וָעֹז: הָבוּ לַיהוה כְּבוֹד שְׁמוֹ,
שְׂאוּ־מִנְחָה וּבֹאוּ לְחַצְרוֹתָיו: הִשְׁתַּחֲווּ לַיהוה בְּהַדְרַת־קֹדֶשׁ,
חִילוּ מִפָּנָיו כָּל־הָאָרֶץ: אִמְרוּ בַגּוֹיִם יהוה מָלָךְ, אַף־תִּכּוֹן תֵּבֵל
בַּל־תִּמּוֹט, יָדִין עַמִּים בְּמֵישָׁרִים: ◂ יִשְׂמְחוּ הַשָּׁמַיִם וְתָגֵל הָאָרֶץ,
יִרְעַם הַיָּם וּמְלֹאוֹ: יַעֲלֹז שָׂדַי וְכָל־אֲשֶׁר־בּוֹ, אָז יְרַנְּנוּ כָּל־עֲצֵי־
יָעַר: לִפְנֵי יהוה כִּי בָא, כִּי בָא לִשְׁפֹּט הָאָרֶץ, יִשְׁפֹּט־תֵּבֵל בְּצֶדֶק,
וְעַמִּים בֶּאֱמוּנָתוֹ:

... A THOUSAND WORDS

CONNECTION

"The Sabbath is the lived enactment of the messianic age, a world of peace in which striving and conflict are (temporarily) at an end and all creation sings a song of being to its Creator." (Rabbi Jonathan Sacks, *The Jonathan Sacks Haggada*)

This psalm envisions a time when a new song will be sung; the entire world will sing about the glory of God in the messianic age. It is fitting that we sing about this on Shabbat, a time when we live in anticipation of this era.

יהוה מָלָךְ The LORD reigns, let the earth be glad. Let the many islands rejoice. Clouds and thick darkness surround Him; righteousness and justice are the foundation of His throne. Fire goes ahead of Him, consuming His enemies on every side. His lightning lights up the world; the earth sees and trembles. Mountains melt like wax before the LORD, before the LORD of all the earth. The heavens declare His righteousness, and all the peoples see His glory. All who worship images and boast in idols are put to shame. Bow down to Him, all you heavenly powers. Zion hears and rejoices, and the towns of Judah are glad because of your judgments, LORD. For You, LORD, are supreme over all the earth; You are great far above all heavenly powers. ▸ Let those who love the LORD hate evil, for He protects the lives of his devoted ones, delivering them from the hand of the wicked. Light is sown for the righteous, and joy for the upright in heart. Rejoice in the LORD, you who are righteous, and give thanks to His holy name. Ps. 97

---

that which is proper, still gets "down" at times. He feels troubled at times, and he hopes that, with the help of God, he will be able to continue on the correct path. That is why the "light" for the righteous is merely "sown"; when he has reached a higher level of self-improvement, this light will blossom into an overwhelming happiness. On the other hand, one who is upright (*yashar*) has worked on himself to the point that his evil inclination ceases to bother him. He knows that he has what he needs to serve God properly. Therefore, he is able to experience true joy upon doing that which is proper, as he feels sure that he will not stumble in the future.

CONNECTION

Rachel Fraenkel, mother of Naftali Fraenkel who was kidnapped and murdered in Israel in the summer of 2014, said: "People from all over were saying, 'These are not just your boys, these are our children.' Sometimes I ask myself, was this just an illusion? I have this image of a person walking in the dark and it's raining and they're stumbling and they're figuring out their way. They don't see anything and then for a second there's lightning and in that lightning they see the reality of their surroundings. It helps them guide their way. We had days and days of lightning. It's no illusion what we saw there, ourselves. We're part of something huge. We're part of a people, of a true family that's for real."

תהלים צז
יהוה מָלָךְ תָּגֵל הָאָרֶץ, יִשְׂמְחוּ אִיִּים רַבִּים: עָנָן וַעֲרָפֶל סְבִיבָיו,
צֶדֶק וּמִשְׁפָּט מְכוֹן כִּסְאוֹ: אֵשׁ לְפָנָיו תֵּלֵךְ, וּתְלַהֵט סָבִיב צָרָיו:
הֵאִירוּ בְרָקָיו תֵּבֵל, רָאֲתָה וַתָּחֵל הָאָרֶץ: הָרִים כַּדּוֹנַג נָמַסּוּ
מִלִּפְנֵי יהוה, מִלִּפְנֵי אֲדוֹן כָּל־הָאָרֶץ: הִגִּידוּ הַשָּׁמַיִם צִדְקוֹ, וְרָאוּ
כָל־הָעַמִּים כְּבוֹדוֹ: יֵבֹשׁוּ כָּל־עֹבְדֵי פֶסֶל הַמִּתְהַלְלִים בָּאֱלִילִים,
הִשְׁתַּחֲווּ־לוֹ כָּל־אֱלֹהִים: שָׁמְעָה וַתִּשְׂמַח צִיּוֹן, וַתָּגֵלְנָה בְּנוֹת
יְהוּדָה, לְמַעַן מִשְׁפָּטֶיךָ יהוה: כִּי־אַתָּה יהוה עֶלְיוֹן עַל־כָּל־הָאָרֶץ,
מְאֹד נַעֲלֵיתָ עַל־כָּל־אֱלֹהִים: ‹ אֹהֲבֵי יהוה שִׂנְאוּ רָע, שֹׁמֵר
נַפְשׁוֹת חֲסִידָיו, מִיַּד רְשָׁעִים יַצִּילֵם: אוֹר זָרֻעַ לַצַּדִּיק, וּלְיִשְׁרֵי־לֵב
שִׂמְחָה: שִׂמְחוּ צַדִּיקִים בַּיהוה, וְהוֹדוּ לְזֵכֶר קָדְשׁוֹ:

REFLECTION

What emotions are described in this psalm?

Which emotion describes how you feel toward God now?

What areas in your life would benefit from more "love"?

...A THOUSAND WORDS

LEARNING

Rav Ḥayyim of Volozhin explained a difference between "righteous" and "upright." A righteous person (a *tzaddik*) is a person whose evil inclination works extremely hard to cause him or her to stray from the path of good. This person, even though he knows that he is doing that which is correct, and experiences joy from doing

מִזְמוֹר A Psalm. Sing a new song to the LORD, for He has done wondrous things; He has saved by His right hand and His holy arm. The LORD has made His salvation known; He has displayed His righteousness in the sight of the nations. He remembered His loving-kindness and trustworthiness to the house of Israel; all the ends of the earth have seen the victory of our LORD. Shout for joy to the LORD, all the earth; burst into song, sing with joy, play music. Play music to the LORD on the harp – on the harp with the sound of singing. With trumpets and the sound of the shofar, shout for joy before the LORD, the King. ▸ Let the sea and all that is in it thunder, the world and all who live in it. Let the rivers clap their hands, the mountains sing together for joy – before the LORD, for He is coming to judge the earth. He will judge the world with justice, and the peoples fairly. *Ps. 98*

LEARNING

וְעַתָּה
כִּתְבוּ לָכֶם אֶת־הַשִּׁירָה הַזֹּאת
(דברים לא, יט)

"And now,
write for yourself this song."
(*Devarim* 31:19)

This is the commandment to write down the Torah. We often refer to the Torah as a song, perhaps because the transmission of Torah can be best preserved in song (*Tosafot, Megilla* 32a). Think of how many songs you know by heart – how can you remember so many words? Words of song are imprinted on our hearts and souls which makes them that much easier to remember.

...A THOUSAND WORDS

תהלים צח

מִזְמוֹר, שִׁירוּ לַיהוה שִׁיר חָדָשׁ כִּי־נִפְלָאוֹת עָשָׂה, הוֹשִׁיעָה־לּוֹ יְמִינוֹ וּזְרוֹעַ קָדְשׁוֹ: הוֹדִיעַ יהוה יְשׁוּעָתוֹ, לְעֵינֵי הַגּוֹיִם גִּלָּה צִדְקָתוֹ: זָכַר חַסְדּוֹ וֶאֱמוּנָתוֹ לְבֵית יִשְׂרָאֵל, רָאוּ כָל־אַפְסֵי־אָרֶץ אֵת יְשׁוּעַת אֱלֹהֵינוּ: הָרִיעוּ לַיהוה כָּל־הָאָרֶץ, פִּצְחוּ וְרַנְּנוּ וְזַמֵּרוּ: זַמְּרוּ לַיהוה בְּכִנּוֹר, בְּכִנּוֹר וְקוֹל זִמְרָה: בַּחֲצֹצְרוֹת וְקוֹל שׁוֹפָר, הָרִיעוּ לִפְנֵי הַמֶּלֶךְ יהוה: ׳ יִרְעַם הַיָּם וּמְלֹאוֹ, תֵּבֵל וְיֹשְׁבֵי בָהּ: נְהָרוֹת יִמְחֲאוּ־כָף, יַחַד הָרִים יְרַנֵּנוּ: לִפְנֵי יהוה כִּי בָא לִשְׁפֹּט הָאָרֶץ, יִשְׁפֹּט־תֵּבֵל בְּצֶדֶק, וְעַמִּים בְּמֵישָׁרִים:

CONNECTION

Reb Yosef Friedenson tells the following story:

During the war, he and a group of friends were in a metal shop in a slave labor camp. The day was Shemini Atzeret, and though they were living in constant fear for their lives, they still wanted to celebrate the day in some way. Before receiving their orders from the overseer, a man named Pape, they found a few free moments and despite their bitter situation they broke out in the spirited holiday song, "Ein adir kaHashem, ve'ein barukh keven Amram" – *"There is none as powerful as Hashem, nor blessed as Moshe, the son of Amram."*

Pape walked into the shop and was shocked. Despite the torture, the humiliation, and the endless sense of loss that was their daily existence, these Jews were singing! "Why do you sing?" he asked in bewilderment. "Is life so good that you can sing?"

The group explained the words of the song, going through each stanza, including those that read, "There are no wise men like the scholars of the Torah, and there is no redeemer like Hashem."

Pape was astonished. "After all the pain and torture that you have been through, do you really still believe this?"

Immediately one of the younger members of the group jumped up and cried out, "Yes!" This particular lad wasn't particularly known for his religiosity, yet his voice was emphatic. Immediately others joined him with their endorsement.

Pape was astonished; he shook his head and was heard to say, "I don't know how the Fuhrer will ever get rid of you!"

REFLECTION

What acts make you notice God and His intervention in your life?

What do you want to celebrate?

יהוה מָלָךְ The LORD reigns, let the peoples tremble. He sits enthroned on the Cherubim, let the earth quake. Great is the LORD in Zion, He is elevated over all the peoples. Let them praise Your name, O great and awesome One: He is holy! The King in His might loves justice. You have established fairness. The justice and righteousness in Jacob is Your doing. Elevate the LORD our God, and bow at His footstool: He is holy! Moses and Aaron were among His priests; Samuel was among those who called on His name. They called on the LORD and He answered them. ▸ He spoke to them in a pillar of cloud; they observed His testimonies and the law He gave them. LORD our God, You answered them. You were for them a forgiving God, though You punished their sins. Elevate the LORD our God and bow at His holy mountain, for the LORD our God is holy. *Ps. 99*

CONNECTION

A holy Hasidic Rebbe was conducting his tish. *Hundreds of Hasidim flocked to his table to listen to the words of Torah, to sing the special* niggunim *from their* Ḥasidut *and to share in the delicious fruits that were distributed. In the middle of the* tish, *a poor man made his way to the head of the table where the Rebbe sat. The Hasidim eyed his tattered clothing with interest. The poor man tapped the Rebbe on the shoulder and asked him, "My horse will no longer walk, what should I do?" The Rebbe looked thoughtful and answered the man, "Let him rest, I am sure he will recover." The singing recommenced until the poor man tapped the Rebbe again. "I already rested him," he said. The Hasidim, somewhat impatient and frustrated with the man, tried to hush him. The Rebbe shook his head and smiled at the poor man: "Perhaps take him to have his shoe changed."*

The poor man smiled a wide and appreciative smile, thanked the Rebbe profusely, and shuffled out of the room.

Without waiting for the inevitable questions from his Hasidim, the Rebbe explained: "Questions are attempts at a connection. This man wanted to connect with our Ḥasidut *and this* tish, *and asking questions about his horse was the only way he knew how to approach us. Who am I to turn away anyone seeking to connect?"*

Do you ask questions to connect to someone?
What question do you want to ask God?

תהלים צט

יהוה מָלָךְ יִרְגְּזוּ עַמִּים, יֹשֵׁב כְּרוּבִים תָּנוּט הָאָרֶץ: יהוה בְּצִיּוֹן
גָּדוֹל, וְרָם הוּא עַל־כָּל־הָעַמִּים: יוֹדוּ שִׁמְךָ גָּדוֹל וְנוֹרָא קָדוֹשׁ
הוּא: וְעֹז מֶלֶךְ מִשְׁפָּט אָהֵב, אַתָּה כּוֹנַנְתָּ מֵישָׁרִים, מִשְׁפָּט
וּצְדָקָה בְּיַעֲקֹב אַתָּה עָשִׂיתָ: רוֹמְמוּ יהוה אֱלֹהֵינוּ, וְהִשְׁתַּחֲווּ
לַהֲדֹם רַגְלָיו, קָדוֹשׁ הוּא: מֹשֶׁה וְאַהֲרֹן בְּכֹהֲנָיו, וּשְׁמוּאֵל בְּקֹרְאֵי
שְׁמוֹ, קֹרְאִים אֶל־יהוה וְהוּא יַעֲנֵם: ◂ בְּעַמּוּד עָנָן יְדַבֵּר אֲלֵיהֶם,
שָׁמְרוּ עֵדֹתָיו וְחֹק נָתַן־לָמוֹ: יהוה אֱלֹהֵינוּ אַתָּה עֲנִיתָם, אֵל נֹשֵׂא
הָיִיתָ לָהֶם, וְנֹקֵם עַל־עֲלִילוֹתָם: רוֹמְמוּ יהוה אֱלֹהֵינוּ, וְהִשְׁתַּחֲווּ
לְהַר קָדְשׁוֹ, כִּי־קָדוֹשׁ יהוה אֱלֹהֵינוּ:

...A THOUSAND WORDS

REFLECTION

Does God speak to you?

Do you hear God
in your world?
Where?

What does God say?

In what ways do you think
God can speak to us today?

LEARNING

וּשְׁמוּאֵל בְּקֹרְאֵי שְׁמוֹ Shmuel, possibly the greatest *navi* after Moshe, also led and taught the people in this way. Each of them called upon Hashem in supplication to ask Hashem's forgiveness for the people and He answered them – קֹרְאִים אֶל־ה׳ וְהוּא יַעֲנֵם. Each of these leaders had a special relationship with God and they chose to channel their connection in service of the people. This is what makes them leaders, not simply holy people.

Moshe and Aharon were among His Kohanim – מֹשֶׁה וְאַהֲרֹן בְּכֹהֲנָיו. Kohanim are designated individuals who exert influence through teaching, personal example, and symbolic acts. Moshe officiated as a *Kohen Gadol* during the seven days of the inauguration of the *Mishkan* and Aharon followed until his death. Both had tremendous influence as leaders to help the people connect with God.

The following psalm is said standing:

מִזְמוֹר לְדָוִד A psalm of David. Give to the LORD, you angelic powers, give to the LORD glory and might. Give to the LORD the glory due to His name. Bow to the LORD in the beauty of holi-ness. The LORD's voice echoes over the waters; the God of glory thunders; the LORD is over the mighty waters. The LORD's voice in power, the LORD's voice in beauty, the LORD's voice breaks cedars, the LORD shatters the cedars of Lebanon. He makes Lebanon skip like a calf, Sirion like a young wild ox. The LORD's voice cleaves flames of fire. The LORD's voice makes the desert quake, the LORD shakes the desert of Kadesh. ▸ The LORD's voice makes hinds calve and strips the forests bare, and in His temple all say: "Glory!" The LORD sat enthroned at the Flood, the LORD sits enthroned as King for ever. The LORD will give strength to His people; the LORD will bless His people with peace. *Ps. 29*

REFLECTION

What inspires you to sing?

When does singing inspire you?

... A THOUSAND WORDS

The following psalm is said standing:

מִזְמוֹר לְדָוִד, הָבוּ לַיהוה בְּנֵי אֵלִים, הָבוּ לַיהוה כָּבוֹד וָעֹז: הָבוּ תהלים כט
לַיהוה כְּבוֹד שְׁמוֹ, הִשְׁתַּחֲווּ לַיהוה בְּהַדְרַת־קֹדֶשׁ: קוֹל יהוה
עַל הַמָּיִם, אֵל־הַכָּבוֹד הִרְעִים, יהוה עַל־מַיִם רַבִּים: קוֹל־יהוה
בַּכֹּחַ, קוֹל יהוה בֶּהָדָר: קוֹל יהוה שֹׁבֵר אֲרָזִים, וַיְשַׁבֵּר יהוה אֶת־
אַרְזֵי הַלְּבָנוֹן: וַיַּרְקִידֵם כְּמוֹ־עֵגֶל, לְבָנוֹן וְשִׂרְיֹן כְּמוֹ בֶן־רְאֵמִים:
קוֹל־יהוה חֹצֵב לַהֲבוֹת אֵשׁ: קוֹל יהוה יָחִיל מִדְבָּר, יָחִיל יהוה
מִדְבַּר קָדֵשׁ: › קוֹל יהוה יְחוֹלֵל אַיָּלוֹת וַיֶּחֱשֹׂף יְעָרוֹת, וּבְהֵיכָלוֹ,
כֻּלּוֹ אֹמֵר כָּבוֹד: יהוה לַמַּבּוּל יָשָׁב, וַיֵּשֶׁב יהוה מֶלֶךְ לְעוֹלָם:
יהוה עֹז לְעַמּוֹ יִתֵּן, יהוה יְבָרֵךְ אֶת־עַמּוֹ בַשָּׁלוֹם:

LEARNING

In this psalm, King David recounts stirring impressions of the voice of Hashem as it was heard at critical times during the history of the world, beginning with creation. The voices are heard in places where God's glory is not immediately apparent. These seven voices are a reference to the seven days of the week (Rabbi Tzvi Hersh Weinreb). The Talmud (*Berakhot* 29a) explains that the seven blessings of the Shabbat *Amida* correspond to the seven times the phrase "God's voice" appears in this psalm. The number seven incorporates six – corresponding to the six days of creative activity – plus an additional seventh dimension of direction and purpose (Maharal, *Tiferet Yisrael*, ch. 40). The seven blessings of the Shabbat *Amida* teach that the Shabbat rest is not just the abstention from productive work, but rather the development of our moral faculties and spiritual direction, cultivating our closeness to God and His ways.

CONNECTION

The Gemara (Pesaḥim 117a) *explains the difference between the chapters of* Tehillim *that start with the words* "Mizmor leDavid" *and the ones that start with* "LeDavid mizmor." *When a psalm begins with* "LeDavid mizmor," *King David* received ruaḥ hakodesh *(divine inspiration), and as a result he wrote the song. By contrast, when a psalm starts with* "Mizmor leDavid," *David composed the song himself, and through his own words and music, he was able to receive divine inspiration and to connect with God.*

The following is said in some congregations:

Please, by the power of Your great right hand,
set the captive nation free.
Accept Your people's prayer. Strengthen us, purify us,
You who are feared.
Please, Mighty One, guard like the pupil of the eye
those who seek Your unity.
Bless them, cleanse them, have compassion on them,
grant them Your righteousness always.
Mighty One, Holy One, in Your great goodness
guide Your congregation.
Only One, Great One, turn to Your people,
who declare Your holiness.
Accept our plea and listen to our cry,
You who know all secret thoughts.

Blessed be the name of His glorious kingdom for
ever and all time.

LEARNING

The *Ana BeKho'aḥ* prayer is attributed to the great kabalistic sage Rabbi Neḥunia ben HaKana (first century CE). The mystical prayer was written according to the forty-two-letter name of Hashem and is composed of seven lines, with six words in each line. The first letter of every word spells out the forty-two-letter name, one of the Holy Names of Hashem. Each line corresponds to one day of the week. God's name is not explicitly expressed – just hinted to, encouraging us to look beneath the surface and seek Him out.

CONNECTION

For most Jews, the prayer of Ana BeKho'aḥ *is an appeal for salvation from metaphysical dangers which may impede our prayers from reaching God. However, we can take a moment to consider the soldiers of Israel, who literally lay their lives on the line on behalf of their people, state, and tradition. Their* Ana BeKho'aḥ *might be asking God to physically strengthen the nation. Therefore, it is altogether appropriate for us to think of them and their sacrifices, and join them in an appeal to the Holy One, blessed be He, in the form of the poem Ana* BeKho'aḥ, *to keep them and their families safe from harm.* (Rabbi Yaakov Bieler)

The following is said in some congregations:

אָנָּא, בְּכֹחַ גְּדֻלַּת יְמִינְךָ, תַּתִּיר צְרוּרָה.
קַבֵּל רִנַּת עַמְּךָ, שַׂגְּבֵנוּ, טַהֲרֵנוּ, נוֹרָא.
נָא גִבּוֹר, דּוֹרְשֵׁי יִחוּדְךָ כְּבָבַת שָׁמְרֵם.
בָּרְכֵם, טַהֲרֵם, רַחֲמֵם, צִדְקָתְךָ תָּמִיד גָּמְלֵם.
חֲסִין קָדוֹשׁ, בְּרֹב טוּבְךָ נַהֵל עֲדָתֶךָ.
יָחִיד גֵּאֶה, לְעַמְּךָ פְּנֵה, זוֹכְרֵי קְדֻשָּׁתֶךָ.
שַׁוְעָתֵנוּ קַבֵּל וּשְׁמַע צַעֲקָתֵנוּ, יוֹדֵעַ תַּעֲלוּמוֹת.

בָּרוּךְ שֵׁם כְּבוֹד מַלְכוּתוֹ לְעוֹלָם וָעֶד.

... A THOUSAND WORDS

REFLECTION

Do you know someone who might feel trapped and needs special attention from God?

Who do you want to ask God to help this Shabbat?

Do you know someone serving in the IDF? Where are they this Shabbat?

לְכָה דוֹדִי Come, my Beloved, to greet the bride;
let us welcome the Sabbath.
Come, my Beloved, to greet the bride;
let us welcome the Sabbath.

שָׁמוֹר "Observe" and "Remember" in one act of speech,
the One and Only God made us hear.
The Lord is One and His name is One,
for fame, for splendor, and for praise.
Come, my Beloved, to greet the bride;
let us welcome the Sabbath.

לִקְרַאת To greet the Sabbath, come let us go,
for of blessing, she is the source.
From the outset, as of old, ordained:
last in deed, first in thought.
Come, my Beloved, to greet the bride;
let us welcome the Sabbath.

CONNECTION

"Even in those neighborhoods made up predominantly of religious Jews, one can no longer talk of the 'sanctity of Shabbat.' True, there are Jews in America who observe Shabbat.... But it is not for Shabbat that my heart aches; it is for the forgotten 'erev Shabbat' *(eve of the Sabbath). There are Shabbat-observing Jews in America, but there are no* 'erev Shabbat' *Jews who go out to greet Shabbat with beating hearts and pulsating souls. There are many who observe the precepts with their hands, with their feet, and or with their mouths – but there are few indeed who truly know the meaning of the service of the heart!"* (Rabbi J.B. Soloveitchik, *On Repentance*)

LEARNING

The Talmud (*Shevuot* 20b) explains that when the commandment of Shabbat was given, God spoke one utterance, but we heard two distinct words: *shamor*, representing the prohibitions, and *zakhor*, representing the affirmative commandments. Affirmative commandments are associated with *ahavat Hashem*, love of God, while prohibitions are associated with *yirat Hashem*, fear of God. The reason why they were said simultaneously is to show the equal importance of both. Shabbat is not simply a list of prohibitions, nor is it just about eating good food and making Kiddush. Shabbat is about connecting to God and taking time to find our spiritual core through the combination of these commandments.

לְכָה דוֹדִי לִקְרַאת כַּלָּה, פְּנֵי שַׁבָּת נְקַבְּלָה.
לְכָה דוֹדִי לִקְרַאת כַּלָּה, פְּנֵי שַׁבָּת נְקַבְּלָה.

שָׁמוֹר וְזָכוֹר בְּדִבּוּר אֶחָד
הִשְׁמִיעָנוּ אֵל הַמְיֻחָד
יהוה אֶחָד וּשְׁמוֹ אֶחָד
לְשֵׁם וּלְתִפְאֶרֶת וְלִתְהִלָּה.
לְכָה דוֹדִי לִקְרַאת כַּלָּה, פְּנֵי שַׁבָּת נְקַבְּלָה.

לִקְרַאת שַׁבָּת לְכוּ וְנֵלְכָה
כִּי הִיא מְקוֹר הַבְּרָכָה
מֵרֹאשׁ מִקֶּדֶם נְסוּכָה
סוֹף מַעֲשֶׂה בְּמַחֲשָׁבָה תְּחִלָּה.
לְכָה דוֹדִי לִקְרַאת כַּלָּה, פְּנֵי שַׁבָּת נְקַבְּלָה.

LEARNING

This mystical hymn to the Shabbat was composed by the kabbalist Rabbi Shlomo HaLevi Alkabetz (1500–1580), teacher and brother-in-law of the famed kabbalist Rabbi Moshe Cordovero. Rabbi Alkabetz was one of the esteemed members of the Tzefat circle of scholars and mystics, which included Rabbi Yosef Karo, author of the *Shulḥan Arukh*, Rabbi Moshe Cordovero, and Rabbi Yitzḥak Luria, the famous mystic known as the Holy Ari. The author signed his name "Shlomo HaLevi," in the acrostic formed by the first letters of the first eight stanzas of the hymn.

Only the first two stanzas and the last stanza relate to the Shabbat theme. The rest reflect the Jewish longing for redemption, which includes the restoration of Yerushalayim and the coming of the Mashiaḥ. Each of the other five stanzas describes another stage in the process of redemption.

Imagine the hills and mountains surrounding Tzefat; at the time when this song was written it was the practice of the great scholars to venture out of their *shuls* into the fields, turning toward the west at the time of sunset to literally greet Shabbat.

What do you think is the connection between the two distinct themes of *Lekha Dodi* – Shabbat, and the redemption and restoration of Yerushalayim?

מִקְדַּשׁ Sanctuary of the King, royal city,
arise, go forth from your ruined state.
Too long have you dwelt in the valley of tears.
He will shower compassion on you.

Come, my Beloved, to greet the bride;
let us welcome the Sabbath.

הִתְנַעֲרִי Shake yourself off, arise from the dust!
Put on your clothes of glory, My people.
Through the son of Jesse the Bethlehemite,
draw near to my soul and redeem it.

Come, my Beloved, to greet the bride;
let us welcome the Sabbath.

CONNECTION

"Anyone who feels a true bond in his heart with the life of the nation over many generations, simply will not be able – even if he believes neither in the World to Come nor the Jewish state – to imagine the Jewish people without ***Shabbat Malketa*** *(the Sabbath Queen). It may be said without exaggeration that more than the Jews kept the Sabbath, it was the Sabbath that kept them."* (Aḥad HaAm)

REFLECTION

Do you need to "brush away or shake off" anything from the past week?

Look at your Shabbat clothes. What special feelings for Shabbat do they help you feel?

How can you try to have a positive attitude this Shabbat?

LEARNING

Who is the beloved **דודי** in this beautiful prayer?

Rabbi Yaakovson in *Netiv Bina* says that the *"Dod"* is *Knesset Yisrael*, and we are thus inviting an inter-generational mass of our people to join together in greeting Shabbat. The more common understanding, however, is that of Rabbi S.R. Hirsch and others, that the *"Dod"* is Hashem. We begin the verse by asking Hashem (*"Dodi"*) to go ahead (*"Lekha"*) and greet (*"likrat"*) Shabbat (*"kalla"*), which, when He does, would in turn lead all of the Jews together to accept (*"nekabla"*) the face of Shabbat (*"penei Shabbat"*). Hashem marches ahead at the front of the line to "greet" Shabbat, so to speak, following which we all together accept Shabbat as a nation.

מִקְדַּשׁ מֶלֶךְ עִיר מְלוּכָה
קוּמִי צְאִי מִתּוֹךְ הַהֲפֵכָה
רַב לָךְ שֶׁבֶת בְּעֵמֶק הַבָּכָא
וְהוּא יַחֲמֹל עָלַיִךְ חֶמְלָה.
לְכָה דוֹדִי לִקְרַאת כַּלָּה, פְּנֵי שַׁבָּת נְקַבְּלָה.

הִתְנַעֲרִי, מֵעָפָר קוּמִי
לִבְשִׁי בִּגְדֵי תִפְאַרְתֵּךְ עַמִּי
עַל יַד בֶּן יִשַׁי בֵּית הַלַּחְמִי
קָרְבָה אֶל נַפְשִׁי, גְּאָלָהּ.
לְכָה דוֹדִי לִקְרַאת כַּלָּה, פְּנֵי שַׁבָּת נְקַבְּלָה.

LEARNING

The image of shaking off the dust and dressing in grand clothing is a central metaphor in *Yeshayahu*. It refers to the transition from enslaved captive to royal lady and from abandoned woman mourning her beloved to a remarriage in bridal clothes. **הִתְנַעֲרִי, מֵעָפָר קוּמִי** commands the poet (*Yeshayahu* 52:2) to throw off your depression, regain your dignity and self-respect, and prepare for your liberation from captivity. The Shabbat entrance is correlated with Israel's rise to redemption. The metaphor is the commandment to change our "literal" clothes and our mood as Shabbat approaches and we emerge from the alienation and dusty reality of weekday existence.

Think about something you want to shake off; what difficulty or negativity do you want to rise from as Shabbat enters into our lives?

... A THOUSAND WORDS

הִתְעוֹרְרִי Wake up, wake up,
for your light has come: rise, shine!
Awake, awake, break out in song,
for the LORD's glory is revealed on you.

Come, my Beloved, to greet the bride;
let us welcome the Sabbath.

לֹא תֵבֹשִׁי Do not be ashamed, do not be confused.
Why be discouraged? Why do you mourn?
In you the needy of My people find shelter,
and the city shall be rebuilt on its hill.

Come, my Beloved, to greet the bride;
let us welcome the Sabbath.

CONNECTION

Master of the universe,
grant me always the ability to be alone;
may it ever be my custom to go outdoors each day
among the trees and grasses, among all growing things,
and there may I be alone, and enter into prayer,
to talk with the One to whom I belong.

May I express there everything in my heart,
and may all the foliage of the field (all grasses, trees, and plants)
may they all awake at my coming,
to send the power of their life into the words of my prayer,
so that my prayer and speech are made whole,
through the life and spirit of all growing things,
which are made as one by their transcendent Source.

May they all be gathered into my prayer,
and thus may I be worthy to open my heart fully
in prayer, supplication, and holy speech,
that I pour out the words of my heart
before Your Presence like water, O LORD,
and lift up my hands to You in worship,
on behalf of my own soul, and the souls of my children.

(Rabbi Nachman of Breslov)

הִתְעוֹרְרִי הִתְעוֹרְרִי
כִּי בָא אוֹרֵךְ קוּמִי אוֹרִי
עוּרִי עוּרִי, שִׁיר דַּבֵּרִי
כְּבוֹד יהוה עָלַיִךְ נִגְלָה.
לְכָה דוֹדִי לִקְרַאת כַּלָּה, פְּנֵי שַׁבָּת נְקַבְּלָה.

לֹא תֵבֹשִׁי וְלֹא תִכָּלְמִי
מַה תִּשְׁתּוֹחֲחִי וּמַה תֶּהֱמִי
בָּךְ יֶחֱסוּ עֲנִיֵּי עַמִּי
וְנִבְנְתָה עִיר עַל תִּלָּהּ.
לְכָה דוֹדִי לִקְרַאת כַּלָּה, פְּנֵי שַׁבָּת נְקַבְּלָה.

LEARNING

Just as the *kalla* (bride) appears to her *ḥatan* (groom) dressed beautifully, with jewelry and perfume, Shabbat presents herself to Israel dressed beautifully with jewelry. Just as the *ḥatan* is dressed in magnificent attire, so a person should dress magnificently for Shabbat. Just as the *ḥatan* enjoys pleasures on his wedding day, so a person should indulge in pleasures on Shabbat. Just as the *ḥatan* takes off from work, so does a person refrain from work on Shabbat…. Just as the *ḥatan* refrains from food and drink before the wedding ceremony, one should not eat heavily on Friday afternoon so as to enter Shabbat with an appetite. Just as the *ḥatan* is sanctifies (*Kiddushin*) his bride with wine, so a person should sanctify Shabbat with wine. (*Sefer HaPelia* | 36b)

… A THOUSAND WORDS

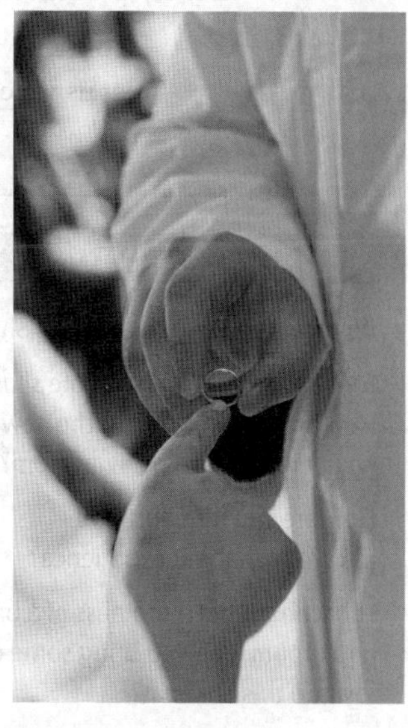

וְהָיוּ Those who plundered you shall be plundered,
and all who devoured you shall be far away.
Your God will rejoice over you
as a bridegroom rejoices over his bride.

Come, my Beloved, to greet the bride;
let us welcome the Sabbath.

יָמִין Right and left you shall spread out,
and the LORD you will fear.
Through the descendant of Peretz,
we shall rejoice and we shall be glad.

Come, my Beloved, to greet the bride;
let us welcome the Sabbath.

Stand and turn to face the door or the rear (usually western side) of the synagogue, as if to greet the incoming bride, bowing at the words "Enter, O bride!," then turn back.

בּוֹאִי Come in peace, O crown of her husband;
come with joy and celebration,
among the faithful of the treasured people.
Enter, O bride! Enter, O bride!

Come, my Beloved, to greet the bride;
let us welcome the Sabbath.

REFLECTION

What will you rejoice over this Shabbat?

Turn and face the back of the *shul* –
How are you welcoming the new week,
what are you turning away from?

How are you bringing God
into your Shabbat experience?

Think about the happiness of a bride and groom. Can you bring some of that joy into this Shabbat?

LEARNING

Maharal writes: "Just as the bridegroom glances excitedly and thinks, 'Come forth bride, come forth bride,' in anticipation and excitement for her arrival to join him under the *ḥuppa* – so do we approach the Shabbat to greet her and excitedly say, 'Come forth bride, come forth bride!'"

וְהָיוּ לִמְשִׁסָּה שֹׁאסָיִךְ
וְרָחֲקוּ כָּל מְבַלְּעָיִךְ
יָשִׂישׂ עָלַיִךְ אֱלֹהָיִךְ
כִּמְשׂוֹשׂ חָתָן עַל כַּלָּה.

לְכָה דוֹדִי לִקְרַאת כַּלָּה, פְּנֵי שַׁבָּת נְקַבְּלָה.

יָמִין וּשְׂמֹאל תִּפְרֹצִי
וְאֶת יהוה תַּעֲרִיצִי
עַל יַד אִישׁ בֶּן פַּרְצִי
וְנִשְׂמְחָה וְנָגִילָה.

לְכָה דוֹדִי לִקְרַאת כַּלָּה, פְּנֵי שַׁבָּת נְקַבְּלָה.

Stand and turn to face the door or the rear (usually western side) of the בית כנסת*, as if to greet the incoming bride, bowing at the words* בּוֹאִי כַלָּה*, then turn back.*

בּוֹאִי בְשָׁלוֹם עֲטֶרֶת בַּעְלָהּ
גַּם בְּשִׂמְחָה וּבְצָהֳלָה
תּוֹךְ אֱמוּנֵי עַם סְגֻלָּה
בּוֹאִי כַלָּה, בּוֹאִי כַלָּה.

לְכָה דוֹדִי לִקְרַאת כַּלָּה, פְּנֵי שַׁבָּת נְקַבְּלָה.

CONNECTION

Have you ever moved to a new house? Or gone away for a long time? Imagine the scene, as you are walking away from your home to take a long trip or to leave for a long time. Something makes you turn back and look. You would not do this if you were simply going to school for the day or to a store.

Why do we turn around at Bo'i be-shalom*? We turn because we are moving away from the past and moving ahead to the next week. When you turn around, you show that you are saying a real goodbye to the week and moving ahead to a new week. Turning back symbolizes a move forward.* (Rabbi Simcha Willig)

Mourners during the week of Shiva return to the synagogue at this point. They are greeted with the following words of consolation:

הַמָּקוֹם May the Almighty comfort you
among the other mourners of Zion and Jerusalem.

On Motza'ei Yom Tov or Shabbat Ḥol HaMo'ed, Kabbalat Shabbat begins here.

מִזְמוֹר A psalm. A song for the Sabbath day. It is good to thank the LORD *Ps. 92*
and sing psalms to Your name, Most High – to tell of Your loving-kindness in the morning and Your trustworthiness at night, to the music of the ten-stringed lyre and the melody of the harp. For You have made me rejoice by Your work, O LORD; I sing for joy at the deeds of Your hands. How great are Your deeds, LORD, and how very deep Your thoughts. A boor cannot know, nor can a fool understand, that though the wicked spring up like grass and all evildoers flourish, it is only that they may be destroyed for ever. But You, LORD, are eternally elevated. For behold Your enemies, LORD, behold Your enemies will perish; all evildoers will be scattered. You have raised my pride like that of a wild ox; I am anointed with fresh oil. My eyes shall look in triumph on my enemies, my ears shall hear the downfall of the wicked who rise against me. ▸ The righteous will flourish like a palm tree and grow tall like a cedar in Lebanon. Planted in the LORD's House, blossoming in our God's courtyards, they will still bear fruit in old age, and stay vigorous and fresh, declaring that the LORD is upright: He is my Rock, in whom there is no wrong.

REFLECTION

What does Shabbat make you thankful for?

What aspect of Shabbat do you feel thankful for this week?

What song of thanks do you want to sing this Shabbat?

...A THOUSAND WORDS

Mourners during the week of שבעה *return to the* בית כנסת *at this point. They are greeted with the following words of consolation:*

הַמָּקוֹם יְנַחֵם אֶתְכֶם בְּתוֹךְ שְׁאָר אֲבֵלֵי צִיּוֹן וִירוּשָׁלָיִם.

On קבלת שבת*,* שבת חול המועד *or* מוצאי יום טוב *begins here.*

תהלים צב

מִזְמוֹר שִׁיר לְיוֹם הַשַּׁבָּת: טוֹב לְהֹדוֹת לַיהוה, וּלְזַמֵּר לְשִׁמְךָ
עֶלְיוֹן: לְהַגִּיד בַּבֹּקֶר חַסְדֶּךָ, וֶאֱמוּנָתְךָ בַּלֵּילוֹת: עֲלֵי־עָשׂוֹר
וַעֲלֵי־נָבֶל, עֲלֵי הִגָּיוֹן בְּכִנּוֹר: כִּי שִׂמַּחְתַּנִי יהוה בְּפָעֳלֶךָ, בְּמַעֲשֵׂי
יָדֶיךָ אֲרַנֵּן: מַה־גָּדְלוּ מַעֲשֶׂיךָ יהוה, מְאֹד עָמְקוּ מַחְשְׁבֹתֶיךָ:
אִישׁ־בַּעַר לֹא יֵדָע, וּכְסִיל לֹא־יָבִין אֶת־זֹאת: בִּפְרֹחַ רְשָׁעִים
כְּמוֹ עֵשֶׂב, וַיָּצִיצוּ כָּל־פֹּעֲלֵי אָוֶן, לְהִשָּׁמְדָם עֲדֵי־עַד: וְאַתָּה
מָרוֹם לְעֹלָם יהוה: כִּי הִנֵּה אֹיְבֶיךָ יהוה, כִּי־הִנֵּה אֹיְבֶיךָ יֹאבֵדוּ,
יִתְפָּרְדוּ כָּל־פֹּעֲלֵי אָוֶן: וַתָּרֶם כִּרְאֵים קַרְנִי, בַּלֹּתִי בְּשֶׁמֶן רַעֲנָן:
וַתַּבֵּט עֵינִי בְּשׁוּרָי, בַּקָּמִים עָלַי מְרֵעִים תִּשְׁמַעְנָה אָזְנָי: ◂ צַדִּיק
כַּתָּמָר יִפְרָח, כְּאֶרֶז בַּלְּבָנוֹן יִשְׂגֶּה: שְׁתוּלִים בְּבֵית יהוה, בְּחַצְרוֹת
אֱלֹהֵינוּ יַפְרִיחוּ: עוֹד יְנוּבוּן בְּשֵׂיבָה, דְּשֵׁנִים וְרַעֲנַנִּים יִהְיוּ: לְהַגִּיד
כִּי־יָשָׁר יהוה, צוּרִי, וְלֹא־עַוְלָתָה בּוֹ:

CONNECTION

In the midst of the destruction of the Warsaw Ghetto, the saintly Alexander Rebbe, Rabbi Yitzḥak Menaḥem Dancyger, delivered to his Hasidim an inspiring message.

"The verse says emunatkha*, 'Your faithfulness,' rather than* emunati*, 'my faith in You.' It's not a Jew's belief in Hashem that gives him life at night. It's the way Hashem believes in us that gives us life. When the night is so dark and endless, what keeps us alive is remembering how much Hashem believes in us. Hashem believes that we will bring the coming day."*

Regardless of whether Shabbat finds us in the morning, בַּבֹּקֶר*, in good times, or* בַּלֵּילוֹת*, in the nights, in times of utter darkness, of night after night without hope of morning, each Shabbat we will proclaim God's loving-kindness in the morning and His faithfulness at night.* (Rabbi S.R. Hirsch)

יהוה מָלָךְ The Lord reigns. He is robed in majesty. The Lord is robed, clothed with strength. The world is firmly established; it cannot be moved. Your throne stands firm as of old; You are eternal. Rivers lift up, Lord, rivers lift up their voice, rivers lift up their crashing waves. ▸ Mightier than the noise of many waters, than the mighty waves of the sea is the Lord on high. Your testimonies are very sure; holiness adorns Your House, Lord, for evermore. *Ps. 93*

REFLECTION

Where do you see God's majesty?

How do you look different on Shabbat?

Have you ever felt Shabbat gave you a taste of something special? What did it feel like?

... A THOUSAND WORDS

יהוה מָלָךְ, גֵּאוּת לָבֵשׁ, לָבֵשׁ יהוה עֹז הִתְאַזָּר, אַף־תִּכּוֹן תֵּבֵל תהלים צג
בַּל־תִּמּוֹט: נָכוֹן כִּסְאֲךָ מֵאָז, מֵעוֹלָם אָתָּה: נָשְׂאוּ נְהָרוֹת יהוה,
נָשְׂאוּ נְהָרוֹת קוֹלָם, יִשְׂאוּ נְהָרוֹת דָּכְיָם: › מִקֹּלוֹת מַיִם רַבִּים,
אַדִּירִים מִשְׁבְּרֵי־יָם, אַדִּיר בַּמָּרוֹם יהוה: עֵדֹתֶיךָ נֶאֶמְנוּ מְאֹד,
לְבֵיתְךָ נַאֲוָה־קֹדֶשׁ, יהוה לְאֹרֶךְ יָמִים:

LEARNING

The psalm talks about a time after the final redemption, the future *Olam HaBa*, the World to Come. The Gemara (*Berakhot* 57b) tells us that Shabbat is a taste of the World to Come. What does this mean? It means that Shabbat is a model or sample of what the world will be like in the messianic age, when the world has been redeemed. The Midrash explains that when God gave Israel the Torah, God promised that if the people would keep His commandments, they would be rewarded with the World to Come. The Israelites hadn't the slightest idea of what God was promising, so He gave them Shabbat as a taste of the World to Come.

CONNECTION

In Warsaw we lived three houses away from the Modzhitzer shtiebel. Generally, I would go to this Modzhitzer shtiebel for seuda shelishit. *Poor Jews would be seated around the table. This was a neighborhood where many Jews worked as porters. I knew these Jews well and I constantly spoke with them. They were sincerely pious Jews who willingly sacrificed for their spiritual commitments. I once spoke with one of them who was frail and short. He constantly carried heavy metal pieces, his face harried and tired, and I wondered where he got the physical strength to support this weight.*

On Shabbat I saw this very Jew and I did not recognize him. He came over to me in his tattered kapoteh. *It was covered in endless patches, even the patches had patches. Yet his face shone with the joy of Shabbat. I recognized in a tangible fashion that a person's Shabbat countenance is totally different than his weekday appearance.* (Adapted from *The Rav: The World of Rabbi Joseph B. Soloveitchik*)

MOURNER'S KADDISH

The following prayer, said by mourners, requires the presence of a minyan. A transliteration can be found on page 1151.

Mourner: יִתְגַּדַּל Magnified and sanctified
may His great name be,
in the world He created by His will.
May He establish His kingdom
in your lifetime and in your days,
and in the lifetime of all the house of Israel,
swiftly and soon –
and say: Amen.

All: May His great name
be blessed for ever and all time.

Mourner: Blessed and praised,
glorified and elevated,
raised and honored,
uplifted and praised
be the name of the Holy One,
blessed be He,
beyond any blessing,
song, praise and consolation
uttered in the world –
and say: Amen.

May there be great peace from heaven,
and life for us and all Israel –
and say: Amen.

Bow, take three steps back, as if taking leave of the Divine Presence, then bow, first left, then right, then center, while saying:

May He who makes peace in His high places,
make peace for us and all Israel –
and say: Amen.

קדיש יתום

The following prayer, said by mourners, requires the presence of a מנין*.*
A transliteration can be found on page 1151.

אבל: יִתְגַּדַּל וְיִתְקַדַּשׁ שְׁמֵהּ רַבָּא (קהל: אָמֵן)
בְּעָלְמָא דִּי בְרָא כִרְעוּתֵהּ
וְיַמְלִיךְ מַלְכוּתֵהּ
בְּחַיֵּיכוֹן וּבְיוֹמֵיכוֹן וּבְחַיֵּי דְכָל בֵּית יִשְׂרָאֵל
בַּעֲגָלָא וּבִזְמַן קָרִיב, וְאִמְרוּ אָמֵן. (קהל: אָמֵן)

קהל ואבל: יְהֵא שְׁמֵהּ רַבָּא מְבָרַךְ לְעָלַם וּלְעָלְמֵי עָלְמַיָּא.

אבל: יִתְבָּרַךְ וְיִשְׁתַּבַּח וְיִתְפָּאַר
וְיִתְרוֹמַם וְיִתְנַשֵּׂא וְיִתְהַדָּר וְיִתְעַלֶּה וְיִתְהַלָּל
שְׁמֵהּ דְּקֻדְשָׁא בְּרִיךְ הוּא (קהל: בְּרִיךְ הוּא)
לְעֵלָּא מִן כָּל בִּרְכָתָא
/ בשבת שובה: לְעֵלָּא לְעֵלָּא מִכָּל בִּרְכָתָא/
וְשִׁירָתָא, תֻּשְׁבְּחָתָא וְנֶחֱמָתָא
דַּאֲמִירָן בְּעָלְמָא, וְאִמְרוּ אָמֵן. (קהל: אָמֵן)

יְהֵא שְׁלָמָא רַבָּא מִן שְׁמַיָּא
וְחַיִּים, עָלֵינוּ וְעַל כָּל יִשְׂרָאֵל
וְאִמְרוּ אָמֵן. (קהל: אָמֵן)

Bow, take three steps back, as if taking leave of the Divine Presence, then bow, first left, then right, then center, while saying:

עֹשֶׂה שָׁלוֹם/ בשבת שובה: הַשָּׁלוֹם/ בִּמְרוֹמָיו
הוּא יַעֲשֶׂה שָׁלוֹם עָלֵינוּ וְעַל כָּל יִשְׂרָאֵל
וְאִמְרוּ אָמֵן. (קהל: אָמֵן)

The following is not said when Shabbat begins the evening immediately after a Yom Tov.

1. בַּמֶּה מַדְלִיקִין With what wicks may we light[1] the Sabbath lamp and with what may we not light? We may not use a wick of cedar bast, or uncombed flax, or raw silk, or a wick made of

א בַּמֶּה מַדְלִיקִין[1] וּבַמָּה אֵין מַדְלִיקִין. אֵין מַדְלִיקִין לֹא

1. ***Ner with kik oil.*** *Samuel said: I asked all the seafarers about it, and they told me that there is a certain bird in the towns of the sea called kik. Rabbi Yitzḥak son of Rav*

CONNECTION

In the mid-nineties, a Jewish advertising executive wondered: what if the New York Times – the "Paper of Record" – printed the Shabbat candle lighting time each week? Imagine the Jewish awareness and pride that might result from such a prominent mention of Shabbateach week. He contacted a Jewish philanthropist and sold him on the idea. It cost nearly two thousand dollars a week but he agreed to fund it. For the next five years, every Friday, Jews around the world would see 'Jewish Women: Shabbat candle lighting time this Friday is ..."

Eventually the philanthropist had to reduce the number of projects he had been funding. And, so, in June 1999, the little Shabbat candle lighting notice made its last appearance in the New York Times. At least that's what people thought.

On January 1, 2000, the NY Times ran a Millennium edition commemorating the paper's 100th anniversary. It was a special issue that featured three front pages. One contained the news from January 1, 1900. The second contained the actual news of the day, January 1, 2000. And the third front page, featured projected headlines of January 1, 2100. It included such stories as a welcome to the fifty-first state: Cuba and a debate over the issue of whether robots should be allowed to vote. And so on. And, in addition to the creative articles, there was one extra piece. Down on the bottom of the Year 2100 front page, was the candle lighting time in New York for January 1, 2100. Nobody asked for it. Nobody paid for it. It was just put in by the Times. The production manager of the New York Times – an Irish Catholic – was asked about this curious entry. His answer speaks to the eternity of our people and to the power of Jewish ritual."We don't know what will happen in the year 2100. It is impossible to predict the future. But of one thing you can be certain. That in the year 2100 Jewish women will be lighting Shabbos candles." (*Rabbi Paysach Krohn*)

willow bast or desert weed, or seaweed. [For oil] we may not use pitch, or wax, or cottonseed oil or [contaminated consecrated] oil that must be destroyed by burning, or fat from sheeps' tails, or tallow. Naḥum the Mede says: We may use boiled tallow. But the sages say: Whether boiled or not boiled, we may not use it.

בְּלֶכֶשׁ, וְלֹא בְחֹסֶן, וְלֹא בְכַלָּךְ, וְלֹא בִּפְתִילַת הָאִידָן, וְלֹא בִּפְתִילַת הַמִּדְבָּר, וְלֹא בִירוֹקָה שֶׁעַל פְּנֵי הַמָּיִם. וְלֹא בְזֶפֶת וְלֹא בְשַׁעֲוָה וְלֹא בְּשֶׁמֶן קִיק וְלֹא בְּשֶׁמֶן שְׂרֵפָה וְלֹא בְאַלְיָה וְלֹא בְחֵלֶב. נַחוּם הַמָּדִי אוֹמֵר: מַדְלִיקִין בְּחֵלֶב מְבֻשָּׁל, וַחֲכָמִים אוֹמְרִים: אֶחָד מְבֻשָּׁל וְאֶחָד שֶׁאֵינוֹ מְבֻשָּׁל, אֵין מַדְלִיקִין בּוֹ.

Yehuda said: It is cotton-seed oil; Resh Lakish said: Oil from Yona's kikayon (Shabbat 21a).

In Bameh Madlikin, Rav Kook sees a parallel between oil and success, and between the wick and an individual. The loftier kind of success we seek is one which fills a person with inner happiness and raises one's life to a higher plane.

This success is akin to the oil which is drawn through the extent of the wick, fully saturating it. Each Talmudic explanation of the term "kik" hints to a success which remains external to the individual.

First, the towns of the sea, though reputably prosperous, were known for their moral corruption. Anyone who pursues success there could be guaranteed that it would not penetrate their inner being nor bring them serenity. True happiness is not found on a distant island, but in the home of every Jew, in a life of modesty, humility and pure-heartedness. The love of family and the Torah awaken the holiest emotions of the heart by the light of the candles in one's home on Shabbat eve.

Second, the cotton plant resembles a grapevine in its form. The grapevine represents happiness, which appears to be internal, but in truth remains external to a person. Ultimately, the heart is empty.

Third, the kikayon of Yona was here today and gone tomorrow. It highlights an ephemeral happiness, which dissipates all too soon. Because there is no inherent connection between material success and an individual, nothing can be harvested in the long term.

Rather, what our souls yearn for in earnest from Shabbat can only be acquired through hard work and a pure heart. This inherent happiness spreads naturally to the downhearted. This is the success we seek, and this is the oil we light.

---

1. משנה שבת, פרק שני – *Mishna Shabbat, chapter 2.*

ב אֵין מַדְלִיקִין בְּשֶׁמֶן שְׂרֵפָה בְּיוֹם טוֹב. רַבִּי יִשְׁמָעֵאל אוֹמֵר: אֵין מַדְלִיקִין בְּעִטְרָן מִפְּנֵי כְּבוֹד הַשַּׁבָּת. וַחֲכָמִים מַתִּירִין בְּכָל הַשְּׁמָנִים, בְּשֶׁמֶן שֻׁמְשְׁמִין, בְּשֶׁמֶן אֱגוֹזִים, בְּשֶׁמֶן צְנוֹנוֹת, בְּשֶׁמֶן דָּגִים, בְּשֶׁמֶן פַּקֻּעוֹת, בְּעִטְרָן וּבְנֵפְט. רַבִּי טַרְפוֹן אוֹמֵר: אֵין מַדְלִיקִין אֶלָּא בְּשֶׁמֶן זַיִת בִּלְבָד.

ג כָּל הַיּוֹצֵא מִן הָעֵץ אֵין מַדְלִיקִין בּוֹ, אֶלָּא פִשְׁתָּן. וְכָל הַיּוֹצֵא מִן הָעֵץ אֵינוֹ מִטַּמֵּא טֻמְאַת אֹהָלִים, אֶלָּא פִשְׁתָּן. פְּתִילַת הַבֶּגֶד שֶׁקִּפְּלָהּ וְלֹא הִבְהֲבָהּ, רַבִּי אֱלִיעֶזֶר אוֹמֵר: טְמֵאָה הִיא, וְאֵין מַדְלִיקִין בָּהּ. רַבִּי עֲקִיבָא אוֹמֵר: טְהוֹרָה הִיא, וּמַדְלִיקִין בָּהּ.

ד לֹא יִקֹּב אָדָם שְׁפוֹפֶרֶת שֶׁל בֵּיצָה וִימַלְּאֶנָּה שֶׁמֶן וְיִתְּנֶנָּה עַל פִּי הַנֵּר,

2. [Contaminated consecrated] oil that must be destroyed by burning may not be used for a festival lamp. Rabbi Yishmael says: We may not use tar out of respect for the honor due to the Sabbath. But the sages permit all these oils: sesame oil, nut oil, radish oil, fish oil, gourd oil, tar or naphtha. Rabbi Tarfon, however, says: We may use only olive oil.

3. No product from a tree may be used as a wick for the Sabbath lamp, except flax. Also no product of a tree can contract "tent" uncleanness, except flax. If a wick was made from a cloth that has been twisted but not singed, Rabbi Eliezer declares, it is susceptible to contamination and may not be used for a Sabbath lamp; but Rabbi Akiva says, it is not susceptible to contamination, and may be used for the Sabbath lamp.

4. One may not pierce an eggshell, fill it with oil, and put it over the mouth of a lamp so that the oil may drip from it into the lamp, even if the vessel is of earthenware, but Rabbi Yehuda permits it. If, however, the potter had originally

2. Rabbi Tarfon says: We only light with olive oil. *The Shabbat lights allude to the enlightenment of the mind, which comes with the holiness of the day of rest. There are many kinds of oil, and there are many kinds of wisdom. Human wisdom can lead to character refinement and can prepare an individual to bring much good to the world. But the purest olive oil, the enlightenment of the Torah, is reserved for Shabbat. It is impervious to confusion and evil intention. The holiest day is dedicated to the pursuit of the wisdom of the Torah.*

attached it to the lamp, it is permitted because it constitutes a single vessel. One may not fill a bowl with oil, put it beside a lamp, and put the end of the wick in it so that it draws oil from the bowl; but Rabbi Yehuda permits this.

בִּשְׁבִיל שֶׁתְּהֵא מְנַטֶּפֶת, וַאֲפִילוּ הִיא שֶׁל חֶרֶס. וְרַבִּי יְהוּדָה מַתִּיר. אֲבָל אִם חִבְּרָהּ הַיּוֹצֵר מִתְּחִלָּה מֻתָּר, מִפְּנֵי שֶׁהוּא כְּלִי אֶחָד. לֹא יְמַלֵּא אָדָם אֶת הַקְּעָרָה שֶׁמֶן וְיִתְּנֶנָּה בְּצַד הַנֵּר וְיִתֵּן רֹאשׁ הַפְּתִילָה בְּתוֹכָהּ, בִּשְׁבִיל שֶׁתְּהֵא שׁוֹאֶבֶת. וְרַבִּי יְהוּדָה מַתִּיר.

5. One who extinguishes a lamp because he is afraid of heathens, robbers, or depression, or to enable a sick person to sleep, is not liable [for violating the Sabbath]. If he did it to spare the lamp, or the oil, or the wick, he is liable. Rabbi Yose absolves him in all these cases except that of sparing the wick, because he thereby turns it into charcoal.

ה הַמְכַבֶּה אֶת הַנֵּר מִפְּנֵי שֶׁהוּא מִתְיָרֵא מִפְּנֵי גוֹיִם, מִפְּנֵי לִסְטִים, מִפְּנֵי רוּחַ רָעָה, אוֹ בִּשְׁבִיל הַחוֹלֶה שֶׁיִּישַׁן, פָּטוּר. כְּחָס עַל הַנֵּר, כְּחָס עַל הַשֶּׁמֶן, כְּחָס עַל הַפְּתִילָה, חַיָּב. רַבִּי יוֹסֵי פּוֹטֵר בְּכֻלָּן חוּץ מִן הַפְּתִילָה, מִפְּנֵי שֶׁהוּא עוֹשָׂהּ פֶּחָם.

ו עַל שָׁלֹשׁ עֲבֵרוֹת נָשִׁים מֵתוֹת בִּשְׁעַת לֵדָתָן, עַל שֶׁאֵינָן זְהִירוֹת בְּנִדָּה, בְּחַלָּה וּבְהַדְלָקַת הַנֵּר.

6. For three transgressions women may die in childbirth: for being careless in observing the laws of menstruation, separating ḥalla [dough-offering], and lighting the Sabbath light.

*6. **For three transgressions women may die in childbirth.** Rav Kook explains that the moment of childbirth signifies the influx of divine energy into a person's home. To bring a new soul into this world, women must first prepare spiritually. The observance of Nidda represents the disruption of a natural animal pattern of sexual engagement in favor of a relationship built on ideals and lofty aspirations. Ḥalla, a portion of dough reserved for the Kohen, shows that a family accepts their interdependence with unique and holy individuals whom they hope will influence their home. The Shabbat lights demonstrate the inner light that a family seeks to reveal in its home through calm interactions. Every heart rests from sadness and anxiety; every simple delight is sanctified and raised up. With these practices, a family is ready to receive the divine light and a new soul.*

7. One should say three things at home on the eve of the Sabbath just before dark: Have you tithed? Have you prepared the Eiruv? Light the Sabbath lamp. If there is doubt whether or not darkness has fallen, we may not tithe the definitely untithed produce, nor immerse [unclean] vessels, nor light the Sabbath lamp. We may tithe the produce about which there is a doubt whether it has been tithed or not, we may prepare an Eiruv, and insulate hot food.

It was taught,[2] Rabbi Ḥanina said: One should examine his clothing on the eve of the Sabbath before nightfall [to ensure that one is not carrying anything], for one may forget and go out. Rabbi Yosef said: This is an important law about the Sabbath [for it is easy to forget, and thus inadvertently violate the holiness of the day].

ז שְׁלֹשָׁה דְבָרִים צָרִיךְ אָדָם לוֹמַר בְּתוֹךְ בֵּיתוֹ עֶרֶב שַׁבָּת עִם חֲשֵׁכָה: עִשַּׂרְתֶּם, עֵרַבְתֶּם, הַדְלִֽיקוּ אֶת הַנֵּר. סָפֵק חֲשֵׁכָה סָפֵק אֵינָהּ חֲשֵׁכָה, אֵין מְעַשְּׂרִין אֶת הַוַּדַּאי, וְאֵין מַטְבִּילִין אֶת הַכֵּלִים, וְאֵין מַדְלִיקִין אֶת הַנֵּרוֹת. אֲבָל מְעַשְּׂרִין אֶת הַדְּמַאי, וּמְעָרְבִין וְטוֹמְנִין אֶת הַחַמִּין.

תַּנְיָא,[2] אָמַר רַבִּי חֲנִינָא: חַיָּב אָדָם לְמַשְׁמֵשׁ בִּגְדָיו בְּעֶרֶב שַׁבָּת עִם חֲשֵׁכָה, שֶׁמָּא יִשְׁכַּח וְיֵצֵא. אָמַר רַב יוֹסֵף: הִלְכְתָא רַבְּתָא לְשַׁבְּתָא.

7. ***One should say three things at home on the eve of Sabbath.*** *Rav Kook emphasizes the importance of attaining certainty that the most important tasks in one's home have been fulfilled. As Shabbat enters and the holiness of Israel shines brightest, the soul which attains certainty that one's home is completely ready shall be engraved with its light.*

Rabbi Ḥanina said: One should examine his clothing. *According to Rav Kook, one of the fundamentals of Shabbat is comparing one's external life with one's inner life. The greater the distance is between the two, the greater the alienation one feels from one's true nature. In our external lives, we are*

2. שבת יב. – *Shabbat 12a.*

Rabbi Elazar said[3] in the name of Rabbi Ḥanina: The disciples of the sages increase peace in the world, as it is said, "And all your children shall be taught of the Lord, and great shall be the peace of your children [*banayikh*]."[4] Read not *banayikh*, "your children," but *bonayikh*, "your builders." Those who love Your Torah have great peace; there is no stumbling block for them. May there be peace within your ramparts, prosperity in your palaces. For the sake of my brothers and friends, I shall say, "Peace be within you."[5] For the sake of the House of the Lord our God, I will seek your good.[6] ▸ May the Lord give strength to His people; may the Lord bless His people with peace.[7]

אָמַר רַבִּי אֶלְעָזָר,[3] אָמַר רַבִּי חֲנִינָא: תַּלְמִידֵי חֲכָמִים מַרְבִּים שָׁלוֹם בָּעוֹלָם, שֶׁנֶּאֱמַר: וְכָל־בָּנַיִךְ לִמּוּדֵי יהוה, וְרַב שְׁלוֹם בָּנָיִךְ:[4] אַל תִּקְרֵי בָּנָיִךְ, אֶלָּא בּוֹנָיִךְ. שָׁלוֹם רָב לְאֹהֲבֵי תוֹרָתֶךָ, וְאֵין־לָמוֹ מִכְשׁוֹל: יְהִי־שָׁלוֹם בְּחֵילֵךְ, שַׁלְוָה בְּאַרְמְנוֹתָיִךְ. לְמַעַן אַחַי וְרֵעָי אֲדַבְּרָה־נָּא שָׁלוֹם בָּךְ:[5] לְמַעַן בֵּית־יהוה אֱלֹהֵינוּ אֲבַקְשָׁה טוֹב לָךְ:[6] ◂ יהוה עֹז לְעַמּוֹ יִתֵּן, יהוה יְבָרֵךְ אֶת־עַמּוֹ בַשָּׁלוֹם:[7]

constantly pulled by others in many different directions. Shabbat is a process not only of accentuating one's inner life, but also of bringing one's two lives in step with each other. Though one would not violate the spiritual dimension of Shabbat if his clothing is not examined, one would not have achieved a refocusing of one's external life, represented by one's clothing. Therefore, in addition to examining one's clothing, special Shabbat clothing is worn to demonstrate the realignment of one's external life.

Adapted by Rabbi Sarna from Rav Kook, Olat Re'iyya. Rabbi Avraham Yitzchak Kook, a renowned Halakhist, Kabbalist, and Jewish thinker was the first Chief Rabbi of Israel.

3. ברכות סד. – *Berakhot 64a*
4. ישעיה נד – *Yeshayahu 54*
5. תהלים קיט – *Tehillim 119*
6. תהלים קכב – *Tehillim 122*
7. תהלים כט – *Tehillim 29*

THE RABBIS' KADDISH

The following prayer, said by mourners, requires the presence of a minyan.
A transliteration can be found on page 1150.

Mourner: יִתְגַּדַּל Magnified and sanctified may His great name be,
in the world He created by His will.
May He establish His kingdom
in your lifetime and in your days,
and in the lifetime of all the house of Israel,
swiftly and soon –
and say: Amen.

All: May His great name be blessed for ever and all time.

Mourner: Blessed and praised, glorified and elevated,
raised and honored, uplifted and praised
be the name of the Holy One, blessed be He,
beyond any blessing, song, praise and consolation
uttered in the world –
and say: Amen.

To Israel, to the teachers,
their disciples and their disciples' disciples,
and to all who engage in the study of Torah,
in this (*In Israel add:* holy) place or elsewhere,
may there come to them and you great peace,
grace, kindness and compassion,
long life, abundant sustenance and deliverance,
from their Father in Heaven –
and say: Amen.

May there be great peace from heaven,
and (good) life for us and all Israel –
and say: Amen.

Bow, take three steps back, as if taking leave of the Divine Presence,
then bow, first left, then right, then center, while saying:

May He who makes peace in His high places,
in His compassion make peace
for us and all Israel –
and say: Amen.

קדיש דרבן

The following prayer, said by mourners, requires the presence of a מנין.
A transliteration can be found on page 1150.
A transliteration can be found on page 1150.

אבל: **יִתְגַּדַּל וְיִתְקַדַּשׁ שְׁמֵהּ רַבָּא** (קהל: אָמֵן)
בְּעָלְמָא דִּי בְרָא כִרְעוּתֵהּ, וְיַמְלִיךְ מַלְכוּתֵהּ
בְּחַיֵּיכוֹן וּבְיוֹמֵיכוֹן וּבְחַיֵּי דְכָל בֵּית יִשְׂרָאֵל
בַּעֲגָלָא וּבִזְמַן קָרִיב, וְאִמְרוּ אָמֵן. (קהל: אָמֵן)

קהל ואבל: **יְהֵא שְׁמֵהּ רַבָּא מְבָרַךְ לְעָלַם וּלְעָלְמֵי עָלְמַיָּא.**

אבל: **יִתְבָּרַךְ וְיִשְׁתַּבַּח וְיִתְפָּאַר וְיִתְרוֹמַם וְיִתְנַשֵּׂא**
וְיִתְהַדָּר וְיִתְעַלֶּה וְיִתְהַלָּל
שְׁמֵהּ דְּקֻדְשָׁא בְּרִיךְ הוּא (קהל: בְּרִיךְ הוּא)
לְעֵלָּא מִן כָּל בִּרְכָתָא / בשבת שובה: **לְעֵלָּא לְעֵלָּא מִכָּל בִּרְכָתָא/**
וְשִׁירָתָא, תֻּשְׁבְּחָתָא וְנֶחֱמָתָא
דַּאֲמִירָן בְּעָלְמָא, וְאִמְרוּ אָמֵן. (קהל: אָמֵן)

עַל יִשְׂרָאֵל וְעַל רַבָּנָן
וְעַל תַּלְמִידֵיהוֹן וְעַל כָּל תַּלְמִידֵי תַלְמִידֵיהוֹן
וְעַל כָּל מָאן דְּעָסְקִין בְּאוֹרַיְתָא
דִּי בְּאַתְרָא (בארץ ישראל: **קַדִּישָׁא**) **הָדֵין, וְדִי בְּכָל אֲתַר וַאֲתַר**
יְהֵא לְהוֹן וּלְכוֹן שְׁלָמָא רַבָּא
חִנָּא וְחִסְדָּא, וְרַחֲמֵי, וְחַיֵּי אֲרִיכֵי, וּמְזוֹנֵי רְוִיחֵי
וּפֻרְקָנָא מִן קֳדָם אֲבוּהוֹן דִּי בִשְׁמַיָּא, וְאִמְרוּ אָמֵן. (קהל: אָמֵן)

יְהֵא שְׁלָמָא רַבָּא מִן שְׁמַיָּא
וְחַיִּים (טוֹבִים) עָלֵינוּ וְעַל כָּל יִשְׂרָאֵל, וְאִמְרוּ אָמֵן. (קהל: אָמֵן)

Bow, take three steps back, as if taking leave of the Divine Presence, then bow, first left, then right, then center, while saying:

עֹשֶׂה שָׁלוֹם/ בשבת שובה: **הַשָּׁלוֹם/ בִּמְרוֹמָיו**
הוּא יַעֲשֶׂה בְרַחֲמָיו שָׁלוֹם
עָלֵינוּ וְעַל כָּל יִשְׂרָאֵל, וְאִמְרוּ אָמֵן. (קהל: אָמֵן)

Ma'ariv for Shabbat

BLESSINGS OF THE SHEMA

The Leader says the following, bowing at "Bless," standing straight at "the LORD." The congregation, followed by the Leader, responds, bowing at "Bless," standing straight at "the LORD."

Leader: **BLESS**
the LORD, the blessed One.

Congregation: Bless the LORD, the blessed One,
for ever and all time.

Leader: Bless the LORD, the blessed One,
for ever and all time.

בָּרוּךְ Blessed are You, LORD our God, King of the Universe,
who by His word brings on evenings,
by His wisdom opens the gates of heaven,
with understanding makes time change and the seasons rotate,
and by His will
orders the stars in their constellations in the sky.
He creates day and night,
rolling away the light before the darkness,
and darkness before the light.
▸ He makes the day pass and brings on night,
distinguishing day from night:
the LORD of multitudes is His name.
May the living and forever enduring God
rule over us for all time.
Blessed are You, LORD, who brings on evenings.

מעריב לשבת

קריאת שמע וברכותיה

The שליח ציבור *says the following, bowing at* בָּרְכוּ*, standing straight at* ה׳*.*
The קהל*, followed by the* שליח ציבור*, responds, bowing at* בָּרוּךְ*, standing straight at* ה׳*.*

ש״ץ: בָּרְכוּ
אֶת יהוה הַמְבֹרָךְ.

קהל: בָּרוּךְ יהוה הַמְבֹרָךְ לְעוֹלָם וָעֶד.
ש״ץ: בָּרוּךְ יהוה הַמְבֹרָךְ לְעוֹלָם וָעֶד.

בָּרוּךְ אַתָּה יהוה אֱלֹהֵינוּ מֶלֶךְ הָעוֹלָם
אֲשֶׁר בִּדְבָרוֹ מַעֲרִיב עֲרָבִים
בְּחָכְמָה פּוֹתֵחַ שְׁעָרִים
וּבִתְבוּנָה מְשַׁנֶּה עִתִּים וּמַחֲלִיף אֶת הַזְּמַנִּים
וּמְסַדֵּר אֶת הַכּוֹכָבִים בְּמִשְׁמְרוֹתֵיהֶם בָּרָקִיעַ כִּרְצוֹנוֹ.
בּוֹרֵא יוֹם וָלַיְלָה, גּוֹלֵל אוֹר מִפְּנֵי חֹשֶׁךְ וְחֹשֶׁךְ מִפְּנֵי אוֹר
◂ וּמַעֲבִיר יוֹם וּמֵבִיא לָיְלָה
וּמַבְדִּיל בֵּין יוֹם וּבֵין לָיְלָה
יהוה צְבָאוֹת שְׁמוֹ.
אֵל חַי וְקַיָּם תָּמִיד, יִמְלֹךְ עָלֵינוּ לְעוֹלָם וָעֶד.
בָּרוּךְ אַתָּה יהוה, הַמַּעֲרִיב עֲרָבִים.

אַהֲבַת עוֹלָם With everlasting love
have You loved Your people, the house of Israel.
You have taught us Torah and commandments,
decrees and laws of justice.
Therefore, LORD our God, when we lie down and when we rise up
we will speak of Your decrees, rejoicing in the words of Your Torah
and Your commandments for ever.
▸ For they are our life and the length of our days;
on them will we meditate day and night.
May You never take away Your love from us.
Blessed are You, LORD, who loves His people Israel.

The Shema must be said with intense concentration.
When not with a minyan, say:
God, faithful King!

The following verse should be said aloud, while covering the eyes with the right hand:

Listen, Israel: the LORD is our God, the LORD is One. *Deut. 6*

Quietly: Blessed be the name of His glorious kingdom for ever and all time.

וְאָהַבְתָּ Love the LORD your God with all your heart, with all your soul, and with all your might. These words which I command you today shall be on your heart. Teach them repeatedly to your children, speaking of them when you sit at home and when you travel on the way, when you lie down and when you rise. Bind them as a sign on your hand, and they shall be a symbol between your eyes. Write them on the doorposts of your house and gates. *Deut. 6*

וְהָיָה If you indeed follow My commandments with which I charge you today, to love the LORD your God and worship Him with all your heart and with all your soul, I will give rain in your land in its season, the early and late rain; and you shall gather in your grain, wine and oil. I will give grass in your field for your cattle, and you shall eat and be satisfied. Be careful lest your heart be tempted and you go astray and worship other gods, bowing down to them. *Deut. 11*

אַהֲבַת עוֹלָם בֵּית יִשְׂרָאֵל עַמְּךָ אָהָבְתָּ
תּוֹרָה וּמִצְוֹת, חֻקִּים וּמִשְׁפָּטִים, אוֹתָנוּ לִמַּדְתָּ
עַל כֵּן יהוה אֱלֹהֵינוּ בְּשָׁכְבֵנוּ וּבְקוּמֵנוּ נָשִׂיחַ בְּחֻקֶּיךָ
וְנִשְׂמַח בְּדִבְרֵי תוֹרָתֶךָ וּבְמִצְוֹתֶיךָ לְעוֹלָם וָעֶד
◄ כִּי הֵם חַיֵּינוּ וְאֹרֶךְ יָמֵינוּ, וּבָהֶם נֶהְגֶּה יוֹמָם וָלָיְלָה.
וְאַהֲבָתְךָ אַל תָּסִיר מִמֶּנּוּ לְעוֹלָמִים.
בָּרוּךְ אַתָּה יהוה, אוֹהֵב עַמּוֹ יִשְׂרָאֵל.

The שמע *must be said with intense concentration.*
When not with a מנין*, say:*

אֵל מֶלֶךְ נֶאֱמָן

The following verse should be said aloud, while covering the eyes with the right hand:

שְׁמַע יִשְׂרָאֵל, יהוה אֱלֹהֵינוּ, יהוה ׀ אֶחָד׃ דברים ו

Quietly בָּרוּךְ שֵׁם כְּבוֹד מַלְכוּתוֹ לְעוֹלָם וָעֶד.

וְאָהַבְתָּ אֵת יהוה אֱלֹהֶיךָ, בְּכָל־לְבָבְךָ וּבְכָל־נַפְשְׁךָ וּבְכָל־ דברים ו
מְאֹדֶךָ׃ וְהָיוּ הַדְּבָרִים הָאֵלֶּה, אֲשֶׁר אָנֹכִי מְצַוְּךָ הַיּוֹם, עַל־לְבָבֶךָ׃
וְשִׁנַּנְתָּם לְבָנֶיךָ וְדִבַּרְתָּ בָּם, בְּשִׁבְתְּךָ בְּבֵיתֶךָ וּבְלֶכְתְּךָ בַדֶּרֶךְ,
וּבְשָׁכְבְּךָ וּבְקוּמֶךָ׃ וּקְשַׁרְתָּם לְאוֹת עַל־יָדֶךָ וְהָיוּ לְטֹטָפֹת בֵּין
עֵינֶיךָ׃ וּכְתַבְתָּם עַל־מְזֻזוֹת בֵּיתֶךָ וּבִשְׁעָרֶיךָ׃

וְהָיָה אִם־שָׁמֹעַ תִּשְׁמְעוּ אֶל־מִצְוֹתַי אֲשֶׁר אָנֹכִי מְצַוֶּה אֶתְכֶם דברים יא
הַיּוֹם, לְאַהֲבָה אֶת־יהוה אֱלֹהֵיכֶם וּלְעָבְדוֹ, בְּכָל־לְבַבְכֶם וּבְכָל־
נַפְשְׁכֶם׃ וְנָתַתִּי מְטַר־אַרְצְכֶם בְּעִתּוֹ, יוֹרֶה וּמַלְקוֹשׁ, וְאָסַפְתָּ
דְגָנֶךָ וְתִירֹשְׁךָ וְיִצְהָרֶךָ׃ וְנָתַתִּי עֵשֶׂב בְּשָׂדְךָ לִבְהֶמְתֶּךָ, וְאָכַלְתָּ
וְשָׂבָעְתָּ׃ הִשָּׁמְרוּ לָכֶם פֶּן־יִפְתֶּה לְבַבְכֶם, וְסַרְתֶּם וַעֲבַדְתֶּם
אֱלֹהִים אֲחֵרִים וְהִשְׁתַּחֲוִיתֶם לָהֶם׃ וְחָרָה אַף־יהוה בָּכֶם, וְעָצַר

Then the LORD's anger will flare against you and He will close the heavens so that there will be no rain. The land will not yield its crops, and you will perish swiftly from the good land that the LORD is giving you. Therefore, set these, My words, on your heart and soul. Bind them as a sign on your hand, and they shall be a symbol between your eyes. Teach them to your children, speaking of them when you sit at home and when you travel on the way, when you lie down and when you rise. Write them on the doorposts of your house and gates, so that you and your children may live long in the land that the LORD swore to your ancestors to give them, for as long as the heavens are above the earth.

וַיֹּאמֶר The LORD spoke to Moses, saying: Speak to the Israelites *Num. 15*
and tell them to make tzitzit on the corners of their garments for all generations. They shall attach to the tzitzit at each corner a thread of blue. This shall be your tzitzit, and you shall see it and remember all of the LORD's commandments and keep them, not straying after your heart and after your eyes, following your own sinful desires. Thus you will be reminded to keep all My commandments, and be holy to your God. I am the LORD your God, who brought you out of the land of Egypt to be your God. I am the LORD your God.

True –

The Leader repeats:

▸ The LORD your God is true –

וֶאֱמוּנָה – and faithful is all this,
and firmly established for us
that He is the LORD our God,
and there is none besides Him,
and that we, Israel, are His people.
He is our King, who redeems us from the hand of kings
and delivers us from the grasp of all tyrants.

אֶת־הַשָּׁמַיִם וְלֹא־יִהְיֶה מָטָר, וְהָאֲדָמָה לֹא תִתֵּן אֶת־יְבוּלָהּ,
וַאֲבַדְתֶּם מְהֵרָה מֵעַל הָאָרֶץ הַטֹּבָה אֲשֶׁר יהוה נֹתֵן לָכֶם:
וְשַׂמְתֶּם אֶת־דְּבָרַי אֵלֶּה עַל־לְבַבְכֶם וְעַל־נַפְשְׁכֶם, וּקְשַׁרְתֶּם
אֹתָם לְאוֹת עַל־יֶדְכֶם, וְהָיוּ לְטוֹטָפֹת בֵּין עֵינֵיכֶם: וְלִמַּדְתֶּם
אֹתָם אֶת־בְּנֵיכֶם לְדַבֵּר בָּם, בְּשִׁבְתְּךָ בְּבֵיתֶךָ וּבְלֶכְתְּךָ בַדֶּרֶךְ,
וּבְשָׁכְבְּךָ וּבְקוּמֶךָ: וּכְתַבְתָּם עַל־מְזוּזוֹת בֵּיתֶךָ וּבִשְׁעָרֶיךָ: לְמַעַן
יִרְבּוּ יְמֵיכֶם וִימֵי בְנֵיכֶם עַל הָאֲדָמָה אֲשֶׁר נִשְׁבַּע יהוה לַאֲבֹתֵיכֶם
לָתֵת לָהֶם, כִּימֵי הַשָּׁמַיִם עַל־הָאָרֶץ:

וַיֹּאמֶר יהוה אֶל־מֹשֶׁה לֵּאמֹר: דַּבֵּר אֶל־בְּנֵי יִשְׂרָאֵל וְאָמַרְתָּ במדבר טו
אֲלֵהֶם, וְעָשׂוּ לָהֶם צִיצִת עַל־כַּנְפֵי בִגְדֵיהֶם לְדֹרֹתָם, וְנָתְנוּ
עַל־צִיצִת הַכָּנָף פְּתִיל תְּכֵלֶת: וְהָיָה לָכֶם לְצִיצִת, וּרְאִיתֶם אֹתוֹ
וּזְכַרְתֶּם אֶת־כָּל־מִצְוֺת יהוה וַעֲשִׂיתֶם אֹתָם, וְלֹא תָתֻרוּ אַחֲרֵי
לְבַבְכֶם וְאַחֲרֵי עֵינֵיכֶם, אֲשֶׁר־אַתֶּם זֹנִים אַחֲרֵיהֶם: לְמַעַן תִּזְכְּרוּ
וַעֲשִׂיתֶם אֶת־כָּל־מִצְוֺתָי, וִהְיִיתֶם קְדֹשִׁים לֵאלֹהֵיכֶם: אֲנִי יהוה
אֱלֹהֵיכֶם, אֲשֶׁר הוֹצֵאתִי אֶתְכֶם מֵאֶרֶץ מִצְרַיִם, לִהְיוֹת לָכֶם
לֵאלֹהִים, אֲנִי יהוה אֱלֹהֵיכֶם:

אֱמֶת

The שליח ציבור *repeats:*

▸ יהוה אֱלֹהֵיכֶם אֱמֶת

וֶאֱמוּנָה כָּל זֹאת וְקַיָּם עָלֵינוּ
כִּי הוּא יהוה אֱלֹהֵינוּ וְאֵין זוּלָתוֹ
וַאֲנַחְנוּ יִשְׂרָאֵל עַמּוֹ.
הַפּוֹדֵנוּ מִיַּד מְלָכִים
מַלְכֵּנוּ הַגּוֹאֲלֵנוּ מִכַּף כָּל הֶעָרִיצִים.

He is our God,
who on our behalf repays our foes
and brings just retribution on our mortal enemies;
who performs great deeds beyond understanding
and wonders beyond number;
who kept us alive, not letting our foot slip; *Ps. 66*
who led us on the high places of our enemies,
raising our pride above all our foes;
who did miracles for us
and brought vengeance against Pharaoh;
who performed signs and wonders
in the land of Ham's children;
who smote in His fury all the firstborn of Egypt,
and brought out His people Israel from their midst
into everlasting freedom;
who led His children through the divided Reed Sea,
plunging their pursuers and enemies into the depths.
When His children saw His might,
they gave praise and thanks to His name,
▸ and willingly accepted His Sovereignty.
Moses and the children of Israel
then sang a song to You with great joy, and they all exclaimed:

"Who is like You, LORD, among the mighty? *Ex. 15*
Who is like You, majestic in holiness,
awesome in praises, doing wonders?"

▸ Your children beheld Your majesty
as You parted the sea before Moses.
"This is my God!" they responded, and then said:

"The LORD shall reign for ever and ever." *Ex. 15*

▸ And it is said,
"For the LORD has redeemed Jacob *Jer. 31*
and rescued him from a power stronger than his own."
Blessed are You, LORD, who redeemed Israel.

הָאֵל הַנִּפְרָע לָֽנוּ מִצָּרֵֽינוּ
וְהַמְשַׁלֵּם גְּמוּל לְכָל אוֹיְבֵי נַפְשֵֽׁנוּ.
הָעוֹשֶׂה גְדוֹלוֹת עַד אֵין חֵֽקֶר, וְנִפְלָאוֹת עַד אֵין מִסְפָּר
הַשָּׂם נַפְשֵֽׁנוּ בַּחַיִּים, וְלֹא־נָתַן לַמּוֹט רַגְלֵֽנוּ: תהלים סו
הַמַּדְרִיכֵֽנוּ עַל בָּמוֹת אוֹיְבֵֽינוּ
וַיָּֽרֶם קַרְנֵֽנוּ עַל כָּל שׂוֹנְאֵֽינוּ.
הָעוֹשֶׂה לָּֽנוּ נִסִּים וּנְקָמָה בְּפַרְעֹה
אוֹתוֹת וּמוֹפְתִים בְּאַדְמַת בְּנֵי חָם.
הַמַּכֶּה בְעֶבְרָתוֹ כָּל בְּכוֹרֵי מִצְרָֽיִם
וַיּוֹצֵא אֶת עַמּוֹ יִשְׂרָאֵל מִתּוֹכָם לְחֵרוּת עוֹלָם.
הַמַּעֲבִיר בָּנָיו בֵּין גִּזְרֵי יַם סוּף
אֶת רוֹדְפֵיהֶם וְאֶת שׂוֹנְאֵיהֶם בִּתְהוֹמוֹת טִבַּע
וְרָאוּ בָנָיו גְּבוּרָתוֹ, שִׁבְּחוּ וְהוֹדוּ לִשְׁמוֹ
◂ וּמַלְכוּתוֹ בְּרָצוֹן קִבְּלוּ עֲלֵיהֶם.
מֹשֶׁה וּבְנֵי יִשְׂרָאֵל, לְךָ עָנוּ שִׁירָה בְּשִׂמְחָה רַבָּה
וְאָמְרוּ כֻלָּם
מִי־כָמֹֽכָה בָּאֵלִם יהוה שמות טו
מִי כָּמֹֽכָה נֶאְדָּר בַּקֹּֽדֶשׁ
נוֹרָא תְהִלֹּת עֹֽשֵׂה פֶֽלֶא:

◂ מַלְכוּתְךָ רָאוּ בָנֶֽיךָ, בּוֹקֵֽעַ יָם לִפְנֵי מֹשֶׁה
זֶה אֵלִי עָנוּ, וְאָמְרוּ
יהוה יִמְלֹךְ לְעֹלָם וָעֶד: שמות טו

◂ וְנֶאֱמַר
כִּי־פָדָה יהוה אֶת־יַעֲקֹב, וּגְאָלוֹ מִיַּד חָזָק מִמֶּֽנּוּ: ירמיהו לא
בָּרוּךְ אַתָּה יהוה, גָּאַל יִשְׂרָאֵל.

הַשְׁכִּיבֵנוּ Help us lie down, O Lord our God, in peace,
and rise up, O our King, to life.
Spread over us Your canopy of peace.
Direct us with Your good counsel,
and save us for the sake of Your name.
Shield us and remove from us every enemy,
plague, sword, famine and sorrow.
Remove the enemy from before and behind us.
Shelter us in the shadow of Your wings,
for You, God, are our Guardian and Deliverer;
You, God, are a gracious and compassionate King.
▸ Guard our going out and our coming in,
for life and peace, from now and for ever.
Spread over us Your canopy of peace.
Blessed are You, Lord, who spreads a canopy of peace over us,
over all His people Israel, and over Jerusalem.

...A THOUSAND WORDS

CONNECTION

On Yom Tov each Jew was commanded to come close to the Shekhina*; this is the mitzva of* aliya laregel*, the festival pilgrimage. He stepped out from his home and walked to Jerusalem in search of the* Shekhina*. But Yom Tov is not the abode of the* Shekhina*. The Torah did not tell a Jew to make a pilgrimage to Jerusalem on Shabbat. There is no need. On Shabbat the* Shekhina *knocks on the door. All we have to do is let Her in.* (Adapted from Rabbi J.B. Soloveitchik, *Siddur Mesorat HaRav*)

Can you feel the *Shekhina* in your home on Shabbat?

Can you think of anything you can do to make the *Shekhina* more present (or felt) in your home this Shabbat?

הַשְׁכִּיבֵנוּ יהוה אֱלֹהֵינוּ לְשָׁלוֹם
וְהַעֲמִידֵנוּ מַלְכֵּנוּ לְחַיִּים
וּפְרֹשׂ עָלֵינוּ סֻכַּת שְׁלוֹמֶךָ
וְתַקְּנֵנוּ בְּעֵצָה טוֹבָה מִלְּפָנֶיךָ
וְהוֹשִׁיעֵנוּ לְמַעַן שְׁמֶךָ.
וְהָגֵן בַּעֲדֵנוּ
וְהָסֵר מֵעָלֵינוּ אוֹיֵב, דֶּבֶר וְחֶרֶב וְרָעָב וְיָגוֹן
וְהָסֵר שָׂטָן מִלְּפָנֵינוּ וּמֵאַחֲרֵינוּ
וּבְצֵל כְּנָפֶיךָ תַּסְתִּירֵנוּ
כִּי אֵל שׁוֹמְרֵנוּ וּמַצִּילֵנוּ אָתָּה
כִּי אֵל מֶלֶךְ חַנּוּן וְרַחוּם אָתָּה.
◂ וּשְׁמֹר צֵאתֵנוּ וּבוֹאֵנוּ לְחַיִּים וּלְשָׁלוֹם מֵעַתָּה וְעַד עוֹלָם.
וּפְרֹשׂ עָלֵינוּ סֻכַּת שְׁלוֹמֶךָ.
בָּרוּךְ אַתָּה יהוה
הַפּוֹרֵשׂ סֻכַּת שָׁלוֹם עָלֵינוּ וְעַל כָּל עַמּוֹ יִשְׂרָאֵל וְעַל יְרוּשָׁלָיִם.

LEARNING

Shabbat is a special time of peace and tranquility. The Shabbat version of this prayer contains in it a different ending than the weekday prayers. The weekday prayer ends with the phrase, "who keeps His people Israel," and the Shabbat version ends with, "who spreads a canopy of peace over us." Rabbi S.R. Hirsch explains that Shabbat is different from the week; it brings its own protection and spreads feelings of tranquility and peace.

REFLECTION

How do you feel when Shabbat comes in?

How can you contribute to peaceful feelings that Shabbat brings?

When you wish someone *"Shabbat shalom"* what are you really wishing them?

The congregation stands and, together with the Leader, says:

וְשָׁמְרוּ The children of Israel must keep the Sabbath, Ex. 31
observing the Sabbath in every generation
as an everlasting covenant.
It is a sign between Me and the children of Israel for ever,
for in six days God made the heavens and the earth,
but on the seventh day He ceased work
and refreshed Himself.

REFLECTION

How are you "keeping" this Shabbat?

Are you able to do something special to "keep" this Shabbat?

How are you feeding and refreshing your soul?

... A THOUSAND WORDS

The קהל *stands and, together with the* שליח ציבור*, says:*

שמות לא

וְשָׁמְרוּ בְנֵי־יִשְׂרָאֵל אֶת־הַשַּׁבָּת
לַעֲשׂוֹת אֶת־הַשַּׁבָּת לְדֹרֹתָם בְּרִית עוֹלָם:
בֵּינִי וּבֵין בְּנֵי יִשְׂרָאֵל, אוֹת הִוא לְעֹלָם
כִּי־שֵׁשֶׁת יָמִים עָשָׂה יהוה אֶת־הַשָּׁמַיִם וְאֶת־הָאָרֶץ
וּבַיּוֹם הַשְּׁבִיעִי שָׁבַת וַיִּנָּפַשׁ:

CONNECTION

In "Shabbat in Space: The Legacy of Ilan Ramon," Rabbi Zvi Konikov describes his first encounter with Ilan Ramon.

I first met Ilan Ramon at an almost clandestine gathering in my hometown of Satellite Beach, Florida. NASA personnel and Israeli security teams had taken extra security precautions to ensure that nothing would go wrong. Even the location had been kept secret until the very day of the meeting.

Ilan addressed the assembled Jewish community leaders. After his speech he approached me. He greeted me with a warm hug and presented me with his request: "Rabbi, I need to talk with you. I want to keep Shabbat while in space, but no one can tell me how to do it!"

And that was how our friendship began.

Ilan was a very special Jew. He often expressed the thought that he saw his trip to space as a mission. "I will represent the entire Jewish people," he would say. As a representative of the Jewish people, he wanted to do everything in the very best possible way Jewishly, including keeping Shabbat and eating only kosher food.

LEARNING

וַיִּנָּפַשׁ takes its root from the word **נֶפֶשׁ**. Shabbat provides space to refresh the soul. The Midrash (*Tanḥuma Tzav*) explains that the word **וַיִּנָּפַשׁ** hints to the idea that on Shabbat a person is given an extra soul. This "*neshama yeteira* – extra soul" provides us with the ability to spiritually connect more easily. This is why, after Shabbat, when we make Havdala, we smell spices to revive ourselves from the loss of our Shabbat *neshama yeteira*.

HALF KADDISH

Leader: יִתְגַּדַּל Magnified and sanctified may His great name be,
in the world He created by His will.
May He establish His kingdom
in your lifetime and in your days,
and in the lifetime of all the house of Israel,
swiftly and soon –
and say: Amen.

All: May His great name be blessed
for ever and all time.

Leader: Blessed and praised, glorified and elevated,
raised and honored, uplifted and praised
be the name of the Holy One,
blessed be He,
beyond any blessing,
song, praise and consolation
uttered in the world –
and say: Amen.

Amida are always the same, on Shabbat, festivals, and weekdays. On Shabbat, however, we do not focus on our material needs, and we replace the thirteen blessings of request of the weekday Amida with one *berakha* that speaks about the holiness of the day. The *Amida* of each of the *tefilla* services on Shabbat – Ma'ariv, Shaḥarit, Mussaf and Minḥa – follows this same pattern.

The middle *berakha* of this *Amida* focuses on Shabbat as the climax of the creation of the universe. It describes Shabbat as holier than the other days of the week. The *berakha* concludes with a prayer that Hashem should accept with favor our observance of Shabbat, help us to fulfill the Torah and the mitzvot that are contained in it, and aid us in keeping the Shabbat.

As you take three steps forward to stand before Hashem, on the holiest day of the week, consider what it means to be like Hashem and to be holy. Can you focus on Torah, mitzvot, and spirituality instead of whatever else you have been thinking about? How can your practice of Shabbat help you achieve that?

For more information on the *Amida* in general turn to page 148.

חצי קדיש

ש״ץ: יִתְגַּדַּל וְיִתְקַדַּשׁ שְׁמֵהּ רַבָּא (קהל: אָמֵן)
בְּעָלְמָא דִּי בְרָא כִרְעוּתֵהּ
וְיַמְלִיךְ מַלְכוּתֵהּ
בְּחַיֵּיכוֹן וּבְיוֹמֵיכוֹן וּבְחַיֵּי דְכָל בֵּית יִשְׂרָאֵל
בַּעֲגָלָא וּבִזְמַן קָרִיב
וְאִמְרוּ אָמֵן. (קהל: אָמֵן)

קהל וש״ץ: יְהֵא שְׁמֵהּ רַבָּא מְבָרַךְ לְעָלַם וּלְעָלְמֵי עָלְמַיָּא.

ש״ץ: יִתְבָּרַךְ וְיִשְׁתַּבַּח וְיִתְפָּאַר וְיִתְרוֹמַם וְיִתְנַשֵּׂא
וְיִתְהַדָּר וְיִתְעַלֶּה וְיִתְהַלָּל
שְׁמֵהּ דְּקֻדְשָׁא בְּרִיךְ הוּא (קהל: בְּרִיךְ הוּא)
לְעֵלָּא מִן כָּל בִּרְכָתָא
/בשבת שובה: לְעֵלָּא לְעֵלָּא מִכָּל בִּרְכָתָא/
וְשִׁירָתָא, תֻּשְׁבְּחָתָא וְנֶחֱמָתָא
דַּאֲמִירָן בְּעָלְמָא
וְאִמְרוּ אָמֵן. (קהל: אָמֵן)

INTRODUCTION TO THE SHABBAT *AMIDA*

The prayers until this point are preparations for the Amida, in which we stand in God's presence. The *Amida* is the pinnacle of our *tefillot*, in which we stand before God and bare our souls. Originally composed by the Men of the Great Assembly, the weekday *Amida* consisted of eighteen blessings, and is often referred to by the name *Shemoneh Esreh*, despite the later addition of a nineteenth blessing. The *Amida* for Shabbat and for festivals has only seven blessings, yet is often still referred to as the *Shemoneh Esreh*.

The weekday *Amida* has its own internal logical structure. The first three *berakhot* are blessings of praise (*shevaḥ*), followed by thirteen requests (*bakashot*), and then the *Amida* concludes with three blessings of thanks (*hoda'a*). The first three and last three *berakhot* of the

THE AMIDA

The following prayer, until "in former years" on page 480, is said silently, standing with feet together. Take three steps forward and at the points indicated by ▾, bend the knees at the first word, bow at the second, and stand straight before saying God's name.

O Lord, open my lips,
so that my mouth may declare Your praise. *Ps. 51*

PATRIARCHS

בָּרוּךְ Blessed are You,
Lord our God and God of our fathers,
God of Abraham, God of Isaac and God of Jacob;
the great, mighty and awesome God, God Most High,
who acts with loving-kindness and creates all,
who remembers the loving-kindness of the fathers
and will bring a Redeemer to their children's children
for the sake of His name, in love.

On Shabbat Shuva: Remember us for life, O King who desires life,
and write us in the book of life –
for Your sake, O God of life.

King, Helper, Savior, Shield:
Blessed are You, Lord, Shield of Abraham.

DIVINE MIGHT

אַתָּה גִּבּוֹר You are eternally mighty, Lord.
You give life to the dead and have great power to save.

The phrase "He makes the wind blow and the rain fall" is added from Simḥat Torah until Pesaḥ. In Israel, the phrase "He causes the dew to fall" is added from Pesaḥ until Shemini Atzeret.

In fall & winter: He makes the wind blow and the rain fall.
In Israel, in spring & summer: He causes the dew to fall.

He sustains the living with loving-kindness,
and with great compassion revives the dead.
He supports the fallen, heals the sick, sets captives free,

עמידה

The following prayer, until קַדְמֹנִיּוֹת *on page 481, is said silently, standing with feet together. Take three steps forward and at the points indicated by* ❜*, bend the knees at the first word, bow at the second, and stand straight before saying God's name.*

אֲדֹנָי, שְׂפָתַי תִּפְתָּח, וּפִי יַגִּיד תְּהִלָּתֶךָ: תהלים נא

אבות

בָּרוּךְ אַתָּה יהוה, אֱלֹהֵינוּ וֵאלֹהֵי אֲבוֹתֵינוּ
אֱלֹהֵי אַבְרָהָם, אֱלֹהֵי יִצְחָק, וֵאלֹהֵי יַעֲקֹב
הָאֵל הַגָּדוֹל הַגִּבּוֹר וְהַנּוֹרָא, אֵל עֶלְיוֹן
גּוֹמֵל חֲסָדִים טוֹבִים, וְקוֹנֵה הַכֹּל
וְזוֹכֵר חַסְדֵי אָבוֹת
וּמֵבִיא גוֹאֵל לִבְנֵי בְנֵיהֶם לְמַעַן שְׁמוֹ בְּאַהֲבָה.

בשבת שובה: זָכְרֵנוּ לְחַיִּים, מֶלֶךְ חָפֵץ בַּחַיִּים
וְכָתְבֵנוּ בְּסֵפֶר הַחַיִּים, לְמַעַנְךָ אֱלֹהִים חַיִּים.

מֶלֶךְ עוֹזֵר וּמוֹשִׁיעַ וּמָגֵן.
בָּרוּךְ אַתָּה יהוה, מָגֵן אַבְרָהָם.

גבורות

אַתָּה גִּבּוֹר לְעוֹלָם, אֲדֹנָי
מְחַיֵּה מֵתִים אַתָּה, רַב לְהוֹשִׁיעַ

The phrase מַשִּׁיב הָרְוּחַ *is added from* שמחת תורה *until* פסח.
In ארץ ישראל *the phrase* מוֹרִיד הַטָּל *is added from* פסח *until* שמיני עצרת.

בחורף: מַשִּׁיב הָרְוּחַ וּמוֹרִיד הַגֶּשֶׁם / בארץ ישראל בקיץ: מוֹרִיד הַטָּל

מְכַלְכֵּל חַיִּים בְּחֶסֶד, מְחַיֵּה מֵתִים בְּרַחֲמִים רַבִּים
סוֹמֵךְ נוֹפְלִים, וְרוֹפֵא חוֹלִים, וּמַתִּיר אֲסוּרִים
וּמְקַיֵּם אֱמוּנָתוֹ לִישֵׁנֵי עָפָר.

and keeps His faith with those who sleep in the dust.
Who is like You, Master of might,
and who can compare to You,
O King who brings death and gives life,
and makes salvation grow?

On Shabbat Shuva: Who is like You, compassionate Father,
who remembers His creatures
in compassion, for life?

Faithful are You to revive the dead.
Blessed are You, LORD, who revives the dead.

HOLINESS

אַתָּה קָדוֹשׁ You are holy and Your name is holy,
and holy ones praise You daily, Selah!
Blessed are You, LORD,
the holy God. / *On Shabbat Shuva:* the holy King./

(*If forgotten, repeat the Amida.*)

HOLINESS OF THE DAY

אַתָּה קִדַּשְׁתָּ You sanctified the seventh day
for Your name's sake,
as the climax of the creation of heaven and earth.
Of all days, You blessed it; of all seasons You sanctified it –
and so it is written in Your Torah:

LEARNING

The difference between Shabbat and Yom Tov is that God Himself blessed and sanctified Shabbat directly. The *kedusha* of Yom Tov, though, is conferred through the Jewish people. The festivals are decided based on the Jewish people's sanctification of the new moon, an act that takes place by the hand of man. Since Shabbat is sanctified directly by God, it is holier than all other times.

CONNECTION

"There are all sorts of inequalities in the world, but there's one thing we all have equally, and that's time itself. Whether we're rich or poor, there are still only twenty-four hours in the day; 365 days in the year; and a span of life that's all too short." (Rabbi Jonathan Sacks, *From Optimism to Hope*)

מִי כָמְוֹךָ, בַּעַל גְּבוּרוֹת, וּמִי דְּוֹמֶה לָּךְ
מֶלֶךְ, מֵמִית וּמְחַיֶּה וּמַצְמִיחַ יְשׁוּעָה.

בשבת שובה: מִי כָמְוֹךָ אַב הָרַחֲמִים
זוֹכֵר יְצוּרָיו לְחַיִּים בְּרַחֲמִים.

וְנֶאֱמָן אַתָּה לְהַחֲיוֹת מֵתִים.
בָּרוּךְ אַתָּה יהוה, מְחַיֵּה הַמֵּתִים.

קדושת השם

אַתָּה קָדוֹשׁ וְשִׁמְךָ קָדוֹשׁ
וּקְדוֹשִׁים בְּכָל יוֹם יְהַלְלְוּךָ סֶּלָה.
בָּרוּךְ אַתָּה יהוה, הָאֵל הַקָּדוֹשׁ. / בשבת שובה: הַמֶּלֶךְ הַקָּדוֹשׁ./

(*If forgotten, repeat the* עמידה.)

קדושת היום

אַתָּה קִדַּשְׁתָּ אֶת יוֹם הַשְּׁבִיעִי לִשְׁמֶךָ
תַּכְלִית מַעֲשֵׂה שָׁמַיִם וָאָרֶץ
וּבֵרַכְתּוֹ מִכָּל הַיָּמִים, וְקִדַּשְׁתּוֹ מִכָּל הַזְּמַנִּים
וְכֵן כָּתוּב בְּתוֹרָתֶךָ

...A THOUSAND WORDS

REFLECTION

Can you think of a time in your life when you felt holiness?
When was it?
Why was it special?

How can we make the time on Shabbat most valuable?

What makes Shabbat holy for you?

וַיְכֻלּוּ Then the heavens and the earth were completed, *Gen. 2*
and all their multitudes.
With the seventh day, God completed the work He had done.
He ceased on the seventh day from all the work He had done.
God blessed the seventh day and declared it holy,
because on it He ceased from all His work
He had created to do.

... A THOUSAND WORDS

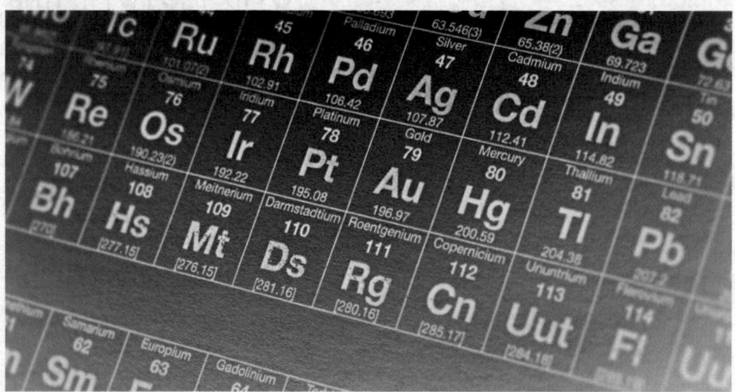

CONNECTION

The Midrash Tanḥuma (Tazria 5) *cites a famous dispute between Rabbi Akiva and the wicked Roman procurator Turnus Rufus. Turnus Rufus asked Rabbi Akiva, "Whose acts are greater, mankind's or God's?" Rabbi Akiva answered him that man's acts are greater.*

Turnus Rufus asked why Jews are circumcised.

Rabbi Akiva responded: Because God gave the mitzvot to the Jewish people in order to refine them, to complete His creations, just as He created wheat for us to mill into flour and bake into bread. God created the world, and left opportunity for us to continue His creation and partner with Him. God created the human body to be perfected by man, leaving us the space to complete His creation. Likewise, God created the world with space for us to perfect it as implied by the word לַעֲשׂוֹת*, "to do," which is written as the infinitive form.*

בראשית ב

וַיְכֻלּוּ הַשָּׁמַיִם וְהָאָרֶץ וְכָל־צְבָאָם:
וַיְכַל אֱלֹהִים בַּיּוֹם הַשְּׁבִיעִי מְלַאכְתּוֹ אֲשֶׁר עָשָׂה
וַיִּשְׁבֹּת בַּיּוֹם הַשְּׁבִיעִי מִכָּל־מְלַאכְתּוֹ אֲשֶׁר עָשָׂה:
וַיְבָרֶךְ אֱלֹהִים אֶת־יוֹם הַשְּׁבִיעִי, וַיְקַדֵּשׁ אֹתוֹ
כִּי בוֹ שָׁבַת מִכָּל־מְלַאכְתּוֹ
אֲשֶׁר־בָּרָא אֱלֹהִים לַעֲשׂוֹת:

REFLECTION

What did you
successfully complete
this week?

Do you have
a sense of closure
on the week?

How will you commit
to being part
of the historical chain
of Shabbat observance?

How will you impact
the world that God created?

LEARNING

The Gemara (*Shabbat* 119b) says: Even if an individual prays alone on the eve of the Sabbath, he must recite וַיְכֻלּוּ, because Rabbi Hamnuna said: "He who prays on the eve of the Sabbath and recites 'Then the heavens and the earth were completed,' it is as though he had become a partner with the Holy One, blessed be He, in the creation, for it is said, וַיְכֻלּוּ [they were completed]; but it can also be read, 'they completed.'" When one recites this paragraph, he testifies that he agrees to partner with God in perfecting creation.

CONNECTION

The infinitive לַעֲשׂוֹת *means that man is now charged to carry on the work that was ended on the seventh day, as creation itself was left incomplete. The existence of evil reflects the imperfection of creation. God gave us the great assignment of participating in the progressive work of creation; Judaism is thus a religion of activism against evil. In the future, God will indeed complete creation; in the meantime, man is assigned the task of combating evil himself.* (Rabbi J.B. Soloveitchik, Commentary on the *Ḥumash*)

אֱלֹהֵינוּ Our God and God of our ancestors,
may You find favor in our rest.
Make us holy through Your commandments
and give us our share in Your Torah.
Satisfy us with Your goodness,
give us joy in Your salvation,
and purify our hearts to serve You in truth.
In love and favor, O LORD our God,
give us as our heritage Your holy Shabbat,
so that Israel, who sanctify Your name,
may find rest on it.
Blessed are You, LORD,
who sanctifies the Sabbath.

TEMPLE SERVICE

רְצֵה Find favor, LORD our God,
in Your people Israel and their prayer.
Restore the service to Your most holy House,
and accept in love and favor
the fire-offerings of Israel and their prayer.
May the service of Your people Israel
always find favor with You.

REFLECTION

How might your rest on Shabbat make God pleased?

What type of rest might displease God?

How might resting on Shabbat help you stay connected to Judaism?

LEARNING

The statement בְּאַהֲבָה, with love, is in keeping with the nature of Shabbat. In fact, the word is repeatedly inserted in various portions of the Yom Tov services when Yom Tov should coincide with Shabbat. For Shabbat is the day on which the creature is reunited with the Creator in purity; it is the day appointed by the Creator so that His creature will not forget Him. Thus the basic characteristic of Shabbat is love, the love of the creature for its Maker and the love of the Maker in turn for His creation. (Rabbi S.R. Hirsch)

אֱלֹהֵינוּ וֵאלֹהֵי אֲבוֹתֵינוּ, רְצֵה בִמְנוּחָתֵנוּ.
קַדְּשֵׁנוּ בְּמִצְוֹתֶיךָ, וְתֵן חֶלְקֵנוּ בְּתוֹרָתֶךָ
שַׂבְּעֵנוּ מִטּוּבֶךָ, וְשַׂמְּחֵנוּ בִּישׁוּעָתֶךָ
וְטַהֵר לִבֵּנוּ לְעָבְדְּךָ בֶּאֱמֶת.
וְהַנְחִילֵנוּ, יהוה אֱלֹהֵינוּ, בְּאַהֲבָה וּבְרָצוֹן שַׁבַּת קָדְשֶׁךָ
וְיָנוּחוּ בָהּ יִשְׂרָאֵל מְקַדְּשֵׁי שְׁמֶךָ.
בָּרוּךְ אַתָּה יהוה, מְקַדֵּשׁ הַשַּׁבָּת.

עבודה

רְצֵה יהוה אֱלֹהֵינוּ בְּעַמְּךָ יִשְׂרָאֵל, וּבִתְפִלָּתָם
וְהָשֵׁב אֶת הָעֲבוֹדָה לִדְבִיר בֵּיתֶךָ
וְאִשֵּׁי יִשְׂרָאֵל וּתְפִלָּתָם בְּאַהֲבָה תְקַבֵּל בְּרָצוֹן
וּתְהִי לְרָצוֹן תָּמִיד עֲבוֹדַת יִשְׂרָאֵל עַמֶּךָ.

...A THOUSAND WORDS

CONNECTION

The Beit HaLevi explains the fundamental difference between the first six days and Shabbat. In the first six days, Hashem was actively creating completely new forms of existence from nothing. On Shabbat, He refrained from creating new things, however He did not sit idly, so to speak, and do nothing. What did He do on Shabbat?

God is constantly recreating the world. We acknowledge this in Birkot Keriat Shema. We say "and in His goodness, He renews the works of creation every day, constantly." This means that Hashem is constantly creating the world anew. If He stopped doing this for one instant, the world would cease to exist. This process began on the first Shabbat of creation, and it is this that is described as Hashem's menuha. *It contrasted with the previous six days in that on Shabbat, Hashem refrained from creating new things,* yesh me'ayin, *rather He recreated the world in its previous form. Thus, Hashem's* menuha *did not constitute a mere refraining of activity, rather it represented a change from creating new things, to recreating them in their previous form. This was the 'creation' of the seventh day.*

On Rosh Ḥodesh and Ḥol HaMo'ed:

אֱלֹהֵינוּ Our God and God of our ancestors, may there rise, come, reach, appear, be favored, heard, regarded and remembered before You, our recollection and remembrance, as well as the remembrance of our ancestors, and of the Messiah son of David Your servant, and of Jerusalem Your holy city, and of all Your people the house of Israel – for deliverance and well-being, grace, loving-kindness and compassion, life and peace, on this day of:

On Rosh Ḥodesh: Rosh Ḥodesh.
On Pesaḥ: the Festival of Matzot.
On Sukkot: the Festival of Sukkot.

On it remember us, Lord our God, for good; recollect us for blessing, and save us for life. In accord with Your promise of salvation and compassion, spare us and be gracious to us; have compassion on us and save us, for our eyes are turned to You because You, God, are a gracious and compassionate King.

וְתֶחֱזֶינָה And may our eyes witness
Your return to Zion in compassion.
Blessed are You, Lord, who restores His Presence to Zion.

THANKSGIVING

מוֹדִים We give thanks to You,
for You are the Lord our God and God of our ancestors
for ever and all time.
You are the Rock of our lives,
Shield of our salvation from generation to generation.
We will thank You and declare Your praise for our lives,
which are entrusted into Your hand;
for our souls, which are placed in Your charge;
for Your miracles which are with us every day;
and for Your wonders and favors
at all times, evening, morning and midday.
You are good – for Your compassion never fails.
You are compassionate – for Your loving-kindnesses never cease.
We have always placed our hope in You.

On ראש חודש and חול המועד:

אֱלֹהֵינוּ וֵאלֹהֵי אֲבוֹתֵינוּ, יַעֲלֶה וְיָבוֹא וְיַגִּיעַ, וְיֵרָאֶה וְיֵרָצֶה וְיִשָּׁמַע, וְיִפָּקֵד וְיִזָּכֵר זִכְרוֹנֵנוּ וּפִקְדּוֹנֵנוּ וְזִכְרוֹן אֲבוֹתֵינוּ, וְזִכְרוֹן מָשִׁיחַ בֶּן דָּוִד עַבְדֶּךָ, וְזִכְרוֹן יְרוּשָׁלַיִם עִיר קָדְשֶׁךָ, וְזִכְרוֹן כָּל עַמְּךָ בֵּית יִשְׂרָאֵל, לְפָנֶיךָ, לִפְלֵיטָה לְטוֹבָה, לְחֵן וּלְחֶסֶד וּלְרַחֲמִים, לְחַיִּים וּלְשָׁלוֹם בְּיוֹם

בראש חודש: רֹאשׁ הַחֹדֶשׁ / בפסח: חַג הַמַּצּוֹת / בסוכות: חַג הַסֻּכּוֹת

הַזֶּה. זָכְרֵנוּ יהוה אֱלֹהֵינוּ בּוֹ לְטוֹבָה, וּפָקְדֵנוּ בוֹ לִבְרָכָה, וְהוֹשִׁיעֵנוּ בוֹ לְחַיִּים. וּבִדְבַר יְשׁוּעָה וְרַחֲמִים, חוּס וְחָנֵּנוּ וְרַחֵם עָלֵינוּ וְהוֹשִׁיעֵנוּ, כִּי אֵלֶיךָ עֵינֵינוּ, כִּי אֵל מֶלֶךְ חַנּוּן וְרַחוּם אָתָּה.

וְתֶחֱזֶינָה עֵינֵינוּ בְּשׁוּבְךָ לְצִיּוֹן בְּרַחֲמִים.
בָּרוּךְ אַתָּה יהוה, הַמַּחֲזִיר שְׁכִינָתוֹ לְצִיּוֹן.

הודאה

מוֹדִים אֲנַחְנוּ לָךְ
שָׁאַתָּה הוּא יהוה אֱלֹהֵינוּ וֵאלֹהֵי אֲבוֹתֵינוּ לְעוֹלָם וָעֶד.
צוּר חַיֵּינוּ, מָגֵן יִשְׁעֵנוּ, אַתָּה הוּא לְדוֹר וָדוֹר.
נוֹדֶה לְּךָ וּנְסַפֵּר תְּהִלָּתֶךָ
עַל חַיֵּינוּ הַמְּסוּרִים בְּיָדֶךָ
וְעַל נִשְׁמוֹתֵינוּ הַפְּקוּדוֹת לָךְ
וְעַל נִסֶּיךָ שֶׁבְּכָל יוֹם עִמָּנוּ
וְעַל נִפְלְאוֹתֶיךָ וְטוֹבוֹתֶיךָ
שֶׁבְּכָל עֵת, עֶרֶב וָבֹקֶר וְצָהֳרָיִם.
הַטּוֹב, כִּי לֹא כָלוּ רַחֲמֶיךָ
וְהַמְרַחֵם, כִּי לֹא תַמּוּ חֲסָדֶיךָ
מֵעוֹלָם קִוִּינוּ לָךְ.

On Ḥanukka:

עַל הַנִּסִּים [We thank You also] for the miracles, the redemption, the mighty deeds, the salvations, and the victories in battle which You performed for our ancestors in those days, at this time.

בִּימֵי מַתִּתְיָהוּ In the days of Mattityahu, son of Yoḥanan, the High Priest, the Hasmonean, and his sons, the wicked Greek kingdom rose up against Your people Israel to make them forget Your Torah and to force them to transgress the laws of Your will. It was then that You in Your great compassion stood by them in the time of their distress. You championed their cause, judged their claim, and avenged their wrong. You delivered the strong into the hands of the weak, the many into the hands of the few, the impure into the hands of the pure, the wicked into the hands of the righteous, and the arrogant into the hands of those who were engaged in the study of Your Torah. You made for Yourself great and holy fame in Your world, and for Your people Israel You performed a great salvation and redemption as of this very day. Your children then entered the holiest part of Your House, cleansed Your Temple, purified Your Sanctuary, kindled lights in Your holy courts, and designated these eight days of Ḥanukka for giving thanks and praise to Your great name.

Continue with "For all these things."

On Shushan Purim in Jerusalem:

עַל הַנִּסִּים [We thank You also] for the miracles, the redemption, the mighty deeds, the salvations, and the victories in battle which You performed for our ancestors in those days, at this time.

בִּימֵי מָרְדְּכַי In the days of Mordekhai and Esther, in Shushan the capital, the
wicked Haman rose up against them and sought to destroy, slay and exterminate *Esther 3*
all the Jews, young and old, children and women, on one day, the thirteenth day of the twelfth month, which is the month of Adar, and to plunder their possessions. Then You in Your great compassion defeated his counsel, frustrated his plans, and caused his scheme to recoil on his own head, so that they hanged him and his sons on the gallows.

Continue with "For all these things."

וְעַל כֻּלָּם For all these things may Your name be blessed and elevated, our King, continually, for ever and all time.

On Shabbat Shuva: And write, for a good life, all the children of Your covenant.

Let all that lives thank You, Selah! and praise Your name in truth,
God, our Savior and Help, Selah!
Blessed are You, LORD,
whose name is "the Good" and to whom thanks are due.

בחנוכה:

עַל הַנִּסִּים וְעַל הַפֻּרְקָן וְעַל הַגְּבוּרוֹת וְעַל הַתְּשׁוּעוֹת וְעַל הַמִּלְחָמוֹת שֶׁעָשִׂיתָ לַאֲבוֹתֵינוּ בַּיָּמִים הָהֵם בַּזְּמַן הַזֶּה.

בִּימֵי מַתִּתְיָהוּ בֶּן יוֹחָנָן כֹּהֵן גָּדוֹל חַשְׁמוֹנַאי וּבָנָיו, כְּשֶׁעָמְדָה מַלְכוּת יָוָן הָרְשָׁעָה עַל עַמְּךָ יִשְׂרָאֵל לְהַשְׁכִּיחָם תּוֹרָתֶךָ וּלְהַעֲבִירָם מֵחֻקֵּי רְצוֹנֶךָ, וְאַתָּה בְּרַחֲמֶיךָ הָרַבִּים עָמַדְתָּ לָהֶם בְּעֵת צָרָתָם, רַבְתָּ אֶת רִיבָם, דַּנְתָּ אֶת דִּינָם, נָקַמְתָּ אֶת נִקְמָתָם, מָסַרְתָּ גִּבּוֹרִים בְּיַד חַלָּשִׁים, וְרַבִּים בְּיַד מְעַטִּים, וּטְמֵאִים בְּיַד טְהוֹרִים, וּרְשָׁעִים בְּיַד צַדִּיקִים, וְזֵדִים בְּיַד עוֹסְקֵי תוֹרָתֶךָ, וּלְךָ עָשִׂיתָ שֵׁם גָּדוֹל וְקָדוֹשׁ בְּעוֹלָמֶךָ, וּלְעַמְּךָ יִשְׂרָאֵל עָשִׂיתָ תְּשׁוּעָה גְדוֹלָה וּפֻרְקָן כְּהַיּוֹם הַזֶּה. וְאַחַר כֵּן בָּאוּ בָנֶיךָ לִדְבִיר בֵּיתֶךָ, וּפִנּוּ אֶת הֵיכָלֶךָ, וְטִהֲרוּ אֶת מִקְדָּשֶׁךָ, וְהִדְלִיקוּ נֵרוֹת בְּחַצְרוֹת קָדְשֶׁךָ, וְקָבְעוּ שְׁמוֹנַת יְמֵי חֲנֻכָּה אֵלּוּ, לְהוֹדוֹת וּלְהַלֵּל לְשִׁמְךָ הַגָּדוֹל.

Continue with וְעַל כֻּלָּם.

בשושן פורים בירושלים:

עַל הַנִּסִּים וְעַל הַפֻּרְקָן וְעַל הַגְּבוּרוֹת וְעַל הַתְּשׁוּעוֹת וְעַל הַמִּלְחָמוֹת שֶׁעָשִׂיתָ לַאֲבוֹתֵינוּ בַּיָּמִים הָהֵם בַּזְּמַן הַזֶּה.

בִּימֵי מָרְדְּכַי וְאֶסְתֵּר בְּשׁוּשַׁן הַבִּירָה, כְּשֶׁעָמַד עֲלֵיהֶם הָמָן הָרָשָׁע, בִּקֵּשׁ לְהַשְׁמִיד לַהֲרֹג וּלְאַבֵּד אֶת־כָּל־הַיְּהוּדִים מִנַּעַר וְעַד־זָקֵן טַף וְנָשִׁים בְּיוֹם אֶחָד, בִּשְׁלוֹשָׁה עָשָׂר לְחֹדֶשׁ שְׁנֵים־עָשָׂר, הוּא־חֹדֶשׁ אֲדָר, וּשְׁלָלָם לָבוֹז: וְאַתָּה בְּרַחֲמֶיךָ הָרַבִּים הֵפַרְתָּ אֶת עֲצָתוֹ, וְקִלְקַלְתָּ אֶת מַחֲשַׁבְתּוֹ, וַהֲשֵׁבוֹתָ לוֹ גְּמוּלוֹ בְּרֹאשׁוֹ, וְתָלוּ אוֹתוֹ וְאֶת בָּנָיו עַל הָעֵץ. (אסתר ג)

Continue with וְעַל כֻּלָּם.

וְעַל כֻּלָּם יִתְבָּרַךְ וְיִתְרוֹמַם שִׁמְךָ מַלְכֵּנוּ תָּמִיד לְעוֹלָם וָעֶד.

בשבת שובה: וּכְתֹב לְחַיִּים טוֹבִים כָּל בְּנֵי בְרִיתֶךָ.

וְכֹל הַחַיִּים יוֹדוּךָ סֶּלָה, וִיהַלְלוּ אֶת שִׁמְךָ בֶּאֱמֶת הָאֵל יְשׁוּעָתֵנוּ וְעֶזְרָתֵנוּ סֶלָה.

בָּרוּךְ אַתָּה יהוה, הַטּוֹב שִׁמְךָ וּלְךָ נָאֶה לְהוֹדוֹת.

PEACE

שָׁלוֹם רָב Give great peace to Your people Israel for ever,
for You are the sovereign LORD of all peace;
and may it be good in Your eyes to bless Your people Israel
at every time, at every hour, with Your peace.

On Shabbat Shuva: In the book of life, blessing, peace and prosperity,
may we and all Your people the house of Israel
be remembered and written before You
for a good life, and for peace.*

Blessed are You, LORD, who blesses His people Israel with peace.

**On Shabbat Shuva outside Israel, many end the blessing:*
Blessed are You, LORD, who makes peace.

Some say the following verse:
May the words of my mouth and the inner thoughts of my heart *Ps. 19*
find favor before You, LORD, my Rock and Redeemer.

אֱלֹהַי My God, *Berakhot 17a*
guard my tongue from evil and my lips from dishonest speech.
To those who curse me, let my soul be silent;
may my soul be to all like the dust.
Open my heart to Your Torah and let my soul pursue Your commandments.
As for all who plan evil against me,
swiftly defeat their counsel and frustrate their plans.
Act for the sake of Your name; act for the sake of Your right hand;
act for the sake of Your holiness; act for the sake of Your Torah.
That Your beloved ones may be rescued, *Ps. 60*
save with Your right hand and answer me.
May the words of my mouth and the inner thoughts of my heart *Ps. 19*
find favor before You, LORD, my Rock and Redeemer.

Bow, take three steps back, then bow, first left, then right, then center, while saying:
May He who makes peace in His high places,
make peace for us and all Israel – and say: Amen.

יְהִי רָצוֹן May it be Your will, LORD our God and God of our ancestors, that the Temple be rebuilt speedily in our days, and give us a share in Your Torah. And there we will serve You with fear, as in the days of old and as in former years. Then the offering *Mal. 3* of Judah and Jerusalem will be pleasing to the LORD as in the days of old and as in former years.

ברכת שלום

שָׁלוֹם רָב עַל יִשְׂרָאֵל עַמְּךָ תָּשִׂים לְעוֹלָם
כִּי אַתָּה הוּא מֶלֶךְ אָדוֹן לְכָל הַשָּׁלוֹם.
וְטוֹב בְּעֵינֶיךָ לְבָרֵךְ אֶת עַמְּךָ יִשְׂרָאֵל
בְּכָל עֵת וּבְכָל שָׁעָה בִּשְׁלוֹמֶךָ.

בשבת שובה: בְּסֵפֶר חַיִּים, בְּרָכָה וְשָׁלוֹם, וּפַרְנָסָה טוֹבָה
נִזָּכֵר וְנִכָּתֵב לְפָנֶיךָ, אֲנַחְנוּ וְכָל עַמְּךָ בֵּית יִשְׂרָאֵל
לְחַיִּים טוֹבִים וּלְשָׁלוֹם.*

בָּרוּךְ אַתָּה יהוה, הַמְבָרֵךְ אֶת עַמּוֹ יִשְׂרָאֵל בַּשָּׁלוֹם.

**On* שבת שובה *in* חוץ לארץ*, many end the blessing:*

בָּרוּךְ אַתָּה יהוה, עוֹשֵׂה הַשָּׁלוֹם.

Some say the following verse:

יִהְיוּ לְרָצוֹן אִמְרֵי־פִי וְהֶגְיוֹן לִבִּי לְפָנֶיךָ, יהוה צוּרִי וְגֹאֲלִי: תהלים יט

אֱלֹהַי, נְצֹר לְשׁוֹנִי מֵרָע וּשְׂפָתַי מִדַּבֵּר מִרְמָה ברכות יז.
וְלִמְקַלְלַי נַפְשִׁי תִדֹּם, וְנַפְשִׁי כֶּעָפָר לַכֹּל תִּהְיֶה.
פְּתַח לִבִּי בְּתוֹרָתֶךָ, וּבְמִצְוֹתֶיךָ תִּרְדֹּף נַפְשִׁי.
וְכָל הַחוֹשְׁבִים עָלַי רָעָה, מְהֵרָה הָפֵר עֲצָתָם וְקַלְקֵל מַחֲשַׁבְתָּם.
עֲשֵׂה לְמַעַן שְׁמֶךָ, עֲשֵׂה לְמַעַן יְמִינֶךָ
עֲשֵׂה לְמַעַן קְדֻשָּׁתֶךָ, עֲשֵׂה לְמַעַן תּוֹרָתֶךָ.
לְמַעַן יֵחָלְצוּן יְדִידֶיךָ, הוֹשִׁיעָה יְמִינְךָ וַעֲנֵנִי: תהלים ס
יִהְיוּ לְרָצוֹן אִמְרֵי־פִי וְהֶגְיוֹן לִבִּי לְפָנֶיךָ, יהוה צוּרִי וְגֹאֲלִי: תהלים יט

Bow, take three steps back, then bow, first left, then right, then center, while saying:

עֹשֶׂה שָׁלוֹם/ בשבת שובה: הַשָּׁלוֹם/ בִּמְרוֹמָיו
הוּא יַעֲשֶׂה שָׁלוֹם עָלֵינוּ וְעַל כָּל יִשְׂרָאֵל, וְאִמְרוּ אָמֵן.

יְהִי רָצוֹן מִלְּפָנֶיךָ יהוה אֱלֹהֵינוּ וֵאלֹהֵי אֲבוֹתֵינוּ, שֶׁיִּבָּנֶה בֵּית הַמִּקְדָּשׁ בִּמְהֵרָה
בְיָמֵינוּ, וְתֵן חֶלְקֵנוּ בְּתוֹרָתֶךָ, וְשָׁם נַעֲבָדְךָ בְּיִרְאָה כִּימֵי עוֹלָם וּכְשָׁנִים קַדְמֹנִיּוֹת.
וְעָרְבָה לַיהוה מִנְחַת יְהוּדָה וִירוּשָׁלָםִ כִּימֵי עוֹלָם וּכְשָׁנִים קַדְמֹנִיּוֹת: מלאכי ג

All stand and say:

וַיְכֻלּוּ Then the heavens and the earth were completed, *Gen. 2*
and all their multitudes.
With the seventh day, God completed the work He had done.
He ceased on the seventh day from all the work He had done.
God blessed the seventh day and declared it holy,
because on it He ceased from all His work He had created to do.

The following until "who sanctifies the Sabbath" on page 486,
is omitted when praying with an occasional minyan or alone.
The Leader continues:

בָּרוּךְ Blessed are You, Lord our God and God of our fathers,
God of Abraham, God of Isaac and God of Jacob,
the great, mighty and awesome God,
God Most High, Creator of heaven and earth.

---

of always reciting them after the *Amida* was instituted every Shabbat, in order to ensure Shabbat is always recognized with these words, and to maintain continuity between one Shabbat and the next.

Another reason we repeat these words together as a community is because they are considered testimony that God created the world and then rested on Shabbat. Since testimony in a Jewish court must be given by at least two witnesses, we repeat this testimony together as a community. For the same reason, we stand while saying this paragraph, just as witnesses in a court of law must stand. There is also the custom for one who was still saying his personal *Amida* when this was recited communally, to join with another person and say this paragraph together, a pair of witnesses giving testimony to an eternal truth.

REFLECTION

When God created the first human beings, God led them around the Garden of Eden and said: "Look at My works! See how beautiful they are – how excellent! For your sake I created them all. See to it that you do not spoil and destroy My world; for if you do, there will be no one else to repair it."
(*Kohelet Raba* 7:13)

If God created the world,
why do we have a responsibility
to look after it?
Do you think Shabbat has a role
to play in our responsibility
to look after creation?
How do you look after the world
in your everyday life?

All stand and say:

בראשית ב

וַיְכֻלּוּ הַשָּׁמַיִם וְהָאָרֶץ וְכָל־צְבָאָם:
וַיְכַל אֱלֹהִים בַּיּוֹם הַשְּׁבִיעִי מְלַאכְתּוֹ אֲשֶׁר עָשָׂה
וַיִּשְׁבֹּת בַּיּוֹם הַשְּׁבִיעִי מִכָּל־מְלַאכְתּוֹ אֲשֶׁר עָשָׂה:
וַיְבָרֶךְ אֱלֹהִים אֶת־יוֹם הַשְּׁבִיעִי, וַיְקַדֵּשׁ אֹתוֹ
כִּי בוֹ שָׁבַת מִכָּל־מְלַאכְתּוֹ, אֲשֶׁר־בָּרָא אֱלֹהִים, לַעֲשׂוֹת:

The following until מְקַדֵּשׁ הַשַּׁבָּת *on page 487, is omitted when praying with an occasional* מנין *or alone.*
The שליח ציבור *continues:*

בָּרוּךְ אַתָּה יהוה, אֱלֹהֵינוּ וֵאלֹהֵי אֲבוֹתֵינוּ
אֱלֹהֵי אַבְרָהָם, אֱלֹהֵי יִצְחָק, וֵאלֹהֵי יַעֲקֹב
הָאֵל הַגָּדוֹל הַגִּבּוֹר וְהַנּוֹרָא, אֵל עֶלְיוֹן, קֹנֵה שָׁמַיִם וָאָרֶץ.

REFLECTION

"Whoever recites this paragraph, it is as if he is a partner with God in the creation of the world." (*Shabbat* 119b)

Is creation "complete"?
Was creation complete after the sixth day or only after Shabbat?
Is the world still being created?
How can you be a partner with God in creation?

LEARNING

To understand how we should keep Shabbat, we must first understand how God kept the first Shabbat. These verses, from the second chapter of *Bereshit*, describe in God's own words the very first Shabbat after the creation of the world. These words were deemed so central to our understanding and experience of Shabbat that we say them three times during the evening's proceedings: once in *Amida* itself; now, immediately following the *Amida*; and then again in Kiddush for the night of Shabbat.

These words are recited once again here by the entire community together for a number of reasons. On a Shabbat that is also a festival (Pesaḥ, Shavuot, and Sukkot) the *Amida* for Shabbat is replaced by one specific for the festival, and it does not include these words. So the practice

The congregation then the Leader:

מָגֵן אָבוֹת By His word, He was the Shield of our ancestors.
By His promise, He will revive the dead.
There is none like the holy God/*On Shabbat Shuva:* the holy King/
who gives rest to His people on His holy Sabbath day,
for He found them worthy of His favor to give them rest.
Before Him we will come in worship with fear and awe,
giving thanks to His name daily, continually, with due blessings.
He is God to whom thanks are due, the LORD of peace
who sanctifies the Sabbath and blesses the seventh day,
and in holiness gives rest to a people filled with delight,
in remembrance of the work of creation.

CONNECTION

At age twenty-two, Yosef Mendelevich participated in an attempted hijacking of a Russian plane to raise awareness about the desperate plight of Soviet Jews, who had no freedom to practice their religion. He was arrested before the plane ever left the ground and served twelve years in the Soviet gulag. In his time in the prison, Rabbi Mendelevich refused to give up on his religious observance despite tremendous hardship, daily beatings, starvation, and isolation. He describes an interrogation in his book:

"Look at yourself," said the KGB major. "There's nothing Jewish about you. You're a Russian; you know more than me of Russian culture, of Pushkin, Lermontov, Dostoyevsky.... Even your face isn't really a Jewish one. Confess that you were mistaken and you'll live; you'll serve six or seven years and be released while you're still young. You mustn't stand on principle. Think about your life."

This bit of "friendly" advice hit Yosef very hard. As he was led back to his cell, he couldn't help but think about what the major had said. "It was like a seduction. I would go back to my cell and think, maybe he is right. I really could get the death penalty. Maybe I should just pretend it was a mistake, and when I come out of prison I can start again." As I struggled with this thought, I realized that in order to survive I must build a wall around myself. I needed to build myself as a Jew right here in this basement. I must become so Jewish that this KGB man would never again even be able to accuse me of not being a Jew!

Mendelevich had been covering his head with a beret before his arrest, but it had been confiscated in prison. At that moment, he pulled a handkerchief from his pocket, tied the corners, and placed it on his head as a kippa.

What shields do you have for your Jewish identity?

The קהל *then the* שליח ציבור:

מָגֵן אָבוֹת בִּדְבָרוֹ, מְחַיֵּה מֵתִים בְּמַאֲמָרוֹ
הָאֵל / בשבת שובה: הַמֶּלֶךְ / הַקָּדוֹשׁ שֶׁאֵין כָּמְוֹהוּ
הַמֵּנִיחַ לְעַמּוֹ בְּיוֹם שַׁבַּת קָדְשׁוֹ
כִּי בָם רָצָה לְהָנִיחַ לָהֶם
לְפָנָיו נַעֲבֹד בְּיִרְאָה וָפַחַד
וְנוֹדֶה לִשְׁמוֹ בְּכָל יוֹם תָּמִיד, מֵעֵין הַבְּרָכוֹת
אֵל הַהוֹדָאוֹת, אֲדוֹן הַשָּׁלוֹם
מְקַדֵּשׁ הַשַּׁבָּת וּמְבָרֵךְ שְׁבִיעִי
וּמֵנִיחַ בִּקְדֻשָּׁה לְעַם מְדֻשְּׁנֵי עֹנֶג
זֵכֶר לְמַעֲשֵׂה בְרֵאשִׁית.

LEARNING

The *Magen Avot* prayer begins with the passage, "*Barukh Ata Hashem*…" and consists of brief summaries of each of the seven *berakhot* of the Friday night *Amida*:

1. **מָגֵן אָבוֹת** refers to the *berakha* of **אָבוֹת**, the first *berakha*;
2. **מְחַיֵּה מֵתִים** is the *berakha* of resurrection, the second *berakha*;
3. **הָאֵל הַקָּדוֹשׁ** is the blessing of holiness, the third *berakha*;
4. **הַמֵּנִיחַ לְעַמּוֹ** is the *berakha* of **קְדֻשַּׁת הַיּוֹם** special for Shabbat;
5. **לְפָנָיו נַעֲבֹד** is the *berakha* of **רְצֵה** asking that God accept our *tefillot*;
6. **וְנוֹדֶה לִשְׁמוֹ** is the *berakha* of **מוֹדִים** giving thanks for His many favors;
7. **אֲדוֹן הַשָּׁלוֹם** is the final *berakha* of peace – **שָׁלוֹם רָב**.

REFLECTION

"To defend a country,
you need an army.
But to defend an identity,
you need a school.
Judaism is the religion
of the book, not the sword."
(Rabbi Jonathan Sacks,
Radical Then, Radical Now)

How did "Hashem's word"
protect our ancestors?

How can we ensure
it protects us today?

How do you protect
the memory
of your ancestors
and the values
by which they lived?

The Leader continues:

אֱלֹהֵינוּ Our God and God of our ancestors,
may You find favor in our rest.
Make us holy through Your commandments
and give us our share in Your Torah.
Satisfy us with Your goodness,
give us joy in Your salvation,
and purify our hearts to serve You in truth.
In love and favor, LORD our God,
give us as our heritage Your holy Sabbath,
so that Israel who sanctify Your name
may find rest on it.
Blessed are You, LORD,
who sanctifies the Sabbath.

CONNECTION

"By telling us how to live, the commandments give us our mission – if we choose to accept it – of bettering, even perfecting, the world God created… I was taught that the Children of Israel became a nation not when they were liberated from slavery, but when the Law was revealed to them on Sinai – because that gave them their reason for being, their national destiny. Those same values give each of us a personal destiny. But you can't be passive about your destiny. It isn't fulfilled unless you decide to work to make it happen.

"The commandment to observe the Sabbath is…at the heart of our destiny. But the Sabbath doesn't automatically enter our lives. We have to decide to bring it in, to seize that part of our destiny. And that can be difficult.

"My religious observance, including my Sabbath observance, has taught me that it's okay to be different… When you choose your own path – whether in faith, politics, or whatever you do – you will not only feel better, but people will respect you for your choice."
(Senator Joe Lieberman)

REFLECTION

Can a long *tefilla*
in a busy synagogue,
learning Torah,
a fun and loud meal
with friends and family,
and hours of playing games
with friends or siblings,
be considered "rest"?
How so?

The שליח ציבור *continues:*

אֱלֹהֵֽינוּ וֵאלֹהֵי אֲבוֹתֵֽינוּ, רְצֵה בִמְנוּחָתֵֽנוּ.
קַדְּשֵֽׁנוּ בְּמִצְוֹתֶֽיךָ וְתֵן חֶלְקֵֽנוּ בְּתוֹרָתֶֽךָ
שַׂבְּעֵֽנוּ מִטּוּבֶֽךָ וְשַׂמְּחֵֽנוּ בִּישׁוּעָתֶֽךָ
וְטַהֵר לִבֵּֽנוּ לְעָבְדְּךָ בֶּאֱמֶת.
וְהַנְחִילֵֽנוּ יהוה אֱלֹהֵֽינוּ בְּאַהֲבָה וּבְרָצוֹן שַׁבַּת קָדְשֶֽׁךָ
וְיָנֽוּחוּ בָהּ יִשְׂרָאֵל מְקַדְּשֵׁי שְׁמֶֽךָ.
בָּרוּךְ אַתָּה יהוה, מְקַדֵּשׁ הַשַּׁבָּת.

LEARNING

Resting seems to be just a lack of activity, but in truth rest is what crowns all achievements and enables every goal. Shabbat represents the perspective of the end goal, which is more significant than the act of creation itself. The *menuḥa* of Shabbat is not merely an absence of work, but *menuḥa* that comes from the attainment of wholeness. (Rav Kook, *Olat Re'iya*)

...A THOUSAND WORDS

FULL KADDISH

Leader: יִתְגַּדַּל Magnified and sanctified
may His great name be,
in the world He created by His will.
May He establish His kingdom
in your lifetime and in your days,
and in the lifetime of all the house of Israel,
swiftly and soon –
and say: Amen.

All: May His great name be blessed for ever and all time.

Leader: Blessed and praised,
glorified and elevated,
raised and honored,
uplifted and praised
be the name of the Holy One,
blessed be He, beyond any blessing,
song, praise and consolation
uttered in the world –
and say: Amen.

May the prayers and pleas of all Israel
be accepted by their Father in heaven –
and say: Amen.

May there be great peace from heaven,
and life for us and all Israel –
and say: Amen.

Bow, take three steps back, as if taking leave of the Divine Presence, then bow, first left, then right, then center, while saying:

May He who makes peace in His high places,
make peace for us and all Israel –
and say: Amen.

קדיש שלם

ש״ץ: יִתְגַּדַּל וְיִתְקַדַּשׁ שְׁמֵהּ רַבָּא (קהל: אָמֵן)

בְּעָלְמָא דִּי בְרָא כִרְעוּתֵהּ

וְיַמְלִיךְ מַלְכוּתֵהּ

בְּחַיֵּיכוֹן וּבְיוֹמֵיכוֹן וּבְחַיֵּי דְכָל בֵּית יִשְׂרָאֵל

בַּעֲגָלָא וּבִזְמַן קָרִיב, וְאִמְרוּ אָמֵן. (קהל: אָמֵן)

קהל וש״ץ: יְהֵא שְׁמֵהּ רַבָּא מְבָרַךְ לְעָלַם וּלְעָלְמֵי עָלְמַיָּא.

ש״ץ: יִתְבָּרַךְ וְיִשְׁתַּבַּח וְיִתְפָּאַר

וְיִתְרוֹמַם וְיִתְנַשֵּׂא וְיִתְהַדָּר וְיִתְעַלֶּה וְיִתְהַלָּל

שְׁמֵהּ דְּקֻדְשָׁא בְּרִיךְ הוּא (קהל: בְּרִיךְ הוּא)

לְעֵלָּא מִן כָּל בִּרְכָתָא

/בשבת שובה: לְעֵלָּא לְעֵלָּא מִכָּל בִּרְכָתָא/

וְשִׁירָתָא, תֻּשְׁבְּחָתָא וְנֶחֱמָתָא

דַּאֲמִירָן בְּעָלְמָא, וְאִמְרוּ אָמֵן. (קהל: אָמֵן)

תִּתְקַבַּל צְלוֹתְהוֹן וּבָעוּתְהוֹן דְּכָל יִשְׂרָאֵל

קֳדָם אֲבוּהוֹן דִּי בִשְׁמַיָּא, וְאִמְרוּ אָמֵן. (קהל: אָמֵן)

יְהֵא שְׁלָמָא רַבָּא מִן שְׁמַיָּא

וְחַיִּים, עָלֵינוּ וְעַל כָּל יִשְׂרָאֵל, וְאִמְרוּ אָמֵן. (קהל: אָמֵן)

Bow, take three steps back, as if taking leave of the Divine Presence, then bow, first left, then right, then center, while saying:

עֹשֶׂה שָׁלוֹם/בשבת שובה: הַשָּׁלוֹם/ בִּמְרוֹמָיו

הוּא יַעֲשֶׂה שָׁלוֹם עָלֵינוּ וְעַל כָּל יִשְׂרָאֵל

וְאִמְרוּ אָמֵן. (קהל: אָמֵן)

KIDDUSH IN THE SYNAGOGUE

The Leader raises a cup of wine and says:

Please pay attention, my masters.

בָּרוּךְ Blessed are You, Lord our God, King of the Universe,
who creates the fruit of the vine.

בָּרוּךְ Blessed are You, Lord our God, King of the Universe,
who has made us holy with His commandments, has favored us,
and in love and favor given us His holy Sabbath as a heritage,
a remembrance of the work of creation.
It is the first among the holy days of assembly,
a remembrance of the exodus from Egypt.
For You chose us and sanctified us from all the peoples,
and in love and favor gave us Your holy Sabbath as a heritage.
Blessed are You, Lord, who sanctifies the Sabbath.

The wine should be drunk by children under the age of Bar/Bat Mitzva or, if there are none, by the Leader.

CONNECTION

Some of my earliest memories of going to shul *were with my father on Friday night. As a four year old, I would hold my Daddy's hand and proudly walk with him to* shul *as Shabbat came in. I would sit next to him, my little legs dangling from the bench, reading my book, and every so often he would point at the page for me to join in with the* ḥazan *and the congregation. As the end of davening approached, my excitement would grow. This was the moment I had been waiting for. As the* ḥazan *started chanting* Magen Avot, *a little old man could be seen at the* bima *preparing the wine for Kiddush. He would slowly take out a shining silver becher and the tiny plastic cups in which he would distribute the Kiddush wine to the children. From that moment, I would repeatedly glance up at my Daddy, anxiously waiting for his quiet nod for me to run to the* bima *and wait together with the other children for my little cup of wine. We would huddle around the* ḥazan *as he sang the Kiddush, each world seeming to last forever. When I finally received my portion I held it carefully with both my hands, careful not to spill even a drop. I will never forget the taste of that sweet wine that I cherished in the synagogue every Friday night.*

... A THOUSAND WORDS

קידוש בבית הכנסת

The שליח ציבור *raises a cup of wine and says:*

סַבְרִי מָרָנָן

בָּרוּךְ אַתָּה יהוה אֱלֹהֵינוּ מֶלֶךְ הָעוֹלָם, בּוֹרֵא פְּרִי הַגָּפֶן.

בָּרוּךְ אַתָּה יהוה אֱלֹהֵינוּ מֶלֶךְ הָעוֹלָם
אֲשֶׁר קִדְּשָׁנוּ בְּמִצְוֹתָיו, וְרָצָה בָנוּ
וְשַׁבַּת קָדְשׁוֹ בְּאַהֲבָה וּבְרָצוֹן הִנְחִילָנוּ
זִכָּרוֹן לְמַעֲשֵׂה בְרֵאשִׁית
כִּי הוּא יוֹם תְּחִלָּה לְמִקְרָאֵי קֹדֶשׁ, זֵכֶר לִיצִיאַת מִצְרָיִם
כִּי בָנוּ בָחַרְתָּ וְאוֹתָנוּ קִדַּשְׁתָּ מִכָּל הָעַמִּים
וְשַׁבַּת קָדְשְׁךָ בְּאַהֲבָה וּבְרָצוֹן הִנְחַלְתָּנוּ.
בָּרוּךְ אַתָּה יהוה, מְקַדֵּשׁ הַשַּׁבָּת.

The wine should be drunk by children under the age of בר מצווה *or* בת מצווה *or, if there are none, by the* שליח ציבור.

LEARNING

Many communities have the custom to recite Kiddush in the synagogue. This custom originated in Talmudic times when people would eat and even sleep in the synagogue if they had need to do so. Today, though the synagogue is no longer used in this way, Kiddush is often recited in *shul* on Friday night, on behalf of those congregants who do not have wine at home. According to the ruling of the *Shulḥan Arukh* (*Oraḥ Ḥayyim* 269:1), if Kiddush is made in the synagogue, the cup should be given to one of the children to drink, since adults have an obligation to make Kiddush in the place where they will eat their meal.

REFLECTION

How do you sanctify Shabbat as a community?

How else can a *shul* be used apart from davening?

Where do you feel most connected to Judaism, in your *beit knesset* or in your home?

What does your community contribute to your Jewish identity that your family cannot?

How does your Shabbat remind you of creation?

How could your Shabbat remind you of the exodus?

From the second night of Pesaḥ until the night before Shavuot,
the Omer is counted here (page 356).

Stand while saying Aleinu.

עָלֵינוּ It is our duty to praise the Master of all,
and ascribe greatness to the Author of creation,
who has not made us like the nations of the lands
nor placed us like the families of the earth;
who has not made our portion like theirs,
nor our destiny like all their multitudes.
(For they worship vanity and emptiness,
and pray to a god who cannot save.)
But we bow in worship
and thank the Supreme King of kings,
the Holy One, blessed be He,
who extends the heavens and establishes the earth,
whose throne of glory is in the heavens above,
and whose power's Presence is in the highest of heights.
He is our God; there is no other.
Truly He is our King, there is none else,
as it is written in His Torah:
"You shall know and take to heart this day *Deut. 4*
that the LORD is God, in heaven above and on earth below.
There is no other."

Therefore, we place our hope in You, LORD our God,
that we may soon see the glory of Your power,
when You will remove abominations from the earth,
and idols will be utterly destroyed,
when the world will be perfected
under the sovereignty of the Almighty,
when all humanity will call on Your name,
to turn all the earth's wicked toward You.
All the world's inhabitants will realize and know
that to You every knee must bow
and every tongue swear loyalty.

From the second night of פסח *until the night before* שבועות*,*
the עומר *is counted here* (*page 357*).

Stand while saying עָלֵינוּ.

עָלֵינוּ לְשַׁבֵּחַ לַאֲדוֹן הַכֹּל, לָתֵת גְּדֻלָּה לְיוֹצֵר בְּרֵאשִׁית
שֶׁלֹּא עָשָׂנוּ כְּגוֹיֵי הָאֲרָצוֹת
וְלֹא שָׂמָנוּ כְּמִשְׁפְּחוֹת הָאֲדָמָה
שֶׁלֹּא שָׂם חֶלְקֵנוּ כָּהֶם וְגוֹרָלֵנוּ כְּכָל הֲמוֹנָם.
(שֶׁהֵם מִשְׁתַּחֲוִים לְהֶבֶל וָרִיק וּמִתְפַּלְּלִים אֶל אֵל לֹא יוֹשִׁיעַ.)
וַאֲנַחְנוּ כּוֹרְעִים וּמִשְׁתַּחֲוִים וּמוֹדִים
לִפְנֵי מֶלֶךְ מַלְכֵי הַמְּלָכִים, הַקָּדוֹשׁ בָּרוּךְ הוּא
שֶׁהוּא נוֹטֶה שָׁמַיִם וְיוֹסֵד אָרֶץ
וּמוֹשַׁב יְקָרוֹ בַּשָּׁמַיִם מִמַּעַל
וּשְׁכִינַת עֻזּוֹ בְּגָבְהֵי מְרוֹמִים.
הוּא אֱלֹהֵינוּ, אֵין עוֹד.
אֱמֶת מַלְכֵּנוּ, אֶפֶס זוּלָתוֹ
כַּכָּתוּב בְּתוֹרָתוֹ
דברים ד
וְיָדַעְתָּ הַיּוֹם וַהֲשֵׁבֹתָ אֶל־לְבָבֶךָ
כִּי יהוה הוּא הָאֱלֹהִים בַּשָּׁמַיִם מִמַּעַל וְעַל־הָאָרֶץ מִתָּחַת
אֵין עוֹד:

עַל כֵּן נְקַוֶּה לְּךָ יהוה אֱלֹהֵינוּ, לִרְאוֹת מְהֵרָה בְּתִפְאֶרֶת עֻזֶּךָ
לְהַעֲבִיר גִּלּוּלִים מִן הָאָרֶץ, וְהָאֱלִילִים כָּרוֹת יִכָּרֵתוּן
לְתַקֵּן עוֹלָם בְּמַלְכוּת שַׁדַּי.
וְכָל בְּנֵי בָשָׂר יִקְרְאוּ בִשְׁמֶךָ לְהַפְנוֹת אֵלֶיךָ כָּל רִשְׁעֵי אָרֶץ.
יַכִּירוּ וְיֵדְעוּ כָּל יוֹשְׁבֵי תֵבֵל
כִּי לְךָ תִּכְרַע כָּל בֶּרֶךְ, תִּשָּׁבַע כָּל לָשׁוֹן.

Before You, LORD our God, they will kneel and bow down
and give honor to Your glorious name.
They will all accept the yoke of Your kingdom,
and You will reign over them soon and for ever.
For the kingdom is Yours,
and to all eternity You will reign in glory,
as it is written in Your Torah:
"The LORD will reign for ever and ever." *Ex. 15*
▸ And it is said: "Then the LORD shall be King over all the earth; *Zech. 14*
on that day the LORD shall be One and His name One."

Some add:

Have no fear of sudden terror or of the ruin when it overtakes the wicked. *Prov. 3*
Devise your strategy, but it will be defeated; *Is. 8*
propose your plan, but it will not stand, for God is with us.
When you grow old, I will still be the same. *Is. 46*
When your hair turns gray, I will still carry you.
I made you, I will bear you, I will carry you, and I will rescue you.

MOURNER'S KADDISH

The following prayer, said by mourners, requires the presence of a minyan.
A transliteration can be found on page 1151.

Mourner: יִתְגַּדַּל Magnified and sanctified
may His great name be,
in the world He created by His will.
May He establish His kingdom
in your lifetime and in your days,
and in the lifetime of all the house of Israel,
swiftly and soon –
and say: Amen.

All: May His great name be blessed
for ever and all time.

Mourner: Blessed and praised, glorified and elevated,
raised and honored, uplifted and praised
be the name of the Holy One,
blessed be He,

לְפָנֶיךָ יהוה אֱלֹהֵינוּ יִכְרְעוּ וְיִפֹּלוּ, וְלִכְבוֹד שִׁמְךָ יְקָר יִתֵּנוּ
וִיקַבְּלוּ כֻלָּם אֶת עֹל מַלְכוּתֶךָ
וְתִמְלֹךְ עֲלֵיהֶם מְהֵרָה לְעוֹלָם וָעֶד.
כִּי הַמַּלְכוּת שֶׁלְּךָ הִיא וּלְעוֹלְמֵי עַד תִּמְלֹךְ בְּכָבוֹד
כַּכָּתוּב בְּתוֹרָתֶךָ, יהוה יִמְלֹךְ לְעֹלָם וָעֶד: שמות טו
◂ וְנֶאֱמַר, וְהָיָה יהוה לְמֶלֶךְ עַל־כָּל־הָאָרֶץ זכריה יד
בַּיּוֹם הַהוּא יִהְיֶה יהוה אֶחָד וּשְׁמוֹ אֶחָד:

Some add:

אַל־תִּירָא מִפַּחַד פִּתְאֹם וּמִשֹּׁאַת רְשָׁעִים כִּי תָבֹא: משלי ג
עֻצוּ עֵצָה וְתֻפָר, דַּבְּרוּ דָבָר וְלֹא יָקוּם, כִּי עִמָּנוּ אֵל: ישעיה ח
וְעַד־זִקְנָה אֲנִי הוּא, וְעַד־שֵׂיבָה אֲנִי אֶסְבֹּל ישעיה מו
אֲנִי עָשִׂיתִי וַאֲנִי אֶשָּׂא וַאֲנִי אֶסְבֹּל וַאֲמַלֵּט:

קדיש יתום

The following prayer, said by mourners, requires the presence of a מנין.
A transliteration can be found on page 1151.

אבל: יִתְגַּדַּל וְיִתְקַדַּשׁ שְׁמֵהּ רַבָּא (קהל: אָמֵן)
בְּעָלְמָא דִּי בְרָא כִרְעוּתֵהּ
וְיַמְלִיךְ מַלְכוּתֵהּ
בְּחַיֵּיכוֹן וּבְיוֹמֵיכוֹן וּבְחַיֵּי דְכָל בֵּית יִשְׂרָאֵל
בַּעֲגָלָא וּבִזְמַן קָרִיב
וְאִמְרוּ אָמֵן. (קהל: אָמֵן)

קהל ואבל: יְהֵא שְׁמֵהּ רַבָּא מְבָרַךְ לְעָלַם וּלְעָלְמֵי עָלְמַיָּא.

אבל: יִתְבָּרַךְ וְיִשְׁתַּבַּח וְיִתְפָּאַר
וְיִתְרוֹמַם וְיִתְנַשֵּׂא וְיִתְהַדָּר וְיִתְעַלֶּה וְיִתְהַלָּל
שְׁמֵהּ דְּקֻדְשָׁא בְּרִיךְ הוּא (קהל: בְּרִיךְ הוּא)

beyond any blessing,
song, praise and consolation uttered in the world –
and say: Amen.

May there be great peace from heaven,
and life for us and all Israel –
and say: Amen.

Bow, take three steps back, as if taking leave of the Divine Presence, then bow, first left, then right, then center, while saying:

May He who makes peace in His high places,
make peace for us and all Israel –
and say: Amen.

From the second day of Rosh Ḥodesh Elul until and including Shemini Atzeret (in Israel until and including Hoshana Raba), the following psalm is said:

לְדָוִד A psalm of David. The Lord is my light and my salvation – whom then shall I fear? The Lord is the stronghold of my life – of whom shall I be afraid? When evil men close in on me to devour my flesh, it is they, my enemies and foes, who stumble and fall. Should an army besiege me, my heart would not fear. Should war break out against me, still I would be confident. One thing I ask of the Lord, only this do I seek: to live in the House of the Lord all the days of my life, to gaze on the beauty of the Lord and worship in His Temple. For He will keep me safe in His pavilion on the day of trouble. He will hide me under the cover of His tent. He will set me high upon a rock. Now my head is high above my enemies who surround me. I will sacrifice in His tent with shouts of joy. I will sing and chant praises to the Lord. Lord, hear my voice when I call. Be gracious to me and answer me. On Your behalf my heart says, "Seek My face." Your face, Lord, will I seek. Do not hide Your face from me. Do not turn Your servant away in anger. You have been my help. Do not reject or abandon me, God, my Savior. Were my father and my mother to abandon me, the Lord would take me in. Teach me Your way, Lord, and lead me on a level path, because of my oppressors. Do not abandon me to the will of my enemies, for false witnesses have risen against me, breathing violence. ▸ Were it not for my faith that I shall see the Lord's goodness in the land of the living. Hope in the Lord. Be strong and of good courage, and hope in the Lord! *Ps. 27*

Mourner's Kaddish (on previous page)

לְעֵלָּא מִן כָּל בִּרְכָתָא / בשבת שובה: לְעֵלָּא לְעֵלָּא מִכָּל בִּרְכָתָא/
וְשִׁירָתָא, תֻּשְׁבְּחָתָא וְנֶחֱמָתָא
דַּאֲמִירָן בְּעָלְמָא, וְאִמְרוּ אָמֵן. (קהל: אָמֵן)

יְהֵא שְׁלָמָא רַבָּא מִן שְׁמַיָּא
וְחַיִּים, עָלֵינוּ וְעַל כָּל יִשְׂרָאֵל, וְאִמְרוּ אָמֵן. (קהל: אָמֵן)

Bow, take three steps back, as if taking leave of the Divine Presence, then bow, first left, then right, then center, while saying:

עֹשֶׂה שָׁלוֹם/ בשבת שובה: הַשָּׁלוֹם/ בִּמְרוֹמָיו
הוּא יַעֲשֶׂה שָׁלוֹם
עָלֵינוּ וְעַל כָּל יִשְׂרָאֵל, וְאִמְרוּ אָמֵן. (קהל: אָמֵן)

From the second day of ראש חודש אלול *until and including* שמיני עצרת (*in* ארץ ישראל *until and including* הושענא רבה), *the following psalm is said:*

תהלים כז
לְדָוִד, יהוה אוֹרִי וְיִשְׁעִי, מִמִּי אִירָא, יהוה מָעוֹז־חַיַּי, מִמִּי אֶפְחָד: בִּקְרֹב עָלַי מְרֵעִים לֶאֱכֹל אֶת־בְּשָׂרִי, צָרַי וְאֹיְבַי לִי, הֵמָּה כָשְׁלוּ וְנָפָלוּ: אִם־תַּחֲנֶה עָלַי מַחֲנֶה, לֹא־יִירָא לִבִּי, אִם־תָּקוּם עָלַי מִלְחָמָה, בְּזֹאת אֲנִי בוֹטֵחַ: אַחַת שָׁאַלְתִּי מֵאֵת־יהוה, אוֹתָהּ אֲבַקֵּשׁ, שִׁבְתִּי בְּבֵית־יהוה כָּל־יְמֵי חַיַּי, לַחֲזוֹת בְּנֹעַם־יהוה, וּלְבַקֵּר בְּהֵיכָלוֹ: כִּי יִצְפְּנֵנִי בְּסֻכֹּה בְּיוֹם רָעָה, יַסְתִּרֵנִי בְּסֵתֶר אָהֳלוֹ, בְּצוּר יְרוֹמְמֵנִי: וְעַתָּה יָרוּם רֹאשִׁי עַל אֹיְבַי סְבִיבוֹתַי, וְאֶזְבְּחָה בְאָהֳלוֹ זִבְחֵי תְרוּעָה, אָשִׁירָה וַאֲזַמְּרָה לַיהוה: שְׁמַע־יהוה קוֹלִי אֶקְרָא, וְחָנֵּנִי וַעֲנֵנִי: לְךָ אָמַר לִבִּי בַּקְּשׁוּ פָנָי, אֶת־פָּנֶיךָ יהוה אֲבַקֵּשׁ: אַל־תַּסְתֵּר פָּנֶיךָ מִמֶּנִּי, אַל תַּט־בְּאַף עַבְדֶּךָ, עֶזְרָתִי הָיִיתָ, אַל־תִּטְּשֵׁנִי וְאַל־תַּעַזְבֵנִי, אֱלֹהֵי יִשְׁעִי: כִּי־אָבִי וְאִמִּי עֲזָבוּנִי, וַיהוה יַאַסְפֵנִי: הוֹרֵנִי יהוה דַּרְכֶּךָ, וּנְחֵנִי בְּאֹרַח מִישׁוֹר, לְמַעַן שׁוֹרְרָי: אַל־תִּתְּנֵנִי בְּנֶפֶשׁ צָרָי, כִּי קָמוּ־בִי עֵדֵי־שֶׁקֶר, וִיפֵחַ חָמָס: › לוּלֵא הֶאֱמַנְתִּי לִרְאוֹת בְּטוּב־יהוה בְּאֶרֶץ חַיִּים: קַוֵּה אֶל־יהוה, חֲזַק וְיַאֲמֵץ לִבֶּךָ, וְקַוֵּה אֶל־יהוה:

קדיש יתום (*on previous page*)

Most congregations sing Yigdal at this point.
In Israel, most congregations sing Adon Olam (*page 26*).

GREAT
is the living God and praised.
He exists, and His existence is beyond time.

He is One, and there is no unity like His.
Unfathomable, His oneness is infinite.

He has neither bodily form nor substance;
His holiness is beyond compare.

He preceded all that was created.
He was first: there was no beginning to His beginning.

Behold He is Master of the Universe; every creature
shows His greatness and majesty.

The rich flow of His prophecy He gave
to His treasured people in whom He gloried.

Never in Israel has there arisen another like Moses,
a prophet who beheld God's image.

God gave His people a Torah of truth
by the hand of His prophet, most faithful of His House.

God will not alter or change His law
for any other, for eternity.

He sees and knows our secret thoughts;
as soon as something is begun, He foresees its end.

He rewards people with loving-kindness according to their deeds;
He punishes the wicked according to his wickedness.

At the end of days He will send our Messiah,
to redeem those who await His final salvation.

God will revive the dead in His great loving-kindness.
Blessed for evermore is His glorious name!

Most congregations sing יגדל *at this point.*
In ארץ ישראל*, most congregations sing* אדון עולם *(page 27).*

יִגְדַּל

אֱלֹהִים חַי וְיִשְׁתַּבַּח, נִמְצָא וְאֵין עֵת אֶל מְצִיאוּתוֹ.

אֶחָד וְאֵין יָחִיד כְּיִחוּדוֹ, נֶעְלָם וְגַם אֵין סוֹף לְאַחְדוּתוֹ.

אֵין לוֹ דְּמוּת הַגּוּף וְאֵינוֹ גוּף, לֹא נַעֲרֹךְ אֵלָיו קְדֻשָּׁתוֹ.

קַדְמוֹן לְכָל דָּבָר אֲשֶׁר נִבְרָא, רִאשׁוֹן וְאֵין רֵאשִׁית לְרֵאשִׁיתוֹ.

הִנּוֹ אֲדוֹן עוֹלָם, וְכָל נוֹצָר יוֹרֶה גְדֻלָּתוֹ וּמַלְכוּתוֹ.

שֶׁפַע נְבוּאָתוֹ נְתָנוֹ אֶל־אַנְשֵׁי סְגֻלָּתוֹ וְתִפְאַרְתּוֹ.

לֹא קָם בְּיִשְׂרָאֵל כְּמֹשֶׁה עוֹד נָבִיא וּמַבִּיט אֶת תְּמוּנָתוֹ.

תּוֹרַת אֱמֶת נָתַן לְעַמּוֹ אֵל עַל יַד נְבִיאוֹ נֶאֱמַן בֵּיתוֹ.

לֹא יַחֲלִיף הָאֵל וְלֹא יָמִיר דָּתוֹ לְעוֹלָמִים לְזוּלָתוֹ.

צוֹפֶה וְיוֹדֵעַ סְתָרֵינוּ, מַבִּיט לְסוֹף דָּבָר בְּקַדְמָתוֹ.

גּוֹמֵל לְאִישׁ חֶסֶד כְּמִפְעָלוֹ, נוֹתֵן לְרָשָׁע רָע כְּרִשְׁעָתוֹ.

יִשְׁלַח לְקֵץ יָמִין מְשִׁיחֵנוּ לִפְדּוֹת מְחַכֵּי קֵץ יְשׁוּעָתוֹ.

מֵתִים יְחַיֶּה אֵל בְּרֹב חַסְדּוֹ, בָּרוּךְ עֲדֵי עַד שֵׁם תְּהִלָּתוֹ.

LEARNING

When an architect dedicates a newly constructed home, it is the orderliness of the design that is celebrated. Shabbat, the day after the creation of the universe, celebrates the world of causality and cosmic order. It is appropriate to rejoice and praise God for His creation of the orderly world as we perceive it daily. (Rabbi J.B. Soloveitchik, *On Pesach, Sefirat ha-Omer and Shavuot*)

Kiddush and Zemirot for Shabbat Evening

BLESSING THE CHILDREN

On the evening of Shabbat, many have the custom to bless their children.

To sons, say:

יְשִׂמְךָ May God make you like Ephraim and Manasseh.

To daughters, say:

יְשִׂימֵךְ May God make you like Sarah, Rebecca, Rachel and Leah.

Gen. 48

יְבָרֶכְךָ May the Lord bless you
and protect you.
May the Lord make His face shine on you
and be gracious to you.
May the Lord turn His face toward you
and give you peace.

Num. 6

REFLECTION

"Shabbat is the day we stand still and let all our blessings catch up with us."
(Rabbi Jonathan Sacks, *Radical Then, Radical Now*)

What blessing do you want your parents to give you?

What do you want to bless your parents with?

What wishes would you want for your future children?

Look at the people around you, choose someone in the room; what *berakha* would you like to give them?

CONNECTION

When we were little children, my parents would bless us every Friday night. In our home, my parents would bless us before we went to sleep. This is not the traditional time or custom but it was what we did every week. Before we would go to bed both my father and my mother would gently touch my head and recite the prayer for me to grow to be as righteous as our matriarchs. As far back as I remember I would reach up to place my hands on my parents' heads as they gave me my berakha *and I would try to think of the most wonderful blessings I could wish for them. After they finished, they would kiss my head and wish me good night.*

קידוש וזמירות לליל שבת

ברכת הבנים

On ליל שבת*, many have the custom to bless their children.*

To sons, say:	*To daughters, say:*	
יְשִׂמְךָ אֱלֹהִים	יְשִׂימֵךְ אֱלֹהִים	בראשית מח
כְּאֶפְרַיִם וְכִמְנַשֶּׁה:	כְּשָׂרָה רִבְקָה רָחֵל וְלֵאָה.	

במדבר ו

יְבָרֶכְךָ יהוה וְיִשְׁמְרֶךָ:
יָאֵר יהוה פָּנָיו אֵלֶיךָ וִיחֻנֶּךָּ:
יִשָּׂא יהוה פָּנָיו אֵלֶיךָ וְיָשֵׂם לְךָ שָׁלוֹם:

... A THOUSAND WORDS

LEARNING

We bless boys to be like Menashe and Ephraim, the first brothers in the Torah to live without rivalry. Ephraim and Menashe were brothers who lived in harmony, for their life focus was the highest example of working for the good of their community and their people. Decisions were not based on what was good for them but rather on what was good for the Jewish people.

We bless girls to be like the four matriarchs, Sarah, Rivka, Rachel, and Leah. Each woman teaches unique lessons about leadership, dignity, self-sacrifice, and motherhood.

The *Birkat HaBanim* also represents the continuity of the Jewish people. Each new generation approaches the one preceding it to accept upon itself the awesome responsibility and blessed privilege of being yet another link in the chain that is the nation of Israel, and vows to emulate the great Jews of generations past who were proud of their heritage and who lovingly and devotedly passed it on to their children. At a time when so many of our brothers and sisters have assimilated and severed that link, what better guarantee of the Jewish people's continuity?

Many people sing each of the four verses of the following song three times:

שָׁלוֹם עֲלֵיכֶם Welcome,
ministering angels, angels of the Most High,
from the Supreme King of kings,
the Holy One, blessed be He.

Enter in peace,
angels of peace, angels of the Most High,
from the Supreme King of kings,
the Holy One, blessed be He.

Bless me with peace,
angels of peace, angels of the Most High,
from the Supreme King of kings,
the Holy One, blessed be He.

Go in peace,
angels of peace, angels of the Most High,
from the Supreme King of kings,
the Holy One, blessed be He.

כִּי מַלְאָכָיו He will command His angels about you, *Ps. 91*
to guard you in all your ways.
May the Lord guard your going out and your return, *Ps. 121*
from now and for all time.

... A THOUSAND WORDS

REFLECTION

What does it mean to bring angels into your home?

How do you contribute to making your home peaceful?

Who are the messengers of God in your life?

Many people sing each of the four verses of the following song three times:

שָׁלוֹם עֲלֵיכֶם
מַלְאֲכֵי הַשָּׁרֵת, מַלְאֲכֵי עֶלְיוֹן
מִמֶּלֶךְ מַלְכֵי הַמְּלָכִים, הַקָּדוֹשׁ בָּרוּךְ הוּא.

בּוֹאֲכֶם לְשָׁלוֹם
מַלְאֲכֵי הַשָּׁלוֹם, מַלְאֲכֵי עֶלְיוֹן
מִמֶּלֶךְ מַלְכֵי הַמְּלָכִים, הַקָּדוֹשׁ בָּרוּךְ הוּא.

בָּרְכוּנִי לְשָׁלוֹם
מַלְאֲכֵי הַשָּׁלוֹם, מַלְאֲכֵי עֶלְיוֹן
מִמֶּלֶךְ מַלְכֵי הַמְּלָכִים, הַקָּדוֹשׁ בָּרוּךְ הוּא.

צֵאתְכֶם לְשָׁלוֹם
מַלְאֲכֵי הַשָּׁלוֹם, מַלְאֲכֵי עֶלְיוֹן
מִמֶּלֶךְ מַלְכֵי הַמְּלָכִים, הַקָּדוֹשׁ בָּרוּךְ הוּא.

תהלים צא כִּי מַלְאָכָיו יְצַוֶּה־לָּךְ, לִשְׁמָרְךָ בְּכָל־דְּרָכֶיךָ:
תהלים קכא יהוה יִשְׁמָר־צֵאתְךָ וּבוֹאֶךָ, מֵעַתָּה וְעַד־עוֹלָם:

LEARNING

It was taught, Rabbi Yose son of Rabbi Yehuda said: Two ministering angels accompany man on the eve of the Sabbath from the synagogue to his home, one good and one evil. When he arrives home, if he finds the Sabbath candles brightly glowing, the table laid, and the home in good peaceful order, the good angel exclaims, "May it be like this next Sabbath also," and the evil angel unwillingly responds, "Amen." But if not, if the home is in disarray, the family is quarrelling, and there is no peace in the home, the evil angel says, "Let it be the Divine Will that the same should be true for another Sabbath," and the good Angel proclaims "Amen" against his will. (*Shabbat* 119b)

Some say:

רִבּוֹן כָּל הָעוֹלָמִים Master of all worlds, Lord of all souls, Lord of peace, mighty, blessed and great King, King who speaks peace, King who is glorious, enduring and pure, King who gives life to worlds, King who is good and does good, King alone and unique, great King who robes Himself in compassion, King who reigns over all kings, who is elevated and supports those who fall, King who is Author of creation, who redeems and rescues, who is radiant and ruddy, King who is holy, high and elevated, King who hears prayer, King whose way is just: I thank You, Lord my God and God of my ancestors, for all the loving-kindness You have done and will do for me, and all the members of my household and all my fellow creatures. Blessed are Your angels, holy and pure, who do Your will. Lord of peace, King to whom peace belongs, bless me with peace, and give me and the members of my household, and all Your people the house of Israel, a good and peaceful life. King elevated over all the heavenly multitudes, who formed me and who formed creation, I ask Your radiant presence, that You find me and all the members of my household worthy of grace and good favor in Your eyes and the eyes of all people and all who see us, that we may serve You. May we be worthy to receive Sabbaths amidst great joy, wealth and honor, and few sins. May You remove from me and all the members of my household and all Your people the house of Israel all sickness and disease, all poverty, hardship and destitution. Give us an upright desire to serve You in truth, awe and love. May we find honor in Your eyes and the eyes of all who see us, for You are the King of honor: to You it belongs, to You it accords. Please, King who reigns over all kings, command Your angels, ministering angels who minister to the Most High, to act compassionately toward me when they enter my house on our holy day, for I have lit my lights, spread my couch and changed my clothes in honor of the Sabbath; I have come to Your House to lay my pleas before You that You remove my sighs; I have testified that in six days You created all things, and said it a second time, and will testify to it a third time over my cup, in joy, as You commanded me to remember it, delighting in the extra soul You have given me. On it [the Sabbath] I shall rest as You have commanded me, thereby to serve You. So too I will declare Your greatness in joyful song, for I have set the Lord before me, that You may have compassion upon me in my exile, redeeming me and awakening my heart to Your love. Then I will keep Your commands and laws without sadness, praying correctly as is right and fitting. Angels of peace, come in peace and bless me with peace; declare blessed the table I have prepared, and go in peace, now and forever. Amen, Selah.

Some say:

רִבּוֹן כָּל הָעוֹלָמִים, אֲדוֹן כָּל הַנְּשָׁמוֹת, אֲדוֹן הַשָּׁלוֹם. מֶלֶךְ אַבִּיר, מֶלֶךְ בָּרוּךְ, מֶלֶךְ גָּדוֹל, מֶלֶךְ דּוֹבֵר שָׁלוֹם, מֶלֶךְ הָדוּר, מֶלֶךְ וָתִיק, מֶלֶךְ זַךְ, מֶלֶךְ חֵי הָעוֹלָמִים, מֶלֶךְ טוֹב וּמֵטִיב, מֶלֶךְ יָחִיד וּמְיֻחָד, מֶלֶךְ כַּבִּיר, מֶלֶךְ לוֹבֵשׁ רַחֲמִים, מֶלֶךְ מַלְכֵי הַמְּלָכִים, מֶלֶךְ נִשְׂגָּב, מֶלֶךְ סוֹמֵךְ נוֹפְלִים, מֶלֶךְ עֹשֶׂה מַעֲשֵׂה בְרֵאשִׁית, מֶלֶךְ פּוֹדֶה וּמַצִּיל, מֶלֶךְ צַח וְאָדֹם, מֶלֶךְ קָדוֹשׁ, מֶלֶךְ רָם וְנִשָּׂא, מֶלֶךְ שׁוֹמֵעַ תְּפִלָּה, מֶלֶךְ תָּמִים דַּרְכּוֹ. מוֹדֶה אֲנִי לְפָנֶיךָ, יהוה אֱלֹהַי וֵאלֹהֵי אֲבוֹתַי, עַל כָּל הַחֶסֶד אֲשֶׁר עָשִׂיתָ עִמָּדִי וַאֲשֶׁר אַתָּה עָתִיד לַעֲשׂוֹת עִמִּי וְעִם כָּל בְּנֵי בֵיתִי וְעִם כָּל בְּרִיּוֹתֶיךָ, בְּנֵי בְרִיתִי. וּבְרוּכִים הֵם מַלְאָכֶיךָ הַקְּדוֹשִׁים וְהַטְּהוֹרִים שֶׁעוֹשִׂים רְצוֹנֶךָ. אֲדוֹן הַשָּׁלוֹם, מֶלֶךְ שֶׁהַשָּׁלוֹם שֶׁלּוֹ, בָּרְכֵנִי בַשָּׁלוֹם, וְתִפְקֹד אוֹתִי וְאֶת כָּל בְּנֵי בֵיתִי וְכָל עַמְּךָ בֵּית יִשְׂרָאֵל לְחַיִּים טוֹבִים וּלְשָׁלוֹם. מֶלֶךְ עֶלְיוֹן עַל כָּל צְבָא מָרוֹם, יוֹצְרֵנוּ, יוֹצֵר בְּרֵאשִׁית, אֲחַלֶּה פָנֶיךָ הַמְּאִירִים, שֶׁתְּזַכֶּה אוֹתִי וְאֶת כָּל בְּנֵי בֵיתִי לִמְצֹא חֵן וְשֵׂכֶל טוֹב בְּעֵינֶיךָ וּבְעֵינֵי כָל בְּנֵי אָדָם וּבְעֵינֵי כָל רוֹאֵינוּ לַעֲבוֹדָתֶךָ. וְזַכֵּנוּ לְקַבֵּל שַׁבָּתוֹת מִתּוֹךְ רֹב שִׂמְחָה וּמִתּוֹךְ עֹשֶׁר וְכָבוֹד וּמִתּוֹךְ מִעוּט עֲוֹנוֹת. וְהָסֵר מִמֶּנִּי וּמִכָּל בְּנֵי בֵיתִי וּמִכָּל עַמְּךָ בֵּית יִשְׂרָאֵל כָּל מִינֵי חֹלִי וְכָל מִינֵי מַדְוֶה וְכָל מִינֵי דַלּוּת וַעֲנִיּוּת וְאֶבְיוֹנוּת. וְתֵן בָּנוּ יֵצֶר טוֹב לְעָבְדְּךָ בֶּאֱמֶת וּבְיִרְאָה וּבְאַהֲבָה. וְנִהְיֶה מְכֻבָּדִים בְּעֵינֶיךָ וּבְעֵינֵי כָל רוֹאֵינוּ, כִּי אַתָּה הוּא מֶלֶךְ הַכָּבוֹד, כִּי לְךָ נָאֶה, כִּי לְךָ יָאֶה. אָנָּא, מֶלֶךְ מַלְכֵי הַמְּלָכִים, צַוֵּה לְמַלְאָכֶיךָ, מַלְאֲכֵי הַשָּׁרֵת, מְשָׁרְתֵי עֶלְיוֹן, שֶׁיִּפְקְדוּנִי בְּרַחֲמִים וִיבָרְכוּנִי בְּבוֹאָם לְבֵיתִי בְּיוֹם קָדְשֵׁנוּ, כִּי הִדְלַקְתִּי נֵרוֹתַי וְהִצַּעְתִּי מִטָּתִי וְהֶחֱלַפְתִּי שִׂמְלוֹתַי לִכְבוֹד יוֹם הַשַּׁבָּת וּבָאתִי לְבֵיתְךָ לְהַפִּיל תְּחִנָּתִי לְפָנֶיךָ, שֶׁתַּעֲבִיר אַנְחָתִי, וָאָעִיד אֲשֶׁר בָּרָאתָ בְשִׁשָּׁה יָמִים כָּל הַיְצוּר, וָאֶשְׁנֶה וַאֲשַׁלֵּשׁ עוֹד לְהָעִיד עַל כּוֹסִי בְּתוֹךְ שִׂמְחָתִי, כַּאֲשֶׁר צִוִּיתַנִי לְזָכְרוֹ וּלְהִתְעַנֵּג בְּיֶתֶר נִשְׁמָתִי אֲשֶׁר נָתַתָּ בִּי. בּוֹ אֶשְׁבֹּת כַּאֲשֶׁר צִוִּיתַנִי לְשָׁרְתֶךָ, וְכֵן אַגִּיד גְּדֻלָּתְךָ בְּרִנָּה, וְשִׁוִּיתִי יהוה לִקְרָאתִי שֶׁתְּרַחֲמֵנִי עוֹד בְּגָלוּתִי לְגָאֳלֵנִי לְעוֹרֵר לִבִּי לְאַהֲבָתֶךָ. וְאָז אֶשְׁמֹר פִּקּוּדֶיךָ וְחֻקֶּיךָ בְּלִי עֶצֶב, וְאֶתְפַּלֵּל כַּדָּת כָּרָאוּי וְכַנָּכוֹן. מַלְאֲכֵי הַשָּׁלוֹם, בּוֹאֲכֶם לְשָׁלוֹם, בָּרְכוּנִי לְשָׁלוֹם, וְאִמְרוּ בָּרוּךְ לְשֻׁלְחָנִי הֶעָרוּךְ, וְצֵאתְכֶם לְשָׁלוֹם מֵעַתָּה וְעַד עוֹלָם, אָמֵן סֶלָה.

אֵשֶׁת־חַיִל A woman of strength, who can find? Her worth is far beyond pearls. *Prov. 31*
Her husband's heart trusts in her, and he has no lack of gain.
She brings him good, not harm, all the days of her life.
She seeks wool and linen, and works with willing hands.
She is like a ship laden with merchandise, bringing her food from afar.
She rises while it is still night, providing food for her household, portions for her maids.
She considers a field and buys it; from her earnings she plants a vineyard.
She clothes herself with strength, and braces her arms for her tasks.
She sees that her business goes well; her lamp does not go out at night.
She holds the distaff in her hand, and grasps the spindle with her palms.
She reaches out her palm to the poor, and extends her hand to the needy.
She has no fear for her family when it snows, for all her household is clothed in crimson wool.
She makes elegant coverings; her clothing is fine linen and purple wool.
Her husband is well known in the gates, where he sits with the elders of the land.
She makes linen garments and sells them, and supplies merchants with sashes.
She is clothed with strength and dignity; she can laugh at the days to come.
She opens her mouth with wisdom, and the law of kindness is on her tongue.
She watches over the ways of her household, and never eats the bread of idleness.
Her children rise and call her happy; her husband also praises her:
"Many women have excelled, but you surpass them all."
Charm is deceptive and beauty vain: it is the God-fearing woman who deserves praise.
Give her the reward she has earned; let her deeds bring her praise in the gates.

CONNECTION

I used to have long conversations with my mother. In fact, it was a monologue rather than a dialogue. She talked and I "happened" to overhear. I used to watch her arranging the house in honor of a holiday. I used to see her recite prayers. I used to watch her recite the sidra *every Friday night and I remember the nostalgic tune. I learned very much from her.*

Most of all, I learned that Judaism expresses itself not only in formal compliance with the law but also in a living experience. She taught me that there is a flavor, a scent, and a warmth to mitzvot. I learned from her the most important thing in life – to feel the presence of the Almighty and the gentle pressure of His hand resting upon my frail shoulders. Without her teachings, which quite often were transmitted to me in silence, I would have grown up a soulless being, dry and insensitive. (Rabbi J.B. Soloveitchik, *"A Tribute to the Rebbetzin of Talne"*)

משלי לא

אֵשֶׁת־חַיִל מִי יִמְצָא, וְרָחֹק מִפְּנִינִים מִכְרָהּ:
בָּטַח בָּהּ לֵב בַּעְלָהּ, וְשָׁלָל לֹא יֶחְסָר:
גְּמָלַתְהוּ טוֹב וְלֹא־רָע, כֹּל יְמֵי חַיֶּיהָ:
דָּרְשָׁה צֶמֶר וּפִשְׁתִּים, וַתַּעַשׂ בְּחֵפֶץ כַּפֶּיהָ:
הָיְתָה כָּאֳנִיּוֹת סוֹחֵר, מִמֶּרְחָק תָּבִיא לַחְמָהּ:
וַתָּקָם בְּעוֹד לַיְלָה, וַתִּתֵּן טֶרֶף לְבֵיתָהּ, וְחֹק לְנַעֲרֹתֶיהָ:
זָמְמָה שָׂדֶה וַתִּקָּחֵהוּ, מִפְּרִי כַפֶּיהָ נָטְעָה כָּרֶם:
חָגְרָה בְעוֹז מָתְנֶיהָ, וַתְּאַמֵּץ זְרוֹעֹתֶיהָ:
טָעֲמָה כִּי־טוֹב סַחְרָהּ, לֹא־יִכְבֶּה בַלַּיְלָ נֵרָהּ:
יָדֶיהָ שִׁלְּחָה בַכִּישׁוֹר, וְכַפֶּיהָ תָּמְכוּ פָלֶךְ:
כַּפָּהּ פָּרְשָׂה לֶעָנִי, וְיָדֶיהָ שִׁלְּחָה לָאֶבְיוֹן:
לֹא־תִירָא לְבֵיתָהּ מִשָּׁלֶג, כִּי כָל־בֵּיתָהּ לָבֻשׁ שָׁנִים:
מַרְבַדִּים עָשְׂתָה־לָּהּ, שֵׁשׁ וְאַרְגָּמָן לְבוּשָׁהּ:
נוֹדָע בַּשְּׁעָרִים בַּעְלָהּ, בְּשִׁבְתּוֹ עִם־זִקְנֵי־אָרֶץ:
סָדִין עָשְׂתָה וַתִּמְכֹּר, וַחֲגוֹר נָתְנָה לַכְּנַעֲנִי:
עוֹז־וְהָדָר לְבוּשָׁהּ, וַתִּשְׂחַק לְיוֹם אַחֲרוֹן:
פִּיהָ פָּתְחָה בְחָכְמָה, וְתוֹרַת־חֶסֶד עַל־לְשׁוֹנָהּ:
צוֹפִיָּה הֲלִיכוֹת בֵּיתָהּ, וְלֶחֶם עַצְלוּת לֹא תֹאכֵל:
קָמוּ בָנֶיהָ וַיְאַשְּׁרוּהָ, בַּעְלָהּ וַיְהַלְלָהּ:
רַבּוֹת בָּנוֹת עָשׂוּ חָיִל, וְאַתְּ עָלִית עַל־כֻּלָּנָה:
שֶׁקֶר הַחֵן וְהֶבֶל הַיֹּפִי, אִשָּׁה יִרְאַת־יהוה הִיא תִתְהַלָּל:
תְּנוּ־לָהּ מִפְּרִי יָדֶיהָ, וִיהַלְלוּהָ בַשְּׁעָרִים מַעֲשֶׂיהָ:

REFLECTION

How does your mother or grandmother make your Shabbat special?

In how many ways does your mother or grandmother make your life special?

What do you want to say thank you to her for?

"The Messiah and the final redemption of the Jewish people will come by the merit of the Jewish woman."
(*Sota* 11)

Some say:

Prepare the feast of perfect faith, joy of the holy King.
Prepare the royal feast.

This is the feast [mystically known as] 'the Field of Holy Apples' –
and 'the Small Face' and 'the Holy Ancient One'
[mystical terms for aspects of the Divine] come to partake in the feast with it.

With songs of praise I will cut away [evil forces],
to enter the holy gates of 'the Field of Apples.'
We now invite Her [the Divine Presence] with a newly prepared table
and a fine candelabrum spreading light upon our heads.
Between right and left is the bride, decked with jewelry, adorned and robed.
Her husband embraces her, and in the joy of their togetherness
[evil forces] are crushed.
Cries and suffering stop and cease; a new face comes upon spirits and souls.
She will have great and doubled joy; light will come, and bounteous blessing.
Come near, dear friends, and prepare delicacies of many kinds, and fish and fowl.
Renewing souls and spirits through the thirty-two [paths of wisdom]
and the three branches [of Scripture].
She [the Divine Presence] has seventy crowns, and above,
the King is crowned with all in the Holy of Holies.
Engraved and hidden with her are all worlds,
but the pestle of the Ancient of Days releases all that is hidden.
May it be His will that the Divine Presence rest on His people who,
for His name's sake, delight in sweet foods and honey.
To the south, I will arrange the candelabrum of hidden [wisdom],
to the north I will set the table with bread.
With wine in the cup, and myrtle clusters for bridegroom and bride,
the weak will be given strength.
Let us make them crowns of precious words, seventy crowns beyond the fifty.
May the Divine Presence be crowned with six loaves on each side, like
the two sets of six loaves [of showbread] and other articles [in the Temple].
[On the Sabbath] impure powers and afflicting angels cease and desist; and
those who are confined have respite.
To break bread the size of an olive or an egg, for there are two ways of
interpreting the *Yod* [of the divine name], restrictively or expansively.
It is like pure olive oil, pressed in a mill, flowing like rivers, whispering secrets.
Let us speak of mysteries, secrets unrevealed, hidden and concealed.
To crown the bride with mysteries above, at this,
the holy angels' wedding celebration.

Some say:

אַתְקִֽינוּ סְעוּדָתָא דִמְהֵימְנוּתָא שְׁלִימְתָא
חֶדְוְתָא דְמַלְכָּא קַדִּישָׁא.
אַתְקִֽינוּ סְעוּדָתָא דְמַלְכָּא.
דָּא הִיא סְעוּדָתָא דַּחֲקַל תַּפּוּחִין קַדִּישִׁין
וּזְעֵיר אַנְפִּין וְעַתִּיקָא קַדִּישָׁא אָתַיִן לְסַעֲדָה בַּהֲדַהּ.

אֲזַמֵּר בִּשְׁבָחִין / לְמֶעַל גּוֹ פִתְחִין / דְּבַחֲקַל תַּפּוּחִין / דְּאִנּוּן קַדִּישִׁין.
נְזַמֵּן לַהּ הַשְׁתָּא / בְּפָתוֹרָא חַדְתָּא / וּבִמְנָרְתָא טָבְתָא / דְּנָהֲרָה עַל רֵישִׁין.
יְמִינָא וּשְׂמָאלָא / וּבֵינַֽיְהוּ כַלָּה / בְּקִשּׁוּטִין אָזְלָא / וּמָנִין וּלְבוּשִׁין.
יְחַבֵּק לַהּ בַּעְלָהּ / וּבִיסוֹדָא דִי לַהּ / דְּעָבֵד נַיְחָא לַהּ / יְהֵא כָתֵשׁ כְּתִישִׁין.
צְוָחִין אוּף עָקְתִין / בְּטִילִין וּשְׁבִיתִין / בְּרַם אַנְפִּין חַדְתִּין / וְרוּחִין עִם נַפְשִׁין.
חֲדוּ סַגִּי יֵיתֵי / וְעַל חֲדָה תַרְתֵּי / נְהוֹרָא לַהּ יַמְטֵי / וּבִרְכָן דִּנְפִישִׁין.
קְרֵֽיבוּ שׁוֹשְׁבִינִין / עֲבִֽידוּ תִקּוּנִין / לְאַפָּשָׁה זֵינִין / וְנוּנִין עִם רַחְשִׁין.
לְמֶעְבַּד נִשְׁמָתִין / וְרוּחִין חַדְתִּין / בְּתַרְתֵּי וּתְלָתִין / וּבִתְלָתָא שִׁבְשִׁין.
וְעִטְרִין שַׁבְעִין לַהּ / וּמַלְכָּא דִלְעֵֽלָּא / דְּיִתְעַטַּר כֹּֽלָּא / בְּקַדִּישׁ קַדִּישִׁין.
רְשִׁימִין וּסְתִימִין / בְּגַוַּהּ כָּל עָלְמִין / בְּרַם עַתִּיק יוֹמִין / הֲלָא בָטֵשׁ בְּטִישִׁין.
יְהֵא רַעֲוָה קַמֵּהּ / דְּתִשְׁרֵי עַל עַמֵּהּ / דְּיִתְעַנַּג לִשְׁמֵהּ / בְּמִתְקִין וְדֻבְשִׁין.
אֲסַדֵּר לִדְרוֹמָא / מְנָרְתָא דִסְתִימָא / וְשֻׁלְחָן עִם נַהֲמָא / בְּצִפּוֹנָא אַדְשִׁין.
בְּחַמְרָא גוֹ כָסָא / וּמַדַּנֵּי אָסָא / לְאָרוּס וַאֲרוּסָה / לְאַתְקָפָא חַלָּשִׁין.
נְעַבֵּד לוֹן כִּתְרִין / בְּמִלִּין יַקִּירִין / בְּשַׁבְעִין עִטּוּרִין / דְּעַל גַּבֵּי חַמְשִׁין.
שְׁכִינְתָא תִתְעַטַּר / בְּשִׁית נַהֲמֵי לִסְטַר / בְּוָוִין תִּתְקַטַּר / וְזֵינִין דִּכְנִישִׁין.
(שְׁבִיתִין וּשְׁבִיקִין / מְסָאֲבִין דְּדָחֲקִין / חֲבִילִין דִּמְעִיקִין / וְכָל זֵינֵי חַרְשִׁין.)
לְמִבְצַע עַל רִיפְתָא / כְּזֵיתָא וּכְבֵיעָתָא / תְּרֵין יוּדִין נָקְטָא / סְתִימִין וּפְרִישִׁין.
מְשַׁח זֵיתָא דָכְיָא / דְּטָחֲנִין רֵיחַיָּא / וְנָגְדִין נַחְלַיָּא / בְּגַוַּהּ בִּלְחִישִׁין.
הֲלָא נֵימָא רָזִין / וּמִלִּין דִּגְנִיזִין / דְּלֵיתֵיהוֹן מִתְחֲזִין / טְמִירִין וּכְבִישִׁין.
לְאַעְטָרָה כַלָּה / בְּרָזִין דִּלְעֵֽלָּא / בְּגוֹ הַאי הִלּוּלָה / דְּעִירִין קַדִּישִׁין.

KIDDUSH FOR SHABBAT EVENING

Quietly: And it was evening, and it was morning – *Gen. 1*
יוֹם הַשִּׁשִּׁי the sixth day.

Then the heavens and the earth were completed, *Gen. 2*
and all their multitudes.
With the seventh day, God completed the work He had done.
He ceased on the seventh day from all the work He had done.
God blessed the seventh day and declared it holy,
because on it He ceased from all His work
He had created to do.

When saying Kiddush for others, add:
Please pay attention, my masters.

Blessed are You, LORD our God, King of the Universe,
who creates the fruit of the vine.

REFLECTION

Close your eyes.
Try to imagine
the very first Shabbat
after creation.
Each of the last days
had seen enormous changes
to the physical universe.
And now,
on the seventh day…
Shabbat.
What does
the world look like?
What would it feel like
to live in the world
on that first Shabbat?

Close your eyes.
Try to imagine
the first Shabbat
after the exodus from Egypt.
For hundreds of years
your people had been slaves,
subject to the cruelest physical labor
and spiritual torment.
And now, following
spectacular miracles and wonders,
your people have freedom at last.
And now…Shabbat.
What does that Shabbat feel like?
What emotions does
that Shabbat bring?

קידוש לליל שבת

Quietly וַיְהִי־עֶרֶב וַיְהִי־בֹקֶר — בראשית א

יוֹם הַשִּׁשִּׁי:

וַיְכֻלּוּ הַשָּׁמַיִם וְהָאָרֶץ וְכָל־צְבָאָם: — בראשית ב

וַיְכַל אֱלֹהִים בַּיּוֹם הַשְּׁבִיעִי מְלַאכְתּוֹ אֲשֶׁר עָשָׂה

וַיִּשְׁבֹּת בַּיּוֹם הַשְּׁבִיעִי מִכָּל־מְלַאכְתּוֹ אֲשֶׁר עָשָׂה:

וַיְבָרֶךְ אֱלֹהִים אֶת־יוֹם הַשְּׁבִיעִי, וַיְקַדֵּשׁ אֹתוֹ

כִּי בוֹ שָׁבַת מִכָּל־מְלַאכְתּוֹ, אֲשֶׁר־בָּרָא אֱלֹהִים, לַעֲשׂוֹת:

When saying קידוש *for others, add:*

סַבְרִי מָרָנָן

בָּרוּךְ אַתָּה יהוה אֱלֹהֵינוּ מֶלֶךְ הָעוֹלָם

בּוֹרֵא פְּרִי הַגָּפֶן.

CONNECTION

The psalmist speaks of the cup of wine as the symbol of redemption: "I will lift up the cup of salvation and call upon God's name" (Tehillim 116:13). *Wine is a symbol of joy, as is written, "Wine gladdens the heart of man"* (Tehillim 104:15)*.... Wine, to be sure, also has a less-than-worthwhile aspect. Our sages understood only too well the dangers inherent in this beverage.... And yet they bid us to begin each Sabbath with Kiddush over wine. This teaches us that the world is not divided into good and bad or holy and profane, but rather into good and not-yet-good, into holy and not-yet-holy. Wine when drunk with moderation can be an instrument for holiness. When abused, it becomes a source of harm and even tragedy. While everything is potentially dangerous, all of creation emanates from the Divine. The Jew is not to shun the physical; his task is to make it sacred, to sanctify every aspect of creation, to suffuse the physical with the spiritual potential in all things and thus make them holy.* (Rabbi Shlomo Riskin, *The Passover Haggadah*)

Blessed are You, Lord our God, King of the Universe,
who has made us holy through His commandments,
who has favored us,
and in love and favor
gave us His holy Sabbath as a heritage,
a remembrance of the work of creation.
It is the first among the holy days of assembly,
a remembrance of the exodus from Egypt.
For You chose us and sanctified us
from all the peoples,
and in love and favor
gave us Your holy Sabbath
as a heritage.
Blessed are You, Lord,
who sanctifies the Sabbath.

On Shabbat Ḥol HaMo'ed Sukkot, if Kiddush is made in the sukka, add:
Blessed are You, Lord our God, King of the Universe,
who has made us holy through his commandments
and has commanded us to live in the sukka.

It is customary for all present to drink of the wine.

---

then rested on the seventh day (*Bereshit* 2:1–3). This is the theme mentioned in connection with Shabbat in the first appearance of the Ten Commandments. By saying these verses we are testifying to the fact that God created the world, and declaring our belief in this. The second section is the *berakha* made over the wine, on which the Kiddush ritual is said. Finally, the third section is a long *berakha* (with an opening and conclusion blessing) in which we sanctify the day. In this section reference is also made to the other central theme of Shabbat that is mentioned in the second appearance of the Ten Commandments in *Devarim* – the exodus from Egypt.

What do creation and the exodus have in common?

בָּרוּךְ אַתָּה יהוה אֱלֹהֵינוּ מֶלֶךְ הָעוֹלָם
אֲשֶׁר קִדְּשָׁנוּ בְּמִצְוֹתָיו, וְרָצָה בָנוּ
וְשַׁבַּת קָדְשׁוֹ בְּאַהֲבָה וּבְרָצוֹן הִנְחִילָנוּ
זִכָּרוֹן לְמַעֲשֵׂה בְרֵאשִׁית
כִּי הוּא יוֹם תְּחִלָּה לְמִקְרָאֵי קֹדֶשׁ
זֵכֶר לִיצִיאַת מִצְרָיִם
כִּי בָנוּ בָחַרְתָּ וְאוֹתָנוּ קִדַּשְׁתָּ מִכָּל הָעַמִּים
וְשַׁבַּת קָדְשְׁךָ בְּאַהֲבָה וּבְרָצוֹן הִנְחַלְתָּנוּ.
בָּרוּךְ אַתָּה יהוה
מְקַדֵּשׁ הַשַּׁבָּת.

On שבת חול המועד סוכות*, if* קידוש *is made in the* סוכה*, add:*

בָּרוּךְ אַתָּה יהוה אֱלֹהֵינוּ מֶלֶךְ הָעוֹלָם
אֲשֶׁר קִדְּשָׁנוּ בְּמִצְוֹתָיו וְצִוָּנוּ לֵישֵׁב בַּסֻּכָּה.

It is customary for all present to drink of the wine.

LEARNING

The Ten Commandments appear in the Torah twice, in *Shemot* and in *Devarim*. The first mention of Shabbat in the list in *Shemot* commands us to "Remember Shabbat" (*Shemot* 20:8), while in *Devarim* the word used for this commandment is "to keep" (*Devarim* 5:12). "Keeping" or "observing" Shabbat refers to the negative mitzvot, the prohibitions that we are commanded not to do on Shabbat. And "remembering Shabbat" refers to the positive mitzvot, and also alludes specifically to recitation of Kiddush, among other mitzvot.

Kiddush on Friday night is made up of three parts. The first is the description of the very first Shabbat of creation, when God completed the universe and

ZEMIROT FOR SHABBAT EVENING

כָּל מְקַדֵּשׁ All who fittingly sanctify the seventh day,
All who protect the Sabbath properly from desecration,
Will have great reward in accord with their deed.
"Each in his own camp, each under his own banner." *Num. 1*

Lovers of the LORD, who await the building of the Temple,
Be glad and joyful on the Sabbath as if receiving the gift of God's inheritance,
Raise your hands in holiness and say to God:
"Blessed is the LORD who has given rest to His people Israel." *I Kings 8*

Seekers of the LORD, offspring of His beloved Abraham,
Who are slow to leave the Sabbath but hasten to enter it,
Who rejoice to keep it and make its *eiruv* –
"This is the day the LORD has made; let us rejoice and be glad in it." *Ps. 118*

Remember Moses' Torah, from which the laws of Sabbath are learned,
Engraved is the seventh day like a bedecked bride between her companions,
The pure inherit it and sanctify it with the words: "All that He had made…
With the seventh day God completed the work He had done." *Gen. 2*

It is a sacred day from beginning to end,
All Jacob's offspring will honor it as the King's word and decree,
Resting on it and rejoicing with delights of food and drink.
"All the congregation of Israel will observe it." *Ex. 12*

Extend Your loving-kindness to those who know You, zealous and retributive God,
Those who keep the seventh day, fulfilling "Remember" and "Observe,"
Give them the joy of Jerusalem rebuilt, make them shine with the light of Your face.
"Fill them with the rich plenty of Your House, give them drink from Your river of delights." *Ps. 36*

Help those who, on the seventh day, rest from plow and harvest,
Who walk slowly, and eat three meals to bless You.
May their righteousness shine like the light of the seven days,
LORD God of Israel, give completion. *I Sam. 14*

זמירות לליל שבת

כָּל מְקַדֵּשׁ שְׁבִיעִי כָּרָאוּי לוֹ
כָּל שׁוֹמֵר שַׁבָּת כַּדָּת, מֵחַלְּלוֹ
שְׂכָרוֹ הַרְבֵּה מְאֹד עַל פִּי פָעֳלוֹ
אִישׁ עַל־מַחֲנֵהוּ וְאִישׁ עַל־דִּגְלוֹ: במדבר א

אוֹהֲבֵי יהוה הַמְחַכִּים לְבִנְיַן אֲרִיאֵל
בְּיוֹם הַשַּׁבָּת שִׂישׂוּ וְשִׂמְחוּ כִּמְקַבְּלֵי מַתַּן נַחֲלִיאֵל
גַּם שְׂאוּ יְדֵיכֶם קֹדֶשׁ וְאִמְרוּ לָאֵל
בָּרוּךְ יהוה אֲשֶׁר נָתַן מְנוּחָה לְעַמּוֹ יִשְׂרָאֵל: מלכים א, ח

דּוֹרְשֵׁי יהוה זֶרַע אַבְרָהָם אוֹהֲבוֹ
הַמְאַחֲרִים לָצֵאת מִן הַשַּׁבָּת וּמְמַהֲרִים לָבוֹא
וּשְׂמֵחִים לְשָׁמְרוֹ וּלְעָרֵב עֵרוּבוֹ
זֶה־הַיּוֹם עָשָׂה יהוה, נָגִילָה וְנִשְׂמְחָה בוֹ: תהלים קיח

זִכְרוּ תּוֹרַת מֹשֶׁה בְּמִצְוַת שַׁבָּת גְּרוּסָה
חֲרוּתָה לַיּוֹם הַשְּׁבִיעִי, כְּכַלָּה בֵּין רֵעוֹתֶיהָ מְשֻׁבָּצָה
טְהוֹרִים יִירָשׁוּהָ, וִיקַדְּשׁוּהָ בְּמַאֲמַר כָּל אֲשֶׁר עָשָׂה
וַיְכַל אֱלֹהִים בַּיּוֹם הַשְּׁבִיעִי מְלַאכְתּוֹ אֲשֶׁר עָשָׂה: בראשית ב

יוֹם קָדוֹשׁ הוּא, מִבּוֹאוֹ וְעַד צֵאתוֹ
כָּל זֶרַע יַעֲקֹב יְכַבְּדוּהוּ, כִּדְבַר הַמֶּלֶךְ וְדָתוֹ
לָנוּחַ בּוֹ וְלִשְׂמֹחַ בְּתַעֲנוּג אָכוֹל וְשָׁתֹה
כָּל־עֲדַת יִשְׂרָאֵל יַעֲשׂוּ אֹתוֹ: שמות יב

מְשֹׁךְ חַסְדְּךָ לְיוֹדְעֶיךָ, אֵל קַנּוֹא וְנוֹקֵם
נוֹטְרֵי יוֹם הַשְּׁבִיעִי זָכוֹר וְשָׁמוֹר לְהָקֵם
שַׂמְּחֵם בְּבִנְיַן שָׁלֵם, בְּאוֹר פָּנֶיךָ תַּבְהִיקֵם
יִרְוְיֻן מִדֶּשֶׁן בֵּיתֶךָ, וְנַחַל עֲדָנֶיךָ תַשְׁקֵם: תהלים לו

עֲזֹר לַשּׁוֹבְתִים בַּשְּׁבִיעִי, בֶּחָרִישׁ וּבַקָּצִיר עוֹלָמִים
פּוֹסְעִים בּוֹ פְּסִיעָה קְטַנָּה, סוֹעֲדִים בּוֹ, לְבָרֵךְ שָׁלֹשׁ פְּעָמִים
צִדְקָתָם תַּצְהִיר כְּאוֹר שִׁבְעַת הַיָּמִים
יהוה אֱלֹהֵי יִשְׂרָאֵל, הָבָה תָמִים: שמואל א, יד

מְנוּחָה וְשִׂמְחָה Rest and joy, light for all Jews,
Is the Sabbath day, day of delights;
Those who keep and recall it bear witness
That in six days all creation was made.

The highest heavens, land and seas,
The multitudes of heaven, high and sublime;
Sea monsters, humans and all wild beasts,
Were created by God, the LORD, who formed all worlds.

It was He who spoke to His treasured people:
"Keep it to make it holy from beginning to end."
The holy Sabbath is His day of delight,
For on it God rested from all His work.

Through the Sabbath commandment
God will give you strength,
Rise, pray to Him, and He will invigorate you.
Recite the Nishmat prayer, and the Kedusha,
Then eat with joy, for He is pleased with you.

With twin loaves, and wine for the Kiddush,
With many delicacies and a willing spirit;
Those who delight in it shall merit great reward:
The coming of the redeemer, and life in the World to Come.

מְנוּחָה וְשִׂמְחָה אוֹר לַיְּהוּדִים
יוֹם שַׁבָּתוֹן, יוֹם מַחֲמַדִּים
שׁוֹמְרָיו וְזוֹכְרָיו הֵמָּה מְעִידִים
כִּי לְשִׁשָּׁה כֹּל בְּרוּאִים וְעוֹמְדִים.

שְׁמֵי שָׁמַיִם, אֶרֶץ וְיַמִּים
כָּל צְבָא מָרוֹם גְּבוֹהִים וְרָמִים
תַּנִּין וְאָדָם וְחַיַּת רְאֵמִים
כִּי בְּיָהּ יהוה צוּר עוֹלָמִים.

הוּא אֲשֶׁר דִּבֶּר לְעַם סְגֻלָּתוֹ
שָׁמוֹר לְקַדְּשׁוֹ מִבּוֹאוֹ עַד צֵאתוֹ
שַׁבַּת קֹדֶשׁ יוֹם חֶמְדָּתוֹ
כִּי בוֹ שָׁבַת אֵל מִכָּל מְלַאכְתּוֹ.

בְּמִצְוַת שַׁבָּת אֵל יַחֲלִיצָךְ
קוּם קְרָא אֵלָיו, יָחִישׁ לְאַמְּצָךְ
נִשְׁמַת כָּל חַי וְגַם נַעֲרִיצָךְ
אֱכֹל בְּשִׂמְחָה כִּי כְבָר רָצָךְ.

בְּמִשְׁנֶה לֶחֶם וְקִדּוּשׁ רַבָּה
בְּרֹב מַטְעַמִּים וְרוּחַ נְדִיבָה
יִזְכּוּ לְרַב טוּב הַמִּתְעַנְּגִים בָּהּ
בְּבִיאַת גּוֹאֵל לְחַיֵּי הָעוֹלָם הַבָּא.

מַה־יְּדִידוּת How beloved is your rest, Sabbath Queen,
We run to greet you: Come, royal bride,
Dressed in fine robes. We light the light with blessing.
All labors end [as is said:] "You shall do no work."
To savor the delights of fowl, quail and fish.

In advance all kinds of tasty food have been prepared,
Fattened chickens made ready while it was still day.
Varied dishes set out, and fragrant wines to drink,
And special delicacies all three times.
To savor the delights of fowl, quail and fish.

They shall inherit Jacob's heritage, a heritage unbounded,
Rich and poor will honor [the Sabbath] and be worthy of redemption,
If you keep the Sabbath day you will be My special treasure,
Six days shall you labor – and on the seventh let us rejoice.
To savor the delights of fowl, quail and fish.

Your secular concerns are forbidden; so too are calculations.
Reflections are permitted, and arranging matches for girls,
And teaching a child a book, and singing songs of praise,
And meditating on fine words at every place and gathering.
To savor the delights of fowl, quail and fish.

Your walk shall be unhurried; you shall call the Sabbath a delight.
Sleep too is praiseworthy, for it refreshes the spirit.
Therefore my soul yearns for you, to rest in you in love,
As if within a fence of roses: on it son and daughter rest.
To savor the delights of fowl, quail and fish.

A foretaste of the World to Come is the day of Sabbath rest.
All who take delight in it will be worthy of great joy.
They will be saved with relief from the birthpangs of the Messiah,
May our redemption spring forth, and sadness and sighing flee away.
To savor the delights of fowl, quail and fish.

מַה־יְּדִידוּת מְנוּחָתֵךְ, אַתְּ שַׁבָּת הַמַּלְכָּה
בְּכֵן נָרוּץ לִקְרָאתֵךְ, בּוֹאִי כַלָּה נְסוּכָה
לְבוּשׁ בִּגְדֵי חֲמוּדוֹת, לְהַדְלִיק נֵר בִּבְרָכָה
וַתֵּכֶל כָּל הָעֲבוֹדוֹת, לֹא תַעֲשׂוּ מְלָאכָה.
לְהִתְעַנֵּג בְּתַעֲנוּגִים בַּרְבּוּרִים וּשְׂלָו וְדָגִים.

מֵעֶרֶב מַזְמִינִים כָּל מִינֵי מַטְעַמִּים
מִבְּעוֹד יוֹם מוּכָנִים תַּרְנְגוֹלִים מְפֻטָּמִים
וְלַעֲרֹךְ כַּמָּה מִינִים, שְׁתוֹת יֵינוֹת מְבֻשָּׂמִים
וְתַפְנוּקֵי מַעֲדַנִּים בְּכָל שָׁלֹשׁ פְּעָמִים.
לְהִתְעַנֵּג בְּתַעֲנוּגִים בַּרְבּוּרִים וּשְׂלָו וְדָגִים.

נַחֲלַת יַעֲקֹב יִירָשׁ, בְּלִי מְצָרִים נַחֲלָה
וִיכַבְּדוּהוּ עָשִׁיר וָרָשׁ, וְתִזְכּוּ לִגְאֻלָּה
יוֹם שַׁבָּת אִם תְּכַבֵּדוּ וִהְיִיתֶם לִי סְגֻלָּה
שֵׁשֶׁת יָמִים תַּעֲבֹדוּ וּבַשְּׁבִיעִי נָגִילָה.
לְהִתְעַנֵּג בְּתַעֲנוּגִים בַּרְבּוּרִים וּשְׂלָו וְדָגִים.

חֲפָצֶיךָ אֲסוּרִים וְגַם לַחְשֹׁב חֶשְׁבּוֹנוֹת
הִרְהוּרִים מֻתָּרִים וּלְשַׁדֵּךְ הַבָּנוֹת
וְתִינוֹק לְלַמְּדוֹ סֵפֶר, לַמְנַצֵּחַ בִּנְגִינוֹת
וְלַהֲגוֹת בְּאִמְרֵי שֶׁפֶר בְּכָל פִּנּוֹת וּמַחֲנוֹת.
לְהִתְעַנֵּג בְּתַעֲנוּגִים בַּרְבּוּרִים וּשְׂלָו וְדָגִים.

הִלּוּכָךְ יְהֵא בְנַחַת, עֹנֶג קְרָא לַשַּׁבָּת
וְהַשֵּׁנָה מְשֻׁבַּחַת כְּדָת נֶפֶשׁ מְשִׁיבַת
בְּכֵן נַפְשִׁי לְךָ עָרְגָה וְלָנוּחַ בְּחִבַּת
כְּשׁוֹשַׁנִּים סוּגָה, בּוֹ יָנוּחוּ בֵּן וּבַת.
לְהִתְעַנֵּג בְּתַעֲנוּגִים בַּרְבּוּרִים וּשְׂלָו וְדָגִים.

מֵעֵין עוֹלָם הַבָּא יוֹם שַׁבָּת מְנוּחָה
כָּל הַמִּתְעַנְּגִים בָּהּ יִזְכּוּ לְרֹב שִׂמְחָה
מֵחֶבְלֵי מָשִׁיחַ יֻצָּלוּ לִרְוָחָה
פְּדוּתֵנוּ תַצְמִיחַ, וְנָס יָגוֹן וַאֲנָחָה.
לְהִתְעַנֵּג בְּתַעֲנוּגִים בַּרְבּוּרִים וּשְׂלָו וְדָגִים.

יוֹם זֶה לְיִשְׂרָאֵל This day for Israel is light and joy,
a Sabbath of serenity.
At the assembly at Sinai You decreed the laws,
Sabbath and the festivals – to keep them all my years;
Setting a table before me with courses of fine food –
A Sabbath of serenity.

This day, for Israel, is light and joy, a Sabbath of serenity.

Heart's delight to a shattered people,
To suffering spirits, an extra soul.
From troubled hearts may it banish sighs –
A Sabbath of serenity.

This day, for Israel, is light and joy, a Sabbath of serenity.

You sanctified and blessed it above all other days.
In six days You finished the making of all worlds.
On it sad souls find quiet and safety –
A Sabbath of serenity.

This day, for Israel, is light and joy, a Sabbath of serenity.

All work is forbidden by the feared One's commandment,
I will merit royal glory if I keep the Sabbath day,
Bringing the awesome One a sweetly scented gift –
A Sabbath of serenity.

This day, for Israel, is light and joy, a Sabbath of serenity.

Renew our Sanctuary, remember the ruined city.
Bestow Your goodness, Savior, on one who is sad,
Yet still she spends the Sabbath in song and praise –
A Sabbath of serenity.

This day, for Israel, is light and joy, a Sabbath of serenity.

יוֹם זֶה לְיִשְׂרָאֵל אוֹרָה וְשִׂמְחָה, שַׁבַּת מְנוּחָה.

צִוִּיתָ פִּקּוּדִים בְּמַעֲמַד סִינַי
שַׁבָּת וּמוֹעֲדִים לִשְׁמֹר בְּכָל שָׁנַי
לַעֲרֹךְ לְפָנַי מַשְׂאֵת וַאֲרוּחָה שַׁבַּת מְנוּחָה.

יוֹם זֶה לְיִשְׂרָאֵל אוֹרָה וְשִׂמְחָה, שַׁבַּת מְנוּחָה.

חֶמְדַּת הַלְּבָבוֹת לְאֻמָּה שְׁבוּרָה
לִנְפָשׁוֹת נִכְאָבוֹת נְשָׁמָה יְתֵרָה
לְנֶפֶשׁ מְצֵרָה יָסִיר אֲנָחָה שַׁבַּת מְנוּחָה.

יוֹם זֶה לְיִשְׂרָאֵל אוֹרָה וְשִׂמְחָה, שַׁבַּת מְנוּחָה.

קִדַּשְׁתָּ בֵּרַכְתָּ אוֹתוֹ מִכָּל יָמִים
בְּשֵׁשֶׁת כִּלִּיתָ מְלֶאכֶת עוֹלָמִים
בּוֹ מָצְאוּ עֲגוּמִים הַשְׁקֵט וּבִטְחָה שַׁבַּת מְנוּחָה.

יוֹם זֶה לְיִשְׂרָאֵל אוֹרָה וְשִׂמְחָה, שַׁבַּת מְנוּחָה.

לְאִסּוּר מְלָאכָה צִוִּיתָנוּ נוֹרָא
אֶזְכֶּה הוֹד מְלוּכָה אִם שַׁבָּת אֶשְׁמְרָה
אַקְרִיב שַׁי לַמּוֹרָא, מִנְחָה מֶרְקָחָה שַׁבַּת מְנוּחָה.

יוֹם זֶה לְיִשְׂרָאֵל אוֹרָה וְשִׂמְחָה, שַׁבַּת מְנוּחָה.

חַדֵּשׁ מִקְדָּשֵׁנוּ, זָכְרָה נֶחֱרֶבֶת
טוּבְךָ, מוֹשִׁיעֵנוּ, תְּנָה לַנֶּעֱצֶבֶת
בְּשַׁבָּת יוֹשֶׁבֶת בְּזֶמֶר וּשְׁבָחָה שַׁבַּת מְנוּחָה.

יוֹם זֶה לְיִשְׂרָאֵל אוֹרָה וְשִׂמְחָה, שַׁבַּת מְנוּחָה.

יָהּ רִבּוֹן Master of all worlds, our God, adored,
King of kings, over all the Lord:
Your wondrous deeds to applaud
We sing to You with one accord.

God of all worlds, our God, adored;
King of kings, over all, the Lord.

Early and late my praise shall ring,
To You, holy Author of every thing:
Beasts of the field, birds that take wing.
Angels and mortals to You shall sing.

God of all worlds, our God, adored;
King of kings, over all, the Lord.

Your great good deeds are vast in scale,
You humble the proud, You lift the frail.
A thousand years would not avail
Of Your works to tell the tale.

God of all worlds, our God, adored;
King of kings, over all, the Lord.

Yours is the glory, the greatness too,
From the lion's jaw, Your flock rescue.
Bring Your exiles home to You:
The people You chose, save anew.

God of all worlds, our God, adored;
King of kings, over all, the Lord.

Come back to Your Temple, Your sacred shrine,
That there in joy our souls may entwine.
In song our voices to combine,
When Jerusalem's beauty again will shine.

God of all worlds, our God, adored;
King of kings, over all, the Lord.

יָהּ רִבּוֹן עָלַם וְעָלְמַיָּא
אַנְתְּ הוּא מַלְכָּא מֶלֶךְ מַלְכַיָּא
עוֹבַד גְּבוּרְתָּךְ וְתִמְהַיָּא
שְׁפַר קֳדָמָךְ לְהַחֲוָיָא.

יָהּ רִבּוֹן עָלַם וְעָלְמַיָּא, אַנְתְּ הוּא מַלְכָּא מֶלֶךְ מַלְכַיָּא.

שְׁבָחִין אֲסַדֵּר צַפְרָא וְרַמְשָׁא
לָךְ אֱלָהָא קַדִּישָׁא דִּי בְרָא כָּל נַפְשָׁא
עִירִין קַדִּישִׁין וּבְנֵי אֱנָשָׁא
חֵיוַת בָּרָא וְעוֹפֵי שְׁמַיָּא.

יָהּ רִבּוֹן עָלַם וְעָלְמַיָּא, אַנְתְּ הוּא מַלְכָּא מֶלֶךְ מַלְכַיָּא.

רַבְרְבִין עוֹבְדָיךְ וְתַקִּיפִין
מָכֵךְ רָמַיָּא וְזָקֵף כְּפִיפִין
לוּ יְחֵי גְבַר שְׁנִין אַלְפִין
לָא יֵעֹל גְּבוּרְתָּךְ בְּחֻשְׁבְּנַיָּא.

יָהּ רִבּוֹן עָלַם וְעָלְמַיָּא, אַנְתְּ הוּא מַלְכָּא מֶלֶךְ מַלְכַיָּא.

אֱלָהָא דִּי לֵהּ יְקָר וּרְבוּתָא
פְּרֹק יַת עָנָךְ מִפֻּם אַרְיְוָתָא
וְאַפֵּק יַת עַמָּךְ מִגּוֹ גָלוּתָא
עַמָּא דִי בְחַרְתְּ מִכָּל אֻמַּיָּא.

יָהּ רִבּוֹן עָלַם וְעָלְמַיָּא, אַנְתְּ הוּא מַלְכָּא מֶלֶךְ מַלְכַיָּא.

לְמִקְדְּשָׁךְ תּוּב וּלְקֹדֶשׁ קֻדְשִׁין
אֲתַר דִּי בֵהּ יֶחֱדוּן רוּחִין וְנַפְשִׁין
וִיזַמְּרוּן לָךְ שִׁירִין וְרַחֲשִׁין
בִּירוּשְׁלֵם קַרְתָּא דְשֻׁפְרַיָּא.

יָהּ רִבּוֹן עָלַם וְעָלְמַיָּא, אַנְתְּ הוּא מַלְכָּא מֶלֶךְ מַלְכַיָּא.

צוּר מִשֶּׁלּוֹ The Rock from whom we have eaten:
Bless Him, my faithful friends;
we have sufficed, we have left over,
just as the LORD said.

He feeds His world – our Shepherd, our Father,
we have eaten of His bread, His wine we have drunk.
So let us thank His name, let us praise Him with our mouths,
saying, singing: None is holy like the LORD.

The Rock from whom we have eaten: Bless Him, my faithful friends;
we have sufficed, we have left over, just as the LORD said.

With song and sound of thanks, we shall bless our God,
for the gift He gave our fathers: A lovely land.
With food and sustenance He has satisfied our souls.
His kindness overwhelms us: True is the LORD.

The Rock from whom we have eaten: Bless Him, my faithful friends;
we have sufficed, we have left over, just as the LORD said.

Have compassion in Your love for Your people, our Rock,
for Zion, Your home of glory, Temple of our splendor.
The son of David Your servant: may he come and redeem us,
breath of our life, anointed of the LORD.

The Rock from whom we have eaten: Bless Him, my faithful friends;
we have sufficed, we have left over, just as the LORD said.

May the Temple be rebuilt, Zion's city full again;
there we will sing a new song as we go up in joy,
to the Compassionate, the Holy One –
may He be blessed and raised on high –
with a full cup of wine, sign of the blessing of the LORD.

The Rock from whom we have eaten: Bless Him, my faithful friends;
we have sufficed, we have left over, just as the LORD said.

צוּר מִשֶּׁלּוֹ אָכַלְנוּ בָּרְכוּ אֱמוּנַי
שָׂבַעְנוּ וְהוֹתַרְנוּ כִּדְבַר יהוה.

הַזָּן אֶת עוֹלָמוֹ רוֹעֵנוּ אָבִינוּ
אָכַלְנוּ אֶת לַחְמוֹ וְיֵינוֹ שָׁתִינוּ
עַל כֵּן נוֹדֶה לִשְׁמוֹ וּנְהַלְּלוֹ בְּפִינוּ
אָמַרְנוּ וְעָנִינוּ אֵין קָדוֹשׁ כַּיהוה.

צוּר מִשֶּׁלּוֹ אָכַלְנוּ, בָּרְכוּ אֱמוּנַי, שָׂבַעְנוּ וְהוֹתַרְנוּ כִּדְבַר יהוה.

בְּשִׁיר וְקוֹל תּוֹדָה נְבָרֵךְ אֱלֹהֵינוּ
עַל אֶרֶץ חֶמְדָּה שֶׁהִנְחִיל לַאֲבוֹתֵינוּ
מָזוֹן וְצֵידָה הִשְׂבִּיעַ לְנַפְשֵׁנוּ
חַסְדּוֹ גָּבַר עָלֵינוּ וֶאֱמֶת יהוה.

צוּר מִשֶּׁלּוֹ אָכַלְנוּ, בָּרְכוּ אֱמוּנַי, שָׂבַעְנוּ וְהוֹתַרְנוּ כִּדְבַר יהוה.

רַחֵם בְּחַסְדֶּךָ עַל עַמְּךָ צוּרֵנוּ
עַל צִיּוֹן מִשְׁכַּן כְּבוֹדֶךָ זְבוּל בֵּית תִּפְאַרְתֵּנוּ
בֶּן דָּוִד עַבְדֶּךָ יָבוֹא וְיִגְאָלֵנוּ
רוּחַ אַפֵּינוּ מְשִׁיחַ יהוה.

צוּר מִשֶּׁלּוֹ אָכַלְנוּ, בָּרְכוּ אֱמוּנַי, שָׂבַעְנוּ וְהוֹתַרְנוּ כִּדְבַר יהוה.

יִבָּנֶה הַמִּקְדָּשׁ עִיר צִיּוֹן תְּמַלֵּא
וְשָׁם נָשִׁיר שִׁיר חָדָשׁ וּבִרְנָנָה נַעֲלֶה
הָרַחֲמָן הַנִּקְדָּשׁ יִתְבָּרַךְ וְיִתְעַלֶּה
עַל כּוֹס יַיִן מָלֵא כְּבִרְכַּת יהוה.

צוּר מִשֶּׁלּוֹ אָכַלְנוּ, בָּרְכוּ אֱמוּנַי, שָׂבַעְנוּ וְהוֹתַרְנוּ כִּדְבַר יהוה.

צָמְאָה נַפְשִׁי My soul thirsts for God, the living God Ps. 42
My heart and flesh will sing joyfully to the living God. Ps. 84
The One God created me, and said "As I live,
No one shall see Me and live."
My soul thirsts for God, the living God
My heart and flesh will sing joyfully to the living God.

He created all with wisdom, design and thought,
Deeply hidden though it is from the eyes of all that live.
His glory is high above all, every mouth makes known His splendor,
Blessed is He in whose hands is the life-force of all that lives.
My soul thirsts for God, the living God
My heart and flesh will sing joyfully to the living God.

He set apart the quiet one's offspring, to teach them decrees,
Which if one performs them, thereby he shall live.
Who can defend himself? We are like specks of dust,
Truly none can defend itself before You, nothing that lives.
My soul thirsts for God, the living God
My heart and flesh will sing joyfully to the living God.

In the heart, the inclination is like a viper's poison,
How then can we return, and be like flesh that lives?
Those who have gone astray, if they wished, could turn from their way,
Before they go to their rest in the place destined for all that lives.
My soul thirsts for God, the living God
My heart and flesh will sing joyfully to the living God.

For everything, I shall thank You, every mouth shall declare Your oneness,
You who open Your hand and satisfy all that lives.
Recall the love of ancient times, and revive those who slumber,
Bring near the days when the Messiah shall live.
My soul thirsts for God, the living God
My heart and flesh will sing joyfully to the living God.

See who is the true mistress, when the handmaid says,
"No, your son is dead while my son lives."
I will bow face down and spread my hands toward you,
When I open my mouth to say: "The soul of all that lives."
My soul thirsts for God, the living God
My heart and flesh will sing joyfully to the living God.

צָמְאָה נַפְשִׁי לֵאלֹהִים לְאֵל חָי: לִבִּי וּבְשָׂרִי יְרַנְּנוּ אֶל אֵל־חָי: תהלים מב תהלים פד
אֵל אֶחָד בְּרָאַנִי, וְאָמַר חַי אָנִי   כִּי לֹא יִרְאַנִי הָאָדָם וָחָי.

צָמְאָה נַפְשִׁי לֵאלֹהִים לְאֵל חָי, לִבִּי וּבְשָׂרִי יְרַנְּנוּ אֶל אֵל־חָי.

בָּרָא כֹל בְּחָכְמָה, בְּעֵצָה וּבִמְזִמָּה   מְאֹד נֶעְלָמָה מֵעֵינֵי כָּל חָי.
רָם עַל כֹּל כְּבוֹדוֹ, כָּל פֶּה יְחַוֶּה הוֹדוֹ   בָּרוּךְ אֲשֶׁר בְּיָדוֹ נֶפֶשׁ כָּל חָי.

צָמְאָה נַפְשִׁי לֵאלֹהִים לְאֵל חָי, לִבִּי וּבְשָׂרִי יְרַנְּנוּ אֶל אֵל־חָי.

הִבְדִּיל נִינֵי תָם, חֻקִּים לְהוֹרוֹתָם   אֲשֶׁר יַעֲשֶׂה אוֹתָם הָאָדָם וָחָי.
מִי זֶה יִצְטַדָּק, נִמְשַׁל לְאָבָק דָּק   אֱמֶת, כִּי לֹא יִצְדַּק לְפָנֶיךָ כָּל חָי.

צָמְאָה נַפְשִׁי לֵאלֹהִים לְאֵל חָי, לִבִּי וּבְשָׂרִי יְרַנְּנוּ אֶל אֵל־חָי.

בְּלֵב יֵצֶר חָשׁוּב כִּדְמוּת חֲמַת עַכְשׁוּב   וְאֵיכָכָה יָשׁוּב הַבָּשָׂר הֶחָי.
נְסוֹגִים אִם אָבוּ, וּמִדַּרְכָּם שָׁבוּ   טֶרֶם יִשְׁכָּבוּ בֵּית מוֹעֵד לְכָל חָי.

צָמְאָה נַפְשִׁי לֵאלֹהִים לְאֵל חָי, לִבִּי וּבְשָׂרִי יְרַנְּנוּ אֶל אֵל־חָי.

עַל כֹּל אֲהוֹדֶךָ, כָּל פֶּה תְּיַחֲדֶךָ   פּוֹתֵחַ אֶת יָדֶךָ וּמַשְׂבִּיעַ לְכָל חָי.
זְכֹר אַהֲבַת קְדוּמִים, וְהַחֲיֵה נִרְדָּמִים   וְקָרֵב הַיָּמִים אֲשֶׁר בֶּן יִשַׁי חָי.

צָמְאָה נַפְשִׁי לֵאלֹהִים לְאֵל חָי, לִבִּי וּבְשָׂרִי יְרַנְּנוּ אֶל אֵל־חָי.

רְאֵה לִגְבֶרֶת אֱמֶת, שִׁפְחָה נוֹאֶמֶת   לֹא כִי, בְּנֵךְ הַמֵּת וּבְנִי הֶחָי.
אֶקֹּד עַל אַפִּי, וְאֶפְרֹשׂ לְךָ כַּפִּי   עֵת אֶפְתַּח פִּי בְּנִשְׁמַת כָּל חָי.

צָמְאָה נַפְשִׁי לֵאלֹהִים לְאֵל חָי, לִבִּי וּבְשָׂרִי יְרַנְּנוּ אֶל אֵל־חָי.

Shaḥarit for Shabbat

Begin as on weekdays, from pages 4–70.

On Hoshana Raba and, in many communites, on Yom HaAtzma'ut and Yom Yerushalayim, Pesukei DeZimra of Yom Tov are said.

A PSALM BEFORE VERSES OF PRAISE

מִזְמוֹר שִׁיר A psalm of David. *Ps. 30*
A song for the dedication of the House.
I will elevate You, Lord, for You have lifted me up,
and not let my enemies rejoice over me.
Lord, my God, I cried to You for help and You healed me.
Lord, You lifted my soul from the grave;
You spared me from going down to the pit.
Sing to the Lord, you His devoted ones,
and give thanks to His holy name.
For His anger is for a moment, but His favor for a lifetime.
At night there may be weeping, but in the morning there is joy.
When I felt secure, I said, "I shall never be shaken."
Lord, when You favored me,
You made me stand firm as a mountain,
but when You hid Your face, I was terrified.
To You, Lord, I called; I pleaded with my Lord:
"What gain would there be if I died
and went down to the grave?
Can dust thank You? Can it declare Your truth?
Hear, Lord, and be generous to me; Lord, be my help."
You have turned my sorrow into dancing.
▸ You have removed my sackcloth and clothed me with joy,
so that my soul may sing to You and not be silent.
Lord my God, for ever will I thank You.

שחרית לשבת

Begin as on weekdays, from pages 5–71.

On יום העצמאות *and, in many communites, on* הושענא רבה *and* יום ירושלים, יום טוב *of* פסוקי דזמרה *are said.*

מזמור לפני פסוקי דזמרה

מִזְמוֹר שִׁיר־חֲנֻכַּת הַבַּיִת לְדָוִד: תהלים ל
אֲרוֹמִמְךָ יהוה כִּי דִלִּיתָנִי, וְלֹא־שִׂמַּחְתָּ אֹיְבַי לִי:
יהוה אֱלֹהָי, שִׁוַּעְתִּי אֵלֶיךָ וַתִּרְפָּאֵנִי:
יהוה, הֶעֱלִיתָ מִן־שְׁאוֹל נַפְשִׁי, חִיִּיתַנִי מִיָּרְדִי־בוֹר:
זַמְּרוּ לַיהוה חֲסִידָיו, וְהוֹדוּ לְזֵכֶר קָדְשׁוֹ:
כִּי רֶגַע בְּאַפּוֹ, חַיִּים בִּרְצוֹנוֹ
בָּעֶרֶב יָלִין בֶּכִי וְלַבֹּקֶר רִנָּה:
וַאֲנִי אָמַרְתִּי בְשַׁלְוִי, בַּל־אֶמּוֹט לְעוֹלָם:
יהוה, בִּרְצוֹנְךָ הֶעֱמַדְתָּה לְהַרְרִי עֹז
הִסְתַּרְתָּ פָנֶיךָ הָיִיתִי נִבְהָל:
אֵלֶיךָ יהוה אֶקְרָא, וְאֶל־אֲדֹנָי אֶתְחַנָּן:
מַה־בֶּצַע בְּדָמִי, בְּרִדְתִּי אֶל שָׁחַת
הֲיוֹדְךָ עָפָר, הֲיַגִּיד אֲמִתֶּךָ:
שְׁמַע־יהוה וְחָנֵּנִי, יהוה הֱיֵה־עֹזֵר לִי:
◄ הָפַכְתָּ מִסְפְּדִי לְמָחוֹל לִי, פִּתַּחְתָּ שַׂקִּי, וַתְּאַזְּרֵנִי שִׂמְחָה:
לְמַעַן יְזַמֶּרְךָ כָבוֹד וְלֹא יִדֹּם
יהוה אֱלֹהַי, לְעוֹלָם אוֹדֶךָּ:

MOURNER'S KADDISH

The following prayer, said by mourners, requires the presence of a minyan. A transliteration can be found on page 1151.

Mourner: יִתְגַּדַּל Magnified and sanctified
may His great name be,
in the world He created by His will.
May He establish His kingdom
in your lifetime and in your days,
and in the lifetime of all the house of Israel,
swiftly and soon –
and say: Amen.

All: May His great name be blessed
for ever and all time.

Mourner: Blessed and praised,
glorified and elevated,
raised and honored,
uplifted and praised
be the name of the Holy One,
blessed be He,
beyond any blessing,
song, praise and consolation
uttered in the world –
and say: Amen.

May there be great peace from heaven,
and life for us and all Israel –
and say: Amen.

Bow, take three steps back, as if taking leave of the Divine Presence, then bow, first left, then right, then center, while saying:

May He who makes peace in His high places,
make peace for us and all Israel –
and say: Amen.

קדיש יתום

The following prayer, said by mourners, requires the presence of a מנין.
A transliteration can be found on page 1151.

אבל: **יִתְגַּדַּל וְיִתְקַדַּשׁ שְׁמֵהּ רַבָּא** (קהל: אָמֵן)
בְּעָלְמָא דִּי בְרָא כִרְעוּתֵהּ
וְיַמְלִיךְ מַלְכוּתֵהּ
בְּחַיֵּיכוֹן וּבְיוֹמֵיכוֹן וּבְחַיֵּי דְכָל בֵּית יִשְׂרָאֵל
בַּעֲגָלָא וּבִזְמַן קָרִיב
וְאִמְרוּ אָמֵן. (קהל: אָמֵן)

קהל ואבל: **יְהֵא שְׁמֵהּ רַבָּא מְבָרַךְ לְעָלַם וּלְעָלְמֵי עָלְמַיָּא.**

אבל: **יִתְבָּרַךְ וְיִשְׁתַּבַּח וְיִתְפָּאַר**
וְיִתְרוֹמַם וְיִתְנַשֵּׂא וְיִתְהַדָּר וְיִתְעַלֶּה וְיִתְהַלָּל
שְׁמֵהּ דְּקֻדְשָׁא בְּרִיךְ הוּא (קהל: בְּרִיךְ הוּא)
לְעֵלָּא מִן כָּל בִּרְכָתָא / בשבת שובה: **לְעֵלָּא לְעֵלָּא מִכָּל בִּרְכָתָא**/
וְשִׁירָתָא, תֻּשְׁבְּחָתָא וְנֶחֱמָתָא
דַּאֲמִירָן בְּעָלְמָא
וְאִמְרוּ אָמֵן. (קהל: אָמֵן)

יְהֵא שְׁלָמָא רַבָּא מִן שְׁמַיָּא
וְחַיִּים, עָלֵינוּ וְעַל כָּל יִשְׂרָאֵל
וְאִמְרוּ אָמֵן. (קהל: אָמֵן)

Bow, take three steps back, as if taking leave of the Divine Presence, then bow, first left, then right, then center, while saying:

עֹשֶׂה שָׁלוֹם/ בשבת שובה: **הַשָּׁלוֹם**/ **בִּמְרוֹמָיו**
הוּא יַעֲשֶׂה שָׁלוֹם עָלֵינוּ וְעַל כָּל יִשְׂרָאֵל
וְאִמְרוּ אָמֵן. (קהל: אָמֵן)

PESUKEI DEZIMRA

The following introductory blessing to the Pesukei DeZimra (Verses of Praise) is said standing, while holding the two front tzitziot of the tallit. They are kissed and released at the end of the blessing at "songs of praise" (below). From the beginning of this prayer to the end of the Amida, conversation is forbidden.

Some say:

I hereby prepare my mouth to thank, praise and applaud my Creator, for the sake of the unification of the Holy One, blessed be He, and His Divine Presence, through that which is hidden and concealed, in the name of all Israel.

BLESSED IS HE WHO SPOKE

and the world came into being, blessed is He.
Blessed is He who creates the universe.
Blessed is He who speaks and acts.
Blessed is He who decrees and fulfills.
Blessed is He who shows compassion to the earth.
Blessed is He who shows compassion to all creatures.
Blessed is He who gives a good reward
to those who fear Him.
Blessed is He who lives for ever
and exists to eternity.
Blessed is He who redeems and saves.
Blessed is His name.

Blessed are You, LORD our God, King of the Universe, God, compassionate Father, celebrated by the mouth of His people, praised and glorified by the tongue of His devoted ones and those who serve Him. With the songs of Your servant David we will praise You, O LORD our God. With praises and psalms we will magnify and praise You, glorify You, Speak Your name and declare Your kingship, our King, our God, ▸ the only One, Giver of life to the worlds the King whose great name is praised and glorified to all eternity. Blessed are You, LORD, the King celebrated with songs of praise.

פסוקי דזמרה

The following introductory blessing to the פסוקי דזמרה *is said standing, while holding the two front* ציציות *of the* טלית*. They are kissed and released at the end of the blessing at* בְּתִשְׁבָּחוֹת *(below). From the beginning of this prayer to the end of the* עמידה*, conversation is forbidden.*

Some say:

הֲרֵינִי מְזַמֵּן אֶת פִּי לְהוֹדוֹת וּלְהַלֵּל וּלְשַׁבֵּחַ אֶת בּוֹרְאִי, לְשֵׁם יִחוּד קֻדְשָׁא בְּרִיךְ הוּא וּשְׁכִינְתֵּהּ עַל יְדֵי הַהוּא טָמִיר וְנֶעְלָם בְּשֵׁם כָּל יִשְׂרָאֵל.

בָּרוּךְ שֶׁאָמַר וְהָיָה הָעוֹלָם, בָּרוּךְ הוּא.

בָּרוּךְ עוֹשֶׂה בְרֵאשִׁית

בָּרוּךְ אוֹמֵר וְעוֹשֶׂה

בָּרוּךְ גּוֹזֵר וּמְקַיֵּם

בָּרוּךְ מְרַחֵם עַל הָאָרֶץ

בָּרוּךְ מְרַחֵם עַל הַבְּרִיּוֹת

בָּרוּךְ מְשַׁלֵּם שָׂכָר טוֹב לִירֵאָיו

בָּרוּךְ חַי לָעַד וְקַיָּם לָנֶצַח

בָּרוּךְ פּוֹדֶה וּמַצִּיל

בָּרוּךְ שְׁמוֹ

בָּרוּךְ אַתָּה יהוה אֱלֹהֵינוּ מֶלֶךְ הָעוֹלָם, הָאֵל הָאָב הָרַחֲמָן הַמְהֻלָּל בְּפִי עַמּוֹ, מְשֻׁבָּח וּמְפֹאָר בִּלְשׁוֹן חֲסִידָיו וַעֲבָדָיו, וּבְשִׁירֵי דָוִד עַבְדֶּךָ, נְהַלֶּלְךָ יהוה אֱלֹהֵינוּ. בִּשְׁבָחוֹת וּבִזְמִירוֹת, נְגַדֶּלְךָ וּנְשַׁבֵּחֲךָ וּנְפָאֶרְךָ, וְנַזְכִּיר שִׁמְךָ וְנַמְלִיכְךָ, מַלְכֵּנוּ אֱלֹהֵינוּ. ‹ יָחִיד חֵי הָעוֹלָמִים, מֶלֶךְ, מְשֻׁבָּח וּמְפֹאָר עֲדֵי עַד שְׁמוֹ הַגָּדוֹל. בָּרוּךְ אַתָּה יהוה, מֶלֶךְ מְהֻלָּל בַּתִּשְׁבָּחוֹת.

הודו Thank the Lord, call on His name, make His acts known among the peoples. Sing to Him, make music to Him, tell of all His wonders. Glory in His holy name; let the hearts of those who seek the Lord rejoice. Search out the Lord and His strength; seek His presence at all times. Remember the wonders He has done, His miracles, and the judgments He pronounced. Descendants of Yisrael His servant, sons of Jacob His chosen ones: He is the Lord our God. His judgments are throughout the earth. Remember His covenant for ever, the word He commanded for a thousand generations. He made it with Abraham, vowed it to Isaac, and confirmed it to Jacob as a law and to Israel as an everlasting covenant, saying, "To you I will give the land of Canaan as your allotted heritage." You were then small in number, few, strangers there, wandering from nation to nation, from one kingdom to another, but He let no man oppress them, and for their sake He rebuked kings: "Do not touch My anointed ones, and do My prophets no harm." Sing to the Lord, all the earth; declare His salvation daily. Declare His glory among the nations, His wonders among all the peoples. For great is the Lord and greatly to be praised; He is awesome beyond all heavenly powers. ▸ For all the gods of the peoples are mere idols; it was the Lord who made the heavens. *I Chr. 16*

Before Him are majesty and splendor; there is strength and beauty in His holy place. Give to the Lord, families of the peoples, give to the Lord honor and might. Give to the Lord the glory due to His name; bring an offering and come before Him; bow down to the Lord in the splendor of holiness. Tremble before Him, all the earth; the world stands firm, it will not be shaken. Let the heavens rejoice and the earth be glad; let them declare among the nations, "The Lord is King." Let the sea roar, and all that is in it; let the fields be jubilant, and all they contain. Then the trees of the forest will sing for joy before the Lord, for He is coming to judge the earth. Thank the Lord for He is good; His loving-kindness is for ever. Say: "Save us, God of our salvation; gather us and rescue us from the nations, to acknowledge Your holy name and glory in Your praise. Blessed is the Lord, God of Israel, from this world to eternity." And let all the people say "Amen" and "Praise the Lord."

דברי הימים א׳ טז

הודו לַיהוה קִרְאוּ בִשְׁמוֹ, הוֹדִיעוּ בָעַמִּים עֲלִילֹתָיו: שִׁירוּ לוֹ, זַמְּרוּ־לוֹ, שִׂיחוּ בְּכָל־נִפְלְאוֹתָיו: הִתְהַלְלוּ בְּשֵׁם קָדְשׁוֹ, יִשְׂמַח לֵב מְבַקְשֵׁי יהוה: דִּרְשׁוּ יהוה וְעֻזּוֹ, בַּקְּשׁוּ פָנָיו תָּמִיד: זִכְרוּ נִפְלְאֹתָיו אֲשֶׁר עָשָׂה, מֹפְתָיו וּמִשְׁפְּטֵי־פִיהוּ: זֶרַע יִשְׂרָאֵל עַבְדּוֹ, בְּנֵי יַעֲקֹב בְּחִירָיו: הוּא יהוה אֱלֹהֵינוּ בְּכָל־הָאָרֶץ מִשְׁפָּטָיו: זִכְרוּ לְעוֹלָם בְּרִיתוֹ, דָּבָר צִוָּה לְאֶלֶף דּוֹר: אֲשֶׁר כָּרַת אֶת־אַבְרָהָם, וּשְׁבוּעָתוֹ לְיִצְחָק: וַיַּעֲמִידֶהָ לְיַעֲקֹב לְחֹק, לְיִשְׂרָאֵל בְּרִית עוֹלָם: לֵאמֹר, לְךָ אֶתֵּן אֶרֶץ־כְּנָעַן, חֶבֶל נַחֲלַתְכֶם: בִּהְיוֹתְכֶם מְתֵי מִסְפָּר, כִּמְעַט וְגָרִים בָּהּ: וַיִּתְהַלְּכוּ מִגּוֹי אֶל־גּוֹי, וּמִמַּמְלָכָה אֶל־עַם אַחֵר: לֹא־הִנִּיחַ לְאִישׁ לְעָשְׁקָם, וַיּוֹכַח עֲלֵיהֶם מְלָכִים: אַל־תִּגְּעוּ בִּמְשִׁיחָי, וּבִנְבִיאַי אַל־תָּרֵעוּ: שִׁירוּ לַיהוה כָּל־הָאָרֶץ, בַּשְּׂרוּ מִיּוֹם־אֶל־יוֹם יְשׁוּעָתוֹ: סַפְּרוּ בַגּוֹיִם אֶת־כְּבוֹדוֹ, בְּכָל־הָעַמִּים נִפְלְאֹתָיו: כִּי גָדוֹל יהוה וּמְהֻלָּל מְאֹד, וְנוֹרָא הוּא עַל־כָּל־אֱלֹהִים: › כִּי כָּל־אֱלֹהֵי הָעַמִּים אֱלִילִים, וַיהוה שָׁמַיִם עָשָׂה:

הוֹד וְהָדָר לְפָנָיו, עֹז וְחֶדְוָה בִּמְקֹמוֹ: הָבוּ לַיהוה מִשְׁפְּחוֹת עַמִּים, הָבוּ לַיהוה כָּבוֹד וָעֹז: הָבוּ לַיהוה כְּבוֹד שְׁמוֹ, שְׂאוּ מִנְחָה וּבֹאוּ לְפָנָיו, הִשְׁתַּחֲווּ לַיהוה בְּהַדְרַת־קֹדֶשׁ: חִילוּ מִלְּפָנָיו כָּל־הָאָרֶץ, אַף־תִּכּוֹן תֵּבֵל בַּל־תִּמּוֹט: יִשְׂמְחוּ הַשָּׁמַיִם וְתָגֵל הָאָרֶץ, וְיֹאמְרוּ בַגּוֹיִם יהוה מָלָךְ: יִרְעַם הַיָּם וּמְלוֹאוֹ, יַעֲלֹץ הַשָּׂדֶה וְכָל־אֲשֶׁר־בּוֹ: אָז יְרַנְּנוּ עֲצֵי הַיָּעַר, מִלִּפְנֵי יהוה, כִּי־בָא לִשְׁפּוֹט אֶת־הָאָרֶץ: הוֹדוּ לַיהוה כִּי טוֹב, כִּי לְעוֹלָם חַסְדּוֹ: וְאִמְרוּ, הוֹשִׁיעֵנוּ אֱלֹהֵי יִשְׁעֵנוּ, וְקַבְּצֵנוּ וְהַצִּילֵנוּ מִן־הַגּוֹיִם, לְהֹדוֹת לְשֵׁם קָדְשֶׁךָ, לְהִשְׁתַּבֵּחַ בִּתְהִלָּתֶךָ: בָּרוּךְ יהוה אֱלֹהֵי יִשְׂרָאֵל מִן־הָעוֹלָם וְעַד־הָעֹלָם, וַיֹּאמְרוּ כָל־הָעָם אָמֵן, וְהַלֵּל לַיהוה:

▸ Elevate the Lord our God and bow before His footstool: He is Ps. 99
holy. Elevate the Lord our God and bow at His holy mountain; for
holy is the Lord our God.

He is compassionate. He forgives wrongdoing and does not Ps. 78
destroy. Repeatedly He suppresses His anger, not rousing His full fury.
You, Lord: do not withhold Your compassion from me. May Your Ps. 40
loving-kindness and truth always guard me. Remember, Lord, Your Ps. 25
acts of compassion and love, for they have existed for ever. Ascribe Ps. 68
power to God, whose majesty is over Israel and whose might is in
the skies. You are awesome, God, in Your holy places. It is the God
of Israel who gives might and strength to the people, may God be
blessed. God of retribution, Lord, God of retribution, appear. Arise, Ps. 94
Judge of the earth, to repay the arrogant their just deserts. Salvation Ps. 3
belongs to the Lord; may Your blessing rest upon Your people, Selah!
▸ The Lord of multitudes is with us, the God of Jacob is our strong- Ps. 46
hold, Selah! Lord of multitudes, happy is the one who trusts in You. Ps. 84
Lord, save! May the King answer us on the day we call. Ps. 20

Save Your people and bless Your heritage; tend them and carry Ps. 28
them for ever. Our soul longs for the Lord; He is our Help and Shield. Ps. 33
For in Him our hearts rejoice, for in His holy name we have trusted.
May Your loving-kindness, Lord, be upon us, as we have put our hope
in You. Show us, Lord, Your loving-kindness and give us Your salva- Ps. 85
tion. Arise, help us and redeem us for the sake of Your love. I am the Ps. 44 Ps. 81
Lord your God who brought you up from the land of Egypt: open
your mouth wide and I will fill it. Happy is the people for whom this Ps. 144
is so; happy is the people whose God the Lord. ▸ As for me, I trust in Ps. 13
Your loving-kindness; my heart rejoices in Your salvation. I will sing
to the Lord for He has been good to me.

*On Hoshana Raba, Yom HaAtzma'ut and Yom Yerushalayim,
the following psalm is said. The custom is to say it standing.*

מִזְמוֹר A psalm of thanksgiving. Shout joyously to the Lord, all the earth. Ps. 100
Serve the Lord with joy. Come before Him with celebration. Know that the Lord is God. He made us and we are His. We are His people and the flock He tends. Enter His gates with thanksgiving, His courts with praise. Thank Him and bless His name. ▸ For the Lord is good, His loving-kindness is everlasting, and His trustworthiness is for every generation.

▸ רוֹמְמוּ יהוה אֱלֹהֵינוּ וְהִשְׁתַּחֲווּ לַהֲדֹם רַגְלָיו, קָדוֹשׁ הוּא: תהלים צט
רוֹמְמוּ יהוה אֱלֹהֵינוּ וְהִשְׁתַּחֲווּ לְהַר קָדְשׁוֹ, כִּי־קָדוֹשׁ יהוה
אֱלֹהֵינוּ:

וְהוּא רַחוּם, יְכַפֵּר עָוֹן וְלֹא־יַשְׁחִית, וְהִרְבָּה לְהָשִׁיב אַפּוֹ, תהלים עח
וְלֹא־יָעִיר כָּל־חֲמָתוֹ: אַתָּה יהוה לֹא־תִכְלָא רַחֲמֶיךָ מִמֶּנִּי, חַסְדְּךָ תהלים מ
וַאֲמִתְּךָ תָּמִיד יִצְּרוּנִי: זְכֹר־רַחֲמֶיךָ יהוה וַחֲסָדֶיךָ, כִּי מֵעוֹלָם תהלים כה
הֵמָּה: תְּנוּ עֹז לֵאלֹהִים, עַל־יִשְׂרָאֵל גַּאֲוָתוֹ, וְעֻזּוֹ בַּשְּׁחָקִים: נוֹרָא תהלים סח
אֱלֹהִים מִמִּקְדָּשֶׁיךָ, אֵל יִשְׂרָאֵל הוּא נֹתֵן עֹז וְתַעֲצֻמוֹת לָעָם, בָּרוּךְ
אֱלֹהִים: אֵל־נְקָמוֹת יהוה, אֵל נְקָמוֹת הוֹפִיעַ: הִנָּשֵׂא שֹׁפֵט הָאָרֶץ, תהלים צד
הָשֵׁב גְּמוּל עַל־גֵּאִים: לַיהוה הַיְשׁוּעָה, עַל־עַמְּךָ בִרְכָתֶךָ סֶּלָה: ▸ תהלים ג
יהוה צְבָאוֹת עִמָּנוּ, מִשְׂגָּב לָנוּ אֱלֹהֵי יַעֲקֹב סֶלָה: יהוה צְבָאוֹת, תהלים מו תהלים פד
אַשְׁרֵי אָדָם בֹּטֵחַ בָּךְ: יהוה הוֹשִׁיעָה, הַמֶּלֶךְ יַעֲנֵנוּ בְיוֹם־קָרְאֵנוּ: תהלים כ
הוֹשִׁיעָה אֶת־עַמֶּךָ, וּבָרֵךְ אֶת־נַחֲלָתֶךָ, וּרְעֵם וְנַשְּׂאֵם עַד־ תהלים כח
הָעוֹלָם: נַפְשֵׁנוּ חִכְּתָה לַיהוה, עֶזְרֵנוּ וּמָגִנֵּנוּ הוּא: כִּי־בוֹ יִשְׂמַח תהלים לג
לִבֵּנוּ, כִּי בְשֵׁם קָדְשׁוֹ בָטָחְנוּ: יְהִי־חַסְדְּךָ יהוה עָלֵינוּ, כַּאֲשֶׁר
יִחַלְנוּ לָךְ: הַרְאֵנוּ יהוה חַסְדֶּךָ, וְיֶשְׁעֲךָ תִּתֶּן־לָנוּ: קוּמָה עֶזְרָתָה תהלים פה תהלים מד
לָּנוּ, וּפְדֵנוּ לְמַעַן חַסְדֶּךָ: אָנֹכִי יהוה אֱלֹהֶיךָ הַמַּעַלְךָ מֵאֶרֶץ תהלים פא
מִצְרָיִם, הַרְחֶב־פִּיךָ וַאֲמַלְאֵהוּ: אַשְׁרֵי הָעָם שֶׁכָּכָה לּוֹ, אַשְׁרֵי תהלים קמד
הָעָם שֶׁיהוה אֱלֹהָיו: ▸ וַאֲנִי בְּחַסְדְּךָ בָטַחְתִּי, יָגֵל לִבִּי בִּישׁוּעָתֶךָ, תהלים יג
אָשִׁירָה לַיהוה, כִּי גָמַל עָלָי:

On הושענא רבה, יום העצמאות *and* יום ירושלים,
the following psalm is said. The custom is to say it standing.

מִזְמוֹר לְתוֹדָה, הָרִיעוּ לַיהוה כָּל־הָאָרֶץ: עִבְדוּ אֶת־יהוה בְּשִׂמְחָה, תהלים ק
בֹּאוּ לְפָנָיו בִּרְנָנָה: דְּעוּ כִּי־יהוה הוּא אֱלֹהִים, הוּא עָשָׂנוּ וְלוֹ אֲנַחְנוּ,
עַמּוֹ וְצֹאן מַרְעִיתוֹ: בֹּאוּ שְׁעָרָיו בְּתוֹדָה, חֲצֵרֹתָיו בִּתְהִלָּה, הוֹדוּ לוֹ,
בָּרְכוּ שְׁמוֹ: ▸ כִּי־טוֹב יהוה, לְעוֹלָם חַסְדּוֹ, וְעַד־דֹּר וָדֹר אֱמוּנָתוֹ:

לַמְנַצֵּחַ For the conductor of music. A psalm of David. The heavens declare the glory of God; the skies declare the work of His hands. Day to day they pour forth speech; night to night they communicate knowledge. There is no speech, there are no words, their voice is not heard. Yet their music carries throughout the earth, their words to the end of the world. In them He has set a tent for the sun. It emerges like a groom from his marriage chamber, rejoicing like a champion about to run a race. It rises at one end of the heaven and makes its circuit to the other: nothing is hidden from its heat. The LORD's Torah is perfect, refreshing the soul. The LORD's testimony is faithful, making the simple wise. The LORD's commands are just, making the heart happy. The LORD's commandment is radiant, giving light to the eyes. The fear of the LORD is pure, enduring for ever. The LORD's judgments are true, altogether righteous. More precious than gold, than much fine gold. They are sweeter than honey, than honey from the comb. Your servant, too, is careful of them, for in observing them there is great reward. Yet who can understand his errors? Cleanse me of hidden faults. Keep Your servant also from deliberate sins; let them not have dominion over me. Then shall I be blameless, and innocent of grave sin. ▸ May the words of my mouth and the inner thoughts of my heart find favor before You, LORD, my Rock and my Redeemer. *Ps. 19*

REFLECTION

How do you connect to God most?

Is it easier for you to connect to God through nature or Torah?

What does the phrase "deafening silence" mean?

When can silence be louder than words?

Can you hear music from the earth? Does it help you connect to God?

LEARNING

There are seven new psalms added to the morning service (in addition to 92 and 93 which are said on Friday night too). According to the Ya'avetz, one psalm is said for each day of the week just like the seven days of *Sheva Berakhot*, the seven blessings said at a wedding. The themes of these psalms include: creation, the exodus, the giving of the Torah (which happened on Shabbat), and the messianic era.

תהלים יט

לַמְנַצֵּחַ מִזְמוֹר לְדָוִד: הַשָּׁמַיִם מְסַפְּרִים כְּבוֹד־אֵל, וּמַעֲשֵׂה יָדָיו מַגִּיד הָרָקִיעַ: יוֹם לְיוֹם יַבִּיעַ אֹמֶר, וְלַיְלָה לְּלַיְלָה יְחַוֶּה־דָּעַת: אֵין־אֹמֶר וְאֵין דְּבָרִים, בְּלִי נִשְׁמָע קוֹלָם: בְּכָל־הָאָרֶץ יָצָא קַוָּם, וּבִקְצֵה תֵבֵל מִלֵּיהֶם, לַשֶּׁמֶשׁ שָׂם־אֹהֶל בָּהֶם: וְהוּא כְּחָתָן יֹצֵא מֵחֻפָּתוֹ, יָשִׂישׂ כְּגִבּוֹר לָרוּץ אֹרַח: מִקְצֵה הַשָּׁמַיִם מוֹצָאוֹ, וּתְקוּפָתוֹ עַל־קְצוֹתָם, וְאֵין נִסְתָּר מֵחַמָּתוֹ: תּוֹרַת יהוה תְּמִימָה, מְשִׁיבַת נָפֶשׁ, עֵדוּת יהוה נֶאֱמָנָה, מַחְכִּימַת פֶּתִי: פִּקּוּדֵי יהוה יְשָׁרִים, מְשַׂמְּחֵי־לֵב, מִצְוַת יהוה בָּרָה, מְאִירַת עֵינָיִם: יִרְאַת יהוה טְהוֹרָה, עוֹמֶדֶת לָעַד, מִשְׁפְּטֵי־יהוה אֱמֶת, צָדְקוּ יַחְדָּו: הַנֶּחֱמָדִים מִזָּהָב וּמִפַּז רָב, וּמְתוּקִים מִדְּבַשׁ וְנֹפֶת צוּפִים: גַּם־עַבְדְּךָ נִזְהָר בָּהֶם, בְּשָׁמְרָם עֵקֶב רָב: שְׁגִיאוֹת מִי־יָבִין, מִנִּסְתָּרוֹת נַקֵּנִי: גַּם מִזֵּדִים חֲשֹׂךְ עַבְדֶּךָ, אַל־יִמְשְׁלוּ־בִי אָז אֵיתָם, וְנִקֵּיתִי מִפֶּשַׁע רָב: ◂ יִהְיוּ לְרָצוֹן אִמְרֵי־פִי וְהֶגְיוֹן לִבִּי לְפָנֶיךָ, יהוה, צוּרִי וְגֹאֲלִי:

... A THOUSAND WORDS

לְדָוִד Of David. When he pretended to be insane before Abimelech, who drove him away, and he left. I will bless the LORD at all times; His praise will be always on my lips. My soul will glory in the LORD; let the lowly hear this and rejoice. Magnify the LORD with me; let us elevate His name together. I sought the LORD, and He answered me; He saved me from all my fears. Those who look to Him are radiant; Their faces are never downcast. This poor man called, and the LORD heard; He saved him from all his troubles. The LORD's angel encamps around those who fear Him, and He rescues them. Taste and see that the LORD is good; happy is the man who takes refuge in Him. Fear the LORD, you His holy ones, for those who fear Him lack nothing. Young lions may grow weak and hungry, but those who seek the LORD lack no good thing. Come, my children, listen to me; I will teach you the fear of the LORD. Who desires life, loving each day to see good? Then guard your tongue from evil and your lips from speaking lies. Turn from evil and do good; seek peace and pursue it. The eyes of the LORD are on the righteous and His ears listen to their cry; The LORD's face is set against those who do evil, to erase their memory from the earth. The righteous cry out, and the LORD hears them; saving them from all their troubles. The LORD is close to the brokenhearted, and saves those who are crushed in spirit. Many troubles may befall the righteous, but the LORD saves him from them all; He protects all his bones, so that none of them will be broken. Evil will slay the wicked; the enemies of the righteous will be condemned. ▸ The LORD redeems His servants; none who take refuge in Him shall be condemned. *Ps. 34*

---

close cannot accept advice, he is too close to it, but when there is distance, he is more open.

"How many times in the yeshiva did I try to talk to you. I tried shouting, I tried speaking kindly, I tried to appease you, nothing would get through; it was all like talking to a wall. But now, what an amazing thing, now that you have left the yeshiva, the words of King David are fulfilled. You are open, listening and willing to learn."

לְדָוִד, בְּשַׁנּוֹתוֹ אֶת־טַעְמוֹ לִפְנֵי אֲבִימֶלֶךְ, וַיְגָרְשֵׁהוּ וַיֵּלַךְ: אֲבָרְכָה תהלים לד
אֶת־יהוה בְּכָל־עֵת, תָּמִיד תְּהִלָּתוֹ בְּפִי: בַּיהוה תִּתְהַלֵּל נַפְשִׁי,
יִשְׁמְעוּ עֲנָוִים וְיִשְׂמָחוּ: גַּדְּלוּ לַיהוה אִתִּי, וּנְרוֹמְמָה שְׁמוֹ יַחְדָּו:
דָּרַשְׁתִּי אֶת־יהוה וְעָנָנִי, וּמִכָּל־מְגוּרוֹתַי הִצִּילָנִי: הִבִּיטוּ אֵלָיו
וְנָהָרוּ, וּפְנֵיהֶם אַל־יֶחְפָּרוּ: זֶה עָנִי קָרָא, וַיהוה שָׁמֵעַ, וּמִכָּל־צָרוֹתָיו
הוֹשִׁיעוֹ: חֹנֶה מַלְאַךְ־יהוה סָבִיב לִירֵאָיו, וַיְחַלְּצֵם: טַעֲמוּ וּרְאוּ
כִּי־טוֹב יהוה, אַשְׁרֵי הַגֶּבֶר יֶחֱסֶה־בּוֹ: יְראוּ אֶת־יהוה קְדֹשָׁיו, כִּי־
אֵין מַחְסוֹר לִירֵאָיו: כְּפִירִים רָשׁוּ וְרָעֵבוּ, וְדֹרְשֵׁי יהוה לֹא־יַחְסְרוּ
כָל־טוֹב: לְכוּ־בָנִים שִׁמְעוּ־לִי, יִרְאַת יהוה אֲלַמֶּדְכֶם: מִי־הָאִישׁ
הֶחָפֵץ חַיִּים, אֹהֵב יָמִים לִרְאוֹת טוֹב: נְצֹר לְשׁוֹנְךָ מֵרָע, וּשְׂפָתֶיךָ
מִדַּבֵּר מִרְמָה: סוּר מֵרָע וַעֲשֵׂה־טוֹב, בַּקֵּשׁ שָׁלוֹם וְרָדְפֵהוּ: עֵינֵי
יהוה אֶל־צַדִּיקִים, וְאָזְנָיו אֶל־שַׁוְעָתָם: פְּנֵי יהוה בְּעֹשֵׂי רָע,
לְהַכְרִית מֵאֶרֶץ זִכְרָם: צָעֲקוּ וַיהוה שָׁמֵעַ, וּמִכָּל־צָרוֹתָם הִצִּילָם:
קָרוֹב יהוה לְנִשְׁבְּרֵי־לֵב, וְאֶת־דַּכְּאֵי־רוּחַ יוֹשִׁיעַ: רַבּוֹת רָעוֹת
צַדִּיק, וּמִכֻּלָּם יַצִּילֶנּוּ יהוה: שֹׁמֵר כָּל־עַצְמוֹתָיו, אַחַת מֵהֵנָּה לֹא
נִשְׁבָּרָה: תְּמוֹתֵת רָשָׁע רָעָה, וְשֹׂנְאֵי צַדִּיק יֶאְשָׁמוּ: ◂ פּוֹדֶה יהוה
נֶפֶשׁ עֲבָדָיו, וְלֹא יֶאְשְׁמוּ כָּל־הַחֹסִים בּוֹ:

CONNECTION

Rav Yitzhak Hutner received a surprising letter from a former student in his yeshiva. He was surprised to receive a question or any correspondence from this particular student because in all his time in the yeshiva, Rabbi Hutner had no success in talking to him. In receiving the letter Rabbi Hutner said that he finally understood something about human interactions through the words in this psalm.

Normally, when we want to talk to someone, offer them guidance or advice, we beckon them close, "Come here I want to talk to you." In our psalm, David says, "Come my children, listen to me…"

Perhaps this is the secret, a soul that is

תְּפִלָּה לְמֹשֶׁה A prayer of Moses, the man of God. LORD, You have been our shelter in every generation. Before the mountains were born, before You brought forth the earth and the world, from everlasting to everlasting You are God. You turn men back to dust, saying, "Return, you children of men." For a thousand years in Your sight are like yesterday when it has passed, like a watch in the night. You sweep men away; they sleep. In the morning they are like grass newly grown: in the morning it flourishes and is new, but by evening it withers and dries up. For we are consumed by Your anger, terrified by Your fury. You have set our wrongdoings before You, our secret sins in the light of Your presence. All our days pass away in Your fury, we spend our years like a sigh. The span of our life is seventy years, or if we are strong, eighty years; but the best of them is trouble and sorrow, for they quickly pass, and we fly away. Who can know the force of Your anger? Your fury matches the fear due to You. Teach us rightly to number our days, that we may gain a heart of wisdom. Relent, O LORD! How much longer? Be sorry for Your servants. Satisfy us in the morning with Your loving-kindness, that we may sing and rejoice all our days. Give us joy for as many days as You have afflicted us, for as many years as we saw trouble. Let Your deeds be seen by Your servants, and Your glory by their children. ▸ May the pleasantness of the LORD our God be upon us. Establish for us the work of our hands, O establish the work of our hands. *Ps. 90*

REFLECTION

What makes a person a "man of God"?

What would you do if you only had one more year to live?

Can you take a moment on this Shabbat to consider how you use your time?

CONNECTION

Steve Jobs: Live each day as if it was your last.

When I was seventeen, I read a quote that went something like: "If you live each day as if it was your last, someday you'll most certainly be right." It made an impression on me, and since then, for the past thirty-three years, I have looked in the mirror every morning and asked myself: "If today were the last day of my life, would I want to do what I am about to do today?" And whenever the answer has been "no" for too many days in a row, I know I need to change something. (Stanford University, 2005)

תהלים צ

תְּפִלָּה לְמֹשֶׁה אִישׁ־הָאֱלֹהִים, אֲדֹנָי, מָעוֹן אַתָּה הָיִיתָ לָּנוּ בְּדֹר וָדֹר: בְּטֶרֶם הָרִים יֻלָּדוּ, וַתְּחוֹלֵל אֶרֶץ וְתֵבֵל, וּמֵעוֹלָם עַד־עוֹלָם אַתָּה אֵל: תָּשֵׁב אֱנוֹשׁ עַד־דַּכָּא, וַתֹּאמֶר שׁוּבוּ בְנֵי־אָדָם: כִּי אֶלֶף שָׁנִים בְּעֵינֶיךָ, כְּיוֹם אֶתְמוֹל כִּי יַעֲבֹר, וְאַשְׁמוּרָה בַלָּיְלָה: זְרַמְתָּם, שֵׁנָה יִהְיוּ, בַּבֹּקֶר כֶּחָצִיר יַחֲלֹף: בַּבֹּקֶר יָצִיץ וְחָלָף, לָעֶרֶב יְמוֹלֵל וְיָבֵשׁ: כִּי־כָלִינוּ בְאַפֶּךָ, וּבַחֲמָתְךָ נִבְהָלְנוּ: שַׁתָּ עֲוֹנֹתֵינוּ לְנֶגְדֶּךָ, עֲלֻמֵנוּ לִמְאוֹר פָּנֶיךָ: כִּי כָל־יָמֵינוּ פָּנוּ בְעֶבְרָתֶךָ, כִּלִּינוּ שָׁנֵינוּ כְמוֹ־הֶגֶה: יְמֵי־שְׁנוֹתֵינוּ בָהֶם שִׁבְעִים שָׁנָה, וְאִם בִּגְבוּרֹת שְׁמוֹנִים שָׁנָה, וְרָהְבָּם עָמָל וָאָוֶן, כִּי־גָז חִישׁ וַנָּעֻפָה: מִי־יוֹדֵעַ עֹז אַפֶּךָ, וּכְיִרְאָתְךָ עֶבְרָתֶךָ, לִמְנוֹת יָמֵינוּ כֵּן הוֹדַע, וְנָבִא לְבַב חָכְמָה: שׁוּבָה יהוה עַד־מָתָי, וְהִנָּחֵם עַל־עֲבָדֶיךָ: שַׂבְּעֵנוּ בַבֹּקֶר חַסְדֶּךָ, וּנְרַנְּנָה וְנִשְׂמְחָה בְּכָל־יָמֵינוּ: שַׂמְּחֵנוּ כִּימוֹת עִנִּיתָנוּ, שְׁנוֹת רָאִינוּ רָעָה: יֵרָאֶה אֶל־עֲבָדֶיךָ פָעֳלֶךָ, וַהֲדָרְךָ עַל־בְּנֵיהֶם: › וִיהִי נֹעַם אֲדֹנָי אֱלֹהֵינוּ עָלֵינוּ, וּמַעֲשֵׂה יָדֵינוּ כּוֹנְנָה עָלֵינוּ, וּמַעֲשֵׂה יָדֵינוּ כּוֹנְנֵהוּ:

LEARNING

The central theme of the *mizmor* is the passage of time, which can be visualized as a flowing river. A person standing on the shore sees the water continually flowing past like the days continually flowing through our lives. The days that have passed are no more. It is as if they have vanished, never to return. However, we are responsible for the harm that we have done in those vanished days. The memory of the past hangs over us, affecting our present and our future. The memory of the past also allows for sincere repentance; this ideal of rebirth is so strong that the Talmud (*Pesaḥim* 54a) teaches that repentance was created before creation itself.

... A THOUSAND WORDS

ישֵׁב בְּסֵתֶר He who lives in the shelter of the Most High lives in the shadow of the Almighty. I say of the LORD, my Refuge and Stronghold, my God in whom I trust, that He will save you from the hunter's trap and the deadly disease. With His outstretched limbs He will cover you, and beneath His wings you will find shelter; His truthfulness is an encircling shield. You need not fear terror by night, nor the arrow that flies by day; not the disease that stalks in darkness, nor the plague that ravages at noon. A thousand may fall at your side, ten thousand at your right hand, but it will not come near you. You will only look with your eyes and see the punishment of the wicked. Because you [have said:] "The LORD is my Refuge," taking the Most High as your shelter, no harm will befall you, no plague will come near your tent, for He will command His angels about you, to guard you in all your ways. They will lift you in their hands, lest your foot stumble on a stone. You will tread on lions and vipers, you will trample on young lions and snakes. [God says] "Because he loves Me, I will rescue him; I will protect him, because he acknowledges My name. When he calls on Me, I will answer him, I will be with him in distress, I will save him and bring him honor. ▸ With long life I will satisfy him, and show him My salvation. *Ps. 91*

With long life I will satisfy him, and show him My salvation."

LEARNING

The Talmud (*Shevuot* 15b) names this psalm "*shir shel pega'im*" – "a song against mishaps." This psalm is often said in times of danger. When Moshe went to heaven to receive the *luḥot* he was afraid of the heavenly angels who were less than happy with his presence in their domain. For this reason, it is recorded, he recited this psalm. (*Midrash Tanḥuma Naso* 23)

REFLECTION

Have you ever felt the presence of God and felt protected by it?

What can you do to feel the presence and protection of God more often?

What do you want to ask God to protect you from?

Has there ever been a time when you felt that God could help you?

תהלים צא

יֹשֵׁב בְּסֵתֶר עֶלְיוֹן, בְּצֵל שַׁדַּי יִתְלוֹנָן: אֹמַר לַיהוה מַחְסִי
וּמְצוּדָתִי, אֱלֹהַי אֶבְטַח־בּוֹ: כִּי הוּא יַצִּילְךָ מִפַּח יָקוּשׁ, מִדֶּבֶר
הַוּוֹת: בְּאֶבְרָתוֹ יָסֶךְ לָךְ, וְתַחַת־כְּנָפָיו תֶּחְסֶה, צִנָּה וְסֹחֵרָה
אֲמִתּוֹ: לֹא־תִירָא מִפַּחַד לָיְלָה, מֵחֵץ יָעוּף יוֹמָם: מִדֶּבֶר בָּאֹפֶל
יַהֲלֹךְ, מִקֶּטֶב יָשׁוּד צָהֳרָיִם: יִפֹּל מִצִּדְּךָ אֶלֶף, וּרְבָבָה מִימִינֶךָ,
אֵלֶיךָ לֹא יִגָּשׁ: רַק בְּעֵינֶיךָ תַבִּיט, וְשִׁלֻּמַת רְשָׁעִים תִּרְאֶה:
כִּי־אַתָּה יהוה מַחְסִי, עֶלְיוֹן שַׂמְתָּ מְעוֹנֶךָ: לֹא־תְאֻנֶּה אֵלֶיךָ
רָעָה, וְנֶגַע לֹא־יִקְרַב בְּאָהֳלֶךָ: כִּי מַלְאָכָיו יְצַוֶּה־לָּךְ, לִשְׁמָרְךָ
בְּכָל־דְּרָכֶיךָ: עַל־כַּפַּיִם יִשָּׂאוּנְךָ, פֶּן־תִּגֹּף בָּאֶבֶן רַגְלֶךָ: עַל־
שַׁחַל וָפֶתֶן תִּדְרֹךְ, תִּרְמֹס כְּפִיר וְתַנִּין: כִּי בִי חָשַׁק וַאֲפַלְּטֵהוּ,
אֲשַׂגְּבֵהוּ כִּי־יָדַע שְׁמִי: יִקְרָאֵנִי וְאֶעֱנֵהוּ, עִמּוֹ אָנֹכִי בְצָרָה,
אֲחַלְּצֵהוּ וַאֲכַבְּדֵהוּ: ‹ אֹרֶךְ יָמִים אַשְׂבִּיעֵהוּ, וְאַרְאֵהוּ בִּישׁוּעָתִי:
אֹרֶךְ יָמִים אַשְׂבִּיעֵהוּ, וְאַרְאֵהוּ בִּישׁוּעָתִי:

CONNECTION

A man once went to the great Maggid of Mezeritch with a question that deeply troubled him. He could not fathom how one could follow the Talmudic counsel that "One should bless God for the bad just as one blesses Him for the good" (Mishna Berakhot 9:5). *Is it possible to be thankful for one's troubles and misery?*

The Maggid replied that he should go seek out his disciple, Reb Zusha of Hanipol, and ask him this question.

The man followed the Maggid's advice and traveled to Rabbi Zusha. The tzaddik received him warmly and invited him into his home. As soon as the guest entered the house, it became obvious that the family was extremely poor. The furnishings were simple and bare, there was little food to eat, and the family members were beset with various afflictions and illnesses. Nevertheless Rabbi Zusha was happy and cheerful. The guest was astonished.

The man posed his question. "I asked the Maggid how is it possible to bless God for the bad just as one blesses Him for the good, and the Maggid told me that only you can help me in this matter."

Reb Zusha replied, "This is indeed a very difficult question. But why did our holy master send you to me? How would I know? He should have sent you to someone who has experienced suffering!"

הַלְלוּיָהּ Halleluya! Praise the name of the Lord. Praise Him, you servants of the Lord who stand in the Lord's House, in the courtyards of the House of our God. Praise the Lord, for the Lord is good; sing praises to His name, for it is lovely. For the Lord has chosen Jacob as His own, Israel as his treasure. For I know that the Lord is great, that our Lord is above all heavenly powers. Whatever pleases the Lord, He does, in heaven and on earth, in the seas and all the depths. He raises clouds from the ends of the earth; He sends lightning with the rain; He brings out the wind from His storehouses. He struck down the firstborn of Egypt, of both man and animals. He sent signs and wonders into your midst, Egypt – against Pharaoh and all his servants. He struck down many nations and slew mighty kings: Siḥon, King of the Amorites, Og, King of Bashan, and all the kingdoms of Canaan, giving their land as a heritage, a heritage for His people Israel. Your name, Lord, endures for ever; Your fame, Lord, for all generations. For the Lord will bring justice to His people, and have compassion on His servants. The idols of the nations are silver and gold, the work of human hands. They have mouths, but cannot speak; eyes, but cannot see; ears, but cannot hear; there is no breath in their mouths. Those who make them will become like them: so will all who trust in them. ▸ House of Israel, bless the Lord. House of Aaron, bless the Lord. House of Levi, bless the Lord. You who fear the Lord, bless the Lord. Blessed is the Lord from Zion, He who is present in Jerusalem. Halleluya! *Ps. 135*

CONNECTION

וַאֲפִלּוּ בְּהַסְתָּרָה שֶׁבְּתוֹךְ הַהַסְתָּרָה
בְּוַדַּאי גַּם שָׁם נִמְצָא הַשֵּׁם יִתְבָּרַךְ

(Rebbe Nahman of Breslov)

Eliezer Rosenfeld, father of 26-year-old Malachi Rosenfeld who was fatally wounded in a terror attack in the summer of 2015, delivered a heart-rending farewell to his son at the funeral.

During the eulogy, the grieving father – supported by two of his remaining seven children – sang a song of faith. "Even in the most concealed of concealed moments," sang the bereaved father, "certainly God, blessed be He, is also found there."

Amid sobs from other mourners, he urged his tearful audience to sing with him as he reached the words, "Even behind the most difficult things that happen to you, He (still) stands, He stands – and we will stand, we will stand with God."

תהלים קלה

הַלְלוּיָהּ, הַלְלוּ אֶת־שֵׁם יהוה, הַלְלוּ עַבְדֵי יהוה: שֶׁעֹמְדִים בְּבֵית יהוה, בְּחַצְרוֹת בֵּית אֱלֹהֵינוּ: הַלְלוּיָהּ כִּי־טוֹב יהוה, זַמְּרוּ לִשְׁמוֹ כִּי נָעִים: כִּי־יַעֲקֹב בָּחַר לוֹ יָהּ, יִשְׂרָאֵל לִסְגֻלָּתוֹ: כִּי אֲנִי יָדַעְתִּי כִּי־גָדוֹל יהוה, וַאֲדֹנֵינוּ מִכָּל־אֱלֹהִים: כָּל אֲשֶׁר־חָפֵץ יהוה עָשָׂה, בַּשָּׁמַיִם וּבָאָרֶץ, בַּיַּמִּים וְכָל־תְּהֹמוֹת: מַעֲלֶה נְשִׂאִים מִקְצֵה הָאָרֶץ, בְּרָקִים לַמָּטָר עָשָׂה, מוֹצֵא־רוּחַ מֵאוֹצְרוֹתָיו: שֶׁהִכָּה בְּכוֹרֵי מִצְרָיִם, מֵאָדָם עַד־בְּהֵמָה: שָׁלַח אוֹתֹת וּמֹפְתִים בְּתוֹכֵכִי מִצְרָיִם, בְּפַרְעֹה וּבְכָל־עֲבָדָיו: שֶׁהִכָּה גּוֹיִם רַבִּים, וְהָרַג מְלָכִים עֲצוּמִים: לְסִיחוֹן מֶלֶךְ הָאֱמֹרִי, וּלְעוֹג מֶלֶךְ הַבָּשָׁן, וּלְכֹל מַמְלְכוֹת כְּנָעַן: וְנָתַן אַרְצָם נַחֲלָה, נַחֲלָה לְיִשְׂרָאֵל עַמּוֹ: יהוה שִׁמְךָ לְעוֹלָם, יהוה זִכְרְךָ לְדֹר־וָדֹר: כִּי־יָדִין יהוה עַמּוֹ, וְעַל־עֲבָדָיו יִתְנֶחָם: עֲצַבֵּי הַגּוֹיִם כֶּסֶף וְזָהָב, מַעֲשֵׂה יְדֵי אָדָם: פֶּה־לָהֶם וְלֹא יְדַבֵּרוּ, עֵינַיִם לָהֶם וְלֹא יִרְאוּ: אָזְנַיִם לָהֶם וְלֹא יַאֲזִינוּ, אַף אֵין־יֶשׁ־רוּחַ בְּפִיהֶם: כְּמוֹהֶם יִהְיוּ עֹשֵׂיהֶם, כֹּל אֲשֶׁר־בֹּטֵחַ בָּהֶם: ‹ בֵּית יִשְׂרָאֵל בָּרְכוּ אֶת־יהוה, בֵּית אַהֲרֹן בָּרְכוּ אֶת־יהוה: בֵּית הַלֵּוִי בָּרְכוּ אֶת־יהוה, יִרְאֵי יהוה בָּרְכוּ אֶת־יהוה: בָּרוּךְ יהוה מִצִּיּוֹן, שֹׁכֵן יְרוּשָׁלָםִ, הַלְלוּיָהּ:

REFLECTION

Look at all the miraculous deeds recorded in this psalm.
Have you ever seen something miraculous?

Take a moment to reflect on the daily miracles you have in your life.
Where do you see God in your life?

How can you find God when He seems hidden to you?

... A THOUSAND WORDS

The custom is to stand for the following psalm.

הודו Thank the LORD for He is good; His loving-kindness is for ever. *Ps. 136*
Thank the God of gods, His loving-kindness is for ever.
Thank the LORD of lords, His loving-kindness is for ever.
To the One who alone
works great wonders, His loving-kindness is for ever.
Who made the heavens with wisdom, His loving-kindness is for ever.
Who spread the earth upon the waters, His loving-kindness is for ever.
Who made the great lights, His loving-kindness is for ever.
The sun to rule by day, His loving-kindness is for ever.
The moon and the stars to rule by night; His loving-kindness is for ever.
Who struck Egypt
through their firstborn, His loving-kindness is for ever.
And brought out Israel from their midst, His loving-kindness is for ever.
With a strong hand
and outstretched arm, His loving-kindness is for ever.

LEARNING

The Gemara (*Pesaḥim* 118a) calls this psalm Hallel HaGadol because it portrays God as enthroned in the heights of the universe giving sustenance to every living thing. It contains twenty-six stanzas which represent the generations between creation and the giving of the Torah, two of the themes of Shabbat. Until the giving of the Torah the world needed to exist on the kindness and mercy of God; after the Torah was given, the world exists on the merit of those who keep the Torah. Maharal explains that we talk about each of the kindnesses in detail, so that we are able to reflect upon and appreciate each act of kindness individually. (*Netivot Olam, Netiv HaAvoda* 18)

CONNECTION

"Mr. Speaker, allow me just one further point. This House should know, it is not necessary to be an observant Jew to appreciate the full historic and sacred aura that enshrines the 'perfect gift' called Shabbat. Its prohibitions are not arbitrary. They provide insulation against corrosive everydayness, they build fences against invasions by the profane, and they enrich the soul by creating a space for sacred time. In a word, one need not be pious to accept the cherished principle of Shabbat. One merely needs to be a proud Jew." (Prime Minister Menachem Begin speaking to the Knesset)

The custom is to stand for the following psalm.

הוֹדוּ לַיהוה כִּי־טוֹב כִּי לְעוֹלָם חַסְדּוֹ: תהלים קלו
הוֹדוּ לֵאלֹהֵי הָאֱלֹהִים כִּי לְעוֹלָם חַסְדּוֹ:
הוֹדוּ לַאֲדֹנֵי הָאֲדֹנִים כִּי לְעוֹלָם חַסְדּוֹ:
לְעֹשֵׂה נִפְלָאוֹת גְּדֹלוֹת לְבַדּוֹ כִּי לְעוֹלָם חַסְדּוֹ:
לְעֹשֵׂה הַשָּׁמַיִם בִּתְבוּנָה כִּי לְעוֹלָם חַסְדּוֹ:
לְרֹקַע הָאָרֶץ עַל־הַמָּיִם כִּי לְעוֹלָם חַסְדּוֹ:
לְעֹשֵׂה אוֹרִים גְּדֹלִים כִּי לְעוֹלָם חַסְדּוֹ:
אֶת־הַשֶּׁמֶשׁ לְמֶמְשֶׁלֶת בַּיּוֹם כִּי לְעוֹלָם חַסְדּוֹ:
אֶת־הַיָּרֵחַ וְכוֹכָבִים לְמֶמְשְׁלוֹת בַּלָּיְלָה כִּי לְעוֹלָם חַסְדּוֹ:
לְמַכֵּה מִצְרַיִם בִּבְכוֹרֵיהֶם כִּי לְעוֹלָם חַסְדּוֹ:
וַיּוֹצֵא יִשְׂרָאֵל מִתּוֹכָם כִּי לְעוֹלָם חַסְדּוֹ:
בְּיָד חֲזָקָה וּבִזְרוֹעַ נְטוּיָה כִּי לְעוֹלָם חַסְדּוֹ:

CONNECTION

Every one of us has been granted special moments; they are what one may call "windows of joy." When we are blessed with such moments we realize that words are futile in describing what our hearts feel.

In this chapter we see many of these "windows of joy" described. This particular chapter is indeed called "Hallel HaGadol," *"the Great Prayer of Praise," because it touches on so many of Hashem's mercies to His nation. These mercies are not always written in large letters; rather they are sometimes lived in the small print that makes up the tapestry that is our lives.* (Rabbi Yitzchak Rubin)

REFLECTION

Think about the details of your life. What small individual detail are you thankful for?

How have you seen God's kindness in your life?

How do you display small acts of kindness?

Who split the Reed Sea into parts,	His loving-kindness is for ever.
And made Israel pass through it,	His loving-kindness is for ever.
Casting Pharaoh and his army into the Reed Sea;	His loving-kindness is for ever.
Who led His people through the wilderness;	His loving-kindness is for ever.
Who struck down great kings,	His loving-kindness is for ever.
And slew mighty kings,	His loving-kindness is for ever.
Siḥon, King of the Amorites,	His loving-kindness is for ever.
And Og, King of Bashan,	His loving-kindness is for ever.
And gave their land as a heritage,	His loving-kindness is for ever.
A heritage for His servant Israel;	His loving-kindness is for ever.
Who remembered us in our lowly state,	His loving-kindness is for ever.
And rescued us from our tormentors,	His loving-kindness is for ever.
▸ Who gives food to all flesh,	His loving-kindness is for ever.
Give thanks to the God of heaven.	His loving-kindness is for ever.

... A THOUSAND WORDS

לְגֹזֵר יַם־סוּף לִגְזָרִים	כִּי לְעוֹלָם חַסְדּוֹ:
וְהֶעֱבִיר יִשְׂרָאֵל בְּתוֹכוֹ	כִּי לְעוֹלָם חַסְדּוֹ:
וְנִעֵר פַּרְעֹה וְחֵילוֹ בְיַם־סוּף	כִּי לְעוֹלָם חַסְדּוֹ:
לְמוֹלִיךְ עַמּוֹ בַּמִּדְבָּר	כִּי לְעוֹלָם חַסְדּוֹ:
לְמַכֵּה מְלָכִים גְּדֹלִים	כִּי לְעוֹלָם חַסְדּוֹ:
וַיַּהֲרֹג מְלָכִים אַדִּירִים	כִּי לְעוֹלָם חַסְדּוֹ:
לְסִיחוֹן מֶלֶךְ הָאֱמֹרִי	כִּי לְעוֹלָם חַסְדּוֹ:
וּלְעוֹג מֶלֶךְ הַבָּשָׁן	כִּי לְעוֹלָם חַסְדּוֹ:
וְנָתַן אַרְצָם לְנַחֲלָה	כִּי לְעוֹלָם חַסְדּוֹ:
נַחֲלָה לְיִשְׂרָאֵל עַבְדּוֹ	כִּי לְעוֹלָם חַסְדּוֹ:
שֶׁבְּשִׁפְלֵנוּ זָכַר לָנוּ	כִּי לְעוֹלָם חַסְדּוֹ:
וַיִּפְרְקֵנוּ מִצָּרֵינוּ	כִּי לְעוֹלָם חַסְדּוֹ:
◂ נֹתֵן לֶחֶם לְכָל־בָּשָׂר	כִּי לְעוֹלָם חַסְדּוֹ:
הוֹדוּ לְאֵל הַשָּׁמָיִם	כִּי לְעוֹלָם חַסְדּוֹ:

REFLECTION

"If we search
for revelation in history,
we will find it,
more compellingly
than anywhere else,
in the history
of that unusual people,
our ancestors."
(Rabbi Jonathan Sacks,
A Letter in the Scroll)

When do you find
Jewish history inspiring?

Does Jewish history
help or hinder
your faith in God?

Today, this Shabbat,
can you see God
in the history we are living
in our lifetime?

רַנְּנוּ Sing joyfully to the LORD, you righteous, for praise from the upright is pleasing. Give thanks to the LORD with the harp; make music to Him on the ten-stringed lute. Sing Him a new song, play skillfully with shouts of joy. For the LORD's word is right, and all His deeds are done in faith. He loves righteousness and justice; the earth is full of the LORD's loving-kindness. By the LORD's word the heavens were made, and all their starry multitudes by the breath of His mouth. He gathers the sea waters as a heap, and places the deep in storehouses. Let all the earth fear the LORD, and all the world's inhabitants stand in awe of Him. For He spoke, and it was; He commanded, and it stood firm. The LORD foils the plans of nations; He defeats the intentions of peoples. The LORD's plans stand for ever, His heart's intents for all generations. Happy is the nation whose God is the LORD, the people He has chosen as His own. From heaven the LORD looks down and sees all mankind; from His dwelling place He oversees all who live on earth. He forms the hearts of all, and understands all their deeds. No king is saved by the size of his army; no warrior is saved by great strength. A horse is a vain hope for deliverance; despite its great strength, it cannot save. The eye of the LORD is on those who fear Him, on those who place their hope in His unfailing love, to rescue their soul from death, and keep them alive in famine. Our soul waits for the LORD; He is our Help and Shield. ▸ In Him our hearts rejoice, for we trust in His holy name. May Your loving-kindness be upon us, LORD, as we have put our hope in You. Ps. 33

REFLECTION

What brings you joy?

How can you spread joy?

Does music bring you joy? How?

How does doing the right and just thing make you feel?

...A THOUSAND WORDS

תהלים לג

רַנְּנוּ צַדִּיקִים בַּיהוה, לַיְשָׁרִים נָאוָה תְהִלָּה: הוֹדוּ לַיהוה בְּכִנּוֹר, בְּנֵבֶל עָשׂוֹר זַמְּרוּ־לוֹ: שִׁירוּ־לוֹ שִׁיר חָדָשׁ, הֵיטִיבוּ נַגֵּן בִּתְרוּעָה: כִּי־יָשָׁר דְּבַר־יהוה, וְכָל־מַעֲשֵׂהוּ בֶּאֱמוּנָה: אֹהֵב צְדָקָה וּמִשְׁפָּט, חֶסֶד יהוה מָלְאָה הָאָרֶץ: בִּדְבַר יהוה שָׁמַיִם נַעֲשׂוּ, וּבְרוּחַ פִּיו כָּל־צְבָאָם: כֹּנֵס כַּנֵּד מֵי הַיָּם, נֹתֵן בְּאוֹצָרוֹת תְּהוֹמוֹת: יִירְאוּ מֵיהוה כָּל־הָאָרֶץ, מִמֶּנּוּ יָגוּרוּ כָּל־יֹשְׁבֵי תֵבֵל: כִּי הוּא אָמַר וַיֶּהִי, הוּא־צִוָּה וַיַּעֲמֹד: יהוה הֵפִיר עֲצַת־גּוֹיִם, הֵנִיא מַחְשְׁבוֹת עַמִּים: עֲצַת יהוה לְעוֹלָם תַּעֲמֹד, מַחְשְׁבוֹת לִבּוֹ לְדֹר וָדֹר: אַשְׁרֵי הַגּוֹי אֲשֶׁר־יהוה אֱלֹהָיו, הָעָם בָּחַר לְנַחֲלָה לוֹ: מִשָּׁמַיִם הִבִּיט יהוה, רָאָה אֶת־כָּל־בְּנֵי הָאָדָם: מִמְּכוֹן־שִׁבְתּוֹ הִשְׁגִּיחַ, אֶל כָּל־יֹשְׁבֵי הָאָרֶץ: הַיֹּצֵר יַחַד לִבָּם, הַמֵּבִין אֶל־כָּל־מַעֲשֵׂיהֶם: אֵין־הַמֶּלֶךְ נוֹשָׁע בְּרָב־חָיִל, גִּבּוֹר לֹא־יִנָּצֵל בְּרָב־כֹּחַ: שֶׁקֶר הַסּוּס לִתְשׁוּעָה, וּבְרֹב חֵילוֹ לֹא יְמַלֵּט: הִנֵּה עֵין יהוה אֶל־יְרֵאָיו, לַמְיַחֲלִים לְחַסְדּוֹ: לְהַצִּיל מִמָּוֶת נַפְשָׁם, וּלְחַיּוֹתָם בָּרָעָב: נַפְשֵׁנוּ חִכְּתָה לַיהוה, עֶזְרֵנוּ וּמָגִנֵּנוּ הוּא: ◂ כִּי־בוֹ יִשְׂמַח לִבֵּנוּ, כִּי בְשֵׁם קָדְשׁוֹ בָטָחְנוּ: יְהִי־חַסְדְּךָ יהוה עָלֵינוּ, כַּאֲשֶׁר יִחַלְנוּ לָךְ:

LEARNING

This *mizmor* is a joyful song of praise to Hashem, designed to be performed by the righteous people who have experienced the joy of doing *teshuva* and being forgiven for their sins. Thus, the *mizmor* begins with the lead singer calling upon his listeners to praise Hashem with inspired singing accompanied by instrumental music.

Rav Kook explained that this line actually describes two different states of relating to God. There is a state of *bitaḥon*, trusting in God and that everything is in His hands and all that He does is ultimately for the best. There is a higher state of relating to God: "In Him our heart will rejoice" – when one experiences pure, elevated *simḥa* (joy) in everything God bestows upon him.

מִזְמוֹר שִׁיר A psalm. A song for the Sabbath day. It is good to thank *Ps. 92*
the Lord and sing psalms to Your name, Most High – to tell of Your loving-kindness in the morning and Your trustworthiness at night, to the music of the ten-stringed lyre and the melody of the harp. For You have made me rejoice by Your work, O Lord; I sing for joy at the deeds of Your hands. How great are Your deeds, Lord, and how very deep Your thoughts. A boor cannot know, nor can a fool understand, that though the wicked spring up like grass and all evildoers flourish, it is only that they may be destroyed for ever. But You, Lord, are eternally great. For behold Your enemies, Lord, behold Your enemies will perish; all evildoers will be scattered. You have raised my pride like that of a wild ox; I am anointed with fresh oil. My eyes shall look in triumph on my enemies, my ears shall hear the downfall of the wicked who rise against me. ▸ The righteous will flourish like a palm tree and grow tall like a cedar in Lebanon. Planted in the Lord's House, blossoming in our God's courtyards, they will still bear fruit in old age, and stay vigorous and fresh, declaring that the Lord is upright: He is my Rock, in whom there is no wrong.

יהוה מָלָךְ The Lord reigns. He is robed in majesty. The Lord is *Ps. 93*
robed, clothed with strength. The world is firmly established; it cannot be moved. Your throne stands firm as of old; You are eternal. Rivers lift up, Lord, rivers lift up their voice, rivers lift up their Crashing waves. ▸ Mightier than the noise of many waters, than the mighty waves of the sea is the Lord on high. Your testimonies are very sure; holiness adorns Your House, Lord, for evermore.

יְהִי כְבוֹד May the Lord's glory be for ever; may the Lord rejoice *Ps. 104*
in His works. May the Lord's name be blessed, now and for ever. *Ps. 113*
From the rising of the sun to its setting, may the Lord's name be
praised. The Lord is high above all nations; His glory is above the
heavens. Lord, Your name is for ever. Your fame, Lord, is for all *Ps. 135*
generations. The Lord has established His throne in heaven; His *Ps. 103*
kingdom rules all. Let the heavens rejoice and the earth be glad. Let *1 Chr. 16*
them say among the nations, "The Lord is King." The Lord is King,

מִזְמוֹר שִׁיר לְיוֹם הַשַּׁבָּת: טוֹב לְהֹדוֹת לַיהוה, וּלְזַמֵּר לְשִׁמְךָ תהלים צב
עֶלְיוֹן: לְהַגִּיד בַּבֹּקֶר חַסְדֶּךָ, וֶאֱמוּנָתְךָ בַּלֵּילוֹת: עֲלֵי־עָשׂוֹר
וַעֲלֵי־נָבֶל, עֲלֵי הִגָּיוֹן בְּכִנּוֹר: כִּי שִׂמַּחְתַּנִי יהוה בְּפָעֳלֶךָ, בְּמַעֲשֵׂי
יָדֶיךָ אֲרַנֵּן: מַה־גָּדְלוּ מַעֲשֶׂיךָ יהוה, מְאֹד עָמְקוּ מַחְשְׁבֹתֶיךָ:
אִישׁ־בַּעַר לֹא יֵדָע, וּכְסִיל לֹא־יָבִין אֶת־זֹאת: בִּפְרֹחַ רְשָׁעִים
כְּמוֹ עֵשֶׂב, וַיָּצִיצוּ כָּל־פֹּעֲלֵי אָוֶן, לְהִשָּׁמְדָם עֲדֵי־עַד: וְאַתָּה
מָרוֹם לְעֹלָם יהוה: כִּי הִנֵּה אֹיְבֶיךָ יהוה, כִּי־הִנֵּה אֹיְבֶיךָ יֹאבֵדוּ,
יִתְפָּרְדוּ כָּל־פֹּעֲלֵי אָוֶן: וַתָּרֶם כִּרְאֵים קַרְנִי, בַּלֹּתִי בְּשֶׁמֶן רַעֲנָן:
וַתַּבֵּט עֵינִי בְּשׁוּרָי, בַּקָּמִים עָלַי מְרֵעִים תִּשְׁמַעְנָה אָזְנָי: ◂ צַדִּיק
כַּתָּמָר יִפְרָח, כְּאֶרֶז בַּלְּבָנוֹן יִשְׂגֶּה: שְׁתוּלִים בְּבֵית יהוה, בְּחַצְרוֹת
אֱלֹהֵינוּ יַפְרִיחוּ: עוֹד יְנוּבוּן בְּשֵׂיבָה, דְּשֵׁנִים וְרַעֲנַנִּים יִהְיוּ: לְהַגִּיד
כִּי־יָשָׁר יהוה, צוּרִי, וְלֹא־עַוְלָתָה בּוֹ:

יהוה מָלָךְ, גֵּאוּת לָבֵשׁ, לָבֵשׁ יהוה עֹז הִתְאַזָּר, אַף־תִּכּוֹן תֵּבֵל תהלים צג
בַּל־תִּמּוֹט: נָכוֹן כִּסְאֲךָ מֵאָז, מֵעוֹלָם אָתָּה: נָשְׂאוּ נְהָרוֹת יהוה,
נָשְׂאוּ נְהָרוֹת קוֹלָם, יִשְׂאוּ נְהָרוֹת דָּכְיָם: ◂ מִקֹּלוֹת מַיִם רַבִּים,
אַדִּירִים מִשְׁבְּרֵי־יָם, אַדִּיר בַּמָּרוֹם יהוה: עֵדֹתֶיךָ נֶאֶמְנוּ מְאֹד
לְבֵיתְךָ נַאֲוָה־קֹדֶשׁ, יהוה לְאֹרֶךְ יָמִים:

יְהִי כְבוֹד יהוה לְעוֹלָם, יִשְׂמַח יהוה בְּמַעֲשָׂיו: יְהִי שֵׁם יהוה תהלים קד / תהלים קיג
מְבֹרָךְ, מֵעַתָּה וְעַד־עוֹלָם: מִמִּזְרַח־שֶׁמֶשׁ עַד־מְבוֹאוֹ, מְהֻלָּל
שֵׁם יהוה: רָם עַל־כָּל־גּוֹיִם יהוה, עַל הַשָּׁמַיִם כְּבוֹדוֹ: יהוה תהלים קלה
שִׁמְךָ לְעוֹלָם, יהוה זִכְרְךָ לְדֹר־וָדֹר: יהוה בַּשָּׁמַיִם הֵכִין כִּסְאוֹ, תהלים קג
וּמַלְכוּתוֹ בַּכֹּל מָשָׁלָה: יִשְׂמְחוּ הַשָּׁמַיִם וְתָגֵל הָאָרֶץ, וְיֹאמְרוּ דברי הימים א׳ טז
בַגּוֹיִם יהוה מָלָךְ: יהוה מֶלֶךְ, יהוה מָלָךְ, יהוה יִמְלֹךְ לְעֹלָם וָעֶד.

the Lord was King, the Lord will be King for ever and all time.
The Lord is King for ever and all time; nations will perish from Ps. 10
His land. The Lord foils the plans of nations; He frustrates the Ps. 33
intentions of peoples. Many are the intentions in a person's mind, Prov. 19
but the Lord's plan prevails. The Lord's plan shall stand for ever, Ps. 33
His mind's intent for all generations. For He spoke and it was; He
commanded and it stood firm. For the Lord has chosen Zion; He Ps. 132
desired it for His dwelling. For the Lord has chosen Jacob, Israel Ps. 135
as His special treasure. For the Lord will not abandon His people; Ps. 94
nor will He abandon His heritage. ▸ He is compassionate. He for- Ps. 78
gives wrongdoing and does not destroy. Repeatedly He suppresses
His anger, not not rousing His full fury. Lord, save! May the King Ps. 20
answer us on the day we call.

The line beginning with "You open Your hand" should be said with special concentration, representing as it does the key idea of this psalm, and of Pesukei DeZimra as a whole, that God is the creator and sustainer of all.

אַשְׁרֵי Happy are those who live in Your House; Ps. 84
they shall continue to praise You, Selah!
Happy are the people for whom this is so; Ps. 144
happy are the people whose God is the Lord.
A song of praise by David. Ps. 145

א I will elevate You, my God, the King, and bless Your name for ever and all time. ב Every day I will bless You, and praise Your name for ever and all time. ג Great is the Lord and greatly to be praised; His greatness is unfathomable. ד One generation will praise Your works to the next, and tell of Your mighty deeds. ה On the glorious splendor of Your majesty I will meditate, and on the acts of Your wonders. ו They shall talk of the power of Your awesome deeds, and I will tell of Your greatness. ז They shall recite the record of Your great goodness, and sing with joy of Your righteousness. ח The Lord is generous and compassionate, slow to anger and great in loving-kindness. ט The Lord is good to all, and His compassion extends to all His works. י All Your works

יהוה מֶלֶךְ עוֹלָם וָעֶד, אָבְדוּ גוֹיִם מֵאַרְצוֹ: יהוה הֵפִיר עֲצַת־גּוֹיִם, תהלים י תהלים לג
הֵנִיא מַחְשְׁבוֹת עַמִּים: רַבּוֹת מַחֲשָׁבוֹת בְּלֶב־אִישׁ, וַעֲצַת יהוה משלי יט
הִיא תָקוּם: עֲצַת יהוה לְעוֹלָם תַּעֲמֹד, מַחְשְׁבוֹת לִבּוֹ לְדֹר וָדֹר: תהלים לג
כִּי הוּא אָמַר וַיֶּהִי, הוּא־צִוָּה וַיַּעֲמֹד: כִּי־בָחַר יהוה בְּצִיּוֹן, אִוָּהּ תהלים קלב
לְמוֹשָׁב לוֹ: כִּי־יַעֲקֹב בָּחַר לוֹ יָהּ, יִשְׂרָאֵל לִסְגֻלָּתוֹ: כִּי לֹא־יִטֹּשׁ תהלים קלה תהלים צד
יהוה עַמּוֹ, וְנַחֲלָתוֹ לֹא יַעֲזֹב: ◂ וְהוּא רַחוּם, יְכַפֵּר עָוֹן וְלֹא־יַשְׁחִית, תהלים עח
וְהִרְבָּה לְהָשִׁיב אַפּוֹ, וְלֹא־יָעִיר כָּל־חֲמָתוֹ: יהוה הוֹשִׁיעָה, הַמֶּלֶךְ תהלים כ
יַעֲנֵנוּ בְיוֹם־קָרְאֵנוּ:

The line beginning with פּוֹתֵחַ אֶת יָדֶךָ *should be said with special concentration, representing as it does the key idea of this psalm, and of* פסוקי דזמרה *as a whole, that God is the creator and sustainer of all.*

אַשְׁרֵי יוֹשְׁבֵי בֵיתֶךָ, עוֹד יְהַלְלוּךָ סֶּלָה: תהלים פד
אַשְׁרֵי הָעָם שֶׁכָּכָה לּוֹ, אַשְׁרֵי הָעָם שֶׁיהוה אֱלֹהָיו: תהלים קמד
תְּהִלָּה לְדָוִד תהלים קמה
אֲרוֹמִמְךָ אֱלוֹהַי הַמֶּלֶךְ, וַאֲבָרְכָה שִׁמְךָ לְעוֹלָם וָעֶד:
בְּכָל־יוֹם אֲבָרְכֶךָּ, וַאֲהַלְלָה שִׁמְךָ לְעוֹלָם וָעֶד:
גָּדוֹל יהוה וּמְהֻלָּל מְאֹד, וְלִגְדֻלָּתוֹ אֵין חֵקֶר:
דּוֹר לְדוֹר יְשַׁבַּח מַעֲשֶׂיךָ, וּגְבוּרֹתֶיךָ יַגִּידוּ:
הֲדַר כְּבוֹד הוֹדֶךָ, וְדִבְרֵי נִפְלְאֹתֶיךָ אָשִׂיחָה:
וֶעֱזוּז נוֹרְאֹתֶיךָ יֹאמֵרוּ, וּגְדוּלָּתְךָ אֲסַפְּרֶנָּה:
זֵכֶר רַב־טוּבְךָ יַבִּיעוּ, וְצִדְקָתְךָ יְרַנֵּנוּ:
חַנּוּן וְרַחוּם יהוה, אֶרֶךְ אַפַּיִם וּגְדָל־חָסֶד:
טוֹב־יהוה לַכֹּל, וְרַחֲמָיו עַל־כָּל־מַעֲשָׂיו:
יוֹדוּךָ יהוה כָּל־מַעֲשֶׂיךָ, וַחֲסִידֶיךָ יְבָרְכוּכָה:

shall thank You, Lord, and Your devoted ones shall bless You. כ They shall talk of the glory of Your kingship, and speak of Your might. ל To make known to mankind His mighty deeds and the glorious majesty of His kingship. מ Your kingdom is an everlasting kingdom, and Your reign is for all generations. ס The Lord supports all who fall, and raises all who are bowed down. ע All raise their eyes to You in hope, and You give them their food in due season. פ You open Your hand, and satisfy every living thing with favor. צ The Lord is righteous in all His ways, and kind in all He does. ק The Lord is close to all who call on Him, to all who call on Him in truth. ר He fulfills the will of those who fear Him; He hears their cry and saves them. ש The Lord guards all who love Him, but all the wicked He will destroy. ת ▸ My mouth shall speak the praise of the Lord, and all creatures shall bless His holy name for ever and all time.

We will bless the Lord now and for ever. Halleluya! *Ps. 115*

הַלְלוּיָהּ Halleluya! Praise the Lord, my soul. I will praise the Lord all my life; I will sing to my God as long as I live. Put not your trust in princes, or in mortal man who cannot save. His breath expires, he returns to the earth; on that day his plans come to an end. Happy is he whose help is the God of Jacob, whose hope is in the Lord his God who made heaven and earth, the sea and all they contain; He who keeps faith for ever. He secures justice for the oppressed. He gives food to the hungry. The Lord sets captives free. The Lord gives sight to the blind. The Lord raises those bowed down. The Lord loves the righteous. The Lord protects the stranger. He gives courage to the orphan and widow. He defeats the way of the wicked. ▸ The Lord shall reign for ever. He is your God, Zion, for all generations. Halleluya! *Ps. 146*

הַלְלוּיָהּ Halleluya! How good it is to sing songs to our God; how pleasant and fitting to praise Him. The Lord rebuilds Jerusalem. He gathers the scattered exiles of Israel. He heals the *Ps. 147*

כְּבוֹד מַלְכוּתְךָ יֹאמֵרוּ, וּגְבוּרָתְךָ יְדַבֵּרוּ:
לְהוֹדִיעַ לִבְנֵי הָאָדָם גְּבוּרֹתָיו, וּכְבוֹד הֲדַר מַלְכוּתוֹ:
מַלְכוּתְךָ מַלְכוּת כָּל־עֹלָמִים, וּמֶמְשַׁלְתְּךָ בְּכָל־דּוֹר וָדֹר:
סוֹמֵךְ יהוה לְכָל־הַנֹּפְלִים, וְזוֹקֵף לְכָל־הַכְּפוּפִים:
עֵינֵי־כֹל אֵלֶיךָ יְשַׂבֵּרוּ, וְאַתָּה נוֹתֵן־לָהֶם אֶת־אָכְלָם בְּעִתּוֹ:
פּוֹתֵחַ אֶת־יָדֶךָ, וּמַשְׂבִּיעַ לְכָל־חַי רָצוֹן:
צַדִּיק יהוה בְּכָל־דְּרָכָיו, וְחָסִיד בְּכָל־מַעֲשָׂיו:
קָרוֹב יהוה לְכָל־קֹרְאָיו, לְכֹל אֲשֶׁר יִקְרָאֻהוּ בֶאֱמֶת:
רְצוֹן־יְרֵאָיו יַעֲשֶׂה, וְאֶת־שַׁוְעָתָם יִשְׁמַע, וְיוֹשִׁיעֵם:
שׁוֹמֵר יהוה אֶת־כָּל־אֹהֲבָיו, וְאֵת כָּל־הָרְשָׁעִים יַשְׁמִיד:
◂ תְּהִלַּת יהוה יְדַבֶּר פִּי, וִיבָרֵךְ כָּל־בָּשָׂר שֵׁם קָדְשׁוֹ לְעוֹלָם וָעֶד:
וַאֲנַחְנוּ נְבָרֵךְ יָהּ מֵעַתָּה וְעַד־עוֹלָם, הַלְלוּיָהּ: תהלים קטו

הַלְלוּיָהּ, הַלְלִי נַפְשִׁי אֶת־יהוה: אֲהַלְלָה יהוה בְּחַיָּי, אֲזַמְּרָה תהלים קמו
לֵאלֹהַי בְּעוֹדִי: אַל־תִּבְטְחוּ בִנְדִיבִים, בְּבֶן־אָדָם שֶׁאֵין לוֹ
תְשׁוּעָה: תֵּצֵא רוּחוֹ, יָשֻׁב לְאַדְמָתוֹ, בַּיּוֹם הַהוּא אָבְדוּ עֶשְׁתֹּנֹתָיו:
אַשְׁרֵי שֶׁאֵל יַעֲקֹב בְּעֶזְרוֹ, שִׂבְרוֹ עַל־יהוה אֱלֹהָיו: עֹשֶׂה שָׁמַיִם
וָאָרֶץ, אֶת־הַיָּם וְאֶת־כָּל־אֲשֶׁר־בָּם, הַשֹּׁמֵר אֱמֶת לְעוֹלָם: עֹשֶׂה
מִשְׁפָּט לָעֲשׁוּקִים, נֹתֵן לֶחֶם לָרְעֵבִים, יהוה מַתִּיר אֲסוּרִים: יהוה
פֹּקֵחַ עִוְרִים, יהוה זֹקֵף כְּפוּפִים, יהוה אֹהֵב צַדִּיקִים: יהוה שֹׁמֵר
אֶת־גֵּרִים, יָתוֹם וְאַלְמָנָה יְעוֹדֵד, וְדֶרֶךְ רְשָׁעִים יְעַוֵּת: ◂ יִמְלֹךְ
יהוה לְעוֹלָם, אֱלֹהַיִךְ צִיּוֹן לְדֹר וָדֹר, הַלְלוּיָהּ:

הַלְלוּיָהּ, כִּי־טוֹב זַמְּרָה אֱלֹהֵינוּ, כִּי־נָעִים נָאוָה תְהִלָּה: בּוֹנֵה תהלים קמז
יְרוּשָׁלַםִ יהוה, נִדְחֵי יִשְׂרָאֵל יְכַנֵּס: הָרוֹפֵא לִשְׁבוּרֵי לֵב, וּמְחַבֵּשׁ

brokenhearted and binds up their wounds. He counts the number of the stars, calling each by name. Great is our LORD and mighty in power; His understanding has no limit. The LORD gives courage to the humble, but casts the wicked to the ground. Sing to the LORD in thanks; make music to our God on the harp. He covers the sky with clouds. He provides the earth with rain and makes grass grow on the hills. He gives food to the cattle and to the ravens when they cry. He does not take delight in the strength of horses nor pleasure in the fleetness of man. The LORD takes pleasure in those who fear Him, who put their hope in His loving care. Praise the LORD, Jerusalem; sing to your God, Zion, for He has strengthened the bars of your gates and blessed your children in your midst. He has brought peace to your borders, and satisfied you with the finest wheat. He sends His commandment to earth; swiftly runs His word. He spreads snow like fleece, sprinkles frost like ashes, scatters hail like crumbs. Who can stand His cold? He sends His word and melts them; He makes the wind blow and the waters flow. ▸ He has declared His words to Jacob, His statutes and laws to Israel. He has done this for no other nation; such laws they do not know. Halleluya!

הַלְלוּיָהּ Halleluya! Praise the LORD from the heavens, praise Him in the heights. Praise Him, all His angels; praise Him, all His multitudes. Praise Him, sun and moon; praise Him, all shining stars. Praise Him, highest heavens and the waters above the heavens. Let them praise the name of the LORD, for He commanded and they were created. He established them for ever and all time, issuing a decree that will never change. Praise the LORD from the earth: sea monsters and all the deep seas; fire and hail, snow and mist, storm winds that obey His word; mountains and all hills, fruit trees and all cedars; wild animals and all cattle, creeping things and winged birds; kings of the earth and all nations, princes and all judges on earth; youths and maidens, *Ps. 148*

לַעַצְּבוֹתָם: מוֹנֶה מִסְפָּר לַכּוֹכָבִים, לְכֻלָּם שֵׁמוֹת יִקְרָא: גָּדוֹל אֲדוֹנֵינוּ וְרַב־כֹּחַ, לִתְבוּנָתוֹ אֵין מִסְפָּר: מְעוֹדֵד עֲנָוִים יהוה, מַשְׁפִּיל רְשָׁעִים עֲדֵי־אָרֶץ: עֱנוּ לַיהוה בְּתוֹדָה, זַמְּרוּ לֵאלֹהֵינוּ בְכִנּוֹר: הַמְכַסֶּה שָׁמַיִם בְּעָבִים, הַמֵּכִין לָאָרֶץ מָטָר, הַמַּצְמִיחַ הָרִים חָצִיר: נוֹתֵן לִבְהֵמָה לַחְמָהּ, לִבְנֵי עֹרֵב אֲשֶׁר יִקְרָאוּ: לֹא בִגְבוּרַת הַסּוּס יֶחְפָּץ, לֹא־בְשׁוֹקֵי הָאִישׁ יִרְצֶה: רוֹצֶה יהוה אֶת־יְרֵאָיו, אֶת־הַמְיַחֲלִים לְחַסְדּוֹ: שַׁבְּחִי יְרוּשָׁלַםִ אֶת־יהוה, הַלְלִי אֱלֹהַיִךְ צִיּוֹן: כִּי־חִזַּק בְּרִיחֵי שְׁעָרָיִךְ, בֵּרַךְ בָּנַיִךְ בְּקִרְבֵּךְ: הַשָּׂם־גְּבוּלֵךְ שָׁלוֹם, חֵלֶב חִטִּים יַשְׂבִּיעֵךְ: הַשֹּׁלֵחַ אִמְרָתוֹ אָרֶץ, עַד־מְהֵרָה יָרוּץ דְּבָרוֹ: הַנֹּתֵן שֶׁלֶג כַּצָּמֶר, כְּפוֹר כָּאֵפֶר יְפַזֵּר: מַשְׁלִיךְ קַרְחוֹ כְפִתִּים, לִפְנֵי קָרָתוֹ מִי יַעֲמֹד: יִשְׁלַח דְּבָרוֹ וְיַמְסֵם, יַשֵּׁב רוּחוֹ יִזְּלוּ־מָיִם: ‹ מַגִּיד דְּבָרָו לְיַעֲקֹב, חֻקָּיו וּמִשְׁפָּטָיו לְיִשְׂרָאֵל: לֹא עָשָׂה כֵן לְכָל־גּוֹי, וּמִשְׁפָּטִים בַּל־יְדָעוּם, הַלְלוּיָהּ:

הַלְלוּיָהּ, הַלְלוּ אֶת־יהוה מִן־הַשָּׁמַיִם, הַלְלוּהוּ בַּמְּרוֹמִים: תהלים קמח
הַלְלוּהוּ כָל־מַלְאָכָיו, הַלְלוּהוּ כָּל־צְבָאָו: הַלְלוּהוּ שֶׁמֶשׁ וְיָרֵחַ, הַלְלוּהוּ כָּל־כּוֹכְבֵי אוֹר: הַלְלוּהוּ שְׁמֵי הַשָּׁמָיִם, וְהַמַּיִם אֲשֶׁר מֵעַל הַשָּׁמָיִם: יְהַלְלוּ אֶת־שֵׁם יהוה, כִּי הוּא צִוָּה וְנִבְרָאוּ: וַיַּעֲמִידֵם לָעַד לְעוֹלָם, חָק־נָתַן וְלֹא יַעֲבוֹר: הַלְלוּ אֶת־יהוה מִן־הָאָרֶץ, תַּנִּינִים וְכָל־תְּהֹמוֹת: אֵשׁ וּבָרָד שֶׁלֶג וְקִיטוֹר, רוּחַ סְעָרָה עֹשָׂה דְבָרוֹ: הֶהָרִים וְכָל־גְּבָעוֹת, עֵץ פְּרִי וְכָל־אֲרָזִים: הַחַיָּה וְכָל־בְּהֵמָה, רֶמֶשׂ וְצִפּוֹר כָּנָף: מַלְכֵי־אֶרֶץ וְכָל־לְאֻמִּים, שָׂרִים וְכָל־שֹׁפְטֵי אָרֶץ: בַּחוּרִים וְגַם־בְּתוּלוֹת, זְקֵנִים עִם־נְעָרִים:

old and young. ‣ Let them praise the name of the LORD, for His name alone is sublime; His majesty is above earth and heaven. He has raised the pride of His people, for the glory of all His devoted ones, the children of Israel, the people close to Him. Halleluya!

הַלְלוּיָהּ Halleluya! Sing to the LORD a new song, His praise in the assembly of the devoted. Let Israel rejoice in its Maker; let the children of Zion delight in their King. Let them praise His name with dancing; sing praises to Him with drum and harp. For the LORD delights in His people; He adorns the humble with salvation. Let the devoted celebrate in glory; let them sing for joy on their beds. Let high praises of God be in their throats, and a two-edged sword in their hand: to impose retribution on the nations, punishment on the peoples, ‣ binding their kings with chains, their nobles with iron shackles, carrying out the judgment written against them. This is the glory of all His devoted ones. Halleluya! *Ps. 149*

הַלְלוּיָהּ Halleluya! *Ps. 150*

Praise God in His holy place;
praise Him in the heavens of His power.
Praise Him for His mighty deeds;
praise Him for His immense greatness.
Praise Him with blasts of the shofar;
praise Him with the harp and lyre.
Praise Him with drum and dance;
praise Him with strings and flute.
Praise Him with clashing cymbals;
praise Him with resounding cymbals.

‣ Let all that breathes praise the LORD. Halleluya!
Let all that breathes praise the LORD. Halleluya!

◂ יְהַלְלוּ אֶת־שֵׁם יהוה, כִּי־נִשְׂגָּב שְׁמוֹ לְבַדּוֹ, הוֹדוֹ עַל־אֶרֶץ וְשָׁמָיִם: וַיָּרֶם קֶרֶן לְעַמּוֹ, תְּהִלָּה לְכָל־חֲסִידָיו, לִבְנֵי יִשְׂרָאֵל עַם קְרֹבוֹ, הַלְלוּיָהּ:

תהלים קמט הַלְלוּיָהּ, שִׁירוּ לַיהוה שִׁיר חָדָשׁ, תְּהִלָּתוֹ בִּקְהַל חֲסִידִים: יִשְׂמַח יִשְׂרָאֵל בְּעֹשָׂיו, בְּנֵי־צִיּוֹן יָגִילוּ בְמַלְכָּם: יְהַלְלוּ שְׁמוֹ בְמָחוֹל, בְּתֹף וְכִנּוֹר יְזַמְּרוּ־לוֹ: כִּי־רוֹצֶה יהוה בְּעַמּוֹ, יְפָאֵר עֲנָוִים בִּישׁוּעָה: יַעְלְזוּ חֲסִידִים בְּכָבוֹד, יְרַנְּנוּ עַל־מִשְׁכְּבוֹתָם: רוֹמְמוֹת אֵל בִּגְרוֹנָם, וְחֶרֶב פִּיפִיּוֹת בְּיָדָם: לַעֲשׂוֹת נְקָמָה בַּגּוֹיִם, תּוֹכֵחוֹת בַּלְאֻמִּים: ◂ לֶאְסֹר מַלְכֵיהֶם בְּזִקִּים, וְנִכְבְּדֵיהֶם בְּכַבְלֵי בַרְזֶל: לַעֲשׂוֹת בָּהֶם מִשְׁפָּט כָּתוּב, הָדָר הוּא לְכָל־חֲסִידָיו, הַלְלוּיָהּ:

תהלים קנ הַלְלוּיָהּ, הַלְלוּ־אֵל בְּקָדְשׁוֹ
הַלְלוּהוּ בִּרְקִיעַ עֻזּוֹ:
הַלְלוּהוּ בִגְבוּרֹתָיו
הַלְלוּהוּ כְּרֹב גֻּדְלוֹ:
הַלְלוּהוּ בְּתֵקַע שׁוֹפָר
הַלְלוּהוּ בְּנֵבֶל וְכִנּוֹר:
הַלְלוּהוּ בְּתֹף וּמָחוֹל
הַלְלוּהוּ בְּמִנִּים וְעֻגָב:
הַלְלוּהוּ בְצִלְצְלֵי־שָׁמַע
הַלְלוּהוּ בְּצִלְצְלֵי תְרוּעָה:
◂ כֹּל הַנְּשָׁמָה תְּהַלֵּל יָהּ, הַלְלוּיָהּ:
כֹּל הַנְּשָׁמָה תְּהַלֵּל יָהּ, הַלְלוּיָהּ:

בָּרוּךְ Blessed be the LORD for ever. Amen and Amen. *Ps. 89*
Blessed from Zion be the LORD *Ps. 135*
who is present in Jerusalem. Halleluya!
Blessed be the LORD, God of Israel, who alone does wonders. *Ps. 72*
▸ Blessed be His glorious name for ever,
and may all the earth be filled with His glory.
Amen and Amen.

Stand until "The soul" on page 570.

וַיְבָרֶךְ David blessed the LORD in front of the entire assembly. David said, "Blessed are You, LORD, God of our father Yisrael, for ever and ever. Yours, LORD, are the greatness and the power, the glory, majesty and splendor, for everything in heaven and earth is Yours. Yours, LORD, is the kingdom; You are elevated as Head over all. Both riches and honor are in Your gift and You reign over all things. In Your hand are strength and might. It is in Your power to make great and give strength to all. Therefore, our God, we thank You and praise Your glorious name." *1 Chr. 29*

You alone are the LORD. You made the heavens, even the highest heavens, and all their multitudes, the earth and all that is on it, the seas and all they contain. You give life to them all, and the multitudes of heaven worship You. ▸ You are the LORD God who chose Abram and brought him out of Ur of the Chaldees, changing his name to Abraham. You found his heart faithful toward You, ◂ and You made a covenant with him to give to his descendants the land of the Canaanites, Hittites, Amorites, Perizzites, Jebusites and Girgashites. You fulfilled Your promise for You are righteous. You saw the suffering of our ancestors in Egypt. You heard their cry at the Sea of Reeds. You sent signs and wonders against Pharaoh, all his servants and all the people of his land, because You knew how arrogantly the Egyptians treated them. You created for Yourself fame that remains to this day. ▸ You divided the sea before them, so that they passed through the sea on dry land, but You cast their pursuers into the depths, like a stone into mighty waters. *Neh. 9*

תהלים פט בָּרוּךְ יהוה לְעוֹלָם, אָמֵן וְאָמֵן:

תהלים קלה בָּרוּךְ יהוה מִצִּיּוֹן, שֹׁכֵן יְרוּשָׁלָםִ, הַלְלוּיָהּ:

תהלים עב בָּרוּךְ יהוה אֱלֹהִים אֱלֹהֵי יִשְׂרָאֵל, עֹשֵׂה נִפְלָאוֹת לְבַדּוֹ:

◄ וּבָרוּךְ שֵׁם כְּבוֹדוֹ לְעוֹלָם, וְיִמָּלֵא כְבוֹדוֹ אֶת־כָּל־הָאָרֶץ אָמֵן וְאָמֵן:

Stand until נִשְׁמַת *on page 571.*

דברי הימים א׳ כט וַיְבָרֶךְ דָּוִיד אֶת־יהוה לְעֵינֵי כָּל־הַקָּהָל, וַיֹּאמֶר דָּוִיד, בָּרוּךְ אַתָּה יהוה, אֱלֹהֵי יִשְׂרָאֵל אָבִינוּ, מֵעוֹלָם וְעַד־עוֹלָם: לְךָ יהוה הַגְּדֻלָּה וְהַגְּבוּרָה וְהַתִּפְאֶרֶת וְהַנֵּצַח וְהַהוֹד, כִּי־כֹל בַּשָּׁמַיִם וּבָאָרֶץ, לְךָ יהוה הַמַּמְלָכָה וְהַמִּתְנַשֵּׂא לְכֹל לְרֹאשׁ: וְהָעֹשֶׁר וְהַכָּבוֹד מִלְּפָנֶיךָ, וְאַתָּה מוֹשֵׁל בַּכֹּל, וּבְיָדְךָ כֹּחַ וּגְבוּרָה, וּבְיָדְךָ לְגַדֵּל וּלְחַזֵּק לַכֹּל: וְעַתָּה אֱלֹהֵינוּ מוֹדִים אֲנַחְנוּ לָךְ, וּמְהַלְלִים לְשֵׁם תִּפְאַרְתֶּךָ:

נחמיה ט אַתָּה־הוּא יהוה לְבַדֶּךָ, אַתָּ עָשִׂיתָ אֶת־הַשָּׁמַיִם, שְׁמֵי הַשָּׁמַיִם וְכָל־צְבָאָם, הָאָרֶץ וְכָל־אֲשֶׁר עָלֶיהָ, הַיַּמִּים וְכָל־אֲשֶׁר בָּהֶם, וְאַתָּה מְחַיֶּה אֶת־כֻּלָּם, וּצְבָא הַשָּׁמַיִם לְךָ מִשְׁתַּחֲוִים: ◄ אַתָּה הוּא יהוה הָאֱלֹהִים אֲשֶׁר בָּחַרְתָּ בְּאַבְרָם, וְהוֹצֵאתוֹ מֵאוּר כַּשְׂדִּים, וְשַׂמְתָּ שְּׁמוֹ אַבְרָהָם: וּמָצָאתָ אֶת־לְבָבוֹ נֶאֱמָן לְפָנֶיךָ, ◄ וְכָרוֹת עִמּוֹ הַבְּרִית לָתֵת אֶת־אֶרֶץ הַכְּנַעֲנִי הַחִתִּי הָאֱמֹרִי וְהַפְּרִזִּי וְהַיְבוּסִי וְהַגִּרְגָּשִׁי, לָתֵת לְזַרְעוֹ, וַתָּקֶם אֶת־דְּבָרֶיךָ, כִּי צַדִּיק אָתָּה: וַתֵּרֶא אֶת־עֳנִי אֲבֹתֵינוּ בְּמִצְרָיִם, וְאֶת־זַעֲקָתָם שָׁמַעְתָּ עַל־יַם־סוּף: וַתִּתֵּן אֹתֹת וּמֹפְתִים בְּפַרְעֹה וּבְכָל־עֲבָדָיו וּבְכָל־עַם אַרְצוֹ, כִּי יָדַעְתָּ כִּי הֵזִידוּ עֲלֵיהֶם, וַתַּעַשׂ־לְךָ שֵׁם כְּהַיּוֹם הַזֶּה: ◄ וְהַיָּם בָּקַעְתָּ לִפְנֵיהֶם, וַיַּעַבְרוּ בְתוֹךְ־הַיָּם בַּיַּבָּשָׁה, וְאֶת־רֹדְפֵיהֶם הִשְׁלַכְתָּ בִמְצוֹלֹת כְּמוֹ־אֶבֶן, בְּמַיִם עַזִּים:

וַיּֽוֹשַׁע That day the LORD saved Israel from the hands of the Egyptians, and Israel saw the Egyptians lying dead on the seashore. ▸ When Israel saw the great power the LORD had displayed against the Egyptians, the people feared the LORD, and believed in the LORD and in His servant, Moses. *Ex. 14*

אָז יָשִׁיר־מֹשֶׁה Then Moses and the Israelites sang this song to the LORD, saying: *Ex. 15*

I will sing to the LORD, for He has triumphed gloriously;
horse and rider He has hurled into the sea.
The LORD is my strength and song; He has become my salvation.
This is my God, and I will beautify Him,
my father's God, and I will elevate Him.
The LORD is a Master of war; LORD is His name.
Pharaoh's chariots and army He cast into the sea;
the best of his officers drowned in the Sea of Reeds.
The deep waters covered them;
they went down to the depths like a stone.
Your right hand, LORD, is majestic in power.
Your right hand, LORD, shatters the enemy.
In the greatness of Your majesty, You overthrew those who rose against You.
You sent out Your fury; it consumed them like straw.
By the blast of Your nostrils the waters piled up.
The surging waters stood straight like a wall;
the deeps congealed in the heart of the sea.
The enemy said, "I will pursue. I will overtake. I will divide the spoil.
My desire shall have its fill of them.
I will draw my sword. My hand will destroy them."
You blew with Your wind; the sea covered them.
They sank in the mighty waters like lead.
Who is like You, LORD, among the mighty? Who is like You –
majestic in holiness, awesome in glory, working wonders?
You stretched out Your right hand, the earth swallowed them.

וַיּוֹשַׁע יהוה בַּיּוֹם הַהוּא אֶת־יִשְׂרָאֵל מִיַּד מִצְרָיִם, וַיַּרְא יִשְׂרָאֵל שמות יד
אֶת־מִצְרַיִם מֵת עַל־שְׂפַת הַיָּם: • וַיַּרְא יִשְׂרָאֵל אֶת־הַיָּד הַגְּדֹלָה
אֲשֶׁר עָשָׂה יהוה בְּמִצְרַיִם, וַיִּירְאוּ הָעָם אֶת־יהוה, וַיַּאֲמִינוּ
בַּיהוה וּבְמֹשֶׁה עַבְדּוֹ:

אָז יָשִׁיר־מֹשֶׁה וּבְנֵי יִשְׂרָאֵל אֶת־הַשִּׁירָה הַזֹּאת לַיהוה, וַיֹּאמְרוּ שמות טו
לֵאמֹר, אָשִׁירָה לַיהוה כִּי־גָאֹה גָּאָה, סוּס
וְרֹכְבוֹ רָמָה בַיָּם: עָזִּי וְזִמְרָת יָהּ וַיְהִי־לִי
לִישׁוּעָה, זֶה אֵלִי וְאַנְוֵהוּ, אֱלֹהֵי
אָבִי וַאֲרֹמְמֶנְהוּ: יהוה אִישׁ מִלְחָמָה, יהוה
שְׁמוֹ: מַרְכְּבֹת פַּרְעֹה וְחֵילוֹ יָרָה בַיָּם, וּמִבְחַר
שָׁלִשָׁיו טֻבְּעוּ בְיַם־סוּף: תְּהֹמֹת יְכַסְיֻמוּ, יָרְדוּ בִמְצוֹלֹת כְּמוֹ־
אָבֶן: יְמִינְךָ יהוה נֶאְדָּרִי בַּכֹּחַ, יְמִינְךָ
יהוה תִּרְעַץ אוֹיֵב: וּבְרֹב גְּאוֹנְךָ תַּהֲרֹס
קָמֶיךָ, תְּשַׁלַּח חֲרֹנְךָ יֹאכְלֵמוֹ כַּקַּשׁ: וּבְרוּחַ
אַפֶּיךָ נֶעֶרְמוּ מַיִם, נִצְּבוּ כְמוֹ־נֵד
נֹזְלִים, קָפְאוּ תְהֹמֹת בְּלֶב־יָם: אָמַר
אוֹיֵב אֶרְדֹּף, אַשִּׂיג, אֲחַלֵּק שָׁלָל, תִּמְלָאֵמוֹ
נַפְשִׁי, אָרִיק חַרְבִּי, תּוֹרִישֵׁמוֹ יָדִי: נָשַׁפְתָּ
בְרוּחֲךָ כִּסָּמוֹ יָם, צָלְלוּ כַּעוֹפֶרֶת בְּמַיִם
אַדִּירִים: מִי־כָמֹכָה בָּאֵלִם יהוה, מִי
כָּמֹכָה נֶאְדָּר בַּקֹּדֶשׁ, נוֹרָא תְהִלֹּת עֹשֵׂה
פֶלֶא: נָטִיתָ יְמִינְךָ תִּבְלָעֵמוֹ אָרֶץ: נָחִיתָ

In Your loving-kindness, You led the people You redeemed.
In Your strength, You guided them to Your holy abode.
Nations heard and trembled;
terror gripped Philistia's inhabitants.
The chiefs of Edom were dismayed,
Moab's leaders were seized with trembling,
the people of Canaan melted away.
Fear and dread fell upon them.
By the power of Your arm, they were still as stone –
until Your people crossed, LORD,
until the people You acquired crossed over.
You will bring them and plant them on the mountain of Your heritage –
the place, LORD, You made for Your presence,
the Sanctuary, LORD, Your hands established.
The LORD will reign for ever and all time.

The LORD will reign for ever and all time.
The LORD's kingship is established for ever and to all eternity.

When Pharaoh's horses, chariots and riders went into the sea,
the LORD brought the waters of the sea back over them, but the Israelites walked on dry land through the sea.

▸ For kingship is the LORD's *Ps. 22*
and He rules over the nations.
Saviors shall go up to Mount Zion *Ob. 1*
to judge Mount Esau,
and the LORD's shall be the kingdom.
Then the LORD shall be King over all the earth; *Zech. 14*
on that day the LORD shall be One and His name One,
(as it is written in Your Torah, saying:
Listen, Israel: the LORD is our God, the LORD is One.) *Deut. 6*

On Hoshana Raba, Yom HaAtzma'ut and Yom Yerushalayim, continue with the weekday service, from "May Your name be praised" on page 116.

בְּחַסְדְּךָ עַם־זוּ גָּאָלְתָּ, נֵהַלְתָּ בְעָזְּךָ אֶל־נְוֵה
קָדְשֶׁךָ: שָׁמְעוּ עַמִּים יִרְגָּזוּן, חִיל
אָחַז יֹשְׁבֵי פְּלָשֶׁת: אָז נִבְהֲלוּ אַלּוּפֵי
אֱדוֹם, אֵילֵי מוֹאָב יֹאחֲזֵמוֹ רָעַד, נָמֹגוּ
כֹּל יֹשְׁבֵי כְנָעַן: תִּפֹּל עֲלֵיהֶם אֵימָתָה
וָפַחַד, בִּגְדֹל זְרוֹעֲךָ יִדְּמוּ כָּאָבֶן, עַד־
יַעֲבֹר עַמְּךָ יהוה, עַד־יַעֲבֹר עַם־זוּ
קָנִיתָ: תְּבִאֵמוֹ וְתִטָּעֵמוֹ בְּהַר נַחֲלָתְךָ, מָכוֹן
לְשִׁבְתְּךָ פָּעַלְתָּ יהוה, מִקְּדָשׁ אֲדֹנָי כּוֹנְנוּ
יָדֶיךָ: יהוה יִמְלֹךְ לְעֹלָם וָעֶד:

יהוה יִמְלֹךְ לְעֹלָם וָעֶד.
יהוה מַלְכוּתֵהּ קָאֵם לְעָלַם וּלְעָלְמֵי עָלְמַיָּא.

כִּי
בָא סוּס פַּרְעֹה בְּרִכְבּוֹ וּבְפָרָשָׁיו בַּיָּם, וַיָּשֶׁב יהוה עֲלֵהֶם אֶת־מֵי
הַיָּם, וּבְנֵי יִשְׂרָאֵל הָלְכוּ בַיַּבָּשָׁה בְּתוֹךְ הַיָּם:

תהלים כב ◂ כִּי לַיהוה הַמְּלוּכָה וּמֹשֵׁל בַּגּוֹיִם:
עובדיה א וְעָלוּ מוֹשִׁעִים בְּהַר צִיּוֹן לִשְׁפֹּט אֶת־הַר עֵשָׂו
וְהָיְתָה לַיהוה הַמְּלוּכָה:
זכריה יד וְהָיָה יהוה לְמֶלֶךְ עַל־כָּל־הָאָרֶץ
בַּיּוֹם הַהוּא יִהְיֶה יהוה אֶחָד וּשְׁמוֹ אֶחָד:
דברים ו (וּבְתוֹרָתְךָ כָּתוּב לֵאמֹר, שְׁמַע יִשְׂרָאֵל, יהוה אֱלֹהֵינוּ יהוה אֶחָד:)

On הושענא רבה, יום העצמאות *and* יום ירושלים *continue with* יִשְׁתַּבַּח *on page 117.*

THE SOUL

of all that lives shall bless Your name, LORD our God,
and the spirit of all flesh shall always glorify
and elevate Your remembrance, our King.
From eternity to eternity You are God.
Without You, we have no king, redeemer or savior,
who liberates, rescues, sustains
and shows compassion in every time of trouble and distress.
We have no king but You, God of the first and last,
God of all creatures, Master of all ages,
celebrated by a multitude of praises,
who guides His world with loving-kindness
and His creatures with compassion.
The LORD neither slumbers nor sleeps.
He rouses the sleepers
and wakens the slumberers.
He makes the dumb speak,
sets the bound free,
supports the fallen,
and raises those bowed down.
To You alone we give thanks:

CONNECTION

"Kuzari King: I have often reflected about you and come to the conclusion that God has some secret design in preserving you, and that He appointed the Shabbat and holidays as the strongest means of preserving your strength and splendor. The nations broke you up and made you their servants on account of your intelligence and purity. They would even have made you their warriors were it not for those festive seasons which you observe so carefully, because they originate with God, and are based on such causes as 'Remembrance of the creation,' 'Remembrance of the exodus from Egypt,' and 'Remembrance of the giving of the Torah.' These are all divine commands, to observe which you are charged." (Rabbi Yehuda HaLevi, *Kuzari*)

נִשְׁמַת

כָּל חַי תְּבָרֵךְ אֶת שִׁמְךָ, יהוה אֱלֹהֵינוּ
וְרוּחַ כָּל בָּשָׂר תְּפָאֵר וּתְרוֹמֵם זִכְרְךָ מַלְכֵּנוּ תָּמִיד.
מִן הָעוֹלָם וְעַד הָעוֹלָם אַתָּה אֵל
וּמִבַּלְעָדֶיךָ אֵין לָנוּ מֶלֶךְ גּוֹאֵל וּמוֹשִׁיעַ
פּוֹדֶה וּמַצִּיל וּמְפַרְנֵס וּמְרַחֵם
בְּכָל עֵת צָרָה וְצוּקָה אֵין לָנוּ מֶלֶךְ אֶלָּא אָתָּה.
אֱלֹהֵי הָרִאשׁוֹנִים וְהָאַחֲרוֹנִים, אֱלוֹהַּ כָּל בְּרִיּוֹת
אֲדוֹן כָּל תּוֹלָדוֹת, הַמְהֻלָּל בְּרֹב הַתִּשְׁבָּחוֹת
הַמְנַהֵג עוֹלָמוֹ בְּחֶסֶד וּבְרִיּוֹתָיו בְּרַחֲמִים.
וַיהוה לֹא יָנוּם וְלֹא יִישָׁן
הַמְעוֹרֵר יְשֵׁנִים וְהַמֵּקִיץ נִרְדָּמִים
וְהַמֵּשִׂיחַ אִלְּמִים וְהַמַּתִּיר אֲסוּרִים
וְהַסּוֹמֵךְ נוֹפְלִים וְהַזּוֹקֵף כְּפוּפִים.
לְךָ לְבַדְּךָ אֲנַחְנוּ מוֹדִים.

CONNECTION

וַיִּפַּח בְּאַפָּיו נִשְׁמַת חַיִּים
וַיְהִי הָאָדָם לְנֶפֶשׁ חַיָּה

"And He blew into his nostrils the breath of life, and man became a living soul."

(Bereshit 2:7)

What is the uniqueness of mankind? The secret can be found in this very verse. Humans have **נִשְׁמַת חַיִּים**, *a living soul, and are therefore unique among all the animals. Rashi explains that this special soul is the unique ability of mankind to be able to think independently and the ability to speak. While nature, by virtue of its beauty, serves as praise of God through its existence alone, man has the unique ability to actually praise Him, by articulating his own words and forming them into coherent speech.*

If our mouths were as full of song as the sea,
and our tongue with celebration as its countless waves,
if our lips were full of praise like the spacious heavens,
and our eyes shone like the sun and moon,
if our hands were outstretched like eagles of the sky,
and our feet as swift as deer –
still we could not thank You enough,
Lord our God and God of our ancestors,
or bless Your name
for even one of the thousand thousands
and myriad myriads of favors
You did for our ancestors and for us.
You redeemed us from Egypt, Lord our God,
and freed us from the house of slavery.
In famine You nourished us;
in times of plenty You sustained us.
You saved us from the sword, saved us from the plague,
and spared us from serious and lasting illness.

... A THOUSAND WORDS

אִלּוּ פִינוּ מָלֵא שִׁירָה כַּיָּם
וּלְשׁוֹנֵנוּ רִנָּה כַּהֲמוֹן גַּלָּיו
וְשִׂפְתוֹתֵינוּ שֶׁבַח כְּמֶרְחֲבֵי רָקִיעַ
וְעֵינֵינוּ מְאִירוֹת כַּשֶּׁמֶשׁ וְכַיָּרֵחַ
וְיָדֵינוּ פְרוּשׂוֹת כְּנִשְׁרֵי שָׁמָיִם
וְרַגְלֵינוּ קַלּוֹת כָּאַיָּלוֹת
אֵין אֲנַחְנוּ מַסְפִּיקִים לְהוֹדוֹת לְךָ
יהוה אֱלֹהֵינוּ וֵאלֹהֵי אֲבוֹתֵינוּ
וּלְבָרֵךְ אֶת שְׁמֶךָ
עַל אַחַת מֵאֶלֶף אֶלֶף אַלְפֵי אֲלָפִים
וְרִבֵּי רְבָבוֹת פְּעָמִים הַטּוֹבוֹת
שֶׁעָשִׂיתָ עִם אֲבוֹתֵינוּ וְעִמָּנוּ.
מִמִּצְרַיִם גְּאַלְתָּנוּ, יהוה אֱלֹהֵינוּ, וּמִבֵּית עֲבָדִים פְּדִיתָנוּ
בְּרָעָב זַנְתָּנוּ וּבְשָׂבָע כִּלְכַּלְתָּנוּ
מֵחֶרֶב הִצַּלְתָּנוּ וּמִדֶּבֶר מִלַּטְתָּנוּ
וּמֵחֳלָיִים רָעִים וְנֶאֱמָנִים דִּלִּיתָנוּ.

LEARNING

There are not enough words to praise God. Even if we could find enough words, words in and of themselves can only give us limited meaning. *Nishmat* explores how we can use all the elements of the body to praise God.

This prayer is an outpouring of praise and gratitude to God, and depicts our utter dependency on His mercy, our total inadequacy to laud Him properly, and our enthusiastic resolve to dedicate ourselves to His service. Even though this prayer, which is recited on Shabbat and Yom Tov, does not contain any mention of the day, it is still appropriate because the additional holiness of the Shabbat and the time it affords for extra contemplation make man better able to understand and express the message of the *Nishmat* prayer.

Until now Your mercies have helped us.
Your love has not abandoned us.
May You, LORD our God, never abandon us.
Therefore the limbs You formed within us,
the spirit and soul You breathed into our nostrils,
and the tongue You placed in our mouth –
they will thank and bless, praise and glorify, elevate and admire,
sanctify and pay tribute to Your name, O our King.
For every mouth shall give thanks to You,
every tongue vow allegiance to You,
every knee shall bend to You,
every upright body shall bow to You,
all hearts shall fear You,
and our innermost being sing praises to Your name,
as is written:

"All my bones shall say: LORD, who is like You? *Ps. 35*
You save the poor from one stronger than him,
the poor and needy from one who would rob him."

Who is like You? Who is equal to You?
Who can be compared to You?
O great, mighty and awesome God, God Most High,
Maker of heaven and earth.
▸ We will applaud, praise and glorify You and bless Your holy name,
as it is said:

"Of David. Bless the LORD, O my soul, *Ps. 103*
and all that is within me bless His holy name."

REFLECTION

Have you ever felt
you do not have the words
to adequately express
how you feel?

How can you say thank you
when you cannot find the right words?

How can you use every part of your body
to serve God?

עַד הֵנָּה עֲזָרוּנוּ רַחֲמֶיךָ, וְלֹא עֲזָבוּנוּ חֲסָדֶיךָ
וְאַל תִּטְּשֵׁנוּ, יהוה אֱלֹהֵינוּ, לָנֶצַח.
עַל כֵּן אֵבָרִים שֶׁפִּלַּגְתָּ בָּנוּ
וְרוּחַ וּנְשָׁמָה שֶׁנָּפַחְתָּ בְּאַפֵּנוּ
וְלָשׁוֹן אֲשֶׁר שַׂמְתָּ בְּפִינוּ
הֵן הֵם יוֹדוּ וִיבָרְכוּ וִישַׁבְּחוּ וִיפָאֲרוּ
וִירוֹמְמוּ וְיַעֲרִיצוּ וְיַקְדִּישׁוּ וְיַמְלִיכוּ אֶת שִׁמְךָ מַלְכֵּנוּ
כִּי כָל פֶּה לְךָ יוֹדֶה
וְכָל לָשׁוֹן לְךָ תִשָּׁבַע
וְכָל בֶּרֶךְ לְךָ תִכְרַע
וְכָל קוֹמָה לְפָנֶיךָ תִשְׁתַּחֲוֶה
וְכָל לְבָבוֹת יִירָאוּךָ
וְכָל קֶרֶב וּכְלָיוֹת יְזַמְּרוּ לִשְׁמֶךָ
כַּדָּבָר שֶׁכָּתוּב
כָּל עַצְמֹתַי תֹּאמַרְנָה יהוה מִי כָמוֹךָ תהלים לה
מַצִּיל עָנִי מֵחָזָק מִמֶּנּוּ
וְעָנִי וְאֶבְיוֹן מִגֹּזְלוֹ:
מִי יִדְמֶה לָּךְ וּמִי יִשְׁוֶה לָּךְ וּמִי יַעֲרָךְ לָךְ
הָאֵל הַגָּדוֹל, הַגִּבּוֹר וְהַנּוֹרָא
אֵל עֶלְיוֹן, קוֹנֵה שָׁמַיִם וָאָרֶץ.
◂ נְהַלֶּלְךָ וּנְשַׁבֵּחֲךָ וּנְפָאֶרְךָ וּנְבָרֵךְ אֶת שֵׁם קָדְשֶׁךָ
כָּאָמוּר
לְדָוִד, בָּרְכִי נַפְשִׁי אֶת־יהוה תהלים קג
וְכָל־קְרָבַי אֶת־שֵׁם קָדְשׁוֹ:

הָאֵל God – in Your absolute power,
Great – in the glory of Your name,
Mighty – for ever,
Awesome – in Your awe-inspiring deeds,
The King – who sits on a throne.
High and lofty

The Leader for Shaharit begins here:

HE INHABITS ETERNITY;
great and holy is His name.
And it is written:

Sing joyfully to the LORD, you righteous, *Ps. 33*
for praise from the upright is pleasing.

▸ By the mouth	of the upright	You shall be praised.
By the words	of the righteous	You shall be blessed.
By the tongue	of the pious	You shall be celebrated,
And in the midst	of the holy	You shall be sanctified.

וּבְמַקְהֲלוֹת And in the assemblies
of tens of thousands of Your people, the house of Israel,
with joyous song shall Your name, our King,
be glorified in every generation.

LEARNING

בָּרוּךְ חֲכַם הָרָזִים
"Blessed are You Hashem the Knower of secrets."

The Gemara (*Berakhot* 58a) states that this blessing should be made if one sees a gathering of 600,000 Jews in one place. In this exceptional *berakha* we refer to Hashem as the *Ḥakham HaRazim*, the One whose wisdom encompasses the knowledge of the secrets.

The Gemara and commentaries explain that when we see so many people in one place we become aware that although their personalities and features are not the same, God knows exactly what is in each and every person's heart and mind. Only when we are surrounded by such a large crowd can we access this awareness to be able to make this unique *berakha*.

הָאֵל בְּתַעֲצוּמוֹת עֻזֶּךָ
הַגָּדוֹל בִּכְבוֹד שְׁמֶךָ
הַגִּבּוֹר לָנֶצַח וְהַנּוֹרָא בְּנוֹרְאוֹתֶיךָ
הַמֶּלֶךְ הַיּוֹשֵׁב עַל כִּסֵּא
רָם וְנִשָּׂא

The שליח ציבור *for* שחרית *begins here:*

שׁוֹכֵן עַד

מָרוֹם וְקָדוֹשׁ שְׁמוֹ
וְכָתוּב
רַנְּנוּ צַדִּיקִים בַּיהוה, לַיְשָׁרִים נָאוָה תְהִלָּה: תהלים לג
◂ בְּפִי יְשָׁרִים תִּתְהַלָּל
וּבְדִבְרֵי צַדִּיקִים תִּתְבָּרַךְ
וּבִלְשׁוֹן חֲסִידִים תִּתְרוֹמָם
וּבְקֶרֶב קְדוֹשִׁים תִּתְקַדָּשׁ

וּבְמַקְהֲלוֹת רִבְבוֹת עַמְּךָ בֵּית יִשְׂרָאֵל
בְּרִנָּה יִתְפָּאַר שִׁמְךָ מַלְכֵּנוּ בְּכָל דּוֹר וָדוֹר

... A THOUSAND WORDS

▸ For this is the duty of all creatures before You,
Lord our God and God of our ancestors:
to thank, praise, applaud, glorify, elevate,
honor, bless, raise high and acclaim –
even beyond all the words of song and praise
of David, son of Jesse, Your servant, Your anointed.

Stand until after "Barekhu" on the next page.

יִשְׁתַּבַּח May Your name be praised for ever, our King,
the great and holy God, King in heaven and on earth.
For to You, Lord our God and God of our ancestors,
it is right to offer song and praise,
hymn and psalm,
strength and dominion,
eternity, greatness and power,
song of praise and glory,
holiness and kingship,
▸ blessings and thanks, from now and for ever.
Blessed are You, Lord,
God and King, great in praises,
God of thanksgivings,
Master of wonders,
who delights in hymns of song,
King, God, Giver of life to the worlds.

On Shabbat Shuva, many congregations open the Ark and say this psalm responsively, verse by verse.

שִׁיר הַמַּעֲלוֹת A song of ascents. From the depths I have called to You, Lord. Lord, hear my voice; let Your ears be attentive to my plea. If You, Lord, should keep account of sins, O Lord, who could stand? But with You there is forgiveness, that You may be held in awe. I wait for the Lord, my soul waits, and in His word I put my hope. My soul waits for the Lord more than watchmen wait for the morning, more than watchmen wait for the morning. Israel, put your hope in the Lord, for with the Lord there is loving-kindness, and great is His power to redeem. It is He who will redeem Israel from all their sins. *Ps. 130*

◂ שֶׁכֵּן חוֹבַת כָּל הַיְצוּרִים
לְפָנֶיךָ יהוה אֱלֹהֵינוּ וֵאלֹהֵי אֲבוֹתֵינוּ
לְהוֹדוֹת, לְהַלֵּל, לְשַׁבֵּחַ, לְפָאֵר, לְרוֹמֵם
לְהַדֵּר, לְבָרֵךְ, לְעַלֵּה וּלְקַלֵּס
עַל כָּל דִּבְרֵי שִׁירוֹת וְתִשְׁבְּחוֹת
דָּוִד בֶּן יִשַׁי, עַבְדְּךָ מְשִׁיחֶךָ.

Stand until after בָּרְכוּ *on the next page.*

יִשְׁתַּבַּח שִׁמְךָ לָעַד, מַלְכֵּנוּ
הָאֵל הַמֶּלֶךְ הַגָּדוֹל וְהַקָּדוֹשׁ בַּשָּׁמַיִם וּבָאָרֶץ
כִּי לְךָ נָאֶה, יהוה אֱלֹהֵינוּ וֵאלֹהֵי אֲבוֹתֵינוּ
שִׁיר וּשְׁבָחָה, הַלֵּל וְזִמְרָה
עֹז וּמֶמְשָׁלָה, נֶצַח, גְּדֻלָּה וּגְבוּרָה
תְּהִלָּה וְתִפְאֶרֶת, קְדֻשָּׁה וּמַלְכוּת
◂ בְּרָכוֹת וְהוֹדָאוֹת, מֵעַתָּה וְעַד עוֹלָם.
בָּרוּךְ אַתָּה יהוה, אֵל מֶלֶךְ גָּדוֹל בַּתִּשְׁבָּחוֹת
אֵל הַהוֹדָאוֹת, אֲדוֹן הַנִּפְלָאוֹת
הַבּוֹחֵר בְּשִׁירֵי זִמְרָה, מֶלֶךְ, אֵל, חֵי הָעוֹלָמִים.

On שבת שובה*, many congregations open the* ארון קודש
and say this psalm responsively, verse by verse.

תהלים קל
שִׁיר הַמַּעֲלוֹת, מִמַּעֲמַקִּים קְרָאתִיךָ יהוה: אֲדֹנָי שִׁמְעָה בְקוֹלִי,
תִּהְיֶינָה אָזְנֶיךָ קַשֻּׁבוֹת לְקוֹל תַּחֲנוּנָי: אִם־עֲוֹנוֹת תִּשְׁמָר־יָהּ, אֲדֹנָי
מִי יַעֲמֹד: כִּי־עִמְּךָ הַסְּלִיחָה, לְמַעַן תִּוָּרֵא: קִוִּיתִי יהוה קִוְּתָה נַפְשִׁי,
וְלִדְבָרוֹ הוֹחָלְתִּי: נַפְשִׁי לַאדֹנָי, מִשֹּׁמְרִים לַבֹּקֶר, שֹׁמְרִים לַבֹּקֶר:
יַחֵל יִשְׂרָאֵל אֶל יהוה, כִּי־עִם־יהוה הַחֶסֶד, וְהַרְבֵּה עִמּוֹ פְדוּת:
וְהוּא יִפְדֶּה אֶת־יִשְׂרָאֵל, מִכֹּל עֲוֹנוֹתָיו:

HALF KADDISH

Leader: יִתְגַּדַּל Magnified and sanctified
may His great name be,
in the world He created by His will.
May He establish His kingdom
in your lifetime and in your days,
and in the lifetime of all the house of Israel,
swiftly and soon – and say: Amen.

All: May His great name be blessed for ever and all time.

Leader: Blessed and praised, glorified and elevated,
raised and honored, uplifted and praised
be the name of the Holy One, blessed be He,
beyond any blessing,
song, praise and consolation
uttered in the world – and say: Amen.

BLESSINGS OF THE SHEMA

The following blessing and response are said only in the presence of a minyan.
They represent a formal summons to the congregation to engage in an act of collective prayer.
The custom of bowing at this point is based on 1 Chronicles 29:20, "David said to the whole assembly, 'Now bless the LORD your God.' All the assembly blessed the LORD God of their fathers and bowed their heads low to the LORD and the King."
The Leader says the following, bowing at "Bless," standing straight at "the LORD."
The congregation, followed by the Leader, responds, bowing at "Bless," standing straight at "the LORD."

Leader: BLESS
the LORD, the blessed One.

Congregation: Bless the LORD, the blessed One,
for ever and all time.

Leader: Bless the LORD, the blessed One,
for ever and all time.

חצי קדיש

ש״ץ: יִתְגַּדַּל וְיִתְקַדַּשׁ שְׁמֵהּ רַבָּא (קהל: אָמֵן)
בְּעָלְמָא דִּי בְרָא כִרְעוּתֵהּ, וְיַמְלִיךְ מַלְכוּתֵהּ
בְּחַיֵּיכוֹן וּבְיוֹמֵיכוֹן וּבְחַיֵּי דְכָל בֵּית יִשְׂרָאֵל
בַּעֲגָלָא וּבִזְמַן קָרִיב, וְאִמְרוּ אָמֵן. (קהל: אָמֵן)

קהל וש״ץ: יְהֵא שְׁמֵהּ רַבָּא מְבָרַךְ לְעָלַם וּלְעָלְמֵי עָלְמַיָּא.

ש״ץ: יִתְבָּרַךְ וְיִשְׁתַּבַּח וְיִתְפָּאַר וְיִתְרוֹמַם וְיִתְנַשֵּׂא
וְיִתְהַדָּר וְיִתְעַלֶּה וְיִתְהַלָּל
שְׁמֵהּ דְּקֻדְשָׁא בְּרִיךְ הוּא (קהל: בְּרִיךְ הוּא)
לְעֵלָּא מִן כָּל בִּרְכָתָא / בשבת שובה: לְעֵלָּא לְעֵלָּא מִכָּל בִּרְכָתָא/
וְשִׁירָתָא, תֻּשְׁבְּחָתָא וְנֶחֱמָתָא, דַּאֲמִירָן בְּעָלְמָא
וְאִמְרוּ אָמֵן. (קהל: אָמֵן)

קריאת שמע וברכותיה

The following blessing and response are said only in the presence of a מנין*.*
They represent a formal summons to the קהל *to engage in an act of collective prayer.*
The custom of bowing at this point is based on דברי הימים א׳ כט, כ*, "David said to the whole assembly, 'Now bless the Lord your God.' All the assembly blessed the Lord God of their fathers and bowed their heads low to the Lord and the King."*
The שליח ציבור *says the following, bowing at* בָּרְכוּ*, standing straight at* ה׳*.*
The קהל*, followed by the* שליח ציבור*, responds, bowing at* בָּרוּךְ*, standing straight at* ה׳*.*

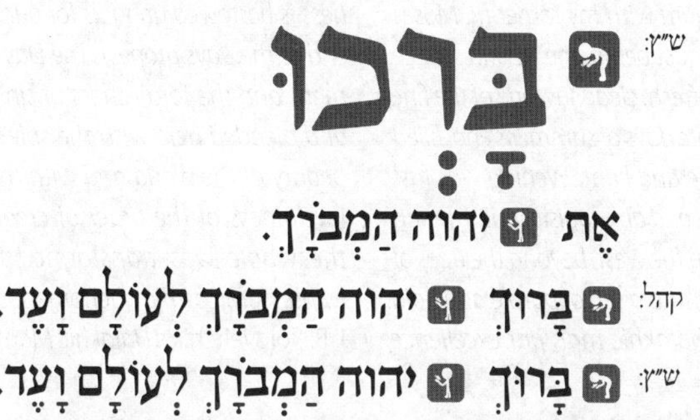
ש״ץ: בָּרְכוּ
אֶת יהוה הַמְבֹרָךְ.
קהל: בָּרוּךְ יהוה הַמְבֹרָךְ לְעוֹלָם וָעֶד.
ש״ץ: בָּרוּךְ יהוה הַמְבֹרָךְ לְעוֹלָם וָעֶד.

The custom is to sit from this point until the Amida, since the predominant emotion of this section of the prayers is love rather than awe. Conversation is forbidden until after the Amida.

בָּרוּךְ Blessed are You, LORD our God, King of the Universe,
who forms light and creates darkness, *Is. 45*
makes peace and creates all.

All will thank You.
All will praise You.
All will declare:
Nothing is as holy as the LORD.
All will elevate You, Selah, You who form all –
the God who daily opens the doors of the gates of the East
and cleaves the windows of the sky,
who brings out the sun from its place
and the moon from its abode,
giving light to the whole world and its inhabitants
whom He created by the attribute of compassion.
In compassion He gives light to the earth and its inhabitants,
and in His goodness daily,
continually, renews the work of creation.

CONNECTION

"I remember how once, on the Day of Atonement, I went outside into the synagogue courtyard with my father [R. Moses Soloveitchik], just before the Ne'ilah service. It had been a fresh, clear day, one of the fine, almost delicate days of summer's end, filled with sunshine and light. Evening was fast approaching, and an exquisite autumn sun was sinking in the west, beyond the trees of the cemetery, into a sea of purple and gold. R. Moses, a halakhic man par excellence, turned to me and said: "This sunset differs from ordinary sunsets for with it forgiveness is bestowed upon us for our sins" (the end of the days atones). The Day of Atonement and the forgiveness of sins merged and blended here with the splendor and beauty of the world and with the hidden lawfulness of the order of creation and the whole was transformed into one living, holy, cosmic phenomenon". (Rabbi J. B. Soloveitchik's *Halakhic Man*)

The custom is to sit from this point until the עמידה*, since the predominant emotion of this section of the prayers is love rather than awe. Conversation is forbidden until after the* עמידה.

בָּרוּךְ אַתָּה יהוה אֱלֹהֵינוּ מֶלֶךְ הָעוֹלָם
יוֹצֵר אוֹר וּבוֹרֵא חֹשֶׁךְ ישעיה מה
עֹשֶׂה שָׁלוֹם וּבוֹרֵא אֶת הַכֹּל.

הַכֹּל יוֹדְוּךָ וְהַכֹּל יְשַׁבְּחוּךָ
וְהַכֹּל יֹאמְרוּ אֵין קָדוֹשׁ כַּיהוה
הַכֹּל יְרוֹמְמוּךָ סֶּלָה, יוֹצֵר הַכֹּל.
הָאֵל הַפּוֹתֵחַ בְּכָל יוֹם דַּלְתוֹת שַׁעֲרֵי מִזְרָח
וּבוֹקֵעַ חַלּוֹנֵי רָקִיעַ
מוֹצִיא חַמָּה מִמְּקוֹמָהּ וּלְבָנָה מִמְּכוֹן שִׁבְתָּהּ
וּמֵאִיר לָעוֹלָם כֻּלּוֹ וּלְיוֹשְׁבָיו
שֶׁבָּרָא בְּמִדַּת הָרַחֲמִים.
הַמֵּאִיר לָאָרֶץ וְלַדָּרִים עָלֶיהָ בְּרַחֲמִים
וּבְטוּבוֹ מְחַדֵּשׁ בְּכָל יוֹם תָּמִיד מַעֲשֵׂה בְרֵאשִׁית.

LEARNING

Just as God created the world from nothing, with His infinite power, so too, ever since then, every day and every moment the world's existence is dependent on the fact that God imbues in it His will, the overflow of a new light. Were He to remove His force for even one moment, the entire world would immediately return to nothingness. This is the meaning of the words of the Men of the Great Assembly, "**מְחַדֵּשׁ בְּכָל יוֹם תָּמִיד מַעֲשֵׂה בְרֵאשִׁית**." (*Nefesh HaḤayyim* 1:2)

REFLECTION

Take a moment to reflect. How does Shabbat give you an opportunity to think about the marvels of creation?

How do you see God recreating each day?

How does Shabbat give you the opportunity to recreate yourself?

He is the King who alone was elevated since time began,
praised, glorified and raised high from days of old.
Eternal God, in Your great compassion, have compassion on us,
LORD of our strength, Rock of our refuge,
Shield of our salvation, Stronghold of our safety.

אֵין כְּעֶרְכֶּךָ None can be compared to You,
there is none besides You;
None without You.
Who is like You?

▸ None can be compared to You,
LORD our God – in this world.
There is none besides You, our King –
in the life of the World to Come.
There is none but You, our Redeemer –
in the days of the Messiah.
There is none like You, our Savior –
at the resurrection of the dead.

אֵל אָדוֹן God, LORD of all creation,
the Blessed, is blessed by every soul.
His greatness and goodness fill the world;
knowledge and wisdom surround Him.

CONNECTION

Rabbi Akiva said: The twenty-two letters of the Torah were engraved with a fiery stylus on the awesome crown of "the Holy One, blessed be He". When Hashem sought to create the world, the letters descended before Him, each one begging that the world might be created through it.

First, the letter tav *approached and said, "Master of the Universe, create the world with me, since through me You will give the Torah to* Benei Yisrael, *as the verse says: 'Torah was commanded to us by Moshe.'"*

Hashem refused tav's *request, since the letter* tav *was destined to be engraved on the brows of the sinners at the time of the* Ḥurban Beit HaMikdash, *marking them for destruction. Dejected by refusal, tav exited, and the letter* shin *entered in its place, only to meet with similar refusal. Each letter entered and was dismissed, until finally the*

"Connection" continues on page 587.

הַמֶּלֶךְ הַמְרוֹמָם לְבַדּוֹ מֵאָז
הַמְשֻׁבָּח וְהַמְפֹאָר וְהַמִּתְנַשֵּׂא מִימוֹת עוֹלָם.
אֱלֹהֵי עוֹלָם, בְּרַחֲמֶיךָ הָרַבִּים רַחֵם עָלֵינוּ
אֲדוֹן עֻזֵּנוּ, צוּר מִשְׂגַּבֵּנוּ
מָגֵן יִשְׁעֵנוּ, מִשְׂגָּב בַּעֲדֵנוּ.

אֵין כְּעֶרְכֶּךָ
וְאֵין זוּלָתֶךָ
אֶפֶס בִּלְתֶּךָ
וּמִי דּוֹמֶה לָּךְ.

› אֵין כְּעֶרְכְּךָ, יהוה אֱלֹהֵינוּ, בָּעוֹלָם הַזֶּה
וְאֵין זוּלָתְךָ, מַלְכֵּנוּ, לְחַיֵּי הָעוֹלָם הַבָּא
אֶפֶס בִּלְתְּךָ, גּוֹאֲלֵנוּ, לִימוֹת הַמָּשִׁיחַ
וְאֵין דּוֹמֶה לְּךָ, מוֹשִׁיעֵנוּ, לִתְחִיַּת הַמֵּתִים.

אֵל אָדוֹן עַל כָּל הַמַּעֲשִׂים
בָּרוּךְ וּמְבֹרָךְ בְּפִי כָּל נְשָׁמָה
גָּדְלוֹ וְטוּבוֹ מָלֵא עוֹלָם
דַּעַת וּתְבוּנָה סוֹבְבִים אוֹתוֹ.

LEARNING

The twenty-two phrases of the אֵל אָדוֹן prayer parallel the twenty-two words of the weekday prayer אֵל בָּרוּךְ. Sometimes, an experience of such overwhelming beauty can fill us with such awe that we find it difficult to describe it with words. The framework of the alphabet allows us to describe this magnificence with one word or one phrase for each letter, symbolizing all encompassing descriptions.

Elevated above the holy Ḥayyot,
adorned in glory on the Chariot;
Merit and right are before His throne,
kindness and compassion before His glory.

Good are the radiant stars our God created;
He formed them with knowledge,
understanding and thought.
He gave them strength and might
to rule throughout the world.

Full of splendor, radiating light,
beautiful is their splendor throughout the world.
Glad as they go forth, joyous as they return,
they fulfill with awe their Creator's will.

Glory and honor they give to His name,
celebration and song at the mention of His majesty.
He called the sun into being and it shone with light.
He looked and fashioned the form of the moon.

All the multitudes on high give Him praise;
the Seraphim, Ophanim and holy Ḥayyot
ascribe glory and greatness –

... A THOUSAND WORDS

REFLECTION

What is the most beautiful thing you have ever seen?

What emotions did you experience when you saw it?

Have you ever seen something so beautiful you were lost for words?

הַמִּתְגָּאֶה עַל חַיּוֹת הַקֹּדֶשׁ
וְנֶהְדָּר בְּכָבוֹד עַל הַמֶּרְכָּבָה
זְכוּת וּמִישׁוֹר לִפְנֵי כִסְאוֹ
חֶסֶד וְרַחֲמִים לִפְנֵי כְבוֹדוֹ.

טוֹבִים מְאוֹרוֹת שֶׁבָּרָא אֱלֹהֵינוּ
יְצָרָם בְּדַעַת בְּבִינָה וּבְהַשְׂכֵּל
כֹּחַ וּגְבוּרָה נָתַן בָּהֶם
לִהְיוֹת מוֹשְׁלִים בְּקֶרֶב תֵּבֵל.

מְלֵאִים זִיו וּמְפִיקִים נֹגַהּ
נָאֶה זִיוָם בְּכָל הָעוֹלָם
שְׂמֵחִים בְּצֵאתָם וְשָׂשִׂים בְּבוֹאָם
עוֹשִׂים בְּאֵימָה רְצוֹן קוֹנָם.

פְּאֵר וְכָבוֹד נוֹתְנִים לִשְׁמוֹ
צָהֳלָה וְרִנָּה לְזֵכֶר מַלְכוּתוֹ
קָרָא לַשֶּׁמֶשׁ וַיִּזְרַח אוֹר
רָאָה וְהִתְקִין צוּרַת הַלְּבָנָה.

שֶׁבַח נוֹתְנִים לוֹ כָּל צְבָא מָרוֹם
תִּפְאֶרֶת וּגְדֻלָּה, שְׂרָפִים וְאוֹפַנִּים וְחַיּוֹת הַקֹּדֶשׁ.

letter bet entered and said, "Master of the Universe, create the world with me, since with me You will be praised each day, 'Barukh Hashem *forever, amen and amen.'"*

Hashem accepted bet's *proposal, and used it to create the world, as the verse says, "Bereshit (in the beginning) Hashem created."* (Yalkut Shimoni, Bereshit *1:1)*

The Rosh writes in his commentary to Nedarim*: "All forms of wisdom and knowledge are hidden in the shapes of the Hebrew letters." From them we learn not only philosophical or kabbalistic concepts, but halakha and* musar *as well.*

לָאֵל To God who rested from all works,
and on the seventh day ascended and sat on His throne of glory.
He robed the day of rest in glory
and called the Sabbath day a delight.
This is the praise of the seventh day,
that on it God rested from all His work.
The seventh day itself gives praise, saying,
"A psalm, a song for the Sabbath day. *Ps. 92*
It is good to give thanks to the LORD."
Therefore let all He has formed glorify and bless God.
Let them give praise, honor and greatness to God,
the King, who formed all things
and in His holiness gave a heritage of rest
to His people Israel on the holy Sabbath day.
May Your name, O LORD our God, be sanctified,
and Your fame, O our King, be glorified
in the heavens above and on earth below.
May You be blessed, our Deliverer,
by the praises of Your handiwork,
and by the radiant lights You have made:
may they glorify You. Selah!

CONNECTION

I had an awesome 8th grade teacher. She was dynamic and fun and made learning Ḥumash *interesting and exciting. She was also famous for the toughest tests, and the kids in 9th grade warned us to study hard for her exams. It was the first test of the year. We sat at our desks, pencils sharpened, anxiously awaiting the dreaded exam paper. Immediately after receiving it, everyone in the class began frantically scribbling answers. Out of the corner of my eye, I noticed my teacher; she was not walking around the room supervising us – she was also frantically scribbling down her answers to the test.*

After the test was over, I raised my hand: "Mora, why were you working on the test you assigned for us?"

She smiled: "Because, my dear class, we are in this together; if you are being tested, then I should be also."

God rests on Shabbat with us, we are in it together.

לָאֵל אֲשֶׁר שָׁבַת מִכָּל הַמַּעֲשִׂים
בַּיּוֹם הַשְּׁבִיעִי נִתְעַלָּה וְיָשַׁב עַל כִּסֵּא כְבוֹדוֹ.
תִּפְאֶרֶת עָטָה לְיוֹם הַמְּנוּחָה
עֹנֶג קָרָא לְיוֹם הַשַּׁבָּת.
זֶה שֶׁבַח שֶׁלְּיוֹם הַשְּׁבִיעִי
שֶׁבּוֹ שָׁבַת אֵל מִכָּל מְלַאכְתּוֹ
וְיוֹם הַשְּׁבִיעִי מְשַׁבֵּחַ וְאוֹמֵר
מִזְמוֹר שִׁיר לְיוֹם הַשַּׁבָּת, טוֹב לְהֹדוֹת לַיהוה: תהלים צב
לְפִיכָךְ יְפָאֲרוּ וִיבָרְכוּ לָאֵל כָּל יְצוּרָיו
שֶׁבַח יְקָר וּגְדֻלָּה יִתְּנוּ לָאֵל מֶלֶךְ יוֹצֵר כֹּל
הַמַּנְחִיל מְנוּחָה לְעַמּוֹ יִשְׂרָאֵל בִּקְדֻשָּׁתוֹ בְּיוֹם שַׁבַּת קֹדֶשׁ.
שִׁמְךָ יהוה אֱלֹהֵינוּ יִתְקַדַּשׁ, וְזִכְרְךָ מַלְכֵּנוּ יִתְפָּאַר
בַּשָּׁמַיִם מִמַּעַל וְעַל הָאָרֶץ מִתָּחַת.
תִּתְבָּרַךְ מוֹשִׁיעֵנוּ עַל שֶׁבַח מַעֲשֵׂה יָדֶיךָ
וְעַל מְאוֹרֵי אוֹר שֶׁעָשִׂיתָ
יְפָאֲרוּךָ סֶּלָה.

REFLECTION

If no one kept Shabbat would it still be Shabbat?

How are you like God?

How can you be more like God?

How do you act like God?

LEARNING

Shabbat was not simply designed so man could have a day of rest and recreation. The true purpose of Shabbat is to remind people of the fact that the first Shabbat was preceded by a work of creation which the Creator completed by resting on the seventh day. Even if all the days of the week were spent in faithful service to God, one must refrain from all labor on the seventh day to contemplate in retrospect what he has accomplished and achieved and to rejoice in the achievements of the week. (Rabbi S.R. Hirsch)

תִּתְבָּרַךְ May You be blessed,
our Rock, King and Redeemer, Creator of holy beings.
May Your name be praised for ever,
our King, Creator of the ministering angels,
all of whom stand in the universe's heights,
declaring together, in awe, aloud,
the words of the living God, the eternal King.
They are all beloved, all pure, all mighty,
and all perform in awe and fear the will of their Maker.
▸ All open their mouths in holiness and purity,
with song and psalm,
and bless, praise, glorify,
fear, sanctify and declare the sovereignty of –
The name of the great, mighty
and awesome God and King,
holy is He.
▸ All accept on themselves,
one from another,
the yoke of the kingdom of heaven,
giving permission to one another
to sanctify the One who formed them,
in serene spirit,
pure speech and sweet melody.
All, as one, declare His holiness,
saying in awe:

All say aloud:

Holy, holy, holy is the Lord of multitudes; *Is. 6*
the whole world is filled with His glory.

▸ Then the Ophanim and the Holy Ḥayyot,
with a roar of noise,
raise themselves toward the Seraphim and,
facing them, give praise, saying:

All say aloud:

Blessed is the Lord's glory from His place. *Ezek. 3*

תִּתְבָּרַךְ
צוּרֵנוּ מַלְכֵּנוּ וְגוֹאֲלֵנוּ, בּוֹרֵא קְדוֹשִׁים
יִשְׁתַּבַּח שִׁמְךָ לָעַד, מַלְכֵּנוּ, יוֹצֵר מְשָׁרְתִים
וַאֲשֶׁר מְשָׁרְתָיו כֻּלָּם עוֹמְדִים בְּרוּם עוֹלָם
וּמַשְׁמִיעִים בְּיִרְאָה יַחַד בְּקוֹל דִּבְרֵי אֱלֹהִים חַיִּים וּמֶלֶךְ עוֹלָם.
כֻּלָּם אֲהוּבִים, כֻּלָּם בְּרוּרִים, כֻּלָּם גִּבּוֹרִים
וְכֻלָּם עוֹשִׂים בְּאֵימָה וּבְיִרְאָה רְצוֹן קוֹנָם
◂ וְכֻלָּם פּוֹתְחִים אֶת פִּיהֶם בִּקְדֻשָּׁה וּבְטָהֳרָה
בְּשִׁירָה וּבְזִמְרָה
וּמְבָרְכִים וּמְשַׁבְּחִים וּמְפָאֲרִים
וּמַעֲרִיצִים וּמַקְדִּישִׁים וּמַמְלִיכִים ◂
אֶת שֵׁם הָאֵל הַמֶּלֶךְ הַגָּדוֹל, הַגִּבּוֹר וְהַנּוֹרָא
קָדוֹשׁ הוּא.
◂ וְכֻלָּם מְקַבְּלִים עֲלֵיהֶם עֹל מַלְכוּת שָׁמַיִם זֶה מִזֶּה
וְנוֹתְנִים רְשׁוּת זֶה לָזֶה
לְהַקְדִּישׁ לְיוֹצְרָם בְּנַחַת רוּחַ, בְּשָׂפָה בְרוּרָה וּבִנְעִימָה
קְדֻשָּׁה כֻּלָּם כְּאֶחָד, עוֹנִים וְאוֹמְרִים בְּיִרְאָה

All say aloud:

ישעיה ו
קָדוֹשׁ, קָדוֹשׁ, קָדוֹשׁ יהוה צְבָאוֹת
מְלֹא כָל־הָאָרֶץ כְּבוֹדוֹ:

◂ וְהָאוֹפַנִּים וְחַיּוֹת הַקֹּדֶשׁ
בְּרַעַשׁ גָּדוֹל מִתְנַשְּׂאִים לְעֻמַּת שְׂרָפִים
לְעֻמָּתָם מְשַׁבְּחִים וְאוֹמְרִים

All say aloud:

יחזקאל ג
בָּרוּךְ כְּבוֹד־יהוה מִמְּקוֹמוֹ:

לָאֵל To the blessed God they offer melodies.
To the King, living and eternal God,
they say psalms and declare praises.
For it is He alone
who does mighty deeds
and creates new things,
who is Master of battles
and sows righteousness,
who makes salvation grow
and creates cures,
who is is feared in praises,
the LORD of wonders,
who in His goodness,
continually renews the work of creation, day after day,
as it is said:
"[Praise] Him who made the great lights, *Ps. 136*
for His love endures for ever."
▸ May You make a new light shine over Zion,
and may we all soon be worthy of its light.
Blessed are You, LORD,
who forms the radiant lights.

אַהֲבָה You have loved us with great love, LORD our God,
and with immense compassion
have You had compassion on us.
Our Father, our King,
for the sake of our ancestors who trusted in You,
and to whom You taught the laws of life,
be gracious also to us and teach us.
Our Father, compassionate Father, ever compassionate,
have compassion on us.
Instill in our hearts the desire to understand and discern,
to listen, learn and teach, to observe, perform and fulfill
all the teachings of Your Torah in love.

לָאֵל בָּרוּךְ נְעִימוֹת יִתֵּנוּ
לַמֶּלֶךְ אֵל חַי וְקַיָּם
זְמִירוֹת יֹאמֵרוּ וְתִשְׁבָּחוֹת יַשְׁמִיעוּ
כִּי הוּא לְבַדּוֹ
פּוֹעֵל גְּבוּרוֹת, עוֹשֶׂה חֲדָשׁוֹת
בַּעַל מִלְחָמוֹת, זוֹרֵעַ צְדָקוֹת
מַצְמִיחַ יְשׁוּעוֹת, בּוֹרֵא רְפוּאוֹת
נוֹרָא תְהִלּוֹת, אֲדוֹן הַנִּפְלָאוֹת
הַמְחַדֵּשׁ בְּטוּבוֹ בְּכָל יוֹם תָּמִיד מַעֲשֵׂה בְרֵאשִׁית
כָּאָמוּר
לְעֹשֵׂה אוֹרִים גְּדֹלִים תהלים קלו
כִּי לְעוֹלָם חַסְדּוֹ:
◄ אוֹר חָדָשׁ עַל צִיּוֹן תָּאִיר וְנִזְכֶּה כֻלָּנוּ מְהֵרָה לְאוֹרוֹ.
בָּרוּךְ אַתָּה יהוה, יוֹצֵר הַמְּאוֹרוֹת.

אַהֲבָה רַבָּה אֲהַבְתָּנוּ, יהוה אֱלֹהֵינוּ
חֶמְלָה גְדוֹלָה וִיתֵרָה חָמַלְתָּ עָלֵינוּ.
אָבִינוּ מַלְכֵּנוּ
בַּעֲבוּר אֲבוֹתֵינוּ שֶׁבָּטְחוּ בְךָ
וַתְּלַמְּדֵם חֻקֵּי חַיִּים, כֵּן תְּחָנֵּנוּ וּתְלַמְּדֵנוּ.
אָבִינוּ, הָאָב הָרַחֲמָן, הַמְרַחֵם
רַחֵם עָלֵינוּ
וְתֵן בְּלִבֵּנוּ לְהָבִין וּלְהַשְׂכִּיל
לִשְׁמֹעַ, לִלְמֹד וּלְלַמֵּד, לִשְׁמֹר וְלַעֲשׂוֹת, וּלְקַיֵּם
אֶת כָּל דִּבְרֵי תַלְמוּד תּוֹרָתֶךָ בְּאַהֲבָה.

Enlighten our eyes in Your Torah
and let our hearts cling to Your commandments.
Unite our hearts to love and fear Your name,
so that we may never be ashamed.
And because we have trusted in Your holy, great and feared name,
may we be glad and rejoice in Your salvation.

At this point, gather the four tzitziot of the tallit, holding them in the left hand.

Bring us back in peace from the four quarters of the earth
and lead us upright to our land.
▸ For You are a God who performs acts of salvation,
and You chose us from all peoples and tongues,
bringing us close to Your great name for ever in truth,
that we may thank You
and declare Your oneness in love.
Blessed are You, LORD, who chooses His people Israel in love.

The Shema must be said with intense concentration. In the first paragraph one should accept, with love, the sovereignty of God; in the second, the mitzvot as the will of God. The end of the third paragraph constitutes fulfillment of the mitzva to remember, morning and evening, the exodus from Egypt.

When not praying with a minyan, say:

God, faithful King!

The following verse should be said aloud, while covering the eyes with the right hand:

Listen, Israel: the LORD is our God, the LORD is One.

Deut. 6

Quietly: Blessed be the name of His glorious kingdom for ever and all time.

וְאָהַבְתָּ Love the LORD your God with all your heart, with all your soul, and with all your might. These words which I command you today shall be on your heart. Teach them repeatedly to your children, speaking of them when you sit at home and when you travel on the way, when you lie down and when you *Deut. 6*

וְהָאֵר עֵינֵינוּ בְּתוֹרָתֶךָ, וְדַבֵּק לִבֵּנוּ בְּמִצְוֹתֶיךָ
וְיַחֵד לְבָבֵנוּ לְאַהֲבָה וּלְיִרְאָה אֶת שְׁמֶךָ
וְלֹא נֵבוֹשׁ לְעוֹלָם וָעֶד.
כִּי בְשֵׁם קָדְשְׁךָ הַגָּדוֹל וְהַנּוֹרָא בָּטָחְנוּ
נָגִילָה וְנִשְׂמְחָה בִּישׁוּעָתֶךָ.

At this point, gather the four ציציות *of the* טלית*, holding them in the left hand.*

וַהֲבִיאֵנוּ לְשָׁלוֹם מֵאַרְבַּע כַּנְפוֹת הָאָרֶץ
וְתוֹלִיכֵנוּ קוֹמְמִיּוּת לְאַרְצֵנוּ.
‣ כִּי אֵל פּוֹעֵל יְשׁוּעוֹת אָתָּה, וּבָנוּ בָחַרְתָּ מִכָּל עַם וְלָשׁוֹן
וְקֵרַבְתָּנוּ לְשִׁמְךָ הַגָּדוֹל סֶלָה, בֶּאֱמֶת
לְהוֹדוֹת לְךָ וּלְיַחֶדְךָ בְּאַהֲבָה.
בָּרוּךְ אַתָּה יהוה, הַבּוֹחֵר בְּעַמּוֹ יִשְׂרָאֵל בְּאַהֲבָה.

The שמע *must be said with intense concentration. In the first paragraph one should accept, with love, the sovereignty of God; in the second, the* מצוות *as the will of God. The end of the third paragraph constitutes fulfillment of the* מצווה *to remember, morning and evening, the exodus from Egypt.*

When not praying with a מנין*, say:*

אֵל מֶלֶךְ נֶאֱמָן

The following verse should be said aloud, while covering the eyes with the right hand:

שְׁמַע יִשְׂרָאֵל, יהוה אֱלֹהֵינוּ, יהוה ׀ אֶחָד: דברים ו

Quietly בָּרוּךְ שֵׁם כְּבוֹד מַלְכוּתוֹ לְעוֹלָם וָעֶד.

וְאָהַבְתָּ אֵת יהוה אֱלֹהֶיךָ, בְּכָל־לְבָבְךָ וּבְכָל־נַפְשְׁךָ וּבְכָל־ דברים ו
מְאֹדֶךָ: וְהָיוּ הַדְּבָרִים הָאֵלֶּה, אֲשֶׁר אָנֹכִי מְצַוְּךָ הַיּוֹם, עַל־לְבָבֶךָ:
וְשִׁנַּנְתָּם לְבָנֶיךָ וְדִבַּרְתָּ בָּם, בְּשִׁבְתְּךָ בְּבֵיתֶךָ וּבְלֶכְתְּךָ בַדֶּרֶךְ,

rise. Bind them as a sign on your hand, and they shall be a symbol between your eyes. Write them on the doorposts of your house and gates.

וְהָיָה If you indeed follow My commandments with which I charge you today, to love the LORD your God and worship Him with all your heart and with all your soul, I will give rain in your land in its season, the early and late rain; and you shall gather in your grain, wine and oil. I will give grass in your field for your cattle, and you shall eat and be satisfied. Be careful lest your heart be tempted and you go astray and worship other gods, bowing down to them. Then the LORD's anger will flare against you and He will close the heavens so that there will be no rain. The land will not yield its crops, and you will perish swiftly from the good land that the LORD is giving you. Therefore, set these, My words, on your heart and soul. Bind them as a sign on your hand, and they shall be a symbol between your eyes. Teach them to your children, speaking of them when you sit at home and when you travel on the way, when you lie down and when you rise. Write them on the doorposts of your house and gates, so that you and your children may live long in the land that the LORD swore to your ancestors to give them, for as long as the heavens are above the earth. *Deut. 11*

Hold the tzitziot in the right hand also (some transfer to the right hand), kissing them at °.

וַיֹּאמֶר The LORD spoke to Moses, saying: Speak to the Israelites and tell them to make °tzitzit on the corners of their garments for all generations. They shall attach to the °tzitzit at each corner a thread of blue. This shall be your °tzitzit, and you shall see it and remember all of the LORD's commandments and keep them, not straying after your heart and after your eyes, following your own sinful desires. Thus you will be reminded to keep all My commandments, and be holy to your God. I am the LORD your *Num. 15*

וּבְשָׁכְבְּךָ וּבְקוּמֶךָ: וּקְשַׁרְתָּם לְאוֹת עַל־יָדֶךָ וְהָיוּ לְטֹטָפֹת בֵּין
עֵינֶיךָ: וּכְתַבְתָּם עַל־מְזֻזוֹת בֵּיתֶךָ וּבִשְׁעָרֶיךָ:

דברים יא וְהָיָה אִם־שָׁמֹעַ תִּשְׁמְעוּ אֶל־מִצְוֹתַי אֲשֶׁר אָנֹכִי מְצַוֶּה אֶתְכֶם
הַיּוֹם, לְאַהֲבָה אֶת־יהוה אֱלֹהֵיכֶם וּלְעָבְדוֹ, בְּכָל־לְבַבְכֶם וּבְכָל־
נַפְשְׁכֶם: וְנָתַתִּי מְטַר־אַרְצְכֶם בְּעִתּוֹ, יוֹרֶה וּמַלְקוֹשׁ, וְאָסַפְתָּ
דְגָנֶךָ וְתִירֹשְׁךָ וְיִצְהָרֶךָ: וְנָתַתִּי עֵשֶׂב בְּשָׂדְךָ לִבְהֶמְתֶּךָ, וְאָכַלְתָּ
וְשָׂבָעְתָּ: הִשָּׁמְרוּ לָכֶם פֶּן־יִפְתֶּה לְבַבְכֶם, וְסַרְתֶּם וַעֲבַדְתֶּם
אֱלֹהִים אֲחֵרִים וְהִשְׁתַּחֲוִיתֶם לָהֶם: וְחָרָה אַף־יהוה בָּכֶם, וְעָצַר
אֶת־הַשָּׁמַיִם וְלֹא־יִהְיֶה מָטָר, וְהָאֲדָמָה לֹא תִתֵּן אֶת־יְבוּלָהּ,
וַאֲבַדְתֶּם מְהֵרָה מֵעַל הָאָרֶץ הַטֹּבָה אֲשֶׁר יהוה נֹתֵן לָכֶם:
וְשַׂמְתֶּם אֶת־דְּבָרַי אֵלֶּה עַל־לְבַבְכֶם וְעַל־נַפְשְׁכֶם, וּקְשַׁרְתֶּם
אֹתָם לְאוֹת עַל־יֶדְכֶם, וְהָיוּ לְטוֹטָפֹת בֵּין עֵינֵיכֶם: וְלִמַּדְתֶּם
אֹתָם אֶת־בְּנֵיכֶם לְדַבֵּר בָּם, בְּשִׁבְתְּךָ בְּבֵיתֶךָ וּבְלֶכְתְּךָ בַדֶּרֶךְ,
וּבְשָׁכְבְּךָ וּבְקוּמֶךָ: וּכְתַבְתָּם עַל־מְזוּזוֹת בֵּיתֶךָ וּבִשְׁעָרֶיךָ: לְמַעַן
יִרְבּוּ יְמֵיכֶם וִימֵי בְנֵיכֶם עַל הָאֲדָמָה אֲשֶׁר נִשְׁבַּע יהוה לַאֲבֹתֵיכֶם
לָתֵת לָהֶם, כִּימֵי הַשָּׁמַיִם עַל־הָאָרֶץ:

Hold the ציציות *in the right hand also (some transfer to the right hand), kissing them at °.*

במדבר טו וַיֹּאמֶר יהוה אֶל־מֹשֶׁה לֵּאמֹר: דַּבֵּר אֶל־בְּנֵי יִשְׂרָאֵל וְאָמַרְתָּ
אֲלֵהֶם, וְעָשׂוּ לָהֶם °צִיצִת עַל־כַּנְפֵי בִגְדֵיהֶם לְדֹרֹתָם, וְנָתְנוּ
°עַל־צִיצִת הַכָּנָף פְּתִיל תְּכֵלֶת: וְהָיָה לָכֶם °לְצִיצִת, וּרְאִיתֶם
אֹתוֹ וּזְכַרְתֶּם אֶת־כָּל־מִצְוֹת יהוה וַעֲשִׂיתֶם אֹתָם, וְלֹא תָתוּרוּ
אַחֲרֵי לְבַבְכֶם וְאַחֲרֵי עֵינֵיכֶם, אֲשֶׁר־אַתֶּם זֹנִים אַחֲרֵיהֶם: לְמַעַן
תִּזְכְּרוּ וַעֲשִׂיתֶם אֶת־כָּל־מִצְוֹתָי, וִהְיִיתֶם קְדֹשִׁים לֵאלֹהֵיכֶם: אֲנִי

God, who brought you out of the land of Egypt to be your God.
I am the LORD your God.

°True –

The Leader repeats:

▸ The LORD your God is true –

וְיַצִּיב And firm, established and enduring,
right, faithful,
beloved, cherished, delightful, pleasant,
awesome, mighty, perfect, accepted,
good and beautiful
is this faith for us for ever.

True is the eternal God, our King,
Rock of Jacob, Shield of our salvation.
He exists and His name exists
through all generations.
His throne is established,
His kingship and trustworthiness endure for ever.

At °, kiss the tzitziot and release them.

His words live and persist,
faithful and desirable
°for ever and all time.
▸ So they were for our ancestors,
so they are for us,
and so they will be for our children
and all our generations
and for all future generations
of the seed of Israel, Your servants.
For the early and the later generations
this faith has proved good
and enduring for ever –

יְהוָה אֱלֹהֵיכֶם, אֲשֶׁר הוֹצֵאתִי אֶתְכֶם מֵאֶרֶץ מִצְרַיִם, לִהְיוֹת לָכֶם לֵאלֹהִים, אֲנִי יְהוָה אֱלֹהֵיכֶם:

°אֱמֶת

The שליח ציבור *repeats:*

◂ יהוה אֱלֹהֵיכֶם אֱמֶת

וְיַצִּיב, וְנָכוֹן וְקַיָּם, וְיָשָׁר וְנֶאֱמָן
וְאָהוּב וְחָבִיב, וְנֶחְמָד וְנָעִים
וְנוֹרָא וְאַדִּיר, וּמְתֻקָּן וּמְקֻבָּל, וְטוֹב וְיָפֶה
הַדָּבָר הַזֶּה עָלֵינוּ לְעוֹלָם וָעֶד.

אֱמֶת אֱלֹהֵי עוֹלָם מַלְכֵּנוּ
צוּר יַעֲקֹב מָגֵן יִשְׁעֵנוּ
לְדוֹר וָדוֹר הוּא קַיָּם וּשְׁמוֹ קַיָּם
וְכִסְאוֹ נָכוֹן
וּמַלְכוּתוֹ וֶאֱמוּנָתוֹ לָעַד קַיֶּמֶת.

At °, kiss the ציציות *and release them.*

וּדְבָרָיו חָיִים וְקַיָּמִים
נֶאֱמָנִים וְנֶחֱמָדִים
°לָעַד וּלְעוֹלְמֵי עוֹלָמִים
◂ עַל אֲבוֹתֵינוּ וְעָלֵינוּ
עַל בָּנֵינוּ וְעַל דּוֹרוֹתֵינוּ
וְעַל כָּל דּוֹרוֹת זֶרַע יִשְׂרָאֵל עֲבָדֶיךָ.
עַל הָרִאשׁוֹנִים וְעַל הָאַחֲרוֹנִים
דָּבָר טוֹב וְקַיָּם לְעוֹלָם וָעֶד

True and faithful, an irrevocable law.

True You are the LORD: our God and God of our ancestors,
▸ our King and King of our ancestors,
our Redeemer and Redeemer of our ancestors,
our Maker,
Rock of our salvation,
our Deliverer and Rescuer:
this has ever been Your name.
There is no God but You.

עֶזְרַת You have always been the help of our ancestors,
Shield and Savior of their children
after them in every generation.
Your presence is in the heights of the universe,
and Your judgments and righteousness
reach to the ends of the earth.
Happy is the one who obeys Your commandments
and takes to heart Your teaching and Your word.

True You are the Master of Your people
and a mighty King
who pleads their cause.

True You are the first and You are the last.
Besides You, we have no king, redeemer or savior.
From Egypt You redeemed us, LORD our God,
and from the slave-house You saved us.
All their firstborn You killed,
but Your firstborn You redeemed.
You split the Sea of Reeds
and drowned the arrogant.
You brought Your beloved ones across.
The water covered their enemies; *Ps. 106*
not one of them was left.

אֱמֶת וֶאֱמוּנָה, חֹק וְלֹא יַעֲבֹר.

אֱמֶת שָׁאַתָּה הוּא יהוה אֱלֹהֵינוּ וֵאלֹהֵי אֲבוֹתֵינוּ
◄ מַלְכֵּנוּ מֶלֶךְ אֲבוֹתֵינוּ
גּוֹאֲלֵנוּ גּוֹאֵל אֲבוֹתֵינוּ
יוֹצְרֵנוּ צוּר יְשׁוּעָתֵנוּ
פּוֹדֵנוּ וּמַצִּילֵנוּ מֵעוֹלָם שְׁמֶךָ
אֵין אֱלֹהִים זוּלָתֶךָ.

עֶזְרַת אֲבוֹתֵינוּ אַתָּה הוּא מֵעוֹלָם
מָגֵן וּמוֹשִׁיעַ לִבְנֵיהֶם אַחֲרֵיהֶם בְּכָל דּוֹר וָדוֹר.
בְּרוּם עוֹלָם מוֹשָׁבֶךָ
וּמִשְׁפָּטֶיךָ וְצִדְקָתְךָ עַד אַפְסֵי אָרֶץ.
אַשְׁרֵי אִישׁ שֶׁיִּשְׁמַע לְמִצְוֹתֶיךָ
וְתוֹרָתְךָ וּדְבָרְךָ יָשִׂים עַל לִבּוֹ.

אֱמֶת אַתָּה הוּא אָדוֹן לְעַמֶּךָ
וּמֶלֶךְ גִּבּוֹר לָרִיב רִיבָם.

אֱמֶת אַתָּה הוּא רִאשׁוֹן וְאַתָּה הוּא אַחֲרוֹן
וּמִבַּלְעָדֶיךָ אֵין לָנוּ מֶלֶךְ גּוֹאֵל וּמוֹשִׁיעַ.
מִמִּצְרַיִם גְּאַלְתָּנוּ, יהוה אֱלֹהֵינוּ
וּמִבֵּית עֲבָדִים פְּדִיתָנוּ
כָּל בְּכוֹרֵיהֶם הָרָגְתָּ, וּבְכוֹרְךָ גָּאָלְתָּ
וְיַם סוּף בָּקַעְתָּ, וְזֵדִים טִבַּעְתָּ
וִידִידִים הֶעֱבַרְתָּ
וַיְכַסּוּ־מַיִם צָרֵיהֶם, אֶחָד מֵהֶם לֹא נוֹתָר: תהלים קו

For this, the beloved ones praised and elevated God,
the cherished ones sang psalms, songs and praises,
blessings and thanksgivings to the King,
the living and enduring God.
High and elevated, great and awesome,
He humbles the arrogant and raises the lowly,
freeing captives and redeeming those in need,
helping the poor
and answering His people when they cry out to Him.

Stand in preparation for the Amida.
Take three steps back before beginning the Amida.

▸ Praises to God Most High,
the Blessed One who is blessed.
Moses and the children of Israel
recited to You a song with great joy,
and they all exclaimed:

"Who is like You, LORD, among the mighty? *Ex. 15*
Who is like You, majestic in holiness,
awesome in praises, doing wonders?"

▸ With a new song, the redeemed people praised
Your name at the seashore.
Together they all gave thanks,
proclaimed Your kingship,
and declared:

"The LORD shall reign for ever and ever." *Ex. 15*

Congregants should end the following blessing together with the Leader so as to be able to move directly from the words "redeemed Israel" to the Amida, without the interruption of saying Amen.

▸ צוּר יִשְׂרָאֵל Rock of Israel! Arise to the help of Israel.
Deliver, as You promised, Judah and Israel.

Our Redeemer, the LORD of multitudes is His name, *Is. 47*
the Holy One of Israel.

Blessed are You, LORD, who redeemed Israel.

עַל זֹאת שִׁבְּחוּ אֲהוּבִים, וְרוֹמְמוּ אֵל
וְנָתְנוּ יְדִידִים זְמִירוֹת, שִׁירוֹת וְתִשְׁבָּחוֹת
בְּרָכוֹת וְהוֹדָאוֹת לַמֶּלֶךְ אֵל חַי וְקַיָּם
רָם וְנִשָּׂא, גָּדוֹל וְנוֹרָא
מַשְׁפִּיל גֵּאִים וּמַגְבִּיהַּ שְׁפָלִים
מוֹצִיא אֲסִירִים, וּפוֹדֶה עֲנָוִים וְעוֹזֵר דַּלִּים
וְעוֹנֶה לְעַמּוֹ בְּעֵת שַׁוְּעָם אֵלָיו.

Stand in preparation for the עמידה*.*
Take three steps back before beginning the עמידה*.*

◂ תְּהִלּוֹת לְאֵל עֶלְיוֹן, בָּרוּךְ הוּא וּמְבֹרָךְ
מֹשֶׁה וּבְנֵי יִשְׂרָאֵל, לְךָ עָנוּ שִׁירָה בְּשִׂמְחָה רַבָּה
וְאָמְרוּ כֻלָּם

שמות טו מִי־כָמֹכָה בָּאֵלִם, יהוה
מִי כָּמֹכָה נֶאְדָּר בַּקֹּדֶשׁ, נוֹרָא תְהִלֹּת, עֹשֵׂה פֶלֶא:

◂ שִׁירָה חֲדָשָׁה שִׁבְּחוּ גְאוּלִים
לְשִׁמְךָ עַל שְׂפַת הַיָּם
יַחַד כֻּלָּם הוֹדוּ וְהִמְלִיכוּ
וְאָמְרוּ

שמות טו יהוה יִמְלֹךְ לְעֹלָם וָעֶד:

The קהל *should end the following blessing together with the* שליח ציבור
so as to be able to move directly from the words גָּאַל יִשְׂרָאֵל *to*
the עמידה*, without the interruption of saying* אמן*.*

◂ צוּר יִשְׂרָאֵל, קוּמָה בְּעֶזְרַת יִשְׂרָאֵל
וּפְדֵה כִנְאֻמֶךָ יְהוּדָה וְיִשְׂרָאֵל.

ישעיה מז גֹּאֲלֵנוּ יהוה צְבָאוֹת שְׁמוֹ, קְדוֹשׁ יִשְׂרָאֵל:
בָּרוּךְ אַתָּה יהוה, גָּאַל יִשְׂרָאֵל.

THE AMIDA

The following prayer, until "in former years" on page 622, is said silently, standing with feet together. If there is a minyan, the Amida is repeated aloud by the Leader. Take three steps forward and at the points indicated by ˚, bend the knees at the first word, bow at the second, and stand straight before saying God's name.

O Lord, open my lips, so that my mouth may declare Your praise. *Ps. 51*

PATRIARCHS

בָּרוּךְ Blessed are You,
Lord our God and God of our fathers,
God of Abraham, God of Isaac and God of Jacob;
the great, mighty and awesome God, God Most High,
who acts with loving-kindness and creates all,
who remembers the loving-kindness of the fathers
and will bring a Redeemer to their children's children
for the sake of His name, in love.

On Shabbat Shuva: Remember us for life, O King who desires life,
and write us in the book of life – for Your sake, O God of life.

King, Helper, Savior, Shield:
Blessed are You, Lord, Shield of Abraham.

DIVINE MIGHT

אַתָּה גִּבּוֹר You are eternally mighty, Lord.
You give life to the dead and have great power to save.

The phrase "He makes the wind blow and the rain fall" is added from Simḥat Torah until Pesaḥ. In Israel the phrase "He causes the dew to fall" is added from Pesaḥ until Shemini Atzeret.

In fall & winter: He makes the wind blow and the rain fall.
In Israel, in spring & summer: He causes the dew to fall.

He sustains the living with loving-kindness,
and with great compassion revives the dead.
He supports the fallen, heals the sick, sets captives free,
and keeps His faith with those who sleep in the dust.
Who is like You, Master of might, and who can compare to You,
O King who brings death and gives life, and makes salvation grow?

On Shabbat Shuva: Who is like You, compassionate Father,
who remembers His creatures in compassion, for life?

עמידה

The following prayer, until קַדְמֹנִיּוֹת *on page 623, is said silently, standing with feet together. If there is a* מנין*, the* עמידה *is repeated aloud by the* שליח ציבור*. Take three steps forward and at the points indicated by* ׳*, bend the knees at the first word, bow at the second, and stand straight before saying God's name.*

אֲדֹנָי, שְׂפָתַי תִּפְתָּח, וּפִי יַגִּיד תְּהִלָּתֶךָ: תהלים נא

אבות

בָּרוּךְ אַתָּה יהוה, אֱלֹהֵינוּ וֵאלֹהֵי אֲבוֹתֵינוּ
אֱלֹהֵי אַבְרָהָם, אֱלֹהֵי יִצְחָק, וֵאלֹהֵי יַעֲקֹב
הָאֵל הַגָּדוֹל הַגִּבּוֹר וְהַנּוֹרָא, אֵל עֶלְיוֹן
גּוֹמֵל חֲסָדִים טוֹבִים, וְקוֹנֵה הַכֹּל, וְזוֹכֵר חַסְדֵי אָבוֹת
וּמֵבִיא גוֹאֵל לִבְנֵי בְנֵיהֶם לְמַעַן שְׁמוֹ בְּאַהֲבָה.

בשבת שובה: זָכְרֵנוּ לְחַיִּים, מֶלֶךְ חָפֵץ בַּחַיִּים
וְכָתְבֵנוּ בְּסֵפֶר הַחַיִּים, לְמַעַנְךָ אֱלֹהִים חַיִּים.

מֶלֶךְ עוֹזֵר וּמוֹשִׁיעַ וּמָגֵן.
בָּרוּךְ אַתָּה יהוה, מָגֵן אַבְרָהָם.

גבורות

אַתָּה גִּבּוֹר לְעוֹלָם, אֲדֹנָי, מְחַיֵּה מֵתִים אַתָּה, רַב לְהוֹשִׁיעַ

The phrase מַשִּׁיב הָרוּחַ *is added from* שמחת תורה *until* פסח*.*
In ארץ ישראל *the phrase* מוֹרִיד הַטָּל *is added from* פסח *until* שמיני עצרת*.*

בחורף: מַשִּׁיב הָרוּחַ וּמוֹרִיד הַגֶּשֶׁם / בארץ ישראל בקיץ: מוֹרִיד הַטָּל

מְכַלְכֵּל חַיִּים בְּחֶסֶד, מְחַיֵּה מֵתִים בְּרַחֲמִים רַבִּים
סוֹמֵךְ נוֹפְלִים, וְרוֹפֵא חוֹלִים, וּמַתִּיר אֲסוּרִים
וּמְקַיֵּם אֱמוּנָתוֹ לִישֵׁנֵי עָפָר.
מִי כָמוֹךָ, בַּעַל גְּבוּרוֹת, וּמִי דּוֹמֶה לָּךְ
מֶלֶךְ, מֵמִית וּמְחַיֶּה וּמַצְמִיחַ יְשׁוּעָה.

בשבת שובה: מִי כָמוֹךָ אַב הָרַחֲמִים, זוֹכֵר יְצוּרָיו לְחַיִּים בְּרַחֲמִים.

Faithful are You to revive the dead.
Blessed are You, LORD, who revives the dead.

When saying the Amida silently, continue with "You are holy" on the next page.

KEDUSHA

During the Leader's Repetition, the following is said standing with feet together, rising on the toes at the words indicated by ▴.

Cong. then Leader: נְקַדֵּשׁ We will sanctify Your name on earth,
as they sanctify it in the highest heavens,
as is written by Your prophet,
"And they [the angels] call to one another saying: *Is. 6*

Cong. then Leader: ▴Holy, ▴holy, ▴holy is the LORD of multitudes
the whole world is filled with His glory."
Then with a sound of mighty noise, majestic and strong,
they make their voice heard,
raising themselves toward the Seraphim,
and facing them say: "Blessed…

Cong. then Leader: ▴"Blessed is the LORD's glory from His place." *Ezek. 3*
Reveal Yourself from Your place,
O our King, and reign over us, for we are waiting for You.
When will You reign in Zion?
May it be soon in our days,
and may You be present there for ever and all time.
May You be great and sanctified in the midst of Jerusalem,
Your city, from generation to generation for evermore.
May our eyes see Your kingdom,
as is said in the songs of Your splendor,
written by David your righteous anointed one:

---

more. We yearn not only for the redemption of time but for the redemption of space. We yearn not only for a moment of redemption but for the ultimate redemption, God's return to Zion.

REFLECTION

Where and when in your life can you experience *kedusha*?
What places have you visited that feel holy?
What people do you know
that you sense are holy?

וְנֶאֱמָן אַתָּה לְהַחֲיוֹת מֵתִים.
בָּרוּךְ אַתָּה יהוה, מְחַיֵּה הַמֵּתִים.

When saying the עמידה *silently, continue with* אַתָּה קָדוֹשׁ *on the next page.*

קדושה

During the חזרת הש״ץ, *the following is said standing with feet together, rising on the toes at the words indicated by* ˄.

קהל *then* ש״ץ: נְקַדֵּשׁ אֶת שִׁמְךָ בָּעוֹלָם, כְּשֵׁם שֶׁמַּקְדִּישִׁים אוֹתוֹ בִּשְׁמֵי מָרוֹם
ישעיה ו כַּכָּתוּב עַל יַד נְבִיאֶךָ: וְקָרָא זֶה אֶל־זֶה וְאָמַר

קהל *then* ש״ץ: ˄קָדוֹשׁ, ˄קָדוֹשׁ, ˄קָדוֹשׁ, יהוה צְבָאוֹת
מְלֹא כָל־הָאָרֶץ כְּבוֹדוֹ:
אָז בְּקוֹל רַעַשׁ גָּדוֹל אַדִּיר וְחָזָק, מַשְׁמִיעִים קוֹל
מִתְנַשְּׂאִים לְעֻמַּת שְׂרָפִים
לְעֻמָּתָם בָּרוּךְ יֹאמֵרוּ

קהל *then* ש״ץ: יחזקאל ג ˄בָּרוּךְ כְּבוֹד־יהוה מִמְּקוֹמוֹ:
מִמְּקוֹמְךָ מַלְכֵּנוּ תוֹפִיעַ וְתִמְלֹךְ עָלֵינוּ
כִּי מְחַכִּים אֲנַחְנוּ לָךְ.
מָתַי תִּמְלֹךְ בְּצִיּוֹן, בְּקָרוֹב בְּיָמֵינוּ לְעוֹלָם וָעֶד תִּשְׁכֹּן
תִּתְגַּדַּל וְתִתְקַדַּשׁ בְּתוֹךְ יְרוּשָׁלַיִם עִירְךָ
לְדוֹר וָדוֹר וּלְנֵצַח נְצָחִים.
וְעֵינֵינוּ תִרְאֶינָה מַלְכוּתֶךָ
כַּדָּבָר הָאָמוּר בְּשִׁירֵי עֻזֶּךָ, עַל יְדֵי דָוִד מְשִׁיחַ צִדְקֶךָ

LEARNING

On Shabbat we experience the redemption of time when we sanctify a moment in the week. In the special *Kedusha* for Shabbat we yearn for something even

At one point in *Kedusha* the question is asked, "When will You, Hashem, return to Jerusalem? When will the *geula* (redemption) come?"

Cong. then Leader: ▲"The Lord shall reign for ever. He is your God, Zion, from generation to generation, Halleluya!" *Ps. 146*

Leader: From generation to generation we will speak of Your greatness,
and we will declare Your holiness for evermore.
Your praise, our God, shall not leave our mouth forever,
for You, God, are a great and holy King.
Blessed are You, Lord, the holy God.
/ *On Shabbat Shuva:* the holy King./

The Leader continues with "Moses rejoiced" on the next page.

HOLINESS

אַתָּה קָדוֹשׁ You are holy and Your name is holy,
and holy ones praise You daily, Selah!
Blessed are You, Lord,
the holy God. / *On Shabbat Shuva:* the holy King./

(*If forgotten, repeat the Amida.*)

... A THOUSAND WORDS

then קהל ש״ץ: יִמְלֹךְ יהוה לְעוֹלָם, אֱלֹהַיִךְ צִיּוֹן לְדֹר וָדֹר, הַלְלוּיָהּ: תהלים קמו

ש״ץ: לְדוֹר וָדוֹר נַגִּיד גָּדְלֶךָ
וּלְנֵצַח נְצָחִים קְדֻשָּׁתְךָ נַקְדִּישׁ
וְשִׁבְחֲךָ אֱלֹהֵינוּ מִפִּינוּ לֹא יָמוּשׁ לְעוֹלָם וָעֶד
כִּי אֵל מֶלֶךְ גָּדוֹל וְקָדוֹשׁ אָתָּה.
בָּרוּךְ אַתָּה יהוה, הָאֵל הַקָּדוֹשׁ./ בשבת שובה: הַמֶּלֶךְ הַקָּדוֹשׁ./

The שליח ציבור *continues with* יִשְׂמַח מֹשֶׁה *on the next page.*

קדושת השם

אַתָּה קָדוֹשׁ וְשִׁמְךָ קָדוֹשׁ
וּקְדוֹשִׁים בְּכָל יוֹם יְהַלְלוּךָ סֶּלָה.
בָּרוּךְ אַתָּה יהוה, הָאֵל הַקָּדוֹשׁ. / בשבת שובה: הַמֶּלֶךְ הַקָּדוֹשׁ./

(*If forgotten, repeat the* עמידה.)

CONNECTION

In what ways is the settler who has his own "place" superior to the nomad who has none of his own? First, the nomad is an exploiter, living off others. He moves from one pasture to another, from one feeding ground to another. When favorable ecological conditions turn, he lifts his tent and travels anew. He has neither the desire nor intent to cultivate his land, for he has no land of his own; and he can always find new pastures. Secondly, the nomad has no mental "bond" with his land. Since he has offered it nothing, it offers him nothing. He does not feel a symbiotic relationship between himself and his land. He has no "place consciousness."

Place consciousness means having a firm identity. The wanderer is tethered to nothing. By having a place the settler can develop a clear and consistent identity.

Relationships with others, particularly with God, can also be characterized as wanderings or settled. We refer to God as HaMakom *(the place) to emphasize the aspect of our relationship with God that gives us identity and stability. We no longer have to wander. God is our place.* (Adapted from Rabbi J.B. Soloveitchik, *Sacred and Profane*)

HOLINESS OF THE DAY

יִשְׂמַח Moses rejoiced at the gift of his portion
when You called him "faithful servant."
A crown of glory You placed on his head
when he stood before You on Mount Sinai.
He brought down in his hands two tablets of stone
on which was engraved the observance of the Sabbath.
So it is written in Your Torah:

וְשָׁמְרוּ The children of Israel must keep the Sabbath, *Ex. 31*
observing the Sabbath in every generation
as an everlasting covenant.
It is a sign between Me and the children of Israel for ever,
for in six days God made the heavens and the earth,
but on the seventh day He ceased work and refreshed Himself.

CONNECTION

Sometimes, I even think my Sabbath observance may actually have helped my political career, although, of course, I did not become Sabbath observant because of a focus group or public opinion poll. For that, I must "blame" my parents and rabbis.

Here's a story that illustrates my point. In the State Senate, I had a Democratic colleague and friend named Con O'Leary, who later became the Senate majority leader. One day in 1988, during my first run for the US Senate, against the incumbent Republican senator Lowell Weicker, Con called and said to me, "Joe, I think you're going to win this election."

"That's great, Con," I said, knowing most people felt otherwise, "Why?"

"I went to visit my mother yesterday," he explained, "and three of her lady friends were with her having afternoon tea. So you had four silver-haired Catholic ladies there. I asked them who they planned to vote for in the presidential race. They said they were going to vote Republican – for Bush, not Dukakis. I argued with them, but I finally gave up and said, 'What about the Senate – Weicker or Lieberman?' And my mother said, 'That's easy, I'm voting for Lieberman.' All the other women said, 'Yes, we're voting for Lieberman.'"

"Why is that such an easy choice?" O'Leary asked his mother.

And Mrs. O'Leary said, "I like the fact that Joe Lieberman is a religious man and keeps his Sabbath." "And," Con concluded, "the three other silver-haired heads nodded."

Thank you Mrs. O'Leary. (*Jewish Action* interview with Senator Joe Lieberman)

קדושת היום

יִשְׂמַח מֹשֶׁה בְּמַתְּנַת חֶלְקוֹ, כִּי עֶבֶד נֶאֱמָן קָרָאתָ לּוֹ
כְּלִיל תִּפְאֶרֶת בְּרֹאשׁוֹ נָתַתָּ לּוֹ בְּעָמְדוֹ לְפָנֶיךָ עַל הַר סִינַי
וּשְׁנֵי לוּחוֹת אֲבָנִים הוֹרִיד בְּיָדוֹ
וְכָתוּב בָּהֶם שְׁמִירַת שַׁבָּת
וְכֵן כָּתוּב בְּתוֹרָתֶךָ

שמות לא

וְשָׁמְרוּ בְנֵי־יִשְׂרָאֵל אֶת־הַשַּׁבָּת
לַעֲשׂוֹת אֶת־הַשַּׁבָּת לְדֹרֹתָם בְּרִית עוֹלָם:
בֵּינִי וּבֵין בְּנֵי יִשְׂרָאֵל אוֹת הִוא לְעֹלָם
כִּי־שֵׁשֶׁת יָמִים עָשָׂה יהוה אֶת־הַשָּׁמַיִם וְאֶת־הָאָרֶץ
וּבַיּוֹם הַשְּׁבִיעִי שָׁבַת וַיִּנָּפַשׁ:

LEARNING

According to Abudraham, "*matnat ḥelko*" refers to the gift of Shabbat.

When the Jewish people were in Egypt, Moshe saw that they had no rest, no break, no respite from their labor, so he said to Pharaoh, "A slave with no rest day is a dead slave."

Pharaoh agreed and Moshe established Shabbat as a day of rest. (*Shemot Raba* 1:1)

How happy must the Jews have been on those Shabbatot in Egypt.

... A THOUSAND WORDS

REFLECTION

Do you see Shabbat as a gift?

What would your life be like without Shabbat?

How do you think the Jews in Egypt felt about Shabbat?

וְלֹא You, O Lord our God, did not give it
to the other nations of the world,
nor did You, our King, give it as a heritage
to those who worship idols.
In its rest the uncircumcised do not live,
for You gave it in love to Israel Your people,
to the descendants of Jacob whom You chose.
May the people who sanctify the seventh day
all find satisfaction and delight in Your goodness,
for You favored the seventh day and made it holy,
calling it the most cherished of days,
a remembrance of the act of creation.

REFLECTION

What makes
the Jewish people
unique?

What do you
love most
about being Jewish?

Does Shabbat make you proud
to be Jewish?
Why?

Can you recall a Shabbat
that made you proud
to be Jewish?

CONNECTION

It is no exaggeration to say that the Jew has survived two thousand years of persecution and humiliation largely because he had the Sabbath. It was one factor that not only made him survive, but kept him alive, both spiritually and morally.

Without the Sabbath, the Jew would have vanished. It has been said that as much as the Jew has kept Shabbat so has Shabbat kept the Jew.

As long as Judaism exists as a vibrant, vital force, the Sabbath is its most outstanding ritual practice.

In order to understand this, you would have to experience a true traditional Shabbat. You would see a change take place, almost like magic. Take the poorest Jew, the most wretched person, and the Sabbath transforms him, as if by a miracle, into a man of dignity and pride. He might be a beggar all week long, but on this one day, he is a true king. (Rabbi Aryeh Kaplan)

וְלֹא נְתַתּוֹ, יהוה אֱלֹהֵינוּ, לְגוֹיֵי הָאֲרָצוֹת
וְלֹא הִנְחַלְתּוֹ, מַלְכֵּנוּ, לְעוֹבְדֵי פְסִילִים
וְגַם בִּמְנוּחָתוֹ לֹא יִשְׁכְּנוּ עֲרֵלִים
כִּי לְיִשְׂרָאֵל עַמְּךָ נְתַתּוֹ בְּאַהֲבָה, לְזֶרַע יַעֲקֹב אֲשֶׁר בָּם בָּחָרְתָּ.
עַם מְקַדְּשֵׁי שְׁבִיעִי
כֻּלָּם יִשְׂבְּעוּ וְיִתְעַנְּגוּ מִטּוּבֶךָ
וּבַשְּׁבִיעִי רָצִיתָ בּוֹ וְקִדַּשְׁתּוֹ
חֶמְדַּת יָמִים אוֹתוֹ קָרָאתָ, זֵכֶר לְמַעֲשֵׂה בְרֵאשִׁית.

LEARNING

Hashem offered us the Torah. However, He did not offer it to the Jews alone, but to all of the nations. First He approached the children of Eisav and asked them, "Do you wish to accept the Torah?" They replied, "What is written in it?"

When God told them about the laws of murder, they refused to accept the Torah.

Next Hashem went to the children of Ammon and Moav, and asked, "Do you wish to accept the Torah?" They asked, "What is written in it?"

When God told them about the laws of immorality, they refused to accept the Torah.

Hashem then went to the children of Yishmael, and asked them, "Do you wish to accept the Torah?" They asked, "What is written in it?"

When God told them about the laws of theft, they too refused to accept the Torah.

There was not a single nation on whose door Hashem did not approach to ask if they were willing to receive the Torah. Finally, when God offered the Torah to the Jewish people, they accepted His gift without question saying, "*Naaseh venishma.*" (*Sifri, VeZot HaBerakha* 343)

...A THOUSAND WORDS

אֱלֹהֵינוּ Our God and God of our ancestors, find favor in our rest.
Make us holy through Your commandments
and give us our share in Your Torah.
Satisfy us with Your goodness, give us joy in Your salvation,
and purify our hearts to serve You in truth.
In love and favor, LORD our God,
give us as our heritage Your holy Sabbath,
so that Israel who sanctify Your name may find rest on it.
Blessed are You, LORD, who sanctifies the Sabbath.

TEMPLE SERVICE

רְצֵה Find favor, LORD our God, in Your people Israel
and their prayer.
Restore the service to Your most holy House,
and accept in love and favor the fire-offerings of Israel
and their prayer.
May the service of Your people Israel always find favor with You.

On Rosh Ḥodesh and Ḥol HaMo'ed, say:

אֱלֹהֵינוּ Our God and God of our ancestors, may there rise, come, reach, appear, be favored, heard, regarded and remembered before You, our recollection and remembrance, as well as the remembrance of our ancestors, and of the Messiah son of David Your servant, and of Jerusalem Your holy city, and of all Your people the house of Israel – for deliverance and well-being, grace, loving-kindness and compassion, life and peace, on this day of:

On Rosh Ḥodesh: Rosh Ḥodesh.
On Pesaḥ: the Festival of Matzot.
On Sukkot: the Festival of Sukkot.

On it remember us, LORD our God, for good; recollect us for blessing, and save us for life. In accord with Your promise of salvation and compassion, spare us and be gracious to us; have compassion on us and save us, for our eyes are turned to You because You, God, are a gracious and compassionate King.

וְתֶחֱזֶינָה And may our eyes witness Your return
to Zion in compassion.
Blessed are You, LORD, who restores His Presence to Zion.

אֱלֹהֵינוּ וֵאלֹהֵי אֲבוֹתֵינוּ, רְצֵה בִמְנוּחָתֵנוּ
קַדְּשֵׁנוּ בְּמִצְוֹתֶיךָ וְתֵן חֶלְקֵנוּ בְּתוֹרָתֶךָ
שַׂבְּעֵנוּ מִטּוּבֶךָ, וְשַׂמְּחֵנוּ בִּישׁוּעָתֶךָ
וְטַהֵר לִבֵּנוּ לְעָבְדְּךָ בֶּאֱמֶת
וְהַנְחִילֵנוּ, יהוה אֱלֹהֵינוּ, בְּאַהֲבָה וּבְרָצוֹן שַׁבַּת קָדְשֶׁךָ
וְיָנוּחוּ בוֹ יִשְׂרָאֵל מְקַדְּשֵׁי שְׁמֶךָ.
בָּרוּךְ אַתָּה יהוה, מְקַדֵּשׁ הַשַּׁבָּת.

עבודה

רְצֵה יהוה אֱלֹהֵינוּ בְּעַמְּךָ יִשְׂרָאֵל, וּבִתְפִלָּתָם
וְהָשֵׁב אֶת הָעֲבוֹדָה לִדְבִיר בֵּיתֶךָ
וְאִשֵּׁי יִשְׂרָאֵל וּתְפִלָּתָם בְּאַהֲבָה תְקַבֵּל בְּרָצוֹן
וּתְהִי לְרָצוֹן תָּמִיד עֲבוֹדַת יִשְׂרָאֵל עַמֶּךָ.

On ראש חודש *and* חול המועד*, say:*

אֱלֹהֵינוּ וֵאלֹהֵי אֲבוֹתֵינוּ, יַעֲלֶה וְיָבוֹא וְיַגִּיעַ, וְיֵרָאֶה וְיֵרָצֶה וְיִשָּׁמַע, וְיִפָּקֵד וְיִזָּכֵר זִכְרוֹנֵנוּ וּפִקְדוֹנֵנוּ וְזִכְרוֹן אֲבוֹתֵינוּ, וְזִכְרוֹן מָשִׁיחַ בֶּן דָּוִד עַבְדֶּךָ, וְזִכְרוֹן יְרוּשָׁלַיִם עִיר קָדְשֶׁךָ, וְזִכְרוֹן כָּל עַמְּךָ בֵּית יִשְׂרָאֵל, לְפָנֶיךָ, לִפְלֵיטָה לְטוֹבָה, לְחֵן וּלְחֶסֶד וּלְרַחֲמִים, לְחַיִּים וּלְשָׁלוֹם בְּיוֹם

בראש חודש: רֹאשׁ הַחֹדֶשׁ / בפסח: חַג הַמַּצּוֹת / בסוכות: חַג הַסֻּכּוֹת

הַזֶּה. זָכְרֵנוּ יהוה אֱלֹהֵינוּ בּוֹ לְטוֹבָה, וּפָקְדֵנוּ בוֹ לִבְרָכָה, וְהוֹשִׁיעֵנוּ בוֹ לְחַיִּים. וּבִדְבַר יְשׁוּעָה וְרַחֲמִים, חוּס וְחָנֵּנוּ וְרַחֵם עָלֵינוּ וְהוֹשִׁיעֵנוּ, כִּי אֵלֶיךָ עֵינֵינוּ, כִּי אֵל מֶלֶךְ חַנּוּן וְרַחוּם אָתָּה.

וְתֶחֱזֶינָה עֵינֵינוּ בְּשׁוּבְךָ לְצִיּוֹן בְּרַחֲמִים.
בָּרוּךְ אַתָּה יהוה, הַמַּחֲזִיר שְׁכִינָתוֹ לְצִיּוֹן.

THANKSGIVING

מוֹדִים We give thanks to You,
for You are the LORD our God
and God of our ancestors
for ever and all time.
You are the Rock of our lives,
Shield of our salvation
from generation to generation.
We will thank You and
declare Your praise for our lives,
which are entrusted into Your hand;
for our souls,
which are placed in Your charge;
for Your miracles
which are with us every day;
and for Your wonders and favors
at all times, evening,
morning and midday.
You are good –
for Your compassion never fails.
You are compassionate –
for Your loving-kindnesses never cease.
We have always placed our hope in You.

During the Leader's Repetition, the congregation says quietly:

מוֹדִים We give thanks
to You, for You are
the LORD our God
and God of our ancestors,
God of all flesh,
who formed us
and formed the universe.
Blessings and thanks
are due to Your great
and holy name for giving us
life and sustaining us.
May You continue
to give us life and sustain us;
and may You gather our
exiles to Your holy courts,
to keep Your decrees,
do Your will and serve You
with a perfect heart,
for it is for us
to give You thanks.
Blessed be God to whom
thanksgiving is due.

On Ḥanukka:

עַל הַנִּסִּים [We thank You also] for the miracles, the redemption, the mighty deeds, the salvations, and the victories in battle which You performed for our ancestors in those days, at this time.

בִּימֵי מַתִּתְיָהוּ In the days of Mattityahu, son of Yoḥanan, the High Priest, the Hasmonean, and his sons, the wicked Greek kingdom rose up against Your people Israel to make them forget Your Torah and to force them to transgress the laws of Your will. It was then that You in Your great compassion stood by them in the time of their distress. You championed their cause, judged their claim, and avenged their wrong. You delivered the strong into the hands of the weak, the many into the hands of the few, the impure into the hands of the pure, the wicked into the hands of the righteous, and the arrogant into the hands of

הודאה

מוֹדִים אֲנַחְנוּ לָךְ
שָׁאַתָּה הוּא יהוה אֱלֹהֵינוּ
וֵאלֹהֵי אֲבוֹתֵינוּ לְעוֹלָם וָעֶד.
צוּר חַיֵּינוּ, מָגֵן יִשְׁעֵנוּ
אַתָּה הוּא לְדוֹר וָדוֹר.
נוֹדֶה לְּךָ וּנְסַפֵּר תְּהִלָּתֶךָ
עַל חַיֵּינוּ הַמְּסוּרִים בְּיָדֶךָ
וְעַל נִשְׁמוֹתֵינוּ הַפְּקוּדוֹת לָךְ
וְעַל נִסֶּיךָ שֶׁבְּכָל יוֹם עִמָּנוּ
וְעַל נִפְלְאוֹתֶיךָ וְטוֹבוֹתֶיךָ
שֶׁבְּכָל עֵת
עֶרֶב וָבֹקֶר וְצָהֳרָיִם.
הַטּוֹב, כִּי לֹא כָלוּ רַחֲמֶיךָ
וְהַמְרַחֵם, כִּי לֹא תַמּוּ חֲסָדֶיךָ
מֵעוֹלָם קִוִּינוּ לָךְ.

During חזרת הש״ץ, *the* קהל *says quietly:*

מוֹדִים אֲנַחְנוּ לָךְ
שָׁאַתָּה הוּא יהוה אֱלֹהֵינוּ
וֵאלֹהֵי אֲבוֹתֵינוּ
אֱלֹהֵי כָל בָּשָׂר
יוֹצְרֵנוּ, יוֹצֵר בְּרֵאשִׁית.
בְּרָכוֹת וְהוֹדָאוֹת
לְשִׁמְךָ הַגָּדוֹל וְהַקָּדוֹשׁ
עַל שֶׁהֶחֱיִיתָנוּ וְקִיַּמְתָּנוּ.
כֵּן תְּחַיֵּנוּ וּתְקַיְּמֵנוּ
וְתֶאֱסֹף גָּלֻיּוֹתֵינוּ
לְחַצְרוֹת קָדְשֶׁךָ
לִשְׁמֹר חֻקֶּיךָ
וְלַעֲשׂוֹת רְצוֹנֶךָ וּלְעָבְדְּךָ
בְּלֵבָב שָׁלֵם
עַל שֶׁאֲנַחְנוּ מוֹדִים לָךְ.
בָּרוּךְ אֵל הַהוֹדָאוֹת.

בחנוכה:

עַל הַנִּסִּים וְעַל הַפֻּרְקָן וְעַל הַגְּבוּרוֹת וְעַל הַתְּשׁוּעוֹת וְעַל הַמִּלְחָמוֹת שֶׁעָשִׂיתָ לַאֲבוֹתֵינוּ בַּיָּמִים הָהֵם בַּזְּמַן הַזֶּה.

בִּימֵי מַתִּתְיָהוּ בֶּן יוֹחָנָן כֹּהֵן גָּדוֹל חַשְׁמוֹנַאי וּבָנָיו, כְּשֶׁעָמְדָה מַלְכוּת יָוָן הָרְשָׁעָה עַל עַמְּךָ יִשְׂרָאֵל לְהַשְׁכִּיחָם תּוֹרָתֶךָ וּלְהַעֲבִירָם מֵחֻקֵּי רְצוֹנֶךָ, וְאַתָּה בְּרַחֲמֶיךָ הָרַבִּים עָמַדְתָּ לָהֶם בְּעֵת צָרָתָם, רַבְתָּ אֶת רִיבָם, דַּנְתָּ אֶת דִּינָם, נָקַמְתָּ אֶת נִקְמָתָם, מָסַרְתָּ גִבּוֹרִים בְּיַד חַלָּשִׁים, וְרַבִּים בְּיַד מְעַטִּים, וּטְמֵאִים בְּיַד טְהוֹרִים, וּרְשָׁעִים בְּיַד צַדִּיקִים, וְזֵדִים בְּיַד עוֹסְקֵי

those who were engaged in the study of Your Torah. You made for Yourself great and holy fame in Your world, and for Your people Israel You performed a great salvation and redemption as of this very day. Your children then entered the holiest part of Your House, cleansed Your Temple, purified Your Sanctuary, kindled lights in Your holy courts, and designated these eight days of Ḥanukka for giving thanks and praise to Your great name.

Continue with "For all these things."

On Shushan Purim in Jerusalem:

עַל הַנִּסִּים [We thank You also] for the miracles, the redemption, the mighty deeds, the salvations, and the victories in battle which You performed for our ancestors in those days, at this time.

בִּימֵי מָרְדְּכַי In the days of Mordekhai and Esther, in Shushan the capital, the
wicked Haman rose up against them and sought to destroy, slay and exterminate *Esther 3*
all the Jews, young and old, children and women, on one day, the thirteenth day of the twelfth month, which is the month of Adar, and to plunder their possessions. Then You in Your great compassion defeated his counsel, frustrated his plans, and caused his scheme to recoil on his own head, so that they hanged him and his sons on the gallows.

Continue with "For all these things."

וְעַל כֻּלָּם For all these things may Your name be blessed and elevated, our King, continually, for ever and all time.

On Shabbat Shuva: And write, for a good life, all the children of Your covenant.

Let all that lives thank You, Selah! and praise Your name in truth, God, our Savior and Help, Selah!
Blessed are You, Lord,
whose name is "the Good" and to whom thanks are due.

The following is said by the Leader during the Repetition of the Amida.
In Israel, if Kohanim bless the congregation, turn to page 1064.

Our God and God of our fathers, bless us with the threefold blessing in the Torah, written by the hand of Moses Your servant and pronounced by Aaron and his sons the priests, Your holy people, as it is said:

May the Lord bless you and protect you. *Num. 6*
Cong: May it be Your will.
May the Lord make His face shine on you and be gracious to you.
Cong: May it be Your will.
May the Lord turn His face toward you, and give you peace.
Cong: May it be Your will.

תּוֹרָתֶךָ, וּלְךָ עָשִׂיתָ שֵׁם גָּדוֹל וְקָדוֹשׁ בְּעוֹלָמֶךָ, וּלְעַמְּךָ יִשְׂרָאֵל עָשִׂיתָ
תְּשׁוּעָה גְדוֹלָה וּפֻרְקָן כְּהַיּוֹם הַזֶּה. וְאַחַר כֵּן בָּאוּ בָנֶיךָ לִדְבִיר בֵּיתֶךָ,
וּפִנּוּ אֶת הֵיכָלֶךָ, וְטִהֲרוּ אֶת מִקְדָּשֶׁךָ, וְהִדְלִיקוּ נֵרוֹת בְּחַצְרוֹת קָדְשֶׁךָ,
וְקָבְעוּ שְׁמוֹנַת יְמֵי חֲנֻכָּה אֵלּוּ, לְהוֹדוֹת וּלְהַלֵּל לְשִׁמְךָ הַגָּדוֹל.

Continue with וְעַל כֻּלָּם.

בשושן פורים בירושלים:

עַל הַנִּסִּים וְעַל הַפֻּרְקָן וְעַל הַגְּבוּרוֹת וְעַל הַתְּשׁוּעוֹת וְעַל הַמִּלְחָמוֹת
שֶׁעָשִׂיתָ לַאֲבוֹתֵינוּ בַּיָּמִים הָהֵם בַּזְּמַן הַזֶּה.

בִּימֵי מָרְדְּכַי וְאֶסְתֵּר בְּשׁוּשַׁן הַבִּירָה, כְּשֶׁעָמַד עֲלֵיהֶם הָמָן הָרָשָׁע,
אסתר ג בִּקֵּשׁ לְהַשְׁמִיד לַהֲרֹג וּלְאַבֵּד אֶת־כָּל־הַיְּהוּדִים מִנַּעַר וְעַד־זָקֵן טַף
וְנָשִׁים בְּיוֹם אֶחָד, בִּשְׁלוֹשָׁה עָשָׂר לְחֹדֶשׁ שְׁנֵים־עָשָׂר, הוּא־חֹדֶשׁ אֲדָר,
וּשְׁלָלָם לָבוֹז: וְאַתָּה בְּרַחֲמֶיךָ הָרַבִּים הֵפַרְתָּ אֶת עֲצָתוֹ, וְקִלְקַלְתָּ אֶת
מַחֲשַׁבְתּוֹ, וַהֲשֵׁבוֹתָ לּוֹ גְּמוּלוֹ בְּרֹאשׁוֹ, וְתָלוּ אוֹתוֹ וְאֶת בָּנָיו עַל הָעֵץ.

Continue with וְעַל כֻּלָּם.

וְעַל כֻּלָּם יִתְבָּרַךְ וְיִתְרוֹמַם שִׁמְךָ מַלְכֵּנוּ תָּמִיד לְעוֹלָם וָעֶד.

בשבת שובה: וּכְתֹב לְחַיִּים טוֹבִים כָּל בְּנֵי בְרִיתֶךָ.

וְכֹל הַחַיִּים יוֹדְוּךָ סֶּלָה, וִיהַלְלוּ אֶת שִׁמְךָ בֶּאֱמֶת
הָאֵל יְשׁוּעָתֵנוּ וְעֶזְרָתֵנוּ סֶלָה.

בָּרוּךְ אַתָּה יהוה, הַטּוֹב שִׁמְךָ וּלְךָ נָאֶה לְהוֹדוֹת.

The following is said by the שליח ציבור *during* חזרת הש״ץ.
In ארץ ישראל, *if* כהנים *say* ברכת כהנים, *turn to page 1065.*

אֱלֹהֵינוּ וֵאלֹהֵי אֲבוֹתֵינוּ, בָּרְכֵנוּ בַבְּרָכָה הַמְשֻׁלֶּשֶׁת בַּתּוֹרָה, הַכְּתוּבָה עַל יְדֵי
מֹשֶׁה עַבְדֶּךָ, הָאֲמוּרָה מִפִּי אַהֲרֹן וּבָנָיו כֹּהֲנִים עַם קְדוֹשֶׁיךָ, כָּאָמוּר

במדבר ו יְבָרֶכְךָ יהוה וְיִשְׁמְרֶךָ: קהל: כֵּן יְהִי רָצוֹן
יָאֵר יהוה פָּנָיו אֵלֶיךָ וִיחֻנֶּךָּ: קהל: כֵּן יְהִי רָצוֹן
יִשָּׂא יהוה פָּנָיו אֵלֶיךָ וְיָשֵׂם לְךָ שָׁלוֹם: קהל: כֵּן יְהִי רָצוֹן

PEACE

שִׂים שָׁלוֹם Give peace, goodness and blessing,
grace, loving-kindness and compassion to us
and all Israel Your people.
Bless us, our Father, all as one, with the light of Your face,
for by the light of Your face You have given us, LORD our God,
the Torah of life and love of kindness,
righteousness, blessing, compassion,
life and peace.
May it be good in Your eyes to bless Your people Israel
at every time, in every hour, with Your peace.

On Shabbat Shuva: In the book of life, blessing,
peace and prosperity,
may we and all Your people
the house of Israel be remembered and written
before You for a good life, and for peace.*

Blessed are You, LORD,
who blesses His people Israel with peace.

**On Shabbat Shuva outside Israel, many end the blessing:*
Blessed are You, LORD, who makes peace.

The following verse concludes the Leader's Repetition of the Amida.
Some also say it here as part of the silent Amida.
May the words of my mouth and the inner thoughts of my heart *Ps. 19*
find favor before You, LORD, my Rock and Redeemer.

אֱלֹהַי My God, *Berakhot 17a*
guard my tongue from evil
and my lips from dishonest speech.
To those who curse me, let my soul be silent;
may my soul be to all like the dust.
Open my heart to Your Torah
and let my soul pursue Your commandments.
As for all who plan evil against me,
swiftly defeat their counsel and frustrate their plans.

ברכת שלום

שִׂים שָׁלוֹם טוֹבָה וּבְרָכָה
חֵן וָחֶסֶד וְרַחֲמִים
עָלֵינוּ וְעַל כָּל יִשְׂרָאֵל עַמֶּךָ.
בָּרְכֵנוּ אָבִינוּ כֻּלָּנוּ כְּאֶחָד בְּאוֹר פָּנֶיךָ
כִּי בְאוֹר פָּנֶיךָ נָתַתָּ לָּנוּ, יהוה אֱלֹהֵינוּ
תּוֹרַת חַיִּים וְאַהֲבַת חֶסֶד
וּצְדָקָה וּבְרָכָה וְרַחֲמִים וְחַיִּים וְשָׁלוֹם.
וְטוֹב בְּעֵינֶיךָ לְבָרֵךְ אֶת עַמְּךָ יִשְׂרָאֵל
בְּכָל עֵת וּבְכָל שָׁעָה בִּשְׁלוֹמֶךָ.

בשבת שובה: בְּסֵפֶר חַיִּים, בְּרָכָה וְשָׁלוֹם, וּפַרְנָסָה טוֹבָה
נִזָּכֵר וְנִכָּתֵב לְפָנֶיךָ, אֲנַחְנוּ וְכָל עַמְּךָ בֵּית יִשְׂרָאֵל
לְחַיִּים טוֹבִים וּלְשָׁלוֹם.*

בָּרוּךְ אַתָּה יהוה, הַמְבָרֵךְ אֶת עַמּוֹ יִשְׂרָאֵל בַּשָּׁלוֹם.

**On* שבת שובה *in* חוץ לארץ*, many end the blessing:*

בָּרוּךְ אַתָּה יהוה, עוֹשֵׂה הַשָּׁלוֹם.

The following verse concludes the חזרת הש״ץ*.*
Some also say it here as part of the silent עמידה*.*

יִהְיוּ לְרָצוֹן אִמְרֵי־פִי וְהֶגְיוֹן לִבִּי לְפָנֶיךָ, יהוה צוּרִי וְגֹאֲלִי: תהלים יט

אֱלֹהַי ברכות יז.

נְצֹר לְשׁוֹנִי מֵרָע, וּשְׂפָתַי מִדַּבֵּר מִרְמָה
וְלִמְקַלְלַי נַפְשִׁי תִדֹּם, וְנַפְשִׁי כֶּעָפָר לַכֹּל תִּהְיֶה.
פְּתַח לִבִּי בְּתוֹרָתֶךָ, וּבְמִצְוֹתֶיךָ תִּרְדֹּף נַפְשִׁי.
וְכָל הַחוֹשְׁבִים עָלַי רָעָה
מְהֵרָה הָפֵר עֲצָתָם וְקַלְקֵל מַחֲשַׁבְתָּם.

Act for the sake of Your name;
act for the sake of Your right hand;
act for the sake of Your holiness;
act for the sake of Your Torah.

That Your beloved ones may be rescued, *Ps. 60*
save with Your right hand and answer me.
May the words of my mouth *Ps. 19*
and the inner thoughts of my heart
find favor before You, LORD, my Rock and Redeemer.

Bow, take three steps back, then bow, first left, then right, then center, while saying:

May He who makes peace in His high places,
make peace for us and all Israel –
and say: Amen.

יְהִי רָצוֹן May it be Your will, LORD our God and God of our ancestors,
that the Temple be rebuilt speedily in our days,
and give us a share in Your Torah.
And there we will serve You with fear,
as in the days of old and as in former years.
Then the offering of Judah and Jerusalem *Mal. 3*
will be pleasing to the LORD
as in the days of old and as in former years.

On Rosh Ḥodesh, Ḥol HaMo'ed and Ḥanukka,
the service continues with Hallel on page 822.

עֲשֵׂה לְמַעַן שְׁמֶךָ
עֲשֵׂה לְמַעַן יְמִינֶךָ
עֲשֵׂה לְמַעַן קְדֻשָּׁתֶךָ
עֲשֵׂה לְמַעַן תּוֹרָתֶךָ.

לְמַעַן יֵחָלְצוּן יְדִידֶיךָ, הוֹשִׁיעָה יְמִינְךָ וַעֲנֵנִי: תהלים ס
יִהְיוּ לְרָצוֹן אִמְרֵי־פִי וְהֶגְיוֹן לִבִּי לְפָנֶיךָ, יהוה צוּרִי וְגֹאֲלִי: תהלים יט

Bow, take three steps back, then bow, first left, then right, then center, while saying:

עֹשֶׂה שָׁלוֹם/ בשבת שובה: הַשָּׁלוֹם/ בִּמְרוֹמָיו
הוּא יַעֲשֶׂה שָׁלוֹם עָלֵינוּ וְעַל כָּל יִשְׂרָאֵל
וְאִמְרוּ אָמֵן.

יְהִי רָצוֹן מִלְּפָנֶיךָ יהוה אֱלֹהֵינוּ וֵאלֹהֵי אֲבוֹתֵינוּ
שֶׁיִּבָּנֶה בֵּית הַמִּקְדָּשׁ בִּמְהֵרָה בְיָמֵינוּ
וְתֵן חֶלְקֵנוּ בְּתוֹרָתֶךָ
וְשָׁם נַעֲבָדְךָ בְּיִרְאָה כִּימֵי עוֹלָם וּכְשָׁנִים קַדְמֹנִיּוֹת.
וְעָרְבָה לַיהוה מִנְחַת יְהוּדָה וִירוּשָׁלָםִ כִּימֵי עוֹלָם וּכְשָׁנִים קַדְמֹנִיּוֹת: מלאכי ג

On ראש חודש, חול המועד *and* חנוכה,
the service continues with הלל *on page 823.*

FULL KADDISH

Leader: יִתְגַּדַּל Magnified and sanctified
may His great name be,
in the world He created by His will.
May He establish His kingdom
in your lifetime and in your days,
and in the lifetime of all the house of Israel,
swiftly and soon –
and say: Amen.

All: May His great name
be blessed for ever and all time.

Leader: Blessed and praised,
glorified and elevated,
raised and honored,
uplifted and praised
be the name of the Holy One,
blessed be He, beyond any blessing,
song, praise and consolation
uttered in the world –
and say: Amen.

May the prayers and pleas of all Israel
be accepted by their Father in heaven –
and say: Amen.

May there be great peace from heaven,
and life for us and all Israel –
and say: Amen.

Bow, take three steps back, as if taking leave of the Divine Presence, then bow, first left, then right, then center, while saying:

May He who makes peace in His high places,
make peace for us and all Israel –
and say: Amen.

קדיש שלם

ש״ץ: יִתְגַּדַּל וְיִתְקַדַּשׁ שְׁמֵהּ רַבָּא (קהל: אָמֵן)
בְּעָלְמָא דִּי בְרָא כִרְעוּתֵהּ
וְיַמְלִיךְ מַלְכוּתֵהּ
בְּחַיֵּיכוֹן וּבְיוֹמֵיכוֹן וּבְחַיֵּי דְכָל בֵּית יִשְׂרָאֵל
בַּעֲגָלָא וּבִזְמַן קָרִיב, וְאִמְרוּ אָמֵן. (קהל: אָמֵן)

קהל וש״ץ: יְהֵא שְׁמֵהּ רַבָּא מְבָרַךְ לְעָלַם וּלְעָלְמֵי עָלְמַיָּא.

ש״ץ: יִתְבָּרַךְ וְיִשְׁתַּבַּח וְיִתְפָּאַר
וְיִתְרוֹמַם וְיִתְנַשֵּׂא וְיִתְהַדָּר וְיִתְעַלֶּה וְיִתְהַלָּל
שְׁמֵהּ דְּקֻדְשָׁא בְּרִיךְ הוּא (קהל: בְּרִיךְ הוּא)
לְעֵלָּא מִן כָּל בִּרְכָתָא
/ בשבת שובה: לְעֵלָּא לְעֵלָּא מִכָּל בִּרְכָתָא/
וְשִׁירָתָא, תֻּשְׁבְּחָתָא וְנֶחֱמָתָא
דַּאֲמִירָן בְּעָלְמָא, וְאִמְרוּ אָמֵן. (קהל: אָמֵן)

תִּתְקַבַּל צְלוֹתְהוֹן וּבָעוּתְהוֹן דְּכָל יִשְׂרָאֵל
קֳדָם אֲבוּהוֹן דִּי בִשְׁמַיָּא, וְאִמְרוּ אָמֵן. (קהל: אָמֵן)

יְהֵא שְׁלָמָא רַבָּא מִן שְׁמַיָּא
וְחַיִּים, עָלֵינוּ וְעַל כָּל יִשְׂרָאֵל, וְאִמְרוּ אָמֵן. (קהל: אָמֵן)

Bow, take three steps back, as if taking leave of the Divine Presence, then bow, first left, then right, then center, while saying:

עֹשֶׂה שָׁלוֹם/ בשבת שובה: הַשָּׁלוֹם/ בִּמְרוֹמָיו
הוּא יַעֲשֶׂה שָׁלוֹם עָלֵינוּ וְעַל כָּל יִשְׂרָאֵל
וְאִמְרוּ אָמֵן. (קהל: אָמֵן)

REMOVING THE TORAH FROM THE ARK

אֵין־כָּמוֹךָ There is none like You among the heavenly powers, *Ps. 86*
LORD, and there are no works like Yours.
Your kingdom is an eternal kingdom, *Ps. 145*
and Your dominion is for all generations.

The LORD is King, the LORD was King,
the LORD shall be King for ever and all time.
The LORD will give strength to His people; *Ps. 29*
the LORD will bless His people with peace.

Father of compassion,
favor Zion with Your goodness; rebuild the walls of Jerusalem. *Ps. 51*
For we trust in You alone, King, God,
high and great, Master of worlds.

REFLECTION

Why do you think we read from the Torah publicly?

Does this ceremonial reading feel different to you from when you read the same words yourself on your own?

How do you think you can connect more to the public reading of the Torah?

Yisrael are called up to the Torah, thus representing the collective of the entire nation. Indeed, the procedure is highly reminiscent of the giving of the Torah at Mount Sinai, when the entire Jewish people heard the voice of God communicate with them. This revelation at Sinai was not to a single prophet but to the complete nation of millions, and each parent passed on what they saw and heard to their children who did the same with their children in a chain of tradition that brings us here today. If one ever wanted proof of the truth of Torah and revelation and God, said Rabbi Yehuda HaLevi in the early twelfth century, then this unbroken, unending chain of tradition is it.

In addition to the set number of people who are called up on Shabbat and holy days, there is another *aliya* that is added at the end, called *Maftir*, or conclusion. This person will also be given the honor of reading the portion from the *Navi*, the book of Prophets that is read subsequent to the Torah reading. He is given an *aliya* for the Torah as well, in deference to the honor of the Torah, lest one think that a reading from the Prophets is equal in status to that of the Torah itself (*Megilla* 23a). (Rabbi Jay Goldmintz, *The Koren Ani Tefilla Shabbat Siddur*)

הוצאת ספר תורה

תהלים פו אֵין־כָּמְוֹךָ בָאֱלֹהִים, אֲדֹנָי, וְאֵין כְּמַעֲשֶׂיךָ:

תהלים קמה מַלְכוּתְךָ מַלְכוּת כָּל־עֹלָמִים

וּמֶמְשַׁלְתְּךָ בְּכָל־דּוֹר וָדֹר:

יהוה מֶלֶךְ, יהוה מָלָךְ, יהוה יִמְלֹךְ לְעֹלָם וָעֶד.

תהלים כט יהוה עֹז לְעַמּוֹ יִתֵּן, יהוה יְבָרֵךְ אֶת־עַמּוֹ בַשָּׁלוֹם:

אַב הָרַחֲמִים

תהלים נא הֵיטִיבָה בִרְצוֹנְךָ אֶת־צִיּוֹן תִּבְנֶה חוֹמוֹת יְרוּשָׁלָםִ:

כִּי בְךָ לְבַד בָּטָחְנוּ, מֶלֶךְ אֵל רָם וְנִשָּׂא, אֲדוֹן עוֹלָמִים.

INTRODUCTION TO *KERIAT HATORAH*

... A THOUSAND WORDS

Tradition has it that Moshe himself decreed that there be a regular Torah reading on Shabbat and all holy days (*Soferim* 10:1). The Torah has fifty-four divisions, or portions, each one called a *parasha*, one for each Shabbat of the year during a leap year. In a non-leap year, some of the portions (*parashot*) are doubled up, so that the entire Torah is completed annually, a collective reaffirmation of our identity.

The portion that is read is itself divided into a different number of sections depending on the sanctity of the occasion, and each section is apportioned to a different person in the congregation. On Shabbat there are seven people called up, on Yom Kippur there are six, on a Yom Tov there are five, on Rosh Ḥodesh and Ḥol HaMo'ed (intermediate days of a festival) there are four, and on regular weekdays there are three (*Megilla* 4:1–2). Each division is called an *aliya*, or ascent, a reference to the physical ascent to the platform where the Torah is read, as well as an echo of the ascent to Mount Sinai where the Torah was given. A minimum of ten verses are read, according to one tradition as a symbolic representation of the Ten Commandments (*Megilla* 21b; Yerushalmi, *Ta'anit* 4:3). A minimum of three people are called up, reminiscent perhaps of Moshe, Aharon, and Miriam, under whose watch the Torah was given. Minimally, a Kohen, Levi, and

The Ark is opened and the congregation stands. All say:

וַיְהִי בִּנְסֹעַ Whenever the Ark set out, Moses would say, *Num. 10*
"Arise, LORD, and may Your enemies be scattered.
May those who hate You flee before You."
For the Torah shall come forth from Zion, *Is. 2*
and the word of the LORD from Jerusalem.
Blessed is He who in His Holiness gave the Torah to His people Israel.

On Shabbat, continue with "Blessed is the name" on page 630.

On Hoshana Raba, say the following verses three times:

יהוה The LORD, the LORD, compassionate and gracious God, *Ex. 34*
slow to anger, abounding in loving-kindness and truth,
extending loving-kindness to a thousand generations, forgiving
wrongdoing, rebellion and sin, and absolving [the guilty who repent].

Master of the Universe, fulfill my requests for good. Satisfy my desire, grant my request, and pardon me for all my wrongdoings and all wrongdoings of the members of my household, with the pardon of loving-kindness and compassion. Purify us from our sins, our wrongdoings and our transgressions; remember us with a memory of favorable deeds before You and be mindful of us in salvation and compassion. Remember us for a good life, for peace, for livelihood and sustenance, for bread to eat and clothes to wear, for wealth, honor and length of days dedicated to Your Torah and its commandments. Give us discernment and understanding that we may understand and discern its deep secrets. Send healing for all our pain, and bless all the work of our hands. Ordain for us decrees of good, salvation and consolation, and nullify all hard and harsh decrees against us. And may the hearts of the government, its advisers and ministers / *in Israel:* And may the hearts of our ministers and their advisers, / be favorable toward us. Amen. May this be Your will.

יִהְיוּ May the words of my mouth and the inner thoughts of my heart *Ps. 19*
find favor before You, LORD, my Rock and Redeemer.

Say the following verse three times:

וַאֲנִי As for me, may my prayer come to You, LORD, at a time of favor. *Ps. 69*
O God, in Your great love, answer me with Your faithful salvation.

---

if it were a bride. If it is desecrated or destroyed, we bury it as if it were a relative or friend. We study it endlessly as if in it were hidden all the secrets of our being. Heinrich Heine once called the Torah the "portable homeland" of the Jewish people, by which he meant that when we lacked a land, we found our home in the Torah's words. More powerfully still, the Ba'al Shem Tov – founder of the Hasidic movement in the eighteenth century – said that the Jewish people is a living sefer Torah, *and every Jew is one of its letters. I am moved by that image, and it invites a question – the question: Will we, in our lifetime, be letters in the scroll of the Jewish people?* (Rabbi Jonathan Sacks, *A Letter in the Scroll*)

The ארון קודש *is opened and the* קהל *stands. All say:*

וַיְהִי בִּנְסֹעַ הָאָרֹן וַיֹּאמֶר מֹשֶׁה במדבר י
קוּמָה יהוה וְיָפֻצוּ אֹיְבֶיךָ וְיָנֻסוּ מְשַׂנְאֶיךָ מִפָּנֶיךָ:
כִּי מִצִּיּוֹן תֵּצֵא תוֹרָה וּדְבַר־יהוה מִירוּשָׁלָםִ: ישעיה ב
בָּרוּךְ שֶׁנָּתַן תּוֹרָה לְעַמּוֹ יִשְׂרָאֵל בִּקְדֻשָּׁתוֹ.

On שבת*, continue with* בְּרִיךְ שְׁמֵהּ *on page 631.*

On הושענא רבה*, say the following verses three times:*

יהוה, יהוה, אֵל רַחוּם וְחַנּוּן, אֶרֶךְ אַפַּיִם וְרַב־חֶסֶד וֶאֱמֶת: שמות לד
נֹצֵר חֶסֶד לָאֲלָפִים, נֹשֵׂא עָוֹן וָפֶשַׁע וְחַטָּאָה, וְנַקֵּה:

רִבּוֹנוֹ שֶׁל עוֹלָם, מַלֵּא מִשְׁאֲלוֹתַי לְטוֹבָה, וְהָפֵק רְצוֹנִי וְתֵן שְׁאֵלָתִי, וּמְחֹל לִי עַל כָּל עֲוֹנוֹתַי וְעַל כָּל עֲוֹנוֹת אַנְשֵׁי בֵיתִי, מְחִילָה בְּחֶסֶד מְחִילָה בְּרַחֲמִים, וְטַהֲרֵנוּ מֵחֲטָאֵינוּ וּמֵעֲוֹנוֹתֵינוּ וּמִפְּשָׁעֵינוּ, וְזָכְרֵנוּ בְּזִכָּרוֹן טוֹב לְפָנֶיךָ, וּפָקְדֵנוּ בִּפְקֻדַּת יְשׁוּעָה וְרַחֲמִים. וְזָכְרֵנוּ לְחַיִּים טוֹבִים וּלְשָׁלוֹם, וּפַרְנָסָה וְכַלְכָּלָה, וְלֶחֶם לֶאֱכֹל וּבֶגֶד לִלְבֹּשׁ, וְעֹשֶׁר וְכָבוֹד, וְאֹרֶךְ יָמִים לַהֲגוֹת בְּתוֹרָתֶךָ וּלְקַיֵּם מִצְוֹתֶיהָ, וְשֵׂכֶל וּבִינָה לְהָבִין וּלְהַשְׂכִּיל עִמְקֵי סוֹדוֹתֶיהָ. וְהָפֵק רְפוּאָה לְכָל מַכְאוֹבֵינוּ, וּבָרֵךְ כָּל מַעֲשֵׂה יָדֵינוּ, וּגְזֹר עָלֵינוּ גְּזֵרוֹת טוֹבוֹת יְשׁוּעוֹת וְנֶחָמוֹת, וּבַטֵּל מֵעָלֵינוּ כָּל גְּזֵרוֹת קָשׁוֹת וְרָעוֹת, וְתֵן בְּלֵב הַמַּלְכוּת וְיוֹעֲצֶיהָ וְשָׂרֶיהָ / בארץ ישראל: וְתֵן בְּלֵב שָׂרֵינוּ וְיוֹעֲצֵיהֶם/ עָלֵינוּ לְטוֹבָה. אָמֵן וְכֵן יְהִי רָצוֹן.

יִהְיוּ לְרָצוֹן אִמְרֵי־פִי וְהֶגְיוֹן לִבִּי לְפָנֶיךָ, יהוה צוּרִי וְגֹאֲלִי: תהלים יט

Say the following verse three times:

וַאֲנִי תְפִלָּתִי־לְךָ יהוה, עֵת רָצוֹן, אֱלֹהִים בְּרָב־חַסְדֶּךָ תהלים סט
עֲנֵנִי בֶּאֱמֶת יִשְׁעֶךָ:

CONNECTION

The holiest object in Judaism is a sefer Torah*, a scroll of the Law. Still written today as it was thousands of years ago, by hand with a quill on parchment, it symbolizes some of Judaism's deepest beliefs: that God is to be found in words, that these words are to be found in the Torah, and that they form the basis of the covenant – the bond of love – between God and the Jewish people.*

I wonder if any people has ever loved a book as we love the Torah. We stand when it passes as if it were a king. We dance with it as

On Shabbat and on Hoshana Raba:

Blessed is the name of the Master of the Universe. Blessed is Your crown and Your place. May Your favor always be with Your people Israel. Show Your people the salvation of Your right hand in Your Temple. Give us the gift of Your good light, and accept our prayers in mercy. May it be Your will to prolong our life in goodness. May I be counted among the righteous, so that You will have compassion on me and protect me and all that is mine and all that is Your people Israel's. You feed all; You sustain all; You rule over all; You rule over kings, for sovereignty is Yours. I am a servant of the Holy One, blessed be He, before whom and before whose glorious Torah I bow at all times. Not in man do I trust, nor on any angel do I rely, but on the God of heaven who is the God of truth, whose Torah is truth, whose prophets speak truth, and who abounds in acts of love and truth. ▸ In Him I trust, and to His holy and glorious name I offer praises. May it be Your will to open my heart to the Torah, and to fulfill the wishes of my heart and of the hearts of all Your people Israel for good, for life, and for peace. *Zohar, Vayak-hel*

The Leader takes the Torah scroll in his right arm. Leader then congregation:

Listen, Israel: the Lord is our God, the Lord is One. *Deut. 6*

Leader then congregation:

One is our God; great is our Master;
holy (*On Hoshana Raba:* and awesome) is His name.

The Leader turns to face the Ark, bows and says:

Magnify the Lord with me,
and let us elevate His name together. *Ps. 34*

Torah deserves as the word of God in our midst. Then, as the *ḥazan* parades the *sefer Torah* through the synagogue, many have the custom to physically demonstrate this honor by approaching the Torah as it passes by, and if possible kissing the *sefer Torah* directly or with one's tzitzit.

On שבת *and on* הושענא רבה*:*

זוהר ויקהל בְּרִיךְ שְׁמֵהּ דְּמָרֵא עָלְמָא, בְּרִיךְ כִּתְרָךְ וְאַתְרָךְ. יְהֵא רְעוּתָךְ עִם עַמָּךְ יִשְׂרָאֵל לְעָלַם, וּפֻרְקַן יְמִינָךְ אַחֲזִי לְעַמָּךְ בְּבֵית מַקְדְּשָׁךְ, וּלְאַמְטוּיֵי לַנָא מִטּוּב נְהוֹרָךְ, וּלְקַבֵּל צְלוֹתַנָא בְּרַחֲמִין. יְהֵא רַעֲוָא קֳדָמָךְ דְּתוֹרִיךְ לַן חַיִּין בְּטִיבוּ, וְלֶהֱוֵי אֲנָא פְקִידָא בְּגוֹ צַדִּיקַיָּא, לְמִרְחַם עֲלַי וּלְמִנְטַר יָתִי וְיַת כָּל דִּי לִי וְדִי לְעַמָּךְ יִשְׂרָאֵל. אַנְתְּ הוּא זָן לְכֹלָּא וּמְפַרְנֵס לְכֹלָּא, אַנְתְּ הוּא שַׁלִּיט עַל כֹּלָּא, אַנְתְּ הוּא דְּשַׁלִּיט עַל מַלְכַיָּא, וּמַלְכוּתָא דִּילָךְ הִיא. אֲנָא עַבְדָּא דְקֻדְשָׁא בְּרִיךְ הוּא, דְּסָגֵדְנָא קַמֵּהּ וּמִקַּמֵּי דִּיקַר אוֹרַיְתֵהּ בְּכָל עִדָּן וְעִדָּן. לָא עַל אֱנָשׁ רָחֵיצְנָא וְלָא עַל בַּר אֱלָהִין סָמִיכְנָא, אֶלָּא בֶּאֱלָהָא דִשְׁמַיָּא, דְּהוּא אֱלָהָא קְשׁוֹט, וְאוֹרַיְתֵהּ קְשׁוֹט, וּנְבִיאוֹהִי קְשׁוֹט, וּמַסְגֵּא לְמֶעְבַּד טַבְוָן וּקְשׁוֹט. ‹ בֵּהּ אֲנָא רָחִיץ, וְלִשְׁמֵהּ קַדִּישָׁא יַקִּירָא אֲנָא אֵמַר תֻּשְׁבְּחָן. יְהֵא רַעֲוָא קֳדָמָךְ דְּתִפְתַּח לִבָּאִי בְּאוֹרַיְתָא, וְתַשְׁלִים מִשְׁאֲלִין דְּלִבָּאִי וְלִבָּא דְכָל עַמָּךְ יִשְׂרָאֵל לְטָב וּלְחַיִּין וְלִשְׁלָם.

The שליח ציבור *takes the* ספר תורה *in his right arm.* שליח ציבור *then* קהל*:*

דברים ו שְׁמַע יִשְׂרָאֵל, יהוה אֱלֹהֵינוּ, יהוה אֶחָד:

שליח ציבור *then* קהל*:*

אֶחָד אֱלֹהֵינוּ, גָּדוֹל אֲדוֹנֵינוּ

קָדוֹשׁ (בהושענא רבה: וְנוֹרָא) שְׁמוֹ.

The שליח ציבור *turns to face the* ארון קודש*, bows and says:*

תהלים לד גַּדְּלוּ לַיהוה אִתִּי וּנְרוֹמְמָה שְׁמוֹ יַחְדָּו:

LEARNING

As the *sefer Torah* is removed from the *aron hakodesh*, the entire community sing in unison, led by the *hazan*, declaring their belief in the greatness of the One God. The drama and majesty of this moment is befitting of the honor the *sefer*

The Ark is closed. The Leader carries the Torah scroll to the bima and the congregation says:

לְךָ Yours, LORD, are the greatness and the power, the glory and the majesty and splendor, for everything in heaven and earth is Yours. Yours, LORD, is the kingdom; You are elevated as Head over all. *I Chr. 29*

רוֹמְמוּ Elevate the LORD our God and bow to His footstool; He is holy. Elevate the LORD our God, and bow at His holy mountain, for holy is the LORD our God. *Ps. 99*

Over all may the name of the Supreme King of kings, the Holy One blessed be He, be magnified and sanctified, praised and glorified, elevated and celebrated, in the worlds that He has created – this world and the World to Come – in accordance with His will, and the will of those who fear Him, and the will of the whole house of Israel. He is the Rock of worlds, LORD of all creatures, God of all souls, who is present in the spacious heights and inhabits the high heavens of old. His holiness is over the Ḥayyot and over the throne of glory. Therefore may Your name, LORD our God, be sanctified among us in the sight of all that lives. Let us sing before Him a new song,
as it is written: "Sing to God, make music for His name, celebrate Him who rides the *Ps. 68*
clouds – the LORD is His name – and rejoice before Him." And may we see Him eye
to eye when He returns to His abode as it is written: "For they shall see eye to eye *Is. 52*
when the LORD returns to Zion." And it is said: "Then will the glory of the LORD be *Is. 40*
revealed, and all mankind together shall see that the mouth of the LORD has spoken."

Father of mercy, have compassion on the people borne by Him. May He remember the covenant with the mighty (patriarchs), and save us from evil times. May He reproach the evil instinct in the people carried by Him, and graciously give that we be an eternal remnant. May He fulfill in good measure our requests for salvation and compassion.

---

decrease in his own pile, and so they repeated the transfer the next night. These nocturnal activities went on for several nights, until one night the brothers bumped into each other. In that instant, in the dark of night, the glow of brotherly love lit up the mountain sky; they each understood what the other had been doing and fell into each other's arms in a loving embrace. According to the legend, when God saw that display of brotherly love, He selected the site for His Temple.

...A THOUSAND WORDS

The ארון קודש *is closed. The* שליח ציבור *carries the* ספר תורה *to the* בימה *and the* קהל *says:*

דברי הימים א׳ כט
לְךָ יהוה הַגְּדֻלָּה וְהַגְּבוּרָה וְהַתִּפְאֶרֶת וְהַנֵּצַח וְהַהוֹד, כִּי־כֹל בַּשָּׁמַיִם וּבָאָרֶץ, לְךָ יהוה הַמַּמְלָכָה וְהַמִּתְנַשֵּׂא לְכֹל לְרֹאשׁ:

תהלים צט
רוֹמְמוּ יהוה אֱלֹהֵינוּ וְהִשְׁתַּחֲווּ לַהֲדֹם רַגְלָיו, קָדוֹשׁ הוּא: רוֹמְמוּ יהוה אֱלֹהֵינוּ וְהִשְׁתַּחֲווּ לְהַר קָדְשׁוֹ, כִּי־קָדוֹשׁ יהוה אֱלֹהֵינוּ:

עַל הַכֹּל יִתְגַּדַּל וְיִתְקַדַּשׁ וְיִשְׁתַּבַּח וְיִתְפָּאַר וְיִתְרוֹמַם וְיִתְנַשֵּׂא שְׁמוֹ שֶׁל מֶלֶךְ מַלְכֵי הַמְּלָכִים הַקָּדוֹשׁ בָּרוּךְ הוּא בָּעוֹלָמוֹת שֶׁבָּרָא, הָעוֹלָם הַזֶּה וְהָעוֹלָם הַבָּא, כִּרְצוֹנוֹ וְכִרְצוֹן יְרֵאָיו וְכִרְצוֹן כָּל בֵּית יִשְׂרָאֵל. צוּר הָעוֹלָמִים, אֲדוֹן כָּל הַבְּרִיּוֹת, אֱלוֹהַּ כָּל הַנְּפָשׁוֹת, הַיּוֹשֵׁב בְּמֶרְחֲבֵי מָרוֹם, הַשּׁוֹכֵן בִּשְׁמֵי שְׁמֵי קֶדֶם, קְדֻשָּׁתוֹ עַל הַחַיּוֹת, וּקְדֻשָּׁתוֹ עַל כִּסֵּא הַכָּבוֹד. וּבְכֵן יִתְקַדַּשׁ שִׁמְךָ בָּנוּ יהוה אֱלֹהֵינוּ לְעֵינֵי
תהלים סח
כָּל חָי, וְנֹאמַר לְפָנָיו שִׁיר חָדָשׁ, כַּכָּתוּב: שִׁירוּ לֵאלֹהִים זַמְּרוּ שְׁמוֹ, סֹלּוּ לָרֹכֵב
ישעיה נב
בָּעֲרָבוֹת, בְּיָהּ שְׁמוֹ, וְעִלְזוּ לְפָנָיו: וְנִרְאֵהוּ עַיִן בְּעַיִן בְּשׁוּבוֹ אֶל נָוֵהוּ, כַּכָּתוּב: כִּי
ישעיה מ
עַיִן בְּעַיִן יִרְאוּ בְּשׁוּב יהוה צִיּוֹן: וְנֶאֱמַר: וְנִגְלָה כְּבוֹד יהוה, וְרָאוּ כָל־בָּשָׂר יַחְדָּו כִּי פִּי יהוה דִּבֵּר:

אַב הָרַחֲמִים הוּא יְרַחֵם עַם עֲמוּסִים, וְיִזְכֹּר בְּרִית אֵיתָנִים, וְיַצִּיל נַפְשׁוֹתֵינוּ מִן הַשָּׁעוֹת הָרָעוֹת, וְיִגְעַר בְּיֵצֶר הָרָע מִן הַנְּשׂוּאִים, וְיָחֹן אוֹתָנוּ לִפְלֵיטַת עוֹלָמִים, וִימַלֵּא מִשְׁאֲלוֹתֵינוּ בְּמִדָּה טוֹבָה יְשׁוּעָה וְרַחֲמִים.

CONNECTION

Long before the Beit HaMikdash *was built, two brothers lived and farmed on that site. One was married and had a large family, while the other was single. They lived in close proximity to each other, and each worked his land growing wheat. When harvest time arrived, each was blessed with a bountiful crop and piled up his grain for long-term storage. The unmarried brother, observing his good fortune, thought to himself that God had blessed him with more than he needed, whereas his brother, who was blessed with a large family, could surely use more. He arose in the middle of the night and secretly took from his grain and put it in his brother's pile. Similarly, the married brother thought to himself that he was fortunate to have children who will care for him in his old age, while his brother will depend on what he saved. He, too, arose in the middle of the night and quietly transferred grain from his pile to his brother's. In the morning, each pondered why there was no noticeable*

The Torah scroll is placed on the bima and the Gabbai calls a Kohen to the Torah.

וְיַעֲזֹר May He help, shield and save all who seek refuge in Him,
and let us say: Amen. Let us all give greatness to our God
and give honor to the Torah. *Let the Kohen come forward.
Arise (*name* son of *father's name*), the Kohen.

**If no Kohen is present, a Levi or Yisrael is called up as follows:*
/As there is no Kohen, arise (*name* son of *father's name*) in place of a Kohen./

Blessed is He who, in His holiness, gave the Torah to His people Israel.

The congregation followed by the Gabbai:

You who cling to the Lord your God are all alive today. *Deut. 4*

The appropriate Torah portion is read.

---

4. There is a custom to hold onto the wooden handles which are called the *atzei ḥayyim* or "trees (lit. wood) of life." (Recall the verse [*Mishlei* 3:18] עֵץ־חַיִּים הִיא לַמַּחֲזִיקִים בָּהּ – "It is a tree of life to those who grasp it.") One reason may be purely practical – you need to open the Torah to find the place (*Megilla* 32a). Another suggestion is that it is as if one is actually receiving the Torah on Mount Sinai (*Orḥot Ḥayyim*). And yet another suggestion is that there is a need to hold onto any article over which one is reciting a blessing, similar to a lulav (*Beit Yosef*). The custom is to keep holding at least one of the handles until one is completely finished with one's *aliya*.
5. The Gemara (*Megilla* 32a) relates a dispute about how one should recite the blessings. Rabbi Meir was concerned that if you look into the *sefer Torah* when reciting the blessings, people might think that the blessings were actually printed inside the Torah and were part of the Torah itself. Those who follow his opinion therefore suggest that one turn one's head to the left (*Magen Avraham* 139:8) or the right (*Arukh HaShulḥan* 139:13), or close one's eyes (*Ḥayyei Adam*), or do anything but look down. Rabbi Yehuda, on the other hand, said that you don't really need to worry about that since most people know the blessings are separate from the Torah itself; according to this view, you may recite the blessing while looking in the Torah (*Baḥ* and *Taz*)
6. Reciting *Barekhu* is in effect an invitation to the community to join with you in learning Torah together, with you as their representative. They, in turn, answer in order to convey their presence and their participation. It is therefore important to recite the words loudly

Continues on page 637.

The ספר תורה *is placed on the* שולחן *and the* גבאי *calls a* כהן *to the* תורה*.*

וְיַעֲזֹר וְיָגֵן וְיוֹשִׁיעַ לְכָל הַחוֹסִים בּוֹ, וְנֹאמַר אָמֵן. הַכֹּל הָבוּ גֹדֶל לֵאלֹהֵינוּ וּתְנוּ כָבוֹד לַתּוֹרָה. *כֹּהֵן קְרַב, יַעֲמֹד (פלוני בֶּן פלוני) **הַכֹּהֵן.**

**If no* כהן *is present, a* לוי *or* ישראל *is called up as follows:*

/אֵין כָּאן כֹּהֵן, יַעֲמֹד (פלוני בֶּן פלוני) **בִּמְקוֹם כֹּהֵן./**

בָּרוּךְ שֶׁנָּתַן תּוֹרָה לְעַמּוֹ יִשְׂרָאֵל בִּקְדֻשָּׁתוֹ.

The קהל *followed by the* גבאי*:*

וְאַתֶּם הַדְּבֵקִים בַּיהוה אֱלֹהֵיכֶם חַיִּים כֻּלְּכֶם הַיּוֹם: דברים ד

The appropriate תורה *portion is read.*

A GUIDE TO GETTING AN *ALIYA*

1. Getting an *aliya* is a big deal. It's important to recall that the *kavod* (honor) is not only yours but the Torah's. In fact Rabbi Yehuda (*Berakhot* 55a) suggested that, except in certain extenuating circumstances, one's life might be shortened, God forbid, if one turns down an *aliya*. After all, the Torah is described as **כִּי הוּא חַיֶּיךָ וְאֹרֶךְ יָמֶיךָ** (*Devarim* 30:20) – "Torah is your life and the length of your days." Why would you want to give it up?
2. In order to show your love of the Torah and what an honor it is to get an *aliya*, and in order that everyone else doesn't have to wait unnecessarily long until you get from your seat to the *bima*, the custom is to take the shortest route to the Torah. If you are equidistant from both sides of the *bima*, the custom is to go up on the right side and leave via the left side. This is just because there is a preference in Judaism for the right (*Yoma* 15b). Hence, some halakhic authorities prefer that you always go up the right side even if the *bima* is further away from you (*Ḥatam Sofer Oraḥ Ḥayyim* 187). The prophet Yeḥezkel (46:9) noted that in the *Beit HaMikdash* the custom was to enter via one gate and leave via another. Consider this *aliya*, then, a kind of going up to the *Beit HaMikdash*.
3. Since you are about to "read" the Torah, it makes sense to see exactly what you are about to "read" before making the blessing. That's why there is a custom for the *ba'al koreh* to show you the place where your *aliya* begins. There is another custom to make a motion to touch that spot with one's tallit or some other material and then kiss it in order to display one's love of Torah and one's excitement at this opportunity.

The Reader shows the oleh the section to be read.
The oleh touches the scroll at that place with the tzitzit of his tallit,
which he then kisses. Holding the handles of the scroll, he says:

Oleh: Bless the LORD, the blessed One.

Cong: Bless the LORD, the blessed One,
for ever and all time.

Oleh: Bless the LORD, the blessed One,
for ever and all time.
Blessed are You, LORD our God, King of the Universe,
who has chosen us from all peoples
and has given us His Torah.
Blessed are You, LORD, Giver of the Torah.

After the reading, the oleh says:

Oleh: Blessed are You, LORD our God, King of the Universe,
who has given us the Torah of truth,
planting everlasting life in our midst.
Blessed are You, LORD, Giver of the Torah.

---

standing beside the *gabbai* until the completion of the next *aliya*. This is considered a fulfillment of giving honor to the Torah by not abandoning it prematurely (*Levush*). While theoretically one could leave once the next person getting an *aliya is* standing in front of the Torah, the custom is to wait until the end of his *aliya* and to try to get back to one's seat before the next *aliya* so that one does not miss any of the reading (*Magen Avraham* 141:8).

9. When returning to one's seat, the custom is to take the longer route back, as if to symbolize your sadness at leaving the Torah (*Levush*) or lest it look like you are trying to make a hasty getaway (*Arukh HaShulḥan*). If the routes are equidistant, then leave from the opposite side you came from.

10. Finally, it is customary for people to wish יְיַשַׁר כֹּחַ (*yishar ko'aḥ/koḥakha*), "May your strength be increased" or "more power to you," to which the traditional reply is בָּרוּךְ תִּהְיֶה – "May you be blessed." In Sephardic tradition the greeting is, "May your strength be increased and may you be blessed," to which the traditional reply is "*Ḥazak ve'ematz* " – "Be strong and courageous." (Rabbi Jay Goldmintz, *The Koren Ani Tefilla Shabbat Siddur*)

The קורא *shows the* עולה *the section to be read.*
The עולה *touches the scroll at that place with the* ציצית *of his* טלית,
which he then kisses. Holding the handles of the scroll, he says:

עולה: בָּרְכוּ אֶת יהוה הַמְבֹרָךְ.

קהל: בָּרוּךְ יהוה הַמְבֹרָךְ לְעוֹלָם וָעֶד.

עולה: בָּרוּךְ יהוה הַמְבֹרָךְ לְעוֹלָם וָעֶד.
בָּרוּךְ אַתָּה יהוה אֱלֹהֵינוּ מֶלֶךְ הָעוֹלָם
אֲשֶׁר בָּחַר בָּנוּ מִכָּל הָעַמִּים
וְנָתַן לָנוּ אֶת תּוֹרָתוֹ.
בָּרוּךְ אַתָּה יהוה, נוֹתֵן הַתּוֹרָה.

After the קריאת התורה, *the* עולה *says:*

עולה: בָּרוּךְ אַתָּה יהוה אֱלֹהֵינוּ מֶלֶךְ הָעוֹלָם
אֲשֶׁר נָתַן לָנוּ תּוֹרַת אֱמֶת
וְחַיֵּי עוֹלָם נָטַע בְּתוֹכֵנוּ.
בָּרוּךְ אַתָּה יהוה, נוֹתֵן הַתּוֹרָה.

---

enough so that everyone (or at least a *minyan*'s worth) can hear you.

7. Ideally, each person is supposed to read the Torah portion for his own *aliya*. But if that were always enforced, then a person who could not read it accurately might be embarrassed (Ran), or he might read it with so many errors that those present would not be fulfilling their obligation to hear the Torah reading (Rosh), or a person who could not read Hebrew would never get an *aliya*, nor could a blind person. As such, the custom evolved to have a *ba'al koreh*, who would be in charge of the reading and act as a *shaliaḥ* or messenger for the person getting the *aliya*. Nevertheless, there is a custom that the person getting an *aliya* should do his best to read along in a whisper with the *ba'al koreh* as if to fulfill his own obligation to read, and so as to reinforce that the blessing he said was on his own reading.

8. Upon completion of the final blessing, the custom is to remain at the *bima*

One who has survived a situation of danger says:

Blessed are You, Lord our God, King of the Universe, who bestows good on the unworthy, who has bestowed on me much good.

The congregation responds:

Amen. May He who bestowed much good on you continue to bestow on you much good, Selah.

After a Bar Mitzva boy has finished the Torah blessing, his father says aloud:

Blessed is He who has released me from the responsibility for this child.

In some congregations, during the week before a yahrzeit, "God, full of mercy" for a relative on page 748.

FOR AN OLEH

May He who blessed our fathers, Abraham, Isaac and Jacob, bless (*name*, son of *father's name*) who has been called up in honor of the All-Present, in honor of the Torah, and in honor of the Sabbath. As a reward for this, may the Holy One, blessed be He, protect and save him from all trouble and distress, all infection and illness, and send blessing and success to all the work of his hands, together with all Israel, his brethren, and let us say: Amen.

FOR A SICK MAN

May He who blessed our fathers, Abraham, Isaac and Jacob, Moses and Aaron, David and Solomon, bless and heal one who is ill, (*sick person's name*, son of *mother's name*), on whose behalf (*name of the one making the offering*) is making a contribution to charity. As a reward for this, may the Holy One, blessed be He, be filled with compassion for him, to restore his health, cure him, strengthen and revive him, sending him a swift and full recovery from heaven to all his 248 organs and 365 sinews, amongst the other sick ones in Israel, a healing of the spirit and a healing of the body – though on Shabbat it is forbidden to cry out, may healing be quick to come – now, swiftly and soon, and let us say: Amen.

FOR A SICK WOMAN

May He who blessed our fathers, Abraham, Isaac and Jacob, Moses and Aaron, David and Solomon, bless and heal one who is ill, (*sick person's name*, daughter of *mother's name*), on whose behalf (*name of the one

One who has survived a situation of danger says:

בָּרוּךְ אַתָּה יהוה אֱלֹהֵינוּ מֶלֶךְ הָעוֹלָם, הַגּוֹמֵל לְחַיָּבִים טוֹבוֹת שֶׁגְּמָלַנִי כָּל טוֹב.

The קהל *responds:*

אָמֵן. מִי שֶׁגְּמָלְךָ כָּל טוֹב הוּא יִגְמָלְךָ כָּל טוֹב, סֶלָה.

After a בר מצווה *has finished the* תורה *blessing, his father says aloud:*

בָּרוּךְ שֶׁפְּטָרַנִי מֵעָנְשׁוֹ שֶׁלָּזֶה.

In some congregations, during the week before a yahrzeit,
אֵל מָלֵא רַחֲמִים *on page 749.*

מי שברך לעולה לתורה

מִי שֶׁבֵּרַךְ אֲבוֹתֵינוּ אַבְרָהָם יִצְחָק וְיַעֲקֹב, הוּא יְבָרֵךְ אֶת (פלוני בֶּן פלוני), בַּעֲבוּר שֶׁעָלָה לִכְבוֹד הַמָּקוֹם וְלִכְבוֹד הַתּוֹרָה וְלִכְבוֹד הַשַּׁבָּת. בִּשְׂכַר זֶה הַקָּדוֹשׁ בָּרוּךְ הוּא יִשְׁמְרֵהוּ וְיַצִּילֵהוּ מִכָּל צָרָה וְצוּקָה וּמִכָּל נֶגַע וּמַחֲלָה, וְיִשְׁלַח בְּרָכָה וְהַצְלָחָה בְּכָל מַעֲשֵׂה יָדָיו עִם כָּל יִשְׂרָאֵל אֶחָיו, וְנֹאמַר אָמֵן.

מי שברך לחולה

מִי שֶׁבֵּרַךְ אֲבוֹתֵינוּ אַבְרָהָם יִצְחָק וְיַעֲקֹב, מֹשֶׁה וְאַהֲרֹן דָּוִד וּשְׁלֹמֹה הוּא יְבָרֵךְ וִירַפֵּא אֶת הַחוֹלֶה (פלוני בֶּן פלונית) בַּעֲבוּר שֶׁ(פלוני בֶּן פלוני) נוֹדֵר צְדָקָה בַּעֲבוּרוֹ. בִּשְׂכַר זֶה הַקָּדוֹשׁ בָּרוּךְ הוּא יִמָּלֵא רַחֲמִים עָלָיו לְהַחֲלִימוֹ וּלְרַפְּאוֹתוֹ וּלְהַחֲזִיקוֹ וּלְהַחֲיוֹתוֹ וְיִשְׁלַח לוֹ מְהֵרָה רְפוּאָה שְׁלֵמָה מִן הַשָּׁמַיִם לִרְמַ״ח אֵבָרָיו וּשְׁסָ״ה גִּידָיו בְּתוֹךְ שְׁאָר חוֹלֵי יִשְׂרָאֵל, רְפוּאַת הַנֶּפֶשׁ וּרְפוּאַת הַגּוּף. שַׁבָּת הִיא מִלִּזְעֹק וּרְפוּאָה קְרוֹבָה לָבוֹא, הַשְׁתָּא בַּעֲגָלָא וּבִזְמַן קָרִיב, וְנֹאמַר אָמֵן.

מי שברך לחולָה

מִי שֶׁבֵּרַךְ אֲבוֹתֵינוּ אַבְרָהָם יִצְחָק וְיַעֲקֹב, מֹשֶׁה וְאַהֲרֹן דָּוִד וּשְׁלֹמֹה הוּא יְבָרֵךְ וִירַפֵּא אֶת הַחוֹלָה (פלונית בַּת פלונית) בַּעֲבוּר שֶׁ(פלוני בֶּן פלוני)

making the offering) is making a contribution to charity. As a reward for this, may the Holy One, blessed be He, be filled with compassion for her, to restore her health, cure her, strengthen and revive her, sending her a swift and full recovery from heaven to all her organs and sinews, amongst the other sick ones in Israel, a healing of the spirit and a healing of the body – though on the Sabbath) it is forbidden to cry out, may healing be quick to come – now, swiftly and soon, and let us say: Amen.

ON THE BIRTH OF A SON

May He who blessed our fathers, Abraham, Isaac and Jacob, Moses and Aaron, David and Solomon, Sarah, Rebecca, Rachel and Leah, bless the woman who has given birth (*name,* daughter of *father's name*), and her son who has been born to her as an auspicious sign. Her husband, the child's father, is making a contribution to charity. As a reward for this, may father and mother merit to bring the child into the covenant of Abraham and to a life of Torah, to the marriage canopy and to good deeds, and let us say: Amen.

ON THE BIRTH OF A DAUGHTER

May He who blessed our fathers, Abraham, Isaac and Jacob, Moses and Aaron, David and Solomon, Sarah, Rebecca, Rachel and Leah, bless the woman who has given birth (*name,* daughter of *father's name*), and her daughter who has been born to her as an auspicious sign; and may her name be called in Israel (*baby's name,* daughter of *father's name*). Her husband, the child's father, is making a contribution to charity. As a reward for this, may father and mother merit to raise her to a life of Torah, to the marriage canopy, and to good deeds, and let us say: Amen.

FOR A BAR MITZVA

May He who blessed our fathers, Abraham, Isaac and Jacob, bless (*name,* son of *father's name*) who has completed thirteen years and attained the age of the commandments, who has been called to the Torah to give praise and thanks to God, may His name be blessed, for all the good He has bestowed on him. May the Holy One, blessed be He, protect and sustain him and direct his heart to be perfect with God, to walk in His ways and keep the commandments all the days of his life, and let us say: Amen.

נוֹדֵר צְדָקָה בַּעֲבוּרָהּ. בִּשְׂכַר זֶה הַקָּדוֹשׁ בָּרוּךְ הוּא יִמָּלֵא רַחֲמִים עָלֶיהָ לְהַחֲלִימָהּ וּלְרַפְּאתָהּ וּלְהַחֲזִיקָהּ וּלְהַחֲיוֹתָהּ וְיִשְׁלַח לָהּ מְהֵרָה רְפוּאָה שְׁלֵמָה מִן הַשָּׁמַיִם לְכָל אֵבָרֶיהָ וּלְכָל גִּידֶיהָ בְּתוֹךְ שְׁאָר חוֹלֵי יִשְׂרָאֵל, רְפוּאַת הַנֶּפֶשׁ וּרְפוּאַת הַגּוּף. שַׁבָּת הִיא מִלִּזְעֹק וּרְפוּאָה קְרוֹבָה לָבוֹא, הַשְׁתָּא בַּעֲגָלָא וּבִזְמַן קָרִיב, וְנֹאמַר אָמֵן.

מי שברך ליולדת בן

מִי שֶׁבֵּרַךְ אֲבוֹתֵינוּ אַבְרָהָם יִצְחָק וְיַעֲקֹב, מֹשֶׁה וְאַהֲרֹן דָּוִד וּשְׁלֹמֹה, שָׂרָה רִבְקָה רָחֵל וְלֵאָה הוּא יְבָרֵךְ אֶת הָאִשָּׁה הַיּוֹלֶדֶת (פלונית בַּת פלוני) וְאֶת בְּנָהּ שֶׁנּוֹלַד לָהּ לְמַזָּל טוֹב בַּעֲבוּר שֶׁבַּעְלָהּ וְאָבִיו נוֹדֵר צְדָקָה בַּעֲדָם. בִּשְׂכַר זֶה יִזְכּוּ אָבִיו וְאִמּוֹ לְהַכְנִיסוֹ בִּבְרִיתוֹ שֶׁל אַבְרָהָם אָבִינוּ וּלְגַדְּלוֹ לְתוֹרָה וּלְחֻפָּה וּלְמַעֲשִׂים טוֹבִים, וְנֹאמַר אָמֵן.

מי שברך ליולדת בת

מִי שֶׁבֵּרַךְ אֲבוֹתֵינוּ אַבְרָהָם יִצְחָק וְיַעֲקֹב, מֹשֶׁה וְאַהֲרֹן דָּוִד וּשְׁלֹמֹה, שָׂרָה רִבְקָה רָחֵל וְלֵאָה הוּא יְבָרֵךְ אֶת הָאִשָּׁה הַיּוֹלֶדֶת (פלונית בַּת פלוני) וְאֶת בִּתָּהּ שֶׁנּוֹלְדָה לָהּ לְמַזָּל טוֹב וְיִקָּרֵא שְׁמָהּ בְּיִשְׂרָאֵל (פלונית בַּת פלוני), בַּעֲבוּר שֶׁבַּעְלָהּ וְאָבִיהָ נוֹדֵר צְדָקָה בַּעֲדָן. בִּשְׂכַר זֶה יִזְכּוּ אָבִיהָ וְאִמָּהּ לְגַדְּלָהּ לְתוֹרָה וּלְחֻפָּה וּלְמַעֲשִׂים טוֹבִים, וְנֹאמַר אָמֵן.

מי שברך לבר מצווה

מִי שֶׁבֵּרַךְ אֲבוֹתֵינוּ אַבְרָהָם יִצְחָק וְיַעֲקֹב הוּא יְבָרֵךְ אֶת (פלוני בֶּן פלוני) שֶׁמָּלְאוּ לוֹ שְׁלֹשׁ עֶשְׂרֵה שָׁנָה וְהִגִּיעַ לְמִצְוֹת, וְעָלָה לַתּוֹרָה, לָתֵת שֶׁבַח וְהוֹדָיָה לְהַשֵּׁם יִתְבָּרַךְ עַל כָּל הַטּוֹבָה שֶׁגָּמַל אִתּוֹ. יִשְׁמְרֵהוּ הַקָּדוֹשׁ בָּרוּךְ הוּא וִיחַיֵּהוּ, וִיכוֹנֵן אֶת לִבּוֹ לִהְיוֹת שָׁלֵם עִם יהוה וְלָלֶכֶת בִּדְרָכָיו וְלִשְׁמֹר מִצְוֹתָיו כָּל הַיָּמִים, וְנֹאמַר אָמֵן.

FOR A BAT MITZVA

May He who blessed our fathers, Abraham, Isaac and Jacob, Sarah, Rebecca, Rachel and Leah, bless (*name*, daughter of *father's name*) who has completed twelve years and attained the age of the commandments, and gives praise and thanks to God, may His name be blessed, for all the good He has bestowed on her. May the Holy One, blessed be He, protect and sustain her and direct her heart to be perfect with God, to walk in His ways and keep the commandments all the days of her life, and let us say: Amen.

HALF KADDISH

Before Maftir is read, the Reader says Half Kaddish:

Reader: יִתְגַּדַּל Magnified and sanctified
may His great name be,
in the world He created by His will.
May He establish His kingdom
in your lifetime and in your days,
and in the lifetime of all the house of Israel,
swiftly and soon –
and say: Amen.

All: May His great name be blessed
for ever and all time.

Reader: Blessed and praised,
glorified and elevated,
raised and honored,
uplifted and praised
be the name of the Holy One,
blessed be He,
beyond any blessing,
song, praise and consolation
uttered in the world –
and say: Amen.

מי שברך לבת מצווה

מִי שֶׁבֵּרַךְ אֲבוֹתֵינוּ אַבְרָהָם יִצְחָק וְיַעֲקֹב, שָׂרָה רִבְקָה רָחֵל וְלֵאָה, הוּא יְבָרֵךְ אֶת (פלונית בַּת פלוני) שֶׁמָּלְאוּ לָהּ שְׁתֵּים עֶשְׂרֵה שָׁנָה וְהִגִּיעָה לְמִצְוֹת, וְנוֹתֶנֶת שֶׁבַח וְהוֹדָיָה לְהַשֵּׁם יִתְבָּרַךְ עַל כָּל הַטּוֹבָה שֶׁגָּמַל אִתָּהּ. יִשְׁמְרֶהָ הַקָּדוֹשׁ בָּרוּךְ הוּא וִיחַיֶּהָ, וִיכוֹנֵן אֶת לִבָּהּ לִהְיוֹת שָׁלֵם עִם יהוה וְלָלֶכֶת בִּדְרָכָיו וְלִשְׁמֹר מִצְוֹתָיו כָּל הַיָּמִים, וְנֹאמַר אָמֵן.

חצי קדיש

Before מפטיר *is read, the* קורא *says* חצי קדיש*:*

קורא: יִתְגַּדַּל וְיִתְקַדַּשׁ שְׁמֵהּ רַבָּא (קהל: אָמֵן)
בְּעָלְמָא דִּי בְרָא כִרְעוּתֵהּ
וְיַמְלִיךְ מַלְכוּתֵהּ
בְּחַיֵּיכוֹן וּבְיוֹמֵיכוֹן וּבְחַיֵּי דְכָל בֵּית יִשְׂרָאֵל
בַּעֲגָלָא וּבִזְמַן קָרִיב
וְאִמְרוּ אָמֵן. (קהל: אָמֵן)

קהל וקורא: יְהֵא שְׁמֵהּ רַבָּא מְבָרַךְ לְעָלַם וּלְעָלְמֵי עָלְמַיָּא.

קורא: יִתְבָּרַךְ וְיִשְׁתַּבַּח וְיִתְפָּאַר וְיִתְרוֹמַם וְיִתְנַשֵּׂא
וְיִתְהַדָּר וְיִתְעַלֶּה וְיִתְהַלָּל
שְׁמֵהּ דְּקֻדְשָׁא בְּרִיךְ הוּא (קהל: בְּרִיךְ הוּא)
לְעֵלָּא מִן כָּל בִּרְכָתָא
/בשבת שובה: לְעֵלָּא לְעֵלָּא מִכָּל בִּרְכָתָא/
וְשִׁירָתָא, תֻּשְׁבְּחָתָא וְנֶחֱמָתָא
דַּאֲמִירָן בְּעָלְמָא
וְאִמְרוּ אָמֵן. (קהל: אָמֵן)

HAGBAHA AND GELILA

The Torah scroll is lifted and the congregation says:

וְזֹאת הַתּוֹרָה This is the Torah *Deut. 4*
that Moses placed before the children of Israel, *Num. 9*
at the LORD's commandment, by the hand of Moses.

Some add: It is a tree of life to those who grasp it, and those who uphold it are happy. *Prov. 3*
Its ways are ways of pleasantness, and all its paths are peace.
Long life is in its right hand; in its left, riches and honor.
It pleased the LORD for the sake of [Israel's] righteousness, *Is. 42*
to make the Torah great and glorious.

The Torah scroll is bound and covered.

BLESSINGS BEFORE AND AFTER READING THE HAFTARA

Before reading the Haftara, the person called up for Maftir says:

בָּרוּךְ Blessed are You, LORD our God, King of the Universe, who chose good prophets and was pleased with their words, spoken in truth. Blessed are You, LORD, who chose the Torah, His servant Moses, His people Israel, and the prophets of truth and righteousness.

---

called up at the end of the Torah reading to make one blessing before and another after that reading (= two blessings), then one blessing before the *Haftara*, then read a minimum of twenty-one verses from a selection of a book of the Prophets that is related in some way to the weekly Torah portion, and then four blessings afterwards for a total of seven blessings.

Finally, there is an opinion which suggests that the public reading from the Prophets is the remnant of an old custom to take time out on Shabbat to do some learning after finishing Shaḥarit, something that is more difficult to do during the week when everyone needs to rush off to work (Rashi). Seen in this light, the reading is a way for us to extend our individual and communal commitment to learning beyond that which some may think of as the minimum. In particular, we focus on the books that are too often ignored in education (Shakh in *Yoreh De'ah* 245:5), the Prophets, whose prophecies and speeches were written down because they have a message not only for their own time but for future generations as well. The essence of our listening intently to this recitation, then, is our ability to discern and internalize those messages, as has been done for generations of Jews since these words were first uttered. (Rabbi Jay Goldmintz, *The Koren Ani Tefilla Shabbat Siddur*)

הגבהה וגלילה

The ספר תורה *is lifted and the* קהל *says:*

וְזֹאת הַתּוֹרָה אֲשֶׁר־שָׂם מֹשֶׁה לִפְנֵי בְּנֵי יִשְׂרָאֵל: דברים ד

עַל־פִּי יהוה בְּיַד מֹשֶׁה: במדבר ט

Some add

עֵץ־חַיִּים הִיא לַמַּחֲזִיקִים בָּהּ וְתֹמְכֶיהָ מְאֻשָּׁר: משלי ג
דְּרָכֶיהָ דַרְכֵי־נֹעַם וְכָל־נְתִיבֹתֶיהָ שָׁלוֹם:
אֹרֶךְ יָמִים בִּימִינָהּ, בִּשְׂמֹאולָהּ עֹשֶׁר וְכָבוֹד:
יהוה חָפֵץ לְמַעַן צִדְקוֹ יַגְדִּיל תּוֹרָה וְיַאְדִּיר: ישעיה מב

The ספר תורה *is bound and covered.*

ברכות ההפטרה

Before reading the הפטרה*, the person called up for* מפטיר *says:*

בָּרוּךְ אַתָּה יהוה אֱלֹהֵינוּ מֶלֶךְ הָעוֹלָם אֲשֶׁר בָּחַר בִּנְבִיאִים טוֹבִים, וְרָצָה בְדִבְרֵיהֶם הַנֶּאֱמָרִים בֶּאֱמֶת. בָּרוּךְ אַתָּה יהוה, הַבּוֹחֵר בַּתּוֹרָה וּבְמֹשֶׁה עַבְדּוֹ וּבְיִשְׂרָאֵל עַמּוֹ וּבִנְבִיאֵי הָאֱמֶת וָצֶדֶק.

INTRODUCTION TO *HAFTARA*

In addition to the weekly Torah portion, there is also a tradition to read a relatively short selection, called the *Haftara*, from a book of the Prophets. The exact source for this custom is not definitively known. One opinion has it that it was instituted by Ezra the Scribe in the fifth century BCE once all of the books of the Bible were canonized.

A more widely accepted theory is that there was a time in Jewish history when the public reading of the Torah was banned by the government (perhaps during the time of the Ḥanukka story in the second century BCE or even later during the time of the Roman Empire). In order to nevertheless keep echoes of the tradition alive, the community resorted to reading a selection of the Prophets that was related in some way (e.g., in theme or language) to what would have been the Torah portion for that week. They established that the selection be a minimum of twenty-one verses long (to correspond to the minimum of three verses of the Torah read by each of the seven people who would have gotten an *aliya*) and that there be seven introductory blessings (to correspond to the missing blessings made by the seven people who would have gotten an *aliya*) (*Mishna Berura* 284:2). When the decree was rescinded, the practice nevertheless continued such that today one person is

After the Haftara, the person called up for Maftir says the following blessings:

בָּרוּךְ Blessed are You, Lord our God, King of the Universe, Rock of all worlds, righteous for all generations, the faithful God who says and does, speaks and fulfills, all of whose words are truth and righteousness. You are faithful, Lord our God, and faithful are Your words, not one of which returns unfulfilled, for You, God, are a faithful (and compassionate) King. Blessed are You, Lord, faithful in all His words.

רַחֵם Have compassion on Zion for it is the source of our life, and save the one grieved in spirit swiftly in our days. Blessed are You, Lord, who makes Zion rejoice in her children.

שַׂמְּחֵנוּ Give us joy, Lord our God, through Elijah the prophet Your servant, and through the kingdom of the house of David Your anointed – may he soon come and make our hearts glad. May no stranger sit on his throne, and may others not continue to inherit his glory, for You promised him by Your holy name that his light would never be extinguished. Blessed are You, Lord, Shield of David.

On Shabbat, including Shabbat Ḥol HaMo'ed Pesaḥ, say:

עַל הַתּוֹרָה For the Torah, for divine worship, for the prophets, and for this Sabbath day which You, Lord our God, have given us for holiness and rest, honor and glory – for all these we thank and bless You, Lord our God, and may Your name be blessed by the mouth of all that lives, continually, for ever and all time. Blessed are You, Lord, who sanctifies the Sabbath.

On Shabbat Ḥol HaMo'ed Sukkot, say:

For the Torah, for divine worship, for the prophets, for this Sabbath day and for this day of the Festival of Sukkot which You, Lord our God, have given us for holiness and rest, for joy and gladness, honor and glory – for all these we thank and bless You, Lord our God, and may Your name be blessed by the mouth of all that lives, continually, for ever and all time. Blessed are You, Lord, who sanctifies the Sabbath, Israel and the festivals.

After the הפטרה*, the person called up for* מפטיר *says the following blessings:*

בָּרוּךְ אַתָּה יהוה אֱלֹהֵינוּ מֶלֶךְ הָעוֹלָם, צוּר כָּל הָעוֹלָמִים, צַדִּיק בְּכָל הַדּוֹרוֹת, הָאֵל הַנֶּאֱמָן, הָאוֹמֵר וְעוֹשֶׂה, הַמְדַבֵּר וּמְקַיֵּם, שֶׁכָּל דְּבָרָיו אֱמֶת וָצֶדֶק. נֶאֱמָן אַתָּה הוּא יהוה אֱלֹהֵינוּ וְנֶאֱמָנִים דְּבָרֶיךָ, וְדָבָר אֶחָד מִדְּבָרֶיךָ אָחוֹר לֹא יָשׁוּב רֵיקָם, כִּי אֵל מֶלֶךְ נֶאֱמָן (וְרַחֲמָן) אָתָּה. בָּרוּךְ אַתָּה יהוה, הָאֵל הַנֶּאֱמָן בְּכָל דְּבָרָיו.

רַחֵם עַל צִיּוֹן כִּי הִיא בֵּית חַיֵּינוּ, וְלַעֲלוּבַת נֶפֶשׁ תּוֹשִׁיעַ בִּמְהֵרָה בְיָמֵינוּ. בָּרוּךְ אַתָּה יהוה, מְשַׂמֵּחַ צִיּוֹן בְּבָנֶיהָ.

שַׂמְּחֵנוּ יהוה אֱלֹהֵינוּ בְּאֵלִיָּהוּ הַנָּבִיא עַבְדֶּךָ, וּבְמַלְכוּת בֵּית דָּוִד מְשִׁיחֶךָ, בִּמְהֵרָה יָבוֹא וְיָגֵל לִבֵּנוּ. עַל כִּסְאוֹ לֹא יֵשֶׁב זָר, וְלֹא יִנְחֲלוּ עוֹד אֲחֵרִים אֶת כְּבוֹדוֹ, כִּי בְשֵׁם קָדְשְׁךָ נִשְׁבַּעְתָּ לּוֹ שֶׁלֹּא יִכְבֶּה נֵרוֹ לְעוֹלָם וָעֶד. בָּרוּךְ אַתָּה יהוה, מָגֵן דָּוִד.

On שבת*, including* שבת חול המועד פסח*, say:*

עַל הַתּוֹרָה וְעַל הָעֲבוֹדָה וְעַל הַנְּבִיאִים וְעַל יוֹם הַשַּׁבָּת הַזֶּה, שֶׁנָּתַתָּ לָּנוּ יהוה אֱלֹהֵינוּ לִקְדֻשָּׁה וְלִמְנוּחָה, לְכָבוֹד וּלְתִפְאָרֶת. עַל הַכֹּל יהוה אֱלֹהֵינוּ אֲנַחְנוּ מוֹדִים לָךְ וּמְבָרְכִים אוֹתָךְ, יִתְבָּרַךְ שִׁמְךָ בְּפִי כָּל חַי תָּמִיד לְעוֹלָם וָעֶד. בָּרוּךְ אַתָּה יהוה, מְקַדֵּשׁ הַשַּׁבָּת.

On שבת חול המועד סוכות*, say:*

עַל הַתּוֹרָה וְעַל הָעֲבוֹדָה וְעַל הַנְּבִיאִים וְעַל יוֹם הַשַּׁבָּת הַזֶּה, וְעַל יוֹם חַג הַסֻּכּוֹת הַזֶּה שֶׁנָּתַתָּ לָּנוּ, יהוה אֱלֹהֵינוּ לִקְדֻשָּׁה וְלִמְנוּחָה, לְשָׂשׂוֹן וּלְשִׂמְחָה, לְכָבוֹד וּלְתִפְאָרֶת. עַל הַכֹּל יהוה אֱלֹהֵינוּ אֲנַחְנוּ מוֹדִים לָךְ וּמְבָרְכִים אוֹתָךְ. יִתְבָּרַךְ שִׁמְךָ בְּפִי כָּל חַי תָּמִיד לְעוֹלָם וָעֶד. בָּרוּךְ אַתָּה יהוה, מְקַדֵּשׁ הַשַּׁבָּת וְיִשְׂרָאֵל וְהַזְּמַנִּים.

The following three paragraphs are only said when praying with a minyan (some say the first paragraph without a minyan).

יְקוּם פֻּרְקָן May deliverance arise from heaven, bringing grace, love and compassion, long life, abundant sustenance and heavenly help, physical health and enlightenment of mind, living and thriving children who will neither interrupt nor cease from the words of the Torah – to our masters and teachers of the holy communities in the land of Israel and Babylon; to the leaders of assemblies and the leaders of communities in exile; to the heads of academies and to the judges in the gates; to all their disciples and their disciples' disciples, and to all who occupy themselves in study of the Torah. May the King of the Universe bless them, prolonging their lives, increasing their days, and adding to their years. May they be redeemed and saved from all distress and illness. May our Master in heaven be their help at all times and seasons; and let us say: Amen.

יְקוּם פֻּרְקָן May deliverance arise from heaven, bringing grace, love and compassion, long life, abundant sustenance and heavenly help, physical health and enlightenment of mind, living and thriving children who will neither interrupt nor cease from the words of the Torah – to all this holy congregation, great and small, women and children. May the King of the Universe bless you, prolonging your lives, increasing your days, and adding to your years. May you be redeemed and saved from all distress and illness. May our Master in heaven be your help at all times and seasons; and let us say: Amen.

מִי שֶׁבֵּרַךְ May He who blessed our fathers, Abraham, Isaac and Jacob, bless all this holy congregation, together with all other holy congregations: them, their wives, their sons and daughters, and all that is theirs. May He bless those who unite to form synagogues for prayer and those who come there to pray; those who provide lamps for light and wine for Kiddush and Havdala, food for visitors and charity for the poor, and all who faithfully occupy themselves with the needs of the community. May the Holy One, blessed be He, give them their reward; may He remove from them all illness, give them complete healing, and forgive all their sins. May He send blessing and success to all the work of their hands, together with all Israel their brethren; and let us say: Amen.

The following three paragraphs are only said when praying with a מנין
(*some say the first paragraph without a* מנין).

יְקוּם פֻּרְקָן מִן שְׁמַיָּא, חִנָּא וְחִסְדָּא וְרַחֲמֵי וְחַיֵּי אֲרִיכֵי וּמְזוֹנֵי רְוִיחֵי, וְסִיַּעְתָּא דִשְׁמַיָּא, וּבַרְיוּת גּוּפָא וּנְהוֹרָא מְעַלְּיָא, זַרְעָא חַיָּא וְקַיָּמָא, זַרְעָא דִּי לָא יִפְסֻק וְדִי לָא יִבְטֻל מִפִּתְגָּמֵי אוֹרַיְתָא, לְמָרָנָן וְרַבָּנָן חֲבוּרָתָא קַדִּישָׁתָא דִּי בְאַרְעָא דְיִשְׂרָאֵל וְדִי בְּבָבֶל, לְרֵישֵׁי כַלָּה, וּלְרֵישֵׁי גַלְוָתָא, וּלְרֵישֵׁי מְתִיבָתָא, וּלְדַיָּנֵי דְבָבָא, לְכָל תַּלְמִידֵיהוֹן, וּלְכָל תַּלְמִידֵי תַלְמִידֵיהוֹן, וּלְכָל מָאן דְּעָסְקִין בְּאוֹרַיְתָא. מַלְכָּא דְעָלְמָא יְבָרֵךְ יָתְהוֹן, יַפֵּשׁ חַיֵּיהוֹן וְיַסְגֵּא יוֹמֵיהוֹן, וְיִתֵּן אַרְכָא לִשְׁנֵיהוֹן, וְיִתְפָּרְקוּן וְיִשְׁתֵּיזְבוּן מִן כָּל עָקָא וּמִן כָּל מַרְעִין בִּישִׁין. מָרָן דִּי בִשְׁמַיָּא יְהֵא בְסַעְדְּהוֹן כָּל זְמַן וְעִדָּן, וְנֹאמַר אָמֵן.

יְקוּם פֻּרְקָן מִן שְׁמַיָּא, חִנָּא וְחִסְדָּא וְרַחֲמֵי וְחַיֵּי אֲרִיכֵי וּמְזוֹנֵי רְוִיחֵי, וְסִיַּעְתָּא דִשְׁמַיָּא, וּבַרְיוּת גּוּפָא וּנְהוֹרָא מְעַלְּיָא, זַרְעָא חַיָּא וְקַיָּמָא, זַרְעָא דִּי לָא יִפְסֻק וְדִי לָא יִבְטֻל מִפִּתְגָּמֵי אוֹרַיְתָא, לְכָל קְהָלָא קַדִּישָׁא הָדֵין, רַבְרְבַיָּא עִם זְעֵרַיָּא, טַפְלָא וּנְשַׁיָּא. מַלְכָּא דְעָלְמָא יְבָרֵךְ יָתְכוֹן, יַפֵּשׁ חַיֵּיכוֹן וְיַסְגֵּא יוֹמֵיכוֹן, וְיִתֵּן אַרְכָא לִשְׁנֵיכוֹן, וְתִתְפָּרְקוּן וְתִשְׁתֵּיזְבוּן מִן כָּל עָקָא וּמִן כָּל מַרְעִין בִּישִׁין. מָרָן דִּי בִשְׁמַיָּא יְהֵא בְסַעְדְּכוֹן כָּל זְמַן וְעִדָּן, וְנֹאמַר אָמֵן.

מִי שֶׁבֵּרַךְ אֲבוֹתֵינוּ אַבְרָהָם יִצְחָק וְיַעֲקֹב, הוּא יְבָרֵךְ אֶת כָּל הַקָּהָל הַקָּדוֹשׁ הַזֶּה עִם כָּל קְהִלּוֹת הַקֹּדֶשׁ, הֵם וּנְשֵׁיהֶם וּבְנֵיהֶם וּבְנוֹתֵיהֶם וְכָל אֲשֶׁר לָהֶם, וּמִי שֶׁמְּיַחֲדִים בָּתֵּי כְנֵסִיּוֹת לִתְפִלָּה, וּמִי שֶׁבָּאִים בְּתוֹכָם לְהִתְפַּלֵּל, וּמִי שֶׁנּוֹתְנִים נֵר לַמָּאוֹר וְיַיִן לְקִדּוּשׁ וּלְהַבְדָּלָה וּפַת לָאוֹרְחִים וּצְדָקָה לָעֲנִיִּים, וְכָל מִי שֶׁעוֹסְקִים בְּצָרְכֵי צִבּוּר בֶּאֱמוּנָה. הַקָּדוֹשׁ בָּרוּךְ הוּא יְשַׁלֵּם שְׂכָרָם, וְיָסִיר מֵהֶם כָּל מַחֲלָה, וְיִרְפָּא לְכָל גּוּפָם, וְיִסְלַח לְכָל עֲוֹנָם, וְיִשְׁלַח בְּרָכָה וְהַצְלָחָה בְּכָל מַעֲשֵׂי יְדֵיהֶם עִם כָּל יִשְׂרָאֵל אֲחֵיהֶם, וְנֹאמַר אָמֵן.

The prayer for the Welfare of the Canadian Government is on the next page.

PRAYER FOR THE WELFARE OF THE AMERICAN GOVERNMENT

The Leader says the following:

הַנּוֹתֵן תְּשׁוּעָה May He who gives salvation to kings and dominion to princes, whose kingdom is an everlasting kingdom, who saves His servant David from the evil sword, who makes a way in the sea and a path through the mighty waters, bless and protect, guard and help, elevate, magnify and uplift the President, Vice President and all officials of this land. May the Supreme King of kings in His mercy put into their hearts and the hearts of all their advisors and officials, to deal kindly with us and all Israel. In their days and in ours, may Judah be saved and Israel live in safety, and may the Redeemer come to Zion. May this be His will, and let us say: Amen.

PRAYER FOR THE SAFETY OF THE AMERICAN MILITARY

The Leader says the following:

אַדִּיר בַּמָּרוֹם God on high who is present in might, the King to whom peace belongs, look down from Your holy habitation and bless the soldiers of the American military forces who risk their lives for the sake of peace on earth. Be their shelter and stronghold, and let them not falter. Give them the strength and courage to thwart the plans of the enemy and end the rule of evil. May their enemies be scattered and their enemies flee before them, and may they rejoice in Your salvation. Bring them back safely to their homes, as is written: "The LORD will guard you from all harm, He will guard your life. The LORD will guard your going and coming, now and for evermore." And may there be fulfilled for us the verse: "Nation shall not lift up sword against nation, nor shall they learn war any more." Let all the inhabitants on earth know that sovereignty is Yours and Your name inspires awe over all You have created – and let us say: Amen.

Ps. 121

Is. 2

The prayer for the Welfare of the Canadian Government is on the next page.

תפילה לשלום המלכות

The שליח ציבור *says the following:*

הַנּוֹתֵן תְּשׁוּעָה לַמְּלָכִים וּמֶמְשָׁלָה לַנְּסִיכִים, מַלְכוּתוֹ מַלְכוּת כָּל עוֹלָמִים, הַפּוֹצֶה אֶת דָּוִד עַבְדּוֹ מֵחֶרֶב רָעָה, הַנּוֹתֵן בַּיָּם דֶּרֶךְ וּבְמַיִם עַזִּים נְתִיבָה, הוּא יְבָרֵךְ וְיִשְׁמֹר וְיִנְצֹר וְיַעֲזֹר וִירוֹמֵם וִיגַדֵּל וִינַשֵּׂא לְמַעְלָה אֶת הַנָּשִׂיא וְאֵת מִשְׁנֵהוּ וְאֶת כָּל שָׂרֵי הָאָרֶץ הַזֹּאת. מֶלֶךְ מַלְכֵי הַמְּלָכִים, בְּרַחֲמָיו יִתֵּן בְּלִבָּם וּבְלֵב כָּל יוֹעֲצֵיהֶם וְשָׂרֵיהֶם לַעֲשׂוֹת טוֹבָה עִמָּנוּ וְעִם כָּל יִשְׂרָאֵל. בִּימֵיהֶם וּבְיָמֵינוּ תִּוָּשַׁע יְהוּדָה, וְיִשְׂרָאֵל יִשְׁכֹּן לָבֶטַח, וּבָא לְצִיּוֹן גּוֹאֵל. וְכֵן יְהִי רָצוֹן, וְנֹאמַר אָמֵן.

תפילה לשלום חיילי צבא ארצות הברית

The שליח ציבור *says the following:*

אַדִּיר בַּמָּרוֹם שׁוֹכֵן בִּגְבוּרָה, מֶלֶךְ שֶׁהַשָּׁלוֹם שֶׁלּוֹ, הַשְׁקִיפָה
מִמְּעוֹן קָדְשְׁךָ, וּבָרֵךְ אֶת חַיָּלֵי צְבָא אַרְצוֹת הַבְּרִית, הַמְחָרְפִים
נַפְשָׁם בְּלֶכְתָּם לָשִׂים שָׁלוֹם בָּאָרֶץ. הֱיֵה נָא לָהֶם מַחֲסֶה וּמָעוֹז,
וְאַל תִּתֵּן לַמּוֹט רַגְלָם, חַזֵּק יְדֵיהֶם וְאַמֵּץ רוּחָם לְהָפֵר עֲצַת
אוֹיֵב וּלְהַעֲבִיר מֶמְשֶׁלֶת זָדוֹן, יָפוּצוּ אוֹיְבֵיהֶם וְיָנוּסוּ מְשַׂנְאֵיהֶם
מִפְּנֵיהֶם, וְיִשְׂמְחוּ בִּישׁוּעָתֶךָ. הֲשִׁיבֵם בְּשָׁלוֹם אֶל בֵּיתָם, כַּכָּתוּב
בְּדִבְרֵי קָדְשֶׁךָ: יְהוָה יִשְׁמָרְךָ מִכָּל־רָע, יִשְׁמֹר אֶת־נַפְשֶׁךָ: יְהוָה תהלים קכא
יִשְׁמָר־צֵאתְךָ וּבוֹאֶךָ, מֵעַתָּה וְעַד־עוֹלָם: וְקַיֵּם בָּנוּ מִקְרָא שֶׁכָּתוּב:
לֹא־יִשָּׂא גוֹי אֶל־גּוֹי חֶרֶב, וְלֹא־יִלְמְדוּ עוֹד מִלְחָמָה: וְיֵדְעוּ כָּל ישעיה ב
יוֹשְׁבֵי תֵבֵל כִּי לְךָ מְלוּכָה יָאֲתָה, וְשִׁמְךָ נוֹרָא עַל כָּל מַה שֶּׁבָּרָאתָ.
וְנֹאמַר אָמֵן.

PRAYER FOR THE WELFARE OF THE CANADIAN GOVERNMENT

The Leader says the following:

הַנּוֹתֵן תְּשׁוּעָה May He who gives salvation to kings and dominion to princes, whose kingdom is an everlasting kingdom, who saves His servant David from the evil sword, who makes a way in the sea and a path through the mighty waters, bless and protect, guard and help, elevate, magnify and uplift the Prime Minister and all the elected and appointed officials of Canada. May the Supreme King of kings in His mercy put into their hearts and the hearts of all their advisors and officials, to deal kindly with us and all Israel. In their days and in ours, may Judah be saved and Israel live in safety, and may the Redeemer come to Zion. May this be His will, and let us say: Amen.

PRAYER FOR THE SAFETY OF THE CANADIAN MILITARY FORCES

The Leader says the following:

אַדִּיר בַּמָּרוֹם God on high who is present in might, the King to whom peace belongs, look down from Your holy habitation and bless the soldiers of the Canadian Forces who risk their lives for the sake of peace on earth. Be their shelter and stronghold, and let them not falter. Give them the strength and courage to defeat the plans of the enemy and end the rule of evil. May their enemies be scattered and their enemies flee before them, and may they rejoice in Your salvation. Bring them back safely to their homes, as is written: "The Lord will guard you from all harm, He will guard your life. The Lord will guard your going and coming, now and for evermore." And may there be fulfilled for us the verse: "Nation shall not lift up sword against nation, nor shall they learn war any more." Let all the inhabitants on earth know that sovereignty is Yours and Your name inspires awe over all You have created – and let us say: Amen.

Ps. 121

Is. 2

תפילה לשלום המלכות

The שליח ציבור *says the following:*

הַנּוֹתֵן תְּשׁוּעָה לַמְּלָכִים וּמֶמְשָׁלָה לַנְּסִיכִים, מַלְכוּתוֹ מַלְכוּת כָּל עוֹלָמִים, הַפּוֹצֶה אֶת דָּוִד עַבְדּוֹ מֵחֶרֶב רָעָה, הַנּוֹתֵן בַּיָּם דֶּרֶךְ וּבְמַיִם עַזִּים נְתִיבָה, הוּא יְבָרֵךְ וְיִשְׁמֹר וְיִנְצֹר וְיַעֲזֹר וִירוֹמֵם וִיגַדֵּל וִינַשֵּׂא לְמַעְלָה אֶת רֹאשׁ הַמֶּמְשָׁלָה וְאֶת כָּל שָׂרֵי הָאָרֶץ הַזֹּאת. מֶלֶךְ מַלְכֵי הַמְּלָכִים, בְּרַחֲמָיו יִתֵּן בְּלִבָּם וּבְלֵב כָּל יוֹעֲצֵיהֶם וְשָׂרֵיהֶם לַעֲשׂוֹת טוֹבָה עִמָּנוּ וְעִם כָּל יִשְׂרָאֵל. בִּימֵיהֶם וּבְיָמֵינוּ תִּוָּשַׁע יְהוּדָה, וְיִשְׂרָאֵל יִשְׁכֹּן לָבֶטַח, וּבָא לְצִיּוֹן גּוֹאֵל. וְכֵן יְהִי רָצוֹן, וְנֹאמַר אָמֵן.

תפילה לשלום חיילי צבא קנדה

The שליח ציבור *says the following:*

אַדִּיר בַּמָּרוֹם שׁוֹכֵן בִּגְבוּרָה, מֶלֶךְ שֶׁהַשָּׁלוֹם שֶׁלּוֹ, הַשְׁקִיפָה מִמְּעוֹן קָדְשְׁךָ, וּבָרֵךְ אֶת חַיָּלֵי צְבָא קָנָדָה, הַמְחָרְפִים נַפְשָׁם בְּלֶכְתָּם לָשִׂים שָׁלוֹם בָּאָרֶץ. הֱיֵה נָא לָהֶם מַחֲסֶה וּמָעוֹז, וְאַל תִּתֵּן לַמּוֹט רַגְלָם, חַזֵּק יְדֵיהֶם וְאַמֵּץ רוּחָם לְהָפֵר עֲצַת אוֹיֵב וּלְהַעֲבִיר מֶמְשֶׁלֶת זָדוֹן, יָפוּצוּ אוֹיְבֵיהֶם וְיָנוּסוּ מְשַׂנְאֵיהֶם מִפְּנֵיהֶם, וְיִשְׂמְחוּ בִּישׁוּעָתֶךָ. הֲשִׁיבֵם בְּשָׁלוֹם אֶל בֵּיתָם, כַּכָּתוּב
בְּדִבְרֵי קָדְשֶׁךָ: יהוה יִשְׁמָרְךָ מִכָּל־רָע, יִשְׁמֹר אֶת־נַפְשֶׁךָ: יהוה תהלים קכא
יִשְׁמָר־צֵאתְךָ וּבוֹאֶךָ, מֵעַתָּה וְעַד־עוֹלָם: וְקַיֵּם בָּנוּ מִקְרָא
שֶׁכָּתוּב: לֹא־יִשָּׂא גוֹי אֶל־גּוֹי חֶרֶב, וְלֹא־יִלְמְדוּ עוֹד מִלְחָמָה: ישעיה ב
וְיֵדְעוּ כָּל יוֹשְׁבֵי תֵבֵל כִּי לְךָ מְלוּכָה יָאֲתָה, וְשִׁמְךָ נוֹרָא עַל כָּל מַה שֶּׁבָּרָאתָ. וְנֹאמַר אָמֵן.

PRAYER FOR THE STATE OF ISRAEL

The Leader says the following prayer:

אָבִינוּ שֶׁבַּשָּׁמַיִם Heavenly Father, Israel's Rock and Redeemer, bless the State of Israel, the first flowering of our redemption. Shield it under the wings of Your loving-kindness and spread over it the canopy of Your peace. Send Your light and truth to its leaders, ministers and advisors, and direct them with good counsel before You.

Strengthen the hands of the defenders of our Holy Land; give them deliverance, our God, and crown them with the crown of victory. Give peace in the land and everlasting joy to its inhabitants.

As for our brothers, the whole house of Israel, remember them in all the lands of our (*In Israel say:* their) dispersion, and swiftly lead us (*In Israel say:* them) upright to Zion Your city, and Jerusalem Your dwelling place, as is written in the Torah of Moses Your servant: "Even if you are scattered to the furthermost lands under the heavens, from there the LORD your God will gather you and take you back. The LORD your God will bring you to the land your ancestors possessed and you will possess it; and He will make you more prosperous and numerous than your ancestors. Then the LORD your God will open up your heart and the heart of your descendants, to love the LORD your God with all your heart and with all your soul, that you may live." *Deut. 30*

Unite our hearts to love and fear Your name and observe all the words of Your Torah, and swiftly send us Your righteous anointed one of the house of David, to redeem those who long for Your salvation.

Appear in Your glorious majesty over all who live on earth, and let all who breathe declare: The LORD God of Israel is King and His kingship has dominion over all. Amen, Selah.

תפילה לשלום מדינת ישראל

The שליח ציבור *says the following prayer:*

אָבִינוּ שֶׁבַּשָּׁמַיִם, צוּר יִשְׂרָאֵל וְגוֹאֲלוֹ, בָּרֵךְ אֶת מְדִינַת יִשְׂרָאֵל, רֵאשִׁית צְמִיחַת גְּאֻלָּתֵנוּ. הָגֵן עָלֶיהָ בְּאֶבְרַת חַסְדֶּךָ וּפְרֹשׂ עָלֶיהָ סֻכַּת שְׁלוֹמֶךָ, וּשְׁלַח אוֹרְךָ וַאֲמִתְּךָ לְרָאשֶׁיהָ, שָׂרֶיהָ וְיוֹעֲצֶיהָ, וְתַקְּנֵם בְּעֵצָה טוֹבָה מִלְּפָנֶיךָ.

חַזֵּק אֶת יְדֵי מְגִנֵּי אֶרֶץ קָדְשֵׁנוּ, וְהַנְחִילֵם אֱלֹהֵינוּ יְשׁוּעָה וַעֲטֶרֶת נִצָּחוֹן תְּעַטְּרֵם, וְנָתַתָּ שָׁלוֹם בָּאָרֶץ וְשִׂמְחַת עוֹלָם לְיוֹשְׁבֶיהָ.

וְאֶת אַחֵינוּ כָּל בֵּית יִשְׂרָאֵל, פְּקָד נָא בְּכָל אַרְצוֹת פְּזוּרֵינוּ,
וְתוֹלִיכֵנוּ / בארץ ישראל: פְּזוּרֵיהֶם, וְתוֹלִיכֵם/ מְהֵרָה קוֹמְמִיּוּת לְצִיּוֹן
עִירֶךָ וְלִירוּשָׁלַיִם מִשְׁכַּן שְׁמֶךָ, כַּכָּתוּב בְּתוֹרַת מֹשֶׁה עַבְדֶּךָ:
אִם־יִהְיֶה נִדַּחֲךָ בִּקְצֵה הַשָּׁמָיִם, מִשָּׁם יְקַבֶּצְךָ יהוה אֱלֹהֶיךָ דברים ל
וּמִשָּׁם יִקָּחֶךָ: וֶהֱבִיאֲךָ יהוה אֱלֹהֶיךָ אֶל־הָאָרֶץ אֲשֶׁר־יָרְשׁוּ
אֲבֹתֶיךָ וִירִשְׁתָּהּ, וְהֵיטִבְךָ וְהִרְבְּךָ מֵאֲבֹתֶיךָ: וּמָל יהוה אֱלֹהֶיךָ
אֶת־לְבָבְךָ וְאֶת־לְבַב זַרְעֶךָ, לְאַהֲבָה אֶת־יהוה אֱלֹהֶיךָ בְּכָל־
לְבָבְךָ וּבְכָל־נַפְשְׁךָ, לְמַעַן חַיֶּיךָ:

וְיַחֵד לְבָבֵנוּ לְאַהֲבָה וּלְיִרְאָה אֶת שְׁמֶךָ, וְלִשְׁמֹר אֶת כָּל דִּבְרֵי תוֹרָתֶךָ, וּשְׁלַח לָנוּ מְהֵרָה בֶּן דָּוִד מְשִׁיחַ צִדְקֶךָ, לִפְדּוֹת מְחַכֵּי קֵץ יְשׁוּעָתֶךָ.

וְהוֹפַע בַּהֲדַר גְּאוֹן עֻזֶּךָ עַל כָּל יוֹשְׁבֵי תֵּבֵל אַרְצֶךָ וְיֹאמַר כֹּל אֲשֶׁר נְשָׁמָה בְאַפּוֹ, יהוה אֱלֹהֵי יִשְׂרָאֵל מֶלֶךְ וּמַלְכוּתוֹ בַּכֹּל מָשָׁלָה, אָמֵן סֶלָה.

PRAYER FOR ISRAEL'S DEFENSE FORCES

The Leader says the following prayer:

מִי שֶׁבֵּרַךְ May He who blessed our ancestors, Abraham, Isaac and Jacob, bless the members of Israel's Defense Forces and its security services who stand guard over our land and the cities of our God from the Lebanese border to the Egyptian desert, from the Mediterranean sea to the approach of the Aravah, and wherever else they are, on land, in air and at sea. May the Lord make the enemies who rise against us be struck down before them. May the Holy One, blessed be He, protect and save them from all trouble and distress, suffering and illness, and send blessing and success to all the work of their hands. May He subdue our enemies under them and crown them with deliverance and victory. And may there be fulfilled in them the verse, "It is the Lord your God who goes with you to fight for you against your enemies, to save you." And let us say: Amen. *Deut. 20*

PRAYER FOR THOSE BEING HELD IN CAPTIVITY

If Israeli soldiers or civilians are being held in captivity, the Leader says the following:

מִי שֶׁבֵּרַךְ May He who blessed our ancestors, Abraham, Isaac and Jacob, Joseph, Moses and Aaron, David and Solomon, bless, protect and guard the members of Israel's Defense Forces missing in action or held captive, and other captives among our brethren, the whole house of Israel, who are in distress or captivity, as we, the members of this holy congregation, pray on their behalf. May the Holy One, blessed be He, have compassion on them and bring them out from darkness and the shadow of death; may He break their bonds, save them from their distress, and bring them swiftly back to their families' embrace. Give thanks to the Lord for His loving-kindness and for the wonders He does for the children of men; and may there be fulfilled in them the verse: "Those redeemed by the Lord will return; they will enter Zion with singing, and everlasting joy will crown their heads. Gladness and joy will overtake them, and sorrow and sighing will flee away." And let us say: Amen. *Ps. 107* *Is. 35*

מי שברך לחיילי צה״ל

The שליח ציבור *says the following prayer:*

מִי שֶׁבֵּרַךְ אֲבוֹתֵינוּ אַבְרָהָם יִצְחָק וְיַעֲקֹב הוּא יְבָרֵךְ אֶת חַיָּלֵי צְבָא הַהֲגָנָה לְיִשְׂרָאֵל וְאַנְשֵׁי כֹּחוֹת הַבִּטָּחוֹן, הָעוֹמְדִים עַל מִשְׁמַר אַרְצֵנוּ וְעָרֵי אֱלֹהֵינוּ, מִגְּבוּל הַלְּבָנוֹן וְעַד מִדְבַּר מִצְרַיִם וּמִן הַיָּם הַגָּדוֹל עַד לְבוֹא הָעֲרָבָה וּבְכָל מָקוֹם שֶׁהֵם, בַּיַּבָּשָׁה, בָּאֲוִיר וּבַיָּם. יִתֵּן יהוה אֶת אוֹיְבֵינוּ הַקָּמִים עָלֵינוּ נִגָּפִים לִפְנֵיהֶם. הַקָּדוֹשׁ בָּרוּךְ הוּא יִשְׁמֹר וְיַצִּיל אֶת חַיָּלֵינוּ מִכָּל צָרָה וְצוּקָה וּמִכָּל נֶגַע וּמַחֲלָה, וְיִשְׁלַח בְּרָכָה וְהַצְלָחָה בְּכָל מַעֲשֵׂי יְדֵיהֶם. יַדְבֵּר שׂוֹנְאֵינוּ תַּחְתֵּיהֶם וִיעַטְּרֵם בְּכֶתֶר יְשׁוּעָה וּבַעֲטֶרֶת נִצָּחוֹן. וִיקֻיַּם בָּהֶם הַכָּתוּב: כִּי יהוה אֱלֹהֵיכֶם הַהֹלֵךְ עִמָּכֶם לְהִלָּחֵם לָכֶם עִם־ (דברים כ)
אֹיְבֵיכֶם לְהוֹשִׁיעַ אֶתְכֶם: וְנֹאמַר אָמֵן.

מי שברך לשבויים

If Israeli soldiers or civilians are being held in captivity, the שליח ציבור *says the following:*

מִי שֶׁבֵּרַךְ אֲבוֹתֵינוּ אַבְרָהָם יִצְחָק וְיַעֲקֹב, יוֹסֵף מֹשֶׁה וְאַהֲרֹן, דָּוִד וּשְׁלֹמֹה, הוּא יְבָרֵךְ וְיִשְׁמֹר וְיִנְצֹר אֶת נֶעְדְּרֵי צְבָא הַהֲגָנָה לְיִשְׂרָאֵל וּשְׁבוּיָו, וְאֶת כָּל אַחֵינוּ הַנְּתוּנִים בְּצָרָה וּבְשִׁבְיָה, בַּעֲבוּר שֶׁכָּל הַקָּהָל הַקָּדוֹשׁ הַזֶּה מִתְפַּלֵּל בַּעֲבוּרָם. הַקָּדוֹשׁ בָּרוּךְ הוּא יִמָּלֵא רַחֲמִים עֲלֵיהֶם, וְיוֹצִיאֵם מֵחֹשֶׁךְ וְצַלְמָוֶת, וּמוֹסְרוֹתֵיהֶם יְנַתֵּק, וּמִמְּצוּקוֹתֵיהֶם יוֹשִׁיעֵם, וִישִׁיבֵם מְהֵרָה לְחֵיק מִשְׁפְּחוֹתֵיהֶם.
יוֹדוּ לַיהוה חַסְדּוֹ וְנִפְלְאוֹתָיו לִבְנֵי אָדָם: וִיקֻיַּם בָּהֶם מִקְרָא (תהלים קז)
שֶׁכָּתוּב: וּפְדוּיֵי יהוה יְשֻׁבוּן, וּבָאוּ צִיּוֹן בְּרִנָּה, וְשִׂמְחַת עוֹלָם (ישעיה לה)
עַל־רֹאשָׁם, שָׂשׂוֹן וְשִׂמְחָה יַשִּׂיגוּ, וְנָסוּ יָגוֹן וַאֲנָחָה: וְנֹאמַר אָמֵן.

BLESSING THE NEW MONTH

On the Shabbat before Rosh Ḥodesh, the following is said by the congregation, and repeated by the Leader:

יְהִי רָצוֹן May it be Your will, LORD our God and God of our fathers, *Berakhot 16b*
to renew for us this coming month for good and blessing.
Give us long life,
a life of peace,
a life of goodness,
a life of blessing,
a life of sustenance,
a life of physical health,
a life marked by fear of heaven and dread of sin,
a life without shame or disgrace,
a life of wealth and honor,
a life in which we have love for the Torah and fear of heaven,
a life in which our hearts' desires are fulfilled for good.
Amen, Selah.

---

upon these declarations; without the declarations, there would be no way of knowing the precise day on which each month began, and therefore no way of knowing on which days the holidays were supposed to occur. In later days, however, the calendar was fixed by a mathematical computation. After the destruction of the *Beit HaMikdash*, sacrifices were no longer available and after the disbandment of the Sanhedrin the declarations of the month were discontinued. Accordingly, the celebration of this festival has substantially diminished. Today, we celebrate Rosh Ḥodesh through singing *Hallel* and extending davening in place of sacrifices.

... A THOUSAND WORDS

REFLECTION

What is your new month's resolution?

What do you want to achieve this month?

For whom do you want to pray?

How can you be at one with the people around you?

ברכת החודש

On the שבת before ראש חודש, the following is said by the קהל, and repeated by the שליח ציבור:

ברכות טז:

יְהִי רָצוֹן מִלְּפָנֶיךָ, יהוה אֱלֹהֵינוּ וֵאלֹהֵי אֲבוֹתֵינוּ
שֶׁתְּחַדֵּשׁ עָלֵינוּ אֶת הַחֹדֶשׁ הַזֶּה לְטוֹבָה וְלִבְרָכָה.
וְתִתֶּן לָנוּ חַיִּים אֲרוּכִים, חַיִּים שֶׁל שָׁלוֹם
חַיִּים שֶׁל טוֹבָה, חַיִּים שֶׁל בְּרָכָה
חַיִּים שֶׁל פַּרְנָסָה, חַיִּים שֶׁל חִלּוּץ עֲצָמוֹת
חַיִּים שֶׁיֵּשׁ בָּהֶם יִרְאַת שָׁמַיִם וְיִרְאַת חֵטְא
חַיִּים שֶׁאֵין בָּהֶם בּוּשָׁה וּכְלִמָּה
חַיִּים שֶׁל עֹשֶׁר וְכָבוֹד
חַיִּים שֶׁתְּהֵא בָנוּ אַהֲבַת תּוֹרָה וְיִרְאַת שָׁמַיִם
חַיִּים שֶׁיִּמָּלְאוּ מִשְׁאֲלוֹת לִבֵּנוּ לְטוֹבָה
אָמֵן סֶלָה.

LEARNING

The Shabbat before Rosh Ḥodesh is known as *Shabbat Mevarekhim*, which means "the Sabbath of blessing." In the times of the *Beit HaMikdash*, Rosh Hodesh was a significant festival day. At that time, Rosh Ḥodesh was determined by the testimony of two witnesses seeing the new moon. Each month began when the first sliver of moon became visible, and observers would watch the sky for any sign of the moon. If they saw the moon, they would report their sightings to the Sanhedrin, which would interrogate them to make sure that they were not mistaken. Where in the sky did the moon appear? Which direction was it pointing? If two independent, reliable eyewitnesses confirmed that the new moon had appeared and described it consistently, the Sanhedrin would declare the new month and send out messengers to tell people when the month began.

The day the moon appeared was a festival, announced with the sounding of the shofar, celebration, and sacrifices. The importance of this holiday in ancient times should not be underestimated. The entire calendar was dependent

The new moon is announced, then the Leader takes the Torah scroll in his right arm and says:

מִי שֶׁעָשָׂה May He who performed miracles for our ancestors
and redeemed them from slavery to freedom, redeem us soon,
and gather in our dispersed people from the four quarters of the earth,
so that all Israel may be united in friendship,
and let us say: Amen.

The Leader, then the congregation:

The new month of (*Hebrew month*) will occur on (*day of week*).
May it come to us and all Israel for good.

The congregation and Leader continue:

Outside Israel:

May the Holy One, blessed be He, renew this new month for us and for all His people, the house of Israel, for life and peace, gladness and joy, salvation and consolation; and let us say: Amen.

In Israel:

May the Holy One, blessed be He,
renew this month for us and for all His people
the house of Israel, wherever they are,
for good and blessing, gladness and joy,
for salvation and consolation,
livelihood and sustenance, for life and peace,
good tidings and good news,
(*In winter:* for rain in its due season,)
for complete healing
and imminent redemption,
and let us say: Amen.

---

commentators discuss the implication of the words "for good and blessing." If it is good isn't it blessed? And if it is blessed isn't it good?

Perhaps we can understand the prayer based on something that the Alter of Kelm, Rav Simha Zissel zt"l *taught regarding a verse in* Tehillim *133:1:* "הִנֵּה מַה־טּוֹב וּמַה־נָּעִים, שֶׁבֶת אַחִים גַּם־יָחַד" *– "Behold how good and sweet it is when brothers come together."*

The Alter remarked that there are many things in this world that are good for us, but are not sweet, like medicine. Similarly, there are many things in this world that are sweet, like candy, but may not be good for us. Something that is both intrinsically good and sweet is when brothers come together.

Our lives can be good but may not feel like a blessing. We pray at the outset of the month that God should bless us with a palpably good month that appears to us like a blessing as well. (Rabbi Ephraim Epstein)

The מולד *is announced, then the* שליח ציבור *takes the* ספר תורה *in his right arm and says:*

מִי שֶׁעָשָׂה נִסִּים לַאֲבוֹתֵינוּ
וְגָאַל אוֹתָם מֵעַבְדוּת לְחֵרוּת
הוּא יִגְאַל אוֹתָנוּ בְּקָרוֹב
וִיקַבֵּץ נִדָּחֵינוּ מֵאַרְבַּע כַּנְפוֹת הָאָרֶץ
חֲבֵרִים כָּל יִשְׂרָאֵל וְנֹאמַר אָמֵן.

The שליח ציבור*, then the* קהל*:*

רֹאשׁ חֹדֶשׁ *month* **יִהְיֶה בְּיוֹם** *day* (**וּבְיוֹם*** *day*)
הַבָּא עָלֵינוּ וְעַל כָּל יִשְׂרָאֵל לְטוֹבָה.

**if the second day falls on Sunday, then substitute:* וּלְמָחֳרָתוֹ בְּיוֹם

The שליח ציבור *and* קהל *continue:*

In ארץ ישראל *say:*	*In* חוץ לארץ *say:*
יְחַדְּשֵׁהוּ הַקָּדוֹשׁ בָּרוּךְ הוּא	יְחַדְּשֵׁהוּ
עָלֵינוּ וְעַל כָּל עַמּוֹ בֵּית יִשְׂרָאֵל	הַקָּדוֹשׁ בָּרוּךְ הוּא
בְּכָל מָקוֹם שֶׁהֵם	עָלֵינוּ
לְטוֹבָה וְלִבְרָכָה, לְשָׂשׂוֹן וּלְשִׂמְחָה	וְעַל כָּל עַמּוֹ
לִישׁוּעָה וּלְנֶחָמָה, לְפַרְנָסָה וּלְכַלְכָּלָה	בֵּית יִשְׂרָאֵל
לְחַיִּים וּלְשָׁלוֹם	לְחַיִּים וּלְשָׁלוֹם
לִשְׁמוּעוֹת טוֹבוֹת וְלִבְשׂוֹרוֹת טוֹבוֹת	לְשָׂשׂוֹן וּלְשִׂמְחָה
(בחורף: וְלִגְשָׁמִים בְּעִתָּם)	לִישׁוּעָה וּלְנֶחָמָה
וְלִרְפוּאָה שְׁלֵמָה, וְלִגְאֻלָּה קְרוֹבָה	
וְנֹאמַר אָמֵן.	וְנֹאמַר אָמֵן.

CONNECTION

In the opening lines of the prayer it says: "May it be Your will, Lord our God and God of our fathers, to renew for us this coming month for good and blessing." The

The following is omitted on days when Taḥanun is not said (see page 206). It is also omitted on a Shabbat before Rosh Ḥodesh (except for the Shabbat before Rosh Ḥodesh Iyar and Rosh Ḥodesh Sivan) and on Shabbat Shekalim, Zakhor, Para and HaḤodesh.

אַב הָרַחֲמִים Father of compassion, who is present on high: may He remember in His compassion the pious, the upright and the blameless – holy communities who sacrificed their lives for the sanctification of God's name. Lovely and pleasant in their lives, in death they were not parted. They were swifter than eagles and stronger than lions to do the will of their Maker and the desire of their Creator. O our God, remember them for good with the other righteous of the world, and may He exact retribution for the shed blood of His servants, as it is written in the Torah of Moses, the man of God: "O nations, acclaim His people, for He will avenge the blood of His servants, wreak vengeance on His enemies, and make clean His people's land." And by Your servants, the prophets, it is written: "I shall cleanse their blood which I have not yet cleansed, says the LORD who is present in Zion." And in the holy Writings it says: "Why should the nations say: Where is their God? Before our eyes, may those nations know that You avenge the shed blood of Your servants." And it also says: "For the Avenger of blood remembers them and does not forget the cry of the afflicted." And it further says: "He will execute judgment among the nations, filled with the dead, crushing rulers far and wide. From the brook by the wayside he will drink, then he will hold his head high."

Deut. 32 · *Joel 4* · *Ps. 79* · *Ps. 9* · *Ps. 110*

---

the national exile that followed. We say *Yizkor*, remembering our personal grief and mourning for deceased loved ones, on all of the major festivals, days when we experience communal joy and ecstasy. No joy is complete when we still live in an imperfect world where people may be killed for the religion they believe in or the community they belong to. And so too on Shabbat we include this *tefilla*, to remember those who were killed *al kiddush Hashem* (sanctifying God's name), despite the joy of Shabbat.

In addition to mourning those who perished while sanctifying God's name, reciting *Av HaRaḥamim* bolsters our hope and faith that the God of Israel is just, and rewards as well as punishes those who deserve it. The Midrash reveals that each time a Jew is tormented and killed for simply being Jewish, God douses His own divine cloak with a measure of blood to match. When God metes out retribution to our enemies, He will wear this holy cloak. The *Yefeh To'ar* explains the Midrash to mean that every Jewish soul is dear to our Father in Heaven and that each and every soul will be remembered and defended.

The following is omitted on days when תחנון *is not said (see page 207).*
It is also omitted on שבת מברכים *(except for the* שבת *before* ראש חודש אייר
and ראש חודש סיון*) and on the "*ארבע פרשיות*,"* שקלים, זכור, פרה *and* החודש.

אַב הָרַחֲמִים שׁוֹכֵן מְרוֹמִים, בְּרַחֲמָיו הָעֲצוּמִים הוּא יִפְקֹד בְּרַחֲמִים
הַחֲסִידִים וְהַיְשָׁרִים וְהַתְּמִימִים, קְהִלּוֹת הַקֹּדֶשׁ שֶׁמָּסְרוּ נַפְשָׁם עַל
קְדֻשַּׁת הַשֵּׁם, הַנֶּאֱהָבִים וְהַנְּעִימִים בְּחַיֵּיהֶם, וּבְמוֹתָם לֹא נִפְרָדוּ,
מִנְּשָׁרִים קַלּוּ וּמֵאֲרָיוֹת גָּבֵרוּ לַעֲשׂוֹת רְצוֹן קוֹנָם וְחֵפֶץ צוּרָם. יִזְכְּרֵם
אֱלֹהֵינוּ לְטוֹבָה עִם שְׁאָר צַדִּיקֵי עוֹלָם, וְיִנְקֹם לְעֵינֵינוּ נִקְמַת דַּם עֲבָדָיו
הַשָּׁפוּךְ, כַּכָּתוּב בְּתוֹרַת מֹשֶׁה אִישׁ הָאֱלֹהִים: הַרְנִינוּ גוֹיִם עַמּוֹ, כִּי דברים לב
דַם־עֲבָדָיו יִקּוֹם, וְנָקָם יָשִׁיב לְצָרָיו, וְכִפֶּר אַדְמָתוֹ עַמּוֹ: וְעַל יְדֵי עֲבָדֶיךָ
הַנְּבִיאִים כָּתוּב לֵאמֹר: וְנִקֵּיתִי, דָּמָם לֹא־נִקֵּיתִי, וַיהוה שֹׁכֵן בְּצִיּוֹן: יואל ד
וּבְכִתְבֵי הַקֹּדֶשׁ נֶאֱמַר: לָמָּה יֹאמְרוּ הַגּוֹיִם אַיֵּה אֱלֹהֵיהֶם, יִוָּדַע בַּגּוֹיִם תהלים עט
לְעֵינֵינוּ נִקְמַת דַּם־עֲבָדֶיךָ הַשָּׁפוּךְ: וְאוֹמֵר: כִּי־דֹרֵשׁ דָּמִים אוֹתָם זָכָר, תהלים ט
לֹא־שָׁכַח צַעֲקַת עֲנָוִים: וְאוֹמֵר: יָדִין בַּגּוֹיִם מָלֵא גְוִיּוֹת, מָחַץ רֹאשׁ תהלים קי
עַל־אֶרֶץ רַבָּה: מִנַּחַל בַּדֶּרֶךְ יִשְׁתֶּה, עַל־כֵּן יָרִים רֹאשׁ:

LEARNING

Av HaRaḥamim, a haunting prayer that memorializes martyrs who were killed for no other reason than that they were Jewish, was probably written around the year 1096, in response to the First Crusade. Originally it was only recited on the Shabbat before Shavuot, as this was the time of year when this tragedy occurred. Later, the custom developed to recite it every Shabbat unless the Shabbat coincides with a happy occasion such as a festival, Rosh Ḥodesh, the blessing of the new month, or an individual's celebration such as a *brit mila* or a *Shabbat ḥatan*. However, even if such an event occurs on Shabbat during the *Sefira* period, which is the actual period that the crusade occurred, *Av HaRaḥamim* is still recited.

It is a quintessentially Jewish approach to joy and celebration to spend a moment, during the height of those emotions, reflecting on our nation's history, both the tragic and the glorious. A *ḥatan* under his *ḥuppa* breaks a glass and places ashes on his forehead remembering at the moment of intense personal joy the destruction of the Temple and

אַשְׁרֵי Happy are those who live in Your House; *Ps. 84*
they shall continue to praise You, Selah!

Happy are the people for whom this is so; *Ps. 144*
happy are the people whose God is the LORD.

A song of praise by David. *Ps. 145*

א I will elevate You, my God, the King, and bless Your name for ever and all time. ב Every day I will bless You, and praise Your name for ever and all time. ג Great is the LORD and greatly to be praised; His greatness is unfathomable. ד One generation will praise Your works to the next, and tell of Your mighty deeds. ה On the glorious splendor of Your majesty I will meditate, and on the acts of Your wonders. ו They shall talk of the power of Your awesome deeds, and I will tell of Your greatness. ז They shall recite the record of Your great goodness, and sing with joy of Your righteousness. ח The LORD is generous and compassionate, slow to anger and great in loving-kindness. ט The LORD is good to all, and His compassion extends to all His works. י All Your works shall thank You, LORD, and Your devoted ones shall bless You. כ They shall talk of the glory of Your kingship, and speak of Your might. ל To make known to mankind His mighty deeds and the glorious majesty of His kingship. מ Your kingdom is an everlasting kingdom, and Your reign is for all generations. ס The LORD supports all who fall, and raises all who are bowed down. ע All raise their eyes to You in hope, and You give them their food in due season. פ You open Your hand, and satisfy every living thing with favor. צ The LORD is righteous in all His ways, and kind in all He does. ק The LORD is close to all who call on Him, to all who call on Him in truth. ר He fulfills the will of those who fear Him; He hears their cry and saves them. ש The LORD guards all who love Him, but all the wicked He will destroy. ת ▸ My mouth shall speak the praise of the LORD, and all creatures shall bless His holy name for ever and all time.

We will bless the LORD now and for ever. Halleluya! *Ps. 115*

אַשְׁרֵי יוֹשְׁבֵי בֵיתֶךָ, עוֹד יְהַלְלוּךָ סֶּלָה: תהלים פד
אַשְׁרֵי הָעָם שֶׁכָּכָה לּוֹ, אַשְׁרֵי הָעָם שֶׁיהוה אֱלֹהָיו: תהלים קמד
תְּהִלָּה לְדָוִד תהלים קמה
אֲרוֹמִמְךָ אֱלוֹהַי הַמֶּלֶךְ, וַאֲבָרְכָה שִׁמְךָ לְעוֹלָם וָעֶד:
בְּכָל־יוֹם אֲבָרְכֶךָּ, וַאֲהַלְלָה שִׁמְךָ לְעוֹלָם וָעֶד:
גָּדוֹל יהוה וּמְהֻלָּל מְאֹד, וְלִגְדֻלָּתוֹ אֵין חֵקֶר:
דּוֹר לְדוֹר יְשַׁבַּח מַעֲשֶׂיךָ, וּגְבוּרֹתֶיךָ יַגִּידוּ:
הֲדַר כְּבוֹד הוֹדֶךָ, וְדִבְרֵי נִפְלְאֹתֶיךָ אָשִׂיחָה:
וֶעֱזוּז נוֹרְאֹתֶיךָ יֹאמֵרוּ, וּגְדוּלָּתְךָ אֲסַפְּרֶנָּה:
זֵכֶר רַב־טוּבְךָ יַבִּיעוּ, וְצִדְקָתְךָ יְרַנֵּנוּ:
חַנּוּן וְרַחוּם יהוה, אֶרֶךְ אַפַּיִם וּגְדָל־חָסֶד:
טוֹב־יהוה לַכֹּל, וְרַחֲמָיו עַל־כָּל־מַעֲשָׂיו:
יוֹדוּךָ יהוה כָּל־מַעֲשֶׂיךָ, וַחֲסִידֶיךָ יְבָרְכוּכָה:
כְּבוֹד מַלְכוּתְךָ יֹאמֵרוּ, וּגְבוּרָתְךָ יְדַבֵּרוּ:
לְהוֹדִיעַ לִבְנֵי הָאָדָם גְּבוּרֹתָיו, וּכְבוֹד הֲדַר מַלְכוּתוֹ:
מַלְכוּתְךָ מַלְכוּת כָּל־עֹלָמִים, וּמֶמְשַׁלְתְּךָ בְּכָל־דּוֹר וָדֹר:
סוֹמֵךְ יהוה לְכָל־הַנֹּפְלִים, וְזוֹקֵף לְכָל־הַכְּפוּפִים:
עֵינֵי־כֹל אֵלֶיךָ יְשַׂבֵּרוּ, וְאַתָּה נוֹתֵן־לָהֶם אֶת־אָכְלָם בְּעִתּוֹ:
פּוֹתֵחַ אֶת־יָדֶךָ, וּמַשְׂבִּיעַ לְכָל־חַי רָצוֹן:
צַדִּיק יהוה בְּכָל־דְּרָכָיו, וְחָסִיד בְּכָל־מַעֲשָׂיו:
קָרוֹב יהוה לְכָל־קֹרְאָיו, לְכֹל אֲשֶׁר יִקְרָאֻהוּ בֶאֱמֶת:
רְצוֹן־יְרֵאָיו יַעֲשֶׂה, וְאֶת־שַׁוְעָתָם יִשְׁמַע, וְיוֹשִׁיעֵם:
שׁוֹמֵר יהוה אֶת־כָּל־אֹהֲבָיו, וְאֵת כָּל־הָרְשָׁעִים יַשְׁמִיד:
◄ תְּהִלַּת יהוה יְדַבֶּר פִּי, וִיבָרֵךְ כָּל־בָּשָׂר שֵׁם קָדְשׁוֹ לְעוֹלָם וָעֶד:
וַאֲנַחְנוּ נְבָרֵךְ יָהּ מֵעַתָּה וְעַד־עוֹלָם, הַלְלוּיָהּ: תהלים קטו

RETURNING THE TORAH TO THE ARK

The Ark is opened. All stand. The Leader takes the Torah scroll and says:

יְהַלְלוּ Let them praise the name of the LORD, *Ps. 148*
for His name alone is sublime.

The congregation responds:

הוֹדוֹ His majesty is above earth and heaven.
He has raised the horn of His people,
for the glory of all His devoted ones,
the children of Israel, the people close to Him.
Halleluya!

While the Torah scroll is being returned to the Ark, say:

מִזְמוֹר לְדָוִד A psalm of David. Give to the LORD, you angelic pow- *Ps. 29*
ers, give to the LORD glory and might. Give to the LORD the glory due to His name. Bow to the LORD in the beauty of holiness. The LORD's voice echoes over the waters; the God of glory thunders; the LORD is over the mighty waters. The LORD's voice in power, the LORD's voice in beauty, the LORD's voice breaks cedars, the LORD

Jews behave, I'm not going to have anything to do with a prayer book."

As Wiesenthal turned to walk away, Rabbi Silver touched him on the shoulder and gently said, "Silly man, why do you look at the Jew who used his siddur to take food out of starving people's mouths? Why don't you look at the many Jews who gave up their last piece of bread in order to be able to use a siddur? That's faith. That's the true power of the siddur." Rabbi Silver then embraced him.

"I went to the services the next day," said Wiesenthal.

CONNECTION

"No people has ever insisted more firmly than the Jews that history has a purpose and humanity a destiny. At a very early stage of their collective existence they believed they had detected a divine scheme for the human race, of which their own society was to be a pilot. They worked out their role in immense detail. They clung to it with heroic persistence in the face of savage suffering.... The Jewish vision became the prototype for many similar grand designs for humanity, both divine and man-made. The Jews, therefore, stand right at the center of the perennial attempt to give human life the dignity of a purpose." (Paul Johnson, *A History of the Jews*)*learning*

הכנסת ספר תורה

The ארון קודש *is opened. All stand. The* שליח ציבור *takes the* ספר תורה *and says:*

תהלים קמח
יְהַלְלוּ אֶת־שֵׁם יהוה, כִּי־נִשְׂגָּב שְׁמוֹ, לְבַדּוֹ

The קהל *responds:*

הוֹדוֹ עַל־אֶרֶץ וְשָׁמָיִם:
וַיָּרֶם קֶרֶן לְעַמּוֹ, תְּהִלָּה לְכָל־חֲסִידָיו
לִבְנֵי יִשְׂרָאֵל עַם קְרֹבוֹ, הַלְלוּיָהּ:

While the ספר תורה *is being returned to the* ארון קודש*, say:*

תהלים כט
מִזְמוֹר לְדָוִד, הָבוּ לַיהוה בְּנֵי אֵלִים, הָבוּ לַיהוה כָּבוֹד וָעֹז: הָבוּ
לַיהוה כְּבוֹד שְׁמוֹ, הִשְׁתַּחֲווּ לַיהוה בְּהַדְרַת־קֹדֶשׁ: קוֹל יהוה עַל־
הַמָּיִם, אֵל־הַכָּבוֹד הִרְעִים, יהוה עַל־מַיִם רַבִּים: קוֹל־יהוה בַּכֹּחַ,
קוֹל יהוה בֶּהָדָר: קוֹל יהוה שֹׁבֵר אֲרָזִים, וַיְשַׁבֵּר יהוה אֶת־אַרְזֵי

CONNECTION

Simon Wiesenthal was a famous Nazi-hunter. He once spoke at a conference of European rabbis in Bratislava, Slovakia, in March 2000. The rabbis presented the 91-year-old Wiesenthal with an award, and he, visibly moved, told them the following story.

It was in Mauthausen, shortly after liberation. The camp was visited by Rabbi Eliezer Silver, head of Agudat Harabanim (Union of Orthodox Rabbis of North America), on a mission to offer aid and comfort to the survivors. Rabbi Silver also organized a special service, and he invited Wiesenthal to join the other survivors in prayer. Wiesenthal declined, and explained why.

"In the camp," Wiesenthal said to Rabbi Silver, "there was one religious man who somehow managed to smuggle in a siddur (prayer book). At first, I greatly admired the man for his courage – that he'd risked his life in order to bring the siddur in. But the next day I realized, to my horror, that this man was 'renting out' this siddur to people in exchange for food. People were giving him their last piece of bread for a few minutes with the prayer book. This man, who was very thin and emaciated when the whole thing started, was soon eating so much that he died before everyone else – his system couldn't handle it."

He continued: "If this is how religious

shatters the cedars of Lebanon. He makes Lebanon skip like a calf, Sirion like a young wild ox. The LORD's voice cleaves flames of fire. The LORD's voice makes the desert quake, the LORD shakes the desert of Kadesh. The LORD's voice makes hinds calve and strips the forests bare, and in His temple all say: "Glory!" The LORD sat enthroned at the Flood, the LORD sits enthroned as King for ever. The LORD will give strength to His people; the LORD will bless His people with peace.

As the Torah scroll is placed into the Ark, all say:

וּבְנֻחֹה יֹאמַר When the Ark came to rest, Moses would say: "Return, *Num. 10*
O LORD, to the countless thousands of Israel." Advance, LORD, *Ps. 132*
to Your resting place, You and Your mighty Ark. Your priests are clothed in righteousness, and Your devoted ones sing in joy. For the
sake of Your servant David, do not reject Your anointed one. For *Prov. 4*
I give you good instruction; do not abandon My Torah. It is a tree *Prov. 3*
of life to those who grasp it, and those who uphold it are happy. Its
ways are ways of pleasantness, and all its paths are peace. ▸ Turn us *Lam. 5*
back, O LORD, to You, and we will return. Renew our days as of old.

The Ark is closed.

HALF KADDISH

Leader: יִתְגַּדַּל Magnified and sanctified may His great name be,
in the world He created by His will.
May He establish His kingdom
in your lifetime and in your days,
and in the lifetime of all the house of Israel,
swiftly and soon – and say: Amen.

All: May His great name be blessed for ever and all time.

Leader: Blessed and praised, glorified and elevated,
raised and honored, uplifted and praised
be the name of the Holy One, blessed be He,
beyond any blessing,
song, praise and consolation uttered in the world –
and say: Amen.

הַלְּבָנוֹן: וַיַּרְקִידֵם כְּמוֹ־עֵגֶל, לְבָנוֹן וְשִׂרְיוֹן כְּמוֹ בֶן־רְאֵמִים: קוֹל־יהוה חֹצֵב לַהֲבוֹת אֵשׁ: קוֹל יהוה יָחִיל מִדְבָּר, יָחִיל יהוה מִדְבַּר קָדֵשׁ: קוֹל יהוה יְחוֹלֵל אַיָּלוֹת וַיֶּחֱשֹׂף יְעָרוֹת, וּבְהֵיכָלוֹ, כֻּלּוֹ אֹמֵר כָּבוֹד: יהוה לַמַּבּוּל יָשָׁב, וַיֵּשֶׁב יהוה מֶלֶךְ לְעוֹלָם: יהוה עֹז לְעַמּוֹ יִתֵּן, יהוה יְבָרֵךְ אֶת־עַמּוֹ בַשָּׁלוֹם:

As the ספר תורה *is placed into the* ארון קודש*, all say:*

וּבְנֻחֹה יֹאמַר, שׁוּבָה יהוה רִבְבוֹת אַלְפֵי יִשְׂרָאֵל: קוּמָה יהוה במדבר י
לִמְנוּחָתֶךָ, אַתָּה וַאֲרוֹן עֻזֶּךָ: כֹּהֲנֶיךָ יִלְבְּשׁוּ־צֶדֶק, וַחֲסִידֶיךָ יְרַנֵּנוּ: תהלים קלב
בַּעֲבוּר דָּוִד עַבְדֶּךָ אַל־תָּשֵׁב פְּנֵי מְשִׁיחֶךָ: כִּי לֶקַח טוֹב נָתַתִּי משלי ד
לָכֶם, תּוֹרָתִי אַל־תַּעֲזֹבוּ: עֵץ־חַיִּים הִיא לַמַּחֲזִיקִים בָּהּ, וְתֹמְכֶיהָ משלי ג
מְאֻשָּׁר: דְּרָכֶיהָ דַרְכֵי־נֹעַם וְכָל־נְתִיבוֹתֶיהָ שָׁלוֹם: ◂ הֲשִׁיבֵנוּ יהוה איכה ה
אֵלֶיךָ וְנָשׁוּבָה, חַדֵּשׁ יָמֵינוּ כְּקֶדֶם:

The ארון קודש *is closed.*

חצי קדיש

ש״ץ: יִתְגַּדַּל וְיִתְקַדַּשׁ שְׁמֵהּ רַבָּא (קהל: אָמֵן)
בְּעָלְמָא דִּי בְרָא כִרְעוּתֵהּ
וְיַמְלִיךְ מַלְכוּתֵהּ
בְּחַיֵּיכוֹן וּבְיוֹמֵיכוֹן וּבְחַיֵּי דְכָל בֵּית יִשְׂרָאֵל
בַּעֲגָלָא וּבִזְמַן קָרִיב, וְאִמְרוּ אָמֵן. (קהל: אָמֵן)

קהל וש״ץ: יְהֵא שְׁמֵהּ רַבָּא מְבָרַךְ לְעָלַם וּלְעָלְמֵי עָלְמַיָּא.

ש״ץ: יִתְבָּרַךְ וְיִשְׁתַּבַּח וְיִתְפָּאַר וְיִתְרוֹמַם וְיִתְנַשֵּׂא
וְיִתְהַדָּר וְיִתְעַלֶּה וְיִתְהַלָּל
שְׁמֵהּ דְּקֻדְשָׁא בְּרִיךְ הוּא (קהל: בְּרִיךְ הוּא)
לְעֵלָּא מִן כָּל בִּרְכָתָא / בשבת שובה: לְעֵלָּא לְעֵלָּא מִכָּל בִּרְכָתָא/
וְשִׁירָתָא, תֻּשְׁבְּחָתָא וְנֶחֱמָתָא
דַּאֲמִירָן בְּעָלְמָא, וְאִמְרוּ אָמֵן. (קהל: אָמֵן)

Musaf for Shabbat

On Shabbat Ḥol HaMo'ed say the Musaf for Ḥol HaMo'ed on page 858.

THE AMIDA

The following prayer, until "in former years" on page 694, is said silently, standing with feet together. If there is a minyan, the Amida is repeated aloud by the Leader. Take three steps forward and at the points indicated by ˅, bend the knees at the first word, bow at the second, and stand straight before saying God's name.

When I declare the LORD's name, give glory to our God. *Deut. 32*
O LORD, open my lips, so that my mouth may declare Your praise. *Ps. 51*

PATRIARCHS

בָּרוּךְ Blessed are You,
LORD our God and God of our fathers,
God of Abraham, God of Isaac and God of Jacob;
the great, mighty and awesome God, God Most High,

...A THOUSAND WORDS

tains a description of the sacrificial service that took place in the Temple on Shabbat. The root of the Hebrew word for sacrifice, קָרְבָּן, is ק־ר־ב, which means close. The spiritual aim of a sacrifice is for it to become a vehicle for coming close to God. Our *tefillot* have the same aim. As we stand before God and dig deep into our souls to present our emotional and spiritual energies to God, we become closer to Him through this act of personal sacrifice and worship.

מוסף לשבת

On שבת חול המועד *say the* מוסף לחול המועד *on page 859.*

עמידה

The following prayer, until קַדְמֹנִיּוֹת *on page 695, is said standing with feet together. If there is a* מנין*, the* עמידה *is repeated aloud by the* שליח ציבור*. Take three steps forward and at the points indicated by* ', *bend the knees at the first word, bow at the second, and stand straight before saying God's name.*

דברים לב   כִּי שֵׁם יהוה אֶקְרָא, הָבוּ גֹדֶל לֵאלֹהֵינוּ:

תהלים נא   אֲדֹנָי, שְׂפָתַי תִּפְתָּח, וּפִי יַגִּיד תְּהִלָּתֶךָ:

אבות

בָּרוּךְ אַתָּה יהוה, אֱלֹהֵינוּ וֵאלֹהֵי אֲבוֹתֵינוּ
אֱלֹהֵי אַבְרָהָם, אֱלֹהֵי יִצְחָק, וֵאלֹהֵי יַעֲקֹב
הָאֵל הַגָּדוֹל הַגִּבּוֹר וְהַנּוֹרָא, אֵל עֶלְיוֹן

INTRODUCTION TO *MUSAF*

In the Talmud (*Berakhot* 26b) there is a disagreement as to the origin of our prayer services. Rabbi Yose was of the opinion that the services were inspired by the Patriarchs. Avraham inaugurated Shaḥarit, Yitzḥak inaugurated Minḥa, and Ya'akov, Ma'ariv. Rabbi Yehoshua disagreed and stated that they were instituted based on the daily offerings in the Temple. The Gemara uses the existence of the *Musaf* service, that has no corresponding forefather associated with it, to arrive at the conclusion to the argument: the prayer services were instituted by our forefathers, but the rabbis based the laws of prayer on the laws of the offerings.

The *Musaf* service on Shabbat, as on Rosh Ḥodesh and festivals, is a replacement for the *musaf* sacrificial service in the Temple. This was an extra sacrifice on these special days brought in addition to the regular daily morning and afternoon offerings. We live in a historical period when we are unable to fulfill the Temple service, and so, instead, we ask God to accept our *tefillot* in place of our sacrifices, fulfilling the words of the prophet Hoshea (14:3): "Receive us graciously that we may offer [the words of] our lips as the sacrifice of bulls."

As well as general Shabbat themes, the *Amida* for *Musaf* of Shabbat con-

who acts with loving-kindness and creates all,
who remembers the loving-kindness of the fathers
and will bring a Redeemer to their children's children
for the sake of His name, in love.

On Shabbat Shuva: Remember us for life, O King who desires life,
and write us in the book of life –
for Your sake, O God of life.

King, Helper, Savior, Shield:
Blessed are You, LORD, Shield of Abraham.

DIVINE MIGHT

אַתָּה גִּבּוֹר You are eternally mighty, LORD.
You give life to the dead and have great power to save.

The phrase "He makes the wind blow and the rain fall" is added from Simḥat Torah until Pesaḥ. In Israel the phrase "He causes the dew to fall" is added from Pesaḥ until Shemini Atzeret.

In fall & winter: He makes the wind blow and the rain fall.
In Israel, in spring & summer: He causes the dew to fall.

He sustains the living with loving-kindness,
and with great compassion revives the dead.
He supports the fallen, heals the sick, sets captives free,
and keeps His faith with those who sleep in the dust.
Who is like You, Master of might,
and who can compare to You,
O King who brings death and gives life,
and makes salvation grow?

On Shabbat Shuva: Who is like You, compassionate Father,
who remembers His creatures
in compassion, for life?

Faithful are You to revive the dead.
Blessed are You, LORD, who revives the dead.

גּוֹמֵל חֲסָדִים טוֹבִים, וְקֹנֵה הַכֹּל
וְזוֹכֵר חַסְדֵי אָבוֹת
וּמֵבִיא גוֹאֵל לִבְנֵי בְנֵיהֶם לְמַעַן שְׁמוֹ בְּאַהֲבָה.

בשבת שובה: זָכְרֵנוּ לְחַיִּים, מֶלֶךְ חָפֵץ בַּחַיִּים
וְכָתְבֵנוּ בְּסֵפֶר הַחַיִּים, לְמַעַנְךָ אֱלֹהִים חַיִּים.

מֶלֶךְ עוֹזֵר וּמוֹשִׁיעַ וּמָגֵן.
בָּרוּךְ אַתָּה יהוה, מָגֵן אַבְרָהָם.

גבורות
אַתָּה גִּבּוֹר לְעוֹלָם, אֲדֹנָי
מְחַיֵּה מֵתִים אַתָּה, רַב לְהוֹשִׁיעַ

The phrase מַשִּׁיב הָרְוּחַ *is added from* שמחת תורה *until* פסח.
In ארץ ישראל *the phrase* מוֹרִיד הַטָּל *is added from* פסח *until* שמיני עצרת.

בחורף: מַשִּׁיב הָרְוּחַ וּמוֹרִיד הַגֶּשֶׁם / בארץ ישראל בקיץ: מוֹרִיד הַטָּל

מְכַלְכֵּל חַיִּים בְּחֶסֶד, מְחַיֵּה מֵתִים בְּרַחֲמִים רַבִּים
סוֹמֵךְ נוֹפְלִים, וְרוֹפֵא חוֹלִים, וּמַתִּיר אֲסוּרִים
וּמְקַיֵּם אֱמוּנָתוֹ לִישֵׁנֵי עָפָר.
מִי כָמְוֹךָ, בַּעַל גְּבוּרוֹת
וּמִי דּוֹמֶה לָּךְ
מֶלֶךְ, מֵמִית וּמְחַיֶּה וּמַצְמִיחַ יְשׁוּעָה.

בשבת שובה: מִי כָמְוֹךָ אַב הָרַחֲמִים
זוֹכֵר יְצוּרָיו לְחַיִּים בְּרַחֲמִים.

וְנֶאֱמָן אַתָּה לְהַחֲיוֹת מֵתִים.
בָּרוּךְ אַתָּה יהוה, מְחַיֵּה הַמֵּתִים.

When saying the Amida silently, continue with "You are holy" on the next page.

KEDUSHA

During the Leader's Repetition, the following is said standing with feet together, rising on the toes at the words indicated by ▴.

Cong. then Leader: נַעֲרִיצְךָ We will fear and sanctify You with the words
uttered by the holy Seraphim
who sanctify Your name in the Sanctuary;
as is written by Your prophet:
"They call out to one another, saying: *Is. 6*

Cong. then Leader: ▴Holy, ▴holy, ▴holy is the LORD of multitudes;
the whole world is filled with His glory."
His glory fills the universe.
His ministering angels ask each other,
"Where is the place of His glory?"
Those facing them reply "Blessed –

Cong. then Leader: ▴"Blessed is the LORD's glory from His place." *Ezek. 3*
From His place may He turn with compassion
and be gracious to the people
who declare the unity of His name,
morning and evening, every day, continually,
twice each day reciting in love the Shema:

LEARNING

The *Kedusha* is a recitation of the praises of God by the angels. Interestingly they ask the question "Where is the place of His Glory?" What does this mean? What are they asking?

There are places where God is not clearly manifest, where we can't see or feel God's presence. When a person is overcome with doubt and he feels distant and he asks "Where is God?" the question itself should not be seen as something negative. Rabbi Nachman explains that just asking the question itself can bring about spirituality. Asking the question is the first step forward from the place of doubt. When the angels say "Where is the place of His glory?" the question itself brings spirituality into a place where it might otherwise not be found. (*Likutei Moharan Tinyana* 12)

When saying the עמידה silently, continue with אַתָּה קָדוֹשׁ on the next page.

קדושה

During the חזרת הש״ץ, the following is said standing with feet together, rising on the toes at the words indicated by ˄.

then קהל ש״ץ: נַעֲרִיצְךָ וְנַקְדִּישְׁךָ כְּסוֹד שִׂיחַ שַׂרְפֵי קֹדֶשׁ
הַמַּקְדִּישִׁים שִׁמְךָ בַּקֹּדֶשׁ
כַּכָּתוּב עַל יַד נְבִיאֶךָ:
וְקָרָא זֶה אֶל־זֶה וְאָמַר ישעיה ו

then קהל ש״ץ: ˄קָדוֹשׁ, ˄קָדוֹשׁ, ˄קָדוֹשׁ, יהוה צְבָאוֹת
מְלֹא כָל הָאָרֶץ כְּבוֹדוֹ:
כְּבוֹדוֹ מָלֵא עוֹלָם, מְשָׁרְתָיו שׁוֹאֲלִים זֶה לָזֶה
אַיֵּה מְקוֹם כְּבוֹדוֹ
לְעֻמָּתָם בָּרוּךְ יֹאמֵרוּ

then קהל ש״ץ: ˄בָּרוּךְ כְּבוֹד־יהוה מִמְּקוֹמוֹ: יחזקאל ג
מִמְּקוֹמוֹ הוּא יִפֶן בְּרַחֲמִים
וְיָחֹן עַם הַמְיַחֲדִים שְׁמוֹ
עֶרֶב וָבֹקֶר בְּכָל יוֹם תָּמִיד
פַּעֲמַיִם בְּאַהֲבָה שְׁמַע אוֹמְרִים

CONNECTION

Yeḥezkel experienced his prophecy and visions not in Jerusalem, nor the Temple, but as a refugee in exile at a time of great suffering for the Jewish people. But despite the fact that it was a time when God seemed to be in hiding, we are told that "the heavens were opened and [Yeḥezkel] saw visions of God" (Yeḥezkel 1:1). When Yeḥezkel declared, "Blessed be the Lord's glory from His place" (ibid. 3:13) he was referring to the huge distance between God and His people. But as Yeḥezkel demonstrated, God is still accessible despite His distance.

Cong. then Leader: "Listen, Israel: the LORD is our God, the LORD is One." *Deut. 6*
He is our God, He is our Father, He is our King,
He is our Savior – and He, in His compassion,
will let us hear a second time
in the presence of all that lives,
His promise to be "Your God." *Num. 15*
"I am the LORD your God."

Leader: And in Your holy Writings it is written:

Cong. then Leader: ▲"The LORD shall reign for ever. He is your God, Zion, *Ps. 146*
from generation to generation, Halleluya!"

Leader: From generation to generation
we will speak of Your greatness,
and we will declare Your holiness for evermore.
Your praise, our God, shall not leave our mouth forever,
for You, God, are a great and holy King.
Blessed are You, LORD,
the holy God. / *On Shabbat Shuva:* the holy King./

The Leader continues on the next page with "You instituted the Sabbath" on Shabbat and "Long ago You formed" on Rosh Ḥodesh.

HOLINESS

אַתָּה קָדוֹשׁ You are holy and Your name is holy,
and holy ones praise You daily, Selah!
Blessed are You, LORD,
the holy God. / *On Shabbat Shuva:* the holy King./
(*If forgotten, repeat the Amida.*)

CONNECTION

"[Moishe] explained to me, with great emphasis, that every question possessed a power that was lost in the answer.... 'And why do you pray, Moishe?' I asked him. 'I pray to the God within me for the strength to ask Him the real questions.'" (Elie Wiesel, *Night*)

then קהל ש״ץ: שְׁמַע יִשְׂרָאֵל, יהוה אֱלֹהֵינוּ, יהוה אֶחָד: דברים ו

הוּא אֱלֹהֵינוּ, הוּא אָבִינוּ, הוּא מַלְכֵּנוּ, הוּא מוֹשִׁיעֵנוּ
וְהוּא יַשְׁמִיעֵנוּ בְּרַחֲמָיו שֵׁנִית לְעֵינֵי כָּל חָי
לִהְיוֹת לָכֶם לֵאלֹהִים במדבר טו
אֲנִי יהוה אֱלֹהֵיכֶם:

ש״ץ: וּבְדִבְרֵי קָדְשְׁךָ כָּתוּב לֵאמֹר

then קהל ש״ץ: יִמְלֹךְ יהוה לְעוֹלָם, אֱלֹהַיִךְ צִיּוֹן לְדֹר וָדֹר, הַלְלוּיָהּ: תהלים קמו

ש״ץ: לְדוֹר וָדוֹר נַגִּיד גָּדְלֶךָ, וּלְנֵצַח נְצָחִים קְדֻשָּׁתְךָ נַקְדִּישׁ
וְשִׁבְחֲךָ אֱלֹהֵינוּ מִפִּינוּ לֹא יָמוּשׁ לְעוֹלָם וָעֶד
כִּי אֵל מֶלֶךְ גָּדוֹל וְקָדוֹשׁ אָתָּה.
בָּרוּךְ אַתָּה יהוה, הָאֵל הַקָּדוֹשׁ./ בשבת שובה: הַמֶּלֶךְ הַקָּדוֹשׁ./

The שליח ציבור *continues on the next page with* תִּכַּנְתָּ שַׁבָּת *on* שבת *and* אַתָּה יָצַרְתָּ *on* ראש חודש.

קדושת השם

אַתָּה קָדוֹשׁ וְשִׁמְךָ קָדוֹשׁ, וּקְדוֹשִׁים בְּכָל יוֹם יְהַלְלוּךָ סֶּלָה.
בָּרוּךְ אַתָּה יהוה, הָאֵל הַקָּדוֹשׁ. / בשבת שובה: **הַמֶּלֶךְ הַקָּדוֹשׁ.**/

(*If forgotten, repeat the* עמידה.)

REFLECTION

Where do you look for God?

What questions do you have for Him?

What do you ask when you can't find God?

... A THOUSAND WORDS

On Shabbat Rosh Ḥodesh say "Long ago You formed" below the line.

HOLINESS OF THE DAY

תִּכַּנְתָּ שַׁבָּת You instituted the Sabbath, You favored its offerings.
You commanded its specific laws
along with the order of its libations.
Those who delight in it inherit eternal glory,
those who relish it merit life,
and those who love its teachings have chosen greatness.
Even before Sinai they were commanded about it.
Then You, LORD our God, commanded us to offer on it
the additional offering of the Sabbath in the proper way.

On Shabbat Rosh Ḥodesh:

אַתָּה יָצַרְתָּ Long ago You formed Your world,
completing Your work on the seventh day.
You loved us. You favored us, raising us above all languages.
You made us holy through Your commandments,
brought us near, O our King, to Your service,
and called us by Your great and holy name.
You also gave us in love, LORD our God,
Sabbaths for rest and New Moons for atonement.
But because we and our ancestors sinned against You,
our city was laid waste, our Sanctuary made desolate,
our splendor exiled, and the glory gone from our House of life.
We can no longer fulfill our obligations in Your chosen House,
the great and holy Temple called by Your name,
because of the hand that was stretched out against Your Sanctuary.

Continue below the line on the next page.

... A THOUSAND WORDS

REFLECTION

Is Shabbat a sacrifice for you?

What do you sacrifice on Shabbat?

What do you gain on Shabbat?

On שבת ראש חודש *say* אַתָּה יָצַרְתָּ *below the line.*

קדושת היום

תִּכַּנְתָּ שַׁבָּת, רָצִיתָ קָרְבְּנוֹתֶיהָ
צִוִּיתָ פֵּרוּשֶׁיהָ עִם סִדּוּרֵי נְסָכֶיהָ
מְעַנְּגֶיהָ לְעוֹלָם כָּבוֹד יִנְחָלוּ, טוֹעֲמֶיהָ חַיִּים זָכוּ
וְגַם הָאוֹהֲבִים דְּבָרֶיהָ גְּדֻלָּה בָּחָרוּ.
אָז מִסִּינַי נִצְטַוּוּ עָלֶיהָ
וַתְּצַוֵּנוּ יהוה אֱלֹהֵינוּ לְהַקְרִיב בָּהּ קָרְבַּן מוּסַף שַׁבָּת כָּרָאוּי.

בשבת ראש חודש:

אַתָּה יָצַרְתָּ עוֹלָמְךָ מִקֶּדֶם, כִּלִּיתָ מְלַאכְתְּךָ בַּיּוֹם הַשְּׁבִיעִי
אָהַבְתָּ אוֹתָנוּ וְרָצִיתָ בָּנוּ, וְרוֹמַמְתָּנוּ מִכָּל הַלְּשׁוֹנוֹת
וְקִדַּשְׁתָּנוּ בְּמִצְוֹתֶיךָ, וְקֵרַבְתָּנוּ מַלְכֵּנוּ לַעֲבוֹדָתֶךָ
וְשִׁמְךָ הַגָּדוֹל וְהַקָּדוֹשׁ עָלֵינוּ קָרָאתָ.
וַתִּתֶּן לָנוּ יהוה אֱלֹהֵינוּ בְּאַהֲבָה, שַׁבָּתוֹת לִמְנוּחָה וְרָאשֵׁי חֳדָשִׁים לְכַפָּרָה.
וּלְפִי שֶׁחָטָאנוּ לְפָנֶיךָ אֲנַחְנוּ וַאֲבוֹתֵינוּ
חָרְבָה עִירֵנוּ, וְשָׁמֵם בֵּית מִקְדָּשֵׁנוּ, וְגָלָה יְקָרֵנוּ, וְנִטַּל כָּבוֹד מִבֵּית חַיֵּינוּ
וְאֵין אֲנַחְנוּ יְכוֹלִים לַעֲשׂוֹת חוֹבוֹתֵינוּ בְּבֵית בְּחִירָתֶךָ
בַּבַּיִת הַגָּדוֹל וְהַקָּדוֹשׁ שֶׁנִּקְרָא שִׁמְךָ עָלָיו, מִפְּנֵי הַיָּד שֶׁנִּשְׁתַּלְּחָה בְּמִקְדָּשֶׁךָ.

Continue below the line on the next page.

LEARNING

This *tefilla* is an acrostic, each word beginning with the next letter of the *Alef-Bet*. While there are many acrostics found in the siddur, some of which run according to the *Alef-Bet*, this is the only one that uses the *Alef-Bet* in the reverse order. Several reasons have been suggested for this. It could merely be a literary device, for beauty or to aid in memorization. Others suggest there is mystical significance, and refer to the style as **תשר״ק**, the last four letters of the *Alef-Bet* in reverse order. This word also means whistle, and hints at the verse in *Zekharia* (10:8) "I will whistle and gather them because I will have redeemed them," connecting this *tefilla* therefore to the final redemption.

יְהִי רָצוֹן May it be Your will,
Lord our God and God of our ancestors,
to lead us back in joy to our land
and to plant us within our borders.
There we will prepare for You our obligatory offerings:
the regular daily offerings in their order,
and the additional offerings according to their laws.

May it be Your will, Lord our God and God of our ancestors,
to lead us back in joy to our land,
and to plant us within our borders.
There we will prepare for You our obligatory offerings:
the regular daily offerings in their order,
and the additional offerings according to their laws.
And the additional offerings
of this Sabbath day,
and of this New Moon day,
we will prepare and offer before You in love,
in accord with Your will's commandment,
as You wrote for us in Your Torah
through Your servant Moses,
by Your own word, as it is said:

Continue below the line on the next page.

REFLECTION

"In the future,
the abundance of knowledge
will spread to and penetrate
even animals…
and the sacrifices,
which will then be from grain,
will be as pleasing to God
as in days of old in yesteryear
[when there were
animal sacrifices]…"
(Rav Kook, *Olat Re'iya*)

Can you imagine
the emotional experience
of bringing a *korban*,
and watching it being sacrificed,
knowing it is in your stead?
Close your eyes and try and experience
those emotions now.

What values are inherent
in the concept of sacrifice?

What could you sacrifice for God today?

יְהִי רָצוֹן מִלְּפָנֶיךָ, יהוה אֱלֹהֵינוּ וֵאלֹהֵי אֲבוֹתֵינוּ
שֶׁתַּעֲלֵנוּ בְשִׂמְחָה לְאַרְצֵנוּ וְתִטָּעֵנוּ בִּגְבוּלֵנוּ
וְשָׁם נַעֲשֶׂה לְפָנֶיךָ אֶת קָרְבְּנוֹת חוֹבוֹתֵינוּ
תְּמִידִים כְּסִדְרָם וּמוּסָפִים כְּהִלְכָתָם.

יְהִי רָצוֹן מִלְּפָנֶיךָ, יהוה אֱלֹהֵינוּ וֵאלֹהֵי אֲבוֹתֵינוּ
שֶׁתַּעֲלֵנוּ בְשִׂמְחָה לְאַרְצֵנוּ וְתִטָּעֵנוּ בִּגְבוּלֵנוּ
וְשָׁם נַעֲשֶׂה לְפָנֶיךָ אֶת קָרְבְּנוֹת חוֹבוֹתֵינוּ
תְּמִידִים כְּסִדְרָם וּמוּסָפִים כְּהִלְכָתָם.
וְאֶת מוּסְפֵי יוֹם הַשַּׁבָּת הַזֶּה וְיוֹם רֹאשׁ הַחֹדֶשׁ הַזֶּה
נַעֲשֶׂה וְנַקְרִיב לְפָנֶיךָ בְּאַהֲבָה כְּמִצְוַת רְצוֹנֶךָ
כְּמוֹ שֶׁכָּתַבְתָּ עָלֵינוּ בְּתוֹרָתֶךָ
עַל יְדֵי מֹשֶׁה עַבְדֶּךָ מִפִּי כְבוֹדֶךָ, כָּאָמוּר

Continue below the line on the next page.

...A THOUSAND WORDS

CONNECTION

If we think of the Sabbath as a "day of rest" from a hard week's work, then these rules do not make any sense at all.... Why are we forbidden to do so many things even when little or no physical work is involved? What does the Torah mean when it says that God rested? Was He tired? Had He worked too hard? Was creation an exhausting task? This is our definition: Work, in the Sabbath sense, is an act that shows man's mastery over the world by means of his intelligence and skill. We can now understand the Sabbath ritual. We must leave nature untouched. We must not demonstrate our mastery over nature, nor change it in any way. We must not intervene in the natural process. Any change or interference, no matter how trivial or small, is a violation of this rest. (Rabbi Aryeh Kaplan)

וְאֶת מוּסַף And the additional offering of this Sabbath day
we will prepare and offer before You in love,
in accord with Your will's commandment,
as You wrote for us in Your Torah
through Your servant Moses, by Your own word,
as it is said:

"On the Sabbath day, *Num. 28*
make an offering of two lambs a year old, without blemish,
together with two-tenths of an ephah of fine flour
mixed with oil as a meal-offering, and its appropriate libation.
This is the burnt-offering for every Sabbath,
in addition to the regular daily burnt-offering and its libation."

"On the Sabbath day,
make an offering of two lambs a year old, without blemish, *Num. 28*
together with two-tenths of an ephah of fine flour
mixed with oil as a meal-offering, and its appropriate libation.
This is the burnt-offering for every Sabbath,
in addition to the regular daily burnt-offering and its libation."

"And on your new moons, present as a burnt-offering to the LORD
two young bulls, one ram, *Num. 28*
and seven yearling lambs without blemish."

And their meal-offerings and wine-libations as ordained:
three-tenths of an ephah for each bull,
two-tenths of an ephah for the ram,
one-tenth of an ephah for each lamb,
wine for the libations,
a male goat for atonement,
and two regular daily offerings according to their law.

Continue below the line on the next page.

REFLECTION

What do you do on Shabbat that is special
that you do not do during the week?
Do you make Shabbat special
or does Shabbat make you special?

What more can you do
to make this Shabbat
special for you
and those around you?

וְאֶת מוּסַף יוֹם הַשַּׁבָּת הַזֶּה
נַעֲשֶׂה וְנַקְרִיב לְפָנֶיךָ בְּאַהֲבָה כְּמִצְוַת רְצוֹנֶךָ
כְּמוֹ שֶׁכָּתַבְתָּ עָלֵינוּ בְּתוֹרָתֶךָ
עַל יְדֵי מֹשֶׁה עַבְדֶּךָ מִפִּי כְבוֹדֶךָ
כָּאָמוּר

במדבר כח
וּבְיוֹם הַשַּׁבָּת שְׁנֵי־כְבָשִׂים בְּנֵי־שָׁנָה תְּמִימִם
וּשְׁנֵי עֶשְׂרֹנִים סֹלֶת מִנְחָה בְּלוּלָה בַשֶּׁמֶן וְנִסְכּוֹ:
עֹלַת שַׁבַּת בְּשַׁבַּתּוֹ, עַל־עֹלַת הַתָּמִיד וְנִסְכָּהּ:

במדבר כח
וּבְיוֹם הַשַּׁבָּת שְׁנֵי־כְבָשִׂים בְּנֵי־שָׁנָה תְּמִימִם
וּשְׁנֵי עֶשְׂרֹנִים סֹלֶת מִנְחָה בְּלוּלָה בַשֶּׁמֶן וְנִסְכּוֹ:
עֹלַת שַׁבַּת בְּשַׁבַּתּוֹ, עַל־עֹלַת הַתָּמִיד וְנִסְכָּהּ:

במדבר כח
וּבְרָאשֵׁי חָדְשֵׁיכֶם תַּקְרִיבוּ עֹלָה לַיהוה
פָּרִים בְּנֵי־בָקָר שְׁנַיִם, וְאַיִל אֶחָד, כְּבָשִׂים בְּנֵי־שָׁנָה שִׁבְעָה, תְּמִימִם:
וּמִנְחָתָם וְנִסְכֵּיהֶם כִּמְדֻבָּר
שְׁלֹשָׁה עֶשְׂרֹנִים לַפָּר, וּשְׁנֵי עֶשְׂרֹנִים לָאַיִל
וְעִשָּׂרוֹן לַכֶּבֶשׂ, וְיַיִן כְּנִסְכּוֹ, וְשָׂעִיר לְכַפֵּר, וּשְׁנֵי תְמִידִים כְּהִלְכָתָם.

Continue below the line on the next page.

... A THOUSAND WORDS

יִשְׂמְחוּ Those who keep the Sabbath and call it a delight
shall rejoice in Your kingship.
The people who sanctify the seventh day shall all be satisfied
and take delight in Your goodness,
for You favored the seventh day and declared it holy.
You called it "most desirable of days"
in remembrance of Creation.

Those who keep the Sabbath and call it a delight
shall rejoice in Your kingship.
The people who sanctify the seventh day shall all be satisfied
and take delight in Your goodness,
for You favored the seventh day and declared it holy.
You called it "most desirable of days"
in remembrance of Creation.

Continue below the line on the next page.

Sleep. *We are a sleep-deprived civilization and Shabbat is certainly a day for catching up. As one of the zemirot declares, "Sleep on Shabbat is a pleasure"* (ta'anug, *from the same root as* oneg*), and some even went so far as to find a biblical justification for doing so!*

Learn Torah. *Set some time aside every Shabbat for learning something new about Judaism. If not on Shabbat, then when will you do it? How will you grow in your knowledge and understanding of Judaism if you don't invest time in it?*

Talk Shabbat. *Language is the primary medium for conveying not only our knowledge but also our values and it can help set the tone for our interactions. Words help create our reality; even the smallest things can make a difference. That is perhaps one reason why on Shabbat we greet one another differently by saying "*Shabbat shalom.*" That greeting can take the place of "hello," "good morning," "good night," or even "goodbye." That's because there is no greater blessing on this day than to wish someone the peace (shalom) and fulfillment (*shlemut*) that Shabbat can bring.*

Treat every Shabbat like it's the first. *Shabbat is not about recreation; rather, it's about re-creation. If on this day we mark the creation of the world, then every Shabbat is like the world was created anew. Every Shabbat is a new experience, a new chance to start all over again. If last Shabbat was not what you wanted it to be, then this Shabbat can be different – because you too are different.* (Rabbi Jay Goldmintz)

יִשְׂמְחוּ בְמַלְכוּתְךָ שׁוֹמְרֵי שַׁבָּת וְקוֹרְאֵי עֹנֶג
עַם מְקַדְּשֵׁי שְׁבִיעִי
כֻּלָּם יִשְׂבְּעוּ וְיִתְעַנְּגוּ מִטּוּבֶךָ
וּבַשְּׁבִיעִי רָצִיתָ בּוֹ וְקִדַּשְׁתּוֹ
חֶמְדַּת יָמִים אוֹתוֹ קָרָאתָ
זֵכֶר לְמַעֲשֵׂה בְרֵאשִׁית.

יִשְׂמְחוּ בְמַלְכוּתְךָ שׁוֹמְרֵי שַׁבָּת וְקוֹרְאֵי עֹנֶג
עַם מְקַדְּשֵׁי שְׁבִיעִי
כֻּלָּם יִשְׂבְּעוּ וְיִתְעַנְּגוּ מִטּוּבֶךָ
וּבַשְּׁבִיעִי רָצִיתָ בּוֹ וְקִדַּשְׁתּוֹ
חֶמְדַּת יָמִים אוֹתוֹ קָרָאתָ
זֵכֶר לְמַעֲשֵׂה בְרֵאשִׁית.

Continue below the line on the next page.

CONNECTION

A GUIDE TO *ONEG SHABBAT*

Oneg Shabbat *is understood to mean enjoying the pleasures of Shabbat. How?*

Eat for Shabbat. *Make the meal special. This need not mean multiple lavish courses and haute cuisine. It simply means doing something different than you would do the rest of the week.*

Sing for Shabbat. Sefer HaḤinukh *says, "Our hearts are affected by our actions." Singing can help us get to a place where thoughts or words alone may not bring us. No wonder, then, that there is such an esteemed history of singing at the Shabbat table. These songs (zemirot) are built around themes related to Shabbat and thereby help provoke and evoke an appreciation of the day.*

Table talk for Shabbat. *Perhaps a true test of whether a meal is for the sake of self-indulgence or for the sake of some loftier value is the table talk that accompanies it. Minimally, food is about survival. On Shabbat, it is especially about enjoyment, and while we inject it with spiritual significance via the blessings recited before and after, sharing words of Torah during the meal lends a different aura and flavor to the festivities.*

אֱלֹהֵינוּ Our God and God of our ancestors, find favor in our rest.
Make us holy through Your commandments
and give us our share in Your Torah.
Satisfy us with Your goodness, give us joy in Your salvation,
and purify our hearts to serve You in truth.
In love and favor, Lord our God,
give us as our heritage Your holy Sabbath,
so that Israel who sanctify Your name may find rest on it.
Blessed are You, Lord, who sanctifies the Sabbath.

Our God and God of our ancestors, find favor in our rest,
and on this Sabbath day renew for us the coming month
for good and blessing, joy and gladness, deliverance and consolation,
sustenance and support, life and peace,
pardon of sin and forgiveness of wrongdoing
(*From Marḥeshvan to Adar II in a Jewish leap year:* and atonement of transgression).
For You have chosen Your people Israel from all nations;
You have made known to them Your holy Sabbath,
and instituted for them rules for the New Moon.
Blessed are You, Lord,
who sanctifies the Sabbath, Israel and the New Moons.

Continue with "Find favor" on the next page.

Ya'aleh VeYavo *in the recitation of* Birkat HaMazon *and the* Amida, *the recitation of the* Musaf *prayer, and a truncated* Hallel.

Yet, Rosh Ḥodesh bears a great and wondrous sanctity. The masters of our tradition ruled that if one did not remember to mention Rosh Ḥodesh in the Shemoneh Esreh, *he must start over. Halakhically there is no difference between one who forgets Rosh Ḥodesh in his prayers and one who neglects to mention Yom Kippur. In both cases he has to repeat his prayer.*

The essence of the sanctity of Rosh Ḥodesh is expressed in modesty and withdrawal. Unlike the sanctity of Shabbat and Yom Tov, on Rosh Ḥodesh the experience of sanctity is instead folded into the depths of one's religious consciousness. However, its modesty does not detract from its sanctity…

Revealed kedusha *does not exceed hidden* kedusha *in its value. Holiness reflects the religious experience in all its complexity, even when it is not given to external expression, when the pursuit of God takes place on a winding road covered in the dust of the weekday routine. The same trumpets which herald the* Simḥat Beit HaSho'eva *on Sukkot are also blown on Rosh Ḥodesh. The echoes of the Rosh Ḥodesh blasts encompass infinity.* (Rabbi J.B. Soloveitchik)

אֱלֹהֵינוּ וֵאלֹהֵי אֲבוֹתֵינוּ, רְצֵה בִמְנוּחָתֵנוּ
קַדְּשֵׁנוּ בְּמִצְוֹתֶיךָ וְתֵן חֶלְקֵנוּ בְּתוֹרָתֶךָ
שַׂבְּעֵנוּ מִטּוּבֶךָ, וְשַׂמְּחֵנוּ בִּישׁוּעָתֶךָ
וְטַהֵר לִבֵּנוּ לְעָבְדְּךָ בֶּאֱמֶת
וְהַנְחִילֵנוּ יהוה אֱלֹהֵינוּ בְּאַהֲבָה וּבְרָצוֹן שַׁבַּת קָדְשֶׁךָ
וְיָנוּחוּ בוֹ יִשְׂרָאֵל מְקַדְּשֵׁי שְׁמֶךָ.
בָּרוּךְ אַתָּה יהוה, מְקַדֵּשׁ הַשַּׁבָּת.

אֱלֹהֵינוּ וֵאלֹהֵי אֲבוֹתֵינוּ, רְצֵה בִמְנוּחָתֵנוּ
וְחַדֵּשׁ עָלֵינוּ בְּיוֹם הַשַּׁבָּת הַזֶּה אֶת הַחֹדֶשׁ הַזֶּה
לְטוֹבָה וְלִבְרָכָה, לְשָׂשׂוֹן וּלְשִׂמְחָה, לִישׁוּעָה וּלְנֶחָמָה
לְפַרְנָסָה וּלְכַלְכָּלָה, לְחַיִּים וּלְשָׁלוֹם, לִמְחִילַת חֵטְא וְלִסְלִיחַת עָוֺן
(*From* מרחשון *to* אדר שני *in a Jewish leap year* וּלְכַפָּרַת פָּשַׁע)
כִּי בְעַמְּךָ יִשְׂרָאֵל בָּחַרְתָּ מִכָּל הָאֻמּוֹת
וְשַׁבַּת קָדְשְׁךָ לָהֶם הוֹדַעְתָּ וְחֻקֵּי רָאשֵׁי חֳדָשִׁים לָהֶם קָבָעְתָּ.
בָּרוּךְ אַתָּה יהוה, מְקַדֵּשׁ הַשַּׁבָּת וְיִשְׂרָאֵל וְרָאשֵׁי חֳדָשִׁים.

Continue with רְצֵה *on the next page.*

LEARNING

There exists a fundamental difference between the holiness of Shabbat and Yom Tov on one hand and the holiness of Rosh Ḥodesh on the other… With every step he takes, the Jew feels the holiness of Shabbat and Yom Tov: it encompasses him and his environment. Shabbat and Yom Tov are days of complete rest, characterized by a neshama yeteira *on the inside and beautiful clothing on the outside… The world of weekday departs and the world of sanctity enters, as demonstrated in one's prayers, meals, clothing, and conduct.*

In contrast, the sanctity of Rosh Ḥodesh is not externally evident. Rosh Ḥodesh is a day like any other. There is no prohibition against performing work… The Jew is dressed in weekday clothes, and worries about his sustenance. He is mired in grayness and the daily monotony. He pours out his prayer in the style that he is used to during the week, detailing the afflictions of his heart in nineteen simple blessings. After the prayer is over, he hurries home to a life of routine. The only difference between Rosh Ḥodesh and weekdays is the mention of

TEMPLE SERVICE

רְצֵה Find favor, Lord our God,
in Your people Israel and their prayer.
Restore the service to Your most holy House,
and accept in love and favor
the fire-offerings of Israel and their prayer.
May the service of Your people Israel always find favor with You.
And may our eyes witness Your return to Zion in compassion.
Blessed are You, Lord, who restores His Presence to Zion.

THANKSGIVING

מוֹדִים We give thanks to You,
for You are the Lord our God
and God of our ancestors
for ever and all time.
You are the Rock of our lives,
Shield of our salvation
from generation to generation.
We will thank You and
declare Your praise for our lives,
which are entrusted into Your hand;
for our souls,
which are placed in Your charge;
for Your miracles
which are with us every day;
and for Your wonders and favors
at all times,
evening, morning and midday.
You are good –
for Your compassion never fails.
You are compassionate –
for Your loving-kindnesses never cease.
We have always placed our hope in You.

During the Leader's Repetition, the congregation says quietly:

מוֹדִים We give thanks
to You, for You are
the Lord our God
and God of our ancestors,
God of all flesh,
who formed us
and formed the universe.
Blessings and thanks
are due to Your great
and holy name for giving us
life and sustaining us.
May You continue
to give us life and sustain us;
and may You gather our
exiles to Your holy courts,
to keep Your decrees,
do Your will and serve You
with a perfect heart,
for it is for us
to give You thanks.
Blessed be God to whom
thanksgiving is due.

עבודה

רְצֵה יהוה אֱלֹהֵינוּ בְּעַמְּךָ יִשְׂרָאֵל, וּבִתְפִלָּתָם
וְהָשֵׁב אֶת הָעֲבוֹדָה לִדְבִיר בֵּיתֶךָ
וְאִשֵּׁי יִשְׂרָאֵל וּתְפִלָּתָם בְּאַהֲבָה תְקַבֵּל בְּרָצוֹן
וּתְהִי לְרָצוֹן תָּמִיד עֲבוֹדַת יִשְׂרָאֵל עַמֶּךָ.
וְתֶחֱזֶינָה עֵינֵינוּ בְּשׁוּבְךָ לְצִיּוֹן בְּרַחֲמִים.
בָּרוּךְ אַתָּה יהוה, הַמַּחֲזִיר שְׁכִינָתוֹ לְצִיּוֹן.

הודאה

מוֹדִים אֲנַחְנוּ לָךְ
שָׁאַתָּה הוּא יהוה אֱלֹהֵינוּ
וֵאלֹהֵי אֲבוֹתֵינוּ לְעוֹלָם וָעֶד.
צוּר חַיֵּינוּ, מָגֵן יִשְׁעֵנוּ
אַתָּה הוּא לְדוֹר וָדוֹר.
נוֹדֶה לְּךָ וּנְסַפֵּר תְּהִלָּתֶךָ
עַל חַיֵּינוּ הַמְּסוּרִים בְּיָדֶךָ
וְעַל נִשְׁמוֹתֵינוּ הַפְּקוּדוֹת לָךְ
וְעַל נִסֶּיךָ שֶׁבְּכָל יוֹם עִמָּנוּ
וְעַל נִפְלְאוֹתֶיךָ וְטוֹבוֹתֶיךָ
שֶׁבְּכָל עֵת
עֶרֶב וָבֹקֶר וְצָהֳרָיִם.
הַטּוֹב, כִּי לֹא כָלוּ רַחֲמֶיךָ
וְהַמְרַחֵם, כִּי לֹא תַמּוּ חֲסָדֶיךָ
מֵעוֹלָם קִוִּינוּ לָךְ.

During חזרת הש״ץ, *the* קהל *says quietly:*

מוֹדִים אֲנַחְנוּ לָךְ
שָׁאַתָּה הוּא יהוה אֱלֹהֵינוּ
וֵאלֹהֵי אֲבוֹתֵינוּ
אֱלֹהֵי כָל בָּשָׂר
יוֹצְרֵנוּ, יוֹצֵר בְּרֵאשִׁית.
בְּרָכוֹת וְהוֹדָאוֹת
לְשִׁמְךָ הַגָּדוֹל וְהַקָּדוֹשׁ
עַל שֶׁהֶחֱיִיתָנוּ וְקִיַּמְתָּנוּ.
כֵּן תְּחַיֵּנוּ וּתְקַיְּמֵנוּ
וְתֶאֱסֹף גָּלֻיּוֹתֵינוּ
לְחַצְרוֹת קָדְשֶׁךָ
לִשְׁמֹר חֻקֶּיךָ
וְלַעֲשׂוֹת רְצוֹנֶךָ וּלְעָבְדְּךָ
בְּלֵבָב שָׁלֵם
עַל שֶׁאֲנַחְנוּ מוֹדִים לָךְ.
בָּרוּךְ אֵל הַהוֹדָאוֹת.

On Ḥanukka:

עַל הַנִּסִּים [We thank You also] for the miracles, the redemption, the mighty deeds, the salvations, and the victories in battle which You performed for our ancestors in those days, at this time.

בִּימֵי מַתִּתְיָהוּ In the days of Mattityahu, son of Yoḥanan, the High Priest, the Hasmonean, and his sons, the wicked Greek kingdom rose up against Your people Israel to make them forget Your Torah and to force them to transgress the laws of Your will. It was then that You in Your great compassion stood by them in the time of their distress. You championed their cause, judged their claim, and avenged their wrong. You delivered the strong into the hands of the weak, the many into the hands of the few, the impure into the hands of the pure, the wicked into the hands of the righteous, and the arrogant into the hands of those who were engaged in the study of Your Torah. You made for Yourself great and holy fame in Your world, and for Your people Israel You performed a great salvation and redemption as of this very day. Your children then entered the holiest part of Your House, cleansed Your Temple, purified Your Sanctuary, kindled lights in Your holy courts, and designated these eight days of Ḥanukka for giving thanks and praise to Your great name.

Continue with "For all these things."

On Shushan Purim in Jerusalem:

עַל הַנִּסִּים [We thank You also] for the miracles, the redemption, the mighty deeds, the salvations, and the victories in battle which You performed for our ancestors in those days at this time.

בִּימֵי מָרְדְּכַי In the days of Mordekhai and Esther, in Shushan the capital, the
wicked Haman rose up against them and sought to destroy, slay and exterminate *Esther 3*
all the Jews, young and old, children and women, on one day, the thirteenth day of the twelfth month, which is the month of Adar, and to plunder their possessions. Then You in Your great compassion defeated his counsel, frustrated his plans, and caused his scheme to recoil on his own head, so that they hanged him and his sons on the gallows.

Continue with "For all these things."

וְעַל כֻּלָּם For all these things may Your name be blessed and elevated, our King, continually, for ever and all time.

On Shabbat Shuva: And write, for a good life, all the children of Your covenant.

Let all that lives thank You, Selah! and praise Your name in truth,
God, our Savior and Help, Selah!
Blessed are You, Lord,
whose name is "the Good" and to whom thanks are due.

בחנוכה:

עַל הַנִּסִּים וְעַל הַפֻּרְקָן וְעַל הַגְּבוּרוֹת וְעַל הַתְּשׁוּעוֹת וְעַל הַמִּלְחָמוֹת שֶׁעָשִׂיתָ לַאֲבוֹתֵינוּ בַּיָּמִים הָהֵם בַּזְּמַן הַזֶּה.

בִּימֵי מַתִּתְיָהוּ בֶּן יוֹחָנָן כֹּהֵן גָּדוֹל חַשְׁמוֹנַאי וּבָנָיו, כְּשֶׁעָמְדָה מַלְכוּת יָוָן הָרְשָׁעָה עַל עַמְּךָ יִשְׂרָאֵל לְהַשְׁכִּיחָם תּוֹרָתֶךָ וּלְהַעֲבִירָם מֵחֻקֵּי רְצוֹנֶךָ, וְאַתָּה בְּרַחֲמֶיךָ הָרַבִּים עָמַדְתָּ לָהֶם בְּעֵת צָרָתָם, רַבְתָּ אֶת רִיבָם, דַּנְתָּ אֶת דִּינָם, נָקַמְתָּ אֶת נִקְמָתָם, מָסַרְתָּ גִבּוֹרִים בְּיַד חַלָּשִׁים, וְרַבִּים בְּיַד מְעַטִּים, וּטְמֵאִים בְּיַד טְהוֹרִים, וּרְשָׁעִים בְּיַד צַדִּיקִים, וְזֵדִים בְּיַד עוֹסְקֵי תוֹרָתֶךָ, וּלְךָ עָשִׂיתָ שֵׁם גָּדוֹל וְקָדוֹשׁ בְּעוֹלָמֶךָ, וּלְעַמְּךָ יִשְׂרָאֵל עָשִׂיתָ תְּשׁוּעָה גְדוֹלָה וּפֻרְקָן כְּהַיּוֹם הַזֶּה. וְאַחַר כֵּן בָּאוּ בָנֶיךָ לִדְבִיר בֵּיתֶךָ, וּפִנּוּ אֶת הֵיכָלֶךָ, וְטִהֲרוּ אֶת מִקְדָּשֶׁךָ, וְהִדְלִיקוּ נֵרוֹת בְּחַצְרוֹת קָדְשֶׁךָ, וְקָבְעוּ שְׁמוֹנַת יְמֵי חֲנֻכָּה אֵלּוּ, לְהוֹדוֹת וּלְהַלֵּל לְשִׁמְךָ הַגָּדוֹל.

Continue with וְעַל כֻּלָּם.

בשושן פורים בירושלים:

עַל הַנִּסִּים וְעַל הַפֻּרְקָן וְעַל הַגְּבוּרוֹת וְעַל הַתְּשׁוּעוֹת וְעַל הַמִּלְחָמוֹת שֶׁעָשִׂיתָ לַאֲבוֹתֵינוּ בַּיָּמִים הָהֵם בַּזְּמַן הַזֶּה.

בִּימֵי מָרְדְּכַי וְאֶסְתֵּר בְּשׁוּשַׁן הַבִּירָה, כְּשֶׁעָמַד עֲלֵיהֶם הָמָן הָרָשָׁע, בִּקֵּשׁ
לְהַשְׁמִיד לַהֲרֹג וּלְאַבֵּד אֶת־כָּל־הַיְּהוּדִים מִנַּעַר וְעַד־זָקֵן טַף וְנָשִׁים בְּיוֹם אסתר ג
אֶחָד, בִּשְׁלוֹשָׁה עָשָׂר לְחֹדֶשׁ שְׁנֵים־עָשָׂר, הוּא־חֹדֶשׁ אֲדָר, וּשְׁלָלָם לָבוֹז: וְאַתָּה בְּרַחֲמֶיךָ הָרַבִּים הֵפַרְתָּ אֶת עֲצָתוֹ, וְקִלְקַלְתָּ אֶת מַחֲשַׁבְתּוֹ, וַהֲשֵׁבוֹתָ לּוֹ גְּמוּלוֹ בְּרֹאשׁוֹ, וְתָלוּ אוֹתוֹ וְאֶת בָּנָיו עַל הָעֵץ.

Continue with וְעַל כֻּלָּם.

וְעַל כֻּלָּם יִתְבָּרַךְ וְיִתְרוֹמַם שִׁמְךָ מַלְכֵּנוּ תָּמִיד לְעוֹלָם וָעֶד.

בשבת שובה: וּכְתֹב לְחַיִּים טוֹבִים כָּל בְּנֵי בְרִיתֶךָ.

וְכֹל הַחַיִּים יוֹדוּךָ סֶּלָה, וִיהַלְלוּ אֶת שִׁמְךָ בֶּאֱמֶת הָאֵל יְשׁוּעָתֵנוּ וְעֶזְרָתֵנוּ סֶלָה.

בָּרוּךְ אַתָּה יהוה, הַטּוֹב שִׁמְךָ וּלְךָ נָאֶה לְהוֹדוֹת.

The following is said by the Leader during the Repetition of the Amida.
In Israel, if Kohanim bless the congregation, *turn to page 1064.*

Our God and God of our fathers, bless us with the threefold blessing in the Torah, written by the hand of Moses Your servant and pronounced by Aaron and his sons the priests, Your holy people, as it is said:

May the LORD bless you and protect you. *Num. 6*
Cong: May it be Your will.
May the LORD make His face shine on you and be gracious to you.
Cong: May it be Your will.
May the LORD turn His face toward you, and give you peace.
Cong: May it be Your will.

PEACE

שִׂים שָׁלוֹם Give peace, goodness and blessing, grace,
loving-kindness and compassion to us
and all Israel Your people.
Bless us, our Father, all as one,
with the light of Your face,
for by the light of Your face You have given us,
LORD our God, the Torah of life and love of kindness,
righteousness, blessing, compassion, life and peace.
May it be good in Your eyes to bless Your people Israel
at every time, in every hour, with Your peace.

On Shabbat Shuva: In the book of life, blessing, peace and prosperity,
may we and all Your people the house of Israel
be remembered and written before You for a good life,
and for peace.*

Blessed are You, LORD, who blesses His people Israel with peace.

**On Shabbat Shuva outside Israel, many end the blessing:*
Blessed are You, LORD, who makes peace.

The following verse concludes the Leader's Repetition of the Amida.
Some also say it here as part of the silent Amida.

May the words of my mouth and the inner thoughts of my heart *Ps. 19*
find favor before You, LORD, my Rock and Redeemer.

The following is said by the שליח ציבור *during* חורת הש״ץ.
In ארץ ישראל *if* כהנים *say* ברכת כהנים *turn to page 1065.*

אֱלֹהֵינוּ וֵאלֹהֵי אֲבוֹתֵינוּ, בָּרְכֵנוּ בַּבְּרָכָה הַמְשֻׁלֶּשֶׁת בַּתּוֹרָה, הַכְּתוּבָה עַל יְדֵי מֹשֶׁה עַבְדֶּךָ, הָאֲמוּרָה מִפִּי אַהֲרֹן וּבָנָיו כֹּהֲנִים עַם קְדוֹשֶׁיךָ, כָּאָמוּר

במדבר ו
יְבָרֶכְךָ יהוה וְיִשְׁמְרֶךָ: קהל: כֵּן יְהִי רָצוֹן
יָאֵר יהוה פָּנָיו אֵלֶיךָ וִיחֻנֶּךָּ: קהל: כֵּן יְהִי רָצוֹן
יִשָּׂא יהוה פָּנָיו אֵלֶיךָ וְיָשֵׂם לְךָ שָׁלוֹם: קהל: כֵּן יְהִי רָצוֹן

ברכת שלום

שִׂים שָׁלוֹם טוֹבָה וּבְרָכָה
חֵן וָחֶסֶד וְרַחֲמִים עָלֵינוּ וְעַל כָּל יִשְׂרָאֵל עַמֶּךָ.
בָּרְכֵנוּ אָבִינוּ כֻּלָּנוּ כְּאֶחָד בְּאוֹר פָּנֶיךָ
כִּי בְאוֹר פָּנֶיךָ נָתַתָּ לָּנוּ, יהוה אֱלֹהֵינוּ
תּוֹרַת חַיִּים וְאַהֲבַת חֶסֶד
וּצְדָקָה וּבְרָכָה וְרַחֲמִים וְחַיִּים וְשָׁלוֹם.
וְטוֹב בְּעֵינֶיךָ לְבָרֵךְ אֶת עַמְּךָ יִשְׂרָאֵל
בְּכָל עֵת וּבְכָל שָׁעָה בִּשְׁלוֹמֶךָ.

בשבת שובה: בְּסֵפֶר חַיִּים, בְּרָכָה וְשָׁלוֹם, וּפַרְנָסָה טוֹבָה
נִזָּכֵר וְנִכָּתֵב לְפָנֶיךָ, אֲנַחְנוּ וְכָל עַמְּךָ בֵּית יִשְׂרָאֵל
לְחַיִּים טוֹבִים וּלְשָׁלוֹם.*

בָּרוּךְ אַתָּה יהוה, הַמְבָרֵךְ אֶת עַמּוֹ יִשְׂרָאֵל בַּשָּׁלוֹם.

**On* שבת שובה *in* חוץ לארץ, *many end the blessing:*

בָּרוּךְ אַתָּה יהוה, עוֹשֵׂה הַשָּׁלוֹם.

The following verse concludes the חורת הש״ץ.
Some also say it here as part of the silent עמידה.

תהלים יט
יִהְיוּ לְרָצוֹן אִמְרֵי־פִי וְהֶגְיוֹן לִבִּי לְפָנֶיךָ, יהוה צוּרִי וְגוֹאֲלִי:

אֱלֹהַי My God, *Berakhot 17a*
guard my tongue from evil and my lips from dishonest speech.
To those who curse me, let my soul be silent;
may my soul be to all like the dust.
Open my heart to Your Torah
and let my soul pursue Your commandments.
As for all who plan evil against me,
swiftly defeat their counsel and frustrate their plans.

Act for the sake of Your name;
act for the sake of Your right hand;
act for the sake of Your holiness;
act for the sake of Your Torah.

That Your beloved ones may be rescued, *Ps. 60*
save with Your right hand and answer me.
May the words of my mouth *Ps. 19*
and the inner thoughts of my heart
find favor before You, LORD, my Rock and Redeemer.

Bow, take three steps back, then bow, first left, then right, then center, while saying:

May He who makes peace in His high places,
make peace for us and all Israel –
and say: Amen.

יְהִי רָצוֹן May it be Your will, LORD our God and God of our ancestors,
that the Temple be rebuilt speedily in our days,
and give us a share in Your Torah.
And there we will serve You with fear,
as in the days of old and as in former years.
Then the offering of Judah and Jerusalem *Mal. 3*
will be pleasing to the LORD
as in the days of old and as in former years.

ברכות יז.

אֱלֹהַי
נְצֹר לְשׁוֹנִי מֵרָע וּשְׂפָתַי מִדַּבֵּר מִרְמָה
וְלִמְקַלְלַי נַפְשִׁי תִדֹּם, וְנַפְשִׁי כֶּעָפָר לַכֹּל תִּהְיֶה.
פְּתַח לִבִּי בְּתוֹרָתֶךָ, וּבְמִצְוֹתֶיךָ תִּרְדֹּף נַפְשִׁי.
וְכָל הַחוֹשְׁבִים עָלַי רָעָה
מְהֵרָה הָפֵר עֲצָתָם וְקַלְקֵל מַחֲשַׁבְתָּם.
עֲשֵׂה לְמַעַן שְׁמֶךָ
עֲשֵׂה לְמַעַן יְמִינֶךָ
עֲשֵׂה לְמַעַן קְדֻשָּׁתֶךָ
עֲשֵׂה לְמַעַן תּוֹרָתֶךָ.

תהלים ס
לְמַעַן יֵחָלְצוּן יְדִידֶיךָ, הוֹשִׁיעָה יְמִינְךָ וַעֲנֵנִי:

תהלים יט
יִהְיוּ לְרָצוֹן אִמְרֵי־פִי וְהֶגְיוֹן לִבִּי לְפָנֶיךָ, יהוה צוּרִי וְגֹאֲלִי:

Bow, take three steps back, then bow, first left, then right, then center, while saying:

עֹשֶׂה שָׁלוֹם/ בשבת שובה: הַשָּׁלוֹם/ בִּמְרוֹמָיו
הוּא יַעֲשֶׂה שָׁלוֹם עָלֵינוּ וְעַל כָּל יִשְׂרָאֵל
וְאִמְרוּ אָמֵן.

יְהִי רָצוֹן מִלְּפָנֶיךָ יהוה אֱלֹהֵינוּ וֵאלֹהֵי אֲבוֹתֵינוּ
שֶׁיִּבָּנֶה בֵּית הַמִּקְדָּשׁ בִּמְהֵרָה בְיָמֵינוּ
וְתֵן חֶלְקֵנוּ בְּתוֹרָתֶךָ
וְשָׁם נַעֲבָדְךָ בְּיִרְאָה כִּימֵי עוֹלָם וּכְשָׁנִים קַדְמוֹנִיּוֹת.

מלאכי ג
וְעָרְבָה לַיהוה מִנְחַת יְהוּדָה וִירוּשָׁלָםִ כִּימֵי עוֹלָם וּכְשָׁנִים קַדְמוֹנִיּוֹת:

FULL KADDISH

Leader: יִתְגַּדַּל Magnified and sanctified
may His great name be,
in the world He created by His will.
May He establish His kingdom
in your lifetime and in your days,
and in the lifetime of all the house of Israel,
swiftly and soon –
and say: Amen.

All: May His great name be blessed for ever and all time.

Leader: Blessed and praised, glorified and elevated,
raised and honored,
uplifted and praised
be the name of the Holy One,
blessed be He,
beyond any blessing,
song, praise and consolation
uttered in the world –
and say: Amen.

May the prayers and pleas of all Israel
be accepted by their Father in heaven –
and say: Amen.

May there be great peace from heaven,
and life for us and all Israel –
and say: Amen.

Bow, take three steps back, as if taking leave of the Divine Presence, then bow, first left, then right, then center, while saying:

May He who makes peace in His high places,
make peace for us and all Israel –
and say: Amen.

קדיש שלם

ש״ץ: יִתְגַּדַּל וְיִתְקַדַּשׁ שְׁמֵהּ רַבָּא (קהל: אָמֵן)
בְּעָלְמָא דִּי בְרָא כִרְעוּתֵהּ
וְיַמְלִיךְ מַלְכוּתֵהּ
בְּחַיֵּיכוֹן וּבְיוֹמֵיכוֹן וּבְחַיֵּי דְכָל בֵּית יִשְׂרָאֵל
בַּעֲגָלָא וּבִזְמַן קָרִיב, וְאִמְרוּ אָמֵן. (קהל: אָמֵן)

קהל וש״ץ: יְהֵא שְׁמֵהּ רַבָּא מְבָרַךְ לְעָלַם וּלְעָלְמֵי עָלְמַיָּא.

ש״ץ: יִתְבָּרַךְ וְיִשְׁתַּבַּח וְיִתְפָּאַר
וְיִתְרוֹמַם וְיִתְנַשֵּׂא וְיִתְהַדָּר וְיִתְעַלֶּה וְיִתְהַלָּל
שְׁמֵהּ דְּקֻדְשָׁא בְּרִיךְ הוּא (קהל: בְּרִיךְ הוּא)
לְעֵלָּא מִן כָּל בִּרְכָתָא
/ בשבת שובה: לְעֵלָּא לְעֵלָּא מִכָּל בִּרְכָתָא/
וְשִׁירָתָא, תֻּשְׁבְּחָתָא וְנֶחֱמָתָא
דַּאֲמִירָן בְּעָלְמָא, וְאִמְרוּ אָמֵן. (קהל: אָמֵן)

תִּתְקַבַּל צְלוֹתְהוֹן וּבָעוּתְהוֹן דְּכָל יִשְׂרָאֵל
קֳדָם אֲבוּהוֹן דִּי בִשְׁמַיָּא, וְאִמְרוּ אָמֵן. (קהל: אָמֵן)

יְהֵא שְׁלָמָא רַבָּא מִן שְׁמַיָּא
וְחַיִּים, עָלֵינוּ וְעַל כָּל יִשְׂרָאֵל, וְאִמְרוּ אָמֵן. (קהל: אָמֵן)

Bow, take three steps back, as if taking leave of the Divine Presence, then bow, first left, then right, then center, while saying:

עֹשֶׂה שָׁלוֹם/ בשבת שובה: הַשָּׁלוֹם/ בִּמְרוֹמָיו
הוּא יַעֲשֶׂה שָׁלוֹם
עָלֵינוּ וְעַל כָּל יִשְׂרָאֵל, וְאִמְרוּ אָמֵן. (קהל: אָמֵן)

אֵין כֵּאלֹהֵינוּ There is none like our God, none like our LORD,
none like our King, none like our Savior.
Who is like our God? Who is like our LORD?
Who is like our King? Who is like our Savior?
We will thank our God, we will thank our LORD,
we will thank our King, we will thank our Savior.
Blessed is our God, blessed is our LORD,
blessed is our King, blessed is our Savior.
You are our God, You are our LORD,
You are our King, You are our Savior.
You are He to whom our ancestors offered the fragrant incense.

פִּטּוּם הַקְּטֹרֶת The incense mixture consisted of balsam, onycha, galbanum and frankincense, each weighing seventy manehs; myrrh, cassia, spikenard and saffron, each weighing sixteen manehs; twelve manehs of costus, three of aromatic bark; nine of cinnamon; nine kabs of Carsina lye; three seahs and three kabs of Cyprus wine. If Cyprus wine was not available, old white wine might be used. A quarter of a kab of Sodom salt, and a minute amount of a smoke-raising herb. Rabbi Nathan says: Also a minute amount of Jordan amber. If one added honey to the mixture, he rendered it unfit for sacred use. If he omitted any one of its ingredients, he is guilty of a capital offense. *Keritot 6a*

LEARNING

The following *tefilla*, אֵין כֵּאלֹהֵינוּ, dates back to the days of the *Geonim*, and acts as an introduction to the final section of the service. It was originally placed in the siddur at the end of Shaḥarit of the weekday and said every day of the week. However, due to the lofty content, which asks us in a poetic way to confront our conception of God and relationship with God, it is now recited in Ashkenazi communities on Shabbat only. This is the time when we are in less of a rush, and have the head space to consider each word and its meaning for us.

The section that follows this, פִּטּוּם הַקְּטֹרֶת, is from the Talmud, and describes the ingredients of the incense that burned in the *Beit HaMikdash* every morning and evening on the smaller altar. Like all other texts that describe the service in the Temple, we consider this a substitute for the real thing, and long for a time when we will be able to reinstitute this service.

אֵין כֵּאלֹהֵינוּ, אֵין כַּאדוֹנֵינוּ, אֵין כְּמַלְכֵּנוּ, אֵין כְּמוֹשִׁיעֵנוּ.
מִי כֵאלֹהֵינוּ, מִי כַאדוֹנֵינוּ, מִי כְמַלְכֵּנוּ, מִי כְמוֹשִׁיעֵנוּ.
נוֹדֶה לֵאלֹהֵינוּ, נוֹדֶה לַאדוֹנֵינוּ, נוֹדֶה לְמַלְכֵּנוּ, נוֹדֶה לְמוֹשִׁיעֵנוּ.
בָּרוּךְ אֱלֹהֵינוּ, בָּרוּךְ אֲדוֹנֵינוּ, בָּרוּךְ מַלְכֵּנוּ, בָּרוּךְ מוֹשִׁיעֵנוּ.
אַתָּה הוּא אֱלֹהֵינוּ, אַתָּה הוּא אֲדוֹנֵינוּ,
אַתָּה הוּא מַלְכֵּנוּ, אַתָּה הוּא מוֹשִׁיעֵנוּ.
אַתָּה הוּא שֶׁהִקְטִירוּ אֲבוֹתֵינוּ לְפָנֶיךָ אֶת קְטֹרֶת הַסַּמִּים.

פִּטּוּם הַקְּטֹרֶת. הַצֳּרִי, וְהַצִּפֹּרֶן, וְהַחֶלְבְּנָה, וְהַלְּבוֹנָה מִשְׁקַל שִׁבְעִים שִׁבְעִים מָנֶה, מֹר, וּקְצִיעָה, שִׁבֹּלֶת נֵרְדְּ, וְכַרְכֹּם מִשְׁקַל שִׁשָּׁה עָשָׂר שִׁשָּׁה עָשָׂר מָנֶה, הַקֹּשְׁטְ שְׁנֵים עָשָׂר, קִלּוּפָה שְׁלֹשָׁה, וְקִנָּמוֹן תִּשְׁעָה, בֹּרִית כַּרְשִׁינָה תִּשְׁעָה קַבִּין, יֵין קַפְרִיסִין סְאִין תְּלָת וְקַבִּין תְּלָתָא, וְאִם אֵין לוֹ יֵין קַפְרִיסִין, מֵבִיא חֲמַר חִוַּרְיָן עַתִּיק. מֶלַח סְדוֹמִית רֹבַע, מַעֲלֶה עָשָׁן כָּל שֶׁהוּא. רַבִּי נָתָן הַבַּבְלִי אוֹמֵר: אַף כִּפַּת הַיַּרְדֵּן כָּל שֶׁהוּא, וְאִם נָתַן בָּהּ דְּבַשׁ פְּסָלָהּ, וְאִם חִסַּר אֶחָד מִכָּל סַמָּנֶיהָ, חַיָּב מִיתָה. כריתות ו.

REFLECTION

Close your eyes.

Clear your mind.

Think about your God.

What do you "see"?

How does God appear to you?

What role does God play in your life?

What would you like to say to your God, now, before the end of *tefilla* this Shabbat morning?

...A THOUSAND WORDS

Rabban Shimon ben Gamliel says: "Balsam" refers to the sap that drips from the balsam tree. The Carsina lye was used for bleaching the onycha to improve it. The Cyprus wine was used to soak the onycha in it to make it pungent. Though urine is suitable for this purpose, it is not brought into the Temple out of respect.

These were the psalms which the Levites used to recite in the Temple: *Mishna, Tamid 7*
On the first day of the week they used to say: "The earth is the LORD's *Ps. 24*
and all it contains, the world and all who live in it."
On the second day they used to say: "Great is the LORD and *Ps. 48*
greatly to be praised in the city of God, on His holy mountain."
On the third day they used to say: "God stands in the divine assembly. *Ps. 82*
Among the judges He delivers judgment."
On the fourth day they used to say: "God of retribution, LORD, *Ps. 94*
God of retribution, appear."
On the fifth day they used to say: "Sing for joy to God, our strength. *Ps. 81*
Shout aloud to the God of Jacob."
On the sixth day they used to say: "The LORD reigns: *Ps. 93*
He is robed in majesty; the LORD is robed, clothed with strength;
the world is firmly established; it cannot be moved."
On the Sabbath they used to say: "A psalm, a song for the Sabbath day" – *Ps. 92*
[meaning] a psalm and song for the time to come,
for the day which will be entirely Sabbath
and rest for life everlasting.

It was taught in the Academy of Elijah: Whoever studies [Torah] laws every day is assured that he will be destined for the World to Come, as it is said, "The ways of the world are His" – read not, "ways" [*halikhot*] but "laws" [*halakhot*]. *Megilla 28b* *Hab. 3*

Rabbi Elazar said in the name of Rabbi Ḥanina: The disciples of the sages increase peace in the world, as it is said, "And all your children shall be taught of the LORD, and great shall be the peace of your children [*banayikh*]." Read not *banayikh*, "your children," but *bonayikh*, "your builders." Those who love Your Torah have great peace; there is no stumbling block for them. May there be peace within your ramparts, prosperity in your palaces. For the sake of my brothers and friends, I shall say, "Peace be within you." For the sake of the House of the LORD our God, I will seek your good. ▸ May the LORD give strength to His people; may the LORD bless His people with peace. *Berakhot 64a* *Is. 54* *Ps. 119* *Ps. 122* *Ps. 29*

רַבָּן שִׁמְעוֹן בֶּן גַּמְלִיאֵל אוֹמֵר: הַצֳּרִי אֵינוֹ אֶלָּא שְׂרָף הַנּוֹטֵף מֵעֲצֵי הַקְּטָף. בֹּרִית כַּרְשִׁינָה שֶׁשָּׁפִין בָּהּ אֶת הַצִּפֹּרֶן כְּדֵי שֶׁתְּהֵא נָאָה, יֵין קַפְרִיסִין שֶׁשּׁוֹרִין בּוֹ אֶת הַצִּפֹּרֶן כְּדֵי שֶׁתְּהֵא עַזָּה, וַהֲלֹא מֵי רַגְלַיִם יָפִין לָהּ, אֶלָּא שֶׁאֵין מַכְנִיסִין מֵי רַגְלַיִם בַּמִּקְדָּשׁ מִפְּנֵי הַכָּבוֹד.

הַשִּׁיר שֶׁהַלְוִיִּם הָיוּ אוֹמְרִים בְּבֵית הַמִּקְדָּשׁ: משנה תמיד ז

בַּיּוֹם הָרִאשׁוֹן הָיוּ אוֹמְרִים

לַיהוה הָאָרֶץ וּמְלוֹאָהּ, תֵּבֵל וְיֹשְׁבֵי בָהּ: תהלים כד

בַּשֵּׁנִי הָיוּ אוֹמְרִים

גָּדוֹל יהוה וּמְהֻלָּל מְאֹד, בְּעִיר אֱלֹהֵינוּ הַר־קָדְשׁוֹ: תהלים מח

בַּשְּׁלִישִׁי הָיוּ אוֹמְרִים

אֱלֹהִים נִצָּב בַּעֲדַת־אֵל, בְּקֶרֶב אֱלֹהִים יִשְׁפֹּט: תהלים פב

בָּרְבִיעִי הָיוּ אוֹמְרִים

אֵל־נְקָמוֹת יהוה, אֵל נְקָמוֹת הוֹפִיעַ: תהלים צד

בַּחֲמִישִׁי הָיוּ אוֹמְרִים

הַרְנִינוּ לֵאלֹהִים עוּזֵּנוּ, הָרִיעוּ לֵאלֹהֵי יַעֲקֹב: תהלים פא

בַּשִּׁשִּׁי הָיוּ אוֹמְרִים

יהוה מָלָךְ גֵּאוּת לָבֵשׁ, לָבֵשׁ יהוה עֹז הִתְאַזָּר תהלים צג

אַף־תִּכּוֹן תֵּבֵל בַּל־תִּמּוֹט:

בַּשַּׁבָּת הָיוּ אוֹמְרִים

מִזְמוֹר שִׁיר לְיוֹם הַשַּׁבָּת: מִזְמוֹר שִׁיר לֶעָתִיד לָבוֹא תהלים צב

לְיוֹם שֶׁכֻּלּוֹ שַׁבָּת וּמְנוּחָה לְחַיֵּי הָעוֹלָמִים.

תָּנָא דְבֵי אֵלִיָּהוּ: כָּל הַשּׁוֹנֶה הֲלָכוֹת בְּכָל יוֹם, מֻבְטָח לוֹ שֶׁהוּא בֶּן עוֹלָם מגילה כח:
הַבָּא, שֶׁנֶּאֱמַר, הֲלִיכוֹת עוֹלָם לוֹ: אַל תִּקְרֵי הֲלִיכוֹת אֶלָּא הֲלָכוֹת. חבקוק ג

אָמַר רַבִּי אֶלְעָזָר, אָמַר רַבִּי חֲנִינָא: תַּלְמִידֵי חֲכָמִים מַרְבִּים שָׁלוֹם בָּעוֹלָם, ברכות סד.
שֶׁנֶּאֱמַר, וְכָל־בָּנַיִךְ לִמּוּדֵי יהוה, וְרַב שְׁלוֹם בָּנָיִךְ: אַל תִּקְרֵי בָּנָיִךְ, אֶלָּא ישעיה נד
בּוֹנָיִךְ. שָׁלוֹם רָב לְאֹהֲבֵי תוֹרָתֶךָ, וְאֵין־לָמוֹ מִכְשׁוֹל: יְהִי־שָׁלוֹם בְּחֵילֵךְ, תהלים קיט תהלים קכב
שַׁלְוָה בְּאַרְמְנוֹתָיִךְ: לְמַעַן אַחַי וְרֵעָי אֲדַבְּרָה־נָּא שָׁלוֹם בָּךְ: לְמַעַן בֵּית־יהוה
אֱלֹהֵינוּ אֲבַקְשָׁה טוֹב לָךְ: ◂ יהוה עֹז לְעַמּוֹ יִתֵּן, יהוה יְבָרֵךְ אֶת־עַמּוֹ בַשָּׁלוֹם: תהלים כט

THE RABBIS' KADDISH

The following prayer, said by mourners, requires the presence of a minyan. A transliteration can be found on page 1150.

Mourner: יִתְגַּדַּל Magnified and sanctified
may His great name be,
in the world He created by His will.
May He establish His kingdom
in your lifetime and in your days,
and in the lifetime of all the house of Israel,
swiftly and soon – and say: Amen.

All: May His great name be blessed for ever and all time.

Mourner: Blessed and praised, glorified and elevated,
raised and honored, uplifted and praised
be the name of the Holy One,
blessed be He,
beyond any blessing,
song, praise and consolation uttered in the world –
and say: Amen.

To Israel, to the teachers,
their disciples and their disciples' disciples,
and to all who engage in the study of Torah,
in this (*in Israel add:* holy) place or elsewhere,
may there come to them and you great peace,
grace, kindness and compassion, long life,
abundant sustenance and deliverance,
from their Father in Heaven –
and say: Amen.

May there be great peace from heaven,
and (good) life for us and all Israel –
and say: Amen.

Bow, take three steps back, as if taking leave of the Divine Presence, then bow, first left, then right, then center, while saying:

May He who makes peace in His high places,
in His compassion make peace for us and all Israel –
and say: Amen.

קדיש דרבנן

The following prayer, said by mourners, requires the presence of a מנין.
A transliteration can be found on page 1150.

אבל: יִתְגַּדַּל וְיִתְקַדַּשׁ שְׁמֵהּ רַבָּא (קהל: אָמֵן)
בְּעָלְמָא דִּי בְרָא כִרְעוּתֵהּ, וְיַמְלִיךְ מַלְכוּתֵהּ
בְּחַיֵּיכוֹן וּבְיוֹמֵיכוֹן וּבְחַיֵּי דְכָל בֵּית יִשְׂרָאֵל
בַּעֲגָלָא וּבִזְמַן קָרִיב, וְאִמְרוּ אָמֵן. (קהל: אָמֵן)

קהל ואבל: יְהֵא שְׁמֵהּ רַבָּא מְבָרַךְ לְעָלַם וּלְעָלְמֵי עָלְמַיָּא.

אבל: יִתְבָּרַךְ וְיִשְׁתַּבַּח וְיִתְפָּאַר וְיִתְרוֹמַם וְיִתְנַשֵּׂא
וְיִתְהַדָּר וְיִתְעַלֶּה וְיִתְהַלָּל
שְׁמֵהּ דְּקֻדְשָׁא בְּרִיךְ הוּא (קהל: בְּרִיךְ הוּא)
לְעֵלָּא מִן כָּל בִּרְכָתָא / בשבת שובה: לְעֵלָּא לְעֵלָּא מִכָּל בִּרְכָתָא/
וְשִׁירָתָא, תֻּשְׁבְּחָתָא וְנֶחֱמָתָא
דַּאֲמִירָן בְּעָלְמָא, וְאִמְרוּ אָמֵן. (קהל: אָמֵן)

עַל יִשְׂרָאֵל וְעַל רַבָּנָן
וְעַל תַּלְמִידֵיהוֹן וְעַל כָּל תַּלְמִידֵי תַלְמִידֵיהוֹן
וְעַל כָּל מָאן דְּעָסְקִין בְּאוֹרַיְתָא
דִּי בְאַתְרָא (בארץ ישראל: קַדִּישָׁא) הָדֵין, וְדִי בְכָל אֲתַר וַאֲתַר
יְהֵא לְהוֹן וּלְכוֹן שְׁלָמָא רַבָּא
חִנָּא וְחִסְדָּא, וְרַחֲמֵי, וְחַיֵּי אֲרִיכֵי, וּמְזוֹנֵי רְוִיחֵי
וּפֻרְקָנָא מִן קֳדָם אֲבוּהוֹן דִּי בִשְׁמַיָּא, וְאִמְרוּ אָמֵן. (קהל: אָמֵן)

יְהֵא שְׁלָמָא רַבָּא מִן שְׁמַיָּא
וְחַיִּים (טוֹבִים) עָלֵינוּ וְעַל כָּל יִשְׂרָאֵל, וְאִמְרוּ אָמֵן. (קהל: אָמֵן)

Bow, take three steps back, as if taking leave of the Divine Presence, then bow, first left, then right, then center, while saying:

עֹשֶׂה שָׁלוֹם/ בשבת שובה: הַשָּׁלוֹם/ בִּמְרוֹמָיו
הוּא יַעֲשֶׂה בְרַחֲמָיו שָׁלוֹם
עָלֵינוּ וְעַל כָּל יִשְׂרָאֵל, וְאִמְרוּ אָמֵן. (קהל: אָמֵן)

Stand while saying Aleinu.

עָלֵינוּ It is our duty to praise the Master of all,
and ascribe greatness to the Author of creation,
who has not made us like the nations of the lands
nor placed us like the families of the earth;
who has not made our portion like theirs,
nor our destiny like all their multitudes.
(For they worship vanity and emptiness,
and pray to a god who cannot save.)
But we bow in worship
and thank the Supreme King of kings, the Holy One, blessed be He,
who extends the heavens and establishes the earth,
whose throne of glory is in the heavens above,
and whose power's Presence is in the highest of heights.
He is our God; there is no other.
Truly He is our King, there is none else,
as it is written in His Torah:
"You shall know and take to heart this day that the LORD is God, *Deut. 4*
in heaven above and on earth below. There is no other."

Therefore, we place our hope in You, LORD our God,
that we may soon see the glory of Your power,
when You will remove abominations from the earth,
and idols will be utterly destroyed,
when the world will be perfected under the sovereignty of the Almighty,
when all humanity will call on Your name,
to turn all the earth's wicked toward You.
All the world's inhabitants will realize and know
that to You every knee must bow and every tongue swear loyalty.
Before You, LORD our God, they will kneel and bow down
and give honor to Your glorious name.
They will all accept the yoke of Your kingdom,
and You will reign over them soon and for ever.
For the kingdom is Yours,
and to all eternity You will reign in glory,
as it is written in Your Torah: "The LORD will reign for ever and ever." *Ex. 15*

Stand while saying עָלֵינוּ.

עָלֵינוּ לְשַׁבֵּחַ לַאֲדוֹן הַכֹּל, לָתֵת גְּדֻלָּה לְיוֹצֵר בְּרֵאשִׁית
שֶׁלֹּא עָשָׂנוּ כְּגוֹיֵי הָאֲרָצוֹת, וְלֹא שָׂמָנוּ כְּמִשְׁפְּחוֹת הָאֲדָמָה
שֶׁלֹּא שָׂם חֶלְקֵנוּ כָּהֶם וְגוֹרָלֵנוּ כְּכָל הֲמוֹנָם.
(שֶׁהֵם מִשְׁתַּחֲוִים לְהֶבֶל וָרִיק וּמִתְפַּלְלִים אֶל אֵל לֹא יוֹשִׁיעַ.)
וַאֲנַחְנוּ כּוֹרְעִים וּמִשְׁתַּחֲוִים וּמוֹדִים
לִפְנֵי מֶלֶךְ מַלְכֵי הַמְּלָכִים, הַקָּדוֹשׁ בָּרוּךְ הוּא
שֶׁהוּא נוֹטֶה שָׁמַיִם וְיוֹסֵד אָרֶץ
וּמוֹשַׁב יְקָרוֹ בַּשָּׁמַיִם מִמַּעַל, וּשְׁכִינַת עֻזּוֹ בְּגָבְהֵי מְרוֹמִים.
הוּא אֱלֹהֵינוּ, אֵין עוֹד.
אֱמֶת מַלְכֵּנוּ, אֶפֶס זוּלָתוֹ, כַּכָּתוּב בְּתוֹרָתוֹ
וְיָדַעְתָּ הַיּוֹם וַהֲשֵׁבֹתָ אֶל־לְבָבֶךָ דברים ד
כִּי יהוה הוּא הָאֱלֹהִים בַּשָּׁמַיִם מִמַּעַל וְעַל־הָאָרֶץ מִתָּחַת
אֵין עוֹד:

עַל כֵּן נְקַוֶּה לְּךָ יהוה אֱלֹהֵינוּ, לִרְאוֹת מְהֵרָה בְּתִפְאֶרֶת עֻזֶּךָ
לְהַעֲבִיר גִּלּוּלִים מִן הָאָרֶץ, וְהָאֱלִילִים כָּרוֹת יִכָּרֵתוּן
לְתַקֵּן עוֹלָם בְּמַלְכוּת שַׁדַּי.
וְכָל בְּנֵי בָשָׂר יִקְרְאוּ בִשְׁמֶךָ לְהַפְנוֹת אֵלֶיךָ כָּל רִשְׁעֵי אָרֶץ.
יַכִּירוּ וְיֵדְעוּ כָּל יוֹשְׁבֵי תֵבֵל
כִּי לְךָ תִּכְרַע כָּל בֶּרֶךְ, תִּשָּׁבַע כָּל לָשׁוֹן.
לְפָנֶיךָ יהוה אֱלֹהֵינוּ יִכְרְעוּ וְיִפֹּלוּ, וְלִכְבוֹד שִׁמְךָ יְקָר יִתֵּנוּ
וִיקַבְּלוּ כֻלָּם אֶת עֹל מַלְכוּתֶךָ
וְתִמְלֹךְ עֲלֵיהֶם מְהֵרָה לְעוֹלָם וָעֶד.
כִּי הַמַּלְכוּת שֶׁלְּךָ הִיא וּלְעוֹלְמֵי עַד תִּמְלֹךְ בְּכָבוֹד
כַּכָּתוּב בְּתוֹרָתֶךָ, יהוה יִמְלֹךְ לְעֹלָם וָעֶד: שמות טו

▸ And it is said: "Then the LORD shall be King over all the earth; *Zech. 14*
on that day the LORD shall be One and His name One."

Some add:

Have no fear of sudden terror or of the ruin when it overtakes the wicked. *Prov. 3*
Devise your strategy, but it will be defeated; *Is. 8*
propose your plan, but it will not stand, for God is with us.
When you grow old, I will still be the same. *Is. 46*
When your hair turns gray, I will still carry you.
I made you, I will bear you, I will carry you, and I will rescue you.

MOURNER'S KADDISH

The following prayer, said by mourners, requires the presence of a minyan.
A transliteration can be found on page 1151.

Mourner: יִתְגַּדַּל Magnified and sanctified may His great name be,
in the world He created by His will.
May He establish His kingdom
in your lifetime and in your days,
and in the lifetime of all the house of Israel,
swiftly and soon –
and say: Amen.

All: May His great name be blessed for ever and all time.

Mourner: Blessed and praised, glorified and elevated,
raised and honored, uplifted and praised
be the name of the Holy One, blessed be He,
beyond any blessing,
song, praise and consolation
uttered in the world –
and say: Amen.

May there be great peace from heaven,
and life for us and all Israel –
and say: Amen.

Bow, take three steps back, as if taking leave of the Divine Presence,
then bow, first left, then right, then center, while saying:

May He who makes peace in His high places,
make peace for us and all Israel –
and say: Amen.

◂ וְנֶאֱמַר, וְהָיָה יהוה לְמֶלֶךְ עַל־כָּל־הָאָרֶץ זכריה יד
בַּיּוֹם הַהוּא יִהְיֶה יהוה אֶחָד וּשְׁמוֹ אֶחָד:

Some add:

אַל־תִּירָא מִפַּחַד פִּתְאֹם וּמִשֹּׁאַת רְשָׁעִים כִּי תָבֹא: משלי ג
עֻצוּ עֵצָה וְתֻפָר, דַּבְּרוּ דָבָר וְלֹא יָקוּם, כִּי עִמָּנוּ אֵל: ישעיה ח
וְעַד־זִקְנָה אֲנִי הוּא, וְעַד־שֵׂיבָה אֲנִי אֶסְבֹּל, אֲנִי עָשִׂיתִי וַאֲנִי אֶשָּׂא וַאֲנִי אֶסְבֹּל וַאֲמַלֵּט: ישעיה מו

קדיש יתום

The following prayer, said by mourners, requires the presence of a מנין*.*
A transliteration can be found on page 1151.

אבל: יִתְגַּדַּל וְיִתְקַדַּשׁ שְׁמֵהּ רַבָּא (קהל: אָמֵן)
בְּעָלְמָא דִּי בְרָא כִרְעוּתֵהּ
וְיַמְלִיךְ מַלְכוּתֵהּ
בְּחַיֵּיכוֹן וּבְיוֹמֵיכוֹן וּבְחַיֵּי דְכָל בֵּית יִשְׂרָאֵל
בַּעֲגָלָא וּבִזְמַן קָרִיב, וְאִמְרוּ אָמֵן. (קהל: אָמֵן)

קהל ואבל: יְהֵא שְׁמֵהּ רַבָּא מְבָרַךְ לְעָלַם וּלְעָלְמֵי עָלְמַיָּא.

אבל: יִתְבָּרַךְ וְיִשְׁתַּבַּח וְיִתְפָּאַר
וְיִתְרוֹמַם וְיִתְנַשֵּׂא וְיִתְהַדָּר וְיִתְעַלֶּה וְיִתְהַלָּל
שְׁמֵהּ דְּקֻדְשָׁא בְּרִיךְ הוּא (קהל: בְּרִיךְ הוּא)
לְעֵלָּא מִן כָּל בִּרְכָתָא / בשבת שובה: לְעֵלָּא לְעֵלָּא מִכָּל בִּרְכָתָא/
וְשִׁירָתָא, תֻּשְׁבְּחָתָא וְנֶחֱמָתָא
דַּאֲמִירָן בְּעָלְמָא, וְאִמְרוּ אָמֵן. (קהל: אָמֵן)

יְהֵא שְׁלָמָא רַבָּא מִן שְׁמַיָּא
וְחַיִּים, עָלֵינוּ וְעַל כָּל יִשְׂרָאֵל, וְאִמְרוּ אָמֵן. (קהל: אָמֵן)

Bow, take three steps back, as if taking leave of the Divine Presence, then bow, first left, then right, then center, while saying:

עֹשֶׂה שָׁלוֹם/ בשבת שובה: הַשָּׁלוֹם/ בִּמְרוֹמָיו, הוּא יַעֲשֶׂה שָׁלוֹם
עָלֵינוּ וְעַל כָּל יִשְׂרָאֵל, וְאִמְרוּ אָמֵן. (קהל: אָמֵן)

On Shabbat continue with the Daily Psalm below.
Many congregations say the Daily Psalm after the Song of Glory, page 712.
(*In Israel on Shabbat Rosh Ḥodesh, some say Barekhi Nafshi, page 772, as the Daily Psalm.*)

Today is the holy Sabbath,
on which the Levites used to say this psalm in the Temple:

מִזְמוֹר A psalm. A song for the Sabbath day. It is good to thank the LORD *Ps. 92*
and sing psalms to Your name, Most High – to tell of Your loving-kindness in the morning and Your trustworthiness at night, to the music of the ten-stringed lyre and the melody of the harp. For You have made me rejoice by Your work, O LORD; I sing for joy at the deeds of Your hands. How great are Your deeds, LORD, and how very deep Your thoughts. A boor cannot know, nor can a fool understand, that though the wicked spring up like grass and all evildoers flourish, it is only that they may be destroyed for ever. But You, LORD, are eternally elevated. For behold Your enemies, LORD, behold Your enemies will perish; all evildoers will be scattered. You have raised my pride like that of a wild ox; I am anointed with fresh oil. My eyes shall look in triumph on my enemies; my ears shall hear the downfall of the wicked who rise against me. The righteous will flourish like a palm tree and grow tall like a cedar in Lebanon. Planted in the LORD's House, blossoming in our God's courtyards, ▸ they will still bear fruit in old age, and stay vigorous and fresh, declaring that the LORD is upright: He is my Rock, in whom there is no wrong.

Mourner's Kaddish (*on the next page*)

On Rosh Ḥodesh, say Barekhi Nafshi on page 772 followed by Mourner's Kaddish.
On Ḥanukka, many congregations add Psalm 30 on page 528 followed by Mourner's Kaddish.

From the second day of Rosh Ḥodesh Elul through Shemini Atzeret
(*in Israel through Hoshana Raba*), *the following psalm is said:*

לְדָוִד A psalm of David. The LORD is my light and my salvation – whom *Ps. 27*
then shall I fear? The LORD is the stronghold of my life – of whom shall I be afraid? When evil men close in on me to devour my flesh, it is they, my enemies and foes, who stumble and fall. Should an army besiege me, my heart would not fear. Should war break out against me, still I would be confident. One thing I ask of the LORD, only this do I seek: to live in the House of the LORD all the days of my life, to gaze on the beauty of the LORD and worship in His Temple. For He will keep me safe in His pavilion on the day of trouble. He will hide me under the cover of His tent. He will set me high upon a rock. Now my head is high above my enemies who surround me. I will sacrifice in His tent with shouts of joy. I will sing and chant praises to the

On שבת *continue with the* שיר של יום *below.*
Many congregations say the שיר של יום *after the* שיר הכבוד, *page 713.*
(*In* ארץ ישראל *on* שבת ראש חודש, *some say* בָּרְכִי נַפְשִׁי, *page 773, as the* שיר של יום.)

הַיּוֹם יוֹם שַׁבַּת קֹדֶשׁ, שֶׁבּוֹ הָיוּ הַלְוִיִּם אוֹמְרִים בְּבֵית הַמִּקְדָּשׁ:

מִזְמוֹר שִׁיר לְיוֹם הַשַּׁבָּת: טוֹב לְהֹדוֹת לַיהוה, וּלְזַמֵּר לְשִׁמְךָ עֶלְיוֹן: תהלים צב
לְהַגִּיד בַּבֹּקֶר חַסְדֶּךָ, וֶאֱמוּנָתְךָ בַּלֵּילוֹת: עֲלֵי־עָשׂוֹר וַעֲלֵי־נָבֶל, עֲלֵי
הִגָּיוֹן בְּכִנּוֹר: כִּי שִׂמַּחְתַּנִי יהוה בְּפָעֳלֶךָ, בְּמַעֲשֵׂי יָדֶיךָ אֲרַנֵּן: מַה־גָּדְלוּ
מַעֲשֶׂיךָ יהוה, מְאֹד עָמְקוּ מַחְשְׁבֹתֶיךָ: אִישׁ־בַּעַר לֹא יֵדָע, וּכְסִיל
לֹא־יָבִין אֶת־זֹאת: בִּפְרֹחַ רְשָׁעִים כְּמוֹ־עֵשֶׂב, וַיָּצִיצוּ כָּל־פֹּעֲלֵי אָוֶן,
לְהִשָּׁמְדָם עֲדֵי־עַד: וְאַתָּה מָרוֹם לְעֹלָם יהוה: כִּי הִנֵּה אֹיְבֶיךָ יהוה,
כִּי־הִנֵּה אֹיְבֶיךָ יֹאבֵדוּ, יִתְפָּרְדוּ כָּל־פֹּעֲלֵי אָוֶן: וַתָּרֶם כִּרְאֵים קַרְנִי,
בַּלֹּתִי בְּשֶׁמֶן רַעֲנָן: וַתַּבֵּט עֵינִי בְּשׁוּרָי, בַּקָּמִים עָלַי מְרֵעִים תִּשְׁמַעְנָה
אָזְנָי: צַדִּיק כַּתָּמָר יִפְרָח, כְּאֶרֶז בַּלְּבָנוֹן יִשְׂגֶּה: שְׁתוּלִים בְּבֵית יהוה,
בְּחַצְרוֹת אֱלֹהֵינוּ יַפְרִיחוּ: › עוֹד יְנוּבוּן בְּשֵׂיבָה, דְּשֵׁנִים וְרַעֲנַנִּים יִהְיוּ:
לְהַגִּיד כִּי־יָשָׁר יהוה, צוּרִי, וְלֹא־עַוְלָתָה בּוֹ:

קדיש יתום (*on the next page*)

On ראש חודש, *say* בָּרְכִי נַפְשִׁי *on page 773 followed by* קדיש יתום.
On חנוכה, *many congregations add* מִזְמוֹר שִׁיר־חֲנֻכַּת הַבַּיִת *page 529 followed by* קדיש יתום.

From the second day of ראש חודש אלול *through* שמיני עצרת
(*in* ארץ ישראל *through* הושענא רבה), *the following psalm is said:*

לְדָוִד, יהוה אוֹרִי וְיִשְׁעִי, מִמִּי אִירָא, יהוה מָעוֹז־חַיַּי, מִמִּי אֶפְחָד: תהלים כז
בִּקְרֹב עָלַי מְרֵעִים לֶאֱכֹל אֶת־בְּשָׂרִי, צָרַי וְאֹיְבַי לִי, הֵמָּה כָשְׁלוּ
וְנָפָלוּ: אִם־תַּחֲנֶה עָלַי מַחֲנֶה, לֹא־יִירָא לִבִּי, אִם־תָּקוּם עָלַי מִלְחָמָה,
בְּזֹאת אֲנִי בוֹטֵחַ: אַחַת שָׁאַלְתִּי מֵאֵת־יהוה, אוֹתָהּ אֲבַקֵּשׁ, שִׁבְתִּי
בְּבֵית־יהוה כָּל־יְמֵי חַיַּי, לַחֲזוֹת בְּנֹעַם־יהוה, וּלְבַקֵּר בְּהֵיכָלוֹ: כִּי
יִצְפְּנֵנִי בְּסֻכֹּה בְּיוֹם רָעָה, יַסְתִּרֵנִי בְּסֵתֶר אָהֳלוֹ, בְּצוּר יְרוֹמְמֵנִי:
וְעַתָּה יָרוּם רֹאשִׁי עַל אֹיְבַי סְבִיבוֹתַי, וְאֶזְבְּחָה בְאָהֳלוֹ זִבְחֵי תְרוּעָה,
אָשִׁירָה וַאֲזַמְּרָה לַיהוה: שְׁמַע־יהוה קוֹלִי אֶקְרָא, וְחָנֵּנִי וַעֲנֵנִי: לְךָ

Lord. Lord, hear my voice when I call. Be gracious to me and answer me. On Your behalf my heart says, "Seek My face." Your face, Lord, will I seek. Do not hide Your face from me. Do not turn Your servant away in anger. You have been my help. Do not reject or abandon me, God, my Savior. Were my father and my mother to abandon me, the Lord would take me in. Teach me Your way, Lord, and lead me on a level path, because of my oppressors. Do not abandon me to the will of my enemies, for false witnesses have risen against me, breathing violence. ▸ Were it not for my faith that I shall see the Lord's goodness in the land of the living. Hope in the Lord. Be strong and of good courage, and hope in the Lord!

MOURNER'S KADDISH

The following prayer, said by mourners, requires the presence of a minyan.
A transliteration can be found on page 1151.

Mourner: יִתְגַּדַּל Magnified and sanctified may His great name be,
in the world He created by His will.
May He establish His kingdom
in your lifetime and in your days,
and in the lifetime of all the house of Israel,
swiftly and soon –
and say: Amen.

All: May His great name be blessed for ever and all time.

Mourner: Blessed and praised, glorified and elevated,
raised and honored, uplifted and praised
be the name of the Holy One, blessed be He,
beyond any blessing, song, praise and consolation
uttered in the world –
and say: Amen.

May there be great peace from heaven,
and life for us and all Israel –
and say: Amen.

Bow, take three steps back, as if taking leave of the Divine Presence,
then bow, first left, then right, then center, while saying:

May He who makes peace in His high places,
make peace for us and all Israel –
and say: Amen.

אָמַר לִבִּי בַּקְּשׁוּ פָנָי, אֶת־פָּנֶיךָ יהוה אֲבַקֵּשׁ: אַל־תַּסְתֵּר פָּנֶיךָ מִמֶּנִּי, אַל תַּט־בְּאַף עַבְדֶּךָ, עֶזְרָתִי הָיִיתָ, אַל־תִּטְּשֵׁנִי וְאַל־תַּעַזְבֵנִי, אֱלֹהֵי יִשְׁעִי: כִּי־אָבִי וְאִמִּי עֲזָבוּנִי, וַיהוה יַאַסְפֵנִי: הוֹרֵנִי יהוה דַּרְכֶּךָ, וּנְחֵנִי בְּאֹרַח מִישׁוֹר, לְמַעַן שׁוֹרְרָי: אַל־תִּתְּנֵנִי בְּנֶפֶשׁ צָרָי, כִּי קָמוּ־בִי עֵדֵי־שֶׁקֶר, וִיפֵחַ חָמָס: ‹ לוּלֵא הֶאֱמַנְתִּי לִרְאוֹת בְּטוּב־יהוה בְּאֶרֶץ חַיִּים: קַוֵּה אֶל־יהוה, חֲזַק וְיַאֲמֵץ לִבֶּךָ, וְקַוֵּה אֶל־יהוה:

קדיש יתום

The following prayer, said by mourners, requires the presence of a מנין.
A transliteration can be found on page 1151.

אבל: יִתְגַּדַּל וְיִתְקַדַּשׁ שְׁמֵהּ רַבָּא (קהל: אָמֵן)
בְּעָלְמָא דִּי בְרָא כִרְעוּתֵהּ, וְיַמְלִיךְ מַלְכוּתֵהּ
בְּחַיֵּיכוֹן וּבְיוֹמֵיכוֹן וּבְחַיֵּי דְכָל בֵּית יִשְׂרָאֵל
בַּעֲגָלָא וּבִזְמַן קָרִיב, וְאִמְרוּ אָמֵן. (קהל: אָמֵן)

קהל ואבל: יְהֵא שְׁמֵהּ רַבָּא מְבָרַךְ לְעָלַם וּלְעָלְמֵי עָלְמַיָּא.

אבל: יִתְבָּרַךְ וְיִשְׁתַּבַּח וְיִתְפָּאַר
וְיִתְרוֹמַם וְיִתְנַשֵּׂא וְיִתְהַדָּר וְיִתְעַלֶּה וְיִתְהַלָּל
שְׁמֵהּ דְּקֻדְשָׁא בְּרִיךְ הוּא (קהל: בְּרִיךְ הוּא)
לְעֵלָּא מִן כָּל בִּרְכָתָא / בשבת שובה: לְעֵלָּא לְעֵלָּא מִכָּל בִּרְכָתָא/
וְשִׁירָתָא, תֻּשְׁבְּחָתָא וְנֶחֱמָתָא
דַּאֲמִירָן בְּעָלְמָא, וְאִמְרוּ אָמֵן. (קהל: אָמֵן)

יְהֵא שְׁלָמָא רַבָּא מִן שְׁמַיָּא
וְחַיִּים, עָלֵינוּ וְעַל כָּל יִשְׂרָאֵל, וְאִמְרוּ אָמֵן. (קהל: אָמֵן)

Bow, take three steps back, as if taking leave of the Divine Presence, then bow, first left, then right, then center, while saying:

עֹשֶׂה שָׁלוֹם/ בשבת שובה: הַשָּׁלוֹם/ בִּמְרוֹמָיו, הוּא יַעֲשֶׂה שָׁלוֹם
עָלֵינוּ וְעַל כָּל יִשְׂרָאֵל, וְאִמְרוּ אָמֵן. (קהל: אָמֵן)

SONG OF GLORY

The Ark is opened and all stand.

Leader: I will sing sweet psalms and I will weave songs,
to You for whom my soul longs.

Cong: My soul yearns for the shelter of Your hand,
that all Your mystic secrets I might understand.

Leader: Whenever I speak of Your glory above,
my heart is yearning for Your love.

Cong: So Your glories I will declare,
and in songs of love give honor to Your name.

Leader: I will tell of Your glory though I have not seen You,
imagine and describe You,
though I have not known You.

Cong: By the hand of Your prophets,
through Your servants' mystery,
You gave a glimpse of Your wondrous majesty.

Leader: Recounting Your greatness and Your glory,
of Your great deeds they told the story.

Cong: They depicted You, though not as You are,
but as You do: Your acts, Your power.

Leader: They represented You in many visions;
through them all
You are One without divisions.

Cong: They saw You, now old, then young,
Your head with gray, with black hair hung.

Leader: Aged on the day of judgment,
yet on the day of war,
a young warrior with mighty hands they saw.

Cong: Triumph like a helmet He wore on his head;
His right hand and holy arm to victory have led.

שיר הכבוד

The ארון קודש *is opened and all stand.*

ש״ץ: אַנְעִים זְמִירוֹת וְשִׁירִים אֶאֱרֹג, כִּי אֵלֶיךָ נַפְשִׁי תַעֲרֹג.
קהל: נַפְשִׁי חָמְדָה בְּצֵל יָדֶךָ, לָדַעַת כָּל רָז סוֹדֶךָ.

ש״ץ: מִדֵּי דַבְּרִי בִּכְבוֹדֶךָ, הוֹמֶה לִבִּי אֶל דּוֹדֶיךָ.
קהל: עַל כֵּן אֲדַבֵּר בְּךָ נִכְבָּדוֹת, וְשִׁמְךָ אֲכַבֵּד בְּשִׁירֵי יְדִידוֹת.

ש״ץ: אֲסַפְּרָה כְבוֹדְךָ וְלֹא רְאִיתִיךָ, אֲדַמְּךָ אֲכַנְּךָ וְלֹא יְדַעְתִּיךָ.
קהל: בְּיַד נְבִיאֶיךָ בְּסוֹד עֲבָדֶיךָ, דִּמִּיתָ הֲדַר כְּבוֹד הוֹדֶךָ.

ש״ץ: גְּדֻלָּתְךָ וּגְבוּרָתֶךָ, כִּנּוּ לְתֹקֶף פְּעֻלָּתֶךָ.
קהל: דִּמּוּ אוֹתְךָ וְלֹא כְּפִי יֶשְׁךָ, וַיְשַׁוּוּךָ לְפִי מַעֲשֶׂיךָ.

ש״ץ: הִמְשִׁילוּךָ בְּרֹב חֶזְיוֹנוֹת, הִנְּךָ אֶחָד בְּכָל דִּמְיוֹנוֹת.
קהל: וַיֶּחֱזוּ בְךָ זִקְנָה וּבַחֲרוּת, וּשְׂעַר רֹאשְׁךָ בְּשֵׂיבָה וְשַׁחֲרוּת.

ש״ץ: זִקְנָה בְּיוֹם דִּין וּבַחֲרוּת בְּיוֹם קְרָב, כְּאִישׁ מִלְחָמוֹת יָדָיו לוֹ רָב.
קהל: חָבַשׁ כּוֹבַע יְשׁוּעָה בְּרֹאשׁוֹ, הוֹשִׁיעָה לּוֹ יְמִינוֹ וּזְרוֹעַ קָדְשׁוֹ.

LEARNING

This prayer explores how limited words are to describe the greatness of God. Yet that is all we have. Mere words. Although in some communities it is said every day, many authorities believe it is too sublime and holy to be said every day, and therefore limited its recitation to Shabbat and Yom Tov, holy days when we have more time to contemplate the abstract and holy ideas contained in the *tefilla*. It has become a widespread custom to have a pre-Bar Mitzva boy to sing the *tefilla*. We are only prepared to entrust the saying of this awe-inspiring *tefilla* to the pure innocence of a young child.

Leader: His curls are filled with dew drops of light,
His locks with fragments of the night.

Cong: He will glory in me, for He delights in me;
My diadem of beauty He shall be.

Leader: His head is like pure beaten gold;
Engraved on His brow, His sacred name behold.

Cong: For grace and glory, beauty and fame,
His people have adorned Him with a crown.

Leader: Like a youth's, His hair in locks unfurls;
Its black tresses flowing in curls.

Cong: Jerusalem, His splendor, is the dwelling place of right;
may He prize it as His highest delight.

Leader: Like a crown in His hand may His treasured people be,
a turban of beauty and of majesty.

Cong: He bore them, carried them, with a crown He adorned them.
They were precious in His sight, and He honored them.

Leader: His glory is on me; my glory is on Him.
He is near to me when I call to Him.

Cong: He is bright and rosy; red will be His dress,
when He comes from Edom, treading the winepress.

Leader: He showed the tefillin-knot to Moses, humble, wise,
when the LORD's likeness was before his eyes.

Cong: He delights in His people; the humble He does raise –
He glories in them; He sits enthroned upon their praise.

CONNECTION

*"The Talmud (*Shabbat 118b*) says that if the Jews were to observe Shabbat twice in a row, the* geula *(redemption) would come immediately. If we could observe Shabbat as it should be, the* geula *would come because there would be no need for* geula. *That would be* geula. *That would be redemption. That would be the messianic time."* (Elie Wiesel)

ש״ץ: טַלְלֵי אוֹרוֹת רֹאשׁוֹ נִמְלָא, קְוֻצּוֹתָיו רְסִיסֵי לָיְלָה.
קהל: יִתְפָּאֵר בִּי כִּי חָפֵץ בִּי, וְהוּא יִהְיֶה לִּי לַעֲטֶרֶת צְבִי.

ש״ץ: כֶּתֶם טָהוֹר פָּז דְּמוּת רֹאשׁוֹ, וְחַק עַל מֵצַח כְּבוֹד שֵׁם קָדְשׁוֹ.
קהל: לְחֵן וּלְכָבוֹד צְבִי תִפְאָרָה, אֻמָּתוֹ לוֹ עִטְּרָה עֲטָרָה.

ש״ץ: מַחְלְפוֹת רֹאשׁוֹ כְּבִימֵי בְחוּרוֹת, קְוֻצּוֹתָיו תַּלְתַּלִּים שְׁחוֹרוֹת.
קהל: נְוֵה הַצֶּדֶק צְבִי תִפְאַרְתּוֹ, יַעֲלֶה נָּא עַל רֹאשׁ שִׂמְחָתוֹ.

ש״ץ: סְגֻלָּתוֹ תְּהִי בְיָדוֹ עֲטֶרֶת, וּצְנִיף מְלוּכָה צְבִי תִפְאֶרֶת.
קהל: עֲמוּסִים נְשָׂאָם, עֲטֶרֶת עִנְּדָם, מֵאֲשֶׁר יָקְרוּ בְעֵינָיו כִּבְּדָם.

ש״ץ: פְּאֵרוֹ עָלַי וּפְאֵרִי עָלָיו, וְקָרוֹב אֵלַי בְּקָרְאִי אֵלָיו.
קהל: צַח וְאָדֹם לִלְבוּשׁוֹ אָדֹם, פּוּרָה בְדָרְכוֹ בְּבוֹאוֹ מֵאֱדוֹם.

ש״ץ: קֶשֶׁר תְּפִלִּין הֶרְאָה לֶעָנָו, תְּמוּנַת יהוה לְנֶגֶד עֵינָיו.
קהל: רוֹצֶה בְעַמּוֹ עֲנָוִים יְפָאֵר, יוֹשֵׁב תְּהִלּוֹת בָּם לְהִתְפָּאֵר.

REFLECTION

Are you sometimes
lost for words?

Do you sometimes
struggle to find
the right words
even though you know
in your heart
what it is you want to say?

If you had the words,
and you were standing
in front of God,
what would you say?

... A THOUSAND WORDS

Leader: Your first word, Your call to every age, is true:
O seek the people who seek You.

Cong: My many songs please take and hear
and may my hymn of joy to You come near.

Leader: May my praise be a crown for Your head,
and like incense before You, the prayers I have said.

Cong: May a poor man's song be precious in Your eyes,
like a song sung over sacrifice.

Leader: To the One who sustains all,
may my blessing take flight:
Creator, Life-Giver, God of right and might.

Cong: And when I offer blessing, to me Your head incline:
accepting it as spice, fragrant and fine.

Leader: May my prayer be to You sweet song.
For You my soul will always long.

The Ark is closed.

Yours, LORD, are the greatness and the power, *1 Chr. 29*
the glory, the majesty and splendor,
for everything in heaven and earth is Yours.
Yours, LORD, is the kingdom;
You are elevated as Head over all.
▸ Who can tell of the mighty acts of the LORD *Ps. 106*
and make all His praise be heard?

Mourner's Kaddish (page 710)

---

the depths of his heart, "My soul wishes to rest in the shade of Your hands, to know all the secrets of all Your enigmas." He was so overcome with yearning for the state that he had been in during this holiest day, that he tried to extend it for a little bit longer, and before he knew it, it was the next day and, his eyes still shut tight, he had not returned home and had not yet broken his fast!

ש״ץ: רֹאשׁ דְּבָרְךָ אֱמֶת קוֹרֵא מֵרֹאשׁ דּוֹר וָדוֹר, עַם דּוֹרֶשְׁךָ דְּרֹשׁ.

קהל: שִׁית הֲמוֹן שִׁירַי נָא עָלֶיךָ, וְרִנָּתִי תִּקְרַב אֵלֶיךָ.

ש״ץ: תְּהִלָּתִי תְּהִי לְרֹאשְׁךָ עֲטֶרֶת, וּתְפִלָּתִי תִּכּוֹן קְטֹרֶת.

קהל: תִּיקַר שִׁירַת רָשׁ בְּעֵינֶיךָ, כַּשִּׁיר יוּשַׁר עַל קָרְבָּנֶיךָ.

ש״ץ: בִּרְכָתִי תַעֲלֶה לְרֹאשׁ מַשְׁבִּיר, מְחוֹלֵל וּמוֹלִיד, צַדִּיק כַּבִּיר.

קהל: וּבְבִרְכָתִי תְנַעֲנַע לִי רֹאשׁ, וְאוֹתָהּ קַח לְךָ כִּבְשָׂמִים רֹאשׁ.

ש״ץ: יֶעֱרַב נָא שִׂיחִי עָלֶיךָ, כִּי נַפְשִׁי תַעֲרֹג אֵלֶיךָ.

The ארון קודש *is closed.*

לְךָ יהוה הַגְּדֻלָּה וְהַגְּבוּרָה וְהַתִּפְאֶרֶת וְהַנֵּצַח וְהַהוֹד דברי הימים א׳ כט
כִּי־כֹל בַּשָּׁמַיִם וּבָאָרֶץ
לְךָ יהוה הַמַּמְלָכָה וְהַמִּתְנַשֵּׂא לְכֹל לְרֹאשׁ:
◂ מִי יְמַלֵּל גְּבוּרוֹת יהוה תהלים קו
יַשְׁמִיעַ כָּל־תְּהִלָּתוֹ:

קדיש יתום (*page 711*)

CONNECTION

The Lubavitcher Rebbe taught a niggun *(Hasidic melody without words) on Simḥat Torah of 1961 (5722). He told his Hasidim there the story of a shtetl, the day after Yom Kippur, when the townspeople came to shul and found a Hasid, still dressed in a white* kittel *and wrapped in his tallit. His eyes were closed tight with joy and pain on his face, as he walked around and around the* bima*, tears streaming from his closed eyes, singing the words to the* Shir HaKavod *(Anim Zemirot). He had spent the entire Yom Kippur in such a lofty spiritual state, completely immersed in "cleaving and yearning" to Hashem, that he had become similar to an angel, singing, from*

Lord of the universe,
who reigned before the birth of any thing –

When by His will all things were made
then was His name declared King.

And when all things shall cease to be
He alone will reign in awe.

He was, He is, and He shall be
glorious for evermore.

He is One, there is none else,
alone, unique, beyond compare;

Without beginning, without end,
His might, His rule are everywhere.

He is my God; my Redeemer lives.
He is the Rock on whom I rely –

My banner and my safe retreat,
my cup, my portion when I cry.

Into His hand my soul I place,
when I awake and when I sleep.

The Lord is with me, I shall not fear;
body and soul from harm will He keep.

אֲדוֹן עוֹלָם

אֲשֶׁר מָלַךְ בְּטֶרֶם כָּל־יְצִיר נִבְרָא.

לְעֵת נַעֲשָׂה בְחֶפְצוֹ כֹּל אֲזַי מֶלֶךְ שְׁמוֹ נִקְרָא.

וְאַחֲרֵי כִּכְלוֹת הַכֹּל לְבַדּוֹ יִמְלֹךְ נוֹרָא.

וְהוּא הָיָה וְהוּא הֹוֶה וְהוּא יִהְיֶה בְּתִפְאָרָה.

וְהוּא אֶחָד וְאֵין שֵׁנִי לְהַמְשִׁיל לוֹ לְהַחְבִּירָה.

בְּלִי רֵאשִׁית בְּלִי תַכְלִית וְלוֹ הָעֹז וְהַמִּשְׂרָה.

וְהוּא אֵלִי וְחַי גּוֹאֲלִי וְצוּר חֶבְלִי בְּעֵת צָרָה.

וְהוּא נִסִּי וּמָנוֹס לִי מְנָת כּוֹסִי בְּיוֹם אֶקְרָא.

בְּיָדוֹ אַפְקִיד רוּחִי בְּעֵת אִישַׁן וְאָעִירָה.

וְעִם רוּחִי גְּוִיָּתִי יהוה לִי וְלֹא אִירָא.

Kiddush and Zemirot for Shabbat Morning

Some say:

אַתְקִינוּ Prepare the feast of perfect faith, joy of the holy King. Prepare the royal feast, this is the feast [mystically known as] "the Holy Ancient One" – and "the Small Face" and "the Field of Holy Apples" [mystical terms for aspects of the Divine] come to partake in the feast with it.

אֲסַדֵּר I will prepare the Sabbath morning feast, and invite to it "the Holy Ancient One." May His radiance shine on it, on the great Kiddush and goodly wine that gladdens the soul. May He send us His splendor; may we see His glory; may He reveal to us His whispered secrets. May He disclose to us the reason for the twelve loaves of bread, which are [the twelve combinations of the letters of] His name, and [the twelve sons of Jacob] the youngest patriarch. May we be united with the One above, who gives life to all; may our strength increase and [our prayers] reach [God's] head. Laborers in the field [of Torah] rejoice with speech and voice, speaking words sweet as honey. Before the Master of the Universe, reveal the meaning of, and give new interpretations to, matters veiled in mystery. To adorn the table with precious secrets, deep, esoteric, not widely to be shared. These words become sky; new heavens, and the sun then is the same. He will be lifted to a higher level, and [God] will take [Israel], from whom He had been separated, as His bride.

חַי יהוה The Lord lives; my Rock is blessed. My soul glories in the Lord.
For the Lord gives light to my lamp; His radiance shines on my head.
The Lord is my Shepherd, I shall not want. He leads me beside the still waters.
He gives food to all flesh; He feeds me my daily bread.
May it be Your will, You, my holy God,
To prepare a table before me, to anoint my head with oil.
Who will lay my rest before the Lord of peace,
and grant that my children stay faithful, [blessed with] life and peace?
May He send His angel before me, to accompany me on the way.
I lift my face with a cup of salvation; my cup is filled to overflowing.
My soul thirsts for the Lord; may He fill my store with plenty.
I lift my eyes to the sages, [celebrating Shabbat] like Hillel, not Shammai.
Most delightful of days and eternity's years; awake, my soul, awake.
Above my head let there shine as one,
the lamp of the commandments and the Torah's light.
Advance, Lord, to where I rest; You and Your mighty Ark.
Please, God, take my blessing and strengthen the shield of Your seer.

קידוש וזמירות ליום שבת

Some say:

אַתְקִֽינוּ סְעוּדְתָא דִמְהֵימְנוּתָא שְׁלִימְתָא, חֶדְוְתָא דְמַלְכָּא קַדִּישָׁא. אַתְקִֽינוּ סְעוּדְתָא דְמַלְכָּא. דָא הִיא סְעוּדְתָא דְעַתִּיקָא קַדִּישָׁא, וּזְעֵיר אַנְפִּין וַחֲקַל תַּפּוּחִין קַדִּישִׁין אָתַיִן לְסַעֲדָה בַּהֲדֵהּ.

אֲסַדֵּר לִסְעוּדְתָא בְּצַפְרָא דְשַׁבַּתָּא   וְאַזְמִין בַּהּ הַשְׁתָּא עַתִּיקָא קַדִּישָׁא.
נְהוֹרֵהּ יִשְׁרֵי בַהּ בְּקִדּוּשָׁא רַבָּה   וּמֵחַמְרָא טָבָא דְּבֵהּ תֶּחֱדֵי נַפְשָׁא.
יְשַׁדַּר לַן שׁוּפְרֵהּ וְנֶחֱזֵי בִּיקָרֵהּ   וְיַחֲוֵי לָן סִתְרֵהּ דְּמִתְאֲמַר בִּלְחִישָׁא.
יְגַלֵּה לַן טַעְמֵי דִּבִתְרֵיסַר נַהֲמֵי   דְּאִנּוּן אָת בִּשְׁמֵהּ כְּפִילָה וּקְלִישָׁא.
צְרוֹרָא דִלְעֵֽלָּא דְבֵהּ חַיֵּי כֹלָּא   וְיִתְרַבֵּי חֵילָא וְתִסַּק עַד רֵישָׁא.
חֲדוּ חַצְדֵי חַקְלָא בְּדִבּוּר וּבְקָלָא   וּמַלְּלוּ מִלָּה מְתִיקָא כְּדֻבְשָׁא.
קֳדָם רִבּוֹן עָלְמִין בְּמִלִּין סְתִימִין   תְּגַלּוּן פִּתְגָמִין וְתֵימְרוּן חִדּוּשָׁא.
לְעַטֵּר פָּתוֹרָא בְּרָזָא יַקִּירָא   עֲמִיקָא וּטְמִירָא וְלָאו מִלְּתָא אֱוְשָׁא.
וְאִלֵּין מִלַּיָּא יְהוֹן לִרְקִיעַיָּא   חֲדָתִין וּשְׁמַיָּא בְּכֵן הַהוּא שִׁמְשָׁא.
רְבוּ יַתִּיר יִסְגֵּי לְעֵילָּא מִן דַּרְגֵּהּ   וְיִסַּב בַּת זוּגֵהּ דַּהֲוַת פְּרִישָׁא.

חַי יהוה וּבָרוּךְ צוּרִי, בַּיהוה תִּתְהַלֵּל נַפְשִׁי
כִּי יהוה יָאִיר נֵרִי, בְּהִלּוֹ נֵרוֹ עֲלֵי רֹאשִׁי.
יהוה רוֹעִי לֹא אֶחְסָר, עַל מֵי מְנוּחוֹת יְנַהֲלֵנִי
נוֹתֵן לֶחֶם לְכָל בָּשָׂר, לֶחֶם חֻקִּי הַטְרִיפֵנִי.
יְהִי רָצוֹן מִלְּפָנֶיךָ, אַתָּה אֱלֹהַי קְדוֹשִׁי
תַּעֲרֹךְ לְפָנַי שֻׁלְחָנֶךָ, תְּדַשֵּׁן בַּשֶּׁמֶן רֹאשִׁי.
מִי יִתֵּן מְנוּחָתִי, לִפְנֵי אֲדוֹן הַשָּׁלוֹם
וְהָיְתָה שְׁלֵמָה מִטָּתִי, הַחַיִּים וְהַשָּׁלוֹם.
יִשְׁלַח מַלְאָכוֹ לְפָנַי, לְלַוּוֹתִי לְוָיָה
בְּכוֹס יְשׁוּעוֹת אֶשָּׂא פָנַי, מְנָת כּוֹסִי רְוָיָה.
צָמְאָה נַפְשִׁי אֶל יהוה, יְמַלֵּא שֹׂבַע אֲסָמַי
אֶל הֶהָרִים אֶשָּׂא עֵינַי, כְּהִלֵּל וְלֹא כְשַׁמַּאי.
חֶדְוַת יָמִים וּשְׁנוֹת עוֹלָמִים, עוּרָה כְבוֹדִי עוּרָה
וְעַל רֹאשִׁי יִהְיוּ תַמִּים, נֵר מִצְוָה וְאוֹר תּוֹרָה.
קוּמָה יהוה לִמְנוּחָתִי, אַתָּה וַאֲרוֹן עֻזֶּךָ
קַח נָא אֵל אֶת בִּרְכָתִי, וְהַחֲזֵק מָגֵן חוֹזֶךָ.

מִזְמוֹר לְדָוִד A psalm of David. The LORD is my Shepherd, I shall not want. *Ps. 23*
He makes me lie down in green pastures. He leads me beside the still waters.
He refreshes my soul.
He guides me in the paths of righteousness for His name's sake.
Though I walk through the valley of the shadow of death,
I will fear no evil, for You are with me; Your rod and Your staff, they comfort me.
You set a table before me in the presence of my enemies;
You anoint my head with oil; my cup is filled to overflowing.
May goodness and kindness follow me all the days of my life,
and may I live in the House of the LORD for evermore.

SHABBAT MORNING KIDDUSH

Some say:

אִם־תָּשִׁיב If you keep your feet from breaking the Sabbath, *Is. 58*
and from pursuing your affairs on My holy day,
if you call the Sabbath a delight, and the LORD's holy day honorable,
and if you honor it by not going your own way
or attending to your own affairs, or speaking idle words,
then you will find joy in the LORD,
and I will cause you to ride on the heights of the earth
and to feast on the inheritance of your father Jacob,
for the mouth of the LORD has spoken.

Most begin Kiddush here.

וְשָׁמְרוּ The children of Israel must keep the Sabbath, *Ex. 31*
observing the Sabbath in every generation
as an everlasting covenant.
It is a sign between Me and the children of Israel for ever,
for in six days the LORD made the heavens and the earth,
but on the seventh day He ceased work and refreshed Himself.

... A THOUSAND WORDS

REFLECTION

- What does it mean that Shabbat is a "sign"?
- If Shabbat is a "sign," what does your Shabbat sign say?
- If Shabbat is our sign to Hashem, does Hashem send us signs as well? What do they say?

תהלים כג

מִזְמוֹר לְדָוִד, יהוה רֹעִי לֹא אֶחְסָר:
בִּנְאוֹת דֶּשֶׁא יַרְבִּיצֵנִי, עַל־מֵי מְנֻחוֹת יְנַהֲלֵנִי:
נַפְשִׁי יְשׁוֹבֵב
יַנְחֵנִי בְמַעְגְּלֵי־צֶדֶק לְמַעַן שְׁמוֹ:
גַּם כִּי־אֵלֵךְ בְּגֵיא צַלְמָוֶת
לֹא־אִירָא רָע, כִּי־אַתָּה עִמָּדִי
שִׁבְטְךָ וּמִשְׁעַנְתֶּךָ הֵמָּה יְנַחֲמֻנִי:
תַּעֲרֹךְ לְפָנַי שֻׁלְחָן נֶגֶד צֹרְרָי
דִּשַּׁנְתָּ בַשֶּׁמֶן רֹאשִׁי, כּוֹסִי רְוָיָה:
אַךְ טוֹב וָחֶסֶד יִרְדְּפוּנִי כָּל־יְמֵי חַיָּי
וְשַׁבְתִּי בְּבֵית־יהוה לְאֹרֶךְ יָמִים:

קידושא רבה

Some say:

ישעיה נח

אִם־תָּשִׁיב מִשַּׁבָּת רַגְלֶךָ עֲשׂוֹת חֲפָצֶךָ בְּיוֹם קָדְשִׁי
וְקָרָאתָ לַשַּׁבָּת עֹנֶג לִקְדוֹשׁ יהוה מְכֻבָּד
וְכִבַּדְתּוֹ מֵעֲשׂוֹת דְּרָכֶיךָ מִמְּצוֹא חֶפְצְךָ וְדַבֵּר דָּבָר:
אָז תִּתְעַנַּג עַל־יהוה
וְהִרְכַּבְתִּיךָ עַל־בָּמֳתֵי אָרֶץ
וְהַאֲכַלְתִּיךָ נַחֲלַת יַעֲקֹב אָבִיךָ
כִּי פִּי יהוה דִּבֵּר:

Most begin קידוש *here.*

שמות לא

וְשָׁמְרוּ בְנֵי־יִשְׂרָאֵל אֶת־הַשַּׁבָּת
לַעֲשׂוֹת אֶת־הַשַּׁבָּת לְדֹרֹתָם בְּרִית עוֹלָם:
בֵּינִי וּבֵין בְּנֵי יִשְׂרָאֵל אוֹת הִוא לְעֹלָם
כִּי־שֵׁשֶׁת יָמִים עָשָׂה יהוה אֶת־הַשָּׁמַיִם וְאֶת־הָאָרֶץ
וּבַיּוֹם הַשְּׁבִיעִי שָׁבַת וַיִּנָּפַשׁ:

זָכוֹר Remember the Sabbath day to keep it holy. *Ex. 20*
Six days you shall labor and do all your work,
but the seventh day is a Sabbath of the LORD your God;
on it you shall not do any work –
you, your son or daughter,
your male or female slave,
or your cattle, or the stranger within your gates.
For in six days the LORD made heaven and earth
and sea and all that is in them,
and rested on the seventh day;
therefore the LORD blessed the Sabbath day
and declared it holy.

When saying Kiddush for others, add:
Please pay attention, my masters.

בָּרוּךְ Blessed are You, LORD our God, King of the Universe,
who creates the fruit of the vine.

On Shabbat Ḥol HaMo'ed Sukkot, if Kiddush is made in the sukka, add:
Blessed are You, LORD our God, King of the Universe,
who has made us holy through His commandments,
and has commanded us to live in the sukka.

CONNECTION

"Shabbat enshrines a social-ethical principle without peer. Shabbat is one of the loftiest values in all of humanity. It originated with us, the Jews. It is all ours. No other civilization in history knew a day of rest. Ancient Egypt had a great culture whose treasures are on view to this day, yet the Egypt of antiquity did not know a day of rest. The Greeks of old excelled in philosophy and the arts, yet they did not know a day of rest. Rome established mighty empires and instituted a system of law which is relevant to this day, yet they did not know a day of rest. Neither did the civilizations of Assyria, Babylon, Persia, India, China – not one of them knew a day of rest." (Prime Minister Menachem Begin)

זָכוֹר אֶת־יוֹם הַשַּׁבָּת לְקַדְּשׁוֹ: שמות כ

שֵׁשֶׁת יָמִים תַּעֲבֹד, וְעָשִׂיתָ כָּל־מְלַאכְתֶּךָ:
וְיוֹם הַשְּׁבִיעִי שַׁבָּת לַיהוה אֱלֹהֶיךָ
לֹא־תַעֲשֶׂה כָל־מְלָאכָה אַתָּה וּבִנְךָ וּבִתֶּךָ
עַבְדְּךָ וַאֲמָתְךָ וּבְהֶמְתֶּךָ, וְגֵרְךָ אֲשֶׁר בִּשְׁעָרֶיךָ:
כִּי שֵׁשֶׁת־יָמִים עָשָׂה יהוה אֶת־הַשָּׁמַיִם וְאֶת־הָאָרֶץ
אֶת־הַיָּם וְאֶת־כָּל־אֲשֶׁר־בָּם
וַיָּנַח בַּיּוֹם הַשְּׁבִיעִי
עַל־כֵּן בֵּרַךְ יהוה אֶת־יוֹם הַשַּׁבָּת וַיְקַדְּשֵׁהוּ:

When saying קידוש *for others, add:*

סַבְרִי מָרָנָן

בָּרוּךְ אַתָּה יהוה אֱלֹהֵינוּ מֶלֶךְ הָעוֹלָם
בּוֹרֵא פְּרִי הַגָּפֶן.

On שבת חול המועד סוכות *if* קידוש *is made in the* סוכה *add:*

בָּרוּךְ אַתָּה יהוה אֱלֹהֵינוּ מֶלֶךְ הָעוֹלָם
אֲשֶׁר קִדְּשָׁנוּ בְּמִצְוֹתָיו וְצִוָּנוּ לֵישֵׁב בַּסֻּכָּה.

LEARNING

Because the Torah commands us to "Remember the Shabbat *day* to keep it holy," the rabbis instituted a rabbinic requirement to also say Kiddush during the day as well as when Shabbat begins the previous evening.

There is no one agreed-upon text for this Kiddush, and in fact one can fulfill one's obligation by merely reciting the *berakha* on wine. There are varying customs as to which verses one should recite before making the *berakha*.

Kiddush is always followed by eating some food, in order to fulfill the obligation of only reciting Kiddush at a meal.

ZEMIROT FOR SHABBAT DAY

בָּרוּךְ Blessed be the Lord who, day by day, carries our burden with salvation and redemption. We will rejoice in His name all day long, and raise our head high in His salvation. For He is a stronghold for the poor and a refuge for the needy.

The Lord's tribes are Israel's testimony: He was distressed in their distress, in their suffering and slavery. Through a pavement of sapphire He showed them the strength of His love, He revealed Himself, lifting them from the depths of the pit. For with the Lord is loving- *Ps. 130*
kindness; He abounds in redemption.

How precious is His loving-kindness; He shelters them under His shade. For their sake He went with them into exile in Babylon. When they went down in ships, He was counted among them. He ensured that they were treated mercifully by those who took them captive. For the Lord will not abandon His people, for the sake of His great name.

In Eilam He placed His throne, to rescue His beloved, to remove from them the stronghold of His rebels. He redeemed His servants from passing under the sword. He raised the pride of His people, for the glory of all His devoted ones. For though He afflicts, He also shows *Lam. 3*
compassion and loving-kindness.

When the he-goat [Greece] extended its power, and the vision of the four ascended to the heights, And in their hearts they intended to destroy those He loved, through His priests He laid low those who rose against Him: The Lord's kindness has not ended nor His *Lam. 3*
compassion ceased.

I was handed over to Edom [Rome] by my quarrelsome friends, who daily fed their appetite with my treasures. His help was with me, supporting my foundations, He will not abandon me all the days of my age. For the Lord does not reject forever. *Lam. 3*

When He comes from Edom with garments stained crimson, there will be slaughter in Botzra, and an execution of traitors, their blood will turn His garments red, in His great strength He will bring the leaders low. With His mighty blast like a day of the east wind. *Is. 27*

When the oppressor from Edom sees how it will be, He will think Botzra to be a refuge like Betzer, giving protection to angels and men, deliberate and accidental sinners alike. Love *Ps. 31*
the Lord, all His devoted ones: all His faithful ones He will guard.

The Rock in His kindness will command His communities to gather, coming together from the four winds, He will settle them upon the high mountains, He will return with us, gathering the dispersed, for it does not say, "He will bring back" but "He will return" and gather.

Blessed is our God who has bestowed good upon us. In His compassion and abundant kindness, He has done great things for us. Like these and those, may He do yet more for us, to magnify His great, mighty and awesome name, by which we are called.

Blessed is our God who created us for His glory, To praise and applaud Him and tell of His majesty, His loving-kindness is greater to us than to any other nation. Therefore with all our heart and soul and might, let us declare His kingship and His unity.

May He to whom peace belongs, send us blessing and peace. From left and right, may Israel have peace. May the Compassionate One bless His people with peace, and may they merit to see children and children's children, occupied with Torah and the commandments, bringing Israel peace. Wondrous Counselor, mighty God, everlasting Father, Prince of peace. *Is. 9*

זמירות ליום שבת

בָּרוּךְ אֲדֹנָי יוֹם יוֹם, יַעֲמָס לָנוּ יֶשַׁע וּפִדְיוֹם, וּבִשְׁמוֹ נָגִיל כָּל הַיּוֹם, וּבִישׁוּעָתוֹ נָרִים
רֹאשׁ עֶלְיוֹן. כִּי הוּא מָעוֹז לַדָּל וּמַחְסֶה לָאֶבְיוֹן.

שִׁבְטֵי יָהּ לְיִשְׂרָאֵל עֵדוּת, בְּצָרָתָם לוֹ צָר בְּסִבְלוּת וּבְעַבְדוּת, בִּלְבְנַת הַסַּפִּיר הֶרְאָם עֹז
יְדִידוּת, וְנִגְלָה לְהַעֲלוֹתָם מֵעֹמֶק בּוֹר וָדוּת. כִּי־עִם־יהוה הַחֶסֶד, וְהַרְבֵּה עִמּוֹ פְדוּת: תהלים קל

מַה יָּקָר חַסְדּוֹ בְּצִלּוֹ לְגוֹנְנֵמוֹ, בְּגָלוּת בָּבֶלָה שֻׁלַּח לְמַעֲנֵמוֹ, לְהוֹרִיד בָּרִיחִים נִמְנָה
בֵינֵימוֹ, וַיִּתְּנֵם לְרַחֲמִים לִפְנֵי שׁוֹבֵימוֹ. כִּי לֹא יִטֹּשׁ יהוה אֶת עַמּוֹ, בַּעֲבוּר הַגָּדוֹל שְׁמוֹ.

עֵילָם שָׁת כִּסְאוֹ לְהַצִּיל יְדִידָיו, לְהַאֲבִיד מִשָּׁם מָעֻזְנֵי מוֹרְדָיו, מֵעֲבוֹר בַּשֶּׁלַח פָּדָה
אֶת עֲבָדָיו, קֶרֶן לְעַמּוֹ יָרִים, תְּהִלָּה לְכָל חֲסִידָיו. כִּי אִם־הוֹגָה, וְרִחַם כְּרֹב חֲסָדָו: איכה ג

וּצְפִיר הָעִזִּים הִגְדִּיל עֲצוּמָיו, וְגַם חָזוּת אַרְבַּע עָלוּ לִמְרוֹמָיו, וּבְלִבָּם דִּמּוּ לְהַשְׁחִית אֶת
רְחוּמָיו, עַל יְדֵי כֹהֲנָיו מִגֵּר מִתְקוֹמְמָיו. חַסְדֵי יהוה כִּי לֹא־תָמְנוּ, כִּי לֹא כָלוּ רַחֲמָיו: איכה ג

נִסְגַּרְתִּי לֶאֱדוֹם בְּיַד רֵעַי מְדָנַי, שֶׁבְּכָל יוֹם מְמַלְּאִים כְּרֵסָם מֵעֲדָנַי, עֶזְרָתוֹ עִמִּי לִסְמֹךְ
אֶת אֲדָנַי, וְלֹא נְטַשְׁתַּנִי כָּל יְמֵי עִדָּנַי. כִּי לֹא יִזְנַח לְעוֹלָם אֲדֹנָי: איכה ג

בְּבוֹאוֹ מֵאֱדוֹם חֲמוּץ בְּגָדִים, זֶבַח לוֹ בְּבָצְרָה וְטֶבַח לוֹ בְּבוֹגְדִים, וְיֵז נִצְחָם מַלְבּוּשָׁיו
לְהַאְדִּים, בְּכֹחוֹ הַגָּדוֹל יִבְצֹר רוּחַ נְגִידִים. הָגָה בְּרוּחוֹ הַקָּשָׁה בְּיוֹם קָדִים: ישעיה כז

רְאוֹתוֹ כִּי כֵן אֲדוֹמִי הָעוֹצֵר, יַחְשֹׁב לוֹ בָּצְרָה תִּקְלֹט כְּבֶצֶר, וּמַלְאָךְ כְּאָדָם בְּתוֹכָהּ
יִנָּצֵר, וּמֵזִיד כַּשּׁוֹגֵג בְּמִקְלָט יֵעָצֵר. אֶהֱבוּ אֶת־יהוה כָּל־חֲסִידָיו, אֱמוּנִים נֹצֵר: תהלים לא

יְצַוֶּה צוּר חַסְדּוֹ קְהִלּוֹתָיו לְקַבֵּץ, מֵאַרְבַּע רוּחוֹת עָדָיו לְהִקָּבֵץ, וּבְהַר מְרוֹם הָרִים
אוֹתָנוּ לְהַרְבֵּץ, וְאִתָּנוּ יָשׁוּב נִדָּחִים קוֹבֵץ. יָשִׁיב לֹא נֶאֱמַר, כִּי אִם וְשָׁב וְקִבֵּץ.

בָּרוּךְ הוּא אֱלֹהֵינוּ אֲשֶׁר טוֹב גְּמָלָנוּ, כְּרַחֲמָיו וּכְרֹב חֲסָדָיו הִגְדִּיל לָנוּ, אֵלֶּה וְכָאֵלֶּה
יוֹסֵף עִמָּנוּ, לְהַגְדִּיל שְׁמוֹ הַגָּדוֹל הַגִּבּוֹר וְהַנּוֹרָא, שֶׁנִּקְרָא עָלֵינוּ.

בָּרוּךְ הוּא אֱלֹהֵינוּ שֶׁבְּרָאָנוּ לִכְבוֹדוֹ, לְהַלְּלוֹ וּלְשַׁבְּחוֹ וּלְסַפֵּר הוֹדוֹ, מִכָּל אֹם גָּבַר
עָלֵינוּ חַסְדּוֹ, לָכֵן בְּכָל לֵב וּבְכָל נֶפֶשׁ וּבְכָל מְאוֹדוֹ, נַמְלִיכוֹ וּנְיַחֲדוֹ.

שֶׁהַשָּׁלוֹם שֶׁלּוֹ יָשִׂים עָלֵינוּ בְּרָכָה וְשָׁלוֹם, מִשְּׂמֹאל וּמִיָּמִין עַל יִשְׂרָאֵל שָׁלוֹם, הָרַחֲמָן
הוּא יְבָרֵךְ אֶת עַמּוֹ בַשָּׁלוֹם, וְיִזְכּוּ לִרְאוֹת בָּנִים וּבְנֵי בָנִים, עוֹסְקִים, בַּתּוֹרָה וּבְמִצְוֹת,
עַל יִשְׂרָאֵל שָׁלוֹם. פֶּלֶא יוֹעֵץ אֵל גִּבּוֹר אֲבִי־עַד שַׂר־שָׁלוֹם: ישעיה ט

בָּרוּךְ אֵל עֶלְיוֹן Blessed is God Most High who has given us rest,
To relieve our souls from distress and pain.
May He seek the good of Zion, the outcast city.
How long must she grieve, her spirits discouraged?
All who keep the Sabbath, man and woman alike, find favor like an offering made to God.

He who rides the heavens, King of worlds,
Gently told His people to rest,
With tasty food and delicacies of all kinds,
With elegant dress, as at a family feast.
All who keep the Sabbath, man and woman alike, find favor like an offering made to God.

Happy are all who await a double reward
From the One who sees all, though He is present in dense dark.
He will give him a heritage in hill and valley,
A heritage and resting place like [Jacob] on whom the sun shone.
All who keep the Sabbath, man and woman alike, find favor like an offering made to God.

Whoever keeps the Sabbath fully, not profaning it,
Shows that he is worthy; holy is his lot.
Happy is he who fulfills the day's duty;
It is like a gift presented to God who fashioned him.
All who keep the Sabbath, man and woman alike, find favor like an offering made to God.

The Rock, my God, called it "Beloved of days."
Happy are the faithful if it is kept intact.
He will set on their head a close-fitting crown.
On them the Rock of Eternity will make His spirit rest.
All who keep the Sabbath, man and woman alike, find favor like an offering made to God.

He who remembers the Sabbath day to keep it holy
Will gain high honor like a diadem on his head.
Therefore let each give to his soul
Delight and joy with which to be elevated.
All who keep the Sabbath, man and woman alike, find favor like an offering made to God.

Let her be holy to you – Sabbath the queen –
Placing a blessing in your home.
In all your dwellings, do no work,
Nor your sons and daughters, your servant or maid.
All who keep the Sabbath, man and woman alike, find favor like an offering made to God.

בָּרוּךְ אֵל עֶלְיוֹן
אֲשֶׁר נָתַן מְנוּחָה, לְנַפְשֵׁנוּ פִּדְיוֹן מִשֵּׁאת וַאֲנָחָה
וְהוּא יִדְרֹשׁ לְצִיּוֹן, עִיר הַנִּדָּחָה, עַד אָנָה תּוּגְיוֹן נֶפֶשׁ נֶאֱנָחָה.

הַשּׁוֹמֵר שַׁבָּת הַבֵּן עִם הַבַּת, לָאֵל יֵרָצוּ כְּמִנְחָה עַל מַחֲבַת.

רוֹכֵב בָּעֲרָבוֹת, מֶלֶךְ עוֹלָמִים, אֶת עַמּוֹ לִשְׁבֹּת אִזֵּן בַּנְּעִימִים
בְּמַאֲכָלוֹת עֲרֵבוֹת בְּמִינֵי מַטְעַמִּים, בְּמַלְבּוּשֵׁי כָבוֹד זֶבַח מִשְׁפָּחָה.

הַשּׁוֹמֵר שַׁבָּת הַבֵּן עִם הַבַּת, לָאֵל יֵרָצוּ כְּמִנְחָה עַל מַחֲבַת.

וְאַשְׁרֵי כָּל חוֹכֶה לְתַשְׁלוּמֵי כֵפֶל, מֵאֵת כֹּל סוֹכֶה, שׁוֹכֵן בָּעֲרָפֶל
נַחֲלָה לוֹ יִזְכֶּה בָּהָר וּבַשָּׁפֶל, נַחֲלָה וּמְנוּחָה כַּשֶּׁמֶשׁ לוֹ זָרְחָה.

הַשּׁוֹמֵר שַׁבָּת הַבֵּן עִם הַבַּת, לָאֵל יֵרָצוּ כְּמִנְחָה עַל מַחֲבַת.

כָּל שׁוֹמֵר שַׁבָּת כַּדָּת מֵחַלְּלוֹ, הֵן הֶכְשַׁר חִבַּת קֹדֶשׁ גּוֹרָלוֹ
וְאִם יֵצֵא חוֹבַת הַיּוֹם, אַשְׁרֵי לוֹ, אֶל אֵל אָדוֹן מְחוֹלְלוֹ מִנְחָה הִיא שְׁלוּחָה.

הַשּׁוֹמֵר שַׁבָּת הַבֵּן עִם הַבַּת, לָאֵל יֵרָצוּ כְּמִנְחָה עַל מַחֲבַת.

חֶמְדַּת הַיָּמִים קְרָאוֹ אֵלִי צוּר, וְאַשְׁרֵי לִתְמִימִים אִם יִהְיֶה נָצוּר
כֶּתֶר הִלּוּמִים עַל רֹאשָׁם יָצוּר, צוּר הָעוֹלָמִים, רוּחוֹ בָּם נָחָה.

הַשּׁוֹמֵר שַׁבָּת הַבֵּן עִם הַבַּת, לָאֵל יֵרָצוּ כְּמִנְחָה עַל מַחֲבַת.

זָכוֹר אֶת יוֹם הַשַּׁבָּת לְקַדְּשׁוֹ, קַרְנוֹ כִּי גָבְהָה נֵזֶר עַל רֹאשׁוֹ
עַל כֵּן יִתֵּן הָאָדָם לְנַפְשׁוֹ, עֹנֶג וְגַם שִׂמְחָה בָּהֶם לְמָשְׁחָה.

הַשּׁוֹמֵר שַׁבָּת הַבֵּן עִם הַבַּת, לָאֵל יֵרָצוּ כְּמִנְחָה עַל מַחֲבַת.

קֹדֶשׁ הִיא לָכֶם שַׁבָּת הַמַּלְכָּה, אֶל תּוֹךְ בָּתֵּיכֶם לְהָנִיחַ בְּרָכָה
בְּכָל מוֹשְׁבוֹתֵיכֶם לֹא תַעֲשׂוּ מְלָאכָה, בְּנֵיכֶם וּבְנוֹתֵיכֶם עֶבֶד וְגַם שִׁפְחָה.

הַשּׁוֹמֵר שַׁבָּת הַבֵּן עִם הַבַּת, לָאֵל יֵרָצוּ כְּמִנְחָה עַל מַחֲבַת.

יוֹם זֶה מְכֻבָּד This day is honored above all others,
For on it He who formed worlds found rest.

For six days, do your work
But the seventh day is God's:
On the Sabbath you shall do no work,
For in six days He made all.

This day is honored above all others,
for on it He who formed worlds found rest.

Foremost among sacred days
Is this day of rest, this holy Sabbath.
So let each say Kiddush over wine,
And break bread over two complete loaves.

This day is honored above all others,
for on it He who formed worlds found rest.

Eat choice food, drink sweet wine,
For God will give to those who cleave to Him
Clothes to wear, due portions of bread,
Meat and fish, and all tasty foods.

This day is honored above all others,
for on it He who formed worlds found rest.

On it you shall lack nothing – so eat,
Be satisfied and bless
The Lord your God, whom you love,
For He has blessed you from all peoples.

This day is honored above all others,
for on it He who formed worlds found rest.

The heavens declare His glory
And the earth is full of His loving-kindness.
See all these things His hand has made
For He is the Rock, His work is perfect.

This day is honored above all others,
for on it He who formed worlds found rest.

יוֹם זֶה מְכֻבָּד מִכָּל יָמִים, כִּי בוֹ שָׁבַת צוּר עוֹלָמִים.

שֵׁשֶׁת יָמִים תַּעֲשֶׂה מְלַאכְתֶּךָ
וְיוֹם הַשְּׁבִיעִי לֵאלֹהֶיךָ
שַׁבָּת לֹא תַעֲשֶׂה בוֹ מְלָאכָה
כִּי כֹל עָשָׂה שֵׁשֶׁת יָמִים.
יוֹם זֶה מְכֻבָּד מִכָּל יָמִים, כִּי בוֹ שָׁבַת צוּר עוֹלָמִים.

רִאשׁוֹן הוּא לְמִקְרָאֵי קֹדֶשׁ
יוֹם שַׁבָּתוֹן יוֹם שַׁבַּת קֹדֶשׁ
עַל כֵּן כָּל אִישׁ בְּיֵינוֹ יְקַדֵּשׁ
עַל שְׁתֵּי לֶחֶם יִבְצְעוּ תְמִימִים.
יוֹם זֶה מְכֻבָּד מִכָּל יָמִים, כִּי בוֹ שָׁבַת צוּר עוֹלָמִים.

אֱכֹל מַשְׁמַנִּים, שְׁתֵה מַמְתַּקִּים
כִּי אֵל יִתֵּן לְכֹל בּוֹ דְבֵקִים
בֶּגֶד לִלְבֹּשׁ, לֶחֶם חֻקִּים
בָּשָׂר וְדָגִים וְכָל מַטְעַמִּים.
יוֹם זֶה מְכֻבָּד מִכָּל יָמִים, כִּי בוֹ שָׁבַת צוּר עוֹלָמִים.

לֹא תֶחְסַר כֹּל בּוֹ, וְאָכַלְתָּ
וְשָׂבָעְתָּ וּבֵרַכְתָּ
אֶת יהוה אֱלֹהֶיךָ אֲשֶׁר אָהַבְתָּ
כִּי בֵרַכְךָ מִכָּל הָעַמִּים.
יוֹם זֶה מְכֻבָּד מִכָּל יָמִים, כִּי בוֹ שָׁבַת צוּר עוֹלָמִים.

הַשָּׁמַיִם מְסַפְּרִים כְּבוֹדוֹ
וְגַם הָאָרֶץ מָלְאָה חַסְדּוֹ
רְאוּ כִּי כָל אֵלֶּה עָשְׂתָה יָדוֹ
כִּי הוּא הַצּוּר פָּעֳלוֹ תָמִים.
יוֹם זֶה מְכֻבָּד מִכָּל יָמִים, כִּי בוֹ שָׁבַת צוּר עוֹלָמִים.

יוֹם שַׁבָּתוֹן The day of rest should not be forgotten, Its memory is like sweet fragrance,
On it the dove found rest, And in it the exhausted rest.

This day is honored by the people of faith. Parents and children guard it with care.
It was engraved on two tablets of stone,
By the greatness of His power and His unfailing strength.

On it the dove found rest, And in it the exhausted rest.

All came together in a covenant: "We will do and we will obey," they said as one.
Then they responded, saying, "The LORD is One" –
Blessed is He who gives the weary strength.

On it the dove found rest, And in it the exhausted rest.

He spoke in His holiness on the Mount of Myrrh [Sinai]:
"Remember and observe the seventh day."
And learn together all His commands: Gird your loins and muster strength.

On it the dove found rest, And in it the exhausted rest.

The people who have wandered like a straying flock –
May He remember the covenant and the oath,
So that no harm should happen to them, As You swore at the end of Noah's flood.

On it the dove found rest, And in it the exhausted rest.

שַׁבָּת הַיּוֹם Today is the Sabbath of the LORD. Celebrate greatly with my songs,
Multiply my delicacies, Keep it like the LORD's command.

Today is the Sabbath of the LORD.

Do not travel beyond boundaries, Do not labor on this day:
Eat, drink, make merry. This is the day the LORD has made.

Today is the Sabbath of the LORD.

If you keep it God will guard you like the pupil of His eye,
You, your son and daughter too. If you call the Sabbath a delight
Then you will find delight before the LORD.

Today is the Sabbath of the LORD.

Eat rich foods and delicacies, Tasty dishes of many kinds,
Soft-shelled nuts and pomegranates: Eat, be satisfied and bless the LORD.

Today is the Sabbath of the LORD.

Make ready on the table delicious bread, And make, this day, three meals.
Bless and thank His glorious name. Take care, observe and do, my sons.

Today is the Sabbath of the LORD.

יוֹם שַׁבָּתוֹן אֵין לִשְׁכֹּחַ, זִכְרוֹ כְּרֵיחַ הַנִּיחֹחַ
יוֹנָה מָצְאָה בוֹ מָנוֹחַ וְשָׁם יָנוּחוּ יְגִיעֵי כֹחַ.

הַיּוֹם נִכְבָּד לִבְנֵי אֱמוּנִים, זְהִירִים לְשָׁמְרוֹ אָבוֹת וּבָנִים
חָקוּק בִּשְׁנֵי לוּחוֹת אֲבָנִים, מֵרֹב אוֹנִים וְאַמִּיץ כֹּחַ.

יוֹנָה מָצְאָה בוֹ מָנוֹחַ וְשָׁם יָנוּחוּ יְגִיעֵי כֹחַ.

וּבָאוּ כֻלָּם בִּבְרִית יַחַד, נַעֲשֶׂה וְנִשְׁמַע אָמְרוּ כְּאֶחָד
וּפָתְחוּ וְעָנוּ יהוה אֶחָד, בָּרוּךְ נֹתֵן לַיָּעֵף כֹּחַ.

יוֹנָה מָצְאָה בוֹ מָנוֹחַ וְשָׁם יָנוּחוּ יְגִיעֵי כֹחַ.

דִּבֶּר בְּקָדְשׁוֹ בְּהַר הַמֹּר, יוֹם הַשְּׁבִיעִי זָכוֹר וְשָׁמוֹר
וְכָל פִּקּוּדָיו יַחַד לִגְמֹר, חַזֵּק מָתְנַיִם וְאַמֵּץ כֹּחַ.

יוֹנָה מָצְאָה בוֹ מָנוֹחַ וְשָׁם יָנוּחוּ יְגִיעֵי כֹחַ.

הָעָם אֲשֶׁר נָע, כַּצֹּאן תָּעָה, יִזְכֹּר לְפָקְדוֹ בְּרִית וּשְׁבוּעָה
לְבַל יַעֲבָר בָּם מִקְרֵה רָעָה, כַּאֲשֶׁר נִשְׁבַּעְתָּ עַל מֵי נֹחַ.

יוֹנָה מָצְאָה בוֹ מָנוֹחַ וְשָׁם יָנוּחוּ יְגִיעֵי כֹחַ.

שַׁבָּת הַיּוֹם לַיהוה, מְאֹד צַהֲלוּ בְּרִנּוּנַי
וְגַם הַרְבּוּ מַעֲדַנַּי, אוֹתוֹ לִשְׁמֹר כְּמִצְוַת יהוה. שַׁבָּת הַיּוֹם לַיהוה.

מֵעֲבֹר דֶּרֶךְ וּגְבוּלִים, מֵעֲשׂוֹת הַיּוֹם פְּעָלִים
לֶאֱכֹל וְלִשְׁתּוֹת בְּהִלּוּלִים, זֶה הַיּוֹם עָשָׂה יהוה. שַׁבָּת הַיּוֹם לַיהוה.

וְאִם תִּשְׁמְרֶנּוּ, יָהּ יִנְצָרְךָ כְּבָבַת, אַתָּה וּבִנְךָ וְגַם הַבַּת
וְקָרָאתָ עֹנֶג לַשַּׁבָּת, אָז תִּתְעַנַּג עַל יהוה. שַׁבָּת הַיּוֹם לַיהוה.

אֱכֹל מַשְׁמַנִּים וּמַעֲדַנִּים, וּמַטְעַמִּים הַרְבֵּה מִינִים
אֱגוֹזֵי פֶרֶךְ וְרִמּוֹנִים, וְאָכַלְתָּ וְשָׂבָעְתָּ וּבֵרַכְתָּ אֶת יהוה. שַׁבָּת הַיּוֹם לַיהוה.

לַעֲרֹךְ בְּשֻׁלְחָן לֶחֶם חֲמוּדוֹת, לַעֲשׂוֹת הַיּוֹם שָׁלֹשׁ סְעוּדוֹת
אֶת הַשֵּׁם הַנִּכְבָּד לְבָרֵךְ וּלְהוֹדוֹת, שִׁקְדוּ וְשִׁמְרוּ וַעֲשׂוּ בָנַי. שַׁבָּת הַיּוֹם לַיהוה.

שִׁמְרוּ שַׁבְּתוֹתַי Observe My Sabbaths, so that you are nourished and fed,
From the radiance of My blessings,
when you come to rest. Borrow on My account, My children,
Delight in My pleasures: Today is the Sabbath of the Lord.

Borrow on My account, My children,
Delight in My pleasures: Today is the Sabbath of the Lord.

Declare freedom from toil, then I will give My blessing,
joining one to the next,
bringing gladness on My day of joy. Wear clothes of fine linen and wool.
And learn from My elders: Today is the Sabbath of the Lord.

Borrow on My account, My children,
Delight in My pleasures: Today is the Sabbath of the Lord.

Quickly bring the portion, obey Esther's command.
Make a reckoning with the Creator,
He will repay you for the food, and more. Trust in Me, My faithful ones,
And drink wine from My plentiful supply. Today is the Sabbath of the Lord.

Borrow on My account, My children,
Delight in My pleasures: Today is the Sabbath of the Lord.

Today is a day of redemption, if you observe the Sabbath;
Then you will be My special treasure.
Stay [for the night of exile], then pass on. Then you will live before Me.
And be filled from My hidden store. Today is the Sabbath of the Lord.

Borrow on My account, My children,
Delight in My pleasures: Today is the Sabbath of the Lord.

Make my city strong, God, the God most high.
Bring back my Temple,
With joy and words of song. There may my singers chant,
My Levites and my priests.
Then you will delight in the Lord. Today is the Sabbath of the Lord.

Borrow on My account, My children,
Delight in My pleasures: Today is the Sabbath of the Lord.

שִׁמְרוּ שַׁבְּתוֹתַי, לְמַעַן תִּינְקוּ וּשְׂבַעְתֶּם, מִזִּיו בִּרְכוֹתַי
אֶל הַמְּנוּחָה כִּי בָאתֶם, וּלְווּ עָלַי בָּנַי, וְעִדְנוּ מַעֲדָנַי

שַׁבָּת הַיּוֹם לַיהוה.

וּלְווּ עָלַי בָּנַי, וְעִדְנוּ מַעֲדָנַי, שַׁבָּת הַיּוֹם לַיהוה.

לְעָמֵל קִרְאוּ דְרוֹר, וְנָתַתִּי אֶת בִּרְכָתִי, אִשָּׁה אֶל אֲחוֹתָהּ לִצְרוֹר
לְגַלּוֹת עַל יוֹם שִׂמְחָתִי, בִּגְדֵי שֵׁשׁ עִם שָׁנִי, וְהִתְבּוֹנְנוּ מִזְּקֵנַי

שַׁבָּת הַיּוֹם לַיהוה.

וּלְווּ עָלַי בָּנַי, וְעִדְנוּ מַעֲדָנַי, שַׁבָּת הַיּוֹם לַיהוה.

מַהֲרוּ אֶת הַמָּנֶה, לַעֲשׂוֹת אֶת דְּבַר אֶסְתֵּר, וְחִשְׁבוּ עִם הַקּוֹנֶה
לְשַׁלֵּם אָכוֹל וְהוֹתֵר, בִּטְחוּ בִי אֱמוּנַי, וּשְׁתוּ יֵין מִשְׁמַנַּי

שַׁבָּת הַיּוֹם לַיהוה.

וּלְווּ עָלַי בָּנַי, וְעִדְנוּ מַעֲדָנַי, שַׁבָּת הַיּוֹם לַיהוה.

הִנֵּה יוֹם גְּאֻלָּה, יוֹם שַׁבָּת אִם תִּשְׁמֹרוּ, וִהְיִיתֶם לִי סְגֻלָּה
לִינוּ וְאַחַר תַּעֲבֹרוּ, וְאָז תִּחְיוּ לְפָנַי, וּתְמַלְאוּ צְפוּנַי

שַׁבָּת הַיּוֹם לַיהוה.

וּלְווּ עָלַי בָּנַי, וְעִדְנוּ מַעֲדָנַי, שַׁבָּת הַיּוֹם לַיהוה.

חַזֵּק קִרְיָתִי, אֵל אֱלֹהִים עֶלְיוֹן, וְהָשֵׁב אֶת נְוָתִי
בְּשִׂמְחָה וּבְהִגָּיוֹן, יְשׁוֹרְרוּ שָׁם רְנָנַי, לְוִיַּי וְכֹהֲנַי, אָז תִּתְעַנַּג עַל יהוה

שַׁבָּת הַיּוֹם לַיהוה.

וּלְווּ עָלַי בָּנַי, וְעִדְנוּ מַעֲדָנַי, שַׁבָּת הַיּוֹם לַיהוה.

כִּי אֶשְׁמְרָה If I keep the Sabbath, God will keep me,
It is an eternal sign between God and me.
It is an eternal sign between God and me.

It is forbidden to engage in business or to travel,
Even to speak about the things we need, or about matters of trade or state.
Instead I will study God's Torah and it will make me wise.
It is an eternal sign between God and me.

On it I always find refreshment for my soul.
See: My Holy One gave the first generation,
A sign, by giving them a double portion on the sixth day.
So may my food be doubled every sixth day!
It is an eternal sign between God and me.

Engraved in God's law is His priests' decree,
To prepare the Show-Bread in His presence.
So, His sages ruled, on it fasting is forbidden, except on sins' Atonement Day.
It is an eternal sign between God and me.

It is a day of honor, a day of delight, with bread and fine wine, meat and fish.
On it those who mourn are turned around,
For it is a joyous day and it will bring me joy.
It is an eternal sign between God and me.

Those who desecrate it by working will, in the end, be cut off.
Therefore I cleanse my heart with it as if with soap.
Evening and morning I will pray to God,
Additional and afternoon prayer also, and He will answer me.
It is an eternal sign between God and me.

דְּרוֹר יִקְרָא God declares freedom to boy and girl,
And guards you like the pupil of His eye.
Your name is pleasant, never will it cease. Rest and be at ease on the Sabbath day.

Seek my Temple and my hall, And show me a sign of salvation.
Plant a shoot in my vineyard. Hear the cry of my people.

Tread the winepress in Botzra, And in Babylon which overpowered.
Crush my enemies in anger and fury, Hear my voice on the day I cry.

God, let there be on the desert mountain, Myrtle, acacia, cypress and box tree.
To one who warns and one who is warned, Let peace flow like river waters.

Crush those who rise against me, zealous God, Melting their heart with grief.
Then we will open and fill our mouths, And tongues with songs of joy to You.

Know what is wisdom for your soul, And it will be a crown for your head.
Keep your Holy One's command, Observe your holy Sabbath day.

כִּי אֶשְׁמְרָה שַׁבָּת אֵל יִשְׁמְרֵנִי. אוֹת הִיא לְעוֹלְמֵי עַד בֵּינוֹ וּבֵינִי.

אוֹת הִיא לְעוֹלְמֵי עַד בֵּינוֹ וּבֵינִי.

אָסוּר מְצֹא חֵפֶץ, עֲשׂוֹת דְּרָכִים, גַּם מִלְּדַבֵּר בּוֹ דִּבְרֵי צְרָכִים
דִּבְרֵי סְחוֹרָה אַף דִּבְרֵי מְלָכִים, אֶהְגֶּה בְּתוֹרַת אֵל וּתְחַכְּמֵנִי.

אוֹת הִיא לְעוֹלְמֵי עַד בֵּינוֹ וּבֵינִי.

בּוֹ אֶמְצָא תָמִיד נֹפֶשׁ לְנַפְשִׁי, הִנֵּה לְדוֹר רִאשׁוֹן נָתַן קְדוֹשִׁי
מוֹפֵת, בְּתֵת לֶחֶם מִשְׁנֶה בַּשִּׁשִּׁי, כָּכָה בְּכָל שִׁשִּׁי יַכְפִּיל מְזוֹנִי.

אוֹת הִיא לְעוֹלְמֵי עַד בֵּינוֹ וּבֵינִי.

רָשַׁם בְּדַת הָאֵל חֹק אֶל סְגָנָיו, בּוֹ לַעֲרֹךְ לֶחֶם פָּנִים בְּפָנָיו
עַל כֵּן לְהִתְעַנּוֹת בּוֹ עַל פִּי נְבוֹנָיו, אָסוּר, לְבַד מִיּוֹם כִּפּוּר עֲוֹנִי.

אוֹת הִיא לְעוֹלְמֵי עַד בֵּינוֹ וּבֵינִי.

הוּא יוֹם מְכֻבָּד, הוּא יוֹם תַּעֲנוּגִים, לֶחֶם וְיַיִן טוֹב, בָּשָׂר וְדָגִים
הַמִּתְאַבְּלִים בּוֹ אָחוֹר נְסוֹגִים, כִּי יוֹם שְׂמָחוֹת הוּא וּתְשַׂמְּחֵנִי.

אוֹת הִיא לְעוֹלְמֵי עַד בֵּינוֹ וּבֵינִי.

מֵחֵל מְלָאכָה בּוֹ סוֹפוֹ לְהַכְרִית, עַל כֵּן אֲכַבֵּס בּוֹ לִבִּי כְּבוֹרִית
וְאֶתְפַּלְּלָה אֶל אֵל עַרְבִית וְשַׁחֲרִית, מוּסָף וְגַם מִנְחָה הוּא יַעֲנֵנִי.

אוֹת הִיא לְעוֹלְמֵי עַד בֵּינוֹ וּבֵינִי.

דְּרוֹר יִקְרָא לְבֵן עִם בַּת, וְיִנְצָרְכֶם כְּמוֹ בָבַת
נְעִים שִׁמְכֶם וְלֹא יֻשְׁבַּת, שְׁבוּ נוּחוּ בְּיוֹם שַׁבָּת

דְּרֹשׁ נָוִי וְאוּלַמִּי, וְאוֹת יֶשַׁע עֲשֵׂה עִמִּי
נְטַע שׂוֹרֵק בְּתוֹךְ כַּרְמִי, שְׁעֵה שַׁוְעַת בְּנֵי עַמִּי.

דְּרֹךְ פּוּרָה בְּתוֹךְ בָּצְרָה, וְגַם בָּבֶל אֲשֶׁר גָּבְרָה
נְתֹץ צָרַי בְּאַף עֶבְרָה, שְׁמַע קוֹלִי בְּיוֹם אֶקְרָא.

אֱלֹהִים תֵּן בַּמִּדְבָּר הַר, הֲדַס שִׁטָּה בְּרוֹשׁ תִּדְהָר
וְלַמַּזְהִיר וְלַנִּזְהָר, שְׁלוֹמִים תֵּן כְּמֵי נָהָר.

הֲדֹךְ קָמַי, אֵל קַנָּא, בְּמוֹג לֵבָב וּבִמְגִנָּה
וְנַרְחִיב פֶּה וּנְמַלְּאֶנָּה, לְשׁוֹנֵנוּ לְךָ רִנָּה.

דְּעֵה חָכְמָה לְנַפְשֶׁךָ, וְהִיא כֶתֶר לְרֹאשֶׁךָ
נְצֹר מִצְוַת קְדוֹשֶׁךָ, שְׁמֹר שַׁבַּת קָדְשֶׁךָ.

Minḥa for Shabbat

אַשְׁרֵי Happy are those who live in Your House; *Ps. 84*
they shall continue to praise You, Selah!
Happy are the people for whom this is so; *Ps. 144*
happy are the people whose God is the LORD.
A song of praise by David. *Ps. 145*

א I will elevate You, my God, the King, and bless Your name for ever and all time. ב Every day I will bless You, and praise Your name for ever and all time. ג Great is the LORD and greatly to be praised; His greatness is unfathomable. ד One generation will praise Your works to the next, and tell of Your mighty deeds. ה On the glorious splendor of Your majesty I will meditate, and on the acts of Your wonders. ו They shall talk of the power of Your awesome deeds, and I will tell of Your greatness. ז They shall recite the record of Your great goodness, and sing with joy of Your righteousness. ח The LORD is generous and compassionate, slow to anger and great in loving-kindness. ט The LORD is good to all, and His compassion extends to all His works. י All Your works shall thank You, LORD, and Your devoted ones shall bless You. כ They shall talk of the glory of Your kingship, and speak of Your might. ל To make known to mankind His mighty deeds and the glorious majesty of His kingship. מ Your kingdom is an everlasting kingdom, and Your reign is for all generations. ס The LORD supports all who fall, and raises all who are bowed down. ע All raise their eyes to You in hope, and You give them their food in due season. פ You open Your hand, and satisfy every living thing with favor. צ The LORD is righteous in all His ways, and kind in all He does. ק The LORD is close to all who call on Him, to all who call on Him in truth. ר He fulfills the will of those who fear Him; He hears their cry and saves them. ש The LORD guards all who love Him, but all the wicked He will destroy. ת ▸ My mouth shall speak the praise of the LORD, and all creatures shall bless His holy name for ever and all time.

We will bless the LORD now and for ever. Halleluya! *Ps. 115*

מנחה לשבת

אַשְׁרֵי יוֹשְׁבֵי בֵיתֶךָ, עוֹד יְהַלְלְוּךָ סֶּלָה: תהלים פד

אַשְׁרֵי הָעָם שֶׁכָּכָה לּוֹ, אַשְׁרֵי הָעָם שֶׁיהוה אֱלֹהָיו: תהלים קמד

תְּהִלָּה לְדָוִד, תהלים קמה

אֲרוֹמִמְךָ אֱלוֹהַי הַמֶּלֶךְ, וַאֲבָרְכָה שִׁמְךָ לְעוֹלָם וָעֶד:

בְּכָל־יוֹם אֲבָרְכֶךָּ, וַאֲהַלְלָה שִׁמְךָ לְעוֹלָם וָעֶד:

גָּדוֹל יהוה וּמְהֻלָּל מְאֹד, וְלִגְדֻלָּתוֹ אֵין חֵקֶר:

דּוֹר לְדוֹר יְשַׁבַּח מַעֲשֶׂיךָ, וּגְבוּרֹתֶיךָ יַגִּידוּ:

הֲדַר כְּבוֹד הוֹדֶךָ, וְדִבְרֵי נִפְלְאוֹתֶיךָ אָשִׂיחָה:

וֶעֱזוּז נוֹרְאוֹתֶיךָ יֹאמֵרוּ, וּגְדוּלָּתְךָ אֲסַפְּרֶנָּה:

זֵכֶר רַב־טוּבְךָ יַבִּיעוּ, וְצִדְקָתְךָ יְרַנֵּנוּ:

חַנּוּן וְרַחוּם יהוה, אֶרֶךְ אַפַּיִם וּגְדָל־חָסֶד:

טוֹב־יהוה לַכֹּל, וְרַחֲמָיו עַל־כָּל־מַעֲשָׂיו:

יוֹדוּךָ יהוה כָּל־מַעֲשֶׂיךָ, וַחֲסִידֶיךָ יְבָרְכוּכָה:

כְּבוֹד מַלְכוּתְךָ יֹאמֵרוּ, וּגְבוּרָתְךָ יְדַבֵּרוּ:

לְהוֹדִיעַ לִבְנֵי הָאָדָם גְּבוּרֹתָיו, וּכְבוֹד הֲדַר מַלְכוּתוֹ:

מַלְכוּתְךָ מַלְכוּת כָּל־עֹלָמִים, וּמֶמְשַׁלְתְּךָ בְּכָל־דּוֹר וָדֹר:

סוֹמֵךְ יהוה לְכָל־הַנֹּפְלִים, וְזוֹקֵף לְכָל־הַכְּפוּפִים:

עֵינֵי־כֹל אֵלֶיךָ יְשַׂבֵּרוּ, וְאַתָּה נוֹתֵן־לָהֶם אֶת־אָכְלָם בְּעִתּוֹ:

פּוֹתֵחַ אֶת־יָדֶךָ, וּמַשְׂבִּיעַ לְכָל־חַי רָצוֹן:

צַדִּיק יהוה בְּכָל־דְּרָכָיו, וְחָסִיד בְּכָל־מַעֲשָׂיו:

קָרוֹב יהוה לְכָל־קֹרְאָיו, לְכֹל אֲשֶׁר יִקְרָאֻהוּ בֶאֱמֶת:

רְצוֹן־יְרֵאָיו יַעֲשֶׂה, וְאֶת־שַׁוְעָתָם יִשְׁמַע, וְיוֹשִׁיעֵם:

שׁוֹמֵר יהוה אֶת־כָּל־אֹהֲבָיו, וְאֵת כָּל־הָרְשָׁעִים יַשְׁמִיד:

◂ תְּהִלַּת יהוה יְדַבֶּר פִּי, וִיבָרֵךְ כָּל־בָּשָׂר שֵׁם קָדְשׁוֹ לְעוֹלָם וָעֶד:

וַאֲנַחְנוּ נְבָרֵךְ יָהּ מֵעַתָּה וְעַד־עוֹלָם, הַלְלוּיָהּ: תהלים קטו

וּבָא לְצִיּוֹן גּוֹאֵל "A redeemer will come to Zion, *Is. 59*
to those of Jacob who repent of their sins," declares the LORD.
"As for Me, this is My covenant with them," says the LORD.
"My spirit, that is on you, and My words I have placed in your mouth will not depart from your mouth, or from the mouth of your children, or from the mouth of their descendants from this time on and for ever," says the LORD.

▸ You are the Holy One, enthroned on the praises of Israel. *Ps. 22*
And [the angels] call to one another, saying, ◂ "Holy, holy, holy is the LORD of multitudes; the whole world is filled with His glory."
And they receive permission from one another, saying: *Targum Yonatan Is. 6*
"Holy in the highest heavens, home of His Presence; holy on earth, the work of His strength; holy for ever and all time is the LORD of multitudes; the whole earth is full of His radiant glory."

▸ Then a wind lifted me up and I heard behind me the sound of a great noise, saying, ◂ "Blessed is the LORD's glory from His place." *Ezek. 3*
Then a wind lifted me up and I heard behind me *Targum Yonatan Ezek. 3*
the sound of a great tempest of those who uttered praise, saying,
"Blessed is the LORD's glory from the place of the home of His Presence."

The LORD shall reign for ever and all time. *Ex. 15*
The LORD's kingdom is established for ever and all time. *Targum Onkelos Ex. 15*

יהוה LORD, God of Abraham, Isaac and Yisrael, our ancestors, may *1 Chr. 29*
You keep this for ever so that it forms the thoughts in Your people's
heart, and directs their heart toward You. He is compassionate. He *Ps. 78*
forgives wrongdoing and does not destroy. Repeatedly He sup-
presses His anger, not not rousing His full fury. For You, my LORD, *Ps. 86*
are good and forgiving, generously kind to all who call on You. Your *Ps. 119*
righteousness is eternally righteous, and Your Torah is truth. Give *Micah 7*
truth to Jacob, loving-kindness to Abraham, as You promised our
ancestors in ancient times. Blessed is my LORD for day after day He *Ps. 68*
burdens us [with His blessings]; is our salvation, Selah! The LORD *Ps. 46*
of multitudes is with us; the God of Jacob is our refuge, Selah! LORD *Ps. 84*
of multitudes, happy is the one who trusts in You. LORD, save. May *Ps. 20*
the King answer us on the day we call.

וּבָא לְצִיּוֹן גּוֹאֵל, וּלְשָׁבֵי פֶשַׁע בְּיַעֲקֹב, נְאֻם יהוה: ישעיה נט
וַאֲנִי זֹאת בְּרִיתִי אוֹתָם, אָמַר יהוה
רוּחִי אֲשֶׁר עָלֶיךָ וּדְבָרַי אֲשֶׁר־שַׂמְתִּי בְּפִיךָ
לֹא־יָמְוּשׁוּ מִפִּיךָ וּמִפִּי זַרְעֲךָ וּמִפִּי זֶרַע זַרְעֲךָ
אָמַר יהוה, מֵעַתָּה וְעַד־עוֹלָם:

◂ וְאַתָּה קָדוֹשׁ יוֹשֵׁב תְּהִלּוֹת יִשְׂרָאֵל: וְקָרָא זֶה אֶל־זֶה וְאָמַר ◂ תהלים כב ישעיה ו
קָדוֹשׁ, קָדוֹשׁ, קָדוֹשׁ, יהוה צְבָאוֹת, מְלֹא כָל־הָאָרֶץ כְּבוֹדוֹ:
וּמְקַבְּלִין דֵּין מִן דֵּין וְאָמְרִין, קַדִּישׁ בִּשְׁמֵי מְרוֹמָא עִלָּאָה בֵּית שְׁכִינְתֵהּ תרגום יונתן ישעיה ו
קַדִּישׁ עַל אַרְעָא עוֹבַד גְּבוּרְתֵהּ, קַדִּישׁ לְעָלַם וּלְעָלְמֵי עָלְמַיָּא
יהוה צְבָאוֹת, מַלְיָא כָל אַרְעָא זִיו יְקָרֵהּ.

◂ וַתִּשָּׂאֵנִי רוּחַ, וָאֶשְׁמַע אַחֲרַי קוֹל רַעַשׁ גָּדוֹל ◂ יחזקאל ג
בָּרוּךְ כְּבוֹד־יהוה מִמְּקוֹמוֹ:
וּנְטָלַתְנִי רוּחָא, וּשְׁמָעִית בַּתְרַי קָל זִיעַ סַגִּיא, דִּמְשַׁבְּחִין וְאָמְרִין תרגום יונתן יחזקאל ג
בְּרִיךְ יְקָרָא דַיהוה מֵאֲתַר בֵּית שְׁכִינְתֵהּ.

יהוה יִמְלֹךְ לְעֹלָם וָעֶד: שמות טו
יהוה מַלְכוּתֵהּ קָאֵם לְעָלַם וּלְעָלְמֵי עָלְמַיָּא. תרגום אונקלוס שמות טו

יהוה אֱלֹהֵי אַבְרָהָם יִצְחָק וְיִשְׂרָאֵל אֲבֹתֵינוּ, שָׁמְרָה־זֹּאת לְעוֹלָם דברי הימים א, כט
לְיֵצֶר מַחְשְׁבוֹת לְבַב עַמֶּךָ, וְהָכֵן לְבָבָם אֵלֶיךָ: וְהוּא רַחוּם יְכַפֵּר עָוֹן תהלים עח
וְלֹא־יַשְׁחִית, וְהִרְבָּה לְהָשִׁיב אַפּוֹ, וְלֹא־יָעִיר כָּל־חֲמָתוֹ: כִּי־אַתָּה תהלים פו
אֲדֹנָי טוֹב וְסַלָּח, וְרַב־חֶסֶד לְכָל־קֹרְאֶיךָ: צִדְקָתְךָ צֶדֶק לְעוֹלָם תהלים קיט
וְתוֹרָתְךָ אֱמֶת: תִּתֵּן אֱמֶת לְיַעֲקֹב, חֶסֶד לְאַבְרָהָם, אֲשֶׁר־נִשְׁבַּעְתָּ מיכה ז
לַאֲבֹתֵינוּ מִימֵי קֶדֶם: בָּרוּךְ אֲדֹנָי יוֹם יוֹם יַעֲמָס־לָנוּ, הָאֵל יְשׁוּעָתֵנוּ תהלים סח
סֶלָה: יהוה צְבָאוֹת עִמָּנוּ, מִשְׂגָּב לָנוּ אֱלֹהֵי יַעֲקֹב סֶלָה: יהוה תהלים מו תהלים כ
צְבָאוֹת, אַשְׁרֵי אָדָם בֹּטֵחַ בָּךְ: יהוה הוֹשִׁיעָה, הַמֶּלֶךְ יַעֲנֵנוּ בְיוֹם־ תהלים פד
קָרְאֵנוּ:

בָּרוּךְ Blessed is He, our God, who created us for His glory, separating us from those who go astray; who gave us the Torah of truth, planting within us eternal life. May He open our heart to His Torah, imbuing our heart with the love and awe of Him, that we may do His will and serve Him with a perfect heart, so that we neither toil in vain nor give birth to confusion.

יְהִי רָצוֹן May it be Your will, O LORD our God and God of our ancestors, that we keep Your laws in this world, and thus be worthy to live, see and inherit goodness and blessing in the Messianic Age and in
the life of the World to Come. So that my soul may sing to You and *Ps. 30*
not be silent. LORD, my God, for ever I will thank You. Blessed is *Jer. 17*
the man who trusts in the LORD, whose trust is in the LORD alone.
Trust in the LORD for evermore, for God, the LORD, is an everlast- *Is. 26*
ing Rock. ▸ Those who know Your name trust in You, for You, LORD, *Ps. 9*
do not abandon those who seek You. The LORD desired, for the *Is. 42*
sake of Israel's merit, to make the Torah great and glorious.

HALF KADDISH

Leader: יִתְגַּדַּל Magnified and sanctified
may His great name be,
in the world He created by His will.
May He establish His kingdom
in your lifetime and in your days,
and in the lifetime of all the house of Israel,
swiftly and soon – and say: Amen.

All: May His great name be blessed for ever and all time.

Leader: Blessed and praised, glorified and elevated,
raised and honored, uplifted and praised
be the name of the Holy One, blessed be He,
beyond any blessing,
song, praise and consolation uttered in the world –
and say: Amen.

בָּרוּךְ הוּא אֱלֹהֵינוּ שֶׁבְּרָאָנוּ לִכְבוֹדוֹ, וְהִבְדִּילָנוּ מִן הַתּוֹעִים, וְנָתַן
לָנוּ תּוֹרַת אֱמֶת, וְחַיֵּי עוֹלָם נָטַע בְּתוֹכֵנוּ. הוּא יִפְתַּח לִבֵּנוּ בְּתוֹרָתוֹ,
וְיָשֵׂם בְּלִבֵּנוּ אַהֲבָתוֹ וְיִרְאָתוֹ וְלַעֲשׂוֹת רְצוֹנוֹ וּלְעָבְדוֹ בְּלֵבָב שָׁלֵם,
לְמַעַן לֹא נִיגַע לָרִיק וְלֹא נֵלֵד לַבֶּהָלָה.

יְהִי רָצוֹן מִלְּפָנֶיךָ יהוה אֱלֹהֵינוּ וֵאלֹהֵי אֲבוֹתֵינוּ, שֶׁנִּשְׁמֹר חֻקֶּיךָ
בָּעוֹלָם הַזֶּה, וְנִזְכֶּה וְנִחְיֶה וְנִרְאֶה וְנִירַשׁ טוֹבָה וּבְרָכָה, לִשְׁנֵי יְמוֹת
הַמָּשִׁיחַ וּלְחַיֵּי הָעוֹלָם הַבָּא. לְמַעַן יְזַמֶּרְךָ כָבוֹד וְלֹא יִדֹּם, יהוה תהלים ל
אֱלֹהַי, לְעוֹלָם אוֹדֶךָּ: בָּרוּךְ הַגֶּבֶר אֲשֶׁר יִבְטַח בַּיהוה, וְהָיָה יהוה ירמיה יז
מִבְטַחוֹ: בִּטְחוּ בַיהוה עֲדֵי־עַד, כִּי בְּיָהּ יהוה צוּר עוֹלָמִים: ◂ וְיִבְטְחוּ ישעיה כו תהלים ט
בְךָ יוֹדְעֵי שְׁמֶךָ, כִּי לֹא־עָזַבְתָּ דֹרְשֶׁיךָ, יהוה: יהוה חָפֵץ לְמַעַן צִדְקוֹ, ישעיה מב
יַגְדִּיל תּוֹרָה וְיַאְדִּיר:

חצי קדיש

ש״ץ: יִתְגַּדַּל וְיִתְקַדַּשׁ שְׁמֵהּ רַבָּא (קהל: אָמֵן)
בְּעָלְמָא דִּי בְרָא כִרְעוּתֵהּ
וְיַמְלִיךְ מַלְכוּתֵהּ
בְּחַיֵּיכוֹן וּבְיוֹמֵיכוֹן וּבְחַיֵּי דְכָל בֵּית יִשְׂרָאֵל
בַּעֲגָלָא וּבִזְמַן קָרִיב, וְאִמְרוּ אָמֵן. (קהל: אָמֵן)

קהל וש״ץ: יְהֵא שְׁמֵהּ רַבָּא מְבָרַךְ לְעָלַם וּלְעָלְמֵי עָלְמַיָּא.

ש״ץ: יִתְבָּרַךְ וְיִשְׁתַּבַּח וְיִתְפָּאַר וְיִתְרוֹמַם וְיִתְנַשֵּׂא
וְיִתְהַדָּר וְיִתְעַלֶּה וְיִתְהַלָּל
שְׁמֵהּ דְּקֻדְשָׁא בְּרִיךְ הוּא (קהל: בְּרִיךְ הוּא)
לְעֵלָּא מִן כָּל בִּרְכָתָא / בשבת שובה: לְעֵלָּא לְעֵלָּא מִכָּל בִּרְכָתָא/
וְשִׁירָתָא, תֻּשְׁבְּחָתָא וְנֶחֱמָתָא
דַּאֲמִירָן בְּעָלְמָא, וְאִמְרוּ אָמֵן. (קהל: אָמֵן)

REMOVING THE TORAH

וַאֲנִי As for me, may my prayer come to You, LORD, Ps. 69
at a time of favor. O God, in Your great love,
answer me with Your faithful salvation.

The Ark is opened and the congregation stands. All say:

וַיְהִי בִּנְסֹעַ Whenever the Ark set out, Moses would say, Num. 10
"Arise, LORD, and may Your enemies be scattered.
May those who hate You flee before You."
For the Torah shall come forth from Zion, Is. 2
and the word of the LORD from Jerusalem.
Blessed is He who in His Holiness
gave the Torah to His people Israel.

Blessed is the name of the Master of the Universe. Blessed is Your crown and Your place. May Your favor always be with Your people Israel. Show Your people the salvation of Your right hand in Your Temple. Give us the gift of Your good light, and accept our prayers in mercy. May it be Your will to prolong our life in goodness. May I be counted among the righteous, so that You will have compassion on me and protect me and all that is mine and all that is Your people Israel's. You feed all; You sustain all; You rule over all; You rule over kings, for sovereignty is Yours. I am a servant of the Holy One, blessed be He, before whom and before whose glorious Torah I bow at all times. Not in man do I trust, nor on any angel do I rely, but on the God of heaven who is the God of truth, whose Torah is truth, whose prophets speak truth, and who abounds in acts of love and truth. ▸ In Him I trust, and to His holy and glorious name I offer praises. May it be Your will to open my heart to the Torah, and to fulfill the wishes of my heart and of the hearts of all Your people Israel for good, for life, and for peace. *Zohar, Vayak-hel*

The Leader takes the Torah scroll in his right arm, bows toward the Ark and says:

Magnify the LORD with me,
and let us elevate His name together. Ps. 34

The Ark is closed.
The Leader carries the Torah scroll to the bima and the congregation says:

לְךָ Yours, LORD, are the greatness and the power, the glory and the majesty and splendor, for everything in heaven and earth is Yours. Yours, LORD, is the kingdom; You are elevated as Head over all. *I Chr. 29*

רוֹמְמוּ Elevate the LORD our God and bow to His footstool; He is holy. Elevate the LORD our God, and bow at His holy mountain, for holy is the LORD our God. *Ps. 99*

הוצאת ספר תורה

וַאֲנִי תְפִלָּתִי־לְךָ יהוה, עֵת רָצוֹן, אֱלֹהִים בְּרָב־חַסְדֶּךָ עֲנֵנִי בֶּאֱמֶת יִשְׁעֶךָ: תהלים סט

The ארון קודש *is opened and the* קהל *stands. All say:*

וַיְהִי בִּנְסֹעַ הָאָרֹן וַיֹּאמֶר מֹשֶׁה במדבר י
קוּמָה יהוה וְיָפֻצוּ אֹיְבֶיךָ וְיָנֻסוּ מְשַׂנְאֶיךָ מִפָּנֶיךָ:
כִּי מִצִּיּוֹן תֵּצֵא תוֹרָה וּדְבַר־יהוה מִירוּשָׁלָםִ: ישעיה ב
בָּרוּךְ שֶׁנָּתַן תּוֹרָה לְעַמּוֹ יִשְׂרָאֵל בִּקְדֻשָּׁתוֹ.

זוהר ויקהל בְּרִיךְ שְׁמֵהּ דְּמָרֵא עָלְמָא, בְּרִיךְ כִּתְרָךְ וְאַתְרָךְ. יְהֵא רְעוּתָךְ עִם עַמָּךְ יִשְׂרָאֵל לְעָלַם, וּפֻרְקַן יְמִינָךְ אַחֲזִי לְעַמָּךְ בְּבֵית מַקְדְּשָׁךְ, וּלְאַמְטוֹיֵי לָנָא מִטּוּב נְהוֹרָךְ, וּלְקַבֵּל צְלוֹתָנָא בְּרַחֲמִין. יְהֵא רַעֲוָא קֳדָמָךְ דְּתוֹרִיךְ לָן חַיִּין בְּטִיבוּ, וְלֶהֱוֵי אֲנָא פְקִידָא בְּגוֹ צַדִּיקַיָּא, לְמִרְחַם עָלַי וּלְמִנְטַר יָתִי וְיַת כָּל דִּי לִי וְדִי לְעַמָּךְ יִשְׂרָאֵל. אַנְתְּ הוּא זָן לְכֹלָּא וּמְפַרְנֵס לְכֹלָּא, אַנְתְּ הוּא שַׁלִּיט עַל כֹּלָּא, אַנְתְּ הוּא דְּשַׁלִּיט עַל מַלְכַיָּא, וּמַלְכוּתָא דִּילָךְ הִיא. אֲנָא עַבְדָּא דְקֻדְשָׁא בְּרִיךְ הוּא, דְּסָגֵדְנָא קַמֵּהּ וּמִקַּמֵּי דִּיקַר אוֹרַיְתֵהּ בְּכָל עִדָּן וְעִדָּן. לָא עַל אֱנָשׁ רָחִיצְנָא וְלָא עַל בַּר אֱלָהִין סָמִיכְנָא, אֶלָּא בֶּאֱלָהָא דִשְׁמַיָּא, דְּהוּא אֱלָהָא קְשׁוֹט, וְאוֹרַיְתֵהּ קְשׁוֹט, וּנְבִיאוֹהִי קְשׁוֹט, וּמַסְגֵּא לְמֶעְבַּד טַבְוָן וּקְשׁוֹט. ◂ בֵּהּ אֲנָא רָחִיץ, וְלִשְׁמֵהּ קַדִּישָׁא יַקִּירָא אֲנָא אֵמַר תֻּשְׁבְּחָן. יְהֵא רַעֲוָא קֳדָמָךְ דְּתִפְתַּח לִבַּאי בְּאוֹרַיְתָא, וְתַשְׁלִים מִשְׁאֲלִין דְּלִבַּאי וְלִבָּא דְכָל עַמָּךְ יִשְׂרָאֵל לְטָב וּלְחַיִּין וְלִשְׁלָם.

The שליח ציבור *takes the* ספר תורה *in his right arm, bows toward the* ארון קודש *and says:*

גַּדְּלוּ לַיהוה אִתִּי וּנְרוֹמְמָה שְׁמוֹ יַחְדָּו: תהלים לד

The ארון קודש *is closed.*
The שליח ציבור *carries the* ספר תורה *to the* בימה *and the* קהל *says:*

דברי הימים א׳ כט לְךָ יהוה הַגְּדֻלָּה וְהַגְּבוּרָה וְהַתִּפְאֶרֶת וְהַנֵּצַח וְהַהוֹד, כִּי־כֹל בַּשָּׁמַיִם וּבָאָרֶץ: לְךָ יהוה הַמַּמְלָכָה וְהַמִּתְנַשֵּׂא לְכֹל לְרֹאשׁ:

תהלים צט רוֹמְמוּ יהוה אֱלֹהֵינוּ וְהִשְׁתַּחֲווּ לַהֲדֹם רַגְלָיו, קָדוֹשׁ הוּא: רוֹמְמוּ יהוה אֱלֹהֵינוּ וְהִשְׁתַּחֲווּ לְהַר קָדְשׁוֹ, כִּי־קָדוֹשׁ יהוה אֱלֹהֵינוּ:

אַב הָרַחֲמִים May the Father of compassion have compassion on the people borne by Him. May He remember the covenant with the mighty [patriarchs], and save us from evil times. May He reproach the evil instinct in the people carried by Him, and graciously give that we be an everlasting remnant. May He fulfill in good measure our requests for salvation and compassion.

The Torah scroll is placed on the bima and the Gabbai calls a Kohen to the Torah.

וְתִגָּלֶה May His kingship over us be soon revealed and seen. May He be gracious to our surviving remnant, the survivors of His people the house of Israel in grace, loving-kindness, compassion and favor, and let us say: Amen. Let us all give greatness to our God and give honor to the Torah. *Let the Kohen come forward. Arise (*name* son of *father's name*), the Kohen.

**If no Kohen is present, a Levi or Yisrael is called up as follows:*

/As there is no Kohen, arise (*name* son of *father's name*) in place of a Kohen./

Blessed is He who, in His holiness, gave the Torah to His people Israel.

The congregation followed by the Gabbai:

You who cling to the LORD your God are all alive today. *Deut. 4*

The appropriate Torah portions are to be found from page 1070.

The Reader shows the oleh the section to be read. The oleh touches the scroll at that place with the tzitzit of his tallit or the fabric belt of the Torah scroll, which he then kisses. Holding the handles of the scroll, he says:

Oleh: Bless the LORD, the blessed One.

Cong: Bless the LORD, the blessed One, for ever and all time.

Oleh: Bless the LORD, the blessed One, for ever and all time.
Blessed are You, LORD our God, King of the Universe, who has chosen us from all peoples and has given us His Torah. Blessed are You, LORD, Giver of the Torah.

After the reading, the oleh says:

Oleh: Blessed are You, LORD our God, King of the Universe, who has given us the Torah of truth, planting everlasting life in our midst. Blessed are You, LORD, Giver of the Torah.

The Torah scroll is lifted and the congregation says:

וְזֹאת הַתּוֹרָה This is the Torah that Moses placed before the children of *Deut. 4*
Israel, at the LORD's commandment, by the hand of Moses. *Num. 9*

Some add: It is a tree of life to those who grasp it, and those who uphold it are happy. Its *Prov. 3* ways are ways of pleasantness, and all its paths are peace. Long life is in its right hand; in its left, riches and honor. It pleased the LORD for the sake of [Israel's] *Is. 42* righteousness, to make the Torah great and glorious.

The Torah scroll is bound and covered.

אַב הָרַחֲמִים הוּא יְרַחֵם עַם עֲמוּסִים, וְיִזְכֹּר בְּרִית אֵיתָנִים, וְיַצִּיל נַפְשׁוֹתֵינוּ מִן הַשָּׁעוֹת הָרָעוֹת, וְיִגְעַר בְּיֵצֶר הָרָע מִן הַנְּשׂוּאִים, וְיָחֹן אוֹתָנוּ לִפְלֵיטַת עוֹלָמִים, וִימַלֵּא מִשְׁאֲלוֹתֵינוּ בְּמִדָּה טוֹבָה יְשׁוּעָה וְרַחֲמִים.

The ספר תורה *is placed on the* שולחן *and the* גבאי *calls a* כהן *to the* תורה.

וְתִגָּלֶה וְתֵרָאֶה מַלְכוּתוֹ עָלֵינוּ בִּזְמַן קָרוֹב, וְיָחֹן פְּלֵיטָתֵנוּ וּפְלֵיטַת עַמּוֹ בֵּית יִשְׂרָאֵל לְחֵן וּלְחֶסֶד וּלְרַחֲמִים וּלְרָצוֹן וְנֹאמַר אָמֵן. הַכֹּל הָבוּ גֹדֶל לֵאלֹהֵינוּ וּתְנוּ כָבוֹד לַתּוֹרָה.
*כֹּהֵן קְרָב, יַעֲמֹד (פלוני בֶּן פלוני) הַכֹּהֵן.

**If no* כהן *is present, a* לוי *or* ישראל *is called up as follows:*

/אֵין כָּאן כֹּהֵן, יַעֲמֹד (פלוני בֶּן פלוני) בִּמְקוֹם כֹּהֵן./

בָּרוּךְ שֶׁנָּתַן תּוֹרָה לְעַמּוֹ יִשְׂרָאֵל בִּקְדֻשָּׁתוֹ.

The קהל *followed by the* גבאי:

דברים ד — וְאַתֶּם הַדְּבֵקִים בַּיהוה אֱלֹהֵיכֶם חַיִּים כֻּלְּכֶם הַיּוֹם:

The appropriate תורה *portions are to be found from page 1070.*

The קורא *shows the* עולה *the section to be read. The* עולה *touches the scroll at that place with the* ציצית *of his* טלית *or the gartel of the* ספר תורה, *which he then kisses. Holding the handles of the scroll, he says:*

עולה: בָּרְכוּ אֶת יהוה הַמְבֹרָךְ.

קהל: בָּרוּךְ יהוה הַמְבֹרָךְ לְעוֹלָם וָעֶד.

עולה: בָּרוּךְ יהוה הַמְבֹרָךְ לְעוֹלָם וָעֶד.
בָּרוּךְ אַתָּה יהוה אֱלֹהֵינוּ מֶלֶךְ הָעוֹלָם, אֲשֶׁר בָּחַר בָּנוּ מִכָּל הָעַמִּים, וְנָתַן לָנוּ אֶת תּוֹרָתוֹ. בָּרוּךְ אַתָּה יהוה, נוֹתֵן הַתּוֹרָה.

After the קריאת התורה, *the* עולה *says:*

עולה: בָּרוּךְ אַתָּה יהוה אֱלֹהֵינוּ מֶלֶךְ הָעוֹלָם, אֲשֶׁר נָתַן לָנוּ תּוֹרַת אֱמֶת, וְחַיֵּי עוֹלָם נָטַע בְּתוֹכֵנוּ. בָּרוּךְ אַתָּה יהוה, נוֹתֵן הַתּוֹרָה.

The ספר תורה *is lifted and the* קהל *says:*

דברים ד — וְזֹאת הַתּוֹרָה אֲשֶׁר־שָׂם מֹשֶׁה לִפְנֵי בְּנֵי יִשְׂרָאֵל:
במדבר ט — עַל־פִּי יהוה בְּיַד מֹשֶׁה:

Some add — משלי ג — עֵץ־חַיִּים הִיא לַמַּחֲזִיקִים בָּהּ וְתֹמְכֶיהָ מְאֻשָּׁר: דְּרָכֶיהָ דַרְכֵי־נֹעַם וְכָל־
נְתִיבוֹתֶיהָ שָׁלוֹם: אֹרֶךְ יָמִים בִּימִינָהּ, בִּשְׂמֹאולָהּ עֹשֶׁר וְכָבוֹד: יהוה חָפֵץ — ישעיה מב
לְמַעַן צִדְקוֹ יַגְדִּיל תּוֹרָה וְיַאְדִּיר:

The ספר תורה *is bound and covered.*

In some congregations, during the week before a yahrzeit, "God, full of mercy" is said.

For a male close relative:

אֵל מָלֵא רַחֲמִים God, full of mercy, who is present on high, give fitting rest on the wings of the Divine Presence, in the heights of the holy and the pure who shine like the radiance of heaven, to the soul of (*name* son of *father's name*) who has gone to his eternal home, and to this I pledge (without formal vow) to give charity in his memory, may his resting place be in the Garden of Eden. Therefore, Master of compassion, shelter him in the shadow of Your wings forever and bind his soul in the bond of everlasting life. The LORD is his heritage; may he rest in peace, and let us say: Amen.

For a female close relative:

אֵל מָלֵא רַחֲמִים God, full of mercy, who is present on high, give fitting rest on the wings of the Divine Presence, in the heights of the holy and the pure who shine like the radiance of heaven, to the soul of (*name* daughter of *father's name*) who has gone to her eternal home, and to this I pledge (without formal vow) to give charity in her memory, may her resting place be in the Garden of Eden. Therefore, Master of compassion, shelter her in the shadow of Your wings forever and bind her soul in the bond of everlasting life. The LORD is her heritage; may she rest in peace, and let us say: Amen.

RETURNING THE TORAH TO THE ARK

The Ark is opened. The Leader takes the Torah scroll and says:

יְהַלְלוּ Let them praise the name of the LORD, for His name alone is sublime. *Ps. 148*

The congregation responds:

הודו His majesty is above earth and heaven. He has raised the horn of His people, for the glory of all His devoted ones, the children of Israel, the people close to Him. Halleluya!

As the Torah scroll is returned to the Ark say:

לְדָוִד מִזְמוֹר A psalm of David. The earth is the LORD's and all it contains, *Ps. 24* the world and all who live in it. For He founded it on the seas and established it on the streams. Who may climb the mountain of the LORD? Who may stand in His holy place? He who has clean hands and a pure heart, who has not taken My name in vain, or sworn dishonestly. He shall receive blessing from the LORD, and just reward from God, his salvation. This is a generation of those who seek Him, the descendants of Jacob who seek Your presence, Selah! Lift up your heads, O gates; be uplifted, eternal doors, so that the King of glory may enter. Who is the

In some congregations, during the week before a yahrzeit, אֵל מָלֵא רַחֲמִים *is said.*

For a male close relative:

אֵל מָלֵא רַחֲמִים, שׁוֹכֵן בַּמְּרוֹמִים, הַמְצֵא מְנוּחָה נְכוֹנָה עַל כַּנְפֵי הַשְּׁכִינָה, בְּמַעֲלוֹת קְדוֹשִׁים וּטְהוֹרִים, כְּזֹהַר הָרָקִיעַ מַזְהִירִים, לְנִשְׁמַת (פלוני בֶּן פלוני) שֶׁהָלַךְ לְעוֹלָמוֹ, בַּעֲבוּר שֶׁבְּלִי נֶדֶר אֶתֵּן צְדָקָה בְּעַד הַזְכָּרַת נִשְׁמָתוֹ, בְּגַן עֵדֶן תְּהֵא מְנוּחָתוֹ. לָכֵן, בַּעַל הָרַחֲמִים יַסְתִּירֵהוּ בְּסֵתֶר כְּנָפָיו לְעוֹלָמִים, וְיִצְרֹר בִּצְרוֹר הַחַיִּים אֶת נִשְׁמָתוֹ, יהוה הוּא נַחֲלָתוֹ, וְיָנְוּחַ בְּשָׁלוֹם עַל מִשְׁכָּבוֹ, וְנֹאמַר אָמֵן.

For a female close relative:

אֵל מָלֵא רַחֲמִים, שׁוֹכֵן בַּמְּרוֹמִים, הַמְצֵא מְנוּחָה נְכוֹנָה עַל כַּנְפֵי הַשְּׁכִינָה, בְּמַעֲלוֹת קְדוֹשִׁים וּטְהוֹרִים, כְּזֹהַר הָרָקִיעַ מַזְהִירִים, לְנִשְׁמַת (פלונית בַּת פלוני) שֶׁהָלְכָה לְעוֹלָמָהּ, בַּעֲבוּר שֶׁבְּלִי נֶדֶר אֶתֵּן צְדָקָה בְּעַד הַזְכָּרַת נִשְׁמָתָהּ, בְּגַן עֵדֶן תְּהֵא מְנוּחָתָהּ. לָכֵן, בַּעַל הָרַחֲמִים יַסְתִּירֶהָ בְּסֵתֶר כְּנָפָיו לְעוֹלָמִים, וְיִצְרֹר בִּצְרוֹר הַחַיִּים אֶת נִשְׁמָתָהּ, יהוה הוּא נַחֲלָתָהּ, וְתָנְוּחַ בְּשָׁלוֹם עַל מִשְׁכָּבָהּ, וְנֹאמַר אָמֵן.

הכנסת ספר תורה

The ארון קודש *is opened. The* שליח ציבור *takes the* ספר תורה *and says:*

יְהַלְלוּ אֶת־שֵׁם יהוה, כִּי־נִשְׂגָּב שְׁמוֹ, לְבַדּוֹ תהלים קמח

The קהל *responds:*

הוֹדוֹ עַל־אֶרֶץ וְשָׁמָיִם: וַיָּרֶם קֶרֶן לְעַמּוֹ, תְּהִלָּה לְכָל־חֲסִידָיו, לִבְנֵי יִשְׂרָאֵל עַם קְרֹבוֹ, הַלְלוּיָהּ:

As the ספר תורה *is returned to the* ארון קודש*, say:*

תהלים כד לְדָוִד מִזְמוֹר, לַיהוה הָאָרֶץ וּמְלוֹאָהּ, תֵּבֵל וְיֹשְׁבֵי בָהּ: כִּי־הוּא עַל־יַמִּים יְסָדָהּ, וְעַל־נְהָרוֹת יְכוֹנְנֶהָ: מִי־יַעֲלֶה בְהַר־יהוה, וּמִי־יָקוּם בִּמְקוֹם קָדְשׁוֹ: נְקִי כַפַּיִם וּבַר־לֵבָב, אֲשֶׁר לֹא־נָשָׂא לַשָּׁוְא נַפְשִׁי וְלֹא נִשְׁבַּע לְמִרְמָה: יִשָּׂא בְרָכָה מֵאֵת יהוה, וּצְדָקָה מֵאֱלֹהֵי יִשְׁעוֹ: זֶה דּוֹר דֹּרְשָׁו, מְבַקְשֵׁי פָנֶיךָ, יַעֲקֹב, סֶלָה: שְׂאוּ שְׁעָרִים רָאשֵׁיכֶם, וְהִנָּשְׂאוּ פִּתְחֵי עוֹלָם, וְיָבוֹא מֶלֶךְ הַכָּבוֹד: מִי זֶה מֶלֶךְ הַכָּבוֹד, יהוה

King of glory? It is the LORD, strong and mighty, the LORD mighty in battle. Lift up your heads, O gates; lift them up, eternal doors, so that the King of glory may enter. Who is He, the King of glory? The LORD of multitudes, He is the King of glory, Selah!

As the Torah scroll is placed into the Ark, say:

וּבְנֻחֹה יֹאמַר When the Ark came to rest, Moses would say: "Return, O *Num. 10*
LORD, to the countless thousands of Israel." Advance, LORD, to Your *Ps. 132*
resting place, You and Your mighty Ark. Your priests are clothed in righteousness, and Your devoted ones sing in joy. For the sake of Your
servant David, do not reject Your anointed one. For I give you good *Prov. 4*
instruction; do not abandon My Torah. It is a tree of life to those who *Prov. 3*
grasp it, and those who uphold it are happy. Its ways are ways of pleasantness, and all its paths are peace. ▸ Turn us back, O LORD, to You, and we *Lam. 5*
will return. Renew our days as of old.

The Ark is closed.

HALF KADDISH

Leader: יִתְגַּדַּל Magnified and sanctified
may His great name be,
in the world He created by His will.
May He establish His kingdom
in your lifetime and in your days,
and in the lifetime of all the house of Israel,
swiftly and soon – and say: Amen.

All: May His great name be blessed
for ever and all time.

Leader: Blessed and praised, glorified and elevated,
raised and honored, uplifted and praised
be the name of the Holy One,
blessed be He,
beyond any blessing,
song, praise and consolation
uttered in the world –
and say: Amen.

עִזּוּז וְגִבּוֹר, יהוה גִּבּוֹר מִלְחָמָה: שְׂאוּ שְׁעָרִים רָאשֵׁיכֶם, וּשְׂאוּ פִּתְחֵי עוֹלָם, וְיָבֹא מֶלֶךְ הַכָּבוֹד: מִי הוּא זֶה מֶלֶךְ הַכָּבוֹד, יהוה צְבָאוֹת הוּא מֶלֶךְ הַכָּבוֹד, סֶלָה:

As the ספר תורה *is placed into the* ארון קודש*, say:*

וּבְנֻחֹה יֹאמַר, שׁוּבָה יהוה רִבְבוֹת אַלְפֵי יִשְׂרָאֵל: קוּמָה יהוה במדבר י
לִמְנוּחָתֶךָ, אַתָּה וַאֲרוֹן עֻזֶּךָ: כֹּהֲנֶיךָ יִלְבְּשׁוּ־צֶדֶק, וַחֲסִידֶיךָ יְרַנֵּנוּ: תהלים קלב
בַּעֲבוּר דָּוִד עַבְדֶּךָ אַל־תָּשֵׁב פְּנֵי מְשִׁיחֶךָ: כִּי לֶקַח טוֹב נָתַתִּי לָכֶם, משלי ד
תּוֹרָתִי אַל־תַּעֲזֹבוּ: עֵץ־חַיִּים הִיא לַמַּחֲזִיקִים בָּהּ, וְתֹמְכֶיהָ מְאֻשָּׁר: משלי ג
דְּרָכֶיהָ דַרְכֵי־נֹעַם וְכָל־נְתִיבוֹתֶיהָ שָׁלוֹם: ◂ הֲשִׁיבֵנוּ יהוה אֵלֶיךָ וְנָשׁוּבָה, איכה ה
חַדֵּשׁ יָמֵינוּ כְּקֶדֶם:

The ארון קודש *is closed.*

חצי קדיש

ש״ץ: יִתְגַּדַּל וְיִתְקַדַּשׁ שְׁמֵהּ רַבָּא (קהל: אָמֵן)
בְּעָלְמָא דִּי בְרָא כִרְעוּתֵהּ
וְיַמְלִיךְ מַלְכוּתֵהּ
בְּחַיֵּיכוֹן וּבְיוֹמֵיכוֹן, וּבְחַיֵּי דְכָל בֵּית יִשְׂרָאֵל
בַּעֲגָלָא וּבִזְמַן קָרִיב, וְאִמְרוּ אָמֵן. (קהל: אָמֵן)

קהל וש״ץ: יְהֵא שְׁמֵהּ רַבָּא מְבָרַךְ לְעָלַם וּלְעָלְמֵי עָלְמַיָּא.

ש״ץ: יִתְבָּרַךְ וְיִשְׁתַּבַּח וְיִתְפָּאַר וְיִתְרוֹמַם וְיִתְנַשֵּׂא
וְיִתְהַדָּר וְיִתְעַלֶּה וְיִתְהַלָּל
שְׁמֵהּ דְּקֻדְשָׁא בְּרִיךְ הוּא (קהל: בְּרִיךְ הוּא)
לְעֵלָּא מִן כָּל בִּרְכָתָא
/בשבת שובה: לְעֵלָּא לְעֵלָּא מִכָּל בִּרְכָתָא/
וְשִׁירָתָא, תֻּשְׁבְּחָתָא וְנֶחֱמָתָא
דַּאֲמִירָן בְּעָלְמָא, וְאִמְרוּ אָמֵן. (קהל: אָמֵן)

THE AMIDA

The following prayer, until "in former years" on page 764, is said silently, standing with feet together. If there is a minyan, the Amida is repeated aloud by the Leader. Take three steps forward and at the points indicated by ▾, bend the knees at the first word, bow at the second, and stand straight before saying God's name.

When I declare the LORD's name, give glory to our God. *Deut. 32*
O LORD, open my lips, so that my mouth may declare Your praise. *Ps. 51*

PATRIARCHS

בָּרוּךְ Blessed are You,
LORD our God and God of our fathers,
God of Abraham, God of Isaac and God of Jacob;
the great, mighty and awesome God, God Most High,
who acts with loving-kindness and creates all,
who remembers the loving-kindness of the fathers
and will bring a Redeemer to their children's children
for the sake of His name, in love.

On Shabbat Shuva: Remember us for life, O King who desires life,
and write us in the book of life –
for Your sake, O God of life.

King, Helper, Savior, Shield:
Blessed are You, LORD, Shield of Abraham.

DIVINE MIGHT

אַתָּה גִּבּוֹר You are eternally mighty, LORD.
You give life to the dead and have great power to save.

The phrase "He makes the wind blow and the rain fall" is added from Simḥat Torah until Pesaḥ. In Israel the phrase "He causes the dew to fall" is added from Pesaḥ until Shemini Atzeret.

In fall & winter: He makes the wind blow and the rain fall.
In Israel, in spring & summer: He causes the dew to fall.

He sustains the living with loving-kindness,
and with great compassion revives the dead.
He supports the fallen, heals the sick, sets captives free,
and keeps His faith with those who sleep in the dust.

עמידה

The following prayer, until קַדְמֹנִיּוֹת *on page 765, is said silently, standing with feet together. If there is a* מנין, *the* עמידה *is repeated aloud by the* שליח ציבור. *Take three steps forward and at the points indicated by* ▾, *bend the knees at the first word, bow at the second, and stand straight before saying God's name.*

כִּי שֵׁם יהוה אֶקְרָא, הָבוּ גֹדֶל לֵאלֹהֵינוּ: דברים לב

אֲדֹנָי, שְׂפָתַי תִּפְתָּח, וּפִי יַגִּיד תְּהִלָּתֶךָ: תהלים נא

אבות

בָּרוּךְ אַתָּה יהוה, אֱלֹהֵינוּ וֵאלֹהֵי אֲבוֹתֵינוּ
אֱלֹהֵי אַבְרָהָם, אֱלֹהֵי יִצְחָק, וֵאלֹהֵי יַעֲקֹב
הָאֵל הַגָּדוֹל הַגִּבּוֹר וְהַנּוֹרָא, אֵל עֶלְיוֹן
גּוֹמֵל חֲסָדִים טוֹבִים, וְקוֹנֵה הַכֹּל
וְזוֹכֵר חַסְדֵי אָבוֹת
וּמֵבִיא גוֹאֵל לִבְנֵי בְנֵיהֶם לְמַעַן שְׁמוֹ בְּאַהֲבָה.

בשבת שובה: זָכְרֵנוּ לְחַיִּים, מֶלֶךְ חָפֵץ בַּחַיִּים
וְכָתְבֵנוּ בְּסֵפֶר הַחַיִּים, לְמַעַנְךָ אֱלֹהִים חַיִּים.

מֶלֶךְ עוֹזֵר וּמוֹשִׁיעַ וּמָגֵן.
בָּרוּךְ אַתָּה יהוה, מָגֵן אַבְרָהָם.

גבורות

אַתָּה גִּבּוֹר לְעוֹלָם, אֲדֹנָי
מְחַיֵּה מֵתִים אַתָּה, רַב לְהוֹשִׁיעַ

The phrase מַשִּׁיב הָרְוּחַ *is added from* שמחת תורה *until* פסח.
In ארץ ישראל, *the phrase* מוֹרִיד הַטָּל *is added from* פסח *until* שמיני עצרת.

בחורף: מַשִּׁיב הָרְוּחַ וּמוֹרִיד הַגֶּשֶׁם / בארץ ישראל בקיץ: מוֹרִיד הַטָּל

מְכַלְכֵּל חַיִּים בְּחֶסֶד, מְחַיֵּה מֵתִים בְּרַחֲמִים רַבִּים
סוֹמֵךְ נוֹפְלִים, וְרוֹפֵא חוֹלִים, וּמַתִּיר אֲסוּרִים
וּמְקַיֵּם אֱמוּנָתוֹ לִישֵׁנֵי עָפָר.

Who is like You, Master of might,
and who can compare to You,
O King who brings death and gives life,
and makes salvation grow?

On Shabbat Shuva: Who is like You, compassionate Father,
who remembers His creatures
in compassion, for life?

Faithful are You to revive the dead.
Blessed are You, LORD, who revives the dead.

When saying the Amida silently, continue with "You are holy" on the next page.

KEDUSHA

During the Leader's Repetition, the following is said standing with feet together, rising on the toes at the words indicated by ▲.

Cong. then Leader: נְקַדֵּשׁ We will sanctify Your name on earth,
as they sanctify it in the highest heavens,
as is written by Your prophet,
"And they [the angels] call to one another saying: *Is. 6*

Cong. then Leader: ▲Holy, ▲holy, ▲holy is the LORD of multitudes
the whole world is filled with His glory."
Those facing them say "Blessed – "

Cong. then Leader: ▲"Blessed is the LORD's glory from His place." *Ezek. 3*
And in Your holy Writings it is written thus:

Cong. then Leader: ▲"The LORD shall reign for ever. He is your God, Zion, *Ps. 146*
from generation to generation, Halleluya!"

Leader: From generation to generation
we will speak of Your greatness,
and we will declare Your holiness for evermore.
Your praise, our God, shall not leave our mouth forever,
for You, God, are a great and holy King.
Blessed are You, LORD, the holy God.
/ *On Shabbat Shuva:* the holy King./

The Leader continues with "You are One" on the next page.

מִי כָמְוֹךָ, בַּעַל גְּבוּרוֹת, וּמִי דּוֹמֶה לָּךְ
מֶלֶךְ, מֵמִית וּמְחַיֶּה וּמַצְמִיחַ יְשׁוּעָה.

בשבת שובה: **מִי כָמְוֹךָ אַב הָרַחֲמִים**
זוֹכֵר יְצוּרָיו לְחַיִּים בְּרַחֲמִים.

וְנֶאֱמָן אַתָּה לְהַחֲיוֹת מֵתִים.
בָּרוּךְ אַתָּה יהוה, מְחַיֵּה הַמֵּתִים.

When saying the עמידה *silently, continue with* אַתָּה קָדוֹשׁ *on the next page.*

קדושה

During the חזרת הש״ץ, *the following is said standing with feet together, rising on the toes at the words indicated by* ⁺.

קהל *then* ש״ץ: **נְקַדֵּשׁ אֶת שִׁמְךָ בָּעוֹלָם, כְּשֵׁם שֶׁמַּקְדִּישִׁים אוֹתוֹ בִּשְׁמֵי מָרוֹם**
כַּכָּתוּב עַל יַד נְבִיאֶךָ:
וְקָרָא זֶה אֶל־זֶה וְאָמַר ישעיה ו

קהל *then* ש״ץ: **⁺קָדוֹשׁ, ⁺קָדוֹשׁ, ⁺קָדוֹשׁ, יהוה צְבָאוֹת**
מְלֹא כָל־הָאָרֶץ כְּבוֹדוֹ:
לְעֻמָּתָם בָּרוּךְ יֹאמֵרוּ

קהל *then* ש״ץ: **⁺בָּרוּךְ כְּבוֹד־יהוה מִמְּקוֹמוֹ:** יחזקאל ג
וּבְדִבְרֵי קָדְשְׁךָ כָּתוּב לֵאמֹר

קהל *then* ש״ץ: **⁺יִמְלֹךְ יהוה לְעוֹלָם, אֱלֹהַיִךְ צִיּוֹן לְדֹר וָדֹר, הַלְלוּיָהּ:** תהלים קמו

ש״ץ: **לְדוֹר וָדוֹר נַגִּיד גָּדְלֶךָ**
וּלְנֵצַח נְצָחִים קְדֻשָּׁתְךָ נַקְדִּישׁ
וְשִׁבְחֲךָ אֱלֹהֵינוּ מִפִּינוּ לֹא יָמוּשׁ לְעוֹלָם וָעֶד
כִּי אֵל מֶלֶךְ גָּדוֹל וְקָדוֹשׁ אָתָּה.
בָּרוּךְ אַתָּה יהוה, הָאֵל הַקָּדוֹשׁ. / בשבת שובה: **הַמֶּלֶךְ הַקָּדוֹשׁ.**/

The שליח ציבור *continues with* אַתָּה אֶחָד *on the next page.*

HOLINESS

אַתָּה קָדוֹשׁ You are holy and Your name is holy,
and holy ones praise You daily, Selah!
Blessed are You, LORD,
the holy God. / *On Shabbat Shuva:* the holy King./
(If forgotten, repeat the Amida.)

HOLINESS OF THE DAY

אַתָּה You are One, Your name is One;
and who is like Your people Israel, a nation unique on earth?
Splendor of greatness and a crown of salvation
is the day of rest and holiness You have given Your people.
Abraham will rejoice, Isaac will sing for joy,
Jacob and his children will find rest in it –
a rest of love and generosity, a rest of truth and faith,
a rest of peace and tranquility, calm and trust;
a complete rest in which You find favor.
May Your children recognize and know
that their rest comes from You,
and that by their rest they sanctify Your name.

The Rebbe went on to give a learned discourse and asked the young man, "Do you understand?"

"Nyet," he replied. The Rebbe then gave a brilliant analogy, interweaving a moving story with mystical symbolism. Again he asked the young man, "Do you understand?" to which he again replied "Nyet." And then the Rebbe started a melody, a wordless song, filled with heartfelt yearning for the Messiah, suffused with love of Torah and desire to joyously hold on to the departing Shabbat.

The disciples danced, and the Russian peasant danced. With tears streaming down his cheeks, the youth turned to the Rebbe and cried out, "Now I understand." (Rabbi Shlomo Riskin)

REFLECTION

As the sun sets
on this Shabbat,
think back over Shabbat.

What was the highlight
for you?

What will you take
in to the week
from this Shabbat?

How have you
been changed
by this week's
Shabbat experience?

קדושת השם

אַתָּה קָדוֹשׁ וְשִׁמְךָ קָדוֹשׁ, וּקְדוֹשִׁים בְּכָל יוֹם יְהַלְלְוּךָ סֶּלָה.
בָּרוּךְ אַתָּה יהוה, הָאֵל הַקָּדוֹשׁ. / בשבת שובה: הַמֶּלֶךְ הַקָּדוֹשׁ./

(*If forgotten, repeat the* עמידה.)

קדושת היום

אַתָּה אֶחָד וְשִׁמְךָ אֶחָד
וּמִי כְּעַמְּךָ יִשְׂרָאֵל גּוֹי אֶחָד בָּאָרֶץ.
תִּפְאֶרֶת גְּדֻלָּה וַעֲטֶרֶת יְשׁוּעָה, יוֹם מְנוּחָה וּקְדֻשָּׁה לְעַמְּךָ נָתָתָּ.
אַבְרָהָם יָגֵל, יִצְחָק יְרַנֵּן, יַעֲקֹב וּבָנָיו יָנְוּחוּ בוֹ
מְנוּחַת אַהֲבָה וּנְדָבָה, מְנוּחַת אֱמֶת וֶאֱמוּנָה
מְנוּחַת שָׁלוֹם וְשַׁלְוָה וְהַשְׁקֵט וָבֶטַח
מְנוּחָה שְׁלֵמָה שֶׁאַתָּה רוֹצֶה בָּהּ.
יַכִּירוּ בָנֶיךָ וְיֵדְעוּ, כִּי מֵאִתְּךָ הִיא מְנוּחָתָם
וְעַל מְנוּחָתָם יַקְדִּישׁוּ אֶת שְׁמֶךָ.

CONNECTION

It was during the last of the Shabbat meals, se'uda shelishit, *that the founder of Chabad Hasidism, Rabbi Shneur Zalman of Liadi, asked his assistant to bring in the young Lithuanian peasant who had been standing outside the synagogue door. In answer to the assistant's questioning look, the Rebbe said, "I feel his Jewish soul; he is one of us." The young man came in and after being asked by the Rebbe about his parentage, explained that he was a foundling, left at the doorstep of a kind Christian couple with no children. But he always felt an affinity toward Jews and Judaism. "You were left by your parents escaping a pogrom and certain death. You are a Jew," said the Rebbe.*

... A THOUSAND WORDS

אֱלֹהֵינוּ Our God and God of our ancestors,
find favor in our rest.
Make us holy through Your commandments
and give us our share in Your Torah.
Satisfy us with Your goodness, give us joy in Your salvation,
and purify our hearts to serve You in truth.
In love and favor, LORD our God,
give us as our heritage Your holy Sabbaths,
so that Israel who sanctify Your name may find rest on them.
Blessed are You, LORD, who sanctifies the Sabbath.

TEMPLE SERVICE

רְצֵה Find favor, LORD our God,
in Your people Israel and their prayer.
Restore the service to Your most holy House,
and accept in love and favor
the fire-offerings of Israel and their prayer.
May the service of Your people Israel always find favor with You.

On Rosh Ḥodesh and Ḥol HaMo'ed:

אֱלֹהֵינוּ Our God and God of our ancestors, may there rise, come, reach, appear, be favored, heard, regarded and remembered before You, our recollection and remembrance, as well as the remembrance of our ancestors, and of the Messiah son of David Your servant, and of Jerusalem Your holy city, and of all Your people the house of Israel – for deliverance and well-being, grace, loving-kindness and compassion, life and peace, on this day of:

On Rosh Ḥodesh: Rosh Ḥodesh.
On Pesaḥ: the Festival of Matzot.
On Sukkot: the Festival of Sukkot.

On it remember us, LORD our God, for good; recollect us for blessing, and save us for life. In accord with Your promise of salvation and compassion, spare us and be gracious to us; have compassion on us and save us, for our eyes are turned to You because You, God, are a gracious and compassionate King.

וְתֶחֱזֶינָה And may our eyes
witness Your return to Zion in compassion.
Blessed are You, LORD, who restores His Presence to Zion.

אֱלֹהֵינוּ וֵאלֹהֵי אֲבוֹתֵינוּ
רְצֵה בִמְנוּחָתֵנוּ
קַדְּשֵׁנוּ בְּמִצְוֹתֶיךָ וְתֵן חֶלְקֵנוּ בְּתוֹרָתֶךָ
שַׂבְּעֵנוּ מִטּוּבֶךָ וְשַׂמְּחֵנוּ בִּישׁוּעָתֶךָ
וְטַהֵר לִבֵּנוּ לְעָבְדְּךָ בֶּאֱמֶת.
וְהַנְחִילֵנוּ יהוה אֱלֹהֵינוּ בְּאַהֲבָה וּבְרָצוֹן שַׁבְּתוֹת קָדְשֶׁךָ
וְיָנוּחוּ בָם יִשְׂרָאֵל מְקַדְּשֵׁי שְׁמֶךָ.
בָּרוּךְ אַתָּה יהוה, מְקַדֵּשׁ הַשַּׁבָּת.

עבודה

רְצֵה יהוה אֱלֹהֵינוּ בְּעַמְּךָ יִשְׂרָאֵל, וּבִתְפִלָּתָם
וְהָשֵׁב אֶת הָעֲבוֹדָה לִדְבִיר בֵּיתֶךָ
וְאִשֵּׁי יִשְׂרָאֵל וּתְפִלָּתָם בְּאַהֲבָה תְקַבֵּל בְּרָצוֹן
וּתְהִי לְרָצוֹן תָּמִיד עֲבוֹדַת יִשְׂרָאֵל עַמֶּךָ.

On ראש חודש *and* חול המועד:

אֱלֹהֵינוּ וֵאלֹהֵי אֲבוֹתֵינוּ, יַעֲלֶה וְיָבוֹא וְיַגִּיעַ, וְיֵרָאֶה וְיֵרָצֶה וְיִשָּׁמַע, וְיִפָּקֵד וְיִזָּכֵר זִכְרוֹנֵנוּ וּפִקְדוֹנֵנוּ וְזִכְרוֹן אֲבוֹתֵינוּ, וְזִכְרוֹן מָשִׁיחַ בֶּן דָּוִד עַבְדֶּךָ, וְזִכְרוֹן יְרוּשָׁלַיִם עִיר קָדְשֶׁךָ, וְזִכְרוֹן כָּל עַמְּךָ בֵּית יִשְׂרָאֵל, לְפָנֶיךָ, לִפְלֵיטָה לְטוֹבָה, לְחֵן וּלְחֶסֶד וּלְרַחֲמִים, לְחַיִּים וּלְשָׁלוֹם בְּיוֹם

בראש חודש: **רֹאשׁ הַחֹדֶשׁ** / בפסח: **חַג הַמַּצּוֹת** / בסוכות: **חַג הַסֻּכּוֹת**

הַזֶּה. זָכְרֵנוּ יהוה אֱלֹהֵינוּ בּוֹ לְטוֹבָה, וּפָקְדֵנוּ בוֹ לִבְרָכָה, וְהוֹשִׁיעֵנוּ בוֹ לְחַיִּים. וּבִדְבַר יְשׁוּעָה וְרַחֲמִים, חוּס וְחָנֵּנוּ וְרַחֵם עָלֵינוּ וְהוֹשִׁיעֵנוּ, כִּי אֵלֶיךָ עֵינֵינוּ, כִּי אֵל מֶלֶךְ חַנּוּן וְרַחוּם אָתָּה.

וְתֶחֱזֶינָה עֵינֵינוּ בְּשׁוּבְךָ לְצִיּוֹן בְּרַחֲמִים.
בָּרוּךְ אַתָּה יהוה, הַמַּחֲזִיר שְׁכִינָתוֹ לְצִיּוֹן.

THANKSGIVING

מוֹדִים We give thanks to You,
for You are the LORD our God
and God of our ancestors
for ever and all time.
You are the Rock of our lives,
Shield of our salvation
from generation to generation.
We will thank You and
declare Your praise for our lives,
which are entrusted into Your hand;
for our souls,
which are placed in Your charge;
for Your miracles
which are with us every day;
and for Your wonders and favors
at all times, evening, morning and midday.
You are good –
for Your compassion never fails.
You are compassionate –
for Your loving-kindnesses never cease.
We have always placed our hope in You.

During the Leader's Repetition, the congregation says quietly:

מוֹדִים We give thanks
to You, for You are
the LORD our God
and God of our ancestors,
God of all flesh, who formed us
and formed the universe.
Blessings and thanks
are due to Your great
and holy name for giving us
life and sustaining us.
May You continue
to give us life and sustain us;
and may You gather our exiles
to Your holy courts,
to keep Your decrees,
do Your will and serve You
with a perfect heart,
for it is for us
to give You thanks.
Blessed be God to whom
thanksgiving is due.

On Ḥanukka:

עַל הַנִּסִּים [We thank You also] for the miracles, the redemption, the mighty deeds, the salvations, and the victories in battle which You performed for our ancestors in those days, at this time.

בִּימֵי מַתִּתְיָהוּ In the days of Mattityahu, son of Yoḥanan, the High Priest, the Hasmonean, and his sons, the wicked Greek kingdom rose up against Your people Israel to make them forget Your Torah and to force them to transgress the laws of Your will. It was then that You in Your great compassion stood by them in the time of their distress. You championed their cause, judged their claim, and avenged their wrong. You delivered the strong into the hands of the weak, the many into the hands of the few, the impure into the hands of the pure, the wicked into the hands of the righteous, and the arrogant into the hands of those who were engaged in the study of Your Torah. You made for Yourself great and holy fame in Your world, and for Your people Israel You performed a great salvation and redemption as of this very day. Your children then entered the holiest part of Your House, cleansed Your Temple, purified Your Sanctuary, kindled lights in Your holy courts, and designated these eight days of Ḥanukka for giving thanks and praise to Your great name.

Continue with "For all these things" on the next page.

הודאה

מוֹדִים אֲנַחְנוּ לָךְ
שָׁאַתָּה הוּא יהוה אֱלֹהֵינוּ
וֵאלֹהֵי אֲבוֹתֵינוּ לְעוֹלָם וָעֶד.
צוּר חַיֵּינוּ, מָגֵן יִשְׁעֵנוּ
אַתָּה הוּא לְדוֹר וָדוֹר.
נוֹדֶה לְּךָ וּנְסַפֵּר תְּהִלָּתֶךָ
עַל חַיֵּינוּ הַמְּסוּרִים בְּיָדֶךָ
וְעַל נִשְׁמוֹתֵינוּ הַפְּקוּדוֹת לָךְ
וְעַל נִסֶּיךָ שֶׁבְּכָל יוֹם עִמָּנוּ
וְעַל נִפְלְאוֹתֶיךָ וְטוֹבוֹתֶיךָ
שֶׁבְּכָל עֵת, עֶרֶב וָבֹקֶר וְצָהֳרָיִם.
הַטּוֹב, כִּי לֹא כָלוּ רַחֲמֶיךָ
וְהַמְרַחֵם, כִּי לֹא תַמּוּ חֲסָדֶיךָ
מֵעוֹלָם קִוִּינוּ לָךְ.

During חזרת הש״ץ, *the* קהל *says quietly:*

מוֹדִים אֲנַחְנוּ לָךְ
שָׁאַתָּה הוּא יהוה אֱלֹהֵינוּ
וֵאלֹהֵי אֲבוֹתֵינוּ
אֱלֹהֵי כָל בָּשָׂר
יוֹצְרֵנוּ, יוֹצֵר בְּרֵאשִׁית.
בְּרָכוֹת וְהוֹדָאוֹת
לְשִׁמְךָ הַגָּדוֹל וְהַקָּדוֹשׁ
עַל שֶׁהֶחֱיִיתָנוּ וְקִיַּמְתָּנוּ.
כֵּן תְּחַיֵּנוּ וּתְקַיְּמֵנוּ
וְתֶאֱסֹף גָּלֻיּוֹתֵינוּ
לְחַצְרוֹת קָדְשֶׁךָ
לִשְׁמֹר חֻקֶּיךָ וְלַעֲשׂוֹת רְצוֹנֶךָ
וּלְעָבְדְּךָ בְּלֵבָב שָׁלֵם
עַל שֶׁאֲנַחְנוּ מוֹדִים לָךְ.
בָּרוּךְ אֵל הַהוֹדָאוֹת.

בחנוכה:

עַל הַנִּסִּים וְעַל הַפֻּרְקָן וְעַל הַגְּבוּרוֹת וְעַל הַתְּשׁוּעוֹת וְעַל הַמִּלְחָמוֹת שֶׁעָשִׂיתָ לַאֲבוֹתֵינוּ בַּיָּמִים הָהֵם בַּזְּמַן הַזֶּה.

בִּימֵי מַתִּתְיָהוּ בֶּן יוֹחָנָן כֹּהֵן גָּדוֹל חַשְׁמוֹנַאי וּבָנָיו, כְּשֶׁעָמְדָה מַלְכוּת יָוָן הָרְשָׁעָה עַל עַמְּךָ יִשְׂרָאֵל לְהַשְׁכִּיחָם תּוֹרָתֶךָ וּלְהַעֲבִירָם מֵחֻקֵּי רְצוֹנֶךָ, וְאַתָּה בְּרַחֲמֶיךָ הָרַבִּים עָמַדְתָּ לָהֶם בְּעֵת צָרָתָם, רַבְתָּ אֶת רִיבָם, דַּנְתָּ אֶת דִּינָם, נָקַמְתָּ אֶת נִקְמָתָם, מָסַרְתָּ גִּבּוֹרִים בְּיַד חַלָּשִׁים, וְרַבִּים בְּיַד מְעַטִּים, וּטְמֵאִים בְּיַד טְהוֹרִים, וּרְשָׁעִים בְּיַד צַדִּיקִים, וְזֵדִים בְּיַד עוֹסְקֵי תוֹרָתֶךָ, וּלְךָ עָשִׂיתָ שֵׁם גָּדוֹל וְקָדוֹשׁ בְּעוֹלָמֶךָ, וּלְעַמְּךָ יִשְׂרָאֵל עָשִׂיתָ תְּשׁוּעָה גְדוֹלָה וּפֻרְקָן כְּהַיּוֹם הַזֶּה. וְאַחַר כֵּן בָּאוּ בָנֶיךָ לִדְבִיר בֵּיתֶךָ, וּפִנּוּ אֶת הֵיכָלֶךָ, וְטִהֲרוּ אֶת מִקְדָּשֶׁךָ, וְהִדְלִיקוּ נֵרוֹת בְּחַצְרוֹת קָדְשֶׁךָ, וְקָבְעוּ שְׁמוֹנַת יְמֵי חֲנֻכָּה אֵלּוּ, לְהוֹדוֹת וּלְהַלֵּל לְשִׁמְךָ הַגָּדוֹל.

Continue with וְעַל כֻּלָּם *on the next page.*

On Shushan Purim in Jerusalem:

עַל הַנִּסִּים [We thank You also] for the miracles, the redemption, the mighty deeds, the salvations, and the victories in battle which You performed for our ancestors in those days, at this time.

בִּימֵי מָרְדְּכַי In the days of Mordekhai and Esther, in Shushan the capital, the wicked Haman rose up against them and sought to destroy, slay and exterminate *Esther 3*
all the Jews, young and old, children and women, on one day, the thirteenth day of the twelfth month, which is the month of Adar, and to plunder their possessions. Then You in Your great compassion defeated his counsel, frustrated his plans, and caused his scheme to recoil on his own head, so that they hanged him and his sons on the gallows.

Continue with "For all these things."

וְעַל כֻּלָּם For all these things may Your name be blessed and elevated, our King, continually, for ever and all time.

On Shabbat Shuva: And write, for a good life,
all the children of Your covenant.

Let all that lives thank You, Selah! and praise Your name in truth,
God, our Savior and Help, Selah!
Blessed are You, LORD,
whose name is "the Good" and to whom thanks are due.

PEACE

שָׁלוֹם רָב Give
great peace
to Your people Israel
for ever,
for You are
the sovereign LORD
of all peace;
and may it be good
in Your eyes
to bless Your people Israel
at every time,
at every hour,
with Your peace.

In Israel:
שִׂים שָׁלוֹם Give peace,
goodness and blessing,
grace, loving-kindness and compassion
to us and all Israel Your people.
Bless us, our Father, all as one,
with the light of Your face,
for by the light of Your face
You have given us, LORD our God,
the Torah of life and love of kindness,
righteousness, blessing, compassion,
life and peace.
May it be good in Your eyes
to bless Your people Israel
at every time, in every hour,
with Your peace.

בשושן פורים בירושלים:
עַל הַנִּסִּים וְעַל הַפֻּרְקָן וְעַל הַגְּבוּרוֹת וְעַל הַתְּשׁוּעוֹת וְעַל הַמִּלְחָמוֹת שֶׁעָשִׂיתָ לַאֲבוֹתֵינוּ בַּיָּמִים הָהֵם בַּזְּמַן הַזֶּה.

בִּימֵי מָרְדְּכַי וְאֶסְתֵּר בְּשׁוּשַׁן הַבִּירָה, כְּשֶׁעָמַד עֲלֵיהֶם הָמָן הָרָשָׁע, בִּקֵּשׁ לְהַשְׁמִיד לַהֲרֹג וּלְאַבֵּד אֶת־כָּל־הַיְּהוּדִים מִנַּעַר וְעַד־זָקֵן טַף וְנָשִׁים בְּיוֹם אסתר ג
אֶחָד, בִּשְׁלוֹשָׁה עָשָׂר לְחֹדֶשׁ שְׁנֵים־עָשָׂר, הוּא־חֹדֶשׁ אֲדָר, וּשְׁלָלָם לָבוֹז: וְאַתָּה בְּרַחֲמֶיךָ הָרַבִּים הֵפַרְתָּ אֶת עֲצָתוֹ, וְקִלְקַלְתָּ אֶת מַחֲשַׁבְתּוֹ, וַהֲשֵׁבוֹתָ לּוֹ גְּמוּלוֹ בְּרֹאשׁוֹ, וְתָלוּ אוֹתוֹ וְאֶת בָּנָיו עַל הָעֵץ.

Continue with וְעַל כֻּלָּם.

וְעַל כֻּלָּם יִתְבָּרַךְ וְיִתְרוֹמַם שִׁמְךָ מַלְכֵּנוּ תָּמִיד לְעוֹלָם וָעֶד.

בשבת שובה: וּכְתֹב לְחַיִּים טוֹבִים כָּל בְּנֵי בְרִיתֶךָ.

וְכֹל הַחַיִּים יוֹדוּךָ סֶּלָה, וִיהַלְלוּ אֶת שִׁמְךָ בֶּאֱמֶת
הָאֵל יְשׁוּעָתֵנוּ וְעֶזְרָתֵנוּ סֶלָה.
בָּרוּךְ אַתָּה יהוה, הַטּוֹב שִׁמְךָ וּלְךָ נָאֶה לְהוֹדוֹת.

ברכת שלום

שָׁלוֹם רָב
עַל יִשְׂרָאֵל עַמְּךָ
תָּשִׂים לְעוֹלָם
כִּי אַתָּה הוּא
מֶלֶךְ אָדוֹן לְכָל הַשָּׁלוֹם.
וְטוֹב בְּעֵינֶיךָ
לְבָרֵךְ אֶת עַמְּךָ יִשְׂרָאֵל
בְּכָל עֵת וּבְכָל שָׁעָה
בִּשְׁלוֹמֶךָ.

In ארץ ישראל:
שִׂים שָׁלוֹם טוֹבָה וּבְרָכָה
חֵן וָחֶסֶד וְרַחֲמִים
עָלֵינוּ וְעַל כָּל יִשְׂרָאֵל עַמֶּךָ.
בָּרְכֵנוּ אָבִינוּ כֻּלָּנוּ כְּאֶחָד בְּאוֹר פָּנֶיךָ
כִּי בְאוֹר פָּנֶיךָ נָתַתָּ לָּנוּ יהוה אֱלֹהֵינוּ
תּוֹרַת חַיִּים וְאַהֲבַת חֶסֶד
וּצְדָקָה וּבְרָכָה וְרַחֲמִים
וְחַיִּים וְשָׁלוֹם.
וְטוֹב בְּעֵינֶיךָ לְבָרֵךְ אֶת עַמְּךָ יִשְׂרָאֵל
בְּכָל עֵת וּבְכָל שָׁעָה בִּשְׁלוֹמֶךָ.

On Shabbat Shuva: In the book of life, blessing, peace and prosperity,
may we and all Your people the house of Israel
be remembered and written before You
for a good life, and for peace.*

Blessed are You, LORD, who blesses His people Israel with peace.

**On Shabbat Shuva outside Israel, many end the blessing:*
Blessed are You, LORD, who makes peace.

The following verse concludes the Leader's Repetition of the Amida. Some also say it here as part of the silent Amida.

May the words of my mouth and the inner thoughts of my heart *Ps. 19*
find favor before You, LORD, my Rock and Redeemer.

אֱלֹהַי My God, *Berakhot 17a*
guard my tongue from evil and my lips from dishonest speech.
To those who curse me, let my soul be silent;
may my soul be to all like the dust.
Open my heart to Your Torah
and let my soul pursue Your commandments.
As for all who plan evil against me,
swiftly defeat their counsel and frustrate their plans.
Act for the sake of Your name; act for the sake of Your right hand;
act for the sake of Your holiness; act for the sake of Your Torah.
That Your beloved ones may be rescued, *Ps. 60*
save with Your right hand and answer me.
May the words of my mouth *Ps. 19*
and the inner thoughts of my heart
find favor before You, LORD, my Rock and Redeemer.

Bow, take three steps back, then bow, first left, then right, then center, while saying:
May He who makes peace in His high places,
make peace for us and all Israel – and say: Amen.

יְהִי רָצוֹן May it be Your will, LORD our God and God of our ancestors,
that the Temple be rebuilt speedily in our days, and give us a share in Your Torah.
And there we will serve You with fear,
as in the days of old and as in former years.
Then the offering of Judah and Jerusalem *Mal. 3*
will be pleasing to the LORD as in the days of old and as in former years.

בשבת שובה: בְּסֵפֶר חַיִּים, בְּרָכָה וְשָׁלוֹם, וּפַרְנָסָה טוֹבָה
נִזָּכֵר וְנִכָּתֵב לְפָנֶיךָ, אֲנַחְנוּ וְכָל עַמְּךָ בֵּית יִשְׂרָאֵל
לְחַיִּים טוֹבִים וּלְשָׁלוֹם.*

בָּרוּךְ אַתָּה יהוה, הַמְבָרֵךְ אֶת עַמּוֹ יִשְׂרָאֵל בַּשָּׁלוֹם.

**On שבת שובה in חוץ לארץ many end the blessing:*

בָּרוּךְ אַתָּה יהוה, עוֹשֶׂה הַשָּׁלוֹם.

The following verse concludes the חזרת הש״ץ.
Some also say it here as part of the silent עמידה.

תהלים יט יִהְיוּ לְרָצוֹן אִמְרֵי־פִי וְהֶגְיוֹן לִבִּי לְפָנֶיךָ, יהוה צוּרִי וְגֹאֲלִי:

ברכות יז. אֱלֹהַי
נְצֹר לְשׁוֹנִי מֵרָע וּשְׂפָתַי מִדַּבֵּר מִרְמָה
וְלִמְקַלְלַי נַפְשִׁי תִדֹּם, וְנַפְשִׁי כֶּעָפָר לַכֹּל תִּהְיֶה.
פְּתַח לִבִּי בְּתוֹרָתֶךָ, וּבְמִצְוֹתֶיךָ תִּרְדֹּף נַפְשִׁי.
וְכָל הַחוֹשְׁבִים עָלַי רָעָה
מְהֵרָה הָפֵר עֲצָתָם וְקַלְקֵל מַחֲשַׁבְתָּם.
עֲשֵׂה לְמַעַן שְׁמֶךָ, עֲשֵׂה לְמַעַן יְמִינֶךָ
עֲשֵׂה לְמַעַן קְדֻשָּׁתֶךָ, עֲשֵׂה לְמַעַן תּוֹרָתֶךָ.
תהלים ס לְמַעַן יֵחָלְצוּן יְדִידֶיךָ, הוֹשִׁיעָה יְמִינְךָ וַעֲנֵנִי:
תהלים יט יִהְיוּ לְרָצוֹן אִמְרֵי־פִי וְהֶגְיוֹן לִבִּי לְפָנֶיךָ, יהוה צוּרִי וְגֹאֲלִי:

Bow, take three steps back, then bow, first left, then right, then center, while saying:

עֹשֶׂה שָׁלוֹם/ בשבת שובה: הַשָּׁלוֹם/ בִּמְרוֹמָיו
הוּא יַעֲשֶׂה שָׁלוֹם עָלֵינוּ וְעַל כָּל יִשְׂרָאֵל, וְאִמְרוּ אָמֵן.

יְהִי רָצוֹן מִלְּפָנֶיךָ יהוה אֱלֹהֵינוּ וֵאלֹהֵי אֲבוֹתֵינוּ
שֶׁיִּבָּנֶה בֵּית הַמִּקְדָּשׁ בִּמְהֵרָה בְיָמֵינוּ, וְתֵן חֶלְקֵנוּ בְּתוֹרָתֶךָ
וְשָׁם נַעֲבָדְךָ בְּיִרְאָה כִּימֵי עוֹלָם וּכְשָׁנִים קַדְמֹנִיּוֹת.
מלאכי ג וְעָרְבָה לַיהוה מִנְחַת יְהוּדָה וִירוּשָׁלָםִ כִּימֵי עוֹלָם וּכְשָׁנִים קַדְמֹנִיּוֹת:

The following is omitted on days when Taḥanun is not said *(see page 206)*.

צִדְקָתְךָ Your righteousness is an everlasting righteousness, and Your Ps. 119
Torah is truth. Your righteousness, O God, reaches to the highest Ps. 71
heights, for You have done great things. O God, who is like You?
Your righteousness is like the mighty mountains; Your judgments Ps. 36
like the great depths. O Lord, You save both man and beast.

FULL KADDISH

Leader: יִתְגַּדַּל Magnified and sanctified may His great name be,
in the world He created by His will.
May He establish His kingdom
in your lifetime and in your days,
and in the lifetime of all the house of Israel,
swiftly and soon – and say: Amen.

All: May His great name be blessed for ever and all time.

Leader: Blessed and praised, glorified and elevated,
raised and honored, uplifted and praised
be the name of the Holy One,
blessed be He,
beyond any blessing,
song, praise and consolation
uttered in the world – and say: Amen.

May the prayers and pleas of all Israel
be accepted by their Father in heaven – and say: Amen.

May there be great peace from heaven,
and life for us and all Israel – and say: Amen.

Bow, take three steps back, as if taking leave of the Divine Presence, then bow, first left, then right, then center, while saying:

May He who makes peace in His high places,
make peace for us and all Israel – and say: Amen.

Between Sukkot and Pesaḥ, some recite Barekhi Nafshi, *page 772**, at this point.*
Between Pesaḥ and Rosh HaShana some recite Ethics of the Fathers, *page 780**, at this point.*

The following is omitted on days when תחנון is not said (see page 207).

צִדְקָתְךָ צֶדֶק לְעוֹלָם וְתוֹרָתְךָ אֱמֶת: וְצִדְקָתְךָ אֱלֹהִים עַד־מָרוֹם, תהלים קיט תהלים עא
אֲשֶׁר־עָשִׂיתָ גְדֹלוֹת, אֱלֹהִים, מִי כָמוֹךָ: צִדְקָתְךָ כְּהַרְרֵי־אֵל, תהלים לו
מִשְׁפָּטֶיךָ תְּהוֹם רַבָּה, אָדָם וּבְהֵמָה תוֹשִׁיעַ יהוה:

קדיש שלם

ש״ץ: יִתְגַּדַּל וְיִתְקַדַּשׁ שְׁמֵהּ רַבָּא (קהל: אָמֵן)
בְּעָלְמָא דִּי בְרָא כִרְעוּתֵהּ, וְיַמְלִיךְ מַלְכוּתֵהּ
בְּחַיֵּיכוֹן וּבְיוֹמֵיכוֹן וּבְחַיֵּי דְכָל בֵּית יִשְׂרָאֵל
בַּעֲגָלָא וּבִזְמַן קָרִיב, וְאִמְרוּ אָמֵן. (קהל: אָמֵן)

קהל וש״ץ: יְהֵא שְׁמֵהּ רַבָּא מְבָרַךְ לְעָלַם וּלְעָלְמֵי עָלְמַיָּא.

ש״ץ: יִתְבָּרַךְ וְיִשְׁתַּבַּח וְיִתְפָּאַר
וְיִתְרוֹמַם וְיִתְנַשֵּׂא וְיִתְהַדָּר וְיִתְעַלֶּה וְיִתְהַלָּל
שְׁמֵהּ דְּקֻדְשָׁא בְּרִיךְ הוּא (קהל: בְּרִיךְ הוּא)
לְעֵלָּא מִן כָּל בִּרְכָתָא / בשבת שובה: לְעֵלָּא לְעֵלָּא מִכָּל בִּרְכָתָא/
וְשִׁירָתָא, תֻּשְׁבְּחָתָא וְנֶחֱמָתָא
דַּאֲמִירָן בְּעָלְמָא, וְאִמְרוּ אָמֵן. (קהל: אָמֵן)

תִּתְקַבַּל צְלוֹתְהוֹן וּבָעוּתְהוֹן דְּכָל יִשְׂרָאֵל
קֳדָם אֲבוּהוֹן דִּי בִשְׁמַיָּא, וְאִמְרוּ אָמֵן. (קהל: אָמֵן)

יְהֵא שְׁלָמָא רַבָּא מִן שְׁמַיָּא
וְחַיִּים, עָלֵינוּ וְעַל כָּל יִשְׂרָאֵל, וְאִמְרוּ אָמֵן. (קהל: אָמֵן)

Bow, take three steps back, as if taking leave of the Divine Presence, then bow, first left, then right, then center, while saying:

עֹשֶׂה שָׁלוֹם/ בשבת שובה: הַשָּׁלוֹם/ בִּמְרוֹמָיו
הוּא יַעֲשֶׂה שָׁלוֹם עָלֵינוּ וְעַל כָּל יִשְׂרָאֵל, וְאִמְרוּ אָמֵן. (קהל: אָמֵן)

Between סוכות and פסח, some recite ברכי נפשי, page 773, at this point.
Between פסח and ראש השנה some recite פרקי אבות, page 781, at this point.

Stand while saying Aleinu.

עָלֵינוּ It is our duty to praise the Master of all,
and ascribe greatness to the Author of creation,
who has not made us like the nations of the lands
nor placed us like the families of the earth;
who has not made our portion like theirs,
nor our destiny like all their multitudes.
(For they worship vanity and emptiness,
and pray to a god who cannot save.)
But we bow in worship
and thank the Supreme King of kings, the Holy One, blessed be He,
who extends the heavens and establishes the earth,
whose throne of glory is in the heavens above,
and whose power's Presence is in the highest of heights.
He is our God; there is no other.
Truly He is our King, there is none else,
as it is written in His Torah:
"You shall know and take to heart this day *Deut. 4*
that the Lord is God,
in heaven above and on earth below. There is no other."

Therefore, we place our hope in You, Lord our God,
that we may soon see the glory of Your power,
when You will remove abominations from the earth,
and idols will be utterly destroyed,
when the world will be perfected
under the sovereignty of the Almighty,
when all humanity will call on Your name,
to turn all the earth's wicked toward You.
All the world's inhabitants will realize and know
that to You every knee must bow and every tongue swear loyalty.
Before You, Lord our God, they will kneel and bow down
and give honor to Your glorious name.
They will all accept the yoke of Your kingdom,
and You will reign over them soon and for ever.
For the kingdom is Yours, and to all eternity You will reign in glory,
as it is written in Your Torah: "The Lord will reign for ever and ever." *Ex. 15*

Stand while saying עָלֵינוּ.

עָלֵינוּ לְשַׁבֵּחַ לַאֲדוֹן הַכֹּל, לָתֵת גְּדֻלָּה לְיוֹצֵר בְּרֵאשִׁית
שֶׁלֹּא עָשָׂנוּ כְּגוֹיֵי הָאֲרָצוֹת, וְלֹא שָׂמָנוּ כְּמִשְׁפְּחוֹת הָאֲדָמָה
שֶׁלֹּא שָׂם חֶלְקֵנוּ כָּהֶם וְגוֹרָלֵנוּ כְּכָל הֲמוֹנָם.
(שֶׁהֵם מִשְׁתַּחֲוִים לְהֶבֶל וָרִיק וּמִתְפַּלְּלִים אֶל אֵל לֹא יוֹשִׁיעַ.)
וַאֲנַחְנוּ כּוֹרְעִים וּמִשְׁתַּחֲוִים וּמוֹדִים
לִפְנֵי מֶלֶךְ מַלְכֵי הַמְּלָכִים, הַקָּדוֹשׁ בָּרוּךְ הוּא
שֶׁהוּא נוֹטֶה שָׁמַיִם וְיוֹסֵד אָרֶץ
וּמוֹשַׁב יְקָרוֹ בַּשָּׁמַיִם מִמַּעַל, וּשְׁכִינַת עֻזּוֹ בְּגָבְהֵי מְרוֹמִים.
הוּא אֱלֹהֵינוּ, אֵין עוֹד.
אֱמֶת מַלְכֵּנוּ, אֶפֶס זוּלָתוֹ
כַּכָּתוּב בְּתוֹרָתוֹ
וְיָדַעְתָּ הַיּוֹם וַהֲשֵׁבֹתָ אֶל־לְבָבֶךָ דברים ד
כִּי יהוה הוּא הָאֱלֹהִים בַּשָּׁמַיִם מִמַּעַל וְעַל־הָאָרֶץ מִתָּחַת
אֵין עוֹד:

עַל כֵּן נְקַוֶּה לְּךָ יהוה אֱלֹהֵינוּ, לִרְאוֹת מְהֵרָה בְּתִפְאֶרֶת עֻזֶּךָ
לְהַעֲבִיר גִּלּוּלִים מִן הָאָרֶץ, וְהָאֱלִילִים כָּרוֹת יִכָּרֵתוּן
לְתַקֵּן עוֹלָם בְּמַלְכוּת שַׁדַּי.
וְכָל בְּנֵי בָשָׂר יִקְרְאוּ בִשְׁמֶךָ לְהַפְנוֹת אֵלֶיךָ כָּל רִשְׁעֵי אָרֶץ.
יַכִּירוּ וְיֵדְעוּ כָּל יוֹשְׁבֵי תֵבֵל
כִּי לְךָ תִּכְרַע כָּל בֶּרֶךְ, תִּשָּׁבַע כָּל לָשׁוֹן.
לְפָנֶיךָ יהוה אֱלֹהֵינוּ יִכְרְעוּ וְיִפֹּלוּ, וְלִכְבוֹד שִׁמְךָ יְקָר יִתֵּנוּ
וִיקַבְּלוּ כֻלָּם אֶת עֹל מַלְכוּתֶךָ
וְתִמְלֹךְ עֲלֵיהֶם מְהֵרָה לְעוֹלָם וָעֶד.
כִּי הַמַּלְכוּת שֶׁלְּךָ הִיא וּלְעוֹלְמֵי עַד תִּמְלֹךְ בְּכָבוֹד
כַּכָּתוּב בְּתוֹרָתֶךָ, יהוה יִמְלֹךְ לְעֹלָם וָעֶד: שמות טו

▸ And it is said: "Then the LORD shall be King over all the earth; on that day the LORD shall be One and His name One." *Zech. 14*

Some add:

Have no fear of sudden terror or of the ruin when it overtakes the wicked. *Prov. 3*
Devise your strategy, but it will be defeated; *Is. 8*
propose your plan, but it will not stand, for God is with us.
When you grow old, I will still be the same. *Is. 46*
When your hair turns gray, I will still carry you.
I made you, I will bear you, I will carry you, and I will rescue you.

MOURNER'S KADDISH

The following prayer, said by mourners, requires the presence of a minyan. A transliteration can be found on page 1151.

Mourner: יִתְגַּדַּל Magnified and sanctified may His great name be,
in the world He created by His will.
May He establish His kingdom in your lifetime
and in your days, and in the lifetime
of all the house of Israel,
swiftly and soon –
and say: Amen.

All: May His great name be blessed for ever and all time.

Mourner: Blessed and praised, glorified and elevated,
raised and honored, uplifted and praised
be the name of the Holy One,
blessed be He,
beyond any blessing,
song, praise and consolation
uttered in the world –
and say: Amen.

May there be great peace from heaven,
and life for us and all Israel –
and say: Amen.

Bow, take three steps back, as if taking leave of the Divine Presence, then bow, first left, then right, then center, while saying:

May He who makes peace in His high places,
make peace for us and all Israel – and say: Amen.

◂ וְנֶאֱמַר, וְהָיָה יהוה לְמֶלֶךְ עַל־כָּל־הָאָרֶץ בַּיּוֹם הַהוּא יִהְיֶה יהוה אֶחָד וּשְׁמוֹ אֶחָד: זכריה יד

Some add:

אַל־תִּירָא מִפַּחַד פִּתְאֹם וּמִשֹּׁאַת רְשָׁעִים כִּי תָבֹא: משלי ג
עֻצוּ עֵצָה וְתֻפָר, דַּבְּרוּ דָבָר וְלֹא יָקוּם, כִּי עִמָּנוּ אֵל: ישעיה ח
וְעַד־זִקְנָה אֲנִי הוּא, וְעַד־שֵׂיבָה אֲנִי אֶסְבֹּל, אֲנִי עָשִׂיתִי וַאֲנִי אֶשָּׂא וַאֲנִי אֶסְבֹּל וַאֲמַלֵּט: ישעיה מו

קדיש יתום

The following prayer, said by mourners, requires the presence of a מנין*.*
A transliteration can be found on page 1151.

אבל: יִתְגַּדַּל וְיִתְקַדַּשׁ שְׁמֵהּ רַבָּא (קהל: אָמֵן)
בְּעָלְמָא דִּי בְרָא כִרְעוּתֵהּ
וְיַמְלִיךְ מַלְכוּתֵהּ
בְּחַיֵּיכוֹן וּבְיוֹמֵיכוֹן וּבְחַיֵּי דְכָל בֵּית יִשְׂרָאֵל
בַּעֲגָלָא וּבִזְמַן קָרִיב, וְאִמְרוּ אָמֵן. (קהל: אָמֵן)

קהל ואבל: יְהֵא שְׁמֵהּ רַבָּא מְבָרַךְ לְעָלַם וּלְעָלְמֵי עָלְמַיָּא.

אבל: יִתְבָּרַךְ וְיִשְׁתַּבַּח וְיִתְפָּאַר
וְיִתְרוֹמַם וְיִתְנַשֵּׂא וְיִתְהַדָּר וְיִתְעַלֶּה וְיִתְהַלָּל
שְׁמֵהּ דְּקֻדְשָׁא בְּרִיךְ הוּא (קהל: בְּרִיךְ הוּא)
לְעֵלָּא מִן כָּל בִּרְכָתָא / בשבת שובה: לְעֵלָּא לְעֵלָּא מִכָּל בִּרְכָתָא/
וְשִׁירָתָא, תֻּשְׁבְּחָתָא וְנֶחֱמָתָא
דַּאֲמִירָן בְּעָלְמָא, וְאִמְרוּ אָמֵן. (קהל: אָמֵן)

יְהֵא שְׁלָמָא רַבָּא מִן שְׁמַיָּא
וְחַיִּים, עָלֵינוּ וְעַל כָּל יִשְׂרָאֵל, וְאִמְרוּ אָמֵן. (קהל: אָמֵן)

Bow, take three steps back, as if taking leave of the Divine Presence, then bow, first left, then right, then center, while saying:

עֹשֶׂה שָׁלוֹם/ בשבת שובה: הַשָּׁלוֹם/ בִּמְרוֹמָיו
הוּא יַעֲשֶׂה שָׁלוֹם עָלֵינוּ וְעַל כָּל יִשְׂרָאֵל, וְאִמְרוּ אָמֵן. (קהל: אָמֵן)

BAREKHI NAFSHI

The following psalms are said from the Shabbat after Simḥat Torah until (but not including) the Shabbat before Pesaḥ.

בָּרְכִי נַפְשִׁי Bless the Lord, my soul. Lord, my God, You are very great, clothed in majesty and splendor, wrapped in a robe of light. You have spread out the heavens like a tent. He has laid the beams of His lofts in the waters. He makes the clouds His chariot, riding on the wings of the wind. He makes the winds His messengers, flames of fire His ministers. He has fixed the earth on its foundations so that it will never be shaken. You covered it with the deep like a cloak; the waters stood above the mountains. At Your rebuke they fled; at the sound of Your thunder they rushed away, flowing over the hills, pouring down into the valleys to the place You appointed for them. You fixed a boundary they were not to pass, so that they would never cover the earth again. He makes springs flow in the valleys; they make their way between the hills, giving drink to all the beasts of the field; the wild donkeys quench their thirst. The birds of the sky live beside them, singing among the foliage. He waters the mountains from His lofts: the earth is filled with the fruit of Your work. He makes grass grow for the cattle, and plants for the use of man, that he may produce bread from the earth, wine to cheer the heart of man, oil to make the face shine, and bread to sustain man's heart. The trees of the Lord drink their fill, the cedars of Lebanon which He planted. There, birds build their nests; the stork makes its home in the cypresses. High hills are for the wild goats; crags are shelter for the badgers. He made the moon to mark the seasons, and makes the sun know when to set. You bring darkness and it is night; then all the beasts of the forests stir. The young lions roar for prey, seeking their food from God. When the sun rises, they slink away and seek rest in their lairs. Man goes out to his work and his labor until evening. How numerous are Your works, Lord; You made them all in wisdom; the earth is full of Your creations. There is the vast, immeasurable sea with its countless swarming creatures, living things great and small. There ships sail. There is Leviathan You formed to sport there. All of them look to You in hope, to give them their food when it is due. What You give them, they gather up. When You open Your hand, they are full with good. When You hide Your face, they are dismayed. When You take away their breath, they die and return to dust. When You send back Your breath, they are created, giving new life to the earth. May the glory of the Lord be for ever; may the Lord rejoice in His works. When He looks at the earth, it trembles. When He touches the mountains, they pour forth smoke. I will sing to the Lord as long as I live; I will sing psalms to my God all my life. May my prayers be pleasing to Him; I shall rejoice in the Lord. May sinners vanish from the earth, and the wicked be no more. Bless the Lord, my soul. Halleluya! *Ps. 104*

ברכי נפשי

The following psalms are said from שבת בראשית *until (but not including)* שבת הגדול.

ברכי נפשי את־יהוה, יהוה אלהי גדלת מאד, הוד והדר לבשת: עטה־ תהלים קד
אור כשלמה, נוטה שמים כיריעה: המקרה במים עליותיו, השם־
עבים רכובו, המהלך על־כנפי־רוח: עשה מלאכיו רוחות, משרתיו
אש להט: יסד־ארץ על־מכוניה, בל־תמוט עולם ועד: תהום כלבוש
כסיתו, על־הרים יעמדו־מים: מן־גערתך ינוסון, מן־קול רעמך יחפזון:
יעלו הרים, ירדו בקעות, אל־מקום זה יסדת להם: גבול־שמת בל־
יעברון, בל־ישבון לכסות הארץ: המשלח מעינים בנחלים, בין הרים
יהלכון: ישקו כל־חיתו שדי, ישברו פראים צמאם: עליהם עוף־השמים
ישכון, מבין עפאים יתנו־קול: משקה הרים מעליותיו, מפרי מעשיך
תשבע הארץ: מצמיח חציר לבהמה, ועשב לעבדת האדם, להוציא
לחם מן־הארץ: ויין ישמח לבב־אנוש, להצהיל פנים משמן, ולחם
לבב־אנוש יסעד: ישבעו עצי יהוה, ארזי לבנון אשר נטע: אשר־שם
צפרים יקננו, חסידה ברושים ביתה: הרים הגבהים ליעלים, סלעים
מחסה לשפנים: עשה ירח למועדים, שמש ידע מבואו: תשת־חשך
ויהי לילה, בו־תרמש כל־חיתו־יער: הכפירים שאגים לטרף, ולבקש
מאל אכלם: תזרח השמש יאספון, ואל־מעונתם ירבצון: יצא אדם
לפעלו, ולעבדתו עדי־ערב: מה־רבו מעשיך יהוה, כלם בחכמה עשית,
מלאה הארץ קנינך: זה הים גדול ורחב ידים, שם־רמש ואין מספר,
חיות קטנות עם־גדלות: שם אניות יהלכון, לויתן זה־יצרת לשחק־
בו: כלם אליך ישברון, לתת אכלם בעתו: תתן להם ילקטון, תפתח
ידך ישבעון טוב: תסתיר פניך יבהלון, תסף רוחם יגועון, ואל־עפרם
ישובון: תשלח רוחך יבראון, ותחדש פני אדמה: יהי כבוד יהוה לעולם,
ישמח יהוה במעשיו: המביט לארץ ותרעד, יגע בהרים ויעשנו: אשירה
ליהוה בחיי, אזמרה לאלהי בעודי: יערב עליו שיחי, אנכי אשמח
ביהוה: יתמו חטאים מן־הארץ, ורשעים עוד אינם, ברכי נפשי את־
יהוה, הללויה:

A song of ascents. I called to the Lord in my distress and He answered me. *Ps. 120*
"Lord, save my soul from lying lips, from a dishonest tongue." What will a dishonest tongue profit you? What will you gain? Only a warrior's sharp arrows, and hot coals of broom-wood. Woe to me that I live in Meshekh, that I live among the tents of Kedar. I have lived too long among those who hate peace. I am for peace, but whenever I speak of it, they are for war.

A song of ascents. I lift my eyes up to the hills; from where will my help come? *Ps. 121*
My help comes from the Lord, Maker of heaven and earth. He will not let your foot stumble; He who guards you does not slumber. See: the Guardian of Israel neither slumbers nor sleeps. The Lord is your Guardian; the Lord is your Shade at your right hand. The sun will not strike you by day, nor the moon by night. The Lord will guard you from all harm; He will guard your life. The Lord will guard your going and coming, now and for evermore.

A song of ascents. Of David. I rejoiced when they said to me, "Let us go to *Ps. 122*
the House of the Lord." Our feet stood within your gates, Jerusalem: Jerusalem built as a city joined together. There the tribes went up, the tribes of the Lord – as a testimony to Israel – to give thanks to the name of the Lord. For there the thrones of justice are set, the thrones of the house of David. Pray for the peace of Jerusalem: "May those who love you prosper. May there be peace within your ramparts, tranquility in your citadels." For the sake of my brothers and my friends, I shall say, "Peace be within you." For the sake of the House of the Lord our God, I shall seek your good.

A song of ascents. To You, enthroned in heaven, I lift my eyes. As the eyes *Ps. 123*
of slaves turn to their master's hand, or the eyes of a slave-girl to the hand of her mistress, so our eyes are turned to the Lord our God, awaiting His favor. Show us favor, Lord, show us favor, for we have suffered more than enough contempt. Too long have we suffered the scorn of the complacent, the contempt of arrogant men.

A song of ascents. Of David. Had the Lord not been on our side – let Israel *Ps. 124*
say it – had the Lord not been on our side when men rose up against us, they would have swallowed us alive when their anger raged against us. The waters would have engulfed us; the torrent would have swept over us; over us would have swept the raging waters. Blessed be the Lord who did not leave us as a prey for their teeth. We escaped like a bird from the hunter's trap; the trap broke and we escaped. Our help is in the name of the Lord, Maker of heaven and earth.

שִׁיר הַמַּעֲלוֹת, אֶל־יהוה בַּצָּרָתָה לִּי, קָרָאתִי וַיַּעֲנֵנִי: יהוה הַצִּילָה נַפְשִׁי תהלים קכ
מִשְּׂפַת־שֶׁקֶר, מִלָּשׁוֹן רְמִיָּה: מַה־יִּתֵּן לְךָ וּמַה־יֹּסִיף לָךְ, לָשׁוֹן רְמִיָּה:
חִצֵּי גִבּוֹר שְׁנוּנִים, עִם גַּחֲלֵי רְתָמִים: אוֹיָה־לִי כִּי־גַרְתִּי מֶשֶׁךְ, שָׁכַנְתִּי
עִם־אָהֳלֵי קֵדָר: רַבַּת שָׁכְנָה־לָּהּ נַפְשִׁי, עִם שׂוֹנֵא שָׁלוֹם: אֲנִי־שָׁלוֹם וְכִי
אֲדַבֵּר, הֵמָּה לַמִּלְחָמָה:

שִׁיר לַמַּעֲלוֹת, אֶשָּׂא עֵינַי אֶל־הֶהָרִים, מֵאַיִן יָבֹא עֶזְרִי: עֶזְרִי מֵעִם יהוה, תהלים קכא
עֹשֵׂה שָׁמַיִם וָאָרֶץ: אַל־יִתֵּן לַמּוֹט רַגְלֶךָ, אַל־יָנוּם שֹׁמְרֶךָ: הִנֵּה לֹא־יָנוּם
וְלֹא יִישָׁן, שׁוֹמֵר יִשְׂרָאֵל: יהוה שֹׁמְרֶךָ, יהוה צִלְּךָ עַל־יַד יְמִינֶךָ: יוֹמָם
הַשֶּׁמֶשׁ לֹא־יַכֶּכָּה, וְיָרֵחַ בַּלָּיְלָה: יהוה יִשְׁמָרְךָ מִכָּל־רָע, יִשְׁמֹר אֶת־נַפְשֶׁךָ:
יהוה יִשְׁמָר־צֵאתְךָ וּבוֹאֶךָ, מֵעַתָּה וְעַד־עוֹלָם:

שִׁיר הַמַּעֲלוֹת לְדָוִד, שָׂמַחְתִּי בְּאֹמְרִים לִי בֵּית יהוה נֵלֵךְ: עֹמְדוֹת הָיוּ תהלים קכב
רַגְלֵינוּ, בִּשְׁעָרַיִךְ יְרוּשָׁלָםִ: יְרוּשָׁלַםִ הַבְּנוּיָה, כְּעִיר שֶׁחֻבְּרָה־לָּהּ יַחְדָּו:
שֶׁשָּׁם עָלוּ שְׁבָטִים שִׁבְטֵי־יָהּ, עֵדוּת לְיִשְׂרָאֵל, לְהֹדוֹת לְשֵׁם יהוה: כִּי
שָׁמָּה יָשְׁבוּ כִסְאוֹת לְמִשְׁפָּט, כִּסְאוֹת לְבֵית דָּוִד: שַׁאֲלוּ שְׁלוֹם יְרוּשָׁלָםִ,
יִשְׁלָיוּ אֹהֲבָיִךְ: יְהִי־שָׁלוֹם בְּחֵילֵךְ, שַׁלְוָה בְּאַרְמְנוֹתָיִךְ: לְמַעַן אַחַי וְרֵעָי,
אֲדַבְּרָה־נָּא שָׁלוֹם בָּךְ: לְמַעַן בֵּית־יהוה אֱלֹהֵינוּ, אֲבַקְשָׁה טוֹב לָךְ:

שִׁיר הַמַּעֲלוֹת, אֵלֶיךָ נָשָׂאתִי אֶת־עֵינַי, הַיֹּשְׁבִי בַּשָּׁמָיִם: הִנֵּה כְעֵינֵי עֲבָדִים תהלים קכג
אֶל־יַד אֲדוֹנֵיהֶם, כְּעֵינֵי שִׁפְחָה אֶל־יַד גְּבִרְתָּהּ, כֵּן עֵינֵינוּ אֶל־יהוה אֱלֹהֵינוּ,
עַד שֶׁיְּחָנֵּנוּ: חָנֵּנוּ יהוה חָנֵּנוּ, כִּי־רַב שָׂבַעְנוּ בוּז: רַבַּת שָׂבְעָה־לָּהּ נַפְשֵׁנוּ,
הַלַּעַג הַשַּׁאֲנַנִּים, הַבּוּז לִגְאֵי יוֹנִים:

שִׁיר הַמַּעֲלוֹת לְדָוִד, לוּלֵי יהוה שֶׁהָיָה לָנוּ, יֹאמַר־נָא יִשְׂרָאֵל: לוּלֵי תהלים קכד
יהוה שֶׁהָיָה לָנוּ, בְּקוּם עָלֵינוּ אָדָם: אֲזַי חַיִּים בְּלָעוּנוּ, בַּחֲרוֹת אַפָּם
בָּנוּ: אֲזַי הַמַּיִם שְׁטָפוּנוּ, נַחְלָה עָבַר עַל־נַפְשֵׁנוּ: אֲזַי עָבַר עַל־נַפְשֵׁנוּ,
הַמַּיִם הַזֵּידוֹנִים: בָּרוּךְ יהוה, שֶׁלֹּא נְתָנָנוּ טֶרֶף לְשִׁנֵּיהֶם: נַפְשֵׁנוּ כְּצִפּוֹר
נִמְלְטָה מִפַּח יוֹקְשִׁים, הַפַּח נִשְׁבָּר וַאֲנַחְנוּ נִמְלָטְנוּ: עֶזְרֵנוּ בְּשֵׁם יהוה,
עֹשֵׂה שָׁמַיִם וָאָרֶץ:

A song of ascents. Those who trust in the Lord are like Mount Zion that *Ps. 125*
cannot be moved, that stands firm for ever. As hills surround Jerusalem so the Lord surrounds His people, now and forever. The scepter of the wicked shall not rest on the land allotted to the righteous, so that the righteous shall not set their hand to wrongdoing. Do good, Lord, to those who are good, to those who are upright in heart. As for those who turn aside to crooked ways, may the Lord make them go the way of evildoers. Peace be on Israel!

A song of ascents. When the Lord brought back the exiles of Zion we were *Ps. 126*
like people who dream. Then were our mouths filled with laughter, and our tongues with songs of joy. Then was it said among the nations, "The Lord has done great things for them." The Lord did do great things for us and we rejoiced. Bring back our exiles, Lord, like streams in a dry land. May those who sowed in tears, reap in joy. May one who goes out weeping, carrying a bag of seed, come back with songs of joy, carrying his sheaves.

A song of ascents. Of Solomon. Unless the Lord builds the house, its build- *Ps. 127*
ers labor in vain. Unless the Lord guards the city, in vain does the guard keep watch. In vain do you rise early and go late to rest, toiling for the bread you eat. He provides for His loved ones while they sleep. Children are a heritage from the Lord; the fruit of the womb, His reward. Like arrows in the hand of a warrior are the sons of one's youth. Happy is the man who fills his quiver with them; they shall not be put to shame when they contend with the enemy at the gate.

A song of ascents. Happy are all who fear the Lord, who walk in His ways. *Ps. 128*
When you eat the fruit of your labor, happy and fortunate are you. Your wife shall be like a fruitful vine within your house; your sons like olive saplings around your table. So shall the man who fears the Lord be blessed. May the Lord bless you from Zion; may you see the good of Jerusalem all the days of your life; and may you live to see your children's children. Peace be on Israel!

A song of ascents. Often since I was young I have been attacked – let Israel now *Ps. 129*
say – often since I was young I have been attacked, but never have my attackers prevailed. Ploughmen ploughed across my back, making long furrows. But the Lord is just; He has cut the bonds of the wicked. Let all who hate Zion be driven back in shame. Let them be like the grass on roofs that fades before it can be pulled up. It will never fill a reaper's hand nor yield an armful for the gatherer of sheaves. No passersby will say to them: "The Lord's blessing be upon you. We bless you in the name of the Lord."

A song of ascents. From the depths I have called to You, O Lord. Lord, hear my *Ps. 130*
voice; let Your ears be attentive to my plea. If You, Lord, should keep account

תהלים קכה

שִׁיר הַמַּעֲלוֹת, הַבֹּטְחִים בַּיהוה, כְּהַר־צִיּוֹן לֹא־יִמּוֹט, לְעוֹלָם יֵשֵׁב: יְרוּשָׁלַםִ, הָרִים סָבִיב לָהּ, וַיהוה סָבִיב לְעַמּוֹ, מֵעַתָּה וְעַד־עוֹלָם: כִּי לֹא יָנוּחַ שֵׁבֶט הָרֶשַׁע עַל גּוֹרַל הַצַּדִּיקִים, לְמַעַן לֹא־יִשְׁלְחוּ הַצַּדִּיקִים בְּעַוְלָתָה יְדֵיהֶם: הֵיטִיבָה יהוה לַטּוֹבִים, וְלִישָׁרִים בְּלִבּוֹתָם: וְהַמַּטִּים עֲקַלְקַלּוֹתָם יוֹלִיכֵם יהוה אֶת־פֹּעֲלֵי הָאָוֶן, שָׁלוֹם עַל־יִשְׂרָאֵל:

תהלים קכו

שִׁיר הַמַּעֲלוֹת, בְּשׁוּב יהוה אֶת־שִׁיבַת צִיּוֹן, הָיִינוּ כְּחֹלְמִים: אָז יִמָּלֵא שְׂחוֹק פִּינוּ וּלְשׁוֹנֵנוּ רִנָּה, אָז יֹאמְרוּ בַגּוֹיִם הִגְדִּיל יהוה לַעֲשׂוֹת עִם־אֵלֶּה: הִגְדִּיל יהוה לַעֲשׂוֹת עִמָּנוּ, הָיִינוּ שְׂמֵחִים: שׁוּבָה יהוה אֶת־שְׁבִיתֵנוּ, כַּאֲפִיקִים בַּנֶּגֶב: הַזֹּרְעִים בְּדִמְעָה בְּרִנָּה יִקְצֹרוּ: הָלוֹךְ יֵלֵךְ וּבָכֹה נֹשֵׂא מֶשֶׁךְ־הַזָּרַע, בֹּא־יָבֹא בְרִנָּה נֹשֵׂא אֲלֻמֹּתָיו:

תהלים קכז

שִׁיר הַמַּעֲלוֹת לִשְׁלֹמֹה, אִם־יהוה לֹא־יִבְנֶה בַיִת, שָׁוְא עָמְלוּ בוֹנָיו בּוֹ, אִם־יהוה לֹא־יִשְׁמָר־עִיר, שָׁוְא שָׁקַד שׁוֹמֵר: שָׁוְא לָכֶם מַשְׁכִּימֵי קוּם מְאַחֲרֵי־שֶׁבֶת, אֹכְלֵי לֶחֶם הָעֲצָבִים, כֵּן יִתֵּן לִידִידוֹ שֵׁנָא: הִנֵּה נַחֲלַת יהוה בָּנִים, שָׂכָר פְּרִי הַבָּטֶן: כְּחִצִּים בְּיַד־גִּבּוֹר כֵּן בְּנֵי הַנְּעוּרִים: אַשְׁרֵי הַגֶּבֶר אֲשֶׁר מִלֵּא אֶת־אַשְׁפָּתוֹ מֵהֶם, לֹא־יֵבֹשׁוּ כִּי־יְדַבְּרוּ אֶת־אוֹיְבִים בַּשָּׁעַר:

תהלים קכח

שִׁיר הַמַּעֲלוֹת, אַשְׁרֵי כָּל־יְרֵא יהוה, הַהֹלֵךְ בִּדְרָכָיו: יְגִיעַ כַּפֶּיךָ כִּי תֹאכֵל, אַשְׁרֶיךָ וְטוֹב לָךְ: אֶשְׁתְּךָ כְּגֶפֶן פֹּרִיָּה בְּיַרְכְּתֵי בֵיתֶךָ, בָּנֶיךָ כִּשְׁתִלֵי זֵיתִים, סָבִיב לְשֻׁלְחָנֶךָ: הִנֵּה כִי־כֵן יְבֹרַךְ גָּבֶר יְרֵא יהוה: יְבָרֶכְךָ יהוה מִצִּיּוֹן, וּרְאֵה בְּטוּב יְרוּשָׁלָםִ, כֹּל יְמֵי חַיֶּיךָ: וּרְאֵה־בָנִים לְבָנֶיךָ, שָׁלוֹם עַל־יִשְׂרָאֵל:

תהלים קכט

שִׁיר הַמַּעֲלוֹת, רַבַּת צְרָרוּנִי מִנְּעוּרַי, יֹאמַר־נָא יִשְׂרָאֵל: רַבַּת צְרָרוּנִי מִנְּעוּרָי, גַּם לֹא־יָכְלוּ לִי: עַל־גַּבִּי חָרְשׁוּ חֹרְשִׁים, הֶאֱרִיכוּ לְמַעֲנִיתָם: יהוה צַדִּיק, קִצֵּץ עֲבוֹת רְשָׁעִים: יֵבֹשׁוּ וְיִסֹּגוּ אָחוֹר כֹּל שֹׂנְאֵי צִיּוֹן: יִהְיוּ כַּחֲצִיר גַּגּוֹת שֶׁקַּדְמַת שָׁלַף יָבֵשׁ: שֶׁלֹּא מִלֵּא כַפּוֹ קוֹצֵר, וְחִצְנוֹ מְעַמֵּר: וְלֹא אָמְרוּ הָעֹבְרִים, בִּרְכַּת־יהוה אֲלֵיכֶם, בֵּרַכְנוּ אֶתְכֶם בְּשֵׁם יהוה:

תהלים קל

שִׁיר הַמַּעֲלוֹת, מִמַּעֲמַקִּים קְרָאתִיךָ יהוה: אֲדֹנָי שִׁמְעָה בְקוֹלִי, תִּהְיֶינָה אָזְנֶיךָ קַשֻּׁבוֹת לְקוֹל תַּחֲנוּנָי: אִם־עֲוֹנוֹת תִּשְׁמָר־יָהּ, אֲדֹנָי מִי יַעֲמֹד: כִּי־

of sins, O LORD, who could stand? But with You there is forgiveness, that You may be held in awe. I wait for the LORD, my soul waits, and in His word I put my hope. My soul waits for the LORD more than watchmen wait for the morning, more than watchmen wait for the morning. Israel, put your hope in the LORD, for with the LORD there is loving-kindness, and great is His power to redeem. It is He who will redeem Israel from all their sins.

A song of ascents. By David. LORD, my heart is not proud, nor are my eyes arrogant. I do not busy myself with great affairs or with things beyond me. But I have made my soul still and quiet, like a weaned child with its mother; like a weaned child is my soul within me. Israel, put your hope in the LORD, now and for evermore. *Ps. 131*

A song of ascents. LORD, remember David and all the hardship he endured. He swore an oath to the LORD and made a vow to the Mighty One of Jacob: "I will not enter my house, nor go to bed; I will not give sleep to my eyes or slumber to my eyelids, until I find a place for the LORD, a dwelling for the Mighty One of Jacob." We heard of it in Efrat, we found it in the fields of Yaar. Let us enter His dwelling, worship at His footstool. Advance, LORD, to Your resting place, You and Your mighty Ark. Your priests are robed in righteousness; Your devoted ones sing for joy. For the sake of Your servant David, do not reject Your anointed one. The LORD swore to David a firm oath that He will not revoke: "One of your own descendants I will set upon your throne. If your sons keep My covenant and My decrees that I teach them, then their sons shall sit upon your throne for all time." For the LORD has chosen Zion; He desired it for His home. This is My resting place for all time; here I will be present, for that is My desire. I will amply bless its store of food; its poor I will satisfy with bread. I will clothe its priests with salvation; its loyal ones shall sing for joy. There I will make David's dynasty flourish; I will prepare a lamp for My anointed one. I will clothe his enemies with shame, but on him will be a shining crown. *Ps. 132*

A song of ascents. By David. How good and pleasant it is when brothers live together. It is like fragrant oil on the head, running down onto the beard, Aaron's beard, that runs down over the collar of his robes. It is like the dew of Hermon that falls on the mountains of Zion. There the LORD bestows His blessing, life for evermore. *Ps. 133*

A song of ascents. Come, bless the LORD, all you servants of the LORD, who nightly stand in the House of the LORD. Lift up your hands toward the Sanctuary and bless the LORD. May the LORD, Maker of heaven and earth, bless you from Zion! *Ps. 134*

עִמְּךָ הַסְּלִיחָה, לְמַעַן תִּוָּרֵא: קִוִּיתִי יהוה קִוְּתָה נַפְשִׁי, וְלִדְבָרוֹ הוֹחָלְתִּי: נַפְשִׁי לַאדֹנָי, מִשֹּׁמְרִים לַבֹּקֶר, שֹׁמְרִים לַבֹּקֶר: יַחֵל יִשְׂרָאֵל אֶל־יהוה, כִּי־עִם־יהוה הַחֶסֶד, וְהַרְבֵּה עִמּוֹ פְדוּת: וְהוּא יִפְדֶּה אֶת־יִשְׂרָאֵל, מִכֹּל עֲוֺנֹתָיו:

תהלים קלא שִׁיר הַמַּעֲלוֹת לְדָוִד, יהוה לֹא־גָבַהּ לִבִּי, וְלֹא־רָמוּ עֵינַי, וְלֹא־הִלַּכְתִּי בִּגְדֹלוֹת וּבְנִפְלָאוֹת מִמֶּנִּי: אִם־לֹא שִׁוִּיתִי וְדוֹמַמְתִּי נַפְשִׁי, כְּגָמֻל עֲלֵי אִמּוֹ, כַּגָּמֻל עָלַי נַפְשִׁי: יַחֵל יִשְׂרָאֵל אֶל־יהוה, מֵעַתָּה וְעַד־עוֹלָם:

תהלים קלב שִׁיר הַמַּעֲלוֹת, זְכוֹר־יהוה לְדָוִד אֵת כָּל־עֻנּוֹתוֹ: אֲשֶׁר נִשְׁבַּע לַיהוה, נָדַר לַאֲבִיר יַעֲקֹב: אִם־אָבֹא בְּאֹהֶל בֵּיתִי, אִם־אֶעֱלֶה עַל־עֶרֶשׂ יְצוּעָי: אִם־אֶתֵּן שְׁנָת לְעֵינָי, לְעַפְעַפַּי תְּנוּמָה: עַד־אֶמְצָא מָקוֹם לַיהוה, מִשְׁכָּנוֹת לַאֲבִיר יַעֲקֹב: הִנֵּה־שְׁמַעֲנוּהָ בְאֶפְרָתָה, מְצָאנוּהָ בִּשְׂדֵי־יָעַר: נָבוֹאָה לְמִשְׁכְּנוֹתָיו, נִשְׁתַּחֲוֶה לַהֲדֹם רַגְלָיו: קוּמָה יהוה לִמְנוּחָתֶךָ, אַתָּה וַאֲרוֹן עֻזֶּךָ: כֹּהֲנֶיךָ יִלְבְּשׁוּ־צֶדֶק, וַחֲסִידֶיךָ יְרַנֵּנוּ: בַּעֲבוּר דָּוִד עַבְדֶּךָ, אַל־תָּשֵׁב פְּנֵי מְשִׁיחֶךָ: נִשְׁבַּע־יהוה לְדָוִד, אֱמֶת לֹא־יָשׁוּב מִמֶּנָּה, מִפְּרִי בִטְנְךָ אָשִׁית לְכִסֵּא־לָךְ: אִם־יִשְׁמְרוּ בָנֶיךָ בְּרִיתִי, וְעֵדֹתִי זוֹ אֲלַמְּדֵם, גַּם־בְּנֵיהֶם עֲדֵי־עַד, יֵשְׁבוּ לְכִסֵּא־לָךְ: כִּי־בָחַר יהוה בְּצִיּוֹן, אִוָּהּ לְמוֹשָׁב לוֹ: זֹאת־מְנוּחָתִי עֲדֵי־עַד, פֹּה אֵשֵׁב כִּי אִוִּתִיהָ: צֵידָהּ בָּרֵךְ אֲבָרֵךְ, אֶבְיוֹנֶיהָ אַשְׂבִּיעַ לָחֶם: וְכֹהֲנֶיהָ אַלְבִּישׁ יֶשַׁע, וַחֲסִידֶיהָ רַנֵּן יְרַנֵּנוּ: שָׁם אַצְמִיחַ קֶרֶן לְדָוִד, עָרַכְתִּי נֵר לִמְשִׁיחִי: אוֹיְבָיו אַלְבִּישׁ בֹּשֶׁת, וְעָלָיו יָצִיץ נִזְרוֹ:

תהלים קלג שִׁיר הַמַּעֲלוֹת לְדָוִד, הִנֵּה מַה־טּוֹב וּמַה־נָּעִים, שֶׁבֶת אַחִים גַּם־יָחַד: כַּשֶּׁמֶן הַטּוֹב עַל־הָרֹאשׁ, יֹרֵד עַל־הַזָּקָן, זְקַן־אַהֲרֹן שֶׁיֹּרֵד עַל־פִּי מִדּוֹתָיו: כְּטַל־חֶרְמוֹן שֶׁיֹּרֵד עַל־הַרְרֵי צִיּוֹן, כִּי שָׁם צִוָּה יהוה אֶת־הַבְּרָכָה, חַיִּים עַד־הָעוֹלָם:

תהלים קלד שִׁיר הַמַּעֲלוֹת, הִנֵּה בָּרְכוּ אֶת־יהוה כָּל־עַבְדֵי יהוה, הָעֹמְדִים בְּבֵית־יהוה בַּלֵּילוֹת: שְׂאוּ־יְדֵכֶם קֹדֶשׁ, וּבָרְכוּ אֶת־יהוה: יְבָרֶכְךָ יהוה מִצִּיּוֹן, עֹשֵׂה שָׁמַיִם וָאָרֶץ:

ETHICS OF THE FATHERS

One of the following chapters is read each Shabbat after Pesaḥ until the Shabbat before Rosh HaShana. On the last three Shabbatot before Rosh HaShana, two chapters are read.

All Israel have a share in the World to Come, as it is said: *Sanhedrin 90a*
"Your people are all righteous; they shall inherit the land for ever; *Is. 60*
they are a shoot of My own planting,
a work of My own hands, that I may be glorified."

CHAPTER I

1. Moses received the Torah at Sinai and handed it on to Joshua; Joshua to the elders; the elders to the prophets; and the prophets handed it on to the men of the Great Assembly. They (the men of the Great Assembly) said three things: Be careful in judgment; raise up many disciples; and make a fence for the Torah.
2. Shimon the Just was one of the last survivors of the Great Assembly. He used to say: On three things the world stands: on the Torah, on divine worship, and on acts of loving-kindness.
3. Antigonos of Sokho received [the Torah tradition] from Shimon the Just. He used to say: Do not be like servants who serve their master on condition of receiving a reward, but be like servants who serve their master not on condition of receiving a reward; and let the fear of Heaven be upon you.
4. Yose ben Yo'ezer of Zereda and Yose ben Yoḥanan of Jerusalem received [the tradition] from them. Yose ben Yo'ezer of Zereda used to say: Let your house be a meeting place for sages; sit in the dust at their feet, and with thirst, drink in their words.
5. Yose ben Yoḥanan of Jerusalem used to say: Let your house be open wide; let the poor join the members of your household; and do not gossip inordinately with women. This was said about one's own wife; all the more so does it apply to another man's wife. Hence the sages say: a man who talks too much with a woman brings trouble on himself, neglects the study of Torah, and in the end will inherit Gehinnom.
6. Yehoshua ben Peraḥya and Nittai the Arbelite received [the tradition] from them. Yehoshua ben Peraḥya used to say: Get yourself a teacher, acquire a companion, and give everyone the benefit of the doubt.
7. Nittai the Arbelite used to say: Keep far from a bad neighbor, do not associate with a bad person, and do not despair of divine retribution.
8. Yehuda ben Tabbai and Shimon ben Shataḥ received [the tradition] from them. Yehuda ben Tabbai used to say: [When sitting as a judge] do not act

פרקי אבות

One of the following chapters is read each שבת *after* פסח *until the* שבת *before* ראש השנה*. On the last three* שבתות *before* ראש השנה*, two chapters are read.*

כָּל יִשְׂרָאֵל יֵשׁ לָהֶם חֵלֶק לָעוֹלָם הַבָּא. שֶׁנֶּאֱמַר: סנהדרין צ.
וְעַמֵּךְ כֻּלָּם צַדִּיקִים, לְעוֹלָם יִירְשׁוּ אָרֶץ ישעיה ס
נֵצֶר מַטָּעַי, מַעֲשֵׂה יָדַי לְהִתְפָּאֵר:

פרק ראשון

א מֹשֶׁה קִבֵּל תּוֹרָה מִסִּינַי וּמְסָרָהּ לִיהוֹשֻׁעַ, וִיהוֹשֻׁעַ לִזְקֵנִים, וּזְקֵנִים לִנְבִיאִים, וּנְבִיאִים מְסָרוּהָ לְאַנְשֵׁי כְנֶסֶת הַגְּדוֹלָה. הֵם אָמְרוּ שְׁלֹשָׁה דְבָרִים: הֱווּ מְתוּנִים בַּדִּין, וְהַעֲמִידוּ תַלְמִידִים הַרְבֵּה, וַעֲשׂוּ סְיָג לַתּוֹרָה.

ב שִׁמְעוֹן הַצַּדִּיק הָיָה מִשְּׁיָרֵי כְנֶסֶת הַגְּדוֹלָה. הוּא הָיָה אוֹמֵר: עַל שְׁלֹשָׁה דְבָרִים הָעוֹלָם עוֹמֵד, עַל הַתּוֹרָה, וְעַל הָעֲבוֹדָה, וְעַל גְּמִילוּת חֲסָדִים.

ג אַנְטִיגְנוֹס אִישׁ סוֹכוֹ קִבֵּל מִשִּׁמְעוֹן הַצַּדִּיק. הוּא הָיָה אוֹמֵר: אַל תִּהְיוּ כַּעֲבָדִים הַמְשַׁמְּשִׁים אֶת הָרַב עַל מְנָת לְקַבֵּל פְּרָס, אֶלָּא הֱווּ כַּעֲבָדִים הַמְשַׁמְּשִׁים אֶת הָרַב שֶׁלֹּא עַל מְנָת לְקַבֵּל פְּרָס, וִיהִי מוֹרָא שָׁמַיִם עֲלֵיכֶם.

ד יוֹסֵי בֶּן יוֹעֶזֶר אִישׁ צְרֵדָה וְיוֹסֵי בֶּן יוֹחָנָן אִישׁ יְרוּשָׁלַיִם קִבְּלוּ מֵהֶם. יוֹסֵי בֶּן יוֹעֶזֶר אִישׁ צְרֵדָה אוֹמֵר: יְהִי בֵיתְךָ בֵּית וַעַד לַחֲכָמִים, וֶהֱוֵי מִתְאַבֵּק בַּעֲפַר רַגְלֵיהֶם, וֶהֱוֵי שׁוֹתֶה בַצָּמָא אֶת דִּבְרֵיהֶם.

ה יוֹסֵי בֶּן יוֹחָנָן אִישׁ יְרוּשָׁלַיִם אוֹמֵר: יְהִי בֵיתְךָ פָּתוּחַ לִרְוָחָה, וְיִהְיוּ עֲנִיִּים בְּנֵי בֵיתֶךָ, וְאַל תַּרְבֶּה שִׂיחָה עִם הָאִשָּׁה. בְּאִשְׁתּוֹ אָמְרוּ, קַל וָחֹמֶר בְּאֵשֶׁת חֲבֵרוֹ. מִכָּאן אָמְרוּ חֲכָמִים: כָּל הַמַּרְבֶּה שִׂיחָה עִם הָאִשָּׁה, גּוֹרֵם רָעָה לְעַצְמוֹ, וּבוֹטֵל מִדִּבְרֵי תוֹרָה, וְסוֹפוֹ יוֹרֵשׁ גֵּיהִנֹּם.

ו יְהוֹשֻׁעַ בֶּן פְּרַחְיָה וְנִתַּאי הָאַרְבֵּלִי קִבְּלוּ מֵהֶם. יְהוֹשֻׁעַ בֶּן פְּרַחְיָה אוֹמֵר: עֲשֵׂה לְךָ רַב, וּקְנֵה לְךָ חָבֵר, וֶהֱוֵי דָן אֶת כָּל הָאָדָם לְכַף זְכוּת.

ז נִתַּאי הָאַרְבֵּלִי אוֹמֵר: הַרְחֵק מִשָּׁכֵן רָע, וְאַל תִּתְחַבֵּר לָרָשָׁע, וְאַל תִּתְיָאֵשׁ מִן הַפֻּרְעָנוּת.

ח יְהוּדָה בֶּן טַבַּאי וְשִׁמְעוֹן בֶּן שָׁטָח קִבְּלוּ מֵהֶם. יְהוּדָה בֶּן טַבַּאי אוֹמֵר: אַל

as an advocate; when the parties to a lawsuit appear before you, regard them both as guilty; but when they leave you, having accepted the verdict, regard them both as innocent.

9. Shimon ben Shataḥ used to say: Examine the witnesses thoroughly, and be careful in your words, lest through them they learn how to lie.

10. Shemaya and Avtalyon received [the tradition] from them. Shemaya used to say: Love work, hate public office, and do not become too intimate with the ruling power.

11. Avtalyon used to say: sages, be careful in what you say, lest you incur the penalty of exile and find yourself banished to a place of evil waters, where your disciples who follow you may drink from them and die, with the result that the name of Heaven will be profaned.

12. Hillel and Shammai received [the tradition] from them. Hillel said: Be among the disciples of Aaron, loving peace and pursuing peace, loving people and drawing them close to the Torah.

13. He used to say: A name made great is a name destroyed. He who does not increase [his knowledge] loses it. He who does not study deserves to die, and he who makes worldly use of the crown [of Torah] passes away.

14. He used to say: If I am not for myself, who will be for me? And if I am only for myself, what am I? And if not now, when?

15. Shammai used to say: Make your Torah study a fixed habit. Say little and do much; and greet everyone cheerfully.

16. Rabban Gamliel used to say: Get yourself a teacher, avoid doubt, and do not make a habit of giving tithes by guessing.

17. Shimon, his son, used to say: All my life I grew up among sages and I found that nothing is better for a person than silence. Not learning but doing is the main thing; and one who talks too much causes sin.

18. Rabban Shimon ben Gamliel used to say: On three things does the world stand – on truth, justice and peace, as it is said, "Administer truth and the judgment of peace in your gates." *Zech. 8*

Rabbi Ḥananya ben Akashya said: The Holy One, blessed be He, wanted to confer merit on Israel. That is why He gave them a copious Torah and many commandments, as it is said, "It pleased the Lord, for the sake of [Israel's] righteousness, to make the Torah great and glorious." *Makkot 23b* *Is. 42*

If there is a minyan, mourners say the Rabbis' Kaddish (page 702).

* * *

תַּעַשׂ עַצְמְךָ כְּעוֹרְכֵי הַדַּיָּנִין, וּכְשֶׁיִּהְיוּ בַּעֲלֵי הַדִּין עוֹמְדִים לְפָנֶיךָ יִהְיוּ בְעֵינֶיךָ כִּרְשָׁעִים, וּכְשֶׁנִּפְטָרִים מִלְּפָנֶיךָ יִהְיוּ בְעֵינֶיךָ כְּזַכָּאִין, כְּשֶׁקִּבְּלוּ עֲלֵיהֶם אֶת הַדִּין.

ט שִׁמְעוֹן בֶּן שָׁטָח אוֹמֵר: הֱוֵי מַרְבֶּה לַחְקֹר אֶת הָעֵדִים, וֶהֱוֵי זָהִיר בִּדְבָרֶיךָ, שֶׁמָּא מִתּוֹכָם יִלְמְדוּ לְשַׁקֵּר.

י שְׁמַעְיָה וְאַבְטַלְיוֹן קִבְּלוּ מֵהֶם. שְׁמַעְיָה אוֹמֵר: אֱהֹב אֶת הַמְּלָאכָה, וּשְׂנָא אֶת הָרַבָּנוּת, וְאַל תִּתְוַדַּע לָרָשׁוּת.

יא אַבְטַלְיוֹן אוֹמֵר: חֲכָמִים הִזָּהֲרוּ בְּדִבְרֵיכֶם, שֶׁמָּא תָחוּבוּ חוֹבַת גָּלוּת, וְתִגְלוּ לִמְקוֹם מַיִם הָרָעִים, וְיִשְׁתּוּ הַתַּלְמִידִים הַבָּאִים אַחֲרֵיכֶם וְיָמוּתוּ, וְנִמְצָא שֵׁם שָׁמַיִם מִתְחַלֵּל.

יב הִלֵּל וְשַׁמַּאי קִבְּלוּ מֵהֶם. הִלֵּל אוֹמֵר: הֱוֵי מִתַּלְמִידָיו שֶׁל אַהֲרֹן, אוֹהֵב שָׁלוֹם וְרוֹדֵף שָׁלוֹם, אוֹהֵב אֶת הַבְּרִיּוֹת וּמְקָרְבָן לַתּוֹרָה.

יג הוּא הָיָה אוֹמֵר: נְגַד שְׁמָא אֲבַד שְׁמֵהּ, וּדְלָא מוֹסִיף יָסֵף, וּדְלָא יָלֵף קְטָלָא חַיָּב, וּדְאִשְׁתַּמַּשׁ בְּתָגָא חֲלָף.

יד הוּא הָיָה אוֹמֵר: אִם אֵין אֲנִי לִי מִי לִי, וּכְשֶׁאֲנִי לְעַצְמִי מָה אֲנִי, וְאִם לֹא עַכְשָׁו אֵימָתָי.

טו שַׁמַּאי אוֹמֵר: עֲשֵׂה תוֹרָתְךָ קֶבַע, אֱמֹר מְעַט וַעֲשֵׂה הַרְבֵּה, וֶהֱוֵי מְקַבֵּל אֶת כָּל הָאָדָם בְּסֵבֶר פָּנִים יָפוֹת.

טז רַבָּן גַּמְלִיאֵל אוֹמֵר: עֲשֵׂה לְךָ רַב, וְהִסְתַּלֵּק מִן הַסָּפֵק, וְאַל תַּרְבֶּה לְעַשֵּׂר אֻמָּדוֹת.

יז שִׁמְעוֹן בְּנוֹ אוֹמֵר: כָּל יָמַי גָּדַלְתִּי בֵּין הַחֲכָמִים, וְלֹא מָצָאתִי לַגּוּף טוֹב מִשְּׁתִיקָה, וְלֹא הַמִּדְרָשׁ עִקָּר אֶלָּא הַמַּעֲשֶׂה, וְכָל הַמַּרְבֶּה דְבָרִים מֵבִיא חֵטְא.

יח רַבָּן שִׁמְעוֹן בֶּן גַּמְלִיאֵל אוֹמֵר: עַל שְׁלֹשָׁה דְבָרִים הָעוֹלָם קַיָּם, עַל הַדִּין,
וְעַל הָאֱמֶת, וְעַל הַשָּׁלוֹם. שֶׁנֶּאֱמַר: אֱמֶת וּמִשְׁפַּט שָׁלוֹם שִׁפְטוּ בְּשַׁעֲרֵיכֶם: זכריה ח

רַבִּי חֲנַנְיָא בֶּן עֲקַשְׁיָא אוֹמֵר: רָצָה הַקָּדוֹשׁ בָּרוּךְ הוּא לְזַכּוֹת אֶת יִשְׂרָאֵל, לְפִיכָךְ מכות כג:
הִרְבָּה לָהֶם תּוֹרָה וּמִצְוֹת. שֶׁנֶּאֱמַר: יהוה חָפֵץ לְמַעַן צִדְקוֹ, יַגְדִּיל תּוֹרָה וְיַאְדִּיר: ישעיה מב

If there is a מנין*, mourners say* קדיש דרבנן *(page 703).*

* * *

All Israel have a share in the World to Come, as it is said: *Sanhedrin 90a*
"Your people are all righteous; they shall inherit the land for ever; *Is. 60*
they are a shoot of My own planting,
a work of My own hands, that I may be glorified."

CHAPTER 2

1. Rabbi [Judah the Prince] said: What is the right path a person should choose for himself? Whatever is honorable to one who chooses it and honorable in the eyes of others. Be as meticulous in the observance of a minor mitzva as a major one, for you do not know the reward for each mitzva. Against the loss that fulfilling a mitzva may entail, reckon its reward, and against the benefit a transgression may bring, reckon the loss it involves. Reflect on three things and you will not fall into transgression: know what is above you – a seeing eye, a hearing ear, and a book in which all your deeds are written.
2. Rabban Gamliel, son of Rabbi Judah the Prince, said: It is good to combine Torah study with a worldly occupation, for the effort involved in both makes one forget sin. Torah study without an occupation will in the end fail and lead to sin. And all who work for the community should do so for the sake of Heaven, for their ancestral merit will support them and their righteousness endures for ever. And as for you [God will say], I count you worthy of great reward as though you yourselves had accomplished it all.
3. Be wary in your dealings with the ruling power, for they only befriend a man when it serves their needs. When it is to their advantage, they appear as friends, but they do not stand by a person in his hour of need.
4. He used to say: Do His will as if it were yours, so that He may do your will as if it were His. Set aside your will for the sake of His, that He may set aside the will of others before yours.
5. Hillel said: Do not separate yourself from the community. Do not be sure of yourself until the day you die. Do not judge your fellow until you have stood in his place. Do not say anything that cannot be understood [at once] in the hope that it will eventually be understood. And do not say, I will study when I have the time, for you may never have the time.
6. He used to say: An uncouth person cannot be sin-fearing, nor can an ignoramus be pious. A shy person cannot learn, nor can an impatient one teach. A person over-occupied in business does not always become wise. In a place where there are no worthy people, strive to be worthy.
7. Seeing a skull floating on the water, he said: "Because you drowned others, they drowned you, and those who drowned you will themselves eventually be drowned."
8. He used to say: The more flesh, the more worms. The more possessions, the more worries. The more wives, the more witchcraft. The more maidservants, the more lewdness. The more menservants, the more robbery. The more Torah,

כָּל יִשְׂרָאֵל יֵשׁ לָהֶם חֵלֶק לָעוֹלָם הַבָּא. שֶׁנֶּאֱמַר: סנהדרין צ.
וְעַמֵּךְ כֻּלָּם צַדִּיקִים, לְעוֹלָם יִירְשׁוּ אָרֶץ ישעיה ס
נֵצֶר מַטָּעַי, מַעֲשֵׂה יָדַי לְהִתְפָּאֵר:

פרק שני

א רַבִּי אוֹמֵר: אֵיזוֹ הִיא דֶרֶךְ יְשָׁרָה שֶׁיָּבֹר לוֹ הָאָדָם, כָּל שֶׁהִיא תִּפְאֶרֶת לְעֹשֶׂיהָ וְתִפְאֶרֶת לוֹ מִן הָאָדָם. וֶהֱוֵי זָהִיר בְּמִצְוָה קַלָּה כְּבַחֲמוּרָה, שֶׁאֵין אַתָּה יוֹדֵעַ מַתַּן שְׂכָרָן שֶׁל מִצְוֹת. וֶהֱוֵי מְחַשֵּׁב הֶפְסֵד מִצְוָה כְּנֶגֶד שְׂכָרָהּ, וּשְׂכַר עֲבֵרָה כְּנֶגֶד הֶפְסֵדָהּ. הִסְתַּכֵּל בִּשְׁלֹשָׁה דְבָרִים, וְאִי אַתָּה בָא לִידֵי עֲבֵרָה. דַּע מַה לְּמַעְלָה מִמְּךָ, עַיִן רוֹאָה, וְאֹזֶן שׁוֹמַעַת, וְכָל מַעֲשֶׂיךָ בַּסֵּפֶר נִכְתָּבִים.

ב רַבָּן גַּמְלִיאֵל בְּנוֹ שֶׁל רַבִּי יְהוּדָה הַנָּשִׂיא אוֹמֵר: יָפֶה תַלְמוּד תּוֹרָה עִם דֶּרֶךְ אֶרֶץ, שֶׁיְּגִיעַת שְׁנֵיהֶם מְשַׁכַּחַת עָוֹן. וְכָל תּוֹרָה שֶׁאֵין עִמָּהּ מְלָאכָה, סוֹפָהּ בְּטֵלָה וְגוֹרֶרֶת עָוֹן. וְכָל הָעוֹסְקִים עִם הַצִּבּוּר, יִהְיוּ עוֹסְקִים עִמָּהֶם לְשֵׁם שָׁמַיִם, שֶׁזְּכוּת אֲבוֹתָם מְסַיַּעְתָּם, וְצִדְקָתָם עוֹמֶדֶת לָעַד. וְאַתֶּם, מַעֲלֶה אֲנִי עֲלֵיכֶם שָׂכָר הַרְבֵּה כְּאִלּוּ עֲשִׂיתֶם.

ג הֱווּ זְהִירִין בָּרָשׁוּת, שֶׁאֵין מְקָרְבִין לוֹ לָאָדָם אֶלָּא לְצֹרֶךְ עַצְמָן. נִרְאִין כְּאוֹהֲבִין בִּשְׁעַת הֲנָאָתָן, וְאֵין עוֹמְדִין לוֹ לָאָדָם בִּשְׁעַת דָּחְקוֹ.

ד הוּא הָיָה אוֹמֵר: עֲשֵׂה רְצוֹנוֹ כִּרְצוֹנְךָ, כְּדֵי שֶׁיַּעֲשֶׂה רְצוֹנְךָ כִּרְצוֹנוֹ. בַּטֵּל רְצוֹנְךָ מִפְּנֵי רְצוֹנוֹ, כְּדֵי שֶׁיְּבַטֵּל רְצוֹן אֲחֵרִים מִפְּנֵי רְצוֹנֶךָ.

ה הִלֵּל אוֹמֵר: אַל תִּפְרֹשׁ מִן הַצִּבּוּר, וְאַל תַּאֲמִין בְּעַצְמְךָ עַד יוֹם מוֹתְךָ, וְאַל תָּדִין אֶת חֲבֵרְךָ עַד שֶׁתַּגִּיעַ לִמְקוֹמוֹ. וְאַל תֹּאמַר דָּבָר שֶׁאִי אֶפְשַׁר לִשְׁמֹעַ, שֶׁסּוֹפוֹ לְהִשָּׁמַע. וְאַל תֹּאמַר לִכְשֶׁאֶפָּנֶה אֶשְׁנֶה, שֶׁמָּא לֹא תִפָּנֶה.

ו הוּא הָיָה אוֹמֵר: אֵין בּוּר יְרֵא חֵטְא, וְלֹא עַם הָאָרֶץ חָסִיד, וְלֹא הַבַּיְשָׁן לָמֵד, וְלֹא הַקַּפְּדָן מְלַמֵּד, וְלֹא כָל הַמַּרְבֶּה בִסְחוֹרָה מַחְכִּים. וּבְמָקוֹם שֶׁאֵין אֲנָשִׁים, הִשְׁתַּדֵּל לִהְיוֹת אִישׁ.

ז אַף הוּא רָאָה גֻּלְגֹּלֶת אַחַת שֶׁצָּפָה עַל פְּנֵי הַמָּיִם. אָמַר לָהּ: עַל דַּאֲטֵפְתְּ אַטְפוּךְ, וְסוֹף מְטִיפַיִךְ יְטוּפוּן.

ח הוּא הָיָה אוֹמֵר: מַרְבֶּה בָשָׂר, מַרְבֶּה רִמָּה. מַרְבֶּה נְכָסִים, מַרְבֶּה דְאָגָה. מַרְבֶּה נָשִׁים, מַרְבֶּה כְשָׁפִים. מַרְבֶּה שְׁפָחוֹת, מַרְבֶּה זִמָּה. מַרְבֶּה עֲבָדִים, מַרְבֶּה גָזֵל. מַרְבֶּה תוֹרָה, מַרְבֶּה חַיִּים. מַרְבֶּה יְשִׁיבָה, מַרְבֶּה חָכְמָה. מַרְבֶּה

the more life. The more study, the more wisdom. The more counsel, the more understanding. The more charity, the more peace. Whoever acquires a good name acquires something for himself. Whoever acquires for himself words of Torah acquires for himself life in the World to Come.

9. Rabban Yoḥanan ben Zakkai received [the tradition] from Hillel and Shammai. He used to say: If you have learnt much Torah, take no special credit for yourself, for it was for this that you were created.

10. Rabban Yoḥanan ben Zakkai had five [pre-eminent] disciples, namely: Rabbi Eliezer ben Hyrcanus, Rabbi Yehoshua ben Ḥananya, Rabbi Yose the Priest, Rabbi Shimon ben Netanel and Rabbi Elazar ben Arakh.

11. He used to recount their praise: Eliezer ben Hyrcanus: a plastered well that never loses a drop. Yehoshua ben Ḥananya: happy the one who gave him birth. Yose the Priest: a pious man. Shimon ben Netanel: a man who fears sin. Elazar ben Arakh: an ever-flowing spring.

12. He used to say: If all the sages of Israel were in one scale of a balance and Eliezer ben Hyrcanus in the other, he would outweigh them all. However, Abba Saul said in his name: If all the sages of Israel, including Eliezer ben Hyrcanus, were in one scale of a balance, and Elazar ben Arakh in the other, he would outweigh them all.

13. He said to them: Go and see which is the right way to which one should cling. Rabbi Eliezer said: a good eye [generosity of spirit]. Rabbi Yehoshua said: a good companion. Rabbi Yose said: a good neighbor. Rabbi Shimon said: one who considers the consequences. Rabbi Elazar said: a good heart. Then he said to them: I prefer the answer of Elazar ben Arakh, for his view includes all of yours.

14. He said to them: Go and see which is the wrong way one should avoid. Rabbi Eliezer said: an evil eye [envy]. Rabbi Yehoshua said: an evil companion. Rabbi Yose said: an evil neighbor. Rabbi Shimon said: one who borrows and does not repay, for borrowing from a person is like borrowing from God, as it is said, "The wicked borrows and does not repay, but the Righteous One is gracious and repays." Rabbi Elazar said: an evil heart. Then he said to them: I prefer the answer of Elazar ben Arakh, for his view includes all of yours. *Ps. 37*

15. Each of the disciples said three things. Rabbi Eliezer said: Let the honor of your fellow be as precious to you as your own. Do not be easily provoked to anger. Repent one day before you die. [He also said:] Warm yourself by the fire of the sages, but be careful of their glowing coals lest you be burnt; for their bite is the bite of a fox, their sting is the sting of a scorpion, their hiss is the hiss of a serpent, and all their words are like fiery coals.

16. Rabbi Yehoshua said: The evil eye [envy], the evil impulse, and hatred of humankind drive a person out of the world.

עֵצָה, מַרְבֶּה תְבוּנָה. מַרְבֶּה צְדָקָה, מַרְבֶּה שָׁלוֹם. קָנָה שֵׁם טוֹב, קָנָה לְעַצְמוֹ. קָנָה לוֹ דִּבְרֵי תוֹרָה, קָנָה לוֹ חַיֵּי הָעוֹלָם הַבָּא.

ט רַבָּן יוֹחָנָן בֶּן זַכַּאי קִבֵּל מֵהִלֵּל וּמִשַּׁמַּאי. הוּא הָיָה אוֹמֵר: אִם לָמַדְתָּ תּוֹרָה הַרְבֵּה, אַל תַּחֲזִיק טוֹבָה לְעַצְמְךָ, כִּי לְכָךְ נוֹצָרְתָּ.

י חֲמִשָּׁה תַלְמִידִים הָיוּ לְרַבָּן יוֹחָנָן בֶּן זַכַּאי. וְאֵלּוּ הֵן: רַבִּי אֱלִיעֶזֶר בֶּן הוֹרְקְנוֹס, רַבִּי יְהוֹשֻׁעַ בֶּן חֲנַנְיָה, רַבִּי יוֹסֵי הַכֹּהֵן, רַבִּי שִׁמְעוֹן בֶּן נְתַנְאֵל, רַבִּי אֶלְעָזָר בֶּן עֲרָךְ.

יא הוּא הָיָה מוֹנֶה שִׁבְחָם: אֱלִיעֶזֶר בֶּן הוֹרְקְנוֹס, בּוֹר סוּד שֶׁאֵינוֹ מְאַבֵּד טִפָּה. יְהוֹשֻׁעַ בֶּן חֲנַנְיָה, אַשְׁרֵי יוֹלַדְתּוֹ. יוֹסֵי הַכֹּהֵן, חָסִיד. שִׁמְעוֹן בֶּן נְתַנְאֵל, יְרֵא חֵטְא. אֶלְעָזָר בֶּן עֲרָךְ, כְּמַעְיָן הַמִּתְגַּבֵּר.

יב הוּא הָיָה אוֹמֵר: אִם יִהְיוּ כָּל חַכְמֵי יִשְׂרָאֵל בְּכַף מֹאזְנַיִם, וֶאֱלִיעֶזֶר בֶּן הוֹרְקְנוֹס בְּכַף שְׁנִיָּה, מַכְרִיעַ אֶת כֻּלָּם. אַבָּא שָׁאוּל אוֹמֵר מִשְּׁמוֹ: אִם יִהְיוּ כָּל חַכְמֵי יִשְׂרָאֵל בְּכַף מֹאזְנַיִם, וֶאֱלִיעֶזֶר בֶּן הוֹרְקְנוֹס אַף עִמָּהֶם, וְאֶלְעָזָר בֶּן עֲרָךְ בְּכַף שְׁנִיָּה, מַכְרִיעַ אֶת כֻּלָּם.

יג אָמַר לָהֶם: צְאוּ וּרְאוּ אֵיזוֹ הִיא דֶּרֶךְ טוֹבָה, שֶׁיִּדְבַּק בָּהּ הָאָדָם. רַבִּי אֱלִיעֶזֶר אוֹמֵר: עַיִן טוֹבָה. רַבִּי יְהוֹשֻׁעַ אוֹמֵר: חָבֵר טוֹב. רַבִּי יוֹסֵי אוֹמֵר: שָׁכֵן טוֹב. רַבִּי שִׁמְעוֹן אוֹמֵר: הָרוֹאֶה אֶת הַנּוֹלָד. רַבִּי אֶלְעָזָר אוֹמֵר: לֵב טוֹב. אָמַר לָהֶם, רוֹאֶה אֲנִי אֶת דִּבְרֵי אֶלְעָזָר בֶּן עֲרָךְ מִדִּבְרֵיכֶם, שֶׁבִּכְלַל דְּבָרָיו דִּבְרֵיכֶם.

יד אָמַר לָהֶם: צְאוּ וּרְאוּ, אֵיזוֹ הִיא דֶּרֶךְ רָעָה, שֶׁיִּתְרַחֵק מִמֶּנָּה הָאָדָם. רַבִּי אֱלִיעֶזֶר אוֹמֵר: עַיִן רָעָה. רַבִּי יְהוֹשֻׁעַ אוֹמֵר: חָבֵר רָע. רַבִּי יוֹסֵי אוֹמֵר: שָׁכֵן רָע. רַבִּי שִׁמְעוֹן אוֹמֵר: הַלֹּוֶה וְאֵינוֹ מְשַׁלֵּם, אֶחָד הַלֹּוֶה מִן הָאָדָם כְּלֹוֶה מִן הַמָּקוֹם, שֶׁנֶּאֱמַר: לֹוֶה רָשָׁע וְלֹא יְשַׁלֵּם, וְצַדִּיק חוֹנֵן וְנוֹתֵן: רַבִּי אֶלְעָזָר אוֹמֵר: לֵב רָע. אָמַר לָהֶם: רוֹאֶה אֲנִי אֶת דִּבְרֵי אֶלְעָזָר בֶּן עֲרָךְ מִדִּבְרֵיכֶם, שֶׁבִּכְלַל דְּבָרָיו דִּבְרֵיכֶם. תהלים לז

טו הֵם אָמְרוּ שְׁלֹשָׁה דְבָרִים. רַבִּי אֱלִיעֶזֶר אוֹמֵר: יְהִי כְבוֹד חֲבֵרְךָ חָבִיב עָלֶיךָ כְּשֶׁלָּךְ, וְאַל תְּהִי נֽוֹחַ לִכְעֹס. וְשׁוּב יוֹם אֶחָד לִפְנֵי מִיתָתְךָ. וֶהֱוֵי מִתְחַמֵּם כְּנֶגֶד אוּרָן שֶׁל חֲכָמִים, וֶהֱוֵי זָהִיר בְּגַחַלְתָּן שֶׁלֹּא תִכָּוֶה, שֶׁנְּשִׁיכָתָן נְשִׁיכַת שׁוּעָל, וַעֲקִיצָתָן עֲקִיצַת עַקְרָב, וּלְחִישָׁתָן לְחִישַׁת שָׂרָף, וְכָל דִּבְרֵיהֶם כְּגַחֲלֵי אֵשׁ.

טז רַבִּי יְהוֹשֻׁעַ אוֹמֵר: עַיִן הָרָע וְיֵצֶר הָרָע וְשִׂנְאַת הַבְּרִיּוֹת, מוֹצִיאִין אֶת הָאָדָם מִן הָעוֹלָם.

17. Rabbi Yose said: Let the property of your fellow be as precious to you as your own. Prepare yourself to study Torah, for it does not come to you as an inheritance. And let all your deeds be for the sake of Heaven.
18. Rabbi Shimon said: Be meticulous in reciting the Shema and the [Amida] prayer. When you pray, do not do so as a fixed routine, but as a plea for mercy and grace before God, as it is said, "For He is gracious and compassionate, slow to anger, abounding in kindness, and renouncing punishment." Do not be evil in your own eyes. *Joel 2*
19. Rabbi Elazar said: Be diligent in the study of Torah. Know how to answer a heretic. Know for whom you labor and who is your Employer who will pay you the reward of your work.
20. Rabbi Tarfon said: The day is short, the task is great, the laborers are lazy, the reward is much, and the Master insistent.
21. He used to say: It is not for you to complete the task, but neither are you free to stand aside from it. If you have studied much Torah, you will be given great reward, for your Employer will faithfully reward your work. Know, though, that the reward of the righteous is granted in the time to come.

Rabbi Ḥananya ben Akashya said: The Holy One, blessed be He, wanted to confer merit on Israel. That is why He gave them a copious Torah and many commandments, as it is said, "It pleased the LORD, for the sake of [Israel's] righteousness, to make the Torah great and glorious." *Makkot 23b* *Is. 42*

If there is a minyan, mourners say the Rabbis' Kaddish (page 702).

* * *

All Israel have a share in the World to Come, as it is said, *Sanhedrin 90a*
"Your people are all righteous; they shall inherit the land for ever; *Is. 60*
they are a shoot of My own planting,
a work of My own hands, that I may be glorified."

CHAPTER 3

1. Akavya ben Mahalalel said: Reflect on three things and you will avoid transgression: Know where you came from, where you are going, and before whom you will have to give an account and reckoning. "Where you came from" – from a putrid drop. "Where you are going" – to a place of dust, worms and maggots. "And before whom you will have to give an account and reckoning" – before the Supreme King of kings, the Holy One, blessed be He.
2. Rabbi Ḥanina, the deputy High Priest, said: Pray for the welfare of the government, for were it not for fear of it, people would swallow one another alive.

יז רַבִּי יוֹסֵי אוֹמֵר: יְהִי מָמוֹן חֲבֵרְךָ חָבִיב עָלֶיךָ כְּשֶׁלָּךְ. וְהַתְקֵן עַצְמְךָ לִלְמֹד
תּוֹרָה, שֶׁאֵינָהּ יְרֻשָּׁה לָךְ. וְכָל מַעֲשֶׂיךָ יִהְיוּ לְשֵׁם שָׁמָיִם.

יח רַבִּי שִׁמְעוֹן אוֹמֵר: הֱוֵי זָהִיר בִּקְרִיאַת שְׁמַע וּבִתְפִלָּה. וּכְשֶׁאַתָּה מִתְפַּלֵּל
אַל תַּעַשׂ תְּפִלָּתְךָ קֶבַע, אֶלָּא רַחֲמִים וְתַחֲנוּנִים לִפְנֵי הַמָּקוֹם, שֶׁנֶּאֱמַר: כִּי יואל ב
חַנּוּן וְרַחוּם הוּא, אֶרֶךְ אַפַּיִם וְרַב־חֶסֶד וְנִחָם עַל־הָרָעָה: וְאַל תְּהִי רָשָׁע
בִּפְנֵי עַצְמְךָ.

יט רַבִּי אֶלְעָזָר אוֹמֵר: הֱוֵי שָׁקוּד לִלְמֹד תּוֹרָה. וְדַע מַה שֶּׁתָּשִׁיב לְאֶפִּיקוֹרוֹס.
וְדַע לִפְנֵי מִי אַתָּה עָמֵל, וּמִי הוּא בַּעַל מְלַאכְתְּךָ, שֶׁיְּשַׁלֶּם לְךָ שְׂכַר פְּעֻלָּתֶךָ.

כ רַבִּי טַרְפוֹן אוֹמֵר: הַיּוֹם קָצֵר, וְהַמְּלָאכָה מְרֻבָּה, וְהַפּוֹעֲלִים עֲצֵלִים, וְהַשָּׂכָר
הַרְבֵּה, וּבַעַל הַבַּיִת דּוֹחֵק.

כא הוּא הָיָה אוֹמֵר: לֹא עָלֶיךָ הַמְּלָאכָה לִגְמֹר, וְלֹא אַתָּה בֶן חוֹרִין לִבָּטֵל מִמֶּנָּה.
אִם לָמַדְתָּ תּוֹרָה הַרְבֵּה, נוֹתְנִין לְךָ שָׂכָר הַרְבֵּה. וְנֶאֱמָן הוּא בַּעַל מְלַאכְתְּךָ,
שֶׁיְּשַׁלֶּם לְךָ שְׂכַר פְּעֻלָּתֶךָ. וְדַע, שֶׁמַּתַּן שְׂכָרָן שֶׁל צַדִּיקִים לֶעָתִיד לָבוֹא.

רַבִּי חֲנַנְיָא בֶּן עֲקַשְׁיָא אוֹמֵר: רָצָה הַקָּדוֹשׁ בָּרוּךְ הוּא לְזַכּוֹת אֶת יִשְׂרָאֵל, לְפִיכָךְ מכות כג:
הִרְבָּה לָהֶם תּוֹרָה וּמִצְוֹת. שֶׁנֶּאֱמַר: יְהוָה חָפֵץ לְמַעַן צִדְקוֹ, יַגְדִּיל תּוֹרָה וְיַאְדִּיר: ישעיה מב

If there is a מנין*, mourners say* קדיש דרבנן *(page 703).*

* * *

כָּל יִשְׂרָאֵל יֵשׁ לָהֶם חֵלֶק לָעוֹלָם הַבָּא. שֶׁנֶּאֱמַר: סנהדרין צ.
וְעַמֵּךְ כֻּלָּם צַדִּיקִים, לְעוֹלָם יִירְשׁוּ אָרֶץ ישעיה ס
נֵצֶר מַטָּעַי, מַעֲשֵׂה יָדַי לְהִתְפָּאֵר:

פרק שלישי

א עֲקַבְיָא בֶּן מַהֲלַלְאֵל אוֹמֵר: הִסְתַּכֵּל בִּשְׁלֹשָׁה דְבָרִים, וְאֵין אַתָּה בָא לִידֵי
עֲבֵרָה. דַּע מֵאַיִן בָּאתָ, וּלְאָן אַתָּה הוֹלֵךְ, וְלִפְנֵי מִי אַתָּה עָתִיד לִתֵּן דִּין
וְחֶשְׁבּוֹן. מֵאַיִן בָּאתָ, מִטִּפָּה סְרוּחָה. וּלְאָן אַתָּה הוֹלֵךְ, לִמְקוֹם עָפָר, רִמָּה
וְתוֹלֵעָה. וְלִפְנֵי מִי אַתָּה עָתִיד לִתֵּן דִּין וְחֶשְׁבּוֹן, לִפְנֵי מֶלֶךְ מַלְכֵי הַמְּלָכִים,
הַקָּדוֹשׁ בָּרוּךְ הוּא.

ב רַבִּי חֲנִינָא סְגַן הַכֹּהֲנִים אוֹמֵר: הֱוֵי מִתְפַּלֵּל בִּשְׁלוֹמָהּ שֶׁל מַלְכוּת, שֶׁאִלְמָלֵא
מוֹרָאָהּ, אִישׁ אֶת רֵעֵהוּ חַיִּים בְּלָעוֹ.

3. Rabbi Ḥanina ben Teradyon said: When two people sit together and no words
of Torah pass between them, they are regarded as a company of scoffers, as it
is said, "He does not sit in the company of scoffers." But when two people sit *Ps. 1*
together and words of Torah do pass between them, the Divine Presence rests
with them, as it is said, "Then those who feared the LORD talked together, and *Mal. 3*
the LORD listened and heard, and a scroll of remembrance was written before
Him concerning those who feared the LORD and cherished His name." This
verse tells me about two people; from where can I learn that even one person
who sits alone and studies Torah, the Holy One, blessed be He, grants him a
reward? From the verse, "Though he sits alone and meditates quietly, He will *Lam. 3*
grant him a reward."

4. Rabbi Shimon said: Three who eat at one table, and do not speak words of
Torah, are as if they had eaten of sacrifices of dead idols, as it is said, "For all the *Is. 28*
tables are full of vomit and filth, when God is absent." However, three who eat
at one table and speak words of Torah, it is as if they had eaten at God's table, as
it is said, "And He spoke to me: This is the table before the LORD." *Ezek. 41*

5. Rabbi Ḥanina ben Ḥakhinai said: One who stays awake at night, travels alone, or turns his mind to idle thoughts, endangers his soul.

6. Rabbi Neḥunya ben HaKanna said: One who takes on himself the yoke of Torah will be spared the yoke of government and the yoke of worldly responsibilities, but one who throws off the yoke of the Torah will bear the yoke of government and the yoke of worldly responsibilities.

7. Rabbi Ḥalafta ben Dosa of Kfar Ḥananya said: When ten people sit together
and study Torah, the Divine Presence rests among them, as it is said, "God *Ps. 82*
stands in the divine assembly." How do we know that the same applies to five?
From the verse, "He has founded His group on the earth." And how do we know *Amos 9*
that it applies even to three? From the verse, "He judges among the judges." How *Ps. 82*
do we know that the same applies even to two? From the verse, "Then those who *Mal. 3*
feared the LORD talked together, and the LORD listened and heard." And how
do we know that it applies even to one? From the verse, "In every place where I *Ex. 20*
cause My name to be mentioned, I will come to you and bless you."

8. Rabbi Elazar of Bartota said: Give Him what is His, for you and yours are
His. This was also said by David: "For all things come from You, and we have *I Chr. 29*
given You only what is Yours."

9. Rabbi Jacob said: One who is reviewing his Torah study while walking on the way, and interrupts his study to say, "What a beautiful tree" or "What a beautiful field," is regarded by Scripture as if he had endangered his soul.

10. Rabbi Dostai of Rabbi Yannai said in the name of Rabbi Meir: One who for-
gets even one thing of his Torah learning, Scripture regards him as if he had
endangered his soul, for it is said, "Only take heed and guard your soul very *Deut. 4*
carefully so that you do not forget the things that your eyes saw." One might

ג רַבִּי חֲנִינָא בֶּן תְּרַדְיוֹן אוֹמֵר: שְׁנַיִם שֶׁיּוֹשְׁבִין, וְאֵין בֵּינֵיהֶם דִּבְרֵי תוֹרָה, הֲרֵי
זֶה מוֹשַׁב לֵצִים, שֶׁנֶּאֱמַר: וּבְמוֹשַׁב לֵצִים לֹא יָשָׁב: אֲבָל שְׁנַיִם שֶׁיּוֹשְׁבִין, תהלים א
וְיֵשׁ בֵּינֵיהֶם דִּבְרֵי תוֹרָה, שְׁכִינָה שְׁרוּיָה בֵינֵיהֶם, שֶׁנֶּאֱמַר: אָז נִדְבְּרוּ יִרְאֵי מלאכי ג
יהוה אִישׁ אֶל־רֵעֵהוּ, וַיַּקְשֵׁב יהוה וַיִּשְׁמָע, וַיִּכָּתֵב סֵפֶר זִכָּרוֹן לְפָנָיו לְיִרְאֵי
יהוה וּלְחֹשְׁבֵי שְׁמוֹ: אֵין לִי אֶלָּא שְׁנַיִם, מִנַּיִן אֲפִלּוּ אֶחָד שֶׁיּוֹשֵׁב וְעוֹסֵק
בַּתּוֹרָה שֶׁהַקָּדוֹשׁ בָּרוּךְ הוּא קוֹבֵעַ לוֹ שָׂכָר, שֶׁנֶּאֱמַר: יֵשֵׁב בָּדָד וְיִדֹּם כִּי נָטַל איכה ג
עָלָיו:

ד רַבִּי שִׁמְעוֹן אוֹמֵר: שְׁלֹשָׁה שֶׁאָכְלוּ עַל שֻׁלְחָן אֶחָד וְלֹא אָמְרוּ עָלָיו דִּבְרֵי
תוֹרָה, כְּאִלּוּ אָכְלוּ מִזִּבְחֵי מֵתִים, שֶׁנֶּאֱמַר: כִּי כָּל־שֻׁלְחָנוֹת מָלְאוּ קִיא ישעיה כח
צֹאָה בְּלִי מָקוֹם: אֲבָל שְׁלֹשָׁה שֶׁאָכְלוּ עַל שֻׁלְחָן אֶחָד, וְאָמְרוּ עָלָיו דִּבְרֵי
תוֹרָה, כְּאִלּוּ אָכְלוּ מִשֻּׁלְחָנוֹ שֶׁל מָקוֹם, שֶׁנֶּאֱמַר: וַיְדַבֵּר אֵלַי, זֶה הַשֻּׁלְחָן יחזקאל מא
אֲשֶׁר לִפְנֵי יהוה:

ה רַבִּי חֲנִינָא בֶּן חֲכִינַאי אוֹמֵר: הַנֵּעוֹר בַּלַּיְלָה, וְהַמְהַלֵּךְ בַּדֶּרֶךְ יְחִידִי, וְהַמְפַנֶּה
לִבּוֹ לְבַטָּלָה, הֲרֵי זֶה מִתְחַיֵּב בְּנַפְשׁוֹ.

ו רַבִּי נְחוּנְיָא בֶּן הַקָּנָה אוֹמֵר: כָּל הַמְקַבֵּל עָלָיו עֹל תּוֹרָה, מַעֲבִירִין מִמֶּנּוּ עֹל
מַלְכוּת וְעֹל דֶּרֶךְ אֶרֶץ. וְכָל הַפּוֹרֵק מִמֶּנּוּ עֹל תּוֹרָה, נוֹתְנִין עָלָיו עֹל מַלְכוּת
וְעֹל דֶּרֶךְ אֶרֶץ.

ז רַבִּי חֲלַפְתָּא בֶּן דּוֹסָא אִישׁ כְּפַר חֲנַנְיָה אוֹמֵר: עֲשָׂרָה שֶׁיּוֹשְׁבִין וְעוֹסְקִין
בַּתּוֹרָה שְׁכִינָה שְׁרוּיָה בֵינֵיהֶם, שֶׁנֶּאֱמַר: אֱלֹהִים נִצָּב בַּעֲדַת־אֵל: וּמִנַּיִן אֲפִלּוּ תהלים פב
חֲמִשָּׁה, שֶׁנֶּאֱמַר: וַאֲגֻדָּתוֹ עַל־אֶרֶץ יְסָדָהּ: וּמִנַּיִן אֲפִלּוּ שְׁלֹשָׁה, שֶׁנֶּאֱמַר: עמוס ט
בְּקֶרֶב אֱלֹהִים יִשְׁפֹּט: וּמִנַּיִן אֲפִלּוּ שְׁנַיִם, שֶׁנֶּאֱמַר: אָז נִדְבְּרוּ יִרְאֵי יהוה אִישׁ תהלים פב מלאכי ג
אֶל־רֵעֵהוּ, וַיַּקְשֵׁב יהוה וַיִּשְׁמָע: וּמִנַּיִן אֲפִלּוּ אֶחָד, שֶׁנֶּאֱמַר: בְּכָל־הַמָּקוֹם שמות כ
אֲשֶׁר אַזְכִּיר אֶת־שְׁמִי, אָבוֹא אֵלֶיךָ וּבֵרַכְתִּיךָ:

ח רַבִּי אֶלְעָזָר אִישׁ בַּרְתּוֹתָא אוֹמֵר: תֶּן לוֹ מִשֶּׁלּוֹ, שֶׁאַתָּה וְשֶׁלְּךָ שֶׁלּוֹ. וְכֵן בְּדָוִד
הוּא אוֹמֵר: כִּי־מִמְּךָ הַכֹּל, וּמִיָּדְךָ נָתַנּוּ לָךְ: דברי הימים א׳ כט

ט רַבִּי יַעֲקֹב אוֹמֵר: הַמְהַלֵּךְ בַּדֶּרֶךְ וְשׁוֹנֶה, וּמַפְסִיק מִמִּשְׁנָתוֹ וְאוֹמֵר, מַה
נָּאֶה אִילָן זֶה, מַה נָּאֶה נִיר זֶה, מַעֲלֶה עָלָיו הַכָּתוּב כְּאִלּוּ מִתְחַיֵּב בְּנַפְשׁוֹ.

י רַבִּי דּוֹסְתַּאי בְּרַבִּי יַנַּאי מִשּׁוּם רַבִּי מֵאִיר אוֹמֵר: כָּל הַשּׁוֹכֵחַ דָּבָר אֶחָד
מִמִּשְׁנָתוֹ, מַעֲלֶה עָלָיו הַכָּתוּב כְּאִלּוּ מִתְחַיֵּב בְּנַפְשׁוֹ, שֶׁנֶּאֱמַר: רַק הִשָּׁמֶר דברים ד
לְךָ וּשְׁמֹר נַפְשְׁךָ מְאֹד, פֶּן־תִּשְׁכַּח אֶת־הַדְּבָרִים אֲשֶׁר־רָאוּ עֵינֶיךָ: יָכוֹל אֲפִלּוּ

think that this applies even to one who finds his studies too hard to remember. Therefore the verse adds, "Lest they be removed from your heart all the days of your life." Thus, one does not endanger his soul unless he deliberately removes teachings from his heart. *Deut. 4*

11. Rabbi Ḥanina ben Dosa said: For one who puts fear of sin before wisdom, wisdom endures. For one who puts wisdom before fear of sin, wisdom does not endure.
12. He also used to say: For one whose good deeds exceed his wisdom, wisdom endures. For one whose wisdom exceeds his good deeds, wisdom does not endure.
13. He also used to say: In one in whom people delight, God delights. In one in whom people do not delight, God does not delight.
14. Rabbi Dosa ben Harkinas said: Sleeping late in the morning, drinking wine at midday, chattering with children and sitting in gatherings of the ignorant – these drive a person from the world.
15. Rabbi Elazar of Modin said: One who desecrates sacred things, despises the festivals, shames his fellow in public, nullifies the covenant of our father Abraham, or attributes meanings to the Torah contrary to normative law, even though he has to his credit Torah and good deeds, has no share in the World to Come.
16. Rabbi Yishmael said: Be yielding to a superior, pleasing to the young, and receive everyone cheerfully.
17. Rabbi Akiva said: Mocking and frivolity lead to immorality. The oral tradition (*Mesora*) is a fence protecting the Torah; tithes are a fence protecting wealth; vows are a fence protecting abstinence. The fence protecting wisdom is silence.
18. He used to say: Beloved is man, for he was created in the image of God. As a gesture of special love, it was made known to him that he was created in the image of God, as it is said, "For in the image of God He made man." *Gen. 9* Beloved are Israel for they are called God's children. As a gesture of special love, it was made known to them that they are called God's children, as it is said, "You are the children of the LORD your God." *Deut. 14* Beloved are Israel, for they were given a precious vessel [the Torah]. As a gesture of special love, it was made known to them that they were given the precious vessel through which the world was created, as it is said, "I have given you good instruction; do not abandon My Torah." *Prov. 4*
19. All is foreseen, yet freedom of choice is given. The world is judged with goodness, but all depends on the majority of one's deeds.
20. He used to say: All is given on collateral, and a net is spread over all the living. The shop is open, the shopkeeper extends credit, the ledger is open, and the hand records. Whoever wishes to borrow may come and borrow. The collectors regularly make their daily rounds and collect payment from a person, whether he realizes it or not. They have [a record] on which they can rely; the judgment is just; and all is prepared for the banquet.

תְּקָפָה עָלָיו מִשְׁנָתוֹ, תַּלְמוּד לוֹמַר: וּפֶן יָסוּרוּ מִלְּבָבְךָ כֹּל יְמֵי חַיֶּיךָ: הָא אֵינוֹ דברים ד
מִתְחַיֵּב בְּנַפְשׁוֹ, עַד שֶׁיֵּשֵׁב וִיסִירֵם מִלִּבּוֹ.

יא רַבִּי חֲנִינָא בֶּן דּוֹסָא אוֹמֵר: כֹּל שֶׁיִּרְאַת חֶטְאוֹ קוֹדֶמֶת לְחָכְמָתוֹ, חָכְמָתוֹ מִתְקַיֶּמֶת. וְכֹל שֶׁחָכְמָתוֹ קוֹדֶמֶת לְיִרְאַת חֶטְאוֹ, אֵין חָכְמָתוֹ מִתְקַיֶּמֶת.

יב הוּא הָיָה אוֹמֵר: כֹּל שֶׁמַּעֲשָׂיו מְרֻבִּין מֵחָכְמָתוֹ, חָכְמָתוֹ מִתְקַיֶּמֶת. וְכֹל שֶׁחָכְמָתוֹ מְרֻבָּה מִמַּעֲשָׂיו, אֵין חָכְמָתוֹ מִתְקַיֶּמֶת.

יג הוּא הָיָה אוֹמֵר: כֹּל שֶׁרְוּחַ הַבְּרִיּוֹת נוֹחָה הֵימֶנּוּ, רְוּחַ הַמָּקוֹם נוֹחָה הֵימֶנּוּ. וְכֹל שֶׁאֵין רְוּחַ הַבְּרִיּוֹת נוֹחָה הֵימֶנּוּ, אֵין רְוּחַ הַמָּקוֹם נוֹחָה הֵימֶנּוּ.

יד רַבִּי דוֹסָא בֶּן הָרְכִּינַס אוֹמֵר: שֵׁנָה שֶׁל שַׁחֲרִית, וְיַיִן שֶׁל צָהֳרַיִם, וְשִׂיחַת הַיְלָדִים, וִישִׁיבַת בָּתֵּי כְנֵסִיּוֹת שֶׁל עַמֵּי הָאָרֶץ, מוֹצִיאִין אֶת הָאָדָם מִן הָעוֹלָם.

טו רַבִּי אֶלְעָזָר הַמּוֹדָעִי אוֹמֵר: הַמְחַלֵּל אֶת הַקֳּדָשִׁים, וְהַמְבַזֶּה אֶת הַמּוֹעֲדוֹת, וְהַמַּלְבִּין פְּנֵי חֲבֵרוֹ בָּרַבִּים, וְהַמֵּפֵר בְּרִיתוֹ שֶׁל אַבְרָהָם אָבִינוּ, וְהַמְגַלֶּה פָנִים בַּתּוֹרָה שֶׁלֹּא כַהֲלָכָה, אַף עַל פִּי שֶׁיֵּשׁ בְּיָדוֹ תּוֹרָה וּמַעֲשִׂים טוֹבִים, אֵין לוֹ חֵלֶק לָעוֹלָם הַבָּא.

טז רַבִּי יִשְׁמָעֵאל אוֹמֵר: הֱוֵי קַל לְרֹאשׁ וְנְוֹחַ לְתִשְׁחֹרֶת, וֶהֱוֵי מְקַבֵּל אֶת כָּל הָאָדָם בְּשִׂמְחָה.

יז רַבִּי עֲקִיבָא אוֹמֵר: שְׂחוֹק וְקַלּוּת רֹאשׁ מַרְגִּילִין אֶת הָאָדָם לְעֶרְוָה. מַסֹּרֶת סְיָג לַתּוֹרָה, מַעַשְׂרוֹת סְיָג לָעֹשֶׁר, נְדָרִים סְיָג לַפְּרִישׁוּת, סְיָג לַחָכְמָה שְׁתִיקָה.

יח הוּא הָיָה אוֹמֵר, חָבִיב אָדָם שֶׁנִּבְרָא בְצֶלֶם, חִבָּה יְתֵרָה נוֹדַעַת לוֹ שֶׁנִּבְרָא
בְּצֶלֶם, שֶׁנֶּאֱמַר: כִּי בְּצֶלֶם אֱלֹהִים עָשָׂה אֶת־הָאָדָם: חֲבִיבִין יִשְׂרָאֵל בראשית ט
שֶׁנִּקְרְאוּ בָנִים לַמָּקוֹם, חִבָּה יְתֵרָה נוֹדַעַת לָהֶם שֶׁנִּקְרְאוּ בָנִים לַמָּקוֹם,
שֶׁנֶּאֱמַר: בָּנִים אַתֶּם לַיהוה אֱלֹהֵיכֶם: חֲבִיבִין יִשְׂרָאֵל שֶׁנִּתַּן לָהֶם כְּלִי דברים יד
חֶמְדָּה, חִבָּה יְתֵרָה נוֹדַעַת לָהֶם שֶׁנִּתַּן לָהֶם כְּלִי חֶמְדָּה שֶׁבּוֹ נִבְרָא הָעוֹלָם,
שֶׁנֶּאֱמַר: כִּי לֶקַח טוֹב נָתַתִּי לָכֶם, תּוֹרָתִי אַל־תַּעֲזֹבוּ: משלי ד

יט הַכֹּל צָפוּי, וְהָרְשׁוּת נְתוּנָה, וּבְטוּב הָעוֹלָם נִדּוֹן, וְהַכֹּל לְפִי רֹב הַמַּעֲשֶׂה.

כ הוּא הָיָה אוֹמֵר: הַכֹּל נָתוּן בְּעֵרָבוֹן, וּמְצוּדָה פְרוּסָה עַל כָּל הַחַיִּים. הֶחָנוּת פְּתוּחָה, וְהַחֶנְוָנִי מַקִּיף, וְהַפִּנְקָס פָּתוּחַ, וְהַיָּד כּוֹתֶבֶת, וְכָל הָרוֹצֶה לִלְווֹת יָבֹא וְיִלְוֶה. וְהַגַּבָּאִין מַחֲזִירִין תָּדִיר בְּכָל יוֹם, וְנִפְרָעִין מִן הָאָדָם מִדַּעְתּוֹ וְשֶׁלֹּא מִדַּעְתּוֹ, וְיֵשׁ לָהֶם עַל מַה שֶּׁיִּסְמֹכוּ. וְהַדִּין, דִּין אֱמֶת. וְהַכֹּל מְתֻקָּן לַסְּעוּדָה.

21. Rabbi Elazar ben Azariah said: If there is no Torah, there is no respect; if there is no respect, there is no Torah. If there is no wisdom, there is no reverence; if there is no reverence, there is no wisdom. If there is no knowledge, there is no understanding; if there is no understanding, there is no knowledge. If there is no flour [sustenance], there is no Torah; if there is no Torah, there is no flour.

22. He used to say: To what may one whose wisdom exceeds his deeds be compared? To a tree with many branches but few roots. When a wind comes, it uproots and overturns it, as it is said, "He shall be like a juniper tree in the desert, which does not sense the coming of good: it is set in the scorched places of the wilderness in a barren, uninhabited land." To what may one whose deeds exceed his wisdom be compared? To a tree with few branches but many roots. Even if all the winds of the world come and blow against it, they cannot dislodge it from its place, as it is said, "He shall be like a tree planted by waters, sending forth its roots by a stream: it does not sense the coming of heat; its leaves are ever fresh; it has no care in a year of drought; it does not cease to bear fruit." *Jer. 17* *Jer. 17*

23. Rabbi Elazar ben Ḥisma said: The laws of bird offerings and the calculation of menstrual periods are essential laws; astronomy and mathematics are adjuncts to wisdom.

Rabbi Ḥananya ben Akashya said: The Holy One, blessed be He, wanted to confer merit on Israel. That is why He gave them a copious Torah and many commandments, as it is said, "It pleased the LORD, for the sake of [Israel's] righteousness, to make the Torah great and glorious." *Makkot 23b* *Is. 42*

If there is a minyan, mourners say the Rabbis' Kaddish (page 702).

* * *

All Israel have a share in the World to Come, as it is said: *Sanhedrin 90a*
"Your people are all righteous; they shall inherit the land for ever; *Is. 60*
they are a shoot of My own planting,
a work of My own hands, that I may be glorified."

CHAPTER 4

1. Ben Zoma said: Who is wise? One who learns from everyone, as it is said, "From all my teachers I have learned, for Your testimonies are my meditation." Who is strong? One who masters his evil impulse, as it is said, "He who is slow to anger is better than the mighty, and he who rules over his spirit is better than he who conquers a city." Who is rich? One who rejoices in what he has, as it is said, "When you eat from the labor of your hands, you will be happy and all will be well with you." "You will be happy" – in this world, "and all will be well with you" – in the World to Come. Who is honored? One who honors others, as it is said, "Those who honor Me, I will honor; but those who scorn Me will be despised." *Ps. 119* *Prov. 16* *Ps. 128* *I Sam. 2*

2. Ben Azzai said: Run to do even a minor mitzva, and flee from sin, for one mitzva leads to another, and one sin leads to another – for the reward of a mitzva is another mitzva, and the recompense of a sin is another sin.

כא רַבִּי אֶלְעָזָר בֶּן עֲזַרְיָה אוֹמֵר: אִם אֵין תּוֹרָה אֵין דֶּרֶךְ אֶרֶץ, אִם אֵין דֶּרֶךְ אֶרֶץ אֵין תּוֹרָה. אִם אֵין חָכְמָה אֵין יִרְאָה, אִם אֵין יִרְאָה אֵין חָכְמָה. אִם אֵין דַּעַת אֵין בִּינָה, אִם אֵין בִּינָה אֵין דַּעַת. אִם אֵין קֶמַח אֵין תּוֹרָה, אִם אֵין תּוֹרָה אֵין קֶמַח.

כב הוּא הָיָה אוֹמֵר: כָּל שֶׁחָכְמָתוֹ מְרֻבָּה מִמַּעֲשָׂיו, לְמָה הוּא דוֹמֶה, לְאִילָן שֶׁעֲנָפָיו מְרֻבִּין וְשָׁרָשָׁיו מֻעָטִין, וְהָרוּחַ בָּאָה וְעוֹקַרְתּוֹ וְהוֹפַכְתּוֹ עַל פָּנָיו. שֶׁנֶּאֱמַר, וְהָיָה כְּעַרְעָר בָּעֲרָבָה, וְלֹא יִרְאֶה כִּי־יָבוֹא טוֹב, וְשָׁכַן חֲרֵרִים בַּמִּדְבָּר, אֶרֶץ מְלֵחָה וְלֹא תֵשֵׁב: אֲבָל כָּל שֶׁמַּעֲשָׂיו מְרֻבִּין מֵחָכְמָתוֹ, לְמָה הוּא דוֹמֶה, לְאִילָן שֶׁעֲנָפָיו מֻעָטִין וְשָׁרָשָׁיו מְרֻבִּין, שֶׁאֲפִלּוּ כָּל הָרוּחוֹת שֶׁבָּעוֹלָם בָּאוֹת וְנוֹשְׁבוֹת בּוֹ, אֵין מְזִיזִין אוֹתוֹ מִמְּקוֹמוֹ. שֶׁנֶּאֱמַר: וְהָיָה כְּעֵץ שָׁתוּל עַל־מַיִם, וְעַל־יוּבַל יְשַׁלַּח שָׁרָשָׁיו, וְלֹא יִרְאֶ כִּי־יָבֹא חֹם, וְהָיָה עָלֵהוּ רַעֲנָן, וּבִשְׁנַת בַּצֹּרֶת לֹא יִדְאָג, וְלֹא יָמִישׁ מֵעֲשׂוֹת פֶּרִי: (ירמיה יז; ירמיה יז)

כג רַבִּי אֶלְעָזָר בֶּן חִסְמָא אוֹמֵר: קִנִּין וּפִתְחֵי נִדָּה הֵן הֵן גּוּפֵי הֲלָכוֹת, תְּקוּפוֹת וְגִימַטְרִיָּאוֹת פַּרְפְּרָאוֹת לַחָכְמָה.

רַבִּי חֲנַנְיָא בֶּן עֲקַשְׁיָא אוֹמֵר: רָצָה הַקָּדוֹשׁ בָּרוּךְ הוּא לְזַכּוֹת אֶת יִשְׂרָאֵל, לְפִיכָךְ הִרְבָּה לָהֶם תּוֹרָה וּמִצְוֹת. שֶׁנֶּאֱמַר: יהוה חָפֵץ לְמַעַן צִדְקוֹ, יַגְדִּיל תּוֹרָה וְיַאְדִּיר: (מכות כג: ; ישעיה מב)

If there is a מנין*, mourners say* קדיש דרבנן *(page 703).*

(page 703)

* * *

כָּל יִשְׂרָאֵל יֵשׁ לָהֶם חֵלֶק לָעוֹלָם הַבָּא. שֶׁנֶּאֱמַר: (סנהדרין צ.)
וְעַמֵּךְ כֻּלָּם צַדִּיקִים, לְעוֹלָם יִירְשׁוּ אָרֶץ (ישעיה ס)
נֵצֶר מַטָּעַי, מַעֲשֵׂה יָדַי לְהִתְפָּאֵר:

פרק רביעי

א בֶּן זוֹמָא אוֹמֵר: אֵיזֶהוּ חָכָם, הַלּוֹמֵד מִכָּל אָדָם, שֶׁנֶּאֱמַר: מִכָּל־מְלַמְּדַי הִשְׂכַּלְתִּי, כִּי עֵדְוֹתֶיךָ שִׂיחָה לִּי: אֵיזֶהוּ גִבּוֹר, הַכּוֹבֵשׁ אֶת יִצְרוֹ, שֶׁנֶּאֱמַר: טוֹב אֶרֶךְ אַפַּיִם מִגִּבּוֹר וּמֹשֵׁל בְּרוּחוֹ מִלֹּכֵד עִיר: אֵיזֶהוּ עָשִׁיר, הַשָּׂמֵחַ בְּחֶלְקוֹ, שֶׁנֶּאֱמַר: יְגִיעַ כַּפֶּיךָ כִּי תֹאכֵל אַשְׁרֶיךָ וְטוֹב לָךְ: אַשְׁרֶיךָ בָּעוֹלָם הַזֶּה וְטוֹב לָךְ לָעוֹלָם הַבָּא. אֵיזֶהוּ מְכֻבָּד, הַמְכַבֵּד אֶת הַבְּרִיּוֹת, שֶׁנֶּאֱמַר: כִּי־מְכַבְּדַי אֲכַבֵּד, וּבֹזַי יֵקָלּוּ: (תהלים קיט; משלי טז; תהלים קכח; שמואל א׳ ב)

ב בֶּן עַזַּאי אוֹמֵר: הֱוֵי רָץ לְמִצְוָה קַלָּה וּבוֹרֵחַ מִן הָעֲבֵרָה. שֶׁמִּצְוָה גוֹרֶרֶת מִצְוָה, וַעֲבֵרָה גוֹרֶרֶת עֲבֵרָה. שֶׁשְּׂכַר מִצְוָה מִצְוָה, וּשְׂכַר עֲבֵרָה עֲבֵרָה.

3. He used to say: Despise no one and disdain nothing, for there is no one who does not have his hour and there is nothing that does not have its place.
4. Rabbi Levitas of Yavne said: Have extreme humility of spirit, for the end of mortal man is the worm [the grave].
5. Rabbi Yoḥanan ben Beroka said: Whoever profanes God's name in secret will be punished in public. Profaning the name is the same whether done inadvertently or deliberately.
6. Rabbi Yishmael his son said: One who learns in order to teach will be given the opportunity to learn and teach. One who learns in order to do will be given the opportunity to learn, teach, keep and do.
7. Rabbi Tzadok said: Do not separate yourself from the community. [When sitting as a judge] do not act as a lawyer. Do not use [the Torah] as a crown for self-glorification, or as a spade with which to dig. Likewise Hillel used to say: One who makes worldly use of the crown [of the Torah] shall fade away. From this you learn that one who seeks personal benefit from the words of Torah risks destroying his life.
8. Rabbi Yose said: One who honors the Torah will be honored by mankind. One who disgraces the Torah will be disgraced by mankind.
9. Rabbi Yishmael his son said: One who avoids serving as a judge spares himself enmity, robbery and false swearing. One who is over-confident in giving decisions is foolish, wicked and arrogant.
10. He used to say: Do not act as a judge alone, for none may judge alone except the One. Do not say "Accept my view"; for they are permitted, not you.
11. Rabbi Yonatan said: Whoever keeps the Torah when poor will eventually keep it in wealth. Whoever neglects the Torah when wealthy will eventually neglect it in poverty.
12. Rabbi Meir said: Limit your business activities and occupy yourself with Torah. Have humility before everyone. If you neglect the Torah, you will have many excuses to neglect it, but if you labor in the Torah, He has great reward to give you.
13. Rabbi Eliezer ben Jacob said: One who performs a single mitzva acquires for himself an advocate. One who commits a single transgression acquires for himself an accuser. Repentance and good deeds are a shield against punishment.
14. Rabbi Yoḥanan the sandal maker said: Every gathering that meets for the sake of heaven will have an enduring effect. One that is not for the sake of heaven will not have an enduring effect.
15. Rabbi Elazar ben Shammua said: Let your student's honor be as precious to you as your own; let your colleague's honor be like the reverence due to your teacher; and let the reverence you have for your teacher be like the reverence due to Heaven.

ג הוּא הָיָה אוֹמֵר: אַל תְּהִי בָז לְכָל אָדָם, וְאַל תְּהִי מַפְלִיג לְכָל דָּבָר. שֶׁאֵין לְךָ אָדָם שֶׁאֵין לוֹ שָׁעָה, וְאֵין לְךָ דָבָר שֶׁאֵין לוֹ מָקוֹם.

ד רַבִּי לְוִיטַס אִישׁ יַבְנֶה אוֹמֵר: מְאֹד מְאֹד הֱוֵי שְׁפַל רוּחַ, שֶׁתִּקְוַת אֱנוֹשׁ רִמָּה.

ה רַבִּי יוֹחָנָן בֶּן בְּרוֹקָא אוֹמֵר: כָּל הַמְּחַלֵּל שֵׁם שָׁמַיִם בַּסֵּתֶר, נִפְרָעִין מִמֶּנּוּ בַּגָּלוּי. אֶחָד שׁוֹגֵג וְאֶחָד מֵזִיד בְּחִלּוּל הַשֵּׁם.

ו רַבִּי יִשְׁמָעֵאל בְּנוֹ אוֹמֵר: הַלּוֹמֵד עַל מְנָת לְלַמֵּד, מַסְפִּיקִין בְּיָדוֹ לִלְמֹד וּלְלַמֵּד. וְהַלּוֹמֵד עַל מְנָת לַעֲשׂוֹת, מַסְפִּיקִין בְּיָדוֹ לִלְמֹד וּלְלַמֵּד, לִשְׁמֹר וְלַעֲשׂוֹת.

ז רַבִּי צָדוֹק אוֹמֵר: אַל תִּפְרֹשׁ מִן הַצִּבּוּר, וְאַל תַּעַשׂ עַצְמְךָ כְּעוֹרְכֵי הַדַּיָּנִין, וְאַל תַּעֲשֶׂהָ עֲטָרָה לְהִתְגַּדֶּל בָּהּ, וְלֹא קַרְדֹּם לַחְפָּר בָּהּ. וְכָךְ הָיָה הִלֵּל אוֹמֵר: וּדְאִשְׁתַּמֵּשׁ בְּתָגָא חֲלָף. הָא לָמַדְתָּ, כָּל הַנֶּהֱנֶה מִדִּבְרֵי תוֹרָה, נוֹטֵל חַיָּיו מִן הָעוֹלָם.

ח רַבִּי יוֹסֵי אוֹמֵר: כָּל הַמְּכַבֵּד אֶת הַתּוֹרָה, גּוּפוֹ מְכֻבָּד עַל הַבְּרִיּוֹת. וְכָל הַמְּחַלֵּל אֶת הַתּוֹרָה, גּוּפוֹ מְחֻלָּל עַל הַבְּרִיּוֹת.

ט רַבִּי יִשְׁמָעֵאל בְּנוֹ אוֹמֵר: הַחוֹשֵׂךְ עַצְמוֹ מִן הַדִּין, פּוֹרֵק מִמֶּנּוּ אֵיבָה וְגָזֵל וּשְׁבוּעַת שָׁוְא. וְהַגַּס לִבּוֹ בְּהוֹרָאָה, שׁוֹטֶה, רָשָׁע וְגַס רוּחַ.

י הוּא הָיָה אוֹמֵר: אַל תְּהִי דָן יְחִידִי, שֶׁאֵין דָּן יְחִידִי אֶלָּא אֶחָד. וְאַל תֹּאמַר קַבְּלוּ דַעְתִּי, שֶׁהֵן רַשָּׁאִין וְלֹא אָתָּה.

יא רַבִּי יוֹנָתָן אוֹמֵר: כָּל הַמְקַיֵּם אֶת הַתּוֹרָה מֵעֹנִי, סוֹפוֹ לְקַיְּמָהּ מֵעֹשֶׁר. וְכָל הַמְבַטֵּל אֶת הַתּוֹרָה מֵעֹשֶׁר, סוֹפוֹ לְבַטְּלָהּ מֵעֹנִי.

יב רַבִּי מֵאִיר אוֹמֵר: הֱוֵי מְמַעֵט בְּעֵסֶק וַעֲסֹק בַּתּוֹרָה, וֶהֱוֵי שְׁפַל רוּחַ בִּפְנֵי כָל אָדָם. וְאִם בָּטַלְתָּ מִן הַתּוֹרָה, יֶשׁ לְךָ בְּטֵלִים הַרְבֵּה כְּנֶגְדָּךְ. וְאִם עָמַלְתָּ בַּתּוֹרָה, יֶשׁ לוֹ שָׂכָר הַרְבֵּה לִתֶּן לָךְ.

יג רַבִּי אֱלִיעֶזֶר בֶּן יַעֲקֹב אוֹמֵר: הָעוֹשֶׂה מִצְוָה אַחַת, קוֹנֶה לּוֹ פְּרַקְלִיט אֶחָד. וְהָעוֹבֵר עֲבֵרָה אַחַת, קוֹנֶה לּוֹ קַטֵּגוֹר אֶחָד. תְּשׁוּבָה וּמַעֲשִׂים טוֹבִים, כִּתְרִיס בִּפְנֵי הַפֻּרְעָנוּת.

יד רַבִּי יוֹחָנָן הַסַּנְדְּלָר אוֹמֵר: כָּל כְּנֵסִיָּה שֶׁהִיא לְשֵׁם שָׁמַיִם, סוֹפָהּ לְהִתְקַיֵּם. וְשֶׁאֵינָהּ לְשֵׁם שָׁמַיִם, אֵין סוֹפָהּ לְהִתְקַיֵּם.

טו רַבִּי אֶלְעָזָר בֶּן שַׁמּוּעַ אוֹמֵר: יְהִי כְבוֹד תַּלְמִידְךָ חָבִיב עָלֶיךָ כְּשֶׁלָּךְ, וּכְבוֹד חֲבֵרְךָ כְּמוֹרָא רַבָּךְ, וּמוֹרָא רַבָּךְ כְּמוֹרָא שָׁמָיִם.

16. Rabbi Judah said: Be careful when you study, for an inadvertent error in study is tantamount to an intentional sin.

17. Rabbi Shimon said: There are three crowns: the crown of Torah, the crown of priesthood, and the crown of kingship – but the crown of a good name surpasses them all.

18. Rabbi Nehorai said: Exile yourself to a place of Torah, and do not assume that it will come after you, for your fellow students will ensure that it will remain with you. "Do not rely on your own understanding." *Prov. 3*

19. Rabbi Yannai said: It is not in our power to explain either the peace of the wicked or the suffering of the righteous.

20. Rabbi Matya ben Ḥarash said: Be first in greeting everyone. Be a tail to lions rather than a head to foxes.

21. Rabbi Jacob said: This world is like an antechamber before the World to Come. Prepare yourself in the antechamber so that you may enter the banqueting hall.

22. He used to say: Better one hour of repentance and good deeds in this world than all the life in the World to Come. Better one hour of bliss in the World to Come than the whole life of this world.

23. Rabbi Shimon ben Elazar said: Do not try to placate your fellow in his hour of anger. Do not try to comfort him while his dead lies before him. Do not question him about his vow at the time he is making it. Do not try to see him in his hour of disgrace.

24. Samuel the Younger used to quote: "If your enemy falls, do not rejoice; if he stumbles, let not your heart be glad; lest the Lord see it and be displeased, and divert His fury from him to you." *Prov. 24*

25. Elisha ben Abuya said: When you learn as a child, what is it like? Like ink written on clean paper. When you learn in old age, what is it like? Like ink written on blotted paper.

26. Rabbi Yose bar Judah of Kfar Bavli said: When you learn from the young, what is it like? Like eating unripe grapes or drinking wine straight from the vat. When you learn from the old, what is it like? Like eating ripe grapes and drinking old wine.

27. Rabbi Meir said: Do not look at the container but at what it contains, for a new flask may contain old wine, and an old flask may not contain anything, even new wine.

28. Rabbi Elazar HaKappar said: Envy, lust, and the seeking of honor, drive a person out of the world.

29. He used to say: Those who are born will one day die, those who die will live again, and the living will be judged. It is for us to know, make known, and confirm that He is God, He is the Maker; He is the Creator; He is the Discerner; He

טו רַבִּי יְהוּדָה אוֹמֵר: הֱוֵי זָהִיר בְּתַלְמוּד, שֶׁשִּׁגְגַת תַּלְמוּד עוֹלָה זָדוֹן.

יז רַבִּי שִׁמְעוֹן אוֹמֵר: שְׁלשָׁה כְתָרִים הֵן, כֶּתֶר תּוֹרָה וְכֶתֶר כְּהֻנָּה וְכֶתֶר מַלְכוּת, וְכֶתֶר שֵׁם טוֹב עוֹלֶה עַל גַּבֵּיהֶן.

יח רַבִּי נְהוֹרָאִי אוֹמֵר: הֱוֵי גוֹלֶה לִמְקוֹם תּוֹרָה. וְאַל תֹּאמַר שֶׁהִיא תָבוֹא אַחֲרֶיךָ,
שֶׁחֲבֵרֶיךָ יְקַיְּמוּהָ בְיָדֶךָ. וְאֶל־בִּינָתְךָ אַל־תִּשָּׁעֵן: משלי ג

יט רַבִּי יַנַּאי אוֹמֵר: אֵין בְּיָדֵינוּ לֹא מִשַּׁלְוַת הָרְשָׁעִים וְאַף לֹא מִיִּסּוּרֵי הַצַּדִּיקִים.

כ רַבִּי מַתְיָא בֶן חָרָשׁ אוֹמֵר: הֱוֵי מַקְדִּים בִּשְׁלוֹם כָּל אָדָם, וֶהֱוֵי זָנָב לָאֲרָיוֹת, וְאַל תְּהִי רֹאשׁ לַשּׁוּעָלִים.

כא רַבִּי יַעֲקֹב אוֹמֵר: הָעוֹלָם הַזֶּה דּוֹמֶה לִפְרוֹזְדוֹר בִּפְנֵי הָעוֹלָם הַבָּא. הַתְקֵן עַצְמְךָ בַפְּרוֹזְדוֹר, כְּדֵי שֶׁתִּכָּנֵס לַטְּרַקְלִין.

כב הוּא הָיָה אוֹמֵר: יָפָה שָׁעָה אַחַת בִּתְשׁוּבָה וּמַעֲשִׂים טוֹבִים בָּעוֹלָם הַזֶּה, מִכָּל חַיֵּי הָעוֹלָם הַבָּא. וְיָפָה שָׁעָה אַחַת שֶׁל קוֹרַת רוּחַ בָּעוֹלָם הַבָּא, מִכָּל חַיֵּי הָעוֹלָם הַזֶּה.

כג רַבִּי שִׁמְעוֹן בֶּן אֶלְעָזָר אוֹמֵר: אַל תְּרַצֶּה אֶת חֲבֵרְךָ בִּשְׁעַת כַּעְסוֹ, וְאַל תְּנַחֲמֶהוּ בְּשָׁעָה שֶׁמֵּתוֹ מֻטָּל לְפָנָיו, וְאַל תִּשְׁאַל לוֹ בִּשְׁעַת נִדְרוֹ, וְאַל תִּשְׁתַּדֵּל לִרְאוֹתוֹ בִּשְׁעַת קַלְקָלָתוֹ.

כד שְׁמוּאֵל הַקָּטָן אוֹמֵר: בִּנְפֹל אוֹיִבְךָ אַל־תִּשְׂמָח, וּבִכָּשְׁלוֹ אַל־יָגֵל לִבֶּךָ: פֶּן־ משלי כד
יִרְאֶה יהוה וְרַע בְּעֵינָיו, וְהֵשִׁיב מֵעָלָיו אַפּוֹ:

כה אֱלִישָׁע בֶּן אֲבוּיָה אוֹמֵר: הַלּוֹמֵד יֶלֶד, לְמָה הוּא דוֹמֶה, לִדְיוֹ כְתוּבָה עַל נְיָר חָדָשׁ. וְהַלּוֹמֵד זָקֵן, לְמָה הוּא דוֹמֶה, לִדְיוֹ כְתוּבָה עַל נְיָר מָחוּק.

כו רַבִּי יוֹסֵי בַר יְהוּדָה אִישׁ כְּפַר הַבַּבְלִי אוֹמֵר: הַלּוֹמֵד מִן הַקְּטַנִּים, לְמָה הוּא דוֹמֶה, לְאוֹכֵל עֲנָבִים קֵהוֹת וְשׁוֹתֶה יַיִן מִגִּתּוֹ. וְהַלּוֹמֵד מִן הַזְּקֵנִים, לְמָה הוּא דוֹמֶה, לְאוֹכֵל עֲנָבִים בְּשׁוּלוֹת וְשׁוֹתֶה יַיִן יָשָׁן.

כז רַבִּי מֵאִיר אוֹמֵר: אַל תִּסְתַּכֵּל בְּקַנְקַן, אֶלָּא בְמַה שֶּׁיֵּשׁ בּוֹ. יֵשׁ קַנְקַן חָדָשׁ מָלֵא יָשָׁן, וְיָשָׁן שֶׁאֲפִלּוּ חָדָשׁ אֵין בּוֹ.

כח רַבִּי אֶלְעָזָר הַקַּפָּר אוֹמֵר: הַקִּנְאָה וְהַתַּאֲוָה וְהַכָּבוֹד, מוֹצִיאִין אֶת הָאָדָם מִן הָעוֹלָם.

כט הוּא הָיָה אוֹמֵר: הַיִּלּוֹדִים לָמוּת, וְהַמֵּתִים לִחְיוֹת, וְהַחַיִּים לִדּוֹן, לֵידַע וּלְהוֹדִיעַ וּלְהִוָּדַע, שֶׁהוּא אֵל, הוּא הַיּוֹצֵר, הוּא הַבּוֹרֵא, הוּא הַמֵּבִין, הוּא

is the Judge; He is the Witness; He is the Plaintiff; and He will deliver the judgment. Blessed is He before whom there is no unrighteousness, no forgetfulness, no favoritism and no taking of bribes; and know that all is according to a strict reckoning. Do not let your evil impulse persuade you that the grave is, for you, a place of refuge: for without your consent you were formed, without your consent you were born, without your consent you live, without your consent you will die, and without your consent you will in the future have to give an account and reckoning before the Supreme King of kings, the Holy One, blessed be He.

Rabbi Ḥananya ben Akashya said: The Holy One, blessed be He, wanted to confer merit on Israel. That is why He gave them a copious Torah and many commandments, as it is said, "It pleased the Lord, for the sake of [Israel's] righteousness, to make the Torah great and glorious." *Makkot 23b* *Is. 42*

If there is a minyan, mourners say the Rabbis' Kaddish (page 702).

* * *

All Israel have a share in the World to Come, as it is said, *Sanhedrin 90a*
"Your people are all righteous; they shall inherit the land for ever; *Is. 60*
they are a shoot of My own planting,
a work of My own hands, that I may be glorified."

CHAPTER 5

1. By ten acts of speech the world was created. What does this teach us? Could not the world have been created by a single act of speech? It is to exact punishment from the wicked who destroy a world created by ten acts of speech, and richly to reward the righteous who sustain the world created by ten acts of speech.
2. There were ten generations from Adam to Noah, to make known how patient God is, for all those generations increasingly provoked Him until He brought on them the waters of the Flood.
3. There were ten generations from Noah to Abraham, to make known how patient God is, for all those generations increasingly provoked Him until Abraham our father came and received the reward which could have been theirs.
4. Abraham our father was tested with ten trials and he withstood all of them, to make known how deep was our father Abraham's love of God.
5. Ten miracles were performed for our ancestors in Egypt, and ten at the Sea. The Holy One, blessed be He, brought ten plagues against the Egyptians in Egypt, and ten at the Sea.
6. With ten trials our ancestors tried the patience of the Holy One, blessed be He, in the wilderness, as it is written, "They have tested Me these ten times, and did not listen to My voice." *Num. 14*
7. Ten miracles were performed for our ancestors in the Temple: (1) No woman miscarried from the aroma of the sacrificial meat; (2) the sacrificial meat never became putrid; (3) no fly was seen in the slaughterhouse;

הַדַּיָּן, הוּא הָעֵד, הוּא בַּעַל דִּין, הוּא עָתִיד לָדוּן. בָּרוּךְ הוּא, שֶׁאֵין לְפָנָיו לֹא עַוְלָה וְלֹא שִׁכְחָה, וְלֹא מַשּׂוֹא פָנִים וְלֹא מִקַּח שֹׁחַד, שֶׁהַכֹּל שֶׁלּוֹ. וְדַע, שֶׁהַכֹּל לְפִי הַחֶשְׁבּוֹן. וְאַל יַבְטִיחֲךָ יִצְרְךָ שֶׁהַשְּׁאוֹל בֵּית מָנוֹס לָךְ, שֶׁעַל כָּרְחֲךָ אַתָּה נוֹצָר, וְעַל כָּרְחֲךָ אַתָּה נוֹלָד, וְעַל כָּרְחֲךָ אַתָּה חַי, וְעַל כָּרְחֲךָ אַתָּה מֵת, וְעַל כָּרְחֲךָ אַתָּה עָתִיד לִתֵּן דִּין וְחֶשְׁבּוֹן לִפְנֵי מֶלֶךְ מַלְכֵי הַמְּלָכִים הַקָּדוֹשׁ בָּרוּךְ הוּא.

רַבִּי חֲנַנְיָא בֶּן עֲקַשְׁיָא אוֹמֵר: רָצָה הַקָּדוֹשׁ בָּרוּךְ הוּא לְזַכּוֹת אֶת יִשְׂרָאֵל, לְפִיכָךְ מכות כג:
הִרְבָּה לָהֶם תּוֹרָה וּמִצְוֹת. שֶׁנֶּאֱמַר: יהוה חָפֵץ לְמַעַן צִדְקוֹ, יַגְדִּיל תּוֹרָה וְיַאְדִּיר: ישעיה מב

If there is a מנין*, mourners say* קדיש דרבנן *(page 703).*

* * *

כָּל יִשְׂרָאֵל יֵשׁ לָהֶם חֵלֶק לָעוֹלָם הַבָּא. שֶׁנֶּאֱמַר: סנהדרין צ.
וְעַמֵּךְ כֻּלָּם צַדִּיקִים, לְעוֹלָם יִירְשׁוּ אָרֶץ ישעיה ס
נֵצֶר מַטָּעַי, מַעֲשֵׂה יָדַי לְהִתְפָּאֵר:

פרק חמישי

א בַּעֲשָׂרָה מַאֲמָרוֹת נִבְרָא הָעוֹלָם. וּמַה תַּלְמוּד לוֹמַר, וַהֲלֹא בְמַאֲמָר אֶחָד יָכוֹל לְהִבָּרְאוֹת, אֶלָּא לְהִפָּרַע מִן הָרְשָׁעִים, שֶׁמְּאַבְּדִין אֶת הָעוֹלָם שֶׁנִּבְרָא בַּעֲשָׂרָה מַאֲמָרוֹת, וְלִתֵּן שָׂכָר טוֹב לַצַּדִּיקִים, שֶׁמְּקַיְּמִין אֶת הָעוֹלָם שֶׁנִּבְרָא בַּעֲשָׂרָה מַאֲמָרוֹת.

ב עֲשָׂרָה דוֹרוֹת מֵאָדָם וְעַד נֹחַ, לְהוֹדִיעַ כַּמָּה אֶרֶךְ אַפַּיִם לְפָנָיו, שֶׁכָּל הַדּוֹרוֹת הָיוּ מַכְעִיסִין וּבָאִין, עַד שֶׁהֵבִיא עֲלֵיהֶם אֶת מֵי הַמַּבּוּל.

ג עֲשָׂרָה דוֹרוֹת מִנֹּחַ וְעַד אַבְרָהָם, לְהוֹדִיעַ כַּמָּה אֶרֶךְ אַפַּיִם לְפָנָיו, שֶׁכָּל הַדּוֹרוֹת הָיוּ מַכְעִיסִין וּבָאִין, עַד שֶׁבָּא אַבְרָהָם אָבִינוּ וְקִבֵּל שְׂכַר כֻּלָּם.

ד עֲשָׂרָה נִסְיוֹנוֹת נִתְנַסָּה אַבְרָהָם אָבִינוּ וְעָמַד בְּכֻלָּם, לְהוֹדִיעַ כַּמָּה חִבָּתוֹ שֶׁל אַבְרָהָם אָבִינוּ.

ה עֲשָׂרָה נִסִּים נַעֲשׂוּ לַאֲבוֹתֵינוּ בְּמִצְרַיִם, וַעֲשָׂרָה עַל הַיָּם. עֶשֶׂר מַכּוֹת הֵבִיא הַקָּדוֹשׁ בָּרוּךְ הוּא עַל הַמִּצְרִיִּים בְּמִצְרַיִם, וְעֶשֶׂר עַל הַיָּם.

ו עֲשָׂרָה נִסְיוֹנוֹת נִסּוּ אֲבוֹתֵינוּ אֶת הַקָּדוֹשׁ בָּרוּךְ הוּא בַּמִּדְבָּר, שֶׁנֶּאֱמַר: וַיְנַסּוּ במדבר יד
אֹתִי זֶה עֶשֶׂר פְּעָמִים, וְלֹא שָׁמְעוּ בְּקוֹלִי:

ז עֲשָׂרָה נִסִּים נַעֲשׂוּ לַאֲבוֹתֵינוּ בְּבֵית הַמִּקְדָּשׁ. לֹא הִפִּילָה אִשָּׁה מֵרֵיחַ בְּשַׂר הַקֹּדֶשׁ, וְלֹא הִסְרִיחַ בְּשַׂר הַקֹּדֶשׁ מֵעוֹלָם, וְלֹא נִרְאָה זְבוּב בְּבֵית

(4) the High Priest never suffered ritual pollution on Yom Kippur; (5) rain never extinguished the fire of the wood-pile on the altar; (6) the wind never blew away the column of smoke that rose from the altar; (7) no defect was ever found in the Omer, the Two Loaves, or the Showbread; (8) the people stood crowded together, yet there was ample space when they prostrated themselves; (9) no serpent or scorpion ever harmed anyone in Jerusalem; and (10) no one ever said to his fellow, "There is no room for me to stay overnight in Jerusalem."

8. Ten things were created on the eve of the Sabbath at twilight. They were: (1) the mouth of the earth; (2) the mouth of the well; (3) the mouth of [Balaam's] ass; (4) the rainbow; (5) the manna; (6) the staff; (7) the Shamir; (8) the writing [on the Tablets]; (9) the inscription; and (10) the Tablets. Some say: also the demons, Moses' burial place, and the ram of our father Abraham. And some say: also tongs made with tongs.

9. Seven traits characterize an uncultured person, and seven a sage. A sage: (1) does not speak before one who is wiser than he; (2) does not interrupt the words of his fellow; (3) does not answer impetuously; (4) asks relevant questions and gives appropriate answers; (5) deals with first things first, and last things last; (6) about something he has not heard he says, "I have not heard"; and (7) he acknowledges the truth. The opposites of these characterize an uncultured person.

10. Seven types of punishment come into the world for seven kinds of transgression: (1) If some tithe and others do not, a famine caused by drought occurs, so that some go hungry while others have sufficient. (2) If all decide not to tithe, a famine comes through tumult [of war] as well as drought. (3) If they also decide not to set apart ḥalla, a fatal famine ensues.

11. (4) Pestilence comes to the world for crimes that, according to the Torah, carry the death penalty, but are not the preserve of a human tribunal, and also for violation of the laws relating to produce of the seventh year. (5) The sword comes to the world for delay of justice, the perversion of justice, and for those who give a legal decision in violation of normative Torah law.

12. (6) Wild beasts come to the world because of perjury and the desecration of God's name. (7) Exile comes to the world for idolatry, sexual immorality and bloodshed, and for violating the sabbatical year of the land.

13. At four periods [of the seven-year sabbatical cycle] pestilence increases: in the fourth year, the seventh year, the year following the sabbatical year, and annually at the conclusion of the Festival of Sukkot. In the fourth year, [pestilence increases] because of neglect of the tithe for the poor in the third year; in the seventh year, because of neglect of the tithe for the poor in the sixth year; in the year following the sabbatical year, because of the violation of the laws of the seventh-year produce; and at the conclusion of the Festival of Sukkot, for robbing the poor of their gifts.

14. There are four types of human character: (1) One who says, "What is mine is mine, and what is yours is yours," is an average person, though some say this is a Sodom type. (2) One who says, "What is mine is yours and what is yours is mine," is an ignoramus. (3) One who says, "What is mine is yours and what is yours is yours," is pious. (4) One who says, "What is yours is mine and what is mine is mine," is wicked.

הַמִּטְבָּחַיִם, וְלֹא אֵרַע קֶרִי לְכֹהֵן גָּדוֹל בְּיוֹם הַכִּפּוּרִים, וְלֹא כִבּוּ הַגְּשָׁמִים אֵשׁ שֶׁל עֲצֵי הַמַּעֲרָכָה, וְלֹא נָצְחָה הָרוּחַ אֶת עַמּוּד הֶעָשָׁן, וְלֹא נִמְצָא פְסוּל בָּעֹמֶר וּבִשְׁתֵּי הַלֶּחֶם וּבְלֶחֶם הַפָּנִים, עוֹמְדִים צְפוּפִים וּמִשְׁתַּחֲוִים רְוָחִים, וְלֹא הִזִּיק נָחָשׁ וְעַקְרָב בִּירוּשָׁלַיִם מֵעוֹלָם, וְלֹא אָמַר אָדָם לַחֲבֵרוֹ: צַר לִי הַמָּקוֹם שֶׁאָלִין בִּירוּשָׁלַיִם.

ח עֲשָׂרָה דְבָרִים נִבְרְאוּ בְּעֶרֶב שַׁבָּת בֵּין הַשְּׁמָשׁוֹת. וְאֵלּוּ הֵן, פִּי הָאָרֶץ, פִּי הַבְּאֵר, פִּי הָאָתוֹן, הַקֶּשֶׁת, וְהַמָּן, וְהַמַּטֶּה, וְהַשָּׁמִיר, הַכְּתָב, וְהַמִּכְתָּב, וְהַלּוּחוֹת. וְיֵשׁ אוֹמְרִים, אַף הַמַּזִּיקִין, וּקְבוּרָתוֹ שֶׁל מֹשֶׁה, וְאֵילוֹ שֶׁל אַבְרָהָם אָבִינוּ. וְיֵשׁ אוֹמְרִים, אַף צְבַת בִּצְבַת עֲשׂוּיָה.

ט שִׁבְעָה דְבָרִים בְּגֹלֶם, וְשִׁבְעָה בְּחָכָם. חָכָם אֵינוֹ מְדַבֵּר לִפְנֵי מִי שֶׁגָּדוֹל מִמֶּנּוּ בְּחָכְמָה, וְאֵינוֹ נִכְנָס לְתוֹךְ דִּבְרֵי חֲבֵרוֹ, וְאֵינוֹ נִבְהָל לְהָשִׁיב, שׁוֹאֵל כָּעִנְיָן וּמֵשִׁיב כַּהֲלָכָה, וְאוֹמֵר עַל רִאשׁוֹן רִאשׁוֹן וְעַל אַחֲרוֹן אַחֲרוֹן, וְעַל מַה שֶּׁלֹּא שָׁמַע אוֹמֵר לֹא שָׁמַעְתִּי, וּמוֹדֶה עַל הָאֱמֶת. וְחִלּוּפֵיהֶן בְּגֹלֶם.

י שִׁבְעָה מִינֵי פֻרְעָנֻיּוֹת בָּאִין לָעוֹלָם עַל שִׁבְעָה גוּפֵי עֲבֵרָה. מִקְצָתָן מְעַשְּׂרִין וּמִקְצָתָן אֵינָן מְעַשְּׂרִין, רָעָב שֶׁל בַּצֹּרֶת בָּא, מִקְצָתָן רְעֵבִים וּמִקְצָתָן שְׂבֵעִים. גָּמְרוּ שֶׁלֹּא לְעַשֵּׂר, רָעָב שֶׁל מְהוּמָה וְשֶׁל בַּצֹּרֶת בָּא. וְשֶׁלֹּא לִטּוֹל אֶת הַחַלָּה, רָעָב שֶׁל כְּלָיָה בָּא.

יא דֶּבֶר בָּא לָעוֹלָם עַל מִיתוֹת הָאֲמוּרוֹת בַּתּוֹרָה שֶׁלֹּא נִמְסְרוּ לְבֵית דִּין, וְעַל פֵּרוֹת שְׁבִיעִית. חֶרֶב בָּאָה לָעוֹלָם עַל עִנּוּי הַדִּין, וְעַל עִוּוּת הַדִּין, וְעַל הַמּוֹרִים בַּתּוֹרָה שֶׁלֹּא כַהֲלָכָה.

יב חַיָּה רָעָה בָּאָה לָעוֹלָם עַל שְׁבוּעַת שָׁוְא וְעַל חִלּוּל הַשֵּׁם. גָּלוּת בָּאָה לָעוֹלָם עַל עֲבוֹדָה זָרָה, וְעַל גִּלּוּי עֲרָיוֹת, וְעַל שְׁפִיכוּת דָּמִים, וְעַל שְׁמִטַּת הָאָרֶץ.

יג בְּאַרְבָּעָה פְרָקִים הַדֶּבֶר מִתְרַבֶּה, בָּרְבִיעִית, וּבַשְּׁבִיעִית, וּבְמוֹצָאֵי שְׁבִיעִית, וּבְמוֹצָאֵי הֶחָג שֶׁבְּכָל שָׁנָה וְשָׁנָה. בָּרְבִיעִית, מִפְּנֵי מַעְשַׂר עָנִי שֶׁבַּשְּׁלִישִׁית. בַּשְּׁבִיעִית, מִפְּנֵי מַעְשַׂר עָנִי שֶׁבַּשִּׁשִּׁית. בְּמוֹצָאֵי שְׁבִיעִית, מִפְּנֵי פֵרוֹת שְׁבִיעִית. בְּמוֹצָאֵי הֶחָג שֶׁבְּכָל שָׁנָה וְשָׁנָה, מִפְּנֵי גֶזֶל מַתְּנוֹת עֲנִיִּים.

יד אַרְבַּע מִדּוֹת בָּאָדָם. הָאוֹמֵר שֶׁלִּי שֶׁלִּי וְשֶׁלְּךָ שֶׁלָּךְ, זוֹ מִדָּה בֵינוֹנִית, וְיֵשׁ אוֹמְרִים, זוֹ מִדַּת סְדוֹם. שֶׁלִּי שֶׁלָּךְ וְשֶׁלְּךָ שֶׁלִּי, עַם הָאָרֶץ. שֶׁלִּי שֶׁלָּךְ וְשֶׁלְּךָ שֶׁלָּךְ, חָסִיד. שֶׁלְּךָ שֶׁלִּי וְשֶׁלִּי שֶׁלִּי, רָשָׁע.

15. There are four types of temperament: (1) One who is easily angered and easily pacified – his loss is cancelled by his gain. (2) One who is hard to anger and hard to pacify – his gain is cancelled by his loss. (3) One who is hard to anger and easily pacified is pious. (4) One who is easily angered and hard to pacify is wicked.

16. There are four types of student: (1) One who learns quickly and forgets quickly – his gain is cancelled by his loss. (2) One who learns slowly and forgets slowly – his loss is cancelled by his gain. (3) One who learns quickly and forgets slowly – his is a happy lot. (4) One who learns slowly and forgets quickly – his is a sad lot.

17. There are four types of donor to charity: (1) One who wishes to give but does not want others to give, begrudges others. (2) One who wants others to give, but does not himself give, begrudges himself. (3) One who gives and wants others to give is pious. (4) One who does not himself give and does not want others to give is wicked.

18. There are four types among those who attend the House of Study: (1) One who goes but does not practice [what he learns] receives a reward for going. (2) One who practices but does not go receives a reward for practicing. (3) One who goes and also practices is pious. (4) One who neither goes nor practices is wicked.

19. There are four types among those who sit before the sages: the sponge, the funnel, the strainer and the sieve. The sponge absorbs everything. The funnel takes in at one end and lets out at the other. The strainer lets out the wine and retains the sediment. The sieve allows the flour dust to pass through and retains the fine flour.

20. If love depends on a specific cause, when the cause ends, so does the love. If love does not depend on a specific cause, then it never ends. What is an example of love depending on a specific cause? The love of Amnon for Tamar. What is an example of love not dependent on a specific cause? The love of David and Jonathan.

21. Any dispute for the sake of Heaven will have enduring value, but any dispute not for the sake of Heaven will not have enduring value. What is an example of a dispute for the sake of heaven? The dispute between Hillel and Shammai. What is an example of one not for the sake of heaven? The dispute of Koraḥ and all his company.

22. One who brings merit to the many will not be the cause of sin. One who causes the many to sin will be denied the means to repent. Moses attained merit and brought merit to the many; therefore the merit of the many was attributed to him, as it is said, "He carried out the LORD's righteousness and His ordinances with Israel." *Deut. 33* Jeroboam, son of Nebat, sinned and caused the many to sin; therefore the sin of the many was attributed to him, as it is said, "For the sins of Jeroboam that he committed and that he caused Israel to commit." *1 Kings 15*

23. Whoever possesses these three traits is one of the disciples of our father Abraham; whoever possesses the three opposite traits is one of the disciples of the wicked Balaam. A generous eye, a modest demeanor and a humble soul are the traits of the disciples of our father Abraham. An evil eye, an arrogant demeanor and an

טו אַרְבַּע מִדּוֹת בַּדֵּעוֹת. נוֹחַ לִכְעֹס וְנוֹחַ לִרְצוֹת, יָצָא הֶפְסֵדוֹ בִּשְׂכָרוֹ. קָשֶׁה לִכְעֹס וְקָשֶׁה לִרְצוֹת, יָצָא שְׂכָרוֹ בְּהֶפְסֵדוֹ. קָשֶׁה לִכְעֹס וְנוֹחַ לִרְצוֹת, חָסִיד. נוֹחַ לִכְעֹס וְקָשֶׁה לִרְצוֹת, רָשָׁע.

טז אַרְבַּע מִדּוֹת בַּתַּלְמִידִים. מָהִיר לִשְׁמֹעַ וּמָהִיר לְאַבֵּד, יָצָא שְׂכָרוֹ בְּהֶפְסֵדוֹ. קָשֶׁה לִשְׁמֹעַ וְקָשֶׁה לְאַבֵּד, יָצָא הֶפְסֵדוֹ בִּשְׂכָרוֹ. מָהִיר לִשְׁמֹעַ וְקָשֶׁה לְאַבֵּד, זֶה חֵלֶק טוֹב. קָשֶׁה לִשְׁמֹעַ וּמָהִיר לְאַבֵּד, זֶה חֵלֶק רָע.

יז אַרְבַּע מִדּוֹת בְּנוֹתְנֵי צְדָקָה. הָרוֹצֶה שֶׁיִּתֵּן וְלֹא יִתְּנוּ אֲחֵרִים, עֵינוֹ רָעָה בְּשֶׁל אֲחֵרִים. יִתְּנוּ אֲחֵרִים וְהוּא לֹא יִתֵּן, עֵינוֹ רָעָה בְּשֶׁלּוֹ. יִתֵּן וְיִתְּנוּ אֲחֵרִים, חָסִיד. לֹא יִתֵּן וְלֹא יִתְּנוּ אֲחֵרִים, רָשָׁע.

יח אַרְבַּע מִדּוֹת בְּהוֹלְכֵי בֵית הַמִּדְרָשׁ. הוֹלֵךְ וְאֵינוֹ עוֹשֶׂה, שְׂכַר הֲלִיכָה בְּיָדוֹ. עוֹשֶׂה וְאֵינוֹ הוֹלֵךְ, שְׂכַר מַעֲשֶׂה בְּיָדוֹ. הוֹלֵךְ וְעוֹשֶׂה, חָסִיד. לֹא הוֹלֵךְ וְלֹא עוֹשֶׂה, רָשָׁע.

יט אַרְבַּע מִדּוֹת בְּיוֹשְׁבִים לִפְנֵי חֲכָמִים, סְפוֹג, וּמַשְׁפֵּךְ, מְשַׁמֶּרֶת, וְנָפָה. סְפוֹג, שֶׁהוּא סוֹפֵג אֶת הַכֹּל. וּמַשְׁפֵּךְ, שֶׁמַּכְנִיס בְּזוֹ וּמוֹצִיא בְזוֹ. מְשַׁמֶּרֶת, שֶׁמּוֹצִיאָה אֶת הַיַּיִן וְקוֹלֶטֶת אֶת הַשְּׁמָרִים. וְנָפָה, שֶׁמּוֹצִיאָה אֶת הַקֶּמַח וְקוֹלֶטֶת אֶת הַסֹּלֶת.

כ כָּל אַהֲבָה שֶׁהִיא תְלוּיָה בְדָבָר, בָּטֵל דָּבָר, בְּטֵלָה אַהֲבָה. וְשֶׁאֵינָהּ תְּלוּיָה בְדָבָר, אֵינָהּ בְּטֵלָה לְעוֹלָם. אֵיזוֹ הִיא אַהֲבָה שֶׁהִיא תְלוּיָה בְדָבָר, זוֹ אַהֲבַת אַמְנוֹן וְתָמָר. וְשֶׁאֵינָהּ תְּלוּיָה בְדָבָר, זוֹ אַהֲבַת דָּוִד וִיהוֹנָתָן.

כא כָּל מַחֲלֹקֶת שֶׁהִיא לְשֵׁם שָׁמַיִם, סוֹפָהּ לְהִתְקַיֵּם. וְשֶׁאֵינָהּ לְשֵׁם שָׁמַיִם, אֵין סוֹפָהּ לְהִתְקַיֵּם. אֵיזוֹ הִיא מַחֲלֹקֶת שֶׁהִיא לְשֵׁם שָׁמַיִם, זוֹ מַחֲלֹקֶת הִלֵּל וְשַׁמַּאי. וְשֶׁאֵינָהּ לְשֵׁם שָׁמַיִם, זוֹ מַחֲלֹקֶת קֹרַח וְכָל עֲדָתוֹ.

כב כָּל הַמְזַכֶּה אֶת הָרַבִּים, אֵין חֵטְא בָּא עַל יָדוֹ. וְכָל הַמַּחֲטִיא אֶת הָרַבִּים, אֵין מַסְפִּיקִין בְּיָדוֹ לַעֲשׂוֹת תְּשׁוּבָה. מֹשֶׁה זָכָה וְזִכָּה אֶת הָרַבִּים, זְכוּת הָרַבִּים תָּלוּי בוֹ, שֶׁנֶּאֱמַר: צִדְקַת יהוה עָשָׂה וּמִשְׁפָּטָיו עִם־יִשְׂרָאֵל: יָרָבְעָם בֶּן נְבָט, דברים לג
חָטָא וְהֶחֱטִיא אֶת הָרַבִּים, חֵטְא הָרַבִּים תָּלוּי בוֹ, שֶׁנֶּאֱמַר: עַל־חַטֹּאות מלכים א׳ טו
יָרָבְעָם אֲשֶׁר חָטָא וַאֲשֶׁר הֶחֱטִיא אֶת־יִשְׂרָאֵל:

כג כָּל מִי שֶׁיֵּשׁ בּוֹ שְׁלֹשָׁה דְבָרִים הַלָּלוּ, הוּא מִתַּלְמִידָיו שֶׁל אַבְרָהָם אָבִינוּ, וּשְׁלֹשָׁה דְבָרִים אֲחֵרִים, הוּא מִתַּלְמִידָיו שֶׁל בִּלְעָם הָרָשָׁע. עַיִן טוֹבָה, וְרוּחַ נְמוּכָה, וְנֶפֶשׁ שְׁפָלָה, תַּלְמִידָיו שֶׁל אַבְרָהָם אָבִינוּ. עַיִן רָעָה, וְרוּחַ גְּבוֹהָה

insatiable soul are attributes of the disciples of the wicked Balaam. What is the difference between our father Abraham's disciples and those of the wicked Balaam? Our father Abraham's disciples enjoy this world and inherit the World to Come, as it is said, "That I may cause those who love me to inherit substance and so that I may fill their treasures." The wicked Balaam's disciples inherit Gehinnom and go down to the pit of destruction, as it is said, "But You, God, will bring them down to the pit of destruction; bloodthirsty and dishonest men shall not live out half their days; but I trust in You."

Prov. 8

Ps. 55

24. Judah ben Tema said: Be strong as a leopard, light as an eagle, swift as a gazelle, and brave as a lion, to do the will of your Father in heaven. He used to say: The shameless go to Gehinnom; those who have a sense of shame are destined for the Garden of Eden. May it be Your will, O LORD our God and God of our ancestors that the Temple be speedily rebuilt in our days; and grant us our portion in Your Torah.

25. He used to say: Five years old is the age to begin studying Scripture; ten for Mishna; thirteen for the obligation of the commandments; fifteen for the study of Talmud; eighteen for marriage; twenty for seeking a livelihood; thirty for full strength; forty for understanding; fifty for giving counsel; sixty for old age; seventy for ripe old age; eighty for exceptional strength; and ninety for a bent back; at a hundred, one is as if he were dead and had left and gone from the world.

26. Ben Bag-Bag said: Turn it [the Torah] over and over, for everything is in it. Reflect on it, grow old and gray in it and do not stir from it, for there is no better portion for you than this. Ben Heh-Heh said: According to the effort is the reward.

Rabbi Ḥananya ben Akashya said: The Holy One, blessed be He, wanted to confer merit on Israel. That is why He gave them a copious Torah and many commandments, as it is said, "It pleased the LORD, for the sake of [Israel's] righteousness, to make the Torah great and glorious."

Makkot 23b

Is. 42

If there is a minyan, mourners say the Rabbis' Kaddish (page 702).

* * *

Sanhedrin 90a

All Israel have a share in the World to Come, as it is said,
"Your people are all righteous; they shall inherit the land for ever;
they are a shoot of My own planting,
a work of My own hands, that I may be glorified."

Is. 60

CHAPTER 6

The sages taught the following in the style of the Mishna – blessed be He who chose them and their teaching.

1. Rabbi Meir said: Whoever engages in Torah study for its own sake merits many things; moreover, the whole world is worthwhile for his sake alone. He is called friend, beloved, a lover of God and a lover of mankind. He brings joy to God; he

וְנֶפֶשׁ רְחָבָה, תַּלְמִידָיו שֶׁל בִּלְעָם הָרָשָׁע. מַה בֵּין תַּלְמִידָיו שֶׁל אַבְרָהָם
אָבִינוּ לְתַלְמִידָיו שֶׁל בִּלְעָם הָרָשָׁע. תַּלְמִידָיו שֶׁל אַבְרָהָם אָבִינוּ אוֹכְלִין
בָּעוֹלָם הַזֶּה וְנוֹחֲלִין הָעוֹלָם הַבָּא, שֶׁנֶּאֱמַר: לְהַנְחִיל אֹהֲבַי יֵשׁ וְאֹצְרֹתֵיהֶם משלי ח
אֲמַלֵּא: אֲבָל תַּלְמִידָיו שֶׁל בִּלְעָם הָרָשָׁע יוֹרְשִׁין גֵּיהִנָּם וְיוֹרְדִין לִבְאֵר שַׁחַת,
שֶׁנֶּאֱמַר: וְאַתָּה אֱלֹהִים תּוֹרִדֵם לִבְאֵר שַׁחַת, אַנְשֵׁי דָמִים וּמִרְמָה לֹא־יֶחֱצוּ תהלים נה
יְמֵיהֶם, וַאֲנִי אֶבְטַח־בָּךְ:

כד יְהוּדָה בֶּן תֵּימָא אוֹמֵר: הֱוֵי עַז כַּנָּמֵר וְקַל כַּנֶּשֶׁר, רָץ כַּצְּבִי וְגִבּוֹר כָּאֲרִי,
לַעֲשׂוֹת רְצוֹן אָבִיךָ שֶׁבַּשָּׁמַיִם. הוּא הָיָה אוֹמֵר: עַז פָּנִים לְגֵיהִנָּם, וּבֹשֶׁת
פָּנִים לְגַן עֵדֶן. יְהִי רָצוֹן מִלְּפָנֶיךָ, יהוה אֱלֹהֵינוּ וֵאלֹהֵי אֲבוֹתֵינוּ, שֶׁיִּבָּנֶה בֵּית
הַמִּקְדָּשׁ בִּמְהֵרָה בְיָמֵינוּ, וְתֵן חֶלְקֵנוּ בְּתוֹרָתֶךָ.

כה הוּא הָיָה אוֹמֵר: בֶּן חָמֵשׁ שָׁנִים לַמִּקְרָא, בֶּן עֶשֶׂר שָׁנִים לַמִּשְׁנָה, בֶּן שְׁלֹשׁ
עֶשְׂרֵה לַמִּצְוֹת, בֶּן חֲמֵשׁ עֶשְׂרֵה לַגְּמָרָא, בֶּן שְׁמוֹנֶה עֶשְׂרֵה לַחֻפָּה, בֶּן עֶשְׂרִים
לִרְדֹּף, בֶּן שְׁלֹשִׁים לַכֹּחַ, בֶּן אַרְבָּעִים לַבִּינָה, בֶּן חֲמִשִּׁים לָעֵצָה, בֶּן שִׁשִּׁים
לַזִּקְנָה, בֶּן שִׁבְעִים לַשֵּׂיבָה, בֶּן שְׁמוֹנִים לַגְּבוּרָה, בֶּן תִּשְׁעִים לָשׁוּחַ, בֶּן מֵאָה
כְּאִלּוּ מֵת וְעָבַר וּבָטֵל מִן הָעוֹלָם.

כו בֶּן בַּג בַּג אוֹמֵר: הֲפֹךְ בָּהּ וַהֲפֹךְ בָּהּ דְּכֹלָּא בָהּ, וּבַהּ תֶּחֱזֵי, וְסִיב וּבְלֵה בַהּ,
וּמִנַּהּ לָא תְזוּעַ, שֶׁאֵין לְךָ מִדָּה טוֹבָה הֵימֶנָּה. בֶּן הֵא הֵא אוֹמֵר: לְפוּם
צַעֲרָא אַגְרָא.

רַבִּי חֲנַנְיָא בֶּן עֲקַשְׁיָא אוֹמֵר: רָצָה הַקָּדוֹשׁ בָּרוּךְ הוּא לְזַכּוֹת אֶת יִשְׂרָאֵל, לְפִיכָךְ מכות כג:
הִרְבָּה לָהֶם תּוֹרָה וּמִצְוֹת. שֶׁנֶּאֱמַר: יהוה חָפֵץ לְמַעַן צִדְקוֹ, יַגְדִּיל תּוֹרָה וְיַאְדִּיר: ישעיה מב

If there is a מנין*, mourners say* קדיש דרבנן *(page 703).*

* * *

כָּל יִשְׂרָאֵל יֵשׁ לָהֶם חֵלֶק לָעוֹלָם הַבָּא. שֶׁנֶּאֱמַר: סנהדרין צ.
וְעַמֵּךְ כֻּלָּם צַדִּיקִים, לְעוֹלָם יִירְשׁוּ אָרֶץ ישעיה ס
נֵצֶר מַטָּעַי, מַעֲשֵׂה יָדַי לְהִתְפָּאֵר:

פרק ששי

שָׁנוּ חֲכָמִים בִּלְשׁוֹן הַמִּשְׁנָה, בָּרוּךְ שֶׁבָּחַר בָּהֶם וּבְמִשְׁנָתָם.

א רַבִּי מֵאִיר אוֹמֵר: כָּל הָעוֹסֵק בַּתּוֹרָה לִשְׁמָהּ, זוֹכֶה לִדְבָרִים הַרְבֵּה. וְלֹא עוֹד,
אֶלָּא שֶׁכָּל הָעוֹלָם כֻּלּוֹ כְּדַאי הוּא לוֹ. נִקְרָא רֵעַ, אָהוּב, אוֹהֵב אֶת הַמָּקוֹם,

brings joy to mankind. [The Torah] clothes him with humility and reverence. It prepares him to be righteous, pious, upright and faithful. It keeps him far from sin and near to virtue. People benefit from his advice and wisdom, understanding and courage, as it is said, "Mine are counsel and wisdom; I am understanding, courage is mine." It gives him sovereignty, dominion and understanding judgment. To him the secrets of the Torah are revealed. He becomes like a never-failing fountain, like a river that never runs dry. He becomes modest and patient; he forgives insults. It makes him great, elevating him above all things. *Prov. 8*

2. Rabbi Yehoshua ben Levi said: Every day a heavenly voice resounds from Mount Horeb, declaring and saying: "Woe to mankind for their contempt of the Torah!" For whoever does not occupy himself with the Torah is called reprehensible, as it is said, "Like a gold ring in the snout of a pig is a beautiful woman bereft of sense." It also says, "The tablets were the work of God, and the writing was the writing of God, engraved (*ḥarut*) on the tablets." Read not *ḥarut* ("engraved") but *ḥerut* ("freedom"), for the only person who is truly free is one who occupies himself with Torah study; and whoever occupies himself with Torah study will be elevated, as it is said, "And from Mattana to Naḥaliel, and from Naḥaliel to Bamot." *Prov. 11* *Ex. 32* *Num. 21*

3. Whoever learns from someone else a single chapter, a single law, a single verse, a single word, even a single letter, must treat him with honor, for so we find in the case of David, King of Israel, who learned only two things from Aḥitophel, yet he called him his teacher, his guide, and his close friend, for so it says, "But it is you, my equal, my guide, my close friend." The following inference can be derived: If David, King of Israel, who learned only two things from Aḥitophel, called him his teacher, guide and close friend, how much more must one who learns from someone else a chapter, a law, a verse, a word or even a single letter, treat him with honor! And honor is due only to Torah, as it is written, "The wise shall inherit honor," and "The wholehearted shall attain good," and "good" signifies Torah, as it is said, "I have given you good instruction; do not abandon My Torah." *Ps. 55* *Prov. 3* *Prov. 28* *Prov. 4*

4. This is the way of Torah: Eat bread with salt, drink water by measure, sleep on the ground, live a life of hardship, but toil in the Torah! If you do so, "You will be happy and it will be well with you": "You will be happy" in this world, "and it shall be well with you" in the World to Come.

5. Do not seek greatness for yourself, and do not long for honor. Let your deeds exceed your learning. Do not crave the table of kings, for your table is greater than theirs, your crown is greater than their crown, and your Employer can be relied upon to pay you your labor's reward.

6. The Torah is greater than priesthood and kingship, for kingship is acquired with thirty attainments, and priesthood is endowed with twenty-four [gifts],

אוהֵב אֶת הַבְּרִיּוֹת, מְשַׂמֵּחַ אֶת הַמָּקוֹם, מְשַׂמֵּחַ אֶת הַבְּרִיּוֹת, וּמַלְבַּשְׁתּוֹ עֲנָוָה וְיִרְאָה, וּמַכְשַׁרְתּוֹ לִהְיוֹת צַדִּיק, חָסִיד, יָשָׁר, וְנֶאֱמָן, וּמְרַחַקְתּוֹ מִן הַחֵטְא, וּמְקָרַבְתּוֹ לִידֵי זְכוּת, וְנֶהֱנִין מִמֶּנּוּ עֵצָה וְתוּשִׁיָּה, בִּינָה וּגְבוּרָה, שֶׁנֶּאֱמַר:
משלי ח לִי־עֵצָה וְתוּשִׁיָּה, אֲנִי בִינָה, לִי גְבוּרָה: וְנוֹתֶנֶת לוֹ מַלְכוּת וּמֶמְשָׁלָה, וְחִקּוּר דִּין, וּמְגַלִּין לוֹ רָזֵי תוֹרָה, וְנַעֲשֶׂה כְּמַעְיָן הַמִּתְגַּבֵּר וּכְנָהָר שֶׁאֵינוֹ פּוֹסֵק, וְהֹוֶה צָנוּעַ, וְאֶרֶךְ רוּחַ, וּמוֹחֵל עַל עֶלְבּוֹנוֹ, וּמְגַדַּלְתּוֹ וּמְרוֹמַמְתּוֹ עַל כָּל הַמַּעֲשִׂים.

ב אָמַר רַבִּי יְהוֹשֻׁעַ בֶּן לֵוִי: בְּכָל יוֹם וָיוֹם, בַּת קוֹל יוֹצֵאת מֵהַר חוֹרֵב וּמַכְרֶזֶת וְאוֹמֶרֶת, אוֹי לָהֶם לַבְּרִיּוֹת מֵעֶלְבּוֹנָהּ שֶׁל תּוֹרָה, שֶׁכָּל מִי שֶׁאֵינוֹ עוֹסֵק
משלי יא בַּתּוֹרָה נִקְרָא נָזוּף, שֶׁנֶּאֱמַר: נֶזֶם זָהָב בְּאַף חֲזִיר, אִשָּׁה יָפָה וְסָרַת טָעַם:
שמות לב וְאוֹמֵר: וְהַלֻּחֹת מַעֲשֵׂה אֱלֹהִים הֵמָּה, וְהַמִּכְתָּב מִכְתַּב אֱלֹהִים הוּא, חָרוּת עַל־הַלֻּחֹת: אַל תִּקְרָא חָרוּת אֶלָּא חֵרוּת, שֶׁאֵין לְךָ בֶּן חוֹרִין אֶלָּא מִי שֶׁעוֹסֵק בְּתַלְמוּד תּוֹרָה. וְכָל מִי שֶׁעוֹסֵק בְּתַלְמוּד תּוֹרָה, הֲרֵי זֶה מִתְעַלֶּה, שֶׁנֶּאֱמַר:
במדבר כא וּמִמַּתָּנָה נַחֲלִיאֵל, וּמִנַּחֲלִיאֵל בָּמוֹת:

ג הַלּוֹמֵד מֵחֲבֵרוֹ פֶּרֶק אֶחָד, אוֹ הֲלָכָה אַחַת, אוֹ פָּסוּק אֶחָד, אוֹ דִבּוּר אֶחָד, אוֹ אֲפִלּוּ אוֹת אַחַת, צָרִיךְ לִנְהָג בּוֹ כָּבוֹד. שֶׁכֵּן מָצִינוּ בְּדָוִד מֶלֶךְ יִשְׂרָאֵל, שֶׁלֹּא לָמַד מֵאֲחִיתֹפֶל אֶלָּא שְׁנֵי דְבָרִים בִּלְבָד, קְרָאוֹ רַבּוֹ אַלּוּפוֹ וּמְיֻדָּעוֹ,
תהלים נה שֶׁנֶּאֱמַר: וְאַתָּה אֱנוֹשׁ כְּעֶרְכִּי, אַלּוּפִי וּמְיֻדָּעִי: וַהֲלֹא דְבָרִים קַל וָחֹמֶר. וּמָה דָּוִד מֶלֶךְ יִשְׂרָאֵל, שֶׁלֹּא לָמַד מֵאֲחִיתֹפֶל אֶלָּא שְׁנֵי דְבָרִים בִּלְבָד, קְרָאוֹ רַבּוֹ אַלּוּפוֹ וּמְיֻדָּעוֹ, הַלּוֹמֵד מֵחֲבֵרוֹ פֶּרֶק אֶחָד, אוֹ הֲלָכָה אַחַת, אוֹ פָּסוּק אֶחָד, אוֹ דִבּוּר אֶחָד, אוֹ אֲפִלּוּ אוֹת אַחַת, עַל אַחַת כַּמָּה וְכַמָּה שֶׁצָּרִיךְ
משלי ג לִנְהָג בּוֹ כָּבוֹד. וְאֵין כָּבוֹד אֶלָּא תוֹרָה, שֶׁנֶּאֱמַר: כָּבוֹד חֲכָמִים יִנְחָלוּ:
משלי כח / משלי ד וּתְמִימִים יִנְחֲלוּ־טוֹב: וְאֵין טוֹב אֶלָּא תוֹרָה, שֶׁנֶּאֱמַר: כִּי לֶקַח טוֹב נָתַתִּי לָכֶם, תּוֹרָתִי אַל־תַּעֲזֹבוּ:

ד כָּךְ הִיא דַּרְכָּהּ שֶׁל תּוֹרָה. פַּת בְּמֶלַח תֹּאכַל, וּמַיִם בִּמְשׂוּרָה תִּשְׁתֶּה, וְעַל הָאָרֶץ תִּישַׁן, וְחַיֵּי צַעַר תִּחְיֶה, וּבַתּוֹרָה אַתָּה עָמֵל. אִם אַתָּה עוֹשֶׂה כֵּן, אַשְׁרֶיךָ וְטוֹב לָךְ, אַשְׁרֶיךָ בָּעוֹלָם הַזֶּה, וְטוֹב לָךְ לָעוֹלָם הַבָּא.

ה אַל תְּבַקֵּשׁ גְּדֻלָּה לְעַצְמְךָ, וְאַל תַּחְמֹד כָּבוֹד. יוֹתֵר מִלִּמּוּדְךָ עֲשֵׂה. וְאַל תִּתְאַוֶּה לְשֻׁלְחָנָם שֶׁל מְלָכִים, שֶׁשֻּׁלְחָנְךָ גָּדוֹל מִשֻּׁלְחָנָם, וְכִתְרְךָ גָּדוֹל מִכִּתְרָם. וְנֶאֱמָן הוּא בַּעַל מְלַאכְתְּךָ, שֶׁיְּשַׁלֶּם לְךָ שְׂכַר פְּעֻלָּתֶךָ.

ו גְּדוֹלָה תוֹרָה יוֹתֵר מִן הַכְּהֻנָּה וּמִן הַמַּלְכוּת. שֶׁהַמַּלְכוּת נִקְנֵית בִּשְׁלֹשִׁים

but the Torah is acquired by forty-eight virtues. They are: study, attentive listening, well-ordered speech, intuitive understanding, awe, reverence, humility, joy, purity, serving the wise, association with colleagues, debate with students, serenity, knowledge of Scripture and Mishna; minimizing time spent on business, worldly matters, pleasure, sleep, small talk or laughter; patience, a kindly heart, faith in the sages, and acceptance of suffering; knowing one's place, being happy with one's lot, restraining one's words, and claiming no credit for oneself; being loved, loving God, loving mankind and loving righteousness, justice and admonishment; shunning honors, avoiding arrogance in one's learning or delight in giving decisions; sharing someone else's burden, giving him the benefit of the doubt, guiding him to truth and peace; concentrating on one's study, asking and answering questions, listening and adding to one's knowledge; learning in order to teach, learning in order to do, making one's teacher wiser, being precise in one's studies, and reporting a saying in the name of the one who said it. For you have learned: Whoever reports a saying in the name of the one who said it brings deliverance to the world, as it is said, "And Esther told the king in the name of Mordekhai." *Esther 2*

7. Great is Torah for it gives life to its practitioners in both this world and the World to Come, as it is said, "For they are life to those that find them, and *Prov. 4* healing to all their flesh"; and it says, "It shall be healing for your body and *Prov. 3* marrow for your bones"; and it says, "It is a tree of life to those who grasp it, and those who support it shall be happy"; and it says, "They shall be a garland *Prov. 1* of grace on your head, and pendants for your neck"; and it says, "It will adorn *Prov. 4* your head with a garland of grace, and bestow on you a crown of glory"; and it says, "Through me shall your days increase, and years of life shall be added *Prov. 9* to you"; and it says, "At its right hand is length of days; in its left, riches and *Prov. 3* honor"; and it says, "For length of days and years of life and peace shall they *Prov. 3* add to you."

8. Rabbi Shimon ben Menasya said in the name of Rabbi Shimon ben Yoḥai: Beauty, strength, wealth, honor, wisdom, old age, gray hair, and children are fitting for the righteous and for the world, as it is said: "Gray hair is a crown *Prov. 16* of glory; it is attained by the way of righteousness"; and it says, "The crown *Prov. 14* of the wise is their wealth"; and it says, "Grandchildren are the crown of *Prov. 17* their elders; the glory of children is their parents"; and it says, "The glory of *Prov. 20* the young is their strength; the majesty of the old is their gray hair"; and it says, "Then the moon shall be ashamed and the sun shall be abashed, for the *Is. 24* LORD of multitudes will reign on Mount Zion and in Jerusalem, and glory shall be before His elders." Rabbi Shimon ben Menasya said: These seven qualities which the sages attributed to the righteous were all present in Rabbi [Judah the Prince] and his sons.

מַעֲלוֹת, וְהַכְּהֻנָּה בְּעֶשְׂרִים וְאַרְבַּע, וְהַתּוֹרָה נִקְנֵית בְּאַרְבָּעִים וּשְׁמוֹנָה
דְבָרִים. וְאֵלּוּ הֵן, בְּתַלְמוּד, בִּשְׁמִיעַת הָאֹזֶן, בַּעֲרִיכַת שְׂפָתָיִם, בְּבִינַת הַלֵּב,
בְּאֵימָה, בְּיִרְאָה, בַּעֲנָוָה, בְּשִׂמְחָה, בְּטָהֳרָה, בְּשִׁמּוּשׁ חֲכָמִים, בְּדִקְדּוּק
חֲבֵרִים, בְּפִלְפּוּל הַתַּלְמִידִים, בְּיִשּׁוּב, בְּמִקְרָא, בְּמִשְׁנָה, בְּמִעוּט סְחוֹרָה,
בְּמִעוּט דֶּרֶךְ אֶרֶץ, בְּמִעוּט תַּעֲנוּג, בְּמִעוּט שֵׁנָה, בְּמִעוּט שִׂיחָה, בְּמִעוּט
שְׂחוֹק, בְּאֶרֶךְ אַפַּיִם, בְּלֵב טוֹב, בֶּאֱמוּנַת חֲכָמִים, בְּקַבָּלַת הַיִּסּוּרִין, הַמַּכִּיר
אֶת מְקוֹמוֹ, וְהַשָּׂמֵחַ בְּחֶלְקוֹ, וְהָעוֹשֶׂה סְיָג לִדְבָרָיו, וְאֵינוֹ מַחֲזִיק טוֹבָה
לְעַצְמוֹ, אָהוּב, אוֹהֵב אֶת הַמָּקוֹם, אוֹהֵב אֶת הַבְּרִיּוֹת, אוֹהֵב אֶת הַצְּדָקוֹת,
אוֹהֵב אֶת הַמֵּישָׁרִים, אוֹהֵב אֶת הַתּוֹכָחוֹת, וּמִתְרַחֵק מִן הַכָּבוֹד, וְלֹא מֵגִיס
לִבּוֹ בְּתַלְמוּדוֹ, וְאֵינוֹ שָׂמֵחַ בְּהוֹרָאָה, נוֹשֵׂא בְעֹל עִם חֲבֵרוֹ, וּמַכְרִיעוֹ לְכַף
זְכוּת, וּמַעֲמִידוֹ עַל הָאֱמֶת, וּמַעֲמִידוֹ עַל הַשָּׁלוֹם, וּמִתְיַשֵּׁב לִבּוֹ בְּתַלְמוּדוֹ,
שׁוֹאֵל וּמֵשִׁיב, שׁוֹמֵעַ וּמוֹסִיף, הַלּוֹמֵד עַל מְנָת לְלַמֵּד, וְהַלּוֹמֵד עַל מְנָת
לַעֲשׂוֹת, הַמַּחְכִּים אֶת רַבּוֹ, וְהַמְכַוֵּן אֶת שְׁמוּעָתוֹ, וְהָאוֹמֵר דָּבָר בְּשֵׁם אוֹמְרוֹ.
הָא לָמַדְתָּ, כָּל הָאוֹמֵר דָּבָר בְּשֵׁם אוֹמְרוֹ, מֵבִיא גְאֻלָּה לָעוֹלָם, שֶׁנֶּאֱמַר:
וַתֹּאמֶר אֶסְתֵּר לַמֶּלֶךְ בְּשֵׁם מָרְדֳּכָי: אסתר ב

ז גְּדוֹלָה תוֹרָה, שֶׁהִיא נוֹתֶנֶת חַיִּים לְעֹשֶׂיהָ בָּעוֹלָם הַזֶּה וּבָעוֹלָם הַבָּא,
שֶׁנֶּאֱמַר: כִּי־חַיִּים הֵם לְמֹצְאֵיהֶם, וּלְכָל־בְּשָׂרוֹ מַרְפֵּא: וְאוֹמֵר: רִפְאוּת תְּהִי משלי ד / משלי ג
לְשָׁרֶּךָ, וְשִׁקּוּי לְעַצְמוֹתֶיךָ: וְאוֹמֵר: עֵץ־חַיִּים הִיא לַמַּחֲזִיקִים בָּהּ, וְתֹמְכֶיהָ
מְאֻשָּׁר: וְאוֹמֵר: כִּי לִוְיַת חֵן הֵם לְרֹאשֶׁךָ, וַעֲנָקִים לְגַרְגְּרֹתֶךָ: וְאוֹמֵר: תִּתֵּן משלי א / משלי ד
לְרֹאשְׁךָ לִוְיַת־חֵן, עֲטֶרֶת תִּפְאֶרֶת תְּמַגְּנֶךָּ: וְאוֹמֵר: כִּי־בִי יִרְבּוּ יָמֶיךָ, וְיוֹסִיפוּ משלי ט
לְךָ שְׁנוֹת חַיִּים: וְאוֹמֵר: אֹרֶךְ יָמִים בִּימִינָהּ, בִּשְׂמֹאולָהּ עֹשֶׁר וְכָבוֹד: משלי ג
וְאוֹמֵר: כִּי אֹרֶךְ יָמִים וּשְׁנוֹת חַיִּים וְשָׁלוֹם יוֹסִיפוּ לָךְ: משלי ג

ח רַבִּי שִׁמְעוֹן בֶּן מְנַסְיָא מִשּׁוּם רַבִּי שִׁמְעוֹן בֶּן יוֹחָאי אוֹמֵר: הַנּוֹי, וְהַכֹּחַ,
וְהָעֹשֶׁר, וְהַכָּבוֹד, וְהַחָכְמָה, וְהַזִּקְנָה, וְהַשֵּׂיבָה, וְהַבָּנִים, נָאֶה לַצַּדִּיקִים וְנָאֶה
לָעוֹלָם, שֶׁנֶּאֱמַר: עֲטֶרֶת תִּפְאֶרֶת שֵׂיבָה, בְּדֶרֶךְ צְדָקָה תִּמָּצֵא: וְאוֹמֵר: עֲטֶרֶת משלי טז / משלי יד
חֲכָמִים עָשְׁרָם: וְאוֹמֵר: עֲטֶרֶת זְקֵנִים בְּנֵי בָנִים, וְתִפְאֶרֶת בָּנִים אֲבוֹתָם: משלי יז
וְאוֹמֵר: תִּפְאֶרֶת בַּחוּרִים כֹּחָם, וַהֲדַר זְקֵנִים שֵׂיבָה: וְאוֹמֵר: וְחָפְרָה הַלְּבָנָה משלי כ / ישעיה כד
וּבוֹשָׁה הַחַמָּה, כִּי־מָלַךְ יהוה צְבָאוֹת בְּהַר צִיּוֹן וּבִירוּשָׁלַיִם, וְנֶגֶד זְקֵנָיו כָּבוֹד:
רַבִּי שִׁמְעוֹן בֶּן מְנַסְיָא אוֹמֵר: אֵלּוּ שֶׁבַע מִדּוֹת שֶׁמָּנוּ חֲכָמִים לַצַּדִּיקִים, כֻּלָּם
נִתְקַיְּמוּ בְּרַבִּי וּבְבָנָיו.

9. Rabbi Yose ben Kisma said: Once I was walking along the road when a man met
and greeted me, and I returned his greeting. He said to me, "Rabbi, where do
you come from?" I replied, "I come from a great city of sages and scribes." He
said to me, "Rabbi, if you are willing to live with us in our place I will give you a
million gold dinars, as well as precious stones and pearls." I replied, "Were you
to give me all the silver and gold and precious stones and pearls in the world,
I would not live anywhere except in a place of Torah, for so it is written in the
book of Psalms by David, King of Israel, 'I prefer the Torah of your mouth to *Ps. 119*
thousands of gold and silver pieces.' Furthermore, when a person departs from
this world, neither silver nor gold nor precious stones nor pearls accompany
him, but only Torah and good deeds, as it is said, 'When you walk, it will lead *Prov. 6*
you; when you lie down, it will watch over you; and when you awake, it will
talk with you.' 'When you walk, it will lead you' – in this world; 'when you lie
down, it will watch over you' – in the grave; 'and when you awake, it will speak
for you' – in the World to Come. And it says, 'Mine is the silver, and Mine is *Hag. 2*
the gold, says the Lord of multitudes.'"

10. Five possessions did the Holy One, blessed be He, declare as His own in His
world, and they are: the Torah, heaven and earth, Abraham, Israel and the
Temple. How do we know this about the Torah? Because it is written, "The *Prov. 8*
Lord created me at the beginning of His way, as the first of His works in days of
old." How do we know it about heaven and earth? Because it is written, "So says *Is. 66*
the Lord: the heaven is My throne, and the earth is My footstool; what house
can you build for Me, and where is the place for My rest?"; and it also says, "How *Ps. 104*
numerous are Your works, Lord; You made them all in wisdom; the earth is full
of Your creations." How do we know it about Abraham? Because it is written,
"And He blessed him and said, Blessed be Abram of God the Most High, owner of *Gen. 14*
heaven and earth." How do we know it about Israel? Because it is written, "Until *Ex. 15*
Your people pass over, O Lord, until this people You acquired pass over"; and
it also says, "As for the holy ones who are on earth and for the mighty, all My *Ps. 16*
delight is in them." How do we know it about the Temple? Because it is written,
"Your dwelling place which You, Lord, have made; the Temple, O Lord, which *Ex. 15*
Your hands established"; and it also says, "He brought them to His holy realm, *Ps. 78*
the mountain His right hand had acquired."

11. All that the Holy One, blessed be He, created in His world, He created solely
for His glory, as it is said, "All that is called by My name, it is for My glory that *Is. 43*
I created it, formed it and made it"; and it also says, "The Lord shall reign for *Ex. 15*
ever and ever."

Rabbi Ḥananya ben Akashya said: The Holy One, blessed be He, wanted to *Makkot 23b*
confer merit on Israel. That is why He gave them a copious Torah and many
commandments, as it is said, "It pleased the Lord, for the sake of [Israel's] *Is. 42*
righteousness, to make the Torah great and glorious."

If there is a minyan, mourners say the Rabbis' Kaddish (page 702).

ט אָמַר רַבִּי יוֹסֵי בֶּן קִסְמָא: פַּעַם אַחַת הָיִיתִי מְהַלֵּךְ בַּדֶּרֶךְ, וּפָגַע בִּי אָדָם
אֶחָד, וְנָתַן לִי שָׁלוֹם וְהֶחֱזַרְתִּי לוֹ שָׁלוֹם. אָמַר לִי, רַבִּי, מֵאֵיזֶה מָקוֹם אָתָּה.
אָמַרְתִּי לוֹ, מֵעִיר גְּדוֹלָה שֶׁל חֲכָמִים וְשֶׁל סוֹפְרִים אָנִי. אָמַר לִי, רַבִּי, רְצוֹנְךָ
שֶׁתָּדוּר עִמָּנוּ בִּמְקוֹמֵנוּ, וַאֲנִי אֶתֵּן לְךָ אֶלֶף אֲלָפִים דִּינְרֵי זָהָב וַאֲבָנִים
טוֹבוֹת וּמַרְגָּלִיּוֹת. אָמַרְתִּי לוֹ, אִם אַתָּה נוֹתֵן לִי כָּל כֶּסֶף וְזָהָב וַאֲבָנִים
טוֹבוֹת וּמַרְגָּלִיּוֹת שֶׁבָּעוֹלָם, אֵינִי דָר אֶלָּא בִּמְקוֹם תּוֹרָה, וְכֵן כָּתוּב בְּסֵפֶר
תְּהִלִּים עַל יְדֵי דָוִד מֶלֶךְ יִשְׂרָאֵל: טוֹב־לִי תוֹרַת־פִּיךָ מֵאַלְפֵי זָהָב וָכָסֶף: תהלים קיט
וְלֹא עוֹד, אֶלָּא שֶׁבִּשְׁעַת פְּטִירָתוֹ שֶׁל אָדָם, אֵין מְלַוִּין לוֹ לְאָדָם לֹא כֶסֶף
וְלֹא זָהָב וְלֹא אֲבָנִים טוֹבוֹת וּמַרְגָּלִיּוֹת, אֶלָּא תּוֹרָה וּמַעֲשִׂים טוֹבִים בִּלְבַד,
שֶׁנֶּאֱמַר: בְּהִתְהַלֶּכְךָ תַּנְחֶה אֹתָךְ, בְּשָׁכְבְּךָ תִּשְׁמֹר עָלֶיךָ, וַהֲקִיצוֹתָ הִיא משלי ו
תְשִׂיחֶךָ: בְּהִתְהַלֶּכְךָ תַּנְחֶה אֹתָךְ, בָּעוֹלָם הַזֶּה. בְּשָׁכְבְּךָ תִּשְׁמֹר עָלֶיךָ,
בַּקֶּבֶר. וַהֲקִיצוֹתָ הִיא תְשִׂיחֶךָ, לָעוֹלָם הַבָּא. וְאוֹמֵר: לִי הַכֶּסֶף וְלִי הַזָּהָב, חגי ב
נְאֻם יהוה צְבָאוֹת:

י חֲמִשָּׁה קִנְיָנִים קָנָה הַקָּדוֹשׁ בָּרוּךְ הוּא בְּעוֹלָמוֹ. וְאֵלּוּ הֵן, תּוֹרָה קִנְיָן אֶחָד,
שָׁמַיִם וָאָרֶץ קִנְיָן אֶחָד, אַבְרָהָם קִנְיָן אֶחָד, יִשְׂרָאֵל קִנְיָן אֶחָד, בֵּית הַמִּקְדָּשׁ
קִנְיָן אֶחָד. תּוֹרָה מִנַּיִן, דִּכְתִיב: יהוה קָנָנִי רֵאשִׁית דַּרְכּוֹ, קֶדֶם מִפְעָלָיו מֵאָז: משלי ח
שָׁמַיִם וָאָרֶץ מִנַּיִן, דִּכְתִיב: כֹּה אָמַר יהוה הַשָּׁמַיִם כִּסְאִי וְהָאָרֶץ הֲדֹם רַגְלָי, ישעיה סו
אֵי־זֶה בַיִת אֲשֶׁר תִּבְנוּ־לִי, וְאֵי־זֶה מָקוֹם מְנוּחָתִי: וְאוֹמֵר: מָה־רַבּוּ מַעֲשֶׂיךָ תהלים קד
יהוה, כֻּלָּם בְּחָכְמָה עָשִׂיתָ, מָלְאָה הָאָרֶץ קִנְיָנֶךָ: אַבְרָהָם מִנַּיִן, דִּכְתִיב:
וַיְבָרְכֵהוּ וַיֹּאמַר, בָּרוּךְ אַבְרָם לְאֵל עֶלְיוֹן, קֹנֵה שָׁמַיִם וָאָרֶץ: יִשְׂרָאֵל מִנַּיִן, בראשית יד
דִּכְתִיב: עַד־יַעֲבֹר עַמְּךָ יהוה, עַד־יַעֲבֹר עַם־זוּ קָנִיתָ: וְאוֹמֵר: לִקְדוֹשִׁים שמות טו תהלים טז
אֲשֶׁר־בָּאָרֶץ הֵמָּה, וְאַדִּירֵי כָּל־חֶפְצִי־בָם: בֵּית הַמִּקְדָּשׁ מִנַּיִן, דִּכְתִיב: מָכוֹן שמות טו
לְשִׁבְתְּךָ פָּעַלְתָּ יהוה, מִקְּדָשׁ אֲדֹנָי כּוֹנְנוּ יָדֶיךָ: וְאוֹמֵר: וַיְבִיאֵם אֶל־גְּבוּל תהלים עח
קָדְשׁוֹ, הַר־זֶה קָנְתָה יְמִינוֹ:

יא כָּל מַה שֶּׁבָּרָא הַקָּדוֹשׁ בָּרוּךְ הוּא בְּעוֹלָמוֹ, לֹא בְרָאוֹ אֶלָּא לִכְבוֹדוֹ, שֶׁנֶּאֱמַר:
כֹּל הַנִּקְרָא בִשְׁמִי וְלִכְבוֹדִי בְּרָאתִיו, יְצַרְתִּיו אַף־עֲשִׂיתִיו: וְאוֹמֵר: יהוה ישעיה מג שמות טו
יִמְלֹךְ לְעֹלָם וָעֶד:

רַבִּי חֲנַנְיָא בֶּן עֲקַשְׁיָא אוֹמֵר: רָצָה הַקָּדוֹשׁ בָּרוּךְ הוּא לְזַכּוֹת אֶת יִשְׂרָאֵל, לְפִיכָךְ מכות כג:
הִרְבָּה לָהֶם תּוֹרָה וּמִצְוֹת. שֶׁנֶּאֱמַר: יהוה חָפֵץ לְמַעַן צִדְקוֹ, יַגְדִּיל תּוֹרָה וְיַאְדִּיר: ישעיה מב

If there is a מנין, *mourners say* קדיש דרבנן *(page 703).*

Se'uda Shelishit for Shabbat

אַתְקִינוּ Prepare the feast of perfect faith, joy of the holy King.
Prepare the Royal feast,
this is the feast [mystically known as] "the Small Face,"
and "the Holy Ancient One" and "the Field of Holy Apples"
[mystical terms for aspects of the Divine]
come to partake in the feast with it.

Children of the palace
who yearn to see the radiance of "the Small Face,"
be here at this table in which the King is engraved.
Long to join this gathering together with the winged angels.
Rejoice now at this time of favor when there is no displeasure.
Come close to me, see my strength, for there are no harsh judgments:
Those brazen dogs are outside, unable to enter.
So I invite the holy Ancient of Days, His brow of desire
as the moment fades,
And His will is revealed, to annul all forces of impurity.
Hurl them into the abyss, hide them in the clefts of rocks,
For now, at Minḥa-time, is a time of joy for "the Small Face."

מִזְמוֹר לְדָוִד A psalm of David. *Ps. 23*
The Lord is my Shepherd, I shall not want.
He makes me lie down in green pastures.
He leads me beside the still waters. He refreshes my soul.
He guides me in the paths of righteousness
for His name's sake.
Though I walk through the valley of the shadow of death,
I will fear no evil, for You are with me;
Your rod and Your staff, they comfort me.
You set a table before me in the presence of my enemies;
You anoint my head with oil; my cup is filled to overflowing.
May goodness and kindness follow me all the days of my life,
and may I live in the House of the Lord for evermore.

סעודה שלישית של שבת

אַתְקֵינוּ סְעוּדָתָא דִמְהֵימְנוּתָא שְׁלִימְתָא, חֶדְוְתָא דְמַלְכָּא קַדִּישָׁא.
אַתְקֵינוּ סְעוּדָתָא דְמַלְכָּא.
דָּא הִיא סְעוּדָתָא דִזְעֵיר אַנְפִּין
וְעַתִּיקָא קַדִּישָׁא וַחֲקַל תַּפּוּחִין קַדִּישִׁין אָתַיִן לְסַעֲדָה בַּהֲדֵהּ.

בְּנֵי הֵיכְלָא, דִּכְסִיפִין לְמֶחֱזֵי זִיו זְעֵיר אַנְפִּין
יְהוֹן הָכָא, בְּהַאי תַּכָא, דְּבֵהּ מַלְכָּא בְּגִלּוּפִין.
צְבוּ לַחֲדָא, בְּהַאי וַעֲדָא, בְּגוֹ עִירִין וְכָל גַּדְפִּין.
חֲדוּ הַשְׁתָּא, בְּהַאי שַׁעְתָּא, דְּבֵהּ רַעֲוָא וְלֵית זַעֲפִין.
קְרִיבוּ לִי, חֲזוּ חֵילִי, דְּלֵית דִּינִין דְּתַקִּיפִין.
לְבַר נַטְלִין, וְלָא עָלִין, הָנֵי כַלְבִּין דַּחֲצִיפִין.
וְהָא אַזְמִין עַתִּיק יוֹמִין, לְמִצְחֵהּ עֲדֵי יְהוֹן חָלְפִין.
רְעוּ דִּי לֵהּ, דְּגַלֵּי לֵהּ, לְבַטָּלָה בְּכָל קְלִיפִין.
יְשַׁוֵּי לוֹן, בְּנִקְבְּהוֹן, וִיטַמְּרוּן בְּגוֹ כֵפִין.
אֲרֵי הַשְׁתָּא, בְּמִנְחָתָא, בְּחֶדְוְתָא דִזְעֵיר אַנְפִּין.

מִזְמוֹר לְדָוִד, יהוה רֹעִי לֹא אֶחְסָר: תהלים כג
בִּנְאוֹת דֶּשֶׁא יַרְבִּיצֵנִי, עַל־מֵי מְנֻחוֹת יְנַהֲלֵנִי:
נַפְשִׁי יְשׁוֹבֵב, יַנְחֵנִי בְמַעְגְּלֵי־צֶדֶק לְמַעַן שְׁמוֹ:
גַּם כִּי־אֵלֵךְ בְּגֵיא צַלְמָוֶת לֹא־אִירָא רָע, כִּי־אַתָּה עִמָּדִי
שִׁבְטְךָ וּמִשְׁעַנְתֶּךָ הֵמָּה יְנַחֲמֻנִי:
תַּעֲרֹךְ לְפָנַי שֻׁלְחָן נֶגֶד צֹרְרָי
דִּשַּׁנְתָּ בַשֶּׁמֶן רֹאשִׁי, כּוֹסִי רְוָיָה:
אַךְ טוֹב וָחֶסֶד יִרְדְּפוּנִי כָּל־יְמֵי חַיָּי
וְשַׁבְתִּי בְּבֵית־יהוה לְאֹרֶךְ יָמִים:

יְדִיד Beloved of the soul, Father of compassion, draw Your servant close to Your will. Like a deer will Your servant run and bow before Your beauty. To him Your love is sweeter than honey from the comb, than any taste.

הָדוּר Glorious, beautiful, radiance of the world, my soul is sick with love for You. Please, God, heal her now by showing her Your tender radiance. Then she will recover her strength and be healed, Be Your servant for eternity.

וָתִיק Ancient of Days, let Your mercy be aroused; please have pity on Your beloved child. How long have I yearned to see the glory of Your strength. Please, my God, my heart's desire – be quick; do not hide Yourself.

הִגָּלֵה Reveal Yourself, beloved, and spread over me the canopy of Your peace. Let the earth shine with Your glory, let us be overjoyed and rejoice in You. Hurry, beloved, for the appointed time has come, and be gracious to me as in the times of old.

אֵל מִסְתַּתֵּר God hides Himself in the beauty of concealment, His wisdom opaque to all human thought; Cause of causes, adorned with the highest crown, they [the angels] give You, LORD, a crown. / In the beginning was Your primordial Torah, inscribed with Your hermetic wisdom. Where can it be found? It is hidden. Wisdom begins in awe of the LORD. / Wider than a river, like never-ending streams, deep waters, that only an understanding man can draw, its outcomes are the fifty gates of understanding. The faithful are guarded by the LORD. / Great God, all eyes are turned toward You. Your great kindness is higher than the heavens. God of Abraham, remember Your servant, I will tell of the LORD's kindness, sing praises to the LORD. / Sublime, majestic in strength and might, who brings forth unparalleled light, "Awe of Isaac," make our judgment light. Forever, LORD, is Your might. / Who is like You, God, doing great deeds, Mighty One of Jacob, awesome in praise, Splendor of Israel, who listens to prayers, LORD who listens to those in need. / God, may the merit of the fathers be our shield. Eternal One of Israel, redeem us from distress. Draw us, raise us, from the pit of exile, that we may loudly sing in service at the House of the LORD. / From right and left the prophets were inspired, finding within them Eternity and Glory, known by the names of Yakhin and Boaz, and all your children shall be learned of the LORD. / Foundation, the Righteous, is hidden in Seven, the sign of the covenant to the world. Source of blessing, Righteous, Foundation of the world, righteous are You, LORD. / Restore, please, David and Solomon's kingdom, with the crown with which his mother crowned it. The congregation of Israel is sweetly called a bride, a crown of splendor in the hand of the LORD. / Mighty One, unite the ten Sefirot as one. Those who divide them from the LORD will see no light. Together they shine like sapphire. Bring my song close to You, the LORD.

Birkat HaMazon can be found on page 1028.
For Ma'ariv turn to page 366. For Havdala turn to page 382.

יְדִיד נֶפֶשׁ, אָב הָרַחֲמָן, מְשֹׁךְ עַבְדְּךָ אֶל רְצוֹנָךְ
יָרוּץ עַבְדְּךָ כְּמוֹ אַיָּל, יִשְׁתַּחֲוֶה מוּל הֲדָרָךְ
כִּי יֶעֱרַב לוֹ יְדִידוּתָךְ, מִנֹּפֶת צוּף וְכָל טָעַם.

הָדוּר, נָאֶה, זִיו הָעוֹלָם, נַפְשִׁי חוֹלַת אַהֲבָתָךְ
אָנָּא, אֵל נָא, רְפָא נָא לָהּ, בְּהַרְאוֹת לָהּ נֹעַם זִיוָךְ
אָז תִּתְחַזֵּק וְתִתְרַפֵּא, וְהָיְתָה לָךְ שִׁפְחַת עוֹלָם.

וָתִיק, יֶהֱמוּ רַחֲמֶיךָ, וְחוּס נָא עַל בֵּן אוֹהֲבָךְ
כִּי זֶה כַּמֶּה נִכְסֹף נִכְסַף לִרְאוֹת בְּתִפְאֶרֶת עֻזָּךְ
אָנָּא, אֵלִי, מַחְמַד לִבִּי, חוּשָׁה נָּא, וְאַל תִּתְעַלָּם.

הִגָּלֶה נָא וּפְרֹשׂ, חָבִיב, עָלַי אֶת סֻכַּת שְׁלוֹמָךְ
תָּאִיר אֶרֶץ מִכְּבוֹדָךְ, נָגִילָה וְנִשְׂמְחָה בָךְ
מַהֵר, אָהוּב, כִּי בָא מוֹעֵד, וְחָנֵּנִי כִּימֵי עוֹלָם.

אֵל מִסְתַּתֵּר בְּשַׁפְרִיר חֶבְיוֹן, הַשֵּׂכֶל הַנֶּעְלָם מִכָּל רַעְיוֹן, עִלַּת הָעִלּוֹת מֻכְתָּר בְּכֶתֶר עֶלְיוֹן, כֶּתֶר יִתְּנוּ לְךָ יהוה. / בְּרֵאשִׁית תּוֹרָתְךָ הַקְּדוּמָה, רְשׁוּמָה חָכְמָתְךָ הַסְּתוּמָה, מֵאַיִן תִּמָּצֵא וְהִיא נֶעְלָמָה, רֵאשִׁית חָכְמָה יִרְאַת יהוה. / רְחוֹבוֹת הַנָּהָר נַחֲלֵי אֱמוּנָה, מַיִם עֲמֻקִּים יִדְלֵם אִישׁ תְּבוּנָה, תּוֹצְאוֹתֶיהָ חֲמִשִּׁים שַׁעֲרֵי בִינָה, אֱמוּנִים נוֹצֵר יהוה. / הָאֵל הַגָּדוֹל עֵינֵי כֹל נֶגְדֶּךָ, רַב חֶסֶד גָּדוֹל עַל הַשָּׁמַיִם חַסְדֶּךָ, אֱלֹהֵי אַבְרָהָם זְכֹר לְעַבְדֶּךָ, חַסְדֵי יהוה אַזְכִּיר תְּהִלּוֹת יהוה. / מָרוֹם נֶאְדָּר בְּכֹחַ וּגְבוּרָה, מוֹצִיא אוֹרָה מֵאֵין תְּמוּרָה, פַּחַד יִצְחָק מִשְׁפָּטֵנוּ הָאִירָה, אַתָּה גִּבּוֹר לְעוֹלָם יהוה. / מִי אֵל כָּמוֹךָ עוֹשֶׂה גְדוֹלוֹת, אֲבִיר יַעֲקֹב נוֹרָא תְהִלּוֹת, תִּפְאֶרֶת יִשְׂרָאֵל שׁוֹמֵעַ תְּפִלּוֹת, כִּי שׁוֹמֵעַ אֶל אֶבְיוֹנִים יהוה. / יְהִי, זְכוּת אָבוֹת יָגֵן עָלֵינוּ, נֶצַח יִשְׂרָאֵל מִצָּרוֹתֵינוּ גְּאָלֵנוּ, וּמִבּוֹר גָּלוּת דְּלֵנוּ וְהַעֲלֵנוּ, לְנַצֵּחַ עַל מְלֶאכֶת בֵּית יהוה. / מִיָּמִין וּמִשְּׂמֹאל יְנִיקַת הַנְּבִיאִים, נֶצַח וָהוֹד מֵהֶם נִמְצָאִים, יָכִין וּבֹעַז בְּשֵׁם נִקְרָאִים, וְכָל בָּנַיִךְ לִמּוּדֵי יהוה. / יְסוֹד צַדִּיק בְּשִׁבְעָה נֶעְלָם, אוֹת בְּרִית הוּא לְעוֹלָם, מַעְיַן הַבְּרָכָה צַדִּיק יְסוֹד עוֹלָם, צַדִּיק אַתָּה יהוה. / נָא הָקֵם מַלְכוּת דָּוִד וּשְׁלֹמֹה, בָּעֲטָרָה שֶׁעִטְּרָה לּוֹ אִמּוֹ, כְּנֶסֶת יִשְׂרָאֵל כַּלָּה קְרוּאָה בִּנְעִימָה, עֲטֶרֶת תִּפְאֶרֶת בְּיַד יהוה. / חָזָק מְיַחֵד כְּאֶחָד עֶשֶׂר סְפִירוֹת, וּמַפְרִיד אַלּוּף לֹא יִרְאֶה מְאוֹרוֹת, סַפִּיר גִּזְרָתָם יַחַד מְאִירוֹת, תִּקְרַב רִנָּתִי לְפָנֶיךָ יהוה.

ברכת המזון *can be found on page 1029.*
For מעריב *turn to page 367. For* הבדלה *turn to page 383.*

מועדים
MO'ADIM

Blessing on Taking the Lulav

On Sukkot, except on Shabbat, the lulav and etrog are taken before Hallel.

Some say the following:

יְהִי רָצוֹן May it be Your will, LORD my God and God of my fathers, that through the fruit of the citron tree, the palm frond, the myrtle branches and willows of the brook, the letters of Your unique name draw close to one another and become united in my hand. Make it known I am called by Your name, so that [evil] will fear to come close to me. When I wave them, may a rich flow of blessings flow from the supreme Source of wisdom to the place of the Tabernacle and the site of the House of our God. May the command of these four species be considered by You as if I had fulfilled it in all its details and roots, as well as the 613 commandments dependent on it, for it is my intention to unify the name of the Holy One, blessed be He, and His Divine Presence, with fear and love, to unify the name *Yod-Heh* with *Vav-Heh*, in perfect unity in the name of all Israel, Amen. Blessed is the LORD forever, Amen and Amen. *Ps. 89*

The lulav is taken in the right hand, with the myrtle leaves on the right, willow leaves on the left. The etrog is taken in the left hand, with its pointed end toward the floor. Then say the following blessing:

בָּרוּךְ Blessed are You, LORD our God, King of the Universe,
who has made us holy through His commandments,
and has commanded us about taking the lulav.

On the first day the lulav is taken, add:

בָּרוּךְ Blessed are You, LORD our God, King of the Universe,
who has given us life, sustained us and brought us to this time.

Invert the etrog, so that its pointed end is facing up.
Face the front of the synagogue and wave the lulav and etrog
in the following sequence, three times in each direction:
ahead, right, back, left, up, down.
Continue to hold the lulav and etrog during Hallel.

סדר נטילת לולב

On סוכות*, except on* שבת*, the* לולב *and* אתרוג *are taken before* הלל*.*

Some say the following:

יְהִי רָצוֹן מִלְּפָנֶיךָ יהוה אֱלֹהַי וֵאלֹהֵי אֲבוֹתַי, בִּפְרִי עֵץ הָדָר וְכַפֹּת תְּמָרִים וַעֲנַף עֵץ עָבֹת וְעַרְבֵי נַחַל, אוֹתִיּוֹת שִׁמְךָ הַמְיֻחָד תְּקָרֵב אֶחָד אֶל אֶחָד וְהָיוּ לַאֲחָדִים בְּיָדִי, וְלֵידַע אֵיךְ שִׁמְךָ נִקְרָא עָלַי וְיִירְאוּ מִגֶּשֶׁת אֵלַי. וּבְנַעֲנוּעִי אוֹתָם תַּשְׁפִּיעַ שֶׁפַע בְּרָכוֹת מִדַּעַת עֶלְיוֹן לִנְוֵה אַפִּרְיוֹן לִמְכוֹן בֵּית אֱלֹהֵינוּ. וּתְהֵא חֲשׁוּבָה לְפָנֶיךָ מִצְוַת אַרְבָּעָה מִינִים אֵלּוּ כְּאִלּוּ קִיַּמְתִּיהָ בְּכָל פְּרָטוֹתֶיהָ וְשָׁרָשֶׁיהָ וְתַרְיַ״ג מִצְוֹת הַתְּלוּיוֹת בָּהּ, כִּי כַוָּנָתִי לְיַחֲדָא שְׁמָא דְקֻדְשָׁא בְּרִיךְ הוּא וּשְׁכִינְתֵּהּ בִּדְחִילוּ וּרְחִימוּ, לְיַחֵד שֵׁם י״ה בו״ה בְּיִחוּדָא שְׁלִים בְּשֵׁם כָּל יִשְׂרָאֵל, אָמֵן. בָּרוּךְ יהוה לְעוֹלָם, אָמֵן וְאָמֵן: תהלים פט

The לולב *is taken in the right hand, with the* הדסים *on the right,* ערבות *on the left. The* אתרוג *is taken in the left hand, with its pointed end toward the floor. Then say the following blessing:*

בָּרוּךְ אַתָּה יהוה אֱלֹהֵינוּ מֶלֶךְ הָעוֹלָם
אֲשֶׁר קִדְּשָׁנוּ בְּמִצְוֹתָיו וְצִוָּנוּ עַל נְטִילַת לוּלָב.

On the first day the לולב *is taken, add:*

בָּרוּךְ אַתָּה יהוה אֱלֹהֵינוּ מֶלֶךְ הָעוֹלָם
שֶׁהֶחֱיָנוּ וְקִיְּמָנוּ וְהִגִּיעָנוּ לַזְּמַן הַזֶּה.

Invert the אתרוג*, so that its pointed end is facing up.*
Face the front of the בית כנסת *and wave the* לולב *and* אתרוג
in the following sequence, three times in each direction:
ahead, right, back, left, up, down.
Continue to hold the לולב *and* אתרוג *during* הלל*.*

Hallel

On Ḥanukka, Ḥol HaMo'ed Sukkot, Yom HaAtzma'ut and Yom Yerushalayim, Full Hallel is said. On Ḥol HaMo'ed Pesaḥ and on Rosh Ḥodesh Half Hallel is said.

בָּרוּךְ Blessed are You, LORD our God, King of the Universe,
who has made us holy through His commandments
and has commanded us to recite the Hallel.

הַלְלוּיָהּ Halleluya! Servants of the LORD, give praise; praise the name of the LORD. Blessed be the name of the LORD now and for evermore. From the rising of the sun to its setting, may the LORD's name be praised. High is the LORD above all nations; His glory is above the heavens. Who is like the LORD our God, who sits enthroned so high, yet turns so low to see the heavens and the earth? ▸ He raises the poor from the dust and the needy from the refuse heap, giving them a place alongside princes, the princes of His people. He makes the woman in a childless house a happy mother of children. Halleluya! *Ps. 113*

LEARNING

Hallel is a collection of chapters from the book of *Tehillim*, containing praise of Hashem and His role in history, that we say on festivals throughout the year. These days are: Pesaḥ, Shavuot, Sukkot, Ḥanukka, Yom HaAtzma'ut, and Yom Yerushalayim. On the last six days of Pesaḥ and Rosh Ḥodesh, the third and fifth paragraph (*Tehillim* 115:1–11 and 116:1–11) are not said. This is called "Half Hallel."

CONNECTION

"The sanctity of time spreads throughout the entire span of time – blessed is the LORD every single day – and the rays of the lights of holiness are drawn in a concealed fashion until they become manifest in sacred times: in the sanctity of Shabbat, the first of the holy convocations, the source of sanctity which showers holiness upon the world and Israel; and in the sanctity of the festivals, which receive the emanation of holiness through Israel, who sanctify the festivals."

(Rav Kook, *Orot HaKodesh* II)

סדר הלל

On חנוכה, חול המועד סוכות, יום העצמאות *and* יום ירושלים, הלל שלם *is said.*
On ראש חודש *and on* חול המועד פסח, הלל בדילוג *is said.*

בָּרוּךְ אַתָּה יהוה אֱלֹהֵינוּ מֶלֶךְ הָעוֹלָם
אֲשֶׁר קִדְּשָׁנוּ בְּמִצְוֹתָיו וְצִוָּנוּ לִקְרֹא אֶת הַהַלֵּל.

הַלְלוּיָהּ, הַלְלוּ עַבְדֵי יהוה, הַלְלוּ אֶת־שֵׁם יהוה: יְהִי שֵׁם יהוה תהלים קיג
מְבֹרָךְ, מֵעַתָּה וְעַד־עוֹלָם: מִמִּזְרַח־שֶׁמֶשׁ עַד־מְבוֹאוֹ, מְהֻלָּל
שֵׁם יהוה: רָם עַל־כָּל־גּוֹיִם יהוה, עַל הַשָּׁמַיִם כְּבוֹדוֹ: מִי כַּיהוה
אֱלֹהֵינוּ, הַמַּגְבִּיהִי לָשָׁבֶת: הַמַּשְׁפִּילִי לִרְאוֹת, בַּשָּׁמַיִם וּבָאָרֶץ:
› מְקִימִי מֵעָפָר דָּל, מֵאַשְׁפֹּת יָרִים אֶבְיוֹן: לְהוֹשִׁיבִי עִם־נְדִיבִים,
עִם נְדִיבֵי עַמּוֹ: מוֹשִׁיבִי עֲקֶרֶת הַבַּיִת, אֵם־הַבָּנִים שְׂמֵחָה,
הַלְלוּיָהּ:

REFLECTION

"God is where you let Him in."
(The Kotzker Rebbe)

Where is God?

When is God?

Where is God in your life?

... A THOUSAND WORDS

בְּצֵאת When Israel came out of Egypt, the house of Jacob from a people of foreign tongue, Judah became His sanctuary, Israel His dominion. The sea saw and fled; the Jordan turned back. The mountains skipped like rams, the hills like lambs. ▸ Why was it, sea, that you fled? Jordan, why did you turn back? Why, mountains, did you skip like rams, and you, hills, like lambs? It was at the presence of the Lord, Creator of the earth, at the presence of the God of Jacob, who turned the rock into a pool of water, flint into a flowing spring. *Ps. 114*

REFLECTION

What do the festivals tell us about the essence of Judaism?

What is your favorite festival? Why?

... A THOUSAND WORDS

תהלים קיד בְּצֵאת יִשְׂרָאֵל מִמִּצְרָיִם, בֵּית יַעֲקֹב מֵעַם לֹעֵז: הָיְתָה יְהוּדָה
לְקָדְשׁוֹ, יִשְׂרָאֵל מַמְשְׁלוֹתָיו: הַיָּם רָאָה וַיָּנֹס, הַיַּרְדֵּן יִסֹּב לְאָחוֹר:
הֶהָרִים רָקְדוּ כְאֵילִים, גְּבָעוֹת כִּבְנֵי־צֹאן: ◂ מַה־לְּךָ הַיָּם כִּי תָנוּס,
הַיַּרְדֵּן תִּסֹּב לְאָחוֹר: הֶהָרִים תִּרְקְדוּ כְאֵילִים, גְּבָעוֹת כִּבְנֵי־צֹאן:
מִלִּפְנֵי אָדוֹן חוּלִי אָרֶץ, מִלִּפְנֵי אֱלוֹהַּ יַעֲקֹב: הַהֹפְכִי הַצּוּר אֲגַם־
מָיִם, חַלָּמִישׁ לְמַעְיְנוֹ־מָיִם:

CONNECTION

Every drop of rain that falls in Sahara Desert says it all,
It's a miracle,
All God's creations great and small, the Golden Gate and the Taj Mahal,
That's a miracle,
Test tube babies being born, mothers, fathers dead and gone,
It's a miracle,
We're having a miracle on earth, mother nature does it all for us,
The wonders of this world go on, the hanging Gardens of Babylon,
Captain Cook and Cain and Abel, Jimi Hendrix to the Tower of Babel
It's a miracle, it's a miracle, it's a miracle, it's a miracle,
The one thing we're all waiting for, is peace on earth – an end to war,
It's a miracle we need – the miracle, the miracle we're all waiting for today,
If every leaf on every tree, could tell a story that would be a miracle,
If every child on every street, had clothes to wear and food to eat,
That's a miracle,
If all God's people could be free, to live in perfect harmony,
It's a miracle, we're having a miracle on earth,
Mother nature does it all for us
Open hearts and surgery, Sunday mornings with a cup of tea,
Super powers always fighting,
But Mona Lisa just keeps on smiling,
The wonders of this world go on,
It's a miracle, it's a miracle, it's a miracle, it's a miracle,
The one thing we're all waiting for, is peace on earth and an end to war,
It's a miracle we need, the miracle, the miracle,
Peace on earth and end to war today,
That time will come one day you'll see when we can all be friends…

(Queen, "The Miracle")

Omit on Rosh Ḥodesh (except on Ḥanukka) and on Ḥol HaMo'ed Pesaḥ:

לֹא לָנוּ Not to us, LORD, not to us, but to Your name give glory, for Your love, for Your truthfulness. Why should the nations say, "Where now is their God?" Our God is in heaven; whatever He wills He does. Their idols are silver and gold, made by human hands. They have mouths but cannot speak; eyes but cannot see. They have ears but cannot hear; noses but cannot smell. They have hands but cannot feel; feet but cannot walk. No sound comes from their throat. Those who make them become like them; so will all who trust in them. ‣ Israel, trust in the LORD – He is their Help and their Shield. House of Aaron, trust in the LORD – He is their Help and their Shield. You who fear the LORD, trust in the LORD – He is their Help and their Shield. Ps. 115

יהוה זְכָרָנוּ The LORD remembers us and will bless us. He will bless the house of Israel. He will bless the house of Aaron. He will bless those who fear the LORD, small and great alike. May the LORD give you increase: you and your children. May you be blessed by the LORD, Maker of heaven and earth. ‣ The heavens are the LORD's, but the earth He has given over to mankind. It is not the dead who praise the LORD, nor those who go down to the silent grave. But we will bless the LORD, now and for ever. Halleluya!

---

from you," he exclaimed. Yehoshua stepped forward and said to him, "Tell me about the modern-day army of the Jewish People; I heard they say it is one of the most powerful armies in the world!" Rabbi Yosef Karo called out, "I want to hear about how halakha has developed over the last 450 years!" Einstein then stepped forward and said, "I want to hear about the amazing advances in science that your generation has achieved, and if my theories have been proved correct." Rabbi Akiva took the boy's hand and said, "My son, I dreamed of the time when the biblical prophecies of a return to Eretz Yisrael *would be fulfilled, and you are living through it. Tell me about it!" And the boy realized just how lucky he was to be a Jew at the beginning of the twenty-first century.*

REFLECTION

"The earth and all its contents is the LORD's, the world, and all its inhabitants."
(*Tehillim* 24:1)

"The LORD God took the man, and placed him in the Garden of Eden to cultivate it and to keep it."
(*Bereshit* 2:15)

To whom does the earth really belong? Us or Hashem?

What are the practical ramifications of the way we answer this question?

Omit on ראש חודש (*except on* חנוכה) *and on* חול המועד פסח:

תהלים קטו

לֹא לָנוּ יהוה לֹא לָנוּ, כִּי־לְשִׁמְךָ תֵּן כָּבוֹד, עַל־חַסְדְּךָ עַל־אֲמִתֶּךָ: לָמָּה יֹאמְרוּ הַגּוֹיִם אַיֵּה־נָא אֱלֹהֵיהֶם: וֵאלֹהֵינוּ בַשָּׁמָיִם, כֹּל אֲשֶׁר־חָפֵץ עָשָׂה: עֲצַבֵּיהֶם כֶּסֶף וְזָהָב, מַעֲשֵׂה יְדֵי אָדָם: פֶּה־לָהֶם וְלֹא יְדַבֵּרוּ, עֵינַיִם לָהֶם וְלֹא יִרְאוּ: אָזְנַיִם לָהֶם וְלֹא יִשְׁמָעוּ, אַף לָהֶם וְלֹא יְרִיחוּן: יְדֵיהֶם וְלֹא יְמִישׁוּן, רַגְלֵיהֶם וְלֹא יְהַלֵּכוּ, לֹא־יֶהְגּוּ בִּגְרוֹנָם: כְּמוֹהֶם יִהְיוּ עֹשֵׂיהֶם, כֹּל אֲשֶׁר־בֹּטֵחַ בָּהֶם: ◂ יִשְׂרָאֵל בְּטַח בַּיהוה, עֶזְרָם וּמָגִנָּם הוּא: בֵּית אַהֲרֹן בִּטְחוּ בַיהוה, עֶזְרָם וּמָגִנָּם הוּא: יִרְאֵי יהוה בִּטְחוּ בַיהוה, עֶזְרָם וּמָגִנָּם הוּא:

יהוה זְכָרָנוּ יְבָרֵךְ, יְבָרֵךְ אֶת־בֵּית יִשְׂרָאֵל, יְבָרֵךְ אֶת־בֵּית אַהֲרֹן: יְבָרֵךְ יִרְאֵי יהוה, הַקְּטַנִּים עִם־הַגְּדֹלִים: יֹסֵף יהוה עֲלֵיכֶם, עֲלֵיכֶם וְעַל־בְּנֵיכֶם: בְּרוּכִים אַתֶּם לַיהוה, עֹשֵׂה שָׁמַיִם וָאָרֶץ: ◂ הַשָּׁמַיִם שָׁמַיִם לַיהוה, וְהָאָרֶץ נָתַן לִבְנֵי־אָדָם: לֹא הַמֵּתִים יְהַלְלוּ־יָהּ, וְלֹא כָּל־יֹרְדֵי דוּמָה: וַאֲנַחְנוּ נְבָרֵךְ יָהּ, מֵעַתָּה וְעַד־עוֹלָם, הַלְלוּיָהּ:

CONNECTION

There was once a boy who had a dream. In the dream he dreamt that he was walking down a long and winding path, and at every turn in the path stood a familiar character from Jewish history. First Avraham, then Moshe, then Yehoshua, then Devora, then David, Shlomo, Eliyahu HaNavi, Ezra, and Esther. Each time the boy stopped to converse with a character he had learnt so much about, and ask them the questions he had always wished he could. The path continued to wind its way. Rabbi Akiva, Hillel and Shamai, Rashi, Rambam, Rabbi Yosef Karo, and the Ba'al Shem Tov. Each time he would jump with excitement as he told the character how much he wished he had lived in their period of Jewish history. As he walked on, the faces became more familiar to him, as he had seen photographs and needed no introduction, to Herzl, David Ben-Gurion, Albert Einstein, Golda Meir, and Rabbi Soloveitchik. As he neared the end of the path he saw a crowd waiting for him, every personality he had met along the way was waiting for him at the end. But this time they were eager to ask him questions. About his life, and Jewish life in the twenty-first century. He was puzzled at their interest and excitement. "Why are you interested in me and my age?" he asked them. "You lived in the most important periods of Jewish history, I have so much more to learn

Omit on Rosh Ḥodesh (except on Ḥanukka) and on Ḥol HaMo'ed Pesaḥ:

אָהַבְתִּי I love the LORD, for He hears my voice, my pleas. He turns His ear to me whenever I call. The bonds of death encompassed me, the anguish of the grave came upon me, I was overcome by trouble and sorrow. Then I called on the name of the LORD: "LORD, I pray, save my life." Generous is the LORD, and righteous; our God is full of compassion. The LORD protects the simple hearted. When I was brought low, He saved me. My soul, be at peace once more, for the LORD has been good to you. For You have rescued me from death, my eyes from weeping, my feet from stumbling. ‣ I shall walk in the presence of the LORD in the land of the living. I had faith, even when I said, "I am greatly afflicted," even when I said rashly, "All men are liars." Ps. 116

מָה־אָשִׁיב How can I repay the LORD for all His goodness to me? I will lift the cup of salvation and call on the name of the LORD. I will fulfill my vows to the LORD in the presence of all His people. Grievous in the LORD's sight is the death of His devoted ones. Truly, LORD, I am Your servant; I am Your servant, the son of Your maidservant. You set me free from my chains. ‣ To You I shall bring a thanksgiving-offering and call on the LORD by name. I will fulfill my vows to the LORD in the presence of all His people, in the courts of the House of the LORD, in your midst, Jerusalem. Halleluya!

הַלְלוּ Praise the LORD, all nations; acclaim Him, all you peoples; Ps. 117
for His loving-kindness to us is strong,
and the LORD's truthfulness is everlasting.
Halleluya!

REFLECTION

"Man creates many coins from one press and each coin is exactly the same. But Hashem, the King of kings, creates all of mankind from one man [Adam], and each person is totally unique!"
(*Mishna Sanhedrin* 4:5)

Are all religions the same?

Are all people the same?

What makes us different?

What makes us the same?

Omit on ראש חודש (*except on* חנוכה) *and on* חול המועד פסח:

תהלים קטז אָהַבְתִּי, כִּי־יִשְׁמַע יהוה, אֶת־קוֹלִי תַּחֲנוּנָי: כִּי־הִטָּה אָזְנוֹ לִי, וּבְיָמַי
אֶקְרָא: אֲפָפוּנִי חֶבְלֵי־מָוֶת, וּמְצָרֵי שְׁאוֹל מְצָאוּנִי, צָרָה וְיָגוֹן אֶמְצָא:
וּבְשֵׁם־יהוה אֶקְרָא, אָנָּה יהוה מַלְּטָה נַפְשִׁי: חַנּוּן יהוה וְצַדִּיק, וֵאלֹהֵינוּ
מְרַחֵם: שֹׁמֵר פְּתָאִים יהוה, דַּלּוֹתִי וְלִי יְהוֹשִׁיעַ: שׁוּבִי נַפְשִׁי לִמְנוּחָיְכִי,
כִּי־יהוה גָּמַל עָלָיְכִי: כִּי חִלַּצְתָּ נַפְשִׁי מִמָּוֶת, אֶת־עֵינִי מִן־דִּמְעָה, אֶת־
רַגְלִי מִדֶּחִי: › אֶתְהַלֵּךְ לִפְנֵי יהוה, בְּאַרְצוֹת הַחַיִּים: הֶאֱמַנְתִּי כִּי אֲדַבֵּר,
אֲנִי עָנִיתִי מְאֹד: אֲנִי אָמַרְתִּי בְחָפְזִי, כָּל־הָאָדָם כֹּזֵב:

מָה־אָשִׁיב לַיהוה, כָּל־תַּגְמוּלוֹהִי עָלָי: כּוֹס־יְשׁוּעוֹת אֶשָּׂא, וּבְשֵׁם
יהוה אֶקְרָא: נְדָרַי לַיהוה אֲשַׁלֵּם, נֶגְדָה־נָּא לְכָל־עַמּוֹ: יָקָר בְּעֵינֵי
יהוה, הַמָּוְתָה לַחֲסִידָיו: אָנָּה יהוה כִּי־אֲנִי עַבְדֶּךָ, אֲנִי־עַבְדְּךָ
בֶּן־אֲמָתֶךָ, פִּתַּחְתָּ לְמוֹסֵרָי: › לְךָ־אֶזְבַּח זֶבַח תּוֹדָה, וּבְשֵׁם יהוה
אֶקְרָא: נְדָרַי לַיהוה אֲשַׁלֵּם, נֶגְדָה־נָּא לְכָל־עַמּוֹ: בְּחַצְרוֹת בֵּית
יהוה, בְּתוֹכֵכִי יְרוּשָׁלָםִ, הַלְלוּיָהּ:

תהלים קיז הַלְלוּ אֶת־יהוה כָּל־גּוֹיִם, שַׁבְּחוּהוּ כָּל־הָאֻמִּים:
כִּי גָבַר עָלֵינוּ חַסְדּוֹ, וֶאֱמֶת־יהוה לְעוֹלָם, הַלְלוּיָהּ:

… A THOUSAND WORDS

The following verses are chanted by the Leader. At the end of each verse, the congregation responds, "Thank the Lord for He is good; His loving-kindness is for ever."

On Sukkot, the lulav and etrog are waved, three waves for each word of the verse (except God's name). On the first word, wave forward, then, on the following words, wave right, back, left, up and down respectively. The Leader waves only for the first two verses. The congregation waves each time the first verse is said in response.

הודו Thank the Lord for He is good; His loving-kindness is for ever. Ps. 118
Let Israel say His loving-kindness is for ever.
Let the house of Aaron say His loving-kindness is for ever.
Let those who fear the Lord say His loving-kindness is for ever.

מִן־הַמֵּצַר In my distress I called on the Lord. The Lord answered me and set me free. The Lord is with me; I will not be afraid. What can man do to me? The Lord is with me. He is my Helper. I will see the downfall of my enemies. It is better to take refuge in the Lord than to trust in man. It is better to take refuge in the Lord than to trust in princes. The nations all surrounded me, but in the Lord's name I drove them off. They surrounded me on every side, but in the Lord's name I drove them off. They surrounded me like bees, they attacked me as fire attacks brushwood, but in the Lord's name I drove them off. They thrust so hard against me, I nearly fell, but the Lord came to my help. The Lord is my strength and my song; He has become my salvation. Sounds of song and salvation resound in the tents of the righteous: "The Lord's right hand has done mighty deeds. The Lord's right hand is lifted high. The Lord's right hand has done mighty deeds." I will not die but live, and tell what the Lord has done. The Lord has punished me severely, but He has not given me over to death. ▸ Open for me the gates of righteousness that I may enter them and thank the Lord. This is the gateway to the Lord; through it, the righteous shall enter.

... A THOUSAND WORDS

LEARNING

The word **הודו** (*hodu*) means thank (as in **תּוֹדָה**/*toda*) and is related to the name Yehuda. Leah chose this name for her son to thank God for his birth (*Bereshit* 29:35). The Hebrew word for a "Jew" is *Yehudi*. The implication is clear – to be a Jew means to be thankful!

The following verses are chanted by the שליח ציבור.
At the end of each verse, the קהל *responds:* הוֹדוּ לַיהוה כִּי־טוֹב, כִּי לְעוֹלָם חַסְדּוֹ.
On סוכות, *the* לולב *and* אתרוג *are waved, three waves for each word of the verse (except God's name). On the first word, wave forward, then, on the following words, wave right, back, left, up and down respectively. The* שליח ציבור *waves only for the first two verses. The* קהל *waves each time the first verse is said in response.*

תהלים קיח

הוֹדוּ לַיהוה כִּי־טוֹב כִּי לְעוֹלָם חַסְדּוֹ:
יֹאמַר־נָא יִשְׂרָאֵל כִּי לְעוֹלָם חַסְדּוֹ:
יֹאמְרוּ־נָא בֵית־אַהֲרֹן כִּי לְעוֹלָם חַסְדּוֹ:
יֹאמְרוּ־נָא יִרְאֵי יהוה כִּי לְעוֹלָם חַסְדּוֹ:

מִן־הַמֵּצַר קָרָֽאתִי יָּהּ, עָנָֽנִי בַמֶּרְחָב יָהּ: יהוה לִי לֹא אִירָא, מַה־יַּעֲשֶׂה לִי אָדָם: יהוה לִי בְּעֹזְרָי, וַאֲנִי אֶרְאֶה בְשֹׂנְאָי: טוֹב לַחֲסוֹת בַּיהוה, מִבְּטֹחַ בָּאָדָם: טוֹב לַחֲסוֹת בַּיהוה, מִבְּטֹחַ בִּנְדִיבִים: כָּל־גּוֹיִם סְבָבוּנִי, בְּשֵׁם יהוה כִּי אֲמִילַם: סַבּוּנִי גַם־סְבָבוּנִי, בְּשֵׁם יהוה כִּי אֲמִילַם: סַבּוּנִי כִדְבֹרִים, דֹּעֲכוּ כְּאֵשׁ קוֹצִים, בְּשֵׁם יהוה כִּי אֲמִילַם: דָּחֹה דְחִיתַֽנִי לִנְפֹּל, וַיהוה עֲזָרָֽנִי: עָזִּי וְזִמְרָת יָהּ, וַיְהִי־לִי לִישׁוּעָה: קוֹל רִנָּה וִישׁוּעָה בְּאָהֳלֵי צַדִּיקִים, יְמִין יהוה עֹֽשָׂה חָֽיִל: יְמִין יהוה רוֹמֵמָה, יְמִין יהוה עֹֽשָׂה חָֽיִל: לֹא־אָמוּת כִּי־אֶחְיֶה, וַאֲסַפֵּר מַעֲשֵׂי יָהּ: יַסֹּר יִסְּרַֽנִּי יָּהּ, וְלַמָּֽוֶת לֹא נְתָנָֽנִי: › פִּתְחוּ־לִי שַׁעֲרֵי־צֶֽדֶק, אָבֹא־בָם אוֹדֶה יָהּ: זֶה־הַשַּֽׁעַר לַיהוה, צַדִּיקִים יָבֹֽאוּ בוֹ:

CONNECTION

"The catastrophe which recently befell the Jewish People – the massacre of millions of Jews in Europe – was another clear demonstration of the urgency of solving the problem of its homelessness by re-establishing in Eretz-Israel the Jewish State, which would open the gates of the homeland wide to every Jew and confer upon the Jewish People the status of a fully privileged member of the comity of nations.

"Survivors of the Nazi holocaust in Europe, as well as Jews from other parts of the world, continued to migrate to Eretz-Israel, undaunted by difficulties, restrictions and dangers, and never ceased to assert their right to a life of dignity, freedom and honest toil in their national homeland."

(Excerpt from "The Declaration of the Establishment of the State of Israel," May 14, 1948)

אוֹדְךָ I will thank You, for You answered me, and became my salvation.
I will thank You, for You answered me, and became my salvation.

The stone the builders rejected has become the main cornerstone.
The stone the builders rejected has become the main cornerstone.

This is the LORD's doing; it is miraculous in our eyes.
This is the LORD's doing; it is miraculous in our eyes.

This is the day the LORD has made; let us rejoice and be glad in it.
This is the day the LORD has made; let us rejoice and be glad in it.

On Sukkot, the lulav and etrog are waved while saying "LORD, please, save us," three waves for each word of the verse (except God's name). On the first word, wave forward and right; third word: back and left; fourth word: up and down.

Leader followed by congregation:

אָנָּא LORD, please, save us.
LORD, please, save us.
LORD, please, give us success.
LORD, please, give us success.

CONNECTION

"...[The Holy Land is] a desolate country whose soil is rich enough, but is given over wholly to weeds...a silent mournful expanse...a desolation...we never saw a human being on the whole route...hardly a tree or shrub anywhere. Even the olive tree and the cactus, those fast friends of a worthless soil, had almost deserted the country."

(Mark Twain, *Innocents Abroad*, 1869)

Today, the State of Israel has a population of more than eight million people. Israel boasts three major metropolitan areas, Tel Aviv, Haifa, and Be'er Sheva, in addition to its capital and Israel's largest city, Jerusalem. Dozens of Israeli cities now have a population of over 100,000 people. Israel's economy is one of the fastest growing and most stable in the world, with the second largest number of start-up companies and NASDAQ-listed companies outside of the United States. Despite having limited natural resources, intensive development of the agricultural and industrial sectors has made Israel largely self-sufficient in food production. Israel's population is one of the most educated in the world, and leads the world in various areas of scientific and technological research. Not to mention the pride Israelis take in their culture and arts. A lot has changed in the last 150 years...

אוֹדְךָ כִּי עֲנִיתָנִי, וַתְּהִי־לִי לִישׁוּעָה:
אוֹדְךָ כִּי עֲנִיתָנִי, וַתְּהִי־לִי לִישׁוּעָה:
אֶבֶן מָאֲסוּ הַבּוֹנִים, הָיְתָה לְרֹאשׁ פִּנָּה:
אֶבֶן מָאֲסוּ הַבּוֹנִים, הָיְתָה לְרֹאשׁ פִּנָּה:
מֵאֵת יהוה הָיְתָה זֹּאת, הִיא נִפְלָאת בְּעֵינֵינוּ:
מֵאֵת יהוה הָיְתָה זֹּאת, הִיא נִפְלָאת בְּעֵינֵינוּ:
זֶה־הַיּוֹם עָשָׂה יהוה, נָגִילָה וְנִשְׂמְחָה בוֹ:
זֶה־הַיּוֹם עָשָׂה יהוה, נָגִילָה וְנִשְׂמְחָה בוֹ:

On סוכות*, the* לולב *and* אתרוג *are waved while saying* אָנָּא יהוה הוֹשִׁיעָה נָּא*, three waves for each word of the verse (except God's name). On the first word, wave forward and right; third word: back and left; fourth word: up and down.*

שליח ציבור *followed by* קהל*:*

אָנָּא יהוה הוֹשִׁיעָה נָּא:
אָנָּא יהוה הוֹשִׁיעָה נָּא:
אָנָּא יהוה הַצְלִיחָה נָּא:
אָנָּא יהוה הַצְלִיחָה נָּא:

REFLECTION

Which are the days
in your personal calendar
you most want to thank
Hashem for?

Which are the days
in our national calendar
you most want to thank
Hashem for?

...A THOUSAND WORDS

בָּרוּךְ Blessed is one who comes in the name of the Lord;
we bless you from the House of the Lord.
Blessed is one who comes in the name of the Lord;
we bless you from the House of the Lord.

The Lord is God; He has given us light. Bind the festival offering
with thick cords [and bring it] to the horns of the altar.
The Lord is God; He has given us light. Bind the festival offering
with thick cords [and bring it] to the horns of the altar.

You are my God and I will thank You; You are my God, I will elevate You.
You are my God and I will thank You; You are my God, I will elevate You.

Thank the Lord for He is good; His loving-kindness is for ever.
Thank the Lord for He is good; His loving-kindness is for ever.

יְהַלְלוּךָ All Your works will praise You, Lord our God,
and Your devoted ones –
the righteous who do Your will,
together with all Your people the house of Israel –
will joyously thank, bless, praise, glorify,
elevate, fear, sanctify, and declare
the sovereignty of Your name, our King.
▸ For it is good to thank You and fitting to sing psalms to Your name,
for from eternity to eternity You are God.
Blessed are You, Lord, King who is celebrated with praises.

On Rosh Ḥodesh and Ḥol HaMo'ed, say Full Kaddish on page 244 and continue the service with the Reading of the Torah on page 220 (on Hoshana Raba on page 626).

On Sukkot some say at this point Hoshanot on page 880, then Full Kaddish on page 244.

On Shabbat the service continues with Full Kaddish on page 624.

On weekday Ḥanukka (except Rosh Ḥodesh Tevet), Yom HaAtzma'ut and Yom Yerushalayim, the service continues with Half Kaddish on page 218.

are meant to be read. But *Tehillim*, Psalms, are meant to be said. Traditionally, *Tehillim* are recited, unlike any of the other books of the Bible.... People have historically turned to *Tehillim* in times of woe as well as in times of joy." (Rabbi Tzvi Hersh Weinreb)

בָּרוּךְ הַבָּא בְּשֵׁם יהוה, בֵּרַכְנוּכֶם מִבֵּית יהוה:
בָּרוּךְ הַבָּא בְּשֵׁם יהוה, בֵּרַכְנוּכֶם מִבֵּית יהוה:

אֵל יהוה וַיָּאֶר לָנוּ, אִסְרוּ־חַג בַּעֲבֹתִים עַד־קַרְנוֹת הַמִּזְבֵּחַ:
אֵל יהוה וַיָּאֶר לָנוּ, אִסְרוּ־חַג בַּעֲבֹתִים עַד־קַרְנוֹת הַמִּזְבֵּחַ:

אֵלִי אַתָּה וְאוֹדֶךָּ, אֱלֹהַי אֲרוֹמְמֶךָּ:
אֵלִי אַתָּה וְאוֹדֶךָּ, אֱלֹהַי אֲרוֹמְמֶךָּ:

הוֹדוּ לַיהוה כִּי־טוֹב, כִּי לְעוֹלָם חַסְדּוֹ:
הוֹדוּ לַיהוה כִּי־טוֹב, כִּי לְעוֹלָם חַסְדּוֹ:

יְהַלְלְוּךָ יהוה אֱלֹהֵינוּ כָּל מַעֲשֶׂיךָ
וַחֲסִידֶיךָ צַדִּיקִים עוֹשֵׂי רְצוֹנֶךָ
וְכָל עַמְּךָ בֵּית יִשְׂרָאֵל
בְּרִנָּה יוֹדוּ וִיבָרְכוּ וִישַׁבְּחוּ וִיפָאֲרוּ וִירוֹמְמוּ וְיַעֲרִיצוּ וְיַקְדִּישׁוּ
וְיַמְלִיכוּ אֶת שִׁמְךָ מַלְכֵּנוּ
◂ כִּי לְךָ טוֹב לְהוֹדוֹת וּלְשִׁמְךָ נָאֶה לְזַמֵּר
כִּי מֵעוֹלָם וְעַד עוֹלָם אַתָּה אֵל.
בָּרוּךְ אַתָּה יהוה, מֶלֶךְ מְהֻלָּל בַּתִּשְׁבָּחוֹת.

On ראש חודש *and* חול המועד, *say* קדיש שלם *on page 245*
and continue the service with קריאת התורה *on page 221 (on* הושענא רבה *on page 627).*

On סוכות *some say at this point* הושענות *on page 881,*
then קדיש שלם *on page 245.*

On שבת *the service continues with* קדיש שלם *on page 625.*

On weekday חנוכה *(except* ראש חודש טבת*),* יום העצמאות *and* יום ירושלים*,*
the service continues with חצי קדיש *on page 219.*

LEARNING

"It has been said that the Five Books of the Torah are meant to be studied, the Prophets are meant to be heard, the [Writings,] Ketuvim such as Job or the book of Esther

Musaf for Rosh Ḥodesh

THE AMIDA

The following prayer, until "in former years" on page 852, is said silently, standing with feet together. If there is a minyan, the Amida is repeated aloud by the Leader. Take three steps forward as if formally entering the place of the Divine Presence.

When I declare the LORD's name, give glory to our God. Deut. 32

O LORD, open my lips, so that my mouth may declare Your praise. Ps. 51

PATRIARCHS

בָּרוּךְ Blessed are You,
LORD our God and God of our fathers,
God of Abraham, God of Isaac and God of Jacob;
the great, mighty and awesome God, God Most High,
who acts with loving-kindness and creates all,
who remembers the loving-kindness of the fathers and will bring a Redeemer to their children's children
for the sake of His name, in love.
King, Helper, Savior, Shield:
Blessed are You, LORD, Shield of Abraham.

DIVINE MIGHT

אַתָּה גִּבּוֹר You are eternally mighty, LORD.
You give life to the dead and have great power to save.

---

the testimony of two witnesses who testified that they actually saw the first sliver of the newly reborn moon in the sky. There is a strong message contained in this ritual process. The new month, and thereby the festivals and the Jewish calendar, are established by man – not by God, or by nature. Through the power of the calendar, God has placed control of the Jewish People's identity and unity in its own hands.

In the time of the *Beit HaMikdash* all biblical festivals, including Rosh Ḥodesh, had an additional sacrificial service called *musaf*. Since the destruction of the *Beit HaMikdash* the *musaf* offering has been replaced with the Musaf service. The Musaf service for Rosh Ḥodesh consists of an *Amida* prayer that has a central *berakha* that expresses our yearning to return to Jerusalem and contains the biblical verses that describe the Rosh Ḥodesh offering, and a prayer that the new month will be blessed for good.

מוסף לראש חודש

עמידה

The following prayer, until קַדְמוֹנִיּוֹת *on page 853, is said silently, standing with feet together. If there is a* מנין*, the* עמידה *is repeated aloud by the* שליח ציבור*. Take three steps forward as if formally entering the place of the Divine Presence.*

כִּי שֵׁם יהוה אֶקְרָא, הָבוּ גֹדֶל לֵאלֹהֵינוּ: דברים לב
אֲדֹנָי, שְׂפָתַי תִּפְתָּח, וּפִי יַגִּיד תְּהִלָּתֶךָ: תהלים נא

אבות

בָּרוּךְ אַתָּה יהוה, אֱלֹהֵינוּ וֵאלֹהֵי אֲבוֹתֵינוּ
אֱלֹהֵי אַבְרָהָם, אֱלֹהֵי יִצְחָק, וֵאלֹהֵי יַעֲקֹב
הָאֵל הַגָּדוֹל הַגִּבּוֹר וְהַנּוֹרָא, אֵל עֶלְיוֹן
גּוֹמֵל חֲסָדִים טוֹבִים, וְקוֹנֵה הַכֹּל, וְזוֹכֵר חַסְדֵי אָבוֹת
וּמֵבִיא גוֹאֵל לִבְנֵי בְנֵיהֶם לְמַעַן שְׁמוֹ בְּאַהֲבָה.
מֶלֶךְ עוֹזֵר וּמוֹשִׁיעַ וּמָגֵן.
בָּרוּךְ אַתָּה יהוה, מָגֵן אַבְרָהָם.

גבורות

אַתָּה גִּבּוֹר לְעוֹלָם, אֲדֹנָי
מְחַיֵּה מֵתִים אַתָּה, רַב לְהוֹשִׁיעַ

LEARNING

INTRODUCTION TO MUSAF FOR ROSH HODESH

The very first mitzva that *Benei Yisrael* were given, even before they left Egypt, was the mitzva of establishing the Jewish calendar. It is the calendar that creates a national identity and unity. A unified calendar causes a synchronization of time consciousness – the entire people keep the same time rhythm, and commemorate the same festivals at the same time.

The calendar itself revolves around the monthly minor festival of Rosh Ḥodesh – the sanctification of the new moon. When there was a Sanhedrin, Rosh Ḥodesh had to be declared by the court on the basis of

The phrase "He makes the wind blow and the rain fall" is added from Simḥat Torah until Pesaḥ. In Israel the phrase "He causes the dew to fall" is added from Pesaḥ until Shemini Atzeret.

In fall & winter: He makes the wind blow and the rain fall.

In Israel, in spring & summer: He causes the dew to fall.

He sustains the living with loving-kindness,
and with great compassion revives the dead.
He supports the fallen, heals the sick, sets captives free,
and keeps His faith with those who sleep in the dust.
Who is like You, Master of might,
and who can compare to You,
O King who brings death and gives life,
and makes salvation grow?
Faithful are You to revive the dead.
Blessed are You, LORD, who revives the dead.

When saying the Amida silently, continue with "You are holy" on the next page.

KEDUSHA

During the Leader's Repetition, the following is said standing with feet together, rising on the toes at the words indicated by ▲.

Cong. then Leader: נְקַדֵּשׁ We will sanctify Your name on earth, as they sanctify it in the highest heavens, as is written by Your prophet,
"And they [the angels] call to one another saying: *Is. 6*

Cong. then Leader: ▲Holy, ▲holy, ▲holy is the LORD of multitudes
the whole world is filled with His glory."
Those facing them say "Blessed – "

Cong. then Leader: ▲"Blessed is the LORD's glory from His place." *Ezek. 3*
And in Your holy Writings it is written thus:

Cong. then Leader: ▲"The LORD shall reign for ever. He is your God, Zion, *Ps. 146*
from generation to generation, Halleluya!"

Leader: From generation to generation we will speak of Your greatness,
and we will declare Your holiness for evermore.
Your praise, our God, shall not leave our mouth forever,
for You, God, are a great and holy King.
Blessed are You, LORD, the holy God.

The Leader continues with "You have given New Moons" on the next page.

The phrase מַשִּׁיב הָרְוּחַ *is added from* שמחת תורה *until* פסח.
In ארץ ישראל *the phrase* מוֹרִיד הַטָּל *is added from* פסח *until* שמיני עצרת.

בחורף: מַשִּׁיב הָרְוּחַ וּמוֹרִיד הַגֶּשֶׁם / בארץ ישראל בקיץ: מוֹרִיד הַטָּל

מְכַלְכֵּל חַיִּים בְּחֶסֶד, מְחַיֵּה מֵתִים בְּרַחֲמִים רַבִּים
סוֹמֵךְ נוֹפְלִים, וְרוֹפֵא חוֹלִים, וּמַתִּיר אֲסוּרִים
וּמְקַיֵּם אֱמוּנָתוֹ לִישֵׁנֵי עָפָר.
מִי כָמְוֹךָ, בַּעַל גְּבוּרוֹת, וּמִי דְּוֹמֶה לָּךְ
מֶלֶךְ, מֵמִית וּמְחַיֶּה וּמַצְמִיחַ יְשׁוּעָה.
וְנֶאֱמָן אַתָּה לְהַחֲיוֹת מֵתִים.
בָּרוּךְ אַתָּה יהוה, מְחַיֵּה הַמֵּתִים.

When saying the עמידה *silently, continue with* אַתָּה קָדוֹשׁ *on the next page.*

קדושה

During the חזרת הש״ץ, *the following is said standing with feet together, rising on the toes at the words indicated by* ˄.

then קהל ש״ץ: נְקַדֵּשׁ אֶת שִׁמְךָ בָּעוֹלָם, כְּשֵׁם שֶׁמַּקְדִּישִׁים אוֹתוֹ בִּשְׁמֵי מָרוֹם
כַּכָּתוּב עַל יַד נְבִיאֶךָ: וְקָרָא זֶה אֶל־זֶה וְאָמַר — ישעיה ו

then קהל ש״ץ: ˄קָדוֹשׁ, ˄קָדוֹשׁ, ˄קָדוֹשׁ, יהוה צְבָאוֹת, מְלֹא כָל־הָאָרֶץ כְּבוֹדוֹ:
לְעֻמָּתָם בָּרוּךְ יֹאמֵרוּ

then קהל ש״ץ: ˄בָּרוּךְ כְּבוֹד־יהוה מִמְּקוֹמוֹ: — יחזקאל ג
וּבְדִבְרֵי קָדְשְׁךָ כָּתוּב לֵאמֹר

then קהל ש״ץ: ˄יִמְלֹךְ יהוה לְעוֹלָם, אֱלֹהַיִךְ צִיּוֹן לְדֹר וָדֹר, הַלְלוּיָהּ: — תהלים קמו

ש״ץ: לְדוֹר וָדוֹר נַגִּיד גָּדְלֶךָ, וּלְנֵצַח נְצָחִים קְדֻשָּׁתְךָ נַקְדִּישׁ
וְשִׁבְחֲךָ אֱלֹהֵינוּ מִפִּינוּ לֹא יָמוּשׁ לְעוֹלָם וָעֶד
כִּי אֵל מֶלֶךְ גָּדוֹל וְקָדוֹשׁ אָתָּה.
בָּרוּךְ אַתָּה יהוה הָאֵל הַקָּדוֹשׁ.

The שליח ציבור *continues with* רָאשֵׁי חֳדָשִׁים *on the next page.*

HOLINESS

אַתָּה קָדוֹשׁ You are holy and Your name is holy,
and holy ones praise You daily, Selah!
Blessed are You, LORD, the holy God.

HOLINESS OF THE DAY

רָאשֵׁי חֳדָשִׁים You have given New Moons to Your people
as a time of atonement for all their offspring.
They would bring You offerings of goodwill,
and goats as sin-offerings for atonement.
May it serve as a remembrance for them all,
and a deliverance of their lives from the hand of the enemy.
May You establish a new altar in Zion,
and may we offer on it the New Moon burnt-offering,
and prepare goats in favor.
May we all rejoice in the Temple service,
and may the songs of David Your servant,
be heard in Your city,
chanted before Your altar.
Bring them everlasting love,
and remember the covenant of the fathers for their children.

Olympic champion. When he got home his goal was to walk just 100 meters. One step at a time. Each day a little more. Six months later, he ran the Jerusalem half-marathon. He didn't tell a soul until the morning of the race. Not even his family. He just wanted to prove to the world he was still alive. Prove to himself. And after that there was no turning back. Joshua just kept moving forward. In the five years that followed, Joshua ran eighteen marathons and twelve ultramarathons. And he shows no sign of slowing down. He enjoys every minute of his newly reborn life. And with every step he takes forward he thanks God for giving him this second chance at life.

REFLECTION

If you could be reborn
into another life, would you?
What would that life
look like?

Can you make anything
like that happen
in your actual life?

Can you reboot your life?
What would it look like
if you did?
Do you sometimes want to?

קדושת השם

אַתָּה קָדוֹשׁ וְשִׁמְךָ קָדוֹשׁ
וּקְדוֹשִׁים בְּכָל יוֹם יְהַלְלוּךָ סֶּלָה.
בָּרוּךְ אַתָּה יהוה, הָאֵל הַקָּדוֹשׁ.

קדושת היום

רָאשֵׁי חֳדָשִׁים לְעַמְּךָ נָתַתָּ
זְמַן כַּפָּרָה לְכָל תּוֹלְדוֹתָם
בִּהְיוֹתָם מַקְרִיבִים לְפָנֶיךָ זִבְחֵי רָצוֹן
וּשְׂעִירֵי חַטָּאת לְכַפֵּר בַּעֲדָם.
זִכָּרוֹן לְכֻלָּם יִהְיוּ, וּתְשׁוּעַת נַפְשָׁם מִיַּד שׂוֹנֵא.
מִזְבֵּחַ חָדָשׁ בְּצִיּוֹן תָּכִין
וְעוֹלַת רֹאשׁ חֹדֶשׁ נַעֲלֶה עָלָיו
וּשְׂעִירֵי עִזִּים נַעֲשֶׂה בְרָצוֹן
וּבַעֲבוֹדַת בֵּית הַמִּקְדָּשׁ נִשְׂמַח כֻּלָּנוּ
וּבְשִׁירֵי דָוִד עַבְדְּךָ הַנִּשְׁמָעִים בְּעִירֶךָ
הָאֲמוּרִים לִפְנֵי מִזְבְּחֶךָ.
אַהֲבַת עוֹלָם תָּבִיא לָהֶם, וּבְרִית אָבוֹת לַבָּנִים תִּזְכֹּר.

CONNECTION

Aged 49, Joshua underwent open-heart surgery at Shaare Zedek Medical Center. Before that day he had never gone out for a run. Exercise was not part of his life at all. In the days following the surgery he could barely move. The first time he tried to get out of his hospital bed a nurse offered him a wheelchair. As he sat there staring at the ceiling he made himself a promise. He would get his life back. And more. A reborn Joshua. And it was going to start that day. To start with he was going to walk down the hospital hallway. Through sheer willpower he pushed himself to walk all the way to the window at the other end. And when he reached it he felt like an

וַהֲבִיאֵנוּ Bring us back, with song, to Zion Your city,
and to Jerusalem Your Sanctuary with everlasting joy.
There we will prepare for You our obligatory offerings:
the regular daily offerings in their order,
and the additional offerings according to their law.

וְאֶת מוּסַף The additional offering of this New Moon day
we will prepare and offer to You
with love according to Your will's commandment,
as You have written for us in Your Torah
by Your own word, through Your servant Moses,
as it is said:

"On your new moons, *Num. 28*
present as a burnt-offering to the LORD,
two young bulls, one ram,
and seven yearling lambs
without blemish."

CONNECTION

Michael Levin grew up in Philadelphia like any other American teenager, but he had a dream. At the age of sixteen he announced to his parents that he was going to make aliya *and enlist in a combat unit in the IDF and serve the Jewish People, and three years later that's exactly what he did. As a 'lone soldier,' a soldier with no immediate family in Israel, he was entitled to extra time off from the army to visit his family back in America. In the summer of 2006 he took this time and was enjoying spending it with his family when he heard about the outbreak of war on Israel's northern border – the Second Lebanon War. Michael was entitled to stay for longer with his family, but all he could think about was rejoining his comrades on the front line. Without a second thought for his safety, he got on the first flight back to Israel and went to join his paratroopers unit in Lebanon. Four days later he died a hero during a fierce battle with terrorists in southern Lebanon. To this day Michael is an inspiration to so many, remembered as someone who made the ultimate sacrifice for his commitment and loyalty to his comrades and to his people. His legacy lives on through the work of the Lone Soldier Center in Memory of Michael Levin, providing a home and support to lone soldiers in the IDF from all over the world.*

וַהֲבִיאֵנוּ לְצִיּוֹן עִירְךָ בְּרִנָּה
וְלִירוּשָׁלַיִם בֵּית מִקְדָּשְׁךָ בְּשִׂמְחַת עוֹלָם
וְשָׁם נַעֲשֶׂה לְפָנֶיךָ אֶת קָרְבְּנוֹת חוֹבוֹתֵינוּ
תְּמִידִים כְּסִדְרָם וּמוּסָפִים כְּהִלְכָתָם.

וְאֶת מוּסַף יוֹם רֹאשׁ הַחֹדֶשׁ הַזֶּה
נַעֲשֶׂה וְנַקְרִיב לְפָנֶיךָ בְּאַהֲבָה כְּמִצְוַת רְצוֹנֶךָ
כְּמוֹ שֶׁכָּתַבְתָּ עָלֵינוּ בְּתוֹרָתֶךָ
עַל יְדֵי מֹשֶׁה עַבְדֶּךָ מִפִּי כְבוֹדֶךָ
כָּאָמוּר
וּבְרָאשֵׁי חָדְשֵׁיכֶם תַּקְרִיבוּ עֹלָה לַיהוה במדבר כח
פָּרִים בְּנֵי־בָקָר שְׁנַיִם
וְאַיִל אֶחָד
כְּבָשִׂים בְּנֵי־שָׁנָה שִׁבְעָה
תְּמִימִם:

...A THOUSAND WORDS

REFLECTION

"The most sublime act is to set another before you."
(William Blake)

We no longer have animal sacrifices as a form of worship. But are there still areas of your life where you sacrifice for Hashem?

Where and what will you sacrifice this month?

וּמִנְחָתָם And their meal-offerings
and wine-libations as ordained:
three-tenths of an ephah for each bull,
two-tenths of an ephah for the ram,
one-tenth of an ephah for each lamb,
wine for the libations,
a male goat for atonement,
and two regular daily offerings
according to their law.

אֱלֹהֵינוּ O God and God of our ancestors,
renew for us the coming month for good and blessing,
joy and gladness, deliverance and consolation,
sustenance and support, life and peace,
pardon of sin and forgiveness of wrongdoing
(*From Marḥeshvan to Adar II in a Jewish leap year* and atonement of crimes).
For You have chosen Your people Israel from all nations,
and have instituted for them rules for the New Moon.
Blessed are You, LORD, who sanctifies Israel and the New Moons.

CONNECTION

"The fifteenth-century Jewish diplomat and scholar Don Isaac Abrabanel, chancellor to King Ferdinand and Queen Isabella of Castile, was once asked by the king how much he owned. He named a certain sum. 'But surely,' the king said, 'you own much more than that.' 'You asked me,' Abrabanel replied, 'how much I owned. The property I have, I do not own. Your majesty may seize it from me tomorrow. At best I am its temporary guardian. The sum I mentioned is what I have given away in charity. That merit alone, neither you nor any earthly power can take away from me.' We own what we are willing to share.

"There is a strange feature of the geography of the Holy Land. Israel contains two seas: the Dead Sea and the Sea of Galilee. The latter is full of life: fish, birds, vegetation. The former, as its name suggests, contains no life at all. Yet they are both fed by the same river, the Jordan. The difference is that the Sea of Galilee receives water at one end and gives out water at the other. The Dead Sea receives but does not give. The Jordan ends there. To receive without reciprocating is a kind of death. To live is to give."

(Rabbi Jonathan Sacks)

וּמִנְחָתָם וְנִסְכֵּיהֶם כִּמְדֻבָּר
שְׁלֹשָׁה עֶשְׂרֹנִים לַפָּר
וּשְׁנֵי עֶשְׂרֹנִים לָאָיִל
וְעִשָּׂרוֹן לַכֶּבֶשׂ
וְיַיִן כְּנִסְכּוֹ, וְשָׂעִיר לְכַפֵּר
וּשְׁנֵי תְמִידִים כְּהִלְכָתָם.

אֱלֹהֵינוּ וֵאלֹהֵי אֲבוֹתֵינוּ
חַדֵּשׁ עָלֵינוּ אֶת הַחֹדֶשׁ הַזֶּה לְטוֹבָה וְלִבְרָכָה
לְשָׂשׂוֹן וּלְשִׂמְחָה, לִישׁוּעָה וּלְנֶחָמָה
לְפַרְנָסָה וּלְכַלְכָּלָה, לְחַיִּים וּלְשָׁלוֹם
לִמְחִילַת חֵטְא וְלִסְלִיחַת עָוֹן
(*From* מרחשון *to* אדר שני *in a Jewish leap year* וּלְכַפָּרַת פָּשַׁע)
כִּי בְעַמְּךָ יִשְׂרָאֵל בָּחַרְתָּ מִכָּל הָאֻמּוֹת
וְחֻקֵּי רָאשֵׁי חֳדָשִׁים לָהֶם קָבָעְתָּ.
בָּרוּךְ אַתָּה יהוה, מְקַדֵּשׁ יִשְׂרָאֵל וְרָאשֵׁי חֳדָשִׁים.

REFLECTION

What would you like this month to hold in store for yourself?

What would you like this month to hold in store for your family?

What would you like this month to hold in store for your people?

...A THOUSAND WORDS

TEMPLE SERVICE

רְצֵה Find favor, LORD our God,
in Your people Israel and their prayer.
Restore the service to Your most holy House,
and accept in love and favor
the fire-offerings of Israel and their prayer.
May the service of Your people Israel
always find favor with You
And may our eyes witness Your return
to Zion in compassion.
Blessed are You, LORD,
who restores His Presence to Zion.

...A THOUSAND WORDS

עבודה

רְצֵה יהוה אֱלֹהֵינוּ בְּעַמְּךָ יִשְׂרָאֵל וּבִתְפִלָּתָם
וְהָשֵׁב אֶת הָעֲבוֹדָה לִדְבִיר בֵּיתֶךָ
וְאִשֵּׁי יִשְׂרָאֵל וּתְפִלָּתָם בְּאַהֲבָה תְקַבֵּל בְּרָצוֹן
וּתְהִי לְרָצוֹן תָּמִיד עֲבוֹדַת יִשְׂרָאֵל עַמֶּךָ.
וְתֶחֱזֶינָה עֵינֵינוּ בְּשׁוּבְךָ לְצִיּוֹן בְּרַחֲמִים.
בָּרוּךְ אַתָּה יהוה, הַמַּחֲזִיר שְׁכִינָתוֹ לְצִיּוֹן.

LEARNING

"Each time the moon finds the sun again, each time it receives its rays of light afresh, God wants His people to find Him again, to be illuminated with fresh rays of light, whenever and however, in running their course, they have had to pass through periods of darkness and obscurity." (Rabbi S.R. Hirsch)

Chazal (*Menaḥot* 110a) tell us that even though there is no *Beit HaMikdash*, when one recites the *korbanot* and longs to offer them, he is credited as if he brought them. We learn that King David longed to build the *Mikdash* itself and thus he is credited as if he had built it even though it was his son Shlomo HaMelekh who actually built it.

CONNECTION

Ten miracles were performed for our ancestors in the Beit HaMikdash*:*

1) *No pregnant woman ever miscarried from the aroma.*
2) *The meat of the* korbanot *never decomposed.*
3) *No flies were ever seen in the slaughterhouse.*
4) *The* Kohen Gadol *never became ritually impure on Yom Kippur.*
5) *Rain never extinguished the flame on the wood-pile on the* mizbe'aḥ.
6) *The wind never blew the straight column of smoke that rose from the* mizbe'aḥ.
7) *No defect was ever found in the Omer, Two Loaves, or Showbread.*
8) *The people who had come to the* Beit HaMikdash *stood crowded tightly together, yet when it came to bowing on the ground there was plenty of room.*
9) *No snake or scorpion ever harmed anyone in Yerushalayim.*
10) *No one who made a pilgrimage to Yerushalayim ever had cause to say, "There is no room for me to stay overnight here."*

(*Avot* 5:7)

THANKSGIVING

מוֹדִים We give thanks to You,
for You are the LORD our God
and God of our ancestors
for ever and all time.
You are the Rock of our lives,
Shield of our salvation
from generation to generation.
We will thank You and
declare Your praise for our lives,
which are entrusted into Your hand;
for our souls,
which are placed in Your charge;
for Your miracles
which are with us every day;
and for Your wonders and favors
at all times, evening,
morning and midday.
You are good –
for Your compassion never fails.
You are compassionate –
for Your loving-kindnesses never cease.
We have always placed our hope in You.

During the Leader's Repetition, the congregation says quietly:

מוֹדִים We give thanks
to You, for You are
the LORD our Godand
God of our ancestors,
God of all flesh,
who formed us
and formed the universe.
Blessings and thanks
are due to Your great
and holy name for giving us
life and sustaining us.
May You continue
to give us life and sustain us;
and may You gather our
exiles to Your holy courts,
to keep Your decrees,
do Your will and serve You
with a perfect heart,
for it is for us
to give You thanks.
Blessed be God to whom
thanksgiving is due.

On Ḥanukka:

עַל הַנִּסִּים [We thank You also] for the miracles, the redemption, the mighty deeds, the salvations, and the victories in battle which You performed for our ancestors in those days, at this time.

בִּימֵי מַתִּתְיָהוּ In the days of Mattityahu, son of Yoḥanan, the High Priest, the Hasmonean, and his sons, the wicked Greek kingdom rose up against Your people Israel to make them forget Your Torah and to force them to transgress the laws of Your will. It was then that You in Your great compassion stood by them in the time of their distress. You championed their cause, judged their claim, and avenged their wrong. You delivered the strong into the hands of the weak, the many into the hands of the few, the impure into the hands of the pure, the wicked into

הודאה

ק מוֹדִים אֲנַחְנוּ לָךְ
שָׁאַתָּה הוּא ק יהוה אֱלֹהֵינוּ
וֵאלֹהֵי אֲבוֹתֵינוּ לְעוֹלָם וָעֶד.
צוּר חַיֵּינוּ, מָגֵן יִשְׁעֵנוּ
אַתָּה הוּא לְדוֹר וָדוֹר.
נוֹדֶה לְּךָ וּנְסַפֵּר תְּהִלָּתֶךָ
עַל חַיֵּינוּ הַמְּסוּרִים בְּיָדֶךָ
וְעַל נִשְׁמוֹתֵינוּ הַפְּקוּדוֹת לָךְ
וְעַל נִסֶּיךָ שֶׁבְּכָל יוֹם עִמָּנוּ
וְעַל נִפְלְאוֹתֶיךָ וְטוֹבוֹתֶיךָ
שֶׁבְּכָל עֵת
עֶרֶב וָבֹקֶר וְצָהֳרָיִם.
הַטּוֹב, כִּי לֹא כָלוּ רַחֲמֶיךָ
וְהַמְרַחֵם, כִּי לֹא תַמּוּ חֲסָדֶיךָ
מֵעוֹלָם קִוִּינוּ לָךְ.

During the חזרת הש״ץ*, the* קהל *says quietly:*

ק מוֹדִים אֲנַחְנוּ לָךְ
שָׁאַתָּה הוּא ק יהוה אֱלֹהֵינוּ
וֵאלֹהֵי אֲבוֹתֵינוּ
אֱלֹהֵי כָל בָּשָׂר
יוֹצְרֵנוּ, יוֹצֵר בְּרֵאשִׁית.
בְּרָכוֹת וְהוֹדָאוֹת
לְשִׁמְךָ הַגָּדוֹל וְהַקָּדוֹשׁ
עַל שֶׁהֶחֱיִיתָנוּ וְקִיַּמְתָּנוּ.
כֵּן תְּחַיֵּנוּ וּתְקַיְּמֵנוּ
וְתֶאֱסֹף גָּלֻיּוֹתֵינוּ
לְחַצְרוֹת קָדְשֶׁךָ
לִשְׁמֹר חֻקֶּיךָ
וְלַעֲשׂוֹת רְצוֹנֶךָ וּלְעָבְדְּךָ
בְּלֵבָב שָׁלֵם
עַל שֶׁאֲנַחְנוּ מוֹדִים לָךְ.
בָּרוּךְ אֵל הַהוֹדָאוֹת.

בחנוכה:
עַל הַנִּסִּים וְעַל הַפֻּרְקָן וְעַל הַגְּבוּרוֹת וְעַל הַתְּשׁוּעוֹת וְעַל הַמִּלְחָמוֹת שֶׁעָשִׂיתָ לַאֲבוֹתֵינוּ בַּיָּמִים הָהֵם בַּזְּמַן הַזֶּה.

בִּימֵי מַתִּתְיָהוּ בֶּן יוֹחָנָן כֹּהֵן גָּדוֹל חַשְׁמוֹנַאי וּבָנָיו, כְּשֶׁעָמְדָה מַלְכוּת יָוָן הָרְשָׁעָה עַל עַמְּךָ יִשְׂרָאֵל לְהַשְׁכִּיחָם תּוֹרָתֶךָ וּלְהַעֲבִירָם מֵחֻקֵּי רְצוֹנֶךָ, וְאַתָּה בְּרַחֲמֶיךָ הָרַבִּים עָמַדְתָּ לָהֶם בְּעֵת צָרָתָם, רַבְתָּ אֶת רִיבָם, דַּנְתָּ אֶת דִּינָם, נָקַמְתָּ אֶת נִקְמָתָם, מָסַרְתָּ גִבּוֹרִים בְּיַד חַלָּשִׁים, וְרַבִּים בְּיַד מְעַטִּים, וּטְמֵאִים בְּיַד טְהוֹרִים, וּרְשָׁעִים בְּיַד צַדִּיקִים,

the hands of the righteous, and the arrogant into the hands of those who were engaged in the study of Your Torah. You made for Yourself a great and holy reputation in Your world, and for Your people Israel You performed a great salvation and redemption as of this very day. Your children then entered the holiest part of Your House, cleansed Your Temple, purified Your Sanctuary, kindled lights in Your holy courts, and designated these eight days of Ḥanukka for giving thanks and praise to Your great name.

Continue with "For all these things."

וְעַל כֻּלָּם For all these things may Your name be blessed and elevated, our King, continually, for ever and all time.
Let all that lives thank You, Selah! and praise Your name in truth, God, our Savior and Help, Selah!
Blessed are You, Lord,
whose name is "the Good" and to whom thanks are due.

When saying the Amida silently, continue with "Give peace" below.

The following is said by the Leader during the Repetition of the Amida.
In Israel, if Kohanim bless the congregation, turn to page 1064.

Our God and God of our fathers, bless us with the threefold blessing in the Torah, written by the hand of Moses Your servant and pronounced by Aaron and his sons the priests, Your holy people, as it is said:

May the Lord bless you and protect you. *Num. 6*
Cong: May it be Your will.
May the Lord make His face shine on you and be generous to you.
Cong: May it be Your will.
May the Lord turn His face toward you, and give you peace.
Cong: May it be Your will.

The Leader continues with "Give peace" below.

PEACE

שִׂים שָׁלוֹם Give peace, goodness and blessing,
grace, loving-kindness and compassion
to us and all Israel Your people.
Bless us, our Father, all as one, with the light of Your face,
for by the light of Your face You have given us, Lord our God,
the Torah of life and love of kindness,
righteousness, blessing, compassion, life and peace.

וְזֵדִים בְּיַד עוֹסְקֵי תוֹרָתֶךָ, וּלְךָ עָשִׂיתָ שֵׁם גָּדוֹל וְקָדוֹשׁ בְּעוֹלָמֶךָ, וּלְעַמְּךָ יִשְׂרָאֵל עָשִׂיתָ תְּשׁוּעָה גְדוֹלָה וּפֻרְקָן כְּהַיּוֹם הַזֶּה. וְאַחַר כֵּן בָּאוּ בָנֶיךָ לִדְבִיר בֵּיתֶךָ, וּפִנּוּ אֶת הֵיכָלֶךָ, וְטִהֲרוּ אֶת מִקְדָּשֶׁךָ, וְהִדְלִיקוּ נֵרוֹת בְּחַצְרוֹת קָדְשֶׁךָ, וְקָבְעוּ שְׁמוֹנַת יְמֵי חֲנֻכָּה אֵלּוּ, לְהוֹדוֹת וּלְהַלֵּל לְשִׁמְךָ הַגָּדוֹל.

Continue with וְעַל כֻּלָּם.

וְעַל כֻּלָּם יִתְבָּרַךְ וְיִתְרוֹמַם שִׁמְךָ מַלְכֵּנוּ תָּמִיד לְעוֹלָם וָעֶד.
וְכֹל הַחַיִּים יוֹדוּךָ סֶּלָה, וִיהַלְלוּ אֶת שִׁמְךָ בֶּאֱמֶת
הָאֵל יְשׁוּעָתֵנוּ וְעֶזְרָתֵנוּ סֶלָה.
בָּרוּךְ אַתָּה יהוה, הַטּוֹב שִׁמְךָ וּלְךָ נָאֶה לְהוֹדוֹת.

When saying the עמידה *silently, continue with* שִׂים שָׁלוֹם *below.*

The following is said by the שליח ציבור *during the* חזרת הש״ץ.
In ארץ ישראל, *if* כוהנים *say* ברכת כוהנים, *turn to page 1065.*

אֱלֹהֵינוּ וֵאלֹהֵי אֲבוֹתֵינוּ, בָּרְכֵנוּ בַּבְּרָכָה הַמְשֻׁלֶּשֶׁת בַּתּוֹרָה, הַכְּתוּבָה עַל יְדֵי מֹשֶׁה עַבְדֶּךָ, הָאֲמוּרָה מִפִּי אַהֲרֹן וּבָנָיו כֹּהֲנִים עַם קְדוֹשֶׁיךָ, כָּאָמוּר

במדבר ו
יְבָרֶכְךָ יהוה וְיִשְׁמְרֶךָ: קהל: כֵּן יְהִי רָצוֹן
יָאֵר יהוה פָּנָיו אֵלֶיךָ וִיחֻנֶּךָּ: קהל: כֵּן יְהִי רָצוֹן
יִשָּׂא יהוה פָּנָיו אֵלֶיךָ וְיָשֵׂם לְךָ שָׁלוֹם: קהל: כֵּן יְהִי רָצוֹן

The שליח ציבור *continues with* שִׂים שָׁלוֹם *below.*

ברכת שלום

שִׂים שָׁלוֹם טוֹבָה וּבְרָכָה
חֵן וָחֶסֶד וְרַחֲמִים עָלֵינוּ וְעַל כָּל יִשְׂרָאֵל עַמֶּךָ.
בָּרְכֵנוּ אָבִינוּ כֻּלָּנוּ כְּאֶחָד בְּאוֹר פָּנֶיךָ
כִּי בְאוֹר פָּנֶיךָ נָתַתָּ לָּנוּ יהוה אֱלֹהֵינוּ
תּוֹרַת חַיִּים וְאַהֲבַת חֶסֶד
וּצְדָקָה וּבְרָכָה וְרַחֲמִים וְחַיִּים וְשָׁלוֹם.

May it be good in Your eyes to bless Your people Israel
at every time, in every hour, with Your peace.
Blessed are You, Lord, who blesses His people Israel with peace.

The following verse concludes the Leader's Repetition of the Amida.
Some also say it here as part of the silent Amida.

May the words of my mouth and the inner thoughts of my heart *Ps. 19*
find favor before You, Lord, my Rock and Redeemer.

אֱלֹהַי My God, guard my tongue from evil *Berakhot 17a*
and my lips from dishonest speech.
To those who curse me, let my soul be silent;
may my soul be to all like the dust.
Open my heart to Your Torah
and let my soul pursue Your commandments.
As for all who plan evil against me,
swiftly defeat their counsel and frustrate their plans.

Act for the sake of Your name;
act for the sake of Your right hand;
act for the sake of Your holiness;
act for the sake of Your Torah.

That Your beloved ones may be rescued, *Ps. 60*
save with Your right hand and answer me.
May the words of my mouth and the inner thoughts of my heart *Ps. 19*
find favor before You, Lord, my Rock and Redeemer.

Bow, take three steps back, then bow, first left, then right, then center, while saying:

May He who makes peace in His high places,
make peace for us and all Israel – and say: Amen.

יְהִי רָצוֹן May it be Your will, Lord our God and God of our ancestors,
that the Temple be rebuilt speedily in our days,
and give us a share in Your Torah.
And there we will serve You with fear,
as in the days of old and as in former years.
Then the offering of Judah and Jerusalem will be pleasing to the Lord *Mal. 3*
as in the days of old and as in former years.

After the Leader's Repetition, the service continues with Full Kaddish (page 245), followed by Aleinu (page 246), the Daily Psalm (page 252) and Barekhi Nafshi (page 264).

וְטוֹב בְּעֵינֶיךָ לְבָרֵךְ אֶת עַמְּךָ יִשְׂרָאֵל
בְּכָל עֵת וּבְכָל שָׁעָה בִּשְׁלוֹמֶךָ.
בָּרוּךְ אַתָּה יהוה, הַמְבָרֵךְ אֶת עַמּוֹ יִשְׂרָאֵל בַּשָּׁלוֹם.

The following verse concludes the חזרת הש״ץ.
Some also say it here as part of the silent עמידה.

תהלים יט יִהְיוּ לְרָצוֹן אִמְרֵי־פִי וְהֶגְיוֹן לִבִּי לְפָנֶיךָ, יהוה צוּרִי וְגֹאֲלִי:

ברכות יז. אֱלֹהַי
נְצֹר לְשׁוֹנִי מֵרָע וּשְׂפָתַי מִדַּבֵּר מִרְמָה
וְלִמְקַלְלַי נַפְשִׁי תִדֹּם, וְנַפְשִׁי כֶּעָפָר לַכֹּל תִּהְיֶה.
פְּתַח לִבִּי בְּתוֹרָתֶךָ, וּבְמִצְוֹתֶיךָ תִּרְדֹּף נַפְשִׁי.
וְכָל הַחוֹשְׁבִים עָלַי רָעָה
מְהֵרָה הָפֵר עֲצָתָם וְקַלְקֵל מַחֲשַׁבְתָּם.
עֲשֵׂה לְמַעַן שְׁמֶךָ, עֲשֵׂה לְמַעַן יְמִינֶךָ
עֲשֵׂה לְמַעַן קְדֻשָּׁתֶךָ, עֲשֵׂה לְמַעַן תּוֹרָתֶךָ.
תהלים ס לְמַעַן יֵחָלְצוּן יְדִידֶיךָ, הוֹשִׁיעָה יְמִינְךָ וַעֲנֵנִי:
תהלים יט יִהְיוּ לְרָצוֹן אִמְרֵי־פִי וְהֶגְיוֹן לִבִּי לְפָנֶיךָ, יהוה צוּרִי וְגֹאֲלִי:

Bow, take three steps back, then bow, first left, then right, then center, while saying:

עֹשֶׂה שָׁלוֹם בִּמְרוֹמָיו
הוּא יַעֲשֶׂה שָׁלוֹם עָלֵינוּ וְעַל כָּל יִשְׂרָאֵל, וְאִמְרוּ אָמֵן.

יְהִי רָצוֹן מִלְּפָנֶיךָ יהוה אֱלֹהֵינוּ וֵאלֹהֵי אֲבוֹתֵינוּ
שֶׁיִּבָּנֶה בֵּית הַמִּקְדָּשׁ בִּמְהֵרָה בְיָמֵינוּ
וְתֵן חֶלְקֵנוּ בְּתוֹרָתֶךָ
וְשָׁם נַעֲבָדְךָ בְּיִרְאָה כִּימֵי עוֹלָם וּכְשָׁנִים קַדְמֹנִיּוֹת.
מלאכי ג וְעָרְבָה לַיהוה מִנְחַת יְהוּדָה וִירוּשָׁלָםִ כִּימֵי עוֹלָם וּכְשָׁנִים קַדְמֹנִיּוֹת:

After the חזרת הש״ץ, *the service continues with* קדיש שלם *(page 245),*
followed by עָלֵינוּ *(page 247),* שיר של יום *(page 253) and* בָּרְכִי נַפְשִׁי *(page 265).*

Meditation in the Sukka

הֲרֵינִי I am hereby prepared and ready to fulfill the commandment of Sukka, as the Creator, blessed be His name has commanded me: "You shall live in booths for seven days; every citizen in Israel shall live in booths so that future generations will know that I made the Israelites live in booths when I brought them out of Egypt. I am the LORD your God." *Lev. 23*

Sit, sit, esteemed guests. Sit, sit, holy guests. Sit, sit, guests in faith. Sit in the shade of the Holy One, blessed be He. Worthy is the portion of Israel, as is written, "For the LORD's portion is His people, Jacob His allotted inheritance." *Deut. 32*

May it be Your will, LORD my God and God of my fathers, that You cause Your Divine Presence to rest among us and that You spread over us the canopy of Your peace, in the merit of the commandment of Sukka which we are fulfilling to unify the name of the Holy One, blessed be He, and His Divine Presence, in fear and love, to unify the name *Yod-Heh* with *Vav-Heh*, in perfect unity in the name of all Israel. May You surround it with the radiance of Your holy and pure glory, spread above their heads like an eagle that stirs up its nest, and from there may a rich flow of life stream down on your servant (*name* son of *mother's name*, Your servant). In the merit of leaving my house to go outside, running in the way of Your commandments, may I be considered as if I had wandered far. Cleanse me thoroughly from my wrongdoing and purify me from my sin. From the esteemed guests, the guests in faith, may Your ears attend to much blessing. To the hungry and thirsty give unfailing food and drink. Give me the privilege of sitting and taking refuge under the shadow of Your wings when I take leave of this world, taking refuge from stream and rain when You rain fiery coals on the wicked. May this command of Sukka that I am fulfilling be considered by You as if I had fulfilled it in all its specifics, details and conditions, as well as all the commandments dependent on it. May the sealing of our fate be for good, and give us the merit of living for many years on the soil of the Holy Land, serving You and revering You. Blessed is the LORD forever, Amen and Amen. *Ps. 89*

תפילה כשנכנסין לסוכה

הֲרֵינִי מוּכָן וּמְזֻמָּן לְקַיֵּם מִצְוַת סֻכָּה, כַּאֲשֶׁר צִוַּנִי הַבּוֹרֵא יִתְבָּרַךְ שְׁמוֹ: בַּסֻּכֹּת תֵּשְׁבוּ שִׁבְעַת יָמִים, כָּל־הָאֶזְרָח בְּיִשְׂרָאֵל יֵשְׁבוּ בַּסֻּכֹּת: לְמַעַן יֵדְעוּ דֹרֹתֵיכֶם, כִּי בַסֻּכּוֹת הוֹשַׁבְתִּי אֶת־בְּנֵי יִשְׂרָאֵל, בְּהוֹצִיאִי אוֹתָם מֵאֶרֶץ מִצְרָיִם: ויקרא כג

תִּיבוּ תִּיבוּ אֻשְׁפִּיזִין עִלָּאִין, תִּיבוּ תִּיבוּ אֻשְׁפִּיזִין קַדִּישִׁין, תִּיבוּ תִּיבוּ אֻשְׁפִּיזִין דִּמְהֵימְנוּתָא. זַכָּאָה חֻלָקְהוֹן דְּיִשְׂרָאֵל, דִּכְתִיב: כִּי חֵלֶק יהוה עַמּוֹ, יַעֲקֹב חֶבֶל נַחֲלָתוֹ: דברים לב

יְהִי רָצוֹן מִלְּפָנֶיךָ יהוה אֱלֹהַי וֵאלֹהֵי אֲבוֹתַי, שֶׁתַּשְׁרֶה שְׁכִינָתְךָ בֵּינֵינוּ, וְתִפְרֹס עָלֵינוּ סֻכַּת שְׁלוֹמֶךָ, בִּזְכוּת מִצְוַת סֻכָּה שֶׁאֲנַחְנוּ מְקַיְּמִין לְיַחֲדָא שְׁמָא דְקֻדְשָׁא בְּרִיךְ הוּא וּשְׁכִינְתֵּהּ בִּדְחִילוּ וּרְחִימוּ, לְיַחֲדָא שֵׁם י״ה בו״ה בְּיִחוּדָא שְׁלִים בְּשֵׁם כָּל יִשְׂרָאֵל, וּלְהַקִּיף אוֹתָהּ מִזִּיו כְּבוֹדְךָ הַקָּדוֹשׁ וְהַטָּהוֹר, נָטוּי עַל רָאשֵׁיהֶם מִלְמַעְלָה כְּנֶשֶׁר יָעִיר קִנּוֹ, וּמִשָּׁם יַשְׁפַּע שֶׁפַע הַחַיִּים לְעַבְדְּךָ (פלוני בֶּן פלונית אֲמָתֶךָ). וּבִזְכוּת צֵאתִי מִבֵּיתִי הַחוּצָה וְדֶרֶךְ מִצְוֹתֶיךָ אָרוּצָה, יֵחָשֵׁב לִי זֹאת כְּאִלּוּ הִרְחַקְתִּי נְדוֹד, וְהֶרֶב כַּבְּסֵנִי מֵעֲוֹנִי וּמֵחַטָּאתִי טַהֲרֵנִי, וּמֵאֻשְׁפִּיזִין עִלָּאִין אֻשְׁפִּיזִין דִּמְהֵימְנוּתָא תִּהְיֶינָה אָזְנֶיךָ קַשֻּׁבוֹת רַב בְּרָכוֹת, וְלָרְעֵבִים גַּם צְמֵאִים תֶּן לַחְמָם וּמֵימָם הַנֶּאֱמָנִים, וְתִתֶּן לִי זְכוּת לָשֶׁבֶת וְלַחֲסוֹת בְּסֵתֶר צֵל כְּנָפֶיךָ בְּעֵת פְּטִירָתִי מִן הָעוֹלָם, וְלַחֲסוֹת מִזֶּרֶם וּמִמָּטָר, כִּי תַמְטִיר עַל רְשָׁעִים פַּחִים. וּתְהֵא חֲשׁוּבָה מִצְוַת סֻכָּה זוֹ שֶׁאֲנִי מְקַיֵּם, כְּאִלּוּ קִיַּמְתִּיהָ בְּכָל פְּרָטֶיהָ וְדִקְדּוּקֶיהָ וּתְנָאֶיהָ וְכָל מִצְוֹת הַתְּלוּיוֹת בָּהּ. וְתֵיטִיב לָנוּ הַחֲתִימָה, וּתְזַכֵּנוּ לֵישֵׁב יָמִים רַבִּים עַל הָאֲדָמָה אַדְמַת קֹדֶשׁ, בַּעֲבוֹדָתְךָ וּבְיִרְאָתֶךָ. בָּרוּךְ יהוה לְעוֹלָם אָמֵן וְאָמֵן: תהלים פט

On entering the sukka and before saying Kiddush, many have the custom to welcome "guests" from the biblical past, who are said to join us as we sit in the sukka:

אֻשְׁפִּיזִין I invite to my meal the exalted guests,
Abraham, Isaac, Jacob, Joseph, Moses, Aaron, and David.

On the first day I pray you, Abraham, exalted guest,
that all the other exalted guests
may sit here with me and you:
Isaac, Jacob, Joseph, Moses, Aaron, and David.

On the second day I pray you, Isaac, exalted guest,
that all the other exalted guests
may sit here with me and you:
Abraham, Jacob, Joseph, Moses, Aaron, and David.

On the third day I pray you, Jacob, exalted guest,
that all the other exalted guests
may sit here with me and you:
Abraham, Isaac, Joseph, Moses, Aaron, and David.

On the fourth day I pray you, Joseph, exalted guest,
that all the other exalted guests
may sit here with me and you:
Abraham, Isaac, Jacob, Moses, Aaron, and David.

On the fifth day I pray you, Moses, exalted guest,
that all the other exalted guests
may sit here with me and you:
Abraham, Isaac, Jacob, Joseph, Aaron, and David.

On the sixth day I pray you, Aaron, exalted guest,
that all the other exalted guests
may sit here with me and you:
Abraham, Isaac, Jacob, Joseph, Moses, and David.

On Hoshana Raba I pray you, David, exalted guest,
that all the other exalted guests
may sit here with me and you:
Abraham, Isaac, Jacob, Joseph, Moses and Aaron.

On the last day of Sukkot, on leaving the sukka:

May it be Your will, Lord our God and God of our fathers, that as I have fulfilled [Your commandment] and sat in this sukka, so next year may I have the privilege of sitting in the sukka made of the skin of Leviathan.

On entering the סוכה *and before saying* קידוש*, many have the custom to welcome "guests" from the biblical past, who are said to join us as we sit in the* סוכה*:*

אֲזַמִּין לִסְעוּדָתִי אֻשְׁפִּיזִין עִלָּאִין
אַבְרָהָם יִצְחָק יַעֲקֹב יוֹסֵף מֹשֶׁה אַהֲרֹן וְדָוִד.

On the first day
בְּמָטוּ מִנָּךְ אַבְרָהָם אֻשְׁפִּיזִי עִלָּאִי דְּיֵתִיב עִמִּי
וְעִמָּךְ כָּל אֻשְׁפִּיזֵי עִלָּאֵי:
יִצְחָק יַעֲקֹב יוֹסֵף מֹשֶׁה אַהֲרֹן וְדָוִד.

On the second day
בְּמָטוּ מִנָּךְ יִצְחָק אֻשְׁפִּיזִי עִלָּאִי דְּיֵתִיב עִמִּי
וְעִמָּךְ כָּל אֻשְׁפִּיזֵי עִלָּאֵי:
אַבְרָהָם יַעֲקֹב יוֹסֵף מֹשֶׁה אַהֲרֹן וְדָוִד.

On the third day
בְּמָטוּ מִנָּךְ יַעֲקֹב אֻשְׁפִּיזִי עִלָּאִי דְּיֵתִיב עִמִּי
וְעִמָּךְ כָּל אֻשְׁפִּיזֵי עִלָּאֵי:
אַבְרָהָם יִצְחָק יוֹסֵף מֹשֶׁה אַהֲרֹן וְדָוִד.

On the fourth day
בְּמָטוּ מִנָּךְ יוֹסֵף אֻשְׁפִּיזִי עִלָּאִי דְּיֵתִיב עִמִּי
וְעִמָּךְ כָּל אֻשְׁפִּיזֵי עִלָּאֵי:
אַבְרָהָם יִצְחָק יַעֲקֹב מֹשֶׁה אַהֲרֹן וְדָוִד.

On the fifth day
בְּמָטוּ מִנָּךְ מֹשֶׁה אֻשְׁפִּיזִי עִלָּאִי דְּיֵתִיב עִמִּי
וְעִמָּךְ כָּל אֻשְׁפִּיזֵי עִלָּאֵי:
אַבְרָהָם יִצְחָק יַעֲקֹב יוֹסֵף אַהֲרֹן וְדָוִד.

On the sixth day
בְּמָטוּ מִנָּךְ אַהֲרֹן אֻשְׁפִּיזִי עִלָּאִי דְּיֵתִיב עִמִּי
וְעִמָּךְ כָּל אֻשְׁפִּיזֵי עִלָּאֵי:
אַבְרָהָם יִצְחָק יַעֲקֹב יוֹסֵף מֹשֶׁה וְדָוִד.

On הושענא רבה
בְּמָטוּ מִנָּךְ דָּוִד אֻשְׁפִּיזִי עִלָּאִי דְּיֵתִיב עִמִּי
וְעִמָּךְ כָּל אֻשְׁפִּיזֵי עִלָּאֵי:
אַבְרָהָם יִצְחָק יַעֲקֹב יוֹסֵף מֹשֶׁה וְאַהֲרֹן.

On the last day of סוכות *on leaving the* סוכה*:*

יְהִי רָצוֹן מִלְּפָנֶיךָ יהוה אֱלֹהֵינוּ וֵאלֹהֵי אֲבוֹתֵינוּ
כְּשֵׁם שֶׁקִּיַּמְתִּי וְיָשַׁבְתִּי בְּסֻכָּה זוֹ
כֵּן אֶזְכֶּה לַשָּׁנָה הַבָּאָה לֵישֵׁב בְּסֻכַּת עוֹרוֹ שֶׁל לִוְיָתָן.

Musaf for Ḥol HaMo'ed

The following prayer, until "in former years" on page 878, is said silently, standing with feet together. If there is a minyan, the Amida is repeated aloud by the Leader. Take three steps forward as if formally entering the place of the Divine Presence.

When I declare the LORD's name, give glory to our God. *Deut. 32*
O LORD, open my lips, so that my mouth may declare Your praise. *Ps. 51*

PATRIARCHS

בָּרוּךְ Blessed are You,
LORD our God and God of our fathers,
God of Abraham, God of Isaac and God of Jacob;
the great, mighty and awesome God, God Most High,
who acts with loving-kindness and creates all,
who remembers the loving-kindness of the fathers
and will bring a Redeemer to their children's children
for the sake of His name, in love. King, Helper, Savior, Shield:
Blessed are You, LORD, Shield of Abraham.

DIVINE MIGHT

אַתָּה גִּבּוֹר You are eternally mighty, LORD.
You give life to the dead and have great power to save.
In Israel: He causes the dew to fall.
He sustains the living with loving-kindness,
and with great compassion revives the dead.
He supports the fallen, heals the sick, sets captives free,
and keeps His faith with those who sleep in the dust.
Who is like You, Master of might,
and who can compare to You,
O King who brings death and gives life, and makes salvation grow?
Faithful are You to revive the dead.
Blessed are You, LORD, who revives the dead.

*When saying the Amida silently, continue with "You are holy" on page 862.
The Kedusha for Shabbat Ḥol HaMo'ed and Ḥoshana Raba is on the next page;
the Kedusha for Ḥol HaMo'ed is on page 862.*

מוסף לחול המועד

The following prayer, until קַדְמֹנִיּוֹת *on page 879, is said silently, standing with feet together. If there is a* מנין*, the* עמידה *is repeated aloud by the* שליח ציבור*. Take three steps forward as if formally entering the place of the Divine Presence.*

כִּי שֵׁם יהוה אֶקְרָא, הָבוּ גֹדֶל לֵאלֹהֵינוּ: דברים לב
אֲדֹנָי, שְׂפָתַי תִּפְתָּח, וּפִי יַגִּיד תְּהִלָּתֶךָ: תהלים נא

אבות

בָּרוּךְ אַתָּה יהוה, אֱלֹהֵינוּ וֵאלֹהֵי אֲבוֹתֵינוּ
אֱלֹהֵי אַבְרָהָם, אֱלֹהֵי יִצְחָק, וֵאלֹהֵי יַעֲקֹב
הָאֵל הַגָּדוֹל הַגִּבּוֹר וְהַנּוֹרָא, אֵל עֶלְיוֹן
גּוֹמֵל חֲסָדִים טוֹבִים, וְקוֹנֵה הַכֹּל, וְזוֹכֵר חַסְדֵי אָבוֹת
וּמֵבִיא גוֹאֵל לִבְנֵי בְנֵיהֶם לְמַעַן שְׁמוֹ בְּאַהֲבָה.
מֶלֶךְ עוֹזֵר וּמוֹשִׁיעַ וּמָגֵן.
בָּרוּךְ אַתָּה יהוה, מָגֵן אַבְרָהָם.

גבורות

אַתָּה גִּבּוֹר לְעוֹלָם, אֲדֹנָי
מְחַיֵּה מֵתִים אַתָּה, רַב לְהוֹשִׁיעַ
בארץ ישראל: מוֹרִיד הַטָּל
מְכַלְכֵּל חַיִּים בְּחֶסֶד, מְחַיֵּה מֵתִים בְּרַחֲמִים רַבִּים
סוֹמֵךְ נוֹפְלִים, וְרוֹפֵא חוֹלִים, וּמַתִּיר אֲסוּרִים
וּמְקַיֵּם אֱמוּנָתוֹ לִישֵׁנֵי עָפָר.
מִי כָמוֹךָ, בַּעַל גְּבוּרוֹת, וּמִי דּוֹמֶה לָּךְ
מֶלֶךְ, מֵמִית וּמְחַיֶּה וּמַצְמִיחַ יְשׁוּעָה.
וְנֶאֱמָן אַתָּה לְהַחֲיוֹת מֵתִים.
בָּרוּךְ אַתָּה יהוה, מְחַיֵּה הַמֵּתִים.

When saying the עמידה *silently, continue with* אַתָּה קָדוֹשׁ *on page 863.*
The קדושה *for* שבת חול המועד *and* הושענא רבה *is on the next page;*
the קדושה *for* חול המועד *is on page 863.*

KEDUSHA FOR SHABBAT ḤOL HAMO'ED AND HOSHANA RABA

The following is said standing with feet together, rising on the toes at the words indicated by ▴.

Cong. then Leader: נַעֲרִיצְךָ We will fear and sanctify You with the words
uttered by the holy Seraphim who sanctify Your name
in the Sanctuary; as is written by Your prophet:
"They call out to one another, saying: *Is. 6*

Cong. then Leader: ▴Holy, ▴holy, ▴holy is the LORD of multitudes;
the whole world is filled with His glory."
His glory fills the universe.
His ministering angels ask each other,
"Where is the place of His glory?"
Those facing them reply "Blessed –

Cong. then Leader: ▴"Blessed is the LORD's glory from His place." *Ezek. 3*
From His place may He turn with compassion
and be generous to the people who declare the unity of His name,
morning and evening, every day, continually,
twice each day reciting in love the Shema:

Cong. then Leader: "Listen, Israel, the LORD is our God, the LORD is One." *Deut. 6*
He is our God, He is our Father, He is our King, He is our Savior –
and He, in His compassion, will let us hear a second time
in the presence of all that lives, His promise "to be Your God. *Num. 15*
I am the LORD your God."

On Shabbat Ḥol HaMo'ed, the following paragraph is omitted:

Cong. then Leader: Glorious is our Glorious One, LORD our Master, *Ps. 8*
and glorious is Your name throughout the earth.
Then the LORD shall be King over all the earth; *Zech. 14*
on that day the LORD shall be One and His name One.

Leader: And in Your holy Writings it is written:

Cong. then Leader: ▴"The LORD shall reign for ever. He is your God, Zion, *Ps. 146*
from generation to generation, Halleluya!"

Leader: From generation to generation we will speak of Your greatness,
and we will declare Your holiness for evermore.
Your praise, our God, shall not leave our mouth forever,
for You, God, are a great and holy King.
Blessed are You, LORD, the holy God.

The Leader continues with "You have chosen us" on the next page.

קדושה לשבת חול המועד ולהושענא רבה

The following is said standing with feet together, rising on the toes at the words indicated by ▲.

קהל *then* ש״ץ: נַעֲרִיצְךָ וְנַקְדִּישְׁךָ כְּסוֹד שִׂיחַ שַׂרְפֵי קֹדֶשׁ
הַמַּקְדִּישִׁים שִׁמְךָ בַּקֹּדֶשׁ
כַּכָּתוּב עַל יַד נְבִיאֶךָ: וְקָרָא זֶה אֶל־זֶה וְאָמַר ישעיה ו

קהל *then* ש״ץ: ▲קָדוֹשׁ, ▲קָדוֹשׁ, ▲קָדוֹשׁ, יהוה צְבָאוֹת, מְלֹא כָל הָאָרֶץ כְּבוֹדוֹ:
כְּבוֹדוֹ מָלֵא עוֹלָם, מְשָׁרְתָיו שׁוֹאֲלִים זֶה לָזֶה, אַיֵּה מְקוֹם כְּבוֹדוֹ
לְעֻמָּתָם בָּרוּךְ יֹאמֵרוּ

קהל *then* ש״ץ: ▲בָּרוּךְ כְּבוֹד־יהוה מִמְּקוֹמוֹ: יחזקאל ג
מִמְּקוֹמוֹ הוּא יִפֶן בְּרַחֲמִים, וְיָחֹן עַם הַמְיַחֲדִים שְׁמוֹ
עֶרֶב וָבֹקֶר בְּכָל יוֹם תָּמִיד
פַּעֲמַיִם בְּאַהֲבָה שְׁמַע אוֹמְרִים

קהל *then* ש״ץ: שְׁמַע יִשְׂרָאֵל, יהוה אֱלֹהֵינוּ, יהוה אֶחָד: דברים ו
הוּא אֱלֹהֵינוּ, הוּא אָבִינוּ, הוּא מַלְכֵּנוּ, הוּא מוֹשִׁיעֵנוּ
וְהוּא יַשְׁמִיעֵנוּ בְּרַחֲמָיו שֵׁנִית לְעֵינֵי כָּל חָי, לִהְיוֹת לָכֶם לֵאלֹהִים במדבר טו
אֲנִי יהוה אֱלֹהֵיכֶם:

On שבת חול המועד*, the following paragraph is omitted:*

קהל *then* ש״ץ: אַדִּיר אַדִּירֵנוּ, יהוה אֲדֹנֵינוּ, מָה־אַדִּיר שִׁמְךָ בְּכָל־הָאָרֶץ: תהלים ח
וְהָיָה יהוה לְמֶלֶךְ עַל־כָּל־הָאָרֶץ זכריה יד
בַּיּוֹם הַהוּא יִהְיֶה יהוה אֶחָד וּשְׁמוֹ אֶחָד:

ש״ץ: וּבְדִבְרֵי קָדְשְׁךָ כָּתוּב לֵאמֹר

קהל *then* ש״ץ: ▲יִמְלֹךְ יהוה לְעוֹלָם, אֱלֹהַיִךְ צִיּוֹן לְדֹר וָדֹר, הַלְלוּיָהּ: תהלים קמו

ש״ץ: לְדוֹר וָדוֹר נַגִּיד גָּדְלֶךָ, וּלְנֵצַח נְצָחִים קְדֻשָּׁתְךָ נַקְדִּישׁ
וְשִׁבְחֲךָ אֱלֹהֵינוּ מִפִּינוּ לֹא יָמוּשׁ לְעוֹלָם וָעֶד
כִּי אֵל מֶלֶךְ גָּדוֹל וְקָדוֹשׁ אָתָּה.
בָּרוּךְ אַתָּה יהוה, הָאֵל הַקָּדוֹשׁ.

The שליח ציבור *continues with* אַתָּה בְחַרְתָּנוּ *on the next page.*

KEDUSHA FOR ḤOL HAMO'ED

During the Leader's Repetition, the following is said standing with feet together, rising on the toes at the words indicated by ▲.

Cong. then Leader: נְקַדֵּשׁ We will sanctify Your name on earth,
as they sanctify it in the highest heavens,
as is written by Your prophet,
"And they [the angels] call to one another saying: *Is. 6*

Cong. then Leader: ▲Holy, ▲holy, ▲holy is the LORD of multitudes
the whole world is filled with His glory."
Those facing them say "Blessed – "

Cong. then Leader: ▲"Blessed is the LORD's glory from His place." *Ezek. 3*
And in Your holy Writings it is written thus:

Cong. then Leader: ▲"The LORD shall reign for ever. *Ps. 146*
He is your God, Zion, from generation to generation,
Halleluya!"

Leader: From generation to generation we will speak of Your greatness,
and we will declare Your holiness for evermore.
Your praise, our God, shall not leave our mouth forever,
for You, God, are a great and holy King.
Blessed are You, LORD, the holy God.

The Leader continues with "You have chosen us" below.

When saying the Amida silently, continue here with "You are holy":

HOLINESS

אַתָּה קָדוֹשׁ You are holy and Your name is holy,
and holy ones praise You daily, Selah!
Blessed are You, LORD, the holy God.

HOLINESS OF THE DAY

אַתָּה בְחַרְתָּנוּ You have chosen us from among all peoples.
You have loved and favored us.
You have raised us above all tongues.
You have made us holy through Your commandments.
You have brought us near, our King, to Your service,
and have called us by Your great and holy name.

קדושה לחול המועד

During the חזרת הש״ץ, *the following is said standing with feet together, rising on the toes at the words indicated by* ▴.

then קהל ש״ץ: נְקַדֵּשׁ אֶת שִׁמְךָ בָּעוֹלָם, כְּשֵׁם שֶׁמַּקְדִּישִׁים אוֹתוֹ בִּשְׁמֵי מָרוֹם
כַּכָּתוּב עַל יַד נְבִיאֶךָ: וְקָרָא זֶה אֶל־זֶה וְאָמַר ישעיה ו

then קהל ש״ץ: ▴קָדוֹשׁ, ▴קָדוֹשׁ, ▴קָדוֹשׁ, יהוה צְבָאוֹת, מְלֹא כָל־הָאָרֶץ כְּבוֹדוֹ:
לְעֻמָּתָם בָּרוּךְ יֹאמֵרוּ

then קהל ש״ץ: ▴בָּרוּךְ כְּבוֹד־יהוה מִמְּקוֹמוֹ: יחזקאל ג
וּבְדִבְרֵי קָדְשְׁךָ כָּתוּב לֵאמֹר

then קהל ש״ץ: ▴יִמְלֹךְ יהוה לְעוֹלָם, אֱלֹהַיִךְ צִיּוֹן לְדֹר וָדֹר, הַלְלוּיָהּ: תהלים קמו

ש״ץ: לְדוֹר וָדוֹר נַגִּיד גָּדְלֶךָ, וּלְנֵצַח נְצָחִים קְדֻשָּׁתְךָ נַקְדִּישׁ
וְשִׁבְחֲךָ אֱלֹהֵינוּ מִפִּינוּ לֹא יָמוּשׁ לְעוֹלָם וָעֶד
כִּי אֵל מֶלֶךְ גָּדוֹל וְקָדוֹשׁ אָתָּה.
בָּרוּךְ אַתָּה יהוה, הָאֵל הַקָּדוֹשׁ.

The שליח ציבור *continues with* אַתָּה בְחַרְתָּנוּ *below.*

When saying the עמידה *silently, continue here with* אַתָּה קָדוֹשׁ:

קדושת השם

אַתָּה קָדוֹשׁ וְשִׁמְךָ קָדוֹשׁ, וּקְדוֹשִׁים בְּכָל יוֹם יְהַלְלוּךָ סֶּלָה.
בָּרוּךְ אַתָּה יהוה, הָאֵל הַקָּדוֹשׁ.

קדושת היום

אַתָּה בְחַרְתָּנוּ מִכָּל הָעַמִּים
אָהַבְתָּ אוֹתָנוּ וְרָצִיתָ בָּנוּ
וְרוֹמַמְתָּנוּ מִכָּל הַלְּשׁוֹנוֹת
וְקִדַּשְׁתָּנוּ בְּמִצְוֹתֶיךָ
וְקֵרַבְתָּנוּ מַלְכֵּנוּ לַעֲבוֹדָתֶךָ
וְשִׁמְךָ הַגָּדוֹל וְהַקָּדוֹשׁ עָלֵינוּ קָרָאתָ.

On Shabbat, add the words in parentheses:

וַתִּתֶּן לָנוּ And You, LORD our God, have given us in love
(Sabbaths for rest and) festivals for rejoicing,
holy days and seasons for joy,
(this Sabbath day and) this day of:

On Pesaḥ: the festival of Matzot,
the time of our freedom
On Sukkot: the festival of Sukkot,
our time of rejoicing

(with love), a holy assembly
in memory of the exodus from Egypt.

וּמִפְּנֵי חֲטָאֵינוּ But because of our sins we were exiled from our land
and driven far from our country.
We cannot go up to appear and bow before You,
and to perform our duties in Your chosen House,
the great and holy Temple that was called by Your name,
because of the hand that was stretched out against Your Sanctuary.
May it be Your will, LORD our God and God of our ancestors,
merciful King,
that You in Your abounding compassion may once more
have mercy on us and on Your Sanctuary,
rebuilding it swiftly and adding to its glory.
Our Father, our King,
reveal the glory of Your kingdom to us swiftly.
Appear and be great over us in the sight of all that lives.
Bring back our scattered ones from among the nations,
and gather our dispersed people from the ends of the earth.
Lead us to Zion, Your city, in celebration,
and to Jerusalem, home of Your Temple, with everlasting joy.
There we will prepare for You our obligatory offerings:
the regular daily offerings in their order
and the additional offerings according to their law.

On שבת*, add the words in parentheses:*

וַתִּתֶּן לָנוּ יהוה אֱלֹהֵינוּ בְּאַהֲבָה
(שַׁבָּתוֹת לִמְנוּחָה וּ) מוֹעֲדִים לְשִׂמְחָה
חַגִּים וּזְמַנִּים לְשָׂשׂוֹן
אֶת יוֹם (הַשַּׁבָּת הַזֶּה וְאֶת יוֹם)

בפסח: חַג הַמַּצּוֹת הַזֶּה, זְמַן חֵרוּתֵנוּ

בסוכות: חַג הַסֻּכּוֹת הַזֶּה, זְמַן שִׂמְחָתֵנוּ

(בְּאַהֲבָה) מִקְרָא קֹדֶשׁ, זֵכֶר לִיצִיאַת מִצְרָיִם.

וּמִפְּנֵי חֲטָאֵינוּ גָּלִינוּ מֵאַרְצֵנוּ, וְנִתְרַחַקְנוּ מֵעַל אַדְמָתֵנוּ
וְאֵין אֲנַחְנוּ יְכוֹלִים לַעֲלוֹת וְלֵרָאוֹת וּלְהִשְׁתַּחֲווֹת לְפָנֶיךָ
וְלַעֲשׂוֹת חוֹבוֹתֵינוּ בְּבֵית בְּחִירָתֶךָ
בַּבַּיִת הַגָּדוֹל וְהַקָּדוֹשׁ שֶׁנִּקְרָא שִׁמְךָ עָלָיו
מִפְּנֵי הַיָּד שֶׁנִּשְׁתַּלְּחָה בְּמִקְדָּשֶׁךָ.
יְהִי רָצוֹן מִלְּפָנֶיךָ יהוה אֱלֹהֵינוּ וֵאלֹהֵי אֲבוֹתֵינוּ
מֶלֶךְ רַחֲמָן
שֶׁתָּשׁוּב וּתְרַחֵם עָלֵינוּ וְעַל מִקְדָּשְׁךָ בְּרַחֲמֶיךָ הָרַבִּים
וְתִבְנֵהוּ מְהֵרָה וּתְגַדֵּל כְּבוֹדוֹ.
אָבִינוּ מַלְכֵּנוּ, גַּלֵּה כְּבוֹד מַלְכוּתְךָ עָלֵינוּ מְהֵרָה
וְהוֹפַע וְהִנָּשֵׂא עָלֵינוּ לְעֵינֵי כָּל חַי
וְקָרֵב פְּזוּרֵינוּ מִבֵּין הַגּוֹיִם, וּנְפוּצוֹתֵינוּ כַּנֵּס מִיַּרְכְּתֵי אָרֶץ.
וַהֲבִיאֵנוּ לְצִיּוֹן עִירְךָ בְּרִנָּה
וְלִירוּשָׁלַיִם בֵּית מִקְדָּשְׁךָ בְּשִׂמְחַת עוֹלָם
וְשָׁם נַעֲשֶׂה לְפָנֶיךָ אֶת קָרְבְּנוֹת חוֹבוֹתֵינוּ
תְּמִידִים כְּסִדְרָם וּמוּסָפִים כְּהִלְכָתָם

And the additional offering(s of this Sabbath day and) of this day of:

On Pesaḥ: the festival of Matzot.

On Sukkot: the festival of Sukkot.

we will prepare and offer before You in love,
in accord with Your will's commandment,
as You wrote for us in Your Torah
through Your servant Moses, by Your own word, as it is said:

On Shabbat add:

וּבְיוֹם הַשַּׁבָּת On the Sabbath day, make an offering of two lambs a year old, without blemish, together with two-tenths of an ephah of fine flour mixed with oil as a meal-offering, and its appropriate libation. This is the burnt-offering for every Sabbath, in addition to the regular daily burnt-offering and its libation. *Num. 28*

On Ḥol HaMo'ed Pesaḥ say:

וְהִקְרַבְתֶּם And you shall bring an offering consumed by fire, a burnt-offering to the Lord: two young bullocks, one ram, and seven yearling male lambs; they shall be to you unblemished. And their meal-offerings and wine-libations as ordained: three-tenths of an ephah for each bull, two-tenths of an ephah for the ram, one-tenth of an ephah for each lamb, wine for the libations, a male goat for atonement, and two regular daily offerings according to their law. *Num. 28*

On weekdays, continue with "Our God and God of our ancestors" on page 870.
On Shabbat, continue with "Those who keep the Sabbath" on page 870.

On the first day of Ḥol HaMo'ed Sukkot,
say the following two paragraphs (in Israel say only the first):

וּבַיּוֹם הַשֵּׁנִי On the second day you shall offer twelve young bullocks, two rams, fourteen yearling male lambs without blemish. And their meal-offerings and wine-libations as ordained: three-tenths of an ephah for each bull, two-tenths of an ephah for each ram, one-tenth of an ephah for each lamb, wine for the libations, a male goat for atonement, and two regular daily offerings according to their law. *Num. 29*

וּבַיּוֹם הַשְּׁלִישִׁי On the third day you shall offer eleven bullocks, two rams, fourteen yearling male lambs without blemish. And their meal-offerings and wine-libations as ordained: three-tenths of an ephah for each bull, two-tenths of an ephah for the ram, one-tenth of an ephah for each lamb, wine for the libations, a male goat for atonement, and two regular daily offerings according to their law. *Num. 29*

On weekdays, continue with "Our God and God of our ancestors" on page 870.
On Shabbat, continue with "Those who keep the Sabbath" on page 870.

וְאֶת מוּסַף יוֹם / שבת: וְאֶת מוּסְפֵי יוֹם הַשַּׁבָּת הַזֶּה וְיוֹם/

בפסח: חַג הַמַּצּוֹת הַזֶּה

בסוכות: חַג הַסֻּכּוֹת הַזֶּה

נַעֲשֶׂה וְנַקְרִיב לְפָנֶיךָ בְּאַהֲבָה כְּמִצְוַת רְצוֹנֶךָ

כְּמוֹ שֶׁכָּתַבְתָּ עָלֵינוּ בְּתוֹרָתֶךָ

עַל יְדֵי מֹשֶׁה עַבְדֶּךָ מִפִּי כְבוֹדֶךָ, כָּאָמוּר

On שבת add:

במדבר כח וּבְיוֹם הַשַּׁבָּת, שְׁנֵי־כְבָשִׂים בְּנֵי־שָׁנָה תְּמִימִם, וּשְׁנֵי עֶשְׂרֹנִים סֹלֶת מִנְחָה בְּלוּלָה בַשֶּׁמֶן וְנִסְכּוֹ: עֹלַת שַׁבַּת בְּשַׁבַּתּוֹ, עַל־עֹלַת הַתָּמִיד וְנִסְכָּהּ:

On חול המועד פסח *say:*

במדבר כח וְהִקְרַבְתֶּם אִשֶּׁה עֹלָה לַיהוה, פָּרִים בְּנֵי־בָקָר שְׁנַיִם וְאַיִל אֶחָד, וְשִׁבְעָה כְבָשִׂים בְּנֵי שָׁנָה, תְּמִימִם יִהְיוּ לָכֶם: וּמִנְחָתָם וְנִסְכֵּיהֶם כִּמְדֻבָּר, שְׁלֹשָׁה עֶשְׂרֹנִים לַפָּר וּשְׁנֵי עֶשְׂרֹנִים לָאָיִל, וְעִשָּׂרוֹן לַכֶּבֶשׂ, וְיַיִן כְּנִסְכּוֹ, וְשָׂעִיר לְכַפֵּר, וּשְׁנֵי תְמִידִים כְּהִלְכָתָם.

On weekdays, continue with אֱלֹהֵינוּ וֵאלֹהֵי אֲבוֹתֵינוּ *on page 871.*
On שבת*, continue with* יִשְׂמְחוּ בְמַלְכוּתְךָ *on page 871.*

On the first day of חול המועד סוכות*,*
say the following two paragraphs (in ארץ ישראל *say only the first):*

במדבר כט וּבַיּוֹם הַשֵּׁנִי, פָּרִים בְּנֵי־בָקָר שְׁנֵים עָשָׂר, אֵילִם שְׁנָיִם, כְּבָשִׂים בְּנֵי־שָׁנָה אַרְבָּעָה עָשָׂר, תְּמִימִם: וּמִנְחָתָם וְנִסְכֵּיהֶם כִּמְדֻבָּר, שְׁלֹשָׁה עֶשְׂרֹנִים לַפָּר, וּשְׁנֵי עֶשְׂרֹנִים לָאָיִל, וְעִשָּׂרוֹן לַכֶּבֶשׂ, וְיַיִן כְּנִסְכּוֹ, וְשָׂעִיר לְכַפֵּר, וּשְׁנֵי תְמִידִים כְּהִלְכָתָם.

במדבר כט וּבַיּוֹם הַשְּׁלִישִׁי, פָּרִים עַשְׁתֵּי־עָשָׂר, אֵילִם שְׁנָיִם, כְּבָשִׂים בְּנֵי־שָׁנָה אַרְבָּעָה עָשָׂר, תְּמִימִם: וּמִנְחָתָם וְנִסְכֵּיהֶם כִּמְדֻבָּר, שְׁלֹשָׁה עֶשְׂרֹנִים לַפָּר, וּשְׁנֵי עֶשְׂרֹנִים לָאָיִל, וְעִשָּׂרוֹן לַכֶּבֶשׂ, וְיַיִן כְּנִסְכּוֹ, וְשָׂעִיר לְכַפֵּר, וּשְׁנֵי תְמִידִים כְּהִלְכָתָם.

On weekdays, continue with אֱלֹהֵינוּ וֵאלֹהֵי אֲבוֹתֵינוּ *on page 871.*
On שבת*, continue with* יִשְׂמְחוּ בְמַלְכוּתְךָ *on page 871.*

On the second day of Ḥol HaMo'ed Sukkot, say the following two paragraphs (in Israel say only the first):

וּבַיּוֹם הַשְּׁלִישִׁי On the third day you shall offer eleven bullocks, two rams, fourteen yearling male lambs without blemish. And their meal-offerings and wine-libations as ordained: three-tenths of an ephah for each bull, two-tenths of an ephah for each ram, one-tenth of an ephah for each lamb, wine for the libations, a male goat for atonement, and two regular daily offerings according to their law. *Num. 29*

וּבַיּוֹם הָרְבִיעִי On the fourth day you shall offer ten bullocks, two rams, fourteen yearling male lambs without blemish. And their meal-offerings and wine-libations as ordained: three-tenths of an ephah for each bull, two-tenths of an ephah for each ram, one-tenth of an ephah for each lamb, wine for the libations, a male goat for atonement, and two regular daily offerings according to their law. *Num. 29*

On weekdays, continue with "Our God and God of our ancestors" on the next page. On Shabbat, continue with "Those who keep the Sabbath" on the next page.

On the third day of Ḥol HaMo'ed Sukkot, say the following two paragraphs (in Israel say only the first):

וּבַיּוֹם הָרְבִיעִי On the fourth day you shall offer ten bullocks, two rams, fourteen yearling male lambs without blemish. And their meal-offerings and wine-libations as ordained: three-tenths of an ephah for each bull, two-tenths of an ephah for each ram, one-tenth of an ephah for each lamb, wine for the libations, a male goat for atonement, and two regular daily offerings according to their law. *Num. 29*

וּבַיּוֹם הַחֲמִישִׁי On the fifth day you shall offer nine bullocks, two rams, fourteen yearling male lambs without blemish. And their meal-offerings and wine-libations as ordained: three-tenths of an ephah for each bull, two-tenths of an ephah for each ram, one-tenth of an ephah for each lamb, wine for the libations, a male goat for atonement, and two regular daily offerings according to their law. *Num. 29*

On weekdays, continue with "Our God and God of our ancestors" on the next page. On Shabbat, continue with "Those who keep the Sabbath" on the next page.

On the fourth day of Ḥol HaMo'ed Sukkot, say the following two paragraphs (in Israel say only the first):

וּבַיּוֹם הַחֲמִישִׁי On the fifth day you shall offer nine bullocks, two rams, fourteen yearling male lambs without blemish. And their meal-offerings and wine-libations as ordained: three-tenths of an ephah for each bull, two-tenths of an ephah for each ram, one-tenth of an ephah for each lamb, wine for the libations, a male goat for atonement, and two regular daily offerings according to their law. *Num. 29*

Continue with "On the sixth day" at the top of the next page.

On the second day of חול המועד סוכות*,*
say the following two paragraphs (in ארץ ישראל *say only the first):*

במדבר כט
וּבַיּוֹם הַשְּׁלִישִׁי, פָּרִים עַשְׁתֵּי־עָשָׂר, אֵילִם שְׁנָיִם, כְּבָשִׂים בְּנֵי־שָׁנָה אַרְבָּעָה עָשָׂר, תְּמִימִם: וּמִנְחָתָם וְנִסְכֵּיהֶם כִּמְדֻבָּר, שְׁלֹשָׁה עֶשְׂרֹנִים לַפָּר, וּשְׁנֵי עֶשְׂרֹנִים לָאָיִל, וְעִשָּׂרוֹן לַכֶּבֶשׂ, וְיַיִן כְּנִסְכּוֹ, וְשָׂעִיר לְכַפֵּר, וּשְׁנֵי תְמִידִים כְּהִלְכָתָם.

במדבר כט
וּבַיּוֹם הָרְבִיעִי, פָּרִים עֲשָׂרָה, אֵילִם שְׁנָיִם, כְּבָשִׂים בְּנֵי־שָׁנָה אַרְבָּעָה עָשָׂר, תְּמִימִם: וּמִנְחָתָם וְנִסְכֵּיהֶם כִּמְדֻבָּר, שְׁלֹשָׁה עֶשְׂרֹנִים לַפָּר, וּשְׁנֵי עֶשְׂרֹנִים לָאָיִל, וְעִשָּׂרוֹן לַכֶּבֶשׂ, וְיַיִן כְּנִסְכּוֹ, וְשָׂעִיר לְכַפֵּר, וּשְׁנֵי תְמִידִים כְּהִלְכָתָם.

On weekdays, continue with אֱלֹהֵינוּ וֵאלֹהֵי אֲבוֹתֵינוּ *on the next page.*
On שבת*, continue with* יִשְׂמְחוּ בְמַלְכוּתְךָ *on the next page.*

On the third day of חול המועד סוכות*,*
say the following two paragraphs (in ארץ ישראל *say only the first):*

במדבר כט
וּבַיּוֹם הָרְבִיעִי, פָּרִים עֲשָׂרָה, אֵילִם שְׁנָיִם, כְּבָשִׂים בְּנֵי־שָׁנָה אַרְבָּעָה עָשָׂר, תְּמִימִם: וּמִנְחָתָם וְנִסְכֵּיהֶם כִּמְדֻבָּר, שְׁלֹשָׁה עֶשְׂרֹנִים לַפָּר, וּשְׁנֵי עֶשְׂרֹנִים לָאָיִל, וְעִשָּׂרוֹן לַכֶּבֶשׂ, וְיַיִן כְּנִסְכּוֹ, וְשָׂעִיר לְכַפֵּר, וּשְׁנֵי תְמִידִים כְּהִלְכָתָם.

במדבר כט
וּבַיּוֹם הַחֲמִישִׁי, פָּרִים תִּשְׁעָה, אֵילִם שְׁנָיִם, כְּבָשִׂים בְּנֵי־שָׁנָה אַרְבָּעָה עָשָׂר, תְּמִימִם: וּמִנְחָתָם וְנִסְכֵּיהֶם כִּמְדֻבָּר, שְׁלֹשָׁה עֶשְׂרֹנִים לַפָּר, וּשְׁנֵי עֶשְׂרֹנִים לָאָיִל, וְעִשָּׂרוֹן לַכֶּבֶשׂ, וְיַיִן כְּנִסְכּוֹ, וְשָׂעִיר לְכַפֵּר, וּשְׁנֵי תְמִידִים כְּהִלְכָתָם.

On weekdays, continue with אֱלֹהֵינוּ וֵאלֹהֵי אֲבוֹתֵינוּ *on the next page.*
On שבת*, continue with* יִשְׂמְחוּ בְמַלְכוּתְךָ *on the next page.*

On the fourth day of חול המועד סוכות*, say the following*
two paragraphs (in ארץ ישראל *say only the first):*

במדבר כט
וּבַיּוֹם הַחֲמִישִׁי, פָּרִים תִּשְׁעָה, אֵילִם שְׁנָיִם, כְּבָשִׂים בְּנֵי־שָׁנָה אַרְבָּעָה עָשָׂר, תְּמִימִם: וּמִנְחָתָם וְנִסְכֵּיהֶם כִּמְדֻבָּר, שְׁלֹשָׁה עֶשְׂרֹנִים לַפָּר, וּשְׁנֵי עֶשְׂרֹנִים לָאָיִל, וְעִשָּׂרוֹן לַכֶּבֶשׂ, וְיַיִן כְּנִסְכּוֹ, וְשָׂעִיר לְכַפֵּר, וּשְׁנֵי תְמִידִים כְּהִלְכָתָם.

Continue with וּבַיּוֹם הַשִּׁשִּׁי *at the top of the next page.*

וּבַיּוֹם הַשִּׁשִּׁי On the sixth day you shall offer eight bullocks, two rams, fourteen yearling male lambs without blemish. And their meal-offerings and wine-libations as ordained: three-tenths of an ephah for each bull, two-tenths of an ephah for each ram, one-tenth of an ephah for each lamb, wine for the libations, a male goat for atonement, and two regular daily offerings according to their law. *Num. 29*

On weekdays, continue with "Our God and God of our ancestors" below.
On Shabbat, continue with "Those who keep the Sabbath" below.

On Hoshana Raba, say the following two paragraphs.
In Israel, say the first paragraph on the fifth day of Ḥol HaMo'ed and the second on Hoshana Raba.

וּבַיּוֹם הַשִּׁשִּׁי On the sixth day you shall offer eight bullocks, two rams, fourteen yearling male lambs without blemish. And their meal-offerings and wine-libations as ordained: three-tenths of an ephah for each bull, two-tenths of an ephah for each ram, one-tenth of an ephah for each lamb, wine for the libations, a male goat for atonement, and two regular daily offerings according to their law. *Num. 29*

וּבַיּוֹם הַשְּׁבִיעִי On the seventh day you shall offer seven bullocks, two rams, fourteen yearling male lambs without blemish. And their meal-offerings and wine-libations as ordained: three-tenths of an ephah for each bull, two-tenths of an ephah for each ram, one-tenth of an ephah for each lamb, wine for the libations, a male goat for atonement, and two regular daily offerings according to their law. *Num. 29*

Continue with "Our God and God of our ancestors" below.

On Shabbat say:

יִשְׂמְחוּ Those who keep the Sabbath and call it a delight shall rejoice in Your kingship. The people who sanctify the seventh day shall all be satisfied and take delight in Your goodness, for You favored the seventh day and declared it holy. You called it "most desirable of days" in remembrance of Creation.

אֱלֹהֵינוּ Our God and God of our ancestors,
merciful King, have compassion upon us.
You who are good and do good, respond to our call.
Return to us in Your abounding mercy
for the sake of our fathers who did Your will.
Rebuild Your Temple as at the beginning,
and establish Your Sanctuary on its site.
Let us witness its rebuilding and gladden us by its restoration.
Bring the priests back to their service,
the Levites to their song and music,
and the Israelites to their homes.

במדבר כט וּבַיּוֹם הַשִּׁשִּׁי, פָּרִים שְׁמֹנָה, אֵילִם שְׁנָיִם, כְּבָשִׂים בְּנֵי־שָׁנָה אַרְבָּעָה עָשָׂר, תְּמִימִם: וּמִנְחָתָם וְנִסְכֵּיהֶם כִּמְדֻבָּר, שְׁלֹשָׁה עֶשְׂרֹנִים לַפָּר, וּשְׁנֵי עֶשְׂרֹנִים לָאָיִל, וְעִשָּׂרוֹן לַכֶּבֶשׂ, וְיַיִן כְּנִסְכּוֹ, וְשָׂעִיר לְכַפֵּר, וּשְׁנֵי תְמִידִים כְּהִלְכָתָם.

On weekdays, continue with אֱלֹהֵינוּ וֵאלֹהֵי אֲבוֹתֵינוּ *below.*
On שבת*, continue with* יִשְׂמְחוּ בְמַלְכוּתְךָ *below.*

On הושענא רבה*, say the following two paragraphs.*
In ארץ ישראל*, say the first paragraph on the fifth day of* חול המועד
and the second on הושענא רבה*:*

במדבר כט וּבַיּוֹם הַשִּׁשִּׁי, פָּרִים שְׁמֹנָה, אֵילִם שְׁנָיִם, כְּבָשִׂים בְּנֵי־שָׁנָה אַרְבָּעָה עָשָׂר, תְּמִימִם: וּמִנְחָתָם וְנִסְכֵּיהֶם כִּמְדֻבָּר, שְׁלֹשָׁה עֶשְׂרֹנִים לַפָּר, וּשְׁנֵי עֶשְׂרֹנִים לָאָיִל, וְעִשָּׂרוֹן לַכֶּבֶשׂ, וְיַיִן כְּנִסְכּוֹ, וְשָׂעִיר לְכַפֵּר, וּשְׁנֵי תְמִידִים כְּהִלְכָתָם.

במדבר כט וּבַיּוֹם הַשְּׁבִיעִי, פָּרִים שִׁבְעָה, אֵילִם שְׁנָיִם, כְּבָשִׂים בְּנֵי־שָׁנָה אַרְבָּעָה עָשָׂר, תְּמִימִם: וּמִנְחָתָם וְנִסְכֵּיהֶם כִּמְדֻבָּר, שְׁלֹשָׁה עֶשְׂרֹנִים לַפָּר, וּשְׁנֵי עֶשְׂרֹנִים לָאָיִל, וְעִשָּׂרוֹן לַכֶּבֶשׂ, וְיַיִן כְּנִסְכּוֹ, וְשָׂעִיר לְכַפֵּר, וּשְׁנֵי תְמִידִים כְּהִלְכָתָם.

Continue with אֱלֹהֵינוּ וֵאלֹהֵי אֲבוֹתֵינוּ *below.*

On שבת *say:*

יִשְׂמְחוּ בְמַלְכוּתְךָ שׁוֹמְרֵי שַׁבָּת וְקוֹרְאֵי עֹנֶג. עַם מְקַדְּשֵׁי שְׁבִיעִי כֻּלָּם יִשְׂבְּעוּ וְיִתְעַנְּגוּ מִטּוּבֶךָ, וּבַשְּׁבִיעִי רָצִיתָ בּוֹ וְקִדַּשְׁתּוֹ, חֶמְדַּת יָמִים אוֹתוֹ קָרָאתָ, זֵכֶר לְמַעֲשֵׂה בְרֵאשִׁית.

אֱלֹהֵינוּ וֵאלֹהֵי אֲבוֹתֵינוּ
מֶלֶךְ רַחֲמָן רַחֵם עָלֵינוּ, טוֹב וּמֵטִיב הִדָּרֶשׁ לָנוּ
שׁוּבָה אֵלֵינוּ בַּהֲמוֹן רַחֲמֶיךָ, בִּגְלַל אָבוֹת שֶׁעָשׂוּ רְצוֹנֶךָ.
בְּנֵה בֵיתְךָ כְּבַתְּחִלָּה, וְכוֹנֵן מִקְדָּשְׁךָ עַל מְכוֹנוֹ
וְהַרְאֵנוּ בְּבִנְיָנוֹ, וְשַׂמְּחֵנוּ בְּתִקּוּנוֹ
וְהָשֵׁב כֹּהֲנִים לַעֲבוֹדָתָם
וּלְוִיִּם לְשִׁירָם וּלְזִמְרָם
וְהָשֵׁב יִשְׂרָאֵל לִנְוֵיהֶם.

וְשָׁם נַעֲלֶה There we will go up and appear and bow before You
on the three pilgrimage festivals, as is written in Your Torah:

"Three times in the year *Deut. 16*
all your men will appear before the LORD your God
at the place He will choose:
on Pesaḥ, Shavuot and Sukkot.
They shall not appear before the LORD empty-handed.
Each shall bring such a gift as he can,
in proportion to the blessing
that the LORD your God gives you."

וְהַשִּׂיאֵנוּ Bring us, LORD our God,
the blessing of Your festivals
for life and peace, joy and gladness,
as You desired and promised to bless us.
Make us holy through Your commandments
and give us a share in Your Torah;
satisfy us with Your goodness,
gladden us with Your salvation,
and purify our hearts to serve You in truth.
And give us a heritage, LORD our God,
with joy and gladness Your holy festivals.
May Israel, who sanctify Your name, rejoice in You.
Blessed are You, LORD,
who sanctifies Israel, and the festive seasons.

TEMPLE SERVICE

רְצֵה Find favor, LORD our God,
in Your people Israel and their prayer.
Restore the service to Your most holy House,
and accept in love and favor
the fire-offerings of Israel and their prayer.
May the service of Your people Israel
always find favor with You.

וְשָׁם נַעֲלֶה וְנֵרָאֶה וְנִשְׁתַּחֲוֶה לְפָנֶיךָ בְּשָׁלֹשׁ פַּעֲמֵי רְגָלֵינוּ
כַּכָּתוּב בְּתוֹרָתֶךָ

שָׁלוֹשׁ פְּעָמִים בַּשָּׁנָה יֵרָאֶה כָל־זְכוּרְךָ אֶת־פְּנֵי יהוה אֱלֹהֶיךָ דברים טז
בַּמָּקוֹם אֲשֶׁר יִבְחָר
בְּחַג הַמַּצּוֹת, וּבְחַג הַשָּׁבֻעוֹת, וּבְחַג הַסֻּכּוֹת
וְלֹא יֵרָאֶה אֶת־פְּנֵי יהוה רֵיקָם:
אִישׁ כְּמַתְּנַת יָדוֹ
כְּבִרְכַּת יהוה אֱלֹהֶיךָ אֲשֶׁר נָתַן־לָךְ:

וְהַשִּׂיאֵנוּ יהוה אֱלֹהֵינוּ אֶת בִּרְכַּת מוֹעֲדֶיךָ
לְחַיִּים וּלְשָׁלוֹם, לְשִׂמְחָה וּלְשָׂשׂוֹן
כַּאֲשֶׁר רָצִיתָ וְאָמַרְתָּ לְבָרְכֵנוּ.
קַדְּשֵׁנוּ בְּמִצְוֹתֶיךָ, וְתֵן חֶלְקֵנוּ בְּתוֹרָתֶךָ
שַׂבְּעֵנוּ מִטּוּבֶךָ, וְשַׂמְּחֵנוּ בִּישׁוּעָתֶךָ
וְטַהֵר לִבֵּנוּ לְעָבְדְּךָ בֶּאֱמֶת
וְהַנְחִילֵנוּ יהוה אֱלֹהֵינוּ
בְּשִׂמְחָה וּבְשָׂשׂוֹן מוֹעֲדֵי קָדְשֶׁךָ
וְיִשְׂמְחוּ בְךָ יִשְׂרָאֵל מְקַדְּשֵׁי שְׁמֶךָ.
בָּרוּךְ אַתָּה יהוה, מְקַדֵּשׁ יִשְׂרָאֵל וְהַזְּמַנִּים.

עבודה

רְצֵה יהוה אֱלֹהֵינוּ בְּעַמְּךָ יִשְׂרָאֵל וּבִתְפִלָּתָם
וְהָשֵׁב אֶת הָעֲבוֹדָה לִדְבִיר בֵּיתֶךָ
וְאִשֵּׁי יִשְׂרָאֵל וּתְפִלָּתָם בְּאַהֲבָה תְקַבֵּל בְּרָצוֹן
וּתְהִי לְרָצוֹן תָּמִיד עֲבוֹדַת יִשְׂרָאֵל עַמֶּךָ.

And may our eyes witness Your return to Zion in compassion.
Blessed are You, LORD, who restores His Presence to Zion.

THANKSGIVING

מוֹדִים We give thanks to You,
for You are the LORD our God
and God of our ancestors
for ever and all time.
You are the Rock of our lives,
Shield of our salvation
from generation to generation.
We will thank You and
declare Your praise for our lives,
which are entrusted into Your hand;
for our souls,
which are placed in Your charge;
for Your miracles
which are with us every day;
and for Your wonders and favors
at all times,
evening, morning and midday.
You are good –
for Your compassion never fails.
You are compassionate –
for Your loving-kindnesses never cease.
We have always placed our hope in You.

During the Leader's Repetition, the congregation says quietly:
מוֹדִים We give thanks
to You, for You are
the LORD our God
and God of our ancestors,
God of all flesh,
who formed us
and formed the universe.
Blessings and thanks
are due to Your great
and holy name for giving us
life and sustaining us.
May You continue
to give us life and sustain us;
and may You gather
our exiles
to Your holy courts,
to keep Your decrees,
do Your will and serve You
with a perfect heart,
for it is for us
to give You thanks.
Blessed be God
to whom thanksgiving is due.

וְעַל כֻּלָּם For all these things may Your name be blessed and elevated,
our King, continually, for ever and all time.
Let all that lives thank You, Selah! and praise Your name in truth,
God, our Savior and Help, Selah!
Blessed are You, LORD,
whose name is "the Good" and to whom thanks are due.

וְתֶחֱזֶינָה עֵינֵינוּ בְּשׁוּבְךָ לְצִיּוֹן בְּרַחֲמִים.
בָּרוּךְ אַתָּה יהוה, הַמַּחֲזִיר שְׁכִינָתוֹ לְצִיּוֹן.

הודאה

מוֹדִים אֲנַחְנוּ לָךְ
שָׁאַתָּה הוּא יהוה אֱלֹהֵינוּ
וֵאלֹהֵי אֲבוֹתֵינוּ לְעוֹלָם וָעֶד.
צוּר חַיֵּינוּ, מָגֵן יִשְׁעֵנוּ
אַתָּה הוּא לְדוֹר וָדוֹר.
נוֹדֶה לְּךָ וּנְסַפֵּר תְּהִלָּתֶךָ
עַל חַיֵּינוּ הַמְּסוּרִים בְּיָדֶךָ
וְעַל נִשְׁמוֹתֵינוּ הַפְּקוּדוֹת לָךְ
וְעַל נִסֶּיךָ שֶׁבְּכָל יוֹם עִמָּנוּ
וְעַל נִפְלְאוֹתֶיךָ וְטוֹבוֹתֶיךָ
שֶׁבְּכָל עֵת
עֶרֶב וָבֹקֶר וְצָהֳרָיִם.
הַטּוֹב, כִּי לֹא כָלוּ רַחֲמֶיךָ
וְהַמְרַחֵם, כִּי לֹא תַמּוּ חֲסָדֶיךָ
מֵעוֹלָם קִוִּינוּ לָךְ.

During the חזרת הש״ץ, *the* קהל *says quietly:*

מוֹדִים אֲנַחְנוּ לָךְ
שָׁאַתָּה הוּא יהוה אֱלֹהֵינוּ
וֵאלֹהֵי אֲבוֹתֵינוּ
אֱלֹהֵי כָל בָּשָׂר
יוֹצְרֵנוּ, יוֹצֵר בְּרֵאשִׁית.
בְּרָכוֹת וְהוֹדָאוֹת
לְשִׁמְךָ הַגָּדוֹל וְהַקָּדוֹשׁ
עַל שֶׁהֶחֱיִיתָנוּ וְקִיַּמְתָּנוּ.
כֵּן תְּחַיֵּנוּ וּתְקַיְּמֵנוּ
וְתֶאֱסֹף גָּלֻיּוֹתֵינוּ
לְחַצְרוֹת קָדְשֶׁךָ
לִשְׁמֹר חֻקֶּיךָ
וְלַעֲשׂוֹת רְצוֹנֶךָ וּלְעָבְדְּךָ
בְּלֵבָב שָׁלֵם
עַל שֶׁאֲנַחְנוּ מוֹדִים לָךְ.
בָּרוּךְ אֵל הַהוֹדָאוֹת.

וְעַל כֻּלָּם יִתְבָּרַךְ וְיִתְרוֹמַם שִׁמְךָ מַלְכֵּנוּ תָּמִיד לְעוֹלָם וָעֶד.
וְכֹל הַחַיִּים יוֹדוּךָ סֶּלָה, וִיהַלְלוּ אֶת שִׁמְךָ בֶּאֱמֶת
הָאֵל יְשׁוּעָתֵנוּ וְעֶזְרָתֵנוּ סֶלָה.
בָּרוּךְ אַתָּה יהוה, הַטּוֹב שִׁמְךָ וּלְךָ נָאֶה לְהוֹדוֹת.

The following is said by the Leader during the Repetition of the Amida,
In Israel, if Kohanim bless the congregation, *turn to page 1064.*

Our God and God of our fathers, bless us with the threefold blessing in the Torah, written by the hand of Moses Your servant and pronounced by Aaron and his sons the priests, Your holy people, as it is said:

May the LORD bless you and protect you. (*Cong:* May it be Your will.) *Num. 6*
May the LORD make His face shine on you and be generous to you.
(*Cong:* May it be Your will.)
May the LORD turn His face toward you, and give you peace.
(*Cong:* May it be Your will.)

PEACE

שִׂים שָׁלוֹם Give peace, goodness and blessing,
grace, loving-kindness and compassion
to us and all Israel Your people.
Bless us, our Father, all as one, with the light of Your face,
for by the light of Your face You have given us, LORD our God,
the Torah of life and love of kindness,
righteousness, blessing, compassion, life and peace.
May it be good in Your eyes to bless Your people Israel
at every time, in every hour, with Your peace.
Blessed are You, LORD,
who blesses His people Israel with peace.

The following verse concludes the Leader's Repetition of the Amida.
Some also say it here as part of the silent Amida.

May the words of my mouth and the inner thoughts of my heart *Ps. 19*
find favor before You, LORD, my Rock and Redeemer.

אֱלֹהַי My God, *Berakhot 17a*
guard my tongue from evil and my lips from dishonest speech.
To those who curse me, let my soul be silent;
may my soul be to all like the dust.
Open my heart to Your Torah and let my soul
pursue Your commandments.
As for all who plan evil against me,
swiftly defeat their counsel and frustrate their plans.

The following is said by the שליח ציבור *during* חזרת הש״ץ.
In ארץ ישראל *if* כוהנים *say* ברכת כוהנים *turn to page 1065.*

אֱלֹהֵינוּ וֵאלֹהֵי אֲבוֹתֵינוּ, בָּרְכֵנוּ בַּבְּרָכָה הַמְשֻׁלֶּשֶׁת בַּתּוֹרָה, הַכְּתוּבָה עַל יְדֵי מֹשֶׁה עַבְדֶּךָ, הָאֲמוּרָה מִפִּי אַהֲרֹן וּבָנָיו כֹּהֲנִים עַם קְדוֹשֶׁיךָ, כָּאָמוּר

במדבר ו
יְבָרֶכְךָ יהוה וְיִשְׁמְרֶךָ: קהל: כֵּן יְהִי רָצוֹן
יָאֵר יהוה פָּנָיו אֵלֶיךָ וִיחֻנֶּךָּ: קהל: כֵּן יְהִי רָצוֹן
יִשָּׂא יהוה פָּנָיו אֵלֶיךָ וְיָשֵׂם לְךָ שָׁלוֹם: קהל: כֵּן יְהִי רָצוֹן

ברכת שלום

שִׂים שָׁלוֹם טוֹבָה וּבְרָכָה
חֵן וָחֶסֶד וְרַחֲמִים, עָלֵינוּ וְעַל כָּל יִשְׂרָאֵל עַמֶּךָ.
בָּרְכֵנוּ אָבִינוּ כֻּלָּנוּ כְּאֶחָד בְּאוֹר פָּנֶיךָ
כִּי בְאוֹר פָּנֶיךָ נָתַתָּ לָּנוּ יהוה אֱלֹהֵינוּ
תּוֹרַת חַיִּים וְאַהֲבַת חֶסֶד
וּצְדָקָה וּבְרָכָה וְרַחֲמִים וְחַיִּים וְשָׁלוֹם.
וְטוֹב בְּעֵינֶיךָ לְבָרֵךְ אֶת עַמְּךָ יִשְׂרָאֵל
בְּכָל עֵת וּבְכָל שָׁעָה בִּשְׁלוֹמֶךָ.
בָּרוּךְ אַתָּה יהוה, הַמְבָרֵךְ אֶת עַמּוֹ יִשְׂרָאֵל בַּשָּׁלוֹם.

The following verse concludes the חזרת הש״ץ.
Some also say it here as part of the silent עמידה.

תהלים יט
יִהְיוּ לְרָצוֹן אִמְרֵי־פִי וְהֶגְיוֹן לִבִּי לְפָנֶיךָ, יהוה צוּרִי וְגֹאֲלִי:

ברכות יז.
אֱלֹהַי
נְצֹר לְשׁוֹנִי מֵרָע וּשְׂפָתַי מִדַּבֵּר מִרְמָה
וְלִמְקַלְלַי נַפְשִׁי תִדֹּם, וְנַפְשִׁי כֶּעָפָר לַכֹּל תִּהְיֶה.
פְּתַח לִבִּי בְּתוֹרָתֶךָ, וּבְמִצְוֹתֶיךָ תִּרְדֹּף נַפְשִׁי.
וְכָל הַחוֹשְׁבִים עָלַי רָעָה
מְהֵרָה הָפֵר עֲצָתָם וְקַלְקֵל מַחֲשַׁבְתָּם.

Act for the sake of Your name;
act for the sake of Your right hand;
act for the sake of Your holiness;
act for the sake of Your Torah.

That Your beloved ones may be rescued, *Ps. 60*
save with Your right hand and answer me.
May the words of my mouth and the inner thoughts of my heart *Ps. 19*
find favor before You, LORD, my Rock and Redeemer.

Bow, take three steps back, then bow, first left, then right, then center, while saying:

May He who makes peace in His high places,
make peace for us and all Israel –
and say: Amen.

יְהִי רָצוֹן May it be Your will, LORD our God and God of our ancestors,
that the Temple be rebuilt speedily in our days,
and give us a share in Your Torah.
And there we will serve You with fear,
as in the days of old and as in former years.
Then the offering of Judah and Jerusalem will be pleasing to the LORD *Mal. 3*
as in the days of old and as in former years.

On Ḥol HaMo'ed Sukkot, Hoshanot on the next page are said at this point (the Hoshanot for Hoshana Raba are on page 895).

On Shabbat Ḥol HaMo'ed, Full Kaddish (page 696) is said and the service continues with "There is none like our God" on page 698.

On Ḥol HaMo'ed Pesaḥ, Full Kaddish (page 244) is said and the service continues with Aleinu (page 246).

עֲשֵׂה לְמַעַן שְׁמֶךָ
עֲשֵׂה לְמַעַן יְמִינֶךָ
עֲשֵׂה לְמַעַן קְדֻשָּׁתֶךָ
עֲשֵׂה לְמַעַן תּוֹרָתֶךָ.
תהלים ס לְמַעַן יֵחָלְצוּן יְדִידֶיךָ, הוֹשִׁיעָה יְמִינְךָ וַעֲנֵנִי:
תהלים יט יִהְיוּ לְרָצוֹן אִמְרֵי־פִי וְהֶגְיוֹן לִבִּי לְפָנֶיךָ, יהוה צוּרִי וְגֹאֲלִי:

Bow, take three steps back, then bow, first left, then right, then center, while saying:

עֹשֶׂה שָׁלוֹם בִּמְרוֹמָיו
הוּא יַעֲשֶׂה שָׁלוֹם עָלֵינוּ וְעַל כָּל יִשְׂרָאֵל, וְאִמְרוּ אָמֵן.

יְהִי רָצוֹן מִלְּפָנֶיךָ יהוה אֱלֹהֵינוּ וֵאלֹהֵי אֲבוֹתֵינוּ
שֶׁיִּבָּנֶה בֵּית הַמִּקְדָּשׁ בִּמְהֵרָה בְיָמֵינוּ
וְתֵן חֶלְקֵנוּ בְּתוֹרָתֶךָ
וְשָׁם נַעֲבָדְךָ בְּיִרְאָה כִּימֵי עוֹלָם וּכְשָׁנִים קַדְמוֹנִיּוֹת.
מלאכי ג וְעָרְבָה לַיהוה מִנְחַת יְהוּדָה וִירוּשָׁלָםִ כִּימֵי עוֹלָם וּכְשָׁנִים קַדְמֹנִיּוֹת:

On חול המועד סוכות, הושענות *on the next page are said at this point (the* הושענות *for* הושענא רבה *are on page 895).*

On שבת חול המועד, קדיש שלם *(page 697) is said and the service continues with* אֵין כֵּאלֹהֵינוּ *on page 699.*

On חול המועד פסח, קדיש שלם *(page 245) is said and the service continues with* עָלֵינוּ *(page 247).*

Hoshanot

Hoshanot are said after the Leader's Repetition of the Amida of Musaf (and in some congregations after Hallel) on every day of Sukkot.

On weekdays, the Ark is opened, and a Torah scroll is taken to the Bima. Members of the congregation who have a Lulav and Etrog make a circuit around the Bima and say Hoshanot. Mourners do not participate in the circuit.

At the conclusion of the Hoshanot, the Torah scroll is returned to the Ark, which is then closed.

On Shabbat, turn to page 888. On Hoshana Raba, turn to page 894.

If first day of Sukkot falls on	*On first day*	*On second day*	*On third day*	*On fourth day*	*On fifth day*	*On sixth day*
Monday	For the sake of Your truth	The Foundation Stone	I shall lay out my prayer	"I am a wall," said the people	God of all salvation	A people guarded
Tuesday	For the sake of Your truth	The Foundation Stone	I shall lay out my prayer	God of all salvation	A people guarded	Master who saves
Thursday	For the sake of Your truth	The Foundation Stone	A people guarded	I shall lay out my prayer	God of all salvation	Master who saves
Shabbat	A people guarded	For the sake of Your truth	I shall lay out my prayer	The Foundation Stone	God of all salvation	Master who saves

Leader then congregation:

הוֹשַׁע נָא Save us, please for Your sake, our God, save us please.

Leader then congregation:

Save us, please for Your sake, our Creator, save us, please.

Leader then congregation:

Save us, please for Your sake, our Redeemer, save us, please.

Leader then congregation:

Save us, please for Your sake, You who seek us, save us, please.

הושענות

The הושענות *are said after the* חזרת הש״ץ *of the* מוסף עמידה
(and in some congregations after הלל*) on every day of* סוכות.
The ארון קודש *is opened, and a* ספר תורה *is taken to the* בימה.
Members of the קהל *who have a* לולב *and* אתרוג *make a circuit around the* בימה *and say* הושענות. *Mourners do not participate in the circuit.*
At the conclusion of the הושענות, *the* ספר תורה *is returned to the* ארון קודש, *which is then closed.*

On שבת, *turn to page 889. On* הושענא רבה, *turn to page 895.*

On sixth day	*On fifth day*	*On fourth day*	*On third day*	*On second day*	*If first day of* סוכות *falls on*
אֹם נְצוּרָה	אֵל לְמוֹשָׁעוֹת	אֹם אֲנִי חוֹמָה	אֶעֱרֹךְ שׁוּעִי	אֶבֶן שְׁתִיָּה	*Monday*
אָדוֹן הַמּוֹשִׁיעַ	אֹם נְצוּרָה	אֵל לְמוֹשָׁעוֹת	אֶעֱרֹךְ שׁוּעִי	אֶבֶן שְׁתִיָּה	*Tuesday*
אָדוֹן הַמּוֹשִׁיעַ	אֵל לְמוֹשָׁעוֹת	אֶעֱרֹךְ שׁוּעִי	אֹם נְצוּרָה	אֶבֶן שְׁתִיָּה	*Thursday*
אָדוֹן הַמּוֹשִׁיעַ	אֵל לְמוֹשָׁעוֹת	אֶבֶן שְׁתִיָּה	אֶעֱרֹךְ שׁוּעִי	לְמַעַן אֲמִתָּךְ	שבת

קהל *then* שליח ציבור:

הוֹשַׁע נָא   לְמַעַנְךָ אֱלֹהֵינוּ   הוֹשַׁע נָא.

קהל *then* שליח ציבור:

הוֹשַׁע נָא   לְמַעַנְךָ בּוֹרְאֵנוּ   הוֹשַׁע נָא.

קהל *then* שליח ציבור:

הוֹשַׁע נָא   לְמַעַנְךָ גּוֹאֲלֵנוּ   הוֹשַׁע נָא.

קהל *then* שליח ציבור:

הוֹשַׁע נָא   לְמַעַנְךָ דּוֹרְשֵׁנוּ   הוֹשַׁע נָא.

Save us, please –

לְמַעַן אֲמִתָּךְ For the sake of Your truth – for the sake of Your covenant – for the sake of Your greatness and glory – for the sake of Your Law – for the sake of Your majesty – for the sake of Your promise – for the sake of Your remembrance – for the sake of Your love – for the sake of Your goodness – for the sake of Your Oneness – for the sake of Your honor – for the sake of Your wisdom – for the sake of Your kingship – for the sake of Your eternity – for the sake of Your mystery – for the sake of Your might – for the sake of Your splendor – for the sake of Your righteousness – for the sake of Your holiness – for the sake of Your great compassion – for the sake of Your Presence – for the sake of Your praise – Save us, please.

Continue with "I and HE: save us, please." on the next page.

Save us, please –

אֶבֶן שְׁתִיָּה The Foundation Stone – the House You chose – the threshing-floor of Ornan – the hidden Shrine – Mount Moriah – where He shall be seen – Your glorious Sanctuary – where David camped – the best of Lebanon – the Beauty of Heights, Joy of all the earth – the Place of Perfect Beauty – the Lodge of Goodness – the Place of Your dwelling – the Shelter of Shalem – the tribes' Pilgrimage – the precious Cornerstone – shining Zion – the Holy of Holies – [the walls] lined with love – Residence of Your glory – the Hill toward which all mouths pray – Save us, please.

Continue with "I and HE: save us, please." on the next page.

Save us, please –

אֶעֱרֹךְ שׁוּעִי I shall lay out my prayer – in the house of my prayer – I found my sin, fasting – I seek You from there, to save me – listen to the sound of my prayer – and rise up to my aid – remember with compassion, my Savior – making life my delight – Beneficent One, hear my groaning – quickly, bring my savior – put an end to my accuser – that he condemn me no more – quickly, God of my salvation – make eternal my salvation – bear the wrongdoing of my wickedness – pass over my sin – turn to me and save me – righteous Rock, my Savior – receive, please, my prayer – raise the horn of my salvation – Almighty One, my Savior – come, show Yourself and save me – Save us, please.

Continue with "I and HE: save us, please" on the next page.

Save us, please –

אוֹם אֲנִי חוֹמָה "I am a wall," said the people – bright as the sun – exiled and reviled – fair like a date palm – killed on account of You – like sheep to the slaughter – dispersed among tormentors – wrapped in Your embrace, clinging to You – bearing Your yoke – the one to know Your Oneness – beaten down in exile – learning the awe of You – our faces scratched – given over to the violent – weighed

הוֹשַׁע נָא

לְמַעַן אֲמִתָּךְ. לְמַעַן בְּרִיתָךְ. לְמַעַן גָּדְלָךְ וְתִפְאַרְתָּךְ. לְמַעַן דָּתָךְ. לְמַעַן הוֹדָךְ. לְמַעַן וִעוּדָךְ. לְמַעַן זִכְרָךְ. לְמַעַן חַסְדָּךְ. לְמַעַן טוּבָךְ. לְמַעַן יִחוּדָךְ. לְמַעַן כְּבוֹדָךְ. לְמַעַן לִמּוּדָךְ. לְמַעַן מַלְכוּתָךְ. לְמַעַן נִצְחָךְ. לְמַעַן סוֹדָךְ. לְמַעַן עֻזָּךְ. לְמַעַן פְּאֵרָךְ. לְמַעַן צִדְקָתָךְ. לְמַעַן קְדֻשָּׁתָךְ. לְמַעַן רַחֲמֶיךָ הָרַבִּים. לְמַעַן שְׁכִינָתָךְ. לְמַעַן תְּהִלָּתָךְ. הוֹשַׁע נָא.

Continue with אֲנִי וָהוֹ הוֹשִׁיעָה נָּא *on the next page.*

הוֹשַׁע נָא

אֶבֶן שְׁתִיָּה. בֵּית הַבְּחִירָה. גֹּרֶן אָרְנָן. דְּבִיר הַמֻּצְנָע. הַר הַמּוֹרִיָּה. וְהַר יֵרָאֶה. זְבוּל תִּפְאַרְתֶּךָ. חָנָה דָוִד. טוֹב הַלְּבָנוֹן. יְפֵה נוֹף מְשׂוֹשׂ כָּל הָאָרֶץ. כְּלִילַת יֹפִי. לִינַת הַצֶּדֶק. מָכוֹן לְשִׁבְתֶּךָ. נָוֶה שַׁאֲנָן. סֻכַּת שָׁלֵם. עֲלִיַּת שְׁבָטִים. פִּנַּת יִקְרַת. צִיּוֹן הַמְצֻיֶּנֶת. קֹדֶשׁ הַקֳּדָשִׁים. רָצוּף אַהֲבָה. שְׁכִינַת כְּבוֹדֶךָ. תֵּל תַּלְפִּיּוֹת. הוֹשַׁע נָא.

Continue with אֲנִי וָהוֹ הוֹשִׁיעָה נָּא *on the next page.*

הוֹשַׁע נָא

אֶעֱרֹךְ שׁוּעִי. בְּבֵית שַׁוְעִי. גִּלִּיתִי בַצּוֹם פִּשְׁעִי. דְּרַשְׁתִּיךָ בּוֹ לְהוֹשִׁיעִי. הַקְשִׁיבָה לְקוֹל שַׁוְעִי. וְקוּמָה וְהוֹשִׁיעִי. זְכֹר וְרַחֵם מוֹשִׁיעִי. חַי כֵּן תְּשַׁעְשְׁעִי. טוֹב בְּאֹנֶק שְׁעִי. יוֹחַשׁ מוֹשִׁיעִי. כַּלֵּה מַרְשִׁיעִי. לְבַל עוֹד יַרְשִׁיעִי. מַהֵר אֱלֹהֵי יִשְׁעִי. נֶצַח לְהוֹשִׁיעִי. שָׂא נָא עֲוֹן רִשְׁעִי. עֲבֹר עַל פִּשְׁעִי. פְּנֵה נָא לְהוֹשִׁיעִי. צוּר צַדִּיק מוֹשִׁיעִי. קַבֵּל נָא שַׁוְעִי. רוֹמֵם קֶרֶן יִשְׁעִי. שַׁדַּי מוֹשִׁיעִי. תּוֹפִיעַ וְתוֹשִׁיעִי. הוֹשַׁע נָא.

Continue with אֲנִי וָהוֹ הוֹשִׁיעָה נָּא *on the next page.*

הוֹשַׁע נָא

אֹם אֲנִי חוֹמָה. בָּרָה כַּחַמָּה. גּוֹלָה וְסוּרָה. דָּמְתָה לְתָמָר. הַהֲרוּגָה עָלֶיךָ. וְנֶחְשֶׁבֶת כְּצֹאן טִבְחָה. זְרוּיָה בֵּין מַכְעִיסֶיהָ. חֲבוּקָה וּדְבוּקָה בָךְ. טוֹעֶנֶת עֻלָּךְ. יְחִידָה לְיַחֲדָךְ. כְּבוּשָׁה בַגּוֹלָה. לוֹמֶדֶת יִרְאָתָךְ. מְרוּטַת לֶחִי. נְתוּנָה

down beneath Your burden – oppressed and in turmoil – redeemed by [Moses] Toviya – holy flock – the communities of Jacob – marked out with Your name – roaring, "Save us, please!" – leaning on You – Save us, please.

Continue with "I and HE: save us, please" below.

Save us, please –

אֵל לְמוֹשָׁעוֹת God of all salvation – for keeping our four vows – we who draw close in prayer – who come knocking to lay out our prayer – who speak Your words of delight – who rejoice in their questions – crying out to be heard – we who watch for the Redemption – hear those who hold on to You – who understand Your calendar – who bow to You and pray – to comprehend Your message – as it comes from Your mouth – (You who give salvation) – telling their stories – making known Your testament – You who work salvation – bring a righteous [leader] for the saved – bring close our salvations – with noise, amid thundering – in three brief hours – speed us our salvation – Save us, please.

Continue with "I and HE: save us, please" below.

Save us, please –

אָדוֹן הַמּוֹשִׁיעַ Master who saves – there is no one else – mighty, with great power to save – when I was brought low, He saved me – God who saves – who delivers and saves – save those who cry out to You – those who yet watch for You – nourish Your young lambs – make the harvest lavish – sprout every growing thing and save us – do not condemn this valley – make the good fruits sweet and save us – carry the clouds to us – shake down the raindrops – do not hold back the clouds – You who open Your hand and satisfy – relieve those who thirst for You – save those who call to You – save those You have loved – rescue those who rise to seek You – save Your innocent ones – Save us, please.

I and HE: save us, please.

כְּהוֹשַׁעְתָּ As You saved the mighty ones in Lud with You,
coming down for Your people's deliverance – save us, please.

As You saved nation and God together,
[the people] called for God's salvation – save us, please.

As You saved the crowding multitudes,
and angelic multitudes along with them – save us, please.

לְמַכִּים. סוֹבֶלֶת סִבְלָךְ. עֲנִיָּה סוֹעֲרָה. פְּדוּיַת טוֹבִיָּה. צֹאן קָדָשִׁים. קְהִלּוֹת יַעֲקֹב. רְשׁוּמִים בִּשְׁמֶךָ. שׁוֹאֲגִים הוֹשַׁע נָא. תְּמוּכִים עָלֶיךָ. הוֹשַׁע נָא.

Continue with אֲנִי וָהוֹ הוֹשִׁיעָה נָּא *below.*

הוֹשַׁע נָא

אֵל לְמוֹשָׁעוֹת. בְּאַרְבַּע שְׁבוּעוֹת. נָּשִׁים בְּשַׁוְעוֹת. דּוֹפְקֵי עֶרֶךְ שׁוּעוֹת. הוֹגֵי שַׁעֲשׁוּעוֹת. וְחִידוֹת מִשְׁתַּעַשְׁעוֹת. זוֹעֲקִים לְהַשְׁעוֹת. חוֹכֵי יְשׁוּעוֹת. טְפוּלִים בְּךָ שְׁעוֹת. יוֹדְעֵי בֵּין שָׁעוֹת. כּוֹרְעֶיךָ בְּשַׁוְעוֹת. לְהָבִין שְׁמוּעוֹת. מִפִּיךָ נִשְׁמָעוֹת. נוֹתֵן תְּשׁוּעוֹת. סְפוּרוֹת מַשְׁמָעוֹת. עֵדוֹת מַשְׁמִיעוֹת. פּוֹעֵל יְשׁוּעוֹת. צַדִּיק נוֹשָׁעוֹת. קִרְיַת תְּשׁוּעוֹת. רֶגֶשׁ תְּשׁוּאוֹת. שָׁלֹשׁ שָׁעוֹת. תָּחִישׁ לִתְשׁוּעוֹת. הוֹשַׁע נָא.

Continue with אֲנִי וָהוֹ הוֹשִׁיעָה נָּא *below.*

הוֹשַׁע נָא

אָדוֹן הַמּוֹשִׁיעַ. בִּלְתְּךָ אֵין לְהוֹשִׁיעַ. גִּבּוֹר וְרַב לְהוֹשִׁיעַ. דַּלּוֹתִי וְלִי יְהוֹשִׁיעַ. הָאֵל הַמּוֹשִׁיעַ. וּמַצִּיל וּמוֹשִׁיעַ. זוֹעֲקֶיךָ תּוֹשִׁיעַ. חוֹכֶיךָ הוֹשִׁיעַ. טְלָאֶיךָ תַּשְׂבִּיעַ. יְבוּל לְהַשְׁפִּיעַ. כָּל שִׂיחַ תַּדְשֵׁא וְתוֹשִׁיעַ. לְגֵיא בַּל תַּרְשִׁיעַ. מְגָדִים תַּמְתִּיק וְתוֹשִׁיעַ. נְשִׂיאִים לְהַסִּיעַ. שְׂעִירִים לְהָנִיעַ. עֲנָנִים מִלְּהַמְנִיעַ. פּוֹתֵחַ יָד וּמַשְׂבִּיעַ. צְמֵאֶיךָ תַּשְׂבִּיעַ. קוֹרְאֶיךָ תּוֹשִׁיעַ. רְחוּמֶיךָ תּוֹשִׁיעַ. שׁוֹחֲרֶיךָ הוֹשִׁיעַ. תְּמִימֶיךָ תּוֹשִׁיעַ. הוֹשַׁע נָא.

אֲנִי וָהוֹ הוֹשִׁיעָה נָּא.

כְּהוֹשַׁעְתָּ אֵלִים בְּלוּד עִמָּךְ.
בְּצֵאתְךָ לְיֵשַׁע עַמָּךְ. כֵּן הוֹשַׁע נָא.

כְּהוֹשַׁעְתָּ גּוֹי וֵאלֹהִים.
דְּרוּשִׁים לְיֵשַׁע אֱלֹהִים. כֵּן הוֹשַׁע נָא.

כְּהוֹשַׁעְתָּ הֲמוֹן צְבָאוֹת.
וְעִמָּם מַלְאֲכֵי צְבָאוֹת. כֵּן הוֹשַׁע נָא.

As You saved pure ones from the grip of slavery,
Gracious One; enslaved in cruel hands – save us, please.

As You saved those submerged betwe5en slices of the deep,
and brought Your own glory through it with them –
save us, please.

As You saved the stem as they sang "And God saved" –
but the Deliverer reads it, "God was saved" – save us, please.

As You saved, and You said, "I took you out,"
but let it be pointed, "I was taken out with you" – save us, please.

As You saved those who encompassed the Altar,
bearing their willows to encircle the Altar – save us, please.

As You saved the Ark of wonders that was wronged,
tormenting Philistia with fury, and saving it – save us, please.

As You saved the communities You sent away to Babylon,
being sent too, for them, Your compassionate Self –
save us, please.

As You saved the returning exiles of the tribes of Jacob,
so come back and return the exiles of the tents of Jacob –
and save us, please.

As You saved those who kept Your commandments and waited for
salvation, / God of all salvation – and save us, please.

I and *HE*: save us, please.

The Torah scroll is returned to the Ark.

הוֹשִׁיעָה Save Your people; bless Your legacy; tend them and carry them forever. *Ps. 28* Let these words with which I have pleaded with the *1 Kings 8* Lord be close to the Lord our God day and night, that He may do justice for His servant, and justice for His people Israel, day after day; so that all the peoples of the earth will know that the Lord is God. There is no other.

The Ark is closedand the service continues with Full Kaddish *on page 244*

כְּהוֹשַׁעְתָּ זַכִּים מִבֵּית עֲבָדִים.
חַנּוּן בְּיָדָם מַעֲבִידִים. כֵּן הוֹשַׁע נָא.
כְּהוֹשַׁעְתָּ טְבוּעִים בְּצוּל גְּזָרִים.
יְקָרְךָ עִמָּם מַעֲבִירִים. כֵּן הוֹשַׁע נָא.
כְּהוֹשַׁעְתָּ כַּנָּה מְשׁוֹרֶרֶת וַיּוֹשַׁע.
לְגוֹחָה מְצֻיֶּנֶת וַיִּוָּשַׁע. כֵּן הוֹשַׁע נָא.
כְּהוֹשַׁעְתָּ מַאֲמָר וְהוֹצֵאתִי אֶתְכֶם.
נָקוּב וְהוּצֵאתִי אִתְּכֶם. כֵּן הוֹשַׁע נָא.
כְּהוֹשַׁעְתָּ סוֹבְבֵי מִזְבֵּחַ.
עוֹמְסֵי עֲרָבָה לְהַקִּיף מִזְבֵּחַ. כֵּן הוֹשַׁע נָא.
כְּהוֹשַׁעְתָּ פִּלְאֵי אָרוֹן כְּהֻפְשַׁע.
צִעֵר פְּלֶשֶׁת בַּחֲרוֹן אַף, וְנוֹשַׁע. כֵּן הוֹשַׁע נָא.
כְּהוֹשַׁעְתָּ קְהִלּוֹת בָּבֶלָה שִׁלַּחְתָּ.
רַחוּם לְמַעֲנָם שֻׁלַּחְתָּ. כֵּן הוֹשַׁע נָא.
כְּהוֹשַׁעְתָּ שְׁבוּת שִׁבְטֵי יַעֲקֹב.
תָּשׁוּב וְתָשִׁיב שְׁבוּת אָהֳלֵי יַעֲקֹב. וְהוֹשִׁיעָה נָּא.
כְּהוֹשַׁעְתָּ שׁוֹמְרֵי מִצְוֹת וְחוֹכֵי יְשׁוּעוֹת.
אֵל לְמוֹשָׁעוֹת. וְהוֹשִׁיעָה נָּא.

אֲנִי וָהוֹ הוֹשִׁיעָה נָּא.

The ספר תורה *is returned to the* ארון קודש.

הוֹשִׁיעָה אֶת־עַמֶּךָ, וּבָרֵךְ אֶת־נַחֲלָתֶךָ, וּרְעֵם וְנַשְּׂאֵם עַד־הָעוֹלָם: וְיִהְיוּ תהלים כח
דְבָרַי אֵלֶּה, אֲשֶׁר הִתְחַנַּנְתִּי לִפְנֵי יהוה, קְרֹבִים אֶל־יהוה אֱלֹהֵינוּ יוֹמָם מלכים א׳ ח
וָלָיְלָה, לַעֲשׂוֹת מִשְׁפַּט עַבְדּוֹ וּמִשְׁפַּט עַמּוֹ יִשְׂרָאֵל, דְּבַר־יוֹם בְּיוֹמוֹ:
לְמַעַן דַּעַת כָּל־עַמֵּי הָאָרֶץ כִּי יהוה הוּא הָאֱלֹהִים, אֵין עוֹד:

The ארון קודש *is closed and the service continues with* קדיש שלם *on page 245.*

HOSHANOT FOR SHABBAT

The Ark is opened but no Torah scrolls are taken out.
The congregation does not walk around the Bima.

Leader then congregation:

הוֹשַׁע נָא Save us, please for Your sake, our God, save us please.

Leader then congregation:

Save us, please for Your sake, our Creator, save us, please.

Leader then congregation:

Save us, please for Your sake, our Redeemer, save us, please.

Leader then congregation:

Save us, please for Your sake, You who seek us, save us, please.

Save us, please –

אֹם נְצוּרָה כְּבָבַת A people guarded like the pupil of Your eye – who understand the Law that refreshes the spirit – who learn through all the laws of the Sabbath – who unfold the rules of carrying on the Sabbath – who fix two thousand cubits as our boundary for the Sabbath – and keep our feet from breaking the Sabbath – who remember early and keep hold of the Sabbath – and speed to hasten in the Sabbath – who for six days work hard for the Sabbath – who sit patiently on before ending the Sabbath – who call her an honor, delight, our Sabbath – who change their clothes, and dress for the Sabbath – who prepare themselves feast and drink for the Sabbath – laying a spread of sweet things on the Sabbath – holding three festive meals for the Sabbath – who break bread over two loaves on the Sabbath – distinguishing four domains on the Sabbath – who light the candles for the command, for the Sabbath – who sanctify the day on the Sabbath – who speak seven blessings [in the Amida] of the Sabbath – who read seven portions of Torah on the Sabbath – bring us into what is ours, the day that will be entirely Sabbath – Save us, please.

I and *HE*: save us, please.

כְּהוֹשַׁעְתָּ As You saved Adam, formed in Your hands, and protected him, making the holy Sabbath his ransom, clemency – so, save us, please.

הושענות לשבת

The ארון קודש *is opened but no* ספרי תורה *are taken out.*
The קהל *does not walk around the* בימה*.*

קהל *then* שליח ציבור*:*

הוֹשַׁע נָא לְמַעַנְךָ אֱלֹהֵינוּ הוֹשַׁע נָא.

קהל *then* שליח ציבור*:*

הוֹשַׁע נָא לְמַעַנְךָ בּוֹרְאֵנוּ הוֹשַׁע נָא.

קהל *then* שליח ציבור*:*

הוֹשַׁע נָא לְמַעַנְךָ גּוֹאֲלֵנוּ הוֹשַׁע נָא.

קהל *then* שליח ציבור*:*

הוֹשַׁע נָא לְמַעַנְךָ דּוֹרְשֵׁנוּ הוֹשַׁע נָא.

הוֹשַׁע נָא

אֹם נְצוּרָה כְּבָבַת. בּוֹנֶנֶת בְּדָת נֶפֶשׁ מְשִׁיבַת. גּוֹמֶרֶת הִלְכוֹת שַׁבָּת. דּוֹרֶשֶׁת מַשְׂאַת שַׁבָּת. הַקּוֹבַעַת אַלְפַּיִם תְּחוּם שַׁבָּת. וּמְשִׁיבַת רֶגֶל מִשַּׁבָּת. זָכוֹר וְשָׁמוֹר מְקַיֶּמֶת בַּשַּׁבָּת. חָשָׁה לְמַהֵר בִּיאַת שַׁבָּת. טוֹרַחַת כָּל מִשְׁנֶה לַשַּׁבָּת. יוֹשֶׁבֶת וּמַמְתֶּנֶת עַד כְּלוֹת שַׁבָּת. כָּבוֹד וָעֹנֶג קוֹרְאָה לַשַּׁבָּת. לְבוּשׁ וּכְסוּת מַחֲלֶפֶת בַּשַּׁבָּת. מַאֲכָל וּמִשְׁתֶּה מְכִינָה לַשַּׁבָּת. נֹעַם מְגָדִים מַנְעֶמֶת לַשַּׁבָּת. סְעוּדוֹת שָׁלֹשׁ מְקַיֶּמֶת בַּשַּׁבָּת. עַל שְׁתֵּי כִכָּרוֹת בּוֹצַעַת בַּשַּׁבָּת. פּוֹרֶטֶת אַרְבַּע רְשֻׁיּוֹת שַׁבָּת. צִוּוּי הַדְלָקַת נֵר מַדְלֶקֶת בַּשַּׁבָּת. קִדּוּשׁ הַיּוֹם מְקַדֶּשֶׁת בַּשַּׁבָּת. רָן שֶׁבַע מְפַלֶּלֶת בַּשַּׁבָּת. שִׁבְעָה בַּדָּת קוֹרְאָה בַּשַּׁבָּת. תַּנְחִילֶנָּה לְיוֹם שֶׁכֻּלּוֹ שַׁבָּת. הוֹשַׁע נָא.

אֲנִי וָהוּ הוֹשִׁיעָה נָּא.

כְּהוֹשַׁעְתָּ אָדָם יְצִיר כַּפֶּיךָ לְגוֹנְנָה.
בְּשַׁבַּת קֹדֶשׁ הִמְצֵאתוֹ כֹּפֶר וַחֲנִינָה. כֵּן הוֹשַׁע נָא.

As You saved the people who remained distinct while longing for freedom –
in their thoughts already marking out the seventh day for rest –
so, save us, please.

As You saved the people You led and guided as Your flock,
and gave a Law at Mara, by the still waters – so, save us, please.

As You saved those who received Your gift in the Wilderness of Sin, the camp,
who were taught and collected two-fold bread on a Friday –
so, save us, please.

As You saved those who clung to You, who learned of their own mind to
prepare for the Sabbath, / and [Moses] their shepherd blessed their
strength and concurred – so, save us, please.

As You saved those who ate [manna] stored up on [their day of] delight,
and it looked no different and its scent had not spoiled –
so, save us, please.

As You saved those who learned every law of a journey on the Sabbath,
who rested, stopped, and kept the boundaries of domain and
encampment – so, save us, please.

As You saved those who could hear the fourth commandment at Sinai:
both "Remember" and "Keep" to make the seventh day holy –
so, save us, please.

As You saved those commanded to march seven times round Jericho,
besieging her to strike until she fell on the Sabbath –
so, save us, please.

As You saved Kohelet [Solomon] and his people in the eternal House,
when they came to please You for seven days and seven –
so, save us, please.

As You saved those who returned, rising up from Exile, redeemed,
as they read Your Torah on this Festival, each day – so, save us, please.

As You saved those who rejoiced for You in the second House, renewed,
in the Sanctuary where they took up the lulav all seven days –
so, save us, please.

As You saved those whose willow beating overrode the Sabbath,
who placed branches from Motza at the base of the Altar –
so, save us, please.

כְּהוֹשַׁעְתָּ גּוֹי מְצֻיָּן מִקַּוִּים חֹפֶשׁ.
דֵּעָה כִּוְּנוּ לָבֹר שְׁבִיעִי לְנֹפֶשׁ. כֵּן הוֹשַׁע נָא.

כְּהוֹשַׁעְתָּ הָעָם נִהַגְתָּ כַּצֹּאן לְהַנְחוֹת.
וְחֹק שַׂמְתָּ בְּמָרָה עַל מֵי מְנוּחוֹת. כֵּן הוֹשַׁע נָא.

כְּהוֹשַׁעְתָּ זְבוּדֶיךָ בְּמִדְבַּר סִין בַּמַּחֲנֶה.
חָכְמוּ וְלָקְטוּ בַּשִּׁשִּׁי לֶחֶם מִשְׁנֶה. כֵּן הוֹשַׁע נָא.

כְּהוֹשַׁעְתָּ טְפוּלֶיךָ הוֹרוּ הֲכָנָה בַּמַּדָּעִם.
יָשַׁר כֹּחָם, וְהוֹדָה לָמוֹ רוֹעָם. כֵּן הוֹשַׁע נָא.

כְּהוֹשַׁעְתָּ כִּלְכְּלוּ בְּעֹנֶג מָן הַמִּשְׁמָר.
לֹא הָפַךְ עֵינוֹ וְרֵיחוֹ לֹא נָמָר. כֵּן הוֹשַׁע נָא.

כְּהוֹשַׁעְתָּ מִשְׁפְּטֵי מַשָּׂאוֹת שַׁבָּת גָּמָרוּ.
נָחוּ וְשָׁבְתוּ, רְשֻׁיּוֹת וּתְחוּמִים שָׁמָרוּ. כֵּן הוֹשַׁע נָא.

כְּהוֹשַׁעְתָּ סִינַי הָשְׁמְעוּ בְּדִבּוּר רְבִיעִי.
עִנְיַן זָכוֹר וְשָׁמוֹר לְקַדֵּשׁ שְׁבִיעִי. כֵּן הוֹשַׁע נָא.

כְּהוֹשַׁעְתָּ פְּקֻדּוּ יְרִיחוֹ שֶׁבַע לְהַקֵּף.
צָרוּ עַד רִדְתָּהּ בַּשַּׁבָּת לְתַקֵּף. כֵּן הוֹשַׁע נָא.

כְּהוֹשַׁעְתָּ קֹהֶלֶת וְעַמּוֹ בְּבֵית עוֹלָמִים.
רִצּוּךְ בְּחָגְגָם שִׁבְעָה וְשִׁבְעָה יָמִים. כֵּן הוֹשַׁע נָא.

כְּהוֹשַׁעְתָּ שָׁבִים עוֹלֵי גוֹלָה לְפִדְיוֹם.
תּוֹרָתְךָ בְּקָרְאָם בֶּחָג יוֹם יוֹם. כֵּן הוֹשַׁע נָא.

כְּהוֹשַׁעְתָּ מְשַׂמְּחֶיךָ בְּבִנְיַן שֵׁנִי הַמְחֻדָּשׁ.
נוֹטְלִין לוּלָב כָּל שִׁבְעָה בַּמִּקְדָּשׁ. כֵּן הוֹשַׁע נָא.

כְּהוֹשַׁעְתָּ חִבּוּט עֲרָבָה שַׁבָּת מַדְחִים.
מְרֻבִּיּוֹת מוֹצָא לִיסוֹד מִזְבֵּחַ מַנִּיחִים. כֵּן הוֹשַׁע נָא.

As You saved those who rejoiced with supple, long, high willows,
as they parted from the place calling "Praise to you, Altar!" –
so, save us, please.

As You saved those who gave thanks and who prayed and were true to their words, / all of them repeating "We are the Lord's and to Him our eyes are turned" – so, save us, please.

As You saved those circling [the Altar,] the wine-vat You carved out, with luscious willows, / as they sang out, "*I* and *HE*: save us, please" –
so, save us, please.

As You saved the eager legion [of priests], hastening to serve on the day of rest, / bringing a double Sabbath offering, burnt-offering and meal-offering – so, save us, please.

As You saved Your Levites, making them many on their platform,
singing "A psalm. A song for the Sabbath day" – so, save us, please.

As You saved those You comforted, always delighting in Your commands,
and desired and delivered them, bringing them safe to respite
and peace – so, save us, please.

As You saved the returning exiles of the tribes of Jacob,
so come back and return the exiles of the tents of Jacob –
and save us, please.

As You saved those who kept Your commandments and waited for salvation,
God of all salvation – save us, please.

I and *HE*: save us, please.

הוֹשִׁיעָה Save Your people; bless Your legacy; tend them and carry them forever. Let these words with which I have pleaded with the Lord be close to the Lord our God day and night, that He may do justice for His servant, and justice for His people Israel, day after day; so that all the peoples of the earth will know that the Lord is God. There is no other. *Ps. 28* *I Kings 8*

The Ark is closed
and the Leader continues the service with Full Kaddish on page 696.

כְּהוֹשַׁעְתָּ בְּרֻכּוֹת וַאֲרֻכּוֹת וּגְבוֹהוֹת מְעֻלָּסִים.
בְּפְטִירָתָן יֹפִי לְךָ מִזְבֵּחַ מְקַלְּסִים. כֵּן הוֹשַׁע נָא.

כְּהוֹשַׁעְתָּ מוֹדִים וּמְיַחֲלִים וְלֹא מְשַׁנִּים.
כֻּלָּנוּ אֲנוּ לְיָהּ וְעֵינֵינוּ לְיָהּ שׁוֹנִים. כֵּן הוֹשַׁע נָא.

כְּהוֹשַׁעְתָּ יֶקֶב מֵחֲצֵבֶיךָ סוֹבְבִים בִּרְנָנָה.
רוֹנְנִים אֲנִי וָהוּ הוֹשִׁיעָה נָּא. כֵּן הוֹשַׁע נָא.

כְּהוֹשַׁעְתָּ חֵיל זְרִיזִים מְשָׁרְתִים בִּמְנוּחָה.
קָרְבַּן שַׁבָּת כָּפוּל, עוֹלָה וּמִנְחָה. כֵּן הוֹשַׁע נָא.

כְּהוֹשַׁעְתָּ לְוִיֶּיךָ עַל דּוּכָנָם לְהַרְבַּת.
אוֹמְרִים מִזְמוֹר שִׁיר לְיוֹם הַשַּׁבָּת. כֵּן הוֹשַׁע נָא.

כְּהוֹשַׁעְתָּ נְחוּמֶיךָ בְּמִצְוֹתֶיךָ תָּמִיד יִשְׁתַּעְשְׁעוּן.
וּרְצֵם וְהַחֲלִיצֵם בְּשׁוּבָה וָנַחַת יִוָּשֵׁעוּן. כֵּן הוֹשַׁע נָא.

כְּהוֹשַׁעְתָּ שְׁבוּת שִׁבְטֵי יַעֲקֹב.
תָּשׁוּב וְתָשִׁיב שְׁבוּת אָהֳלֵי יַעֲקֹב. וְהוֹשִׁיעָה נָּא.

כְּהוֹשַׁעְתָּ שׁוֹמְרֵי מִצְוֹת וְחוֹכֵי יְשׁוּעוֹת.
אֵל לְמוֹשָׁעוֹת. וְהוֹשִׁיעָה נָּא.

אֲנִי וָהוּ הוֹשִׁיעָה נָּא.

הוֹשִׁיעָה אֶת־עַמֶּךָ, וּבָרֵךְ אֶת־נַחֲלָתֶךָ, וּרְעֵם וְנַשְּׂאֵם עַד־הָעוֹלָם: וְיִהְיוּ תהלים כח מלכים א׳ ח
דְבָרַי אֵלֶּה, אֲשֶׁר הִתְחַנַּנְתִּי לִפְנֵי יהוה, קְרֹבִים אֶל־יהוה אֱלֹהֵינוּ יוֹמָם
וָלָיְלָה, לַעֲשׂוֹת מִשְׁפַּט עַבְדּוֹ וּמִשְׁפַּט עַמּוֹ יִשְׂרָאֵל, דְּבַר־יוֹם בְּיוֹמוֹ:
לְמַעַן דַּעַת כָּל־עַמֵּי הָאָרֶץ כִּי יהוה הוּא הָאֱלֹהִים, אֵין עוֹד:

The ארון קודש *is closed*
and the שליח ציבור *continues the service with* קדיש שלם *on page 697.*

HOSHANOT FOR HOSHANA RABA

It is the custom to leave the Ark open until the end of the Hoshanot. All of the Torah scrolls are held on the Bima. Members of the congregation who have a Lulav and Etrog circle the Bima seven times while the Hoshanot are read. After finishing the first circuit, say "For I said" and immediately proceed to make another circuit, saying "The Foundation Stone," etc.

Leader then congregation:

הוֹשַׁע נָא Save us, please for Your sake, our God, save us please.

Leader then congregation:

Save us, please for Your sake, our Creator, save us, please.

Leader then congregation:

Save us, please for Your sake, our Redeemer, save us, please.

Leader then congregation:

Save us, please for Your sake, You who seek us, save us, please.

Save us, please –

First Hakafa:

לְמַעַן אֲמִתָּךְ For the sake of Your truth – for the sake of Your covenant – for the sake of Your greatness and glory – for the sake of Your Law – for the sake of Your majesty – for the sake of Your promise – for the sake of Your remembrance – for the sake of Your love – for the sake of Your goodness – for the sake of Your Oneness – for the sake of Your honor – for the sake of Your wisdom – for the sake of Your kingship – for the sake of Your eternity – for the sake of Your mystery – for the sake of Your might – for the sake of Your splendor – for the sake of Your righteousness – for the sake of Your holiness – for the sake of Your great compassion – for the sake of Your Presence – for the sake of Your praise – Save us, please.

After circling the Bima the first time, say:

For I said, *Ps. 89*
the world is built by loving-kindness.

הושענות להושענא רבה

It is the custom to leave the ארון קודש *open until the end of the* הושענות.

All of the ספרי תורה *are held on the* בימה.
Members of the קהל *who have a* לולב *and* אתרוג *circle the* בימה
seven times while the הושענות *are read. After finishing the first circuit,*
say כִּי־אָמַרְתִּי *and immediately proceed to make another circuit, saying* אֶבֶן שְׁתִיָּה*, etc.*

קהל *then* שליח ציבור:

הוֹשַׁע נָא   לְמַעַנְךָ אֱלֹהֵינוּ   הוֹשַׁע נָא.

קהל *then* שליח ציבור:

הוֹשַׁע נָא   לְמַעַנְךָ בּוֹרְאֵנוּ   הוֹשַׁע נָא.

קהל *then* שליח ציבור:

הוֹשַׁע נָא   לְמַעַנְךָ גּוֹאֲלֵנוּ   הוֹשַׁע נָא.

קהל *then* שליח ציבור:

הוֹשַׁע נָא   לְמַעַנְךָ דּוֹרְשֵׁנוּ   הוֹשַׁע נָא.

הוֹשַׁע נָא

First הקפה:

לְמַעַן אֲמִתָּךְ. לְמַעַן בְּרִיתָךְ. לְמַעַן גָּדְלָךְ וְתִפְאַרְתָּךְ. לְמַעַן דָּתָךְ.
לְמַעַן הוֹדָךְ. לְמַעַן וִעוּדָךְ. לְמַעַן זִכְרָךְ. לְמַעַן חַסְדָּךְ. לְמַעַן טוּבָךְ.
לְמַעַן יִחוּדָךְ. לְמַעַן כְּבוֹדָךְ. לְמַעַן לִמּוּדָךְ. לְמַעַן מַלְכוּתָךְ. לְמַעַן נִצְחָךְ.
לְמַעַן סוֹדָךְ. לְמַעַן עֻזָּךְ. לְמַעַן פְּאֵרָךְ. לְמַעַן צִדְקָתָךְ. לְמַעַן קְדֻשָּׁתָךְ.
לְמַעַן רַחֲמֶיךָ הָרַבִּים. לְמַעַן שְׁכִינָתָךְ. לְמַעַן תְּהִלָּתָךְ. הוֹשַׁע נָא.

After circling the בימה *the first time, say:*

תהלים פט   כִּי־אָמַרְתִּי עוֹלָם חֶסֶד יִבָּנֶה:

Save us, please –

Second Hakafa:

אֶבֶן שְׁתִיָּה The Foundation Stone – the House You chose – the threshing-floor of Arnan – the hidden Shrine – Mount Moriah – where He shall be seen – Your glorious Sanctuary – where David camped – the best of Lebanon – the Beauty of Heights, Joy of all the earth – the Place of Perfect Beauty – the Lodge of Goodness – the Place of Your dwelling – the Shelter of Shalem – the tribes' Pilgrimage – the precious Cornerstone – shining Zion – the Holy of Holies – [the walls] lined with love – Residence of Your glory – the Hill toward which all mouths pray – Save us, please.

After circling the Bima the second time, say:

A strong arm is Yours, might is Yours; *Ps. 89*
Your hand holds its power, Your right hand raised.

Save us, please –

Third Hakafa:

אוֹם אֲנִי חוֹמָה "I am a wall," said the people – bright as the sun – exiled and reviled – fair like a date palm – killed on account of You – like sheep to the slaughter – dispersed among tormentors – wrapped in Your embrace, clinging to You – bearing Your yoke – the one to know Your Oneness – beaten down in exile – learning the awe of You – our faces scratched – given over to the violent – weighed down beneath Your burden – oppressed and in turmoil – redeemed by [Moses] Toviya – holy flock – the communities of Jacob – marked out with Your name – roaring, "Save us, please!" – leaning on You – Save us, please.

After circling the Bima the third time, say:

Give truth to Jacob, loving-kindness to Abraham. *Mic. 7*

Save us, please –

Fourth Hakafa:

אָדוֹן הַמּוֹשִׁיעַ Master who saves – there is no one else – mighty, with great power to save – when I was brought low, He saved me – God who saves – who delivers and saves – save those who cry out to You – those who yet watch for You – nourish Your young lambs – make the harvest lavish – sprout every growing thing and save us – do not condemn this valley – make the good fruits sweet and save us – carry the clouds to us – shake down the raindrops

הוֹשַׁע נָא

Second הקפה:

אֶבֶן שְׁתִיָּה. בֵּית הַבְּחִירָה. גֹּרֶן אָרְנָן. דְּבִיר הַמֻּצְנָע. הַר הַמּוֹרִיָּה. וְהַר יֵרָאֶה. זְבוּל תִּפְאַרְתֶּךָ. חָנָה דָוִד. טוֹב הַלְּבָנוֹן. יְפֵה נוֹף מְשׂוֹשׂ כָּל הָאָרֶץ. כְּלִילַת יֹפִי. לִינַת הַצֶּדֶק. מָכוֹן לְשִׁבְתֶּךָ. נָוֶה שַׁאֲנָן. סֻכַּת שָׁלֵם. עֲלִיַּת שְׁבָטִים. פִּנַּת יִקְרַת. צִיּוֹן הַמְצֻיֶּנֶת. קֹדֶשׁ הַקֳּדָשִׁים. רָצוּף אַהֲבָה. שְׁכִינַת כְּבוֹדֶךָ. תֵּל תַּלְפִּיּוֹת. הוֹשַׁע נָא.

After circling the בימה *the second time, say:*

לְךָ זְרוֹעַ עִם־גְּבוּרָה, תָּעֹז יָדְךָ תָּרוּם יְמִינֶךָ: תהלים פט

הוֹשַׁע נָא

Third הקפה:

אֹם אֲנִי חוֹמָה. בָּרָה כַּחַמָּה. גּוֹלָה וְסוּרָה. דָּמְתָה לְתָמָר. הַהֲרוּגָה עָלֶיךָ. וְנֶחְשֶׁבֶת כְּצֹאן טִבְחָה. זְרוּיָה בֵּין מַכְעִיסֶיהָ. חֲבוּקָה וּדְבוּקָה בָךְ. טוֹעֶנֶת עֻלָּךְ. יְחִידָה לְיַחֲדָךְ. כְּבוּשָׁה בַּגּוֹלָה. לוֹמֶדֶת יִרְאָתָךְ. מְרוּטַת לֶחִי. נְתוּנָה לְמַכִּים. סוֹבֶלֶת סִבְלָךְ. עֲנִיָּה סוֹעֲרָה. פְּדוּיַת טוֹבִיָּה. צֹאן קָדָשִׁים. קְהִלּוֹת יַעֲקֹב. רְשׁוּמִים בִּשְׁמֶךָ. שׁוֹאֲגִים הוֹשַׁע נָא. תְּמוּכִים עָלֶיךָ. הוֹשַׁע נָא.

After circling the בימה *the third time, say:*

תִּתֵּן אֱמֶת לְיַעֲקֹב, חֶסֶד לְאַבְרָהָם: מיכה ז

הוֹשַׁע נָא

Fourth הקפה:

אָדוֹן הַמּוֹשִׁיעַ. בִּלְתְּךָ אֵין לְהוֹשִׁיעַ. גִּבּוֹר וְרַב לְהוֹשִׁיעַ. דַּלּוֹתִי וְלִי יְהוֹשִׁיעַ. הָאֵל הַמּוֹשִׁיעַ. וּמַצִּיל וּמוֹשִׁיעַ. זוֹעֲקֶיךָ תּוֹשִׁיעַ. חוֹכֶיךָ הוֹשִׁיעַ. טְלָאֶיךָ תַּשְׂבִּיעַ. יְבוּל לְהַשְׁפִּיעַ. כָּל שִׂיחַ תַּדְשֵׁא וְתוֹשִׁיעַ. לְגֵיא בַּל תַּרְשִׁיעַ. מְגָדִים תַּמְתִּיק וְתוֹשִׁיעַ. נְשִׂיאִים לְהַסִּיעַ. שְׂעִירִים לְהָנִיעַ.

– do not hold back the clouds – You who open Your hand and satisfy – relieve those who thirst for You – save those who call to You – save those You have loved – rescue those who rise to seek You – save Your innocent ones – Save us, please.

After circling the Bima the fourth time, say:

At Your hand, bliss for evermore. *Ps. 16*

Save us, please –

Fifth Hakafa:

אָדָם וּבְהֵמָה Man and beast – body, spirit and soul – muscle, bone, skin – likeness and image woven – glory reduced to mere breath – likened to beasts that fall silent – light and beauty and stature – renew the face of the land – planting trees on desolate ground – winepress and bounty of meadows – vineyard and sycamore fig – bring to the land renowned – mighty rain to scent spices – to recover a devastated place – to raise up the shrub – to make the delightful fruits robust – to make the land glorious with flowers – to soak the plants with rain – to make cool waters flow – to fill out the raindrops – to raise up the earth – the earth that is hung over nothingness – Save us, please.

After circling the Bima the fifth time, say:

Lord our Master, how majestic is Your name throughout the earth, *Ps. 8*
Your glory over all the heavens.

Save us, please –

Sixth Hakafa:

אֲדָמָה מֵאֶרֶר Save earth from cursedness – save cattle from miscarriage – save threshing floor from pest – save grain from burning – save wealth from want – save sustenance from terror – save olive from windfall – save wheat from grasshopper – save food from vermin – save wine-vat from maggot – save vineyard from worm – save late harvest from locust – save bounty from crickets – save souls from horror – save abundance from insects – save herds from infirmity – save fruits from the gales – save flocks from destruction – save crops from the curse – save plenty from poverty – save the wheat-ears from leanness – save produce from disease – Save us, please.

After circling the Bima the sixth time, say:

The Lord is righteous in all His ways, *Ps. 145*
and kind in all He does.

עֲנָנִים מִלְּהַמְנִיעַ. פּוֹתֵחַ יָד וּמַשְׂבִּיעַ. צְמֵאֶיךָ תַּשְׂבִּיעַ. קוֹרְאֶיךָ תּוֹשִׁיעַ. רְחוּמֶיךָ תּוֹשִׁיעַ. שׁוֹחֲרֶיךָ הוֹשִׁיעַ. תְּמִימֶיךָ תּוֹשִׁיעַ. הוֹשַׁע נָא.

After circling the בימה *the fourth time, say:*

תהלים טז

נְעִמוֹת בִּימִינְךָ נֶצַח:

הוֹשַׁע נָא

Fifth הקפה:

אָדָם וּבְהֵמָה. בָּשָׂר וְרוּחַ וּנְשָׁמָה. גִּיד וְעֶצֶם וְקַרְמָה. דְּמוּת וְצֶלֶם וְרִקְמָה. הוֹד לַהֶבֶל דָּמָה. וְנִמְשַׁל כַּבְּהֵמוֹת נִדְמָה. זִיו וְתֹאַר וְקוֹמָה. חִדּוּשׁ פְּנֵי אֲדָמָה. טִיעַת עֲצֵי נְשַׁמָּה. יְקָבִים וְקָמָה. כְּרָמִים וְשִׁקְמָה. לְתֵבֵל הַמְסֻיָּמָה. מְטָרוֹת עֹז לְסַמְּמָה. נְשִׁיָּה לְקַיְּמָה. שִׂיחִים לְקוֹמְמָה. עֲדָנִים לְעָצְמָה. פְּרָחִים לְהַעֲצִימָה. צְמָחִים לְגָשְׁמָה. קָרִים לְזָרְמָה. רְבִיבִים לְשַׁלְּמָה. שְׁתִיָּה לְרוֹמְמָה. תְּלוּיָה עַל בְּלִימָה. הוֹשַׁע נָא.

After circling the בימה *the fifth time, say:*

תהלים ח

יהוה אֲדֹנֵינוּ מָה־אַדִּיר שִׁמְךָ בְּכָל־הָאָרֶץ
אֲשֶׁר־תְּנָה הוֹדְךָ עַל־הַשָּׁמָיִם:

הוֹשַׁע נָא

Sixth הקפה:

אֲדָמָה מֵאֶרֶר. בְּהֵמָה מִמְּשַׁכֶּלֶת. גֹּרֶן מִגָּזָם. דָּגָן מִדַּלֶּקֶת. הוֹן מִמְּאֵרָה. וְאֹכֶל מִמְּהוּמָה. זַיִת מִנֶּשֶׁל. חִטָּה מֵחָגָב. טֶרֶף מִגּוֹבַי. יֶקֶב מִיֶּלֶק. כֶּרֶם מִתּוֹלַעַת. לֶקֶשׁ מֵאַרְבֶּה. מֶגֶד מִצְּלָצַל. נֶפֶשׁ מִבֶּהָלָה. שֹׂבַע מִסָּלְעָם. עֲדָרִים מִדַּלּוּת. פֵּרוֹת מִשִּׁדָּפוֹן. צֹאן מִצְּמִיתוּת. קָצִיר מִקְּלָלָה. רֹב מֵרָזוֹן. שִׁבֹּלֶת מִצִּנָּמוֹן. תְּבוּאָה מֵחָסִיל. הוֹשַׁע נָא.

After circling the בימה *the sixth time, say:*

תהלים קמה

צַדִּיק יהוה בְּכָל־דְּרָכָיו, וְחָסִיד בְּכָל־מַעֲשָׂיו:

Save us, please –

Seventh Hakafa:

לְמַעַן אֵיתָן For the sake of steadfast [Abraham], who was thrown into flames of fire –
for the sake of his son [Isaac] who was bound on the wood of the fire –
for the sake of the mighty [Jacob] who struggled with a prince of fire –
for the sake of the flags [of the tribes] You led in light and a cloud of fire –
for the sake of one who was raised up to the heights and rose, like an angel of fire –
for the sake of one who is to You like a deputy among erelim of fire –
for the sake of the gift of commandments made in fire –
for the sake of the curtained Tent [of Meeting] and its cloud of fire –
for the sake of that scene on the mountain, of Your coming down to it in fire –
for the sake of the loveliness of that House You preferred above heavens of fire –
for the sake of [Moses] who yearned until the dying of the fire –
for the sake of [Aaron] who took a fire pan to quell a rage of fire –
for the sake of [Pinehas] who burned with a great jealousy, Your fire –
for the sake of [Joshua] who raised his hand and brought down stones of fire –
for the sake of [Samuel] who burned a milk lamb wholly in the fire –
for the sake of [David] who stood in the threshing floor and found favor again through fire –
for the sake of [Solomon] who spoke in the Courtyard and down came fire –
for the sake of Your messenger [Elijah] who rose and was raised up in a chariot with horses of fire –
for the sake of [Hananiah, Mishael and Azariah,] the holy ones flung into fire –
for the sake of [Daniel] who saw the thousands of countless [angels], the rivers of fire –
for the sake of the desolate remains of Your city burnt up by fire –
for the sake of the past of these clans of Judah whom You shall make as a basin of fire – Save us, please.

After circling the Bima the seventh time, say:

לְךָ Yours, Lord, are the greatness and the power, *1 Chr. 29*
the glory and the majesty and splendor,
for everything in heaven and earth is Yours.
Yours, Lord, is the kingdom; You are elevated as Head over all.
Then the Lord shall be King over all the earth; *Zech. 14*
on that day the Lord shall be One and His name One.
And in Your Torah it is written:
Listen, Israel: the Lord is our God, the Lord is One. *Deut. 6*
Blessed be the name of His glorious kingdom for ever and all time.

הוֹשַׁע נָא

Seventh הקפה:

לְמַעַן אֵיתָן הַנִּזְרָק בְּלַהַב אֵשׁ.
לְמַעַן בֵּן הַנֶּעֱקַד עַל עֵצִים וָאֵשׁ.
לְמַעַן גִּבּוֹר הַנֶּאֱבַק עִם שַׂר אֵשׁ.
לְמַעַן דְּגָלִים נָחִיתָ בְּאוֹר וַעֲנַן אֵשׁ.
לְמַעַן הָעֳלָה לַמָּרוֹם, וְנִתְעַלָּה כְּמַלְאֲכֵי אֵשׁ.
לְמַעַן וְהוּא לָךְ כְּסֶגֶן בְּאֶרְאֶלֵּי אֵשׁ.
לְמַעַן זֶבֶד דִּבְּרוֹת הַנְּתוּנוֹת מֵאֵשׁ.
לְמַעַן חִפּוּי יְרִיעוֹת וַעֲנַן אֵשׁ.
לְמַעַן טֶכֶס הַר יָרַדְתָּ עָלָיו בָּאֵשׁ.
לְמַעַן יְדִידוּת בַּיִת אֲשֶׁר אָהַבְתָּ מִשְּׁמֵי אֵשׁ.
לְמַעַן כָּמַהּ עַד שָׁקְעָה הָאֵשׁ.
לְמַעַן לָקַח מַחְתַּת אֵשׁ וְהֵסִיר חֲרוֹן אֵשׁ.
לְמַעַן מְקַנֵּא קִנְאָה גְדוֹלָה בָּאֵשׁ.
לְמַעַן נָף יָדוֹ וְיָרְדוּ אַבְנֵי אֵשׁ.
לְמַעַן שָׂם טְלֵה חָלָב כְּלִיל אֵשׁ.
לְמַעַן עָמַד בַּגֹּרֶן וְנִתְרַצָּה בָאֵשׁ.
לְמַעַן פִּלֵּל בָּעֲזָרָה וְיָרְדָה הָאֵשׁ.
לְמַעַן צִיר עָלָה וְנִתְעַלָּה בְּרֶכֶב וְסוּסֵי אֵשׁ.
לְמַעַן קְדוֹשִׁים מֻשְׁלָכִים בָּאֵשׁ.
לְמַעַן רִבּוֹ רִבְבָן חָז וְנַהֲרֵי אֵשׁ.
לְמַעַן שְׁמֵמוֹת עִירְךָ הַשְּׂרוּפָה בָאֵשׁ.
לְמַעַן תּוֹלְדוֹת אַלּוּפֵי יְהוּדָה, תָּשִׂים כְּכִיּוֹר אֵשׁ. הוֹשַׁע נָא.

After circling the בימה *the seventh time, say:*

דברי הימים א׳ כט
לְךָ יהוה הַגְּדֻלָּה וְהַגְּבוּרָה וְהַתִּפְאֶרֶת וְהַנֵּצַח וְהַהוֹד, כִּי־כֹל בַּשָּׁמַיִם וּבָאָרֶץ
לְךָ יהוה הַמַּמְלָכָה וְהַמִּתְנַשֵּׂא לְכֹל לְרֹאשׁ:

זכריה יד
וְהָיָה יהוה לְמֶלֶךְ עַל־כָּל־הָאָרֶץ, בַּיּוֹם הַהוּא יִהְיֶה יהוה אֶחָד וּשְׁמוֹ אֶחָד:

דברים ו
וּבְתוֹרָתְךָ כָּתוּב לֵאמֹר: שְׁמַע יִשְׂרָאֵל, יהוה אֱלֹהֵינוּ, יהוה אֶחָד:
בָּרוּךְ שֵׁם כְּבוֹד מַלְכוּתוֹ לְעוֹלָם וָעֶד.

I and *HE*: save us, please.

כְּהוֹשַׁעְתָּ As You saved the mighty ones in Lud with You,
coming down for Your people's deliverance – save us, please.

As You saved nation and God together,
[the people] called for God's salvation – save us, please.

As You saved the crowding multitudes,
and angelic multitudes along with them – save us, please.

As You saved pure ones from the grip of slavery,
Gracious One; enslaved in cruel hands – save us, please.

As You saved those submerged between slices of the deep,
and brought Your own glory through it with them –
save us, please.

As You saved the stem as they sang "And God saved" –
but the Deliverer reads it, "God was saved" – save us, please.

As You saved, and You said, "I took you out,"
but let it be pointed, "I was taken out with you" – save us, please.

As You saved those who encompassed the Altar,
bearing their willows to encircle the Altar – save us, please.

As You saved the Ark of wonders that was wronged,
tormenting Philistia with fury, and saving it – save us, please.

As You saved the communities You sent away to Babylon,
being sent too, for them, Your compassionate Self –
save us, please.

As You saved the returning exiles of the tribes of Jacob,
so come back and return the exiles of the tents of Jacob –
and save us, please.

As You saved those who kept Your commandments and waited for
salvation, / God of all salvation – and save us, please.

אֲנִי וָהוֹ הוֹשִׁיעָה נָּא.

כְּהוֹשַׁעְתָּ אֵלִים בְּלוּד עִמָּךְ.
בְּצֵאתְךָ לְיֵשַׁע עַמָּךְ. כֵּן הוֹשַׁע נָא.

כְּהוֹשַׁעְתָּ גּוֹי וֵאלֹהִים.
דְּרוּשִׁים לְיֵשַׁע אֱלֹהִים. כֵּן הוֹשַׁע נָא.

כְּהוֹשַׁעְתָּ הֲמוֹן צְבָאוֹת.
וְעִמָּם מַלְאֲכֵי צְבָאוֹת. כֵּן הוֹשַׁע נָא.

כְּהוֹשַׁעְתָּ זַכִּים מִבֵּית עֲבָדִים.
חַנּוּן בְּיָדָם מַעֲבִידִים. כֵּן הוֹשַׁע נָא.

כְּהוֹשַׁעְתָּ טְבוּעִים בְּצוּל גְּזָרִים.
יְקָרְךָ עִמָּם מַעֲבִירִים. כֵּן הוֹשַׁע נָא.

כְּהוֹשַׁעְתָּ כַּנָּה מְשׁוֹרֶרֶת וַיּוֹשַׁע.
לְגוֹחָה מְצֻיֶּנֶת וַיִּוָּשַׁע. כֵּן הוֹשַׁע נָא.

כְּהוֹשַׁעְתָּ מַאֲמַר וְהוֹצֵאתִי אֶתְכֶם.
נָקוּב וְהוּצֵאתִי אִתְּכֶם. כֵּן הוֹשַׁע נָא.

כְּהוֹשַׁעְתָּ סוֹבְבֵי מִזְבֵּחַ.
עוֹמְסֵי עֲרָבָה לְהַקִּיף מִזְבֵּחַ. כֵּן הוֹשַׁע נָא.

כְּהוֹשַׁעְתָּ פִּלְאֵי אָרוֹן כְּהֻפְשַׁע.
צִעֵר פְּלֶשֶׁת בַּחֲרוֹן אַף, וְנוֹשַׁע. כֵּן הוֹשַׁע נָא.

כְּהוֹשַׁעְתָּ קְהִלּוֹת בָּבֶלָה שִׁלַּחְתָּ.
רַחוּם לְמַעֲנָם שֻׁלַּחְתָּ. כֵּן הוֹשַׁע נָא.

כְּהוֹשַׁעְתָּ שְׁבוּת שִׁבְטֵי יַעֲקֹב.
תָּשׁוּב וְתָשִׁיב שְׁבוּת אָהֳלֵי יַעֲקֹב. וְהוֹשִׁיעָה נָּא.

כְּהוֹשַׁעְתָּ שׁוֹמְרֵי מִצְוֹת וְחוֹכֵי יְשׁוּעוֹת.
אֵל לְמוֹשָׁעוֹת. וְהוֹשִׁיעָה נָּא.

I and *HE*: save us, please.

תְּתְּנֵנוּ לְשֵׁם Give us name and honor; / return us to our home, our land; / raise us up, up above; / gather us to the House of prayer; / plant us as a tree on streams of water; / redeem us from infection and illness; / crown us with bridal love; / have us rejoice in the House of prayer; / lead us beside the still waters forever; / fill us with wisdom and insight; / clothe us with strength and dignity; / crown us with the finest crown; / guide us straight along a paved avenue; / set us down upon a straight pathway; / grace us with compassion and mercy; / remember us, "Who is this rising?" / save us, to the end, to Redemption; / have us glow with the splendor of the crowd; / bind us about You like a loincloth girt; / make us greater with Your great hand; / bring us to Your House in song, in celebration; / make us majestic with salvation and joy; / strengthen us in Your relief and rescue; / sweep our hearts up in the building of Your city anew; / awaken us to Zion in her completion; / give us the honor to see the city rebuilt on its hill; / set us down to pasture in happiness and joy; / strengthen us, God of Jacob, always –

Save us, please.

Leader then congregation:

Please: save us, please.

אָנָּא Please – listen to the plea of those who hunger for Your rescue,
as they bring willows of the stream to delight You –
and save us, please.

Please – redeem this stem You planted,
as You sweep away Duma [the regime that rules us]–
and save us, please.

Please – look to the covenant You have sealed in us,
as You destroy the dark places of this earth –
and save us, please.

Please – remember for our sake our father] Abraham [who knew You,
as You make Your love known to [the others] –
and save us, please.

אֲנִי וָהוֹ הוֹשִׁיעָה נָּא.

תְּתְּנֵנוּ לְשֵׁם וְלִתְהִלָּה.	תְּחָנֵנוּ בְּרַחֲמִים וּבְחֶמְלָה.
תְּשִׁיבֵנוּ אֶל הַחֶבֶל וְאֶל הַנַּחֲלָה.	תִּזְכְּרֵנוּ בְּמִי זֹאת עוֹלָה.
תְּרוֹמְמֵנוּ לְמַעְלָה לְמָעְלָה.	תּוֹשִׁיעֵנוּ לְקֵץ הַגְּאֻלָּה.
תְּקַבְּצֵנוּ לְבֵית הַתְּפִלָּה.	תְּהַדְּרֵנוּ בְּזִיו הַמְּלָה.
תְּצִיבֵנוּ כְּעֵץ עַל פַּלְגֵי מַיִם שְׁתוּלָה.	תַּדְבִּיקֵנוּ כְּאֵזוֹר חֲתוּלָה.
תִּפְדֵּנוּ מִכָּל נֶגַע וּמַחֲלָה.	תְּגַדְּלֵנוּ בְּיָד הַגְּדוֹלָה.
תְּעַטְּרֵנוּ בְּאַהֲבָה כְלוּלָה.	תְּבִיאֵנוּ לְבֵיתְךָ בְּרִנָּה וְצָהֳלָה.
תְּשַׂמְּחֵנוּ בְּבֵית הַתְּפִלָּה.	תְּאַדְּרֵנוּ בְּיֶשַׁע וְגִילָה.
תְּנַהֲלֵנוּ עַל מֵי מְנוּחוֹת סֶלָה.	תְּאַמְּצֵנוּ בְּרֶוַח וְהַצָּלָה.
תְּמַלְּאֵנוּ חָכְמָה וְשִׂכְלָה.	תְּלַבְּבֵנוּ בְּבִנְיַן עִירְךָ כְּבַתְּחִלָּה.
תַּלְבִּישֵׁנוּ עֹז וּגְדֻלָּה.	תְּעוֹרְרֵנוּ לְצִיּוֹן בְּשִׁכְלוּלָהּ.
תַּכְתִּירֵנוּ בְּכֶתֶר כְּלוּלָה.	תִּזַכֵּנוּ בִּנְבְנְתָה הָעִיר עַל תִּלָּהּ.
תְּיַשְּׁרֵנוּ בְּאֹרַח סְלוּלָה.	תַּרְבִּיצֵנוּ בְּשָׂשׂוֹן וְגִילָה.
תִּטָּעֵנוּ בְּיֹשֶׁר מְסִלָּה.	תְּחַזְּקֵנוּ אֱלֹהֵי יַעֲקֹב סֶלָה.

הוֹשַׁע נָא.

קהל *then* שליח ציבור:

אָנָּא, הוֹשִׁיעָה נָּא.

אָנָּא אֱזוֹן חִין תַּאֲבֵי יִשְׁעָךְ.
בְּעַרְבֵי נַחַל לְשַׁעְשְׁעָךְ. וְהוֹשִׁיעָה נָּא.

אָנָּא גְּאַל כַּנַּת נִטְעָךְ.
דּוֹמָה בְּטַאטְאָךְ. וְהוֹשִׁיעָה נָּא.

אָנָּא הַבֵּט לִבְרִית טִבְעָךְ.
וּמַחֲשַׁכֵּי אֶרֶץ בְּהַטְבִּיעָךְ. וְהוֹשִׁיעָה נָּא.

אָנָּא זְכָר לָנוּ אָב יְדָעָךְ.
חַסְדְּךָ לָמוֹ בְּהוֹדִיעָךְ. וְהוֹשִׁיעָה נָּא.

Please – as You perform miracles for the pure of heart,
make it known that these are Your own wonders –
and save us, please.

Please – You whose strength is immense, give us Your salvation,
as You swore to our forefathers – and save us, please.

Please – answer the wishes of the people who beg of You,
like the prayer of [Isaac] bound on the Mountain of
Myrrh – and save us, please.

Please – strengthen [Israel,] the tamarisks You planted,
as You push aside oppressors – and save us, please.

Please – open for us Your treasuries of rain,
as from them You water arid land – and save us, please.

Please – when You shake the earth, lead those who call on You
to pasture in the best of Your meadows – and save us, please.

Please – lift the gates of Your [House] from their destruction,
as You raise the ruins each mouth prays towards –
and save us, please.

Leader then congregation:

Please; God, please;
save, please; save us, please.

אֵל נָא God, please; we have gone astray like lost sheep;
do not erase our name from Your book – save, please; save us, please.

God, please; tend the flock destined to slaughter,
raged against, killed in Your name – save, please; save us, please.

God, please; Your flock, the flock You tend,
Your creation, Your beloved – save, please; save us, please.

God, please; the poorest of the flock –
answer their prayer at a time of favor – save, please; save us, please.

אָנָּא טְהוֹרֵי לֵב בְּהַפְלִיאָךְ.
יוֹדַע כִּי הוּא פִּלְאָךְ. וְהוֹשִׁיעָה נָּא.

אָנָּא כַּבִּיר כֹּחַ תֶּן לָנוּ יִשְׁעָךְ.
לַאֲבוֹתֵינוּ כְּהִשָּׁבְעָךְ. וְהוֹשִׁיעָה נָּא.

אָנָּא מָלֵא מִשְׁאֲלוֹת עַם מְשַׁוְּעָךְ.
נֶעֱקַד בְּהַר מוֹר כְּמוֹ שַׁוְעָךְ. וְהוֹשִׁיעָה נָּא.

אָנָּא סַגֵּב אֶשְׁלֵי נִטְעָךְ.
עָרִיצִים בְּהֵנִיעָךְ. וְהוֹשִׁיעָה נָּא.

אָנָּא פְּתַח לָנוּ אוֹצְרוֹת רִבְעָךְ.
צִיָּה מֵהֶם בְּהַרְבִּיעָךְ. וְהוֹשִׁיעָה נָּא.

אָנָּא קוֹרְאֶיךָ אֶרֶץ בְּרוֹעֲעָךְ.
רְעֵם בְּטוּב מִרְעָךְ. וְהוֹשִׁיעָה נָּא.

אָנָּא שְׁעָרֶיךָ תַּעַל מִמְּשׁוֹאָךְ.
תֵּל תַּלְפִּיּוֹת בְּהַשִּׂיאָךְ. וְהוֹשִׁיעָה נָּא.

קהל *then* שליח ציבור:

אָנָּא, אֵל נָא, הוֹשַׁע נָא וְהוֹשִׁיעָה נָּא.

אֵל נָא תָּעִינוּ כְּשֶׂה אוֹבֵד
שְׁמֵנוּ מִסִּפְרְךָ אַל תְּאַבֵּד הוֹשַׁע נָא וְהוֹשִׁיעָה נָּא.

אֵל נָא רְעֵה אֶת צֹאן הַהֲרֵגָה
קְצוּפָה, וְעָלֶיךָ הֲרוּגָה הוֹשַׁע נָא וְהוֹשִׁיעָה נָּא.

אֵל נָא צֹאנְךָ וְצֹאן מַרְעִיתֶךָ
פְּעֻלָּתְךָ וְרַעְיָתֶךָ הוֹשַׁע נָא וְהוֹשִׁיעָה נָּא.

אֵל נָא עֲנִיֵּי הַצֹּאן
שִׂיחָם עֲנֵה בְּעֵת רָצוֹן הוֹשַׁע נָא וְהוֹשִׁיעָה נָּא.

God, please; those who raise their eyes to You –
may those who rise against You be as nothing beside them –
save, please; save us, please.

God, please; those who pour water out before You –
from the wellsprings of salvation, let them draw water –
save, please; save us, please.

God, please; let the redeemers go up to Zion,
leaning upon You, saved in Your name – save, please; save us, please.

God, please; Your clothes red with blood,
rage and shake away all those who betray –
save, please; save us, please.

God, please; surely remember,
those sold away for a letekh of grain, for a kor –
save, please; save us, please.

God, please; those who seek You with stems of willow,
hear their weeping from the highest heaven –
save, please; save us, please.

God, please; crown this year with blessing,
and hear my words as I pray, on the day of Hoshana –
save, please; save us, please.

Leader then congregation:

Please; God, please;
save, please; save us, please; You are our Father.

לְמַעַן For the sake of one perfect in his generation,
who escaped in his righteousness,
saved from the flood, when there came down a deluge of water –
the people that says "I am a wall" –
save, please: save us, please: You are our Father.

For the sake of one whole in all his doings, tested with ten trials,
who saw angels and said, "Please, bring a little water" –
the people shining like the sun –
save, please: save us, please: You are our Father.

אֵל נָא נוֹשְׂאֵי לְךָ עַיִן
מִתְקוֹמְמֶיךָ יִהְיוּ כְּאַיִן הוֹשַׁע נָא וְהוֹשִׁיעָה נָּא.

אֵל נָא לִמְנַסְּכֵי לְךָ מַיִם
כְּמִמַּעַיְנֵי הַיְשׁוּעָה יִשְׁאֲבוּן מַיִם הוֹשַׁע נָא וְהוֹשִׁיעָה נָּא.

אֵל נָא יַעֲלוּ לְצִיּוֹן מוֹשִׁיעִים
טְפוּלִים בְּךָ וּבְשִׁמְךָ נוֹשָׁעִים הוֹשַׁע נָא וְהוֹשִׁיעָה נָּא.

אֵל נָא חֲמוּץ בְּגָדִים
זְעוֹם לִנְעֹר כָּל בּוֹגְדִים הוֹשַׁע נָא וְהוֹשִׁיעָה נָּא.

אֵל נָא וְזָכוֹר תִּזְכֹּר
הַנְּכוּרִים בְּלֶתֶךְ וָכֹר הוֹשַׁע נָא וְהוֹשִׁיעָה נָּא.

אֵל נָא דּוֹרְשֶׁיךָ בְּעַנְפֵי עֲרָבוֹת
גֹּעִים שְׁעֵה מֵעֲרָבוֹת הוֹשַׁע נָא וְהוֹשִׁיעָה נָּא.

אֵל נָא בָּרֵךְ בְּעִטּוּר שָׁנָה
אִמְרֵי רְצֵה בְּפִלּוּלֵי בְּיוֹם הוֹשַׁעְנָא הוֹשַׁע נָא וְהוֹשִׁיעָה נָּא.

then קהל שליח ציבור:

אָנָּא, אֵל נָא

הוֹשַׁע נָא וְהוֹשִׁיעָה נָּא, אָבִינוּ אָתָּה.

לְמַעַן תָּמִים בְּדוֹרוֹתָיו, הַנִּמְלָט בְּרֹב צִדְקוֹתָיו
מֻצָּל מִשֶּׁטֶף בְּבוֹא מַבּוּל מַיִם.
לְאֹם אֲנִי חוֹמָה הוֹשַׁע נָא וְהוֹשִׁיעָה נָּא, אָבִינוּ אָתָּה.

לְמַעַן שָׁלֵם בְּכָל מַעֲשִׂים, הַמְנֻסֶּה בַּעֲשָׂרָה נִסִּים
כְּשֶׂר מַלְאָכִים, נָם יֻקַּח נָא מְעַט מַיִם.
לְבָרָה כַּחַמָּה הוֹשַׁע נָא וְהוֹשִׁיעָה נָּא, אָבִינוּ אָתָּה.

For the sake of a tender, only child, young fruit borne to a man of a hundred,
who cried out, "Where is the lamb for the burnt offering?!"
Whose servants brought him news: "We have found water!" –
the people expelled and banished –
save, please: save us, please: You are our Father.

For the sake of one who came in first to bear blessing,
who gained a foe and waited for salvation by Your name;
who made goats fertile with branches, by troughs of water –
the people likened to a date palm –
save, please: save us, please: You are our Father.

For the sake of the one righteous enough to be chosen as Your priest,
serving You like a bridegroom adorned,
tested at Masa, by the Mei Meriva water –
the good mountain – save, please: save us, please: You are our Father.

For the sake of the one raised to be master of his brothers,
Judah who became the most powerful of brothers,
numerous as dust; his pail overflows with water –
not for us, but for Your sake –
save, please: save us, please: You are our Father.

For the sake of the humblest of men, the most faithful,
for whose righteous sake the manna fell,
pulled to be redeemer, drawn forth from the water –
this people, gazing out – save, please: save us, please: You are our Father.

For the sake of one You raised like angels of the heights, clad with the urim and tumim, commanded to come into the Temple with sanctified hands and feet, bathed in water –
this people sick with love –
save, please: save us, please: You are our Father.

For the sake of the prophetess who danced between the camps;
to whom the people on their yearning journey raised their eyes [to lead them]; for her sake it moved, it rose and it rested, the well of water –
the people of the goodly tents –
save, please: save us, please: You are our Father.

For the sake of the servant who never left the Tent, over whom the holy spirit rested, for whose sake the Jordan parted its water –
the people beautiful and shining –
save, please: save us, please: You are our Father.

לְמַעַן רַךְ וְיָחִיד נֶחֱנַט פְּרִי לְמֵאָה, זָעַק אַיֵּה הַשֶּׂה לְעֹלָה
בִּשְּׂרוּהוּ עֲבָדָיו מָצָאנוּ מַיִם.
לְגוֹלָה וְסוּרָה הוֹשַׁע נָא וְהוֹשִׁיעָה נָּא, אָבִינוּ אָתָּה.

לְמַעַן קָדַם שְׂאֵת בְּרָכָה, הַנִּשְׂטָם וּלְשִׁמְךָ חִכָּה
מְיַחֵם בְּמַקְלוֹת בְּשִׁקְתוֹת הַמָּיִם.
לְדָמְתָה לְתָמָר הוֹשַׁע נָא וְהוֹשִׁיעָה נָּא, אָבִינוּ אָתָּה.

לְמַעַן צָדַק הֱיוֹת לְךָ לְכֹהֵן, כְּחָתָן פְּאֵר יְכַהֵן
מְנֻסֶּה בְּמַסָּה בְּמֵי מְרִיבַת מַיִם.
לְהָהָר הַטּוֹב הוֹשַׁע נָא וְהוֹשִׁיעָה נָּא, אָבִינוּ אָתָּה.

לְמַעַן פְּאֵר הֱיוֹת גְּבִיר לְאֶחָיו, יְהוּדָה אֲשֶׁר גָּבַר בְּאֶחָיו
מִסְפַּר רֹבַע מִדָּלְיָו יִזַּל מַיִם.
לֹא לָנוּ כִּי אִם לְמַעַנְךָ הוֹשַׁע נָא וְהוֹשִׁיעָה נָּא, אָבִינוּ אָתָּה.

לְמַעַן עָנָו מִכֹּל וְנֶאֱמָן, אֲשֶׁר בְּצִדְקוֹ כִּלְכֵּל הַמָּן
מָשׁוּךְ לְגוֹאֵל וּמָשׁוּי מִמַּיִם.
לְזֹאת הַנִּשְׁקָפָה הוֹשַׁע נָא וְהוֹשִׁיעָה נָּא, אָבִינוּ אָתָּה.

לְמַעַן שַׂמְתּוֹ כְּמַלְאֲכֵי מְרוֹמִים, הַלּוֹבֵשׁ אוּרִים וְתֻמִּים
מְצֻוֶּה לָבוֹא בְּמִקְדָּשׁ בְּקִדּוּשׁ יָדַיִם וְרַגְלַיִם וּרְחִיצַת מַיִם.
לְחוֹלַת אַהֲבָה הוֹשַׁע נָא וְהוֹשִׁיעָה נָּא, אָבִינוּ אָתָּה.

לְמַעַן נְבִיאָה מְחוֹלַת מַחֲנַיִם, לְכַמְהֵי לֵב הוּשְׂמָה עֵינַיִם
לְרַגְלָהּ רָצָה עָלוֹת וְרֶדֶת בְּאֵר מַיִם.
לְטוֹבוּ אֹהָלָיו הוֹשַׁע נָא וְהוֹשִׁיעָה נָּא, אָבִינוּ אָתָּה.

לְמַעַן מְשָׁרֵת לֹא מָשׁ מֵאֹהֶל, וְרוּחַ הַקֹּדֶשׁ עָלָיו אִהֵל
בְּעָבְרוֹ בַּיַּרְדֵּן נִכְרְתוּ הַמַּיִם.
לְיָפָה וּבָרָה הוֹשַׁע נָא וְהוֹשִׁיעָה נָּא, אָבִינוּ אָתָּה.

For the sake of the one taught to read a sign of good things,
who cried out, "Where are the wonders now?"
But later wrung rain from the wool – a whole bowl full of water –
the bride of Lebanon –
save, please: save us, please: You are our Father.

For the sake of one who ground his enemies alone, dedicated from the womb
a Nazirite, from the hollow of a jawbone You brought him forth water –
for Your holy name's sake –
save, please: save us, please: You are our Father.

For the sake of those included in the army of Your war,
at whose hands You gave Your salvation,
marked out from the people as from their hands they lapped up water –
those who never betrayed –
save, please: save us, please: You are our Father.

For the sake of the good child growing more and more,
who never allowed himself to take from the people;
when the people repented he said, "Draw forth water!" –
the people, lovely as Jerusalem –
save, please: save us, please: You are our Father.

For the sake of one who laughed and danced in song,
who taught the Torah through any instrument of music,
who libated before You, though he longed to drink water –
those who placed their hope in You –
save, please: save us, please: You are our Father.

For the sake of the pure one who went up in a storm cloud,
who was jealous for You and who turned back Your rage,
at whose word down came fire to lick the dust and water –
the people whose eyes are like pools –
save, please: save us, please: You are our Father.

For the sake of one who served his teacher truly,
and was assigned a double measure of his spirit.
When he called the musician to play, the pools were filled with water –
those who said "Who is like You?" –
save, please: save us, please: You are our Father.

לְמַעַן לָמַד רְאוֹת לְטוֹבָה אוֹת, זָעַק אַיֵּה נִפְלָאוֹת
מְצֵה טַל מִגִּזָּה מְלֹא הַסֵּפֶל מָיִם.
לְכַלַּת לְבָנוֹן הוֹשַׁע נָא וְהוֹשִׁיעָה נָּא, אָבִינוּ אָתָּה.

לְמַעַן כְּלוּלֵי עֲשׂוֹת מִלְחַמְתֶּךָ, אֲשֶׁר בְּיָדָם תַּתָּה יְשׁוּעָתֶךָ
צְרוּפֵי מִגּוֹי בְּלָקְקָם בְּיָדָם מָיִם.
לְלֹא בָגְדוּ בָךְ הוֹשַׁע נָא וְהוֹשִׁיעָה נָּא, אָבִינוּ אָתָּה.

לְמַעַן יְחִיד צוֹרְרִים דָּשׁ, אֲשֶׁר מֵרֶחֶם לְנְזִיר הֻקְדָּשׁ
מִמַּכְתֵּשׁ לֶחִי הִבְקַעְתָּ לוֹ מָיִם.
לְמַעַן שֵׁם קָדְשֶׁךָ הוֹשַׁע נָא וְהוֹשִׁיעָה נָּא, אָבִינוּ אָתָּה.

לְמַעַן טוֹב הוֹלֵךְ וְגָדֵל, אֲשֶׁר מֵעֹשֶׁק עֵדָה חִדֵּל
בְּשׁוּב עַם מֵחֵטְא צִוָּה שְׁאֹב מָיִם.
לְנָאוָה כִּירוּשָׁלָיִם הוֹשַׁע נָא וְהוֹשִׁיעָה נָּא, אָבִינוּ אָתָּה.

לְמַעַן חִיֵּךְ מְכַרְכֵּר בְּשִׁיר, הַמְלַמֵּד תּוֹרָה בְּכָל כְּלֵי שִׁיר
מְנַסֵּךְ לְפָנֶיךָ כְּתָאַב שְׁתוֹת מָיִם.
לְשָׁמוּ בָךְ סִבְרָם הוֹשַׁע נָא וְהוֹשִׁיעָה נָּא, אָבִינוּ אָתָּה.

לְמַעַן זָךְ עָלָה בִּסְעָרָה, הַמְקַנֵּא וּמֵשִׁיב עֶבְרָה
לִפְלוּלוֹ יָרְדָה אֵשׁ וְלִחֲכָה עָפָר וּמָיִם.
לְעֵינֶיהָ בְּרֵכוֹת הוֹשַׁע נָא וְהוֹשִׁיעָה נָּא, אָבִינוּ אָתָּה.

לְמַעַן מְשָׁרֵת בֶּאֱמֶת לְרַבּוֹ, פִּי שְׁנַיִם בְּרוּחוֹ נֶאֱצַל בּוֹ
בְּקַחְתּוֹ מְנַגֵּן נִתְמַלְּאוּ גֵבִים מָיִם.
לְפָצוּ מִי כָמֹכָה הוֹשַׁע נָא וְהוֹשִׁיעָה נָּא, אָבִינוּ אָתָּה.

For the sake of one who thought to do Your will,
who declared repentance to all Your flock;
then, when the blasphemer came, he stopped up all springs of water –
Zion, perfect beauty –
save, please: save us, please: You are our Father.

For the sake of those who sought You from the heart of Exile,
to whom Your secrets were revealed,
and not to be tainted [by meat and wine]
they asked for grains and water –
those who cry out to You from their distress –
save, please: save us, please: You are our Father.

For the sake of one who learned wisdom and insight,
the keen-minded scribe who set forth a pledge,
the one who made us wiser with words deep as oceans of water –
the [city that] flocked with people –
save, please: save us, please: You are our Father.

For the sake of those who come to You today with all their hearts,
who pour out their words without two minds,
who ask of You Your mighty torrents of water –
those who sang at the sea –
save, please: save us, please: You are our Father.

For the sake of those who say "May Your name be declared great" –
and they are Your inheritance, Your people;
who thirst for Your salvation as an arid land thirsts water –
those for whom You sought out a resting place –
save, please: save us, please: You are our Father.

Leader then congregation:

Save, please, God, please,
save us, please.

Save, please, please forgive
and give us success, please.

Save us, God who is our Refuge.

Put down the Lulav and Etrog and pick up the Hoshanot.

לְמַעַן הִרְהֵר עֲשׂוֹת רְצוֹנֶךָ, הַמַּכְרִיז תְּשׁוּבָה לְצֹאנֶךָ
אָז בְּבוֹא מְחָרֵף סָתַם עֵינוֹת מַיִם.
לְצִיּוֹן מִכְלַל יֹפִי הוֹשַׁע נָא וְהוֹשִׁיעָה נָּא, אָבִינוּ אָתָּה.

לְמַעַן דָּרְשׁוּךָ בְּתוֹךְ הַגּוֹלָה, וְסוֹדְךָ לָמוֹ נִגְלָה
בְּלִי לְהִתְגָּאֵל דָּרְשׁוּ זֵרְעוֹנִים וּמַיִם.
לְקוֹרְאֶיךָ בַּצָּר הוֹשַׁע נָא וְהוֹשִׁיעָה נָּא, אָבִינוּ אָתָּה.

לְמַעַן גְּמַר חָכְמָה וּבִינָה, סוֹפֵר מָהִיר מְפַלֵּשׂ אֲמָנָה
מַחְכִּימֵנוּ אֲמָרִים הַמְּשׁוּלִים בְּרַחֲבֵי מַיִם.
לְרַבּוֹתֵי עָם הוֹשַׁע נָא וְהוֹשִׁיעָה נָּא, אָבִינוּ אָתָּה.

לְמַעַן בָּאֵי לְךָ הַיּוֹם בְּכָל לֵב, שׁוֹפְכִים לְךָ שִׂיחַ בְּלֹא לֵב וָלֵב
שׁוֹאֲלִים מִמְּךָ עֹז מְטָרוֹת מַיִם.
לְשׁוֹרְרוּ בַיָּם הוֹשַׁע נָא וְהוֹשִׁיעָה נָּא, אָבִינוּ אָתָּה.

לְמַעַן אוֹמְרֵי יִגְדַּל שְׁמֶךָ, וְהֵם נַחֲלָתְךָ וְעַמֶּךָ
צְמֵאִים לְיִשְׁעֲךָ כְּאֶרֶץ עֲיֵפָה לַמַּיִם.
לְתֵרֶת לָמוֹ מְנוּחָה הוֹשַׁע נָא וְהוֹשִׁיעָה נָּא, אָבִינוּ אָתָּה.

שליח ציבור then קהל:

הוֹשַׁע נָא, אֵל נָא
אָנָּא הוֹשִׁיעָה נָּא.

הוֹשַׁע נָא, סְלַח נָא
וְהַצְלִיחָה נָא

וְהוֹשִׁיעֵנוּ אֵל מָעֻזֵּנוּ.

Put down the לולב *and* אתרוג *and pick up the* הושענות.

תַּעֲנֶה Answer the faithful ones who pour out their hearts
to You like water – and save us, please;
for the sake of [Abraham] who came through
fire and water – and grant us success, please;
He gave the order and said, "Please, bring
a little water" – save us, God our Refuge.

Answer the flagged tribes who went swift through the split sea – and save us, please;
for the sake of [Isaac who was] bound at the
gate of heaven – and grant us success, please;
he who yet lived to return and to dig out
wells of water – save us, God our Refuge.

Answer the pure ones encamped on the water – and save us, please;
for the sake of smooth-skinned [Jacob] who
peeled branches by troughs of water – and grant us success, please;
he who heaved and rolled a rock from the
well of water – save us, God our Refuge.

Answer the beloved ones, heirs to a Law likened to water – and save us, please;
for the sake of those [princes in the wilderness]
whose staffs drew forth water – and grant us success, please;
to prepare for them and for their children –
water – save us, God our Refuge.

Answer those who plead as in the wilderness for water – and save us, please;
for the sake of [Moses], trusted in Your household,
who provided the people with water – and grant us success, please;
he hit the rock and out flowed water – save us, God our Refuge.

Answer those who sang in the wilderness, "Spring up, well
of water!" – and save us, please;
for the sake of [Aaron,] commanded at the
Mei Meriva water – and grant us success, please;
commanded to give those who thirsted, water – save us, God our Refuge.

Answer the holy ones who pour before You water – and save us, please;
for the sake of [David] father of song-makers
who longed to drink water – and grant us success, please;
but who held back and poured before You water –
save us, God our Refuge.

Answer those who come to beseech You with four species
grown by water – and save us, please;
for the sake of the Hill of ruins all mouths pray
towards, the source of water – and grant us success, please;
open up the earth and let the heavens rain down water –
and save us, God our Refuge.

תַּעֲנֶה אֱמוּנִים שׁוֹפְכִים לְךָ לֵב כַּמַּיִם וְהוֹשִׁיעָה נָּא.
לְמַעַן בָּא בָאֵשׁ וּבַמַּיִם וְהַצְלִיחָה נָא.
גָּזַר וְנָם יֻקַּח נָא מְעַט מַיִם וְהוֹשִׁיעֵנוּ אֵל מָעֻזֵּנוּ.

תַּעֲנֶה דְגָלִים גָּזוּ גִּזְרֵי מַיִם וְהוֹשִׁיעָה נָּא.
לְמַעַן הַנֶּעֱקַד בְּשַׁעַר הַשָּׁמַיִם וְהַצְלִיחָה נָא.
וְשָׁב וְחָפַר בְּאֵרוֹת מַיִם וְהוֹשִׁיעֵנוּ אֵל מָעֻזֵּנוּ.

תַּעֲנֶה זַכִּים חוֹנִים עֲלֵי מַיִם וְהוֹשִׁיעָה נָּא.
לְמַעַן חָלָק מְפַצֵּל מַקְלוֹת בְּשִׁקְתוֹת הַמַּיִם וְהַצְלִיחָה נָא.
טָעַן וְגָל אֶבֶן מִבְּאֵר מַיִם וְהוֹשִׁיעֵנוּ אֵל מָעֻזֵּנוּ.

תַּעֲנֶה יְדִידִים נוֹחֲלֵי דָת מְשׁוּלַת מַיִם וְהוֹשִׁיעָה נָּא.
לְמַעַן כָּרוּ בְּמִשְׁעֲנוֹתָם מַיִם וְהַצְלִיחָה נָא.
לְהָכִין לָמוֹ וּלְצֶאֱצָאֵימוֹ מַיִם וְהוֹשִׁיעֵנוּ אֵל מָעֻזֵּנוּ.

תַּעֲנֶה מִתְחַנְּנִים כְּבִישִׁימוֹן עֲלֵי מַיִם וְהוֹשִׁיעָה נָּא.
לְמַעַן נֶאֱמַן בַּיִת מַסְפִּיק לָעָם מַיִם וְהַצְלִיחָה נָא.
סֶלַע הָךְ וַיָּזוּבוּ מַיִם וְהוֹשִׁיעֵנוּ אֵל מָעֻזֵּנוּ.

תַּעֲנֶה עוֹנִים עֲלֵי בְאֵר מַיִם וְהוֹשִׁיעָה נָּא.
לְמַעַן פָּקַד בְּמֵי מְרִיבַת מַיִם וְהַצְלִיחָה נָא.
צְמֵאִים לְהַשְׁקוֹת מַיִם וְהוֹשִׁיעֵנוּ אֵל מָעֻזֵּנוּ.

תַּעֲנֶה קְדוֹשִׁים מְנַסְּכִים לְךָ מַיִם וְהוֹשִׁיעָה נָּא.
לְמַעַן רֹאשׁ מְשׁוֹרְרִים כְּתָאֵב שְׁתוֹת מַיִם וְהַצְלִיחָה נָא.
שָׁב וְנָסַךְ לְךָ מַיִם וְהוֹשִׁיעֵנוּ אֵל מָעֻזֵּנוּ.

תַּעֲנֶה שׁוֹאֲלִים בְּרִבּוּעַ אֶשְׁלֵי מַיִם וְהוֹשִׁיעָה נָּא.
לְמַעַן תֵּל תַּלְפִּיּוֹת מוֹצָא מַיִם וְהַצְלִיחָה נָא.
תִּפְתַּח אֶרֶץ וְתַרְעִיף שָׁמַיִם וְהוֹשִׁיעֵנוּ אֵל מָעֻזֵּנוּ.

Leader then congregation:

Have compassion, please,
for the community of the people of Yeshurun;
forgive and pardon their wrongdoing,
and save us, God of our salvation.

אָז As the eyes of slaves are raised / to their masters' hands,
we come before You, judged, save us, God of our salvation.

Proud Masters of masters, / they have brought us to conflict;
they have trampled us; other masters have mastered us,
so save us, God of our salvation.

We have come today, pleading – / before You, Compassionate and Gracious One,
telling and repeating Your wondrous acts, now save us, God of our salvation.

Please do not dry up / what flowed with milk and honey;
heal the land's pain with clouds full of water and save us, God of our salvation.

Plant us in luscious land, / at the hand of the seven shepherds, the eight princes,
righteous, upright God of faithfulness, yes, save us, God of our salvation.

You forged a covenant with the land / for as long as the earth will be,
never to break it apart again, so save us, God of our salvation.

Those who plead with You for water / as willows thirst over streams of water –
remember for them the libation of water and save us, God of our salvation.

As they plead they carry with them / plants, held straight as they grow;
answer their prayer, their voice and save us, God of our salvation.

You who work salvations, / turn to hear their prayers,
and defend them, God of salvation, to save us, God of our salvation.

Listen to the voice of their crowds who come, / and open the earth, to bear
fruit of salvation, You who are great in saving, who desire no evil,
save us, God of our salvation.

Open the gates of heaven, / and throw open Your treasury of good.
Save us, and do not press Your claims against us
but save us, God of our salvation.

Leader then congregation:

Open the gates of heaven,
and Your treasure-house of goodness – open for us.
Save us and do not extend judgment against us –
and save us, God of our salvation.

קהל *then* שליח ציבור:

רַחֵם נָא קְהַל עֲדַת יְשׁוּרוּן, סְלַח וּמְחַל עֲוֹנָם
וְהוֹשִׁיעֵנוּ אֱלֹהֵי יִשְׁעֵנוּ.

אָז כְּעֵינֵי עֲבָדִים אֶל יַד אֲדוֹנִים
בָּאנוּ לְפָנֶיךָ נְדוֹנִים. וְהוֹשִׁיעֵנוּ אֱלֹהֵי יִשְׁעֵנוּ.
גָּאֶה אֲדוֹנֵי הָאֲדוֹנִים, נִתְגָּרוּ בָנוּ מְדָנִים
דְּשׁוּנוּ וּבְעָלוּנוּ זוּלָתְךָ אֲדוֹנִים. וְהוֹשִׁיעֵנוּ אֱלֹהֵי יִשְׁעֵנוּ.
הֵן גַּשְׁנוּ הַיּוֹם בְּתַחֲנוּן, עָדֶיךָ רַחוּם וְחַנּוּן
וְסִפַּרְנוּ נִפְלְאוֹתֶיךָ בְּשִׁנּוּן. וְהוֹשִׁיעֵנוּ אֱלֹהֵי יִשְׁעֵנוּ.
זָבַת חָלָב וּדְבַשׁ, נָא אַל תִּיבַשׁ
חֲשְׁרַת מַיִם כְּאַבָּה תְּחֻבַּשׁ. וְהוֹשִׁיעֵנוּ אֱלֹהֵי יִשְׁעֵנוּ.
טָעֲנוּ בִשְׁמֹנָה, בְּיַד שִׁבְעָה וּשְׁמוֹנָה
יָשָׁר צַדִּיק אֵל אֱמוּנָה. וְהוֹשִׁיעֵנוּ אֱלֹהֵי יִשְׁעֵנוּ.
כָּרַתָּ בְּרִית לָאָרֶץ, עוֹד כָּל יְמֵי הָאָרֶץ
לְבִלְתִּי פְּרָץ בָּהּ פֶּרֶץ. וְהוֹשִׁיעֵנוּ אֱלֹהֵי יִשְׁעֵנוּ.
מִתְחַנְּנִים עֲלֵי מַיִם, כַּעֲרָבִים עַל יִבְלֵי מַיִם
נָא זְכָר לָמוֹ נִסּוּךְ הַמַּיִם. וְהוֹשִׁיעֵנוּ אֱלֹהֵי יִשְׁעֵנוּ.
שִׂיחִים בְּדֶרֶךְ מַטְעָתָם, עוֹמְסִים בְּשַׁוְעָתָם
עֲנֵם בְּקוֹל פְּגִיעָתָם. וְהוֹשִׁיעֵנוּ אֱלֹהֵי יִשְׁעֵנוּ.
פּוֹעֵל יְשׁוּעוֹת, פְּנֵה לִפְלוּלָם שְׁעוֹת
צַדְּקֵם אֵל לְמוֹשָׁעוֹת. וְהוֹשִׁיעֵנוּ אֱלֹהֵי יִשְׁעֵנוּ.
קוֹל רִגְשָׁם תִּשַׁע, תִּפְתַּח אֶרֶץ וְיִפְרוּ יֶשַׁע
רַב לְהוֹשִׁיעַ וְלֹא חָפֵץ רֶשַׁע. וְהוֹשִׁיעֵנוּ אֱלֹהֵי יִשְׁעֵנוּ.

קהל *then* שליח ציבור:

שַׁעֲרֵי שָׁמַיִם פְּתַח, וְאוֹצָרְךָ הַטּוֹב לָנוּ תִפְתַּח.
תּוֹשִׁיעֵנוּ וְרִיב אַל תִּמְתַּח. וְהוֹשִׁיעֵנוּ אֱלֹהֵי יִשְׁעֵנוּ.

Leader then congregation:

The voice of the herald, he heralds and says –

אֹמֶן Your true salvation is coming; / the voice of my Beloved, here He is
coming – heralding, saying. / A voice: He is coming with myriad [heavenly]
legions, / coming to stand on the Mount of Olives – heralding, saying. /
A voice: He is coming to sound the shofar, / as the mount is broken in half
beneath Him – heralding, saying. / A voice: He knocks, He looks, He shines
out, / and half the mount is moved from the east – heralding, saying. /
A voice: He is fulfilling the words He spoke / and coming, and all His holy
ones with Him – heralding, saying. / A voice: and for all who have come
into this world, / the echo is heard in all the world – heralding, saying. /
A voice: the children borne of His womb, / were born in a day like a child
of his mother – heralding, saying. / A voice: she labored and bore – who is
this? / Who has heard of anything like this? – heralding, saying. / A voice: *Is. 66*
the Pure One who wrought all this – / and who has seen anything like this? – *Ibid.*
heralding, saying. / A voice: salvation, its time already set; / can the land give *Ibid.*
birth all in a day? – heralding, saying. / A voice: the One mighty above and
below, / can a nation be born all in one birth? – heralding, saying. / A voice: *Ibid.*
when the shining One redeems His people, / as evening falls, there shall be *Zech. 14*
light – heralding, saying. / A voice: saviors shall go up to Mount Zion: / for
Zion has labored and has given birth – heralding, saying. / A voice is heard *Is. 66*
throughout your borders: / "Broaden the spread of your tents!" – heralding, *Is. 54*
saying. / A voice: "Let your home extend as far as Damascus; / receive your
sons and your daughters" – heralding, saying. / A voice: "Be joyful, dune
flower of the coast; / for the [forebears] who slept in Hebron are awoken" –
heralding, saying. / A voice: "Turn to Me and be saved; / today, if you listen *Is. 45*
to My voice" – heralding, saying. / A voice: a [savior] has grown up, Tzemaḥ
his name, / and he is none other than David himself – heralding, saying. /
A voice: "Rise up, you who lie in the ashes; / awaken and sing, you who sleep *Is. 26*
in the dust" – heralding, saying. / A voice: the city flocking with people for
his crowning: / a tower of salvation, His own king – heralding, saying. / *II Sam. 22*
A voice to silence the names of the wicked; / dealing kindly with his anointed, *Ibid.*
David – heralding, saying. / A voice: grant salvation to an eternal people; / *Ibid.*
to David and his descendants forever – heralding, saying.

The Leader says three times, then the congregation repeats three times:

The voice of the herald, he heralds and says –

קהל *then* שליח ציבור:

קוֹל מְבַשֵּׂר מְבַשֵּׂר וְאוֹמֵר.

אֹמֶן יִשְׁעֲךָ בָּא, קוֹל דּוֹדִי הִנֵּה זֶה בָּא. מְבַשֵּׂר וְאוֹמֵר.

בָּא בְּרִבְבוֹת כִּתִּים, לַעֲמֹד עַל הַר הַזֵּיתִים. מְבַשֵּׂר וְאוֹמֵר.

גִּשְׁתּוֹ בַּשּׁוֹפָר לִתְקֹעַ, תַּחְתָּיו הַר יִבָּקֵעַ. מְבַשֵּׂר וְאוֹמֵר.

דָּפַק וְהֵצִיץ וְזָרַח, וּמָשׁ חֲצִי הָהָר מִמִּזְרָח. מְבַשֵּׂר וְאוֹמֵר.

הֵקִים מִלּוּל נְאֻמוֹ, וּבָא הוּא וְכָל קְדוֹשָׁיו עִמּוֹ. מְבַשֵּׂר וְאוֹמֵר.

וּלְכָל בָּאֵי הָעוֹלָם, בַּת קוֹל יִשָּׁמַע בָּעוֹלָם. מְבַשֵּׂר וְאוֹמֵר.

זֶרַע עֲמוּסֵי רַחְמוֹ, נוֹלְדוּ כְּיֶלֶד מִמְּעֵי אִמּוֹ. מְבַשֵּׂר וְאוֹמֵר.

חָלָה וְיָלְדָה מִי זֹאת, מִי־שָׁמַע כָּזֹאת. מְבַשֵּׂר וְאוֹמֵר. ישעיה סו

טָהוֹר פָּעַל כָּל אֵלֶּה, מִי רָאָה כָּאֵלֶּה. מְבַשֵּׂר וְאוֹמֵר. שם

יֶשַׁע וּזְמַן הוּחַד, הֲיוּחַל אֶרֶץ בְּיוֹם אֶחָד. מְבַשֵּׂר וְאוֹמֵר. שם

כַּבִּיר רוּם וָתַחַת, אִם־יִוָּלֵד גּוֹי פַּעַם אֶחָת. מְבַשֵּׂר וְאוֹמֵר. שם

לְעֵת יִגְאַל עַמּוֹ נָאוֹר, וְהָיָה לְעֶת־עֶרֶב יִהְיֶה־אוֹר. מְבַשֵּׂר וְאוֹמֵר. זכריה יד

מוֹשִׁיעִים יַעֲלוּ לְהַר צִיּוֹן, כִּי־חָלָה גַּם־יָלְדָה צִיּוֹן. מְבַשֵּׂר וְאוֹמֵר. ישעיה סו

נִשְׁמַע בְּכָל גְּבוּלֵךְ, הַרְחִיבִי מְקוֹם אָהֳלֵךְ. מְבַשֵּׂר וְאוֹמֵר. ישעיה נד

שִׂימִי עַד דַּמֶּשֶׂק מִשְׁכְּנוֹתַיִךְ, קַבְּלִי בָנַיִךְ וּבְנוֹתַיִךְ. מְבַשֵּׂר וְאוֹמֵר.

עִלְזִי חֲבַצֶּלֶת הַשָּׁרוֹן, כִּי קָמוּ יְשֵׁנֵי חֶבְרוֹן. מְבַשֵּׂר וְאוֹמֵר.

פְּנוּ אֵלַי וְהִוָּשְׁעוּ, הַיּוֹם אִם בְּקֹלִי תִשְׁמָעוּ. מְבַשֵּׂר וְאוֹמֵר. ישעיה מה

צֶמַח אִישׁ צֶמַח שְׁמוֹ, הוּא דָוִד בְּעַצְמוֹ. מְבַשֵּׂר וְאוֹמֵר.

קוּמוּ כְּפוּשֵׁי עָפָר, הָקִיצוּ וְרַנְּנוּ שֹׁכְנֵי עָפָר. מְבַשֵּׂר וְאוֹמֵר. ישעיה כו

רַבָּתִי עָם בְּהַמְלִיכוֹ, מִגְדּוֹל יְשׁוּעוֹת מַלְכּוֹ. מְבַשֵּׂר וְאוֹמֵר. שמואל ב׳ כב

שֵׁם רְשָׁעִים לְהַאֲבִיד, עֹשֶׂה־חֶסֶד לִמְשִׁיחוֹ לְדָוִד. מְבַשֵּׂר וְאוֹמֵר. שם

תְּנָה יְשׁוּעוֹת לְעַם עוֹלָם, לְדָוִד וּלְזַרְעוֹ עַד־עוֹלָם. מְבַשֵּׂר וְאוֹמֵר. שם

שליח ציבור *says three times then* קהל *repeats three times:*

קוֹל מְבַשֵּׂר מְבַשֵּׂר וְאוֹמֵר.

Beat the Hoshanot against a chair or the floor five times, then say the following:

הוֹשִׁיעָה Save Your people; bless Your legacy; *Ps. 28*
tend them and carry them forever.
Let these words with which I have pleaded with the Lord *1 Kings 8*
be close to the Lord our God day and night,
that they may do justice for His servant,
and justice for His people Israel, day after day;
so that all the peoples of the earth will know
that the Lord is God.
There is no other.

The Torah scrolls are returned to the Ark, which is then closed.

May it be Your will, Lord our God, God of our ancestors, who chooses good prophets, and their good customs – to receive our prayers and our circlings with compassion and favor. Remember for us the merit of Your seven perfect ones, and remove the wall of iron that separates us from You, and hear our pleas, and seal us with a good judgment – You who suspends the world over nothingness. And seal us in the book of good life.

On this day, invest Your mighty Presence with the five sweetened powers – by means of the beating of the willows, the custom of Your holy prophets – and let love be awakened among them. Kiss us with the kisses of Your mouth, which sweetens all might and all judgments. Shine light upon Your mighty Presence, by the name *Yod-Heh-Vav*, which is the dew that is a dew of light. And from that place, emanate plenty to Your servant, who prays here before You; lengthen his life and forgive him his sins and wrongdoings and rebellions. And extend Your hand, Your right hand, to receive him in full repentance before You. Open Your treasury of good, to satisfy the yearning soul with water, as it is written, "The Lord will open His good treasury for You, *Deut. 28*
open the heavens, to give your land its rain in its right time, and to bless all the work of your hands:" Amen.

The Leader continues with Full Kaddish on page 244.

Beat the הושענות *against a chair or the floor five times, then say the following:*

הוֹשִֽׁיעָה אֶת־עַמֶּֽךָ, וּבָרֵךְ אֶת־נַחֲלָתֶֽךָ תהלים כח
וּרְעֵם וְנַשְּׂאֵם עַד־הָעוֹלָם:
וְיִהְיוּ דְבָרַי אֵֽלֶּה, אֲשֶׁר הִתְחַנַּֽנְתִּי לִפְנֵי יהוה מלכים א׳ ח
קְרֹבִים אֶל־יהוה אֱלֹהֵֽינוּ יוֹמָם וָלָֽיְלָה
לַעֲשׂוֹת מִשְׁפַּט עַבְדּוֹ וּמִשְׁפַּט עַמּוֹ יִשְׂרָאֵל
דְּבַר־יוֹם בְּיוֹמוֹ:
לְמַֽעַן דַּֽעַת כָּל־עַמֵּי הָאָֽרֶץ כִּי יהוה הוּא הָאֱלֹהִים
אֵין עוֹד:

The ספרי תורה *are returned to the* ארון קודש*, which is then closed.*

יְהִי רָצוֹן מִלְּפָנֶֽיךָ יהוה אֱלֹהֵֽינוּ וֵאלֹהֵי אֲבוֹתֵֽינוּ, הַבּוֹחֵר בִּנְבִיאִים טוֹבִים וּבְמִנְהֲגֵיהֶם הַטּוֹבִים, שֶׁתְּקַבֵּל בְּרַחֲמִים וּבְרָצוֹן אֶת תְּפִלָּתֵֽנוּ וְהַקָּפוֹתֵֽינוּ. וּזְכׇר לָֽנוּ זְכוּת שִׁבְעַת תְּמִימֶֽיךָ, וְתָסִיר מְחִצַּת הַבַּרְזֶל הַמַּפְסֶֽקֶת בֵּינֵֽינוּ וּבֵינֶֽךָ, וְתַאֲזִין שַׁוְעָתֵֽנוּ, וְתֵיטִיב לָֽנוּ הַחֲתִימָה, תּוֹלֶה אֶֽרֶץ עַל בְּלִימָה, וְחׇתְמֵֽנוּ בְּסֵֽפֶר חַיִּים טוֹבִים.

וְהַיּוֹם הַזֶּה תִּתֵּן בִּשְׁכִינַת עֻזֶּֽךָ חָמֵשׁ גְּבוּרוֹת מְמֻתָּקוֹת, עַל יְדֵי חֲבִיטַת עֲרָבָה מִנְהַג נְבִיאֶֽיךָ הַקְּדוֹשִׁים, וְתִתְעוֹרֵר הָאַהֲבָה בֵּינֵיהֶם. וְתִשָּׁקֵֽנוּ מִנְּשִׁיקוֹת פִּֽיךָ, מְמַתֶּֽקֶת כׇּל הַגְּבוּרוֹת וְכׇל הַדִּינִין. וְתָאִיר לִשְׁכִינַת עֻזְּךָ בְּשֵׁם יוּ״ד הֵ״א וָא״ו שֶׁהוּא טַל אוֹרוֹת טַלֶּֽךָ, וּמִשָּׁם תַּשְׁפִּֽיעַ שֶֽׁפַע לְעַבְדְּךָ הַמִּתְפַּלֵּל לְפָנֶֽיךָ, שֶׁתַּאֲרִיךְ יָמָיו וְתִמְחַל לוֹ חֲטָאָיו וַעֲוֹנוֹתָיו וּפְשָׁעָיו. וְתִפְשֹׁט יְמִינְךָ וְיָדְךָ לְקַבְּלוֹ בִּתְשׁוּבָה שְׁלֵמָה לְפָנֶֽיךָ. וְאוֹצָרְךָ הַטּוֹב תִּפְתַּח לְהַשְׂבִּֽיעַ מַֽיִם נֶֽפֶשׁ שׁוֹקֵקָה, כְּמוֹ שֶׁכָּתוּב: יִפְתַּח יהוה דברים כח
לְךָ אֶת־אוֹצָרוֹ הַטּוֹב אֶת־הַשָּׁמַֽיִם לָתֵת מְטַר־אַרְצְךָ בְּעִתּוֹ, וּלְבָרֵךְ אֵת כׇּל־מַעֲשֵׂה יָדֶֽךָ: אָמֵן.

The שליח ציבור *continues with* קדיש שלם *on page 245.*

ANNULMENT OF VOWS

On the morning before Rosh HaShana, one should annul vows before three men, who sit as judges, saying:

שִׁמְעוּ נָא Listen, please, my masters (expert judges): every vow or oath or prohibition or restriction or ban that I have vowed or sworn, whether awake or in a dream, or that I swore with one of the holy names that may not be erased, or by the holy four-letter name of God, blessed be He, or any naziriteship that I accepted on myself, even a naziriteship like that of Samson, or any prohibition, even against enjoyment, whether I forbade it to myself or others, by any expression of prohibition, whether using the language of prohibition or restriction or ban, or any positive commitment, even to perform a [non-obligatory] commandment, that I undertook by way of a vow or voluntary undertaking or oath or naziriteship or any other such expression, whether it was done by handshake or vow or voluntary undertaking or commandment-mandated custom I have customarily practiced, or any utterance that I have verbalized, or any non-obligatory commandment or good practice or conduct I have vowed and resolved in my heart to do, and have done three times without specifying that it does not have the force of a vow, whether it relates to myself or others, both those known to me and those I have already forgotten – regarding all of them, I hereby express my retroactive regret, and ask and seek their annulment from you, my eminences. For I fear that I may stumble and be trapped, Heaven forbid, in the sin of vows, oaths, naziriteships, bans, prohibitions, restrictions and agreements. I do not regret, Heaven forbid, the performance of the good deeds I have done. I regret, rather, having accepted them on myself in the language of vow, oath, naziriteship, prohibition, ban, restriction, agreement or acceptance of the heart.

Therefore I request annulment for them all.

I regret all these things I have mentioned, whether they related to monetary matters, or to the body or to the soul.

התרת נדרים

On the morning before ראש השנה*, one should annul vows before three men, who sit as judges, saying:*

שִׁמְעוּ נָא רַבּוֹתַי (דַּיָּנִים מֻמְחִים), כָּל נֶדֶר אוֹ שְׁבוּעָה אוֹ אִסָּר אוֹ קוֹנָם אוֹ חֵרֶם שֶׁנָּדַרְתִּי אוֹ נִשְׁבַּעְתִּי בְּהָקִיץ אוֹ בַחֲלוֹם, אוֹ נִשְׁבַּעְתִּי בְּשֵׁמוֹת הַקְּדוֹשִׁים שֶׁאֵינָם נִמְחָקִים וּבְשֵׁם הוי״ה בָּרוּךְ הוּא, וְכָל מִינֵי נְזִירוּת שֶׁקִּבַּלְתִּי עָלַי וַאֲפִלּוּ נְזִירוּת שִׁמְשׁוֹן, וְכָל שׁוּם אִסּוּר וַאֲפִלּוּ אִסּוּר הֲנָאָה שֶׁאָסַרְתִּי עָלַי אוֹ עַל אֲחֵרִים בְּכָל לָשׁוֹן שֶׁל אִסּוּר בֵּין בִּלְשׁוֹן אִסּוּר אוֹ חֵרֶם אוֹ קוֹנָם, וְכָל שׁוּם קַבָּלָה אֲפִלּוּ שֶׁל מִצְוָה שֶׁקִּבַּלְתִּי עָלַי בֵּין בִּלְשׁוֹן נֶדֶר בֵּין בִּלְשׁוֹן נְדָבָה בֵּין בִּלְשׁוֹן שְׁבוּעָה בֵּין בִּלְשׁוֹן נְזִירוּת בֵּין בְּכָל לָשׁוֹן, וְגַם הַנַּעֲשֶׂה בִּתְקִיעַת כָּף. בֵּין כָּל נֶדֶר וּבֵין כָּל נְדָבָה וּבֵין שׁוּם מִנְהָג שֶׁל מִצְוָה שֶׁנָּהַגְתִּי אֶת עַצְמִי, וְכָל מוֹצָא שְׂפָתַי שֶׁיָּצָא מִפִּי אוֹ שֶׁנָּדַרְתִּי וְגָמַרְתִּי בְּלִבִּי לַעֲשׂוֹת שׁוּם מִצְוָה מֵהַמִּצְוֹת אוֹ אֵיזוֹ הַנְהָגָה טוֹבָה אוֹ אֵיזֶה דָבָר טוֹב שֶׁנָּהַגְתִּי שָׁלֹשׁ פְּעָמִים, וְלֹא הִתְנֵיתִי שֶׁיְּהֵא בְּלִי נֶדֶר. הֵן דָּבָר שֶׁעָשִׂיתִי, הֵן עַל עַצְמִי הֵן עַל אֲחֵרִים, הֵן אוֹתָן הַיְדוּעִים לִי הֵן אוֹתָן שֶׁכְּבָר שָׁכַחְתִּי. בְּכֻלְּהוֹן אִתְחֲרַטְנָא בְהוֹן מֵעִקָּרָא, וְשׁוֹאֵל וּמְבַקֵּשׁ אֲנִי מִמַּעֲלַתְכֶם הַתָּרָה עֲלֵיהֶם, כִּי יָרֵאתִי פֶּן אֶכָּשֵׁל וְנִלְכַּדְתִּי, חַס וְשָׁלוֹם, בַּעֲוֹן נְדָרִים וּשְׁבוּעוֹת וּנְזִירוֹת וַחֲרָמוֹת וְאִסּוּרִין וְקוֹנָמוֹת וְהַסְכָּמוֹת. וְאֵין אֲנִי תוֹהֵא, חַס וְשָׁלוֹם, עַל קִיּוּם הַמַּעֲשִׂים הַטּוֹבִים הָהֵם שֶׁעָשִׂיתִי, רַק אֲנִי מִתְחָרֵט עַל קַבָּלַת הָעִנְיָנִים בִּלְשׁוֹן נֶדֶר אוֹ שְׁבוּעָה אוֹ נְזִירוּת אוֹ אִסּוּר אוֹ חֵרֶם אוֹ קוֹנָם אוֹ הַסְכָּמָה אוֹ קַבָּלָה בְלֵב, וּמִתְחָרֵט אֲנִי עַל זֶה שֶׁלֹּא אָמַרְתִּי הִנְנִי עוֹשֶׂה דָבָר זֶה בְּלִי נֶדֶר וּשְׁבוּעָה וּנְזִירוּת וְחֵרֶם וְאִסּוּר וְקוֹנָם וְקַבָּלָה בְלֵב.

לָכֵן אֲנִי שׁוֹאֵל הַתָּרָה בְּכֻלְּהוֹן.

אֲנִי מִתְחָרֵט עַל כָּל הַנִּזְכָּר, בֵּין אִם הָיוּ הַמַּעֲשִׂים מִדְּבָרִים הַנּוֹגְעִים בְּמָמוֹן, בֵּין מֵהַדְּבָרִים הַנּוֹגְעִים בְּגוּף, בֵּין מֵהַדְּבָרִים הַנּוֹגְעִים אֶל הַנְּשָׁמָה.

In relation to them all, I regret the language of vow, oath, naziriteship, prohibition, ban, penalty, and acceptance of the heart.

To be sure, according to the law, one who regrets and seeks annulment must specify the vow [from which he seeks release]. But please know, my masters, that it is impossible to specify them, for they are many. I do not seek release from vows that cannot be annulled. Therefore, may it be in your eyes as if I had specified them.

The judges say the following three times:

May all be permitted to you. May all be forgiven you. May all be allowed to you. There is now no vow, oath, naziriteship, ban, prohibition, penalty, ostracism, excommunication, or curse. There is now pardon, forgiveness and atonement. And just as the earthly court has given permission, so may the heavenly court give permission.

The one seeking annulment of vows says:

Behold I make a formal declaration before you that I cancel from now onward all vows and all oaths, naziriteships, prohibitions, penalties, bans, agreements and acceptances of the heart that I may accept upon myself, whether awake or in a dream, except a vow to fast that I undertake at the time of the afternoon prayer. If I forget the conditions of this declaration and make a vow from this day onward, as of now I retroactively regret them and declare them to be null and void, without effect or validity, and they shall have no force whatsoever. Regarding them all, I regret them from now and for ever.

בְּכֻלְּהוֹן אֲנִי מִתְחָרֵט עַל לְשׁוֹן נֶדֶר וּשְׁבוּעָה וּנְזִירוּת וְאִסּוּר וְחֵרֶם וְקוֹנָם וְקַבָּלָה בְלֵב.

וְהִנֵּה מִצַּד הַדִּין הַמִּתְחָרֵט וְהַמְבַקֵּשׁ הַתָּרָה צָרִיךְ לִפְרֹט הַנֶּדֶר, אַךְ דְּעוּ נָא רַבּוֹתַי, כִּי אִי אֶפְשָׁר לְפָרְטָם, כִּי רַבִּים הֵם. וְאֵין אֲנִי מְבַקֵּשׁ הַתָּרָה עַל אוֹתָם הַנְּדָרִים שֶׁאֵין לְהַתִּיר אוֹתָם, עַל כֵּן יִהְיוּ נָא בְעֵינֵיכֶם כְּאִלּוּ הָיִיתִי פוֹרְטָם.

The judges say the following three times:

הַכֹּל יִהְיוּ מֻתָּרִים לָךְ, הַכֹּל מְחוּלִים לָךְ, הַכֹּל שְׁרוּיִים לָךְ. אֵין כָּאן לֹא נֶדֶר וְלֹא שְׁבוּעָה וְלֹא נְזִירוּת וְלֹא חֵרֶם וְלֹא אִסּוּר וְלֹא קוֹנָם וְלֹא נִדּוּי וְלֹא שַׁמְתָּא וְלֹא אָרוּר. אֲבָל יֵשׁ כָּאן מְחִילָה וּסְלִיחָה וְכַפָּרָה. וּכְשֵׁם שֶׁמַּתִּירִים בְּבֵית דִּין שֶׁל מַטָּה, כָּךְ יִהְיוּ מֻתָּרִים מִבֵּית דִּין שֶׁל מַעְלָה.

The one seeking annulment of vows says:

הֲרֵי אֲנִי מוֹסֵר מוֹדָעָה לִפְנֵיכֶם, וַאֲנִי מְבַטֵּל מִכָּאן וּלְהַבָּא כָּל הַנְּדָרִים וְכָל שְׁבוּעוֹת וּנְזִירוּת וְאִסּוּרִין וְקוֹנָמוֹת וַחֲרָמוֹת וְהַסְכָּמוֹת וְקַבָּלָה בְלֵב שֶׁאֲקַבֵּל עָלַי בְּעַצְמִי, הֵן בְּהָקִיץ הֵן בַּחֲלוֹם, חוּץ מִנִּדְרֵי תַעֲנִית בִּשְׁעַת מִנְחָה. וּבְאִם אֶשְׁכַּח לִתְנַאי מוֹדָעָה הַזֹּאת וְאֶדֹּר מֵהַיּוֹם עוֹד, מֵעַתָּה אֲנִי מִתְחָרֵט עֲלֵיהֶם וּמַתְנֶה עֲלֵיהֶם שֶׁיִּהְיוּ כֻלָּן בְּטֵלִין וּמְבֻטָּלִין, לָא שְׁרִירִין וְלָא קַיָּמִין, וְלָא יְהוֹן חָלִין כְּלָל וּכְלָל. בְּכֻלָּן אִתְחֲרַטְנָא בְּהוֹן מֵעַתָּה וְעַד עוֹלָם.

KAPAROT

Taking a rooster (men), or a hen (women) in the right hand (alternatively one may use money), say the following paragraph three times:

בְּנֵי אָדָם Children of men,
those who sat in darkness and the shadow of death, *Ps. 107*
cruelly bound in iron chains –
He brought them out from darkness
and the shadow of death and broke open their chains.
Some were fools with sinful ways,
and suffered affliction because of their wrongdoings.
They found all food repulsive, and came close to the gates of death.
Then they cried to the LORD in their trouble,
and He saved them from their distress.
He sent His word and healed them;
He rescued them from their destruction.
Let them thank the LORD for his loving-kindness
and His miracles for humankind.
If there is one angel out of a thousand in his defense, *Job 33*
to declare his righteousness on his behalf, He will be kind to him
and say, "Spare him from going down to the pit; I have found atonement."

A man revolves the rooster around his head and says:

זֶה חֲלִיפָתִי Let this be my exchange, let this be my substitute,
let this rooster go to death
while I go and enter a good, long life and peace.

A woman revolves the hen around her head and says:

זֹאת חֲלִיפָתִי Let this be my exchange, let this be my substitute,
let this hen go to death
while I go and enter a good, long life and peace.

If money is used, then revolve the money around the head and say:

אֵלּוּ חֲלִיפָתִי Let this be my exchange, let this be my substitute,
let this money go to charity
while I go and enter a good, long life and peace.

סדר כפרות

Taking a rooster (men), or a hen (women) in the right hand (alternatively one may use money), say the following paragraph three times:

בְּנֵי אָדָם

יֹשְׁבֵי חֹשֶׁךְ וְצַלְמָוֶת, אֲסִירֵי עֳנִי וּבַרְזֶל: תהלים קז

יוֹצִיאֵם מֵחֹשֶׁךְ וְצַלְמָוֶת, וּמוֹסְרוֹתֵיהֶם יְנַתֵּק:

אֱוִלִים מִדֶּרֶךְ פִּשְׁעָם, וּמֵעֲוֺנֹתֵיהֶם יִתְעַנּוּ:

כָּל־אֹכֶל תְּתַעֵב נַפְשָׁם, וַיַּגִּיעוּ עַד־שַׁעֲרֵי מָוֶת:

וַיִּזְעֲקוּ אֶל־יהוה בַּצַּר לָהֶם, מִמְּצֻקוֹתֵיהֶם יוֹשִׁיעֵם:

יִשְׁלַח דְּבָרוֹ וְיִרְפָּאֵם, וִימַלֵּט מִשְּׁחִיתוֹתָם:

יוֹדוּ לַיהוה חַסְדּוֹ, וְנִפְלְאוֹתָיו לִבְנֵי אָדָם:

אִם־יֵשׁ עָלָיו מַלְאָךְ מֵלִיץ אֶחָד מִנִּי־אָלֶף, לְהַגִּיד לְאָדָם יָשְׁרוֹ: איוב לג

וַיְחֻנֶּנּוּ, וַיֹּאמֶר פְּדָעֵהוּ מֵרֶדֶת שַׁחַת, מָצָאתִי כֹפֶר:

A man revolves the rooster around his head and says:

זֶה חֲלִיפָתִי, זֶה תְּמוּרָתִי, זֶה כַּפָּרָתִי.
זֶה הַתַּרְנְגוֹל יֵלֵךְ לְמִיתָה
וַאֲנִי אֵלֵךְ וְאֶכָּנֵס לְחַיִּים טוֹבִים אֲרֻכִּים וּלְשָׁלוֹם.

A woman revolves the hen around her head and says:

זֹאת חֲלִיפָתִי, זֹאת תְּמוּרָתִי, זֹאת כַּפָּרָתִי.
זֹאת הַתַּרְנְגֹלֶת תֵּלֵךְ לְמִיתָה
וַאֲנִי אֵלֵךְ וְאֶכָּנֵס לְחַיִּים טוֹבִים אֲרֻכִּים וּלְשָׁלוֹם.

If money is used, then revolve the money around the head and say:

אֵלּוּ חֲלִיפָתִי, אֵלּוּ תְּמוּרָתִי, אֵלּוּ כַּפָּרָתִי.
אֵלּוּ הַמָּעוֹת יֵלְכוּ לִצְדָקָה
וַאֲנִי אֵלֵךְ וְאֶכָּנֵס לְחַיִּים טוֹבִים אֲרֻכִּים וּלְשָׁלוֹם.

VIDUY FOR MINḤA OF EREV YOM KIPPUR

The following is said on Erev Yom Kippur (and by a bride and groom on the eve of their wedding), in the Amida before "My God, guard":

אֱלֹהֵינוּ Our God and God of our fathers,
let our prayer come before You,
and do not hide Yourself from our plea,
for we are not so arrogant or obstinate as to say before You,
Lord, our God and God of our fathers,
we are righteous and have not sinned,
for in truth, we and our fathers have sinned.

Strike the left side of the chest with the right fist while saying each of the sins:

אָשַׁמְנוּ We have sinned, we have acted treacherously,
we have robbed, we have spoken slander.
We have acted perversely, we have acted wickedly,
we have acted presumptuously, we have been violent, we have framed lies.
We have given bad advice, we have deceived, we have scorned,
we have rebelled, we have provoked, we have turned away,
we have committed wrongdoing, we have transgressed,
we have persecuted, we have been obstinate.
We have acted wickedly, we have corrupted,
we have acted abominably, we have strayed, we have led others astray.

סַרְנוּ We have turned away from Your commandments and good laws,
to no avail, for You are just in all that has befallen us,
for You have acted faithfully while we have done wickedly.

מַה נֹּאמַר What can we say before You, You who is present on high?
What can we declare before You, You who abide in heaven?
Do You not know all, the hidden and revealed alike?

אַתָּה יוֹדֵעַ You know the mysteries of the universe,
and the hidden secrets of all that lives.
You search the inmost being, and test the heart and mind.
Nothing is hidden from You, nor is anything concealed from Your eyes.
Therefore may it be Your will, Lord our God and God of our fathers,
to give atonement for all our sins,
forgive all our wrongdoings,
and pardon all our crimes.

וידוי למנחה בערב יום הכיפורים

The following is said on ערב יום הכיפורים *(and by a* חתן *and* כלה *on the eve of their wedding), in the Amida before* אֱלֹהַי, נְצֹר*:*

אֱלֹהֵינוּ וֵאלֹהֵי אֲבוֹתֵינוּ
תָּבוֹא לְפָנֶיךָ תְּפִלָּתֵנוּ, וְאַל תִּתְעַלַּם מִתְּחִנָּתֵנוּ.
שֶׁאֵין אֲנַחְנוּ עַזֵּי פָנִים וּקְשֵׁי עֹרֶף לוֹמַר לְפָנֶיךָ
יהוה אֱלֹהֵינוּ וֵאלֹהֵי אֲבוֹתֵינוּ
צַדִּיקִים אֲנַחְנוּ וְלֹא חָטָאנוּ. אֲבָל אֲנַחְנוּ וַאֲבוֹתֵינוּ חָטָאנוּ.

Strike the left side of the chest with the right fist while saying each of the sins:

אָשַׁמְנוּ, בָּגַדְנוּ, גָּזַלְנוּ, דִּבַּרְנוּ דֹפִי
הֶעֱוִינוּ, וְהִרְשַׁעְנוּ, זַדְנוּ, חָמַסְנוּ, טָפַלְנוּ שֶׁקֶר
יָעַצְנוּ רָע, כִּזַּבְנוּ, לַצְנוּ, מָרַדְנוּ, נִאַצְנוּ, סָרַרְנוּ
עָוִינוּ, פָּשַׁעְנוּ, צָרַרְנוּ, קִשִּׁינוּ עֹרֶף
רָשַׁעְנוּ, שִׁחַתְנוּ, תִּעַבְנוּ, תָּעִינוּ, תִּעְתָּעְנוּ.

סַרְנוּ מִמִּצְוֹתֶיךָ וּמִמִּשְׁפָּטֶיךָ הַטּוֹבִים, וְלֹא שָׁוָה לָנוּ.
וְאַתָּה צַדִּיק עַל כָּל הַבָּא עָלֵינוּ
כִּי אֱמֶת עָשִׂיתָ, וַאֲנַחְנוּ הִרְשָׁעְנוּ.

מַה נֹּאמַר לְפָנֶיךָ יוֹשֵׁב מָרוֹם, וּמַה נְּסַפֵּר לְפָנֶיךָ שׁוֹכֵן שְׁחָקִים
הֲלֹא כָּל הַנִּסְתָּרוֹת וְהַנִּגְלוֹת אַתָּה יוֹדֵעַ.

אַתָּה יוֹדֵעַ רָזֵי עוֹלָם וְתַעֲלוּמוֹת סִתְרֵי כָל חָי.
אַתָּה חוֹפֵשׂ כָּל חַדְרֵי בָטֶן וּבוֹחֵן כְּלָיוֹת וָלֵב.
אֵין דָּבָר נֶעְלָם מִמֶּךָּ וְאֵין נִסְתָּר מִנֶּגֶד עֵינֶיךָ.
וּבְכֵן, יְהִי רָצוֹן מִלְּפָנֶיךָ, יהוה אֱלֹהֵינוּ וֵאלֹהֵי אֲבוֹתֵינוּ
שֶׁתְּכַפֵּר לָנוּ עַל כָּל חַטֹּאתֵינוּ
וְתִסְלַח לָנוּ עַל כָּל עֲוֹנוֹתֵינוּ
וְתִמְחַל לָנוּ עַל כָּל פְּשָׁעֵינוּ.

Strike the left side of the chest with the right fist while saying each of the sins.

עַל חֵטְא For the sin we have sinned before You under duress or freewill,
and for the sin we have sinned before You in hardness of heart.

For the sin we have sinned before You unwittingly,
and for the sin we have sinned before You by an utterance of our lips.

For the sin we have sinned before You by unchastity,
and for the sin we have sinned before You openly or secretly.

For the sin we have sinned before You knowingly and dishonestly,
and for the sin we have sinned before You in speech.

For the sin we have sinned before You by wronging a neighbor,
and for the sin we have sinned before You by thoughts of the heart.

For the sin we have sinned before You in a gathering for immorality,
and for the sin we have sinned before You by insincere confession.

For the sin we have sinned before You by contempt for parents and teachers,
and for the sin we have sinned before You intentionally or in error.

For the sin we have sinned before You by force,
and for the sin we have sinned before You by desecrating Your name.

For the sin we have sinned before You by impure lips,
and for the sin we have sinned before You by foolish speech.

For the sin we have sinned before You by the evil inclination,
and for the sin we have sinned before You knowingly or unwittingly.

For all these, God of forgiveness,
forgive us, pardon us, give us atonement.

Strike the left side of the chest with the right fist while saying each of the sins.

עַל חֵטְא שֶׁחָטָאנוּ לְפָנֶיךָ בְּאֹנֶס וּבְרָצוֹן

וְעַל חֵטְא שֶׁחָטָאנוּ לְפָנֶיךָ בְּאִמּוּץ הַלֵּב

עַל חֵטְא שֶׁחָטָאנוּ לְפָנֶיךָ בִּבְלִי דָעַת

וְעַל חֵטְא שֶׁחָטָאנוּ לְפָנֶיךָ בְּבִטּוּי שְׂפָתָיִם

עַל חֵטְא שֶׁחָטָאנוּ לְפָנֶיךָ בְּגִלּוּי עֲרָיוֹת

וְעַל חֵטְא שֶׁחָטָאנוּ לְפָנֶיךָ בְּגָלוּי וּבַסָּתֶר

עַל חֵטְא שֶׁחָטָאנוּ לְפָנֶיךָ בְּדַעַת וּבְמִרְמָה

וְעַל חֵטְא שֶׁחָטָאנוּ לְפָנֶיךָ בְּדִבּוּר פֶּה

עַל חֵטְא שֶׁחָטָאנוּ לְפָנֶיךָ בְּהוֹנָאַת רֵעַ

וְעַל חֵטְא שֶׁחָטָאנוּ לְפָנֶיךָ בְּהַרְהוֹר הַלֵּב

עַל חֵטְא שֶׁחָטָאנוּ לְפָנֶיךָ בִּוְעִידַת זְנוּת

וְעַל חֵטְא שֶׁחָטָאנוּ לְפָנֶיךָ בְּוִדּוּי פֶּה

עַל חֵטְא שֶׁחָטָאנוּ לְפָנֶיךָ בְּזִלְזוּל הוֹרִים וּמוֹרִים

וְעַל חֵטְא שֶׁחָטָאנוּ לְפָנֶיךָ בְּזָדוֹן וּבִשְׁגָגָה

עַל חֵטְא שֶׁחָטָאנוּ לְפָנֶיךָ בְּחֹזֶק יָד

וְעַל חֵטְא שֶׁחָטָאנוּ לְפָנֶיךָ בְּחִלּוּל הַשֵּׁם

עַל חֵטְא שֶׁחָטָאנוּ לְפָנֶיךָ בְּטֻמְאַת שְׂפָתָיִם

וְעַל חֵטְא שֶׁחָטָאנוּ לְפָנֶיךָ בְּטִפְּשׁוּת פֶּה

עַל חֵטְא שֶׁחָטָאנוּ לְפָנֶיךָ בְּיֵצֶר הָרָע

וְעַל חֵטְא שֶׁחָטָאנוּ לְפָנֶיךָ בְּיוֹדְעִים וּבְלֹא יוֹדְעִים

וְעַל כֻּלָּם אֱלוֹהַּ סְלִיחוֹת סְלַח לָנוּ, מְחַל לָנוּ, כַּפֶּר לָנוּ.

For the sin we have sinned before You by dishonesty and lies,
and for the sin we have sinned before You by bribery.

For the sin we have sinned before You by scorn,
and for the sin we have sinned before You by evil speech.

For the sin we have sinned before You in business,
and for the sin we have sinned before You with food and drink.

For the sin we have sinned before You by interest and extortion,
and for the sin we have sinned before You by being arrogant.

For the sin we have sinned before You by the idle chatter of our lips,
and for the sin we have sinned before You by prying eyes.

For the sin we have sinned before You by arrogance,
and for the sin we have sinned before You by insolence.

For all these, God of forgiveness,
forgive us, pardon us, give us atonement.

For the sin we have sinned before You by casting off the yoke,
and for the sin we have sinned before You by perverting judgment.

For the sin we have sinned before You by entrapping a neighbor,
and for the sin we have sinned before You by envy.

For the sin we have sinned before You by lack of seriousness,
and for the sin we have sinned before You by obstinacy.

For the sin we have sinned before You by running to do evil,
and for the sin we have sinned before You by gossip.

עַל חֵטְא שֶׁחָטָאנוּ לְפָנֶיךָ בְּכַחַשׁ וּבְכָזָב
וְעַל חֵטְא שֶׁחָטָאנוּ לְפָנֶיךָ בְּכַפַּת שֹׁחַד

עַל חֵטְא שֶׁחָטָאנוּ לְפָנֶיךָ בְּלָצוֹן
וְעַל חֵטְא שֶׁחָטָאנוּ לְפָנֶיךָ בְּלָשׁוֹן הָרָע

עַל חֵטְא שֶׁחָטָאנוּ לְפָנֶיךָ בְּמַשָּׂא וּבְמַתָּן
וְעַל חֵטְא שֶׁחָטָאנוּ לְפָנֶיךָ בְּמַאֲכָל וּבְמִשְׁתֶּה

עַל חֵטְא שֶׁחָטָאנוּ לְפָנֶיךָ בְּנֶשֶׁךְ וּבְמַרְבִּית
וְעַל חֵטְא שֶׁחָטָאנוּ לְפָנֶיךָ בִּנְטִיַּת גָּרוֹן

עַל חֵטְא שֶׁחָטָאנוּ לְפָנֶיךָ בְּשִׂיחַ שִׂפְתוֹתֵינוּ
וְעַל חֵטְא שֶׁחָטָאנוּ לְפָנֶיךָ בְּשִׂקּוּר עָיִן

עַל חֵטְא שֶׁחָטָאנוּ לְפָנֶיךָ בְּעֵינַיִם רָמוֹת
וְעַל חֵטְא שֶׁחָטָאנוּ לְפָנֶיךָ בְּעַזּוּת מֶצַח

וְעַל כֻּלָּם אֱלוֹהַּ סְלִיחוֹת סְלַח לָנוּ, מְחַל לָנוּ, כַּפֶּר לָנוּ.

עַל חֵטְא שֶׁחָטָאנוּ לְפָנֶיךָ בִּפְרִיקַת עֹל
וְעַל חֵטְא שֶׁחָטָאנוּ לְפָנֶיךָ בִּפְלִילוּת

עַל חֵטְא שֶׁחָטָאנוּ לְפָנֶיךָ בִּצְדִיַּת רֵעַ
וְעַל חֵטְא שֶׁחָטָאנוּ לְפָנֶיךָ בְּצָרוּת עָיִן

עַל חֵטְא שֶׁחָטָאנוּ לְפָנֶיךָ בְּקַלּוּת רֹאשׁ
וְעַל חֵטְא שֶׁחָטָאנוּ לְפָנֶיךָ בְּקַשְׁיוּת עֹרֶף

עַל חֵטְא שֶׁחָטָאנוּ לְפָנֶיךָ בְּרִיצַת רַגְלַיִם לְהָרַע
וְעַל חֵטְא שֶׁחָטָאנוּ לְפָנֶיךָ בִּרְכִילוּת

For the sin we have sinned before You by vain oath,
and for the sin we have sinned before You by baseless hatred.

For the sin we have sinned before You by breach of trust,
and for the sin we have sinned before You by confusion of heart.

For all these, God of forgiveness,
forgive us, pardon us, give us atonement.

וְעַל חֲטָאִים And for the sins for which we are liable to bring a burnt-offering,
and for the sins for which we are liable to bring a sin-offering,
and for the sins for which we are liable to bring an offering according to our means,
and for the sins for which we are liable to bring a guilt-offering for certain or possible sin,
and for the sins for which we are liable to lashes for rebellion,
and for the sins for which we are liable to forty lashes,
and for the sins for which we are liable to death by the hands of Heaven,
and for the sins for which we are liable to be cut off and childless,
and for the sins for which we are liable to the four death penalties inflicted by the court: stoning, burning, beheading and strangling.

For positive and negative commandments,
whether they can be remedied by an act or not,
for sins known to us and for those that are unknown –
for those that are known,
we have already declared them before You and confessed them to You;
and for those that are unknown,
before You they are revealed and known,
as it is said, "The secret things belong to the LORD our God, *Deut. 29*
but the things that are revealed are for us and our children for ever,
that we may fulfill all the words of this Torah."
For You are He who forgives Israel
and pardons the tribes of Yeshurun in every generation,
and besides You we have no king who pardons and forgives, only You.

עַל חֵטְא שֶׁחָטָאנוּ לְפָנֶיךָ בִּשְׁבוּעַת שָׁוְא
וְעַל חֵטְא שֶׁחָטָאנוּ לְפָנֶיךָ בְּשִׂנְאַת חִנָּם

עַל חֵטְא שֶׁחָטָאנוּ לְפָנֶיךָ בִּתְשׂוּמֶת יָד
וְעַל חֵטְא שֶׁחָטָאנוּ לְפָנֶיךָ בְּתִמְהוֹן לֵבָב

וְעַל כֻּלָּם אֱלוֹהַּ סְלִיחוֹת סְלַח לָנוּ, מְחַל לָנוּ, כַּפֶּר לָנוּ.

וְעַל חֲטָאִים שֶׁאָנוּ חַיָּבִים עֲלֵיהֶם עוֹלָה
וְעַל חֲטָאִים שֶׁאָנוּ חַיָּבִים עֲלֵיהֶם חַטָּאת
וְעַל חֲטָאִים שֶׁאָנוּ חַיָּבִים עֲלֵיהֶם קָרְבָּן עוֹלֶה וְיוֹרֵד
וְעַל חֲטָאִים שֶׁאָנוּ חַיָּבִים עֲלֵיהֶם אָשָׁם וַדַּאי וְתָלוּי
וְעַל חֲטָאִים שֶׁאָנוּ חַיָּבִים עֲלֵיהֶם מַכַּת מַרְדּוּת
וְעַל חֲטָאִים שֶׁאָנוּ חַיָּבִים עֲלֵיהֶם מַלְקוּת אַרְבָּעִים
וְעַל חֲטָאִים שֶׁאָנוּ חַיָּבִים עֲלֵיהֶם מִיתָה בִּידֵי שָׁמַיִם
וְעַל חֲטָאִים שֶׁאָנוּ חַיָּבִים עֲלֵיהֶם כָּרֵת וַעֲרִירִי
וְעַל חֲטָאִים שֶׁאָנוּ חַיָּבִים עֲלֵיהֶם אַרְבַּע מִיתוֹת בֵּית דִּין
סְקִילָה, שְׂרֵפָה, הֶרֶג, וְחֶנֶק.
עַל מִצְוַת עֲשֵׂה וְעַל מִצְוַת לֹא תַעֲשֶׂה.
בֵּין שֶׁיֵּשׁ בָּהּ קוּם עֲשֵׂה וּבֵין שֶׁאֵין בָּהּ קוּם עֲשֵׂה.
אֶת הַגְּלוּיִים לָנוּ וְאֶת שֶׁאֵינָם גְּלוּיִים לָנוּ
אֶת הַגְּלוּיִים לָנוּ, כְּבָר אֲמַרְנוּם לְפָנֶיךָ, וְהוֹדִינוּ לְךָ עֲלֵיהֶם
וְאֶת שֶׁאֵינָם גְּלוּיִים לָנוּ, לְפָנֶיךָ הֵם גְּלוּיִים וִידוּעִים
כַּדָּבָר שֶׁנֶּאֱמַר
הַנִּסְתָּרֹת לַיהוה אֱלֹהֵינוּ דברים כט
וְהַנִּגְלֹת לָנוּ וּלְבָנֵינוּ עַד־עוֹלָם
לַעֲשׂוֹת אֶת־כָּל־דִּבְרֵי הַתּוֹרָה הַזֹּאת:
כִּי אַתָּה סָלְחָן לְיִשְׂרָאֵל וּמָחֳלָן לְשִׁבְטֵי יְשֻׁרוּן בְּכָל דּוֹר וָדוֹר
וּמִבַּלְעָדֶיךָ אֵין לָנוּ מֶלֶךְ מוֹחֵל וְסוֹלֵחַ אֶלָּא אָתָּה.

אֱלֹהַי My God,
before I was formed I was unworthy,
and now that I have been formed it is as if I had not been formed.
I am dust while alive,
how much more so when I am dead.
See, I am before You like a vessel filled with shame and disgrace.
May it be Your will, Lord my God and God of my fathers,
that I may sin no more,
and as for the sins I have committed before You,
erase them in Your great compassion,
but not by suffering or severe illness.

אֱלֹהַי My God, *Berakhot 17a*
guard my tongue from evil
and my lips from dishonest speech.
To those who curse me, let my soul be silent;
may my soul be to all like the dust.
Open my heart to Your Torah
and let my soul pursue Your commandments.
As for all who plan evil against me,
swiftly defeat their counsel and frustrate their plans.

Act for the sake of Your name; act for the sake of Your right hand;
act for the sake of Your holiness; act for the sake of Your Torah.

That Your beloved ones may be rescued, *Ps. 60*
save with Your right hand and answer me.
May the words of my mouth and the inner thoughts of my heart *Ps. 19*
find favor before You, Lord, my Rock and Redeemer.

Bow, take three steps back, then bow, first left, then right, then center, while saying:

May He who makes peace in His high places,
make peace for us and all Israel – and say: Amen.

יְהִי רָצוֹן May it be Your will, Lord our God and God of our ancestors,
that the Temple be rebuilt speedily in our days,
and give us a share in Your Torah.
And there we will serve You with fear,
as in the days of old and as in former years.
Then the offering of Judah and Jerusalem *Mal. 3*
will be pleasing to the Lord as in the days of old and as in former years.

אֱלֹהַי
עַד שֶׁלֹּא נוֹצַרְתִּי אֵינִי כְדַאי
וְעַכְשָׁיו שֶׁנּוֹצַרְתִּי, כְּאִלּוּ לֹא נוֹצַרְתִּי
עָפָר אֲנִי בְּחַיַּי, קַל וָחֹמֶר בְּמִיתָתִי.
הֲרֵי אֲנִי לְפָנֶיךָ כִּכְלִי מָלֵא בוּשָׁה וּכְלִמָּה.
יְהִי רָצוֹן מִלְּפָנֶיךָ, יהוה אֱלֹהַי וֵאלֹהֵי אֲבוֹתַי
שֶׁלֹּא אֶחֱטָא עוֹד.
וּמַה שֶּׁחָטָאתִי לְפָנֶיךָ, מְחֹק בְּרַחֲמֶיךָ הָרַבִּים
אֲבָל לֹא עַל יְדֵי יִסּוּרִים וָחֳלָיִם רָעִים.

אֱלֹהַי ברכות יז.
נְצֹר לְשׁוֹנִי מֵרָע וּשְׂפָתַי מִדַּבֵּר מִרְמָה
וְלִמְקַלְלַי נַפְשִׁי תִדֹּם, וְנַפְשִׁי כֶּעָפָר לַכֹּל תִּהְיֶה.
פְּתַח לִבִּי בְּתוֹרָתֶךָ, וּבְמִצְוֹתֶיךָ תִּרְדֹּף נַפְשִׁי.
וְכָל הַחוֹשְׁבִים עָלַי רָעָה
מְהֵרָה הָפֵר עֲצָתָם וְקַלְקֵל מַחֲשַׁבְתָּם.
עֲשֵׂה לְמַעַן שְׁמֶךָ, עֲשֵׂה לְמַעַן יְמִינֶךָ
עֲשֵׂה לְמַעַן קְדֻשָּׁתֶךָ, עֲשֵׂה לְמַעַן תּוֹרָתֶךָ.
לְמַעַן יֵחָלְצוּן יְדִידֶיךָ, הוֹשִׁיעָה יְמִינְךָ וַעֲנֵנִי: תהלים ס
יִהְיוּ לְרָצוֹן אִמְרֵי פִי וְהֶגְיוֹן לִבִּי לְפָנֶיךָ, יהוה צוּרִי וְגֹאֲלִי: תהלים יט

Bow, take three steps back, then bow, first left, then right, then center, while saying:

עֹשֶׂה שָׁלוֹם / בעשרת ימי תשובה: הַשָּׁלוֹם/ בִּמְרוֹמָיו
הוּא יַעֲשֶׂה שָׁלוֹם עָלֵינוּ וְעַל כָּל יִשְׂרָאֵל וְאִמְרוּ אָמֵן.

יְהִי רָצוֹן מִלְּפָנֶיךָ יהוה אֱלֹהֵינוּ וֵאלֹהֵי אֲבוֹתֵינוּ
שֶׁיִּבָּנֶה בֵּית הַמִּקְדָּשׁ בִּמְהֵרָה בְיָמֵינוּ, וְתֵן חֶלְקֵנוּ בְּתוֹרָתֶךָ
וְשָׁם נַעֲבָדְךָ בְּיִרְאָה כִּימֵי עוֹלָם וּכְשָׁנִים קַדְמוֹנִיּוֹת.
וְעָרְבָה לַיהוה מִנְחַת יְהוּדָה וִירוּשָׁלָיִם כִּימֵי עוֹלָם וּכְשָׁנִים קַדְמוֹנִיּוֹת: מלאכי ג

SERVICE FOR ḤANUKKA

On each of the eight nights of Ḥanukka, the lights of the menora are lit: one on the first night, two on the second, and so on. On the first night, the rightmost branch of the menora is used; on each following night, an additional light is added to the left. Each night, the new light is lit first, then the others, moving rightwards. If possible, the menora should be displayed near a window so that it is visible from the street.

The lights are lit using a separate flame known as the shamash. The lighting should be carried out as soon as possible after nightfall. On Friday night, it must be done before the beginning of Shabbat. Before lighting the Ḥanukka lights, say:

בָּרוּךְ Blessed are You, LORD our God, King of the Universe,
who has made us holy through His commandments,
and has commanded us to light the Ḥanukka lights.

בָּרוּךְ Blessed are You, LORD our God, King of the Universe,
who performed miracles for our ancestors in those days,
at this time.

On the first night, add:

בָּרוּךְ Blessed are You, LORD our God, King of the Universe,
who has given us life, sustained us, and brought us to this time.

After lighting the first light, say:

הַנֵּרוֹת הַלָּלוּ We light these lights *Soferim ch. 20*
because of the miracles and wonders,
deliverances and victories
You performed for our ancestors
in those days, at this time,
through Your holy priests.

Throughout the eight days of Ḥanukka
these lights are holy
and we are not permitted
to make any other use of them,
except to look at them,

that we may give thanks and praise to Your great name
for Your miracles, Your wonders and Your deliverances.

סדר הדלקת נרות חנוכה

On each of the eight nights of חנוכה*, the lights of the* חנוכיה *are lit: one on the first night, two on the second, and so on. On the first night, the rightmost branch of the* חנוכיה *is used; on each following night, an additional light is added to the left. Each night, the new light is lit first, then the others, moving rightwards. If possible, the* חנוכיה *should be displayed near a window so that it is visible from the street. The lights are lit using a separate flame known as the* שמש*. The lighting should be carried out as soon as possible after nightfall. On Friday night, it must be done before the beginning of* שבת*. Before lighting the* חנוכה *lights, say:*

בָּרוּךְ אַתָּה יהוה אֱלֹהֵינוּ מֶלֶךְ הָעוֹלָם
אֲשֶׁר קִדְּשָׁנוּ בְּמִצְוֹתָיו וְצִוָּנוּ לְהַדְלִיק נֵר שֶׁל חֲנֻכָּה.

בָּרוּךְ אַתָּה יהוה אֱלֹהֵינוּ מֶלֶךְ הָעוֹלָם
שֶׁעָשָׂה נִסִּים לַאֲבוֹתֵינוּ בַּיָּמִים הָהֵם בַּזְּמַן הַזֶּה.

On the first night, add:

בָּרוּךְ אַתָּה יהוה אֱלֹהֵינוּ מֶלֶךְ הָעוֹלָם
שֶׁהֶחֱיָנוּ וְקִיְּמָנוּ וְהִגִּיעָנוּ לַזְּמַן הַזֶּה.

After lighting the first light, say:

מסכת סופרים פרק כ

הַנֵּרוֹת הַלָּלוּ אָנוּ מַדְלִיקִים
עַל הַנִּסִּים וְעַל הַנִּפְלָאוֹת וְעַל הַתְּשׁוּעוֹת וְעַל הַמִּלְחָמוֹת
שֶׁעָשִׂיתָ לַאֲבוֹתֵינוּ בַּיָּמִים הָהֵם בַּזְּמַן הַזֶּה
עַל יְדֵי כֹּהֲנֶיךָ הַקְּדוֹשִׁים.
וְכָל שְׁמוֹנַת יְמֵי חֲנֻכָּה
הַנֵּרוֹת הַלָּלוּ קֹדֶשׁ הֵם
וְאֵין לָנוּ רְשׁוּת לְהִשְׁתַּמֵּשׁ בָּהֶם
אֶלָּא לִרְאוֹתָם בִּלְבָד
כְּדֵי לְהוֹדוֹת וּלְהַלֵּל לְשִׁמְךָ הַגָּדוֹל
עַל נִסֶּיךָ וְעַל נִפְלְאוֹתֶיךָ וְעַל יְשׁוּעָתֶךָ.

After all the lights are lit:

מָעוֹז צוּר Refuge, Rock of my salvation:
to You it is a delight to give praise.
Restore my House of prayer, so that there I may offer You thanksgiving.
When You silence the loud-mouthed enemy,
then will I complete, with song and psalm, the altar's dedication.

רָעוֹת Troubles filled my soul; my strength was spent with sorrow.
They embittered my life with hardship,
when I was enslaved under Egyptian rule.
But God with His great power brought out His treasured people,
while Pharaoh's multitudes and followers sank like a stone into the deep.

דְּבִיר He brought me to His holy abode, but even there I found no rest.
The oppressor came and exiled me,
because I had served strange gods.
I had drunk poisoned wine. I almost perished.
Then Babylon fell, Zerubbabel came: within seventy years I was saved.

כְּרֹת The Agagite, son of Hammedatha,
sought to cut down the tall fir tree,
but it became a trap to him, and his arrogance was brought to an end.
You raised the head of the Benjaminite,
and the enemy's name You blotted out.
His many sons and his household You hanged on the gallows.

יְוָנִים Then the Greeks gathered against me,
in the days of the Hasmoneans.
They broke down the walls of my towers, and defiled all the oils.
But from the last remaining flask
a miracle was wrought for Your beloved.
Therefore the sages ordained these eight days for song and praise.

חֲשֹׂף Bare Your holy arm, and hasten the time of salvation.
Take retribution against the evil nation
on behalf of Your servants,
for the hour [of deliverance] has been too long delayed;
there seems no end to the evil days.
Thrust the enemy into the darkness of death,
and establish for us the seven Shepherds.

After all the lights are lit:

מָעוֹז צוּר יְשׁוּעָתִי   לְךָ נָאֶה לְשַׁבֵּחַ
תִּכּוֹן בֵּית תְּפִלָּתִי   וְשָׁם תּוֹדָה נְזַבֵּחַ
לְעֵת תָּכִין מַטְבֵּחַ   מִצָּר הַמְנַבֵּחַ
אָז אֶגְמֹר   בְּשִׁיר מִזְמוֹר   חֲנֻכַּת הַמִּזְבֵּחַ.

רָעוֹת שָׂבְעָה נַפְשִׁי   בְּיָגוֹן כֹּחִי כָּלָה
חַיַּי מֵרְרוּ בְקֹשִׁי   בְּשִׁעְבּוּד מַלְכוּת עֶגְלָה
וּבְיָדוֹ הַגְּדוֹלָה   הוֹצִיא אֶת הַסְּגֻלָּה
חֵיל פַּרְעֹה   וְכָל זַרְעוֹ   יָרְדוּ כְּאֶבֶן מְצוּלָה.

דְּבִיר קָדְשׁוֹ הֱבִיאַנִי   וְגַם שָׁם לֹא שָׁקַטְתִּי
וּבָא נוֹגֵשׂ וְהִגְלַנִי   כִּי זָרִים עָבַדְתִּי
וְיֵין רַעַל מָסַכְתִּי   כִּמְעַט שֶׁעָבַרְתִּי
קֵץ בָּבֶל   זְרֻבָּבֶל   לְקֵץ שִׁבְעִים נוֹשַׁעְתִּי.

כְּרֹת קוֹמַת בְּרוֹשׁ בִּקֵּשׁ   אֲגָגִי בֶּן הַמְּדָתָא
וְנִהְיָתָה לּוֹ לְפַח וּלְמוֹקֵשׁ   וְגַאֲוָתוֹ נִשְׁבָּתָה
רֹאשׁ יְמִינִי נִשֵּׂאתָ   וְאוֹיֵב שְׁמוֹ מָחִיתָ
רֹב בָּנָיו   וְקִנְיָנָיו   עַל הָעֵץ תָּלִיתָ.

יְוָנִים נִקְבְּצוּ עָלַי   אֲזַי בִּימֵי חַשְׁמַנִּים
וּפָרְצוּ חוֹמוֹת מִגְדָּלַי   וְטִמְּאוּ כָּל הַשְּׁמָנִים
וּמִנּוֹתַר קַנְקַנִּים   נַעֲשָׂה נֵס לַשּׁוֹשַׁנִּים
בְּנֵי בִינָה   יְמֵי שְׁמוֹנָה   קָבְעוּ שִׁיר וּרְנָנִים.

חֲשׂוֹף זְרוֹעַ קָדְשֶׁךָ   וְקָרֵב קֵץ הַיְשׁוּעָה
נְקֹם נִקְמַת עֲבָדֶיךָ   מֵאֻמָּה הָרְשָׁעָה
כִּי אָרְכָה לָנוּ הַשָּׁעָה   וְאֵין קֵץ לִימֵי הָרָעָה
דְּחֵה אַדְמוֹן   בְּצֵל צַלְמוֹן   הָקֵם לָנוּ רוֹעִים שִׁבְעָה.

SERVICE FOR PURIM

Before the reading of the Megilla, the congregation stands and the Reader says the following three blessings:

בָּרוּךְ Blessed are You, Lord our God, King of the Universe,
who has made us holy through His commandments,
and has commanded us about reading the Megilla.

בָּרוּךְ Blessed are You, Lord our God, King of the Universe,
who performed miracles for our ancestors
in those days at this time.

בָּרוּךְ Blessed are You, Lord our God, King of the Universe,
who has given us life, sustained us, and brought us to this time.

The Megilla is read. When the reading is completed, the scroll is rolled up and, if a minyan is present, the Reader continues:

בָּרוּךְ Blessed are You, Lord our God, King of the Universe,
who pleads our cause, judges our claim, avenges our wrong,
brings retribution to our enemies, and punishes our enemies.
Blessed are You, Lord, who on behalf of His people Israel,
exacts punishment from all their enemies, the God who brings salvation.

The following is said after the night reading of the Megilla:

אֲשֶׁר הֵנִיא [God] frustrated the plan of the nations,
defeated the intentions of the crafty.
An evil man rose up against us,
an arrogant branch of Amalek's tree,
arrogant, rich, he dug his own pit.
His pride became his own trap.
He was trapped in the trap he set for others.
Seeking to destroy, he was destroyed.
Haman shared his ancestors' hate,
and stirred against children the hostility of brothers.
He did not remember Saul's act of mercy,
his pity for Agag, through which a new enemy was born.
The wicked planned to cut off the righteous,
but the impure were defeated by the pure.

סדר קריאת המגילה בפורים

Before the reading of the מגילה, the קהל stands and the קורא says the following three blessings:

בָּרוּךְ אַתָּה יהוה אֱלֹהֵינוּ מֶלֶךְ הָעוֹלָם
אֲשֶׁר קִדְּשָׁנוּ בְּמִצְוֹתָיו וְצִוָּנוּ עַל מִקְרָא מְגִלָּה.

בָּרוּךְ אַתָּה יהוה אֱלֹהֵינוּ מֶלֶךְ הָעוֹלָם
שֶׁעָשָׂה נִסִּים לַאֲבוֹתֵינוּ בַּיָּמִים הָהֵם בַּזְּמַן הַזֶּה.

בָּרוּךְ אַתָּה יהוה אֱלֹהֵינוּ מֶלֶךְ הָעוֹלָם
שֶׁהֶחֱיָנוּ וְקִיְּמָנוּ וְהִגִּיעָנוּ לַזְּמַן הַזֶּה.

The מגילה is read. When the reading is completed, the scroll is rolled up and, if a מנין is present, the קורא continues:

בָּרוּךְ אַתָּה יהוה אֱלֹהֵינוּ מֶלֶךְ הָעוֹלָם
הָרָב אֶת רִיבֵנוּ, וְהַדָּן אֶת דִּינֵנוּ, וְהַנּוֹקֵם אֶת נִקְמָתֵנוּ
וְהַמְשַׁלֵּם גְּמוּל לְכָל אוֹיְבֵי נַפְשֵׁנוּ, וְהַנִּפְרָע לָנוּ מִצָּרֵינוּ.
בָּרוּךְ אַתָּה יהוה
הַנִּפְרָע לְעַמּוֹ יִשְׂרָאֵל מִכָּל צָרֵיהֶם, הָאֵל הַמּוֹשִׁיעַ.

The following is said after the night reading of the מגילה:

אֲשֶׁר הֵנִיא עֲצַת גּוֹיִם, וַיָּפֶר מַחְשְׁבוֹת עֲרוּמִים.
בְּקוּם עָלֵינוּ אָדָם רָשָׁע, נֵצֶר זָדוֹן מִזֶּרַע עֲמָלֵק.
גָּאָה בְעָשְׁרוֹ וְכָרָה לוֹ בּוֹר, וּגְדֻלָּתוֹ יָקְשָׁה לוֹ לָכֶד.
דִּמָּה בְנַפְשׁוֹ לִלְכֹּד וְנִלְכַּד, בִּקֵּשׁ לְהַשְׁמִיד וְנִשְׁמַד מְהֵרָה.
הָמָן הוֹדִיעַ אֵיבַת אֲבוֹתָיו, וְעוֹרֵר שִׂנְאַת אַחִים לַבָּנִים.
וְלֹא זָכַר רַחֲמֵי שָׁאוּל, כִּי בְחֶמְלָתוֹ עַל אֲגָג נוֹלַד אוֹיֵב.
זָמַם רָשָׁע לְהַכְרִית צַדִּיק, וְנִלְכַּד טָמֵא בִּידֵי טָהוֹר.

[Mordekhai's] goodness overcame the father's [Saul's] error,
  but the evil [Haman] piled sin upon sin.
He hid in his heart his cunning schemes,
  intent on his evildoing.
He stretched out his hand against God's holy ones;
  he spent his wealth to destroy every memory of them.
When Mordekhai saw the fury go forth,
  and Haman's decrees issued in Shushan,
he put on sackcloth, wrapped himself in mourning,
  decreed a fast and sat on ashes.
"Who will arise to atone for error,
  and find forgiveness for our ancestors' sins?"
A flower blossomed from the palm tree;
  Hadassa arose to wake those who slept.
Her servants hastened Haman to come,
  to serve him wine with the venom of serpents.
He had risen by his wealth, but fell by his evil.
  He made the very gallows by which he was hanged.
All the inhabitants of the world were amazed
  when Haman's ploy (*pur*) became our joy (*Purim*).
The righteous was saved from evil hands,
  the perpetrator suffered the fate of his intended victim.
They undertook to celebrate Purim,
  and to rejoice on it year after year.
You heard the prayer of Mordekhai and Esther;
  and Haman and his sons were hanged on the gallows.

The following is said after both night and morning readings of the Megilla:

שׁוֹשַׁנַּת יַעֲקֹב The lily of Jacob rejoiced and was glad,
When, together, they saw Mordekhai robed in royal blue.
You have been their eternal salvation, their hope in every generation;
To make known that all who hope in You will not be put to shame,
All who trust in You will never be humiliated.
Cursed be Haman who sought to destroy me. Blessed be Mordekhai the Yehudi.
Cursed be Zeresh, wife of him who terrified me.
Blessed be Esther [whose actions saved] me.
Cursed be all the wicked; blessed be all Israel.
And may Ḥarbona, too, be remembered for good.

After the reading of the megilla at night, Ma'ariv continues with "You are Holy" to "great and glorious" on pages 370–372 (on Motza'ei Shabbat, begin with "May the pleasantness" on page 368). The Leader then continues with Full Kaddish on page 374 (omitting the line "May the prayers and pleas"). (On Motza'ei Shabbat, continue with "May God give you" on page 376.) The service continues with Aleinu and Mourner's Kaddish.

In the morning, continue with Ashrei on page 236.

חֶסֶד גָּבַר עַל שִׁגְגַת אָב, וְרָשָׁע הוֹסִיף חֵטְא עַל חֲטָאָיו.
טָמַן בְּלִבּוֹ מַחְשְׁבוֹת עֲרוּמָיו, וַיִּתְמַכֵּר לַעֲשׂוֹת רָעָה.
יָדוֹ שָׁלַח בִּקְדוֹשֵׁי אֵל, כַּסְפּוֹ נָתַן לְהַכְרִית זִכְרָם.
כִּרְאוֹת מָרְדְּכַי כִּי יָצָא קֶצֶף, וְדָתֵי הָמָן נִתְּנוּ בְשׁוּשָׁן.
לָבַשׁ שַׂק וְקָשַׁר מִסְפֵּד וְגָזַר צוֹם וַיֵּשֶׁב עַל הָאֵפֶר.
מִי זֶה יַעֲמֹד לְכַפֵּר שְׁגָגָה, וְלִמְחֹל חַטַּאת עֲוֹן אֲבוֹתֵינוּ.
נֵץ פֶּרַח מִלּוּלָב, הֵן הֲדַסָּה עָמְדָה לְעוֹרֵר יְשֵׁנִים.
סָרִיסֶיהָ הִבְהִילוּ לְהָמָן, לְהַשְׁקוֹתוֹ יֵין חֲמַת תַּנִּינִים.
עָמַד בְּעָשְׁרוֹ וְנָפַל בְּרִשְׁעוֹ, עָשָׂה לוֹ עֵץ וְנִתְלָה עָלָיו.
פִּיהֶם פָּתְחוּ כָּל יוֹשְׁבֵי תֵבֵל, כִּי פוּר הָמָן נֶהְפַּךְ לְפוּרֵנוּ.
צַדִּיק נֶחֱלַץ מִיַּד רָשָׁע, אוֹיֵב נִתַּן תַּחַת נַפְשׁוֹ.
קִיְּמוּ עֲלֵיהֶם לַעֲשׂוֹת פּוּרִים וְלִשְׂמֹחַ בְּכָל שָׁנָה וְשָׁנָה.
רָאִיתָ אֶת תְּפִלַּת מָרְדְּכַי וְאֶסְתֵּר, הָמָן וּבָנָיו עַל הָעֵץ תָּלִיתָ.

The following is said after both night and morning readings of the מגילה:

שׁוֹשַׁנַּת יַעֲקֹב צָהֲלָה וְשָׂמֵחָה
בִּרְאוֹתָם יַחַד תְּכֵלֶת מָרְדְּכָי.
תְּשׁוּעָתָם הָיִיתָ לָנֶצַח, וְתִקְוָתָם בְּכָל דּוֹר וָדוֹר.
לְהוֹדִיעַ שֶׁכָּל קֹוֶיךָ לֹא יֵבֹשׁוּ
וְלֹא יִכָּלְמוּ לָנֶצַח כָּל הַחוֹסִים בָּךְ.
אָרוּר הָמָן אֲשֶׁר בִּקֵּשׁ לְאַבְּדִי
בָּרוּךְ מָרְדְּכַי הַיְּהוּדִי.
אֲרוּרָה זֶרֶשׁ אֵשֶׁת מַפְחִידִי
בְּרוּכָה אֶסְתֵּר בַּעֲדִי.
אֲרוּרִים כָּל הָרְשָׁעִים, בְּרוּכִים כָּל יִשְׂרָאֵל
וְגַם חַרְבוֹנָה זָכוּר לַטּוֹב.

After the reading of the מגילה *at night,* מעריב *continues with* וַיְאַדִּיר *to* וְאַתָּה קָדוֹשׁ *on pages 371–373 (on* מוצאי שבת*, begin with* וִיהִי נֹעַם *on page 369). The* שליח ציבור *then continues with* קדיש שלם *on page 375 (omitting the line* תִּתְקַבַּל*). (On* מוצאי שבת*, continue with* וְיִתֶּן־לְךָ *on page 377.) The service continues with* עָלֵינוּ *and* קדיש יתום*.*

In the morning, continue with אַשְׁרֵי *on page 237.*

Shaḥarit for Yom HaZikaron

At the end of Shaḥarit, after Full Kaddish, the Ark is opened and the following is said by some congregations:

לַמְנַצֵּחַ For the conductor of music. Upon the death of Labben. A psalm of David. *Ps. 9*
I will thank You, LORD, with all my heart; I will tell of all Your wonders.
I will rejoice and celebrate in You; I will sing praise to Your name, Most High.
My enemies retreat; they stumble and perish before You.
For You have upheld my case and my cause; You have sat enthroned as righteous Judge.
You have rebuked nations and destroyed the wicked, blotting out their name for ever and all time.
The enemy are finished, ruined forever; You have overthrown their cities; even the memory of them is lost.
But the LORD abides forever; He has established His throne for judgment.
He will judge the world with righteousness, and try the cause of peoples with justice.
The LORD is a refuge for the oppressed, a stronghold in times of trouble.
Those who know Your name trust in You, for You, LORD, do not abandon those who seek You.
Sing praise to the LORD who is present in Zion; tell the peoples of His deeds.
For He who avenges blood remembers; He does not forget the cry of the afflicted.
Have mercy on me, LORD, see how my enemies afflict me. Lift me up from the gates of death,
That in the gates of the Daughter of Zion I may tell all Your praises and rejoice in Your deliverance.
The nations have fallen into the pit they dug; their feet are caught in the net they hid.
The LORD is known by His justice; the wicked is ensnared by the work of his own hands. Reflect on this, Selah.
The wicked return to the grave, all the nations that forget God.
The needy will not be forgotten forever, nor the hope of the afflicted ever be lost.
Arise, LORD, let not man have power; let the nations be judged in Your presence.
Strike them with fear, LORD; let the nations know they are only men. Selah.

The Ark is closed.

שחרית ליום הזיכרון

At the end of שחרית*, after* קדיש שלם*, the* ארון קודש *is opened and the following is said by some congregations:*

לַמְנַצֵּחַ עַל־מוּת לַבֵּן מִזְמוֹר לְדָוִד: תהלים ט
אוֹדֶה יהוה בְּכָל־לִבִּי, אֲסַפְּרָה כָּל־נִפְלְאוֹתֶיךָ:
אֶשְׂמְחָה וְאֶעֶלְצָה בָךְ, אֲזַמְּרָה שִׁמְךָ עֶלְיוֹן:
בְּשׁוּב־אוֹיְבַי אָחוֹר, יִכָּשְׁלוּ וְיֹאבְדוּ מִפָּנֶיךָ:
כִּי־עָשִׂיתָ מִשְׁפָּטִי וְדִינִי, יָשַׁבְתָּ לְכִסֵּא שׁוֹפֵט צֶדֶק:
גָּעַרְתָּ גוֹיִם אִבַּדְתָּ רָשָׁע, שְׁמָם מָחִיתָ לְעוֹלָם וָעֶד:
הָאוֹיֵב תַּמּוּ חֳרָבוֹת לָנֶצַח, וְעָרִים נָתַשְׁתָּ, אָבַד זִכְרָם הֵמָּה:
וַיהוה לְעוֹלָם יֵשֵׁב, כּוֹנֵן לַמִּשְׁפָּט כִּסְאוֹ:
וְהוּא יִשְׁפֹּט־תֵּבֵל בְּצֶדֶק, יָדִין לְאֻמִּים בְּמֵישָׁרִים:
וִיהִי יהוה מִשְׂגָּב לַדָּךְ, מִשְׂגָּב לְעִתּוֹת בַּצָּרָה:
וְיִבְטְחוּ בְךָ יוֹדְעֵי שְׁמֶךָ, כִּי לֹא־עָזַבְתָּ דֹרְשֶׁיךָ, יהוה:
זַמְּרוּ לַיהוה יֹשֵׁב צִיּוֹן, הַגִּידוּ בָעַמִּים עֲלִילוֹתָיו:
כִּי־דֹרֵשׁ דָּמִים אוֹתָם זָכָר, לֹא־שָׁכַח צַעֲקַת עֲנָוִים:
חָנְנֵנִי יהוה רְאֵה עָנְיִי מִשֹּׂנְאָי, מְרוֹמְמִי מִשַּׁעֲרֵי־מָוֶת:
לְמַעַן אֲסַפְּרָה כָּל־תְּהִלָּתֶיךָ, בְּשַׁעֲרֵי בַת־צִיּוֹן אָגִילָה בִּישׁוּעָתֶךָ:
טָבְעוּ גוֹיִם בְּשַׁחַת עָשׂוּ, בְּרֶשֶׁת־זוּ טָמָנוּ נִלְכְּדָה רַגְלָם:
נוֹדַע יהוה מִשְׁפָּט עָשָׂה, בְּפֹעַל כַּפָּיו נוֹקֵשׁ רָשָׁע, הִגָּיוֹן סֶלָה:
יָשׁוּבוּ רְשָׁעִים לִשְׁאוֹלָה, כָּל־גּוֹיִם שְׁכֵחֵי אֱלֹהִים:
כִּי לֹא לָנֶצַח יִשָּׁכַח אֶבְיוֹן, תִּקְוַת עֲנִיִּים תֹּאבַד לָעַד:
קוּמָה יהוה אַל־יָעֹז אֱנוֹשׁ, יִשָּׁפְטוּ גוֹיִם עַל־פָּנֶיךָ:
שִׁיתָה יהוה מוֹרָה לָהֶם, יֵדְעוּ גוֹיִם, אֱנוֹשׁ הֵמָּה סֶּלָה:

The ארון קודש *is closed.*

Memorial Prayer for Fallen Israeli Soldiers

אָבִינוּ שֶׁבַּשָּׁמַיִם Heavenly Father, God, Source of the spirits of all flesh,
remember, we pray You, the pure souls of our sons and daughters
who heroically gave their lives
in defense of the people and the Land.
Swifter than eagles, stronger than lions,
they fought for the liberation of their people and homeland,
sacrificing their lives for Israel's rebirth in its holy land.
They breathed a spirit of strength and courage
into the whole house of Israel,
in the Land and the Diaspora,
inspiring it to go forward toward its redemption and liberation.
Remember them, our God, for good,
together with the countless holy ones
and heroes of Israel from ancient times.
May their souls be bound in the bonds of everlasting life,
may the Garden of Eden be their resting place, may they rest in peace
and receive their reward at the End of Days.
Amen.

לְדָוִד Of David. Blessed is the LORD, my Rock, who trains my hands for war, *Ps. 144*
my fingers for battle. He is my Benefactor, my Fortress, my Stronghold and my Refuge, my Shield in whom I trust, He who subdues nations under me. LORD, what is man that You care for him, what are mortals that You think of them? Man is no more than a breath, his days like a fleeting shadow. LORD, part Your heavens and come down; touch the mountains so that they pour forth smoke. Flash forth lightning and scatter them; shoot Your arrows and panic them. Reach out Your hand from on high; save me and rescue me from the mighty waters, from the hands of strangers, whose every word is worthless, whose right hands are raised in falsehood. To You, God, I will sing a new song; to You I will play music on a ten-stringed harp. He who gives salvation to kings, who saved His servant David from the cruel sword: may He save me and rescue me from the hands of strangers, whose every word is worthless, whose right hands are raised in falsehood. Then our sons will be like saplings, well nurtured in their youth. Our daughters will be like pillars carved for a palace. Our barns will be filled with every kind of provision. Our sheep will increase by thousands, even tens of thousands in our fields. Our oxen will draw heavy loads. There will be no breach in the walls, no going into captivity, no cries of distress in our streets. Happy are the people for whom this is so; happy are the people whose God is the LORD.

Memorial Prayer for Fallen Israeli Soldiers

אָבִינוּ שֶׁבַּשָּׁמַיִם, אֵל אֱלֹהֵי הָרוּחוֹת לְכָל בָּשָׂר
זְכֹר נָא אֶת הַנְּשָׁמוֹת הַזַּכּוֹת וְהַטְּהוֹרוֹת שֶׁל בָּנֵינוּ וּבְנוֹתֵינוּ
אֲשֶׁר הֶעֱרוּ אֶת נַפְשָׁם לַמָּוֶת מוֹת גִּבּוֹרִים
בְּהֵחָלְצָם לְעֶזְרַת הָעָם וְהָאָרֶץ.
מִנְּשָׁרִים קַלּוּ מֵאֲרָיוֹת גָּבֵרוּ
בְּמִלְחַמְתָּם לְמַעַן שִׁחְרוּר עַמָּם וּמוֹלַדְתָּם.
בַּעֲלוֹתָם עַל מִזְבַּח תְּקוּמַת יִשְׂרָאֵל בְּאֶרֶץ קָדְשׁוֹ
הֵפִיחוּ רוּחַ עֹז וּגְבוּרָה בְּכָל בֵּית יִשְׂרָאֵל בָּאָרֶץ וּבַתְּפוּצוֹת
וַיִּתְעוֹרֵר לִקְרַאת גְּאֻלָּתוֹ וּפְדוּת נַפְשׁוֹ.
יִזְכְּרֵם אֱלֹהֵינוּ לְטוֹבָה
עִם רִבְבוֹת אַלְפֵי קְדוֹשֵׁי יִשְׂרָאֵל וְגִבּוֹרָיו מִימֵי עוֹלָם
בִּצְרוֹר הַחַיִּים יִצְרֹר אֶת נִשְׁמָתָם
בְּגַן עֵדֶן תְּהֵא מְנוּחָתָם
וְיָנוּחוּ בְשָׁלוֹם עַל מִשְׁכְּבָם
וְיַעַמְדוּ לְגוֹרָלָם לְקֵץ הַיָּמִין
אָמֵן.

תהלים קמד

לְדָוִד בָּרוּךְ יהוה צוּרִי הַמְלַמֵּד יָדַי לַקְרָב, אֶצְבְּעוֹתַי לַמִּלְחָמָה: חַסְדִּי וּמְצוּדָתִי
מִשְׂגַּבִּי וּמְפַלְטִי לִי מָגִנִּי וּבוֹ חָסִיתִי הָרוֹדֵד עַמִּי תַחְתָּי: יהוה מָה־אָדָם וַתֵּדָעֵהוּ,
בֶּן־אֱנוֹשׁ וַתְּחַשְּׁבֵהוּ: אָדָם לַהֶבֶל דָּמָה יָמָיו כְּצֵל עוֹבֵר: יהוה הַט־שָׁמֶיךָ וְתֵרֵד
גַּע בֶּהָרִים וְיֶעֱשָׁנוּ: בְּרוֹק בָּרָק וּתְפִיצֵם, שְׁלַח חִצֶּיךָ וּתְהֻמֵּם: שְׁלַח יָדֶיךָ מִמָּרוֹם
פְּצֵנִי וְהַצִּילֵנִי מִמַּיִם רַבִּים מִיַּד בְּנֵי נֵכָר: אֲשֶׁר פִּיהֶם דִּבֶּר־שָׁוְא, וִימִינָם יְמִין
שָׁקֶר: אֱלֹהִים שִׁיר חָדָשׁ אָשִׁירָה לָּךְ, בְּנֵבֶל עָשׂוֹר אֲזַמְּרָה־לָּךְ: הַנּוֹתֵן תְּשׁוּעָה
לַמְּלָכִים הַפּוֹצֶה אֶת־דָּוִד עַבְדּוֹ מֵחֶרֶב רָעָה: פְּצֵנִי וְהַצִּילֵנִי מִיַּד בְּנֵי־נֵכָר אֲשֶׁר־
פִּיהֶם דִּבֶּר־שָׁוְא וִימִינָם יְמִין שָׁקֶר: אֲשֶׁר בָּנֵינוּ כִּנְטִעִים מְגֻדָּלִים בִּנְעוּרֵיהֶם
בְּנוֹתֵינוּ כְזָוִיֹּת מְחֻטָּבוֹת תַּבְנִית הֵיכָל: מְזָוֵינוּ מְלֵאִים מְפִיקִים מִזַּן אֶל־זַן צֹאונֵנוּ
מַאֲלִיפוֹת מְרֻבָּבוֹת בְּחוּצוֹתֵינוּ: אַלּוּפֵינוּ מְסֻבָּלִים אֵין פֶּרֶץ וְאֵין יוֹצֵאת וְאֵין
צְוָחָה בִּרְחֹבֹתֵינוּ: אַשְׁרֵי הָעָם שֶׁכָּכָה לּוֹ אַשְׁרֵי הָעָם שֶׁיהוה אֱלֹהָיו:

Ma'ariv for Yom HaAtzma'ut

In many communities, the following is said before Ma'ariv:

הֹדוּ Thank the LORD for He is good; His loving-kindness is for ever. *Ps. 107*
Let those the LORD redeemed say this – those He redeemed from the enemy's hand, those He gathered from the lands, from east and west, from north and south. Some lost their way in desert wastelands, finding no way to a city where they could live. They were hungry and thirsty, and their spirit grew faint. Then they cried out to the LORD in their trouble, and He rescued them from their distress. He led them by a straight path to a city where they could live. Let them thank the LORD for His loving-kindness and His miracles for humankind, for He satisfies the thirsty and fills the hungry with good. Some sat in darkness and the shadow of death, cruelly bound in iron chains, for they had rebelled against God's words and despised the counsel of the Most High. He humbled their hearts

---

Jewish refugees from around the world, finding them places to live, food to eat, and jobs to do. Two-thirds of this tiny country is arid uninhabitable desert. Yet Israel has managed to settle thousands of people there, and "make the desert bloom," growing crops and vegetation, using ingenious computerized irrigation systems. Israel has become one of the world's most educated populations, with one of the fastest growing economies of the world, inventing many of the products that we all take for granted, such as the computer chip, the technology behind the cell phone, the disk-on-key, and the cherry tomato! And all of this while continuously having to fight for its very existence.

In 1967, Israel faced the most critical threat in its short history before and since that year, in the Six-Day War. Again, far superior armies massed on Israel's borders and threatened to wipe it off the map. In six miraculous days those armies were comprehensively defeated and Israel's existence and security was ensured once again. And now with Yerushalayim, Israel's eternal capital, once again united and unified, Judaism's holiest sites were finally accessible to the whole Jewish People. The events of this period are celebrated and commemorated in much the same way as Yom HaAtzma'ut on Yom Yerushalayim, which falls on the 28th of Iyar every year.

In the words of Rabbi Sacks, "Jews were the first to see God in history, to see the unfolding of events as a meaningful narrative, the ongoing story of the covenant between God and His people. The celebration of Yom HaAtzma'ut as a religious festival is part of this faith."

מעריב ליום העצמאות

In many communities, the following is said before מעריב*:*

הֹדוּ לַיהוה כִּי־טוֹב, כִּי לְעוֹלָם חַסְדּוֹ: יֹאמְרוּ גְּאוּלֵי יהוה, אֲשֶׁר תהלים קז
גְּאָלָם מִיַּד־צָר: וּמֵאֲרָצוֹת קִבְּצָם, מִמִּזְרָח וּמִמַּעֲרָב, מִצָּפוֹן
וּמִיָּם: תָּעוּ בַמִּדְבָּר, בִּישִׁימוֹן דָּרֶךְ, עִיר מוֹשָׁב לֹא מָצָאוּ:
רְעֵבִים גַּם־צְמֵאִים, נַפְשָׁם בָּהֶם תִּתְעַטָּף: וַיִּצְעֲקוּ אֶל־יהוה
בַּצַּר לָהֶם, מִמְּצוּקוֹתֵיהֶם יַצִּילֵם: וַיַּדְרִיכֵם בְּדֶרֶךְ יְשָׁרָה, לָלֶכֶת
אֶל־עִיר מוֹשָׁב: יוֹדוּ לַיהוה חַסְדּוֹ, וְנִפְלְאוֹתָיו לִבְנֵי אָדָם:
כִּי־הִשְׂבִּיעַ נֶפֶשׁ שֹׁקֵקָה, וְנֶפֶשׁ רְעֵבָה מִלֵּא־טוֹב: יֹשְׁבֵי חֹשֶׁךְ
וְצַלְמָוֶת, אֲסִירֵי עֳנִי וּבַרְזֶל: כִּי־הִמְרוּ אִמְרֵי־אֵל, וַעֲצַת עֶלְיוֹן

LEARNING

INTRODUCTION TO YOM HAATZMA'UT AND YOM YERUSHALAYIM

"This is the day the Lord has made; let us rejoice and be glad in it."
(*Tehillim* 118:24)

This verse, in some ways a climax to the Hallel service, provides a microcosm of the Jewish approach to history. When we see God's hand in Jewish history we proclaim it. And we sing about it. Loudly!

After almost two thousand years of painful exile, on the 5th of Iyar 5708 (1948) the Jewish People reestablished themselves as a sovereign nation in their historical homeland. On that first Yom HaAtzma'ut, Independence Day, the Jewish People had finally come home.

So every year, on the 5th of Iyar, we celebrate Israel's creation on Yom HaAtzma'ut as a religious day of joy and celebration, and thanks and praise to Hashem for His guiding of the historical process. Since that time, too, the miracles have not ceased and we say Hallel for that too.

David Ben-Gurion, Israel's first prime minister, once said that to be a realistic person in Israel, you have to believe in miracles! And this little country has produced miracle after miracle in its short history. In 1948, this young country with its tiny, inexperienced, ill-equipped, and under-trained army managed to fend off five Arab armies bent on its destruction. Once the fighting was over in 1949, this brand-new country of just 600,000 people took in more than a million

with hard labor; they stumbled, and there was none to help. Then they cried to the LORD in their trouble, and He saved them from their distress. He brought them out from darkness and the shadow of death and broke open their chains. Let them thank the LORD for His loving-kindness and His miracles for humankind, for He shattered gates of bronze and broke their iron bars. Some were fools with sinful ways, and suffered affliction because of their wrongdoing. They found all food repulsive, and came close to the gates of death. Then they cried to the LORD in their trouble, and He saved them from their distress. He sent His word and healed them; He rescued them from their destruction. Let them thank the LORD for His loving-kindness and His miracles for humankind. Let them sacrifice thanksgiving-offerings and tell His deeds with songs of joy. Those who go to sea in ships, plying their trade in the mighty waters, have seen the works of the LORD, His miracles in the deep. He spoke and stirred up a tempest that lifted high the waves. They rose to the heavens and plunged down to the depths; their souls melted in misery. They reeled and staggered like drunkards; all their skill was to no avail. Then they cried to the LORD in their trouble, and He brought them out of their distress. He stilled the storm to a whisper, and the waves of the sea grew calm. They rejoiced when all was quiet, then He guided them to their destination. Let them thank the LORD for His loving-kindness and His miracles for humankind. Let them elevate Him in the assembly of the people and praise Him in the council of the elders. He turns rivers into a desert, springs of water into parched land, fruitful land into a salt marsh, because of the wickedness of its inhabitants. He turns the desert into pools of water, parched land into flowing springs; He brings the hungry to live there, they build themselves a town in which to live. They sow fields and plant vineyards that yield a fruitful harvest; He blesses them, and they increase greatly, their herds do not decrease, though they had been few and brought low by oppression, adversity and sorrow. He pours contempt on nobles and makes them wander in a pathless waste.
▸ He lifts the destitute from poverty and enlarges their families like flocks. The upright see and rejoice, but the mouth of all wrongdoers is stopped. Whoever is wise, let him lay these things to heart, and reflect on the loving-kindness of the LORD.

נָאֱצוּ: וַיַּכְנַע בֶּעָמָל לִבָּם, כָּשְׁלוּ וְאֵין עֹזֵר: וַיִּזְעֲקוּ אֶל־יהוה בַּצַּר לָהֶם, מִמְּצֻקוֹתֵיהֶם יוֹשִׁיעֵם: יוֹצִיאֵם מֵחֹשֶׁךְ וְצַלְמָוֶת, וּמוֹסְרוֹתֵיהֶם יְנַתֵּק: יוֹדוּ לַיהוה חַסְדּוֹ, וְנִפְלְאוֹתָיו לִבְנֵי אָדָם: כִּי־שִׁבַּר דַּלְתוֹת נְחֹשֶׁת, וּבְרִיחֵי בַרְזֶל גִּדֵּעַ: אֱוִלִים מִדֶּרֶךְ פִּשְׁעָם, וּמֵעֲוֹנֹתֵיהֶם יִתְעַנּוּ: כָּל־אֹכֶל תְּתַעֵב נַפְשָׁם, וַיַּגִּיעוּ עַד־שַׁעֲרֵי מָוֶת: וַיִּזְעֲקוּ אֶל־יהוה בַּצַּר לָהֶם, מִמְּצֻקוֹתֵיהֶם יוֹשִׁיעֵם: יִשְׁלַח דְּבָרוֹ וְיִרְפָּאֵם, וִימַלֵּט מִשְּׁחִיתוֹתָם: יוֹדוּ לַיהוה חַסְדּוֹ, וְנִפְלְאוֹתָיו לִבְנֵי אָדָם: וְיִזְבְּחוּ זִבְחֵי תוֹדָה וִיסַפְּרוּ מַעֲשָׂיו בְּרִנָּה: יוֹרְדֵי הַיָּם בָּאֳנִיּוֹת, עֹשֵׂי מְלָאכָה בְּמַיִם רַבִּים: הֵמָּה רָאוּ מַעֲשֵׂי יהוה, וְנִפְלְאוֹתָיו בִּמְצוּלָה: וַיֹּאמֶר, וַיַּעֲמֵד רוּחַ סְעָרָה, וַתְּרוֹמֵם גַּלָּיו: יַעֲלוּ שָׁמַיִם, יֵרְדוּ תְהוֹמוֹת, נַפְשָׁם בְּרָעָה תִתְמוֹגָג: יָחוֹגּוּ וְיָנוּעוּ כַּשִּׁכּוֹר, וְכָל־חָכְמָתָם תִּתְבַּלָּע: וַיִּצְעֲקוּ אֶל־יהוה בַּצַּר לָהֶם, וּמִמְּצוּקֹתֵיהֶם יוֹצִיאֵם: יָקֵם סְעָרָה לִדְמָמָה, וַיֶּחֱשׁוּ גַּלֵּיהֶם: וַיִּשְׂמְחוּ כִי־יִשְׁתֹּקוּ, וַיַּנְחֵם אֶל־מְחוֹז חֶפְצָם: יוֹדוּ לַיהוה חַסְדּוֹ, וְנִפְלְאוֹתָיו לִבְנֵי אָדָם: וִירוֹמְמוּהוּ בִּקְהַל־עָם, וּבְמוֹשַׁב זְקֵנִים יְהַלְלוּהוּ: יָשֵׂם נְהָרוֹת לְמִדְבָּר, וּמֹצָאֵי מַיִם לְצִמָּאוֹן: אֶרֶץ פְּרִי לִמְלֵחָה, מֵרָעַת יוֹשְׁבֵי בָהּ: יָשֵׂם מִדְבָּר לַאֲגַם־מַיִם, וְאֶרֶץ צִיָּה לְמֹצָאֵי מָיִם: וַיּוֹשֶׁב שָׁם רְעֵבִים, וַיְכוֹנְנוּ עִיר מוֹשָׁב: וַיִּזְרְעוּ שָׂדוֹת, וַיִּטְּעוּ כְרָמִים, וַיַּעֲשׂוּ פְּרִי תְבוּאָה: וַיְבָרְכֵם וַיִּרְבּוּ מְאֹד, וּבְהֶמְתָּם לֹא יַמְעִיט: וַיִּמְעֲטוּ וַיָּשֹׁחוּ, מֵעֹצֶר רָעָה וְיָגוֹן: שֹׁפֵךְ בּוּז עַל־נְדִיבִים, וַיַּתְעֵם בְּתֹהוּ לֹא־דָרֶךְ: ◂ וַיְשַׂגֵּב אֶבְיוֹן מֵעוֹנִי, וַיָּשֶׂם כַּצֹּאן מִשְׁפָּחוֹת: יִרְאוּ יְשָׁרִים וְיִשְׂמָחוּ, וְכָל־עַוְלָה קָפְצָה פִּיהָ: מִי־חָכָם וְיִשְׁמָר־אֵלֶּה, וְיִתְבּוֹנְנוּ חַסְדֵי יהוה:

יהוה מָלָךְ The LORD reigns, let the earth be glad. Let the many islands rejoice. Clouds and thick darkness surround Him; righteousness and justice are the foundation of His throne. Fire goes ahead of Him, consuming His enemies on every side. His lightning lights up the world; the earth sees and trembles. Mountains melt like wax before the LORD, before the LORD of all the earth. The heavens declare His righteousness, and all the peoples see His glory. All who worship images and boast in idols are put to shame. Bow down to Him, all you heavenly powers. Zion hears and rejoices, and the towns of Judah are glad because of Your judgments, LORD. For You, LORD, are supreme over all the earth; You are great far above all heavenly powers. Let those who love the LORD hate evil, for He protects the lives of His devoted ones, delivering them from the hand of the wicked. ▸ Light is sown for the righteous, and joy for the upright in heart. Rejoice in the LORD, you who are righteous, and give thanks to His holy name. *Ps. 97*

The Leader and the Congregation say this psalm responsively, verse by verse

מִזְמוֹר A Psalm. Sing a new song to the LORD, *Ps. 98*
for He has done miracles;
He has saved by His right hand and His holy arm.
The LORD has made His salvation known;
He has displayed His righteousness in the sight of the nations.
He remembered His loving-kindness and trustworthiness
to the house of Israel;
all the ends of the earth have seen the victory of our LORD.
Shout for joy to the LORD, all the earth;
burst into song, sing with joy, play music.
Play music to the LORD on the harp –
on the harp with the sound of singing.
With trumpets and the sound of the shofar,
shout for joy before the LORD, the King.
▸ Let the sea and all that is in it thunder,
the world and all who live in it.
Let the rivers clap their hands, the mountains sing together for joy –
before the LORD, for He is coming to judge the earth.
He will judge the world with justice, and the peoples fairly.

יהוה מָלָךְ תָּגֵל הָאָֽרֶץ, יִשְׂמְחוּ אִיִּים רַבִּים: עָנָן וַעֲרָפֶל סְבִיבָיו, תהלים צז
צֶֽדֶק וּמִשְׁפָּט מְכוֹן כִּסְאוֹ: אֵשׁ לְפָנָיו תֵּלֵךְ, וּתְלַהֵט סָבִיב צָרָיו:
הֵאִֽירוּ בְרָקָיו תֵּבֵל, רָאֲתָה וַתָּחֵל הָאָֽרֶץ: הָרִים כַּדּוֹנַג נָמַֽסּוּ
מִלִּפְנֵי יהוה, מִלִּפְנֵי אֲדוֹן כָּל־הָאָֽרֶץ: הִגִּידוּ הַשָּׁמַֽיִם צִדְקוֹ,
וְרָאוּ כָל־הָעַמִּים כְּבוֹדוֹ: יֵבֹֽשׁוּ כָּל־עֹֽבְדֵי פֶֽסֶל הַמִּתְהַלְלִים
בָּאֱלִילִים, הִשְׁתַּחֲווּ־לוֹ כָּל־אֱלֹהִים: שָׁמְעָה וַתִּשְׂמַח צִיּוֹן,
וַתָּגֵֽלְנָה בְּנוֹת יְהוּדָה, לְמַֽעַן מִשְׁפָּטֶֽיךָ יהוה: כִּי־אַתָּה יהוה
עֶלְיוֹן עַל־כָּל־הָאָֽרֶץ, מְאֹד נַעֲלֵֽיתָ עַל־כָּל־אֱלֹהִים: אֹהֲבֵי יהוה
שִׂנְאוּ רָע, שֹׁמֵר נַפְשׁוֹת חֲסִידָיו, מִיַּד רְשָׁעִים יַצִּילֵם: ◂ אוֹר
זָרֻֽעַ לַצַּדִּיק, וּלְיִשְׁרֵי־לֵב שִׂמְחָה: שִׂמְחוּ צַדִּיקִים בַּיהוה, וְהוֹדוּ
לְזֵֽכֶר קָדְשׁוֹ:

The שליח ציבור *and the* קהל *say this psalm responsively, verse by verse*

מִזְמוֹר, שִׁירוּ לַיהוה שִׁיר חָדָשׁ כִּי־נִפְלָאוֹת עָשָׂה תהלים צח
הוֹשִֽׁיעָה־לּוֹ יְמִינוֹ וּזְרוֹעַ קָדְשׁוֹ:
הוֹדִֽיעַ יהוה יְשׁוּעָתוֹ, לְעֵינֵי הַגּוֹיִם גִּלָּה צִדְקָתוֹ:
זָכַר חַסְדּוֹ וֶאֱמוּנָתוֹ לְבֵית יִשְׂרָאֵל
רָאוּ כָל־אַפְסֵי־אָֽרֶץ אֵת יְשׁוּעַת אֱלֹהֵֽינוּ:
הָרִֽיעוּ לַיהוה כָּל־הָאָֽרֶץ, פִּצְחוּ וְרַנְּנוּ וְזַמֵּֽרוּ:
זַמְּרוּ לַיהוה בְּכִנּוֹר, בְּכִנּוֹר וְקוֹל זִמְרָה:
בַּחֲצֹצְרוֹת וְקוֹל שׁוֹפָר, הָרִֽיעוּ לִפְנֵי הַמֶּֽלֶךְ יהוה:
◂ יִרְעַם הַיָּם וּמְלֹאוֹ, תֵּבֵל וְיֹֽשְׁבֵי בָהּ:
נְהָרוֹת יִמְחֲאוּ־כָף, יַֽחַד הָרִים יְרַנֵּֽנוּ:
לִפְנֵי־יהוה כִּי בָא לִשְׁפֹּט הָאָֽרֶץ
יִשְׁפֹּט־תֵּבֵל בְּצֶֽדֶק, וְעַמִּים בְּמֵישָׁרִים:

It is customary to sing:

הִתְעוֹרְרִי Wake up, wake up,
For your light has come: rise, shine!
Awake, awake, break out in song,
For the LORD's glory is revealed on you.
This is the day the LORD has made; Ps. 118
let us rejoice and be glad in it.

לֹא תֵבֹשִׁי Do not be ashamed, do not be confused.
Why be discouraged? Why do you mourn?
In you the needy of My people find shelter,
And the city shall be rebuilt on its hill.
This is the day the LORD has made;
let us rejoice and be glad in it.

יָמִין Right and left you shall spread out,
And God you will fear.
Through the descendant of Peretz,
We shall rejoice and we shall be glad.
This is the day the LORD has made;
let us rejoice and be glad in it.

Ma'ariv for Weekdays (page 312) is said at this point, in the Yom Tov melody. After Full Kaddish, the Ark is opened and the following is said responsively by the Leader and congregation.

Listen, Israel: the LORD is our God, the LORD is One. *Deut. 6*

The following is said three times responsively:

The LORD, He is God.

The Leader says the following which is repeated by the congregation.

מִי שֶׁעָשָׂה May He who performed miracles for our ancestors and for us,
redeeming us from slavery to freedom,
give us a complete redemption soon,
and gather in our dispersed people
from the four quarters of the earth,
so that all Israel may be united in friendship,
and let us say: Amen.

The Ark is closed.

It is customary to sing:

הִתְעוֹרְרִי הִתְעוֹרְרִי
כִּי בָא אוֹרֵךְ קוּמִי אוֹרִי
עוּרִי עוּרִי, שִׁיר דַּבֵּרִי
כְּבוֹד יהוה עָלַיִךְ נִגְלָה.

תהלים קיח זֶה־הַיּוֹם עָשָׂה יהוה, נָגִילָה וְנִשְׂמְחָה בוֹ:

לֹא תֵבֹשִׁי וְלֹא תִכָּלְמִי
מַה תִּשְׁתּוֹחֲחִי וּמַה תֶּהֱמִי
בָּךְ יֶחֱסוּ עֲנִיֵּי עַמִּי
וְנִבְנְתָה עִיר עַל תִּלָּהּ.
זֶה־הַיּוֹם עָשָׂה יהוה, נָגִילָה וְנִשְׂמְחָה בוֹ:

יָמִין וּשְׂמֹאל תִּפְרֹצִי
וְאֶת יהוה תַּעֲרִיצִי
עַל יַד אִישׁ בֶּן פַּרְצִי
וְנִשְׂמְחָה וְנָגִילָה.
זֶה־הַיּוֹם עָשָׂה יהוה, נָגִילָה וְנִשְׂמְחָה בוֹ:

קדיש שלם מעריב לחול (page 313) is said at this point, in the יום טוב melody. After קדיש שלם, the ארון קודש is opened and the following is said responsively by the שליח ציבור and the קהל.

דברים ו **שְׁמַע יִשְׂרָאֵל, יהוה אֱלֹהֵינוּ, יהוה אֶחָד:**

The following is said three times responsively:

יהוה הוּא הָאֱלֹהִים.

The שליח ציבור says the following which is repeated by the קהל.

מִי שֶׁעָשָׂה נִסִּים לַאֲבוֹתֵינוּ וְלָנוּ
וּגְאָלָנוּ מֵעַבְדוּת לְחֵרוּת
הוּא יִגְאָלֵנוּ גְּאֻלָּה שְׁלֵמָה בְּקָרוֹב
וִיקַבֵּץ נִדָּחֵינוּ מֵאַרְבַּע כַּנְפוֹת הָאָרֶץ
חֲבֵרִים כָּל יִשְׂרָאֵל, וְנֹאמַר אָמֵן.

The ארון קודש is closed.

The Leader continues:

וְכִי־תָבֹאוּ When you go into battle in your land against an enemy who is attacking you, sound a staccato blast on the trumpets. Then you will be remembered by the LORD your God and you will be saved from your enemies. On your days of rejoicing – your festivals and new moon celebrations – you shall sound a note on the trumpets over your burnt- and peace-offerings, and they will be a remembrance for you before your God. I am the LORD your God. *Num. 10*

The shofar is sounded with a Tekia Gedola and the following is said aloud:

Next year in Jerusalem rebuilt.

All:

May it be Your will, LORD our God and God of our fathers,
That as we have merited to witness the beginning of redemption,
So may we merit to hear the sound of the shofar
of our righteous anointed one, swiftly in our days.

All sing:

שִׁיר הַמַּעֲלוֹת A song of ascents. When the LORD brought back the exiles of Zion we were like people who dream. Then were our mouths filled with laughter, and our tongues with songs of joy. Then was it said among the nations, "The LORD has done great things for them." The LORD did do great things for us and we rejoiced. Bring back our exiles, LORD, like streams in a dry land. May those who sowed in tears, reap in joy. May one who goes out weeping, carrying a bag of seed, come back with songs of joy, carrying his sheaves. *Ps. 126*

*The Omer is counted (**page 356**), followed by Aleinu (**page 350**).*

All sing:

אֲנִי מַאֲמִין I believe with perfect faith
in the coming of the Messiah,
and though he may delay,
I wait daily for his coming.

It is customary to greet each other with the following phrase:

Happy festival; to a complete redemption!

The שליח ציבור *continues:*

וְכִי־תָבֹאוּ מִלְחָמָה בְּאַרְצְכֶם עַל־הַצַּר הַצֹּרֵר אֶתְכֶם, וַהֲרֵעֹתֶם במדבר י
בַּחֲצֹצְרֹת, וְנִזְכַּרְתֶּם לִפְנֵי יהוה אֱלֹהֵיכֶם, וְנוֹשַׁעְתֶּם מֵאֹיְבֵיכֶם:
וּבְיוֹם שִׂמְחַתְכֶם וּבְמוֹעֲדֵיכֶם וּבְרָאשֵׁי חָדְשֵׁכֶם, וּתְקַעְתֶּם
בַּחֲצֹצְרֹת עַל עֹלֹתֵיכֶם וְעַל זִבְחֵי שַׁלְמֵיכֶם, וְהָיוּ לָכֶם לְזִכָּרוֹן
לִפְנֵי אֱלֹהֵיכֶם, אֲנִי יהוה אֱלֹהֵיכֶם:

The שופר *is sounded with a* תקיעה גדולה *and the following is said aloud:*

לַשָּׁנָה הַבָּאָה בִּירוּשָׁלַיִם הַבְּנוּיָה.

All:

יְהִי רָצוֹן מִלְּפָנֶיךָ יהוה אֱלֹהֵינוּ וֵאלֹהֵי אֲבוֹתֵינוּ
שֶׁכְּשֵׁם שֶׁזָּכִינוּ לְאַתְחַלְתָּא דִגְאֻלָּה
כֵּן נִזְכֶּה לִשְׁמֹעַ קוֹל שׁוֹפָרוֹ שֶׁל מְשִׁיחַ צִדְקֵנוּ בִּמְהֵרָה בְיָמֵינוּ.

All sing:

שִׁיר הַמַּעֲלוֹת, בְּשׁוּב יהוה אֶת־שִׁיבַת צִיּוֹן, הָיִינוּ כְּחֹלְמִים: אָז יִמָּלֵא תהלים קכו
שְׂחוֹק פִּינוּ וּלְשׁוֹנֵנוּ רִנָּה, אָז יֹאמְרוּ בַגּוֹיִם הִגְדִּיל יהוה לַעֲשׂוֹת עִם־אֵלֶּה:
הִגְדִּיל יהוה לַעֲשׂוֹת עִמָּנוּ, הָיִינוּ שְׂמֵחִים: שׁוּבָה יהוה אֶת־שְׁבִיתֵנוּ,
כַּאֲפִיקִים בַּנֶּגֶב: הַזֹּרְעִים בְּדִמְעָה בְּרִנָּה יִקְצֹרוּ: הָלוֹךְ יֵלֵךְ וּבָכֹה נֹשֵׂא
מֶשֶׁךְ־הַזָּרַע, בֹּא־יָבֹא בְרִנָּה נֹשֵׂא אֲלֻמֹּתָיו:

The עומר *is counted (page 357), followed by* עָלֵינוּ *(page 351).*

All sing:

אֲנִי מַאֲמִין בֶּאֱמוּנָה שְׁלֵמָה בְּבִיאַת הַמָּשִׁיחַ
וְאַף עַל פִּי שֶׁיִּתְמַהְמֵהַּ
עִם כָּל זֶה אֲחַכֶּה לּוֹ בְּכָל יוֹם שֶׁיָּבוֹא.

It is customary to greet each other with the following phrase:

מוֹעֲדִים לְשִׂמְחָה לִגְאֻלָּה שְׁלֵמָה

Shaḥarit for Yom HaAtzma'ut

Begin as on weekdays, from pages 4–70.
In many communities, Pesukei DeZimra of Yom Tov are said (page 528). Some communities recite Shirat HaYam (page 566) responsively verse by verse. After the Leader's Repetition, Full Hallel (page 822) is said followed by Half Kaddish (page 218). On Thursdays the Torah is read (page 220). On all days, the following Haftara is read.

עוֹד הַיּוֹם This day he will halt at Nob; he will wave his hand, mountain of the daughter of Zion, hill of Jerusalem. See, the sovereign LORD of multitudes will lop off the boughs with an axe. The tall trees will be felled, the lofty ones laid low. He will cut down the forest thickets with an axe. Lebanon will fall before the Mighty One. A shoot will grow from the stump of Jesse; from his roots a branch will bear fruit. The spirit of the LORD will rest on him – a spirit of wisdom and understanding, a spirit of counsel and power, a spirit of knowledge and the fear of the LORD, and he will delight in the fear of the LORD. He will not judge by what his eyes see, or decide by what his ears hear; with justice he will judge the poor, and with fairness defend humble in the land. He will strike the earth with the rod of his mouth; with the breath of his lips he will slay the wicked. Justice will be his belt and trustworthiness the sash around his waist. The wolf will live with the lamb, the leopard will lie down with the kid, the calf and the lion and the yearling together; and a little child will lead them. The cow will graze with the bear, their young will lie down together, and the lion will eat straw like the ox. An infant will play near the cobra's hole, and a young child put his hand into the viper's nest. They will neither harm nor destroy on all My holy mountain, for the earth will be full of the knowledge of the LORD as the waters cover the sea. On that day the stock of Jesse will stand as a banner for the peoples; nations will rally to him, and his place of rest will be glorious. On that day the LORD will reach out His hand a second time to reclaim the remnant that is left of His people from Assyria, Lower Egypt, Pathros, Cush, Elam, Shinar, Hamath and the islands of the sea. He will raise a banner for the nations and gather the exiles of Israel; He will assemble the scattered people of Judah from the four quarters of the earth. Ephraim's jealousy will vanish,

Is. 10:32–12:6

שחרית ליום העצמאות

Begin as on weekdays, from pages 5–71.

In many communities, פסוקי דזמרה *of* יום טוב *are said (page 529). Some communities recite* שירת הים *(page 567) responsively verse by verse. After* חזרת הש״ץ, הלל שלם *(page 823) is said followed by* חצי קדיש *(page 219). On Thursdays the* תורה *is read (page 221). On all days, the following* הפטרה *is read.*

ישעיה י:לב–יב:ו

עוֹד הַיּוֹם בְּנֹב לַעֲמֹד יְנֹפֵף יָדוֹ הַר בַּת־צִיּוֹן גִּבְעַת יְרוּשָׁלִָם׃ הִנֵּה הָאָדוֹן יהוה צְבָאוֹת מְסָעֵף פֻּארָה בְּמַעֲרָצָה וְרָמֵי הַקּוֹמָה גְּדֻעִים וְהַגְּבֹהִים יִשְׁפָּלוּ׃ וְנִקַּף סִבְכֵי הַיַּעַר בַּבַּרְזֶל וְהַלְּבָנוֹן בְּאַדִּיר יִפּוֹל׃

וְיָצָא חֹטֶר מִגֵּזַע יִשָׁי וְנֵצֶר מִשָּׁרָשָׁיו יִפְרֶה׃ וְנָחָה עָלָיו רוּחַ יהוה רוּחַ חָכְמָה וּבִינָה רוּחַ עֵצָה וּגְבוּרָה רוּחַ דַּעַת וְיִרְאַת יהוה׃ וַהֲרִיחוֹ בְּיִרְאַת יהוה וְלֹא־לְמַרְאֵה עֵינָיו יִשְׁפּוֹט וְלֹא־לְמִשְׁמַע אָזְנָיו יוֹכִיחַ׃ וְשָׁפַט בְּצֶדֶק דַּלִּים וְהוֹכִיחַ בְּמִישׁוֹר לְעַנְוֵי־אָרֶץ וְהִכָּה־אֶרֶץ בְּשֵׁבֶט פִּיו וּבְרוּחַ שְׂפָתָיו יָמִית רָשָׁע׃ וְהָיָה צֶדֶק אֵזוֹר מָתְנָיו וְהָאֱמוּנָה אֵזוֹר חֲלָצָיו׃ וְגָר זְאֵב עִם־כֶּבֶשׂ וְנָמֵר עִם־גְּדִי יִרְבָּץ וְעֵגֶל וּכְפִיר וּמְרִיא יַחְדָּו וְנַעַר קָטֹן נֹהֵג בָּם׃ וּפָרָה וָדֹב תִּרְעֶינָה יַחְדָּו יִרְבְּצוּ יַלְדֵיהֶן וְאַרְיֵה כַּבָּקָר יֹאכַל־תֶּבֶן׃ וְשִׁעֲשַׁע יוֹנֵק עַל־חֻר פָּתֶן וְעַל מְאוּרַת צִפְעוֹנִי גָּמוּל יָדוֹ הָדָה׃ לֹא־יָרֵעוּ וְלֹא־יַשְׁחִיתוּ בְּכָל־הַר קָדְשִׁי כִּי־מָלְאָה הָאָרֶץ דֵּעָה אֶת־יהוה כַּמַּיִם לַיָּם מְכַסִּים׃

וְהָיָה בַּיּוֹם הַהוּא שֹׁרֶשׁ יִשַׁי אֲשֶׁר עֹמֵד לְנֵס עַמִּים אֵלָיו גּוֹיִם יִדְרֹשׁוּ וְהָיְתָה מְנֻחָתוֹ כָּבוֹד׃

וְהָיָה ׀ בַּיּוֹם הַהוּא יוֹסִיף אֲדֹנָי ׀ שֵׁנִית יָדוֹ לִקְנוֹת אֶת־שְׁאָר עַמּוֹ אֲשֶׁר יִשָּׁאֵר מֵאַשּׁוּר וּמִמִּצְרַיִם וּמִפַּתְרוֹס וּמִכּוּשׁ וּמֵעֵילָם וּמִשִּׁנְעָר וּמֵחֲמָת וּמֵאִיֵּי הַיָּם׃ וְנָשָׂא נֵס לַגּוֹיִם וְאָסַף נִדְחֵי יִשְׂרָאֵל וּנְפֻצוֹת יְהוּדָה יְקַבֵּץ מֵאַרְבַּע כַּנְפוֹת הָאָרֶץ׃ וְסָרָה קִנְאַת אֶפְרַיִם וְצֹרְרֵי

and Judah's harassment will end. Ephraim will not be jealous of Judah, nor will Judah be hostile toward Ephraim. They will swoop down on the slopes of Philistia to the west; together they will plunder the people to the east. Edom and Moab will be subject to them, and the Ammonites shall obey them. The LORD will dry up the gulf of the Egyptian sea; with a scorching wind He will sweep His hand over the Euphrates River. He will break it up into seven streams so that people can cross over in sandals. There will be a highway for the survivors of His people that is left from Assyria, as there was for Israel when they came up from Egypt. In that day you will say: "I will praise You, O LORD. Although You were angry with me, Your anger has turned away and You have comforted me. Surely God is my salvation; I will trust and not be afraid. The LORD, the LORD, is my strength and my song; He has become my salvation." With joy you will draw water from the wells of salvation. In that day you will say: "Give thanks to the LORD, call on His name; make known among the nations what He has done, and declare that His name is great. Sing to the LORD, for He has done glorious things; let this be known to all the world. Shout aloud and sing for joy, people of Zion, for great is the Holy One of Israel among you."

PRAYER FOR THE STATE OF ISRAEL

The Leader says the following prayer:

אָבִינוּ שֶׁבַּשָּׁמַיִם Heavenly Father, Israel's Rock and Redeemer, bless the State of Israel, the first flowering of our redemption. Shield it under the wings of Your loving-kindness and spread over it the canopy of Your peace. Send Your light and truth to its leaders, ministers and advisors, and direct them with good counsel before You.

Strengthen the hands of the defenders of our Holy Land; give them deliverance, our God, and crown them with the crown of victory. Give peace in the land and everlasting joy to its inhabitants.

As for our brothers, the whole house of Israel, remember them in all the lands of our (*In Israel say:* their) dispersion, and swiftly lead us

יְהוּדָה יִכָּרֵתוּ אֶפְרַיִם לֹא־יְקַנֵּא אֶת־יְהוּדָה וִיהוּדָה לֹא־יָצֹר אֶת־אֶפְרָיִם׃ וְעָפוּ בְכָתֵף פְּלִשְׁתִּים יָמָּה יַחְדָּו יָבֹזּוּ אֶת־בְּנֵי־קֶדֶם אֱדוֹם וּמוֹאָב מִשְׁלוֹחַ יָדָם וּבְנֵי עַמּוֹן מִשְׁמַעְתָּם׃ וְהֶחֱרִים יהוה אֵת לְשׁוֹן יָם־מִצְרַיִם וְהֵנִיף יָדוֹ עַל־הַנָּהָר בַּעְיָם רוּחוֹ וְהִכָּהוּ לְשִׁבְעָה נְחָלִים וְהִדְרִיךְ בַּנְּעָלִים׃ וְהָיְתָה מְסִלָּה לִשְׁאָר עַמּוֹ אֲשֶׁר יִשָּׁאֵר מֵאַשּׁוּר כַּאֲשֶׁר הָיְתָה לְיִשְׂרָאֵל בְּיוֹם עֲלֹתוֹ מֵאֶרֶץ מִצְרָיִם׃ וְאָמַרְתָּ בַּיּוֹם הַהוּא אוֹדְךָ יהוה כִּי אָנַפְתָּ בִּי יָשֹׁב אַפְּךָ וּתְנַחֲמֵנִי׃ הִנֵּה אֵל יְשׁוּעָתִי אֶבְטַח וְלֹא אֶפְחָד כִּי־עָזִּי וְזִמְרָת יָהּ יהוה וַיְהִי־לִי לִישׁוּעָה׃ וּשְׁאַבְתֶּם־מַיִם בְּשָׂשׂוֹן מִמַּעַיְנֵי הַיְשׁוּעָה׃ וַאֲמַרְתֶּם בַּיּוֹם הַהוּא הוֹדוּ לַיהוה קִרְאוּ בִשְׁמוֹ הוֹדִיעוּ בָעַמִּים עֲלִילֹתָיו הַזְכִּירוּ כִּי נִשְׂגָּב שְׁמוֹ׃ זַמְּרוּ יהוה כִּי גֵאוּת עָשָׂה מוּדַעַת זֹאת בְּכָל־הָאָרֶץ׃ צַהֲלִי וָרֹנִּי יוֹשֶׁבֶת צִיּוֹן כִּי־גָדוֹל בְּקִרְבֵּךְ קְדוֹשׁ יִשְׂרָאֵל׃

תפילה לשלום מדינת ישראל

The שליח ציבור *says the following prayer:*

אָבִינוּ שֶׁבַּשָּׁמַיִם, צוּר יִשְׂרָאֵל וְגוֹאֲלוֹ, בָּרֵךְ אֶת מְדִינַת יִשְׂרָאֵל, רֵאשִׁית צְמִיחַת גְּאֻלָּתֵנוּ. הָגֵן עָלֶיהָ בְּאֶבְרַת חַסְדֶּךָ וּפְרֹשׂ עָלֶיהָ סֻכַּת שְׁלוֹמֶךָ, וּשְׁלַח אוֹרְךָ וַאֲמִתְּךָ לְרָאשֶׁיהָ, שָׂרֶיהָ וְיוֹעֲצֶיהָ, וְתַקְּנֵם בְּעֵצָה טוֹבָה מִלְּפָנֶיךָ.

חַזֵּק אֶת יְדֵי מְגִנֵּי אֶרֶץ קָדְשֵׁנוּ, וְהַנְחִילֵם אֱלֹהֵינוּ יְשׁוּעָה וַעֲטֶרֶת נִצָּחוֹן תְּעַטְּרֵם, וְנָתַתָּ שָׁלוֹם בָּאָרֶץ וְשִׂמְחַת עוֹלָם לְיוֹשְׁבֶיהָ.

וְאֶת אַחֵינוּ כָּל בֵּית יִשְׂרָאֵל, פְּקָד נָא בְּכָל אַרְצוֹת פְּזוּרֵינוּ, וְתוֹלִיכֵנוּ / בארץ ישראל: פְּזוּרֵיהֶם, וְתוֹלִיכֵם / מְהֵרָה קוֹמְמִיּוּת לְצִיּוֹן

(*In Israel say:* them) upright to Zion Your city, and Jerusalem Your dwelling place, as is written in the Torah of Moses Your servant: "Even if you are scattered to the furthermost lands under the heavens, from there the LORD your God will gather you and take you back. The LORD your God will bring you to the land your ancestors possessed and you will possess it; and He will make you more prosperous and numerous than your ancestors. Then the LORD your God will open up your heart and the heart of your descendants, to love the LORD your God with all your heart and with all your soul, that you may live." *Deut. 30*

Unite our hearts to love and fear Your name and observe all the words of Your Torah, and swiftly send us Your righteous anointed one of the house of David, to redeem those who long for Your salvation.

Appear in Your glorious majesty over all who live on earth, and let all who breathe declare: The LORD God of Israel is King and His kingship has dominion over all. Amen, Selah.

The Memorial Prayer for Fallen Israeli Soldiers (page 950) is said.
The service then continues with Ashrei (page 236) until the end of Shaḥarit.
At the end of the service, sing:

אֲנִי מַאֲמִין I believe with perfect faith
in the coming of the Messiah,
and though he may delay,
I wait daily for his coming.

YOM YERUSHALAYIM

At Minḥa before Yom Yerushalayim, Taḥanun is omitted. In the evening, Ma'ariv for weekdays is said in the Yom Tov melody. The Omer is counted. Many have the custom to add prayers of thanksgiving at the end of Ma'ariv.

In Shaḥarit, many communities say the Pesukei DeZimra of Yom Tov (page 528). After the Leader's Repetition, Full Hallel (page 822) is said and the regular service continues.

עִירֶךָ וְלִירוּשָׁלַיִם מִשְׁכַּן שְׁמֶךָ, כַּכָּתוּב בְּתוֹרַת מֹשֶׁה עַבְדֶּךָ:
אִם־יִהְיֶה נִדַּחֲךָ בִּקְצֵה הַשָּׁמָיִם, מִשָּׁם יְקַבֶּצְךָ יהוה אֱלֹהֶיךָ דברים ל
וּמִשָּׁם יִקָּחֶךָ: וֶהֱבִיאֲךָ יהוה אֱלֹהֶיךָ אֶל־הָאָרֶץ אֲשֶׁר־יָרְשׁוּ
אֲבֹתֶיךָ וִירִשְׁתָּהּ, וְהֵיטִבְךָ וְהִרְבְּךָ מֵאֲבֹתֶיךָ: וּמָל יהוה אֱלֹהֶיךָ
אֶת־לְבָבְךָ וְאֶת־לְבַב זַרְעֶךָ, לְאַהֲבָה אֶת־יהוה אֱלֹהֶיךָ בְּכָל־
לְבָבְךָ וּבְכָל־נַפְשְׁךָ, לְמַעַן חַיֶּיךָ:

וְיַחֵד לְבָבֵנוּ לְאַהֲבָה וּלְיִרְאָה אֶת שְׁמֶךָ, וְלִשְׁמֹר אֶת כָּל דִּבְרֵי תוֹרָתֶךָ, וּשְׁלַח לָנוּ מְהֵרָה בֶּן דָּוִד מְשִׁיחַ צִדְקֶךָ, לִפְדּוֹת מְחַכֵּי קֵץ יְשׁוּעָתֶךָ.

וְהוֹפַע בַּהֲדַר גְּאוֹן עֻזֶּךָ עַל כָּל יוֹשְׁבֵי תֵבֵל אַרְצֶךָ וְיֹאמַר כֹּל אֲשֶׁר נְשָׁמָה בְאַפּוֹ, יהוה אֱלֹהֵי יִשְׂרָאֵל מֶלֶךְ וּמַלְכוּתוֹ בַּכֹּל מָשָׁלָה, אָמֵן סֶלָה.

The אזכרה *for Fallen Israeli Soldiers (page 951) is said.*
The service then continues with אַשְׁרֵי *(page 237) until the end of* שחרית.
At the end of the service, sing:

אֲנִי מַאֲמִין בֶּאֱמוּנָה שְׁלֵמָה, בְּבִיאַת הַמָּשִׁיחַ
וְאַף עַל פִּי שֶׁיִּתְמַהְמֵהַּ
עִם כָּל זֶה אֲחַכֶּה לּוֹ בְּכָל יוֹם שֶׁיָּבוֹא.

יום חירות ירושלים

At מנחה *before* יום ירושלים, תחנון *is omitted.*
In the evening, מעריב לחול *is said in the* יום טוב *melody. The* עומר *is counted.*
Many have the custom to add prayers of thanksgiving at the end of מעריב.

In שחרית *many communities say the* פסוקי דזמרה *of* יום טוב *(page 529).*
After חזרת הש״ץ, הלל שלם *(page 823) is said and the regular service continues.*

Seliḥot

Seliḥot are said on Fast Days. On Tisha B'Av, Kinot are said instead.
On the Fast of Gedalya, the Seliḥot for the Ten Days of Repentance are said.

SELIḤOT FOR THE TENTH OF TEVET

סְלַח לָנוּ Forgive us, our Father, for in our great foolishness we have blundered. Pardon us, our King, for our wrongdoings are many.

אֵל אֶרֶךְ You are a God slow to anger, You are called the Master of Compassion, and You have taught the way of repentance. May You remember today and every day the greatness of Your compassion and kindness, for the sake of the descendants of Your beloved ones. Turn toward us in compassion, for You are the Master of Compassion. We come before You in plea and prayer, as You in ancient times showed the humble one [Moses]. Turn from Your fierce anger, as is written in Your Torah. In the shadow of Your wings may we shelter and abide, as on the day when the LORD descended in the cloud. ▸ Overlook sin and wipe away guilt, as on the day when "He stood beside him there." Give ear to our pleading and listen to our speech, as on the day when "he called upon the name of the LORD," and in that place is said –

Congregation then Leader:

And the LORD passed by before him and declared: *Ex. 34*

All say aloud:

יהוה The LORD, the LORD, compassionate and generous God, slow to anger, abounding in loving-kindness and truth, extending loving-kindness to a thousand generations, forgiving wrongdoing, rebellion and sin, and absolving [the guilty who repent]. Forgive us our wrongdoing and our sin, and take us as Your inheritance.

Continue:

סְלַח לָנוּ Forgive us, our Father, for we have sinned. Pardon us, our King, for we have transgressed. For You, LORD, are good and forgiving, abounding in *Ps. 86*
loving-kindness to all who call on You.

For with the LORD there is loving-kindness, and great is His power to redeem. *Ps. 130*
LORD, save Israel from all its troubles. It is He who will redeem Israel from *Ps. 25* *Ps. 130*
all its sins. The LORD redeems His servants; those who take refuge in Him *Ps. 34*
shall not be condemned.

כְּרַחֵם As a father has compassion for his children, so, LORD, have compassion for us.
Salvation is the LORD's; on Your people is Your blessing, Selah! *Ps. 3*

סליחות

סליחות are said on Fast Days. On תשעה באב*,* קינות *are said instead.*
On צום גדליה*, the* סליחות *for the* עשרת ימי תשובה *are said.*

סליחות לעשרה בטבת

סלח לנו, אבינו, כי ברב אולתנו שגינו.
מחל לנו, מלכנו, כי רבו עונינו.

אל ארך אפים אתה, ובעל הרחמים נקראת, ודרך תשובה הורית. גדלת רחמיך וחסדיך, תזכר היום ובכל יום לזרע ידידיך. תפן אלינו ברחמים, כי אתה הוא בעל הרחמים. בתחנון ובתפלה פניך נקדם, כהודעת לענו מקדם. מחרון אפך שוב, כמו בתורתך כתוב. ובצל כנפיך נחסה ונתלונן, כיום וירד יהוה בענן. ‹ תעבר על פשע ותמחה אשם, כיום ויתיצב עמו שם. תאזין שועתנו ותקשיב מנו מאמר, כיום ויקרא בשם יהוה, ושם נאמר

*:*שליח ציבור *then* קהל

שמות לד ויעבר יהוה על־פניו ויקרא

All say aloud:

יהוה, יהוה, אל רחום וחנון, ארך אפים, ורב־חסד ואמת: נצר חסד לאלפים, נשא עון ופשע וחטאה, ונקה: וסלחת לעוננו ולחטאתנו, ונחלתנו:

Continue:

תהלים פו סלח לנו אבינו כי חטאנו, מחל לנו מלכנו כי פשענו. כי־אתה אדני טוב וסלח, ורב־חסד לכל־קראיך:

תהלים קל / תהלים כה / תהלים קל / תהלים לד
כי־עם־יהוה החסד, והרבה עמו פדות: פדה אלהים את־ישראל מכל צרותיו: והוא יפדה את־ישראל מכל עונותיו: פודה יהוה נפש עבדיו, ולא יאשמו כל־החסים בו:

כרחם אב על בנים, כן תרחם יהוה עלינו.
תהלים ג ליהוה הישועה, על־עמך ברכתך סלה:

The LORD of multitudes is with us, the God of Jacob is our stronghold, Selah! *Ps. 46*
LORD of multitudes, happy is the one who trusts in You. *Ps. 84*
LORD, save! May the King answer us on the day we call. *Ps. 20*

▸ Forgive, please, this people's wrongdoing, *Num. 14*
in the abundance of Your kindness,
and as You have forgiven this people from the time of Egypt until now,
and there it is written:

Congregation then Leader:

And the LORD said, I have forgiven as you asked.

Continue:

הַטֵּה Give ear, my God and hear; open Your eyes and see our desolation, and the city that bears Your name, for it is not on the strength of our righteousness that we throw down our pleadings before You, but on the strength of Your great compassion. LORD, hear me; LORD, forgive; LORD, listen and act and do not delay – for Your sake, my God; for Your city and Your people bear Your name. *Dan. 9*

Our God and God of our fathers:

אֶזְכְּרָה I shall recall the anguish that came to me;
He inflicted three blows upon me in this month.
He cut me off, He veered me aside, He beat me –
but now He has finally drained me out. *Job 16*

On the eighth of the month He darkened my right and my left;
I marked out all three days for fasting.
The king of Greece forced me to write the Torah in his tongue.
The ploughmen have ploughed across my back;
they made the furrows long.

I raged, on the ninth, in shame and disgrace,
my mantle of glory and my wreath were taken from me.
The man who gave us the words of Heaven
was torn from us on that day –
that was Ezra the Scribe.

On the tenth, Ezekiel the Seer, son of Buzi was commanded,
"Write this happening in the scroll,
for the remembrance of a people melted away and disgraced;
write this very day." *Ezek. 24*

יהוה צְבָאוֹת עִמָּנוּ, מִשְׂגָּב לָנוּ אֱלֹהֵי יַעֲקֹב סֶלָה: תהלים מו
יהוה צְבָאוֹת, אַשְׁרֵי אָדָם בֹּטֵחַ בָּךְ: תהלים פד
יהוה הוֹשִׁיעָה, הַמֶּלֶךְ יַעֲנֵנוּ בְיוֹם־קָרְאֵנוּ: תהלים כ

◂ סְלַח־נָא לַעֲוֹן הָעָם הַזֶּה כְּגֹדֶל חַסְדֶּךָ במדבר יד
וְכַאֲשֶׁר נָשָׂאתָה לָעָם הַזֶּה מִמִּצְרַיִם וְעַד־הֵנָּה:
וְשָׁם נֶאֱמַר

שליח ציבור then קהל:

וַיֹּאמֶר יהוה, סָלַחְתִּי כִּדְבָרֶךָ:

Continue:

הַטֵּה אֱלֹהַי אָזְנְךָ וּשְׁמָע, פְּקַח עֵינֶיךָ וּרְאֵה שֹׁמְמֹתֵינוּ וְהָעִיר אֲשֶׁר־נִקְרָא דניאל ט
שִׁמְךָ עָלֶיהָ, כִּי לֹא עַל־צִדְקֹתֵינוּ אֲנַחְנוּ מַפִּילִים תַּחֲנוּנֵינוּ לְפָנֶיךָ, כִּי עַל־
רַחֲמֶיךָ הָרַבִּים: אֲדֹנָי שְׁמָעָה, אֲדֹנָי סְלָחָה, אֲדֹנָי הַקְשִׁיבָה וַעֲשֵׂה אַל־תְּאַחַר,
לְמַעַנְךָ אֱלֹהַי, כִּי־שִׁמְךָ נִקְרָא עַל־עִירְךָ וְעַל־עַמֶּךָ:

אֱלֹהֵינוּ וֵאלֹהֵי אֲבוֹתֵינוּ
אֶזְכְּרָה מָצוֹק אֲשֶׁר קְרָאַנִי.
בְּשָׁלֹשׁ מַכּוֹת בַּחֹדֶשׁ הַזֶּה הִכַּנִי.
גִּדְּעַנִי הֱנִיאַנִי הִכְאַנִי.
אַךְ־עַתָּה הֶלְאָנִי: איוב טז
דְּעָכַנִי בִּשְׁמוֹנָה בוֹ שְׂמָאלִית וִימָנִית.
הֲלֹא שְׁלָשְׁתָּן קָבַעְתִּי תַעֲנִית.
וּמֶלֶךְ יָוָן אֲנָסַנִי לִכְתֹּב דָּת, יְוָנִית.
עַל גַּבִּי חָרְשׁוּ חוֹרְשִׁים, הֶאֱרִיכוּ מַעֲנִית.
זֹעַמְתִּי בְּתִשְׁעָה בוֹ בִּכְלִמָּה וְחֵפֶר.
חָשַׂךְ מֵעָלַי מְעִיל הוֹד וְצֶפֶר.
טָרֹף טֹרַף בּוֹ הַנּוֹתֵן אִמְרֵי שֶׁפֶר.
הוּא עֶזְרָא הַסּוֹפֵר.
יוֹם עֲשִׂירִי, צֻוָּה בֶן בּוּזִי הַחוֹזֶה.
כְּתָב לְךָ בְּסֵפֶר הַמַּחֲזֶה.
לְזִכָּרוֹן לְעַם נָמֵס וְנִבְזֶה.
אֶת־עֶצֶם הַיּוֹם הַזֶּה: יחזקאל כד

The tenth was listed last among the fasts
to show the order of the months.
My own mouth gapes open with weeping and wailing,
and this chronicle of troubles burns within my heart –
as the fugitive came to me and said, "The city is crushed."

For these things I have scattered dust upon my face.
I have spoken now of all four –
would that I could shoot an arrow through my heart.
For these great torments, I have dug my own grave.
"The LORD is righteous; I have rebelled against His word." *Lam. 1*

I have called out Your name as I grieve my troubles.
Witness my oppression and hear my voice in its entreaty.
Hear my pleading, please, hasten my salvation. *Lam. 3*
Do not block Your ears to my sighing, to my cry.

‣ In the month of Tevet I was stricken sorely.
The world changed its course, from where I stand.
I was stubborn, I sinned –
yet may He reveal His goodness to me;
the One who told the ocean, "Only thus far, come."

אֵל מֶלֶךְ God, King who sits upon a throne of compassion, who acts with loving-kindness, who pardons the wrongdoings of His people, passing them before Him in order; who forgives sinners and pardons transgressors; who performs righteousness with all flesh and spirit, do not repay their bad actions in kind. ‣ God, You taught us to speak thirteen attributes: recall for us today the covenant of the thirteen attributes, as You in ancient times showed the humble one [Moses], as is written: The LORD descended in the cloud *Ex. 34* and stood with him there, and declared in the name of the LORD:

Congregation then Leader:

And the LORD passed by before him and declared: *Ex. 34*

All say aloud:

יהוה The LORD, the LORD, compassionate and generous God, slow to anger, abounding in loving-kindness and truth, extending loving-kindness to a thousand generations, forgiving wrongdoing, rebellion and sin, and absolving [the guilty who repent]. Forgive us our wrongdoing and our sin, and take us as Your inheritance.

מִנְיַן סֵדֶר חֳדָשִׁים בַּעֲשָׂרָה בּוֹ הֵעִיר.
נְהִי וִילֵל בָּמוֹ פִּי אַפְעִיר.
סֵדֶר פֻּרְעָנִיּוֹת בְּתוֹךְ לְבָבִי יִבְעִיר.
בְּבֹא אֵלַי הַפָּלִיט לֵאמֹר הֻכְּתָה הָעִיר.
עַל אֵלֶּה, עַל פְּנֵי אֲבַק זֵרִיתִי.
פַּצְתִּי עַל אַרְבַּעְתָּן, לוֹ חֵץ בְּלִבִּי יָרִיתִי.
צָרוֹת עַל אֵלֶּה, קֶבֶר לִי כָּרִיתִי.
צַדִּיק הוּא יהוה, כִּי פִיהוּ מָרִיתִי: איכה א
קָרָאתִי שִׁמְךָ, מִתְנַחֵם עַל רָעָתִי.
רְאֵה עָנְיִי וּשְׁמַע קוֹל פְּגִיעָתִי.
שְׁמַע תְּחִנָּתִי, חִישׁ נָא יְשׁוּעָתִי.
אַל־תַּעְלֵם אָזְנְךָ לְרַוְחָתִי לְשַׁוְעָתִי: איכה ג
› יֶרַח טֵבֵת, מְאֹד לָקִיתִי בּוֹ.
וְנִשְׂתָּרְגוּ עָלַי סִדְרֵי נְתִיבוֹ.
סָרַרְתִּי, פָּשַׁעְתִּי, יְגַלֶּה לִי טוּבוֹ.
הָאוֹמֵר לַיָּם עַד פֹּה תָבוֹא.

אֵל מֶלֶךְ יוֹשֵׁב עַל כִּסֵּא רַחֲמִים, מִתְנַהֵג בַּחֲסִידוּת. מוֹחֵל עֲוֹנוֹת עַמּוֹ, מַעֲבִיר רִאשׁוֹן רִאשׁוֹן. מַרְבֶּה מְחִילָה לְחַטָּאִים, וּסְלִיחָה לְפוֹשְׁעִים. עֹשֶׂה צְדָקוֹת עִם כָּל בָּשָׂר וָרוּחַ, לֹא כְרָעָתָם תִּגְמֹל. › אֵל, הוֹרֵיתָ לָּנוּ לוֹמַר שְׁלֹשׁ עֶשְׂרֵה, וּזְכָר לָנוּ הַיּוֹם בְּרִית שְׁלֹשׁ עֶשְׂרֵה, כְּמוֹ שֶׁהוֹדַעְתָּ לֶעָנָו מִקֶּדֶם, כְּמוֹ שֶׁכָּתוּב: וַיֵּרֶד יהוה בֶּעָנָן, וַיִּתְיַצֵּב עִמּוֹ שָׁם, וַיִּקְרָא בְשֵׁם, יהוה: שמות לד

שליח ציבור *then* קהל:

וַיַּעֲבֹר יהוה עַל־פָּנָיו וַיִּקְרָא שמות לד

All say aloud:

יהוה, יהוה, אֵל רַחוּם וְחַנּוּן, אֶרֶךְ אַפַּיִם, וְרַב־חֶסֶד וֶאֱמֶת: נֹצֵר חֶסֶד לָאֲלָפִים, נֹשֵׂא עָוֺן וָפֶשַׁע וְחַטָּאָה, וְנַקֵּה: וְסָלַחְתָּ לַעֲוֺנֵנוּ וּלְחַטָּאתֵנוּ, וּנְחַלְתָּנוּ:

Continue:

סְלַח לָנוּ Forgive us, our Father, for we have sinned. Pardon us, our King, for we have transgressed. For You, LORD, are good and forgiving, abounding in loving-kindness to all who call on You. *Ps. 86*

God, nations came into Your inheritance, they made Your holy Sanctuary impure, they reduced Jerusalem to ruins. God, wanton people came up against us and a gang of oppressors sought out our lives, and did not place You before them. *Ps. 79*

כְּרַחֵם As a father has compassion for his children,
so, LORD, have compassion for us.
Salvation is the LORD's; on Your people is Your blessing, Selah! *Ps. 3*
The LORD of multitudes is with us, the God of Jacob is our stronghold, Selah! *Ps. 46*
LORD of multitudes, happy is the one who trusts in You. *Ps. 84*
LORD, save! May the King answer us on the day we call. *Ps. 20*

Our God and God of our fathers:

אֶבֶן הָרֹאשָׁה The Temple, Top Stone,
is laid to ruin and ploughed over,
and the Torah's heirs, Israel, a derision among nations.

Within me an aching heart, sickened and pained –
we are left as if fatherless, become like orphans.

Israel, delicate and refined, fenced by lilies of the Law,
has now become mournful, given over to assailants.

The faithful city has become like a widow,
the countless descendants of Jacob
have been sold for no price.

Refined and delicate, worthy of royalty,
they have been ploughed across in long furrows
over many years and days.

The house of Jacob is given over to plunder,
to jeering and slander,
and the joyous city to plantations of vines.

Doused in poison by lawless ones,
is the people once desired like offerings,
like fragrant incense.

Continue:

סְלַח לָנוּ אָבִינוּ כִּי חָטָאנוּ, מְחַל לָנוּ מַלְכֵּנוּ כִּי פָשָׁעְנוּ. כִּי־אַתָּה אֲדֹנָי טוֹב וְסַלָּח, וְרַב־חֶסֶד לְכָל־קֹרְאֶיךָ: תהלים פו

אֱלֹהִים בָּאוּ גוֹיִם בְּנַחֲלָתֶךָ, טִמְּאוּ אֶת־הֵיכַל קָדְשֶׁךָ, שָׂמוּ אֶת־יְרוּשָׁלַםִ לְעִיִּים: אֱלֹהִים, זֵדִים קָמוּ עָלֵינוּ, וַעֲדַת עָרִיצִים בִּקְשׁוּ נַפְשֵׁנוּ, וְלֹא שָׂמוּךָ לְנֶגְדָּם. תהלים עט

כְּרַחֵם אָב עַל בָּנִים, כֵּן תְּרַחֵם יהוה עָלֵינוּ.

לַיהוה הַיְשׁוּעָה, עַל־עַמְּךָ בִרְכָתֶךָ סֶּלָה: תהלים ג

יהוה צְבָאוֹת עִמָּנוּ, מִשְׂגָּב לָנוּ אֱלֹהֵי יַעֲקֹב סֶלָה: תהלים מו

יהוה צְבָאוֹת, אַשְׁרֵי אָדָם בֹּטֵחַ בָּךְ: תהלים פד

יהוה הוֹשִׁיעָה, הַמֶּלֶךְ יַעֲנֵנוּ בְיוֹם־קָרְאֵנוּ: תהלים כ

אֱלֹהֵינוּ וֵאלֹהֵי אֲבוֹתֵינוּ

אֶבֶן הָרֹאשָׁה, לְעִיִּים וְלַחֲרִישָׁה
וְנוּחֲלֵי מוֹרָשָׁה, מְנוֹד רֹאשׁ בַּלְאֻמִּים.

בְּקִרְבִּי לֵב נִכְאָב, נִדְוֶה וְנִדְאָב
נִשְׁאַרְנוּ כְּאֵין אָב, וְהָיִינוּ כִּיתוֹמִים.

רַכָּה וַעֲנֻגָּה, בְּשׁוֹשַׁנִּים סוּגָה
וְעַתָּה הִיא נוּגָה, מְסוּרָה בְּיַד קָמִים.

הָיְתָה כְּאַלְמָנָה, קִרְיָה נֶאֱמָנָה
וְזֶרַע מִי מָנָה, נִמְכְּרוּ בְּלֹא דָמִים.

מְעֻנָּגָה וְרַכָּה, צָלְחָה לִמְלוּכָה
וּמְעֻנִּיתָהּ אָרְכָה, זֶה כַּמָּה שָׁנִים וְיָמִים.

בֵּית יַעֲקֹב לְבִזָּה, לְלַעַג וְלַעֲזָה
וְהָעִיר הָעַלִּיזָה, לְמַטְּעֵי כְרָמִים.

רְוּוּיָה תַרְעֵלָה, בְּיַד בְּנֵי עַוְלָה
הָרְצוּיָה כְּעוֹלָה, וְכִקְטֹרֶת הַסַּמִּים.

They have despised and neglected the Torah of Moses Avi-Zanoaḥ,
they can find no rest by night or by day.

Awesome, highest God, may the desire arise in You
to bring a year of recompense for Israel's strife.

Renew our days as of old, Dwelling Place who is our God of old.
And wash our red guilt white as wool; our stains as snow.

▸ Strengthen us in awe of You, and in the keeping of Your Law.
And come to us, in Your salvation, God who is full of compassion.

אֵל מֶלֶךְ God, King who sits upon a throne of compassion, who acts with loving-kindness, who pardons the wrongdoings of His people, passing them before Him in order; who forgives sinners and pardons transgressors; who performs righteousness with all flesh and spirit, do not repay their bad actions in kind. ▸ God, You taught us to speak thirteen attributes: recall for us today the covenant of the thirteen attributes, as You in ancient times showed the humble one [Moses], as is written: The Lord descended in the cloud and stood with him there, and declared in the name of the Lord: *Ex. 34*

Congregation then Leader:

And the Lord passed by before him and declared: *Ex. 34*

All say aloud:

יהוה The Lord, the Lord, compassionate and generous God, slow to anger, abounding in loving-kindness and truth, extending loving-kindness to a thousand generations, forgiving wrongdoing, rebellion and sin, and absolving [the guilty who repent]. Forgive us our wrongdoing and our sin, and take us as Your inheritance.

Continue:

סְלַח לָנוּ Forgive us, our Father, for we have sinned. Pardon us, our King, for we have transgressed. For You, Lord, are good and forgiving, abounding in loving-kindness to all who call on You. *Ps. 86*

The following is said responsively:

אֲבוֹתַי When my forebears trusted in the name of God, my Rock,
they grew and were successful and also gave forth fruit.
And from the time when they were drawn away
to walk with Him in enmity,
they diminished and diminished until the tenth month. *Gen. 8*

מָאֲסָה לְזְנַח, תּוֹרַת אֲבִי זָנְוֹחַ
וְלֹא מָצְאָה מָנְוֹחַ, לֵילוֹת וְגַם יָמִים.
נוֹרָא אֵל עֶלְיוֹן, מִמְּךָ יְהִי צִבְיוֹן
לְהָשִׁיב לְרִיב צִיּוֹן, שְׁנַת שִׁלּוּמִים.

חַדֵּשׁ יָמֵינוּ כְּקֶדֶם, מְעוֹנָה אֱלֹהֵי קֶדֶם
וּלְבֵן כְּצֶמֶר אָדֹם, וּכְשֶׁלֶג כְּתָמִים.
› חַזְּקֵנוּ בְּיִרְאָתֶךָ, וּבְקִיּוּם תּוֹרָתֶךָ
וּפָקְדֵנוּ בִּישׁוּעָתֶךָ, אֵל מָלֵא רַחֲמִים.

אֵל מֶלֶךְ יוֹשֵׁב עַל כִּסֵּא רַחֲמִים, מִתְנַהֵג בַּחֲסִידוּת. מוֹחֵל עֲוֹנוֹת עַמּוֹ,
מַעֲבִיר רִאשׁוֹן רִאשׁוֹן. מַרְבֶּה מְחִילָה לְחַטָּאִים, וּסְלִיחָה לְפוֹשְׁעִים. עֹשֶׂה
צְדָקוֹת עִם כָּל בָּשָׂר וָרְוּחַ, לֹא כְרָעָתָם תִּגְמֹל. › אֵל, הוֹרֵיתָ לָּנוּ לוֹמַר שְׁלֹשׁ
עֶשְׂרֵה, וּזְכָר לָנוּ הַיּוֹם בְּרִית שְׁלֹשׁ עֶשְׂרֵה, כְּמוֹ שֶׁהוֹדַעְתָּ לֶעָנָו מִקֶּדֶם,
כְּמוֹ שֶׁכָּתוּב: וַיֵּרֶד יהוה בֶּעָנָן, וַיִּתְיַצֵּב עִמּוֹ שָׁם, וַיִּקְרָא בְשֵׁם, יהוה: שמות לד

שליח ציבור then קהל:

וַיַּעֲבֹר יהוה עַל־פָּנָיו וַיִּקְרָא שמות לד

All say aloud:

יהוה, יהוה, אֵל רַחוּם וְחַנּוּן, אֶרֶךְ אַפַּיִם, וְרַב־חֶסֶד וֶאֱמֶת: נֹצֵר
חֶסֶד לָאֲלָפִים, נֹשֵׂא עָוֹן וָפֶשַׁע וְחַטָּאָה, וְנַקֵּה: וְסָלַחְתָּ לַעֲוֹנֵנוּ
וּלְחַטָּאתֵנוּ, וּנְחַלְתָּנוּ:

Continue:

סְלַח לָנוּ אָבִינוּ כִּי חָטָאנוּ, מְחַל לָנוּ מַלְכֵּנוּ כִּי פָשָׁעְנוּ. כִּי־אַתָּה אֲדֹנָי טוֹב תהלים פו
וְסַלָּח, וְרַב־חֶסֶד לְכָל־קֹרְאֶיךָ:

The following is said responsively:

אֲבוֹתַי כִּי בָטְחוּ בְּשֵׁם אֱלֹהֵי צוּרִי
גָּדְלוּ וְהִצְלִיחוּ וְגַם עָשׂוּ פֶרִי
וּמֵעֵת הֻדְּחוּ וְהָלְכוּ עִמּוֹ קֶרִי
הָיוּ הָלוֹךְ וְחָסוֹר עַד הַחֹדֶשׁ הָעֲשִׂירִי. בראשית ח

On the tenth, the king of Babylon laid siege on the city,
and beleaguered it. The chief of the army arrived,
and I was yielded to be trampled,
was tormented in shackles,
and from month to month my harp turned to grief.

Once like the first figs of a new tree,
they were the very first to be destroyed.
They spoke the names of others, and sin closed their destiny.
They did not recognize God's face and were swept off by the flood –
agony like that of a first childbirth, soars up as high as Heaven.

God brought us a day of evil and siege,
ordered enemies about me to harvest my last fruits.
The day my heart was quelled, no strength to resist,
and He said to the prophet,
"Preach this to the rebellious house."

He took the cloak of authority from the judges at the gate.
His rage burned like fire and He raised the crown away,
and He cast down the splendor of the Temple, Forest of Lebanon,
and rushing wind and storm make my flesh bristle and shiver.

Once you were called most beautiful;
now you are darkened,
for you have stumbled over wrongdoing
and your heart has turned back.
You have been attacked from behind,
have been weakened, once, then twice,
and even the slightest dressing or balm not offered you.

The Righteous One, perfect Rock,
who forgives wrongdoing almost too great to bear,
flew from the cherubs to the threshold,
and from there to a corner of the roof,
because of the wrongdoing marked out; the scream of it rose up,
their evil as great as a fruit-tree's crop.

The One who weighs the actions of people,
strengthened all my attackers,
for my days had been filled with malignant deeds,

בַּעֲשִׂירִי לַחֹדֶשׁ סָמַךְ מֶלֶךְ בָּבֶל
וְצָר עַל עִיר הַקֹּדֶשׁ, וְנִקְרַב רַב הַחוֹבֵל
נִתַּתִּי הֲדֵשׁ וְעֻנֵּיתִי בַכֶּבֶל
וְהָיָה מִדֵּי חֹדֶשׁ לְאֵבֶל כִּנּוֹרִי.

רֵאשִׁית בִּכּוּרָה לְרֵאשִׁית הַחֵרֶם
שָׂם אֲחֵרִים הִזְכִּירָה, וְהֶעָוֹן גּוֹרֵם
פְּנֵי אֵל לֹא הִכִּירָה, וְשָׁטְפָה בְּזֶרֶם
צָרָה כִּמְבַכִּירָה כָּעֵת בַּמָּרוֹם תַּמְרִיא.

הָאֱלֹהִים הֵבִיא יוֹם רָעָה וּמָצוֹר
צִוָּה צָרֵי סְבִיבַי עוֹלָלַי לִבְצוֹר
יוֹם הֵרַךְ לְבָבִי וְאֵין כֹּחַ לַעֲצוֹר
וְדִבֶּר אֶל נָבִיא, מְשֹׁל אֶל בֵּית הַמֶּרִי.

מִיּוֹשְׁבֵי שַׁעַר הֶעֱבִיר אַדֶּרֶת
חֲמָתוֹ כָּאֵשׁ בָּעַר, וְהֵרִים עֲטֶרֶת
וּמִלְּבָנוֹן יַעַר הִשְׁלִיךְ תִּפְאֶרֶת
וְרוּחַ סוֹעָה וָסַעַר תְּסַמֵּר שַׂעֲרַת בְּשָׂרִי.

יְפֵיפִית נִמְשַׁלְתְּ, וְעַתָּה קְדוֹרַנִּית
בְּעָוֹן כִּי כָשַׁלְתְּ, וְלִבֵּךְ אֲחוֹרַנִּית
זֻנְּבוּךְ וְנֶחְשַׁלְתְּ רִאשׁוֹנָה וְשֵׁנִית
וְהַחְתֵּל לֹא חֻתַּלְתְּ מְעַט צֳרִי.

צַדִּיק הַצּוּר תָּם, נָשָׂא עָוֹן נִלְאָה
מִכְּרוּב לְמִפְתָּן, לְפִנַּת גַּג דָּאָה
מֵעָוֹן הִנְכִּתָם, וְצַעֲקָתָם בָּאָה
רַבָּה רָעָתָם כְּעֵץ עֹשֶׂה פֶּרִי.

חִזֵּק כָּל קָמַי, תּוֹכֵן הָעֲלִילוֹת
כִּי מָלְאוּ יָמַי בְּרֹעַ מִפְעָלוֹת

and in the shamefulness of my youth
I forgot the good given me,
and the One who gives me my bread and water,
my flax and my wool.

My attackers opened wide their mouths and swallowed up my legacy.
They overcame me utterly, drank my blood and gulped it down.
Strangers became my enemies, they injured my brothers –
strangers who called out, "Destroy, destroy!"
Descendants of Seir the Horite.

They said, "Come, let us finish them off,
and put an end to their memory."
Jealous, vengeful God, give retribution;
let them load the burden of their own ruin.
Pay them back for their actions
and have their hopes disgrace them,
like the baker who dreamt his dream
of three baskets of white bread.

My wound was not softened, my bruise enough to kill me,
and my eyes have grown dim with watching for my bright-faced Love.
Is His anger even now not forever forgotten?
Why has He done this; why this burning rage?

This God of mine is compassionate; He shall not forever reject.
The days of my grief have grown long and still my heart sighs.
Return, God, to my tent; do not abandon Your place.
Close the days of my grief. Bring my recompense.

LORD who is the portion allotted to me,
come to me quickly, help me,
and loosen my sackcloth,
wrap me around in joy,
and dazzle my darkness with Your light – light up
the twilight I once longed for, for it is You who are my lamp.

Redeem my soul from anguish and sighing,
give Your people remission, my King and my Holy One.
And turn into relief the fast of Av;
into gladness and joy, the fast of Tammuz and the fast of Tevet.

Continue with "God, King who sits" on page 1012.

וּמִבֹּשֶׁת עֲלוּמַי שָׁכַחְתִּי גְמוּלוֹת
נוֹתֵן לַחְמִי וּמֵימַי, פִּשְׁתִּי וְצַמְרִי.

קָמַי פִּיהֶם פָּעֲרוּ וְנַחֲלָתִי בָּלְעוּ
מְאֹד עָלַי גָּבְרוּ וְדָמַי שָׁתוּ וְלָעוּ
נָכְרִים עָלַי צָרוּ וְאֶת אַחַי הֵרֵעוּ
הָאוֹמְרִים עָרוּ עָרוּ, בְּנֵי שֵׂעִיר הַחֹרִי.

אָמְרוּ לְכוּ נַכְלִם, וְנַשְׁבִּיתָה זִכְרָם
אֵל קַנּוֹא וְנוֹקֵם, גְּמָלֵם, יִשְׂאוּ אֶת שִׁבְרָם
כְּמַעֲשֵׂיהֶם שַׁלֵּם וְיֵבוֹשׁוּ מִשִּׁבְרָם
כְּאִישׁ חָלוּם חוֹלֵם שְׁלֹשָׁה סַלֵּי חֹרִי.

פְּצָעַי לֹא רֻכְּכָה וְחַבּוּרוֹתַי רֶצַח
וְעֵינִי הַכֵּהֲתָה, צוֹפָה לְדוֹדִי צַח
הַעוֹד לֹא שָׁכְכָה חֲמָתוֹ לָנֶצַח
עַל מֶה עָשָׂה כָּכָה וּמֶה חֳרִי.

רַחוּם זֶה אֵלִי, אַל לָעַד תִּזְנַח
אָרְכוּ יְמֵי אֶבְלִי וְעוֹד לִבִּי נֶאֱנַח
שׁוּבָה אֶל לְאָהֳלִי, מְקוֹמְךָ אַל תַּנַּח
שַׁלֵּם יְמֵי אֶבְלִי כִּי תָבוֹא עַל שְׂכָרִי.

יהוה מְנָת חֶלְקִי, חוּשָׁה לִּי לְעֶזְרָה
וּפִתַּחְתָּ שַׂקִּי, שִׂמְחָה לִי לְאַזְרָה
וְתַגִּיהַּ אֶת חָשְׁכִּי בְּאוֹרְךָ לְהָאִירָה
אֶת נֶשֶׁף חִשְׁקִי, כִּי אַתָּה נֵרִי.

מִיגוֹן וַאֲנָחָה, פְּדֵה אֵל אֶת נַפְשִׁי
עֲשֵׂה לְעַמְּךָ הֲנָחָה, מַלְכִּי וּקְדוֹשִׁי
תַּהֲפוֹךְ לִרְוָחָה אֶת צוֹם הַחֲמִישִׁי
לְשָׂשׂוֹן וּלְשִׂמְחָה, צוֹם הָרְבִיעִי וְצוֹם הָעֲשִׂירִי.

Continue with אֵל מֶלֶךְ יוֹשֵׁב *on page 1013.*

SELIḤOT FOR THE FAST OF ESTHER

סְלַח לָנוּ Forgive us, our Father, for in our great foolishness we have blundered. Pardon us, our King, for our wrongdoings are many.

אֵל אֶרֶךְ You are a God slow to anger, You are called the Master of Compassion, and You have taught the way of repentance. May You remember today and every day the greatness of Your compassion and kindness, for the sake of the descendants of Your beloved ones. Turn toward us in compassion, for You are the Master of Compassion. We come before You in plea and prayer, as You in ancient times showed the humble one [Moses]. Turn from Your fierce anger, as is written in Your Torah. In the shadow of Your wings may we shelter and abide, as on the day when the Lord descended in the cloud. ▸ Disregard crimes and erase guilt as on the day You stood with him [Moses] there. Hear our cry and listen to our word, as on the day You declared in the name of the Lord, and there it is written:

Congregation then Leader:

And the Lord passed by before him and declared: *Ex. 34*

All say aloud:

יהוה The Lord, the Lord, compassionate and generous God, slow to anger, abounding in loving-kindness and truth, extending loving-kindness to a thousand generations, forgiving wrongdoing, rebellion and sin, and absolving [the guilty who repent]. Forgive us our wrongdoing and our sin, and take us as Your inheritance.

Continue:

סְלַח לָנוּ Forgive us, our Father, for we have sinned. Pardon us, our King, for we have transgressed. For You, Lord, are good and forgiving, abounding in *Ps. 86*
loving-kindness to all who call on You.

We have waited patiently for the Lord, and He has turned toward us and heard *Is. 26*
our cry. And on the path of Your laws, Lord, we have waited for You, for it is Your name and Your memory that are our souls' desire.

כְּרַחֵם As a father has compassion for his children,
so, Lord, have compassion for us.
Salvation is the Lord's; on Your people is Your blessing, Selah! *Ps. 3*
The Lord of multitudes is with us, the God of Jacob is our stronghold, Selah! *Ps. 46*
Lord of multitudes, happy is the one who trusts in You. *Ps. 84*
Lord, save! May the King answer us on the day we call. *Ps. 20*

סליחות לתענית אסתר

סְלַח לָנוּ, אָבִינוּ, כִּי בְּרֹב אִוַּלְתֵּנוּ שָׁגִינוּ.
מְחַל לָנוּ, מַלְכֵּנוּ, כִּי רַבּוּ עֲוֹנֵינוּ.

אֵל אֶרֶךְ אַפַּיִם אַתָּה, וּבַעַל הָרַחֲמִים נִקְרֵאתָ, וְדֶרֶךְ תְּשׁוּבָה הוֹרֵיתָ. גְּדֻלַּת רַחֲמֶיךָ וַחֲסָדֶיךָ, תִּזְכֹּר הַיּוֹם וּבְכָל יוֹם לְזֶרַע יְדִידֶיךָ. תֵּפֶן אֵלֵינוּ בְּרַחֲמִים, כִּי אַתָּה הוּא בַּעַל הָרַחֲמִים. בְּתַחֲנוּן וּבִתְפִלָּה פָּנֶיךָ נְקַדֵּם, כְּהוֹדַעְתָּ לֶעָנָו מִקֶּדֶם. מֵחֲרוֹן אַפְּךָ שׁוּב, כְּמוֹ בְּתוֹרָתְךָ כָּתוּב. וּבְצֵל כְּנָפֶיךָ נֶחֱסֶה וְנִתְלוֹנָן, כְּיוֹם וַיֵּרֶד יהוה בֶּעָנָן. ‹ תַּעֲבֹר עַל פֶּשַׁע וְתִמְחֶה אָשָׁם, כְּיוֹם וַיִּתְיַצֵּב עִמּוֹ שָׁם. תַּאֲזִין שַׁוְעָתֵנוּ וְתַקְשִׁיב מֶנּוּ מַאֲמָר, כְּיוֹם וַיִּקְרָא בְשֵׁם יהוה, וְשָׁם נֶאֱמַר

קהל then שליח ציבור:

וַיַּעֲבֹר יהוה עַל־פָּנָיו וַיִּקְרָא שמות לד

All say aloud:

יהוה, יהוה, אֵל רַחוּם וְחַנּוּן, אֶרֶךְ אַפַּיִם, וְרַב־חֶסֶד וֶאֱמֶת: נֹצֵר חֶסֶד לָאֲלָפִים, נֹשֵׂא עָוֹן וָפֶשַׁע וְחַטָּאָה, וְנַקֵּה: וְסָלַחְתָּ לַעֲוֹנֵנוּ וּלְחַטָּאתֵנוּ, וּנְחַלְתָּנוּ:

Continue:

סְלַח לָנוּ אָבִינוּ כִּי חָטָאנוּ, מְחַל לָנוּ מַלְכֵּנוּ כִּי פָשָׁעְנוּ. כִּי־אַתָּה אֲדֹנָי טוֹב וְסַלָּח, וְרַב־חֶסֶד לְכָל־קֹרְאֶיךָ: תהלים פו

קַוֵּה קִוִּינוּ יהוה, וַיֵּט אֵלֵינוּ וַיִּשְׁמַע שַׁוְעָתֵנוּ. אַף אֹרַח מִשְׁפָּטֶיךָ יהוה קִוִּינוּךָ, לְשִׁמְךָ וּלְזִכְרְךָ תַּאֲוַת־נָפֶשׁ: ישעיה כו

כְּרַחֵם אָב עַל בָּנִים, כֵּן תְּרַחֵם יהוה עָלֵינוּ.
לַיהוה הַיְשׁוּעָה, עַל־עַמְּךָ בִרְכָתֶךָ סֶּלָה: תהלים ג
יהוה צְבָאוֹת עִמָּנוּ, מִשְׂגָּב לָנוּ אֱלֹהֵי יַעֲקֹב סֶלָה: תהלים מו
יהוה צְבָאוֹת, אַשְׁרֵי אָדָם בֹּטֵחַ בָּךְ: תהלים פד
יהוה הוֹשִׁיעָה, הַמֶּלֶךְ יַעֲנֵנוּ בְיוֹם־קָרְאֵנוּ: תהלים כ

▸ Forgive, please, this people's wrongdoing, in the abundance of Your kindness, *Num. 14*
and as You have forgiven this people from the time of Egypt until now,
and there it is written:

Congregation then Leader:

And the LORD said, I have forgiven as you asked.

Continue:

הַטֵּה Give ear, my God and hear; open Your eyes and see our desolation, and the city that bears Your name, for it is not on the strength of our righteousness that we throw down our pleadings before You, but on the strength of Your great compassion. LORD, hear me; LORD, forgive, LORD, listen and act and do not delay – for Your sake, my God; for Your city and Your people bear Your name. *Dan. 9*

Our God and God of our fathers:

אָדָם When a man rose up against us, convulsions of trembling seized us.
When he attached himself to a government of flattery, we almost stumbled and fell.
They cheerfully closed an agreement to sell us,
as a person with an unwanted mound gives it away quite freely
to one with an unwanted pit.
There was no defense.
They said, "Come, let us annihilate them from among nations: *Ps. 83*
the name of Israel shall be recalled no more."

My eyes turned heavenward and I called on You to curse my enemies:
"Cut off name and remnant; expunge their name, let it rot.
And be Enemy to my enemies; bring them down in the very deceptions
with which they deceived the people of Jacob."
And they said, "The LORD will not see; *Ps. 94*
the God of Jacob will not comprehend."

Yet God tormented the scattered ones and made them mournful –
but did not mean to destroy them utterly.
They were guilty on the face of things, and so He terrorized them.
By the taking off of a ring, He made them tremble.
But God fulfilled the good of His word, raising them up in the view of nations.
"In their enemies' land He did not reject them, *Lev. 26*
and did not detest them to the point of destruction."

He revealed the premonition of events for a nation begrimed and scratched over.
He wrote "I shall surely hide (*astir*) Myself" to hint at Esther,
and fragrant "pure myrrh," translated "mar-dokh," to hint at Mordekhai;
all to put an end to Haman on the morrow, "From (*hamin*) the tree" foreshadowing his gallows.
"In place of the thorn bush, shall rise up a cypress, *Is. 55*
and in place of the nettle, shall rise up myrtle."

סְלַח־נָא לַעֲוֹן הָעָם הַזֶּה כְּגֹדֶל חַסְדֶּךָ במדבר יד
וְכַאֲשֶׁר נָשָׂאתָה לָעָם הַזֶּה מִמִּצְרַיִם וְעַד־הֵנָּה:
וְשָׁם נֶאֱמַר

קהל *then* שליח ציבור:

וַיֹּאמֶר יהוה, סָלַחְתִּי כִּדְבָרֶךָ:

Continue:

הַטֵּה אֱלֹהַי אָזְנְךָ וּשְׁמָע, פְּקַח עֵינֶיךָ וּרְאֵה שֹׁמְמֹתֵינוּ וְהָעִיר אֲשֶׁר־נִקְרָא דניאל ט
שִׁמְךָ עָלֶיהָ, כִּי לֹא עַל־צִדְקֹתֵינוּ אֲנַחְנוּ מַפִּילִים תַּחֲנוּנֵינוּ לְפָנֶיךָ, כִּי עַל־
רַחֲמֶיךָ הָרַבִּים: אֲדֹנָי שְׁמָעָה, אֲדֹנָי סְלָחָה, אֲדֹנָי הַקְשִׁיבָה וַעֲשֵׂה אַל־
תְּאַחַר, לְמַעַנְךָ אֱלֹהַי, כִּי־שִׁמְךָ נִקְרָא עַל־עִירְךָ וְעַל־עַמֶּךָ:

אֱלֹהֵינוּ וֵאלֹהֵי אֲבוֹתֵינוּ

אָדָם בְּקוּם עָלֵינוּ, חִיל אֲחָזָתְנוּ לִרְעֹד.
בְּהִסְתַּפְּחוֹ לְמַלְכוּת חָנֵף, כִּמְעַט כָּשַׁלְנוּ לִמְעֹד.
גָּמְרוּ לְמָכְרֵנוּ כְּתָל וְחָרִיץ בְּלִי מִסְעוֹד.
אָמְרוּ לְכוּ וְנַכְחִידֵם מִגּוֹי, וְלֹא־יִזָּכֵר שֵׁם־יִשְׂרָאֵל עוֹד: תהלים פג

דַּלּוּ עֵינַי לַמָּרוֹם, קְרָאתִיךָ אוֹיְבַי לָקֹב.
הַכְרֵת שֵׁם וּשְׁאָר, וּמְחוֹת שֵׁם לִרְקֹב.
וְצָר צוֹרְרֵי בְּנִכְלֵיהֶם אֲשֶׁר נִכְּלוּ לַעֲקֹב.
וַיֹּאמְרוּ, לֹא יִרְאֶה־יָּהּ, וְלֹא־יָבִין אֱלֹהֵי יַעֲקֹב: תהלים צד

זְרוּיִים עָנָה וְיָגָה, וְלֹא מִלֵּב לְכַלּוֹתָם.
חָבוּ לְפָנִים, וְרָדָם בַּהֲסָרַת טַבַּעַת לְהַחֲלוֹתָם.
טוּב דְּבָרוֹ הֵקִים לְעֵינֵי הַגּוֹיִם לְהַעֲלוֹתָם.
בִּהְיוֹתָם בְּאֶרֶץ אֹיְבֵיהֶם לֹא־מְאַסְתִּים וְלֹא־גְעַלְתִּים לְכַלֹּתָם: ויקרא כו

יָדַע רֶמֶז הַקּוֹרוֹת לָעָם מֵעֵפֶר וּמֵהֲדָס.
כָּתַב הַסֵּתֶר אֶסְתֵּיר וּמָר דְּרוֹר מְפֻרְדָּס.
לְשַׁבֵּת הָמָן מִמָּחֳרָת, הַמָּן הָעֵץ קִנְדָּס.
תַּחַת הַנַּעֲצוּץ יַעֲלֶה בְרוֹשׁ וְתַחַת הַסִּרְפַּד יַעֲלֶה הֲדַס: ישעיה נה

The king who listened to lies, dictated accusation and sorrow.
He wrapped himself in priestly clothes, Ahasuerus,
having mistaken his reckoning of the End.
He ordered "other vessels" to be used,
from the Quarry from which the world was hewn;
and the devil too, came and placed himself among them. *Job 2*

When the people in Shushan ate of their destroyer's meat,
the king opened his mouth wide to accuse them,
to give them over into the hands of the one who was ready to pay their price.
The Rock, meanwhile, agreed to write a letter to destroy their hope;
"I said that I would yield them up, *Deut. 32*
would put an end to their memory among mankind."

The angels, messengers of peace, wept bitterly, crying out,
"Compassionate One, look to the covenant and do not break it, pushing it away!"
The Torah, too, heard of it and put on clothes of widowhood and sorrow;
and she laid her hands upon her head and walked along, *II Sam. 13*
crying as she went.

[Elijah] The Tishbite wrapped a covering of sackcloth around his waist.
He hurried and told the three fathers who sleep in the Cave of Makhpelah,
and then hastened to the Shepherd, [Moses] –
"What do you mean by sleeping?
Rouse yourself! Get up and call out to your God – *Jonah 1*
perhaps He may change His mind!"

He told [Mordekhai] Bilshan of the pronouncement
that had been sealed in clay – but not in blood.
They learnt from the example of Nineveh
how to overturn anger after a decree;
the son of Kish knocked at the door of the school,
and covered himself in sackcloth and sat down on the earth. *Jonah 3*

For three days he gathered the children before him –
thirsty, hidden from by God – so that, in the voice of Jacob,
they might weaken the hand of the bold-faced king.
His hands raised steadily to God, Mordekhai prayed,
"Save us now from insult;
that he should not come and slaughter us, *Gen. 32*
mothers and children together."

Those and those, from all sides, the children of my mighty ones and teachers,
all cried out, and their plea rose up to the Lord.
And God, when those plaintive calls reached Him, asked,
"And what is this bleating of sheep that meets My ears?" *I Sam. 15*

מַקְשִׁיב דְּבַר שֶׁקֶר כָּתַב שִׂטְנָה וָעֶצֶב.
נִתְעַטֵּף בְּבִגְדֵי שְׂרָד כְּטֹעֶה בְּמִנְיַן קֶצֶב.
סִדֵּר לְהִשְׁתַּמֵּשׁ בְּשׁוֹנִים כְּלֵי הַמַּחְצֵב.
וַיָּבוֹא גַם־הַשָּׂטָן בְּתֹכָם לְהִתְיַצֵּב: איוב ב

עִם הַנִּמְצָאִים בְּשׁוּשַׁן, בְּאָכְלָם מִזֶּבַח עוֹכְרָם.
פָּעַר פִּיו לְהַשְׂטִינָם, וּלְהַסְגִּירָם בְּיַד נוֹתֵן מִכְרָם.
צוֹר הִסְכִּים לִכְתֹּב אִגֶּרֶת לְאַבֵּד שִׁבְרָם.
אָמַרְתִּי אַפְאֵיהֶם, אַשְׁבִּיתָה מֵאֱנוֹשׁ זִכְרָם: דברים לב

קְדוֹשִׁים מַלְאֲכֵי שָׁלוֹם מַר יִבְכָּיוּן בִּצְעָקָה.
רַחוּם הַבֵּט לַבְּרִית וְאַל תָּפֵר לְהַרְחִיקָה.
שָׁמְעָה מוֹרָשָׁה, וַתִּלְבַּשׁ בִּגְדֵי אַלְמְנוּת וּמוּעָקָה.
וַתָּשֶׂם יָדָהּ עַל־רֹאשָׁהּ, וַתֵּלֶךְ הָלוֹךְ וְזָעָקָה: שמואל ב׳ יג

תִּשְׁבִּי שָׂם אֵזוֹר שַׂק בְּמָתְנָיו תַּחְבֹּשֶׁת.
מִהֵר וְהוֹדִיעַ יְשֵׁנֵי מַכְפֵּל, אָבוֹת שְׁלֹשֶׁת.
נָחַץ לְרוֹעֶה, מַה לְּךָ נִרְדָּם לְהִתְעַשֵּׁת.
קוּם קְרָא אֶל־אֱלֹהֶיךָ, אוּלַי יִתְעַשֵּׁת: יונה א

חוֹתַם טִיט אֲשֶׁר נַעֲשָׂה, לְבִלְשָׁן סִפֵּר.
מִנִּינְוֵה לָמְדוּ לְאַחַר גְּזֵרָה כַּעַס לְהָפֵר.
בֶּן קִישׁ הִקִּישׁ דַּלְתוֹת בֵּית הַסֵּפֶר.
וַיְכַס שַׂק, וַיֵּשֶׁב עַל־הָאֵפֶר: יונה ג

רִבֵּץ תִּינוֹקוֹת לְפָנָיו יָמִים שְׁלֹשָׁה, צְמֵאִים וּמְכֻפָּנִים.
בְּקוֹל יַעֲקֹב לְחַלֵּשׁ יְדֵי עַז פָּנִים.
יָדָיו אֱמוּנָה לָאֵל, הַצִּילֵנִי נָא מֵעֲלָבוֹנִים.
פֶּן־יָבוֹא וְהִכַּנִי אֵם עַל־בָּנִים: בראשית לב

מִזֶּה אֵלֶּה וּמִזֶּה אֵלֶּה, בְּנֵי אֵיתָנַי וְרַבָּנַי.
כֻּלָּם צָעֲקוּ, וַתַּעַל שַׁוְעָתָם אֶל יהוה.
יָהּ, לְקוֹל רִנּוּן כָּבוֹא, שָׁאַל לְפָנָי.
וּמֶה קוֹל־הַצֹּאן הַזֶּה בְּאָזְנָי: שמואל א׳ טו

The shepherd Moses answered Him,
"These are the little ones of the holy offspring.
LORD, save ones condemned to die, from the evil enemy."
The compassion of the Generous One was stirred,
and He was moved to weep for what had happened.
And so it was that when the King of Israel read the letter, *II Kings 5*
He tore it to pieces.

The Jew suspended sons below and father above.
Each man covered three *amot*; the fourth *amah* above was space exposed.
Mordekhai saw a double revenge, was delighted, and spoke praises:
"I was returned to my post and he was hanged!" *Gen. 41*

Esther wrote with emphasis,
that a Hallel of thanks should be read on that day;
and what the beloved ones accepted down below was established above.
A banner shall be raised by those who bear witness,
to make the wonder known now, as it was then.
And at this time – may relief and salvation rise up for the Jews. *Esther 4*

אֵל מֶלֶךְ God, King who sits upon a throne of compassion, who acts with loving-kindness, who pardons the wrongdoings of His people, passing them before Him in order; who forgives sinners and pardons transgressors; who performs righteousness with all flesh and spirit, do not repay their bad actions in kind. God, You taught us to speak thirteen attributes: recall for us today the covenant of the thirteen attributes, as You in ancient times showed the humble one [Moses], as is written: The LORD descended in the cloud and stood with him there, and declared in the name of the LORD:

Congregation then Leader:

And the LORD passed by before him and declared: *Ex. 34*

All say aloud:

יהוה The LORD, the LORD, compassionate and generous God, slow to anger, abounding in loving-kindness and truth, extending loving-kindness to a thousand generations, forgiving wrongdoing, rebellion and sin, and absolving [the guilty who repent]. Forgive us our wrongdoing and our sin, and take us as Your inheritance.

Continue:

סְלַח לָנוּ Forgive us, our Father, for we have sinned. Pardon us, our King, for we have transgressed. For You, LORD, are good and forgiving, abounding in loving-kindness to all who call on You. *Ps. 86*

רוֹעֶה הֱשִׁיבוֹ, הֵם קְטַנֵּי קֹדֶשׁ זֶרַע.
יָהּ, הַצֵּל לְקוּחִים לַמָּוֶת מֵאוֹיֵב הָרָע.
חַנּוּן נִכְמְרוּ רַחֲמָיו וַיְבַקֵּשׁ לִבְכּוֹת הַמְאֹרָע.
מלכים ב׳ ה וַיְהִי כִּקְרֹא מֶלֶךְ־יִשְׂרָאֵל אֶת־הַסֵּפֶר, וַיִּקְרַע:

יְהוּדִי הוֹקִיעַ, יְלָדָיו לְמַטָּה וַאֲבִיהֶם לְמַעְלָה.
אִישׁ אִישׁ בְּשָׁלֹשׁ אַמּוֹת, וְהָרְבִיעִית אֲוִיר מְגֻלָּה.
מִשְׁנֶה נָקַם חָזָה, וְדָתָה וְשָׂמַח וְשָׂשׂ תְּהִלָּה.
בראשית מא אֹתִי הֵשִׁיב עַל־כַּנִּי וְאֹתוֹ תָלָה:

◂ וַתִּכְתֹּב אֶסְתֵּר תֹּקֶף, לִקְרֹא כְּבְהַלֵּל מְהוֹדִים.
מִלְמַעְלָה קִיְּמוּ מַה שֶּׁקִּבְּלוּ לְמַטָּה דוֹדִים.
נֵס יְנוֹסֵס לְפַרְסֵם כְּאָז פְּלָאוֹ מְסַהֲדִים.
אסתר ד בָּעֵת הַזֹּאת רֶוַח וְהַצָּלָה יַעֲמוֹד לַיְּהוּדִים:

אֵל מֶלֶךְ יוֹשֵׁב עַל כִּסֵּא רַחֲמִים, מִתְנַהֵג בַּחֲסִידוּת. מוֹחֵל עֲוֹנוֹת עַמּוֹ, מַעֲבִיר רִאשׁוֹן רִאשׁוֹן. מַרְבֶּה מְחִילָה לְחַטָּאִים, וּסְלִיחָה לְפוֹשְׁעִים. עֹשֶׂה צְדָקוֹת עִם כָּל בָּשָׂר וָרוּחַ, לֹא כְרָעָתָם תִּגְמֹל. ◂ אֵל, הוֹרֵיתָ לָּנוּ לוֹמַר שְׁלשׁ עֶשְׂרֵה, וּזְכָר לָנוּ הַיּוֹם בְּרִית שְׁלשׁ עֶשְׂרֵה, כְּמוֹ שֶׁהוֹדַעְתָּ לֶעָנָו מִקֶּדֶם, כְּמוֹ שֶׁכָּתוּב: וַיֵּרֶד יהוה בֶּעָנָן, וַיִּתְיַצֵּב עִמּוֹ שָׁם, וַיִּקְרָא בְשֵׁם, יהוה:

קהל then שליח ציבור:

שמות לד וַיַּעֲבֹר יהוה עַל־פָּנָיו וַיִּקְרָא

All say aloud:

יהוה, יהוה, אֵל רַחוּם וְחַנּוּן, אֶרֶךְ אַפַּיִם, וְרַב־חֶסֶד וֶאֱמֶת: נֹצֵר חֶסֶד לָאֲלָפִים, נֹשֵׂא עָוֹן וָפֶשַׁע וְחַטָּאָה, וְנַקֵּה: וְסָלַחְתָּ לַעֲוֹנֵנוּ וּלְחַטָּאתֵנוּ, וּנְחַלְתָּנוּ:

Continue:

תהלים פו סְלַח לָנוּ אָבִינוּ כִּי חָטָאנוּ, מְחַל לָנוּ מַלְכֵּנוּ כִּי פָשָׁעְנוּ. כִּי־אַתָּה אֲדֹנָי טוֹב וְסַלָּח, וְרַב־חֶסֶד לְכָל־קֹרְאֶיךָ:

כִּי־עִמְּךָ For in You there is a wellspring of life; in Your light shall we see light. *Ps. 36*
As we call You, God of our righteousness, answer us. In a narrow place You
have opened out our horizon; be generous to us and hear our prayer. And *Num. 14*
now let the strength of the LORD be great, as You have said.

כְּרַחֵם As a father has compassion for his children,
so, LORD, have compassion for us.
Salvation is the LORD's; on Your people is Your blessing, Selah! *Ps. 3*
The LORD of multitudes is with us, *Ps. 46*
the God of Jacob is our stronghold, Selah!
LORD of multitudes, happy is the one who trusts in You. *Ps. 84*
LORD, save! May the King answer us on the day we call. *Ps. 20*

Our God and God of our fathers:

אַתָּה הָאֵל It is You who are the God of wonders.
You have made known among nations
Your terrifying strength.
You redeemed Your people by might from torments,
suppressed their enemies with ignominious death.

When the enemy rose to awaken strife,
and seemed about to cut down the exquisite flowers, Israel,
he plotted to measure out into the masters' treasuries,
a hundred times the silver talents
of the sockets in the Tabernacle.

You warned Your lambs
to announce the shekel offering early;
You knew what would be.
You warned us to be punctual,
and to find a way to douse the fire
of ones who sought to burn us.
And so, those once condemned to death –
are marked out for resurrection.

When (for appearances,) they worshiped a narrow image,
they were yielded up to be clipped off:
all those offshoots and grapes.
Traps surrounded them on all sides;
they turned their eyes to You,
they were concealed in Your hiddenness.

כִּי־עִמְּךָ מְקוֹר חַיִּים, בְּאוֹרְךָ נִרְאֶה־אוֹר: בְּקָרְאֵנוּ עֲנֵנוּ אֱלֹהֵי צִדְקֵנוּ, תהלים לו
בַּצָּר הִרְחַבְתָּ לָּנוּ, חָנֵּנוּ וּשְׁמַע תְּפִלָּתֵנוּ. וְעַתָּה יִגְדַּל־נָא כֹּחַ אֲדֹנָי, כַּאֲשֶׁר במדבר יד
דִּבַּרְתָּ לֵאמֹר:

כְּרַחֵם אָב עַל בָּנִים, כֵּן תְּרַחֵם יהוה עָלֵינוּ.
לַיהוה הַיְשׁוּעָה, עַל־עַמְּךָ בִרְכָתֶךָ סֶּלָה: תהלים ג
יהוה צְבָאוֹת עִמָּנוּ, מִשְׂגָּב לָנוּ אֱלֹהֵי יַעֲקֹב סֶלָה: תהלים מו
יהוה צְבָאוֹת, אַשְׁרֵי אָדָם בֹּטֵחַ בָּךְ: תהלים פד
יהוה הוֹשִׁיעָה, הַמֶּלֶךְ יַעֲנֵנוּ בְיוֹם־קָרְאֵנוּ: תהלים כ

אֱלֹהֵינוּ וֵאלֹהֵי אֲבוֹתֵינוּ

אַתָּה הָאֵל עוֹשֵׂה פְלָאוֹת
בָּעַמִּים הוֹדַעְתָּ עֹז נוֹרָאוֹת
גָּאַלְתָּ בִּזְרוֹעַ עַמְּךָ מִתְּלָאוֹת
דִּכִּיתָ צָרֵיהֶם בְּמוֹתֵי תַחֲלוּאוֹת.

הָאוֹיֵב בְּקוּמוֹ לְעוֹרֵר מְדָנִים
וְדִמָּה לְהַכְרִית פִּרְחֵי עֲדָנִים
זָמַם לִשְׁקֹל לְגִנְזֵי אֲדוֹנִים
חֲלִיפֵי מְאַת כִּכְּרֵי אֲדָנִים.

טְלָאֶיךָ הִזְהַרְתָּ שִׁקְלֵיהֶם לְהַקְדִּים
יָדַעְתָּ הָעֲתִידוֹת וְדָרַשְׁתָּ נִשְׁקָדִים
כְּבוּי לְהַמְצִיא לְלַהַב יוֹקְדִים
לְקוּחִים לַמָּוֶת לְתֶחִי נִפְקָדִים.

מְסִבָּה צָרָה בְּעָבְדָם לְפָנִים
נִמְסְרוּ לְהַתֵּז קְנוֹקְנוֹת וּגְפָנִים
סְבָבוּם מוֹקְשִׁים בְּכָל דְּפָנִים
עֵינֵיהֶם לְךָ תוֹלִים וּבְסִתְרְךָ נִצְפָּנִים.

The lots were overturned,
they ruled over their enemies,
and the gallows was prepared to receive
Haman the Agagite.
God struck and swallowed the façade
of covering that covered,
and He entombed His people's enemies in darkness.

Peace and truth were written on all sides;
power of salvation, steady rock and fortress.
The plunderer was plundered,
he was caught in his own trap.
The one who spoke against me was swept away;
destroyed; eyed disdainfully.

The people made celebrations,
and these were fixed for all generations.
Amalek had entered the Scriptures three times –
how could there be a fourth?
Yet on High it was agreed and here below it was sealed,
and the reason for all that had been fixed,
was inscribed in the scroll.

Your hand is lifted high to forgive sinners.
You set Mordekhai the Jew and Hadassah Esther
in their place as saviors,
and now their righteousness remains forever to delight us,
and the study of their honor
to recall to You those who were saved.

Be zealous for Your name, Awesome and Sanctified One.
Witness Your vineyard, destroyed, trampled;
gather our scattered ones
and their song to You will be renewed.
Sustain them and revive them with the building of the Temple.

▸ And as You did awe-inspiring things in those days,
so perform with us the wonder of salvation for all time.
Find in Your presence our ransom, our appeasement –
God, King who sits upon a throne of compassion.

פּוּר נֶהְפַּךְ בְּאוֹיְבִים לִשְׁלֹט
צְלִיבָה הוּכַן אֲגָגִי לִקְלֹט
קְלַע וּבְלַע פְּנֵי הַלּוֹט הַלּוֹט
רִיבִי עַם בְּאַשְׁמַנִּים לַעֲלֹט.

שָׁלוֹם וֶאֱמֶת נִכְתַּב מִכָּל צַד
תְּקֹף יֶשַׁע סֶלַע וּמְצָד
שׁוֹדֵד הַשֻּׁדַּד וּבְרִשְׁתּוֹ נוֹצַד
מְדָנֵי נִסְחַף נִצְמַת וְנִרְצַד.

עָשׂוּ שִׂמְחוֹת וּלְדוֹרוֹת קְבָעוּם
וּמִקְרָאוֹת שְׁלֹשׁוּם וְלֹא רִבְּעוּם
נִסְכְּמוּ מִמַּעַל וּלְמַטָּה טְבָעוּם
בְּסֵפֶר נֶחְקַק עַל מָה קְבָעוּם.

רָמָה יָדְךָ לִסְלֹחַ לַפּוֹשְׁעִים
יְהוּדִי וַהֲדַסָּה הֻקְמַת מוֹשִׁיעִים
צִדְקָתָם עוֹמֶדֶת לָעַד לְשַׁעֲשׁוּעִים
חֵקֶר כְּבוֹדָם לְהִזָּכֵר לְנוֹשָׁעִים.

קַנֵּא לְשִׁמְךָ נוֹרָא וְנִקְדָּשׁ
חָזֵה כַּרְמְךָ נֶהֱרָס וְנָדָשׁ
זֵרוּיֵינוּ קַבֵּץ וְשִׁיר לְךָ יְחֻדָּשׁ
קִיְּמֵם וְהַחַיִּם בְּבִנְיַן בֵּית הַמִּקְדָּשׁ.

‹ וּכְעָשׂוּתְךָ נוֹרָאוֹת בְּאוֹתָן הַיָּמִים
אִתָּנוּ הַפְלֵא תְּשׁוּעַת עוֹלָמִים
מְצוֹא לְפָנֶיךָ כֹּפֶר וְתַנְחוּמִים
אֵל מֶלֶךְ יוֹשֵׁב עַל כִּסֵּא רַחֲמִים.

God, King who sits upon a throne of compassion, who acts with loving-kindness, who pardons the wrongdoings of His people, passing them before Him in order; who forgives sinners and pardons transgressors; who performs righteousness with all flesh and spirit, do not repay their bad actions in kind. ▸ God, You taught us to speak thirteen attributes: recall for us today the covenant of the thirteen attributes, as You in ancient times showed the humble one [Moses], as is written: The LORD descended in the cloud and stood with him there, and declared in the name of the LORD:

Congregation then Leader:

And the LORD passed by before him and declared: *Ex. 34*

All say aloud:

יהוה The LORD, the LORD, compassionate and generous God, slow to anger, abounding in loving-kindness and truth, extending loving-kindness to a thousand generations, forgiving wrongdoing, rebellion and sin, and absolving [the guilty who repent]. Forgive us our wrongdoing and our sin, and take us as Your inheritance.

Continue:

סְלַח לָנוּ Forgive us, our Father, for we have sinned. Pardon us, our King, for we have transgressed. For You, LORD, are good and forgiving, abounding in loving-kindness to all who call on You. *Ps. 86*

The following is said responsively:

Small of number we stand pleading before You:
do not block Your ears to the cry of people crushed.
Listen to their entreaty from the Heaven where You are present,
as You saved Your children
in the days of Myrrh and Myrtle [Mordekhai and Esther].

> On Israel's praises You sit enthroned, hearing their cry,
> listening to their prayer.
> Bringing healing even before the blow,
> counting it out to help the ones You have acquired;
> to settle their homes again.

A foe and enemy fixed his eyes like knives on Israel;
he opened wide his mouth to swallow up the humble man.
He deliberated within him to destroy Mordekhai's great community;
in the letter, he etched his intent to destroy the treasured people.

אֵל מֶלֶךְ יוֹשֵׁב עַל כִּסֵּא רַחֲמִים, מִתְנַהֵג בַּחֲסִידוּת. מוֹחֵל עֲוֹנוֹת עַמּוֹ, מַעֲבִיר רִאשׁוֹן רִאשׁוֹן. מַרְבֶּה מְחִילָה לְחַטָּאִים, וּסְלִיחָה לְפוֹשְׁעִים. עֹשֶׂה צְדָקוֹת עִם כָּל בָּשָׂר וָרְוּחַ, לֹא כְרָעָתָם תִּגְמֹל. ◀ אֵל, הוֹרֵיתָ לָנוּ לוֹמַר שְׁלֹשׁ עֶשְׂרֵה, וּזְכָר לָנוּ הַיּוֹם בְּרִית שְׁלֹשׁ עֶשְׂרֵה, כְּמוֹ שֶׁהוֹדַעְתָּ לֶעָנָו מִקֶּדֶם, כְּמוֹ שֶׁכָּתוּב: וַיֵּרֶד יהוה בֶּעָנָן, וַיִּתְיַצֵּב עִמּוֹ שָׁם, וַיִּקְרָא בְשֵׁם, יהוה:

שליח ציבור then קהל:

וַיַּעֲבֹר יהוה עַל־פָּנָיו וַיִּקְרָא שמות לד

All say aloud:

יהוה, יהוה, אֵל רַחוּם וְחַנּוּן, אֶרֶךְ אַפַּיִם, וְרַב־חֶסֶד וֶאֱמֶת: נֹצֵר חֶסֶד לָאֲלָפִים, נֹשֵׂא עָוֹן וָפֶשַׁע וְחַטָּאָה, וְנַקֵּה: וְסָלַחְתָּ לַעֲוֹנֵנוּ וּלְחַטָּאתֵנוּ, וּנְחַלְתָּנוּ:

Continue:

סְלַח לָנוּ אָבִינוּ כִּי חָטָאנוּ, מְחַל לָנוּ מַלְכֵּנוּ כִּי פָשָׁעְנוּ. כִּי־אַתָּה אֲדֹנָי טוֹב וְסַלָּח, וְרַב־חֶסֶד לְכָל־קֹרְאֶיךָ: תהלים פו

The following is said responsively:

בְּמַתֵי מִסְפָּר חִלִּינוּ פָנֶיךָ.
לְשַׁוְעַת נְכָאִים אַל תַּעְלֵם אָזְנֶךָ.
הַקְשֵׁב תַּחֲנוּנָתָם מִשְּׁמֵי מְעוֹנֶךָ.
כְּבִימֵי מֹר וַהֲדַס הוֹשַׁעְתָּ בָנֶיךָ.

תְּהִלּוֹת יִשְׂרָאֵל אַתָּה יוֹשֵׁב.
שַׁוְעָתָם מַאֲזִין וְרִנָּתָם קוֹשֵׁב.
רְפָאוּת לְמַחַץ מַקְדִּים וּמְחַשֵּׁב.
קְנוּיֶיךָ לְהֵיטִיב וּנְוֵיהֶם לְיַשֵּׁב.

צַר וְאוֹיֵב הִלְטִישׁ עֵינָיו.
פִּיהוּ פָּעַר לִשְׁאֹף עָנָו.
עֶשֶׁת בְּשִׁלְיוֹ לְהַשְׁמִיד קְהַל הֲמוֹנָיו.
סֶגֶל לְאַבֵּד חָרַת בְּנִשְׁתְּוָנָיו.

You who take revenge upon foes
and persist in Your claim against enemies;
You measured them out with the very measure
they used against Your loved ones.
The fighter and his descendants were hanged, suspended;
they were strung up together, like fish on a thread.

On the day on which the enemies hoped
to lay carnage among the people You harbor,
the rule was overturned and bodies fell;
they bore the brunt and fury of Your rage –
they were trodden underfoot and washed away.

And so may Your name be raised up, great.
Your glory covers all the highest heavens.
As You lift the downtrodden,
those yielded up as plunder,
Your praise fills up the valleys to their very ends.

Consider our thoughts, now,
and witness our suffering.
Rise up, in Your rage, against the bitter enemy.
Master, we have called You from a narrow place.
Please, take us out into the open,
and release us from anguish.

Bring us much, generous pardon.
Hear our prayer,
and what is crude in us – pass over.
Bring down those who press us
and fill them with horror.
And as for us –
do not forever withhold Your compassion.

Continue with "God, King who sits" on page 1012.

נוֹקֵם לְצָרִים וְנוֹטֵר לְאוֹיְבִים.
מְדַדְתָּ מִדָּתָם כְּזְדוּ לַאֲהוּבִים.
לוֹחֵם וּבָנָיו הָתְלוּ מְצֻלָּבִים.
כְּבַחֲרֹזֶת דָּגִים חֹרְזוּ תְחוּבִים.

יוֹם אֲשֶׁר שִׁבְּרוּ צוֹרְרִים.
טִבְחָה לָשִׁית בְּעַם נְצוּרִים.
חֻלְּפָה הַדָּת וְנָפְלוּ פְגָרִים.
זִלְעֲפוּ זְעֵמוּ מוּבָסִים מְגֻרִים.

וּבְכֵן יִתְעַלֶּה שִׁמְךָ וְיִתְנַשָּׂא.
הוֹדְךָ שְׁמֵי שָׁמַיִם כִּסָּה.
דַּכִּים בְּרוֹמִמְךָ נְתוּנִים לִמְשִׁסָּה.
גַּיְא וַאֲפְסֶיהָ תְּהִלָּתְךָ מְכַסָּה.

בִּינָה הֲגִיגֵנוּ עַתָּה, וּרְאֵה בְצָר.
בְּאַפְּךָ קוּמָה עַל צוֹרֵר הַצָּר.
אָדוֹן, קְרָאנוּךָ מִן הַמֵּצַר.
אָנָּא הוֹצִיאֵנוּ לַמֶּרְחָב וְחַלְּצֵנוּ מִצָּר.

מְאֹד תַּרְבֶּה לָנוּ מְחִילָה.
שְׁמַע תְּפִלָּה, וְהַעֲבֵר תִּפְלָה.
לוֹחֲצֵינוּ הַמְעֵד וּמַלְּאֵם חַלְחָלָה.
מִמֶּנּוּ רַחֲמֶיךָ לָעַד לֹא תִּכְלָא.

Continue with אֵל מֶלֶךְ יוֹשֵׁב *on page 1013.*

SELIḤOT FOR THE SEVENTEENTH OF TAMMUZ

סְלַח לָנוּ Forgive us, our Father, for in our great foolishness we have blundered. Pardon us, our King, for our wrongdoings are many.

אֵל אֶרֶךְ You are a God slow to anger, You are called the Master of Compassion, and You have taught the way of repentance. May You remember today and every day the greatness of Your compassion and kindness, for the sake of the descendants of Your beloved ones. Turn toward us in compassion, for You are the Master of Compassion. We come before You in plea and prayer, as You in ancient times showed the humble one [Moses]. Turn from Your fierce anger, as is written in Your Torah. In the shadow of Your wings may we shelter and abide, as on the day when the LORD descended in the cloud. ▸ Disregard crimes and erase guilt as on the day You stood with him [Moses] there. Hear our cry and listen to our word, as on the day You declared in the name of the LORD, and there it is written:

Congregation then Leader:

And the LORD passed by before him and declared: *Ex. 34*

All say aloud:

יהוה The LORD, the LORD, compassionate and generous God, slow to anger, abounding in loving-kindness and truth, extending loving-kindness to a thousand generations, forgiving wrongdoing, rebellion and sin, and absolving [the guilty who repent]. Forgive us our wrongdoing and our sin, and take us as Your inheritance.

Continue:

סְלַח לָנוּ Forgive us, our Father, for we have sinned. Pardon us, our King, for we have transgressed. For You, LORD, are good and forgiving, abounding in *Ps. 86* loving-kindness to all who call on You.

And do not let Him rest, until He establishes, until He makes Jerusalem the *Is. 62* praise of all the earth. For in You there is a wellspring of life; in Your light shall *Ps. 36* we see light. Our God, we are ashamed of our actions, distraught at our sins.

כְּרַחֵם As a father has compassion for his children,
so, LORD, have compassion for us.
Salvation is the LORD's; on Your people is Your blessing, Selah! *Ps. 3*
The LORD of multitudes is with us, the God of Jacob is our stronghold, Selah! *Ps. 46*
LORD of multitudes, happy is the one who trusts in You. *Ps. 84*
LORD, save! May the King answer us on the day we call. *Ps. 20*

סליחות לשבעה עשר בתמוז

סְלַח לָנוּ, אָבִינוּ, כִּי בְּרֹב אִוַּלְתֵּנוּ שָׁגִינוּ.
מְחַל לָנוּ, מַלְכֵּנוּ, כִּי רַבּוּ עֲוֹנֵינוּ.

אֵל אֶרֶךְ אַפַּיִם אַתָּה, וּבַעַל הָרַחֲמִים נִקְרֵאתָ, וְדֶרֶךְ תְּשׁוּבָה הוֹרֵיתָ. גְּדֻלַּת רַחֲמֶיךָ וַחֲסָדֶיךָ, תִּזְכֹּר הַיּוֹם וּבְכָל יוֹם לְזֶרַע יְדִידֶיךָ. תֵּפֶן אֵלֵינוּ בְּרַחֲמִים, כִּי אַתָּה הוּא בַּעַל הָרַחֲמִים. בְּתַחֲנוּן וּבִתְפִלָּה פָּנֶיךָ נְקַדֵּם, כְּהוֹדַעְתָּ לֶעָנָו מִקֶּדֶם. מֵחֲרוֹן אַפְּךָ שׁוּב, כְּמוֹ בְּתוֹרָתְךָ כָּתוּב. וּבְצֵל כְּנָפֶיךָ נֶחֱסֶה וְנִתְלוֹנָן, כְּיוֹם וַיֵּרֶד יהוה בֶּעָנָן. ‹ תַּעֲבֹר עַל פֶּשַׁע וְתִמְחֶה אָשָׁם, כְּיוֹם וַיִּתְיַצֵּב עִמּוֹ שָׁם. תַּאֲזִין שַׁוְעָתֵנוּ וְתַקְשִׁיב מֶנּוּ מַאֲמָר, כְּיוֹם וַיִּקְרָא בְשֵׁם יהוה, וְשָׁם נֶאֱמַר

קהל then שליח ציבור:

וַיַּעֲבֹר יהוה עַל־פָּנָיו וַיִּקְרָא שמות לד

All say aloud:

יהוה, יהוה, אֵל רַחוּם וְחַנּוּן, אֶרֶךְ אַפַּיִם, וְרַב־חֶסֶד וֶאֱמֶת: נֹצֵר חֶסֶד לָאֲלָפִים, נֹשֵׂא עָוֹן וָפֶשַׁע וְחַטָּאָה, וְנַקֵּה: וְסָלַחְתָּ לַעֲוֹנֵנוּ וּלְחַטָּאתֵנוּ, וּנְחַלְתָּנוּ:

Continue:

סְלַח לָנוּ אָבִינוּ כִּי חָטָאנוּ, מְחַל לָנוּ מַלְכֵּנוּ כִּי פָשָׁעְנוּ. כִּי־אַתָּה אֲדֹנָי טוֹב וְסַלָּח, וְרַב־חֶסֶד לְכָל־קֹרְאֶיךָ: תהלים פו

וְאַל־תִּתְּנוּ דֳמִי לוֹ, עַד־יְכוֹנֵן וְעַד־יָשִׂים אֶת־יְרוּשָׁלַםִ תְּהִלָּה בָּאָרֶץ: כִּי־ ישעיה סב / תהלים לו
עִמְּךָ מְקוֹר חַיִּים, בְּאוֹרְךָ נִרְאֶה־אוֹר: אֱלֹהֵינוּ, בֹּשְׁנוּ בְּמַעֲשֵׂינוּ וְנִכְלַמְנוּ בַּעֲוֹנֵינוּ.

כְּרַחֵם אָב עַל בָּנִים, כֵּן תְּרַחֵם יהוה עָלֵינוּ.
לַיהוה הַיְשׁוּעָה, עַל־עַמְּךָ בִרְכָתֶךָ סֶּלָה: תהלים ג
יהוה צְבָאוֹת עִמָּנוּ, מִשְׂגָּב לָנוּ אֱלֹהֵי יַעֲקֹב סֶלָה: תהלים מו
יהוה צְבָאוֹת, אַשְׁרֵי אָדָם בֹּטֵחַ בָּךְ: תהלים פד
יהוה הוֹשִׁיעָה, הַמֶּלֶךְ יַעֲנֵנוּ בְיוֹם־קָרְאֵנוּ: תהלים כ

▸ Forgive, please, this people's wrongdoing, *Num. 14*
in the abundance of Your kindness,
and as You have forgiven this people from the time of Egypt until now,
and there it is written:

Congregation then Leader:

And the LORD said, I have forgiven as you asked.

Continue:

הַטֵּה Give ear, my God and hear; open Your eyes and see our desolation, and *Dan. 9* the city that bears Your name, for it is not on the strength of our righteousness that we throw down our pleadings before You, but on the strength of Your great compassion. LORD, hear me; LORD, forgive; LORD, listen and act and do not delay – for Your sake, my God; for Your city and Your people bear Your name.

Our God and God of our fathers:

אָתָנוּ We come before You, Former of the winds.
In our many wrongdoings our sighs have grown heavy;
the decrees against us powerful and our screams so many –
for on the Seventeenth of Tammuz,
the Tablets were smashed.

We have been exiled from the House of Your choosing;
our judgment was sealed, the decree laid down.
And the light has darkened over us –
for on the Seventeenth of Tammuz,
the Torah scroll was burnt.

Our enemies destroyed the Sanctuary,
the Divine Presence fled from Its corner,
and we were yielded up to the hands of the wanton,
to be consumed –
for on the Seventeenth of Tammuz,
an idol was set up in the Temple.

We were scattered from city to city,
and old and young of us were seized.
The place of our delight was destroyed,
and fire raged through her –
for on the Seventeenth of Tammuz
the city was broken through.

◂ סְלַח־נָא לַעֲוֺן הָעָם הַזֶּה כְּגֹדֶל חַסְדֶּךָ במדבר יד
וְכַאֲשֶׁר נָשָׂאתָה לָעָם הַזֶּה מִמִּצְרַיִם וְעַד־הֵנָּה:
וְשָׁם נֶאֱמַר

then שליח ציבור קהל:

וַיֹּאמֶר יהוה, סָלַחְתִּי כִּדְבָרֶךָ:

Continue:

הַטֵּה אֱלֹהַי אָזְנְךָ וּשְׁמָע, פְּקַח עֵינֶיךָ וּרְאֵה שֹׁמְמֹתֵינוּ וְהָעִיר אֲשֶׁר־נִקְרָא דניאל ט
שִׁמְךָ עָלֶיהָ, כִּי לֹא עַל־צִדְקֹתֵינוּ אֲנַחְנוּ מַפִּילִים תַּחֲנוּנֵינוּ לְפָנֶיךָ, כִּי
עַל־רַחֲמֶיךָ הָרַבִּים: אֲדֹנָי שְׁמָעָה, אֲדֹנָי סְלָחָה, אֲדֹנָי הַקְשִׁיבָה וַעֲשֵׂה
אַל־תְּאַחַר, לְמַעַנְךָ אֱלֹהַי, כִּי־שִׁמְךָ נִקְרָא עַל־עִירְךָ וְעַל־עַמֶּךָ:

אֱלֹהֵינוּ וֵאלֹהֵי אֲבוֹתֵינוּ

אָתָנוּ לְךָ יוֹצֵר רוּחוֹת
בְּרוֹב עֲוֺנֵינוּ כָּבְדוּ אֲנָחוֹת
גְּזֵרוֹת עָצְמוּ וְרַבּוּ צְרִיחוֹת
כִּי בְּשִׁבְעָה עָשָׂר בְּתַמּוּז נִשְׁתַּבְּרוּ הַלֻּחוֹת.

גָּלִינוּ מִבֵּית הַבְּחִירָה
דִּינֵנוּ נֶחְתַּם וְנִגְזְרָה גְזֵרָה
וְחָשַׁךְ בַּעֲדֵנוּ אוֹרָה
כִּי בְּשִׁבְעָה עָשָׂר בְּתַמּוּז נִשְׂרְפָה הַתּוֹרָה.

הָרְסוּ אוֹיְבֵינוּ הַהֵיכָל
וּבָרְחָה שְׁכִינָה מִזָּוִית הֵיכָל
וְנִמְסַרְנוּ בִּידֵי זֵדִים לְהִתְאַכָּל
כִּי בְּשִׁבְעָה עָשָׂר בְּתַמּוּז הָעֳמַד צֶלֶם בַּהֵיכָל.

זֹרֵינוּ מֵעִיר אֶל עִיר
וְנִלְכַּד מִמֶּנּוּ רַב וְצָעִיר
חָרְבָה מְשׂוֹשֵׂנוּ וְאֵשׁ בָּהּ הִבְעִיר
כִּי בְּשִׁבְעָה עָשָׂר בְּתַמּוּז הָבְקְעָה הָעִיר.

The lethal enemy took hold of our Temple, and the cherubs,
bride and bridegroom were deprived of all their ornament.
Because we angered You
we were given up to destruction –
for on the Seventeenth of Tammuz,
the daily offering ceased.

All glory and praise there ended.
The enemy drew his sword
and brandished its point against us;
small children and babies were prepared for the slaughter –
for on the Seventeenth of Tammuz,
the offerings and sacrifices ceased.

We rebelled against the One who inhabits the Heavens,
and so we were dispersed to all the corners of the world.
All our dancing was turned to lament –
for on the Seventeenth of Tammuz,
the Temple service ended.

We acted obstinately with You
in the discord of tongues,
and so our own tongue has learnt lamentation;
we have been abandoned in countless numbers –
for on the Seventeenth of Tammuz,
sin decided our destiny.

We have been dispersed and found no relief,
and so our sighs have multiplied within us;
Rock, see how our souls have been bowed low –
and turn our Seventeenth of Tammuz
into gladness and joy.

We have been obstinate
and many calamities have met us;
and so we have been yielded up to the plunder,
have been pushed into the mud.
See, Lord, and release us from disaster –
and turn our Seventeenth of Tammuz
into joy and gladness.

טָפַשׁ מִקְדָּשֵׁנוּ צַר הַמַּשְׁמִיד
וְנִטַּל מֵחָתָן וְכַלָּה אֶצְעָדָה וְצָמִיד
יַעַן כִּעַסְנוּךָ נִתַּנּוּ לְהַשְׁמִיד
כִּי בְּשִׁבְעָה עָשָׂר בְּתַמּוּז בְּטַל הַתָּמִיד.

כָּלָה מִנּוּ כָּל הוֹד וָשֶׁבַח
חַרְבּוֹ שָׁלַף אוֹיֵב עָלֵינוּ לְאִבְחָה
לִהְיוֹת עוֹלָלִים וְיוֹנְקִים מוּכָנִים לַטֶּבַח
כִּי בְּשִׁבְעָה עָשָׂר בְּתַמּוּז בָּטְלוּ עוֹלָה וָזֶבַח.

מָרַדְנוּ לְשׁוֹכֵן מְעוֹנוֹת
לָכֵן נִתְפַּזַּרְנוּ בְּכָל פִּנּוֹת
נֶהְפַּךְ מְחוֹלֵנוּ לְקִינוֹת
כִּי בְּשִׁבְעָה עָשָׂר בְּתַמּוּז בָּטְלוּ קָרְבָּנוֹת.

סָרַרְנוּ לְפָנֶיךָ מֵרִיב לְשׁוֹנוֹת
לָכֵן לָמְדָה לְשׁוֹנֵנוּ לוֹמַר קִינוֹת
עֲזָבָנוּ בְּלִי לְהִמָּנוֹת
כִּי בְּשִׁבְעָה עָשָׂר בְּתַמּוּז גָּרְמוּ לָנוּ עֲוֹנוֹת.

פֻּזַּרְנוּ בְּלִי מְצוֹא רְוָחָה
לָכֵן רָבְתָה בָּנוּ אֲנָחָה
צוּר רְאֵה נַפְשֵׁנוּ כִּי שָׁחָה
וְשִׁבְעָה עָשָׂר בְּתַמּוּז הֲפָךְ לָנוּ לְשָׂשׂוֹן וּלְשִׂמְחָה.

קָשִׁינוּ עֹרֶף וְרָבְתָה בָּנוּ אָסוֹן
לָכֵן נִתַּנּוּ לִמְשִׁסָּה וְרִפְשׁוֹן
רְאֵה יהוה וְחַלְּצֵנוּ מֵאָסוֹן
וְשִׁבְעָה עָשָׂר בְּתַמּוּז הֲפָךְ לָנוּ לְשִׂמְחָה וּלְשָׂשׂוֹן.

▸ Turn to us, You who reside on High,
and gather in our scattered ones from the very ends of the earth.
Say to Zion, "Come, get up," –
and turn our Seventeenth of Tammuz
to a day of salvation and comfort.

אֵל מֶלֶךְ God, King who sits upon a throne of compassion, who acts with loving-kindness, who pardons the wrongdoings of His people, passing them before Him in order; who forgives sinners and pardons transgressors; who performs righteousness with all flesh and spirit, do not repay their bad actions in kind. ▸ God, You taught us to speak thirteen attributes: recall for us today the covenant of the thirteen attributes, as You in ancient times showed the humble one [Moses], as is written: The Lord descended in the cloud and stood with him there, and declared in the name of the Lord.

Congregation then Leader:

And the Lord passed by before him and declared: *Ex. 34*

All say aloud:

יהוה The Lord, the Lord, compassionate and generous God, slow to anger, abounding in loving-kindness and truth, extending loving-kindness to a thousand generations, forgiving wrongdoing, rebellion and sin, and absolving [the guilty who repent]. Forgive us our wrongdoing and our sin, and take us as Your inheritance.

Continue:

סְלַח לָנוּ Forgive us, our Father, for we have sinned. Pardon us, our King, for
we have transgressed. For You, Lord, are good and forgiving, abounding in *Ps. 86*
loving-kindness to all who call on You.

God, do not rest, do not be silent and do not be still, for Your enemies *Ps. 83*
clamor and those who hate You hold their heads high. God of retribution, *Ps. 94*
Lord; God of retribution, appear

כְּרַחֵם As a father has compassion for his children,
so, Lord, have compassion for us.
Salvation is the Lord's; on Your people is Your blessing, Selah! *Ps. 3*
The Lord of multitudes is with us, *Ps. 46*
the God of Jacob is our stronghold, Selah!
Lord of multitudes: happy is the one who trusts in You. *Ps. 84*
Lord, save! May the King answer us on the day we call. *Ps. 20*

‹ שְׁעֵנוּ שׁוֹכֵן רוּמָה
וְקַבֵּץ נְפוּצוֹתֵינוּ מִקַּצְוֹת אֲדָמָה
תֹּאמַר לְצִיּוֹן קוּמָה
וְשִׁבְעָה עָשָׂר בְּתַמּוּז הֲפָךְ לָנוּ לְיוֹם יְשׁוּעָה וְנֶחָמָה.

אֵל מֶלֶךְ יוֹשֵׁב עַל כִּסֵּא רַחֲמִים, מִתְנַהֵג בַּחֲסִידוּת. מוֹחֵל עֲוֹנוֹת עַמּוֹ, מַעֲבִיר רִאשׁוֹן רִאשׁוֹן. מַרְבֶּה מְחִילָה לְחַטָּאִים, וּסְלִיחָה לְפוֹשְׁעִים. עֹשֶׂה צְדָקוֹת עִם כָּל בָּשָׂר וָרוּחַ, לֹא כְרָעָתָם תִּגְמֹל. ‹ אֵל, הוֹרֵיתָ לָּנוּ לוֹמַר שְׁלֹשׁ עֶשְׂרֵה, וּזְכֹר לָנוּ הַיּוֹם בְּרִית שְׁלֹשׁ עֶשְׂרֵה, כְּמוֹ שֶׁהוֹדַעְתָּ לֶעָנָו מִקֶּדֶם, כְּמוֹ שֶׁכָּתוּב: וַיֵּרֶד יהוה בֶּעָנָן, וַיִּתְיַצֵּב עִמּוֹ שָׁם, וַיִּקְרָא בְשֵׁם, יהוה:

:שליח ציבור then קהל

שמות לד וַיַּעֲבֹר יהוה עַל־פָּנָיו וַיִּקְרָא

All say aloud:

יהוה, יהוה, אֵל רַחוּם וְחַנּוּן, אֶרֶךְ אַפַּיִם, וְרַב־חֶסֶד וֶאֱמֶת: נֹצֵר חֶסֶד לָאֲלָפִים, נֹשֵׂא עָוֹן וָפֶשַׁע וְחַטָּאָה, וְנַקֵּה: וְסָלַחְתָּ לַעֲוֹנֵנוּ וּלְחַטָּאתֵנוּ, וּנְחַלְתָּנוּ:

Continue:

תהלים פו סְלַח לָנוּ אָבִינוּ כִּי חָטָאנוּ, מְחַל לָנוּ מַלְכֵּנוּ כִּי פָשָׁעְנוּ. כִּי־אַתָּה אֲדֹנָי טוֹב וְסַלָּח, וְרַב־חֶסֶד לְכָל־קֹרְאֶיךָ:

תהלים פג אֱלֹהִים אַל־דֳּמִי־לָךְ, אַל־תֶּחֱרַשׁ וְאַל־תִּשְׁקֹט אֵל: כִּי־הִנֵּה אוֹיְבֶיךָ יֶהֱמָיוּן,
וּמְשַׂנְאֶיךָ נָשְׂאוּ רֹאשׁ: אֵל־נְקָמוֹת יהוה, אֵל נְקָמוֹת הוֹפִיעַ: תהלים צד

כְּרַחֵם אָב עַל בָּנִים, כֵּן תְּרַחֵם יהוה עָלֵינוּ.
תהלים ג לַיהוה הַיְשׁוּעָה, עַל־עַמְּךָ בִרְכָתֶךָ סֶּלָה:
תהלים מו יהוה צְבָאוֹת עִמָּנוּ, מִשְׂגָּב לָנוּ אֱלֹהֵי יַעֲקֹב סֶלָה:
תהלים פד יהוה צְבָאוֹת, אַשְׁרֵי אָדָם בֹּטֵחַ בָּךְ:
תהלים כ יהוה הוֹשִׁיעָה, הַמֶּלֶךְ יַעֲנֵנוּ בְיוֹם־קָרְאֵנוּ:

Our God and God of our fathers:

אֲמָרֵר It is bitterly that I weep, over the Hand raised against our ruins.
I blasphemed Him in His House,
in my unfaithfulness and thieving.
The Holy Presence broke out and fled,
flew ten stretches and rose up to the seventh Heaven.

God cut me off, tormented me, burnt me, in the fourth month.
He closed the time set for Him to break those young boys,
who were like boughs just sprouting.
He shot us with His arrows twice, melted and weakened us,
as heedless women wept for Tammuz in the Temple.
He condemned me and became Enemy to me,
then, in the month of Tammuz.

Five traps were laid for me, deep in the Scripture of sufferings sent.
Those people overcame me for my impurity
on the seventeenth of the month.
For I was ensnared like a wretched bride,
unfaithful beneath a wedding canopy of peace and success.
I did not wait for Moses, my shepherd, until the sixth hour,
and the Tablets were smashed.

From His hand was I ornamented
with jewelry of fine gold, brooch and bracelet.
They flowed away on the day of His rage,
when I corrupted my way, and denounced my faith.
I broke off the order of His service and the constant supplies of the altar –
from the Chamber of the Lambs, the daily offering is ended.

Israel is crumbled to pieces, scattered, storm battered, oppressed.
Likened to a ship without a captain, tossed about like a boat.
You have taken her by the head for her sins,
exposed her twice over to mourning and moaning.
Her enemies waged war on her on this day,
and the city was broken through again.

She fled out like a chased gazelle to hide, when none sought her.
They sharpened their tongues, they made her like a lamb,
and left her wool and milk for all takers.
She cries out for the cherished thing with which she was crowned:
the beloved of her eyes eluded her as Apostomus burnt the Torah.

אֱלֹהֵינוּ וֵאלֹהֵי אֲבוֹתֵינוּ

אֶמְרוֹר בִּבְכִי מִפְּנֵי יָד שְׁלוּחָה בְּעִי.
בְּנָאֲצִי בְּתוֹךְ בֵּיתוֹ בִּבְגָדַי וְקָבְעִי.
גָּח וּבָרַח וְנָסַע עָשָׂר וְעָלָה לַשְּׁבִיעִי.
דִּמָּנִי הֱצִיקַנִי הִשִּׂיקַנִי בַּחֹדֶשׁ הָרְבִיעִי.

הֵבִיא מוֹעֵד בִּמְלֹאתוֹ לִשְׁבֹּר בַּחוּרַי גְּמוּז.
וְרִבָּה בוֹ פְּעָמִים בְּמִסְמוּס וּמִזְמוּז.
זְבוּלוֹ כְּשֶׁר שַׁאֲנַנּוֹת מְבַכּוֹת אֶת הַתַּמּוּז.
חִיְּבַנִי וְאִיְּבַנִי אֲזַי בְּיֶרַח תַּמּוּז.

טָמְנוּ פַּחִים חֲמִשָּׁה בְּמִקְרָא תְּלָאוֹת מְשֻׁלָּחוֹת.
יְכַלּוּ לִי בְּשִׁבְעָה עָשָׂר בּוֹ בַּאֲלִיחוֹת.
כִּי נוֹקַשְׁתִּי כְּכַלָּה עֲלוּבָה בְּחֻפַּת שַׁלְוָה וְהַצְלָחוֹת.
לְרוֹעִי לֹא הִמְתַּנְתִּי שֵׁשׁ, וְנִשְׁתַּבְּרוּ הַלֻּחוֹת.

מִיָּדוֹ עֲדִיתִי חֲלִי כֶתֶם, אֶצְעָדָה וְצָמִיד.
נִגְרוֹת בְּיוֹם אַפּוֹ, כְּשִׁחַתִּי דְרָכַי לְהַשְׁמִיד.
סֵדֶר עֲבוֹדָתוֹ וְקֵיץ מִזְבְּחוֹ קָצְתִּי לְהַעֲמִיד.
עַל כֵּן מִלִּשְׁכַּת הַטְּלָאִים בֻּטַּל הַתָּמִיד.

פּוֹר הִתְפּוֹרְרָה וְנִתְפַּזְּרָה סֹעֲרָה עֲנִיָּה.
צִי נִמְשְׁלָה מִבְּלִי חוֹבֵל, וְנִטְרְפָה כָּאֳנִיָּה.
קָחְתָה בְּחַטָּאתָהּ בְּרֹאשָׁהּ, וּבְכֶפֶל תַּאֲנִיָּה וַאֲנִיָּה.
רִיבוּהָ צָרֶיהָ כְּהַיּוֹם, וְהָבְקְעָה הָעִיר בַּשְּׁנִיָּה.

שִׁלְּחָה כִּצְבִי מֻדָּח מֵאֵין דּוֹרֵשׁ לְהַסְתִּירָה.
שָׁנְנוּ לְשׁוֹנָם וּנְתָנוּהָ כְּשֶׁה, צְמֻרָה וְחֻלְבָּה לְהַתִּירָה.
תִּצְעַק עַל כְּלִי חֶמְדָּה שֶׁבּוֹ נִכְתָּרָה.
תַּחֲמוֹד עֵינֶיהָ נִצַּל כְּשָׂרַף אַפּוֹסְטְמוֹס הַתּוֹרָה.

A fool cursed those oppressed and broken to vex them;
he taunted abject people: "They shall be consumed;"
"God shall hide His face from seeing."
When idols were placed in the Temple,
God avenged one's hand at the hand of the other, a disgusting item consumed.
This, at the time when He gathered anguish over us;
for an image was set up in the Sanctuary of God.

Miserable and plagued are these children, who were once the very first.
Their troubles have come close on one another's heels these many years;
stricken as if by the stings of bees and scorpions.
They think their hope is gone,
that as they sit in this darkness they have no more chance.

▸ Zealous God, in Your restraint toward those who anger You
they have flourished fat and succulent.
Raise up those who still await You;
let them stand firm always,
like something planted, or carved out with love.
It is on fast days that truth and peace are hewn out.
May they become forever times of joy and celebration – festive days.

אֵל מֶלֶךְ God, King who sits upon a throne of compassion, who acts with loving-kindness, who pardons the wrongdoings of His people, passing them before Him in order; who forgives sinners and pardons transgressors; who performs righteousness with all flesh and spirit, do not repay their bad actions in kind. ▸ God, You taught us to speak thirteen attributes: recall for us today the covenant of the thirteen attributes, as You in ancient times showed the humble one [Moses], as is written: The Lord descended in the cloud and stood with him there, and declared in the name of the Lord:

Congregation then Leader:

And the Lord passed by before him and declared: *Ex. 34*

All say aloud:

יהוה The Lord, the Lord, compassionate and generous God, slow to anger, abounding in loving-kindness and truth, extending loving-kindness to a thousand generations, forgiving wrongdoing, rebellion and sin, and absolving [the guilty who repent]. Forgive us our wrongdoing and our sin, and take us as Your inheritance.

חֵרֶף עֲשׁוּקִים וּרְצוּצִים בַּעֲבוּר הַרְעִימָם סָכָל.
יְרוּדִים בּוֹהִיָּה לְאֵכֶל וּבְהַסְתֵּר פָּנִים מִלְּהִסְתַּכָּל.
יָד הִשְׁלִים מִכְּנַף שִׁקּוּצִים נֶאֱכָל.
עֵת צָרָה כְּהִתְכַּנֵּס וְהֶעֱמַד צֶלֶם בַּהֵיכָל.

דְּוּוִים סְגוּפִים בָּנִים הָהִיוּ מִקֶּדֶם רִאשׁוֹנִים.
סְמוּכוֹת צָרוֹתֵיהֶם זוֹ לְזוֹ כַּמָּה שָׁנִים.
לוֹקִים כַּאֲשֶׁר תַּעֲשֶׂינָה הַדְּבוֹרִים, וְהָעַקְרַבִּים שׁוֹנִים.
הוֹגִים אָבַד שִׁבְרָם וּבָטֵל סִכּוּיָם בָּאִישׁוֹנִים.

› אֵל קַנָּא, בְּהִתְאַפֵּק בִּמְקַנְאֶיךָ דְּשֵׁנִים רְטֻבִּים.
מְחַכִּים תָּקִים עוֹמְדִים לְעוֹלָמִים, כִּנְטִיעִים מְחֻטָּבִים בָּאֲהָבִים.
הָאֱמֶת וְהַשָּׁלוֹם בְּצוֹמוֹת חֲטוּבִים.
נֶצַח הֱיוֹתָם לְשִׂמְחָה וּלְשָׂשׂוֹן וּלְמוֹעֲדִים טוֹבִים.

אֵל מֶלֶךְ יוֹשֵׁב עַל כִּסֵּא רַחֲמִים, מִתְנַהֵג בַּחֲסִידוּת. מוֹחֵל עֲוֹנוֹת עַמּוֹ, מַעֲבִיר רִאשׁוֹן רִאשׁוֹן. מַרְבֶּה מְחִילָה לְחַטָּאִים, וּסְלִיחָה לְפוֹשְׁעִים. עֹשֶׂה צְדָקוֹת עִם כָּל בָּשָׂר וָרוּחַ, לֹא כְרָעָתָם תִּגְמֹל. › אֵל, הוֹרֵיתָ לָּנוּ לוֹמַר שְׁלֹשׁ עֶשְׂרֵה, וּזְכָר לָנוּ הַיּוֹם בְּרִית שְׁלֹשׁ עֶשְׂרֵה, כְּמוֹ שֶׁהוֹדַעְתָּ לֶעָנָו מִקֶּדֶם, כְּמוֹ שֶׁכָּתוּב: וַיֵּרֶד יהוה בֶּעָנָן, וַיִּתְיַצֵּב עִמּוֹ שָׁם, וַיִּקְרָא בְשֵׁם, יהוה:

then שליח ציבור *:*קהל

שמות לד וַיַּעֲבֹר יהוה עַל־פָּנָיו וַיִּקְרָא

All say aloud:

יהוה, יהוה, אֵל רַחוּם וְחַנּוּן, אֶרֶךְ אַפַּיִם, וְרַב־חֶסֶד וֶאֱמֶת: נֹצֵר חֶסֶד לָאֲלָפִים, נֹשֵׂא עָוֹן וָפֶשַׁע וְחַטָּאָה, וְנַקֵּה: וְסָלַחְתָּ לַעֲוֹנֵנוּ וּלְחַטָּאתֵנוּ, וּנְחַלְתָּנוּ:

Continue:

סְלַח לָנוּ Forgive us, our Father, for we have sinned. Pardon us, our King, for we have transgressed. For You, LORD, are good and forgiving, abounding in loving-kindness to all who call on You. *Ps. 86*

The following is said responsively:

Turn to this prisoner who has been yielded up,
to the hand of Babylon and then of Seir;
to You he has been calling all these years,
and he pleads like a small child,
on the day the enemy prevailed and the city was broken through.

And so I bow myself and strike my hands together,
on this day of five disasters that scattered me about,
for at the time of the golden calf, the Tablets left me.
And the daily offering was annulled,
and they brought me away in a cage.
And an idol was placed in the Sanctuary that was my crowning glory,
and I was deprived of His counsel.
The meal-offering was ended, and Your Law –
the enemy sent it up in flames,
on the day the enemy prevailed and the city was broken through.

I tremble terribly, I stand horrified, on the day the LORD pushed me aside,
And Sennacherib, the Viper of the north, swept me away like a deluge.
My light grew dark, and Sheshakh [Babylon] too, tossed me about like a ball.
And the hunter stretched out his hand, and the goat of Greece,
the hairy one of Rome,
on the day the enemy prevailed and the city was broken through.

The glory of my heart, my Stronghold, will Your rage fume forever?
Will You not see this tired nation, blackened as if by the furnace?
Close, with the descendant of Peretz, the breach in my fence,
and, from among the thorns, pick out the lily.
Build the Temple, and return the borders of the Carmel and of Bashan.
And open Your eyes, exact vengeance from Etzer and Dishan.
Judge a people struck dumb, so that the damages be paid,
by the one who destroys, the one who burns –
on the day the enemy prevailed and the city was broken through.

Continue:

סְלַח לָנוּ אָבִינוּ כִּי חָטָאנוּ, מְחַל לָנוּ מַלְכֵּנוּ כִּי פָשָׁעְנוּ. כִּי־אַתָּה אֲדֹנָי טוֹב תהלים פו
וְסַלָּח, וְרַב־חֶסֶד לְכָל־קֹרְאֶיךָ:

The following is said responsively:

שְׁעֵה נֶאֱסַר, אֲשֶׁר נִמְסַר, בְּיַד בָּבֶל וְגַם שֵׂעִיר.
לְךָ יֶהֱמֶה, זֶה כַּמֶּה, וְיִתְחַנֵּן כְּבֶן צָעִיר.
יוֹם גָּבַר הָאוֹיֵב וַתִּבָּקַע הָעִיר.

לְזֹאת אִכַּף, וְאֶסְפֹּק כַּף, בְּיוֹם חֲמֵשׁ פִּזְּרוּנִי.
וְעַל רֶגֶל הָעֵגֶל, הַלֻּחוֹת יְצָאוּנִי.
וְגַם הִשְׁמִיד הַתָּמִיד, וּבַסּוּגַר הֱבִיאַנִי.
וְהוּשַׂם אֱלִיל בְּהֵיכַל כְּלִיל, וּמֵעֲצָתוֹ כְּלָאַנִי.
וְהַמִּנְחָה הוּנְחָה, וְדָתְךָ, צָר בָּאֵשׁ הִבְעִיר.
יוֹם גָּבַר הָאוֹיֵב וַתִּבָּקַע הָעִיר.

מְאֹד אֶתְחַל, וְאֶתְחַלְחַל, בְּיוֹם שַׁדַּי דְּחָפַנִי.
וְהַשְּׁפִיפוֹן מִצָּפוֹן, כְּשִׁבֹּלֶת שְׁטָפַנִי.
מְאוֹר חָשַׁךְ, וְגַם שֵׁשַׁךְ, כְּמוֹ כַדּוּר צְנָפַנִי.
וְהַצַּיָּד שָׁלַח יָד, וְהַצָּפִיר וְהַשָּׂעִיר.
יוֹם גָּבַר הָאוֹיֵב וַתִּבָּקַע הָעִיר.

הוֹד לִבִּי וּמִשְׂגַּבִּי, הֲלָעַד אַפְּךָ יֶעְשַׁן.
הֲלֹא תִרְאֶה עַם נִלְאֶה, אֲשֶׁר הָשְׁחַר כְּמוֹ כִבְשָׁן.
גְּדֹר פִּרְצִי בְּבֶן פַּרְצִי, וּמֵחֵדֶק לְקֹט שׁוֹשָׁן.
בְּנֵה בֵּית זְבוּל, וְהָשֵׁב גְּבוּל הַכַּרְמֶל וְהַבָּשָׁן.
וְעַיִן פְּקַח, וְנָקָם קַח מֵאֱצֶר וּמִדִּישָׁן.
שְׁפֹט אֵלֶם, וְאָז יְשַׁלֵּם הַמַּבְעֶה וְהַמַּבְעִיר.
יוֹם גָּבַר הָאוֹיֵב וַתִּבָּקַע הָעִיר.

On all days continue:

אֵל מֶלֶךְ God, King who sits upon a throne of compassion, who acts with loving-kindness, who pardons the wrongdoings of His people, passing them before Him in order; who forgives sinners and pardons transgressors; who performs righteousness with all flesh and spirit, do not repay their bad actions in kind. God, You taught us to speak thirteen attributes: recall for us today the covenant of the thirteen attributes, as You in ancient times showed the humble one [Moses], as is written: The LORD descended in the cloud and stood with him there, and declared in the name of the LORD:

Congregation then Leader:

And the LORD passed by before him and declared: *Ex. 34*

All say aloud:

יהוה The LORD, the LORD, compassionate and generous God, slow to anger, abounding in loving-kindness and truth, extending loving-kindness to a thousand generations, forgiving wrongdoing, rebellion and sin, and absolving [the guilty who repent]. Forgive us our wrongdoing and our sin, and take us as Your inheritance.

Continue:

סְלַח לָנוּ Forgive us, our Father, for we have sinned. Pardon us, our King, for we have transgressed. For You, LORD, are good and forgiving, abounding in *Ps. 86*
loving-kindness to all who call on You.

זְכֹר Remember, LORD, Your compassion and loving-kindness, *Ps. 25*
for they are everlasting. Remember us, LORD, in favoring Your people;
redeem us with Your salvation.

זְכֹר Remember Your congregation, the one that You acquired long ago, *Ps. 74*
the tribe of Your inheritance that You redeemed,
this Mount Zion that You have dwelt in.

זְכֹר Remember, LORD, the fondness of Jerusalem; do not forever forget the
love of Zion. You shall rise up and have compassion for Zion, *Ps. 102*
for now it is right to be generous, for the time has come.

זְכֹר Remember, LORD, what the Edomites did on the day Jerusalem fell. *Ps. 137*
They said, "Tear it down, tear it down to its very foundations!"

זְכֹר Remember Abraham, Isaac and Jacob, to whom You swore by Your *Ex. 32*
own self, when You said to them, "I shall make Your descendants
as numerous as the stars in the sky, and I shall give all this Land that
I spoke of to your descendants, and they shall inherit it forever."

זְכֹר Remember Your servants, Abraham, Isaac and Jacob; do not attend to *Deut. 9*
the stubbornness of this people, to their wickedness or sinfulness.

On all days continue:

אֵל מֶלֶךְ יוֹשֵׁב עַל כִּסֵּא רַחֲמִים, מִתְנַהֵג בַּחֲסִידוּת. מוֹחֵל עֲוֹנוֹת עַמּוֹ, מַעֲבִיר רִאשׁוֹן רִאשׁוֹן. מַרְבֶּה מְחִילָה לְחַטָּאִים, וּסְלִיחָה לְפוֹשְׁעִים. עֹשֶׂה צְדָקוֹת עִם כָּל בָּשָׂר וָרוּחַ, לֹא כְרָעָתָם תִּגְמֹל. ◄ אֵל, הוֹרֵיתָ לָּנוּ לוֹמַר שְׁלֹשׁ עֶשְׂרֵה, וּזְכֹר לָנוּ הַיּוֹם בְּרִית שְׁלֹשׁ עֶשְׂרֵה, כְּמוֹ שֶׁהוֹדַעְתָּ לֶעָנָו מִקֶּדֶם, כְּמוֹ שֶׁכָּתוּב: וַיֵּרֶד יהוה בֶּעָנָן, וַיִּתְיַצֵּב עִמּוֹ שָׁם, וַיִּקְרָא בְשֵׁם, יהוה:

שליח ציבור then קהל:

וַיַּעֲבֹר יהוה עַל־פָּנָיו וַיִּקְרָא שמות לד

All say aloud:

יהוה, יהוה, אֵל רַחוּם וְחַנּוּן, אֶרֶךְ אַפַּיִם, וְרַב־חֶסֶד וֶאֱמֶת: נֹצֵר חֶסֶד לָאֲלָפִים, נֹשֵׂא עָוֹן וָפֶשַׁע וְחַטָּאָה, וְנַקֵּה: וְסָלַחְתָּ לַעֲוֹנֵנוּ וּלְחַטָּאתֵנוּ, וּנְחַלְתָּנוּ:

Continue:

סְלַח לָנוּ אָבִינוּ כִּי חָטָאנוּ, מְחַל לָנוּ מַלְכֵּנוּ כִּי פָשָׁעְנוּ. כִּי־אַתָּה אֲדֹנָי טוֹב תהלים פו
וְסַלָּח, וְרַב־חֶסֶד לְכָל־קֹרְאֶיךָ:

זְכֹר־רַחֲמֶיךָ יהוה וַחֲסָדֶיךָ, כִּי מֵעוֹלָם הֵמָּה: תהלים כה
זָכְרֵנוּ יהוה בִּרְצוֹן עַמֶּךָ, פָּקְדֵנוּ בִּישׁוּעָתֶךָ.
זְכֹר עֲדָתְךָ קָנִיתָ קֶּדֶם, גָּאַלְתָּ שֵׁבֶט נַחֲלָתֶךָ תהלים עד
הַר־צִיּוֹן זֶה שָׁכַנְתָּ בּוֹ:
זְכֹר יהוה חִבַּת יְרוּשָׁלָיִם, אַהֲבַת צִיּוֹן אַל תִּשְׁכַּח לָנֶצַח.
אַתָּה תָקוּם תְּרַחֵם צִיּוֹן, כִּי־עֵת לְחֶנְנָהּ, כִּי־בָא מוֹעֵד: תהלים קב
זְכֹר יהוה לִבְנֵי אֱדוֹם אֵת יוֹם יְרוּשָׁלָיִם תהלים קלז
הָאֹמְרִים עָרוּ עָרוּ, עַד הַיְסוֹד בָּהּ:
זְכֹר לְאַבְרָהָם לְיִצְחָק וּלְיִשְׂרָאֵל עֲבָדֶיךָ, אֲשֶׁר נִשְׁבַּעְתָּ לָהֶם בָּךְ שמות לב
וַתְּדַבֵּר אֲלֵהֶם, אַרְבֶּה אֶת־זַרְעֲכֶם כְּכוֹכְבֵי הַשָּׁמָיִם
וְכָל־הָאָרֶץ הַזֹּאת אֲשֶׁר אָמַרְתִּי אֶתֵּן לְזַרְעֲכֶם, וְנָחֲלוּ לְעֹלָם:
זְכֹר לַעֲבָדֶיךָ לְאַבְרָהָם לְיִצְחָק וּלְיַעֲקֹב דברים ט
אַל־תֵּפֶן אֶל־קְשִׁי הָעָם הַזֶּה וְאֶל־רִשְׁעוֹ וְאֶל־חַטָּאתוֹ:

אַל־נָא Please, do not hold against us the sin Num. 12
that we committed so foolishly, that we have sinned.
We have sinned, our Rock; forgive us, our Creator.

Some say responsively (all continue with "Remember the covenant" on the next page):

אֵל נָא God, please, heal please, the diseases of this fruitful vine,
ashamed, disgraced and miserable are her fruits.
Redeem her from destruction and from the seeping wound;
answer us as You answered our father Abraham on Mount Moriah –
We have sinned, our Rock;
forgive us, our Creator.

Let the flags of the people redeemed by Your revealed arm,
be spared from plague; let them not be cut down,
and answer our call, and desire the creations of Your hands.
Answer us as You answered our fathers at the Reed Sea –
We have sinned, our Rock;
forgive us, our Creator.

Reveal now the merit of Abraham and Sarah,
the rock from which we were hewn.
Spare us from rage and lead us on a straight path.
Clear our impurity, and open our eyes to the light of Your Torah.
Answer us as You answered Joshua at Gilgal –
We have sinned, our Rock;
forgive us, our Creator.

Lord, witness the ashes of bound Isaac; make our cure spring up.
Put an end to plunder and brokenness, tempest and storm.
Teach us and make us wise with Your perfect word.
Answer us as You answered Samuel at Mitzpah –
We have sinned, our Rock;
forgive us, our Creator.

Jacob who emerged perfect from the womb – do not let his roots dry up.
Cleanse us of all stain and blemish, and do not have us wither.
Help us and we shall be saved,
and receive of Your ways of kindness.
Answer us as You answered Elijah on Mount Carmel –
We have sinned, our Rock;
forgive us, our Creator.

אַל־נָא תָשֵׁת עָלֵינוּ חַטָּאת אֲשֶׁר נוֹאַלְנוּ וַאֲשֶׁר חָטָאנוּ: במדבר יב

חָטָאנוּ צוּרֵנוּ, סְלַח לָנוּ יוֹצְרֵנוּ.

Some say responsively (all continue with זְכָר לָנוּ בְּרִית *on the next page):*

אֵל נָא, רְפָא נָא תַּחֲלוּאֵי גֶּפֶן פּוֹרִיָּה
בּוֹשָׁה וְחָפְרָה, וְאֻמְלַל פִּרְיָהּ
גָּאֳלֶנָּה מִשַּׁחַת וּמִמַּכָּה טְרִיָּה.
עֲנֵנוּ כְּשֶׁעָנִיתָ לְאַבְרָהָם אָבִינוּ בְּהַר הַמּוֹרִיָּה.
חָטָאנוּ צוּרֵנוּ, סְלַח לָנוּ יוֹצְרֵנוּ.

דִּגְלֵי עָם, פְּדוּיֵי בִּזְרוֹעַ חָשׂוּף
הַצֵּל מִנֶּגֶף וְאַל יִהְיוּ לִשְׁסוּף
וְתַעֲנֶה קְרִיאָתֵנוּ וּלְמַעֲשֵׂה יָדֶיךָ תִּכְסֹף
עֲנֵנוּ כְּשֶׁעָנִיתָ לַאֲבוֹתֵינוּ עַל יַם סוּף.
חָטָאנוּ צוּרֵנוּ, סְלַח לָנוּ יוֹצְרֵנוּ.

זְכוּת צוּר חֻצַּב הַיּוֹם לָנוּ תְגַל
חֲשָׂכֵנוּ מֵאֶנֶף וּנְחֵנוּ בְּיֹשֶׁר מַעְגָּל
טַהֵר טֻמְאָתֵנוּ וְלִמְאוֹר תּוֹרָתְךָ עֵינֵינוּ גַּל
עֲנֵנוּ כְּשֶׁעָנִיתָ לִיהוֹשֻׁעַ בַּגִּלְגָּל.
חָטָאנוּ צוּרֵנוּ, סְלַח לָנוּ יוֹצְרֵנוּ.

יָהּ, רְאֵה דֶּשֶׁן עָקוּד, וְהַצְמַח לָנוּ תְרוּפָה
כַּלֵּה שֹׁד וָשֶׁבֶר, סַעַר וְסוּפָה
לַמְּדֵנוּ וְחַכְּמֵנוּ אִמְרָתְךָ הַצְּרוּפָה
עֲנֵנוּ כְּשֶׁעָנִיתָ לִשְׁמוּאֵל בַּמִּצְפָּה.
חָטָאנוּ צוּרֵנוּ, סְלַח לָנוּ יוֹצְרֵנוּ.

מְתֹמָם מְרַחֵם, שָׁרָשָׁיו אַל תְּקַמֵּל
נָקֵנוּ מִכֶּתֶם וְשֶׁמֶץ, וְלֹא נֶאֱמַל
סַעֲדֵנוּ וְנִוָּשֵׁעָה, וְאָרְחוֹת חֲסָדֶיךָ נִגְמַל
עֲנֵנוּ כְּשֶׁעָנִיתָ לְאֵלִיָּהוּ בְּהַר הַכַּרְמֶל.
חָטָאנוּ צוּרֵנוּ, סְלַח לָנוּ יוֹצְרֵנוּ.

Strengthen us by the righteousness of Moses, drawn from water,
and atone our crimes, wanton or foolish.
Free us from the terror of death that thrusts us back,
rule for our salvation; do not let us melt away in our sins.
Answer us as You answered Jonah in the belly of the fish –
We have sinned, our Rock;
forgive us, our Creator.

Remember Your devoted Aaron's sanctity,
for the sake of Israel of the pleasing steps.
Awaken Your compassion, for we are doubly stricken.
Return us resolutely to our awe of You, do not expose us.
Answer us as You answered David, and Solomon his son in Jerusalem –
We have sinned, our Rock;
forgive us, our Creator.

On the Fast of Esther add:
Answer those who call You; listen out from Your residence.
Hear the cry of those who call out to You, You who listen to the destitute.
Have compassion for Your children, as a father has for his.
Answer us as You answered Mordekhai and Esther:
and on a fifty-cubit gallows they hanged father and sons –
We have sinned, our Rock.
Forgive us, our Creator.

All continue:

זְכֹר Remember the covenant of our fathers, as You have said,
"I shall remember My covenant with Jacob, and My covenant *Lev. 26*
with Isaac, and I shall remember My covenant with Abraham,
and I shall remember the Land."

זְכֹר Remember the covenant of the early ones, as You have said,
"I shall remember for them the covenant of the early ones, *Lev. 26*
those I took out of the Land of Egypt before the eyes of the nations,
in order to be their God: I am the Lord."

עֲשֵׂה Deal kindly with us as You have promised, "Even so, when they are in the land of their enemies I shall not reject them and shall not detest them to the point of destruction, to the point of breaking My covenant with them, for I am the Lord their God." Restore our fortunes, and have compassion for us as is written, "And God shall restore your fortunes and have compassion for you, and shall return and gather you in from all the nations among whom the Lord

Lev. 26 — *Deut. 30*

עוֹדְדֵנוּ בְּצֶדֶק מָשׁוּי מִמַּיִם, וְכַפֵּר זָדוֹן וּמְשׁוּגָה
פְּדֵנוּ מִמְּהוּמַת מָוֶת, וְאָחוֹר בַּל נִסּוֹגָה
צַוֵּה יְשׁוּעָתֵנוּ, וּבַעֲוֹנוֹתֵינוּ אַל נִתְמוֹגְגָה
עֲנֵנוּ כְּשֶׁעָנִיתָ לְיוֹנָה בִּמְעֵי הַדָּגָה.
חָטָאנוּ צוּרֵנוּ, סְלַח לָנוּ יוֹצְרֵנוּ.

קְדֻשַּׁת אִישׁ חֲסִידֶךָ זְכֹר לִיפַת פְּעָמִים
רַחֲמֶיךָ תְּעוֹרֵר כִּי לָקִינוּ בְּכִפְלַיִם
שׁוּבֵנוּ תֹּקֶף לְיִרְאָתֶךָ וְלֹא נֶחְשַׂף שׁוּלַיִם
עֲנֵנוּ כְּשֶׁעָנִיתָ לְדָוִד וְלִשְׁלֹמֹה בְנוֹ בִּירוּשָׁלַיִם.
חָטָאנוּ צוּרֵנוּ, סְלַח לָנוּ יוֹצְרֵנוּ.

On תענית אסתר *add:*

תַּעֲנֶה לְקוֹרְאֶיךָ, וְהַסְכֵּת מִמְּעוֹנִים
תִּשְׁמַע שַׁוְעַת צוֹעֲקֶיךָ, שׁוֹמֵעַ אֶל אֶבְיוֹנִים
תְּרַחֵם עַל בָּנֶיךָ כְּרַחֵם אָב עַל בָּנִים
עֲנֵנוּ כְּמוֹ שֶׁעָנִיתָ לְמָרְדְּכַי וְאֶסְתֵּר
וְתָלוּ עַל עֵץ־חֲמִשִּׁים הָאָב עִם בָּנִים.
חָטָאנוּ צוּרֵנוּ, סְלַח לָנוּ יוֹצְרֵנוּ.

All continue:

ויקרא כו זְכֹר לָנוּ בְּרִית אָבוֹת כַּאֲשֶׁר אָמַרְתָּ: וְזָכַרְתִּי אֶת־בְּרִיתִי יַעֲקוֹב
וְאַף אֶת־בְּרִיתִי יִצְחָק וְאַף אֶת־בְּרִיתִי אַבְרָהָם אֶזְכֹּר
וְהָאָרֶץ אֶזְכֹּר:
ויקרא כו זְכֹר לָנוּ בְּרִית רִאשׁוֹנִים כַּאֲשֶׁר אָמַרְתָּ: וְזָכַרְתִּי לָהֶם בְּרִית רִאשֹׁנִים
אֲשֶׁר הוֹצֵאתִי־אֹתָם מֵאֶרֶץ מִצְרַיִם לְעֵינֵי הַגּוֹיִם
לִהְיוֹת לָהֶם לֵאלֹהִים, אֲנִי יהוה:
ויקרא כו עֲשֵׂה עִמָּנוּ כְּמָה שֶׁהִבְטַחְתָּנוּ: וְאַף גַּם־זֹאת בִּהְיוֹתָם בְּאֶרֶץ אֹיְבֵיהֶם,
לֹא־מְאַסְתִּים וְלֹא־גְעַלְתִּים לְכַלֹּתָם, לְהָפֵר בְּרִיתִי אִתָּם, כִּי אֲנִי יהוה
דברים ל אֱלֹהֵיהֶם: הָשֵׁב שְׁבוּתֵנוּ וְרַחֲמֵנוּ כְּמָה שֶׁכָּתוּב: וְשָׁב יהוה אֱלֹהֶיךָ אֶת־

has scattered you." Gather those of us who have been distanced, as is written,
"If your distanced ones are at the very ends of the heavens, from there shall *Deut. 30*
the Lord your God gather you; from there shall He bring You." Wipe out our
crimes as if they were a cloud, as if they were a haze, as is written, "I have wiped *Is. 44*
out your crimes like a cloud, and as a haze your sins; come back to Me for I have
redeemed you." Wipe out our crimes for Your sake, as You have said, "I, I am the *Is. 43*
one who shall wipe out your crimes for My sake, and I shall not recall your sins."
Whiten our sins as snow and as wool, as is written, "Come now, let us reason *Is. 1*
together, says the Lord; If your sins are like scarlet, they shall be whitened like
snow; should they be as red as crimson, they shall become like wool." Throw
over us pure waters and purify us, as is written, "I shall throw pure waters over *Ezek. 36*
you and you shall be pure. I shall purify you of all your impurities and of all your
idolatry." Have compassion for us and do not destroy us, as is written, "For the *Deut. 4*
Lord your God is a compassionate God; He will not cease to hold you and
He will not destroy you, and will not forget the covenant of your fathers that
He pledged to them." Circumcise our hearts to love Your name, as is written,
"And the Lord will circumcise your heart and the heart of your descendants to *Deut. 30*
love the Lord your God with all your heart and with all your soul, so that you
shall live." Let us find You when we seek You, as is written, "And if from there *Deut. 4*
you seek the Lord your God, you shall find Him, when you seek Him out with
all your heart and with all your soul." Bring us to Your holy mountain, and let
us rejoice in Your house of prayer, as is written, "I shall bring them to My holy *Is. 56*
mountain, and I shall make them rejoice in My house of prayer; their offerings
and their sacrifices will be accepted, desired on My altar, for My House will be
called a house of prayer for all peoples."

The Ark is opened. The following until ◂ is said responsively, verse by verse:

שְׁמַע קוֹלֵנוּ Listen to our voice, Lord our God. Spare us and have compassion
on us, and in compassion and favor accept our prayer. Turn us back, O Lord, *Lam. 5*
to You, and we will return. Renew our days as of old. Do not cast us away from
You, and do not take Your holy spirit from us. Do not cast us away in our old
age; when our strength is gone do not desert us.◂ Do not desert us, Lord; our
God, do not be distant from us. Give us a sign of good things, and those who
hate us shall see it and be ashamed, for You, Lord, will help us and console us.
Hear our speech, Lord, consider our thoughts. May the words of our mouths
and the thoughts within our hearts be pleasing to You, Lord, our Rock and
our Redeemer. For it is You, Lord, that we have longed for; You shall answer
us, Lord our God.

The Ark is closed.

שְׁבוּתְךָ וְרִחֲמֶךָ, וְשָׁב וְקִבֶּצְךָ מִכָּל־הָעַמִּים אֲשֶׁר הֱפִיצְךָ יהוה אֱלֹהֶיךָ
שָׁמָּה: קַבֵּץ נִדָּחֵינוּ כְּמָה שֶׁכָּתוּב: אִם־יִהְיֶה נִדַּחֲךָ בִּקְצֵה הַשָּׁמָיִם, מִשָּׁם דברים ל
יְקַבֶּצְךָ יהוה אֱלֹהֶיךָ וּמִשָּׁם יִקָּחֶךָ: מְחֵה פְשָׁעֵינוּ כָּעָב וְכֶעָנָן כְּמָה שֶׁכָּתוּב:
מָחִיתִי כָעָב פְּשָׁעֶיךָ וְכֶעָנָן חַטֹּאותֶיךָ, שׁוּבָה אֵלַי כִּי גְאַלְתִּיךָ: מְחֵה פְשָׁעֵינוּ ישעיה מד
לְמַעַנְךָ כַּאֲשֶׁר אָמַרְתָּ: אָנֹכִי אָנֹכִי הוּא מֹחֶה פְשָׁעֶיךָ לְמַעֲנִי, וְחַטֹּאתֶיךָ ישעיה מג
לֹא אֶזְכֹּר: הַלְבֵּן חֲטָאֵינוּ כַּשֶּׁלֶג וְכַצֶּמֶר כְּמָה שֶׁכָּתוּב: לְכוּ־נָא וְנִוָּכְחָה ישעיה א
יֹאמַר יהוה, אִם־יִהְיוּ חֲטָאֵיכֶם כַּשָּׁנִים כַּשֶּׁלֶג יַלְבִּינוּ, אִם־יַאְדִּימוּ כַתּוֹלָע
כַּצֶּמֶר יִהְיוּ: זְרֹק עָלֵינוּ מַיִם טְהוֹרִים וְטַהֲרֵנוּ כְּמָה שֶׁכָּתוּב: וְזָרַקְתִּי עֲלֵיכֶם יחזקאל לו
מַיִם טְהוֹרִים וּטְהַרְתֶּם, מִכֹּל טֻמְאוֹתֵיכֶם וּמִכָּל־גִּלּוּלֵיכֶם אֲטַהֵר אֶתְכֶם:
רַחֵם עָלֵינוּ וְאַל תַּשְׁחִיתֵנוּ כְּמָה שֶׁכָּתוּב: כִּי אֵל רַחוּם יהוה אֱלֹהֶיךָ, לֹא דברים ד
יַרְפְּךָ וְלֹא יַשְׁחִיתֶךָ, וְלֹא יִשְׁכַּח אֶת־בְּרִית אֲבֹתֶיךָ אֲשֶׁר נִשְׁבַּע לָהֶם: מוֹל
אֶת לְבָבֵנוּ לְאַהֲבָה אֶת שְׁמֶךָ כְּמָה שֶׁכָּתוּב: וּמָל יהוה אֱלֹהֶיךָ אֶת־לְבָבְךָ דברים ל
וְאֶת־לְבַב זַרְעֶךָ, לְאַהֲבָה אֶת־יהוה אֱלֹהֶיךָ בְּכָל־לְבָבְךָ וּבְכָל־נַפְשְׁךָ,
לְמַעַן חַיֶּיךָ: הִמָּצֵא לָנוּ בְּבַקָּשָׁתֵנוּ כְּמָה שֶׁכָּתוּב: וּבִקַּשְׁתֶּם מִשָּׁם אֶת־ דברים ד
יהוה אֱלֹהֶיךָ וּמָצָאתָ, כִּי תִדְרְשֶׁנּוּ בְּכָל־לְבָבְךָ וּבְכָל־נַפְשֶׁךָ: תְּבִיאֵנוּ אֶל
הַר קָדְשֶׁךָ וְשַׂמְּחֵנוּ בְּבֵית תְּפִלָּתֶךָ כְּמָה שֶׁכָּתוּב: וַהֲבִיאוֹתִים אֶל־הַר ישעיה נו
קָדְשִׁי וְשִׂמַּחְתִּים בְּבֵית תְּפִלָּתִי, עוֹלֹתֵיהֶם וְזִבְחֵיהֶם לְרָצוֹן עַל־מִזְבְּחִי,
כִּי בֵיתִי בֵּית־תְּפִלָּה יִקָּרֵא לְכָל־הָעַמִּים:

The ארון קודש *is opened. The following until ▸ is said responsively, verse by verse:*

שְׁמַע קוֹלֵנוּ, יהוה אֱלֹהֵינוּ, חוּס וְרַחֵם עָלֵינוּ וְקַבֵּל בְּרַחֲמִים וּבְרָצוֹן אֶת
תְּפִלָּתֵנוּ. הֲשִׁיבֵנוּ יהוה אֵלֶיךָ וְנָשׁוּבָה, חַדֵּשׁ יָמֵינוּ כְּקֶדֶם: אַל תַּשְׁלִיכֵנוּ איכה ה
מִלְּפָנֶיךָ, וְרוּחַ קָדְשְׁךָ אַל תִּקַּח מִמֶּנּוּ. אַל תַּשְׁלִיכֵנוּ לְעֵת זִקְנָה, כִּכְלוֹת
כֹּחֵנוּ אַל תַּעַזְבֵנוּ. ▸ אַל תַּעַזְבֵנוּ יהוה, אֱלֹהֵינוּ אַל תִּרְחַק מִמֶּנּוּ. עֲשֵׂה
עִמָּנוּ אוֹת לְטוֹבָה, וְיִרְאוּ שׂוֹנְאֵינוּ וְיֵבֹשׁוּ, כִּי אַתָּה יהוה עֲזַרְתָּנוּ וְנִחַמְתָּנוּ.
אֲמָרֵינוּ הַאֲזִינָה יהוה, בִּינָה הֲגִיגֵנוּ. יִהְיוּ לְרָצוֹן אִמְרֵי פִינוּ וְהֶגְיוֹן לִבֵּנוּ
לְפָנֶיךָ, יהוה צוּרֵנוּ וְגוֹאֲלֵנוּ. כִּי לְךָ יהוה הוֹחָלְנוּ, אַתָּה תַעֲנֶה אֲדֹנָי אֱלֹהֵינוּ.

The ארון קודש *is closed.*

CONFESSION

אֱלֹהֵינוּ Our God and God of our fathers,
let our prayer come before You, and do not hide Yourself from our plea,
for we are not so arrogant or obstinate as to say before You,
Lord, our God and God of our fathers,
we are righteous and have not sinned,
for in truth, we and our fathers have sinned.

Strike the left side of the chest with the right fist while saying each of the sins.

אָשַׁמְנוּ We have been guilty, we have acted treacherously, we have robbed, we have spoken slander. We have acted perversely, we have acted wickedly, we have acted presumptuously, we have been violent, we have framed lies. We have given bad advice, we have deceived, we have scorned, we have rebelled, we have provoked, we have turned away, we have committed wrongdoing, we have transgressed, we have persecuted, we have been obstinate. We have acted wickedly, we have corrupted, we have acted abominably, we have strayed, we have led others astray.

סַרְנוּ We have turned away from Your commandments, and good laws, to no avail, for You are just in all that has befallen us, for You have acted faithfully *Neh. 9*
while we have done wickedly.

הִרְשַׁעְנוּ We have been wicked and we have done wrong, and so we have not been saved. Place it in our hearts to abandon the way of wickedness, and hasten our salvation, as is written by Your prophet, "Let each wicked person *Is. 55*
abandon his ways, each man of wrongdoing his thoughts, and let him come back to the Lord and He will have compassion for him; back to our God for He will forgive generously."

מָשִׁיחַ Your righteous anointed one said to You, "Who can understand his own *Ps. 19*
mistakes? Cleanse me of my hidden faults." Cleanse us, Lord our God, of all our sins, and purify us of all our impurities and throw clear waters over us to purify us, as was written by Your prophet, "I shall throw clear waters over you *Ezek. 36*
and you shall be pure. I shall purify you of all your impurities and of all your idolatry." Your people, Your inheritance, famished of Your good, thirsting for Your loving-kindness, craving Your salvation – they shall recognize and know that compassion and forgiveness belong to the Lord our God.

On days when Taḥanun is not said (such as on the morning of a Brit Mila, or when a bridegroom is present), continue with Avinu Malkenu *on page 200 followed by Half Kaddish (page 218).*

וידוי

אֱלֹהֵינוּ וֵאלֹהֵי אֲבוֹתֵינוּ
תָּבֹא לְפָנֶיךָ תְּפִלָּתֵנוּ, וְאַל תִּתְעַלַּם מִתְּחִנָּתֵנוּ.
שֶׁאֵין אֲנוּ עַזֵּי פָנִים וּקְשֵׁי עֹרֶף לוֹמַר לְפָנֶיךָ
יהוה אֱלֹהֵינוּ וֵאלֹהֵי אֲבוֹתֵינוּ, צַדִּיקִים אֲנַחְנוּ וְלֹא חָטָאנוּ.
אֲבָל אֲנַחְנוּ וַאֲבוֹתֵינוּ חָטָאנוּ.

Strike the left side of the chest with the right fist while saying each of the sins.

אָשַׁמְנוּ, בָּגַדְנוּ, גָּזַלְנוּ, דִּבַּרְנוּ דֹפִי. הֶעֱוִינוּ, וְהִרְשַׁעְנוּ, זַדְנוּ, חָמַסְנוּ, טָפַלְנוּ שֶׁקֶר. יָעַצְנוּ רָע, כִּזַּבְנוּ, לַצְנוּ, מָרַדְנוּ, נִאַצְנוּ, סָרַרְנוּ, עָוִינוּ, פָּשַׁעְנוּ, צָרַרְנוּ, קִשִּׁינוּ עֹרֶף. רָשַׁעְנוּ, שִׁחַתְנוּ, תִּעַבְנוּ, תָּעִינוּ, תִּעְתָּעְנוּ.

נחמיה ט
סַרְנוּ מִמִּצְוֹתֶיךָ וּמִמִּשְׁפָּטֶיךָ הַטּוֹבִים, וְלֹא שָׁוָה לָנוּ. וְאַתָּה צַדִּיק עַל כָּל־הַבָּא עָלֵינוּ, כִּי־אֱמֶת עָשִׂיתָ וַאֲנַחְנוּ הִרְשָׁעְנוּ.

הִרְשַׁעְנוּ וּפָשַׁעְנוּ לָכֵן לֹא נוֹשָׁעְנוּ. וְתֵן בְּלִבֵּנוּ לַעֲזֹב דֶּרֶךְ רֶשַׁע, וְחִישׁ
ישעיה נה
לָנוּ יֶשַׁע, כַּכָּתוּב עַל יַד נְבִיאֶךָ: יַעֲזֹב רָשָׁע דַּרְכּוֹ וְאִישׁ אָוֶן מַחְשְׁבֹתָיו, וְיָשֹׁב אֶל־יהוה וִירַחֲמֵהוּ וְאֶל־אֱלֹהֵינוּ כִּי־יַרְבֶּה לִסְלוֹחַ:

תהלים יט
מְשִׁיחַ צִדְקֶךָ אָמַר לְפָנֶיךָ: שְׁגִיאוֹת מִי־יָבִין, מִנִּסְתָּרוֹת נַקֵּנִי: נַקֵּנוּ יהוה אֱלֹהֵינוּ מִכָּל פְּשָׁעֵינוּ וְטַהֲרֵנוּ מִכָּל טֻמְאוֹתֵינוּ וּזְרֹק עָלֵינוּ מַיִם טְהוֹרִים
יחזקאל לו
וְטַהֲרֵנוּ, כַּכָּתוּב עַל יַד נְבִיאֶךָ: וְזָרַקְתִּי עֲלֵיכֶם מַיִם טְהוֹרִים וּטְהַרְתֶּם, מִכֹּל טֻמְאוֹתֵיכֶם וּמִכָּל־גִּלּוּלֵיכֶם אֲטַהֵר אֶתְכֶם: עַמְּךָ וְנַחֲלָתְךָ רְעֵבֵי טוּבְךָ, צְמֵאֵי חַסְדְּךָ, תְּאֵבֵי יִשְׁעֶךָ, יַכִּירוּ וְיֵדְעוּ, כִּי לַיהוה אֱלֹהֵינוּ הָרַחֲמִים וְהַסְּלִיחוֹת.

On days when תחנון *is not said (such as on the morning of a* ברית מילה*, or when a* חתן *is present), continue with* אבינו מלכנו *on page 201 followed by* חצי קדיש *(page 219).*

אֵל רַחוּם Compassionate God is Your name; Generous God is Your name. We are called by Your name; Lord, act for the sake of Your name. Act for the sake of Your truth. Act for the sake of Your covenant. Act for the sake of Your greatness and glory. Act for the sake of Your Law. Act for the sake of Your majesty. Act for the sake of Your promise. Act for the sake of Your remembrance. Act for the sake of Your loving-kindness. Act for the sake of Your goodness. Act for the sake of Your oneness. Act for the sake of Your honor. Act for the sake of Your wisdom. Act for the sake of Your kingship. Act for the sake of Your eternity. Act for the sake of Your mystery. Act for the sake of Your might. Act for the sake of Your splendor. Act for the sake of Your righteousness. Act for the sake of Your holiness. Act for the sake of Your great compassion. Act for the sake of Your Presence. Act for the sake of Your praise. Act for the sake of those who loved You, who now live in the dust. Act for the sake of Abraham, Isaac and Jacob. Act for the sake of Moses and Aaron. Act for the sake of David and Solomon. Act for the sake of Jerusalem, Your holy city. Act for the sake of Zion, the dwelling place of Your glory. Act for the sake of the desolate site of Your Temple. Act for the sake of the ruins of Your altar. Act for the sake of those killed in sanctification of Your name. Act for the sake of those slaughtered over Your unity. Act for the sake of those who have gone through fire and water in sanctification of Your name. Act for the sake of suckling infants who have not sinned. Act for the sake of little ones just weaned who have done no wrong. Act for the sake of schoolchildren. Act for Your own sake if not for ours. Act for Your own sake, and save us.

עֲנֵנוּ Answer us, Lord, answer us. Answer us, our God, answer us. Answer us, our Father, answer us. Answer us, our Creator, answer us. Answer us, our Redeemer, answer us. Answer us, You who seek us, answer us. Answer us, God who is faithful, answer us. Answer us, You who are ancient and kind, answer us. Answer us, You who are pure and upright, answer us. Answer us, You who are alive and remain, answer us. Answer us, You who are good and do good, answer us. Answer us, You who know our impulses, answer us. Answer us, You who conquer rage, answer us. Answer us, You who clothe Yourself in righteousness, answer us. Answer us, Supreme King of kings, answer us. Answer us, You who are awesome and elevated, answer us. Answer us, You who forgive and pardon, answer us. Answer us, You who answer in times of trouble, answer us. Answer us, You who redeem and save, answer us. Answer us, You who are righteous and straightforward, answer us. Answer us, You who are close to those who call, answer us. Answer us, You who are compassionate and generous, answer us. Answer us, You who listen to the destitute, answer us. Answer us, You who support the innocent, answer us. Answer us, God of our fathers, answer us. Answer us, God of Abraham, answer us. Answer us, Terror of Isaac, answer us. Answer us, Champion of Jacob, answer us. Answer us, Help of the tribes, answer us. Answer us, Stronghold of the mothers, answer us. Answer us, You who are slow to anger, answer us. Answer us, You who are lightly appeased, answer us. Answer us, You who answer at times of favor, answer us. Answer us, Father of orphans, answer us. Answer us, Justice of widows, answer us.

אֵל רַחוּם שְׁמֶךָ. אֵל חַנּוּן שְׁמֶךָ. בָּנוּ נִקְרָא שְׁמֶךָ. יהוה עֲשֵׂה לְמַעַן שְׁמֶךָ. עֲשֵׂה לְמַעַן אֲמִתָּךְ. עֲשֵׂה לְמַעַן בְּרִיתָךְ. עֲשֵׂה לְמַעַן גָּדְלָךְ וְתִפְאַרְתָּךְ. עֲשֵׂה לְמַעַן דָּתָךְ. עֲשֵׂה לְמַעַן הוֹדָךְ. עֲשֵׂה לְמַעַן וַעוּדָךְ. עֲשֵׂה לְמַעַן זִכְרָךְ. עֲשֵׂה לְמַעַן חַסְדָּךְ. עֲשֵׂה לְמַעַן טוּבָךְ. עֲשֵׂה לְמַעַן יִחוּדָךְ. עֲשֵׂה לְמַעַן כְּבוֹדָךְ. עֲשֵׂה לְמַעַן לִמּוּדָךְ. עֲשֵׂה לְמַעַן מַלְכוּתָךְ. עֲשֵׂה לְמַעַן נִצְחָךְ. עֲשֵׂה לְמַעַן סוֹדָךְ. עֲשֵׂה לְמַעַן עֻזָּךְ. עֲשֵׂה לְמַעַן פְּאֵרָךְ. עֲשֵׂה לְמַעַן צִדְקָתָךְ. עֲשֵׂה לְמַעַן קְדֻשָּׁתָךְ. עֲשֵׂה לְמַעַן רַחֲמֶיךָ הָרַבִּים. עֲשֵׂה לְמַעַן שְׁכִינָתָךְ. עֲשֵׂה לְמַעַן תְּהִלָּתָךְ. עֲשֵׂה לְמַעַן אוֹהֲבֶיךָ שׁוֹכְנֵי עָפָר. עֲשֵׂה לְמַעַן אַבְרָהָם יִצְחָק וְיַעֲקֹב. עֲשֵׂה לְמַעַן מֹשֶׁה וְאַהֲרֹן. עֲשֵׂה לְמַעַן דָּוִד וּשְׁלֹמֹה. עֲשֵׂה לְמַעַן יְרוּשָׁלַיִם עִיר קָדְשֶׁךָ. עֲשֵׂה לְמַעַן צִיּוֹן מִשְׁכַּן כְּבוֹדֶךָ. עֲשֵׂה לְמַעַן שִׁמְמוֹת הֵיכָלֶךָ. עֲשֵׂה לְמַעַן הֲרִיסוּת מִזְבְּחֶךָ. עֲשֵׂה לְמַעַן הֲרוּגִים עַל שֵׁם קָדְשֶׁךָ. עֲשֵׂה לְמַעַן טְבוּחִים עַל יִחוּדֶךָ. עֲשֵׂה לְמַעַן בָּאֵי בָאֵשׁ וּבַמַּיִם עַל קִדּוּשׁ שְׁמֶךָ. עֲשֵׂה לְמַעַן יוֹנְקֵי שָׁדַיִם שֶׁלֹּא חָטְאוּ. עֲשֵׂה לְמַעַן גְּמוּלֵי חָלָב שֶׁלֹּא פָשְׁעוּ. עֲשֵׂה לְמַעַן תִּינוֹקוֹת שֶׁל בֵּית רַבָּן. עֲשֵׂה לְמַעַנְךָ אִם לֹא לְמַעֲנֵנוּ. עֲשֵׂה לְמַעַנְךָ וְהוֹשִׁיעֵנוּ.

עֲנֵנוּ יהוה עֲנֵנוּ. עֲנֵנוּ אֱלֹהֵינוּ עֲנֵנוּ. עֲנֵנוּ אָבִינוּ עֲנֵנוּ. עֲנֵנוּ בּוֹרְאֵנוּ עֲנֵנוּ. עֲנֵנוּ גּוֹאֲלֵנוּ עֲנֵנוּ. עֲנֵנוּ דּוֹרְשֵׁנוּ עֲנֵנוּ. עֲנֵנוּ הָאֵל הַנֶּאֱמָן עֲנֵנוּ. עֲנֵנוּ וָתִיק וְחָסִיד עֲנֵנוּ. עֲנֵנוּ זַךְ וְיָשָׁר עֲנֵנוּ. עֲנֵנוּ חַי וְקַיָּם עֲנֵנוּ. עֲנֵנוּ טוֹב וּמֵטִיב עֲנֵנוּ. עֲנֵנוּ יוֹדֵעַ יֵצֶר עֲנֵנוּ. עֲנֵנוּ כּוֹבֵשׁ כְּעָסִים עֲנֵנוּ. עֲנֵנוּ לוֹבֵשׁ צְדָקוֹת עֲנֵנוּ. עֲנֵנוּ מֶלֶךְ מַלְכֵי הַמְּלָכִים עֲנֵנוּ. עֲנֵנוּ נוֹרָא וְנִשְׂגָּב עֲנֵנוּ. עֲנֵנוּ סוֹלֵחַ וּמוֹחֵל עֲנֵנוּ. עֲנֵנוּ עוֹנֶה בְּעֵת צָרָה עֲנֵנוּ. עֲנֵנוּ פּוֹדֶה וּמַצִּיל עֲנֵנוּ. עֲנֵנוּ צַדִּיק וְיָשָׁר עֲנֵנוּ. עֲנֵנוּ קָרוֹב לְקוֹרְאָיו עֲנֵנוּ. עֲנֵנוּ רַחוּם וְחַנּוּן עֲנֵנוּ. עֲנֵנוּ שׁוֹמֵעַ אֶל אֶבְיוֹנִים עֲנֵנוּ. עֲנֵנוּ תּוֹמֵךְ תְּמִימִים עֲנֵנוּ. עֲנֵנוּ אֱלֹהֵי אֲבוֹתֵינוּ עֲנֵנוּ. עֲנֵנוּ אֱלֹהֵי אַבְרָהָם עֲנֵנוּ. עֲנֵנוּ פַּחַד יִצְחָק עֲנֵנוּ. עֲנֵנוּ אֲבִיר יַעֲקֹב עֲנֵנוּ. עֲנֵנוּ עֶזְרַת הַשְּׁבָטִים עֲנֵנוּ. עֲנֵנוּ מִשְׂגַּב אִמָּהוֹת עֲנֵנוּ. עֲנֵנוּ קָשֶׁה לִכְעֹס עֲנֵנוּ. עֲנֵנוּ רַךְ לִרְצוֹת עֲנֵנוּ. עֲנֵנוּ עוֹנֶה בְּעֵת רָצוֹן עֲנֵנוּ. עֲנֵנוּ אֲבִי יְתוֹמִים עֲנֵנוּ. עֲנֵנוּ דַּיַּן אַלְמָנוֹת עֲנֵנוּ.

מִי שֶׁעָנָה The One who answered Abraham our father on Mount Moriah – answer us.

The One who answered Isaac his son, when he was bound upon the altar – answer us.

The One who answered Jacob in Beth-El – answer us.

The One who answered Joseph in prison – answer us.

The One who answered our fathers at the Reed Sea – answer us.

The One who answered Moses at Horeb – answer us.

The One who answered Aaron over his firepan – answer us.

The One who answered Pinehas when he stood up from among the congregation – answer us.

The One who answered Joshua at Gilgal – answer us.

The One who answered Samuel at Mitzpah – answer us.

The One who answered David and Solomon his son in Jerusalem – answer us.

The One who answered Elijah on Mount Carmel – answer us.

The One who answered Elisha at Jericho – answer us.

The One who answered Jonah in the belly of the fish – answer us.

The One who answered Hezekiah the king of Judah in his illness – answer us.

The One who answered Hananiah, Mishael and Azariah in the furnace of fire – answer us.

The One who answered Daniel in the lions' den – answer us.

The One who answered Mordekhai and Esther in Shushan the capital city – answer us.

The One who answered Ezra in his exile – answer us.

The One who answered so many righteous, devoted, innocent and upright people – answer us.

רַחֲמָנָא Loving God, who answers the oppressed: answer us.

Loving God, who answers the broken hearted: answer us.

Loving God, who answers those of humbled spirit: answer us.

Loving God, answer us.

Loving God, spare; Loving God, release; Loving God, save us.

Loving God, have compassion for us now, swiftly, at a time soon coming.

Continue with "Avinu Malkenu" on page 200.

מִי שֶׁעָנָה לְאַבְרָהָם אָבִינוּ בְּהַר הַמּוֹרִיָּה, הוּא יַעֲנֵנוּ.
מִי שֶׁעָנָה לְיִצְחָק בְּנוֹ כְּשֶׁנֶּעֱקַד עַל גַּבֵּי הַמִּזְבֵּחַ, הוּא יַעֲנֵנוּ.
מִי שֶׁעָנָה לְיַעֲקֹב בְּבֵית אֵל, הוּא יַעֲנֵנוּ.
מִי שֶׁעָנָה לְיוֹסֵף בְּבֵית הָאֲסוּרִים, הוּא יַעֲנֵנוּ.
מִי שֶׁעָנָה לַאֲבוֹתֵינוּ עַל יַם סוּף, הוּא יַעֲנֵנוּ.
מִי שֶׁעָנָה לְמֹשֶׁה בְּחוֹרֵב, הוּא יַעֲנֵנוּ.
מִי שֶׁעָנָה לְאַהֲרֹן בַּמַּחְתָּה, הוּא יַעֲנֵנוּ.
מִי שֶׁעָנָה לְפִינְחָס בְּקוּמוֹ מִתּוֹךְ הָעֵדָה, הוּא יַעֲנֵנוּ.
מִי שֶׁעָנָה לִיהוֹשֻׁעַ בַּגִּלְגָּל, הוּא יַעֲנֵנוּ.
מִי שֶׁעָנָה לִשְׁמוּאֵל בַּמִּצְפָּה, הוּא יַעֲנֵנוּ.
מִי שֶׁעָנָה לְדָוִד וּשְׁלֹמֹה בְנוֹ בִּירוּשָׁלָיִם, הוּא יַעֲנֵנוּ.
מִי שֶׁעָנָה לְאֵלִיָּהוּ בְּהַר הַכַּרְמֶל, הוּא יַעֲנֵנוּ.
מִי שֶׁעָנָה לֶאֱלִישָׁע בִּירִיחוֹ, הוּא יַעֲנֵנוּ.
מִי שֶׁעָנָה לְיוֹנָה בִּמְעֵי הַדָּגָה, הוּא יַעֲנֵנוּ.
מִי שֶׁעָנָה לְחִזְקִיָּהוּ מֶלֶךְ יְהוּדָה בְּחָלְיוֹ, הוּא יַעֲנֵנוּ.
מִי שֶׁעָנָה לַחֲנַנְיָה מִישָׁאֵל וַעֲזַרְיָה בְּתוֹךְ כִּבְשַׁן הָאֵשׁ, הוּא יַעֲנֵנוּ.
מִי שֶׁעָנָה לְדָנִיֵּאל בְּגוֹב הָאֲרָיוֹת, הוּא יַעֲנֵנוּ.
מִי שֶׁעָנָה לְמָרְדְּכַי וְאֶסְתֵּר בְּשׁוּשַׁן הַבִּירָה, הוּא יַעֲנֵנוּ.
מִי שֶׁעָנָה לְעֶזְרָא בַּגּוֹלָה, הוּא יַעֲנֵנוּ.
מִי שֶׁעָנָה לְכָל הַצַּדִּיקִים וְהַחֲסִידִים וְהַתְּמִימִים וְהַיְשָׁרִים, הוּא יַעֲנֵנוּ.

רַחֲמָנָא דְּעָנֵי לַעֲנִיֵּי עֲנֵינָן.
רַחֲמָנָא דְּעָנֵי לִתְבִירֵי לִבָּא עֲנֵינָן.
רַחֲמָנָא דְּעָנֵי לְמַכִּיכֵי רוּחָא עֲנֵינָן.
רַחֲמָנָא עֲנֵינָן.
רַחֲמָנָא חוּס, רַחֲמָנָא פְּרֹק, רַחֲמָנָא שֵׁיזִב.
רַחֲמָנָא רַחֵם עֲלָן, הַשְׁתָּא בַּעֲגָלָא וּבִזְמַן קָרִיב.

Continue with אבינו מלכנו *on page 201.*

ברכות
GIVING THANKS

THE MEAL AND ITS BLESSINGS

On washing hands before eating bread:

Blessed are You, Lord our God, King of the Universe,
who has made us holy through His commandments,
and has commanded us about washing hands.

Before eating bread:

Blessed are You, Lord our God, King of the Universe,
who brings forth bread from the earth.

BIRKAT HAMAZON / GRACE AFTER MEALS

On days when Taḥanun is said:

עַל־נַהֲרוֹת By the rivers of Babylon *Ps. 137*
we sat and wept as we remembered Zion.
There on the willow trees we hung up our harps,

---

where "the eyes of God are always upon it. From the beginning of the year until the end of the year" and "if you keep My mitzvot" then "I will give the rain in its season."

The halakha also has a system to encourage continual awareness of the source of our blessings. It is a thorough system of *berakhot* that are said both before and after we partake of and enjoy God's beautiful world. Every time a piece of food passes our lips, every time we smell a pleasant fragrance, every time we see a wondrous aspect of nature, we make a *berakha*, to acknowledge God's role in bringing the wonder of His world to us for our benefit.

Birkat HaMazon, Grace after Meals, is mandated in the Torah as a way to avoid the pitfalls of arrogance and vanity when you are satiated and no longer hungry. "You will eat and be satisfied, and you shall bless the Lord your God..., lest you forget the Lord your God..." (*Devarim* 8:10–11).

Birkat HaMazon, as prescribed in the Torah, was originally three *berakhot*, each one moving in sequence from the universal to the particular. The first, the Blessing for Nourishment, speaks of the universal need of all of God's creation for sustenance. The second *berakha*, the Blessing of the Land, focuses on the unique elements of Jewish life and identity, the Land of Israel, the covenant between us and Hashem, and the Torah. The third blessing, the Blessing for Jerusalem, turns our attention to the future of the Jewish People in messianic times. A fourth *berakha*, the Blessing of God's Goodness, was added at a later date, and over time was expanded to include several other requests and *tefillot*.

סדר סעודה וברכותיה

On washing hands before eating bread:

בָּרוּךְ אַתָּה יהוה אֱלֹהֵינוּ מֶלֶךְ הָעוֹלָם
אֲשֶׁר קִדְּשָׁנוּ בְּמִצְוֹתָיו וְצִוָּנוּ עַל נְטִילַת יָדָיִם.

Before eating bread:

בָּרוּךְ אַתָּה יהוה אֱלֹהֵינוּ מֶלֶךְ הָעוֹלָם
הַמּוֹצִיא לֶחֶם מִן הָאָרֶץ.

ברכת המזון

On days when תחנון *is said:*

תהלים קלז

עַל־נַהֲרוֹת בָּבֶל, שָׁם יָשַׁבְנוּ גַּם־בָּכִינוּ, בְּזָכְרֵנוּ אֶת־צִיּוֹן:
עַל־עֲרָבִים בְּתוֹכָהּ תָּלִינוּ כִּנֹּרוֹתֵינוּ:

LEARNING

INTRODUCTION TO *BERAKHOT* AND *BIRKAT HAMAZON*

Wealth comes with grave risk. The wealthier you are, the more successful you are, and the less you have to worry about where your next meal will come from, the less chance there is you will have perspective on that wealth, and gratitude for its source. When you have achieved these things through your own hard work, there is a danger you will say, "My power and the might of my hand made me this prosperity" (*Devarim* 8:17).

The Torah contrasts *Eretz Yisrael* with Egypt by describing it as a hilly land dependent on rain (which we all know is unreliable in that part of the world) as opposed to Egypt which is fertile like a vegetable garden that can be easily irrigated (*Devarim* 11:10–14). Ramban asks the obvious question. Shouldn't the Torah be comparing the Land of Israel favorably to Egypt, from where God had just taken His people to lead them to the Promised Land? But these verses do not read that way. Ramban explains that Israel's unreliable water source is in fact Israel's unique quality. But it is a spiritual quality. This challenging agricultural setting encourages the inhabitants of this land to continually remember the source of their prosperity, and inspires them to feel wonder and gratitude, focusing them continually on the blessings they have in their lives and where they have come from. The Land of Israel is a land

for there our captors asked us for songs, our tormentors, for amusement, said:
"Sing us one of the songs of Zion!"
How can we sing the LORD's song on foreign soil?
If I forget you, Jerusalem, may my right hand forget its skill.
May my tongue cling to the roof of my mouth
if I do not remember you,
if I do not set Jerusalem above my highest joy.
Remember, LORD, what the Edomites did on the day Jerusalem fell.
They said, "Tear it down, tear it down to its very foundations!"
Daughter of Babylon, doomed to destruction,
happy is he who repays you for what you have done to us,
who seizes your infants and dashes them against the rocks.

On days when Taḥanun is omitted (see full list on page 206):

שִׁיר הַמַּעֲלוֹת A song of ascents. *Ps. 126*
When the LORD brought back the exiles of Zion
we were like people who dream.
Then were our mouths filled with laughter,
and our tongues with songs of joy.
Then was it said among the nations,
"The LORD has done great things for them."
The LORD did do great things for us and we rejoiced.
Bring back our exiles, LORD, like streams in a dry land.
May those who sowed in tears, reap in joy.
May one who goes out weeping, carrying a bag of seed,
come back with songs of joy, carrying his sheaves.

Some say:

תְּהִלַּת My mouth shall speak the praise of God, *Ps. 145*
and all creatures shall bless His holy name for ever and all time.
We will bless God now and for ever. Halleluya! *Ps. 115*
Thank the LORD for He is good; *Ps. 136*
His loving-kindness is for ever.
Who can tell of the LORD's mighty acts *Ps. 106*
and make all His praise be heard?

כִּי שָׁם שְׁאֵלוּנוּ שׁוֹבֵינוּ דִּבְרֵי־שִׁיר וְתוֹלָלֵינוּ שִׂמְחָה
שִׁירוּ לָנוּ מִשִּׁיר צִיּוֹן:
אֵיךְ נָשִׁיר אֶת־שִׁיר־יהוה עַל אַדְמַת נֵכָר:
אִם־אֶשְׁכָּחֵךְ יְרוּשָׁלָםִ, תִּשְׁכַּח יְמִינִי:
תִּדְבַּק לְשׁוֹנִי לְחִכִּי אִם־לֹא אֶזְכְּרֵכִי
אִם־לֹא אַעֲלֶה אֶת־יְרוּשָׁלַםִ עַל רֹאשׁ שִׂמְחָתִי:
זְכֹר יהוה לִבְנֵי אֱדוֹם אֵת יוֹם יְרוּשָׁלָםִ
הָאֹמְרִים עָרוּ עָרוּ עַד הַיְסוֹד בָּהּ:
בַּת־בָּבֶל הַשְּׁדוּדָה, אַשְׁרֵי שֶׁיְשַׁלֶּם־לָךְ אֶת־גְּמוּלֵךְ שֶׁגָּמַלְתְּ לָנוּ:
אַשְׁרֵי שֶׁיֹּאחֵז, וְנִפֵּץ אֶת־עֹלָלַיִךְ אֶל־הַסָּלַע:

On days when תחנון *is omitted (see full list on page 207):*

תהלים קכו
שִׁיר הַמַּעֲלוֹת
בְּשׁוּב יהוה אֶת־שִׁיבַת צִיּוֹן, הָיִינוּ כְּחֹלְמִים:
אָז יִמָּלֵא שְׂחוֹק פִּינוּ וּלְשׁוֹנֵנוּ רִנָּה
אָז יֹאמְרוּ בַגּוֹיִם הִגְדִּיל יהוה לַעֲשׂוֹת עִם־אֵלֶּה:
הִגְדִּיל יהוה לַעֲשׂוֹת עִמָּנוּ, הָיִינוּ שְׂמֵחִים:
שׁוּבָה יהוה אֶת־שְׁבִיתֵנוּ, כַּאֲפִיקִים בַּנֶּגֶב:
הַזֹּרְעִים בְּדִמְעָה בְּרִנָּה יִקְצֹרוּ:
הָלוֹךְ יֵלֵךְ וּבָכֹה נֹשֵׂא מֶשֶׁךְ־הַזָּרַע
בֹּא־יָבֹא בְרִנָּה נֹשֵׂא אֲלֻמֹּתָיו:

Some say:

תהלים קמה
תְּהִלַּת יהוה יְדַבֶּר פִּי
וִיבָרֵךְ כָּל־בָּשָׂר שֵׁם קָדְשׁוֹ לְעוֹלָם וָעֶד:
תהלים קטו
וַאֲנַחְנוּ נְבָרֵךְ יָהּ מֵעַתָּה וְעַד־עוֹלָם, הַלְלוּיָהּ:
תהלים קלו
הוֹדוּ לַיהוה כִּי־טוֹב, כִּי לְעוֹלָם חַסְדּוֹ:
תהלים קו
מִי יְמַלֵּל גְּבוּרוֹת יהוה, יַשְׁמִיעַ כָּל־תְּהִלָּתוֹ:

ZIMMUN / INVITATION

When three or more men say Birkat HaMazon together, the following zimmun is said. When three or more women say Birkat HaMazon, substitute "Friends" for "Gentlemen." The leader should ask permission from those with precedence to lead the Birkat HaMazon.

Leader Gentlemen, let us say grace.

Others May the name of the LORD be blessed
from now and for ever. *Ps. 113*

Leader May the name of the LORD be blessed
from now and for ever.
With your permission,
(my father and teacher / my mother and teacher /
the Kohanim present / our teacher the Rabbi /
the master of this house / the mistress of this house)
my masters and teachers,
let us bless (*in a minyan:* our God,) the One
from whose food we have eaten.

Others Blessed be (*in a minyan:* our God,) the One
from whose food we have eaten,
and by whose goodness we live.

**People present who have not taken part in the meal say:*
*Blessed be (*in a minyan:* our God,) the One
whose name is continually blessed
for ever and all time.

Leader Blessed be (*in a minyan:* our God,) the One
from whose food we have eaten,
and by whose goodness we live.

Blessed be He, and blessed be His name.

סדר הזימון

When three or more men say ברכת המזון together, the following זימון is said. When three or more women say ברכת המזון, substitute חֲבֵרוֹתַי for רַבּוֹתַי. The leader should ask permission from those with precedence to lead the ברכת המזון.

Leader רַבּוֹתַי, נְבָרֵךְ.

Others יְהִי שֵׁם יהוה מְבֹרָךְ מֵעַתָּה וְעַד־עוֹלָם: תהלים קיג

Leader יְהִי שֵׁם יהוה מְבֹרָךְ מֵעַתָּה וְעַד־עוֹלָם:

בִּרְשׁוּת

(אָבִי מוֹרִי / אִמִּי מוֹרָתִי /
כֹּהֲנִים / מוֹרֵנוּ הָרַב /
בַּעַל הַבַּיִת הַזֶּה / בַּעֲלַת הַבַּיִת הַזֶּה)

מָרָנָן וְרַבָּנָן וְרַבּוֹתַי
נְבָרֵךְ (במנין: אֱלֹהֵינוּ) שֶׁאָכַלְנוּ מִשֶּׁלּוֹ.

Others בָּרוּךְ (במנין: אֱלֹהֵינוּ) שֶׁאָכַלְנוּ מִשֶּׁלּוֹ
וּבְטוּבוֹ חָיִינוּ.

**People present who have not taken part in the meal say:*

*בָּרוּךְ (במנין: אֱלֹהֵינוּ) וּמְבֹרָךְ שְׁמוֹ
תָּמִיד לְעוֹלָם וָעֶד.

Leader בָּרוּךְ (במנין: אֱלֹהֵינוּ) שֶׁאָכַלְנוּ מִשֶּׁלּוֹ
וּבְטוּבוֹ חָיִינוּ.

בָּרוּךְ הוּא וּבָרוּךְ שְׁמוֹ.

BLESSING OF NOURISHMENT

בָּרוּךְ Blessed are You, LORD our God, King of the Universe,
who in His goodness feeds the whole world
with grace, kindness and compassion.
He gives food to all living things,
for His kindness is for ever.
Because of His continual great goodness,
we have never lacked food,
nor may we ever lack it,
for the sake of His great name.
For He is God
who feeds and sustains all,
does good to all,
and prepares food for all creatures He has created.
Blessed are You, LORD,
who feeds all.

REFLECTION

"There is enough food in the world today for everyone to have the nourishment necessary for a healthy and productive life." (World Food Program)

Have you ever been hungry?
Have you ever not had enough food to eat?
Is there a difference?

Are there homeless people living in your hometown?

If God provides for all His creatures,
then how can there be poverty and hunger
in the world?

CONNECTION

"Sometimes I want to ask God why He allows poverty, famine, and injustice when He could do something about it, but I'm afraid He might just ask me the same question."

ברכת הזן

בָּרוּךְ אַתָּה יהוה אֱלֹהֵינוּ מֶלֶךְ הָעוֹלָם
הַזָּן אֶת הָעוֹלָם כֻּלּוֹ בְּטוּבוֹ
בְּחֵן בְּחֶסֶד וּבְרַחֲמִים
הוּא נוֹתֵן לֶחֶם לְכָל בָּשָׂר
כִּי לְעוֹלָם חַסְדּוֹ.
וּבְטוּבוֹ הַגָּדוֹל, תָּמִיד לֹא חָסַר לָֽנוּ
וְאַל יֶחְסַר לָֽנוּ מָזוֹן לְעוֹלָם וָעֶד
בַּעֲבוּר שְׁמוֹ הַגָּדוֹל.
כִּי הוּא אֵל זָן וּמְפַרְנֵס לַכֹּל וּמֵטִיב לַכֹּל
וּמֵכִין מָזוֹן לְכָל בְּרִיּוֹתָיו אֲשֶׁר בָּרָא.
בָּרוּךְ אַתָּה יהוה, הַזָּן אֶת הַכֹּל.

... A THOUSAND WORDS

BLESSING OF LAND

נוֹדֶה We thank You, Lord our God,
for having given as a heritage to our ancestors
a desirable, good and spacious land;
for bringing us out, Lord our God, from the land of Egypt,
freeing us from the house of slavery;
for Your covenant which You sealed in our flesh;
for Your Torah which You taught us;
for Your laws which You made known to us;
for the life, grace and kindness
You have given us;
and for the food by which You continually feed and sustain us,
every day, every season, every hour.

On Ḥanukka:

עַל הַנִּסִּים [We thank You also] for the miracles, the redemption, the mighty deeds, the salvations, and the victories in battle which You performed for our ancestors in those days, at this time.

בִּימֵי מַתִּתְיָהוּ In the days of Mattityahu, son of Yoḥanan, the High Priest, the Hasmonean, and his sons, the wicked Greek kingdom rose up against Your people Israel to make them forget Your Torah and to force them to transgress the laws of Your will. It was then that You in Your great compassion stood by them in the time of their distress. You championed their cause, judged their claim, and avenged their wrong. You delivered the strong into the hands of the weak, the many into the hands of the few, the impure into the hands of the pure, the wicked into the hands of the righteous, and the arrogant into the hands of those who were engaged in the study of Your Torah. You made for Yourself a great and holy reputation in Your world, and for Your people Israel You performed a great salvation and redemption as of this very day. Your children then entered the holiest part of Your House, cleansed Your Temple, purified Your Sanctuary, kindled lights in Your holy courts, and designated these eight days of Ḥanukka for giving thanks and praise to Your great name.

Continue with "For all this."

ברכת הארץ

נוֹדֶה לְּךָ, יהוה אֱלֹהֵינוּ
עַל שֶׁהִנְחַלְתָּ לַאֲבוֹתֵינוּ אֶרֶץ חֶמְדָּה טוֹבָה וּרְחָבָה
וְעַל שֶׁהוֹצֵאתָנוּ יהוה אֱלֹהֵינוּ מֵאֶרֶץ מִצְרַיִם
וּפְדִיתָנוּ מִבֵּית עֲבָדִים
וְעַל בְּרִיתְךָ שֶׁחָתַמְתָּ בִּבְשָׂרֵנוּ
וְעַל תּוֹרָתְךָ שֶׁלִּמַּדְתָּנוּ
וְעַל חֻקֶּיךָ שֶׁהוֹדַעְתָּנוּ
וְעַל חַיִּים חֵן וָחֶסֶד שֶׁחוֹנַנְתָּנוּ
וְעַל אֲכִילַת מָזוֹן שָׁאַתָּה זָן וּמְפַרְנֵס אוֹתָנוּ תָּמִיד
בְּכָל יוֹם וּבְכָל עֵת וּבְכָל שָׁעָה.

בחנוכה:

עַל הַנִּסִּים וְעַל הַפֻּרְקָן וְעַל הַגְּבוּרוֹת וְעַל הַתְּשׁוּעוֹת וְעַל הַמִּלְחָמוֹת שֶׁעָשִׂיתָ לַאֲבוֹתֵינוּ בַּיָּמִים הָהֵם בַּזְּמַן הַזֶּה.

בִּימֵי מַתִּתְיָהוּ בֶּן יוֹחָנָן כֹּהֵן גָּדוֹל חַשְׁמוֹנַאי וּבָנָיו, כְּשֶׁעָמְדָה מַלְכוּת יָוָן הָרְשָׁעָה עַל עַמְּךָ יִשְׂרָאֵל לְהַשְׁכִּיחָם תּוֹרָתֶךָ וּלְהַעֲבִירָם מֵחֻקֵּי רְצוֹנֶךָ, וְאַתָּה בְּרַחֲמֶיךָ הָרַבִּים עָמַדְתָּ לָהֶם בְּעֵת צָרָתָם, רַבְתָּ אֶת רִיבָם, דַּנְתָּ אֶת דִּינָם, נָקַמְתָּ אֶת נִקְמָתָם, מָסַרְתָּ גִבּוֹרִים בְּיַד חַלָּשִׁים, וְרַבִּים בְּיַד מְעַטִּים, וּטְמֵאִים בְּיַד טְהוֹרִים, וּרְשָׁעִים בְּיַד צַדִּיקִים, וְזֵדִים בְּיַד עוֹסְקֵי תוֹרָתֶךָ, וּלְךָ עָשִׂיתָ שֵׁם גָּדוֹל וְקָדוֹשׁ בְּעוֹלָמֶךָ, וּלְעַמְּךָ יִשְׂרָאֵל עָשִׂיתָ תְּשׁוּעָה גְדוֹלָה וּפֻרְקָן כְּהַיּוֹם הַזֶּה. וְאַחַר כֵּן בָּאוּ בָנֶיךָ לִדְבִיר בֵּיתֶךָ, וּפִנּוּ אֶת הֵיכָלֶךָ, וְטִהֲרוּ אֶת מִקְדָּשֶׁךָ, וְהִדְלִיקוּ נֵרוֹת בְּחַצְרוֹת קָדְשֶׁךָ, וְקָבְעוּ שְׁמוֹנַת יְמֵי חֲנֻכָּה אֵלּוּ, לְהוֹדוֹת וּלְהַלֵּל לְשִׁמְךָ הַגָּדוֹל.

Continue with וְעַל הַכֹּל.

On Purim:

עַל הַנִּסִּים [We thank You also] for the miracles, the redemption, the mighty deeds, the salvations, and the victories in battle which You performed for our ancestors in those days, at this time.

בִּימֵי מָרְדְּכַי In the days of Mordekhai and Esther, in Shushan the capital, the wicked Haman rose up against them and sought to destroy, slay and exterminate all the Jews, young and old, children and women, on one day, the thirteenth day of the twelfth month, which is the month of Adar, and to plunder their possessions. Then You in Your great compassion defeated his counsel, frustrated his plans, and caused his scheme to recoil on his own head, so that they hanged him and his sons on the gallows. *Esther 3*

Continue with "For all this."

וְעַל הַכֹּל For all this, Lord our God, we thank and bless You.
May Your name be blessed continually
by the mouth of all that lives, for ever and all time –
for so it is written:
"You will eat and be satisfied, *Deut. 8*
then you shall bless the Lord your God
for the good land He has given you."
Blessed are You, Lord,
for the land and for the food.

... A THOUSAND WORDS

בפורים:

עַל הַנִּסִּים וְעַל הַפֻּרְקָן וְעַל הַגְּבוּרוֹת וְעַל הַתְּשׁוּעוֹת וְעַל הַמִּלְחָמוֹת שֶׁעָשִׂיתָ לַאֲבוֹתֵינוּ בַּיָּמִים הָהֵם בַּזְּמַן הַזֶּה.

בִּימֵי מָרְדְּכַי וְאֶסְתֵּר בְּשׁוּשַׁן הַבִּירָה, כְּשֶׁעָמַד עֲלֵיהֶם הָמָן הָרָשָׁע,
אסתר ג בִּקֵּשׁ לְהַשְׁמִיד לַהֲרֹג וּלְאַבֵּד אֶת־כָּל־הַיְּהוּדִים מִנַּעַר וְעַד־זָקֵן טַף
וְנָשִׁים בְּיוֹם אֶחָד, בִּשְׁלוֹשָׁה עָשָׂר לְחֹדֶשׁ שְׁנֵים־עָשָׂר, הוּא־חֹדֶשׁ אֲדָר,
וּשְׁלָלָם לָבוֹז: וְאַתָּה בְּרַחֲמֶיךָ הָרַבִּים הֵפַרְתָּ אֶת עֲצָתוֹ, וְקִלְקַלְתָּ אֶת
מַחֲשַׁבְתּוֹ, וַהֲשֵׁבוֹתָ לּוֹ גְּמוּלוֹ בְּרֹאשׁוֹ, וְתָלוּ אוֹתוֹ וְאֶת בָּנָיו עַל הָעֵץ.

Continue with וְעַל הַכֹּל.

וְעַל הַכֹּל, יהוה אֱלֹהֵינוּ
אֲנַחְנוּ מוֹדִים לָךְ וּמְבָרְכִים אוֹתָךְ
יִתְבָּרַךְ שִׁמְךָ בְּפִי כָּל חַי תָּמִיד לְעוֹלָם וָעֶד
כַּכָּתוּב:

דברים ח וְאָכַלְתָּ וְשָׂבָעְתָּ, וּבֵרַכְתָּ אֶת־יהוה אֱלֹהֶיךָ
עַל־הָאָרֶץ הַטֹּבָה אֲשֶׁר נָתַן־לָךְ:
בָּרוּךְ אַתָּה יהוה, עַל הָאָרֶץ וְעַל הַמָּזוֹן.

CONNECTION

"Come to Israel, come and see the splendor of a desirable land, the splendor of the Carmel and the Sharon, the splendor of the pleasant and beautiful azure skies, the magnificence of the clear, pure, and temperate air that reigns in its majesty and glory, even in Tevet [the cold and rainy season]. Delight and rejoice in this desirable, fair, and pleasing land. A land of life, a land whose air is the wellspring of the spirit. How beautiful and how graceful she is!"

(Rav Kook)

REFLECTION

Where does your food come from?

Do you have an idea
how many people contributed
in some way to getting it
onto your plate?

Do you think
we are less connected to the earth
now that we live
in an industrialized society?

How do you think
we can reconnect?

BLESSING FOR JERUSALEM

רַחֶם נָא Have compassion, please, LORD our God,
on Israel Your people,
on Jerusalem Your city,
on Zion the dwelling place of Your glory,
on the royal house of David Your anointed,
and on the great and holy House that bears Your name.
Our God, our Father,
tend us, feed us, sustain us and support us,
relieve us and send us relief,
LORD our God, swiftly from all our troubles.
Please, LORD our God, do not make us dependent
on the gifts or loans of other people,
but only on Your full, open, holy and generous hand
so that we may suffer neither shame nor humiliation
for ever and all time.

CONNECTION

A girl once asked her teacher to explain the difference between heaven and hell. The teacher began to explain what hell looked like. "Hell is a magnificent banquet hall with ornate gold-leaf decorations and beautiful painted ceilings. At the center of the large hall," he continued, "there is the largest table you have ever seen, creaking under the weight of the most sumptuous feast of every kind of delicacy. A feast fit for a king! All the people surrounding the table, eyes wide at the sight, mouths watering in anticipation of the delicious food they are about to eat."

The young girl challenged, "This doesn't sound much like hell."

"Ah," replied her teacher. "But they can't enjoy even a small bite."

"Whyever not?" cried the girl.

"Because they cannot bend their arms, and so have no way to feed themselves."

"Now tell me about heaven," she asked.

"Heaven is a magnificent banquet hall and at the center of the large hall is the largest table you have ever seen, creaking under the weight of the most sumptuous feast of every kind of delicacy."

Puzzled, the girl exclaimed, "but that is exactly the same as hell!"

"Ah," said her teacher, with a gentle smile, "but in heaven they feed each other!"

ברכת ירושלים

רַחֶם נָא, יהוה אֱלֹהֵינוּ
עַל יִשְׂרָאֵל עַמֶּךָ
וְעַל יְרוּשָׁלַיִם עִירֶךָ
וְעַל צִיּוֹן מִשְׁכַּן כְּבוֹדֶךָ
וְעַל מַלְכוּת בֵּית דָּוִד מְשִׁיחֶךָ
וְעַל הַבַּיִת הַגָּדוֹל וְהַקָּדוֹשׁ שֶׁנִּקְרָא שִׁמְךָ עָלָיו.
אֱלֹהֵינוּ, אָבִינוּ
רְעֵנוּ, זוּנֵנוּ, פַּרְנְסֵנוּ וְכַלְכְּלֵנוּ
וְהַרְוִיחֵנוּ, וְהַרְוַח לָנוּ יהוה אֱלֹהֵינוּ מְהֵרָה מִכָּל צָרוֹתֵינוּ.
וְנָא אַל תַּצְרִיכֵנוּ, יהוה אֱלֹהֵינוּ
לֹא לִידֵי מַתְּנַת בָּשָׂר וָדָם
וְלֹא לִידֵי הַלְוָאָתָם
כִּי אִם לְיָדְךָ הַמְּלֵאָה, הַפְּתוּחָה, הַקְּדוֹשָׁה וְהָרְחָבָה
שֶׁלֹּא נֵבוֹשׁ וְלֹא נִכָּלֵם לְעוֹלָם וָעֶד.

REFLECTION

"It shall be, in the end of days,
the mountain of the house of the Lord
will be established at the top of the mountains,
and it will be elevated from the hills, and
all nations will flow to it. ... He will adjudicate
between the nations, and will rebuke many
peoples; they will beat their swords into
plowshares, and their spears into pruning hooks,
nation will not lift sword against nation, and they
will not learn war any longer."

(*Yeshayahu* 2:2–4)

What role do you think Jerusalem will play in bringing Messianic times closer?

What do you think it means to "beat swords into plowshares"?

What could that mean in our age?

On Shabbat, say:

רְצֵה Favor and strengthen us, LORD our God, through Your commandments, especially through the commandment of the seventh day, this great and holy Sabbath. For it is, for You, a great and holy day. On it we cease work and rest in love in accord with Your will's commandment. May it be Your will, LORD our God, to give us rest without distress, grief, or lament on our day of rest. May You show us the consolation of Zion Your city, and the rebuilding of Jerusalem Your holy city, for You are the Master of salvation and consolation.

On Rosh Ḥodesh and Ḥol HaMo'ed, say:

אֱלֹהֵינוּ Our God and God of our ancestors, may there rise, come, reach, appear, be favored, heard, regarded and remembered before You, our recollection and remembrance, as well as the remembrance of our ancestors, and of the Messiah son of David Your servant, and of Jerusalem Your holy city, and of all Your people the house of Israel – for deliverance and well-being, grace, loving-kindness and compassion, life and peace, on this day of:

On Rosh Ḥodesh: Rosh Ḥodesh.
On Pesaḥ: the Festival of Matzot.
On Sukkot: the Festival of Sukkot.

On it remember us, LORD our God, for good; recollect us for blessing, and save us for life. In accord with Your promise of salvation and compassion, spare us and be generous to us; have compassion on us and save us, for our eyes are turned to You because You are God, generous and compassionate.

וּבְנֵה And may Jerusalem the holy city be rebuilt soon, in our time.
Blessed are You, LORD, who in His compassion
will rebuild Jerusalem. Amen.

... A THOUSAND WORDS

On שבת*, say:*

רְצֵה וְהַחֲלִיצֵנוּ, יהוה אֱלֹהֵינוּ, בְּמִצְוֹתֶיךָ
וּבְמִצְוַת יוֹם הַשְּׁבִיעִי הַשַּׁבָּת הַגָּדוֹל וְהַקָּדוֹשׁ הַזֶּה
כִּי יוֹם זֶה גָּדוֹל וְקָדוֹשׁ הוּא לְפָנֶיךָ
לִשְׁבָּת בּוֹ, וְלָנוּחַ בּוֹ בְּאַהֲבָה כְּמִצְוַת רְצוֹנֶךָ
וּבִרְצוֹנְךָ הָנִיחַ לָנוּ, יהוה אֱלֹהֵינוּ
שֶׁלֹּא תְהֵא צָרָה וְיָגוֹן וַאֲנָחָה בְּיוֹם מְנוּחָתֵנוּ
וְהַרְאֵנוּ, יהוה אֱלֹהֵינוּ, בְּנֶחָמַת צִיּוֹן עִירֶךָ
וּבְבִנְיַן יְרוּשָׁלַיִם עִיר קָדְשֶׁךָ
כִּי אַתָּה הוּא בַּעַל הַיְשׁוּעוֹת וּבַעַל הַנֶּחָמוֹת.

On ראש חודש *and* חול המועד*, say:*

אֱלֹהֵינוּ וֵאלֹהֵי אֲבוֹתֵינוּ
יַעֲלֶה וְיָבוֹא וְיַגִּיעַ, וְיֵרָאֶה וְיֵרָצֶה וְיִשָּׁמַע
וְיִפָּקֵד וְיִזָּכֵר זִכְרוֹנֵנוּ וּפִקְדוֹנֵנוּ, וְזִכְרוֹן אֲבוֹתֵינוּ
וְזִכְרוֹן מָשִׁיחַ בֶּן דָּוִד עַבְדֶּךָ, וְזִכְרוֹן יְרוּשָׁלַיִם עִיר קָדְשֶׁךָ
וְזִכְרוֹן כָּל עַמְּךָ בֵּית יִשְׂרָאֵל
לְפָנֶיךָ, לִפְלֵיטָה לְטוֹבָה
לְחֵן וּלְחֶסֶד וּלְרַחֲמִים, לְחַיִּים וּלְשָׁלוֹם בְּיוֹם

בראש חודש: רֹאשׁ הַחֹדֶשׁ הַזֶּה.
בפסח: חַג הַמַּצּוֹת הַזֶּה.
בסוכות: חַג הַסֻּכּוֹת הַזֶּה.

זָכְרֵנוּ יהוה אֱלֹהֵינוּ בּוֹ לְטוֹבָה
וּפָקְדֵנוּ בוֹ לִבְרָכָה, וְהוֹשִׁיעֵנוּ בוֹ לְחַיִּים.
וּבִדְבַר יְשׁוּעָה וְרַחֲמִים, חוּס וְחָנֵּנוּ וְרַחֵם עָלֵינוּ, וְהוֹשִׁיעֵנוּ
כִּי אֵלֶיךָ עֵינֵינוּ, כִּי אֵל חַנּוּן וְרַחוּם אָתָּה.

וּבְנֵה יְרוּשָׁלַיִם עִיר הַקֹּדֶשׁ בִּמְהֵרָה בְיָמֵינוּ.
בָּרוּךְ אַתָּה יהוה, בּוֹנֵה בְרַחֲמָיו יְרוּשָׁלָיִם, אָמֵן.

BLESSING OF GOD'S GOODNESS

בָּרוּךְ Blessed are You, LORD our God, King of the Universe –
God our Father, our King, our Sovereign,
our Creator, our Redeemer, our Maker,
our Holy One, the Holy One of Jacob.
He is our Shepherd, Israel's Shepherd,
the good King who does good to all.
Every day He has done, is doing, and will do good to us.
He has acted, is acting, and will always act kindly
toward us for ever,
giving us grace, kindness and compassion, relief and rescue, prosperity, blessing, redemption and comfort,
sustenance and support,
compassion, life, peace and all good things,
and of all good things may He never let us lack.

CONNECTION

The interpretation of "The LORD God commanded the man, saying: From every tree of the garden you may eat" (Bereshit 2:16), is that it is a commandment, a requirement, to eat freely and enjoy from everything in the garden, as the Talmud states, "In the future, a person is required to give an accounting for every opportunity he had to enjoy this world from which he refrained." (Yerushalmi, Kiddushin 4:12)

The story is told that at the end of his life, Rabbi Samson Raphael Hirsch, the great nineteenth-century leader of German Jewry, traveled to Switzerland. When his students tried to dissuade him from risking his health to travel, Rabbi Hirsch explained to them, "When I come before Hashem, I will have to answer for many things. But what will I tell Him when He asks me, 'Have you seen My Alps?'"

... A THOUSAND WORDS

ברכת הטוב והמטיב

בָּרוּךְ אַתָּה יהוה אֱלֹהֵינוּ מֶלֶךְ הָעוֹלָם
הָאֵל אָבִינוּ, מַלְכֵּנוּ, אַדִּירֵנוּ
בּוֹרְאֵנוּ, גּוֹאֲלֵנוּ, יוֹצְרֵנוּ, קְדוֹשֵׁנוּ, קְדוֹשׁ יַעֲקֹב
רוֹעֵנוּ, רוֹעֵה יִשְׂרָאֵל, הַמֶּלֶךְ הַטּוֹב וְהַמֵּטִיב לַכֹּל
שֶׁבְּכָל יוֹם וָיוֹם
הוּא הֵטִיב, הוּא מֵטִיב, הוּא יֵיטִיב לָנוּ
הוּא גְמָלָנוּ, הוּא גוֹמְלֵנוּ, הוּא יִגְמְלֵנוּ לָעַד
לְחֵן וּלְחֶסֶד וּלְרַחֲמִים, וּלְרֶוַח, הַצָּלָה וְהַצְלָחָה
בְּרָכָה וִישׁוּעָה, נֶחָמָה, פַּרְנָסָה וְכַלְכָּלָה
וְרַחֲמִים וְחַיִּים וְשָׁלוֹם וְכָל טוֹב
וּמִכָּל טוּב לְעוֹלָם אַל יְחַסְּרֵנוּ.

REFLECTION

What do the following roles all have in common?

- Father
- King
- Creator
- Redeemer
- Shepherd

Which of these do you most relate to?

Is God something else to you, too?

LEARNING

This fourth *berakha* of *Birkat HaMazon* was later added by the rabbis of the Talmud during the period after the Bar Kokhba rebellion against the Romans (132–136 CE), and refers to God's goodness toward us. The first *berakha* of *Birkat HaMazon* focuses on the present, where we thank Hashem for the food that is before us. The second *berakha* focuses us on God's gifts to us in the past, including the Land of Israel and the Torah He gave us. The third *berakha* looks toward the future and has us praying for our future redemption and the rebuilding of Jerusalem and the *Beit HaMikdash*. This final *berakha* of *Birkat HaMazon* uses all three tenses, as it describes how God has, does, and will provide goodness in our life. God is beyond time, and His relationship with us is eternal.

ADDITIONAL REQUESTS

הָרַחֲמָן May the Compassionate One
reign over us for ever and all time.

May the Compassionate One
be blessed in heaven and on earth.

May the Compassionate One
be praised from generation to generation,
be glorified by us to all eternity,
and honored among us for ever and all time.

May the Compassionate One
give us an honorable livelihood.

May the Compassionate One
break the yoke from our neck and lead us upright to our land.

May the Compassionate One
send us many blessings to this house
and this table at which we have eaten.

May the Compassionate One
send us Elijah the prophet – may he be remembered for good –
to bring us good tidings of salvation and consolation.

May the Compassionate One
bless the State of Israel, first flowering of our redemption.

May the Compassionate One
bless the members of Israel's Defense Forces,
who stand guard over our land.

A guest says:

יְהִי רָצוֹן May it be Your will that the master of this house shall not suffer shame in this world, nor humiliation in the World to Come. May all he owns prosper greatly, and may his and our possessions be successful and close to hand. Let not the Accuser hold sway over his deeds or ours, and may no thought of sin, wrongdoing or crimes enter him or us from now and for evermore.

בקשות נוספות

הָרַחֲמָן הוּא יִמְלֹךְ עָלֵינוּ לְעוֹלָם וָעֶד.

הָרַחֲמָן הוּא יִתְבָּרַךְ בַּשָּׁמַיִם וּבָאָרֶץ.

הָרַחֲמָן הוּא יִשְׁתַּבַּח לְדוֹר דּוֹרִים
וְיִתְפָּאַר בָּנוּ לָעַד וּלְנֵצַח נְצָחִים
וְיִתְהַדַּר בָּנוּ לָעַד וּלְעוֹלְמֵי עוֹלָמִים.

הָרַחֲמָן הוּא יְפַרְנְסֵנוּ בְּכָבוֹד.

הָרַחֲמָן הוּא יִשְׁבֹּר עֻלֵּנוּ מֵעַל צַוָּארֵנוּ
וְהוּא יוֹלִיכֵנוּ קוֹמְמִיּוּת לְאַרְצֵנוּ.

הָרַחֲמָן הוּא יִשְׁלַח לָנוּ בְּרָכָה מְרֻבָּה בַּבַּיִת הַזֶּה
וְעַל שֻׁלְחָן זֶה שֶׁאָכַלְנוּ עָלָיו.

הָרַחֲמָן הוּא יִשְׁלַח לָנוּ אֶת אֵלִיָּהוּ הַנָּבִיא זָכוּר לַטּוֹב
וִיבַשֶּׂר לָנוּ בְּשׂוֹרוֹת טוֹבוֹת יְשׁוּעוֹת וְנֶחָמוֹת.

הָרַחֲמָן הוּא יְבָרֵךְ אֶת מְדִינַת יִשְׂרָאֵל
רֵאשִׁית צְמִיחַת גְּאֻלָּתֵנוּ.

הָרַחֲמָן הוּא יְבָרֵךְ אֶת חַיָּלֵי צְבָא הַהֲגָנָה לְיִשְׂרָאֵל
הָעוֹמְדִים עַל מִשְׁמַר אַרְצֵנוּ.

A guest says:

יְהִי רָצוֹן שֶׁלֹּא יֵבוֹשׁ בַּעַל הַבַּיִת בָּעוֹלָם הַזֶּה, וְלֹא יִכָּלֵם לָעוֹלָם הַבָּא, וְיַצְלִיחַ מְאֹד בְּכָל נְכָסָיו, וְיִהְיוּ נְכָסָיו וּנְכָסֵינוּ מֻצְלָחִים וּקְרוֹבִים לָעִיר, וְאַל יִשְׁלֹט שָׂטָן לֹא בְּמַעֲשֵׂה יָדָיו וְלֹא בְּמַעֲשֵׂה יָדֵינוּ. וְאַל יִזְדַּקֵּק לֹא לְפָנָיו וְלֹא לְפָנֵינוּ שׁוּם דְּבַר הִרְהוּר חֵטְא עֲבֵרָה וְעָוֹן, מֵעַתָּה וְעַד עוֹלָם.

הָרַחֲמָן May the Compassionate One bless –

When eating at one's own table, say (include the words in parentheses that apply):

me, (my wife/husband, / my father, my teacher / my mother, my teacher/ my children,) and all that is mine,

A guest at someone else's table says (include the words in parentheses that apply):

the master of this house, him (and his wife, the mistress of this house / and his children,) and all that is his,

Children at their parents' table say (include the words in parentheses that apply):

my father, my teacher, (master of this house,) and my mother, my teacher, (mistress of this house,) them, their household, their children, and all that is theirs.

For all other guests, add:

and all the diners here,

אוֹתָנוּ – together with us and all that is ours.
Just as our forefathers
Abraham, Isaac and Jacob were blessed in all, from all, with all,
so may He bless all of us together
with a complete blessing,
and let us say: Amen.

בַּמָּרוֹם On high, may grace be invoked for them and for us,
as a safeguard of peace.
May we receive a blessing from the Lord
and a just reward from the God of our salvation,
and may we find grace and good favor
in the eyes of God and man.

On Shabbat: May the Compassionate One let us inherit the time, that will be entirely Shabbat and rest for life everlasting.

On Rosh Ḥodesh: May the Compassionate One renew this month for us, for good and blessing.

On Sukkot: May the Compassionate One restore for us, the fallen Tabernacle of David.

הָרַחֲמָן הוּא יְבָרֵךְ

When eating at one's own table, say (include the words in parentheses that apply):

אוֹתִי (וְאֶת אִשְׁתִּי / וְאֶת בַּעְלִי / וְאֶת אָבִי מוֹרִי /
וְאֶת אִמִּי מוֹרָתִי / וְאֶת זַרְעִי) וְאֶת כָּל אֲשֶׁר לִי.

A guest at someone else's table says (include the words in parentheses that apply):

אֶת בַּעַל הַבַּיִת הַזֶּה, אוֹתוֹ (וְאֶת אִשְׁתּוֹ בַּעֲלַת הַבַּיִת
הַזֶּה / וְאֶת זַרְעוֹ) וְאֶת כָּל אֲשֶׁר לוֹ.

Children at their parents' table say (include the words in parentheses that apply):

אֶת אָבִי מוֹרִי (בַּעַל הַבַּיִת הַזֶּה), וְאֶת אִמִּי מוֹרָתִי (בַּעֲלַת
הַבַּיִת הַזֶּה), אוֹתָם וְאֶת בֵּיתָם וְאֶת זַרְעָם וְאֶת כָּל אֲשֶׁר
לָהֶם

For all other guests, add:

וְאֶת כָּל הַמְסֻבִּין כָּאן

אוֹתָנוּ וְאֶת כָּל אֲשֶׁר לָנוּ, כְּמוֹ שֶׁנִּתְבָּרְכוּ אֲבוֹתֵינוּ
אַבְרָהָם יִצְחָק וְיַעֲקֹב, בַּכֹּל, מִכֹּל, כֹּל
כֵּן יְבָרֵךְ אוֹתָנוּ כֻּלָּנוּ יַחַד בִּבְרָכָה שְׁלֵמָה, וְנֹאמַר אָמֵן.

בַּמָּרוֹם יְלַמְּדוּ עֲלֵיהֶם וְעָלֵינוּ זְכוּת
שֶׁתְּהֵא לְמִשְׁמֶרֶת שָׁלוֹם
וְנִשָּׂא בְרָכָה מֵאֵת יהוה וּצְדָקָה מֵאֱלֹהֵי יִשְׁעֵנוּ
וְנִמְצָא חֵן וְשֵׂכֶל טוֹב בְּעֵינֵי אֱלֹהִים וְאָדָם.

בשבת: הָרַחֲמָן הוּא יַנְחִילֵנוּ, יוֹם שֶׁכֻּלּוֹ שַׁבָּת וּמְנוּחָה לְחַיֵּי הָעוֹלָמִים.

בראש חודש: הָרַחֲמָן הוּא יְחַדֵּשׁ עָלֵינוּ, אֶת הַחֹדֶשׁ הַזֶּה לְטוֹבָה וְלִבְרָכָה.

בסוכות: הָרַחֲמָן הוּא יָקִים לָנוּ אֶת סֻכַּת דָּוִד הַנּוֹפֶלֶת.

הָרַחֲמָן May the Compassionate One make us worthy
of the Messianic Age and life in the World to Come.
He gives great / *On Shabbat, Rosh Ḥodesh and Ḥol HaMo'ed:* He is a tower of / *II Sam. 22*
salvation to His king, showing kindness to His anointed,
to David and his descendants for ever.
He who makes peace in His high places,
may He make peace for us and all Israel, and let us say: Amen.

יְראוּ Fear the LORD, you His holy ones; *Ps. 34*
those who fear Him lack nothing.
Young lions may grow weak and hungry,
but those who seek the LORD lack no good thing.
Thank the LORD for He is good; His loving-kindness is for ever. *Ps. 118*
You open Your hand, and satisfy every living thing with favor. *Ps. 145*
Blessed is the person who trusts in the LORD, *Jer. 17*
whose trust is in the LORD alone.
Once I was young, and now I am old, *Ps. 37*
yet I have never watched a righteous man abandoned
or his children begging for bread.
The LORD will give His people strength. *Ps. 29*
The LORD will bless His people with peace.

CONNECTION

Rabbi Elimelech Goldberg has dedicated his life to helping children across the world fight cancer. By literally kicking it! He founded the world renowned organization Kids Kicking Cancer, which provides free martial arts classes focused on breathing techniques and meditation for children battling serious illnesses. After his own daughter Sarah died from leukemia at the age of 2, Rabbi Goldberg has always wanted to help children with the disease. Once, while trying to soothe a young boy in pain from cancer treatment, he offered to teach the boy Choi Kwang-Do, in which Rabbi Goldberg is a black belt. He taught the boy some breathing techniques, and realized then how martial arts can help as a platform for meditation, for relaxation, and to allow children to gain the tools to face the fear and anger that accompanies pain. In 2014 Rabbi Goldberg was voted a Top 10 CNN Hero of the Year, and his story was shared among millions of people.

הָרַחֲמָן הוּא יְזַכֵּנוּ לִימוֹת הַמָּשִׁיחַ וּלְחַיֵּי הָעוֹלָם הַבָּא

שמואל ב׳ כב מַגְדִּל / חול המועד and ראש חודש ,שבת On מִגְדּוֹל / יְשׁוּעוֹת מַלְכּוֹ

וְעֹשֶׂה־חֶסֶד לִמְשִׁיחוֹ, לְדָוִד וּלְזַרְעוֹ עַד־עוֹלָם:

עֹשֶׂה שָׁלוֹם בִּמְרוֹמָיו

הוּא יַעֲשֶׂה שָׁלוֹם עָלֵינוּ וְעַל כָּל יִשְׂרָאֵל, וְאִמְרוּ אָמֵן.

תהלים לד יְראוּ אֶת־יהוה קְדֹשָׁיו, כִּי־אֵין מַחְסוֹר לִירֵאָיו:

כְּפִירִים רָשׁוּ וְרָעֵבוּ, וְדֹרְשֵׁי יהוה לֹא־יַחְסְרוּ כָל־טוֹב:

תהלים קיח הוֹדוּ לַיהוה כִּי־טוֹב, כִּי לְעוֹלָם חַסְדּוֹ:

תהלים קמה פּוֹתֵחַ אֶת־יָדֶךָ, וּמַשְׂבִּיעַ לְכָל־חַי רָצוֹן:

ירמיה יז בָּרוּךְ הַגֶּבֶר אֲשֶׁר יִבְטַח בַּיהוה, וְהָיָה יהוה מִבְטַחוֹ:

תהלים לז נַעַר הָיִיתִי גַּם־זָקַנְתִּי

וְלֹא־רָאִיתִי צַדִּיק נֶעֱזָב וְזַרְעוֹ מְבַקֶּשׁ־לָחֶם:

תהלים כט יהוה עֹז לְעַמּוֹ יִתֵּן, יהוה יְבָרֵךְ אֶת־עַמּוֹ בַשָּׁלוֹם:

... A THOUSAND WORDS

LEARNING

The standard translation of this verse (*Tehilim* 37:25) is "I was young and now I am old and I have not seen the righteous forsaken or his children searching for bread," but Rabbi Sacks translates the word רָאִיתִי as "watched" rather than "seen" based on the use of the same word in *Megillat Ester* (8:6) "For how can I watch the evil that will come unto my people?" This means that according to Rabbi Sacks the verse here really means "I have never stood by silently and watched when a righteous person was forsaken or his children begging for bread." This reading places the responsibility on us to make sure there is justice in the world and that all people are taken care of.

Before eating food, other than bread or matza,
made from the five species of grain (wheat, barley, rye, oats and spelt), or rice:

Blessed are You, the Lord our God, King of the Universe,
who creates the various kinds of nourishment.

Before drinking wine or grape juice:

Blessed are You, Lord our God, King of the Universe,
who creates the fruit of the vine.

Before eating fruit that grows on trees:

Blessed are You, Lord our God, King of the Universe,
who creates the fruit of the tree.

Before eating vegetables, or fruit that does not grow on trees:

Blessed are You, Lord our God, King of the Universe,
who creates the fruit of the ground.

Before eating other food or drinking other liquids:

Blessed are You, Lord our God, King of the Universe,
by whose word all things came to be.

Before eating fruit for the first time in a season, the following is said.
This blessing is also said when buying or wearing a new garment of significant value (e.g. a dress or suit); entering a new home for the first time; or hearing personal good news.

Blessed are You, Lord our God, King of the Universe,
who has given us life, sustained us, and brought us to this time.

BLESSING AFTER FOOD – AL HAMIḤYA

Grace after eating from the "seven species" of produce with which Israel is blessed: food made from the five grains (but not bread); wine or grape juice; grapes, figs, pomegranates, olives, or dates.

בָּרוּךְ Blessed are You, Lord our God, King of the Universe,

After grain products (but not bread or matza):
for the nourishment and sustenance,

After wine or grape juice:
for the vine and the fruit of the vine,

After grapes, figs, olives, pomegranates or dates:
for the tree and the fruit of the tree,

After grain products (but not bread or matza), and wine or grape juice:

for the nourishment and sustenance
and for the vine and the fruit of the vine,

and for the produce of the field; for the desirable, good and spacious land that You willingly gave as heritage to our ancestors, that they might eat of its

Before eating food, other than bread or מצה,
made from the five species of grain (wheat, barley, rye, oats and spelt), or rice:

בָּרוּךְ אַתָּה יהוה אֱלֹהֵינוּ מֶלֶךְ הָעוֹלָם, בּוֹרֵא מִינֵי מְזוֹנוֹת.

Before drinking wine or grape juice:

בָּרוּךְ אַתָּה יהוה אֱלֹהֵינוּ מֶלֶךְ הָעוֹלָם, בּוֹרֵא פְּרִי הַגָּפֶן.

Before eating fruit that grows on trees:

בָּרוּךְ אַתָּה יהוה אֱלֹהֵינוּ מֶלֶךְ הָעוֹלָם, בּוֹרֵא פְּרִי הָעֵץ.

Before eating vegetables, or fruit that does not grow on trees:

בָּרוּךְ אַתָּה יהוה אֱלֹהֵינוּ מֶלֶךְ הָעוֹלָם, בּוֹרֵא פְּרִי הָאֲדָמָה.

Before eating other food or drinking other liquids:

בָּרוּךְ אַתָּה יהוה אֱלֹהֵינוּ מֶלֶךְ הָעוֹלָם, שֶׁהַכֹּל נִהְיָה בִּדְבָרוֹ.

Before eating fruit for the first time in a season, the following שֶׁהֶחֱיָנוּ is said.
This blessing is also said when buying or wearing a new garment of significant value (e.g. a dress or suit); entering a new home for the first time; or hearing personal good news.

בָּרוּךְ אַתָּה יהוה אֱלֹהֵינוּ מֶלֶךְ הָעוֹלָם
שֶׁהֶחֱיָנוּ וְקִיְּמָנוּ וְהִגִּיעָנוּ לַזְּמַן הַזֶּה.

ברכה מעין שלוש

Grace after eating from the "seven species" of produce with which Israel is blessed: food made from the five grains (but not bread); wine or grape juice; grapes, figs, pomegranates, olives, or dates.

בָּרוּךְ אַתָּה יהוה אֱלֹהֵינוּ מֶלֶךְ הָעוֹלָם, עַל

After grain products (but not bread or מצה):	*After wine or grape juice:*	*After grapes, figs, olives, pomegranates or dates:*
הַמִּחְיָה וְעַל הַכַּלְכָּלָה	הַגֶּפֶן וְעַל פְּרִי הַגֶּפֶן	הָעֵץ וְעַל פְּרִי הָעֵץ

After grain products (but not bread or מצה), and wine or grape juice:

הַמִּחְיָה וְעַל הַכַּלְכָּלָה וְעַל הַגֶּפֶן וְעַל פְּרִי הַגֶּפֶן

וְעַל תְּנוּבַת הַשָּׂדֶה וְעַל אֶרֶץ חֶמְדָּה טוֹבָה וּרְחָבָה, שֶׁרָצִיתָ וְהִנְחַלְתָּ לַאֲבוֹתֵינוּ לֶאֱכֹל מִפִּרְיָהּ וְלִשְׂבֹּעַ מִטּוּבָהּ. רַחֶם נָא יהוה אֱלֹהֵינוּ עַל יִשְׂרָאֵל

fruit and be satisfied with its goodness. Have compassion, please, Lord our God, on Israel Your people, on Jerusalem, Your city, on Zion the home of Your glory, on Your altar and Your Temple. May You rebuild Jerusalem, the holy city swiftly in our time, and may You bring us back there, rejoicing in its rebuilding, eating from its fruit, satisfied by its goodness, and blessing You for it in holiness and purity.

On Shabbat: Be pleased to refresh us on this Sabbath Day.
On Rosh Ḥodesh: Remember us for good on this day of the New Moon.
On Pesaḥ: Give us joy on this Festival of Matzot.
On Sukkot: Give us joy on this Festival of Sukkot.

For You, God, are good and do good to all and we thank You for the land

After grain products (but not bread or matza):
and for the nourishment. Blessed are You, Lord, for the land and for the nourishment.

After wine or grape juice:
and for the fruit of the vine.* Blessed are You, Lord, for the land and for the fruit of the vine.*

After grapes, figs, olives, pomegranates or dates:
and for the fruit.** Blessed are You, Lord, for the land and for the fruit.**

After grain products (but not bread or matza), and wine or grape juice:

and for the nourishment and for the fruit of the vine.*
Blessed are You, Lord, for the land and for the nourishment
and the fruit of the vine.*

* *If the wine is from Israel, then substitute "her vine" for "the vine."*
** *If the fruit is from Israel, then substitute "her fruit" for "the fruit."*

BLESSING AFTER FOOD – BOREH NEFASHOT

After food or drink that does not require Birkat HaMazon or Al HaMiḥya – such as meat, fish, dairy products, vegetables, beverages, or fruit other than grapes, figs, pomegranates, olives or dates – say:

בָּרוּךְ Blessed are You, Lord our God, King of the Universe,
who creates the many forms of life and their needs.
For all You have created
to sustain the life of all that lives,
blessed be He, Giver of life to the worlds.

עַמֶּךָ וְעַל יְרוּשָׁלַיִם עִירֶךָ וְעַל צִיּוֹן מִשְׁכַּן כְּבוֹדֶךָ וְעַל מִזְבְּחֶךָ וְעַל הֵיכָלֶךָ.
וּבְנֵה יְרוּשָׁלַיִם עִיר הַקֹּדֶשׁ בִּמְהֵרָה בְיָמֵינוּ, וְהַעֲלֵנוּ לְתוֹכָהּ וְשַׂמְּחֵנוּ
בְּבִנְיָנָהּ וְנֹאכַל מִפִּרְיָהּ וְנִשְׂבַּע מִטּוּבָהּ, וּנְבָרֶכְךָ עָלֶיהָ בִּקְדֻשָּׁה וּבְטָהֳרָה.

בשבת: וּרְצֵה וְהַחֲלִיצֵנוּ בְּיוֹם הַשַּׁבָּת הַזֶּה

בראש חודש: וְזָכְרֵנוּ לְטוֹבָה בְּיוֹם רֹאשׁ הַחֹדֶשׁ הַזֶּה

בפסח: וְשַׂמְּחֵנוּ בְּיוֹם חַג הַמַּצּוֹת הַזֶּה

בסוכות: וְשַׂמְּחֵנוּ בְּיוֹם חַג הַסֻּכּוֹת הַזֶּה

כִּי אַתָּה יהוה טוֹב וּמֵטִיב לַכֹּל, וְנוֹדֶה לְּךָ עַל הָאָרֶץ

After grain products (but not bread or מצה):

וְעַל הַמִּחְיָה.
בָּרוּךְ אַתָּה יהוה עַל
הָאָרֶץ וְעַל הַמִּחְיָה.

After wine or grape juice:

וְעַל פְּרִי הַגֶּפֶן.*
בָּרוּךְ אַתָּה יהוה עַל
הָאָרֶץ וְעַל פְּרִי הַגֶּפֶן.*

After grapes, figs, olives, pomegranates or dates:

וְעַל הַפֵּרוֹת.**
בָּרוּךְ אַתָּה יהוה עַל
הָאָרֶץ וְעַל הַפֵּרוֹת.**

After grain products (but not bread or מצה), and wine or grape juice:

וְעַל הַמִּחְיָה וְעַל פְּרִי הַגֶּפֶן.*
בָּרוּךְ אַתָּה יהוה, עַל הָאָרֶץ וְעַל הַמִּחְיָה וְעַל פְּרִי הַגֶּפֶן.*

**If the wine is from ארץ ישראל, then substitute גַּפְנָהּ for הַגֶּפֶן.*
***If the fruit is from ארץ ישראל, then substitute פֵּרוֹתֶיהָ for הַפֵּרוֹת.*

בורא נפשות

After food or drink that does not require ברכת המזון or מעין שלוש – such as meat, fish, dairy products, vegetables, beverages, or fruit other than grapes, figs, pomegranates, olives or dates – say:

בָּרוּךְ אַתָּה יהוה אֱלֹהֵינוּ מֶלֶךְ הָעוֹלָם
בּוֹרֵא נְפָשׁוֹת רַבּוֹת וְחֶסְרוֹנָן, עַל כָּל מַה שֶּׁבָּרָאתָ
לְהַחֲיוֹת בָּהֶם נֶפֶשׁ כָּל חָי.
בָּרוּךְ חֵי הָעוֹלָמִים.

BLESSINGS

BLESSINGS ON MITZVOT

In Israel on separating teruma and first tithe (if there is doubt as to whether the teruma and first tithe have been taken, the following blessing is not said, but the following declaration is):

Blessed are You, LORD our God, King of the Universe,
who has made us holy through His commandments,
and has commanded us to separate *terumot* and tithes.

Whatever [of the allocated portion] is more than one in a hundred of everything here, is hereby declared to be *teruma gedola* [the priestly portion] and is the northern portion. The one in a hundred that remains here, together with nine equal portions on the upper side of this produce are declared to be the first [levitical] tithe. The one in a hundred I have made first tithe is hereby declared to be *terumat maaser* [the tithe-of-the-tithe set aside for the priests]. Nine other equal portions on the lower side of the produce are declared to be second tithe, but if this produce must have the tithe of the poor separated from it, let them be the tithe of the poor.

In Israel on separating and redeeming the second tithe (if there is doubt as to whether the second tithe has been taken, the following blessing is not said, but the following declaration is):

Blessed are You, LORD our God, King of the Universe,
who has made us holy through His commandments,
and has commanded us about the redemption of the second tithe.

This second tithe, together with its additional fifth, is hereby redeemed by one *peruta* of the coins I have set aside for the redemption of the second tithe.

On taking ḥalla:

Blessed are You, LORD our God, King of the Universe,
who has made us holy through His commandments,
and has commanded us to set aside ḥalla from the dough.

On redeeming fourth-year fruit:

Blessed are You, LORD our God, King of the Universe,
who has made us holy through His commandments,
and has commanded us about the redemption of fruit of the fourth year.

On fixing a mezuza to the doorpost:

Blessed are You, LORD our God, King of the Universe,
who has made us holy through His commandments,
and has commanded us to affix the mezuza.

On making a protective railing around one's roof, or a fence around a pit:

Blessed are You, LORD our God, King of the Universe,
who has made us holy through His commandments,
and has commanded us to to affix a guard-rail.

ברכות

ברכות המצוות

In ארץ ישראל *on separating* תרומה *and* מעשר ראשון (*if there is doubt as to whether the* תרומה *and* מעשר ראשון *have been taken, the following blessing is not said, but the following declaration is*):

בָּרוּךְ אַתָּה יהוה אֱלֹהֵינוּ מֶלֶךְ הָעוֹלָם, אֲשֶׁר קִדְּשָׁנוּ בְּמִצְוֹתָיו וְצִוָּנוּ לְהַפְרִישׁ תְּרוּמוֹת וּמַעַשְׂרוֹת.

מַה שֶּׁהוּא יוֹתֵר מֵאֶחָד מִמֵּאָה מִן הַכֹּל שֶׁיֵּשׁ כָּאן, הֲרֵי הוּא תְּרוּמָה גְדוֹלָה בִּצְפוֹנוֹ, וְהָאֶחָד מִמֵּאָה שֶׁנִּשְׁאַר כָּאן עִם תִּשְׁעָה חֲלָקִים כָּמְוֹהוּ בְּצַד הָעֶלְיוֹן שֶׁל הַפֵּרוֹת הַלָּלוּ, הֲרֵי הֵם מַעֲשֵׂר רִאשׁוֹן. אוֹתוֹ הָאֶחָד מִמֵּאָה שֶׁעֲשִׂיתִיו מַעֲשֵׂר רִאשׁוֹן הֲרֵי הוּא תְּרוּמַת מַעֲשֵׂר. עוֹד תִּשְׁעָה חֲלָקִים כָּאֵלֶּה בְּצַד הַתַּחְתּוֹן שֶׁל הַפֵּרוֹת הֲרֵי הֵם מַעֲשֵׂר שֵׁנִי, וְאִם הֵם חַיָּבִים בְּמַעֲשַׂר עָנִי, הֲרֵי הֵם מַעֲשַׂר עָנִי.

In ארץ ישראל *on separating and redeeming the* מעשר שני (*if there is doubt as to whether the* מעשר שני *has been taken, the following blessing is not said, but the following declaration is*):

בָּרוּךְ אַתָּה יהוה אֱלֹהֵינוּ מֶלֶךְ הָעוֹלָם, אֲשֶׁר קִדְּשָׁנוּ בְּמִצְוֹתָיו וְצִוָּנוּ עַל פִּדְיוֹן מַעֲשֵׂר שֵׁנִי.

מַעֲשֵׂר שֵׁנִי זֶה, הוּא וְחֻמְשׁוֹ, הֲרֵי הוּא מְחֻלָּל עַל פְּרוּטָה אַחַת מִן הַמַּטְבֵּעַ שֶׁיִּחַדְתִּי לְפִדְיוֹן מַעֲשֵׂר שֵׁנִי.

On taking חלה:

בָּרוּךְ אַתָּה יהוה אֱלֹהֵינוּ מֶלֶךְ הָעוֹלָם, אֲשֶׁר קִדְּשָׁנוּ בְּמִצְוֹתָיו וְצִוָּנוּ לְהַפְרִישׁ חַלָּה מִן הָעִסָּה.

On redeeming נטע רבעי:

בָּרוּךְ אַתָּה יהוה אֱלֹהֵינוּ מֶלֶךְ הָעוֹלָם, אֲשֶׁר קִדְּשָׁנוּ בְּמִצְוֹתָיו וְצִוָּנוּ עַל פִּדְיוֹן נֶטַע רְבָעִי.

On fixing a מזוזה *to the doorpost:*

בָּרוּךְ אַתָּה יהוה אֱלֹהֵינוּ מֶלֶךְ הָעוֹלָם, אֲשֶׁר קִדְּשָׁנוּ בְּמִצְוֹתָיו וְצִוָּנוּ לִקְבֹּעַ מְזוּזָה.

On making a protective railing around one's roof, or a fence around a pit:

בָּרוּךְ אַתָּה יהוה אֱלֹהֵינוּ מֶלֶךְ הָעוֹלָם, אֲשֶׁר קִדְּשָׁנוּ בְּמִצְוֹתָיו וְצִוָּנוּ לַעֲשׂוֹת מַעֲקֶה.

On immersing utensils made by or bought from a gentile:

Blessed are You, LORD our God, King of the Universe,
who has made us holy through His commandments,
and has commanded us about immersing a vessel (vessels).

BLESSINGS ON PLEASURES, SIGHTS AND SOUNDS

On wearing new clothes:

Blessed are You, LORD our God, King of the Universe,
who clothes the naked.

On smelling fragrant shrubs or trees:

Blessed are You, LORD our God, King of the Universe,
who creates fragrant trees.

On smelling fragrant herbs, grasses or flowers:

Blessed are You, LORD our God, King of the Universe,
who creates fragrant plants.

On smelling fragrant fruit:

Blessed are You, LORD our God, King of the Universe,
who gives pleasant fragrance to fruits.

On smelling persimmon oil:

Blessed are You, LORD our God, King of the Universe,
who creates pleasing perfume.

On all other scents:

Blessed are You, LORD our God, King of the Universe,
who creates the various spices.

On seeing the wonders of nature, such as lightning, and on the 28-year solar cycle:

Blessed are You, LORD our God, King of the Universe,
Author of creation.

On hearing thunder or experiencing a hurricane:

Blessed are You, LORD our God, King of the Universe,
whose power and might fill the world.

On seeing a rainbow:

Blessed are You, LORD our God, King of the Universe,
who remembers the covenant, is faithful to the covenant,
and fulfills His word.

On seeing the ocean or the Mediterranean Sea for the first time in thirty days:

Blessed are You, LORD our God, King of the Universe,
who has made the great sea.

On immersing utensils made by or bought from a gentile:

בָּרוּךְ אַתָּה יהוה אֱלֹהֵינוּ מֶלֶךְ הָעוֹלָם, אֲשֶׁר קִדְּשָׁנוּ בְּמִצְוֹתָיו
וְצִוָּנוּ עַל טְבִילַת כֶּלִי (כֵּלִים).

ברכות הנהנין, הראייה והשמיעה

On wearing new clothes:

בָּרוּךְ אַתָּה יהוה אֱלֹהֵינוּ מֶלֶךְ הָעוֹלָם, מַלְבִּישׁ עֲרֻמִּים.

On smelling fragrant shrubs or trees:

בָּרוּךְ אַתָּה יהוה אֱלֹהֵינוּ מֶלֶךְ הָעוֹלָם, בּוֹרֵא עֲצֵי בְשָׂמִים.

On smelling fragrant herbs, grasses or flowers:

בָּרוּךְ אַתָּה יהוה אֱלֹהֵינוּ מֶלֶךְ הָעוֹלָם, בּוֹרֵא עִשְׂבֵי בְשָׂמִים.

On smelling fragrant fruit:

בָּרוּךְ אַתָּה יהוה אֱלֹהֵינוּ מֶלֶךְ הָעוֹלָם, הַנּוֹתֵן רֵיחַ טוֹב בַּפֵּרוֹת.

On smelling persimmon oil:

בָּרוּךְ אַתָּה יהוה אֱלֹהֵינוּ מֶלֶךְ הָעוֹלָם, בּוֹרֵא שֶׁמֶן עָרֵב.

On all other scents:

בָּרוּךְ אַתָּה יהוה אֱלֹהֵינוּ מֶלֶךְ הָעוֹלָם, בּוֹרֵא מִינֵי בְשָׂמִים.

On seeing the wonders of nature, such as lightning, and ברכת החמה:

בָּרוּךְ אַתָּה יהוה אֱלֹהֵינוּ מֶלֶךְ הָעוֹלָם, עוֹשֶׂה מַעֲשֵׂה בְרֵאשִׁית.

On hearing thunder or experiencing a hurricane:

בָּרוּךְ אַתָּה יהוה אֱלֹהֵינוּ מֶלֶךְ הָעוֹלָם, שֶׁכֹּחוֹ וּגְבוּרָתוֹ מָלֵא עוֹלָם.

On seeing a rainbow:

בָּרוּךְ אַתָּה יהוה אֱלֹהֵינוּ מֶלֶךְ הָעוֹלָם
זוֹכֵר הַבְּרִית וְנֶאֱמָן בִּבְרִיתוֹ וְקַיָּם בְּמַאֲמָרוֹ.

On seeing the ocean or the Mediterranean Sea for the first time in thirty days:

בָּרוּךְ אַתָּה יהוה אֱלֹהֵינוּ מֶלֶךְ הָעוֹלָם, שֶׁעָשָׂה אֶת הַיָּם הַגָּדוֹל.

On seeing trees blossoming for the first time in the year:
Blessed are You, LORD our God, King of the Universe,
who has withheld nothing from His world, but has created in it
beautiful creatures and trees for human beings to enjoy.

On seeing beautiful scenes of nature:
Blessed are You, LORD our God, King of the Universe,
who has [created] such things in His world.

On seeing unusual people or animals:
Blessed are You, LORD our God, King of the Universe,
who makes [all] creatures different.

On hearing good news from which others as well as oneself will benefit:
Blessed are You, LORD our God, King of the Universe,
who is good and does good.

On hearing bad news, and said by a mourner before the ritual tearing of the garment:
Blessed are You, LORD our God, King of the Universe,
the true Judge.

On seeing an outstanding Torah scholar:
Blessed are You, LORD our God, King of the Universe,
who has shared of His wisdom with those who fear Him.

On seeing an outstanding secular scholar:
Blessed are You, LORD our God, King of the Universe,
who has given of His wisdom with human beings.

On seeing a Monarch or Head of State:
Blessed are You, LORD our God, King of the Universe,
who has given of His glory to human beings.

On seeing 600,000 Jews together in Israel:
Blessed are You, LORD our God, King of the Universe,
who knows all secrets.

On seeing Jewish settlements in Israel:
Blessed are You, LORD our God, King of the Universe,
who establishes the border of the widow.

On seeing the place where miracles occurred to the Jewish People:
Blessed are You, LORD our God, King of the Universe,
who performed miracles for our ancestors in this place.

On seeing the place where miracles occurred to oneself or one's family (insert the relevant words):
Blessed are You, LORD our God, King of the Universe,
who performed a miracle for me (my father / my mother / my ancestors)
in this place.

On seeing trees blossoming for the first time in the year:

בָּרוּךְ אַתָּה יהוה אֱלֹהֵינוּ מֶלֶךְ הָעוֹלָם, שֶׁלֹּא חִסַּר בְּעוֹלָמוֹ כְּלוּם
וּבָרָא בוֹ בְּרִיּוֹת טוֹבוֹת וְאִילָנוֹת טוֹבִים לְהַנּוֹת בָּהֶם בְּנֵי אָדָם.

On seeing beautiful scenes of nature:

בָּרוּךְ אַתָּה יהוה אֱלֹהֵינוּ מֶלֶךְ הָעוֹלָם, שֶׁכָּכָה לוֹ בְּעוֹלָמוֹ.

On seeing unusual people or animals:

בָּרוּךְ אַתָּה יהוה אֱלֹהֵינוּ מֶלֶךְ הָעוֹלָם, מְשַׁנֶּה הַבְּרִיּוֹת.

On hearing good news from which others as well as oneself will benefit:

בָּרוּךְ אַתָּה יהוה אֱלֹהֵינוּ מֶלֶךְ הָעוֹלָם, הַטּוֹב וְהַמֵּטִיב.

On hearing bad news, and said by a mourner before the ritual tearing of the garment:

בָּרוּךְ אַתָּה יהוה אֱלֹהֵינוּ מֶלֶךְ הָעוֹלָם, דַּיַּן הָאֱמֶת.

On seeing an outstanding Torah scholar:

בָּרוּךְ אַתָּה יהוה אֱלֹהֵינוּ מֶלֶךְ הָעוֹלָם, שֶׁחָלַק מֵחָכְמָתוֹ לִירֵאָיו.

On seeing an outstanding secular scholar:

בָּרוּךְ אַתָּה יהוה אֱלֹהֵינוּ מֶלֶךְ הָעוֹלָם, שֶׁנָּתַן מֵחָכְמָתוֹ לְבָשָׂר וָדָם.

On seeing a Monarch or Head of State:

בָּרוּךְ אַתָּה יהוה אֱלֹהֵינוּ מֶלֶךְ הָעוֹלָם, שֶׁנָּתַן מִכְּבוֹדוֹ לְבָשָׂר וָדָם.

On seeing 600,000 Jews together in ארץ ישראל*:*

בָּרוּךְ אַתָּה יהוה אֱלֹהֵינוּ מֶלֶךְ הָעוֹלָם, חֲכַם הָרָזִים.

On seeing Jewish settlements in ארץ ישראל*:*

בָּרוּךְ אַתָּה יהוה אֱלֹהֵינוּ מֶלֶךְ הָעוֹלָם
מַצִּיב גְּבוּל אַלְמָנָה.

On seeing the place where miracles occurred to the Jewish People:

בָּרוּךְ אַתָּה יהוה אֱלֹהֵינוּ מֶלֶךְ הָעוֹלָם
שֶׁעָשָׂה נִסִּים לַאֲבוֹתֵינוּ בַּמָּקוֹם הַזֶּה.

On seeing the place where miracles occurred to oneself or one's family (insert the relevant words):

בָּרוּךְ אַתָּה יהוה אֱלֹהֵינוּ מֶלֶךְ הָעוֹלָם
שֶׁעָשָׂה לִי (לְאָבִי/לְאִמִּי/לַאֲבוֹתַי) נֵס בַּמָּקוֹם הַזֶּה.

ADDITIONAL BLESSINGS

After relieving oneself and washing one's hands, say:

Blessed are You, LORD our God, King of the Universe, who formed man in wisdom and created in him many openings and cavities. It is revealed and known before the throne of Your glory that were one of them to be ruptured or blocked, it would be impossible to survive and stand before You. Blessed are You, LORD, Healer of all flesh who does miracles.

On visiting a cemetery, or seeing a Jewish grave, for the first time in thirty days:

Blessed are You, LORD our God, King of the Universe, who formed you in judgment, who nourished and sustained you in judgment, who brought death on you in judgment, who knows the number of you all in judgment, and who in the future will restore you to life in judgment. Blessed are You, LORD, who revives the dead.

You are eternally mighty, LORD. You give life to the dead and have great power to save. He sustains the living with loving-kindness, and with great compassion revives the dead. He supports the fallen, heals the sick, sets captives free, and keeps His faith with those who sleep in the dust. Who is like You, Master of might, and who can compare to You, O King who brings death and gives life, and makes salvation grow? Faithful are You to revive the dead.

In special cases of urgency only, the following short form of the Amida may be said. First say the first three blessings of the Amida from "O LORD" on page 150 until "the holy God" page 159, then say:

הֲבִינֵנוּ Give us understanding, LORD our God, to know Your ways. Sensitize our hearts so that we may fear You, and forgive us so that we may be redeemed. Keep us far from suffering and satisfy us with the pastures of Your land. Gather our scattered people from the four quarters of the earth. May those who go astray be judged according to Your will: raise Your hand against the wicked. May the righteous rejoice in the rebuilding of Your city, the restoration of Your Temple, the flowering of Your servant David's glory, and the radiant light of the son of Jesse, Your anointed. May You answer us even before we call. Blessed are You, LORD, who hears prayer.

Continue with the final three blessings from "Find favor" on page 186 until the end.

In extreme cases where there is no time to say the abbreviated Amida above, one may say the following. However, if prayer is then possible at a later time, one should say the complete Amida.

צָרְכֵי The needs of Your people Israel are many, and their patience is thin. May it be Your will, LORD our God and God of our ancestors, to give each one of them enough to sustain him, and to every single body, all that it lacks – and perform what is right in Your eyes. Blessed are You, LORD, who listens to prayer.

ברכות נוספות

After relieving oneself and washing one's hands, say:

בָּרוּךְ אַתָּה יהוה אֱלֹהֵינוּ מֶלֶךְ הָעוֹלָם, אֲשֶׁר יָצַר אֶת הָאָדָם בְּחָכְמָה, וּבָרָא בוֹ נְקָבִים נְקָבִים, חֲלוּלִים חֲלוּלִים. גָּלוּי וְיָדְוּעַ לִפְנֵי כִסֵּא כְבוֹדֶךָ, שֶׁאִם יִפָּתֵחַ אֶחָד מֵהֶם אוֹ יִסָּתֵם אֶחָד מֵהֶם, אִי אֶפְשַׁר לְהִתְקַיֵּם וְלַעֲמֹד לְפָנֶיךָ. בָּרוּךְ אַתָּה יהוה, רוֹפֵא כָל בָּשָׂר וּמַפְלִיא לַעֲשׂוֹת.

On visiting a cemetery, or seeing a Jewish grave, for the first time in thirty days:

בָּרוּךְ אַתָּה יהוה אֱלֹהֵינוּ מֶלֶךְ הָעוֹלָם, אֲשֶׁר יָצַר אֶתְכֶם בַּדִּין, וְזָן וְכִלְכֵּל אֶתְכֶם בַּדִּין, וְהֵמִית אֶתְכֶם בַּדִּין, וְיוֹדֵעַ מִסְפַּר כֻּלְּכֶם בַּדִּין, וְהוּא עָתִיד לְהַחֲיוֹתְכֶם וּלְקַיֵּם אֶתְכֶם בַּדִּין. בָּרוּךְ אַתָּה יהוה, מְחַיֵּה הַמֵּתִים.

אַתָּה גִּבּוֹר לְעוֹלָם אֲדֹנָי, מְחַיֵּה מֵתִים אַתָּה, רַב לְהוֹשִׁיעַ, מְכַלְכֵּל חַיִּים בְּחֶסֶד, מְחַיֵּה מֵתִים בְּרַחֲמִים רַבִּים, סוֹמֵךְ נוֹפְלִים, וְרוֹפֵא חוֹלִים, וּמַתִּיר אֲסוּרִים, וּמְקַיֵּם אֱמוּנָתוֹ לִישֵׁנֵי עָפָר. מִי כָמְוֹךָ בַּעַל גְּבוּרוֹת וּמִי דְּוֹמֶה לָּךְ, מֶלֶךְ מֵמִית וּמְחַיֶּה וּמַצְמִיחַ יְשׁוּעָה, וְנֶאֱמָן אַתָּה לְהַחֲיוֹת מֵתִים.

In special cases of urgency only, the following short form of the עמידה *may be said. First say the first three* ברכות *of the* עמידה *from* אֲדֹנָי, שְׂפָתַי תִּפְתָּח *on page 151 until* הַקָּדוֹשׁ *on page 159, then say:*

הֲבִינֵנוּ יהוה אֱלֹהֵינוּ לָדַעַת דְּרָכֶיךָ, וּמוֹל אֶת לְבָבֵנוּ לְיִרְאָתֶךָ, וְתִסְלַח לָנוּ לִהְיוֹת גְּאוּלִים, וְרַחֲקֵנוּ מִמַּכְאוֹב, וְדַשְּׁנֵנוּ בִּנְאוֹת אַרְצֶךָ, וּנְפוּצוֹתֵינוּ מֵאַרְבַּע תְּקַבֵּץ, וְהַתּוֹעִים עַל דַּעְתְּךָ יִשָּׁפֵטוּ, וְעַל הָרְשָׁעִים תָּנִיף יָדֶךָ, וְיִשְׂמְחוּ צַדִּיקִים בְּבִנְיַן עִירֶךָ וּבְתִקּוּן הֵיכָלֶךָ, וּבִצְמִיחַת קֶרֶן לְדָוִד עַבְדֶּךָ וּבַעֲרִיכַת נֵר לְבֶן יִשַׁי מְשִׁיחֶךָ, טֶרֶם נִקְרָא אַתָּה תַעֲנֶה. בָּרוּךְ אַתָּה יהוה, שׁוֹמֵעַ תְּפִלָּה.

Continue with the final three ברכות*, from* רְצֵה *on page 187 until the end.*

In extreme cases where there is no time to say the abbreviated עמידה *above, one may say the following. However, if prayer is then possible at a later time, one should say the complete* עמידה*.*

צָרְכֵי עַמְּךָ יִשְׂרָאֵל מְרֻבִּים וְדַעְתָּם קְצָרָה. יְהִי רָצוֹן מִלְּפָנֶיךָ יהוה אֱלֹהֵינוּ וֵאלֹהֵי אֲבוֹתֵינוּ, שֶׁתִּתֵּן לְכָל אֶחָד וְאֶחָד כְּדֵי פַרְנָסָתוֹ, וּלְכָל גְּוִיָּה וּגְוִיָּה דֵּי מַחְסוֹרָהּ, וְהַטּוֹב בְּעֵינֶיךָ עֲשֵׂה. בָּרוּךְ אַתָּה יהוה, שׁוֹמֵעַ תְּפִלָּה.

**In times of drought in Israel, add:*

וַעֲנֵנוּ And answer us through the attribute of compassion, Creator of the universe who chooses His people Israel to make known His greatness and majestic glory. You who listen to prayer, provide dew and rain on the face of the earth, satisfying the whole universe from Your goodness. Fill our hands from Your blessings and Your hand's rich gift. Guard and deliver this year from all evil, all kinds of destruction and punishment, and give it hope and a peaceful end. Spare us and have compassion on us and on all our produce and fruit, blessing us with rains of blessing. May we merit life, plenty and peace as in the good years. Remove from us plague, sword and famine, wild animals, captivity and plunder, the evil instinct and serious and dangerous illnesses and events. Decree for us goodly decrees, and may Your compassion prevail over Your other attributes, that You may act toward Your children through the attribute of compassion, and in compassion and favor accept our prayer.

BIRKAT KOHANIM IN ISRAEL

In Israel, the following is said by the Leader during the Repetition of the Amida when Kohanim bless the congregation. If there is more than one Kohen, a member of the congregation calls:

Kohanim!

The Kohanim respond:

Blessed are You, Lord our God, King of the Universe, who has made us holy with the holiness of Aaron, and has commanded us to bless His people Israel with love.

The Leader calls word by word, followed by the Kohanim:

יְבָרֶכְךָ May the LORD bless you and protect you. (*Cong:* Amen.) *Num. 6*
May the LORD make His face shine on you
and be generous to you. (*Cong:* Amen.)
May the LORD turn His face toward you,
and give you peace. (*Cong:* Amen.)

The Leader continues with the Blessing of Peace.
On weekdays, at Shaḥarit on page 196 and at Minḥa on page 294. On Shabbat, at Shaḥarit on page 620 and at Musaf on page 692. On Ḥol HaMo'ed, at Musaf on page 876

The congregation says:

אַדִּיר Majestic One on high who is present in power: You are peace and Your name is peace. May it be Your will to bring us and Your people the house of Israel, life and blessing as a safeguard for peace.

The Kohanim say:

רִבּוֹנוֹ Master of the Universe: we have done what You have decreed for us. So too may You deal with us as You have promised us. Look down from Your holy dwelling place, from heaven, and bless Your people Israel and the land You have given us as You promised on oath to our ancestors, a land flowing with milk and honey. *Deut. 26*

**In times of drought in* ארץ ישראל*, add:*

וַעֲנֵנוּ בּוֹרֵא עוֹלָם בְּמִדַּת הָרַחֲמִים, בּוֹחֵר בְּעַמּוֹ יִשְׂרָאֵל לְהוֹדִיעַ גָּדְלוֹ וְהַדְרַת כְּבוֹדוֹ. שׁוֹמֵעַ תְּפִלָּה, תֵּן טַל וּמָטָר עַל פְּנֵי הָאֲדָמָה, וְתַשְׂבִּיעַ אֶת הָעוֹלָם כֻּלּוֹ מִטּוּבֶךָ, וּמַלֵּא יָדֵינוּ מִבִּרְכוֹתֶיךָ וּמֵעֹשֶׁר מַתְּנַת יָדֶךָ. שְׁמֹר וְהַצֵּל שָׁנָה זוֹ מִכָּל דָּבָר רָע, וּמִכָּל מִינֵי מַשְׁחִית וּמִכָּל מִינֵי פֻרְעָנִיּוֹת, וַעֲשֵׂה לָהּ תִּקְוָה וְאַחֲרִית שָׁלוֹם. חוּס וְרַחֵם עָלֵינוּ וְעַל כָּל תְּבוּאָתֵנוּ וּפֵרוֹתֵינוּ, וּבָרְכֵנוּ בְּגִשְׁמֵי בְרָכָה, וְנִזְכֶּה לְחַיִּים וָשֹׂבַע וְשָׁלוֹם כַּשָּׁנִים הַטּוֹבוֹת. וְהָסֵר מִמֶּנּוּ דֶּבֶר וְחֶרֶב וְרָעָב, וְחַיָּה רָעָה וּשְׁבִי וּבִזָּה, וְיֵצֶר הָרָע וָחֳלָיִים רָעִים וְקָשִׁים וּמְאֹרָעוֹת רָעִים וְקָשִׁים. וּגְזֹר עָלֵינוּ גְּזֵרוֹת טוֹבוֹת מִלְּפָנֶיךָ, וְיִגֹּלּוּ רַחֲמֶיךָ עַל מִדּוֹתֶיךָ, וְתִתְנַהֵג עִם בָּנֶיךָ בְּמִדַּת הָרַחֲמִים, וְקַבֵּל בְּרַחֲמִים וּבְרָצוֹן אֶת תְּפִלָּתֵנוּ.

ברכת כוהנים בארץ ישראל

In ארץ ישראל*, the following is said by the* שליח ציבור *during the* חזרת הש״ץ *when* כוהנים *say* ברכת כוהנים*. If there is more than one* כוהן*, a member of the* קהל *calls:*

כֹּהֲנִים

The כוהנים *respond:*

בָּרוּךְ אַתָּה יהוה אֱלֹהֵינוּ מֶלֶךְ הָעוֹלָם, אֲשֶׁר קִדְּשָׁנוּ בִּקְדֻשָּׁתוֹ שֶׁל אַהֲרֹן וְצִוָּנוּ לְבָרֵךְ אֶת עַמּוֹ יִשְׂרָאֵל בְּאַהֲבָה.

The שליח ציבור *calls word by word, followed by the* כוהנים*:*

יְבָרֶכְךָ יהוה וְיִשְׁמְרֶךָ: קהל: אָמֵן במדבר ו
יָאֵר יהוה פָּנָיו אֵלֶיךָ וִיחֻנֶּךָּ: קהל: אָמֵן
יִשָּׂא יהוה פָּנָיו אֵלֶיךָ וְיָשֵׂם לְךָ שָׁלוֹם: קהל: אָמֵן

The שליח ציבור *continues with* ברכת שלום*.*
On weekdays, at שחרית *on page 197 and at* מנחה *on page 295. On* שבת*, at* שחרית *on page 621 and at* מוסף *on page 693. On* חול המועד*, at* מוסף *on page 877.*

The קהל *says:*

אַדִּיר בַּמָּרוֹם שׁוֹכֵן בִּגְבוּרָה, אַתָּה שָׁלוֹם וְשִׁמְךָ שָׁלוֹם. יְהִי רָצוֹן שֶׁתָּשִׂים עָלֵינוּ וְעַל כָּל עַמְּךָ בֵּית יִשְׂרָאֵל חַיִּים וּבְרָכָה לְמִשְׁמֶרֶת שָׁלוֹם.

The כוהנים *say:*

רִבּוֹנוֹ שֶׁל עוֹלָם, עָשִׂינוּ מַה שֶּׁגָּזַרְתָּ עָלֵינוּ, אַף אַתָּה
עֲשֵׂה עִמָּנוּ כְּמוֹ שֶׁהִבְטַחְתָּנוּ. הַשְׁקִיפָה מִמְּעוֹן דברים כו
קָדְשְׁךָ מִן־הַשָּׁמַיִם, וּבָרֵךְ אֶת־עַמְּךָ אֶת־יִשְׂרָאֵל,
וְאֵת הָאֲדָמָה אֲשֶׁר נָתַתָּה לָנוּ, כַּאֲשֶׁר נִשְׁבַּעְתָּ
לַאֲבֹתֵינוּ, אֶרֶץ זָבַת חָלָב וּדְבָשׁ:

THE TRAVELER'S PRAYER

If one intends to return home on the same day, add the words in parentheses:

יְהִי רָצוֹן May it be Your will,
Lord our God and God of our fathers,
to lead us to peace, direct our steps to peace,
guide us to peace, and bring us to our desired destination in life,
joy and peace
(and bring us back to our home in peace).
Rescue us from any enemy or ambush on the way,
and from all suffering that troubles the world.
Send blessing to the work of our hands,
and let us find grace, kindness and compassion
from You and from all who see us.
Hear our pleas,
for You are a God who hears prayer and pleas.
Blessed are You, Lord, who listens to prayer.

May the Lord guard your going out and your return, *Ps. 121*
from now and for all time.

Repeat three times:

וְיַעֲקֹב And Jacob went on his way *Gen. 32*
and angels of God met him.
When he saw them, Jacob said, "This is God's camp"
and he named the place Maḥanaim [two camps].

Repeat three times:

יְבָרֶכְךָ May the Lord bless you and protect you. *Num. 6*
May the Lord make His face shine on you and be generous to you.
May the Lord turn His face toward you and give you peace.

שִׁיר לַמַּעֲלוֹת A song of ascents. I lift my eyes up to the hills; from where will *Ps. 121* my help come? My help comes from the Lord, Maker of heaven and earth. He will not let your foot stumble; He who guards you does not slumber. See: the Guardian of Israel neither slumbers nor sleeps. The Lord is your Guardian; the Lord is your Shade at your right hand. The sun will not strike you by day, nor the moon by night. The Lord will guard you from all harm; He will guard your life. The Lord will guard your going and coming, now and for evermore.

תפילת הדרך

If one intends to return home on the same day, add the words in parentheses:

יְהִי רָצוֹן מִלְּפָנֶיךָ, יהוה אֱלֹהֵינוּ וֵאלֹהֵי אֲבוֹתֵינוּ
שֶׁתּוֹלִיכֵנוּ לְשָׁלוֹם, וְתַצְעִידֵנוּ לְשָׁלוֹם, וְתַדְרִיכֵנוּ לְשָׁלוֹם
וְתַגִּיעֵנוּ לִמְחוֹז חֶפְצֵנוּ לְחַיִּים וּלְשִׂמְחָה וּלְשָׁלוֹם
(וְתַחֲזִירֵנוּ לְבֵיתֵנוּ לְשָׁלוֹם)
וְתַצִּילֵנוּ מִכַּף כָּל אוֹיֵב וְאוֹרֵב בַּדֶּרֶךְ
וּמִכָּל מִינֵי פֻרְעָנִיּוֹת הַמִּתְרַגְּשׁוֹת לָבוֹא לָעוֹלָם
וְתִשְׁלַח בְּרָכָה בְּמַעֲשֵׂה יָדֵינוּ
וְתִתְּנֵנוּ לְחֵן וּלְחֶסֶד וּלְרַחֲמִים בְּעֵינֶיךָ וּבְעֵינֵי כָל רוֹאֵינוּ
וְתִשְׁמַע קוֹל תַּחֲנוּנֵינוּ
כִּי אֵל שׁוֹמֵעַ תְּפִלָּה וְתַחֲנוּן אָתָּה.
בָּרוּךְ אַתָּה יהוה, שׁוֹמֵעַ תְּפִלָּה.

יהוה יִשְׁמָר־צֵאתְךָ וּבוֹאֶךָ, מֵעַתָּה וְעַד־עוֹלָם: תהלים קכא

Repeat three times:

וְיַעֲקֹב הָלַךְ לְדַרְכּוֹ, וַיִּפְגְּעוּ־בוֹ מַלְאֲכֵי אֱלֹהִים: בראשית לב
וַיֹּאמֶר יַעֲקֹב כַּאֲשֶׁר רָאָם, מַחֲנֵה אֱלֹהִים זֶה
וַיִּקְרָא שֵׁם־הַמָּקוֹם הַהוּא מַחֲנָיִם:

Repeat three times:

יְבָרֶכְךָ יהוה וְיִשְׁמְרֶךָ: במדבר ו
יָאֵר יהוה פָּנָיו אֵלֶיךָ וִיחֻנֶּךָּ:
יִשָּׂא יהוה פָּנָיו אֵלֶיךָ וְיָשֵׂם לְךָ שָׁלוֹם:

שִׁיר לַמַּעֲלוֹת, אֶשָּׂא עֵינַי אֶל־הֶהָרִים, מֵאַיִן יָבֹא עֶזְרִי: עֶזְרִי מֵעִם יהוה, תהלים קכא
עֹשֵׂה שָׁמַיִם וָאָרֶץ: אַל־יִתֵּן לַמּוֹט רַגְלֶךָ, אַל־יָנוּם שֹׁמְרֶךָ: הִנֵּה לֹא־יָנוּם
וְלֹא יִישָׁן, שׁוֹמֵר יִשְׂרָאֵל: יהוה שֹׁמְרֶךָ, יהוה צִלְּךָ עַל־יַד יְמִינֶךָ: יוֹמָם
הַשֶּׁמֶשׁ לֹא־יַכֶּכָּה, וְיָרֵחַ בַּלָּיְלָה: יהוה יִשְׁמָרְךָ מִכָּל־רָע, יִשְׁמֹר אֶת־נַפְשֶׁךָ:
יהוה יִשְׁמָר־צֵאתְךָ וּבוֹאֶךָ, מֵעַתָּה וְעַד־עוֹלָם:

קריאת התורה
TORAH READINGS

קריאת התורה לימי שני וחמישי ובמנחה של שבת

THE READING OF THE TORAH FOR MONDAYS, THURSDAYS, AND SHABBAT MINḤA

BERESHIT בראשית

בראשית א: א-כג

FIRST ALIYA: 1:1–5
The first day of creation: Light and darkness, day and night.

בְּרֵאשִׁ֖ית בָּרָ֣א אֱלֹהִ֑ים אֵ֥ת הַשָּׁמַ֖יִם וְאֵ֥ת הָאָֽרֶץ׃ וְהָאָ֗רֶץ הָיְתָ֥ה תֹ֙הוּ֙ וָבֹ֔הוּ וְחֹ֖שֶׁךְ עַל־פְּנֵ֣י תְה֑וֹם וְר֣וּחַ אֱלֹהִ֔ים מְרַחֶ֖פֶת עַל־פְּנֵ֥י הַמָּֽיִם׃ וַיֹּ֥אמֶר אֱלֹהִ֖ים יְהִ֣י א֑וֹר וַֽיְהִי־אֽוֹר׃ וַיַּ֧רְא אֱלֹהִ֛ים אֶת־הָא֖וֹר כִּי־ט֑וֹב וַיַּבְדֵּ֣ל אֱלֹהִ֔ים בֵּ֥ין הָא֖וֹר וּבֵ֥ין הַחֹֽשֶׁךְ׃ וַיִּקְרָ֨א אֱלֹהִ֤ים ׀ לָאוֹר֙ י֔וֹם וְלַחֹ֖שֶׁךְ קָ֣רָא לָ֑יְלָה וַֽיְהִי־עֶ֥רֶב וַֽיְהִי־בֹ֖קֶר י֥וֹם אֶחָֽד׃

לוי

SECOND ALIYA: 1:6–8
The second day of creation: Heaven.

וַיֹּ֣אמֶר אֱלֹהִ֔ים יְהִ֥י רָקִ֖יעַ בְּת֣וֹךְ הַמָּ֑יִם וִיהִ֣י מַבְדִּ֔יל בֵּ֥ין מַ֖יִם לָמָֽיִם׃ וַיַּ֣עַשׂ אֱלֹהִים֮ אֶת־הָרָקִיעַ֒ וַיַּבְדֵּ֗ל בֵּ֤ין הַמַּ֙יִם֙ אֲשֶׁר֙ מִתַּ֣חַת לָרָקִ֔יעַ וּבֵ֣ין הַמַּ֔יִם אֲשֶׁ֖ר מֵעַ֣ל לָרָקִ֑יעַ וַֽיְהִי־כֵֽן׃ וַיִּקְרָ֧א אֱלֹהִ֛ים לָֽרָקִ֖יעַ שָׁמָ֑יִם וַֽיְהִי־עֶ֥רֶב וַֽיְהִי־בֹ֖קֶר י֥וֹם שֵׁנִֽי׃

ישראל

THIRD ALIYA: 1:9–13
The third day of creation: Land and sea; vegetation.

וַיֹּ֣אמֶר אֱלֹהִ֗ים יִקָּו֨וּ הַמַּ֜יִם מִתַּ֤חַת הַשָּׁמַ֙יִם֙ אֶל־מָק֣וֹם אֶחָ֔ד וְתֵרָאֶ֖ה הַיַּבָּשָׁ֑ה וַֽיְהִי־כֵֽן׃ וַיִּקְרָ֨א אֱלֹהִ֤ים ׀ לַיַּבָּשָׁה֙ אֶ֔רֶץ וּלְמִקְוֵ֥ה הַמַּ֖יִם קָרָ֣א יַמִּ֑ים וַיַּ֥רְא אֱלֹהִ֖ים כִּי־טֽוֹב׃ וַיֹּ֣אמֶר אֱלֹהִ֗ים תַּֽדְשֵׁ֤א הָאָ֙רֶץ֙ דֶּ֗שֶׁא עֵ֚שֶׂב מַזְרִ֣יעַ זֶ֔רַע עֵ֣ץ פְּרִ֞י עֹ֤שֶׂה פְּרִי֙ לְמִינ֔וֹ אֲשֶׁ֥ר זַרְעוֹ־ב֖וֹ עַל־הָאָ֑רֶץ וַֽיְהִי־כֵֽן׃ וַתּוֹצֵ֨א הָאָ֜רֶץ דֶּ֠שֶׁא עֵ֣שֶׂב מַזְרִ֤יעַ זֶ֙רַע֙ לְמִינֵ֔הוּ וְעֵ֧ץ עֹֽשֶׂה־פְּרִ֛י אֲשֶׁ֥ר זַרְעוֹ־ב֖וֹ לְמִינֵ֑הוּ וַיַּ֥רְא אֱלֹהִ֖ים כִּי־טֽוֹב׃ וַֽיְהִי־עֶ֥רֶב וַֽיְהִי־בֹ֖קֶר י֥וֹם שְׁלִישִֽׁי׃

Some extend the ישראל *portion on the Thursday reading:*

וַיֹּ֣אמֶר אֱלֹהִ֗ים יְהִ֤י מְאֹרֹת֙ בִּרְקִ֣יעַ הַשָּׁמַ֔יִם לְהַבְדִּ֕יל בֵּ֥ין הַיּ֖וֹם וּבֵ֣ין הַלָּ֑יְלָה וְהָי֤וּ לְאֹתֹת֙ וּלְמ֣וֹעֲדִ֔ים וּלְיָמִ֖ים וְשָׁנִֽים׃

וְהָיוּ לִמְאוֹרֹת בִּרְקִיעַ הַשָּׁמַיִם לְהָאִיר עַל־הָאָרֶץ וַיְהִי־כֵן׃
וַיַּעַשׂ אֱלֹהִים אֶת־שְׁנֵי הַמְּאֹרֹת הַגְּדֹלִים אֶת־הַמָּאוֹר הַגָּדֹל
לְמֶמְשֶׁלֶת הַיּוֹם וְאֶת־הַמָּאוֹר הַקָּטֹן לְמֶמְשֶׁלֶת הַלַּיְלָה
וְאֵת הַכּוֹכָבִים׃ וַיִּתֵּן אֹתָם אֱלֹהִים בִּרְקִיעַ הַשָּׁמָיִם לְהָאִיר
עַל־הָאָרֶץ׃ וְלִמְשֹׁל בַּיּוֹם וּבַלַּיְלָה וּלְהַבְדִּיל בֵּין הָאוֹר וּבֵין
הַחֹשֶׁךְ וַיַּרְא אֱלֹהִים כִּי־טוֹב׃ וַיְהִי־עֶרֶב וַיְהִי־בֹקֶר יוֹם
רְבִיעִי׃
וַיֹּאמֶר אֱלֹהִים יִשְׁרְצוּ הַמַּיִם שֶׁרֶץ נֶפֶשׁ חַיָּה וְעוֹף יְעוֹפֵף עַל־
הָאָרֶץ עַל־פְּנֵי רְקִיעַ הַשָּׁמָיִם׃ וַיִּבְרָא אֱלֹהִים אֶת־הַתַּנִּינִם
הַגְּדֹלִים וְאֵת כָּל־נֶפֶשׁ הַחַיָּה ׀ הָרֹמֶשֶׂת אֲשֶׁר שָׁרְצוּ הַמַּיִם
לְמִינֵהֶם וְאֵת כָּל־עוֹף כָּנָף לְמִינֵהוּ וַיַּרְא אֱלֹהִים כִּי־טוֹב׃
וַיְבָרֶךְ אֹתָם אֱלֹהִים לֵאמֹר פְּרוּ וּרְבוּ וּמִלְאוּ אֶת־הַמַּיִם בַּיַּמִּים
וְהָעוֹף יִרֶב בָּאָרֶץ׃ וַיְהִי־עֶרֶב וַיְהִי־בֹקֶר יוֹם חֲמִישִׁי׃

NOAH נח

בראשית ו: ט–כב

FIRST ALIYA: 6:9–16
Noah was righteous and walked with God. The population of the world had become corrupt and violent. God decrees He will destroy the world with a flood, and commands Noah to build an ark.

SECOND ALIYA: 6:17–19
God enacts a covenant with Noah to save him and his family and two of each species, male and female, in order to repopulate the world.

אֵלֶּה תּוֹלְדֹת נֹחַ נֹחַ אִישׁ צַדִּיק תָּמִים הָיָה בְּדֹרֹתָיו אֶת־
הָאֱלֹהִים הִתְהַלֶּךְ־נֹחַ׃ וַיּוֹלֶד נֹחַ שְׁלֹשָׁה בָנִים אֶת־שֵׁם אֶת־
חָם וְאֶת־יָפֶת׃ וַתִּשָּׁחֵת הָאָרֶץ לִפְנֵי הָאֱלֹהִים וַתִּמָּלֵא הָאָרֶץ
חָמָס׃ וַיַּרְא אֱלֹהִים אֶת־הָאָרֶץ וְהִנֵּה נִשְׁחָתָה כִּי־הִשְׁחִית
כָּל־בָּשָׂר אֶת־דַּרְכּוֹ עַל־הָאָרֶץ׃ וַיֹּאמֶר אֱלֹהִים
לְנֹחַ קֵץ כָּל־בָּשָׂר בָּא לְפָנַי כִּי־מָלְאָה הָאָרֶץ חָמָס מִפְּנֵיהֶם
וְהִנְנִי מַשְׁחִיתָם אֶת־הָאָרֶץ׃ עֲשֵׂה לְךָ תֵּבַת עֲצֵי־גֹפֶר קִנִּים
תַּעֲשֶׂה אֶת־הַתֵּבָה וְכָפַרְתָּ אֹתָהּ מִבַּיִת וּמִחוּץ בַּכֹּפֶר׃ וְזֶה
אֲשֶׁר תַּעֲשֶׂה אֹתָהּ שְׁלֹשׁ מֵאוֹת אַמָּה אֹרֶךְ הַתֵּבָה חֲמִשִּׁים
אַמָּה רָחְבָּהּ וּשְׁלֹשִׁים אַמָּה קוֹמָתָהּ׃ צֹהַר ׀ תַּעֲשֶׂה לַתֵּבָה
וְאֶל־אַמָּה תְּכַלֶּנָּה מִלְמַעְלָה וּפֶתַח הַתֵּבָה בְּצִדָּהּ תָּשִׂים
תַּחְתִּיִּם שְׁנִיִּם וּשְׁלִשִׁים תַּעֲשֶׂהָ׃ *וַאֲנִי הִנְנִי מֵבִיא אֶת־הַמַּבּוּל לוי
מַיִם עַל־הָאָרֶץ לְשַׁחֵת כָּל־בָּשָׂר אֲשֶׁר־בּוֹ רוּחַ חַיִּים מִתַּחַת

הַשָּׁמַיִם כֹּל אֲשֶׁר־בָּאָרֶץ יִגְוָע: וַהֲקִמֹתִי אֶת־בְּרִיתִי אִתָּךְ
וּבָאתָ אֶל־הַתֵּבָה אַתָּה וּבָנֶיךָ וְאִשְׁתְּךָ וּנְשֵׁי־בָנֶיךָ אִתָּךְ:
וּמִכָּל־הָחַי מִכָּל־בָּשָׂר שְׁנַיִם מִכֹּל תָּבִיא אֶל־הַתֵּבָה לְהַחֲיֹת
אִתָּךְ זָכָר וּנְקֵבָה יִהְיוּ: *מֵהָעוֹף לְמִינֵהוּ וּמִן־הַבְּהֵמָה לְמִינָהּ ישראל
מִכֹּל רֶמֶשׂ הָאֲדָמָה לְמִינֵהוּ שְׁנַיִם מִכֹּל יָבֹאוּ אֵלֶיךָ לְהַחֲיוֹת:
וְאַתָּה קַח־לְךָ מִכָּל־מַאֲכָל אֲשֶׁר יֵאָכֵל וְאָסַפְתָּ אֵלֶיךָ וְהָיָה
לְךָ וְלָהֶם לְאָכְלָה: וַיַּעַשׂ נֹחַ כְּכֹל אֲשֶׁר צִוָּה אֹתוֹ אֱלֹהִים
כֵּן עָשָׂה:

THIRD ALIYA: 6:20–22
Noah did as he had been commanded by God.

לך לך LEKH LEKHA

בראשית יב: א–יג

וַיֹּאמֶר יְהוָה אֶל־אַבְרָם לֶךְ־לְךָ מֵאַרְצְךָ וּמִמּוֹלַדְתְּךָ וּמִבֵּית
אָבִיךָ אֶל־הָאָרֶץ אֲשֶׁר אַרְאֶךָּ: וְאֶעֶשְׂךָ לְגוֹי גָּדוֹל וַאֲבָרֶכְךָ
וַאֲגַדְּלָה שְׁמֶךָ וֶהְיֵה בְּרָכָה: וַאֲבָרְכָה מְבָרְכֶיךָ וּמְקַלֶּלְךָ אָאֹר
וְנִבְרְכוּ בְךָ כֹּל מִשְׁפְּחֹת הָאֲדָמָה: *וַיֵּלֶךְ אַבְרָם כַּאֲשֶׁר דִּבֶּר לוי
אֵלָיו יְהוָה וַיֵּלֶךְ אִתּוֹ לוֹט וְאַבְרָם בֶּן־חָמֵשׁ שָׁנִים וְשִׁבְעִים
שָׁנָה בְּצֵאתוֹ מֵחָרָן: וַיִּקַּח אַבְרָם אֶת־שָׂרַי אִשְׁתּוֹ וְאֶת־
לוֹט בֶּן־אָחִיו וְאֶת־כָּל־רְכוּשָׁם אֲשֶׁר רָכָשׁוּ וְאֶת־הַנֶּפֶשׁ
אֲשֶׁר־עָשׂוּ בְחָרָן וַיֵּצְאוּ לָלֶכֶת אַרְצָה כְּנַעַן וַיָּבֹאוּ אַרְצָה
כְּנָעַן: וַיַּעֲבֹר אַבְרָם בָּאָרֶץ עַד מְקוֹם שְׁכֶם עַד אֵלוֹן מוֹרֶה
וְהַכְּנַעֲנִי אָז בָּאָרֶץ: וַיֵּרָא יְהוָה אֶל־אַבְרָם וַיֹּאמֶר לְזַרְעֲךָ
אֶתֵּן אֶת־הָאָרֶץ הַזֹּאת וַיִּבֶן שָׁם מִזְבֵּחַ לַיהוָה הַנִּרְאֶה אֵלָיו:
וַיַּעְתֵּק מִשָּׁם הָהָרָה מִקֶּדֶם לְבֵית־אֵל וַיֵּט אָהֳלֹה בֵּית־אֵל
מִיָּם וְהָעַי מִקֶּדֶם וַיִּבֶן־שָׁם מִזְבֵּחַ לַיהוָה וַיִּקְרָא בְּשֵׁם יְהוָה:
וַיִּסַּע אַבְרָם הָלוֹךְ וְנָסוֹעַ הַנֶּגְבָּה:

FIRST ALIYA: 12:1–3
God's call to Avram to migrate to *Eretz Yisrael*; God promises Avram blessings and progeny.

SECOND ALIYA: 12:4–9
Avram and his entourage make the journey to *Eretz Yisrael*. God appears to Avram and promises this land to his progeny.

וַיְהִי רָעָב בָּאָרֶץ וַיֵּרֶד אַבְרָם מִצְרַיְמָה לָגוּר שָׁם כִּי־כָבֵד ישראל
הָרָעָב בָּאָרֶץ: וַיְהִי כַּאֲשֶׁר הִקְרִיב לָבוֹא מִצְרָיְמָה וַיֹּאמֶר
אֶל־שָׂרַי אִשְׁתּוֹ הִנֵּה־נָא יָדַעְתִּי כִּי אִשָּׁה יְפַת־מַרְאֶה אָתְּ:
וְהָיָה כִּי־יִרְאוּ אֹתָךְ הַמִּצְרִים וְאָמְרוּ אִשְׁתּוֹ זֹאת וְהָרְגוּ אֹתִי
וְאֹתָךְ יְחַיּוּ: אִמְרִי־נָא אֲחֹתִי אָתְּ לְמַעַן יִיטַב־לִי בַעֲבוּרֵךְ
וְחָיְתָה נַפְשִׁי בִּגְלָלֵךְ:

THIRD ALIYA: 12:10–13
Avram and Sarai are forced to leave *Eretz Yisrael* for Egypt due to famine in the land.

VAYERA וירא

בראשית יח: א–יד

FIRST ALIYA: 18:1–5
Avraham is visited by three strangers, who, unbeknown to him, are angels.

וַיֵּרָא אֵלָיו יְהוָה בְּאֵלֹנֵי מַמְרֵא וְהוּא יֹשֵׁב פֶּתַח־הָאֹהֶל
כְּחֹם הַיּוֹם: וַיִּשָּׂא עֵינָיו וַיַּרְא וְהִנֵּה שְׁלֹשָׁה אֲנָשִׁים נִצָּבִים
עָלָיו וַיַּרְא וַיָּרָץ לִקְרָאתָם מִפֶּתַח הָאֹהֶל וַיִּשְׁתַּחוּ אָרְצָה:
וַיֹּאמַר אֲדֹנָי אִם־נָא מָצָאתִי חֵן בְּעֵינֶיךָ אַל־נָא תַעֲבֹר מֵעַל
עַבְדֶּךָ: יֻקַּח־נָא מְעַט־מַיִם וְרַחֲצוּ רַגְלֵיכֶם וְהִשָּׁעֲנוּ תַּחַת
הָעֵץ: וְאֶקְחָה פַת־לֶחֶם וְסַעֲדוּ לִבְּכֶם אַחַר תַּעֲבֹרוּ כִּי־עַל־
כֵּן עֲבַרְתֶּם עַל־עַבְדְּכֶם וַיֹּאמְרוּ כֵּן תַּעֲשֶׂה כַּאֲשֶׁר דִּבַּרְתָּ:

SECOND ALIYA: 18:6–8
Avraham shows the angels hospitality in his home.

לוי *וַיְמַהֵר אַבְרָהָם הָאֹהֱלָה אֶל־שָׂרָה וַיֹּאמֶר מַהֲרִי שְׁלֹשׁ
סְאִים קֶמַח סֹלֶת לוּשִׁי וַעֲשִׂי עֻגוֹת: וְאֶל־הַבָּקָר רָץ אַבְרָהָם
וַיִּקַּח בֶּן־בָּקָר רַךְ וָטוֹב וַיִּתֵּן אֶל־הַנַּעַר וַיְמַהֵר לַעֲשׂוֹת אֹתוֹ:
וַיִּקַּח חֶמְאָה וְחָלָב וּבֶן־הַבָּקָר אֲשֶׁר עָשָׂה וַיִּתֵּן לִפְנֵיהֶם

THIRD ALIYA: 18:9–14
The angels deliver God's promise that Sara will have a son. Sara is disbelieving due to her advanced age, and laughs to herself.

ישראל וְהוּא עֹמֵד עֲלֵיהֶם תַּחַת הָעֵץ וַיֹּאכֵלוּ: *וַיֹּאמְרוּ אֵלָיו אַיֵּה
שָׂרָה אִשְׁתֶּךָ וַיֹּאמֶר הִנֵּה בָאֹהֶל: וַיֹּאמֶר שׁוֹב אָשׁוּב אֵלֶיךָ
כָּעֵת חַיָּה וְהִנֵּה־בֵן לְשָׂרָה אִשְׁתֶּךָ וְשָׂרָה שֹׁמַעַת פֶּתַח
הָאֹהֶל וְהוּא אַחֲרָיו: וְאַבְרָהָם וְשָׂרָה זְקֵנִים בָּאִים בַּיָּמִים
חָדַל לִהְיוֹת לְשָׂרָה אֹרַח כַּנָּשִׁים: וַתִּצְחַק שָׂרָה בְּקִרְבָּהּ
לֵאמֹר אַחֲרֵי בְלֹתִי הָיְתָה־לִּי עֶדְנָה וַאדֹנִי זָקֵן: וַיֹּאמֶר יְהוָה
אֶל־אַבְרָהָם לָמָּה זֶּה צָחֲקָה שָׂרָה לֵאמֹר הַאַף אֻמְנָם אֵלֵד
וַאֲנִי זָקַנְתִּי: הֲיִפָּלֵא מֵיְהוָה דָּבָר לַמּוֹעֵד אָשׁוּב אֵלֶיךָ כָּעֵת
חַיָּה וּלְשָׂרָה בֵן:

HAYYEI SARA חיי שרה

בראשית כג: א–טז

FIRST ALIYA: 23:1–7
Sara dies. Avraham negotiates to buy her a burial plot in Ḥevron.

וַיִּהְיוּ חַיֵּי שָׂרָה מֵאָה שָׁנָה וְעֶשְׂרִים שָׁנָה וְשֶׁבַע שָׁנִים שְׁנֵי
חַיֵּי שָׂרָה: וַתָּמָת שָׂרָה בְּקִרְיַת אַרְבַּע הִוא חֶבְרוֹן בְּאֶרֶץ
כְּנָעַן וַיָּבֹא אַבְרָהָם לִסְפֹּד לְשָׂרָה וְלִבְכֹּתָהּ: וַיָּקָם אַבְרָהָם
מֵעַל פְּנֵי מֵתוֹ וַיְדַבֵּר אֶל־בְּנֵי־חֵת לֵאמֹר: גֵּר־וְתוֹשָׁב אָנֹכִי
עִמָּכֶם תְּנוּ לִי אֲחֻזַּת־קֶבֶר עִמָּכֶם וְאֶקְבְּרָה מֵתִי מִלְּפָנָי:
וַיַּעֲנוּ בְנֵי־חֵת אֶת־אַבְרָהָם לֵאמֹר לוֹ: שְׁמָעֵנוּ ׀ אֲדֹנִי נְשִׂיא
אֱלֹהִים אַתָּה בְּתוֹכֵנוּ בְּמִבְחַר קְבָרֵינוּ קְבֹר אֶת־מֵתֶךָ אִישׁ

מִמֶּ֔נּוּ אֶת־קִבְר֖וֹ לֹֽא־יִכְלֶ֥ה מִמְּךָ֖ מִקְּבֹ֥ר מֵתֶֽךָ׃ וַיָּ֧קָם אַבְרָהָ֛ם
לוי וַיִּשְׁתַּ֥חוּ לְעַם־הָאָ֖רֶץ לִבְנֵי־חֵֽת׃ *וַיְדַבֵּ֥ר אִתָּ֖ם לֵאמֹ֑ר אִם־
יֵ֣שׁ אֶֽת־נַפְשְׁכֶ֗ם לִקְבֹּ֤ר אֶת־מֵתִי֙ מִלְּפָנַ֔י שְׁמָע֕וּנִי וּפִגְעוּ־לִ֖י
בְּעֶפְר֥וֹן בֶּן־צֹֽחַר׃ וְיִתֶּן־לִ֗י אֶת־מְעָרַ֤ת הַמַּכְפֵּלָה֙ אֲשֶׁר־ל֔וֹ
אֲשֶׁ֖ר בִּקְצֵ֣ה שָׂדֵ֑הוּ בְּכֶ֨סֶף מָלֵ֜א יִתְּנֶ֥נָּה לִּ֛י בְּתוֹכְכֶ֖ם לַאֲחֻזַּת־
קָֽבֶר׃ וְעֶפְר֥וֹן יֹשֵׁ֖ב בְּת֣וֹךְ בְּנֵי־חֵ֑ת וַיַּעַן֩ עֶפְר֨וֹן הַחִתִּ֤י אֶת־
אַבְרָהָם֙ בְּאָזְנֵ֣י בְנֵי־חֵ֔ת לְכֹ֛ל בָּאֵ֥י שַֽׁעַר־עִיר֖וֹ לֵאמֹֽר׃ לֹֽא־
אֲדֹנִ֣י שְׁמָעֵ֔נִי הַשָּׂדֶה֙ נָתַ֣תִּי לָ֔ךְ וְהַמְּעָרָ֛ה אֲשֶׁר־בּ֖וֹ לְךָ֣ נְתַתִּ֑יהָ
לְעֵינֵ֧י בְנֵי־עַמִּ֛י נְתַתִּ֥יהָ לָּ֖ךְ קְבֹ֥ר מֵתֶֽךָ׃ וַיִּשְׁתַּ֙חוּ֙ אַבְרָהָ֔ם לִפְנֵ֖י
ישראל עַם־הָאָֽרֶץ׃ *וַיְדַבֵּ֨ר אֶל־עֶפְר֜וֹן בְּאָזְנֵ֤י עַם־הָאָ֙רֶץ֙ לֵאמֹ֔ר אַ֛ךְ
אִם־אַתָּ֥ה ל֖וּ שְׁמָעֵ֑נִי נָתַ֜תִּי כֶּ֤סֶף הַשָּׂדֶה֙ קַ֣ח מִמֶּ֔נִּי וְאֶקְבְּרָ֥ה
אֶת־מֵתִ֖י שָֽׁמָּה׃ וַיַּ֧עַן עֶפְר֛וֹן אֶת־אַבְרָהָ֖ם לֵאמֹ֥ר לֽוֹ׃ אֲדֹנִ֣י
שְׁמָעֵ֔נִי אֶ֠רֶץ אַרְבַּ֨ע מֵאֹ֧ת שֶֽׁקֶל־כֶּ֛סֶף בֵּינִ֥י וּבֵינְךָ֖ מַה־הִ֑וא
וְאֶת־מֵתְךָ֖ קְבֹֽר׃ וַיִּשְׁמַ֣ע אַבְרָהָם֮ אֶל־עֶפְרוֹן֒ וַיִּשְׁקֹ֤ל אַבְרָהָם֙
לְעֶפְרֹ֔ן אֶת־הַכֶּ֕סֶף אֲשֶׁ֥ר דִּבֶּ֖ר בְּאָזְנֵ֣י בְנֵי־חֵ֑ת אַרְבַּ֤ע מֵאוֹת֙
שֶׁ֣קֶל כֶּ֔סֶף עֹבֵ֖ר לַסֹּחֵֽר׃

SECOND ALIYA: 23:8–12
The negotiations continue between Avraham and Efron, the owner of the field.

THIRD ALIYA: 23:13–16
Negotiations are concluded successfully and Avraham purchases the field for the inflated price of four hundred silver shekels.

TOLEDOT תולדות

בראשית כה:יט–כו:ה

וְאֵ֛לֶּה תּוֹלְדֹ֥ת יִצְחָ֖ק בֶּן־אַבְרָהָ֑ם אַבְרָהָ֖ם הוֹלִ֥יד אֶת־יִצְחָֽק׃
וַיְהִ֤י יִצְחָק֙ בֶּן־אַרְבָּעִ֣ים שָׁנָ֔ה בְּקַחְתּ֣וֹ אֶת־רִבְקָ֗ה בַּת־בְּתוּאֵל֙
הָֽאֲרַמִּ֔י מִפַּדַּ֖ן אֲרָ֑ם אֲח֛וֹת לָבָ֥ן הָאֲרַמִּ֖י ל֥וֹ לְאִשָּֽׁה׃ וַיֶּעְתַּ֨ר
יִצְחָ֤ק לַיהוָה֙ לְנֹ֣כַח אִשְׁתּ֔וֹ כִּ֥י עֲקָרָ֖ה הִ֑וא וַיֵּעָ֤תֶר לוֹ֙ יְהוָ֔ה
וַתַּ֖הַר רִבְקָ֥ה אִשְׁתּֽוֹ׃ וַיִּתְרֹֽצְצ֤וּ הַבָּנִים֙ בְּקִרְבָּ֔הּ וַתֹּ֣אמֶר אִם־
לוי כֵּ֔ן לָ֥מָּה זֶּ֖ה אָנֹ֑כִי וַתֵּ֖לֶךְ לִדְרֹ֥שׁ אֶת־יְהוָֽה׃ *וַיֹּאמֶר֩ יְהוָ֨ה לָ֜הּ
גוים שְׁנֵ֤י גֹיִים֙ בְּבִטְנֵ֔ךְ וּשְׁנֵ֣י לְאֻמִּ֔ים מִמֵּעַ֖יִךְ יִפָּרֵ֑דוּ וּלְאֹם֙ מִלְאֹ֣ם
יֶֽאֱמָ֔ץ וְרַ֖ב יַעֲבֹ֥ד צָעִֽיר׃ וַיִּמְלְא֥וּ יָמֶ֖יהָ לָלֶ֑דֶת וְהִנֵּ֥ה תוֹמִ֖ם
בְּבִטְנָֽהּ׃ וַיֵּצֵ֤א הָרִאשׁוֹן֙ אַדְמוֹנִ֔י כֻּלּ֖וֹ כְּאַדֶּ֣רֶת שֵׂעָ֑ר וַיִּקְרְא֥וּ
שְׁמ֖וֹ עֵשָֽׂו׃ וְאַחֲרֵי־כֵ֞ן יָצָ֣א אָחִ֗יו וְיָד֤וֹ אֹחֶ֙זֶת֙ בַּעֲקֵ֣ב עֵשָׂ֔ו
וַיִּקְרָ֥א שְׁמ֖וֹ יַעֲקֹ֑ב וְיִצְחָ֛ק בֶּן־שִׁשִּׁ֥ים שָׁנָ֖ה בְּלֶ֥דֶת אֹתָֽם׃

FIRST ALIYA: 25:19–22
Yitzḥak marries Rivka, who cannot have children. He prays to God and she becomes pregnant with twins.

SECOND ALIYA: 25:23–26
The twin boys are born, first Eisav, then Yaakov.

ישראל

THIRD ALIYA: 25:27–26:5
Eisav becomes a hunter and Yaakov a wholesome man. After an exhausting day hunting, Yaakov gives Eisav a stew he was making, in exchange for his birthright.

★ויגדלו הנערים ויהי עשו איש ידע ציד איש שדה ויעקב
איש תם ישב אהלים: ויאהב יצחק את־עשו כי־ציד בפיו
ורבקה אהבת את־יעקב: ויזד יעקב נזיד ויבא עשו מן־
השדה והוא עיף: ויאמר עשו אל־יעקב הלעיטני נא מן־
האדם האדם הזה כי עיף אנכי על־כן קרא־שמו אדום:
ויאמר יעקב מכרה כיום את־בכרתך לי: ויאמר עשו הנה
אנכי הולך למות ולמה־זה לי בכרה: ויאמר יעקב השבעה
לי כיום וישבע לו וימכר את־בכרתו ליעקב: ויעקב נתן
לעשו לחם ונזיד עדשים ויאכל וישת ויקם וילך ויבז עשו
את־הבכרה:

ויהי רעב בארץ מלבד הרעב הראשון אשר היה בימי
אברהם וילך יצחק אל־אבימלך מלך־פלשתים גררה:
וירא אליו יהוה ויאמר אל־תרד מצרימה שכן בארץ אשר
אמר אליך: גור בארץ הזאת ואהיה עמך ואברכך כי־לך
ולזרעך אתן את־כל־הארצת האל והקמתי את־השבעה
אשר נשבעתי לאברהם אביך: והרביתי את־זרעך ככוכבי
השמים ונתתי לזרעך את כל־הארצת האל והתברכו
בזרעך כל גויי הארץ: עקב אשר־שמע אברהם בקלי
וישמר משמרתי מצותי חקותי ותורתי:

ויצא
VAYETZEH

FIRST ALIYA: 28:10–12
Yaakov flees Eisav, and on his way dreams of a ladder with angels ascending and descending.

SECOND ALIYA: 28:13–17
God appears to him in this dream and promises him that the land will be inherited by his descendants.

בראשית כח:י–כב

ויצא יעקב מבאר שבע וילך חרנה: ויפגע במקום וילן שם
כי־בא השמש ויקח מאבני המקום וישם מראשתיו וישכב
במקום ההוא: ויחלם והנה סלם מצב ארצה וראשו מגיע
השמימה והנה מלאכי אלהים עלים וירדים בו: ★והנה
לוי
יהוה נצב עליו ויאמר אני יהוה אלהי אברהם אביך ואלהי
יצחק הארץ אשר אתה שכב עליה לך אתננה ולזרעך:
והיה זרעך כעפר הארץ ופרצת ימה וקדמה וצפנה ונגבה
ונברכו בך כל־משפחת האדמה ובזרעך: והנה אנכי עמך

וּשְׁמַרְתִּיךָ בְּכֹל אֲשֶׁר־תֵּלֵךְ וַהֲשִׁבֹתִיךָ אֶל־הָאֲדָמָה הַזֹּאת
כִּי לֹא אֶעֱזָבְךָ עַד אֲשֶׁר אִם־עָשִׂיתִי אֵת אֲשֶׁר־דִּבַּרְתִּי לָךְ׃
וַיִּיקַץ יַעֲקֹב מִשְּׁנָתוֹ וַיֹּאמֶר אָכֵן יֵשׁ יְהוָה בַּמָּקוֹם הַזֶּה
וְאָנֹכִי לֹא יָדָעְתִּי׃ וַיִּירָא וַיֹּאמַר מַה־נּוֹרָא הַמָּקוֹם הַזֶּה אֵין
ישראל זֶה כִּי אִם־בֵּית אֱלֹהִים וְזֶה שַׁעַר הַשָּׁמָיִם׃ *וַיַּשְׁכֵּם יַעֲקֹב
בַּבֹּקֶר וַיִּקַּח אֶת־הָאֶבֶן אֲשֶׁר־שָׂם מְרַאֲשֹׁתָיו וַיָּשֶׂם אֹתָהּ
מַצֵּבָה וַיִּצֹק שֶׁמֶן עַל־רֹאשָׁהּ׃ וַיִּקְרָא אֶת־שֵׁם־הַמָּקוֹם
הַהוּא בֵּית־אֵל וְאוּלָם לוּז שֵׁם־הָעִיר לָרִאשֹׁנָה׃ וַיִּדַּר יַעֲקֹב
נֶדֶר לֵאמֹר אִם־יִהְיֶה אֱלֹהִים עִמָּדִי וּשְׁמָרַנִי בַּדֶּרֶךְ הַזֶּה
אֲשֶׁר אָנֹכִי הוֹלֵךְ וְנָתַן־לִי לֶחֶם לֶאֱכֹל וּבֶגֶד לִלְבֹּשׁ׃ וְשַׁבְתִּי
בְשָׁלוֹם אֶל־בֵּית אָבִי וְהָיָה יְהוָה לִי לֵאלֹהִים׃ וְהָאֶבֶן הַזֹּאת
אֲשֶׁר־שַׂמְתִּי מַצֵּבָה יִהְיֶה בֵּית אֱלֹהִים וְכֹל אֲשֶׁר תִּתֶּן־לִי
עַשֵּׂר אֲעַשְּׂרֶנּוּ לָךְ׃

THIRD ALIYA: 28:18–22
In the morning, Yaakov builds a stone monument, and names the place Bet-El.

VAYISHLAH וישלח

בראשית לב:ג-יב
וַיִּשְׁלַח יַעֲקֹב מַלְאָכִים לְפָנָיו אֶל־עֵשָׂו אָחִיו אַרְצָה שֵׂעִיר
שְׂדֵה אֱדוֹם׃ וַיְצַו אֹתָם לֵאמֹר כֹּה תֹאמְרוּן לַאדֹנִי לְעֵשָׂו
כֹּה אָמַר עַבְדְּךָ יַעֲקֹב עִם־לָבָן גַּרְתִּי וָאֵחַר עַד־עָתָּה׃ וַיְהִי־
לִי שׁוֹר וַחֲמוֹר צֹאן וְעֶבֶד וְשִׁפְחָה וָאֶשְׁלְחָה לְהַגִּיד לַאדֹנִי
לוי לִמְצֹא־חֵן בְּעֵינֶיךָ׃ *וַיָּשֻׁבוּ הַמַּלְאָכִים אֶל־יַעֲקֹב לֵאמֹר
בָּאנוּ אֶל־אָחִיךָ אֶל־עֵשָׂו וְגַם הֹלֵךְ לִקְרָאתְךָ וְאַרְבַּע־
מֵאוֹת אִישׁ עִמּוֹ׃ וַיִּירָא יַעֲקֹב מְאֹד וַיֵּצֶר לוֹ וַיַּחַץ אֶת־
הָעָם אֲשֶׁר־אִתּוֹ וְאֶת־הַצֹּאן וְאֶת־הַבָּקָר וְהַגְּמַלִּים לִשְׁנֵי
מַחֲנוֹת׃ וַיֹּאמֶר אִם־יָבוֹא עֵשָׂו אֶל־הַמַּחֲנֶה הָאַחַת וְהִכָּהוּ
ישראל וְהָיָה הַמַּחֲנֶה הַנִּשְׁאָר לִפְלֵיטָה׃ *וַיֹּאמֶר יַעֲקֹב אֱלֹהֵי אָבִי
אַבְרָהָם וֵאלֹהֵי אָבִי יִצְחָק יְהוָה הָאֹמֵר אֵלַי שׁוּב לְאַרְצְךָ
וּלְמוֹלַדְתְּךָ וְאֵיטִיבָה עִמָּךְ׃ קָטֹנְתִּי מִכֹּל הַחֲסָדִים וּמִכָּל־
הָאֱמֶת אֲשֶׁר עָשִׂיתָ אֶת־עַבְדֶּךָ כִּי בְמַקְלִי עָבַרְתִּי אֶת־
הַיַּרְדֵּן הַזֶּה וְעַתָּה הָיִיתִי לִשְׁנֵי מַחֲנוֹת׃ הַצִּילֵנִי נָא מִיַּד אָחִי

FIRST ALIYA: 32:4–6
Yaakov sends an advance party ahead to Eisav to prepare for their meeting.

SECOND ALIYA: 32:7–9
They returned with news that Eisav is approaching with four hundred men by his side. Yaakov divides his camp into two in a defensive formation.

THIRD ALIYA: 32:10–13
Yaakov prays to Hashem to save him in the impending confrontation.

מִיַּד עֵשָׂו כִּי־יָרֵא אָנֹכִי אֹתוֹ פֶּן־יָבוֹא וְהִכַּנִי אֵם עַל־בָּנִים׃
וְאַתָּה אָמַרְתָּ הֵיטֵב אֵיטִיב עִמָּךְ וְשַׂמְתִּי אֶת־זַרְעֲךָ כְּחוֹל
הַיָּם אֲשֶׁר לֹא־יִסָּפֵר מֵרֹב׃

וישב VAYESHEV

בראשית לז:א–יא

FIRST ALIYA: 37:1–3 Yaakov loved Yosef more than his other children and made for him a colorful woolen tunic.

SECOND ALIYA: 37:4–7 Yosef's brothers were jealous of him. Their jealousy increased when he related his first dream, where their sheaves of wheat bowed down to his sheaf.

THIRD ALIYA: 37:8–11 In Yosef's second dream, the sun and the moon and eleven stars (representing his father, mother and brothers) bow down to Yosef.

וַיֵּשֶׁב יַעֲקֹב בְּאֶרֶץ מְגוּרֵי אָבִיו בְּאֶרֶץ כְּנָעַן׃ אֵלֶּה ׀ תֹּלְדוֹת
יַעֲקֹב יוֹסֵף בֶּן־שְׁבַע־עֶשְׂרֵה שָׁנָה הָיָה רֹעֶה אֶת־אֶחָיו בַּצֹּאן
וְהוּא נַעַר אֶת־בְּנֵי בִלְהָה וְאֶת־בְּנֵי זִלְפָּה נְשֵׁי אָבִיו וַיָּבֵא יוֹסֵף
אֶת־דִּבָּתָם רָעָה אֶל־אֲבִיהֶם׃ וְיִשְׂרָאֵל אָהַב אֶת־יוֹסֵף מִכָּל־
לוי בָּנָיו כִּי־בֶן־זְקֻנִים הוּא לוֹ וְעָשָׂה לוֹ כְּתֹנֶת פַּסִּים׃ *וַיִּרְאוּ
אֶחָיו כִּי־אֹתוֹ אָהַב אֲבִיהֶם מִכָּל־אֶחָיו וַיִּשְׂנְאוּ אֹתוֹ וְלֹא
יָכְלוּ דַּבְּרוֹ לְשָׁלֹם׃ וַיַּחֲלֹם יוֹסֵף חֲלוֹם וַיַּגֵּד לְאֶחָיו וַיּוֹסִפוּ
עוֹד שְׂנֹא אֹתוֹ׃ וַיֹּאמֶר אֲלֵיהֶם שִׁמְעוּ־נָא הַחֲלוֹם הַזֶּה
אֲשֶׁר חָלָמְתִּי׃ וְהִנֵּה אֲנַחְנוּ מְאַלְּמִים אֲלֻמִּים בְּתוֹךְ הַשָּׂדֶה
וְהִנֵּה קָמָה אֲלֻמָּתִי וְגַם־נִצָּבָה וְהִנֵּה תְסֻבֶּינָה אֲלֻמֹּתֵיכֶם
ישראל וַתִּשְׁתַּחֲוֶיןָ לַאֲלֻמָּתִי׃ *וַיֹּאמְרוּ לוֹ אֶחָיו הֲמָלֹךְ תִּמְלֹךְ עָלֵינוּ
אִם־מָשׁוֹל תִּמְשֹׁל בָּנוּ וַיּוֹסִפוּ עוֹד שְׂנֹא אֹתוֹ עַל־חֲלֹמֹתָיו
וְעַל־דְּבָרָיו׃ וַיַּחֲלֹם עוֹד חֲלוֹם אַחֵר וַיְסַפֵּר אֹתוֹ לְאֶחָיו
וַיֹּאמֶר הִנֵּה חָלַמְתִּי חֲלוֹם עוֹד וְהִנֵּה הַשֶּׁמֶשׁ וְהַיָּרֵחַ וְאַחַד
עָשָׂר כּוֹכָבִים מִשְׁתַּחֲוִים לִי׃ וַיְסַפֵּר אֶל־אָבִיו וְאֶל־אֶחָיו
וַיִּגְעַר־בּוֹ אָבִיו וַיֹּאמֶר לוֹ מָה הַחֲלוֹם הַזֶּה אֲשֶׁר חָלָמְתָּ
הֲבוֹא נָבוֹא אֲנִי וְאִמְּךָ וְאַחֶיךָ לְהִשְׁתַּחֲוֹת לְךָ אָרְצָה׃
וַיְקַנְאוּ־בוֹ אֶחָיו וְאָבִיו שָׁמַר אֶת־הַדָּבָר׃

מקץ MIKETZ

בראשית מא:א–יד

FIRST ALIYA: 41:1–4 Pharaoh has a dream seven healthy cows ascend from the River Nile, followed by seven starved cows.

וַיְהִי מִקֵּץ שְׁנָתַיִם יָמִים וּפַרְעֹה חֹלֵם וְהִנֵּה עֹמֵד עַל־הַיְאֹר׃
וְהִנֵּה מִן־הַיְאֹר עֹלֹת שֶׁבַע פָּרוֹת יְפוֹת מַרְאֶה וּבְרִיאֹת
בָּשָׂר וַתִּרְעֶינָה בָּאָחוּ׃ וְהִנֵּה שֶׁבַע פָּרוֹת אֲחֵרוֹת עֹלוֹת
אַחֲרֵיהֶן מִן־הַיְאֹר רָעוֹת מַרְאֶה וְדַקּוֹת בָּשָׂר וַתַּעֲמֹדְנָה

אֵ֥צֶל הַפָּר֖וֹת עַל־שְׂפַ֥ת הַיְאֹֽר׃ וַתֹּאכַ֣לְנָה הַפָּר֗וֹת רָע֤וֹת
הַמַּרְאֶה֙ וְדַקֹּ֣ת הַבָּשָׂ֔ר אֵ֚ת שֶׁ֣בַע הַפָּר֔וֹת יְפֹ֥ת הַמַּרְאֶ֖ה
לוי וְהַבְּרִיאֹ֑ת וַיִּיקַ֖ץ פַּרְעֹֽה׃ *וַיִּישָׁ֕ן וַֽיַּחֲלֹ֖ם שֵׁנִ֑ית וְהִנֵּ֣ה ׀ שֶׁ֣בַע
שִׁבֳּלִ֗ים עֹל֛וֹת בְּקָנֶ֥ה אֶחָ֖ד בְּרִיא֥וֹת וְטֹבֽוֹת׃ וְהִנֵּה֙ שֶׁ֣בַע
שִׁבֳּלִ֔ים דַּקּ֖וֹת וּשְׁדוּפֹ֣ת קָדִ֑ים צֹֽמְח֖וֹת אַחֲרֵיהֶֽן׃ וַתִּבְלַ֙עְנָה֙
הַשִּׁבֳּלִ֣ים הַדַּקּ֔וֹת אֵ֚ת שֶׁ֣בַע הַשִּׁבֳּלִ֔ים הַבְּרִיא֖וֹת וְהַמְּלֵא֑וֹת
ישראל וַיִּיקַ֥ץ פַּרְעֹ֖ה וְהִנֵּ֥ה חֲלֽוֹם׃ *וַיְהִ֤י בַבֹּ֙קֶר֙ וַתִּפָּ֣עֶם רוּח֔וֹ וַיִּשְׁלַ֗ח
וַיִּקְרָ֛א אֶת־כָּל־חַרְטֻמֵּ֥י מִצְרַ֖יִם וְאֶת־כָּל־חֲכָמֶ֑יהָ וַיְסַפֵּ֨ר
פַּרְעֹ֤ה לָהֶם֙ אֶת־חֲלֹמ֔וֹ וְאֵין־פּוֹתֵ֥ר אוֹתָ֖ם לְפַרְעֹֽה׃ וַיְדַבֵּר֙
שַׂ֣ר הַמַּשְׁקִ֔ים אֶת־פַּרְעֹ֖ה לֵאמֹ֑ר אֶת־חֲטָאַ֕י אֲנִ֖י מַזְכִּ֥יר
הַיּֽוֹם׃ פַּרְעֹ֖ה קָצַ֣ף עַל־עֲבָדָ֑יו וַיִּתֵּ֨ן אֹתִ֜י בְּמִשְׁמַ֗ר בֵּ֚ית שַׂ֣ר
הַטַּבָּחִ֔ים אֹתִ֕י וְאֵ֖ת שַׂ֥ר הָאֹפִֽים׃ וַנַּחַלְמָ֥ה חֲל֛וֹם בְּלַ֥יְלָה
אֶחָ֖ד אֲנִ֣י וָה֑וּא אִ֛ישׁ כְּפִתְר֥וֹן חֲלֹמ֖וֹ חָלָֽמְנוּ׃ וְשָׁ֨ם אִתָּ֜נוּ
נַ֣עַר עִבְרִ֗י עֶ֚בֶד לְשַׂ֣ר הַטַּבָּחִ֔ים וַנְּסַפֶּר־ל֔וֹ וַיִּפְתָּר־לָ֖נוּ אֶת־
חֲלֹמֹתֵ֑ינוּ אִ֥ישׁ כַּחֲלֹמ֖וֹ פָּתָֽר׃ וַיְהִ֛י כַּאֲשֶׁ֥ר פָּֽתַר־לָ֖נוּ כֵּ֣ן הָיָ֑ה
אֹתִ֛י הֵשִׁ֥יב עַל־כַּנִּ֖י וְאֹת֥וֹ תָלָֽה׃ וַיִּשְׁלַ֤ח פַּרְעֹה֙ וַיִּקְרָ֣א אֶת־
יוֹסֵ֔ף וַיְרִיצֻ֖הוּ מִן־הַבּ֑וֹר וַיְגַלַּח֙ וַיְחַלֵּ֣ף שִׂמְלֹתָ֔יו וַיָּבֹ֖א אֶל־
פַּרְעֹֽה׃

SECOND ALIYA: 41:5–7
In Pharaoh's second dream a stalk of wheat had seven ears of healthy grain, and following them seven dry grains.

THIRD ALIYA: 41:8–14
Pharaoh asked his ministers to find an interpretation, but none could. His head butler recalled Yosef and his ability to interpret dreams.

VAYIGASH ויגש

בראשית מד:יח–ל

וַיִּגַּ֨שׁ אֵלָ֜יו יְהוּדָ֗ה וַיֹּאמֶר֮ בִּ֣י אֲדֹנִי֒ יְדַבֶּר־נָ֨א עַבְדְּךָ֤ דָבָר֙
בְּאָזְנֵ֣י אֲדֹנִ֔י וְאַל־יִ֥חַר אַפְּךָ֖ בְּעַבְדֶּ֑ךָ כִּ֥י כָמ֖וֹךָ כְּפַרְעֹֽה׃ אֲדֹנִ֣י
שָׁאַ֔ל אֶת־עֲבָדָ֖יו לֵאמֹ֑ר הֲיֵשׁ־לָכֶ֥ם אָ֖ב אוֹ־אָֽח׃ וַנֹּ֙אמֶר֙ אֶל־
אֲדֹנִ֔י יֶשׁ־לָ֙נוּ֙ אָ֣ב זָקֵ֔ן וְיֶ֥לֶד זְקֻנִ֖ים קָטָ֑ן וְאָחִ֣יו מֵ֗ת וַיִּוָּתֵ֨ר ה֧וּא
לוי לְבַדּ֛וֹ לְאִמּ֖וֹ וְאָבִ֥יו אֲהֵבֽוֹ׃ *וַתֹּ֙אמֶר֙ אֶל־עֲבָדֶ֔יךָ הוֹרִדֻ֖הוּ אֵלָ֑י
וְאָשִׂ֥ימָה עֵינִ֖י עָלָֽיו׃ וַנֹּ֙אמֶר֙ אֶל־אֲדֹנִ֔י לֹא־יוּכַ֥ל הַנַּ֖עַר לַעֲזֹ֣ב
אֶת־אָבִ֑יו וְעָזַ֥ב אֶת־אָבִ֖יו וָמֵֽת׃ וַתֹּ֙אמֶר֙ אֶל־עֲבָדֶ֔יךָ אִם־לֹ֥א
יֵרֵ֛ד אֲחִיכֶ֥ם הַקָּטֹ֖ן אִתְּכֶ֑ם לֹ֥א תֹסִפ֖וּן לִרְא֥וֹת פָּנָֽי׃ וַיְהִי֙ כִּ֣י

FIRST ALIYA: 44:18–20
Yehuda steps forward to try to convince Yosef to let Binyamin go free and take him in his stead.

SECOND ALIYA: 44:21–24
Yehuda explains to Yosef the impact Binyamin's incarceration will have on his father Yaakov.

ישראל

THIRD ALIYA: 44:25–30
Yehuda explains that the situation is made worse for his father because he has already lost a son (Yosef who is lost to him).

עָלִ֔ינוּ אֶל־עַבְדְּךָ֖ אָבִ֑י וַנַּ֨גֶּד־ל֔וֹ אֵ֖ת דִּבְרֵ֥י אֲדֹנִֽי׃ *וַיֹּ֖אמֶר
אָבִ֑ינוּ שֻׁ֖בוּ שִׁבְרוּ־לָ֥נוּ מְעַט־אֹֽכֶל׃ וַנֹּ֕אמֶר לֹ֥א נוּכַ֖ל לָרֶ֑דֶת
אִם־יֵשׁ֩ אָחִ֨ינוּ הַקָּטֹ֤ן אִתָּ֙נוּ֙ וְיָרַ֔דְנוּ כִּי־לֹ֣א נוּכַ֗ל לִרְאוֹת֙ פְּנֵ֣י
הָאִ֔ישׁ וְאָחִ֥ינוּ הַקָּטֹ֖ן אֵינֶ֥נּוּ אִתָּֽנוּ׃ וַיֹּ֛אמֶר עַבְדְּךָ֥ אָבִ֖י אֵלֵ֑ינוּ
אַתֶּ֣ם יְדַעְתֶּ֔ם כִּ֥י שְׁנַ֖יִם יָֽלְדָה־לִּ֥י אִשְׁתִּֽי׃ וַיֵּצֵ֤א הָֽאֶחָד֙ מֵֽאִתִּ֔י
וָאֹמַ֕ר אַ֖ךְ טָרֹ֣ף טֹרָ֑ף וְלֹ֥א רְאִיתִ֖יו עַד־הֵֽנָּה׃ וּלְקַחְתֶּ֧ם גַּם־
אֶת־זֶ֛ה מֵעִ֥ם פָּנַ֖י וְקָרָ֣הוּ אָס֑וֹן וְהוֹרַדְתֶּ֧ם אֶת־שֵׂיבָתִ֛י בְּרָעָ֖ה
שְׁאֹֽלָה׃ וְעַתָּ֗ה כְּבֹאִי֙ אֶל־עַבְדְּךָ֣ אָבִ֔י וְהַנַּ֖עַר אֵינֶ֣נּוּ אִתָּ֑נוּ
וְנַפְשׁ֖וֹ קְשׁוּרָ֥ה בְנַפְשֽׁוֹ׃

ויחי VAYHI

בראשית
מז:כח–מח:ט

FIRST ALIYA: 47:28–31
Yaakov nears the end of his life. He makes Yosef promise to bury him in *Eretz Yisrael* and not in Egypt.

וַיְחִ֤י יַעֲקֹב֙ בְּאֶ֣רֶץ מִצְרַ֔יִם שְׁבַ֥ע עֶשְׂרֵ֖ה שָׁנָ֑ה וַיְהִ֤י יְמֵֽי־
יַעֲקֹב֙ שְׁנֵ֣י חַיָּ֔יו שֶׁ֣בַע שָׁנִ֔ים וְאַרְבָּעִ֥ים וּמְאַ֖ת שָׁנָֽה׃ וַיִּקְרְב֣וּ
יְמֵֽי־יִשְׂרָאֵל֮ לָמוּת֒ וַיִּקְרָ֣א ׀ לִבְנ֣וֹ לְיוֹסֵ֗ף וַיֹּ֤אמֶר לוֹ֙ אִם־נָ֨א
מָצָ֤אתִי חֵן֙ בְּעֵינֶ֔יךָ שִֽׂים־נָ֥א יָדְךָ֖ תַּ֣חַת יְרֵכִ֑י וְעָשִׂ֤יתָ עִמָּדִי֙
חֶ֣סֶד וֶאֱמֶ֔ת אַל־נָ֥א תִקְבְּרֵ֖נִי בְּמִצְרָֽיִם׃ וְשָֽׁכַבְתִּי֙ עִם־אֲבֹתַ֔י
וּנְשָׂאתַ֙נִי֙ מִמִּצְרַ֔יִם וּקְבַרְתַּ֖נִי בִּקְבֻרָתָ֑ם וַיֹּאמַ֕ר אָנֹכִ֖י אֶעֱשֶׂ֥ה
כִדְבָרֶֽךָ׃ וַיֹּ֗אמֶר הִשָּֽׁבְעָה֙ לִ֔י וַיִּשָּׁבַ֖ע ל֑וֹ וַיִּשְׁתַּ֥חוּ יִשְׂרָאֵ֖ל
עַל־רֹ֥אשׁ הַמִּטָּֽה׃

לוי

SECOND ALIYA: 48:1–3
Yosef brings his sons Efraim and Menashe to receive a blessing from Yaakov before he dies.

וַיְהִ֗י אַחֲרֵי֙ הַדְּבָרִ֣ים הָאֵ֔לֶּה וַיֹּ֣אמֶר לְיוֹסֵ֔ף הִנֵּ֥ה אָבִ֖יךָ חֹלֶ֑ה
וַיִּקַּ֞ח אֶת־שְׁנֵ֤י בָנָיו֙ עִמּ֔וֹ אֶת־מְנַשֶּׁ֖ה וְאֶת־אֶפְרָֽיִם׃ וַיַּגֵּ֣ד
לְיַעֲקֹ֔ב וַיֹּ֕אמֶר הִנֵּ֛ה בִּנְךָ֥ יוֹסֵ֖ף בָּ֣א אֵלֶ֑יךָ וַיִּתְחַזֵּק֙ יִשְׂרָאֵ֔ל
וַיֵּ֖שֶׁב עַל־הַמִּטָּֽה׃ וַיֹּ֤אמֶר יַעֲקֹב֙ אֶל־יוֹסֵ֔ף אֵ֥ל שַׁדַּ֛י נִרְאָֽה־
אֵלַ֥י בְּל֖וּז בְּאֶ֣רֶץ כְּנָ֑עַן וַיְבָ֖רֶךְ אֹתִֽי׃ *וַיֹּ֣אמֶר אֵלַ֗י הִנְנִ֤י מַפְרְךָ֙

ישראל

THIRD ALIYA: 48:4–9
Yaakov informs Yosef that Efraim and Menashe will be considered his sons, and will each have a tribe in their own right.

וְהִרְבִּיתִ֔ךָ וּנְתַתִּ֖יךָ לִקְהַ֣ל עַמִּ֑ים וְנָ֨תַתִּ֜י אֶת־הָאָ֧רֶץ הַזֹּ֛את
לְזַרְעֲךָ֥ אַחֲרֶ֖יךָ אֲחֻזַּ֥ת עוֹלָֽם׃ וְעַתָּ֡ה שְׁנֵֽי־בָנֶ֩יךָ֩ הַנּוֹלָדִ֨ים
לְךָ֜ בְּאֶ֣רֶץ מִצְרַ֗יִם עַד־בֹּאִ֥י אֵלֶ֛יךָ מִצְרַ֖יְמָה לִי־הֵ֑ם אֶפְרַ֙יִם֙
וּמְנַשֶּׁ֔ה כִּרְאוּבֵ֥ן וְשִׁמְע֖וֹן יִֽהְיוּ־לִֽי׃ וּמוֹלַדְתְּךָ֛ אֲשֶׁר־הוֹלַ֥דְתָּ

אחריהם לך יהיו על שם אחיהם יקראו בנחלתם: ואני
בבאי מפדן מתה עלי רחל בארץ כנען בדרך בעוד כברת־
ארץ לבא אפרתה ואקברה שם בדרך אפרת הוא בית
לחם: וירא ישראל את־בני יוסף ויאמר מי־אלה: ויאמר
יוסף אל־אביו בני הם אשר־נתן־לי אלהים בזה ויאמר
קחם־נא אלי ואברכם:

SHEMOT שמות

ואלה שמות בני ישראל הבאים מצרימה את יעקב איש שמות א:א-יז
וביתו באו: ראובן שמעון לוי ויהודה: יששכר זבולן
ובנימן: דן ונפתלי גד ואשר: ויהי כל־נפש יצאי ירך־יעקב
שבעים נפש ויוסף היה במצרים: וימת יוסף וכל־אחיו וכל
הדור ההוא: ובני ישראל פרו וישרצו וירבו ויעצמו במאד
מאד ותמלא הארץ אתם:
ויקם מלך־חדש על־מצרים אשר לא־ידע את־יוסף: לוי
ויאמר אל־עמו הנה עם בני ישראל רב ועצום ממנו:
הבה נתחכמה לו פן־ירבה והיה כי־תקראנה מלחמה
ונוסף גם־הוא על־שנאינו ונלחם־בנו ועלה מן־הארץ:
וישימו עליו שרי מסים למען ענתו בסבלתם ויבן ערי
מסכנות לפרעה את־פתם ואת־רעמסס: וכאשר יענו
אתו כן ירבה וכן יפרץ ויקצו מפני בני ישראל: *ויעבדו ישראל
מצרים את־בני ישראל בפרך: וימררו את־חייהם בעבדה
קשה בחמר ובלבנים ובכל־עבדה בשדה את כל־עבדתם
אשר־עבדו בהם בפרך: ויאמר מלך מצרים למילדת
העברית אשר שם האחת שפרה ושם השנית פועה:
ויאמר בילדכן את־העבריות וראיתן על־האבנים אם־
בן הוא והמתן אתו ואם־בת הוא וחיה: ותיראן המילדת

FIRST ALIYA: 1:1–7
Transition from the seventy souls descended from Yaakov who settled in Egypt, to a populous and mighty Jewish People living amongst the Egyptians.

SECOND ALIYA: 1:8–12
A new Pharaoh comes to power who does not feel indebted to Yosef and his people, and feels threatened by their number and strength. The enslavement begins.

THIRD ALIYA: 1:13–17
A system is established of crushing national enslavement, and male infanticide. The midwives of Egypt refuse to implement the policy.

אֶת־הָאֱלֹהִים וְלֹא עָשׂוּ כַּאֲשֶׁר דִּבֶּר אֲלֵיהֶן מֶלֶךְ מִצְרָיִם
וַתְּחַיֶּיןָ אֶת־הַיְלָדִים׃

VA'ERA וארא

שמות ו:ב–יג

FIRST ALIYA: 6:2–5
God reassures Moshe that He has heard the Israelites suffering, and remembered His covenant to bring them out of Egypt to the Land of Israel.

SECOND ALIYA: 6:6–9
God asks Moshe to deliver this message to the Israelites, in the form of four expressions of redemption.

THIRD ALIYA: 6:10–13
Moshe is concerned about his ability to deliver the message to Pharaoh.

וַיְדַבֵּר אֱלֹהִים אֶל־מֹשֶׁה וַיֹּאמֶר אֵלָיו אֲנִי יהוה׃ וָאֵרָא
אֶל־אַבְרָהָם אֶל־יִצְחָק וְאֶל־יַעֲקֹב בְּאֵל שַׁדָּי וּשְׁמִי יהוה
לֹא נוֹדַעְתִּי לָהֶם׃ וְגַם הֲקִמֹתִי אֶת־בְּרִיתִי אִתָּם לָתֵת לָהֶם
אֶת־אֶרֶץ כְּנָעַן אֵת אֶרֶץ מְגֻרֵיהֶם אֲשֶׁר־גָּרוּ בָהּ׃ וְגַם ׀ אֲנִי
שָׁמַעְתִּי אֶת־נַאֲקַת בְּנֵי יִשְׂרָאֵל אֲשֶׁר מִצְרַיִם מַעֲבִדִים
לוי אֹתָם וָאֶזְכֹּר אֶת־בְּרִיתִי׃ *לָכֵן אֱמֹר לִבְנֵי־יִשְׂרָאֵל אֲנִי יהוה
וְהוֹצֵאתִי אֶתְכֶם מִתַּחַת סִבְלֹת מִצְרַיִם וְהִצַּלְתִּי אֶתְכֶם
מֵעֲבֹדָתָם וְגָאַלְתִּי אֶתְכֶם בִּזְרוֹעַ נְטוּיָה וּבִשְׁפָטִים גְּדֹלִים׃
וְלָקַחְתִּי אֶתְכֶם לִי לְעָם וְהָיִיתִי לָכֶם לֵאלֹהִים וִידַעְתֶּם כִּי
אֲנִי יהוה אֱלֹהֵיכֶם הַמּוֹצִיא אֶתְכֶם מִתַּחַת סִבְלוֹת מִצְרָיִם׃
וְהֵבֵאתִי אֶתְכֶם אֶל־הָאָרֶץ אֲשֶׁר נָשָׂאתִי אֶת־יָדִי לָתֵת
אֹתָהּ לְאַבְרָהָם לְיִצְחָק וּלְיַעֲקֹב וְנָתַתִּי אֹתָהּ לָכֶם מוֹרָשָׁה
אֲנִי יהוה׃ וַיְדַבֵּר מֹשֶׁה כֵּן אֶל־בְּנֵי יִשְׂרָאֵל וְלֹא שָׁמְעוּ אֶל־
מֹשֶׁה מִקֹּצֶר רוּחַ וּמֵעֲבֹדָה קָשָׁה׃
ישראל וַיְדַבֵּר יהוה אֶל־מֹשֶׁה לֵּאמֹר׃ בֹּא דַבֵּר אֶל־פַּרְעֹה מֶלֶךְ
מִצְרָיִם וִישַׁלַּח אֶת־בְּנֵי־יִשְׂרָאֵל מֵאַרְצוֹ׃ וַיְדַבֵּר מֹשֶׁה לִפְנֵי
יהוה לֵאמֹר הֵן בְּנֵי־יִשְׂרָאֵל לֹא־שָׁמְעוּ אֵלַי וְאֵיךְ יִשְׁמָעֵנִי
פַרְעֹה וַאֲנִי עֲרַל שְׂפָתָיִם׃
וַיְדַבֵּר יהוה אֶל־מֹשֶׁה וְאֶל־אַהֲרֹן וַיְצַוֵּם אֶל־בְּנֵי יִשְׂרָאֵל
וְאֶל־פַּרְעֹה מֶלֶךְ מִצְרָיִם לְהוֹצִיא אֶת־בְּנֵי־יִשְׂרָאֵל מֵאֶרֶץ
מִצְרָיִם׃

BO בא

FIRST ALIYA: 10:1–3
Prologue to the eighth plague: God sends Moshe and Aharon back to Pharaoh.

שמות י:א–יא

וַיֹּאמֶר יהוה אֶל־מֹשֶׁה בֹּא אֶל־פַּרְעֹה כִּי־אֲנִי הִכְבַּדְתִּי אֶת־
לִבּוֹ וְאֶת־לֵב עֲבָדָיו לְמַעַן שִׁתִי אֹתֹתַי אֵלֶּה בְּקִרְבּוֹ׃ וּלְמַעַן

תספר באזני בנך ובן־בנך את אשר התעללתי במצרים
ואת־אתתי אשר־שמתי בם וידעתם כי־אני יהוה: ויבא
משה ואהרן אל־פרעה ויאמרו אליו כה־אמר יהוה אלהי
העברים עד־מתי מאנת לענת מפני שלח עמי ויעבדני:
*כי אם־מאן אתה לשלח את־עמי הנני מביא מחר ארבה לוי
בגבלך: וכסה את־עין הארץ ולא יוכל לראת את־הארץ
ואכל ׀ את־יתר הפלטה הנשארת לכם מן־הברד ואכל
את־כל־העץ הצמח לכם מן־השדה: ומלאו בתיך ובתי
כל־עבדיך ובתי כל־מצרים אשר לא־ראו אבתיך ואבות
אבתיך מיום היותם על־האדמה עד היום הזה ויפן ויצא
מעם פרעה: *ויאמרו עבדי פרעה אליו עד־מתי יהיה זה ישראל
לנו למוקש שלח את־האנשים ויעבדו את־יהוה אלהיהם
הטרם תדע כי אבדה מצרים: ויושב את־משה ואת־אהרן
אל־פרעה ויאמר אלהם לכו עבדו את־יהוה אלהיכם מי
ומי ההלכים: ויאמר משה בנערינו ובזקנינו נלך בבנינו
ובבנותנו בצאננו ובבקרנו נלך כי חג־יהוה לנו: ויאמר
אלהם יהי כן יהוה עמכם כאשר אשלח אתכם ואת־טפכם
ראו כי רעה נגד פניכם: לא כן לכו־נא הגברים ועבדו את־
יהוה כי אתה אתם מבקשים ויגרש אתם מאת פני פרעה:

SECOND ALIYA: 10:4–6
Moshe and Aharon warn Pharaoh of the impending eighth plague: locusts.

THIRD ALIYA: 10:7–11
Pharaoh refuses to let the entire people go.

BESHALLAH בשלח

ויהי בשלח פרעה את־העם ולא־נחם אלהים דרך ארץ שמות יג:יז–יח:ח
פלשתים כי קרוב הוא כי ׀ אמר אלהים פן־ינחם העם
בראתם מלחמה ושבו מצרימה: ויסב אלהים ׀ את־העם
דרך המדבר ים־סוף וחמשים עלו בני־ישראל מארץ
מצרים: ויקח משה את־עצמות יוסף עמו כי השבע
השביע את־בני ישראל לאמר פקד יפקד אלהים אתכם
והעליתם את־עצמתי מזה אתכם: ויסעו מסכת ויחנו
באתם בקצה המדבר: ויהוה הלך לפניהם יומם בעמוד

FIRST ALIYA: 13:17–22
God led the Israelites on a longer route to the Land of Israel, in order to avoid the land of the Philistines.

עָנָן לַנְחֹתָם הַדֶּרֶךְ וְלַיְלָה בְּעַמּוּד אֵשׁ לְהָאִיר לָהֶם לָלֶכֶת
יוֹמָם וָלָיְלָה: לֹא־יָמִישׁ עַמּוּד הֶעָנָן יוֹמָם וְעַמּוּד הָאֵשׁ
לָיְלָה לִפְנֵי הָעָם:

SECOND ALIYA: 14:1–4
God strengthens Pharaoh's heart and he changes his mind.

וַיְדַבֵּר יהוה אֶל־מֹשֶׁה לֵּאמֹר: דַּבֵּר אֶל־בְּנֵי יִשְׂרָאֵל וְיָשֻׁבוּ לוי
וְיַחֲנוּ לִפְנֵי פִּי הַחִירֹת בֵּין מִגְדֹּל וּבֵין הַיָּם לִפְנֵי בַּעַל צְפֹן
נִכְחוֹ תַחֲנוּ עַל־הַיָּם: וְאָמַר פַּרְעֹה לִבְנֵי יִשְׂרָאֵל נְבֻכִים
הֵם בָּאָרֶץ סָגַר עֲלֵיהֶם הַמִּדְבָּר: וְחִזַּקְתִּי אֶת־לֵב־פַּרְעֹה
וְרָדַף אַחֲרֵיהֶם וְאִכָּבְדָה בְּפַרְעֹה וּבְכָל־חֵילוֹ וְיָדְעוּ מִצְרַיִם

THIRD ALIYA: 14:5–8
Pharaoh orders his forces to pursue the Israelites.

כִּי־אֲנִי יהוה וַיַּעֲשׂוּ־כֵן: *וַיֻּגַּד לְמֶלֶךְ מִצְרַיִם כִּי בָרַח הָעָם ישראל
וַיֵּהָפֵךְ לְבַב פַּרְעֹה וַעֲבָדָיו אֶל־הָעָם וַיֹּאמְרוּ מַה־זֹּאת
עָשִׂינוּ כִּי־שִׁלַּחְנוּ אֶת־יִשְׂרָאֵל מֵעָבְדֵנוּ: וַיֶּאְסֹר אֶת־רִכְבּוֹ
וְאֶת־עַמּוֹ לָקַח עִמּוֹ: וַיִּקַּח שֵׁשׁ־מֵאוֹת רֶכֶב בָּחוּר וְכֹל
רֶכֶב מִצְרָיִם וְשָׁלִשִׁם עַל־כֻּלּוֹ: וַיְחַזֵּק יהוה אֶת־לֵב פַּרְעֹה
מֶלֶךְ מִצְרַיִם וַיִּרְדֹּף אַחֲרֵי בְּנֵי יִשְׂרָאֵל וּבְנֵי יִשְׂרָאֵל יֹצְאִים
בְּיָד רָמָה:

YITRO יתרו

FIRST ALIYA: 18:1–4
Yitro, the father in law of Moshe, heard all that God did for the Israelites in Egypt.

שמות יח:א־יב

וַיִּשְׁמַע יִתְרוֹ כֹהֵן מִדְיָן חֹתֵן מֹשֶׁה אֵת כָּל־אֲשֶׁר עָשָׂה
אֱלֹהִים לְמֹשֶׁה וּלְיִשְׂרָאֵל עַמּוֹ כִּי־הוֹצִיא יהוה אֶת־יִשְׂרָאֵל
מִמִּצְרָיִם: וַיִּקַּח יִתְרוֹ חֹתֵן מֹשֶׁה אֶת־צִפֹּרָה אֵשֶׁת מֹשֶׁה
אַחַר שִׁלּוּחֶיהָ: וְאֵת שְׁנֵי בָנֶיהָ אֲשֶׁר שֵׁם הָאֶחָד גֵּרְשֹׁם
כִּי אָמַר גֵּר הָיִיתִי בְּאֶרֶץ נָכְרִיָּה: וְשֵׁם הָאֶחָד אֱלִיעֶזֶר כִּי־

SECOND ALIYA: 18:5–8
Yitro takes his daughter Tzippora (Moshe's wife) and her two sons, and joins Moshe and the Israelites.

אֱלֹהֵי אָבִי בְּעֶזְרִי וַיַּצִּלֵנִי מֵחֶרֶב פַּרְעֹה: *וַיָּבֹא יִתְרוֹ חֹתֵן לוי
מֹשֶׁה וּבָנָיו וְאִשְׁתּוֹ אֶל־מֹשֶׁה אֶל־הַמִּדְבָּר אֲשֶׁר־הוּא חֹנֶה
שָׁם הַר הָאֱלֹהִים: וַיֹּאמֶר אֶל־מֹשֶׁה אֲנִי חֹתֶנְךָ יִתְרוֹ בָּא
אֵלֶיךָ וְאִשְׁתְּךָ וּשְׁנֵי בָנֶיהָ עִמָּהּ: וַיֵּצֵא מֹשֶׁה לִקְרַאת חֹתְנוֹ
וַיִּשְׁתַּחוּ וַיִּשַּׁק־לוֹ וַיִּשְׁאֲלוּ אִישׁ־לְרֵעֵהוּ לְשָׁלוֹם וַיָּבֹאוּ
הָאֹהֱלָה: וַיְסַפֵּר מֹשֶׁה לְחֹתְנוֹ אֵת כָּל־אֲשֶׁר עָשָׂה יהוה
לְפַרְעֹה וּלְמִצְרַיִם עַל אוֹדֹת יִשְׂרָאֵל אֵת כָּל־הַתְּלָאָה אֲשֶׁר

ישראל מצאתם בדרך ויצלם יהוה: *ויחד יתרו על כל-הטובה
אשר-עשה יהוה לישראל אשר הצילו מיד מצרים: ויאמר
יתרו ברוך יהוה אשר הציל אתכם מיד מצרים ומיד
פרעה אשר הציל את-העם מתחת יד-מצרים: עתה
ידעתי כי-גדול יהוה מכל-האלהים כי בדבר אשר זדו
עליהם: ויקח יתרו חתן משה עלה וזבחים לאלהים ויבא
אהרן וכל | זקני ישראל לאכל-לחם עם-חתן משה לפני
האלהים:

THIRD ALIYA: 18:9–12
Yitro rejoiced in everything that God had done in Egypt, and offered sacrifices to Him in thanks.

MISHPATIM משפטים

שמות כא: א–יט ואלה המשפטים אשר תשים לפניהם: כי תקנה עבד עברי
שש שנים יעבד ובשבעת יצא לחפשי חנם: אם-בגפו יבא
בגפו יצא אם-בעל אשה הוא ויצאה אשתו עמו: אם-אדניו
יתן-לו אשה וילדה-לו בנים או בנות האשה וילדיה תהיה
לאדניה והוא יצא בגפו: ואם-אמר יאמר העבד אהבתי
את-אדני את-אשתי ואת-בני לא אצא חפשי: והגישו
אדניו אל-האלהים והגישו אל-הדלת או אל-המזוזה ורצע
לוי אדניו את-אזנו במרצע ועבדו לעלם: *וכי-
ימכר איש את-בתו לאמה לא תצא כצאת העבדים:
לו אם-רעה בעיני אדניה אשר-לא יעדה והפדה לעם נכרי
לא-ימשל למכרה בבגדו-בה: ואם-לבנו ייעדנה כמשפט
הבנות יעשה-לה: אם-אחרת יקח-לו שארה כסותה
וענתה לא יגרע: ואם-שלש-אלה לא יעשה לה ויצאה
ישראל חנם אין כסף: *מכה איש ומת מות יומת:
ואשר לא צדה והאלהים אנה לידו ושמתי לך מקום
אשר ינוס שמה: וכי-יזד איש על-רעהו
להרגו בערמה מעם מזבחי תקחנו למות: ומכה
אביו ואמו מות יומת: וגנב איש ומכרו ונמצא
בידו מות יומת: ומקלל אביו ואמו מות

FIRST ALIYA: 21:1–6
The laws of Jewish slaves.

SECOND ALIYA: 21:7–11
The father's rights and responsibilities to his daughter when she is sold as a slave.

THIRD ALIYA: 21:12–19
The laws of murder, manslaughter, and the infliction of bodily injury.

יוּמָת׃ וְכִי־יְרִיבֻן אֲנָשִׁים וְהִכָּה־אִישׁ אֶת־
רֵעֵהוּ בְּאֶבֶן אוֹ בְאֶגְרֹף וְלֹא יָמוּת וְנָפַל לְמִשְׁכָּב׃ אִם־יָקוּם
וְהִתְהַלֵּךְ בַּחוּץ עַל־מִשְׁעַנְתּוֹ וְנִקָּה הַמַּכֶּה רַק שִׁבְתּוֹ יִתֵּן
וְרַפֹּא יְרַפֵּא׃

TERUMA — תרומה

שמות כה:א–טז

FIRST ALIYA: 25:1–5 The funding of the Tabernacle.

SECOND ALIYA: 25:6–9 God commands the building of the Tabernacle.

THIRD ALIYA: 25:10–16 Instructions of how to make the Ark.

וַיְדַבֵּר יְהוָה אֶל־מֹשֶׁה לֵּאמֹר׃ דַּבֵּר אֶל־בְּנֵי יִשְׂרָאֵל וְיִקְחוּ־
לִי תְּרוּמָה מֵאֵת כָּל־אִישׁ אֲשֶׁר יִדְּבֶנּוּ לִבּוֹ תִּקְחוּ אֶת־
תְּרוּמָתִי׃ וְזֹאת הַתְּרוּמָה אֲשֶׁר תִּקְחוּ מֵאִתָּם זָהָב וָכֶסֶף
וּנְחֹשֶׁת׃ וּתְכֵלֶת וְאַרְגָּמָן וְתוֹלַעַת שָׁנִי וְשֵׁשׁ וְעִזִּים׃ וְעֹרֹת
לוי אֵילִם מְאָדָּמִים וְעֹרֹת תְּחָשִׁים וַעֲצֵי שִׁטִּים׃ *שֶׁמֶן לַמָּאֹר
בְּשָׂמִים לְשֶׁמֶן הַמִּשְׁחָה וְלִקְטֹרֶת הַסַּמִּים׃ אַבְנֵי־שֹׁהַם
וְאַבְנֵי מִלֻּאִים לָאֵפֹד וְלַחֹשֶׁן׃ וְעָשׂוּ לִי מִקְדָּשׁ וְשָׁכַנְתִּי
בְּתוֹכָם׃ כְּכֹל אֲשֶׁר אֲנִי מַרְאֶה אוֹתְךָ אֵת תַּבְנִית הַמִּשְׁכָּן
ישראל וְאֵת תַּבְנִית כָּל־כֵּלָיו וְכֵן תַּעֲשׂוּ׃ *וְעָשׂוּ אֲרוֹן
עֲצֵי שִׁטִּים אַמָּתַיִם וָחֵצִי אָרְכּוֹ וְאַמָּה וָחֵצִי רָחְבּוֹ וְאַמָּה וָחֵצִי
קֹמָתוֹ׃ וְצִפִּיתָ אֹתוֹ זָהָב טָהוֹר מִבַּיִת וּמִחוּץ תְּצַפֶּנּוּ וְעָשִׂיתָ
עָלָיו זֵר זָהָב סָבִיב׃ וְיָצַקְתָּ לּוֹ אַרְבַּע טַבְּעֹת זָהָב וְנָתַתָּה
עַל אַרְבַּע פַּעֲמֹתָיו וּשְׁתֵּי טַבָּעֹת עַל־צַלְעוֹ הָאֶחָת וּשְׁתֵּי
טַבָּעֹת עַל־צַלְעוֹ הַשֵּׁנִית׃ וְעָשִׂיתָ בַדֵּי עֲצֵי שִׁטִּים וְצִפִּיתָ
אֹתָם זָהָב׃ וְהֵבֵאתָ אֶת־הַבַּדִּים בַּטַּבָּעֹת עַל צַלְעֹת הָאָרֹן
לָשֵׂאת אֶת־הָאָרֹן בָּהֶם׃ בְּטַבְּעֹת הָאָרֹן יִהְיוּ הַבַּדִּים לֹא
יָסֻרוּ מִמֶּנּוּ׃ וְנָתַתָּ אֶל־הָאָרֹן אֵת הָעֵדֻת אֲשֶׁר אֶתֵּן אֵלֶיךָ׃

TETZAVEH — תצוה

שמות כז:כ–כח:יב

FIRST ALIYA: 27:20–28:5 Instruction on how to make the oil for the menora in the Tabernacle, and the priestly garments.

וְאַתָּה תְּצַוֶּה ׀ אֶת־בְּנֵי יִשְׂרָאֵל וְיִקְחוּ אֵלֶיךָ שֶׁמֶן זַיִת זָךְ כָּתִית
לַמָּאוֹר לְהַעֲלֹת נֵר תָּמִיד׃ בְּאֹהֶל מוֹעֵד מִחוּץ לַפָּרֹכֶת אֲשֶׁר
עַל־הָעֵדֻת יַעֲרֹךְ אֹתוֹ אַהֲרֹן וּבָנָיו מֵעֶרֶב עַד־בֹּקֶר לִפְנֵי יְהוָה
חֻקַּת עוֹלָם לְדֹרֹתָם מֵאֵת בְּנֵי יִשְׂרָאֵל׃ וְאַתָּה

הקרב אליך את־אהרן אחיך ואת־בניו אתו מתוך בני
ישראל לכהנו־לי אהרן נדב ואביהוא אלעזר ואיתמר בני
אהרן: ועשית בגדי־קדש לאהרן אחיך לכבוד ולתפארת:
ואתה תדבר אל־כל־חכמי־לב אשר מלאתיו רוח חכמה
ועשו את־בגדי אהרן לקדשו לכהנו־לי: ואלה הבגדים
אשר יעשו חשן ואפוד ומעיל וכתנת תשבץ מצנפת
ואבנט ועשו בגדי־קדש לאהרן אחיך ולבניו לכהנו־לי:
והם יקחו את־הזהב ואת־התכלת ואת־הארגמן ואת־
תולעת השני ואת־השש:

לוי ועשו את־האפד זהב תכלת וארגמן תולעת שני ושש
משזר מעשה חשב: שתי כתפת חברת יהיה־לו אל־

SECOND ALIYA: 28:6–9
Instructions on the making of the High Priest's garments and breastplate.

שני קצותיו וחבר: וחשב אפדתו אשר עליו כמעשהו
ממנו יהיה זהב תכלת וארגמן ותולעת שני ושש משזר:
ולקחת את־שתי אבני־שהם ופתחת עליהם שמות בני
ישראל ישראל: *ששה משמתם על האבן האחת ואת־שמות

THIRD ALIYA: 28:10–12
The details of the twelve precious stones in the High Priest's breastplate.

הששה הנותרים על־האבן השנית כתולדתם: מעשה
חרש אבן פתוחי חתם תפתח את־שתי האבנים על־שמת
בני ישראל מסבת משבצות זהב תעשה אתם: ושמת
את־שתי האבנים על כתפת האפד אבני זכרן לבני ישראל
ונשא אהרן את־שמותם לפני יהוה על־שתי כתפיו לזכרן:

KI TISSA — כי תשא

FIRST ALIYA: 30:11–13
The census of the Jewish People will be carried out through the giving of a half shekel.

שמות ל:יא–כא וידבר יהוה אל־משה לאמר: כי תשא את־ראש בני־
ישראל לפקדיהם ונתנו איש כפר נפשו ליהוה בפקד
אתם ולא־יהיה בהם נגף בפקד אתם: זה ׀ יתנו כל־העבר
על־הפקדים מחצית השקל בשקל הקדש עשרים גרה
לוי השקל מחצית השקל תרומה ליהוה: *כל העבר על־

SECOND ALIYA: 30:14–16
All men above the age of twenty will be counted in the census.

הפקדים מבן עשרים שנה ומעלה יתן תרומת יהוה:
העשיר לא־ירבה והדל לא ימעיט ממחצית השקל לתת

אֶת־תְּרוּמַת יְהוָה לְכַפֵּר עַל־נַפְשֹׁתֵיכֶם׃ וְלָקַחְתָּ אֶת־כֶּסֶף
הַכִּפֻּרִים מֵאֵת בְּנֵי יִשְׂרָאֵל וְנָתַתָּ אֹתוֹ עַל־עֲבֹדַת אֹהֶל
מוֹעֵד וְהָיָה לִבְנֵי יִשְׂרָאֵל לְזִכָּרוֹן לִפְנֵי יְהוָה לְכַפֵּר עַל־
נַפְשֹׁתֵיכֶם׃

ישראל

THIRD ALIYA: 30:17–21
Instructions of the making of the copper basin for the priests to wash in the Tabernacle.

וַיְדַבֵּר יְהוָה אֶל־מֹשֶׁה לֵּאמֹר׃ וְעָשִׂיתָ כִּיּוֹר נְחֹשֶׁת וְכַנּוֹ
נְחֹשֶׁת לְרָחְצָה וְנָתַתָּ אֹתוֹ בֵּין־אֹהֶל מוֹעֵד וּבֵין הַמִּזְבֵּחַ
וְנָתַתָּ שָׁמָּה מָיִם׃ וְרָחֲצוּ אַהֲרֹן וּבָנָיו מִמֶּנּוּ אֶת־יְדֵיהֶם וְאֶת־
רַגְלֵיהֶם׃ בְּבֹאָם אֶל־אֹהֶל מוֹעֵד יִרְחֲצוּ־מַיִם וְלֹא יָמֻתוּ
אוֹ בְגִשְׁתָּם אֶל־הַמִּזְבֵּחַ לְשָׁרֵת לְהַקְטִיר אִשֶּׁה לַיהוָה׃
וְרָחֲצוּ יְדֵיהֶם וְרַגְלֵיהֶם וְלֹא יָמֻתוּ וְהָיְתָה לָהֶם חָק־עוֹלָם
לוֹ וּלְזַרְעוֹ לְדֹרֹתָם׃

ויקהל VAYAK-HEL

שמות
לה:א–כ

FIRST ALIYA: 35:1–3
Shabbat: you may work for six days and must rest on the seventh which is a holy day.

וַיַּקְהֵל מֹשֶׁה אֶת־כָּל־עֲדַת בְּנֵי יִשְׂרָאֵל וַיֹּאמֶר אֲלֵהֶם אֵלֶּה
הַדְּבָרִים אֲשֶׁר־צִוָּה יְהוָה לַעֲשֹׂת אֹתָם׃ שֵׁשֶׁת יָמִים תֵּעָשֶׂה
מְלָאכָה וּבַיּוֹם הַשְּׁבִיעִי יִהְיֶה לָכֶם קֹדֶשׁ שַׁבַּת שַׁבָּתוֹן
לַיהוָה כָּל־הָעֹשֶׂה בוֹ מְלָאכָה יוּמָת׃ לֹא־תְבַעֲרוּ אֵשׁ בְּכֹל
מֹשְׁבֹתֵיכֶם בְּיוֹם הַשַּׁבָּת׃

לוי

SECOND ALIYA: 35:4–10
Donations to the Tabernacle.

וַיֹּאמֶר מֹשֶׁה אֶל־כָּל־עֲדַת בְּנֵי־יִשְׂרָאֵל לֵאמֹר זֶה הַדָּבָר
אֲשֶׁר־צִוָּה יְהוָה לֵאמֹר׃ קְחוּ מֵאִתְּכֶם תְּרוּמָה לַיהוָה כֹּל
נְדִיב לִבּוֹ יְבִיאֶהָ אֵת תְּרוּמַת יְהוָה זָהָב וָכֶסֶף וּנְחֹשֶׁת׃
וּתְכֵלֶת וְאַרְגָּמָן וְתוֹלַעַת שָׁנִי וְשֵׁשׁ וְעִזִּים׃ וְעֹרֹת אֵילִם
מְאָדָּמִים וְעֹרֹת תְּחָשִׁים וַעֲצֵי שִׁטִּים׃ וְשֶׁמֶן לַמָּאוֹר וּבְשָׂמִים
לְשֶׁמֶן הַמִּשְׁחָה וְלִקְטֹרֶת הַסַּמִּים׃ וְאַבְנֵי־שֹׁהַם וְאַבְנֵי
מִלֻּאִים לָאֵפוֹד וְלַחֹשֶׁן׃ וְכָל־חֲכַם־לֵב בָּכֶם יָבֹאוּ וְיַעֲשׂוּ

ישראל

THIRD ALIYA: 35:11–20
The construction of the Tabernacle.

אֵת כָּל־אֲשֶׁר צִוָּה יְהוָה׃ *אֶת־הַמִּשְׁכָּן אֶת־אָהֳלוֹ וְאֶת־
מִכְסֵהוּ אֶת־קְרָסָיו וְאֶת־קְרָשָׁיו אֶת־בְּרִיחָו אֶת־עַמֻּדָיו
וְאֶת־אֲדָנָיו׃ אֶת־הָאָרֹן וְאֶת־בַּדָּיו אֶת־הַכַּפֹּרֶת וְאֵת פָּרֹכֶת
הַמָּסָךְ׃ אֶת־הַשֻּׁלְחָן וְאֶת־בַּדָּיו וְאֶת־כָּל־כֵּלָיו וְאֵת לֶחֶם

הַפָּנִים׃ וְאֶת־מְנֹרַת הַמָּאוֹר וְאֶת־כֵּלֶיהָ וְאֶת־נֵרֹתֶיהָ וְאֵת
שֶׁמֶן הַמָּאוֹר׃ וְאֶת־מִזְבַּח הַקְּטֹרֶת וְאֶת־בַּדָּיו וְאֵת שֶׁמֶן
הַמִּשְׁחָה וְאֵת קְטֹרֶת הַסַּמִּים וְאֶת־מָסַךְ הַפֶּתַח לְפֶתַח
הַמִּשְׁכָּן׃ אֵת ׀ מִזְבַּח הָעֹלָה וְאֶת־מִכְבַּר הַנְּחֹשֶׁת אֲשֶׁר־
לוֹ אֶת־בַּדָּיו וְאֶת־כָּל־כֵּלָיו אֶת־הַכִּיֹּר וְאֶת־כַּנּוֹ׃ אֵת קַלְעֵי
הֶחָצֵר אֶת־עַמֻּדָיו וְאֶת־אֲדָנֶיהָ וְאֵת מָסַךְ שַׁעַר הֶחָצֵר׃
אֶת־יִתְדֹת הַמִּשְׁכָּן וְאֶת־יִתְדֹת הֶחָצֵר וְאֶת־מֵיתְרֵיהֶם׃
אֶת־בִּגְדֵי הַשְּׂרָד לְשָׁרֵת בַּקֹּדֶשׁ אֶת־בִּגְדֵי הַקֹּדֶשׁ לְאַהֲרֹן
הַכֹּהֵן וְאֶת־בִּגְדֵי בָנָיו לְכַהֵן׃ וַיֵּצְאוּ כָּל־עֲדַת בְּנֵי־יִשְׂרָאֵל
מִלִּפְנֵי מֹשֶׁה׃

PEKUDEI פקודי

שמות לח:כא–לט:א

FIRST ALIYA: 38:21–23
An introduction to the accounts of the donations to the Tabernacle.

אֵלֶּה פְקוּדֵי הַמִּשְׁכָּן מִשְׁכַּן הָעֵדֻת אֲשֶׁר פֻּקַּד עַל־פִּי מֹשֶׁה
עֲבֹדַת הַלְוִיִּם בְּיַד אִיתָמָר בֶּן־אַהֲרֹן הַכֹּהֵן׃ וּבְצַלְאֵל בֶּן־
אוּרִי בֶן־חוּר לְמַטֵּה יְהוּדָה עָשָׂה אֵת כָּל־אֲשֶׁר־צִוָּה
יְהוָה אֶת־מֹשֶׁה׃ וְאִתּוֹ אָהֳלִיאָב בֶּן־אֲחִיסָמָךְ לְמַטֵּה־
דָן חָרָשׁ וְחֹשֵׁב וְרֹקֵם בַּתְּכֵלֶת וּבָאַרְגָּמָן וּבְתוֹלַעַת הַשָּׁנִי
וּבַשֵּׁשׁ׃

לוי

SECOND ALIYA: 38:24–27
Summary of the materials used in the construction of the Tabernacle.

*כָּל־הַזָּהָב הֶעָשׂוּי לַמְּלָאכָה בְּכֹל
מְלֶאכֶת הַקֹּדֶשׁ וַיְהִי ׀ זְהַב הַתְּנוּפָה תֵּשַׁע וְעֶשְׂרִים כִּכָּר
וּשְׁבַע מֵאוֹת וּשְׁלֹשִׁים שֶׁקֶל בְּשֶׁקֶל הַקֹּדֶשׁ׃ וְכֶסֶף פְּקוּדֵי
הָעֵדָה מְאַת כִּכָּר וְאֶלֶף וּשְׁבַע מֵאוֹת וַחֲמִשָּׁה וְשִׁבְעִים
שֶׁקֶל בְּשֶׁקֶל הַקֹּדֶשׁ׃ בֶּקַע לַגֻּלְגֹּלֶת מַחֲצִית הַשֶּׁקֶל בְּשֶׁקֶל
הַקֹּדֶשׁ לְכֹל הָעֹבֵר עַל־הַפְּקֻדִים מִבֶּן עֶשְׂרִים שָׁנָה וָמַעְלָה
לְשֵׁשׁ־מֵאוֹת אֶלֶף וּשְׁלֹשֶׁת אֲלָפִים וַחֲמֵשׁ מֵאוֹת וַחֲמִשִּׁים׃
וַיְהִי מְאַת כִּכַּר הַכֶּסֶף לָצֶקֶת אֵת אַדְנֵי הַקֹּדֶשׁ וְאֵת אַדְנֵי
הַפָּרֹכֶת מְאַת אֲדָנִים לִמְאַת הַכִּכָּר כִּכָּר לָאָדֶן׃

ישראל

THIRD ALIYA: 38:28–39:1
Continuation of the summary of the materials used in the construction of the Tabernacle.

*וְאֶת־
הָאֶלֶף וּשְׁבַע הַמֵּאוֹת וַחֲמִשָּׁה וְשִׁבְעִים עָשָׂה וָוִים לָעַמּוּדִים
וְצִפָּה רָאשֵׁיהֶם וְחִשַּׁק אֹתָם׃ וּנְחֹשֶׁת הַתְּנוּפָה שִׁבְעִים
כִּכָּר וְאַלְפַּיִם וְאַרְבַּע־מֵאוֹת שָׁקֶל׃ וַיַּעַשׂ בָּהּ אֶת־אַדְנֵי

פתח אהל מועד ואת מזבח הנחשת ואת־מכבר הנחשת
אשר־לו ואת כל־כלי המזבח: ואת־אדני החצר סביב ואת־
אדני שער החצר ואת כל־יתדת המשכן ואת־כל־יתדת
החצר סביב: ומן־התכלת והארגמן ותולעת השני עשו
בגדי־שרד לשרת בקדש ויעשו את־בגדי הקדש אשר
לאהרן כאשר צוה יהוה את־משה:

VAYIKRA ויקרא

ויקרא א:א–יג ויקרא אל־משה וידבר יהוה אליו מאהל מועד לאמר:
דבר אל־בני ישראל ואמרת אלהם אדם כי־יקריב מכם

FIRST ALIYA: 1:1–4
The laws of a burnt offering.

קרבן ליהוה מן־הבהמה מן־הבקר ומן־הצאן תקריבו את־
קרבנכם: אם־עלה קרבנו מן־הבקר זכר תמים יקריבנו
אל־פתח אהל מועד יקריב אתו לרצנו לפני יהוה: וסמך
לוי ידו על ראש העלה ונרצה לו לכפר עליו: *ושחט את־בן

SECOND ALIYA: 1:5–9
Continuation of the laws of an elevation offering.

הבקר לפני יהוה והקריבו בני אהרן הכהנים את־הדם
וזרקו את־הדם על־המזבח סביב אשר־פתח אהל מועד:
והפשיט את־העלה ונתח אתה לנתחיה: ונתנו בני אהרן
הכהן אש על־המזבח וערכו עצים על־האש: וערכו בני
אהרן הכהנים את הנתחים את־הראש ואת־הפדר על־
העצים אשר על־האש אשר על־המזבח: וקרבו וכרעיו
ירחץ במים והקטיר הכהן את־הכל המזבחה עלה אשה
ישראל ריח־ניחוח ליהוה: *ואם־מן־הצאן קרבנו מן־

THIRD ALIYA: 1:10–13
Elevation offerings from sheep and goats.

הכשבים או מן־העזים לעלה זכר תמים יקריבנו: ושחט
אתו על ירך המזבח צפנה לפני יהוה וזרקו בני אהרן
הכהנים את־דמו על־המזבח סביב: ונתח אתו לנתחיו
ואת־ראשו ואת־פדרו וערך הכהן אתם על־העצים אשר
על־האש אשר על־המזבח: והקרב והכרעים ירחץ במים
והקריב הכהן את־הכל והקטיר המזבחה עלה הוא אשה
ריח ניחח ליהוה:

TZAV צו

ויקרא ו:א–יא

וידבר יהוה אל־משה לאמר: צו את־אהרן ואת־בניו לאמר
זאת תורת העלה הוא העלה על מוקדה על־המזבח כל־
הלילה עד־הבקר ואש המזבח תוקד בו: ולבש הכהן מדו
בד ומכנסי־בד ילבש על־בשרו והרים את־הדשן אשר
תאכל האש את־העלה על־המזבח ושמו אצל המזבח:

FIRST ALIYA: 6:1–3 Elevation offerings should burn all night.

לוי

*ופשט את־בגדיו ולבש בגדים אחרים והוציא את־הדשן
אל־מחוץ למחנה אל־מקום טהור: והאש על־המזבח
תוקד־בו לא תכבה ובער עליה הכהן עצים בבקר בבקר
וערך עליה העלה והקטיר עליה חלבי השלמים: אש
תמיד תוקד על־המזבח לא תכבה:

SECOND ALIYA: 6:4–6 The ash must be removed to outside the camp.

ישראל

*וזאת
תורת המנחה הקרב אתה בני־אהרן לפני יהוה אל־פני
המזבח: והרים ממנו בקמצו מסלת המנחה ומשמנה
ואת כל־הלבנה אשר על־המנחה והקטיר המזבח ריח
ניחח אזכרתה ליהוה: והנותרת ממנה יאכלו אהרן ובניו
מצות תאכל במקום קדש בחצר אהל־מועד יאכלוה: לא
תאפה חמץ חלקם נתתי אתה מאשי קדש קדשים הוא
כחטאת וכאשם: כל־זכר בבני אהרן יאכלנה חק־עולם
לדרתיכם מאשי יהוה כל אשר־יגע בהם יקדש:

THIRD ALIYA: 6:7–11 The laws of the meal offering.

SHEMINI שמיני

ויקרא ט:א–טז

ויהי ביום השמיני קרא משה לאהרן ולבניו ולזקני ישראל:
ויאמר אל־אהרן קח־לך עגל בן־בקר לחטאת ואיל לעלה
תמימם והקרב לפני יהוה: ואל־בני ישראל תדבר לאמר
קחו שעיר־עזים לחטאת ועגל וכבש בני־שנה תמימם
לעלה: ושור ואיל לשלמים לזבח לפני יהוה ומנחה
בלולה בשמן כי היום יהוה נראה אליכם: ויקחו את
אשר צוה משה אל־פני אהל מועד ויקרבו כל־העדה
ויעמדו לפני יהוה: ויאמר משה זה הדבר אשר־צוה יהוה

FIRST ALIYA: 9:1–5 Moshe gives instructions about the inauguration of the priestly service in the Tabernacle.

SECOND ALIYA: 9:6–10
The priestly service is inaugurated in the Tabernacle.

לוי
תַּעֲשׂוּ וְיֵרָא אֲלֵיכֶם כְּבוֹד יהוה: *וַיֹּאמֶר מֹשֶׁה אֶל־אַהֲרֹן
קְרַב אֶל־הַמִּזְבֵּחַ וַעֲשֵׂה אֶת־חַטָּאתְךָ וְאֶת־עֹלָתֶךָ וְכַפֵּר
בַּעַדְךָ וּבְעַד הָעָם וַעֲשֵׂה אֶת־קָרְבַּן הָעָם וְכַפֵּר בַּעֲדָם
כַּאֲשֶׁר צִוָּה יהוה: וַיִּקְרַב אַהֲרֹן אֶל־הַמִּזְבֵּחַ וַיִּשְׁחַט אֶת־
עֵגֶל הַחַטָּאת אֲשֶׁר־לוֹ: וַיַּקְרִבוּ בְּנֵי אַהֲרֹן אֶת־הַדָּם אֵלָיו
וַיִּטְבֹּל אֶצְבָּעוֹ בַּדָּם וַיִּתֵּן עַל־קַרְנוֹת הַמִּזְבֵּחַ וְאֶת־הַדָּם
יָצַק אֶל־יְסוֹד הַמִּזְבֵּחַ: וְאֶת־הַחֵלֶב וְאֶת־הַכְּלָיֹת וְאֶת־
הַיֹּתֶרֶת מִן־הַכָּבֵד מִן־הַחַטָּאת הִקְטִיר הַמִּזְבֵּחָה כַּאֲשֶׁר

THIRD ALIYA: 9:11–16
Aharon conducts the priestly service in the Tabernacle.

ישראל
צִוָּה יהוה אֶת־מֹשֶׁה: *וְאֶת־הַבָּשָׂר וְאֶת־הָעוֹר שָׂרַף בָּאֵשׁ
מִחוּץ לַמַּחֲנֶה: וַיִּשְׁחַט אֶת־הָעֹלָה וַיַּמְצִאוּ בְּנֵי אַהֲרֹן אֵלָיו
אֶת־הַדָּם וַיִּזְרְקֵהוּ עַל־הַמִּזְבֵּחַ סָבִיב: וְאֶת־הָעֹלָה הִמְצִיאוּ
אֵלָיו לִנְתָחֶיהָ וְאֶת־הָרֹאשׁ וַיַּקְטֵר עַל־הַמִּזְבֵּחַ: וַיִּרְחַץ
אֶת־הַקֶּרֶב וְאֶת־הַכְּרָעָיִם וַיַּקְטֵר עַל־הָעֹלָה הַמִּזְבֵּחָה:
וַיַּקְרֵב אֵת קָרְבַּן הָעָם וַיִּקַּח אֶת־שְׂעִיר הַחַטָּאת אֲשֶׁר לָעָם
וַיִּשְׁחָטֵהוּ וַיְחַטְּאֵהוּ כָּרִאשׁוֹן: וַיַּקְרֵב אֶת־הָעֹלָה וַיַּעֲשֶׂהָ
כַּמִּשְׁפָּט:

תזריע TAZRIA

ויקרא
יב:א–יג:ה

FIRST ALIYA: 12:1–4
The laws concerning post-childbirth.

וַיְדַבֵּר יהוה אֶל־מֹשֶׁה לֵּאמֹר: דַּבֵּר אֶל־בְּנֵי יִשְׂרָאֵל לֵאמֹר
אִשָּׁה כִּי תַזְרִיעַ וְיָלְדָה זָכָר וְטָמְאָה שִׁבְעַת יָמִים כִּימֵי נִדַּת
דְּוֺתָהּ תִּטְמָא: וּבַיּוֹם הַשְּׁמִינִי יִמּוֹל בְּשַׂר עָרְלָתוֹ: וּשְׁלֹשִׁים
יוֹם וּשְׁלֹשֶׁת יָמִים תֵּשֵׁב בִּדְמֵי טָהֳרָה בְּכָל־קֹדֶשׁ לֹא־תִגָּע

SECOND ALIYA: 12:5–8
Post-childbirth offerings.

לוי
וְאֶל־הַמִּקְדָּשׁ לֹא תָבֹא עַד־מְלֹאת יְמֵי טָהֳרָהּ: *וְאִם־נְקֵבָה
תֵלֵד וְטָמְאָה שְׁבֻעַיִם כְּנִדָּתָהּ וְשִׁשִּׁים יוֹם וְשֵׁשֶׁת יָמִים
תֵּשֵׁב עַל־דְּמֵי טָהֳרָה: וּבִמְלֹאת ׀ יְמֵי טָהֳרָהּ לְבֵן אוֹ לְבַת
תָּבִיא כֶּבֶשׂ בֶּן־שְׁנָתוֹ לְעֹלָה וּבֶן־יוֹנָה אוֹ־תֹר לְחַטָּאת
אֶל־פֶּתַח אֹהֶל־מוֹעֵד אֶל־הַכֹּהֵן: וְהִקְרִיבוֹ לִפְנֵי יהוה וְכִפֶּר
עָלֶיהָ וְטָהֲרָה מִמְּקֹר דָּמֶיהָ זֹאת תּוֹרַת הַיֹּלֶדֶת לַזָּכָר אוֹ
לַנְּקֵבָה: וְאִם־לֹא תִמְצָא יָדָהּ דֵּי שֶׂה וְלָקְחָה שְׁתֵּי־תֹרִים

אוֹ שְׁנֵי בְּנֵי יוֹנָה אֶחָד לְעֹלָה וְאֶחָד לְחַטָּאת וְכִפֶּר עָלֶיהָ
הַכֹּהֵן וְטָהֵרָה׃
ישראל וַיְדַבֵּר יְהוָה אֶל־מֹשֶׁה וְאֶל־אַהֲרֹן לֵאמֹר׃ אָדָם כִּי־יִהְיֶה
בְעוֹר־בְּשָׂרוֹ שְׂאֵת אוֹ־סַפַּחַת אוֹ בַהֶרֶת וְהָיָה בְעוֹר־בְּשָׂרוֹ
לְנֶגַע צָרָעַת וְהוּבָא אֶל־אַהֲרֹן הַכֹּהֵן אוֹ אֶל־אַחַד מִבָּנָיו
הַכֹּהֲנִים׃ וְרָאָה הַכֹּהֵן אֶת־הַנֶּגַע בְּעוֹר־הַבָּשָׂר וְשֵׂעָר בַּנֶּגַע
הָפַךְ ׀ לָבָן וּמַרְאֵה הַנֶּגַע עָמֹק מֵעוֹר בְּשָׂרוֹ נֶגַע צָרַעַת הוּא
וְרָאָהוּ הַכֹּהֵן וְטִמֵּא אֹתוֹ׃ וְאִם־בַּהֶרֶת לְבָנָה הִוא בְּעוֹר
בְּשָׂרוֹ וְעָמֹק אֵין־מַרְאֶהָ מִן־הָעוֹר וּשְׂעָרָה לֹא־הָפַךְ לָבָן
וְהִסְגִּיר הַכֹּהֵן אֶת־הַנֶּגַע שִׁבְעַת יָמִים׃ וְרָאָהוּ הַכֹּהֵן בַּיּוֹם
הַשְּׁבִיעִי וְהִנֵּה הַנֶּגַע עָמַד בְּעֵינָיו לֹא־פָשָׂה הַנֶּגַע בָּעוֹר
וְהִסְגִּירוֹ הַכֹּהֵן שִׁבְעַת יָמִים שֵׁנִית׃

THIRD ALIYA: 13:1–5
The laws of *Tzara'at*.

METZORA מצורע

ויקרא יד:א–יב
וַיְדַבֵּר יְהוָה אֶל־מֹשֶׁה לֵּאמֹר׃ זֹאת תִּהְיֶה תּוֹרַת הַמְּצֹרָע
בְּיוֹם טָהֳרָתוֹ וְהוּבָא אֶל־הַכֹּהֵן׃ וְיָצָא הַכֹּהֵן אֶל־מִחוּץ
לַמַּחֲנֶה וְרָאָה הַכֹּהֵן וְהִנֵּה נִרְפָּא נֶגַע־הַצָּרַעַת מִן־הַצָּרוּעַ׃
וְצִוָּה הַכֹּהֵן וְלָקַח לַמִּטַּהֵר שְׁתֵּי־צִפֳּרִים חַיּוֹת טְהֹרוֹת
וְעֵץ אֶרֶז וּשְׁנִי תוֹלַעַת וְאֵזֹב׃ וְצִוָּה הַכֹּהֵן וְשָׁחַט אֶת־הַצִּפּוֹר
לוי הָאֶחָת אֶל־כְּלִי־חֶרֶשׂ עַל־מַיִם חַיִּים׃ *אֶת־הַצִּפֹּר הַחַיָּה
יִקַּח אֹתָהּ וְאֶת־עֵץ הָאֶרֶז וְאֶת־שְׁנִי הַתּוֹלַעַת וְאֶת־הָאֵזֹב
וְטָבַל אוֹתָם וְאֵת ׀ הַצִּפֹּר הַחַיָּה בְּדַם הַצִּפֹּר הַשְּׁחֻטָה
עַל הַמַּיִם הַחַיִּים׃ וְהִזָּה עַל הַמִּטַּהֵר מִן־הַצָּרַעַת שֶׁבַע
פְּעָמִים וְטִהֲרוֹ וְשִׁלַּח אֶת־הַצִּפֹּר הַחַיָּה עַל־פְּנֵי הַשָּׂדֶה׃
וְכִבֶּס הַמִּטַּהֵר אֶת־בְּגָדָיו וְגִלַּח אֶת־כָּל־שְׂעָרוֹ וְרָחַץ בַּמַּיִם
וְטָהֵר וְאַחַר יָבוֹא אֶל־הַמַּחֲנֶה וְיָשַׁב מִחוּץ לְאָהֳלוֹ שִׁבְעַת
יָמִים׃ וְהָיָה בַיּוֹם הַשְּׁבִיעִי יְגַלַּח אֶת־כָּל־שְׂעָרוֹ אֶת־רֹאשׁוֹ
וְאֶת־זְקָנוֹ וְאֵת גַּבֹּת עֵינָיו וְאֶת־כָּל־שְׂעָרוֹ יְגַלֵּחַ וְכִבֶּס אֶת־
ישראל בְּגָדָיו וְרָחַץ אֶת־בְּשָׂרוֹ בַּמַּיִם וְטָהֵר׃ *וּבַיּוֹם הַשְּׁמִינִי יִקַּח

FIRST ALIYA: 14:1–5
The first stage of purification from *Tzara'at*.

SECOND ALIYA: 14:6–9
The second stage of purification from *Tzara'at*.

THIRD ALIYA: 14:10–12
The final stage of purification from *Tzara'at*.

שְׁנֵי־כְבָשִׂים תְּמִימִם וְכַבְשָׂה אַחַת בַּת־שְׁנָתָהּ תְּמִימָה
וּשְׁלֹשָׁה עֶשְׂרֹנִים סֹלֶת מִנְחָה בְּלוּלָה בַשֶּׁמֶן וְלֹג אֶחָד שָׁמֶן׃
וְהֶעֱמִיד הַכֹּהֵן הַמְטַהֵר אֵת הָאִישׁ הַמִּטַּהֵר וְאֹתָם לִפְנֵי
יהוה פֶּתַח אֹהֶל מוֹעֵד׃ וְלָקַח הַכֹּהֵן אֶת־הַכֶּבֶשׂ הָאֶחָד
וְהִקְרִיב אֹתוֹ לְאָשָׁם וְאֶת־לֹג הַשָּׁמֶן וְהֵנִיף אֹתָם תְּנוּפָה
לִפְנֵי יהוה׃

AḤAREI MOT אחרי מות

FIRST ALIYA: 16:1–6
The High Priest's preparation for the Yom Kippur service.

וַיְדַבֵּר יהוה אֶל־מֹשֶׁה אַחֲרֵי מוֹת שְׁנֵי בְּנֵי אַהֲרֹן בְּקָרְבָתָם ויקרא טז:א–יז
לִפְנֵי־יהוה וַיָּמֻתוּ׃ וַיֹּאמֶר יהוה אֶל־מֹשֶׁה דַּבֵּר אֶל־אַהֲרֹן
אָחִיךָ וְאַל־יָבֹא בְכָל־עֵת אֶל־הַקֹּדֶשׁ מִבֵּית לַפָּרֹכֶת אֶל־
פְּנֵי הַכַּפֹּרֶת אֲשֶׁר עַל־הָאָרֹן וְלֹא יָמוּת כִּי בֶּעָנָן אֵרָאֶה
עַל־הַכַּפֹּרֶת׃ בְּזֹאת יָבֹא אַהֲרֹן אֶל־הַקֹּדֶשׁ בְּפַר בֶּן־בָּקָר
לְחַטָּאת וְאַיִל לְעֹלָה׃ כְּתֹנֶת־בַּד קֹדֶשׁ יִלְבָּשׁ וּמִכְנְסֵי־בַד
יִהְיוּ עַל־בְּשָׂרוֹ וּבְאַבְנֵט בַּד יַחְגֹּר וּבְמִצְנֶפֶת בַּד יִצְנֹף בִּגְדֵי־
קֹדֶשׁ הֵם וְרָחַץ בַּמַּיִם אֶת־בְּשָׂרוֹ וּלְבֵשָׁם׃ וּמֵאֵת עֲדַת בְּנֵי
יִשְׂרָאֵל יִקַּח שְׁנֵי־שְׂעִירֵי עִזִּים לְחַטָּאת וְאַיִל אֶחָד לְעֹלָה׃
וְהִקְרִיב אַהֲרֹן אֶת־פַּר הַחַטָּאת אֲשֶׁר־לוֹ וְכִפֶּר בַּעֲדוֹ וּבְעַד

SECOND ALIYA: 16:7–11
The Yom Kippur service: The lots and the goat for Azazel.

בֵּיתוֹ׃ *וְלָקַח אֶת־שְׁנֵי הַשְּׂעִירִם וְהֶעֱמִיד אֹתָם לִפְנֵי יהוה לוי
פֶּתַח אֹהֶל מוֹעֵד׃ וְנָתַן אַהֲרֹן עַל־שְׁנֵי הַשְּׂעִירִם גֹּרָלוֹת
גּוֹרָל אֶחָד לַיהוה וְגוֹרָל אֶחָד לַעֲזָאזֵל׃ וְהִקְרִיב אַהֲרֹן
אֶת־הַשָּׂעִיר אֲשֶׁר עָלָה עָלָיו הַגּוֹרָל לַיהוה וְעָשָׂהוּ חַטָּאת׃
וְהַשָּׂעִיר אֲשֶׁר עָלָה עָלָיו הַגּוֹרָל לַעֲזָאזֵל יָעֳמַד־חַי לִפְנֵי
יהוה לְכַפֵּר עָלָיו לְשַׁלַּח אֹתוֹ לַעֲזָאזֵל הַמִּדְבָּרָה׃ וְהִקְרִיב
אַהֲרֹן אֶת־פַּר הַחַטָּאת אֲשֶׁר־לוֹ וְכִפֶּר בַּעֲדוֹ וּבְעַד בֵּיתוֹ

THIRD ALIYA: 16:12–17
The Yom Kippur service: The incense service and the goat offering for the people.

וְשָׁחַט אֶת־פַּר הַחַטָּאת אֲשֶׁר־לוֹ׃ *וְלָקַח מְלֹא־הַמַּחְתָּה ישראל
גַחֲלֵי־אֵשׁ מֵעַל הַמִּזְבֵּחַ מִלִּפְנֵי יהוה וּמְלֹא חָפְנָיו קְטֹרֶת
סַמִּים דַּקָּה וְהֵבִיא מִבֵּית לַפָּרֹכֶת׃ וְנָתַן אֶת־הַקְּטֹרֶת עַל־
הָאֵשׁ לִפְנֵי יהוה וְכִסָּה ׀ עֲנַן הַקְּטֹרֶת אֶת־הַכַּפֹּרֶת אֲשֶׁר

עַל־הָעֵד֖וּת וְלֹ֥א יָמֽוּת׃ וְלָקַח֙ מִדַּ֣ם הַפָּ֔ר וְהִזָּ֧ה בְאֶצְבָּע֛וֹ
עַל־פְּנֵ֥י הַכַּפֹּ֖רֶת קֵ֑דְמָה וְלִפְנֵ֣י הַכַּפֹּ֗רֶת יַזֶּ֛ה שֶֽׁבַע־פְּעָמִ֥ים
מִן־הַדָּ֖ם בְּאֶצְבָּעֽוֹ׃ וְשָׁחַ֞ט אֶת־שְׂעִ֤יר הַחַטָּאת֙ אֲשֶׁ֣ר לָעָ֔ם
וְהֵבִיא֙ אֶת־דָּמ֔וֹ אֶל־מִבֵּ֖ית לַפָּרֹ֑כֶת וְעָשָׂ֣ה אֶת־דָּמ֗וֹ כַּאֲשֶׁ֤ר
עָשָׂה֙ לְדַ֣ם הַפָּ֔ר וְהִזָּ֥ה אֹת֛וֹ עַל־הַכַּפֹּ֖רֶת וְלִפְנֵ֥י הַכַּפֹּֽרֶת׃
וְכִפֶּ֣ר עַל־הַקֹּ֗דֶשׁ מִטֻּמְאֹת֙ בְּנֵ֣י יִשְׂרָאֵ֔ל וּמִפִּשְׁעֵיהֶ֖ם לְכָל־
חַטֹּאתָ֑ם וְכֵ֤ן יַעֲשֶׂה֙ לְאֹ֣הֶל מוֹעֵ֔ד הַשֹּׁכֵ֣ן אִתָּ֔ם בְּת֖וֹךְ
טֻמְאֹתָֽם׃ וְכָל־אָדָ֞ם לֹא־יִהְיֶ֣ה ׀ בְּאֹ֣הֶל מוֹעֵ֗ד בְּבֹא֛וֹ לְכַפֵּ֥ר
בַּקֹּ֖דֶשׁ עַד־צֵאת֑וֹ וְכִפֶּ֤ר בַּעֲדוֹ֙ וּבְעַ֣ד בֵּית֔וֹ וּבְעַ֖ד כָּל־קְהַ֥ל
יִשְׂרָאֵֽל׃

KEDOSHIM קדושים

וַיְדַבֵּ֥ר יְהוָ֖ה אֶל־מֹשֶׁ֥ה לֵּאמֹֽר׃ דַּבֵּ֞ר אֶל־כָּל־עֲדַ֧ת בְּנֵֽי־ ויקרא יט:א–יד
יִשְׂרָאֵ֛ל וְאָמַרְתָּ֥ אֲלֵהֶ֖ם קְדֹשִׁ֣ים תִּהְי֑וּ כִּ֣י קָד֔וֹשׁ אֲנִ֖י יְהוָ֥ה
אֱלֹהֵיכֶֽם׃ אִ֣ישׁ אִמּ֤וֹ וְאָבִיו֙ תִּירָ֔אוּ וְאֶת־שַׁבְּתֹתַ֖י תִּשְׁמֹ֑רוּ אֲנִ֖י
יְהוָ֥ה אֱלֹהֵיכֶֽם׃ אַל־תִּפְנוּ֙ אֶל־הָ֣אֱלִילִ֔ם וֵאלֹהֵי֙ מַסֵּכָ֔ה לֹ֥א
תַעֲשׂ֖וּ לָכֶ֑ם אֲנִ֖י יְהוָ֥ה אֱלֹהֵיכֶֽם׃ *וְכִ֧י תִזְבְּח֛וּ זֶ֥בַח שְׁלָמִ֖ים לוי
לַֽיהוָ֑ה לִֽרְצֹנְכֶ֖ם תִּזְבָּחֻֽהוּ׃ בְּי֧וֹם זִבְחֲכֶ֛ם יֵאָכֵ֖ל וּמִֽמָּחֳרָ֑ת
וְהַנּוֹתָר֙ עַד־י֣וֹם הַשְּׁלִישִׁ֔י בָּאֵ֖שׁ יִשָּׂרֵֽף׃ וְאִ֛ם הֵאָכֹ֥ל יֵאָכֵ֖ל
בַּיּ֣וֹם הַשְּׁלִישִׁ֑י פִּגּ֥וּל ה֖וּא לֹ֥א יֵרָצֶֽה׃ וְאֹֽכְלָיו֙ עֲוֺנ֣וֹ יִשָּׂ֔א
כִּֽי־אֶת־קֹ֥דֶשׁ יְהוָ֖ה חִלֵּ֑ל וְנִכְרְתָ֛ה הַנֶּ֥פֶשׁ הַהִ֖וא מֵעַמֶּֽיהָ׃
וּֽבְקֻצְרְכֶם֙ אֶת־קְצִ֣יר אַרְצְכֶ֔ם לֹ֧א תְכַלֶּ֛ה פְּאַ֥ת שָׂדְךָ֖ לִקְצֹ֑ר
וְלֶ֥קֶט קְצִֽירְךָ֖ לֹ֥א תְלַקֵּֽט׃ וְכַרְמְךָ֙ לֹ֣א תְעוֹלֵ֔ל וּפֶ֥רֶט כַּרְמְךָ֖
לֹ֣א תְלַקֵּ֑ט לֶֽעָנִ֤י וְלַגֵּר֙ תַּעֲזֹ֣ב אֹתָ֔ם אֲנִ֖י יְהוָ֥ה אֱלֹהֵיכֶֽם׃
*לֹ֖א תִּגְנֹ֑בוּ וְלֹא־תְכַחֲשׁ֥וּ וְלֹֽא־תְשַׁקְּר֖וּ אִ֥ישׁ בַּעֲמִיתֽוֹ׃ וְלֹֽא־ ישראל
תִשָּׁבְע֥וּ בִשְׁמִ֖י לַשָּׁ֑קֶר וְחִלַּלְתָּ֛ אֶת־שֵׁ֥ם אֱלֹהֶ֖יךָ אֲנִ֥י יְהוָֽה׃
לֹא־תַעֲשֹׁ֥ק אֶת־רֵֽעֲךָ֖ וְלֹ֣א תִגְזֹ֑ל לֹֽא־תָלִ֞ין פְּעֻלַּ֥ת שָׂכִ֛יר
אִתְּךָ֖ עַד־בֹּֽקֶר׃ לֹא־תְקַלֵּ֣ל חֵרֵ֔שׁ וְלִפְנֵ֣י עִוֵּ֔ר לֹ֥א תִתֵּ֖ן מִכְשֹׁ֑ל
וְיָרֵ֥אתָ מֵּאֱלֹהֶ֖יךָ אֲנִ֥י יְהוָֽה׃

FIRST ALIYA: 19:1–4
The mitzvot of respecting one's parents, keeping Shabbat, and the prohibition of idolatry.

SECOND ALIYA: 19:5–11
Rejected offerings and agricultural laws that protect the poor.

THIRD ALIYA: 19:12–14
The prohibition against stealing and lying, against swearing falsely in God's name, the laws of honest business practice, and laws that protect the deaf and blind.

אמור EMOR

ויקרא כא:א–טו

FIRST ALIYA: 21:1–6
The laws of being a priest: laws ensuring priestly holiness is maintained.

וַיֹּאמֶר יְהוָה אֶל־מֹשֶׁה אֱמֹר אֶל־הַכֹּהֲנִים בְּנֵי אַהֲרֹן וְאָמַרְתָּ
אֲלֵהֶם לְנֶפֶשׁ לֹא־יִטַּמָּא בְּעַמָּיו׃ כִּי אִם־לִשְׁאֵרוֹ הַקָּרֹב אֵלָיו
לְאִמּוֹ וּלְאָבִיו וְלִבְנוֹ וּלְבִתּוֹ וּלְאָחִיו׃ וְלַאֲחֹתוֹ הַבְּתוּלָה
הַקְּרוֹבָה אֵלָיו אֲשֶׁר לֹא־הָיְתָה לְאִישׁ לָהּ יִטַּמָּא׃ לֹא יִטַּמָּא
בַּעַל בְּעַמָּיו לְהֵחַלּוֹ׃ לֹא־יקרחה קָרְחָה בְּרֹאשָׁם וּפְאַת (יִקְרְחוּ)
זְקָנָם לֹא יְגַלֵּחוּ וּבִבְשָׂרָם לֹא יִשְׂרְטוּ שָׂרָטֶת׃ קְדֹשִׁים יִהְיוּ
לֵאלֹהֵיהֶם וְלֹא יְחַלְּלוּ שֵׁם אֱלֹהֵיהֶם כִּי אֶת־אִשֵּׁי יְהוָה לֶחֶם
אֱלֹהֵיהֶם הֵם מַקְרִיבִם וְהָיוּ קֹדֶשׁ׃ *אִשָּׁה זֹנָה וַחֲלָלָה לֹא (לוי)

SECOND ALIYA: 21:7–12
Priestly marital laws and the laws of the High Priest.

יִקָּחוּ וְאִשָּׁה גְּרוּשָׁה מֵאִישָׁהּ לֹא יִקָּחוּ כִּי־קָדֹשׁ הוּא לֵאלֹהָיו׃
וְקִדַּשְׁתּוֹ כִּי־אֶת־לֶחֶם אֱלֹהֶיךָ הוּא מַקְרִיב קָדֹשׁ יִהְיֶה־לָּךְ
כִּי קָדוֹשׁ אֲנִי יְהוָה מְקַדִּשְׁכֶם׃ וּבַת אִישׁ כֹּהֵן כִּי תֵחֵל לִזְנוֹת
אֶת־אָבִיהָ הִיא מְחַלֶּלֶת בָּאֵשׁ תִּשָּׂרֵף׃ וְהַכֹּהֵן
הַגָּדוֹל מֵאֶחָיו אֲשֶׁר־יוּצַק עַל־רֹאשׁוֹ ׀ שֶׁמֶן הַמִּשְׁחָה וּמִלֵּא
אֶת־יָדוֹ לִלְבֹּשׁ אֶת־הַבְּגָדִים אֶת־רֹאשׁוֹ לֹא יִפְרָע וּבְגָדָיו
לֹא יִפְרֹם׃ וְעַל כָּל־נַפְשֹׁת מֵת לֹא יָבֹא לְאָבִיו וּלְאִמּוֹ לֹא
יִטַּמָּא׃ וּמִן־הַמִּקְדָּשׁ לֹא יֵצֵא וְלֹא יְחַלֵּל אֵת מִקְדַּשׁ אֱלֹהָיו
כִּי נֵזֶר שֶׁמֶן מִשְׁחַת אֱלֹהָיו עָלָיו אֲנִי יְהוָה׃ *וְהוּא אִשָּׁה (ישראל)

THIRD ALIYA: 21:13–15
Marital laws concerning the High Priest.

בִבְתוּלֶיהָ יִקָּח׃ אַלְמָנָה וּגְרוּשָׁה וַחֲלָלָה זֹנָה אֶת־אֵלֶּה לֹא
יִקָּח כִּי אִם־בְּתוּלָה מֵעַמָּיו יִקַּח אִשָּׁה׃ וְלֹא־יְחַלֵּל זַרְעוֹ
בְּעַמָּיו כִּי אֲנִי יְהוָה מְקַדְּשׁוֹ׃

בהר BEHAR

ויקרא כה:א–יג

FIRST ALIYA: 25:1–3
During the *shemitta* year, which is the seventh year in the cycle, the land will rest.

וַיְדַבֵּר יְהוָה אֶל־מֹשֶׁה בְּהַר סִינַי לֵאמֹר׃ דַּבֵּר אֶל־בְּנֵי
יִשְׂרָאֵל וְאָמַרְתָּ אֲלֵהֶם כִּי תָבֹאוּ אֶל־הָאָרֶץ אֲשֶׁר אֲנִי נֹתֵן
לָכֶם וְשָׁבְתָה הָאָרֶץ שַׁבָּת לַיהוָה׃ שֵׁשׁ שָׁנִים תִּזְרַע שָׂדֶךָ
וְשֵׁשׁ שָׁנִים תִּזְמֹר כַּרְמֶךָ וְאָסַפְתָּ אֶת־תְּבוּאָתָהּ׃ *וּבַשָּׁנָה (לוי)

SECOND ALIYA: 25:4–7
During this year the land must not be farmed, and produce must not be sold.

הַשְּׁבִיעִת שַׁבַּת שַׁבָּתוֹן יִהְיֶה לָאָרֶץ שַׁבָּת לַיהוָה שָׂדְךָ
לֹא תִזְרָע וְכַרְמְךָ לֹא תִזְמֹר׃ אֵת סְפִיחַ קְצִירְךָ לֹא תִקְצוֹר

וְאֶת־עִנְּבֵי נְזִירֶךָ לֹא תִבְצֹר שְׁנַת שַׁבָּתוֹן יִהְיֶה לָאָרֶץ:
וְהָיְתָה שַׁבַּת הָאָרֶץ לָכֶם לְאָכְלָה לְךָ וּלְעַבְדְּךָ וְלַאֲמָתֶךָ
וְלִשְׂכִירְךָ וּלְתוֹשָׁבְךָ הַגָּרִים עִמָּךְ: וְלִבְהֶמְתְּךָ וְלַחַיָּה אֲשֶׁר
ישראל בְּאַרְצֶךָ תִּהְיֶה כָל־תְּבוּאָתָהּ לֶאֱכֹל: *וְסָפַרְתָּ
לְךָ שֶׁבַע שַׁבְּתֹת שָׁנִים שֶׁבַע שָׁנִים שֶׁבַע פְּעָמִים וְהָיוּ לְךָ
יְמֵי שֶׁבַע שַׁבְּתֹת הַשָּׁנִים תֵּשַׁע וְאַרְבָּעִים שָׁנָה: וְהַעֲבַרְתָּ
שׁוֹפַר תְּרוּעָה בַּחֹדֶשׁ הַשְּׁבִעִי בֶּעָשׂוֹר לַחֹדֶשׁ בְּיוֹם הַכִּפֻּרִים
תַּעֲבִירוּ שׁוֹפָר בְּכָל־אַרְצְכֶם: וְקִדַּשְׁתֶּם אֵת שְׁנַת הַחֲמִשִּׁים
שָׁנָה וּקְרָאתֶם דְּרוֹר בָּאָרֶץ לְכָל־יֹשְׁבֶיהָ יוֹבֵל הִוא תִּהְיֶה
לָכֶם וְשַׁבְתֶּם אִישׁ אֶל־אֲחֻזָּתוֹ וְאִישׁ אֶל־מִשְׁפַּחְתּוֹ תָּשֻׁבוּ:
יוֹבֵל הִוא שְׁנַת הַחֲמִשִּׁים שָׁנָה תִּהְיֶה לָכֶם לֹא תִזְרָעוּ
וְלֹא תִקְצְרוּ אֶת־סְפִיחֶיהָ וְלֹא תִבְצְרוּ אֶת־נְזִרֶיהָ: כִּי יוֹבֵל
הִוא קֹדֶשׁ תִּהְיֶה לָכֶם מִן־הַשָּׂדֶה תֹּאכְלוּ אֶת־תְּבוּאָתָהּ:
בִּשְׁנַת הַיּוֹבֵל הַזֹּאת תָּשֻׁבוּ אִישׁ אֶל־אֲחֻזָּתוֹ:

THIRD ALIYA: 25:8–13
The fiftieth *Yovel* year, after seven cycles of seven *shemitta* years, will be another year of rest for the land, and ancestral land will return to original owners.

BEHUKKOTAI בחוקותי

ויקרא כו:ג–יג אִם־בְּחֻקֹּתַי תֵּלֵכוּ וְאֶת־מִצְוֹתַי תִּשְׁמְרוּ וַעֲשִׂיתֶם אֹתָם:
וְנָתַתִּי גִשְׁמֵיכֶם בְּעִתָּם וְנָתְנָה הָאָרֶץ יְבוּלָהּ וְעֵץ הַשָּׂדֶה
יִתֵּן פִּרְיוֹ: וְהִשִּׂיג לָכֶם דַּיִשׁ אֶת־בָּצִיר וּבָצִיר יַשִּׂיג אֶת־
זָרַע וַאֲכַלְתֶּם לַחְמְכֶם לָשֹׂבַע וִישַׁבְתֶּם לָבֶטַח בְּאַרְצְכֶם:
לוי *וְנָתַתִּי שָׁלוֹם בָּאָרֶץ וּשְׁכַבְתֶּם וְאֵין מַחֲרִיד וְהִשְׁבַּתִּי חַיָּה
רָעָה מִן־הָאָרֶץ וְחֶרֶב לֹא־תַעֲבֹר בְּאַרְצְכֶם: וּרְדַפְתֶּם אֶת־
אֹיְבֵיכֶם וְנָפְלוּ לִפְנֵיכֶם לֶחָרֶב: וְרָדְפוּ מִכֶּם חֲמִשָּׁה מֵאָה
וּמֵאָה מִכֶּם רְבָבָה יִרְדֹּפוּ וְנָפְלוּ אֹיְבֵיכֶם לִפְנֵיכֶם לֶחָרֶב:
וּפָנִיתִי אֲלֵיכֶם וְהִפְרֵיתִי אֶתְכֶם וְהִרְבֵּיתִי אֶתְכֶם וַהֲקִימֹתִי
ישראל אֶת־בְּרִיתִי אִתְּכֶם: *וַאֲכַלְתֶּם יָשָׁן נוֹשָׁן וְיָשָׁן מִפְּנֵי חָדָשׁ
תּוֹצִיאוּ: וְנָתַתִּי מִשְׁכָּנִי בְּתוֹכְכֶם וְלֹא־תִגְעַל נַפְשִׁי אֶתְכֶם:
וְהִתְהַלַּכְתִּי בְּתוֹכְכֶם וְהָיִיתִי לָכֶם לֵאלֹהִים וְאַתֶּם תִּהְיוּ־
לִי לְעָם: אֲנִי יְהוָה אֱלֹהֵיכֶם אֲשֶׁר הוֹצֵאתִי אֶתְכֶם מֵאֶרֶץ

FIRST ALIYA: 26:3–5
Blessing: If the Jewish People obey God's commands, then they will be blessed with rain and prosperity.

SECOND ALIYA: 26:6–10
Blessing continued: You will live in tranquility on the land.

THIRD ALIYA: 26:11–13
Blessing: God's presence will be felt among the people in the land.

מִצְרַיִם מִהְיֹת לָהֶם עֲבָדִים וָאֶשְׁבֹּר מֹטֹת עֻלְּכֶם וָאוֹלֵךְ
אֶתְכֶם קוֹמְמִיּוּת:

במדבר BEMIDBAR

במדבר א:א–יט

FIRST ALIYA: 1:1–4
The census: every family will be counted according to the men of military age (from twenty years and above).

וַיְדַבֵּר יְהוָה אֶל־מֹשֶׁה בְּמִדְבַּר סִינַי בְּאֹהֶל מוֹעֵד בְּאֶחָד
לַחֹדֶשׁ הַשֵּׁנִי בַּשָּׁנָה הַשֵּׁנִית לְצֵאתָם מֵאֶרֶץ מִצְרַיִם לֵאמֹר:
שְׂאוּ אֶת־רֹאשׁ כָּל־עֲדַת בְּנֵי־יִשְׂרָאֵל לְמִשְׁפְּחֹתָם לְבֵית
אֲבֹתָם בְּמִסְפַּר שֵׁמוֹת כָּל־זָכָר לְגֻלְגְּלֹתָם: מִבֶּן עֶשְׂרִים
שָׁנָה וָמַעְלָה כָּל־יֹצֵא צָבָא בְּיִשְׂרָאֵל תִּפְקְדוּ אֹתָם לְצִבְאֹתָם
אַתָּה וְאַהֲרֹן: וְאִתְּכֶם יִהְיוּ אִישׁ אִישׁ לַמַּטֶּה אִישׁ רֹאשׁ
לוי לְבֵית־אֲבֹתָיו הוּא: *וְאֵלֶּה שְׁמוֹת הָאֲנָשִׁים אֲשֶׁר יַעַמְדוּ

SECOND ALIYA: 1:5–16
The tribal leaders, one from each tribe, will assist Moshe and Aharon in this task.

אִתְּכֶם לִרְאוּבֵן אֱלִיצוּר בֶּן־שְׁדֵיאוּר: לְשִׁמְעוֹן שְׁלֻמִיאֵל
בֶּן־צוּרִישַׁדָּי: לִיהוּדָה נַחְשׁוֹן בֶּן־עַמִּינָדָב: לְיִשָּׂשכָר נְתַנְאֵל
בֶּן־צוּעָר: לִזְבוּלֻן אֱלִיאָב בֶּן־חֵלֹן: לִבְנֵי יוֹסֵף לְאֶפְרַיִם
אֱלִישָׁמָע בֶּן־עַמִּיהוּד לִמְנַשֶּׁה גַּמְלִיאֵל בֶּן־פְּדָהצוּר: לְבִנְיָמִן
אֲבִידָן בֶּן־גִּדְעֹנִי: לְדָן אֲחִיעֶזֶר בֶּן־עַמִּישַׁדָּי: לְאָשֵׁר פַּגְעִיאֵל
בֶּן־עָכְרָן: לְגָד אֶלְיָסָף בֶּן־דְּעוּאֵל: לְנַפְתָּלִי אֲחִירַע בֶּן־עֵינָן:
קְרוּאֵי אֵלֶּה קריאי הָעֵדָה נְשִׂיאֵי מַטּוֹת אֲבוֹתָם רָאשֵׁי אַלְפֵי
ישראל יִשְׂרָאֵל הֵם: *וַיִּקַּח מֹשֶׁה וְאַהֲרֹן אֵת הָאֲנָשִׁים הָאֵלֶּה אֲשֶׁר

THIRD ALIYA: 1:17–19
The entire populace gathered together arranged according to their genealogy for this purpose.

נִקְּבוּ בְּשֵׁמוֹת: וְאֵת כָּל־הָעֵדָה הִקְהִילוּ בְּאֶחָד לַחֹדֶשׁ
הַשֵּׁנִי וַיִּתְיַלְדוּ עַל־מִשְׁפְּחֹתָם לְבֵית אֲבֹתָם בְּמִסְפַּר שֵׁמוֹת
מִבֶּן עֶשְׂרִים שָׁנָה וָמַעְלָה לְגֻלְגְּלֹתָם: כַּאֲשֶׁר צִוָּה יְהוָה אֶת־
מֹשֶׁה וַיִּפְקְדֵם בְּמִדְבַּר סִינָי:

נשא NASO

במדבר ד:כא–לז

FIRST ALIYA: 4:21–24
Census of the priestly family of Gershon.

וַיְדַבֵּר יְהוָה אֶל־מֹשֶׁה לֵּאמֹר: נָשֹׂא אֶת־רֹאשׁ בְּנֵי גֵרְשׁוֹן גַּם־
הֵם לְבֵית אֲבֹתָם לְמִשְׁפְּחֹתָם: מִבֶּן שְׁלֹשִׁים שָׁנָה וָמַעְלָה
עַד בֶּן־חֲמִשִּׁים שָׁנָה תִּפְקֹד אוֹתָם כָּל־הַבָּא לִצְבֹא צָבָא
לַעֲבֹד עֲבֹדָה בְּאֹהֶל מוֹעֵד: זֹאת עֲבֹדַת מִשְׁפְּחֹת הַגֵּרְשֻׁנִּי

לוי

לַעֲבֹד וּלְמַשָּׂא: *וְנָשְׂאוּ אֶת־יְרִיעֹת הַמִּשְׁכָּן וְאֶת־אֹהֶל מוֹעֵד מִכְסֵהוּ וּמִכְסֵה הַתַּחַשׁ אֲשֶׁר־עָלָיו מִלְמָעְלָה וְאֶת־מָסַךְ פֶּתַח אֹהֶל מוֹעֵד: וְאֵת קַלְעֵי הֶחָצֵר וְאֶת־מָסַךְ ׀ פֶּתַח ׀ שַׁעַר הֶחָצֵר אֲשֶׁר עַל־הַמִּשְׁכָּן וְעַל־הַמִּזְבֵּחַ סָבִיב וְאֵת מֵיתְרֵיהֶם וְאֶת־כָּל־כְּלֵי עֲבֹדָתָם וְאֵת כָּל־אֲשֶׁר יֵעָשֶׂה לָהֶם וְעָבָדוּ: עַל־פִּי אַהֲרֹן וּבָנָיו תִּהְיֶה כָּל־עֲבֹדַת בְּנֵי הַגֵּרְשֻׁנִּי לְכָל־מַשָּׂאָם וּלְכֹל עֲבֹדָתָם וּפְקַדְתֶּם עֲלֵהֶם בְּמִשְׁמֶרֶת אֵת כָּל־מַשָּׂאָם: זֹאת עֲבֹדַת מִשְׁפְּחֹת בְּנֵי הַגֵּרְשֻׁנִּי בְּאֹהֶל מוֹעֵד וּמִשְׁמַרְתָּם בְּיַד אִיתָמָר בֶּן־אַהֲרֹן הַכֹּהֵן: *בְּנֵי מְרָרִי לְמִשְׁפְּחֹתָם לְבֵית־אֲבֹתָם

ישראל

תִּפְקֹד אֹתָם: מִבֶּן שְׁלֹשִׁים שָׁנָה וָמַעְלָה וְעַד בֶּן־חֲמִשִּׁים שָׁנָה תִּפְקְדֵם כָּל־הַבָּא לַצָּבָא לַעֲבֹד אֶת־עֲבֹדַת אֹהֶל מוֹעֵד: וְזֹאת מִשְׁמֶרֶת מַשָּׂאָם לְכָל־עֲבֹדָתָם בְּאֹהֶל מוֹעֵד קַרְשֵׁי הַמִּשְׁכָּן וּבְרִיחָיו וְעַמּוּדָיו וַאֲדָנָיו: וְעַמּוּדֵי הֶחָצֵר סָבִיב וְאַדְנֵיהֶם וִיתֵדֹתָם וּמֵיתְרֵיהֶם לְכָל־כְּלֵיהֶם וּלְכֹל עֲבֹדָתָם וּבְשֵׁמֹת תִּפְקְדוּ אֶת־כְּלֵי מִשְׁמֶרֶת מַשָּׂאָם: זֹאת עֲבֹדַת מִשְׁפְּחֹת בְּנֵי מְרָרִי לְכָל־עֲבֹדָתָם בְּאֹהֶל מוֹעֵד בְּיַד אִיתָמָר בֶּן־אַהֲרֹן הַכֹּהֵן:

SECOND ALIYA: 4:25–28
The responsibilities of the family of Gershon during the process of dismantling and transporting of the Tabernacle.

THIRD ALIYA: 4:29–37
The census and responsibilities of the family of Marari during the process of dismantling and transporting of the Tabernacle.

Some extend the ישראל *portion:*

וַיִּפְקֹד מֹשֶׁה וְאַהֲרֹן וּנְשִׂיאֵי הָעֵדָה אֶת־בְּנֵי הַקְּהָתִי לְמִשְׁפְּחֹתָם וּלְבֵית אֲבֹתָם: מִבֶּן שְׁלֹשִׁים שָׁנָה וָמַעְלָה וְעַד בֶּן־חֲמִשִּׁים שָׁנָה כָּל־הַבָּא לַצָּבָא לַעֲבֹדָה בְּאֹהֶל מוֹעֵד: וַיִּהְיוּ פְקֻדֵיהֶם לְמִשְׁפְּחֹתָם אַלְפַּיִם שְׁבַע מֵאוֹת וַחֲמִשִּׁים: אֵלֶּה פְקוּדֵי מִשְׁפְּחֹת הַקְּהָתִי כָּל־הָעֹבֵד בְּאֹהֶל מוֹעֵד אֲשֶׁר פָּקַד מֹשֶׁה וְאַהֲרֹן עַל־פִּי יהוה בְּיַד־מֹשֶׁה:

BEHA'ALOTEKHA בהעלותך

במדבר ח:א–יד

וַיְדַבֵּר יהוה אֶל־מֹשֶׁה לֵּאמֹר: דַּבֵּר אֶל־אַהֲרֹן וְאָמַרְתָּ אֵלָיו בְּהַעֲלֹתְךָ אֶת־הַנֵּרֹת אֶל־מוּל פְּנֵי הַמְּנוֹרָה יָאִירוּ שִׁבְעַת

FIRST ALIYA: 8:1–4
The Menora in the Tabernacle lit by Aharon.

הנרות: ויעש כן אהרן אל־מול פני המנורה העלה נרתיה
כאשר צוה יהוה את־משה: וזה מעשה המנרה מקשה
זהב עד־ירכה עד־פרחה מקשה הוא כמראה אשר הראה
יהוה את־משה כן עשה את־המנרה:
וידבר יהוה אל־משה לאמר: קח את־הלוים מתוך בני לוי

SECOND ALIYA: 8:5–9
The consecration of the Levites.

ישראל וטהרת אתם: וכה־תעשה להם לטהרם הזה
עליהם מי חטאת והעבירו תער על־כל־בשרם וכבסו
בגדיהם והטהרו: ולקחו פר בן־בקר ומנחתו סלת
בלולה בשמן ופר־שני בן־בקר תקח לחטאת: והקרבת
את־הלוים לפני אהל מועד והקהלת את־כל־עדת בני
ישראל: *והקרבת את־הלוים לפני יהוה וסמכו בני־ ישראל

THIRD ALIYA: 8:10–14
The offerings given as part of the service of consecrating the Levites.

ישראל את־ידיהם על־הלוים: והניף אהרן את־הלוים
תנופה לפני יהוה מאת בני ישראל והיו לעבד את־
עבדת יהוה: והלוים יסמכו את־ידיהם על ראש הפרים
ועשה את־האחד חטאת ואת־האחד עלה ליהוה לכפר
על־הלוים: והעמדת את־הלוים לפני אהרן ולפני בניו
והנפת אתם תנופה ליהוה: והבדלת את־הלוים מתוך בני
ישראל והיו לי הלוים:

שלח SHELAH

וידבר יהוה אל־משה לאמר: שלח־לך אנשים ויתרו במדבר יג:א–כ

FIRST ALIYA: 13:1–3
God commands Moshe to send spies to gather information on the Land of Israel.

את־ארץ כנען אשר־אני נתן לבני ישראל איש אחד
איש אחד למטה אבתיו תשלחו כל נשיא בהם: וישלח
אתם משה ממדבר פארן על־פי יהוה כלם אנשים ראשי
בני־ישראל המה: *ואלה שמותם למטה ראובן שמוע לוי

SECOND ALIYA: 13:4–16
The names of the spies, each a distinguished man of his tribe.

בן־זכור: למטה שמעון שפט בן־חורי: למטה יהודה כלב
בן־יפנה: למטה יששכר יגאל בן־יוסף: למטה אפרים
הושע בן־נון: למטה בנימן פלטי בן־רפוא: למטה זבולן
גדיאל בן־סודי: למטה יוסף למטה מנשה גדי בן־סוסי:

לְמַטֵּה דָן עַמִּיאֵל בֶּן־גְּמַלִּי: לְמַטֵּה אָשֵׁר סְתוּר בֶּן־מִיכָאֵל:
לְמַטֵּה נַפְתָּלִי נַחְבִּי בֶּן־וָפְסִי: לְמַטֵּה גָד גְּאוּאֵל בֶּן־מָכִי:
אֵלֶּה שְׁמוֹת הָאֲנָשִׁים אֲשֶׁר־שָׁלַח מֹשֶׁה לָתוּר אֶת־הָאָרֶץ
ישראל וַיִּקְרָא מֹשֶׁה לְהוֹשֵׁעַ בִּן־נוּן יְהוֹשֻׁעַ: *וַיִּשְׁלַח אֹתָם מֹשֶׁה
לָתוּר אֶת־אֶרֶץ כְּנָעַן וַיֹּאמֶר אֲלֵהֶם עֲלוּ זֶה בַּנֶּגֶב וַעֲלִיתֶם
אֶת־הָהָר: וּרְאִיתֶם אֶת־הָאָרֶץ מַה־הִוא וְאֶת־הָעָם
הַיֹּשֵׁב עָלֶיהָ הֶחָזָק הוּא הֲרָפֶה הַמְעַט הוּא אִם־רָב: וּמָה
הָאָרֶץ אֲשֶׁר־הוּא יֹשֵׁב בָּהּ הֲטוֹבָה הִוא אִם־רָעָה וּמָה
הֶעָרִים אֲשֶׁר־הוּא יוֹשֵׁב בָּהֵנָּה הַבְּמַחֲנִים אִם בְּמִבְצָרִים:
וּמָה הָאָרֶץ הַשְּׁמֵנָה הִוא אִם־רָזָה הֲיֵשׁ־בָּהּ עֵץ אִם־אַיִן
וְהִתְחַזַּקְתֶּם וּלְקַחְתֶּם מִפְּרִי הָאָרֶץ וְהַיָּמִים יְמֵי בִּכּוּרֵי
עֲנָבִים:

THIRD ALIYA: 13:17–20
Moshe delivers the mission to the spies.

KORAH קורח

במדבר טז:א–יג וַיִּקַּח קֹרַח בֶּן־יִצְהָר בֶּן־קְהָת בֶּן־לֵוִי וְדָתָן וַאֲבִירָם בְּנֵי
אֱלִיאָב וְאוֹן בֶּן־פֶּלֶת בְּנֵי רְאוּבֵן: וַיָּקֻמוּ לִפְנֵי מֹשֶׁה וַאֲנָשִׁים
מִבְּנֵי־יִשְׂרָאֵל חֲמִשִּׁים וּמָאתָיִם נְשִׂיאֵי עֵדָה קְרִאֵי מוֹעֵד
אַנְשֵׁי־שֵׁם: וַיִּקָּהֲלוּ עַל־מֹשֶׁה וְעַל־אַהֲרֹן וַיֹּאמְרוּ אֲלֵהֶם
רַב־לָכֶם כִּי כָל־הָעֵדָה כֻּלָּם קְדֹשִׁים וּבְתוֹכָם יהוה וּמַדּוּעַ
לוי תִּתְנַשְּׂאוּ עַל־קְהַל יהוה: *וַיִּשְׁמַע מֹשֶׁה וַיִּפֹּל עַל־פָּנָיו:
וַיְדַבֵּר אֶל־קֹרַח וְאֶל־כָּל־עֲדָתוֹ לֵאמֹר בֹּקֶר וְיֹדַע יהוה אֶת־
אֲשֶׁר־לוֹ וְאֶת־הַקָּדוֹשׁ וְהִקְרִיב אֵלָיו וְאֵת אֲשֶׁר יִבְחַר־בּוֹ
יַקְרִיב אֵלָיו: זֹאת עֲשׂוּ קְחוּ־לָכֶם מַחְתּוֹת קֹרַח וְכָל־עֲדָתוֹ:
וּתְנוּ־בָהֵן ׀ אֵשׁ וְשִׂימוּ עֲלֵיהֶן ׀ קְטֹרֶת לִפְנֵי יהוה מָחָר וְהָיָה
הָאִישׁ אֲשֶׁר־יִבְחַר יהוה הוּא הַקָּדוֹשׁ רַב־לָכֶם בְּנֵי לֵוִי:
ישראל *וַיֹּאמֶר מֹשֶׁה אֶל־קֹרַח שִׁמְעוּ־נָא בְּנֵי לֵוִי: הַמְעַט מִכֶּם
כִּי־הִבְדִּיל אֱלֹהֵי יִשְׂרָאֵל אֶתְכֶם מֵעֲדַת יִשְׂרָאֵל לְהַקְרִיב
אֶתְכֶם אֵלָיו לַעֲבֹד אֶת־עֲבֹדַת מִשְׁכַּן יהוה וְלַעֲמֹד לִפְנֵי
הָעֵדָה לְשָׁרְתָם: וַיַּקְרֵב אֹתְךָ וְאֶת־כָּל־אַחֶיךָ בְנֵי־לֵוִי אִתָּךְ

FIRST ALIYA: 16:1–3
Koraḥ, Datan, and Aviram, together with 250 men, rebel against Moshe and Aharon.

SECOND ALIYA: 16:4–7
Moshe sets up the stand-off, invoking God to prove who has the legitimate claim.

THIRD ALIYA: 16:8–13
Moshe tries to deescalate the situation, but to no avail.

וּבִקַּשְׁתֶּם גַּם־כְּהֻנָּה: לָכֵן אַתָּה וְכָל־עֲדָתְךָ הַנֹּעָדִים עַל־
יְהוָה וְאַהֲרֹן מַה־הוּא כִּי תלונו עָלָיו: וַיִּשְׁלַח מֹשֶׁה לִקְרֹא תַּלִּינוּ
לְדָתָן וְלַאֲבִירָם בְּנֵי אֱלִיאָב וַיֹּאמְרוּ לֹא נַעֲלֶה: הַמְעַט כִּי
הֶעֱלִיתָנוּ מֵאֶרֶץ זָבַת חָלָב וּדְבַשׁ לַהֲמִיתֵנוּ בַּמִּדְבָּר כִּי־
תִשְׂתָּרֵר עָלֵינוּ גַּם־הִשְׂתָּרֵר:

HUKAT חוקת

במדבר יט:א–יז

FIRST ALIYA: 19:1–6
The laws of the Red Heifer.

וַיְדַבֵּר יְהוָה אֶל־מֹשֶׁה וְאֶל־אַהֲרֹן לֵאמֹר: זֹאת חֻקַּת הַתּוֹרָה
אֲשֶׁר־צִוָּה יְהוָה לֵאמֹר דַּבֵּר | אֶל־בְּנֵי יִשְׂרָאֵל וְיִקְחוּ אֵלֶיךָ
פָרָה אֲדֻמָּה תְּמִימָה אֲשֶׁר אֵין־בָּהּ מוּם אֲשֶׁר לֹא־עָלָה
עָלֶיהָ עֹל: וּנְתַתֶּם אֹתָהּ אֶל־אֶלְעָזָר הַכֹּהֵן וְהוֹצִיא אֹתָהּ
אֶל־מִחוּץ לַמַּחֲנֶה וְשָׁחַט אֹתָהּ לְפָנָיו: וְלָקַח אֶלְעָזָר הַכֹּהֵן
מִדָּמָהּ בְּאֶצְבָּעוֹ וְהִזָּה אֶל־נֹכַח פְּנֵי אֹהֶל־מוֹעֵד מִדָּמָהּ שֶׁבַע
פְּעָמִים: וְשָׂרַף אֶת־הַפָּרָה לְעֵינָיו אֶת־עֹרָהּ וְאֶת־בְּשָׂרָהּ
וְאֶת־דָּמָהּ עַל־פִּרְשָׁהּ יִשְׂרֹף: וְלָקַח הַכֹּהֵן עֵץ אֶרֶז וְאֵזוֹב
לוי וּשְׁנִי תוֹלַעַת וְהִשְׁלִיךְ אֶל־תּוֹךְ שְׂרֵפַת הַפָּרָה: *וְכִבֶּס בְּגָדָיו

SECOND ALIYA: 19:7–10
The post ritual purification of the serving priest.

הַכֹּהֵן וְרָחַץ בְּשָׂרוֹ בַּמַּיִם וְאַחַר יָבֹא אֶל־הַמַּחֲנֶה וְטָמֵא
הַכֹּהֵן עַד־הָעָרֶב: וְהַשֹּׂרֵף אֹתָהּ יְכַבֵּס בְּגָדָיו בַּמַּיִם וְרָחַץ
בְּשָׂרוֹ בַּמָּיִם וְטָמֵא עַד־הָעָרֶב: וְאָסַף | אִישׁ טָהוֹר אֵת
אֵפֶר הַפָּרָה וְהִנִּיחַ מִחוּץ לַמַּחֲנֶה בְּמָקוֹם טָהוֹר וְהָיְתָה
לַעֲדַת בְּנֵי־יִשְׂרָאֵל לְמִשְׁמֶרֶת לְמֵי נִדָּה חַטָּאת הִוא:
ישראל *וְכִבֶּס הָאֹסֵף אֶת־אֵפֶר הַפָּרָה אֶת־בְּגָדָיו וְטָמֵא עַד־הָעָרֶב

THIRD ALIYA: 19:11–17
The laws of ritual contamination from a corpse.

וְהָיְתָה לִבְנֵי יִשְׂרָאֵל וְלַגֵּר הַגָּר בְּתוֹכָם לְחֻקַּת עוֹלָם: הַנֹּגֵעַ
בְּמֵת לְכָל־נֶפֶשׁ אָדָם וְטָמֵא שִׁבְעַת יָמִים: הוּא יִתְחַטָּא־
בוֹ בַּיּוֹם הַשְּׁלִישִׁי וּבַיּוֹם הַשְּׁבִיעִי יִטְהָר וְאִם־לֹא יִתְחַטָּא
בַּיּוֹם הַשְּׁלִישִׁי וּבַיּוֹם הַשְּׁבִיעִי לֹא יִטְהָר: כָּל־הַנֹּגֵעַ בְּמֵת
בְּנֶפֶשׁ הָאָדָם אֲשֶׁר־יָמוּת וְלֹא יִתְחַטָּא אֶת־מִשְׁכַּן יְהוָה
טִמֵּא וְנִכְרְתָה הַנֶּפֶשׁ הַהִוא מִיִּשְׂרָאֵל כִּי מֵי נִדָּה לֹא־זֹרַק
עָלָיו טָמֵא יִהְיֶה עוֹד טֻמְאָתוֹ בוֹ: זֹאת הַתּוֹרָה אָדָם כִּי־

יָמ֑וּת בְּאֹ֔הֶל כָּל־הַבָּ֤א אֶל־הָאֹ֙הֶל֙ וְכָל־אֲשֶׁ֣ר בָּאֹ֔הֶל יִטְמָ֖א
שִׁבְעַ֥ת יָמִֽים׃ וְכֹל֙ כְּלִ֣י פָת֔וּחַ אֲשֶׁ֛ר אֵין־צָמִ֥יד פָּתִ֖יל עָלָ֑יו
טָמֵ֖א הֽוּא׃ וְכֹ֨ל אֲשֶׁר־יִגַּ֜ע עַל־פְּנֵ֣י הַשָּׂדֶ֗ה בַּֽחֲלַל־חֶ֙רֶב֙
א֣וֹ בְמֵ֔ת אֽוֹ־בְעֶ֥צֶם אָדָ֖ם א֣וֹ בְקָ֑בֶר יִטְמָ֖א שִׁבְעַ֥ת יָמִֽים׃
וְלָֽקְחוּ֙ לַטָּמֵ֔א מֵעֲפַ֖ר שְׂרֵפַ֣ת הַֽחַטָּ֑את וְנָתַ֥ן עָלָ֛יו מַ֥יִם חַיִּ֖ים
אֶל־כֶּֽלִי׃

בלק BALAK

במדבר כב:ב–יב וַיַּ֥רְא בָּלָ֖ק בֶּן־צִפּ֑וֹר אֵ֛ת כָּל־אֲשֶׁר־עָשָׂ֥ה יִשְׂרָאֵ֖ל לָֽאֱמֹרִֽי׃
וַיָּ֨גָר מוֹאָ֜ב מִפְּנֵ֥י הָעָ֛ם מְאֹ֖ד כִּ֣י רַב־ה֑וּא וַיָּ֣קָץ מוֹאָ֔ב מִפְּנֵ֖י
בְּנֵ֥י יִשְׂרָאֵֽל׃ וַיֹּ֨אמֶר מוֹאָ֜ב אֶל־זִקְנֵ֣י מִדְיָ֗ן עַתָּ֞ה יְלַחֲכ֤וּ הַקָּהָל֙
אֶת־כָּל־סְבִיבֹתֵ֔ינוּ כִּלְחֹ֣ךְ הַשּׁ֔וֹר אֵ֖ת יֶ֣רֶק הַשָּׂדֶ֑ה וּבָלָ֧ק
לוי בֶּן־צִפּ֛וֹר מֶ֥לֶךְ לְמוֹאָ֖ב בָּעֵ֥ת הַהִֽוא׃ *וַיִּשְׁלַ֨ח מַלְאָכִ֜ים
אֶל־בִּלְעָ֣ם בֶּן־בְּעֹ֗ר פְּ֠ת֠וֹרָה אֲשֶׁ֧ר עַל־הַנָּהָ֛ר אֶ֥רֶץ בְּנֵֽי־
עַמּ֖וֹ לִקְרֹא־ל֑וֹ לֵאמֹ֗ר הִנֵּה֩ עַ֨ם יָצָ֤א מִמִּצְרַ֙יִם֙ הִנֵּ֤ה כִסָּה֙
אֶת־עֵ֣ין הָאָ֔רֶץ וְה֥וּא יֹשֵׁ֖ב מִמֻּלִֽי׃ וְעַתָּה֩ לְכָה־נָּ֨א אָֽרָה־לִּ֜י
אֶת־הָעָ֣ם הַזֶּ֗ה כִּֽי־עָצ֥וּם הוּא֙ מִמֶּ֔נִּי אוּלַ֤י אוּכַל֙ נַכֶּה־בּ֔וֹ
וַאֲגָרְשֶׁ֖נּוּ מִן־הָאָ֑רֶץ כִּ֣י יָדַ֗עְתִּי אֵ֤ת אֲשֶׁר־תְּבָרֵךְ֙ מְבֹרָ֔ךְ
וַאֲשֶׁ֥ר תָּאֹ֖ר יוּאָֽר׃ וַיֵּ֨לְכ֜וּ זִקְנֵ֤י מוֹאָב֙ וְזִקְנֵ֣י מִדְיָ֔ן וּקְסָמִ֖ים
ישראל בְּיָדָ֑ם וַיָּבֹ֙אוּ֙ אֶל־בִּלְעָ֔ם וַיְדַבְּר֥וּ אֵלָ֖יו דִּבְרֵ֥י בָלָֽק׃ *וַיֹּ֣אמֶר
אֲלֵיהֶ֗ם לִ֤ינוּ פֹה֙ הַלַּ֔יְלָה וַהֲשִׁבֹתִ֤י אֶתְכֶם֙ דָּבָ֔ר כַּאֲשֶׁ֛ר יְדַבֵּ֥ר
יְהוָ֖ה אֵלָ֑י וַיֵּשְׁב֥וּ שָׂרֵֽי־מוֹאָ֖ב עִם־בִּלְעָֽם׃ וַיָּבֹ֥א אֱלֹהִ֖ים אֶל־
בִּלְעָ֑ם וַיֹּ֕אמֶר מִ֛י הָאֲנָשִׁ֥ים הָאֵ֖לֶּה עִמָּֽךְ׃ וַיֹּ֥אמֶר בִּלְעָ֖ם
אֶל־הָאֱלֹהִ֑ים בָּלָ֧ק בֶּן־צִפֹּ֛ר מֶ֥לֶךְ מוֹאָ֖ב שָׁלַ֥ח אֵלָֽי׃ הִנֵּ֤ה
הָעָם֙ הַיֹּצֵ֣א מִמִּצְרַ֔יִם וַיְכַ֖ס אֶת־עֵ֣ין הָאָ֑רֶץ עַתָּ֗ה לְכָ֤ה
קָֽבָה־לִּי֙ אֹת֔וֹ אוּלַ֥י אוּכַ֛ל לְהִלָּ֥חֶם בּ֖וֹ וְגֵרַשְׁתִּֽיו׃ וַיֹּ֤אמֶר
אֱלֹהִים֙ אֶל־בִּלְעָ֔ם לֹ֥א תֵלֵ֖ךְ עִמָּהֶ֑ם לֹ֤א תָאֹר֙ אֶת־הָעָ֔ם כִּ֥י
בָר֖וּךְ הֽוּא׃

FIRST ALIYA: 22:2–4
Balak, the king of Moav, becomes intimidated and fearful of the powerful numerous Israelites.

SECOND ALIYA: 22:5–7
He sends messengers to Balaam the prophet to attempt to employ him in pronouncing a curse on the Jewish People.

THIRD ALIYA: 22:8–12
Balaam enquires of God as to whether he can perform this role, and is denied.

FIRST ALIYA: 25:10–12
Pineḥas receives from God eternal priesthood for his descendants, and a "Covenant of Peace" as a reward for his zealousness.

SECOND ALIYA: 25:13–18
God commands Moshe to initiate a military campaign against Midyan in response to their attempt to corrupt the Israelites.

THIRD ALIYA: 26:1–4
After the plague that punished those Israelites that were corrupted by Midyan, a census was carried out.

PINEḤAS פינחס

במדבר כה:י–כו:ד

וַיְדַבֵּר יְהוָה אֶל־מֹשֶׁה לֵּאמֹר: פִּינְחָס בֶּן־אֶלְעָזָר בֶּן־אַהֲרֹן הַכֹּהֵן הֵשִׁיב אֶת־חֲמָתִי מֵעַל בְּנֵי־יִשְׂרָאֵל בְּקַנְאוֹ אֶת־קִנְאָתִי בְּתוֹכָם וְלֹא־כִלִּיתִי אֶת־בְּנֵי־יִשְׂרָאֵל בְּקִנְאָתִי: לָכֵן אֱמֹר הִנְנִי נֹתֵן לוֹ אֶת־בְּרִיתִי שָׁלוֹם:

לוי

*וְהָיְתָה לּוֹ וּלְזַרְעוֹ אַחֲרָיו בְּרִית כְּהֻנַּת עוֹלָם תַּחַת אֲשֶׁר קִנֵּא לֵאלֹהָיו וַיְכַפֵּר עַל־בְּנֵי יִשְׂרָאֵל: וְשֵׁם אִישׁ יִשְׂרָאֵל הַמֻּכֶּה אֲשֶׁר הֻכָּה אֶת־הַמִּדְיָנִית זִמְרִי בֶּן־סָלוּא נְשִׂיא בֵית־אָב לַשִּׁמְעֹנִי: וְשֵׁם הָאִשָּׁה הַמֻּכָּה הַמִּדְיָנִית כָּזְבִּי בַת־צוּר רֹאשׁ אֻמּוֹת בֵּית־אָב בְּמִדְיָן הוּא:

ישראל

וַיְדַבֵּר יְהוָה אֶל־מֹשֶׁה לֵּאמֹר: צָרוֹר אֶת־הַמִּדְיָנִים וְהִכִּיתֶם אוֹתָם: כִּי־צֹרְרִים הֵם לָכֶם בְּנִכְלֵיהֶם אֲשֶׁר־נִכְּלוּ לָכֶם עַל־דְּבַר פְּעוֹר וְעַל־דְּבַר כָּזְבִּי בַת־נְשִׂיא מִדְיָן אֲחֹתָם הַמֻּכָּה בְיוֹם־הַמַּגֵּפָה עַל־דְּבַר פְּעוֹר: וַיְהִי אַחֲרֵי הַמַּגֵּפָה

וַיֹּאמֶר יְהוָה אֶל־מֹשֶׁה וְאֶל אֶלְעָזָר בֶּן־אַהֲרֹן הַכֹּהֵן לֵאמֹר: שְׂאוּ אֶת־רֹאשׁ ׀ כָּל־עֲדַת בְּנֵי־יִשְׂרָאֵל מִבֶּן עֶשְׂרִים שָׁנָה וָמַעְלָה לְבֵית אֲבֹתָם כָּל־יֹצֵא צָבָא בְּיִשְׂרָאֵל: וַיְדַבֵּר מֹשֶׁה וְאֶלְעָזָר הַכֹּהֵן אֹתָם בְּעַרְבֹת מוֹאָב עַל־יַרְדֵּן יְרֵחוֹ לֵאמֹר: מִבֶּן עֶשְׂרִים שָׁנָה וָמָעְלָה כַּאֲשֶׁר צִוָּה יְהוָה אֶת־מֹשֶׁה וּבְנֵי יִשְׂרָאֵל הַיֹּצְאִים מֵאֶרֶץ מִצְרָיִם:

FIRST ALIYA: 30:2–9
The laws of vows and oaths.

MATOT מטות

במדבר ל:ב–ט

וַיְדַבֵּר מֹשֶׁה אֶל־רָאשֵׁי הַמַּטּוֹת לִבְנֵי יִשְׂרָאֵל לֵאמֹר זֶה הַדָּבָר אֲשֶׁר צִוָּה יְהוָה: אִישׁ כִּי־יִדֹּר נֶדֶר לַיהוָה אוֹ־הִשָּׁבַע שְׁבֻעָה לֶאְסֹר אִסָּר עַל־נַפְשׁוֹ לֹא יַחֵל דְּבָרוֹ כְּכָל־הַיֹּצֵא מִפִּיו יַעֲשֶׂה: וְאִשָּׁה כִּי־תִדֹּר נֶדֶר לַיהוָה וְאָסְרָה אִסָּר בְּבֵית אָבִיהָ בִּנְעֻרֶיהָ: וְשָׁמַע אָבִיהָ אֶת־נִדְרָהּ וֶאֱסָרָהּ אֲשֶׁר אָסְרָה עַל־נַפְשָׁהּ וְהֶחֱרִישׁ לָהּ אָבִיהָ וְקָמוּ כָּל־נְדָרֶיהָ

וְכָל־אִסָּר אֲשֶׁר־אָסְרָה עַל־נַפְשָׁהּ יָקוּם: וְאִם־הֵנִיא אָבִיהָ
אֹתָהּ בְּיוֹם שָׁמְעוֹ כָּל־נְדָרֶיהָ וֶאֱסָרֶיהָ אֲשֶׁר־אָסְרָה עַל־
נַפְשָׁהּ לֹא יָקוּם וַיהוה יִסְלַח־לָהּ כִּי־הֵנִיא אָבִיהָ אֹתָהּ:
וְאִם־הָיוֹ תִהְיֶה לְאִישׁ וּנְדָרֶיהָ עָלֶיהָ אוֹ מִבְטָא שְׂפָתֶיהָ
אֲשֶׁר אָסְרָה עַל־נַפְשָׁהּ: וְשָׁמַע אִישָׁהּ בְּיוֹם שָׁמְעוֹ וְהֶחֱרִישׁ
לָהּ וְקָמוּ נְדָרֶיהָ וֶאֱסָרֶהָ אֲשֶׁר־אָסְרָה עַל־נַפְשָׁהּ יָקֻמוּ:
וְאִם בְּיוֹם שְׁמֹעַ אִישָׁהּ יָנִיא אוֹתָהּ וְהֵפֵר אֶת־נִדְרָהּ אֲשֶׁר
עָלֶיהָ וְאֵת מִבְטָא שְׂפָתֶיהָ אֲשֶׁר אָסְרָה עַל־נַפְשָׁהּ וַיהוה
לוי יִסְלַח־לָהּ: ★וְנֵדֶר אַלְמָנָה וּגְרוּשָׁה כֹּל אֲשֶׁר־אָסְרָה עַל־
נַפְשָׁהּ יָקוּם עָלֶיהָ: וְאִם־בֵּית אִישָׁהּ נָדָרָה אוֹ־אָסְרָה
אִסָּר עַל־נַפְשָׁהּ בִּשְׁבֻעָה: וְשָׁמַע אִישָׁהּ וְהֶחֱרִשׁ לָהּ לֹא
הֵנִיא אֹתָהּ וְקָמוּ כָּל־נְדָרֶיהָ וְכָל־אִסָּר אֲשֶׁר־אָסְרָה עַל־
נַפְשָׁהּ יָקוּם: וְאִם־הָפֵר יָפֵר אֹתָם | אִישָׁהּ בְּיוֹם שָׁמְעוֹ
כָּל־מוֹצָא שְׂפָתֶיהָ לִנְדָרֶיהָ וּלְאִסַּר נַפְשָׁהּ לֹא יָקוּם אִישָׁהּ
ישראל הֲפֵרָם וַיהוה יִסְלַח־לָהּ: ★כָּל־נֵדֶר וְכָל־שְׁבֻעַת אִסָּר לְעַנֹּת
נָפֶשׁ אִישָׁהּ יְקִימֶנּוּ וְאִישָׁהּ יְפֵרֶנּוּ: וְאִם־הַחֲרֵשׁ יַחֲרִישׁ
לָהּ אִישָׁהּ מִיּוֹם אֶל־יוֹם וְהֵקִים אֶת־כָּל־נְדָרֶיהָ אוֹ אֶת־
כָּל־אֱסָרֶיהָ אֲשֶׁר עָלֶיהָ הֵקִים אֹתָם כִּי־הֶחֱרִשׁ לָהּ בְּיוֹם
שָׁמְעוֹ: וְאִם־הָפֵר יָפֵר אֹתָם אַחֲרֵי שָׁמְעוֹ וְנָשָׂא אֶת־עֲוֹנָהּ:
אֵלֶּה הַחֻקִּים אֲשֶׁר צִוָּה יהוה אֶת־מֹשֶׁה בֵּין אִישׁ לְאִשְׁתּוֹ
בֵּין־אָב לְבִתּוֹ בִּנְעֻרֶיהָ בֵּית אָבִיהָ:

SECOND ALIYA: 30:10–13
The laws of vows made by a widow or divorcee.

THIRD ALIYA: 30:14–17
The laws of oaths and vows made by a wife.

MASEI מסעי

במדבר לג:א–נג
אֵלֶּה מַסְעֵי בְנֵי־יִשְׂרָאֵל אֲשֶׁר יָצְאוּ מֵאֶרֶץ מִצְרַיִם לְצִבְאֹתָם
בְּיַד־מֹשֶׁה וְאַהֲרֹן: וַיִּכְתֹּב מֹשֶׁה אֶת־מוֹצָאֵיהֶם לְמַסְעֵיהֶם
עַל־פִּי יהוה וְאֵלֶּה מַסְעֵיהֶם לְמוֹצָאֵיהֶם: וַיִּסְעוּ מֵרַעְמְסֵס
בַּחֹדֶשׁ הָרִאשׁוֹן בַּחֲמִשָּׁה עָשָׂר יוֹם לַחֹדֶשׁ הָרִאשׁוֹן
מִמָּחֳרַת הַפֶּסַח יָצְאוּ בְנֵי־יִשְׂרָאֵל בְּיָד רָמָה לְעֵינֵי כָּל־
לוי מִצְרָיִם: ★וּמִצְרַיִם מְקַבְּרִים אֵת אֲשֶׁר הִכָּה יהוה בָּהֶם כָּל־

FIRST ALIYA: 33:1–3
A summary of the journeys of the Israelites when they left Egypt.

SECOND ALIYA: 33:4–6
The journeys from Ramses to Eitam.

THIRD ALIYA: 33:7–10
The journeys from Eitam to the Reed Sea.

בְּכ֑וֹר וּבֵאלֹ֣הֵיהֶ֔ם עָשָׂ֥ה יְהוָ֖ה שְׁפָטִֽים׃ וַיִּסְע֥וּ בְנֵֽי־יִשְׂרָאֵ֖ל
מֵֽרַעְמְסֵ֑ס וַֽיַּחֲנ֖וּ בְּסֻכֹּֽת׃ וַיִּסְע֖וּ מִסֻּכֹּ֑ת וַיַּחֲנ֣וּ בְאֵתָ֔ם אֲשֶׁ֖ר
בִּקְצֵ֥ה הַמִּדְבָּֽר׃ *וַיִּסְעוּ֙ מֵאֵתָ֔ם וַיָּ֙שָׁב֙ עַל־פִּ֣י הַחִירֹ֔ת אֲשֶׁ֥ר ישראל
עַל־פְּנֵ֖י בַּ֣עַל צְפ֑וֹן וַֽיַּחֲנ֖וּ לִפְנֵ֥י מִגְדֹּֽל׃ וַיִּסְעוּ֙ מִפְּנֵ֣י הַחִירֹ֔ת
וַיַּעַבְר֥וּ בְתוֹךְ־הַיָּ֖ם הַמִּדְבָּ֑רָה וַיֵּ֨לְכ֜וּ דֶּ֣רֶךְ שְׁלֹ֤שֶׁת יָמִים֙
בְּמִדְבַּ֣ר אֵתָ֔ם וַֽיַּחֲנ֖וּ בְּמָרָֽה׃ וַיִּסְעוּ֙ מִמָּרָ֔ה וַיָּבֹ֖אוּ אֵילִ֑מָה
וּ֠בְאֵילִם שְׁתֵּ֨ים עֶשְׂרֵ֜ה עֵינֹ֥ת מַ֛יִם וְשִׁבְעִ֥ים תְּמָרִ֖ים וַיַּֽחֲנוּ־
שָֽׁם׃ וַיִּסְע֖וּ מֵאֵילִ֑ם וַיַּחֲנ֖וּ עַל־יַם־סֽוּף׃

Some extend the לוי *portion:*

וַיִּסְע֖וּ מִיַּם־ס֑וּף וַיַּחֲנ֖וּ בְּמִדְבַּר־סִֽין׃ וַיִּסְע֖וּ מִמִּדְבַּר־סִ֑ין וַֽיַּחֲנ֖וּ
בְּדָפְקָֽה׃ וַיִּסְע֖וּ מִדָּפְקָ֑ה וַֽיַּחֲנ֖וּ בְּאָלֽוּשׁ׃ וַיִּסְע֖וּ מֵֽאָל֑וּשׁ וַֽיַּחֲנוּ֙
בִּרְפִידִ֔ם וְלֹא־הָ֨יָה שָׁ֥ם מַ֛יִם לָעָ֖ם לִשְׁתּֽוֹת׃ וַיִּסְע֖וּ מֵרְפִידִ֑ם
וַֽיַּחֲנ֖וּ בְּמִדְבַּ֥ר סִינָֽי׃ וַיִּסְע֖וּ מִמִּדְבַּ֣ר סִינָ֑י וַֽיַּחֲנ֖וּ בְּקִבְרֹ֥ת
הַֽתַּאֲוָֽה׃ וַיִּסְע֖וּ מִקִּבְרֹ֣ת הַֽתַּאֲוָ֑ה וַֽיַּחֲנ֖וּ בַּחֲצֵרֹֽת׃ וַיִּסְע֖וּ
מֵחֲצֵרֹ֑ת וַֽיַּחֲנ֖וּ בְּרִתְמָֽה׃ וַיִּסְע֖וּ מֵרִתְמָ֑ה וַֽיַּחֲנ֖וּ בְּרִמֹּ֥ן פָּֽרֶץ׃
וַיִּסְע֖וּ מֵרִמֹּ֣ן פָּ֑רֶץ וַֽיַּחֲנ֖וּ בְּלִבְנָֽה׃ וַיִּסְע֖וּ מִלִּבְנָ֑ה וַֽיַּחֲנ֖וּ בְּרִסָּֽה׃
וַיִּסְע֖וּ מֵרִסָּ֑ה וַֽיַּחֲנ֖וּ בִּקְהֵלָֽתָה׃ וַיִּסְע֖וּ מִקְּהֵלָ֑תָה וַֽיַּחֲנ֖וּ בְּהַר־
שָֽׁפֶר׃ וַיִּסְע֖וּ מֵהַר־שָׁ֑פֶר וַֽיַּחֲנ֖וּ בַּחֲרָדָֽה׃ וַיִּסְע֖וּ מֵחֲרָדָ֑ה וַֽיַּחֲנ֖וּ
בְּמַקְהֵלֹֽת׃ וַיִּסְע֖וּ מִמַּקְהֵלֹ֑ת וַֽיַּחֲנ֖וּ בְּתָֽחַת׃ וַיִּסְע֖וּ מִתָּ֑חַת
וַֽיַּחֲנ֖וּ בְּתָֽרַח׃ וַיִּסְע֖וּ מִתָּ֑רַח וַֽיַּחֲנ֖וּ בְּמִתְקָֽה׃ וַיִּסְע֖וּ מִמִּתְקָ֑ה
וַֽיַּחֲנ֖וּ בְּחַשְׁמֹנָֽה׃ וַיִּסְע֖וּ מֵחַשְׁמֹנָ֑ה וַֽיַּחֲנ֖וּ בְּמֹסֵרֽוֹת׃ וַיִּסְע֖וּ
מִמֹּסֵר֑וֹת וַֽיַּחֲנ֖וּ בִּבְנֵ֥י יַעֲקָֽן׃ וַיִּסְע֖וּ מִבְּנֵ֣י יַעֲקָ֑ן וַֽיַּחֲנ֖וּ בְּחֹ֥ר
הַגִּדְגָּֽד׃ וַיִּסְע֖וּ מֵחֹ֣ר הַגִּדְגָּ֑ד וַֽיַּחֲנ֖וּ בְּיָטְבָֽתָה׃ וַיִּסְע֖וּ מִיָּטְבָ֑תָה
וַֽיַּחֲנ֖וּ בְּעַבְרֹנָֽה׃ וַיִּסְע֖וּ מֵעַבְרֹנָ֑ה וַֽיַּחֲנ֖וּ בְּעֶצְיֹ֥ן גָּֽבֶר׃ וַיִּסְע֖וּ
מֵעֶצְיֹ֣ן גָּ֑בֶר וַיַּחֲנ֥וּ בְמִדְבַּר־צִ֖ן הִ֥וא קָדֵֽשׁ׃ וַיִּסְע֖וּ מִקָּדֵ֑שׁ
וַֽיַּחֲנוּ֙ בְּהֹ֣ר הָהָ֔ר בִּקְצֵ֖ה אֶ֥רֶץ אֱדֽוֹם׃ וַיַּעַל֩ אַהֲרֹ֨ן הַכֹּהֵ֜ן
אֶל־הֹ֥ר הָהָ֛ר עַל־פִּ֥י יְהוָ֖ה וַיָּ֣מָת שָׁ֑ם בִּשְׁנַ֣ת הָֽאַרְבָּעִ֗ים
לְצֵ֤את בְּנֵֽי־יִשְׂרָאֵל֙ מֵאֶ֣רֶץ מִצְרַ֔יִם בַּחֹ֥דֶשׁ הַחֲמִישִׁ֖י בְּאֶחָ֥ד
לַחֹֽדֶשׁ׃ וְאַהֲרֹ֔ן בֶּן־שָׁלֹ֛שׁ וְעֶשְׂרִ֥ים וּמְאַ֖ת שָׁנָ֑ה בְּמֹת֖וֹ בְּהֹ֥ר

הָהָר: וַיִּשְׁמַע הַכְּנַעֲנִי מֶלֶךְ עֲרָד וְהוּא־יֹשֵׁב
בַּנֶּגֶב בְּאֶרֶץ כְּנָעַן בְּבֹא בְּנֵי יִשְׂרָאֵל: וַיִּסְעוּ מֵהֹר הָהָר
וַיַּחֲנוּ בְּצַלְמֹנָה: וַיִּסְעוּ מִצַּלְמֹנָה וַיַּחֲנוּ בְּפוּנֹן: וַיִּסְעוּ מִפּוּנֹן
וַיַּחֲנוּ בְּאֹבֹת: וַיִּסְעוּ מֵאֹבֹת וַיַּחֲנוּ בְּעִיֵּי הָעֲבָרִים בִּגְבוּל
מוֹאָב: וַיִּסְעוּ מֵעִיִּים וַיַּחֲנוּ בְּדִיבֹן גָּד: וַיִּסְעוּ מִדִּיבֹן גָּד וַיַּחֲנוּ
בְּעַלְמֹן דִּבְלָתָיְמָה: וַיִּסְעוּ מֵעַלְמֹן דִּבְלָתָיְמָה וַיַּחֲנוּ בְּהָרֵי
הָעֲבָרִים לִפְנֵי נְבוֹ: וַיִּסְעוּ מֵהָרֵי הָעֲבָרִים וַיַּחֲנוּ בְּעַרְבֹת
מוֹאָב עַל יַרְדֵּן יְרֵחוֹ: וַיַּחֲנוּ עַל־הַיַּרְדֵּן מִבֵּית הַיְשִׁמֹת
ישראל עַד אָבֵל הַשִּׁטִּים בְּעַרְבֹת מוֹאָב: *וַיְדַבֵּר
יְהוָה אֶל־מֹשֶׁה בְּעַרְבֹת מוֹאָב עַל־יַרְדֵּן יְרֵחוֹ לֵאמֹר: דַּבֵּר
אֶל־בְּנֵי יִשְׂרָאֵל וְאָמַרְתָּ אֲלֵהֶם כִּי אַתֶּם עֹבְרִים אֶת־הַיַּרְדֵּן
אֶל־אֶרֶץ כְּנָעַן: וְהוֹרַשְׁתֶּם אֶת־כָּל־יֹשְׁבֵי הָאָרֶץ מִפְּנֵיכֶם
וְאִבַּדְתֶּם אֵת כָּל־מַשְׂכִּיֹּתָם וְאֵת כָּל־צַלְמֵי מַסֵּכֹתָם תְּאַבֵּדוּ
וְאֵת כָּל־בָּמוֹתָם תַּשְׁמִידוּ: וְהוֹרַשְׁתֶּם אֶת־הָאָרֶץ וִישַׁבְתֶּם־
בָּהּ כִּי לָכֶם נָתַתִּי אֶת־הָאָרֶץ לָרֶשֶׁת אֹתָהּ:

DEVARIM דברים

דברים א:א-יא אֵלֶּה הַדְּבָרִים אֲשֶׁר דִּבֶּר מֹשֶׁה אֶל־כָּל־יִשְׂרָאֵל בְּעֵבֶר
הַיַּרְדֵּן בַּמִּדְבָּר בָּעֲרָבָה מוֹל סוּף בֵּין־פָּארָן וּבֵין־תֹּפֶל וְלָבָן
וַחֲצֵרֹת וְדִי זָהָב: אַחַד עָשָׂר יוֹם מֵחֹרֵב דֶּרֶךְ הַר־שֵׂעִיר
עַד קָדֵשׁ בַּרְנֵעַ: וַיְהִי בְּאַרְבָּעִים שָׁנָה בְּעַשְׁתֵּי־עָשָׂר חֹדֶשׁ
בְּאֶחָד לַחֹדֶשׁ דִּבֶּר מֹשֶׁה אֶל־בְּנֵי יִשְׂרָאֵל כְּכֹל אֲשֶׁר צִוָּה
לוי יְהוָה אֹתוֹ אֲלֵהֶם: *אַחֲרֵי הַכֹּתוֹ אֵת סִיחֹן מֶלֶךְ הָאֱמֹרִי
אֲשֶׁר יוֹשֵׁב בְּחֶשְׁבּוֹן וְאֵת עוֹג מֶלֶךְ הַבָּשָׁן אֲשֶׁר־יוֹשֵׁב
בְּעַשְׁתָּרֹת בְּאֶדְרֶעִי: בְּעֵבֶר הַיַּרְדֵּן בְּאֶרֶץ מוֹאָב הוֹאִיל
מֹשֶׁה בֵּאֵר אֶת־הַתּוֹרָה הַזֹּאת לֵאמֹר: יְהוָה אֱלֹהֵינוּ דִּבֶּר
אֵלֵינוּ בְּחֹרֵב לֵאמֹר רַב־לָכֶם שֶׁבֶת בָּהָר הַזֶּה: פְּנוּ ׀ וּסְעוּ
לָכֶם וּבֹאוּ הַר הָאֱמֹרִי וְאֶל־כָּל־שְׁכֵנָיו בָּעֲרָבָה בָהָר וּבַשְּׁפֵלָה
וּבַנֶּגֶב וּבְחוֹף הַיָּם אֶרֶץ הַכְּנַעֲנִי וְהַלְּבָנוֹן עַד־הַנָּהָר הַגָּדֹל

FIRST ALIYA: 1:1–3
Moshe begins his farewell speech to his people.

SECOND ALIYA: 1:4–7
Moshe reiterates the promise of the Land of Israel as the premise of the covenant between the Jewish People and God.

THIRD ALIYA: 1:8–11
Moshe describes the multitude that is the Jewish nation.

נְהַר־פְּרָת׃ *רְאֵה נָתַתִּי לִפְנֵיכֶם אֶת־הָאָרֶץ בֹּאוּ וּרְשׁוּ ישראל
אֶת־הָאָרֶץ אֲשֶׁר נִשְׁבַּע יְהוָה לַאֲבֹתֵיכֶם לְאַבְרָהָם לְיִצְחָק
וּלְיַעֲקֹב לָתֵת לָהֶם וּלְזַרְעָם אַחֲרֵיהֶם׃ וָאֹמַר אֲלֵכֶם בָּעֵת
הַהִוא לֵאמֹר לֹא־אוּכַל לְבַדִּי שְׂאֵת אֶתְכֶם׃ יְהוָה אֱלֹהֵיכֶם
הִרְבָּה אֶתְכֶם וְהִנְּכֶם הַיּוֹם כְּכוֹכְבֵי הַשָּׁמַיִם לָרֹב׃ יְהוָה
אֱלֹהֵי אֲבוֹתֵכֶם יֹסֵף עֲלֵיכֶם כָּכֶם אֶלֶף פְּעָמִים וִיבָרֵךְ אֶתְכֶם
כַּאֲשֶׁר דִּבֶּר לָכֶם׃

VA'ET-HANAN ואתחנן

FIRST ALIYA: 3:23–29
Moshe narrates God's refusal of his plea to enter the land and the succession of leadership to Yehoshua.

SECOND ALIYA: 4:1–4
Moshe motivates the people to commit to following God, citing the comeuppance received by those who strayed to worship Ba'al Peor.

דברים ג:כג–ד:ח

וָאֶתְחַנַּן אֶל־יְהוָה בָּעֵת הַהִוא לֵאמֹר׃ אֲדֹנָי יֱהוִה אַתָּה
הַחִלּוֹתָ לְהַרְאוֹת אֶת־עַבְדְּךָ אֶת־גָּדְלְךָ וְאֶת־יָדְךָ הַחֲזָקָה
אֲשֶׁר מִי־אֵל בַּשָּׁמַיִם וּבָאָרֶץ אֲשֶׁר־יַעֲשֶׂה כְמַעֲשֶׂיךָ
וְכִגְבוּרֹתֶךָ׃ אֶעְבְּרָה־נָּא וְאֶרְאֶה אֶת־הָאָרֶץ הַטּוֹבָה אֲשֶׁר
בְּעֵבֶר הַיַּרְדֵּן הָהָר הַטּוֹב הַזֶּה וְהַלְּבָנֹן׃ *וַיִּתְעַבֵּר יְהוָה בִּי לוי
לְמַעַנְכֶם וְלֹא שָׁמַע אֵלָי וַיֹּאמֶר יְהוָה אֵלַי רַב־לָךְ אַל־תּוֹסֶף
דַּבֵּר אֵלַי עוֹד בַּדָּבָר הַזֶּה׃ עֲלֵה ׀ רֹאשׁ הַפִּסְגָּה וְשָׂא עֵינֶיךָ
יָמָּה וְצָפֹנָה וְתֵימָנָה וּמִזְרָחָה וּרְאֵה בְעֵינֶיךָ כִּי־לֹא תַעֲבֹר
אֶת־הַיַּרְדֵּן הַזֶּה׃ וְצַו אֶת־יְהוֹשֻׁעַ וְחַזְּקֵהוּ וְאַמְּצֵהוּ כִּי־הוּא
יַעֲבֹר לִפְנֵי הָעָם הַזֶּה וְהוּא יַנְחִיל אוֹתָם אֶת־הָאָרֶץ אֲשֶׁר
תִּרְאֶה׃ וַנֵּשֶׁב בַּגָּיְא מוּל בֵּית פְּעוֹר׃

וְעַתָּה יִשְׂרָאֵל שְׁמַע אֶל־הַחֻקִּים וְאֶל־הַמִּשְׁפָּטִים אֲשֶׁר
אָנֹכִי מְלַמֵּד אֶתְכֶם לַעֲשׂוֹת לְמַעַן תִּחְיוּ וּבָאתֶם וִירִשְׁתֶּם
אֶת־הָאָרֶץ אֲשֶׁר יְהוָה אֱלֹהֵי אֲבֹתֵיכֶם נֹתֵן לָכֶם׃ לֹא
תֹסִפוּ עַל־הַדָּבָר אֲשֶׁר אָנֹכִי מְצַוֶּה אֶתְכֶם וְלֹא תִגְרְעוּ
מִמֶּנּוּ לִשְׁמֹר אֶת־מִצְוֹת יְהוָה אֱלֹהֵיכֶם אֲשֶׁר אָנֹכִי מְצַוֶּה
אֶתְכֶם׃ עֵינֵיכֶם הָרֹאֹת אֵת אֲשֶׁר־עָשָׂה יְהוָה בְּבַעַל פְּעוֹר
כִּי כָל־הָאִישׁ אֲשֶׁר הָלַךְ אַחֲרֵי בַעַל־פְּעוֹר הִשְׁמִידוֹ יְהוָה
אֱלֹהֶיךָ מִקִּרְבֶּךָ׃ וְאַתֶּם הַדְּבֵקִים בַּיהוָה אֱלֹהֵיכֶם חַיִּים
כֻּלְּכֶם הַיּוֹם׃ *רְאֵה ׀ לִמַּדְתִּי אֶתְכֶם חֻקִּים וּמִשְׁפָּטִים ישראל

THIRD ALIYA: 4:5–8
Moshe urges the people to maintain observance of God's commands.

כַּאֲשֶׁר צִוַּנִי יְהוָה אֱלֹהָי לַעֲשׂוֹת כֵּן בְּקֶרֶב הָאָרֶץ אֲשֶׁר
אַתֶּם בָּאִים שָׁמָּה לְרִשְׁתָּהּ: וּשְׁמַרְתֶּם וַעֲשִׂיתֶם כִּי הִוא
חָכְמַתְכֶם וּבִינַתְכֶם לְעֵינֵי הָעַמִּים אֲשֶׁר יִשְׁמְעוּן אֵת כָּל־
הַחֻקִּים הָאֵלֶּה וְאָמְרוּ רַק עַם־חָכָם וְנָבוֹן הַגּוֹי הַגָּדוֹל
הַזֶּה: כִּי מִי־גוֹי גָּדוֹל אֲשֶׁר־לוֹ אֱלֹהִים קְרֹבִים אֵלָיו כַּיהוָה
אֱלֹהֵינוּ בְּכָל־קָרְאֵנוּ אֵלָיו: וּמִי גּוֹי גָּדוֹל אֲשֶׁר־לוֹ חֻקִּים
וּמִשְׁפָּטִים צַדִּיקִם כְּכֹל הַתּוֹרָה הַזֹּאת אֲשֶׁר אָנֹכִי נֹתֵן
לִפְנֵיכֶם הַיּוֹם:

עקב EKEV

דברים ז:יב–ח:י

FIRST ALIYA: 7:12–21
The promised rewards for the observance of the covenant with God.

וְהָיָה ׀ עֵקֶב תִּשְׁמְעוּן אֵת הַמִּשְׁפָּטִים הָאֵלֶּה וּשְׁמַרְתֶּם
וַעֲשִׂיתֶם אֹתָם וְשָׁמַר יְהוָה אֱלֹהֶיךָ לְךָ אֶת־הַבְּרִית וְאֶת־
הַחֶסֶד אֲשֶׁר נִשְׁבַּע לַאֲבֹתֶיךָ: וַאֲהֵבְךָ וּבֵרַכְךָ וְהִרְבֶּךָ וּבֵרַךְ
פְּרִי־בִטְנְךָ וּפְרִי־אַדְמָתֶךָ דְּגָנְךָ וְתִירֹשְׁךָ וְיִצְהָרֶךָ שְׁגַר־
אֲלָפֶיךָ וְעַשְׁתְּרֹת צֹאנֶךָ עַל הָאֲדָמָה אֲשֶׁר־נִשְׁבַּע לַאֲבֹתֶיךָ
לָתֶת לָךְ: בָּרוּךְ תִּהְיֶה מִכָּל־הָעַמִּים לֹא־יִהְיֶה בְךָ עָקָר
וַעֲקָרָה וּבִבְהֶמְתֶּךָ: וְהֵסִיר יְהוָה מִמְּךָ כָּל־חֹלִי וְכָל־מַדְוֵי
מִצְרַיִם הָרָעִים אֲשֶׁר יָדַעְתָּ לֹא יְשִׂימָם בָּךְ וּנְתָנָם בְּכָל־
שֹׂנְאֶיךָ: וְאָכַלְתָּ אֶת־כָּל־הָעַמִּים אֲשֶׁר יְהוָה אֱלֹהֶיךָ נֹתֵן
לָךְ לֹא־תָחוֹס עֵינְךָ עֲלֵיהֶם וְלֹא תַעֲבֹד אֶת־אֱלֹהֵיהֶם כִּי־
מוֹקֵשׁ הוּא לָךְ: כִּי תֹאמַר בִּלְבָבְךָ רַבִּים הַגּוֹיִם
הָאֵלֶּה מִמֶּנִּי אֵיכָה אוּכַל לְהוֹרִישָׁם: לֹא תִירָא מֵהֶם זָכֹר
תִּזְכֹּר אֵת אֲשֶׁר־עָשָׂה יְהוָה אֱלֹהֶיךָ לְפַרְעֹה וּלְכָל־מִצְרָיִם:
הַמַּסֹּת הַגְּדֹלֹת אֲשֶׁר־רָאוּ עֵינֶיךָ וְהָאֹתֹת וְהַמֹּפְתִים וְהַיָּד
הַחֲזָקָה וְהַזְּרֹעַ הַנְּטוּיָה אֲשֶׁר הוֹצִאֲךָ יְהוָה אֱלֹהֶיךָ כֵּן־
יַעֲשֶׂה יְהוָה אֱלֹהֶיךָ לְכָל־הָעַמִּים אֲשֶׁר־אַתָּה יָרֵא
מִפְּנֵיהֶם: וְגַם אֶת־הַצִּרְעָה יְשַׁלַּח יְהוָה אֱלֹהֶיךָ בָּם עַד־
אֲבֹד הַנִּשְׁאָרִים וְהַנִּסְתָּרִים מִפָּנֶיךָ: לֹא תַעֲרֹץ מִפְּנֵיהֶם

SECOND ALIYA: 7:22–8:3
The promise of enemies delivered, and a historical recap of the journey from Egypt.

כִּי־יְהוָה אֱלֹהֶיךָ בְּקִרְבֶּךָ אֵל גָּדוֹל וְנוֹרָא: *וְנָשַׁל יְהוָה לוי
אֱלֹהֶיךָ אֶת־הַגּוֹיִם הָאֵל מִפָּנֶיךָ מְעַט מְעָט לֹא תוּכַל כַּלֹּתָם
מַהֵר פֶּן־תִּרְבֶּה עָלֶיךָ חַיַּת הַשָּׂדֶה: וּנְתָנָם יְהוָה אֱלֹהֶיךָ
לְפָנֶיךָ וְהָמָם מְהוּמָה גְדֹלָה עַד הִשָּׁמְדָם: וְנָתַן מַלְכֵיהֶם
בְּיָדֶךָ וְהַאֲבַדְתָּ אֶת־שְׁמָם מִתַּחַת הַשָּׁמָיִם לֹא־יִתְיַצֵּב אִישׁ
בְּפָנֶיךָ עַד הִשְׁמִדְךָ אֹתָם: פְּסִילֵי אֱלֹהֵיהֶם תִּשְׂרְפוּן בָּאֵשׁ
לֹא־תַחְמֹד כֶּסֶף וְזָהָב עֲלֵיהֶם וְלָקַחְתָּ לָךְ פֶּן תִּוָּקֵשׁ בּוֹ כִּי
תוֹעֲבַת יְהוָה אֱלֹהֶיךָ הוּא: וְלֹא־תָבִיא תוֹעֵבָה אֶל־בֵּיתֶךָ
וְהָיִיתָ חֵרֶם כָּמֹהוּ שַׁקֵּץ | תְּשַׁקְּצֶנּוּ וְתַעֵב | תְּתַעֲבֶנּוּ כִּי־חֵרֶם
הוּא:

כָּל־הַמִּצְוָה אֲשֶׁר אָנֹכִי מְצַוְּךָ הַיּוֹם תִּשְׁמְרוּן לַעֲשׂוֹת לְמַעַן
תִּחְיוּן וּרְבִיתֶם וּבָאתֶם וִירִשְׁתֶּם אֶת־הָאָרֶץ אֲשֶׁר־נִשְׁבַּע
יְהוָה לַאֲבֹתֵיכֶם: וְזָכַרְתָּ אֶת־כָּל־הַדֶּרֶךְ אֲשֶׁר הוֹלִיכְךָ
יְהוָה אֱלֹהֶיךָ זֶה אַרְבָּעִים שָׁנָה בַּמִּדְבָּר לְמַעַן עַנֹּתְךָ
לְנַסֹּתְךָ לָדַעַת אֶת־אֲשֶׁר בִּלְבָבְךָ הֲתִשְׁמֹר מִצְוֺתָו אִם־
לֹא: וַיְעַנְּךָ וַיַּרְעִבֶךָ וַיַּאֲכִלְךָ אֶת־הַמָּן אֲשֶׁר לֹא־יָדַעְתָּ וְלֹא
יָדְעוּן אֲבֹתֶיךָ לְמַעַן הוֹדִיעֲךָ כִּי לֹא עַל־הַלֶּחֶם לְבַדּוֹ יִחְיֶה
הָאָדָם כִּי עַל־כָּל־מוֹצָא פִי־יְהוָה יִחְיֶה הָאָדָם: *שִׂמְלָתְךָ ישראל
לֹא בָלְתָה מֵעָלֶיךָ וְרַגְלְךָ לֹא בָצֵקָה זֶה אַרְבָּעִים שָׁנָה:
וְיָדַעְתָּ עִם־לְבָבֶךָ כִּי כַּאֲשֶׁר יְיַסֵּר אִישׁ אֶת־בְּנוֹ יְהוָה אֱלֹהֶיךָ
מְיַסְּרֶךָּ: וְשָׁמַרְתָּ אֶת־מִצְוֺת יְהוָה אֱלֹהֶיךָ לָלֶכֶת בִּדְרָכָיו
וּלְיִרְאָה אֹתוֹ: כִּי יְהוָה אֱלֹהֶיךָ מְבִיאֲךָ אֶל־אֶרֶץ טוֹבָה
אֶרֶץ נַחֲלֵי מָיִם עֲיָנֹת וּתְהֹמֹת יֹצְאִים בַּבִּקְעָה וּבָהָר: אֶרֶץ
חִטָּה וּשְׂעֹרָה וְגֶפֶן וּתְאֵנָה וְרִמּוֹן אֶרֶץ־זֵית שֶׁמֶן וּדְבָשׁ:
אֶרֶץ אֲשֶׁר לֹא בְמִסְכֵּנֻת תֹּאכַל־בָּהּ לֶחֶם לֹא־תֶחְסַר כֹּל
בָּהּ אֶרֶץ אֲשֶׁר אֲבָנֶיהָ בַרְזֶל וּמֵהֲרָרֶיהָ תַּחְצֹב נְחֹשֶׁת:
וְאָכַלְתָּ וְשָׂבָעְתָּ וּבֵרַכְתָּ אֶת־יְהוָה אֱלֹהֶיךָ עַל־הָאָרֶץ הַטֹּבָה
אֲשֶׁר נָתַן־לָךְ:

THIRD ALIYA: 8:4–10
The promise of inheriting a wonderful land.

RE'EH
ראה

רְאֵה אָנֹכִי נֹתֵן לִפְנֵיכֶם הַיּוֹם בְּרָכָה וּקְלָלָה: אֶת־ דברים יא:כו–יב:י
הַבְּרָכָה אֲשֶׁר תִּשְׁמְעוּ אֶל־מִצְוֹת יְהוָה אֱלֹהֵיכֶם אֲשֶׁר
אָנֹכִי מְצַוֶּה אֶתְכֶם הַיּוֹם: וְהַקְּלָלָה אִם־לֹא תִשְׁמְעוּ
אֶל־מִצְוֹת יְהוָה אֱלֹהֵיכֶם וְסַרְתֶּם מִן־הַדֶּרֶךְ אֲשֶׁר אָנֹכִי
מְצַוֶּה אֶתְכֶם הַיּוֹם לָלֶכֶת אַחֲרֵי אֱלֹהִים אֲחֵרִים אֲשֶׁר
לֹא־יְדַעְתֶּם: וְהָיָה כִּי יְבִיאֲךָ יְהוָה אֱלֹהֶיךָ אֶל־
הָאָרֶץ אֲשֶׁר־אַתָּה בָא־שָׁמָּה לְרִשְׁתָּהּ וְנָתַתָּה אֶת־הַבְּרָכָה
עַל־הַר גְּרִזִים וְאֶת־הַקְּלָלָה עַל־הַר עֵיבָל: הֲלֹא־הֵמָּה
בְּעֵבֶר הַיַּרְדֵּן אַחֲרֵי דֶּרֶךְ מְבוֹא הַשֶּׁמֶשׁ בְּאֶרֶץ הַכְּנַעֲנִי
הַיֹּשֵׁב בָּעֲרָבָה מוּל הַגִּלְגָּל אֵצֶל אֵלוֹנֵי מֹרֶה: כִּי אַתֶּם
עֹבְרִים אֶת־הַיַּרְדֵּן לָבֹא לָרֶשֶׁת אֶת־הָאָרֶץ אֲשֶׁר־יְהוָה
אֱלֹהֵיכֶם נֹתֵן לָכֶם וִירִשְׁתֶּם אֹתָהּ וִישַׁבְתֶּם־בָּהּ: *וּשְׁמַרְתֶּם לוי
לַעֲשׂוֹת אֵת כָּל־הַחֻקִּים וְאֶת־הַמִּשְׁפָּטִים אֲשֶׁר אָנֹכִי נֹתֵן
לִפְנֵיכֶם הַיּוֹם: אֵלֶּה הַחֻקִּים וְהַמִּשְׁפָּטִים אֲשֶׁר תִּשְׁמְרוּן
לַעֲשׂוֹת בָּאָרֶץ אֲשֶׁר נָתַן יְהוָה אֱלֹהֵי אֲבֹתֶיךָ לְךָ לְרִשְׁתָּהּ
כָּל־הַיָּמִים אֲשֶׁר־אַתֶּם חַיִּים עַל־הָאֲדָמָה: אַבֵּד תְּאַבְּדוּן
אֶת־כָּל־הַמְּקֹמוֹת אֲשֶׁר עָבְדוּ־שָׁם הַגּוֹיִם אֲשֶׁר אַתֶּם
יֹרְשִׁים אֹתָם אֶת־אֱלֹהֵיהֶם עַל־הֶהָרִים הָרָמִים וְעַל־
הַגְּבָעוֹת וְתַחַת כָּל־עֵץ רַעֲנָן: וְנִתַּצְתֶּם אֶת־מִזְבְּחֹתָם
וְשִׁבַּרְתֶּם אֶת־מַצֵּבֹתָם וַאֲשֵׁרֵיהֶם תִּשְׂרְפוּן בָּאֵשׁ וּפְסִילֵי
אֱלֹהֵיהֶם תְּגַדֵּעוּן וְאִבַּדְתֶּם אֶת־שְׁמָם מִן־הַמָּקוֹם הַהוּא:
לֹא־תַעֲשׂוּן כֵּן לַיהוָה אֱלֹהֵיכֶם: כִּי אִם־אֶל־הַמָּקוֹם אֲשֶׁר־
יִבְחַר יְהוָה אֱלֹהֵיכֶם מִכָּל־שִׁבְטֵיכֶם לָשׂוּם אֶת־שְׁמוֹ שָׁם
לְשִׁכְנוֹ תִדְרְשׁוּ וּבָאתָ שָׁמָּה: *וַהֲבֵאתֶם שָׁמָּה עֹלֹתֵיכֶם ישראל
וְזִבְחֵיכֶם וְאֵת מַעְשְׂרֹתֵיכֶם וְאֵת תְּרוּמַת יֶדְכֶם וְנִדְרֵיכֶם
וְנִדְבֹתֵיכֶם וּבְכֹרֹת בְּקַרְכֶם וְצֹאנְכֶם: וַאֲכַלְתֶּם־שָׁם לִפְנֵי
יְהוָה אֱלֹהֵיכֶם וּשְׂמַחְתֶּם בְּכֹל מִשְׁלַח יֶדְכֶם אַתֶּם וּבָתֵּיכֶם
אֲשֶׁר בֵּרַכְךָ יְהוָה אֱלֹהֶיךָ: לֹא תַעֲשׂוּן כְּכֹל אֲשֶׁר אֲנַחְנוּ

FIRST ALIYA: 11:26–31
The ceremony of the blessings and the curses on Mount Gerizim and Mount Eval.

SECOND ALIYA: vv. 11:32–12:5
The command to rid the land of idolatrous altars.

THIRD ALIYA: 12:6–10
Offerings to be brought only at the location designated by God.

עֹשִׂים פֹּה הַיּוֹם אִישׁ כָּל־הַיָּשָׁר בְּעֵינָיו: כִּי לֹא־בָאתֶם
עַד־עָתָּה אֶל־הַמְּנוּחָה וְאֶל־הַנַּחֲלָה אֲשֶׁר־יְהוָה אֱלֹהֶיךָ
נֹתֵן לָךְ: וַעֲבַרְתֶּם אֶת־הַיַּרְדֵּן וִישַׁבְתֶּם בָּאָרֶץ אֲשֶׁר־יְהוָה
אֱלֹהֵיכֶם מַנְחִיל אֶתְכֶם וְהֵנִיחַ לָכֶם מִכָּל־אֹיְבֵיכֶם מִסָּבִיב
וִישַׁבְתֶּם־בֶּטַח:

SHOFETIM — שופטים

דברים טז:יח–יז:יג

FIRST ALIYA: 16:18–20
The establishment of the justice system.

שֹׁפְטִים וְשֹׁטְרִים תִּתֶּן־לְךָ בְּכָל־שְׁעָרֶיךָ אֲשֶׁר יְהוָה אֱלֹהֶיךָ
נֹתֵן לְךָ לִשְׁבָטֶיךָ וְשָׁפְטוּ אֶת־הָעָם מִשְׁפַּט־צֶדֶק: לֹא־
תַטֶּה מִשְׁפָּט לֹא תַכִּיר פָּנִים וְלֹא־תִקַּח שֹׁחַד כִּי הַשֹּׁחַד
יְעַוֵּר עֵינֵי חֲכָמִים וִיסַלֵּף דִּבְרֵי צַדִּיקִם: צֶדֶק צֶדֶק תִּרְדֹּף
לְמַעַן תִּחְיֶה וְיָרַשְׁתָּ אֶת־הָאָרֶץ אֲשֶׁר־יְהוָה אֱלֹהֶיךָ נֹתֵן
לָךְ:

SECOND ALIYA: 16:21–17:10
The laws of blemished sacrifices, and the punishment for idolatry.

לוי *לֹא־תִטַּע לְךָ אֲשֵׁרָה כָּל־עֵץ אֵצֶל מִזְבַּח
יְהוָה אֱלֹהֶיךָ אֲשֶׁר תַּעֲשֶׂה־לָּךְ: וְלֹא־תָקִים לְךָ מַצֵּבָה אֲשֶׁר
שָׂנֵא יְהוָה אֱלֹהֶיךָ: לֹא־תִזְבַּח לַיהוָה אֱלֹהֶיךָ
שׁוֹר וָשֶׂה אֲשֶׁר יִהְיֶה בוֹ מוּם כֹּל דָּבָר רָע כִּי תוֹעֲבַת יְהוָה
אֱלֹהֶיךָ הוּא: כִּי־יִמָּצֵא בְקִרְבְּךָ בְּאַחַד שְׁעָרֶיךָ
אֲשֶׁר־יְהוָה אֱלֹהֶיךָ נֹתֵן לָךְ אִישׁ אוֹ־אִשָּׁה אֲשֶׁר יַעֲשֶׂה
אֶת־הָרַע בְּעֵינֵי יְהוָה־אֱלֹהֶיךָ לַעֲבֹר בְּרִיתוֹ: וַיֵּלֶךְ וַיַּעֲבֹד
אֱלֹהִים אֲחֵרִים וַיִּשְׁתַּחוּ לָהֶם וְלַשֶּׁמֶשׁ | אוֹ לַיָּרֵחַ אוֹ לְכָל־
צְבָא הַשָּׁמַיִם אֲשֶׁר לֹא־צִוִּיתִי: וְהֻגַּד־לְךָ וְשָׁמָעְתָּ וְדָרַשְׁתָּ
הֵיטֵב וְהִנֵּה אֱמֶת נָכוֹן הַדָּבָר נֶעֶשְׂתָה הַתּוֹעֵבָה הַזֹּאת
בְּיִשְׂרָאֵל: וְהוֹצֵאתָ אֶת־הָאִישׁ הַהוּא אוֹ אֶת־הָאִשָּׁה הַהִוא
אֲשֶׁר עָשׂוּ אֶת־הַדָּבָר הָרָע הַזֶּה אֶל־שְׁעָרֶיךָ אֶת־הָאִישׁ אוֹ
אֶת־הָאִשָּׁה וּסְקַלְתָּם בָּאֲבָנִים וָמֵתוּ: עַל־פִּי | שְׁנַיִם עֵדִים
אוֹ שְׁלֹשָׁה עֵדִים יוּמַת הַמֵּת לֹא יוּמַת עַל־פִּי עֵד אֶחָד: יַד
הָעֵדִים תִּהְיֶה־בּוֹ בָרִאשֹׁנָה לַהֲמִיתוֹ וְיַד כָּל־הָעָם בָּאַחֲרֹנָה
וּבִעַרְתָּ הָרָע מִקִּרְבֶּךָ:

כִּי יִפָּלֵא מִמְּךָ דָבָר לַמִּשְׁפָּט בֵּין־דָּם ׀ לְדָם בֵּין־דִּין לְדִין וּבֵין
נֶגַע לָנֶגַע דִּבְרֵי רִיבֹת בִּשְׁעָרֶיךָ וְקַמְתָּ וְעָלִיתָ אֶל־הַמָּקוֹם
אֲשֶׁר יִבְחַר יְהוָה אֱלֹהֶיךָ בּוֹ: וּבָאתָ אֶל־הַכֹּהֲנִים הַלְוִיִּם
וְאֶל־הַשֹּׁפֵט אֲשֶׁר יִהְיֶה בַּיָּמִים הָהֵם וְדָרַשְׁתָּ וְהִגִּידוּ לְךָ
אֵת דְּבַר הַמִּשְׁפָּט: וְעָשִׂיתָ עַל־פִּי הַדָּבָר אֲשֶׁר יַגִּידוּ לְךָ
מִן־הַמָּקוֹם הַהוּא אֲשֶׁר יִבְחַר יְהוָה וְשָׁמַרְתָּ לַעֲשׂוֹת כְּכֹל
אֲשֶׁר יוֹרוּךָ: *עַל־פִּי הַתּוֹרָה אֲשֶׁר יוֹרוּךָ וְעַל־הַמִּשְׁפָּט ישראל
אֲשֶׁר־יֹאמְרוּ לְךָ תַּעֲשֶׂה לֹא תָסוּר מִן־הַדָּבָר אֲשֶׁר־יַגִּידוּ
לְךָ יָמִין וּשְׂמֹאל: וְהָאִישׁ אֲשֶׁר־יַעֲשֶׂה בְזָדוֹן לְבִלְתִּי שְׁמֹעַ
אֶל־הַכֹּהֵן הָעֹמֵד לְשָׁרֶת שָׁם אֶת־יְהוָה אֱלֹהֶיךָ אוֹ אֶל־
הַשֹּׁפֵט וּמֵת הָאִישׁ הַהוּא וּבִעַרְתָּ הָרָע מִיִּשְׂרָאֵל: וְכָל־הָעָם
יִשְׁמְעוּ וְיִרָאוּ וְלֹא יְזִידוּן עוֹד:

THIRD ALIYA: 17:11–13
The laws of the rebellious elder.

KI TETZEH כי תצא

דברים כא:י–כא

כִּי־תֵצֵא לַמִּלְחָמָה עַל־אֹיְבֶיךָ וּנְתָנוֹ יְהוָה אֱלֹהֶיךָ בְּיָדֶךָ
וְשָׁבִיתָ שִׁבְיוֹ: וְרָאִיתָ בַּשִּׁבְיָה אֵשֶׁת יְפַת־תֹּאַר וְחָשַׁקְתָּ
בָהּ וְלָקַחְתָּ לְךָ לְאִשָּׁה: וַהֲבֵאתָהּ אֶל־תּוֹךְ בֵּיתֶךָ וְגִלְּחָה
אֶת־רֹאשָׁהּ וְעָשְׂתָה אֶת־צִפָּרְנֶיהָ: וְהֵסִירָה אֶת־שִׂמְלַת
שִׁבְיָהּ מֵעָלֶיהָ וְיָשְׁבָה בְּבֵיתֶךָ וּבָכְתָה אֶת־אָבִיהָ וְאֶת־
אִמָּהּ יֶרַח יָמִים וְאַחַר כֵּן תָּבוֹא אֵלֶיהָ וּבְעַלְתָּהּ וְהָיְתָה
לְךָ לְאִשָּׁה: וְהָיָה אִם־לֹא חָפַצְתָּ בָּהּ וְשִׁלַּחְתָּהּ לְנַפְשָׁהּ
וּמָכֹר לֹא־תִמְכְּרֶנָּה בַּכָּסֶף לֹא־תִתְעַמֵּר בָּהּ תַּחַת אֲשֶׁר
עִנִּיתָהּ: *כִּי־תִהְיֶיןָ לְאִישׁ שְׁתֵּי נָשִׁים הָאַחַת לוי
אֲהוּבָה וְהָאַחַת שְׂנוּאָה וְיָלְדוּ־לוֹ בָנִים הָאֲהוּבָה וְהַשְּׂנוּאָה
וְהָיָה הַבֵּן הַבְּכֹר לַשְּׂנִיאָה: וְהָיָה בְּיוֹם הַנְחִילוֹ אֶת־בָּנָיו אֵת
אֲשֶׁר־יִהְיֶה לוֹ לֹא יוּכַל לְבַכֵּר אֶת־בֶּן־הָאֲהוּבָה עַל־פְּנֵי בֶן־
הַשְּׂנוּאָה הַבְּכֹר: כִּי אֶת־הַבְּכֹר בֶּן־הַשְּׂנוּאָה יַכִּיר לָתֶת לוֹ פִּי
שְׁנַיִם בְּכֹל אֲשֶׁר־יִמָּצֵא לוֹ כִּי־הוּא רֵאשִׁית אֹנוֹ לוֹ מִשְׁפַּט
הַבְּכֹרָה: *כִּי־יִהְיֶה לְאִישׁ בֵּן סוֹרֵר וּמוֹרֶה אֵינֶנּוּ ישראל

FIRST ALIYA: 21:10–14
The laws of the captive woman in times of war.

SECOND ALIYA: 21:15–17
The rights of the firstborn son.

THIRD ALIYA: 21:18–21
The laws of the rebellious son.

שֹׁמֵעַ בְּקוֹל אָבִיו וּבְקוֹל אִמּוֹ וְיִסְּרוּ אֹתוֹ וְלֹא יִשְׁמַע אֲלֵיהֶם:
וְתָפְשׂוּ בוֹ אָבִיו וְאִמּוֹ וְהוֹצִיאוּ אֹתוֹ אֶל־זִקְנֵי עִירוֹ וְאֶל־שַׁעַר
מְקֹמוֹ: וְאָמְרוּ אֶל־זִקְנֵי עִירוֹ בְּנֵנוּ זֶה סוֹרֵר וּמֹרֶה אֵינֶנּוּ שֹׁמֵעַ
בְּקֹלֵנוּ זוֹלֵל וְסֹבֵא: וּרְגָמֻהוּ כָּל־אַנְשֵׁי עִירוֹ בָאֲבָנִים וָמֵת
וּבִעַרְתָּ הָרָע מִקִּרְבֶּךָ וְכָל־יִשְׂרָאֵל יִשְׁמְעוּ וְיִרָאוּ:

KI TAVO — כי תבוא

דברים כו:א–טו

FIRST ALIYA: 26:1–3
The taking of the first fruits to Jerusalem.

וְהָיָה כִּי־תָבוֹא אֶל־הָאָרֶץ אֲשֶׁר יְהוָה אֱלֹהֶיךָ נֹתֵן לְךָ נַחֲלָה
וִירִשְׁתָּהּ וְיָשַׁבְתָּ בָּהּ: וְלָקַחְתָּ מֵרֵאשִׁית | כָּל־פְּרִי הָאֲדָמָה
אֲשֶׁר תָּבִיא מֵאַרְצְךָ אֲשֶׁר יְהוָה אֱלֹהֶיךָ נֹתֵן לָךְ וְשַׂמְתָּ
בַטֶּנֶא וְהָלַכְתָּ אֶל־הַמָּקוֹם אֲשֶׁר יִבְחַר יְהוָה אֱלֹהֶיךָ לְשַׁכֵּן
שְׁמוֹ שָׁם: וּבָאתָ אֶל־הַכֹּהֵן אֲשֶׁר יִהְיֶה בַּיָּמִים הָהֵם וְאָמַרְתָּ
אֵלָיו הִגַּדְתִּי הַיּוֹם לַיהוָה אֱלֹהֶיךָ כִּי־בָאתִי אֶל־הָאָרֶץ אֲשֶׁר
לוי נִשְׁבַּע יְהוָה לַאֲבֹתֵינוּ לָתֶת לָנוּ: *וְלָקַח הַכֹּהֵן הַטֶּנֶא מִיָּדֶךָ

SECOND ALIYA: 26:4–11
The ceremony of the bringing of the first fruits.

וְהִנִּיחוֹ לִפְנֵי מִזְבַּח יְהוָה אֱלֹהֶיךָ: וְעָנִיתָ וְאָמַרְתָּ לִפְנֵי | יְהוָה
אֱלֹהֶיךָ אֲרַמִּי אֹבֵד אָבִי וַיֵּרֶד מִצְרַיְמָה וַיָּגָר שָׁם בִּמְתֵי מְעָט
וַיְהִי־שָׁם לְגוֹי גָּדוֹל עָצוּם וָרָב: וַיָּרֵעוּ אֹתָנוּ הַמִּצְרִים וַיְעַנּוּנוּ
וַיִּתְּנוּ עָלֵינוּ עֲבֹדָה קָשָׁה: וַנִּצְעַק אֶל־יְהוָה אֱלֹהֵי אֲבֹתֵינוּ
וַיִּשְׁמַע יְהוָה אֶת־קֹלֵנוּ וַיַּרְא אֶת־עָנְיֵנוּ וְאֶת־עֲמָלֵנוּ וְאֶת־
לַחֲצֵנוּ: וַיּוֹצִאֵנוּ יְהוָה מִמִּצְרַיִם בְּיָד חֲזָקָה וּבִזְרֹעַ נְטוּיָה
וּבְמֹרָא גָּדֹל וּבְאֹתוֹת וּבְמֹפְתִים: וַיְבִאֵנוּ אֶל־הַמָּקוֹם הַזֶּה
וַיִּתֶּן־לָנוּ אֶת־הָאָרֶץ הַזֹּאת אֶרֶץ זָבַת חָלָב וּדְבָשׁ: וְעַתָּה
הִנֵּה הֵבֵאתִי אֶת־רֵאשִׁית פְּרִי הָאֲדָמָה אֲשֶׁר־נָתַתָּה לִּי
יְהוָה וְהִנַּחְתּוֹ לִפְנֵי יְהוָה אֱלֹהֶיךָ וְהִשְׁתַּחֲוִיתָ לִפְנֵי יְהוָה
אֱלֹהֶיךָ: וְשָׂמַחְתָּ בְכָל־הַטּוֹב אֲשֶׁר נָתַן־לְךָ יְהוָה אֱלֹהֶיךָ
ישראל וּלְבֵיתֶךָ אַתָּה וְהַלֵּוִי וְהַגֵּר אֲשֶׁר בְּקִרְבֶּךָ: *כִּי

THIRD ALIYA: 26:12–15
The confession said over the bringing of agricultural tithes.

תְכַלֶּה לַעְשֵׂר אֶת־כָּל־מַעְשַׂר תְּבוּאָתְךָ בַּשָּׁנָה הַשְּׁלִישִׁת
שְׁנַת הַמַּעֲשֵׂר וְנָתַתָּה לַלֵּוִי לַגֵּר לַיָּתוֹם וְלָאַלְמָנָה וְאָכְלוּ
בִשְׁעָרֶיךָ וְשָׂבֵעוּ: וְאָמַרְתָּ לִפְנֵי יְהוָה אֱלֹהֶיךָ בִּעַרְתִּי הַקֹּדֶשׁ

מִן־הַבַּיִת וְגַם נְתַתִּיו לַלֵּוִי וְלַגֵּר לַיָּתוֹם וְלָאַלְמָנָה כְּכָל־
מִצְוָתְךָ אֲשֶׁר צִוִּיתָנִי לֹא־עָבַרְתִּי מִמִּצְוֹתֶיךָ וְלֹא שָׁכָחְתִּי׃
לֹא־אָכַלְתִּי בְאֹנִי מִמֶּנּוּ וְלֹא־בִעַרְתִּי מִמֶּנּוּ בְּטָמֵא וְלֹא־
נָתַתִּי מִמֶּנּוּ לְמֵת שָׁמַעְתִּי בְּקוֹל יהוה אֱלֹהָי עָשִׂיתִי כְּכֹל
אֲשֶׁר צִוִּיתָנִי׃ הַשְׁקִיפָה מִמְּעוֹן קָדְשְׁךָ מִן־הַשָּׁמַיִם וּבָרֵךְ
אֶת־עַמְּךָ אֶת־יִשְׂרָאֵל וְאֵת הָאֲדָמָה אֲשֶׁר נָתַתָּה לָנוּ כַּאֲשֶׁר
נִשְׁבַּעְתָּ לַאֲבֹתֵינוּ אֶרֶץ זָבַת חָלָב וּדְבָשׁ׃

נצבים NITZAVIM

אַתֶּם נִצָּבִים הַיּוֹם כֻּלְּכֶם לִפְנֵי יהוה אֱלֹהֵיכֶם רָאשֵׁיכֶם דברים כט:ט–כח
שִׁבְטֵיכֶם זִקְנֵיכֶם וְשֹׁטְרֵיכֶם כֹּל אִישׁ יִשְׂרָאֵל׃ טַפְּכֶם נְשֵׁיכֶם
וְגֵרְךָ אֲשֶׁר בְּקֶרֶב מַחֲנֶיךָ מֵחֹטֵב עֵצֶיךָ עַד שֹׁאֵב מֵימֶיךָ׃
לְעָבְרְךָ בִּבְרִית יהוה אֱלֹהֶיךָ וּבְאָלָתוֹ אֲשֶׁר יהוה אֱלֹהֶיךָ
כֹּרֵת עִמְּךָ הַיּוֹם׃ *לְמַעַן הָקִים־אֹתְךָ הַיּוֹם ׀ לוֹ לְעָם וְהוּא לוי
יִהְיֶה־לְּךָ לֵאלֹהִים כַּאֲשֶׁר דִּבֶּר־לָךְ וְכַאֲשֶׁר נִשְׁבַּע לַאֲבֹתֶיךָ
לְאַבְרָהָם לְיִצְחָק וּלְיַעֲקֹב׃ וְלֹא אִתְּכֶם לְבַדְּכֶם אָנֹכִי כֹּרֵת
אֶת־הַבְּרִית הַזֹּאת וְאֶת־הָאָלָה הַזֹּאת׃ כִּי אֶת־אֲשֶׁר יֶשְׁנוֹ
פֹּה עִמָּנוּ עֹמֵד הַיּוֹם לִפְנֵי יהוה אֱלֹהֵינוּ וְאֵת אֲשֶׁר אֵינֶנּוּ
פֹּה עִמָּנוּ הַיּוֹם׃ *כִּי־אַתֶּם יְדַעְתֶּם אֵת אֲשֶׁר־יָשַׁבְנוּ בְּאֶרֶץ ישראל
מִצְרָיִם וְאֵת אֲשֶׁר־עָבַרְנוּ בְּקֶרֶב הַגּוֹיִם אֲשֶׁר עֲבַרְתֶּם׃
וַתִּרְאוּ אֶת־שִׁקּוּצֵיהֶם וְאֵת גִּלֻּלֵיהֶם עֵץ וָאֶבֶן כֶּסֶף וְזָהָב
אֲשֶׁר עִמָּהֶם׃ פֶּן־יֵשׁ בָּכֶם אִישׁ אוֹ־אִשָּׁה אוֹ מִשְׁפָּחָה אוֹ־
שֵׁבֶט אֲשֶׁר לְבָבוֹ פֹנֶה הַיּוֹם מֵעִם יהוה אֱלֹהֵינוּ לָלֶכֶת
לַעֲבֹד אֶת־אֱלֹהֵי הַגּוֹיִם הָהֵם פֶּן־יֵשׁ בָּכֶם שֹׁרֶשׁ פֹּרֶה רֹאשׁ
וְלַעֲנָה׃ וְהָיָה בְּשָׁמְעוֹ אֶת־דִּבְרֵי הָאָלָה הַזֹּאת וְהִתְבָּרֵךְ
בִּלְבָבוֹ לֵאמֹר שָׁלוֹם יִהְיֶה־לִּי כִּי בִּשְׁרִרוּת לִבִּי אֵלֵךְ לְמַעַן
סְפוֹת הָרָוָה אֶת־הַצְּמֵאָה׃ לֹא־יֹאבֶה יהוה סְלֹחַ לוֹ כִּי אָז
יֶעְשַׁן אַף־יהוה וְקִנְאָתוֹ בָּאִישׁ הַהוּא וְרָבְצָה בּוֹ כָּל־הָאָלָה
הַכְּתוּבָה בַּסֵּפֶר הַזֶּה וּמָחָה יהוה אֶת־שְׁמוֹ מִתַּחַת הַשָּׁמָיִם׃

FIRST ALIYA: 29:9–11
Renewing the covenant between the people and God.

SECOND ALIYA: 29:12–14
The eternal nature of the covenant, with those present at that time as well as future generations.

THIRD ALIYA: 29:15–28
Warnings against idolatrous practices.

וְהִבְדִּילוֹ יְהוָה לְרָעָה מִכֹּל שִׁבְטֵי יִשְׂרָאֵל כְּכֹל אָלוֹת הַבְּרִית
הַכְּתוּבָה בְּסֵפֶר הַתּוֹרָה הַזֶּה: וְאָמַר הַדּוֹר הָאַחֲרוֹן בְּנֵיכֶם
אֲשֶׁר יָקוּמוּ מֵאַחֲרֵיכֶם וְהַנָּכְרִי אֲשֶׁר יָבֹא מֵאֶרֶץ רְחוֹקָה
וְרָאוּ אֶת־מַכּוֹת הָאָרֶץ הַהִוא וְאֶת־תַּחֲלֻאֶיהָ אֲשֶׁר־חִלָּה
יְהוָה בָּהּ: גׇּפְרִית וָמֶלַח שְׂרֵפָה כׇל־אַרְצָהּ לֹא תִזָּרַע וְלֹא
תַצְמִחַ וְלֹא־יַעֲלֶה בָהּ כׇּל־עֵשֶׂב כְּמַהְפֵּכַת סְדֹם וַעֲמֹרָה
אַדְמָה וצביים אֲשֶׁר הָפַךְ יְהוָה בְּאַפּוֹ וּבַחֲמָתוֹ: וְאָמְרוּ כׇּל־ וּצְבוֹיִם
הַגּוֹיִם עַל־מֶה עָשָׂה יְהוָה כָּכָה לָאָרֶץ הַזֹּאת מֶה חֳרִי הָאַף
הַגָּדוֹל הַזֶּה: וְאָמְרוּ עַל אֲשֶׁר עָזְבוּ אֶת־בְּרִית יְהוָה אֱלֹהֵי
אֲבֹתָם אֲשֶׁר כָּרַת עִמָּם בְּהוֹצִיאוֹ אֹתָם מֵאֶרֶץ מִצְרָיִם:
וַיֵּלְכוּ וַיַּעַבְדוּ אֱלֹהִים אֲחֵרִים וַיִּשְׁתַּחֲווּ לָהֶם אֱלֹהִים אֲשֶׁר
לֹא־יְדָעוּם וְלֹא חָלַק לָהֶם: וַיִּחַר־אַף יְהוָה בָּאָרֶץ הַהִוא
לְהָבִיא עָלֶיהָ אֶת־כׇּל־הַקְּלָלָה הַכְּתוּבָה בַּסֵּפֶר הַזֶּה:
וַיִּתְּשֵׁם יְהוָה מֵעַל אַדְמָתָם בְּאַף וּבְחֵמָה וּבְקֶצֶף גָּדוֹל
וַיַּשְׁלִכֵם אֶל־אֶרֶץ אַחֶרֶת כַּיּוֹם הַזֶּה: הַנִּסְתָּרֹת לַיהוָה
אֱלֹהֵינוּ וְהַנִּגְלֹת לָנוּ וּלְבָנֵינוּ עַד־עוֹלָם לַעֲשׂוֹת אֶת־כׇּל־
דִּבְרֵי הַתּוֹרָה הַזֹּאת:

וילך VAYELEKH

דברים לא:א–יג

וַיֵּלֶךְ מֹשֶׁה וַיְדַבֵּר אֶת־הַדְּבָרִים הָאֵלֶּה אֶל־כׇּל־יִשְׂרָאֵל:
וַיֹּאמֶר אֲלֵהֶם בֶּן־מֵאָה וְעֶשְׂרִים שָׁנָה אָנֹכִי הַיּוֹם לֹא־אוּכַל
עוֹד לָצֵאת וְלָבוֹא וַיהוָה אָמַר אֵלַי לֹא תַעֲבֹר אֶת־הַיַּרְדֵּן
הַזֶּה: יְהוָה אֱלֹהֶיךָ הוּא ׀ עֹבֵר לְפָנֶיךָ הוּא־יַשְׁמִיד אֶת־הַגּוֹיִם
הָאֵלֶּה מִלְּפָנֶיךָ וִירִשְׁתָּם יְהוֹשֻׁעַ הוּא עֹבֵר לְפָנֶיךָ כַּאֲשֶׁר דִּבֶּר
יְהוָה: *וְעָשָׂה יְהוָה לָהֶם כַּאֲשֶׁר עָשָׂה לְסִיחוֹן וּלְעוֹג מַלְכֵי לוי
הָאֱמֹרִי וּלְאַרְצָם אֲשֶׁר הִשְׁמִיד אֹתָם: וּנְתָנָם יְהוָה לִפְנֵיכֶם
וַעֲשִׂיתֶם לָהֶם כְּכׇל־הַמִּצְוָה אֲשֶׁר צִוִּיתִי אֶתְכֶם: חִזְקוּ וְאִמְצוּ
אַל־תִּירְאוּ וְאַל־תַּעַרְצוּ מִפְּנֵיהֶם כִּי ׀ יְהוָה אֱלֹהֶיךָ הוּא
הַהֹלֵךְ עִמָּךְ לֹא יַרְפְּךָ וְלֹא יַעַזְבֶךָּ: *וַיִּקְרָא ישראל

FIRST ALIYA: 31:1–3
Moshe begins his final farewell.

SECOND ALIYA: 31:4–6
Moshe delivers words of comfort and inspiration for the coming military campaign to conquer the land.

מֹשֶׁה לִיהוֹשֻׁעַ וַיֹּאמֶר אֵלָיו לְעֵינֵי כָל־יִשְׂרָאֵל חֲזַק וֶאֱמָץ
כִּי אַתָּה תָּבוֹא אֶת־הָעָם הַזֶּה אֶל־הָאָרֶץ אֲשֶׁר נִשְׁבַּע
יהוה לַאֲבֹתָם לָתֵת לָהֶם וְאַתָּה תַּנְחִילֶנָּה אוֹתָם: וַיהוה
הוּא ׀ הַהֹלֵךְ לְפָנֶיךָ הוּא יִהְיֶה עִמָּךְ לֹא יַרְפְּךָ וְלֹא יַעַזְבֶךָּ
לֹא תִירָא וְלֹא תֵחָת: וַיִּכְתֹּב מֹשֶׁה אֶת־הַתּוֹרָה הַזֹּאת
וַיִּתְּנָהּ אֶל־הַכֹּהֲנִים בְּנֵי לֵוִי הַנֹּשְׂאִים אֶת־אֲרוֹן בְּרִית יהוה
וְאֶל־כָּל־זִקְנֵי יִשְׂרָאֵל: וַיְצַו מֹשֶׁה אוֹתָם לֵאמֹר מִקֵּץ ׀ שֶׁבַע
שָׁנִים בְּמֹעֵד שְׁנַת הַשְּׁמִטָּה בְּחַג הַסֻּכּוֹת: בְּבוֹא כָל־יִשְׂרָאֵל
לֵרָאוֹת אֶת־פְּנֵי יהוה אֱלֹהֶיךָ בַּמָּקוֹם אֲשֶׁר יִבְחָר תִּקְרָא
אֶת־הַתּוֹרָה הַזֹּאת נֶגֶד כָּל־יִשְׂרָאֵל בְּאָזְנֵיהֶם: הַקְהֵל אֶת־
הָעָם הָאֲנָשִׁים וְהַנָּשִׁים וְהַטַּף וְגֵרְךָ אֲשֶׁר בִּשְׁעָרֶיךָ לְמַעַן
יִשְׁמְעוּ וּלְמַעַן יִלְמְדוּ וְיָרְאוּ אֶת־יהוה אֱלֹהֵיכֶם וְשָׁמְרוּ
לַעֲשׂוֹת אֶת־כָּל־דִּבְרֵי הַתּוֹרָה הַזֹּאת: וּבְנֵיהֶם אֲשֶׁר לֹא־
יָדְעוּ יִשְׁמְעוּ וְלָמְדוּ לְיִרְאָה אֶת־יהוה אֱלֹהֵיכֶם כָּל־הַיָּמִים
אֲשֶׁר אַתֶּם חַיִּים עַל־הָאֲדָמָה אֲשֶׁר אַתֶּם עֹבְרִים אֶת־הַיַּרְדֵּן
שָׁמָּה לְרִשְׁתָּהּ:

THIRD ALIYA: 31:7–13
Moshe delivers words of inspiration and strength to Yehoshua, and then gives the people the command of *Hak-hel*, the public reading of the Torah in front of the entire people every seven years.

HA'AZINU — האזינו

דברים לב:א-יח

הַאֲזִינוּ הַשָּׁמַיִם וַאֲדַבֵּרָה   וְתִשְׁמַע הָאָרֶץ אִמְרֵי־פִי:
יַעֲרֹף כַּמָּטָר לִקְחִי   תִּזַּל כַּטַּל אִמְרָתִי
כִּשְׂעִירִם עֲלֵי־דֶשֶׁא   וְכִרְבִיבִים עֲלֵי־עֵשֶׂב:
כִּי שֵׁם יהוה אֶקְרָא   הָבוּ גֹדֶל לֵאלֹהֵינוּ:
לוי *הַצּוּר תָּמִים פָּעֳלוֹ   כִּי כָל־דְּרָכָיו מִשְׁפָּט
אֵל אֱמוּנָה וְאֵין עָוֶל   צַדִּיק וְיָשָׁר הוּא:
שִׁחֵת לוֹ לֹא בָּנָיו מוּמָם   דּוֹר עִקֵּשׁ וּפְתַלְתֹּל:
הַ לַיהוה תִּגְמְלוּ־זֹאת   עַם נָבָל וְלֹא חָכָם
הֲלוֹא־הוּא אָבִיךָ קָּנֶךָ   הוּא עָשְׂךָ וַיְכֹנְנֶךָ:

Some start the לוי *portion here:*

ישראל *זְכֹר יְמוֹת עוֹלָם   בִּינוּ שְׁנוֹת דֹּר־וָדֹר

FIRST ALIYA: 32:1–3
Moshe begins his song to inspire his people as he says farewell.

SECOND ALIYA: 32:4–6
Moshe's poetic description of God.

THIRD ALIYA: 32:7–12
Moshe's poetic description of God's role in Jewish history.

שְׁאַל אָבִיךָ וְיַגֵּדְךָ   זְקֵנֶיךָ וְיֹאמְרוּ לָךְ׃
בְּהַנְחֵל עֶלְיוֹן גּוֹיִם   בְּהַפְרִידוֹ בְּנֵי אָדָם
יַצֵּב גְּבֻלֹת עַמִּים   לְמִסְפַּר בְּנֵי יִשְׂרָאֵל׃
כִּי חֵלֶק יהוה עַמּוֹ   יַעֲקֹב חֶבֶל נַחֲלָתוֹ׃
יִמְצָאֵהוּ בְּאֶרֶץ מִדְבָּר   וּבְתֹהוּ יְלֵל יְשִׁמֹן
יְסֹבְבֶנְהוּ יְבוֹנְנֵהוּ   יִצְּרֶנְהוּ כְּאִישׁוֹן עֵינוֹ׃
כְּנֶשֶׁר יָעִיר קִנּוֹ   עַל־גּוֹזָלָיו יְרַחֵף
יִפְרֹשׂ כְּנָפָיו יִקָּחֵהוּ   יִשָּׂאֵהוּ עַל־אֶבְרָתוֹ׃
יהוה בָּדָד יַנְחֶנּוּ   וְאֵין עִמּוֹ אֵל נֵכָר׃

Most finish here; some start the ישראל portion here:

*יַרְכִּבֵהוּ עַל־בָּמוֹתֵי אָרֶץ   וַיֹּאכַל תְּנוּבֹת שָׂדָי   בָּמֳתֵי
וַיֵּנִקֵהוּ דְבַשׁ מִסֶּלַע   וְשֶׁמֶן מֵחַלְמִישׁ צוּר׃
חֶמְאַת בָּקָר וַחֲלֵב צֹאן   עִם־חֵלֶב כָּרִים
וְאֵילִים בְּנֵי־בָשָׁן וְעַתּוּדִים   עִם־חֵלֶב כִּלְיוֹת חִטָּה
וְדַם־עֵנָב תִּשְׁתֶּה־חָמֶר׃   וַיִּשְׁמַן יְשֻׁרוּן וַיִּבְעָט
שָׁמַנְתָּ עָבִיתָ כָּשִׂיתָ   וַיִּטֹּשׁ אֱלוֹהַּ עָשָׂהוּ
וַיְנַבֵּל צוּר יְשֻׁעָתוֹ׃   יַקְנִאֻהוּ בְּזָרִים
בְּתוֹעֵבֹת יַכְעִיסֻהוּ׃   יִזְבְּחוּ לַשֵּׁדִים לֹא אֱלֹהַּ
אֱלֹהִים לֹא יְדָעוּם   חֲדָשִׁים מִקָּרֹב בָּאוּ
לֹא שְׂעָרוּם אֲבֹתֵיכֶם׃   צוּר יְלָדְךָ תֶּשִׁי
וַתִּשְׁכַּח אֵל מְחֹלְלֶךָ׃

VEZOT HABERAKHA   וזאת הברכה

FIRST ALIYA: 33:1–7
Moshe leaves the people with his blessings for the tribes. This sections sees his blessings to Reuven and Yehuda.

דברים לג:א–יז
וְזֹאת הַבְּרָכָה אֲשֶׁר בֵּרַךְ מֹשֶׁה אִישׁ הָאֱלֹהִים אֶת־בְּנֵי
יִשְׂרָאֵל לִפְנֵי מוֹתוֹ׃ וַיֹּאמַר יהוה מִסִּינַי בָּא וְזָרַח מִשֵּׂעִיר
לָמוֹ הוֹפִיעַ מֵהַר פָּארָן וְאָתָה מֵרִבְבֹת קֹדֶשׁ מִימִינוֹ אשדת   אֵשׁ דָּת
לָמוֹ׃ אַף חֹבֵב עַמִּים כָּל־קְדֹשָׁיו בְּיָדֶךָ וְהֵם תֻּכּוּ לְרַגְלֶךָ יִשָּׂא
מִדַּבְּרֹתֶיךָ׃ תּוֹרָה צִוָּה־לָנוּ מֹשֶׁה מוֹרָשָׁה קְהִלַּת יַעֲקֹב׃
וַיְהִי בִישֻׁרוּן מֶלֶךְ בְּהִתְאַסֵּף רָאשֵׁי עָם יַחַד שִׁבְטֵי יִשְׂרָאֵל׃

יְחִי רְאוּבֵן וְאַל־יָמֹת וִיהִי מְתָיו מִסְפָּר: וְזֹאת
לִיהוּדָה֮ וַיֹּאמַר֒ שְׁמַע יהוה קוֹל יְהוּדָה וְאֶל־עַמּוֹ תְּבִיאֶנּוּ
יָדָיו רָב לוֹ וְעֵזֶר מִצָּרָיו תִּהְיֶה:

לוי
וּלְלֵוִי אָמַר תֻּמֶּיךָ וְאוּרֶיךָ לְאִישׁ חֲסִידֶךָ אֲשֶׁר נִסִּיתוֹ בְּמַסָּה
תְּרִיבֵהוּ עַל־מֵי מְרִיבָה: הָאֹמֵר לְאָבִיו וּלְאִמּוֹ לֹא רְאִיתִיו
וְאֶת־אֶחָיו לֹא הִכִּיר וְאֶת־בָּנָו לֹא יָדָע כִּי שָׁמְרוּ אִמְרָתֶךָ
וּבְרִיתְךָ יִנְצֹרוּ: יוֹרוּ מִשְׁפָּטֶיךָ לְיַעֲקֹב וְתוֹרָתְךָ לְיִשְׂרָאֵל
יָשִׂימוּ קְטוֹרָה בְּאַפֶּךָ וְכָלִיל עַל־מִזְבְּחֶךָ: בָּרֵךְ יהוה
חֵילוֹ וּפֹעַל יָדָיו תִּרְצֶה מְחַץ מָתְנַיִם קָמָיו וּמְשַׂנְאָיו מִן־
יְקוּמוּן: לְבִנְיָמִן אָמַר יְדִיד יהוה יִשְׁכֹּן לָבֶטַח עָלָיו

ישראל
חֹפֵף עָלָיו כָּל־הַיּוֹם וּבֵין כְּתֵפָיו שָׁכֵן: *וּלְיוֹסֵף
אָמַר מְבֹרֶכֶת יהוה אַרְצוֹ מִמֶּגֶד שָׁמַיִם מִטָּל וּמִתְּהוֹם
רֹבֶצֶת תָּחַת: וּמִמֶּגֶד תְּבוּאֹת שָׁמֶשׁ וּמִמֶּגֶד גֶּרֶשׁ יְרָחִים:
וּמֵרֹאשׁ הַרְרֵי־קֶדֶם וּמִמֶּגֶד גִּבְעוֹת עוֹלָם: וּמִמֶּגֶד אֶרֶץ
וּמְלֹאָהּ וּרְצוֹן שֹׁכְנִי סְנֶה תָּבוֹאתָה לְרֹאשׁ יוֹסֵף וּלְקָדְקֹד
נְזִיר אֶחָיו: בְּכוֹר שׁוֹרוֹ הָדָר לוֹ וְקַרְנֵי רְאֵם קַרְנָיו בָּהֶם
עַמִּים יְנַגַּח יַחְדָּו אַפְסֵי־אָרֶץ וְהֵם רִבְבוֹת אֶפְרַיִם וְהֵם
אַלְפֵי מְנַשֶּׁה:

SECOND ALIYA: 33:8–12
Moshe's blessings to Levi and Binyamin.

THIRD ALIYA: 33:13–17
Moshe's blessing to Yosef (Efraim and Menashe).

קריאת התורה לראש חודש, לתעניות ציבור, לחנוכה ולפורים

THE READING OF THE TORAH FOR ROSH ḤODESH, FAST DAYS, ḤANUKKA AND PURIM

ROSH ḤODESH — קריאה לראש חודש

For the כהן*, the first three verses are read up to* עֹלָה תָּמִיד*. For the* לוי*, the third verse is repeated and starts with* וְאָמַרְתָּ לָהֶם*. For* שלישי*, continue from* עֹלַת תָּמִיד *up to* וְנִסְכָּהּ*. For* רביעי*, read from* וּבְרָאשֵׁי חָדְשֵׁיכֶם *until the end. In* ארץ ישראל*, some read as follows: For the* כהן *read until* רְבִיעִת הַהִין*, for the* לוי *read from* אֶת־הַכֶּבֶשׂ *until* רֵיחַ נִיחֹחַ לַה׳*, for* שלישי*, the last verse is repeated and starts at* עֹלַת תָּמִיד *up to* וְנִסְכָּהּ*, and for* רביעי*, from* וּבְרָאשֵׁי חָדְשֵׁיכֶם *until the end. On* ראש חודש טבת*, the* כהן *reads until* רְבִיעִת הַהִין*, the* לוי *reads the portion for* שלישי *and the* שלישי *the portion of* רביעי*; the fourth* עולה *reads the appropriate day of* חנוכה *on page 1130.*

במדבר כח:א–טו

FIRST ALIYA: vv. 1–3 The Tamid daily offering.

SECOND ALIYA: vv. 3–5 The details of the Tamid daily offering.

THIRD ALIYA: vv. 6–10 More details of the Tamid, and the Shabbat Musaf offering.

וַיְדַבֵּ֥ר יְהֹוָ֖ה אֶל־מֹשֶׁ֥ה לֵּאמֹֽר׃ צַ֚ו אֶת־בְּנֵ֣י יִשְׂרָאֵ֔ל וְאָמַרְתָּ֖
אֲלֵהֶ֑ם אֶת־קָרְבָּנִ֨י לַחְמִ֜י לְאִשַּׁ֗י רֵ֚יחַ נִיחֹחִ֔י תִּשְׁמְר֖וּ לְהַקְרִ֥יב
לִ֖י בְּמוֹעֲדֽוֹ׃ לוי *וְאָמַרְתָּ֣ לָהֶ֔ם זֶ֚ה הָֽאִשֶּׁ֔ה אֲשֶׁ֥ר תַּקְרִ֖יבוּ לַֽיהֹוָ֑ה
כְּבָשִׂ֨ים בְּנֵֽי־שָׁנָ֧ה תְמִימִ֛ם שְׁנַ֥יִם לַיּ֖וֹם עֹלָ֥ה תָמִֽיד׃ (עד כאן לכהן) *אֶת־
הַכֶּ֥בֶשׂ אֶחָ֖ד תַּעֲשֶׂ֣ה בַבֹּ֑קֶר וְאֵת֙ הַכֶּ֣בֶשׂ הַשֵּׁנִ֔י תַּעֲשֶׂ֖ה בֵּ֥ין
הָעַרְבָּֽיִם׃ וַעֲשִׂירִ֧ית הָאֵיפָ֛ה סֹ֖לֶת לְמִנְחָ֑ה בְּלוּלָ֛ה בְּשֶׁ֥מֶן
כָּתִ֖ית רְבִיעִ֥ת הַהִֽין׃ שלישי *עֹלַ֖ת תָּמִ֑יד הָעֲשֻׂיָה֙ בְּהַ֣ר סִינַ֔י לְרֵ֣יחַ
נִיחֹ֔חַ אִשֶּׁ֖ה לַֽיהֹוָֽה׃ וְנִסְכּוֹ֙ רְבִיעִ֣ת הַהִ֔ין לַכֶּ֖בֶשׂ הָאֶחָ֑ד
בַּקֹּ֗דֶשׁ הַסֵּ֛ךְ נֶ֥סֶךְ שֵׁכָ֖ר לַֽיהֹוָֽה׃ וְאֵת֙ הַכֶּ֣בֶשׂ הַשֵּׁנִ֔י תַּעֲשֶׂ֖ה
בֵּ֣ין הָעַרְבָּ֑יִם כְּמִנְחַ֨ת הַבֹּ֤קֶר וּכְנִסְכּוֹ֙ תַּעֲשֶׂ֔ה אִשֵּׁ֛ה רֵ֥יחַ נִיחֹ֖חַ
לַֽיהֹוָֽה׃

וּבְיוֹם֙ הַשַּׁבָּ֔ת שְׁנֵֽי־כְבָשִׂ֥ים בְּנֵֽי־שָׁנָ֖ה תְּמִימִ֑ם וּשְׁנֵ֣י עֶשְׂרֹנִ֗ים
סֹ֧לֶת מִנְחָ֛ה בְּלוּלָ֥ה בַשֶּׁ֖מֶן וְנִסְכּֽוֹ׃ עֹלַ֥ת שַׁבַּ֖ת בְּשַׁבַּתּ֑וֹ עַל־
עֹלַ֥ת הַתָּמִ֖יד וְנִסְכָּֽהּ׃

רביעי

FOURTH ALIYA: 11–15
The Rosh Ḥodesh offering.

וּבְרָאשֵׁי חָדְשֵׁיכֶם תַּקְרִיבוּ עֹלָה לַיהוה פָּרִים בְּנֵי־בָקָר שְׁנַיִם וְאַיִל אֶחָד כְּבָשִׂים בְּנֵי־שָׁנָה שִׁבְעָה תְּמִימִם: וּשְׁלֹשָׁה עֶשְׂרֹנִים סֹלֶת מִנְחָה בְּלוּלָה בַשֶּׁמֶן לַפָּר הָאֶחָד וּשְׁנֵי עֶשְׂרֹנִים סֹלֶת מִנְחָה בְּלוּלָה בַשֶּׁמֶן לָאַיִל הָאֶחָד: וְעִשָּׂרֹן עִשָּׂרוֹן סֹלֶת מִנְחָה בְּלוּלָה בַשֶּׁמֶן לַכֶּבֶשׂ הָאֶחָד עֹלָה רֵיחַ נִיחֹחַ אִשֶּׁה לַיהוה: וְנִסְכֵּיהֶם חֲצִי הַהִין יִהְיֶה לַפָּר וּשְׁלִישִׁת הַהִין לָאַיִל וּרְבִיעִת הַהִין לַכֶּבֶשׂ יָיִן זֹאת עֹלַת חֹדֶשׁ בְּחָדְשׁוֹ לְחָדְשֵׁי הַשָּׁנָה: וּשְׂעִיר עִזִּים אֶחָד לְחַטָּאת לַיהוה עַל־עֹלַת הַתָּמִיד יֵעָשֶׂה וְנִסְכּוֹ:

READING FOR FAST DAYS קריאה לתענית ציבור

The following is read on a תענית ציבור (*except* תשעה באב) *in both* שחרית *and* מנחה.
At מנחה*, the person called up for* שלישי *also reads the* הפטרה.
It is customary for the קהל *to say aloud the passages marked by arrows, followed by the* קורא.

שמות לב: יא–יד

FIRST ALIYA: vv. 32:11–14
Moshe's successful prayer to God to forgive the people after the sin of the golden calf.

וַיְחַל מֹשֶׁה אֶת־פְּנֵי יהוה אֱלֹהָיו וַיֹּאמֶר לָמָה יהוה יֶחֱרֶה אַפְּךָ בְּעַמֶּךָ אֲשֶׁר הוֹצֵאתָ מֵאֶרֶץ מִצְרַיִם בְּכֹחַ גָּדוֹל וּבְיָד חֲזָקָה: לָמָּה יֹאמְרוּ מִצְרַיִם לֵאמֹר בְּרָעָה הוֹצִיאָם לַהֲרֹג אֹתָם בֶּהָרִים וּלְכַלֹּתָם מֵעַל פְּנֵי הָאֲדָמָה ◂ שׁוּב מֵחֲרוֹן אַפֶּךָ וְהִנָּחֵם עַל־הָרָעָה לְעַמֶּךָ: ◂ זְכֹר לְאַבְרָהָם לְיִצְחָק וּלְיִשְׂרָאֵל עֲבָדֶיךָ אֲשֶׁר נִשְׁבַּעְתָּ לָהֶם בָּךְ וַתְּדַבֵּר אֲלֵהֶם אַרְבֶּה אֶת־זַרְעֲכֶם כְּכוֹכְבֵי הַשָּׁמָיִם וְכָל־הָאָרֶץ הַזֹּאת אֲשֶׁר אָמַרְתִּי אֶתֵּן לְזַרְעֲכֶם וְנָחֲלוּ לְעֹלָם: וַיִּנָּחֶם יהוה עַל־הָרָעָה אֲשֶׁר דִּבֶּר לַעֲשׂוֹת לְעַמּוֹ:

שמות לד: א–י
לוי

SECOND ALIYA: vv. 34:1–3
God instructs Moshe to prepare the second set of tablets of stone.

וַיֹּאמֶר יהוה אֶל־מֹשֶׁה פְּסָל־לְךָ שְׁנֵי־לֻחֹת אֲבָנִים כָּרִאשֹׁנִים וְכָתַבְתִּי עַל־הַלֻּחֹת אֶת־הַדְּבָרִים אֲשֶׁר הָיוּ עַל־הַלֻּחֹת הָרִאשֹׁנִים אֲשֶׁר שִׁבַּרְתָּ: וֶהְיֵה נָכוֹן לַבֹּקֶר וְעָלִיתָ בַבֹּקֶר אֶל־הַר סִינַי וְנִצַּבְתָּ לִי שָׁם עַל־רֹאשׁ הָהָר: וְאִישׁ לֹא־יַעֲלֶה עִמָּךְ וְגַם־אִישׁ אַל־יֵרָא בְּכָל־הָהָר גַּם־הַצֹּאן וְהַבָּקָר אַל־יִרְעוּ

ישראל

THIRD ALIYA: VV. 4–10
God reveals to Moshe the Thirteen Attributes of Mercy.

אֶל־מוּל הָהָר הַהוּא: *וַיִּפְסֹל שְׁנֵי־לֻחֹת אֲבָנִים כָּרִאשֹׁנִים וַיַּשְׁכֵּם מֹשֶׁה בַבֹּקֶר וַיַּעַל אֶל־הַר סִינַי כַּאֲשֶׁר צִוָּה יהוה אֹתוֹ וַיִּקַּח בְּיָדוֹ שְׁנֵי לֻחֹת אֲבָנִים: וַיֵּרֶד יהוה בֶּעָנָן וַיִּתְיַצֵּב עִמּוֹ שָׁם וַיִּקְרָא בְשֵׁם יהוה: וַיַּעֲבֹר יהוה | עַל־פָּנָיו וַיִּקְרָא · יהוה | יהוה אֵל רַחוּם וְחַנּוּן אֶרֶךְ אַפַּיִם וְרַב־חֶסֶד וֶאֱמֶת: נֹצֵר חֶסֶד לָאֲלָפִים נֹשֵׂא עָוֺן וָפֶשַׁע וְחַטָּאָה וְנַקֵּה · לֹא יְנַקֶּה פֹּקֵד | עֲוֺן אָבוֹת עַל־בָּנִים וְעַל־בְּנֵי בָנִים עַל־שִׁלֵּשִׁים וְעַל־רִבֵּעִים: וַיְמַהֵר מֹשֶׁה וַיִּקֹּד אַרְצָה וַיִּשְׁתָּחוּ: וַיֹּאמֶר אִם־נָא מָצָאתִי חֵן בְּעֵינֶיךָ אֲדֹנָי יֵלֶךְ־נָא אֲדֹנָי בְּקִרְבֵּנוּ כִּי עַם־קְשֵׁה־עֹרֶף הוּא · וְסָלַחְתָּ לַעֲוֺנֵנוּ וּלְחַטָּאתֵנוּ וּנְחַלְתָּנוּ: · וַיֹּאמֶר הִנֵּה אָנֹכִי כֹּרֵת בְּרִית נֶגֶד כָּל־עַמְּךָ אֶעֱשֶׂה נִפְלָאֹת אֲשֶׁר לֹא־נִבְרְאוּ בְכָל־הָאָרֶץ וּבְכָל־הַגּוֹיִם וְרָאָה כָל־הָעָם אֲשֶׁר־אַתָּה בְקִרְבּוֹ אֶת־מַעֲשֵׂה יהוה כִּי־נוֹרָא הוּא אֲשֶׁר אֲנִי עֹשֶׂה עִמָּךְ:

ברכות ההפטרה

Before reading the הפטרה*, the person called up for* מפטיר *says:*

בָּרוּךְ אַתָּה יהוה אֱלֹהֵינוּ מֶלֶךְ הָעוֹלָם אֲשֶׁר בָּחַר בִּנְבִיאִים טוֹבִים, וְרָצָה בְדִבְרֵיהֶם הַנֶּאֱמָרִים בֶּאֱמֶת. בָּרוּךְ אַתָּה יהוה, הַבּוֹחֵר בַּתּוֹרָה וּבְמֹשֶׁה עַבְדּוֹ וּבְיִשְׂרָאֵל עַמּוֹ וּבִנְבִיאֵי הָאֱמֶת וָצֶדֶק.

HAFTARA – FAST DAYS הפטרה לתענית ציבור

ישעיה
נה:ו–נו:ח

HAFTARA – FAST DAYS
The Haftara for fast days is taken from Isaiah and has repentance and redemption as its theme.

דִּרְשׁוּ יהוה בְּהִמָּצְאוֹ קְרָאֻהוּ בִּהְיוֹתוֹ קָרוֹב: יַעֲזֹב רָשָׁע דַּרְכּוֹ וְאִישׁ אָוֶן מַחְשְׁבֹתָיו וְיָשֹׁב אֶל־יהוה וִירַחֲמֵהוּ וְאֶל־אֱלֹהֵינוּ כִּי־יַרְבֶּה לִסְלוֹחַ: כִּי לֹא מַחְשְׁבוֹתַי מַחְשְׁבוֹתֵיכֶם וְלֹא דַרְכֵיכֶם דְּרָכָי נְאֻם יהוה: כִּי־גָבְהוּ שָׁמַיִם מֵאָרֶץ כֵּן גָּבְהוּ דְרָכַי מִדַּרְכֵיכֶם וּמַחְשְׁבֹתַי מִמַּחְשְׁבֹתֵיכֶם: כִּי כַּאֲשֶׁר יֵרֵד הַגֶּשֶׁם וְהַשֶּׁלֶג מִן־הַשָּׁמַיִם וְשָׁמָּה לֹא יָשׁוּב כִּי אִם־הִרְוָה אֶת־הָאָרֶץ וְהוֹלִידָהּ וְהִצְמִיחָהּ וְנָתַן זֶרַע לַזֹּרֵעַ וְלֶחֶם

לֶאֹכֵל: כֵּן יִהְיֶה דְבָרִי אֲשֶׁר יֵצֵא מִפִּי לֹא־יָשׁוּב אֵלַי רֵיקָם
כִּי אִם־עָשָׂה אֶת־אֲשֶׁר חָפַצְתִּי וְהִצְלִיחַ אֲשֶׁר שְׁלַחְתִּיו:
כִּי־בְשִׂמְחָה תֵצֵאוּ וּבְשָׁלוֹם תּוּבָלוּן הֶהָרִים וְהַגְּבָעוֹת יִפְצְחוּ
לִפְנֵיכֶם רִנָּה וְכָל־עֲצֵי הַשָּׂדֶה יִמְחֲאוּ־כָף: תַּחַת הַנַּעֲצוּץ
וְתַחַת יַעֲלֶה בְרוֹשׁ תחת הַסִּרְפַּד יַעֲלֶה הֲדַס וְהָיָה לַיהוה לְשֵׁם
לְאוֹת עוֹלָם לֹא יִכָּרֵת: כֹּה אָמַר יהוה שִׁמְרוּ
מִשְׁפָּט וַעֲשׂוּ צְדָקָה כִּי־קְרוֹבָה יְשׁוּעָתִי לָבוֹא וְצִדְקָתִי
לְהִגָּלוֹת: אַשְׁרֵי אֱנוֹשׁ יַעֲשֶׂה־זֹּאת וּבֶן־אָדָם יַחֲזִיק בָּהּ
שֹׁמֵר שַׁבָּת מֵחַלְּלוֹ וְשֹׁמֵר יָדוֹ מֵעֲשׂוֹת כָּל־רָע: וְאַל־יֹאמַר
בֶּן־הַנֵּכָר הַנִּלְוָה אֶל־יהוה לֵאמֹר הַבְדֵּל יַבְדִּילַנִי יהוה מֵעַל
עַמּוֹ וְאַל־יֹאמַר הַסָּרִיס הֵן אֲנִי עֵץ יָבֵשׁ: כִּי־
כֹה ׀ אָמַר יהוה לַסָּרִיסִים אֲשֶׁר יִשְׁמְרוּ אֶת־שַׁבְּתוֹתַי וּבָחֲרוּ
בַּאֲשֶׁר חָפָצְתִּי וּמַחֲזִיקִים בִּבְרִיתִי: וְנָתַתִּי לָהֶם בְּבֵיתִי
וּבְחוֹמֹתַי יָד וָשֵׁם טוֹב מִבָּנִים וּמִבָּנוֹת שֵׁם עוֹלָם אֶתֶּן־לוֹ
אֲשֶׁר לֹא יִכָּרֵת: וּבְנֵי הַנֵּכָר הַנִּלְוִים עַל־יהוה
לְשָׁרְתוֹ וּלְאַהֲבָה אֶת־שֵׁם יהוה לִהְיוֹת לוֹ לַעֲבָדִים כָּל־
שֹׁמֵר שַׁבָּת מֵחַלְּלוֹ וּמַחֲזִיקִים בִּבְרִיתִי: וַהֲבִיאוֹתִים אֶל־
הַר קָדְשִׁי וְשִׂמַּחְתִּים בְּבֵית תְּפִלָּתִי עוֹלֹתֵיהֶם וְזִבְחֵיהֶם
לְרָצוֹן עַל־מִזְבְּחִי כִּי בֵיתִי בֵּית־תְּפִלָּה יִקָּרֵא לְכָל־הָעַמִּים:
נְאֻם אֲדֹנָי יֱהוִה מְקַבֵּץ נִדְחֵי יִשְׂרָאֵל עוֹד אֲקַבֵּץ עָלָיו
לְנִקְבָּצָיו:

After the הפטרה, *the person called up for* מפטיר *says the following blessings:*

בָּרוּךְ אַתָּה יהוה אֱלֹהֵינוּ מֶלֶךְ הָעוֹלָם, צוּר כָּל הָעוֹלָמִים, צַדִּיק בְּכָל הַדּוֹרוֹת, הָאֵל הַנֶּאֱמָן, הָאוֹמֵר וְעוֹשֶׂה, הַמְדַבֵּר וּמְקַיֵּם, שֶׁכָּל דְּבָרָיו אֱמֶת וָצֶדֶק. נֶאֱמָן אַתָּה הוּא יהוה אֱלֹהֵינוּ וְנֶאֱמָנִים דְּבָרֶיךָ, וְדָבָר אֶחָד מִדְּבָרֶיךָ אָחוֹר לֹא יָשׁוּב רֵיקָם, כִּי אֵל מֶלֶךְ נֶאֱמָן (וְרַחֲמָן) אָתָּה. בָּרוּךְ אַתָּה יהוה, הָאֵל הַנֶּאֱמָן בְּכָל דְּבָרָיו.

רַחֵם עַל צִיּוֹן כִּי הִיא בֵּית חַיֵּינוּ, וְלַעֲלוּבַת נֶפֶשׁ תּוֹשִׁיעַ בִּמְהֵרָה בְיָמֵינוּ. בָּרוּךְ אַתָּה יהוה, מְשַׂמֵּחַ צִיּוֹן בְּבָנֶיהָ.

שַׂמְּחֵנוּ יהוה אֱלֹהֵינוּ בְּאֵלִיָּהוּ הַנָּבִיא עַבְדֶּךָ, וּבְמַלְכוּת בֵּית דָּוִד מְשִׁיחֶךָ, בִּמְהֵרָה יָבוֹא וְיָגֵל לִבֵּנוּ. עַל כִּסְאוֹ לֹא יֵשֶׁב זָר, וְלֹא יִנְחֲלוּ עוֹד אֲחֵרִים אֶת כְּבוֹדוֹ, כִּי בְשֵׁם קָדְשְׁךָ נִשְׁבַּעְתָּ לּוֹ שֶׁלֹּא יִכְבֶּה נֵרוֹ לְעוֹלָם וָעֶד. בָּרוּךְ אַתָּה יהוה, מָגֵן דָּוִד.

READING FOR TISHA B'AV קריאה לתשעה באב

The following is read during שחרית *of* תשעה באב*. The person called up for* שלישי *also reads the* הפטרה*. At* מנחה*, the* קריאת התורה *and* הפטרה *are those for regular Fast Days.*

דברים ד:כה–מ

FIRST ALIYA: vv. 25–29 Prophetical prediction that the Jewish People will be exiled from the land.

כִּֽי־תוֹלִ֤יד בָּנִים֙ וּבְנֵ֣י בָנִ֔ים וְנוֹשַׁנְתֶּ֖ם בָּאָ֑רֶץ וְהִשְׁחַתֶּ֗ם
וַעֲשִׂ֤יתֶם פֶּ֙סֶל֙ תְּמ֣וּנַת כֹּ֔ל וַעֲשִׂיתֶ֥ם הָרַ֛ע בְּעֵינֵ֥י־יהוָ֥ה אֱלֹהֶ֖יךָ
לְהַכְעִיסֽוֹ׃ הַעִידֹ֩תִי֩ בָכֶ֨ם הַיּ֜וֹם אֶת־הַשָּׁמַ֣יִם וְאֶת־הָאָ֗רֶץ
כִּֽי־אָבֹ֣ד תֹּאבֵדוּן֮ מַהֵר֒ מֵעַ֣ל הָאָ֔רֶץ אֲשֶׁ֨ר אַתֶּ֜ם עֹבְרִ֧ים אֶת־
הַיַּרְדֵּ֛ן שָׁ֖מָּה לְרִשְׁתָּ֑הּ לֹא־תַאֲרִיכֻ֤ן יָמִים֙ עָלֶ֔יהָ כִּ֥י הִשָּׁמֵ֖ד
תִּשָּׁמֵדֽוּן׃ וְהֵפִ֧יץ יהוָ֛ה אֶתְכֶ֖ם בָּעַמִּ֑ים וְנִשְׁאַרְתֶּם֙ מְתֵ֣י מִסְפָּ֔ר
בַּגּוֹיִ֕ם אֲשֶׁ֨ר יְנַהֵ֧ג יהוָ֛ה אֶתְכֶ֖ם שָֽׁמָּה׃ וַעֲבַדְתֶּם־שָׁ֣ם אֱלֹהִ֔ים
מַעֲשֵׂ֖ה יְדֵ֣י אָדָ֑ם עֵ֣ץ וָאֶ֔בֶן אֲשֶׁ֤ר לֹא־יִרְאוּן֙ וְלֹ֣א יִשְׁמְע֔וּן
וְלֹ֥א יֹֽאכְל֖וּן וְלֹ֥א יְרִיחֻֽן׃ וּבִקַּשְׁתֶּ֥ם מִשָּׁ֛ם אֶת־יהוָ֥ה אֱלֹהֶ֖יךָ
וּמָצָ֑אתָ כִּ֣י תִדְרְשֶׁ֔נּוּ בְּכָל־לְבָבְךָ֖ וּבְכָל־נַפְשֶֽׁךָ׃ *בַּצַּ֣ר לְךָ֔ לוי

SECOND ALIYA: vv. 30–34 God's promise that He will never forget or abandon His people, and will always remember the covenant between God and His people.

וּמְצָא֕וּךָ כֹּ֖ל הַדְּבָרִ֣ים הָאֵ֑לֶּה בְּאַחֲרִית֙ הַיָּמִ֔ים וְשַׁבְתָּ֙ עַד־
יהוָ֣ה אֱלֹהֶ֔יךָ וְשָׁמַעְתָּ֖ בְּקֹלֽוֹ׃ כִּ֣י אֵ֤ל רַחוּם֙ יהוָ֣ה אֱלֹהֶ֔יךָ
לֹ֥א יַרְפְּךָ֖ וְלֹ֣א יַשְׁחִיתֶ֑ךָ וְלֹ֤א יִשְׁכַּח֙ אֶת־בְּרִ֣ית אֲבֹתֶ֔יךָ
אֲשֶׁ֥ר נִשְׁבַּ֖ע לָהֶֽם׃ כִּ֣י שְׁאַל־נָ֠א לְיָמִ֨ים רִאשֹׁנִ֜ים אֲשֶׁר־הָי֣וּ
לְפָנֶ֗יךָ לְמִן־הַיּוֹם֙ אֲשֶׁר֩ בָּרָ֨א אֱלֹהִ֤ים ׀ אָדָם֙ עַל־הָאָ֔רֶץ
וּלְמִקְצֵ֥ה הַשָּׁמַ֖יִם וְעַד־קְצֵ֣ה הַשָּׁמָ֑יִם הֲנִהְיָ֗ה כַּדָּבָ֤ר הַגָּדוֹל֙
הַזֶּ֔ה א֖וֹ הֲנִשְׁמַ֥ע כָּמֹֽהוּ׃ הֲשָׁ֣מַע עָם֩ ק֨וֹל אֱלֹהִ֜ים מְדַבֵּ֤ר
מִתּוֹךְ־הָאֵשׁ֙ כַּאֲשֶׁר־שָׁמַ֥עְתָּ אַתָּ֖ה וַיֶּֽחִי׃ א֣וֹ ׀ הֲנִסָּ֣ה אֱלֹהִ֗ים

לָבוֹא לָקַחַת לוֹ גוֹי מִקֶּרֶב גּוֹי בְּמַסֹּת בְּאֹתֹת וּבְמוֹפְתִים
וּבְמִלְחָמָה וּבְיָד חֲזָקָה וּבִזְרוֹעַ נְטוּיָה וּבְמוֹרָאִים גְּדֹלִים
כְּכֹל אֲשֶׁר־עָשָׂה לָכֶם יְהוָה אֱלֹהֵיכֶם בְּמִצְרַיִם לְעֵינֶיךָ׃
אַתָּה הָרְאֵתָ לָדַעַת כִּי יְהוָה הוּא הָאֱלֹהִים אֵין עוֹד מִלְּבַדּוֹ׃
ישראל *מִן־הַשָּׁמַיִם הִשְׁמִיעֲךָ אֶת־קֹלוֹ לְיַסְּרֶךָּ וְעַל־הָאָרֶץ הֶרְאֲךָ

THIRD ALIYA: vv. 35–40 God's promise that if the people keep the Torah they will live safely in the land.

אֶת־אִשּׁוֹ הַגְּדוֹלָה וּדְבָרָיו שָׁמַעְתָּ מִתּוֹךְ הָאֵשׁ׃ וְתַחַת כִּי
אָהַב אֶת־אֲבֹתֶיךָ וַיִּבְחַר בְּזַרְעוֹ אַחֲרָיו וַיּוֹצִאֲךָ בְּפָנָיו בְּכֹחוֹ
הַגָּדֹל מִמִּצְרָיִם׃ לְהוֹרִישׁ גּוֹיִם גְּדֹלִים וַעֲצֻמִים מִמְּךָ מִפָּנֶיךָ
לַהֲבִיאֲךָ לָתֶת־לְךָ אֶת־אַרְצָם נַחֲלָה כַּיּוֹם הַזֶּה׃ וְיָדַעְתָּ
הַיּוֹם וַהֲשֵׁבֹתָ אֶל־לְבָבֶךָ כִּי יְהוָה הוּא הָאֱלֹהִים בַּשָּׁמַיִם
מִמַּעַל וְעַל־הָאָרֶץ מִתָּחַת אֵין עוֹד׃ וְשָׁמַרְתָּ אֶת־חֻקָּיו
וְאֶת־מִצְוֺתָיו אֲשֶׁר אָנֹכִי מְצַוְּךָ הַיּוֹם אֲשֶׁר יִיטַב לְךָ וּלְבָנֶיךָ
אַחֲרֶיךָ וּלְמַעַן תַּאֲרִיךְ יָמִים עַל־הָאֲדָמָה אֲשֶׁר יְהוָה אֱלֹהֶיךָ
נֹתֵן לְךָ כָּל־הַיָּמִים׃

HAFTARA FOR TISHA B'AV הפטרה לתשעה באב

The blessings before the הפטרה *can be found on page 1121.*

ירמיהו ח:יג–ט:כג

אָסֹף אֲסִיפֵם נְאֻם־יְהוָה אֵין עֲנָבִים בַּגֶּפֶן וְאֵין תְּאֵנִים
בַּתְּאֵנָה וְהֶעָלֶה נָבֵל וָאֶתֵּן לָהֶם יַעַבְרוּם׃ עַל־מָה אֲנַחְנוּ
יֹשְׁבִים הֵאָסְפוּ וְנָבוֹא אֶל־עָרֵי הַמִּבְצָר וְנִדְּמָה־שָּׁם כִּי יְהוָה
אֱלֹהֵינוּ הֲדִמָּנוּ וַיַּשְׁקֵנוּ מֵי־רֹאשׁ כִּי חָטָאנוּ לַיהוָה׃ קַוֵּה
לְשָׁלוֹם וְאֵין טוֹב לְעֵת מַרְפֵּה וְהִנֵּה בְעָתָה׃ מִדָּן נִשְׁמַע
נַחְרַת סוּסָיו מִקּוֹל מִצְהֲלוֹת אַבִּירָיו רָעֲשָׁה כָּל־הָאָרֶץ
וַיָּבוֹאוּ וַיֹּאכְלוּ אֶרֶץ וּמְלוֹאָהּ עִיר וְיֹשְׁבֵי בָהּ׃ כִּי הִנְנִי
מְשַׁלֵּחַ בָּכֶם נְחָשִׁים צִפְעֹנִים אֲשֶׁר אֵין־לָהֶם לָחַשׁ וְנִשְּׁכוּ
אֶתְכֶם נְאֻם־יְהוָה׃ מַבְלִיגִיתִי עֲלֵי יָגוֹן עָלַי לִבִּי
דַוָּי׃ הִנֵּה־קוֹל שַׁוְעַת בַּת־עַמִּי מֵאֶרֶץ מַרְחַקִּים הַיהוָה
אֵין בְּצִיּוֹן אִם־מַלְכָּהּ אֵין בָּהּ מַדּוּעַ הִכְעִסוּנִי בִּפְסִלֵיהֶם

HAFTARA FOR TISHA B'AV The *Haftara* consists of a number of different themes regarding the destruction of the *Beit HaMikdash*.

בְּהַבְלֵי נֵכָר׃ עָבַר קָצִיר כָּלָה קָיִץ וַאֲנַחְנוּ לוֹא נוֹשָׁעְנוּ׃
עַל־שֶׁבֶר בַּת־עַמִּי הָשְׁבָּרְתִּי קָדַרְתִּי שַׁמָּה הֶחֱזִקָתְנִי׃ הַצֳרִי
אֵין בְּגִלְעָד אִם־רֹפֵא אֵין שָׁם כִּי מַדּוּעַ לֹא עָלְתָה אֲרֻכַת
בַּת־עַמִּי׃ מִי־יִתֵּן רֹאשִׁי מַיִם וְעֵינִי מְקוֹר דִּמְעָה
וְאֶבְכֶּה יוֹמָם וָלַיְלָה אֵת חַלְלֵי בַת־עַמִּי׃ מִי־יִתְּנֵנִי בַמִּדְבָּר
מְלוֹן אֹרְחִים וְאֶעֶזְבָה אֶת־עַמִּי וְאֵלְכָה מֵאִתָּם כִּי כֻלָּם
מְנָאֲפִים עֲצֶרֶת בֹּגְדִים׃ וַיַּדְרְכוּ אֶת־לְשׁוֹנָם קַשְׁתָּם שֶׁקֶר
וְלֹא לֶאֱמוּנָה גָּבְרוּ בָאָרֶץ כִּי מֵרָעָה אֶל־רָעָה ׀ יָצָאוּ וְאֹתִי
לֹא־יָדָעוּ נְאֻם־יְהוָה׃ אִישׁ מֵרֵעֵהוּ הִשָּׁמֵרוּ וְעַל־כָּל־אָח אַל־
תִּבְטָחוּ כִּי כָל־אָח עָקוֹב יַעְקֹב וְכָל־רֵעַ רָכִיל יַהֲלֹךְ׃ וְאִישׁ
בְּרֵעֵהוּ יְהָתֵלּוּ וֶאֱמֶת לֹא יְדַבֵּרוּ לִמְּדוּ לְשׁוֹנָם דַּבֶּר־שֶׁקֶר
הַעֲוֵה נִלְאוּ׃ שִׁבְתְּךָ בְּתוֹךְ מִרְמָה בְּמִרְמָה מֵאֲנוּ דַעַת־אוֹתִי
נְאֻם־יְהוָה׃ לָכֵן כֹּה אָמַר יְהוָה צְבָאוֹת הִנְנִי
צוֹרְפָם וּבְחַנְתִּים כִּי־אֵיךְ אֶעֱשֶׂה מִפְּנֵי בַּת־עַמִּי׃ חֵץ שׁוחט שָׁחוּט
לְשׁוֹנָם מִרְמָה דִבֵּר בְּפִיו שָׁלוֹם אֶת־רֵעֵהוּ יְדַבֵּר וּבְקִרְבּוֹ
יָשִׂים אָרְבּוֹ׃ הַעַל־אֵלֶּה לֹא־אֶפְקָד־בָּם נְאֻם־יְהוָה אִם בְּגוֹי
אֲשֶׁר־כָּזֶה לֹא תִתְנַקֵּם נַפְשִׁי׃ עַל־הֶהָרִים אֶשָּׂא
בְכִי וָנֶהִי וְעַל־נְאוֹת מִדְבָּר קִינָה כִּי נִצְּתוּ מִבְּלִי־אִישׁ עֹבֵר
וְלֹא שָׁמְעוּ קוֹל מִקְנֶה מֵעוֹף הַשָּׁמַיִם וְעַד־בְּהֵמָה נָדְדוּ
הָלָכוּ׃ וְנָתַתִּי אֶת־יְרוּשָׁלִַם לְגַלִּים מְעוֹן תַּנִּים וְאֶת־עָרֵי
יְהוּדָה אֶתֵּן שְׁמָמָה מִבְּלִי יוֹשֵׁב׃ מִי־הָאִישׁ
הֶחָכָם וְיָבֵן אֶת־זֹאת וַאֲשֶׁר דִּבֶּר פִּי־יְהוָה אֵלָיו וְיַגִּדָהּ עַל־מָה
אָבְדָה הָאָרֶץ נִצְּתָה כַמִּדְבָּר מִבְּלִי עֹבֵר׃ וַיֹּאמֶר
יְהוָה עַל־עָזְבָם אֶת־תּוֹרָתִי אֲשֶׁר נָתַתִּי לִפְנֵיהֶם וְלֹא־
שָׁמְעוּ בְקוֹלִי וְלֹא־הָלְכוּ בָהּ׃ וַיֵּלְכוּ אַחֲרֵי שְׁרִרוּת לִבָּם
וְאַחֲרֵי הַבְּעָלִים אֲשֶׁר לִמְּדוּם אֲבוֹתָם׃ לָכֵן
כֹּה־אָמַר יְהוָה צְבָאוֹת אֱלֹהֵי יִשְׂרָאֵל הִנְנִי מַאֲכִילָם
אֶת־הָעָם הַזֶּה לַעֲנָה וְהִשְׁקִיתִים מֵי־רֹאשׁ׃ וַהֲפִצוֹתִים

בַּגּוֹיִם אֲשֶׁר לֹא יָדְעוּ הֵמָּה וַאֲבוֹתָם וְשִׁלַּחְתִּי אַחֲרֵיהֶם
אֶת־הַחֶרֶב עַד כַּלּוֹתִי אוֹתָם׃ כֹּה אָמַר יהוה
צְבָאוֹת הִתְבּוֹנְנוּ וְקִרְאוּ לַמְקוֹנְנוֹת וּתְבוֹאֶינָה וְאֶל־
הַחֲכָמוֹת שִׁלְחוּ וְתָבוֹאנָה׃ וּתְמַהֵרְנָה וְתִשֶּׂנָה עָלֵינוּ נֶהִי
וְתֵרַדְנָה עֵינֵינוּ דִּמְעָה וְעַפְעַפֵּינוּ יִזְּלוּ־מָיִם׃ כִּי קוֹל נְהִי
נִשְׁמַע מִצִּיּוֹן אֵיךְ שֻׁדָּדְנוּ בֹּשְׁנוּ מְאֹד כִּי־עָזַבְנוּ אָרֶץ כִּי
הִשְׁלִיכוּ מִשְׁכְּנוֹתֵינוּ׃ כִּי־שְׁמַעְנָה נָשִׁים דְּבַר־
יהוה וְתִקַּח אָזְנְכֶם דְּבַר־פִּיו וְלַמֵּדְנָה בְנוֹתֵיכֶם נֶהִי וְאִשָּׁה
רְעוּתָהּ קִינָה׃ כִּי־עָלָה מָוֶת בְּחַלּוֹנֵינוּ בָּא בְּאַרְמְנוֹתֵינוּ
לְהַכְרִית עוֹלָל מִחוּץ בַּחוּרִים מֵרְחֹבוֹת׃ דַּבֵּר כֹּה נְאֻם־
יהוה וְנָפְלָה נִבְלַת הָאָדָם כְּדֹמֶן עַל־פְּנֵי הַשָּׂדֶה וּכְעָמִיר
מֵאַחֲרֵי הַקֹּצֵר וְאֵין מְאַסֵּף׃ כֹּה ׀ אָמַר יהוה
אַל־יִתְהַלֵּל חָכָם בְּחָכְמָתוֹ וְאַל־יִתְהַלֵּל הַגִּבּוֹר בִּגְבוּרָתוֹ
אַל־יִתְהַלֵּל עָשִׁיר בְּעָשְׁרוֹ׃ כִּי אִם־בְּזֹאת יִתְהַלֵּל הַמִּתְהַלֵּל
הַשְׂכֵּל וְיָדֹעַ אוֹתִי כִּי אֲנִי יהוה עֹשֶׂה חֶסֶד מִשְׁפָּט וּצְדָקָה
בָּאָרֶץ כִּי־בְאֵלֶּה חָפַצְתִּי נְאֻם־יהוה׃

The blessings after the הפטרה *can be found on page 1122.*

קריאה ליום הראשון של חנוכה
FIRST DAY OF ḤANUKKA

במדבר ז:א–יז

וַיְהִי בְּיוֹם כַּלּוֹת מֹשֶׁה לְהָקִים אֶת־הַמִּשְׁכָּן וַיִּמְשַׁח אֹתוֹ
וַיְקַדֵּשׁ אֹתוֹ וְאֶת־כָּל־כֵּלָיו וְאֶת־הַמִּזְבֵּחַ וְאֶת־כָּל־כֵּלָיו
וַיִּמְשָׁחֵם וַיְקַדֵּשׁ אֹתָם׃ וַיַּקְרִיבוּ נְשִׂיאֵי יִשְׂרָאֵל רָאשֵׁי בֵּית
אֲבֹתָם הֵם נְשִׂיאֵי הַמַּטֹּת הֵם הָעֹמְדִים עַל־הַפְּקֻדִים׃ וַיָּבִיאוּ
אֶת־קָרְבָּנָם לִפְנֵי יהוה שֵׁשׁ־עֶגְלֹת צָב וּשְׁנֵי־עָשָׂר בָּקָר עֲגָלָה
עַל־שְׁנֵי הַנְּשִׂאִים וְשׁוֹר לְאֶחָד וַיַּקְרִיבוּ אוֹתָם לִפְנֵי הַמִּשְׁכָּן׃
וַיֹּאמֶר יהוה אֶל־מֹשֶׁה לֵּאמֹר׃ קַח מֵאִתָּם וְהָיוּ לַעֲבֹד
אֶת־עֲבֹדַת אֹהֶל מוֹעֵד וְנָתַתָּה אוֹתָם אֶל־הַלְוִיִּם אִישׁ כְּפִי
עֲבֹדָתוֹ׃ וַיִּקַּח מֹשֶׁה אֶת־הָעֲגָלֹת וְאֶת־הַבָּקָר וַיִּתֵּן אוֹתָם

ḤANUKKA
Introduction to the offerings of the tribal leaders in dedication of the *Mishkan* and the offering of the first tribe – Naḥshon ben Aminadav of the tribe of Yehuda.

אֶל־הַלְוִיִּם׃ אֵת ׀ שְׁתֵּי הָעֲגָלוֹת וְאֵת אַרְבַּעַת הַבָּקָר נָתַן
לִבְנֵי גֵרְשׁוֹן כְּפִי עֲבֹדָתָם׃ וְאֵת ׀ אַרְבַּע הָעֲגָלֹת וְאֵת שְׁמֹנַת
הַבָּקָר נָתַן לִבְנֵי מְרָרִי כְּפִי עֲבֹדָתָם בְּיַד אִיתָמָר בֶּן־אַהֲרֹן
הַכֹּהֵן׃ וְלִבְנֵי קְהָת לֹא נָתָן כִּי־עֲבֹדַת הַקֹּדֶשׁ עֲלֵהֶם בַּכָּתֵף
יִשָּׂאוּ׃ וַיַּקְרִיבוּ הַנְּשִׂאִים אֵת חֲנֻכַּת הַמִּזְבֵּחַ בְּיוֹם הִמָּשַׁח
אֹתוֹ וַיַּקְרִיבוּ הַנְּשִׂיאִם אֶת־קָרְבָּנָם לִפְנֵי הַמִּזְבֵּחַ׃ וַיֹּאמֶר
יהוה אֶל־מֹשֶׁה נָשִׂיא אֶחָד לַיּוֹם נָשִׂיא אֶחָד לַיּוֹם יַקְרִיבוּ
אֶת־קָרְבָּנָם לַחֲנֻכַּת הַמִּזְבֵּחַ׃ *וַיְהִי הַמַּקְרִיב לוי
בַּיּוֹם הָרִאשׁוֹן אֶת־קָרְבָּנוֹ נַחְשׁוֹן בֶּן־עַמִּינָדָב לְמַטֵּה יְהוּדָה׃
וְקָרְבָּנוֹ קַעֲרַת־כֶּסֶף אַחַת שְׁלֹשִׁים וּמֵאָה מִשְׁקָלָהּ מִזְרָק
אֶחָד כֶּסֶף שִׁבְעִים שֶׁקֶל בְּשֶׁקֶל הַקֹּדֶשׁ שְׁנֵיהֶם ׀ מְלֵאִים
סֹלֶת בְּלוּלָה בַשֶּׁמֶן לְמִנְחָה׃ כַּף אַחַת עֲשָׂרָה זָהָב מְלֵאָה
קְטֹרֶת׃ *פַּר אֶחָד בֶּן־בָּקָר אַיִל אֶחָד כֶּבֶשׂ־אֶחָד בֶּן־שְׁנָתוֹ ישראל
לְעֹלָה׃ שְׂעִיר־עִזִּים אֶחָד לְחַטָּאת׃ וּלְזֶבַח הַשְּׁלָמִים בָּקָר
שְׁנַיִם אֵילִם חֲמִשָּׁה עַתּוּדִים חֲמִשָּׁה כְּבָשִׂים בְּנֵי־שָׁנָה
חֲמִשָּׁה זֶה קָרְבַּן נַחְשׁוֹן בֶּן־עַמִּינָדָב׃

קריאה ליום השני של חנוכה

SECOND DAY OF HANUKKA

In ארץ ישראל, *for* שלישי *repeat the first paragraph:* נְתַנְאֵל בֶּן־צוּעָר *until* בַּיּוֹם הַשֵּׁנִי.

במדבר ז: יח–כט

The offering of Netanel ben Tzu'ar of the tribe of Yissakhar.

בַּיּוֹם הַשֵּׁנִי הִקְרִיב נְתַנְאֵל בֶּן־צוּעָר נְשִׂיא יִשָּׂשכָר׃ הִקְרִב
אֶת־קָרְבָּנוֹ קַעֲרַת־כֶּסֶף אַחַת שְׁלֹשִׁים וּמֵאָה מִשְׁקָלָהּ מִזְרָק
אֶחָד כֶּסֶף שִׁבְעִים שֶׁקֶל בְּשֶׁקֶל הַקֹּדֶשׁ שְׁנֵיהֶם ׀ מְלֵאִים
סֹלֶת בְּלוּלָה בַשֶּׁמֶן לְמִנְחָה׃ כַּף אַחַת עֲשָׂרָה זָהָב מְלֵאָה
קְטֹרֶת׃ *פַּר אֶחָד בֶּן־בָּקָר אַיִל אֶחָד כֶּבֶשׂ־אֶחָד בֶּן־שְׁנָתוֹ לוי
לְעֹלָה׃ שְׂעִיר־עִזִּים אֶחָד לְחַטָּאת׃ וּלְזֶבַח הַשְּׁלָמִים בָּקָר
שְׁנַיִם אֵילִם חֲמִשָּׁה עַתֻּדִים חֲמִשָּׁה כְּבָשִׂים בְּנֵי־שָׁנָה חֲמִשָּׁה
זֶה קָרְבַּן נְתַנְאֵל בֶּן־צוּעָר׃

ישראל בַּיּוֹם הַשְּׁלִישִׁי נָשִׂיא לִבְנֵי זְבוּלֻן אֱלִיאָב בֶּן־חֵלֹן׃ קָרְבָּנוֹ
קַעֲרַת־כֶּסֶף אַחַת שְׁלֹשִׁים וּמֵאָה מִשְׁקָלָהּ מִזְרָק אֶחָד
כֶּסֶף שִׁבְעִים שֶׁקֶל בְּשֶׁקֶל הַקֹּדֶשׁ שְׁנֵיהֶם ׀ מְלֵאִים סֹלֶת
בְּלוּלָה בַשֶּׁמֶן לְמִנְחָה׃ כַּף אַחַת עֲשָׂרָה זָהָב מְלֵאָה קְטֹרֶת׃
פַּר אֶחָד בֶּן־בָּקָר אַיִל אֶחָד כֶּבֶשׂ־אֶחָד בֶּן־שְׁנָתוֹ לְעֹלָה׃
שְׂעִיר־עִזִּים אֶחָד לְחַטָּאת׃ וּלְזֶבַח הַשְּׁלָמִים בָּקָר שְׁנַיִם
אֵילִם חֲמִשָּׁה עַתֻּדִים חֲמִשָּׁה כְּבָשִׂים בְּנֵי־שָׁנָה חֲמִשָּׁה זֶה
קָרְבַּן אֱלִיאָב בֶּן־חֵלֹן׃

קריאה ליום השלישי של חנוכה

THIRD DAY OF ḤANUKKA

In ארץ ישראל, *for* שלישי *repeat the first paragraph:* בַּיּוֹם הַשְּׁלִישִׁי *until* אֱלִיאָב בֶּן־חֵלֹן.

במדבר ז:כד–לה

The offering of Eliav ben Ḥelon of the tribe of Zevulun.

בַּיּוֹם הַשְּׁלִישִׁי נָשִׂיא לִבְנֵי זְבוּלֻן אֱלִיאָב בֶּן־חֵלֹן׃ קָרְבָּנוֹ
קַעֲרַת־כֶּסֶף אַחַת שְׁלֹשִׁים וּמֵאָה מִשְׁקָלָהּ מִזְרָק אֶחָד
כֶּסֶף שִׁבְעִים שֶׁקֶל בְּשֶׁקֶל הַקֹּדֶשׁ שְׁנֵיהֶם ׀ מְלֵאִים סֹלֶת
בְּלוּלָה בַשֶּׁמֶן לְמִנְחָה׃ כַּף אַחַת עֲשָׂרָה זָהָב מְלֵאָה קְטֹרֶת׃
לוי *פַּר אֶחָד בֶּן־בָּקָר אַיִל אֶחָד כֶּבֶשׂ־אֶחָד בֶּן־שְׁנָתוֹ לְעֹלָה׃
שְׂעִיר־עִזִּים אֶחָד לְחַטָּאת׃ וּלְזֶבַח הַשְּׁלָמִים בָּקָר שְׁנַיִם
אֵילִם חֲמִשָּׁה עַתֻּדִים חֲמִשָּׁה כְּבָשִׂים בְּנֵי־שָׁנָה חֲמִשָּׁה זֶה
קָרְבַּן אֱלִיאָב בֶּן־חֵלֹן׃

ישראל בַּיּוֹם הָרְבִיעִי נָשִׂיא לִבְנֵי רְאוּבֵן אֱלִיצוּר בֶּן־שְׁדֵיאוּר׃ קָרְבָּנוֹ
קַעֲרַת־כֶּסֶף אַחַת שְׁלֹשִׁים וּמֵאָה מִשְׁקָלָהּ מִזְרָק אֶחָד
כֶּסֶף שִׁבְעִים שֶׁקֶל בְּשֶׁקֶל הַקֹּדֶשׁ שְׁנֵיהֶם ׀ מְלֵאִים סֹלֶת
בְּלוּלָה בַשֶּׁמֶן לְמִנְחָה׃ כַּף אַחַת עֲשָׂרָה זָהָב מְלֵאָה קְטֹרֶת׃
פַּר אֶחָד בֶּן־בָּקָר אַיִל אֶחָד כֶּבֶשׂ־אֶחָד בֶּן־שְׁנָתוֹ לְעֹלָה׃
שְׂעִיר־עִזִּים אֶחָד לְחַטָּאת׃ וּלְזֶבַח הַשְּׁלָמִים בָּקָר שְׁנַיִם
אֵילִם חֲמִשָּׁה עַתֻּדִים חֲמִשָּׁה כְּבָשִׂים בְּנֵי־שָׁנָה חֲמִשָּׁה זֶה
קָרְבַּן אֱלִיצוּר בֶּן־שְׁדֵיאוּר׃

קריאה ליום הרביעי של חנוכה

FOURTH DAY OF ḤANUKKA

In ארץ ישראל, *for* שלישי *repeat the first paragraph:* אֱלִיצוּר בֶּן־שְׁדֵיאוּר *until* בַּיּוֹם הָרְבִיעִי.

The offering of Elitzur ben Shede'ur of the tribe of Reuven.

במדבר ז:ל–מא בַּיּוֹם הָרְבִיעִי נָשִׂיא לִבְנֵי רְאוּבֵן אֱלִיצוּר בֶּן־שְׁדֵיאוּר: קָרְבָּנוֹ
קַעֲרַת־כֶּסֶף אַחַת שְׁלֹשִׁים וּמֵאָה מִשְׁקָלָהּ מִזְרָק אֶחָד
כֶּסֶף שִׁבְעִים שֶׁקֶל בְּשֶׁקֶל הַקֹּדֶשׁ שְׁנֵיהֶם ׀ מְלֵאִים סֹלֶת
בְּלוּלָה בַשֶּׁמֶן לְמִנְחָה: כַּף אַחַת עֲשָׂרָה זָהָב מְלֵאָה קְטֹרֶת:
לוי *פַּר אֶחָד בֶּן־בָּקָר אַיִל אֶחָד כֶּבֶשׂ־אֶחָד בֶּן־שְׁנָתוֹ לְעֹלָה:
שְׂעִיר־עִזִּים אֶחָד לְחַטָּאת: וּלְזֶבַח הַשְּׁלָמִים בָּקָר שְׁנַיִם
אֵילִם חֲמִשָּׁה עַתֻּדִים חֲמִשָּׁה כְּבָשִׂים בְּנֵי־שָׁנָה חֲמִשָּׁה זֶה
קָרְבַּן אֱלִיצוּר בֶּן־שְׁדֵיאוּר:
ישראל בַּיּוֹם הַחֲמִישִׁי נָשִׂיא לִבְנֵי שִׁמְעוֹן שְׁלֻמִיאֵל בֶּן־צוּרִישַׁדָּי:
קָרְבָּנוֹ קַעֲרַת־כֶּסֶף אַחַת שְׁלֹשִׁים וּמֵאָה מִשְׁקָלָהּ מִזְרָק
אֶחָד כֶּסֶף שִׁבְעִים שֶׁקֶל בְּשֶׁקֶל הַקֹּדֶשׁ שְׁנֵיהֶם ׀ מְלֵאִים
סֹלֶת בְּלוּלָה בַשֶּׁמֶן לְמִנְחָה: כַּף אַחַת עֲשָׂרָה זָהָב מְלֵאָה
קְטֹרֶת: פַּר אֶחָד בֶּן־בָּקָר אַיִל אֶחָד כֶּבֶשׂ־אֶחָד בֶּן־שְׁנָתוֹ
לְעֹלָה: שְׂעִיר־עִזִּים אֶחָד לְחַטָּאת: וּלְזֶבַח הַשְּׁלָמִים בָּקָר
שְׁנַיִם אֵילִם חֲמִשָּׁה עַתֻּדִים חֲמִשָּׁה כְּבָשִׂים בְּנֵי־שָׁנָה חֲמִשָּׁה
זֶה קָרְבַּן שְׁלֻמִיאֵל בֶּן־צוּרִישַׁדָּי:

קריאה ליום החמישי של חנוכה

FIFTH DAY OF ḤANUKKA

In ארץ ישראל, *for* שלישי *repeat the first paragraph:* שְׁלֻמִיאֵל בֶּן־צוּרִישַׁדָּי *until* בַּיּוֹם הַחֲמִישִׁי.

The offering of Shelumiel ben Tzurishadai of the tribe of Shimon.

במדבר ז:לו–מז בַּיּוֹם הַחֲמִישִׁי נָשִׂיא לִבְנֵי שִׁמְעוֹן שְׁלֻמִיאֵל בֶּן־צוּרִישַׁדָּי:
קָרְבָּנוֹ קַעֲרַת־כֶּסֶף אַחַת שְׁלֹשִׁים וּמֵאָה מִשְׁקָלָהּ מִזְרָק
אֶחָד כֶּסֶף שִׁבְעִים שֶׁקֶל בְּשֶׁקֶל הַקֹּדֶשׁ שְׁנֵיהֶם ׀ מְלֵאִים
סֹלֶת בְּלוּלָה בַשֶּׁמֶן לְמִנְחָה: כַּף אַחַת עֲשָׂרָה זָהָב מְלֵאָה

לוי קְטֹֽרֶת׃ *פַּ֣ר אֶחָ֞ד בֶּן־בָּקָ֗ר אַ֧יִל אֶחָ֛ד כֶּֽבֶשׂ־אֶחָ֥ד בֶּן־שְׁנָת֖וֹ
לְעֹלָֽה׃ שְׂעִיר־עִזִּ֥ים אֶחָ֖ד לְחַטָּֽאת׃ וּלְזֶ֣בַח הַשְּׁלָמִים֮ בָּקָ֣ר
שְׁנַ֒יִם֒ אֵילִ֤ם חֲמִשָּׁה֙ עַתֻּדִ֣ים חֲמִשָּׁ֔ה כְּבָשִׂ֥ים בְּנֵי־שָׁנָ֖ה חֲמִשָּׁ֑ה
זֶ֛ה קָרְבַּ֥ן שְׁלֻמִיאֵ֖ל בֶּן־צוּרִֽישַׁדָּֽי׃

ישראל בַּיּוֹם֙ הַשִּׁשִּׁ֔י נָשִׂ֖יא לִבְנֵ֣י גָ֑ד אֶלְיָסָ֖ף בֶּן־דְּעוּאֵֽל׃ קָרְבָּנ֞וֹ
קַֽעֲרַת־כֶּ֣סֶף אַחַ֗ת שְׁלֹשִׁ֣ים וּמֵאָה֮ מִשְׁקָלָהּ֒ מִזְרָ֤ק אֶחָד֙
כֶּ֔סֶף שִׁבְעִ֥ים שֶׁ֖קֶל בְּשֶׁ֣קֶל הַקֹּ֑דֶשׁ שְׁנֵיהֶ֣ם ׀ מְלֵאִ֗ים סֹ֛לֶת
בְּלוּלָ֥ה בַשֶּׁ֖מֶן לְמִנְחָֽה׃ כַּ֥ף אַחַ֛ת עֲשָׂרָ֥ה זָהָ֖ב מְלֵאָ֥ה קְטֹֽרֶת׃
פַּ֣ר אֶחָ֞ד בֶּן־בָּקָ֗ר אַ֧יִל אֶחָ֛ד כֶּֽבֶשׂ־אֶחָ֥ד בֶּן־שְׁנָת֖וֹ לְעֹלָֽה׃
שְׂעִיר־עִזִּ֥ים אֶחָ֖ד לְחַטָּֽאת׃ וּלְזֶ֣בַח הַשְּׁלָמִים֮ בָּקָ֣ר שְׁנַ֒יִם֒
אֵילִ֤ם חֲמִשָּׁה֙ עַתֻּדִ֣ים חֲמִשָּׁ֔ה כְּבָשִׂ֥ים בְּנֵי־שָׁנָ֖ה חֲמִשָּׁ֑ה זֶ֛ה
קָרְבַּ֥ן אֶלְיָסָ֖ף בֶּן־דְּעוּאֵֽל׃

קריאה ליום השישי של חנוכה וראש חודש

SIXTH DAY OF ḤANUKKA AND ROSH ḤODESH

The sixth day is ראש חודש טבת. *Two* ספרי תורה *are taken out of the* ארון קודש. *From the first, read the* קריאת התורה *for* ראש חודש *(page 1119)*, *from the second, read* בַּיּוֹם הַשִּׁשִּׁי:

במדבר ז:מב–מז בַּיּוֹם֙ הַשִּׁשִּׁ֔י נָשִׂ֖יא לִבְנֵ֣י גָ֑ד אֶלְיָסָ֖ף בֶּן־דְּעוּאֵֽל׃ קָרְבָּנ֞וֹ
קַֽעֲרַת־כֶּ֣סֶף אַחַ֗ת שְׁלֹשִׁ֣ים וּמֵאָה֮ מִשְׁקָלָהּ֒ מִזְרָ֤ק אֶחָד֙
כֶּ֔סֶף שִׁבְעִ֥ים שֶׁ֖קֶל בְּשֶׁ֣קֶל הַקֹּ֑דֶשׁ שְׁנֵיהֶ֣ם ׀ מְלֵאִ֗ים סֹ֛לֶת
בְּלוּלָ֥ה בַשֶּׁ֖מֶן לְמִנְחָֽה׃ כַּ֥ף אַחַ֛ת עֲשָׂרָ֥ה זָהָ֖ב מְלֵאָ֥ה קְטֹֽרֶת׃
פַּ֣ר אֶחָ֞ד בֶּן־בָּקָ֗ר אַ֧יִל אֶחָ֛ד כֶּֽבֶשׂ־אֶחָ֥ד בֶּן־שְׁנָת֖וֹ לְעֹלָֽה׃
שְׂעִיר־עִזִּ֥ים אֶחָ֖ד לְחַטָּֽאת׃ וּלְזֶ֣בַח הַשְּׁלָמִים֮ בָּקָ֣ר שְׁנַ֒יִם֒
אֵילִ֤ם חֲמִשָּׁה֙ עַתֻּדִ֣ים חֲמִשָּׁ֔ה כְּבָשִׂ֥ים בְּנֵי־שָׁנָ֖ה חֲמִשָּׁ֑ה זֶ֛ה
קָרְבַּ֥ן אֶלְיָסָ֖ף בֶּן־דְּעוּאֵֽל׃

The offering of Elyasaf ben Deu'el of the tribe of Gad

קריאה ליום השביעי של חנוכה וראש חודש

SEVENTH DAY OF ḤANUKKA AND ROSH ḤODESH

If the seventh day is also ראש חודש*, then two* ספרי תורה *are taken out of the* ארון קודש*. From the first, read the* קריאת התורה *for* ראש חודש *(page 1119)**, from the second, read* בַּיּוֹם הַשְּׁבִיעִי*:*

במדבר ז: מח–נג

The offering of Elishama ben Amihud of the tribe of Efraim.

בַּיּוֹם֙ הַשְּׁבִיעִ֔י נָשִׂ֖יא לִבְנֵ֣י אֶפְרָ֑יִם אֱלִֽישָׁמָ֖ע בֶּן־עַמִּיהֽוּד׃ קׇרְבָּנ֞וֹ קַֽעֲרַת־כֶּ֣סֶף אַחַ֗ת שְׁלֹשִׁ֣ים וּמֵאָה֮ מִשְׁקָלָהּ֒ מִזְרָ֤ק אֶחָד֙ כֶּ֔סֶף שִׁבְעִ֥ים שֶׁ֖קֶל בְּשֶׁ֣קֶל הַקֹּ֑דֶשׁ שְׁנֵיהֶ֣ם ׀ מְלֵאִ֗ים סֹ֛לֶת בְּלוּלָ֥ה בַשֶּׁ֖מֶן לְמִנְחָֽה׃ כַּ֥ף אַחַ֛ת עֲשָׂרָ֥ה זָהָ֖ב מְלֵאָ֥ה קְטֹֽרֶת׃ פַּ֣ר אֶחָד֩ בֶּן־בָּקָ֜ר אַ֧יִל אֶחָ֛ד כֶּֽבֶשׂ־אֶחָ֥ד בֶּן־שְׁנָת֖וֹ לְעֹלָֽה׃ שְׂעִיר־עִזִּ֥ים אֶחָ֖ד לְחַטָּֽאת׃ וּלְזֶ֣בַח הַשְּׁלָמִים֮ בָּקָ֣ר שְׁנַ֒יִם֒ אֵילִ֤ם חֲמִשָּׁה֙ עַתֻּדִ֣ים חֲמִשָּׁ֔ה כְּבָשִׂ֥ים בְּנֵֽי־שָׁנָ֖ה חֲמִשָּׁ֑ה זֶ֛ה קׇרְבַּ֥ן אֱלִישָׁמָ֖ע בֶּן־עַמִּיהֽוּד׃

קריאה ליום השביעי של חנוכה

SEVENTH DAY OF ḤANUKKA

If the seventh day is not ראש חודש*, then read as below.*
In ארץ ישראל*, for* שלישי *repeat the first paragraph:*
בַּיּוֹם הַשְּׁבִיעִי *until* אֱלִישָׁמָע בֶּן־עַמִּיהוּד*.*

במדבר ז: מח–נט

בַּיּוֹם֙ הַשְּׁבִיעִ֔י נָשִׂ֖יא לִבְנֵ֣י אֶפְרָ֑יִם אֱלִֽישָׁמָ֖ע בֶּן־עַמִּיהֽוּד׃ קׇרְבָּנ֞וֹ קַֽעֲרַת־כֶּ֣סֶף אַחַ֗ת שְׁלֹשִׁ֣ים וּמֵאָה֮ מִשְׁקָלָהּ֒ מִזְרָ֤ק אֶחָד֙ כֶּ֔סֶף שִׁבְעִ֥ים שֶׁ֖קֶל בְּשֶׁ֣קֶל הַקֹּ֑דֶשׁ שְׁנֵיהֶ֣ם ׀ מְלֵאִ֗ים סֹ֛לֶת בְּלוּלָ֥ה בַשֶּׁ֖מֶן לְמִנְחָֽה׃ כַּ֥ף אַחַ֛ת עֲשָׂרָ֥ה זָהָ֖ב מְלֵאָ֥ה קְטֹֽרֶת׃

לוי ⋆פַּ֣ר אֶחָד֩ בֶּן־בָּקָ֜ר אַ֧יִל אֶחָ֛ד כֶּֽבֶשׂ־אֶחָ֥ד בֶּן־שְׁנָת֖וֹ לְעֹלָֽה׃ שְׂעִיר־עִזִּ֥ים אֶחָ֖ד לְחַטָּֽאת׃ וּלְזֶ֣בַח הַשְּׁלָמִים֮ בָּקָ֣ר שְׁנַ֒יִם֒ אֵילִ֤ם חֲמִשָּׁה֙ עַתֻּדִ֣ים חֲמִשָּׁ֔ה כְּבָשִׂ֥ים בְּנֵֽי־שָׁנָ֖ה חֲמִשָּׁ֑ה זֶ֛ה קׇרְבַּ֥ן אֱלִישָׁמָ֖ע בֶּן־עַמִּיהֽוּד׃

ישראל בַּיּוֹם הַשְּׁמִינִי נָשִׂיא לִבְנֵי מְנַשֶּׁה גַּמְלִיאֵל בֶּן־פְּדָהצוּר: קָרְבָּנוֹ קַעֲרַת־כֶּסֶף אַחַת שְׁלֹשִׁים וּמֵאָה מִשְׁקָלָהּ מִזְרָק אֶחָד כֶּסֶף שִׁבְעִים שֶׁקֶל בְּשֶׁקֶל הַקֹּדֶשׁ שְׁנֵיהֶם ׀ מְלֵאִים סֹלֶת בְּלוּלָה בַשֶּׁמֶן לְמִנְחָה: כַּף אַחַת עֲשָׂרָה זָהָב מְלֵאָה קְטֹרֶת: פַּר אֶחָד בֶּן־בָּקָר אַיִל אֶחָד כֶּבֶשׂ־אֶחָד בֶּן־שְׁנָתוֹ לְעֹלָה: שְׂעִיר־עִזִּים אֶחָד לְחַטָּאת: וּלְזֶבַח הַשְּׁלָמִים בָּקָר שְׁנַיִם אֵילִם חֲמִשָּׁה עַתֻּדִים חֲמִשָּׁה כְּבָשִׂים בְּנֵי־שָׁנָה חֲמִשָּׁה זֶה קָרְבַּן גַּמְלִיאֵל בֶּן־פְּדָהצוּר:

קריאה ליום השמיני של חנוכה

EIGHTH DAY OF HANUKKA

במדבר ז:נד–ח:ד בַּיּוֹם הַשְּׁמִינִי נָשִׂיא לִבְנֵי מְנַשֶּׁה גַּמְלִיאֵל בֶּן־פְּדָהצוּר: קָרְבָּנוֹ קַעֲרַת־כֶּסֶף אַחַת שְׁלֹשִׁים וּמֵאָה מִשְׁקָלָהּ מִזְרָק אֶחָד כֶּסֶף שִׁבְעִים שֶׁקֶל בְּשֶׁקֶל הַקֹּדֶשׁ שְׁנֵיהֶם ׀ מְלֵאִים סֹלֶת בְּלוּלָה בַשֶּׁמֶן לְמִנְחָה: כַּף אַחַת עֲשָׂרָה זָהָב מְלֵאָה קְטֹרֶת:

The reading for the final day of Ḥanukka has the offerings from the remaining tribes.

לוי *פַּר אֶחָד בֶּן־בָּקָר אַיִל אֶחָד כֶּבֶשׂ־אֶחָד בֶּן־שְׁנָתוֹ לְעֹלָה: שְׂעִיר־עִזִּים אֶחָד לְחַטָּאת: וּלְזֶבַח הַשְּׁלָמִים בָּקָר שְׁנַיִם אֵילִם חֲמִשָּׁה עַתֻּדִים חֲמִשָּׁה כְּבָשִׂים בְּנֵי־שָׁנָה חֲמִשָּׁה זֶה קָרְבַּן גַּמְלִיאֵל בֶּן־פְּדָהצוּר:

ישראל בַּיּוֹם הַתְּשִׁיעִי נָשִׂיא לִבְנֵי בִנְיָמִן אֲבִידָן בֶּן־גִּדְעֹנִי: קָרְבָּנוֹ קַעֲרַת־כֶּסֶף אַחַת שְׁלֹשִׁים וּמֵאָה מִשְׁקָלָהּ מִזְרָק אֶחָד כֶּסֶף שִׁבְעִים שֶׁקֶל בְּשֶׁקֶל הַקֹּדֶשׁ שְׁנֵיהֶם ׀ מְלֵאִים סֹלֶת בְּלוּלָה בַשֶּׁמֶן לְמִנְחָה: כַּף אַחַת עֲשָׂרָה זָהָב מְלֵאָה קְטֹרֶת: פַּר אֶחָד בֶּן־בָּקָר אַיִל אֶחָד כֶּבֶשׂ־אֶחָד בֶּן־שְׁנָתוֹ לְעֹלָה: שְׂעִיר־עִזִּים אֶחָד לְחַטָּאת: וּלְזֶבַח הַשְּׁלָמִים בָּקָר שְׁנַיִם אֵילִם חֲמִשָּׁה עַתֻּדִים חֲמִשָּׁה כְּבָשִׂים בְּנֵי־שָׁנָה חֲמִשָּׁה זֶה קָרְבַּן אֲבִידָן בֶּן־גִּדְעֹנִי:

בַּיּוֹם הָעֲשִׂירִי נָשִׂיא לִבְנֵי דָן אֲחִיעֶזֶר בֶּן־עַמִּישַׁדָּי: קָרְבָּנוֹ קַעֲרַת־כֶּסֶף אַחַת שְׁלֹשִׁים וּמֵאָה מִשְׁקָלָהּ מִזְרָק אֶחָד

כֶּ֛סֶף שִׁבְעִ֥ים שֶׁ֖קֶל בְּשֶׁ֣קֶל הַקֹּ֑דֶשׁ שְׁנֵיהֶ֣ם ׀ מְלֵאִ֗ים סֹ֛לֶת בְּלוּלָ֥ה בַשֶּׁ֖מֶן לְמִנְחָֽה׃ כַּ֥ף אַחַ֛ת עֲשָׂרָ֥ה זָהָ֖ב מְלֵאָ֥ה קְטֹֽרֶת׃ פַּ֣ר אֶחָ֞ד בֶּן־בָּקָ֗ר אַ֧יִל אֶחָ֛ד כֶּֽבֶשׂ־אֶחָ֥ד בֶּן־שְׁנָת֖וֹ לְעֹלָֽה׃ שְׂעִיר־עִזִּ֥ים אֶחָ֖ד לְחַטָּֽאת׃ וּלְזֶ֣בַח הַשְּׁלָמִים֮ בָּקָ֣ר שְׁנַ֒יִם֒ אֵילִ֤ם חֲמִשָּׁה֙ עַתֻּדִ֣ים חֲמִשָּׁ֔ה כְּבָשִׂ֥ים בְּנֵֽי־שָׁנָ֖ה חֲמִשָּׁ֑ה זֶ֛ה קָרְבַּ֥ן אֲחִיעֶ֖זֶר בֶּן־עַמִּישַׁדָּֽי׃

בְּיוֹם֙ עַשְׁתֵּ֣י עָשָׂ֣ר י֔וֹם נָשִׂ֖יא לִבְנֵ֣י אָשֵׁ֑ר פַּגְעִיאֵ֖ל בֶּן־עָכְרָֽן׃ קָרְבָּנ֞וֹ קַֽעֲרַת־כֶּ֣סֶף אַחַ֗ת שְׁלֹשִׁ֣ים וּמֵאָה֮ מִשְׁקָלָהּ֒ מִזְרָ֤ק אֶחָד֙ כֶּ֔סֶף שִׁבְעִ֥ים שֶׁ֖קֶל בְּשֶׁ֣קֶל הַקֹּ֑דֶשׁ שְׁנֵיהֶ֣ם ׀ מְלֵאִ֗ים סֹ֛לֶת בְּלוּלָ֥ה בַשֶּׁ֖מֶן לְמִנְחָֽה׃ כַּ֥ף אַחַ֛ת עֲשָׂרָ֥ה זָהָ֖ב מְלֵאָ֥ה קְטֹֽרֶת׃ פַּ֣ר אֶחָ֞ד בֶּן־בָּקָ֗ר אַ֧יִל אֶחָ֛ד כֶּֽבֶשׂ־אֶחָ֥ד בֶּן־שְׁנָת֖וֹ לְעֹלָֽה׃ שְׂעִיר־עִזִּ֥ים אֶחָ֖ד לְחַטָּֽאת׃ וּלְזֶ֣בַח הַשְּׁלָמִים֮ בָּקָ֣ר שְׁנַ֒יִם֒ אֵילִ֤ם חֲמִשָּׁה֙ עַתֻּדִ֣ים חֲמִשָּׁ֔ה כְּבָשִׂ֥ים בְּנֵֽי־שָׁנָ֖ה חֲמִשָּׁ֑ה זֶ֛ה קָרְבַּ֥ן פַּגְעִיאֵ֖ל בֶּן־עָכְרָֽן׃

בְּיוֹם֙ שְׁנֵ֣ים עָשָׂ֣ר י֔וֹם נָשִׂ֖יא לִבְנֵ֣י נַפְתָּלִ֑י אֲחִירַ֖ע בֶּן־עֵינָֽן׃ קָרְבָּנ֞וֹ קַֽעֲרַת־כֶּ֣סֶף אַחַ֗ת שְׁלֹשִׁ֣ים וּמֵאָה֮ מִשְׁקָלָהּ֒ מִזְרָ֤ק אֶחָד֙ כֶּ֔סֶף שִׁבְעִ֥ים שֶׁ֖קֶל בְּשֶׁ֣קֶל הַקֹּ֑דֶשׁ שְׁנֵיהֶ֣ם ׀ מְלֵאִ֗ים סֹ֛לֶת בְּלוּלָ֥ה בַשֶּׁ֖מֶן לְמִנְחָֽה׃ כַּ֥ף אַחַ֛ת עֲשָׂרָ֥ה זָהָ֖ב מְלֵאָ֥ה קְטֹֽרֶת׃ פַּ֣ר אֶחָ֞ד בֶּן־בָּקָ֗ר אַ֧יִל אֶחָ֛ד כֶּֽבֶשׂ־אֶחָ֥ד בֶּן־שְׁנָת֖וֹ לְעֹלָֽה׃ שְׂעִיר־עִזִּ֥ים אֶחָ֖ד לְחַטָּֽאת׃ וּלְזֶ֣בַח הַשְּׁלָמִים֮ בָּקָ֣ר שְׁנַ֒יִם֒ אֵילִ֤ם חֲמִשָּׁה֙ עַתֻּדִ֣ים חֲמִשָּׁ֔ה כְּבָשִׂ֥ים בְּנֵֽי־שָׁנָ֖ה חֲמִשָּׁ֑ה זֶ֛ה קָרְבַּ֥ן אֲחִירַ֖ע בֶּן־עֵינָֽן׃

זֹ֣את ׀ חֲנֻכַּ֣ת הַמִּזְבֵּ֗חַ בְּיוֹם֙ הִמָּשַׁ֣ח אֹת֔וֹ מֵאֵ֖ת נְשִׂיאֵ֣י יִשְׂרָאֵ֑ל קַעֲרֹ֨ת כֶּ֜סֶף שְׁתֵּ֣ים עֶשְׂרֵ֗ה מִֽזְרְקֵי־כֶ֙סֶף֙ שְׁנֵ֣ים עָשָׂ֔ר כַּפּ֥וֹת זָהָ֖ב שְׁתֵּ֥ים עֶשְׂרֵֽה׃ שְׁלֹשִׁ֣ים וּמֵאָ֗ה הַקְּעָרָ֤ה הָֽאַחַת֙ כֶּ֔סֶף וְשִׁבְעִ֖ים הַמִּזְרָ֣ק הָאֶחָ֑ד כֹּ֚ל כֶּ֣סֶף הַכֵּלִ֔ים אַלְפַּ֥יִם וְאַרְבַּע־מֵא֖וֹת בְּשֶׁ֥קֶל הַקֹּֽדֶשׁ׃ כַּפּ֨וֹת זָהָ֤ב שְׁתֵּים־עֶשְׂרֵה֙ מְלֵאֹ֣ת קְטֹ֔רֶת עֲשָׂרָ֧ה עֲשָׂרָ֛ה הַכַּ֖ף בְּשֶׁ֣קֶל הַקֹּ֑דֶשׁ כָּל־זְהַ֥ב הַכַּפּ֖וֹת עֶשְׂרִ֥ים וּמֵאָֽה׃ כָּל־הַבָּקָ֨ר לָעֹלָ֜ה שְׁנֵ֧ים עָשָׂ֣ר פָּרִ֗ים אֵילִ֤ם

שְׁנֵים־עָשָׂר כְּבָשִׂים בְּנֵי־שָׁנָה שְׁנֵים עָשָׂר וּמִנְחָתָם וּשְׂעִירֵי עִזִּים שְׁנֵים עָשָׂר לְחַטָּאת׃ וְכֹל בְּקַר ׀ זֶבַח הַשְּׁלָמִים עֶשְׂרִים וְאַרְבָּעָה פָּרִים אֵילִם שִׁשִּׁים עַתֻּדִים שִׁשִּׁים כְּבָשִׂים בְּנֵי־שָׁנָה שִׁשִּׁים זֹאת חֲנֻכַּת הַמִּזְבֵּחַ אַחֲרֵי הִמָּשַׁח אֹתוֹ׃ וּבְבֹא מֹשֶׁה אֶל־אֹהֶל מוֹעֵד לְדַבֵּר אִתּוֹ וַיִּשְׁמַע אֶת־הַקּוֹל מִדַּבֵּר אֵלָיו מֵעַל הַכַּפֹּרֶת אֲשֶׁר עַל־אֲרֹן הָעֵדֻת מִבֵּין שְׁנֵי הַכְּרֻבִים וַיְדַבֵּר אֵלָיו׃

וַיְדַבֵּר יְהוָה אֶל־מֹשֶׁה לֵּאמֹר׃ דַּבֵּר אֶל־אַהֲרֹן וְאָמַרְתָּ אֵלָיו בְּהַעֲלֹתְךָ אֶת־הַנֵּרֹת אֶל־מוּל פְּנֵי הַמְּנוֹרָה יָאִירוּ שִׁבְעַת הַנֵּרוֹת׃ וַיַּעַשׂ כֵּן אַהֲרֹן אֶל־מוּל פְּנֵי הַמְּנוֹרָה הֶעֱלָה נֵרֹתֶיהָ כַּאֲשֶׁר צִוָּה יְהוָה אֶת־מֹשֶׁה׃ וְזֶה מַעֲשֵׂה הַמְּנֹרָה מִקְשָׁה זָהָב עַד־יְרֵכָהּ עַד־פִּרְחָהּ מִקְשָׁה הִוא כַּמַּרְאֶה אֲשֶׁר הֶרְאָה יְהוָה אֶת־מֹשֶׁה כֵּן עָשָׂה אֶת־הַמְּנֹרָה׃

קריאה לפורים PURIM

שמות יז:ח–טז

FIRST ALIYA: vv. 8–10 Amalek came to attack Israel in Refidim.

וַיָּבֹא עֲמָלֵק וַיִּלָּחֶם עִם־יִשְׂרָאֵל בִּרְפִידִם׃ וַיֹּאמֶר מֹשֶׁה אֶל־יְהוֹשֻׁעַ בְּחַר־לָנוּ אֲנָשִׁים וְצֵא הִלָּחֵם בַּעֲמָלֵק מָחָר אָנֹכִי נִצָּב עַל־רֹאשׁ הַגִּבְעָה וּמַטֵּה הָאֱלֹהִים בְּיָדִי׃ וַיַּעַשׂ יְהוֹשֻׁעַ כַּאֲשֶׁר אָמַר־לוֹ מֹשֶׁה לְהִלָּחֵם בַּעֲמָלֵק וּמֹשֶׁה אַהֲרֹן

לוי וְחוּר עָלוּ רֹאשׁ הַגִּבְעָה׃ *וְהָיָה כַּאֲשֶׁר יָרִים מֹשֶׁה יָדוֹ

SECOND ALIYA: vv. 11–13 Israel's army overcame Amalek when Moshe's arms were held aloft by Aaron and Ḥur.

וְגָבַר יִשְׂרָאֵל וְכַאֲשֶׁר יָנִיחַ יָדוֹ וְגָבַר עֲמָלֵק׃ וִידֵי מֹשֶׁה כְּבֵדִים וַיִּקְחוּ־אֶבֶן וַיָּשִׂימוּ תַחְתָּיו וַיֵּשֶׁב עָלֶיהָ וְאַהֲרֹן וְחוּר תָּמְכוּ בְיָדָיו מִזֶּה אֶחָד וּמִזֶּה אֶחָד וַיְהִי יָדָיו אֱמוּנָה עַד־בֹּא הַשָּׁמֶשׁ׃ וַיַּחֲלֹשׁ יְהוֹשֻׁעַ אֶת־עֲמָלֵק וְאֶת־עַמּוֹ לְפִי־חָרֶב׃

ישראל

THIRD ALIYA: vv. 14–16 The mizva for every generation to erase the memory of Amalek.

וַיֹּאמֶר יְהוָה אֶל־מֹשֶׁה כְּתֹב זֹאת זִכָּרוֹן בַּסֵּפֶר וְשִׂים בְּאָזְנֵי יְהוֹשֻׁעַ כִּי־מָחֹה אֶמְחֶה אֶת־זֵכֶר עֲמָלֵק מִתַּחַת הַשָּׁמָיִם׃ וַיִּבֶן מֹשֶׁה מִזְבֵּחַ וַיִּקְרָא שְׁמוֹ יְהוָה ׀ נִסִּי׃ וַיֹּאמֶר כִּי־יָד עַל־כֵּס יָהּ מִלְחָמָה לַיהוָה בַּעֲמָלֵק מִדֹּר דֹּר׃

קריאת התורה לחול המועד
THE READING OF THE TORAH FOR ḤOL HAMO'ED

חול המועד פסח
ḤOL HAMO'ED PESAḤ

קריאה ליום ראשון דחול המועד בארץ ישראל
FIRST DAY OF ḤOL HAMO'ED IN ISRAEL

Two ספרי תורה *are taken out of the* ארון קודש*. The following* קריאת התורה *is read from the first scroll; the fourth* עלייה *(page 1138) is read from the second scroll.*

FIRST ALIYA: vv. 22:26–23:8 The laws of the Pesaḥ offerings.

ויקרא כב: כו–כג:מד

וידבר יהוה אל־משה לאמר: שור או־כשב או־עז כי
יולד והיה שבעת ימים תחת אמו ומיום השמיני והלאה
ירצה לקרבן אשה ליהוה: ושור או־שה אתו ואת־בנו
לא תשחטו ביום אחד: וכי־תזבחו זבח־תודה ליהוה
לרצנכם תזבחו: ביום ההוא יאכל לא־תותירו ממנו עד־
בקר אני יהוה: ושמרתם מצותי ועשיתם אתם אני יהוה:
ולא תחללו את־שם קדשי ונקדשתי בתוך בני ישראל אני
יהוה מקדשכם: המוציא אתכם מארץ מצרים להיות לכם
לאלהים אני יהוה:

וידבר יהוה אל־משה לאמר: דבר אל־בני ישראל ואמרת
אלהם מועדי יהוה אשר־תקראו אתם מקראי קדש אלה
הם מועדי: ששת ימים תעשה מלאכה וביום השביעי
שבת שבתון מקרא־קדש כל־מלאכה לא תעשו שבת
הוא ליהוה בכל מושבתיכם:

אלה מועדי יהוה מקראי קדש אשר־תקראו אתם במועדם:
בחדש הראשון בארבעה עשר לחדש בין הערבים פסח
ליהוה: ובחמשה עשר יום לחדש הזה חג המצות ליהוה
שבעת ימים מצות תאכלו: ביום הראשון מקרא־קדש

יִהְיֶה לָכֶם כָּל־מְלֶאכֶת עֲבֹדָה לֹא תַעֲשׂוּ׃ וְהִקְרַבְתֶּם אִשֶּׁה לַיהוָה שִׁבְעַת יָמִים בַּיּוֹם הַשְּׁבִיעִי מִקְרָא־קֹדֶשׁ כָּל־מְלֶאכֶת עֲבֹדָה לֹא תַעֲשׂוּ׃

לוי

SECOND ALIYA: vv. 9–14
The Omer offering.

וַיְדַבֵּר יְהוָה אֶל־מֹשֶׁה לֵּאמֹר׃ דַּבֵּר אֶל־בְּנֵי יִשְׂרָאֵל וְאָמַרְתָּ אֲלֵהֶם כִּי־תָבֹאוּ אֶל־הָאָרֶץ אֲשֶׁר אֲנִי נֹתֵן לָכֶם וּקְצַרְתֶּם אֶת־קְצִירָהּ וַהֲבֵאתֶם אֶת־עֹמֶר רֵאשִׁית קְצִירְכֶם אֶל־הַכֹּהֵן׃ וְהֵנִיף אֶת־הָעֹמֶר לִפְנֵי יְהוָה לִרְצֹנְכֶם מִמָּחֳרַת הַשַּׁבָּת יְנִיפֶנּוּ הַכֹּהֵן׃ וַעֲשִׂיתֶם בְּיוֹם הֲנִיפְכֶם אֶת־הָעֹמֶר כֶּבֶשׂ תָּמִים בֶּן־שְׁנָתוֹ לְעֹלָה לַיהוָה׃ וּמִנְחָתוֹ שְׁנֵי עֶשְׂרֹנִים סֹלֶת בְּלוּלָה בַשֶּׁמֶן אִשֶּׁה לַיהוָה רֵיחַ נִיחֹחַ וְנִסְכֹּה יַיִן רְבִיעִת הַהִין׃ וְלֶחֶם וְקָלִי וְכַרְמֶל לֹא תֹאכְלוּ עַד־עֶצֶם הַיּוֹם הַזֶּה עַד הֲבִיאֲכֶם אֶת־קָרְבַּן אֱלֹהֵיכֶם חֻקַּת עוֹלָם לְדֹרֹתֵיכֶם בְּכֹל מֹשְׁבֹתֵיכֶם׃

שלישי

THIRD ALIYA: vv. 15–44
The counting of the Omer, Shavuot, Rosh HaShana and Sukkot offerings.

*וּסְפַרְתֶּם לָכֶם מִמָּחֳרַת הַשַּׁבָּת מִיּוֹם הֲבִיאֲכֶם אֶת־עֹמֶר הַתְּנוּפָה שֶׁבַע שַׁבָּתוֹת תְּמִימֹת תִּהְיֶינָה׃ עַד מִמָּחֳרַת הַשַּׁבָּת הַשְּׁבִיעִת תִּסְפְּרוּ חֲמִשִּׁים יוֹם וְהִקְרַבְתֶּם מִנְחָה חֲדָשָׁה לַיהוָה׃ מִמּוֹשְׁבֹתֵיכֶם תָּבִיאּוּ ׀ לֶחֶם תְּנוּפָה שְׁתַּיִם שְׁנֵי עֶשְׂרֹנִים סֹלֶת תִּהְיֶינָה חָמֵץ תֵּאָפֶינָה בִּכּוּרִים לַיהוָה׃ וְהִקְרַבְתֶּם עַל־הַלֶּחֶם שִׁבְעַת כְּבָשִׂים תְּמִימִם בְּנֵי שָׁנָה וּפַר בֶּן־בָּקָר אֶחָד וְאֵילִם שְׁנָיִם יִהְיוּ עֹלָה לַיהוָה וּמִנְחָתָם וְנִסְכֵּיהֶם אִשֵּׁה רֵיחַ־נִיחֹחַ לַיהוָה׃ וַעֲשִׂיתֶם שְׂעִיר־עִזִּים אֶחָד לְחַטָּאת וּשְׁנֵי כְבָשִׂים בְּנֵי שָׁנָה לְזֶבַח שְׁלָמִים׃ וְהֵנִיף הַכֹּהֵן ׀ אֹתָם עַל לֶחֶם הַבִּכֻּרִים תְּנוּפָה לִפְנֵי יְהוָה עַל־שְׁנֵי כְּבָשִׂים קֹדֶשׁ יִהְיוּ לַיהוָה לַכֹּהֵן׃ וּקְרָאתֶם בְּעֶצֶם ׀ הַיּוֹם הַזֶּה מִקְרָא־קֹדֶשׁ יִהְיֶה לָכֶם כָּל־מְלֶאכֶת עֲבֹדָה לֹא תַעֲשׂוּ חֻקַּת עוֹלָם בְּכָל־מוֹשְׁבֹתֵיכֶם לְדֹרֹתֵיכֶם׃ וּבְקֻצְרְכֶם אֶת־קְצִיר אַרְצְכֶם לֹא־תְכַלֶּה פְּאַת שָׂדְךָ בְּקֻצְרֶךָ וְלֶקֶט קְצִירְךָ לֹא תְלַקֵּט לֶעָנִי וְלַגֵּר תַּעֲזֹב אֹתָם אֲנִי יְהוָה אֱלֹהֵיכֶם׃

וַיְדַבֵּר יְהוָה אֶל־מֹשֶׁה לֵּאמֹר׃ דַּבֵּר אֶל־בְּנֵי יִשְׂרָאֵל

לֵאמֹר בַּחֹדֶשׁ הַשְּׁבִיעִי בְּאֶחָד לַחֹדֶשׁ יִהְיֶה לָכֶם שַׁבָּתוֹן זִכְרוֹן תְּרוּעָה מִקְרָא־קֹדֶשׁ: כָּל־מְלֶאכֶת עֲבֹדָה לֹא תַעֲשׂוּ וְהִקְרַבְתֶּם אִשֶּׁה לַיהוָה: וַיְדַבֵּר יְהוָה אֶל־מֹשֶׁה לֵּאמֹר: אַךְ בֶּעָשׂוֹר לַחֹדֶשׁ הַשְּׁבִיעִי הַזֶּה יוֹם הַכִּפֻּרִים הוּא מִקְרָא־קֹדֶשׁ יִהְיֶה לָכֶם וְעִנִּיתֶם אֶת־נַפְשֹׁתֵיכֶם וְהִקְרַבְתֶּם אִשֶּׁה לַיהוָה: וְכָל־מְלָאכָה לֹא תַעֲשׂוּ בְּעֶצֶם הַיּוֹם הַזֶּה כִּי יוֹם כִּפֻּרִים הוּא לְכַפֵּר עֲלֵיכֶם לִפְנֵי יְהוָה אֱלֹהֵיכֶם: כִּי כָל־הַנֶּפֶשׁ אֲשֶׁר לֹא־תְעֻנֶּה בְּעֶצֶם הַיּוֹם הַזֶּה וְנִכְרְתָה מֵעַמֶּיהָ: וְכָל־הַנֶּפֶשׁ אֲשֶׁר תַּעֲשֶׂה כָּל־מְלָאכָה בְּעֶצֶם הַיּוֹם הַזֶּה וְהַאֲבַדְתִּי אֶת־הַנֶּפֶשׁ הַהִוא מִקֶּרֶב עַמָּהּ: כָּל־מְלָאכָה לֹא תַעֲשׂוּ חֻקַּת עוֹלָם לְדֹרֹתֵיכֶם בְּכֹל מֹשְׁבֹתֵיכֶם: שַׁבַּת שַׁבָּתוֹן הוּא לָכֶם וְעִנִּיתֶם אֶת־נַפְשֹׁתֵיכֶם בְּתִשְׁעָה לַחֹדֶשׁ בָּעֶרֶב מֵעֶרֶב עַד־עֶרֶב תִּשְׁבְּתוּ שַׁבַּתְּכֶם:

וַיְדַבֵּר יְהוָה אֶל־מֹשֶׁה לֵּאמֹר: דַּבֵּר אֶל־בְּנֵי יִשְׂרָאֵל לֵאמֹר בַּחֲמִשָּׁה עָשָׂר יוֹם לַחֹדֶשׁ הַשְּׁבִיעִי הַזֶּה חַג הַסֻּכּוֹת שִׁבְעַת יָמִים לַיהוָה: בַּיּוֹם הָרִאשׁוֹן מִקְרָא־קֹדֶשׁ כָּל־מְלֶאכֶת עֲבֹדָה לֹא תַעֲשׂוּ: שִׁבְעַת יָמִים תַּקְרִיבוּ אִשֶּׁה לַיהוָה בַּיּוֹם הַשְּׁמִינִי מִקְרָא־קֹדֶשׁ יִהְיֶה לָכֶם וְהִקְרַבְתֶּם אִשֶּׁה לַיהוָה עֲצֶרֶת הִוא כָּל־מְלֶאכֶת עֲבֹדָה לֹא תַעֲשׂוּ: אֵלֶּה מוֹעֲדֵי יְהוָה אֲשֶׁר־תִּקְרְאוּ אֹתָם מִקְרָאֵי קֹדֶשׁ לְהַקְרִיב אִשֶּׁה לַיהוָה עֹלָה וּמִנְחָה זֶבַח וּנְסָכִים דְּבַר־יוֹם בְּיוֹמוֹ: מִלְּבַד שַׁבְּתֹת יְהוָה וּמִלְּבַד מַתְּנוֹתֵיכֶם וּמִלְּבַד כָּל־נִדְרֵיכֶם וּמִלְּבַד כָּל־נִדְבֹתֵיכֶם אֲשֶׁר תִּתְּנוּ לַיהוָה: אַךְ בַּחֲמִשָּׁה עָשָׂר יוֹם לַחֹדֶשׁ הַשְּׁבִיעִי בְּאָסְפְּכֶם אֶת־תְּבוּאַת הָאָרֶץ תָּחֹגּוּ אֶת־חַג־יְהוָה שִׁבְעַת יָמִים בַּיּוֹם הָרִאשׁוֹן שַׁבָּתוֹן וּבַיּוֹם הַשְּׁמִינִי שַׁבָּתוֹן: וּלְקַחְתֶּם לָכֶם בַּיּוֹם הָרִאשׁוֹן פְּרִי עֵץ הָדָר כַּפֹּת תְּמָרִים וַעֲנַף עֵץ־עָבֹת וְעַרְבֵי־נָחַל וּשְׂמַחְתֶּם לִפְנֵי יְהוָה אֱלֹהֵיכֶם שִׁבְעַת יָמִים: וְחַגֹּתֶם אֹתוֹ חַג לַיהוָה שִׁבְעַת יָמִים בַּשָּׁנָה

חֻקַּת עוֹלָם לְדֹרֹתֵיכֶם בַּחֹדֶשׁ הַשְּׁבִיעִי תָּחֹגּוּ אֹתוֹ׃ בַּסֻּכֹּת
תֵּשְׁבוּ שִׁבְעַת יָמִים כָּל־הָאֶזְרָח בְּיִשְׂרָאֵל יֵשְׁבוּ בַּסֻּכֹּת׃
לְמַעַן יֵדְעוּ דֹרֹתֵיכֶם כִּי בַסֻּכּוֹת הוֹשַׁבְתִּי אֶת־בְּנֵי יִשְׂרָאֵל
בְּהוֹצִיאִי אוֹתָם מֵאֶרֶץ מִצְרָיִם אֲנִי יְהוָה אֱלֹהֵיכֶם׃ וַיְדַבֵּר
מֹשֶׁה אֶת־מֹעֲדֵי יְהוָה אֶל־בְּנֵי יִשְׂרָאֵל׃

רביעי *is read from the second* ספר תורה*:*

במדבר כח: יט–כה

FOURTH ALIYA: BEMIDBAR 28:19–25
Pesaḥ offerings.

וְהִקְרַבְתֶּם אִשֶּׁה עֹלָה לַיהוָה פָּרִים בְּנֵי־בָקָר שְׁנָיִם וְאַיִל
אֶחָד וְשִׁבְעָה כְבָשִׂים בְּנֵי שָׁנָה תְּמִימִם יִהְיוּ לָכֶם׃ וּמִנְחָתָם
סֹלֶת בְּלוּלָה בַשָּׁמֶן שְׁלֹשָׁה עֶשְׂרֹנִים לַפָּר וּשְׁנֵי עֶשְׂרֹנִים
לָאַיִל תַּעֲשׂוּ׃ עִשָּׂרוֹן עִשָּׂרוֹן תַּעֲשֶׂה לַכֶּבֶשׂ הָאֶחָד לְשִׁבְעַת
הַכְּבָשִׂים׃ וּשְׂעִיר חַטָּאת אֶחָד לְכַפֵּר עֲלֵיכֶם׃ מִלְּבַד עֹלַת
הַבֹּקֶר אֲשֶׁר לְעֹלַת הַתָּמִיד תַּעֲשׂוּ אֶת־אֵלֶּה׃ כָּאֵלֶּה תַּעֲשׂוּ
לַיּוֹם שִׁבְעַת יָמִים לֶחֶם אִשֵּׁה רֵיחַ־נִיחֹחַ לַיהוָה עַל־עוֹלַת
הַתָּמִיד יֵעָשֶׂה וְנִסְכּוֹ׃ וּבַיּוֹם הַשְּׁבִיעִי מִקְרָא־קֹדֶשׁ יִהְיֶה
לָכֶם כָּל־מְלֶאכֶת עֲבֹדָה לֹא תַעֲשׂוּ׃

Continue with חצי קדיש *(page 231).*

קריאה ליום ראשון דחול המועד (ב׳ בארץ ישראל)
FIRST DAY OF ḤOL HAMO'ED (SECOND DAY IN ISRAEL)

שמות יג:א–טז

FIRST ALIYA: vv. 1–4
The mitzva to remember the day Israel left Egypt.

וַיְדַבֵּר יְהוָה אֶל־מֹשֶׁה לֵּאמֹר׃ קַדֶּשׁ־לִי כָל־בְּכוֹר פֶּטֶר כָּל־
רֶחֶם בִּבְנֵי יִשְׂרָאֵל בָּאָדָם וּבַבְּהֵמָה לִי הוּא׃ וַיֹּאמֶר מֹשֶׁה
אֶל־הָעָם זָכוֹר אֶת־הַיּוֹם הַזֶּה אֲשֶׁר יְצָאתֶם מִמִּצְרַיִם מִבֵּית
עֲבָדִים כִּי בְּחֹזֶק יָד הוֹצִיא יְהוָה אֶתְכֶם מִזֶּה וְלֹא יֵאָכֵל
לוי חָמֵץ׃ הַיּוֹם אַתֶּם יֹצְאִים בְּחֹדֶשׁ הָאָבִיב׃ *וְהָיָה כִי־יְבִיאֲךָ
יְהוָה אֶל־אֶרֶץ הַכְּנַעֲנִי וְהַחִתִּי וְהָאֱמֹרִי וְהַחִוִּי וְהַיְבוּסִי אֲשֶׁר
נִשְׁבַּע לַאֲבֹתֶיךָ לָתֶת לָךְ אֶרֶץ זָבַת חָלָב וּדְבָשׁ וְעָבַדְתָּ
אֶת־הָעֲבֹדָה הַזֹּאת בַּחֹדֶשׁ הַזֶּה׃ שִׁבְעַת יָמִים תֹּאכַל מַצֹּת
וּבַיּוֹם הַשְּׁבִיעִי חַג לַיהוָה׃ מַצּוֹת יֵאָכֵל אֵת שִׁבְעַת הַיָּמִים

SECOND ALIYA: vv. 5–10
Eating matza on Pesaḥ and remembering the exodus in the mitzva of *tefillin*.

וְלֹא־יֵרָאֶה לְךָ חָמֵץ וְלֹא־יֵרָאֶה לְךָ שְׂאֹר בְּכָל־גְּבֻלֶךָ:
וְהִגַּדְתָּ לְבִנְךָ בַּיּוֹם הַהוּא לֵאמֹר בַּעֲבוּר זֶה עָשָׂה יהוה
לִי בְּצֵאתִי מִמִּצְרָיִם: וְהָיָה לְךָ לְאוֹת עַל־יָדְךָ וּלְזִכָּרוֹן בֵּין
עֵינֶיךָ לְמַעַן תִּהְיֶה תּוֹרַת יהוה בְּפִיךָ כִּי בְּיָד חֲזָקָה הוֹצִאֲךָ
יהוה מִמִּצְרָיִם: וְשָׁמַרְתָּ אֶת־הַחֻקָּה הַזֹּאת לְמוֹעֲדָהּ מִיָּמִים
יָמִימָה:

שלישי
וְהָיָה כִּי־יְבִאֲךָ יהוה אֶל־אֶרֶץ הַכְּנַעֲנִי כַּאֲשֶׁר נִשְׁבַּע לְךָ
וְלַאֲבֹתֶיךָ וּנְתָנָהּ לָךְ: וְהַעֲבַרְתָּ כָל־פֶּטֶר־רֶחֶם לַיהוה וְכָל־
פֶּטֶר ׀ שֶׁגֶר בְּהֵמָה אֲשֶׁר יִהְיֶה לְךָ הַזְּכָרִים לַיהוה: וְכָל־
פֶּטֶר חֲמֹר תִּפְדֶּה בְשֶׂה וְאִם־לֹא תִפְדֶּה וַעֲרַפְתּוֹ וְכֹל בְּכוֹר
אָדָם בְּבָנֶיךָ תִּפְדֶּה: וְהָיָה כִּי־יִשְׁאָלְךָ בִנְךָ מָחָר לֵאמֹר
מַה־זֹּאת וְאָמַרְתָּ אֵלָיו בְּחֹזֶק יָד הוֹצִיאָנוּ יהוה מִמִּצְרַיִם
מִבֵּית עֲבָדִים: וַיְהִי כִּי־הִקְשָׁה פַרְעֹה לְשַׁלְּחֵנוּ וַיַּהֲרֹג יהוה
כָּל־בְּכוֹר בְּאֶרֶץ מִצְרַיִם מִבְּכֹר אָדָם וְעַד־בְּכוֹר בְּהֵמָה
עַל־כֵּן אֲנִי זֹבֵחַ לַיהוה כָּל־פֶּטֶר רֶחֶם הַזְּכָרִים וְכָל־בְּכוֹר
בָּנַי אֶפְדֶּה: וְהָיָה לְאוֹת עַל־יָדְכָה וּלְטוֹטָפֹת בֵּין עֵינֶיךָ כִּי
בְּחֹזֶק יָד הוֹצִיאָנוּ יהוה מִמִּצְרָיִם:

THIRD ALIYA: vv. 11–16
Redeeming the first born human and animal.

For רביעי *read* וְהִקְרַבְתֶּם *from the second* ספר תורה *(page 1138).*

קריאה ליום שני דחול המועד (ג׳ בארץ ישראל)

SECOND DAY OF ḤOL HAMO'ED (THIRD DAY IN ISRAEL)

If the second day of חול המועד פסח *falls on Sunday, the* קריאת התורה *for the first day of* חול המועד *is read (page 1138).*

FIRST ALIYA: vv. 22:24–26
The laws of lending money and not taking an article of clothing as a deposit.

SECOND ALIYA: vv. 27–23:5
Ethical laws such as not being influenced by the majority and returning the lost animal of your enemy.

שמות כב: כד–כג:יט
אִם־כֶּסֶף ׀ תַּלְוֶה אֶת־עַמִּי אֶת־הֶעָנִי עִמָּךְ לֹא־תִהְיֶה לוֹ כְּנֹשֶׁה
לֹא־תְשִׂימוּן עָלָיו נֶשֶׁךְ: אִם־חָבֹל תַּחְבֹּל שַׂלְמַת רֵעֶךָ עַד־
בֹּא הַשֶּׁמֶשׁ תְּשִׁיבֶנּוּ לוֹ: כִּי הִוא כְסוּתֹה לְבַדָּהּ הִוא שִׂמְלָתוֹ
לְעֹרוֹ בַּמֶּה יִשְׁכָּב וְהָיָה כִּי־יִצְעַק אֵלַי וְשָׁמַעְתִּי כִּי־חַנּוּן
לוי
אָנִי: *אֱלֹהִים לֹא תְקַלֵּל וְנָשִׂיא בְעַמְּךָ לֹא תָאֹר:
מְלֵאָתְךָ וְדִמְעֲךָ לֹא תְאַחֵר בְּכוֹר בָּנֶיךָ תִּתֶּן־לִי: כֵּן־תַּעֲשֶׂה

לְשֹׁרְךָ לְצֹאנֶךָ שִׁבְעַת יָמִים יִהְיֶה עִם־אִמּוֹ בַּיּוֹם הַשְּׁמִינִי
תִּתְּנוֹ־לִי: וְאַנְשֵׁי־קֹדֶשׁ תִּהְיוּן לִי וּבָשָׂר בַּשָּׂדֶה טְרֵפָה לֹא
תֹאכֵלוּ לַכֶּלֶב תַּשְׁלִכוּן אֹתוֹ: לֹא תִשָּׂא שֵׁמַע
שָׁוְא אַל־תָּשֶׁת יָדְךָ עִם־רָשָׁע לִהְיֹת עֵד חָמָס: לֹא־תִהְיֶה
אַחֲרֵי־רַבִּים לְרָעֹת וְלֹא־תַעֲנֶה עַל־רִב לִנְטֹת אַחֲרֵי רַבִּים
לְהַטֹּת: וְדָל לֹא תֶהְדַּר בְּרִיבוֹ: כִּי תִפְגַּע שׁוֹר
אֹיִבְךָ אוֹ חֲמֹרוֹ תֹּעֶה הָשֵׁב תְּשִׁיבֶנּוּ לוֹ: כִּי־
תִרְאֶה חֲמוֹר שֹׂנַאֲךָ רֹבֵץ תַּחַת מַשָּׂאוֹ וְחָדַלְתָּ מֵעֲזֹב לוֹ
עָזֹב תַּעֲזֹב עִמּוֹ: *לֹא תַטֶּה מִשְׁפַּט אֶבְיֹנְךָ בְּרִיבוֹ: שלישי
מִדְּבַר־שֶׁקֶר תִּרְחָק וְנָקִי וְצַדִּיק אַל־תַּהֲרֹג כִּי לֹא־אַצְדִּיק
רָשָׁע: וְשֹׁחַד לֹא תִקָּח כִּי הַשֹּׁחַד יְעַוֵּר פִּקְחִים וִיסַלֵּף דִּבְרֵי
צַדִּיקִים: וְגֵר לֹא תִלְחָץ וְאַתֶּם יְדַעְתֶּם אֶת־נֶפֶשׁ הַגֵּר כִּי־
גֵרִים הֱיִיתֶם בְּאֶרֶץ מִצְרָיִם: וְשֵׁשׁ שָׁנִים תִּזְרַע אֶת־אַרְצֶךָ
וְאָסַפְתָּ אֶת־תְּבוּאָתָהּ: וְהַשְּׁבִיעִת תִּשְׁמְטֶנָּה וּנְטַשְׁתָּהּ
וְאָכְלוּ אֶבְיֹנֵי עַמֶּךָ וְיִתְרָם תֹּאכַל חַיַּת הַשָּׂדֶה כֵּן־תַּעֲשֶׂה
לְכַרְמְךָ לְזֵיתֶךָ: שֵׁשֶׁת יָמִים תַּעֲשֶׂה מַעֲשֶׂיךָ וּבַיּוֹם הַשְּׁבִיעִי
תִּשְׁבֹּת לְמַעַן יָנוּחַ שׁוֹרְךָ וַחֲמֹרֶךָ וְיִנָּפֵשׁ בֶּן־אֲמָתְךָ וְהַגֵּר:
וּבְכֹל אֲשֶׁר־אָמַרְתִּי אֲלֵיכֶם תִּשָּׁמֵרוּ וְשֵׁם אֱלֹהִים אֲחֵרִים
לֹא תַזְכִּירוּ לֹא יִשָּׁמַע עַל־פִּיךָ: שָׁלֹשׁ רְגָלִים תָּחֹג לִי בַּשָּׁנָה:
אֶת־חַג הַמַּצּוֹת תִּשְׁמֹר שִׁבְעַת יָמִים תֹּאכַל מַצּוֹת כַּאֲשֶׁר
צִוִּיתִךָ לְמוֹעֵד חֹדֶשׁ הָאָבִיב כִּי־בוֹ יָצָאתָ מִמִּצְרָיִם וְלֹא־
יֵרָאוּ פָנַי רֵיקָם: וְחַג הַקָּצִיר בִּכּוּרֵי מַעֲשֶׂיךָ אֲשֶׁר תִּזְרַע
בַּשָּׂדֶה וְחַג הָאָסִף בְּצֵאת הַשָּׁנָה בְּאָסְפְּךָ אֶת־מַעֲשֶׂיךָ
מִן־הַשָּׂדֶה: שָׁלֹשׁ פְּעָמִים בַּשָּׁנָה יֵרָאֶה כָּל־זְכוּרְךָ אֶל־פְּנֵי
הָאָדֹן ׀ יְהוָה: לֹא־תִזְבַּח עַל־חָמֵץ דַּם־זִבְחִי וְלֹא־יָלִין חֵלֶב־
חַגִּי עַד־בֹּקֶר: רֵאשִׁית בִּכּוּרֵי אַדְמָתְךָ תָּבִיא בֵּית יְהוָה
אֱלֹהֶיךָ לֹא־תְבַשֵּׁל גְּדִי בַּחֲלֵב אִמּוֹ:

THIRD ALIYA: vv. 5–19 The laws of Shabbat and Shemitta, and a summary of the *Shalosh Regalim*.

For רביעי *read* וְהִקְרַבְתֶּם *from the second* ספר תורה *(page 1138).*

קריאה ליום ליום שלישי דחול המועד
THIRD DAY OF ḤOL HAMO'ED (ד׳ בארץ ישראל) (FOURTH DAY IN ISRAEL)

If the third day of חול המועד פסח *falls on a Monday, the* קריאת התורה *for the second day of* חול המועד *is read* *(page 1139)*.

FIRST ALIYA: vv. 1–3
God instructs Moshe to prepare the second set of tablets of stone.

SECOND ALIYA: vv. 4–10
God reveals to Moshe the Thirteen Attributes of Mercy. Moshe prays for God to forgive Israel.

THIRD ALIYA: vv. 11–26
God warns Israel not to seal a covenant with the inhabitants of the land they are going to, and not to follow in their idolatrous ways.
And... to keep the festival of Pesaḥ.
And... to redeem first born animals.
And... to keep Shabbat.

שמות לד:א–כו
וַיֹּאמֶר יהוה אֶל־מֹשֶׁה פְּסָל־לְךָ שְׁנֵי־לֻחֹת אֲבָנִים כָּרִאשֹׁנִים
וְכָתַבְתִּי עַל־הַלֻּחֹת אֶת־הַדְּבָרִים אֲשֶׁר הָיוּ עַל־הַלֻּחֹת
הָרִאשֹׁנִים אֲשֶׁר שִׁבַּרְתָּ: וֶהְיֵה נָכוֹן לַבֹּקֶר וְעָלִיתָ בַבֹּקֶר
אֶל־הַר סִינַי וְנִצַּבְתָּ לִי שָׁם עַל־רֹאשׁ הָהָר: וְאִישׁ לֹא־
יַעֲלֶה עִמָּךְ וְגַם־אִישׁ אַל־יֵרָא בְּכָל־הָהָר גַּם־הַצֹּאן וְהַבָּקָר
לוי אַל־יִרְעוּ אֶל־מוּל הָהָר הַהוּא: *וַיִּפְסֹל שְׁנֵי־לֻחֹת אֲבָנִים
כָּרִאשֹׁנִים וַיַּשְׁכֵּם מֹשֶׁה בַבֹּקֶר וַיַּעַל אֶל־הַר סִינַי כַּאֲשֶׁר צִוָּה
יהוה אֹתוֹ וַיִּקַּח בְּיָדוֹ שְׁנֵי לֻחֹת אֲבָנִים: וַיֵּרֶד יהוה בֶּעָנָן
וַיִּתְיַצֵּב עִמּוֹ שָׁם וַיִּקְרָא בְשֵׁם יהוה: וַיַּעֲבֹר יהוה ׀ עַל־פָּנָיו
וַיִּקְרָא יהוה ׀ יהוה אֵל רַחוּם וְחַנּוּן אֶרֶךְ אַפַּיִם וְרַב־חֶסֶד
וֶאֱמֶת: נֹצֵר חֶסֶד לָאֲלָפִים נֹשֵׂא עָוֺן וָפֶשַׁע וְחַטָּאָה וְנַקֵּה
לֹא יְנַקֶּה פֹּקֵד ׀ עֲוֺן אָבוֹת עַל־בָּנִים וְעַל־בְּנֵי בָנִים עַל־
שִׁלֵּשִׁים וְעַל־רִבֵּעִים: וַיְמַהֵר מֹשֶׁה וַיִּקֹּד אַרְצָה וַיִּשְׁתָּחוּ:
וַיֹּאמֶר אִם־נָא מָצָאתִי חֵן בְּעֵינֶיךָ אֲדֹנָי יֵלֶךְ־נָא אֲדֹנָי
בְּקִרְבֵּנוּ כִּי עַם־קְשֵׁה־עֹרֶף הוּא וְסָלַחְתָּ לַעֲוֺנֵנוּ וּלְחַטָּאתֵנוּ
וּנְחַלְתָּנוּ: וַיֹּאמֶר הִנֵּה אָנֹכִי כֹּרֵת בְּרִית נֶגֶד כָּל־עַמְּךָ
אֶעֱשֶׂה נִפְלָאֹת אֲשֶׁר לֹא־נִבְרְאוּ בְכָל־הָאָרֶץ וּבְכָל־הַגּוֹיִם
וְרָאָה כָל־הָעָם אֲשֶׁר־אַתָּה בְקִרְבּוֹ אֶת־מַעֲשֵׂה יהוה כִּי־
שלישי נוֹרָא הוּא אֲשֶׁר אֲנִי עֹשֶׂה עִמָּךְ: *שְׁמָר־לְךָ אֵת אֲשֶׁר אָנֹכִי
מְצַוְּךָ הַיּוֹם הִנְנִי גֹרֵשׁ מִפָּנֶיךָ אֶת־הָאֱמֹרִי וְהַכְּנַעֲנִי וְהַחִתִּי
וְהַפְּרִזִּי וְהַחִוִּי וְהַיְבוּסִי: הִשָּׁמֶר לְךָ פֶּן־תִּכְרֹת בְּרִית לְיוֹשֵׁב
הָאָרֶץ אֲשֶׁר אַתָּה בָּא עָלֶיהָ פֶּן־יִהְיֶה לְמוֹקֵשׁ בְּקִרְבֶּךָ:
כִּי אֶת־מִזְבְּחֹתָם תִּתֹּצוּן וְאֶת־מַצֵּבֹתָם תְּשַׁבֵּרוּן וְאֶת־

אשריו תכרתון: כי לא תשתחוה לאל אחר כי יהוה קנא
שמו אל קנא הוא: פן־תכרת ברית ליושב הארץ וזנו ׀
אחרי אלהיהם וזבחו לאלהיהם וקרא לך ואכלת מזבחו:
ולקחת מבנתיו לבניך וזנו בנתיו אחרי אלהיהן והזנו
את־בניך אחרי אלהיהן: אלהי מסכה לא תעשה־לך:
את־חג המצות תשמר שבעת ימים תאכל מצות אשר
צויתך למועד חדש האביב כי בחדש האביב יצאת
ממצרים: כל־פטר רחם לי וכל־מקנך תזכר פטר שור
ושה: ופטר חמור תפדה בשה ואם־לא תפדה וערפתו
כל בכור בניך תפדה ולא־יראו פני ריקם: ששת ימים
תעבד וביום השביעי תשבת בחריש ובקציר תשבת:
וחג שבעת תעשה לך בכורי קציר חטים וחג האסיף
תקופת השנה: שלש פעמים בשנה יראה כל־זכורך את־
פני האדן ׀ יהוה אלהי ישראל: כי־אוריש גוים מפניך
והרחבתי את־גבלך ולא־יחמד איש את־ארצך בעלתך
לראות את־פני יהוה אלהיך שלש פעמים בשנה: לא־
תשחט על־חמץ דם־זבחי ולא־ילין לבקר זבח חג הפסח:
ראשית בכורי אדמתך תביא בית יהוה אלהיך לא־תבשל
גדי בחלב אמו:

For רביעי *read* וְהִקְרַבְתֶּם *from the second* ספר תורה (*page 1138*).

קריאה ליום רביעי דחול המועד (ה׳ בארץ ישראל)
FOURTH DAY OF ḤOL HAMO'ED (FIFTH DAY IN ISRAEL)

במדבר ט:א–יד

וידבר יהוה אל־משה במדבר־סיני בשנה השנית לצאתם
מארץ מצרים בחדש הראשון לאמר: ויעשו בני־ישראל
את־הפסח במועדו: בארבעה עשר־יום בחדש הזה בין
הערבים תעשו אתו במעדו ככל־חקתיו וככל־משפטיו

FIRST ALIYA: VV. 1–5
The laws of the *Korban Pesaḥ*.

תַּעֲשׂוּ אֹתוֹ: וַיְדַבֵּר מֹשֶׁה אֶל־בְּנֵי יִשְׂרָאֵל לַעֲשֹׂת הַפָּסַח:
וַיַּעֲשׂוּ אֶת־הַפֶּסַח בָּרִאשׁוֹן בְּאַרְבָּעָה עָשָׂר יוֹם לַחֹדֶשׁ בֵּין
הָעַרְבַּיִם בְּמִדְבַּר סִינָי כְּכֹל אֲשֶׁר צִוָּה יהוה אֶת־מֹשֶׁה כֵּן
לוי עָשׂוּ בְּנֵי יִשְׂרָאֵל: *וַיְהִי אֲנָשִׁים אֲשֶׁר הָיוּ טְמֵאִים לְנֶפֶשׁ

SECOND ALIYA: vv. 6–8
The laws of Pesaḥ Sheni.

אָדָם וְלֹא־יָכְלוּ לַעֲשֹׂת־הַפֶּסַח בַּיּוֹם הַהוּא וַיִּקְרְבוּ לִפְנֵי
מֹשֶׁה וְלִפְנֵי אַהֲרֹן בַּיּוֹם הַהוּא: וַיֹּאמְרוּ הָאֲנָשִׁים הָהֵמָּה
אֵלָיו אֲנַחְנוּ טְמֵאִים לְנֶפֶשׁ אָדָם לָמָּה נִגָּרַע לְבִלְתִּי הַקְרִיב
אֶת־קָרְבַּן יהוה בְּמֹעֲדוֹ בְּתוֹךְ בְּנֵי יִשְׂרָאֵל: וַיֹּאמֶר אֲלֵהֶם
מֹשֶׁה עִמְדוּ וְאֶשְׁמְעָה מַה־יְצַוֶּה יהוה לָכֶם:
שלישי וַיְדַבֵּר יהוה אֶל־מֹשֶׁה לֵּאמֹר: דַּבֵּר אֶל־בְּנֵי יִשְׂרָאֵל לֵאמֹר

THIRD ALIYA: vv. 9–14
The laws of the *Korban Pesaḥ* continued.

אִישׁ אִישׁ כִּי־יִהְיֶה טָמֵא ׀ לָנֶפֶשׁ אוֹ בְדֶרֶךְ רְחֹקָה לָכֶם אוֹ
לְדֹרֹתֵיכֶם וְעָשָׂה פֶסַח לַיהוה: בַּחֹדֶשׁ הַשֵּׁנִי בְּאַרְבָּעָה עָשָׂר
יוֹם בֵּין הָעַרְבַּיִם יַעֲשׂוּ אֹתוֹ עַל־מַצּוֹת וּמְרֹרִים יֹאכְלֻהוּ:
לֹא־יַשְׁאִירוּ מִמֶּנּוּ עַד־בֹּקֶר וְעֶצֶם לֹא יִשְׁבְּרוּ־בוֹ כְּכָל־חֻקַּת
הַפֶּסַח יַעֲשׂוּ אֹתוֹ: וְהָאִישׁ אֲשֶׁר־הוּא טָהוֹר וּבְדֶרֶךְ לֹא־
הָיָה וְחָדַל לַעֲשׂוֹת הַפֶּסַח וְנִכְרְתָה הַנֶּפֶשׁ הַהִוא מֵעַמֶּיהָ
כִּי ׀ קָרְבַּן יהוה לֹא הִקְרִיב בְּמֹעֲדוֹ חֶטְאוֹ יִשָּׂא הָאִישׁ
הַהוּא: וְכִי־יָגוּר אִתְּכֶם גֵּר וְעָשָׂה פֶסַח לַיהוה כְּחֻקַּת הַפֶּסַח
וּכְמִשְׁפָּטוֹ כֵּן יַעֲשֶׂה חֻקָּה אַחַת יִהְיֶה לָכֶם וְלַגֵּר וּלְאֶזְרַח
הָאָרֶץ:

For רביעי *read* וְהִקְרַבְתֶּם *from the second* ספר תורה *(page 1138).*

קריאה לחול המועד סוכות
ḤOL HAMO'ED SUKKOT

קריאה ליום ראשון דחול המועד סוכות
FIRST DAY OF ḤOL HAMO'ED SUKKOT

In ארץ ישראל*, the first three verses,* וּבַיּוֹם הַשֵּׁנִי *through* וּמִנְחָתָהּ וְנִסְכֵּיהֶם*, are read for each of the four* עליות*.*

FIRST DAY ḤOL HAMO'ED: BEMIDBAR 29:17–25 The offering for the second, third, and fourth days of Sukkot.

במדבר כט:יז–כה
וּבַיּוֹם הַשֵּׁנִי פָּרִים בְּנֵי־בָקָר שְׁנֵים עָשָׂר אֵילִם שְׁנָיִם כְּבָשִׂים בְּנֵי־שָׁנָה אַרְבָּעָה עָשָׂר תְּמִימִם׃ וּמִנְחָתָם וְנִסְכֵּיהֶם לַפָּרִים לָאֵילִם וְלַכְּבָשִׂים בְּמִסְפָּרָם כַּמִּשְׁפָּט׃ וּשְׂעִיר־עִזִּים אֶחָד חַטָּאת מִלְּבַד עֹלַת הַתָּמִיד וּמִנְחָתָהּ וְנִסְכֵּיהֶם׃

לוי
*וּבַיּוֹם הַשְּׁלִישִׁי פָּרִים עַשְׁתֵּי־עָשָׂר אֵילִם שְׁנָיִם כְּבָשִׂים בְּנֵי־שָׁנָה אַרְבָּעָה עָשָׂר תְּמִימִם׃ וּמִנְחָתָם וְנִסְכֵּיהֶם לַפָּרִים לָאֵילִם וְלַכְּבָשִׂים בְּמִסְפָּרָם כַּמִּשְׁפָּט׃ וּשְׂעִיר חַטָּאת אֶחָד מִלְּבַד עֹלַת הַתָּמִיד וּמִנְחָתָהּ וְנִסְכָּהּ׃

שלישי
*וּבַיּוֹם הָרְבִיעִי פָּרִים עֲשָׂרָה אֵילִם שְׁנָיִם כְּבָשִׂים בְּנֵי־שָׁנָה אַרְבָּעָה עָשָׂר תְּמִימִם׃ מִנְחָתָם וְנִסְכֵּיהֶם לַפָּרִים לָאֵילִם וְלַכְּבָשִׂים בְּמִסְפָּרָם כַּמִּשְׁפָּט׃ וּשְׂעִיר־עִזִּים אֶחָד חַטָּאת מִלְּבַד עֹלַת הַתָּמִיד מִנְחָתָהּ וְנִסְכָּהּ׃

רביעי
וּבַיּוֹם הַשֵּׁנִי פָּרִים בְּנֵי־בָקָר שְׁנֵים עָשָׂר אֵילִם שְׁנָיִם כְּבָשִׂים בְּנֵי־שָׁנָה אַרְבָּעָה עָשָׂר תְּמִימִם׃ וּמִנְחָתָם וְנִסְכֵּיהֶם לַפָּרִים לָאֵילִם וְלַכְּבָשִׂים בְּמִסְפָּרָם כַּמִּשְׁפָּט׃ וּשְׂעִיר־עִזִּים אֶחָד חַטָּאת מִלְּבַד עֹלַת הַתָּמִיד וּמִנְחָתָהּ וְנִסְכֵּיהֶם׃ וּבַיּוֹם הַשְּׁלִישִׁי פָּרִים עַשְׁתֵּי־עָשָׂר אֵילִם שְׁנָיִם כְּבָשִׂים בְּנֵי־שָׁנָה אַרְבָּעָה עָשָׂר תְּמִימִם׃ וּמִנְחָתָם וְנִסְכֵּיהֶם לַפָּרִים לָאֵילִם וְלַכְּבָשִׂים בְּמִסְפָּרָם כַּמִּשְׁפָּט׃ וּשְׂעִיר חַטָּאת אֶחָד מִלְּבַד עֹלַת הַתָּמִיד וּמִנְחָתָהּ וְנִסְכָּהּ׃

Continue with חצי קדיש *(page 231).*

קריאה ליום שני דחול המועד סוכות

SECOND DAY OF ḤOL HAMO'ED SUKKOT

In ארץ ישראל*, the first three verses,* וּבַיּוֹם הַשְּׁלִישִׁי *through* וּמִנְחָתָהּ וְנִסְכָּהּ*, are read for each of the four* עליות*.*

SECOND DAY ḤOL HAMO'ED: BEMIDBAR 29:20–28 The offering for the third, fourth, and fifth days of Sukkot.

במדבר כט:כ–כח

וּבַיּ֧וֹם הַשְּׁלִישִׁ֛י פָּרִ֥ים עַשְׁתֵּי־עָשָׂ֖ר אֵילִ֣ם שְׁנָ֑יִם כְּבָשִׂ֧ים
בְּנֵי־שָׁנָ֛ה אַרְבָּעָ֥ה עָשָׂ֖ר תְּמִימִֽם׃ וּמִנְחָתָ֣ם וְנִסְכֵּיהֶ֡ם לַ֠פָּרִ֠ים
לָאֵילִ֧ם וְלַכְּבָשִׂ֛ים בְּמִסְפָּרָ֖ם כַּמִּשְׁפָּֽט׃ וּשְׂעִ֥יר חַטָּ֖את אֶחָ֑ד
מִלְּבַד֙ עֹלַ֣ת הַתָּמִ֔יד וּמִנְחָתָ֖הּ וְנִסְכָּֽהּ׃ ‎*‎וּבַיּ֧וֹם לוי
הָרְבִיעִ֛י פָּרִ֥ים עֲשָׂרָ֖ה אֵילִ֣ם שְׁנָ֑יִם כְּבָשִׂ֧ים בְּנֵי־שָׁנָ֛ה אַרְבָּעָ֥ה
עָשָׂ֖ר תְּמִימִֽם׃ מִנְחָתָ֣ם וְנִסְכֵּיהֶ֗ם לַפָּרִ֜ים לָאֵילִ֧ם וְלַכְּבָשִׂ֛ים
בְּמִסְפָּרָ֖ם כַּמִּשְׁפָּֽט׃ וּשְׂעִיר־עִזִּ֥ים אֶחָ֖ד חַטָּ֑את מִלְּבַד֙ עֹלַ֣ת
הַתָּמִ֔יד מִנְחָתָ֖הּ וְנִסְכָּֽהּ׃ ‎*‎וּבַיּ֧וֹם הַחֲמִישִׁ֛י פָּרִ֥ים שלישי
תִּשְׁעָ֖ה אֵילִ֣ם שְׁנָ֑יִם כְּבָשִׂ֧ים בְּנֵי־שָׁנָ֛ה אַרְבָּעָ֥ה עָשָׂ֖ר תְּמִימִֽם׃
וּמִנְחָתָ֣ם וְנִסְכֵּיהֶ֡ם לַ֠פָּרִ֠ים לָאֵילִ֧ם וְלַכְּבָשִׂ֛ים בְּמִסְפָּרָ֖ם
כַּמִּשְׁפָּֽט׃ וּשְׂעִ֥יר חַטָּ֖את אֶחָ֑ד מִלְּבַד֙ עֹלַ֣ת הַתָּמִ֔יד וּמִנְחָתָ֖הּ
וְנִסְכָּֽהּ׃

וּבַיּ֧וֹם הַשְּׁלִישִׁ֛י פָּרִ֥ים עַשְׁתֵּי־עָשָׂ֖ר אֵילִ֣ם שְׁנָ֑יִם כְּבָשִׂ֧ים רביעי
בְּנֵי־שָׁנָ֛ה אַרְבָּעָ֥ה עָשָׂ֖ר תְּמִימִֽם׃ וּמִנְחָתָ֣ם וְנִסְכֵּיהֶ֡ם לַ֠פָּרִ֠ים
לָאֵילִ֧ם וְלַכְּבָשִׂ֛ים בְּמִסְפָּרָ֖ם כַּמִּשְׁפָּֽט׃ וּשְׂעִ֥יר חַטָּ֖את אֶחָ֑ד
מִלְּבַד֙ עֹלַ֣ת הַתָּמִ֔יד וּמִנְחָתָ֖הּ וְנִסְכָּֽהּ׃ וּבַיּ֧וֹם
הָרְבִיעִ֛י פָּרִ֥ים עֲשָׂרָ֖ה אֵילִ֣ם שְׁנָ֑יִם כְּבָשִׂ֧ים בְּנֵי־שָׁנָ֛ה אַרְבָּעָ֥ה
עָשָׂ֖ר תְּמִימִֽם׃ מִנְחָתָ֣ם וְנִסְכֵּיהֶ֗ם לַפָּרִ֜ים לָאֵילִ֧ם וְלַכְּבָשִׂ֛ים
בְּמִסְפָּרָ֖ם כַּמִּשְׁפָּֽט׃ וּשְׂעִיר־עִזִּ֥ים אֶחָ֖ד חַטָּ֑את מִלְּבַד֙ עֹלַ֣ת
הַתָּמִ֔יד מִנְחָתָ֖הּ וְנִסְכָּֽהּ׃

Continue with חצי קדיש *(page 231).*

קריאה ליום שלישי דחול המועד סוכות

THIRD DAY OF ḤOL HAMO'ED SUKKOT

In ארץ ישראל*, the first three verses,* וּבַיּוֹם הָרְבִיעִי *through* מִנְחָתָהּ וְנִסְכָּהּ*, are read for each of the four* עליות*.*

THIRD DAY ḤOL HAMO'ED: BEMIDBAR 29:23–31 The offering for the fourth, fifth, and sixth days of Sukkot.

במדבר כט:כג–לא

וּבַיּ֧וֹם הָרְבִיעִ֛י פָּרִ֥ים עֲשָׂרָ֖ה אֵילִ֣ם שְׁנָ֑יִם כְּבָשִׂ֧ים בְּנֵי־שָׁנָ֛ה
אַרְבָּעָ֥ה עָשָׂ֖ר תְּמִימִֽם׃ מִנְחָתָ֣ם וְנִסְכֵּיהֶ֗ם לַפָּרִ֜ים לָאֵילִ֧ם

וְלַכְּבָשִׂים בְּמִסְפָּרָם כַּמִּשְׁפָּט: וּשְׂעִיר־עִזִּים אֶחָד חַטָּאת
לוי מִלְּבַד עֹלַת הַתָּמִיד מִנְחָתָהּ וְנִסְכָּהּ: *וּבַיּוֹם
הַחֲמִישִׁי פָּרִים תִּשְׁעָה אֵילִם שְׁנָיִם כְּבָשִׂים בְּנֵי־שָׁנָה
אַרְבָּעָה עָשָׂר תְּמִימִם: וּמִנְחָתָם וְנִסְכֵּיהֶם לַפָּרִים לָאֵילִם
וְלַכְּבָשִׂים בְּמִסְפָּרָם כַּמִּשְׁפָּט: וּשְׂעִיר חַטָּאת אֶחָד מִלְּבַד
שלישי עֹלַת הַתָּמִיד וּמִנְחָתָהּ וְנִסְכָּהּ: *וּבַיּוֹם הַשִּׁשִּׁי
פָּרִים שְׁמֹנָה אֵילִם שְׁנָיִם כְּבָשִׂים בְּנֵי־שָׁנָה אַרְבָּעָה עָשָׂר
תְּמִימִם: וּמִנְחָתָם וְנִסְכֵּיהֶם לַפָּרִים לָאֵילִם וְלַכְּבָשִׂים
בְּמִסְפָּרָם כַּמִּשְׁפָּט: וּשְׂעִיר חַטָּאת אֶחָד מִלְּבַד עֹלַת
הַתָּמִיד מִנְחָתָהּ וּנְסָכֶיהָ:

רביעי וּבַיּוֹם הָרְבִיעִי פָּרִים עֲשָׂרָה אֵילִם שְׁנָיִם כְּבָשִׂים בְּנֵי־שָׁנָה
אַרְבָּעָה עָשָׂר תְּמִימִם: מִנְחָתָם וְנִסְכֵּיהֶם לַפָּרִים לָאֵילִם
וְלַכְּבָשִׂים בְּמִסְפָּרָם כַּמִּשְׁפָּט: וּשְׂעִיר־עִזִּים אֶחָד חַטָּאת
מִלְּבַד עֹלַת הַתָּמִיד מִנְחָתָהּ וְנִסְכָּהּ: וּבַיּוֹם
הַחֲמִישִׁי פָּרִים תִּשְׁעָה אֵילִם שְׁנָיִם כְּבָשִׂים בְּנֵי־שָׁנָה
אַרְבָּעָה עָשָׂר תְּמִימִם: וּמִנְחָתָם וְנִסְכֵּיהֶם לַפָּרִים לָאֵילִם
וְלַכְּבָשִׂים בְּמִסְפָּרָם כַּמִּשְׁפָּט: וּשְׂעִיר חַטָּאת אֶחָד מִלְּבַד
עֹלַת הַתָּמִיד וּמִנְחָתָהּ וְנִסְכָּהּ:

Continue with חצי קדיש *(page 231).*

קריאה ליום רביעי דחול המועד סוכות

FOURTH DAY OF ḤOL HAMO'ED SUKKOT

In ארץ ישראל, *the first three verses,* וּבַיּוֹם הַחֲמִישִׁי *through* וּמִנְחָתָהּ וְנִסְכָּהּ, *are read for each of the four* עליות.

FOURTH DAY ḤOL HAMO'ED: BEMIDBAR 29:26–34 The offering for the fifth, sixth, and seventh days of Sukkot.

במדבר כט: כו–לד

וּבַיּוֹם הַחֲמִישִׁי פָּרִים תִּשְׁעָה אֵילִם שְׁנָיִם כְּבָשִׂים בְּנֵי־
שָׁנָה אַרְבָּעָה עָשָׂר תְּמִימִם: וּמִנְחָתָם וְנִסְכֵּיהֶם לַפָּרִים
לָאֵילִם וְלַכְּבָשִׂים בְּמִסְפָּרָם כַּמִּשְׁפָּט: וּשְׂעִיר חַטָּאת אֶחָד
לוי מִלְּבַד עֹלַת הַתָּמִיד וּמִנְחָתָהּ וְנִסְכָּהּ: *וּבַיּוֹם

הַשִּׁשִּׁי פָּרִים שְׁמֹנָה אֵילִם שְׁנָיִם כְּבָשִׂים בְּנֵי־שָׁנָה אַרְבָּעָה
עָשָׂר תְּמִימִם: וּמִנְחָתָם וְנִסְכֵּיהֶם לַפָּרִים לָאֵילִם וְלַכְּבָשִׂים
בְּמִסְפָּרָם כַּמִּשְׁפָּט: וּשְׂעִיר חַטָּאת אֶחָד מִלְּבַד עֹלַת הַתָּמִיד
מִנְחָתָהּ וּנְסָכֶיהָ: ‎*וּבַיּוֹם הַשְּׁבִיעִי פָּרִים שִׁבְעָה שלישי
אֵילִם שְׁנָיִם כְּבָשִׂים בְּנֵי־שָׁנָה אַרְבָּעָה עָשָׂר תְּמִימִם:
וּמִנְחָתָם וְנִסְכֵּהֶם לַפָּרִים לָאֵילִם וְלַכְּבָשִׂים בְּמִסְפָּרָם
כְּמִשְׁפָּטָם: וּשְׂעִיר חַטָּאת אֶחָד מִלְּבַד עֹלַת הַתָּמִיד
מִנְחָתָהּ וְנִסְכָּהּ:

וּבַיּוֹם הַחֲמִישִׁי פָּרִים תִּשְׁעָה אֵילִם שְׁנָיִם כְּבָשִׂים בְּנֵי־ רביעי
שָׁנָה אַרְבָּעָה עָשָׂר תְּמִימִם: וּמִנְחָתָם וְנִסְכֵּיהֶם לַפָּרִים
לָאֵילִם וְלַכְּבָשִׂים בְּמִסְפָּרָם כַּמִּשְׁפָּט: וּשְׂעִיר חַטָּאת אֶחָד
מִלְּבַד עֹלַת הַתָּמִיד וּמִנְחָתָהּ וְנִסְכָּהּ: וּבַיּוֹם
הַשִּׁשִּׁי פָּרִים שְׁמֹנָה אֵילִם שְׁנָיִם כְּבָשִׂים בְּנֵי־שָׁנָה אַרְבָּעָה
עָשָׂר תְּמִימִם: וּמִנְחָתָם וְנִסְכֵּיהֶם לַפָּרִים לָאֵילִם וְלַכְּבָשִׂים
בְּמִסְפָּרָם כַּמִּשְׁפָּט: וּשְׂעִיר חַטָּאת אֶחָד מִלְּבַד עֹלַת הַתָּמִיד
מִנְחָתָהּ וּנְסָכֶיהָ:

Continue with חצי קדיש *(page 231).*

קריאה ליום החמישי דחול המועד סוכות בארץ ישראל

FIFTH DAY OF ḤOL HAMO'ED SUKKOT IN ISRAEL

In ארץ ישראל*, the following is read for each of the four* עליות*.*

FIFTH DAY ḤOL HAMO'ED IN ISRAEL: BEMIDBAR 29:29–31
The offering for the sixth day of Sukkot.

במדבר כט:כט–לא

וּבַיּוֹם הַשִּׁשִּׁי פָּרִים שְׁמֹנָה אֵילִם שְׁנָיִם כְּבָשִׂים בְּנֵי־שָׁנָה
אַרְבָּעָה עָשָׂר תְּמִימִם: וּמִנְחָתָם וְנִסְכֵּיהֶם לַפָּרִים לָאֵילִם
וְלַכְּבָשִׂים בְּמִסְפָּרָם כַּמִּשְׁפָּט: וּשְׂעִיר חַטָּאת אֶחָד מִלְּבַד
עֹלַת הַתָּמִיד מִנְחָתָהּ וּנְסָכֶיהָ:

Continue with חצי קדיש *(page 231).*

HOSHANA RABA קריאה להושענא רבה

HOSHANA RABA: BEMIDBAR 29:26–34
The offering for the fifth, sixth, and seventh days of Sukkot.

In ארץ ישראל*, the three verses from* וּבַיּוֹם הַשְּׁבִיעִי *through* מִנְחָתָהּ וְנִסְכָּהּ *are read for each of the four* עליות°*.*

במדבר כט:כו–לד
וּבַיּוֹם הַחֲמִישִׁי פָּרִים תִּשְׁעָה אֵילִם שְׁנָיִם כְּבָשִׂים בְּנֵי־
שָׁנָה אַרְבָּעָה עָשָׂר תְּמִימִם: וּמִנְחָתָם וְנִסְכֵּיהֶם לַפָּרִים
לָאֵילִם וְלַכְּבָשִׂים בְּמִסְפָּרָם כַּמִּשְׁפָּט: וּשְׂעִיר חַטָּאת אֶחָד
לוי מִלְּבַד עֹלַת הַתָּמִיד וּמִנְחָתָהּ וְנִסְכָּהּ: *וּבַיּוֹם
הַשִּׁשִּׁי פָּרִים שְׁמֹנָה אֵילִם שְׁנָיִם כְּבָשִׂים בְּנֵי־שָׁנָה אַרְבָּעָה
עָשָׂר תְּמִימִם: וּמִנְחָתָם וְנִסְכֵּיהֶם לַפָּרִים לָאֵילִם וְלַכְּבָשִׂים
בְּמִסְפָּרָם כַּמִּשְׁפָּט: וּשְׂעִיר חַטָּאת אֶחָד מִלְּבַד עֹלַת
שלישי הַתָּמִיד מִנְחָתָהּ וּנְסָכֶיהָ: *וּבַיּוֹם הַשְּׁבִיעִי
פָּרִים שִׁבְעָה אֵילִם שְׁנָיִם כְּבָשִׂים בְּנֵי־שָׁנָה אַרְבָּעָה עָשָׂר
תְּמִימִם: וּמִנְחָתָם וְנִסְכֵּהֶם לַפָּרִים לָאֵילִם וְלַכְּבָשִׂים
בְּמִסְפָּרָם כְּמִשְׁפָּטָם: וּשְׂעִיר חַטָּאת אֶחָד מִלְּבַד עֹלַת
הַתָּמִיד מִנְחָתָהּ וְנִסְכָּהּ:

רביעי וּבַיּוֹם הַשִּׁשִּׁי פָּרִים שְׁמֹנָה אֵילִם שְׁנָיִם כְּבָשִׂים בְּנֵי־שָׁנָה
אַרְבָּעָה עָשָׂר תְּמִימִם: וּמִנְחָתָם וְנִסְכֵּיהֶם לַפָּרִים לָאֵילִם
וְלַכְּבָשִׂים בְּמִסְפָּרָם כַּמִּשְׁפָּט: וּשְׂעִיר חַטָּאת אֶחָד מִלְּבַד
עֹלַת הַתָּמִיד מִנְחָתָהּ וּנְסָכֶיהָ: °וּבַיּוֹם הַשְּׁבִיעִי
פָּרִים שִׁבְעָה אֵילִם שְׁנָיִם כְּבָשִׂים בְּנֵי־שָׁנָה אַרְבָּעָה עָשָׂר
תְּמִימִם: וּמִנְחָתָם וְנִסְכֵּהֶם לַפָּרִים לָאֵילִם וְלַכְּבָשִׂים
בְּמִסְפָּרָם כְּמִשְׁפָּטָם: וּשְׂעִיר חַטָּאת אֶחָד מִלְּבַד עֹלַת
הַתָּמִיד מִנְחָתָהּ וְנִסְכָּהּ:

Continue with חצי קדיש *(page 231).*

RABBIS' KADDISH

Mourner: Yitgadal ve-yitkadash shemeh raba (Cong: Amen)
be-alma di vera khir'uteh, ve-yamlikh malkhuteh
be-ḥayeikhon u-v'yomeikhon
u-v'ḥayei de-khol beit Yisrael,
ba-agala u-vi-zman kariv,
ve-imru Amen. (Cong: Amen)

All: Yeheh shemeh raba mevarakh le-alam u-l'almei almaya.

Mourner: Yitbarakh ve-yishtabaḥ ve-yitpa'ar ve-yitromam ve-yitnasseh
ve-yit'hadar ve-yit'aleh ve-yit'hallal
shemeh de-kudsha, berikh hu. (Cong: Berikh hu)
le-ela min kol birkhata
Between Rosh HaShana & Yom Kippur: le-ela le-ela mi-kol birkhata
ve-shirata, tushbeḥata ve-neḥemata, da-amiran be-alma
ve-imru Amen. (Cong: Amen)

Al Yisrael ve-al rabanan,
ve-al talmideihon ve-al kol talmidei talmideihon
ve-al kol man de-askin be-oraita,
di be-atra (in Israel: kadisha) hadein vedi be-khol atar ve-atar,
yehei lehon u-lekhon shelama raba
ḥina ve-ḥisda ve-raḥamin,
ve-ḥayin arikhin u-mezona revi'ḥa
u-furkana min kodam avuhon di vi-shmaya,
ve-imru Amen. (Cong: Amen)

Yeheh shelama raba min shemaya
ve-ḥayim (tovim) aleinu ve-al kol Yisrael,
ve-imru Amen. (Cong: Amen)

Bow, take three steps back, as if taking leave of the Divine Presence, then bow, first left, then right, then center, while saying:
Oseh shalom (*Between Rosh HaShana & Yom Kippur:* ha-shalom) bi-m'romav,
hu ya'aseh ve-raḥamav shalom aleinu, ve-al kol Yisrael
ve-imru Amen. (Cong: Amen)

RABBIS' KADDISH

Mourner: Yitgadal ve-yitkadash shemeh raba. (*Cong:* Amen)
Be-alema di vera khir'uteh, ve-yamlikh malkhuteh,
be-ḥayyeikhon, uv-yomeikhon,
uv-ḥayyei de-khol beit Yisrael,
ba-agala uvi-zman kariv,
ve-imru Amen. (*Cong:* Amen)

All: Yeheh shemeh raba mevarakh le'alam ul-alemei alemaya.

Mourner: Yitbarakh ve-yishtabaḥ ve-yitpa'ar ve-yitromam ve-yitnaseh
ve-yit-hadar ve-yit'aleh ve-yit-hallal
shemeh dekudsha, berikh hu. (*Cong:* Berikh hu)
Le-ela min kol birkhata
/*Between Rosh HaShana & Yom Kippur:* Le-ela le-ela mi-kol birkhata/
ve-shirata, tushbeḥata ve-neḥemata, da-amiran be-alema,
ve-imru, Amen. (*Cong:* Amen)

Al Yisrael, ve-al rabanan,
ve-al talmideihon, ve-al kol talmidei talmideihon,
ve-al kol man de-asekin be-oraita
di be-atra (*In Israel:* kadisha) ha-dein ve-di be-khol atar va-atar,
yeheh lehon ul-khon shelama raba,
ḥina ve-ḥisda, ve-raḥamei,
ve-ḥayyei arikhei, um-zonei re-viḥei,
u-furkana min kodam avuhon di vish-maya,
ve-imru Amen. (*Cong:* Amen)

Yeheh shelama raba min shemaya
ve-ḥayyim (tovim) aleinu ve-al kol Yisrael,
ve-imru Amen. (*Cong:* Amen)

Bow, take three steps back, as if taking leave of the Divine Presence, then bow, first left, then right, then center, while saying:
Oseh shalom/*Between Rosh HaShana & Yom Kippur:* ha-shalom/
bim-romav,
hu ya'aseh ve-raḥamav shalom aleinu, ve-al kol Yisrael,
ve-imru Amen. (*Cong:* Amen)

MOURNER'S KADDISH

Mourner: Yitgadal ve-yitkadash shemeh raba. (*Cong:* Amen)
Be-alema di vera khir'uteh, ve-yamlikh malkhuteh,
be-ḥayyeikhon, uv-yomeikhon,
uv-ḥayyei de-khol beit Yisrael,
ba-agala uvi-zman kariv,
ve-imru Amen. (*Cong:* Amen)

All: Yeheh shemeh raba mevarakh le'alam ul-alemei alemaya.

Mourner: Yitbarakh ve-yishtabaḥ ve-yitpa'ar ve-yitromam ve-yitnaseh
ve-yit-hadar ve-yit'aleh ve-yit-hallal
shemeh dekudsha, berikh hu. (*Cong:* Berikh hu)
Le-ela min kol birkhata
/ *Between Rosh HaShana & Yom Kippur:* Le-ela le-ela mi-kol birkhata/
ve-shirata, tushbeḥata ve-neḥemata, da-amiran be-alema,
ve-imru, Amen. (*Cong:* Amen)

Yeheh shelama raba min shemaya
ve-ḥayyim aleinu ve-al kol Yisrael,
ve-imru Amen. (*Cong:* Amen)

Bow, take three steps back, as if taking leave of the Divine Presence, then bow, first left, then right, then center, while saying:

Oseh shalom/ *Between Rosh HaShana & Yom Kippur:* ha-shalom/
bim-romav,
hu ya'aseh shalom aleinu, ve-al kol Yisrael,
ve-imru Amen. (*Cong:* Amen)

GUIDE TO THE IMAGES

p. 4: Sunrise on a Sea of Galilee. © maxmacs / Shutterstock.com. A new day dawns and with it endless possibilities.

p. 7: DNA molecules. © vitstudio / Shutterstock.com. The immense and beautiful intricacies of the human body as represented by the DNA structure.

p. 10: The Jewish Bookshelf. © Daniel Rose. The wisdom of Torah takes many shapes and forms and can be seen on any Jewish bookshelf.

p. 14: Tzitzit. © orenhayon. Tzitzit, with *tekhelet,* on a *tallit gadol.*

p. 24: Opening of the IDF's Field Hospital in Nepal. © IDF. There are many definitions of what a Jewish building or a Jewish tent may be.

p. 26: Milky Way Galaxy over Israeli Desert at Night. © Basti Hansen / Shutterstock.com. Hashem is the Lord of the Universe.

p. 30: Jewish man prays at Maimonides tomb. © ChameleonsEye / Shutterstock.com. Rambam authored the Thirteen Principles of Faith, the inspiration for the poem *Yigdal.*

p. 33: Sunset sky with moon. © Jaochainoi / Shutterstock.com. Those beautiful moments when day becomes night.

p. 35: Blurred lights from peak Victoria, Hong Kong. © ESB Professional / Shutterstock.com. Blurry view of Hong Kong: God gives us the ability to see; take a moment to appreciate it.

p. 36: Claire Lomas crossing the finish line. © Lulu Kyriacou / Wikimedia Commons. Claire Lomas became a paraplegic as a result of a riding accident in 2007. She finished the London Marathon in 2012 in 17 days using the ReWalk robotic suit to raise awareness and funds for spinal injury research. God straightens the bent in many ways.

p. 39: Footprints in the Bahamas. © Debbie Stone. God shows us the way, it is up to us if we want to see His path and follow it.

p. 41: Israeli soldier prays at the Western Wall in Jerusalem. © mikhail / Shutterstock.com. A *gibor* prays for *gevura,* for strength to protect the Jewish People.

p. 56: The Ḥatzer. © courtesy of The Temple Institute. An artist's rendition of the courtyard of the Beit HaMikdash where the daily offerings would take place.

p. 70: The Rav and His Talmidim. © Yeshiva University Archives. Rabbi J.B. Soloveitchik, the commensurate rav and teacher, in the act of teaching, appropriately placed on the same page as the words of the Rabbis' Kaddish.

p. 73: Despair. © hikrcn / Shutterstock.com. Sometimes life can feel like a dark tunnel, but when we look to God we can find light and hope at the end of it.

p. 74: Saying Goodbye © Arman Zhenikeyev / Shutterstock.com. The Kaddish prayer gives the mourner a moment to recall the departed, connecting to them once again.

p. 79: Israel Philharmonic Orchestra. © Yeugene/Wikimedia Commons. Music as a language for the soul to praise God.

p. 81: Rav Goren at the Wall. © David Rubinger / Government Press Office. In a text that speaks of miracles and wonders performed by God, and the promise of the Land of Israel to the People of Israel as an everlasting covenant, this is Rabbi Goren, the Chief Rabbi of the IDF, blowing the shofar in 1967 at the Kotel during the Six Day War.

p. 82: New England Autumn Trees Reflection. © Michael Warwick / Shutterstock.com. The beauty of nature itself is singing praise and joy to God.

p. 85: Operation Solomon. © Alpert Nathan / Government Press Office. Non-stop flights of 35 Israeli aircraft transported 14,325 Ethiopian Jews to Israel in 36 hours in a covert Israeli military operation. A modern day fulfillment of the promise to the Jewish People that God will bless them, protect them, and carry them.

p. 87: Lag BaOmer on Har Merom. © david156 / Shutterstock.com. Serving God with joy, and song and dance.

p. 88: The Kinneret. © maxmacs / Shutterstock.com. Stunning nature in the Promised Land: both themes contained in the text.

p. 93: Leket Volunteers. © Leket. Volunteers harvest crops to give to the needy for the organization Leket. God provides for His children. Sometimes through man himself.

p. 95: The Statue of Liberty ©spyarm / Shutterstock.com. The Statue of Liberty represents a society that protects the weak and poor. God promises that He will do the same. Sometimes through man himself.

p. 96: Yerushalayim in the snow. © mikhail / Shutterstock.com. The weather (and snow in particular) and Yerushalayim are two of the themes in this chapter of *Tehillim*.

p. 98: A view of the Dead Sea. © Debbie Stone. The heavens and waters above praise God.

p. 100: Praising God's name with dance. © NCSY Summer Programs. NCSY TJJ participants dancing during Shaḥarit on the top of Massada.

p. 102: Modern Day Instruments. © OSABEE / Shutterstock.com. Praising God through instruments, ancient and modern alike.

p. 104: Thumbs up © Syda Productions / Shutterstock.com. When a person says Amen they show they are in agreement with what has been said.

p. 106: Tzedaka. © Dan Zelazo. A *tzedaka* box built in to a residence in Yerushalayim. Customarily, this point in *tefilla* is a time to give *tzedaka*.

p. 108: View from Rosh Hanikra. © Debbie Stone. God gives life to the earth, sea and everything in it.

p. 111: The Mitla Pass, 1967. © Moshe Milner / Government Press Office. Egyptian tanks destroyed by IAF planes in the Sinai desert in 1967. "That day the Lord saved Israel from the hands of the Egyptians."

p. 117: Musical notation. © Africa Studio / Shutterstock.com. Songs and praise. Like musical notes are a structure to contain the expression of emotion and feelings, so *tefilla* is a structure in which to pour the emotions of praising God.

p. 120: Walking out of the dark into the light. © Alistair Scott / Shutterstock.com. God creates light and darkness, both have a purpose in creation, each new day brings new possibilities.

p. 123: Night sky with stars and nebula. © nienora / Shutterstock.com. The millions of stars that God created give light and warmth to the world.

p. 124: New York City at Sunset. © Matej Kastelic / Shutterstock.com. Manhattan downtown skyline at sunset, illuminated by the last of the sun's rays.

p. 126: The Kohen Gadol performing the *Avoda,* offering *Ketoret* in the *Kodesh HaKodashim,* the holiest service that can be performed by a human being. © courtesy of The Temple Institute. The Aron HaBrit with the *keruvim* that are an earthly representation of the angels, which are a theme of the *tefilla* text.

p. 128: Accepting the yoke of heaven. © Debbie Stone. NCSY TJJ participant praying with intensity in Me'arat HaMakhpela, a place imbued with special holiness.

p. 135: Intergenerational *limmud Torah.* © Daniel Rose. Teach them repeatedly to your children. And grandchildren.

p. 136: The lush crops of a kibbutz field. © Mike Donenfeld / Shutterstock.com. A kibbutz field of lush crops is a fulfillment of the *berakha* in the *Shema.* But the irrigation system hints at the necessary partnership between God and man for this to be achieved.

p. 139: The Ḥilazon. © Natan Slifkin. The Ḥilazon from which the dye to make the color *tekhelet* for *tzitzit* is derived.

p. 140: Eternal Flame in the Hall of Remembrance at Yad Vashem. © Mrbrefast/ Wikimedia Commons. The eternal people, their eternal memory, and their eternal God.

p.143: Generations. © Frank Donnino. Survivor Max Durst holding his first great-grandchild, Harli Glatt. The power of faith passed on from generation to generation.

p. 144: UN Partition Plan vote: 29th November 1947. © Government Press Office. The God of history pleads their cause in the international arena. The first of Rabbi Soloveitchik's six knocks in his essay "Kol Dodi Dofek," the UN votes to create a Jewish State.

p. 147: Oseh Shalom Bimromav. © The Jewish Chronicle. Rabbi Jonathan Sacks, the Shabbaton Choir, and the Moriah Jewish Day School sing a "*shira ḥadasha,*" bringing old and new together in *tefilla* and song.

p. 151: Asking for help from the above. © Debbie Stone. NCSY adviser hiking in northern Israel, finding inspiration from God's beautiful creation.

p. 152: Connecting to our Avot. © Debbie Stone. NCSY TJJ participants praying at the grave of Avraham Avinu in Me'arat HaMakhpela.

p. 155: Rain. © Wolkenengel565 / Shutterstock.com. God provides rain that waters the earth, renewing all life and reviving what would otherwise be dead.

p. 156: The Northern Lights, Greenland. © Vadim Nefedoff / Shutterstock.com.

There is potential holiness in all things. In all of God's creations. The stunning Northern Lights is an especially powerful representation of this, as they are ethereal and incorporeal.

p. 159: Names. © Tani Bayer. What's in a name? A name reflects the essence of a person or thing. The names we use to refer to God express His essence and holiness. Notice some of the names in this list also contain a name of God.

p. 160: The Library of Congress in Washington DC. © Sean Pavone / Shutterstock.com. Knowledge comes in all shapes and forms. We ask God for help to acquire it, but we have to do our part too!

p. 163: Return. © Daniel Rose. The language of repentance in Hebrew is *teshuva*: to return. *Teshuva* returns us to the place where we were before we sinned. To the pristine guiltless condition of a child. This road sign and traffic circle, in Modi'in, Israel, represent return, and the sunrise behind the trees in the background represents rebirth.

p. 164: Remorse. © hikrcn / Shutterstock.com. Saying sorry and asking for forgiveness requires regret and vocalizing what a person has done wrong.

p. 167: Untitled in memory of Marc Weinberg. © Natalie Friedemann-Weinberg. This *berakha* asks for God to redeem us from our personal suffering. Our journey in life can feel like we are a small vulnerable boat riding the waves in the stormy sea. Sometimes we ride the crests of the waves and feel invincible, and sometimes we feel overwhelmed by the sea. We take comfort and find hope in our faith in God, and pray for His help to ride out the storm.

p. 169: Heal the vulnerable. © Iakobchuk Viacheslav / Shutterstock.com. We ask God to heal us in this blessing, physically, emotionally and spiritually.

p. 170: Ripe dates in northern Israel. © Oleg Zaslavsky / Shutterstock.com. We pray for prosperity and financial security, for a year of plenty.

p. 172: Aliya. © ChameleonsEye / Shutterstock.com. Modern *aliya* is the fulfillment of this *berakha*. Jews returning to their homeland from the four corners of the earth, with the notes of the shofar accompanying them.

p. 175: Israel's Supreme Court, Jerusalem. © Israeltourism. We pray for the return of Israel's judicial system from biblical times. While modern-day Israel's legal system is not a total fulfillment of this *berakha*, for the first time since the Sanhedrin we have a Jewish judiciary in *Eretz Yisrael*.

p. 176: Seliḥot at the Kotel. © Wikimedia Commons. This *berakha* was added as a response to sectarian fighting within the Jewish People. The antidote to divisions in the people is unity of this people.

p. 182: The Kotel. © Felix Lipov / Shutterstock.com. Vegetation flowering among the stones of the Kotel. We hope that Messianic times are already on their way, and the nascent buds of redemption are here in our modern Jewish State.

p. 185: Notes to God in the Kotel. © Rasmus Holmboe Dahlused / Shutterstock.com. We ask God to listen to our voice, however we choose to express it.

p. 187: Moon over the Old City of Jerusalem. © mikhail / Shutterstock.com. On this page we have *ḥagim* and the rebuilding of the Temple in Jerusalem. The months of the Jewish calendar, and therefore the dates of the festivals, are calculated by the waxing and waning of the moon.

p. 188: Gratitude. © SceneWalker / Shutterstock.com. A child giving thanks to her mother through a gift. We give thanks for the miracles of nature and the supernatural.

p. 191: A Jewish menora defies the Nazi swastika, 1931. © Yehudah Mansbuch. Celebrating Ḥanukka against all adversity, a menora stands brightly and defiantly against the Nazi flag.

p. 193: Purim in Me'ah She'arim. © ChameleonsEye / Shutterstock.com. Against tremendous odds, the story of Purim turned on its head. We continue to celebrate Purim by dressing up.

p. 196: Statement on wall of First Avenue steps close to UN Headquarters, NYC. © Mike P Shepherd / Alamy Stock Photo. These famous verses from Isaiah have become a universal prayer for peace.

p. 203: Father and son. © Nadezhda1906 / Shutterstock.com. The prayer of *Avinu Malkenu* expresses the emotions of our father-child relationship with God.

p. 215: Delicate and fragile. © Endless Buta / Shutterstock.com. The fragility of our lives in God's hands.

p. 223: Light from the heavens. © Paul Laubach / Shutterstock.com. Give us the gift of Your good light.

p. 230: Hagba'a. © Adiel Lo / Wikimedia Commons. This is the Torah Moshe placed before the Children of Israel.

p. 246: Knesset. © Opachevsky Irina / Shutterstock.com. The flag of the Jewish State flying outside its parliament. Connecting to the particular nature of God's relationship to the Jewish People expressed in the first paragraph of *Aleinu*, and contrasted with the second paragraph.

p. 249: The Jewish flag flies outside the UN. © Andrea Izzotti / Shutterstock.com. The flag of the Jewish State flying outside the UN among the family of nations. Connecting to the universal nature of God's relationship to all nations of the world expressed in the second paragraph of *Aleinu*, and contrasted with the first paragraph.

p. 253: Migdal David, Jerusalem. © Protasov AN / Shutterstock.com. Architectural gate fragment of David's Tower (citadel) in the Old City of Jerusalem: "Lift up your gates... so the glory of God may enter."

p. 254: Ein Avdat. © Debbie Stone. A view of the mountains of Ein Avdat/Ovdat, Israel: "Beautiful in its heights, joy of all the earth."

p. 256: Supreme Court in Washington, DC. © M Dogan / Shutterstock.com. The theme of this *mizmor* is Justice and protecting society's weakest.

p. 259: First Steps. © Valeriya Anufriyeva / Shutterstock.com. God supports us and helps us take our steps; when we are slipping, God holds us up.

p. 260: Compass in the sand. © sergign / Shutterstock.com. God asks us to walk in His ways and promises to protect us always.

p. 263: Banias, Golan Heights. © Protasov AN / Shutterstock.com. Reflective of the language of the psalm: "Rivers lift up their voice, rivers lift up their crashing waves."

p. 265: Early morning moon. © Kent Weakley / Shutterstock.com. The new moon of Rosh Ḥodesh.

p. 266: Finding God in nature © Debbie Stone. NCSY summer participants davening Shaḥarit on Mount Tzefaḥot. "How numerous are Your works, LORD; You made them all in wisdom."

p. 317: Yeshivat Har Etzion Beit Midrash at night. © Gershon Elinson / Yeshivat Har Etzion. Learning Torah day and night.

p. 324: Canopy of peace. © a454 / Shutterstock.com. We pray that God spreads over us a canopy of peace and security.

p. 383: NCSY Havdala. © NCSY.

p. 399: An angel when he is asleep! © Daniel Rose. We pray that God helps us sleep like babies.

p. 412: *Hadlakat Neirot Shabbat.* © Josh Weinberg. An NCSY advisor lighting Shabbat candles with an NCSYer.

p. 414: Lover Under Sunset. © littlesam / Shutterstock.com. A couple enjoying a beautiful sunset – the radiance of the world.

p. 421: Israeli paratroopers stand in front of the of the western Wall, 1967. © David Rubinger / Government Press Office. "Before Him are majesty and splendor; there are strength and beauty in His holy place."

p. 423: Lightning Over a Small Town. © yevjeniy11 / Shutterstock.com. The lightning lights up the darkest of nights. "His lightning lights up the world; the earth sees and trembles."

p. 424: Music at Sunset. © Shlomo Langer. Making music to sing praise to God.

p. 427: Temple Mount in Jerusalem. © Monastyrskyy Mykyta / Shutterstock.com. Robinson's Arch – the continuation of the *Kotel,* to the south-western corner of the Temple Mount.

p. 428: Listening to God Over the Waters. © NCSY. NCSY GIVE girls watch the sunrise over the waters on Har Tzfahot in the Eilat mountain range.

p. 431: Givati infantry brigade soldiers and Armored Brigade cadets participate in an urban warfare training exercise.© Alexi Rosenfeld / IDF. God acts in history through people. We pray (and prayed throughout history) to show strength through His "great right hand" and set our nation free – and we have been blessed to see this in the previous generation, and in our generation, in Israel. God's strength can be seen in the Israel Defense Forces.

p. 435: A little girl enjoying her shabbat dress. © Masha B. Goldman. "Put on your clothes of glory, My people."

p. 437: A *ḥatan* placing the ring on the finger of his *kallah*. © Hello Video and Photo Studio. Lecha dodi describes the welcoming of the shabbat as we welcome a bride.

p. 440: A GIVE West NCSYer celebrating the awesome views of the Grand Canyon © NCSY.

p. 442: Storm at the sea. Dark horizon of the Mediterranean. © Nina Mikryukova / Shutterstock.com. God is even mightier than the noise of the loudest and strongest storms.

p. 462: Shabbat Candles. © Debbie Stone. The shabbat candles symbolize peace and bring peace to the Shabbat home.

p. 464: Milky Way. Night sky with stars and silhouette of a man. © Denis Belitsky / Shutterstock.com. God created the universe in the six days of creation.

p. 471: Hourglass – sand trickling through the bulbs of a crystal sand glass. © Still Life Photography / Shutterstock.com. Time is precious and can be made holy.

p. 472: Periodic table of elements. © isak55 / Shutterstock.com. The building blocks of the completed universe.

p. 475: A goblet or two heads? © imagewriter / Shutterstock.com. White space can be an image, and contain a message. Rest on shabbat is not a mere abstention from something, but rather a positive and holy tangible entity.

p. 487: Spring Nature. Beautiful Landscape. © Subbotina Anna / Shutterstock.com. A moment of tranquility in nature. Sometimes taking a moment to soak in our surroundings helps us to see God's goodness.

p. 490: Ripe grapes on a vine in a vineyard Photographed in Kfar Tabor. © Gal Eitan Photographer / Shutterstock.com.

p. 501: A father blessing his son before his *ḥuppah*. © Hello Video and Photo Studio. Even adults are still their parent's children.

p. 502: Sunset over the Kinneret. © Tuvia Book. A moment of peace and serenity as the sun sets and Shabbat begins.

p. 539: The Torah belongs to us all. © Josh Weinberg. A TJJ teen writes one of the final letters in the NCSY Sefer Torah at Yom NCSY.

p. 543: Yom Hazikaron on Mt. Herzl. © Ohayon Avi / Government Press Office. The soldier mourns the death of a fellow soldier. The verses of tehillim describe the fragility of life, and this is never felt more strongly than when young people die in battle. We are left with no other choice but to trust and have faith in God. While the creation and continued protection of the State of Israel has taken an unimaginable toll in the lives of Jewihs people, if we take a step back and take in the larger picture, the story of gives us faith and comfort that we are living in miraculous times in the shelter of God.

p. 547: Bondi Beach coastal walk, Sydney, Australia. © Debbie Stone. God created and maintains control of the skies and seas all over the world.

p. 550: View of Israel from space. © MarcelClemens / Shutterstock.com (elements of this image furnished by NASA). A view of our inheritance that previous generations could only have dreamed of.

p. 552: Hundreds of teens come together to celebrate Yom NCSY in Israel. © NCSY. "Happy is the nation whose God is the Lord, the people He has chosen as His own."

p. 572: Old, random metal letters. © rangizzz / Shutterstock.com. There are not enough words to praise God.

p. 577: "And in the assemblies of tens of thousands of Your people, the house of Israel, with joyous song shall Your name, our King, be glorified in every generation." © Mikhail / Shutterstock.com.

p. 586: An annular eclipse, May 2012, Tokyo, Japan. © THEJAB / Shutterstock.com. "He called the sun into being and it shone with light."

p. 608: A mother and daughter praising God together. © Alexandra Grossman. "From generation to generation we will speak of Your greatness."

p. 611: Freshly baked *ḥallot*. © Leena Robinson / Shutterstock.com. One of the possible interpretations for why we have two *ḥallot* for the shabbat meals is they represent the two tablets of stone that Moshe brought down from Har Sinai.

p. 613: Little boy with his Sefer Torah. © Shutterstock.com. The love and concern for his sefer Torah reflects the love of Hashem for His people and why He gave them his Torah.

p. 627: Boy reading Torah. © Konstantin Goldenberg / Shutterstock.com.

p. 632: Where heaven and earth meet. . © Yellow531/Wikimedia Commons. "Yours, Lord, are the greatness and the power, the glory and the majesty and splendor, for everything in heaven and earth is Yours."

p. 658: Astronaut's boot print on lunar landing mission. © Castleski / Shutterstock.com. (Elements of this image furnished by NASA.) The Jewish calendar is lunar based, and means we are constantly aware of the moon's cycle.

p. 670: Korbanot in the *Bet Hamikdash*. © courtesy of The Temple Institute. The Musaf service on Shabbat, as on Rosh Ḥodesh and festivals, is a replacement for the musaf sacrifificial service in the Temple.

p. 677: Searching for God. © SFIO CRACHO / Shutterstock.com.

p. 678: Open 24/6. © Benjamin Cohen.

p. 681: A sign reporting that a gas station is closed on Shabbat in Jerusalem. © Yakov/ Wikimedia Commons. Shabbat on a national level.

p. 683: Sofer writes a sefer Torah in Auckland, New Zealand. © ChameleonsEye / Shutterstock.com. "as You wrote for us in Your Torah."

p. 699: Incense. © Roman Schipelev / Shutterstock.com.

p. 715: Moriah College Year 1 students in tefilla. © Nadine Saacks/Moriah College, Sydney, Australia. "We are only prepared to entrust the saying of this awe inspiring tefilla (*Anim Zemirot)* to the pure innocence of a young child."

p. 722: Planet Earth with a spectacular sunset, view on USA and Canada. © janez volmajer / Shutterstock.com (elements of this image furnished by NASA.)

p. 757: "Who is like Your people Israel, a nation unique on earth?" © Tani Bayer (elements of this image furnished by shutterstock.com and alamy.com.)

p. 823: Bonfire. © Tero Hakala / Shutterstock.com. At the time of the Sanhedrin the date of Rosh Ḥodesh was established through the testimony of witnesses who had seen the new moon appear for the first time. This was then communicated to Jewish communities across Israel and beyond through bonfires lit on mountain tops. The date of Rosh Ḥodesh each month in turn establishes when the festivals will occur, and so the entire Jewish calendar.

p. 824: Niagara Falls. © Nikola Bilic / Shutterstock.com. Nature can be so awesome and powerful that sometimes it appears as miraculous and even supernatural in its power and majesty. This chapter of *tehillim* refers to supernatural miracles in nature from Tanakh. Perhaps this scene from nature is just as powerful and awe-inspiring.

p. 829: Humanity. © amelaxa / Shutterstock.com. The universal faith in God of all of humanity.

p. 830: Hagana Ship Exodus 1947. © Shershel Frank / Government Press Office. These verses speak of the highs and lows of Jewish history and the faith that God always saves and protects His people. The ship Exodus 1947 is the most famous illegal-immigrant ship to bring survivors of the Shoah to pre-State Israel against the wishes of the ruling power, Britain. Those immigrants represent the highs and lows of Jewish history in the modern era as they established the modern State of Israel on the back of Jewish history's darkest day. The verse, "In my distress I called on the Lord. The Lord answered me and set me free," translates the Hebrew words מצר and מרחב as "distress" and "free," but they could also be translated as "narrow straits" and "wide spaces." The narrow straits of distress were the Shoah, and the wide space of freedom is the State of Israel.

p. 833: Rosh Pina. © Boris15 / Shutterstock.com. Rosh Pina was an agricultural settlement in the north of Israel established in 1882 during the First Aliya. The founders took its name from the verse in *tehillim* that describes a stone that was rejected by builders (the Jewish People or *Eretz Yisrael*), but later became the cornerstone of a great building. This could refer to the years of national persecution until the Jewish People rightly took their place among the nations